Get Connected.

Intelligent Response Technology

Intelligent Response Technology (IRT) is *Connect Accounting's* new student interface for end-of-chapter assessment content. Intelligent Response Technology provides a general journal application that looks and feels more like what you would find in a general ledger software package, improves answer acceptance to reduce student frustration with formatting issues (such as rounding), and, for select questions, provides an expanded table that guides students through the process of solving the problem.

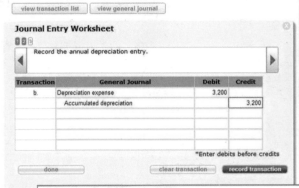

M4-4 Recording Adjusting Entries (Deferred Accounts) LO4-1

In each of the following transactions (a) through (c) for Romney's Marketing Company, use the three-step process illustrated in the chapter to record the adjusting entry at year-end December 31, 2015. The process includes (1) determining if revenue was earned or an expense incurred, (2) determining whether cash was received or paid in the past or will be received or paid in the future, and (3) computing the amount of the adjustment. (If no entry is required for a transaction/event, select "No journal entry required" in the first account field.)

a. Collected $1,200 rent for the period December 1, 2015, to April 1, 2016, which was credited to Unearned Rent Revenue on December 1, 2015.
b. Purchased a machine for $32,000 cash on January 1, 2011. The company estimates annual depreciation at $3,200.
c. Paid $5,000 for a two-year insurance premium on July 1, 2015; debited Prepaid Insurance for that amount.

view transaction list   view general journal

Journal Entry Worksheet

Record the annual depreciation entry.

Transaction	General Journal	Debit	Credit
b.	Depreciation expense	3,200	
	Accumulated depreciation		3,200

*Enter debits before credits

done   clear transaction   record transaction

M2-9 Completing T-Accounts LO2-4

Following are the transactions of Dennen, Inc., for the month of January 2015.

a. Borrowed $30,000 from a local bank.
b. Lent $10,000 to an affiliate; accepted a note due in one year.
c. Sold 100 additional shares of stock with a par value of $0.10 per share to investors for $500 cash.
d. Purchased $15,000 of equipment, paying $5,000 cash and the rest on a note due in one year.
e. Declared and paid $2,000 in dividends to stockholders.

For each of the preceding transactions, record the effects of the transaction in the appropriate T-accounts and determine ending account balances. Beginning balances are provided.

Cash

Beg. Bal.	900		
(a)	30,000	10,000	(b)
(c)	500	5,000	(d)
		2,000	
End. Bal.	14,400		

Notes Receivable

Beg. Bal.	1,000		
(b)	10,000		
End. Bal.	11,000		

Equipment

Beg. Bal.	15,100		
(d)	5,000		
End. Bal.	20,100		

Notes Payable

Beg. Bal.		3,000	
		30,000	(a)
		10,000	(d)
End. Bal.		43,000	

Common Stock

Beg. Bal.		1,000

Additional Paid-in Capital

Beg. Bal.		3,000

E5-5 Preparing a Classified Balance Sheet LO5-3

Campbell Soup Company is the world's leading maker and marketer of soup and sells other well-known brands of food in 120 countries. Presented here are the items listed on its recent balance sheet (dollars in millions) presented in alphabetical order:

Accounts payable	$ 585	Other assets	$ 136	
Accounts receivable	560	Other current assets	152	
Accrued expenses	619	Other current debt	785	
Cash and cash equivalents	484	Other noncurrent liabilities	3,777	
Common stock, $0.0375 par value	351	Property, plant, and equipment, net	2,103	
Intangible assets	2,660	Retained earnings	745	
Inventories	767			

Required:
Prepare a classified consolidated balance sheet for Campbell Soup for the current year (ended July 31). (Enter your answers in millions (i.e., 10,000,000 should be entered as 10).)

CAMPBELL SOUP COMPANY	
Consolidated Balance Sheet	
July 31, Current Year	
(in millions)	
Assets	
Current Assets:	
Cash and cash equivalents	$ 484
Accounts	
Accounts payable	
Accounts receivable	
Total current assets	484
Total assets	$ 484
Liabilities and Stockholders' Equity	
Current liabilities:	

Get Engaged.

eBooks

Connect Plus includes a media-rich eBook that allows you to share your notes with your students. Students can insert and review their own notes, highlight the text, search for specific information, and interact with media resources. Using an eBook with *Connect Plus* gives your students a complete digital solution that allows them to access their materials from any computer.

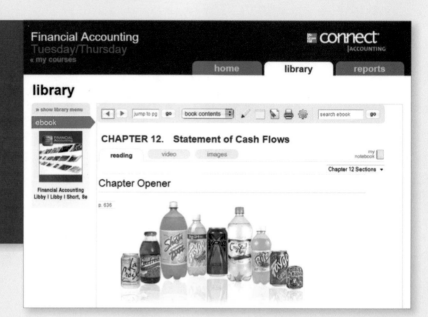

Lecture Capture

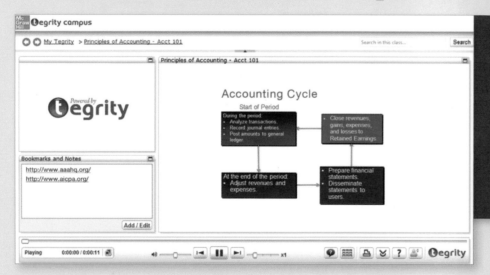

Make your classes available anytime, anywhere. With simple, one-click recording, students can search for a word or phrase and be taken to the exact place in your lecture that they need to review.

EIGHTH EDITION

Financial Accounting

Robert Libby
Cornell University

Patricia A. Libby
Ithaca College

Daniel G. Short
Texas Christian University

Mc
Graw
Hill
Education

To: Jenni, Jon, Emma, and Sophia Drago

Heather and Scott Andresen

Bob and Mary Ann Short, and Maryrose Short

Herman and Doris Hargenrater

Oscar and Selma Libby

Laura Libby

FINANCIAL ACCOUNTING, EIGHTH EDITION

Published by McGraw-Hill Education, 2 Penn Plaza, New York, NY 10121. Copyright © 2014 by McGraw-Hill Education. All rights reserved. Printed in the United States of America. Previous editions © 2011, 2009, and 2007. No part of this publication may be reproduced or distributed in any form or by any means, or stored in a database or retrieval system, without the prior written consent of McGraw-Hill Education, including, but not limited to, in any network or other electronic storage or transmission, or broadcast for distance learning.

Some ancillaries, including electronic and print components, may not be available to customers outside the United States.

This book is printed on acid-free paper.

1 2 3 4 5 6 7 8 9 0 DOW/DOW 1 0 9 8 7 6 5 4 3

ISBN   978-0-07-802555-6
MHID   0-07-802555-9

Senior Vice President, Products & Markets: *Kurt L. Strand*
Vice President, Content Production & Technology Services: *Kimberly Meriwether David*
Director: *Tim Vertovec*
Executive Brand Manager: *James Heine*
Executive Director of Development: *Ann Torbert*
Development Editor: *Rebecca Mann*
Managing Development Editor: *Christina Sanders*
Director of Digital Content: *Patricia Plumb*
Digital Development Editor: *Julie Hankins*
Senior Marketing Manager: *Kathleen Klehr*
Senior Project Manager: *Diane L. Nowaczyk*
Senior Buyer: *Michael R. McCormick*
Interior Designers: *Cara Hawthorne, Pam Verros*
Cover Designer: *Pam Verros*
Senior Content Licensing Specialist: *Jeremy Cheshareck*
Photo Researcher: *Editorial Image, LLC*

Lead Media Project Manager: *Daryl Horrocks*
Media Project Manager: *Ron Nelms*
Typeface: *10.5/12 Times Roman*
Compositor: *Laserwords Private Limited*
Printer: *R. R. Donnelley*
Cover photo credits: Baskets with fresh produce, Digital Vision/Getty Images; Swimming pool, Royalty-Free/CORBIS; Starbucks, The McGraw-Hill Companies, Inc./Jill Braaten, photographer; Front of a motorcycle, Imagestate Media (John Foxx); Apple iPhone menu display, The McGraw-Hill Companies, Inc./Marker Dierker, photographer; National Beverage logo is a registered trademark of National Beverage Corporation and is used with permission; Southwest photo, © AP Photo/Ted S. Warren; AT&T photo, Bloomberg via Getty Images; Kroger, Bloomberg via Getty Images.

All credits appearing on page or at the end of the book are considered to be an extension of the copyright page.

Library of Congress Cataloging-in-Publication Data

Libby, Robert.
  Financial accounting / Robert Libby, Cornell University; Patricia A. Libby, Ithaca College; Daniel G. Short, Texas Christian University.—Eighth edition.
    pages cm
  Includes index.
  ISBN 978-0-07-802555-6 (alk. paper)—ISBN 0-07-802555-9 (alk. paper)
  1. Accounting. 2. Corporations—Accounting. 3. Financial statements. I. Libby, Patricia A. II. Short, Daniel G. III. Title.
  HF5636.L53 2014
  657—dc23

                                                2013006922

The Internet addresses listed in the text were accurate at the time of publication. The inclusion of a website does not indicate an endorsement by the authors or McGraw-Hill Education, and McGraw-Hill Education does not guarantee the accuracy of the information presented at these sites.

www.mhhe.com

ABOUT THE AUTHORS

ROBERT LIBBY

Robert Libby is the David A. Thomas Professor of Accounting at Cornell University, where he teaches the introductory financial accounting course. He previously taught at the University of Illinois, Pennsylvania State University, the University of Texas at Austin, the University of Chicago, and the University of Michigan. He received his BS from Pennsylvania State University and his MAS and PhD from the University of Illinois; he is also a CPA.

Bob is a widely published author and researcher specializing in behavioral accounting. He was selected as the AAA Outstanding Educator in 2000 and received the AAA Outstanding Service Award in 2006 and the AAA Notable Contributions to the Literature Award in 1985 and 1996. He is the only person to have received all three of the Association's highest awards for teaching, service, and research. He has published numerous articles in *The Accounting Review; Journal of Accounting Research; Accounting, Organizations, and Society;* and other accounting journals. He has held a variety of offices, including vice president in the American Accounting Association, and he is a member of the American Institute of CPAs and the editorial boards of *The Accounting Review; Accounting, Organizations, and Society;* and *Journal of Accounting Literature.*

PATRICIA A. LIBBY

Patricia Libby is associate professor of accounting at Ithaca College, where she teaches the undergraduate financial accounting course. She previously taught graduate and undergraduate financial accounting at Eastern Michigan University and the University of Texas. Before entering academe, she was an auditor with Price Waterhouse (now PricewaterhouseCoopers) and a financial administrator at the University of Chicago. She is also faculty advisor to Beta Alpha Psi and Ithaca College Accounting Association. She received her BS from Pennsylvania State University, her MBA from DePaul University, and her PhD from the University of Michigan; she is also a CPA.

Pat conducts research on using cases in the introductory course and other parts of the accounting curriculum. She has published articles in *The Accounting Review, Issues in Accounting Education,* and *The Michigan CPA.*

DANIEL G. SHORT

Daniel Short is professor of accounting and former dean of the M.J. Neeley School of Business at Texas Christian University in Fort Worth, Texas. Before he joined TCU, he was dean at the Richard T. Farmer School of Business at Miami University and the College of Business at Kansas State University. Prior to that, he was associate dean at the University of Texas at Austin, where he taught the undergraduate and graduate financial accounting courses. He also taught at the University of Michigan and the University of Chicago. He received his undergraduate degree from Boston University and his MBA and PhD from the University of Michigan.

Dan has won numerous awards for his outstanding teaching abilities and has published articles in *The Wall Street Journal, The Accounting Review,* the *Journal of Accounting Research,* and other business journals. He has worked with a number of Fortune 500 companies, commercial banks, and investment banks to develop and teach executive education courses on the effective use of accounting information. Dan has also served on boards of directors in several industries, including manufacturing, commercial banking, and medical services.

A TRUSTED LEADER FOR

The award-winning author team of Bob Libby, Pat Libby, and Dan Short has made *Financial Accounting* a best-selling textbook by helping the instructor and student become partners in learning. Libby/Libby/Short uses a remarkable learning approach that keeps students engaged and involved in the material from the first day of class.

Libby/Libby/Short's *Financial Accounting* maintains its leadership by focusing on three key attributes:

THE PIONEERING FOCUS COMPANY APPROACH

The Libby/Libby/Short authors' trademark focus company approach is the best method for helping students understand financial statements and the real-world implications of financial accounting for future managers. **This approach shows that accounting is relevant and motivates students by explaining accounting in a real-world context.** Throughout each chapter, the material is integrated around a familiar focus company, its decisions, and its financial statements. This provides the perfect setting for discussing the importance of accounting and how businesses use accounting information.

A BUILDING-BLOCK APPROACH TO TEACHING TRANSACTION ANALYSIS

Most faculty agree that mastery of the accounting cycle is critical to success in financial accounting. And yet all other financial books introduce and develop transaction analysis in one chapter, bombarding a student early in the course with an overload of new concepts and terms. The authors believe that most faculty take more time with the accounting cycle, but other financial accounting textbooks don't. **By slowing down the introduction of transactions and giving students time to practice and gain mastery, this building-block approach leads to greater student success in their study of later topics in financial accounting such as adjusting entries.**

POWERFUL TECHNOLOGY FOR TEACHING AND STUDY

Students have different learning styles and conflicting time commitments, so they want technology tools that will help them study more efficiently and effectively. The 8th edition includes even more technology features, including McGraw-Hill Connect Accounting, LearnSmart, and Tegrity Campus. See pages xvi–xxi for more details.

STUDENTS AND INSTRUCTORS

"[Libby, Libby, Short] does a **great job explaining financial accounting concepts to college students on an introductory level.**"

—Peggy O'Kelly, Northeastern University

"The text has **some of the best discussions that I have seen in introductory texts of statement of cash flows and financial statement analysis topics**."

—Marilyn Misch, Pepperdine University

"Excellent book with **very good and clear writing, coverage, illustrations** and overall very student friendly."

—Kashi Balachandran, New York University

"The book does an excellent job of using real-world examples to highlight the importance of understanding financial accounting to students who may or may not be interested in pursuing accounting careers. I think this book will hold students' attention, without sacrificing the technical information that provides the foundation for further accounting coursework. **Exceptionally well written and nicely organized**."

—Paul Hribar, University of Iowa

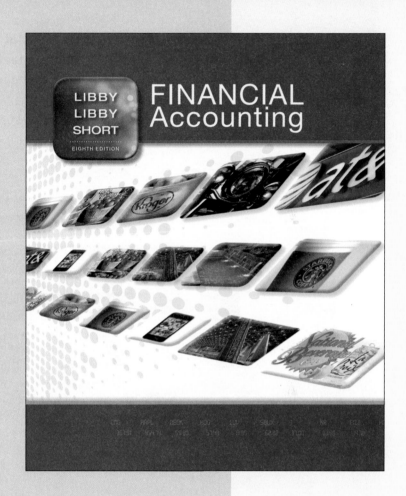

LIBBY
LIBBY
SHORT

EIGHTH EDITION

FINANCIAL
Accounting

MARKET-LEADING PEDAGOGY

Financial Accounting, 8e, offers a host of pedagogical tools that complement the different ways you like to teach and the ways your students like to learn. Some offer information and tips that help you present a complex subject; others highlight issues relevant to what your students read online or see on television. Either way, *Financial Accounting*'s pedagogical support will make a real difference in your course and in your students' learning.

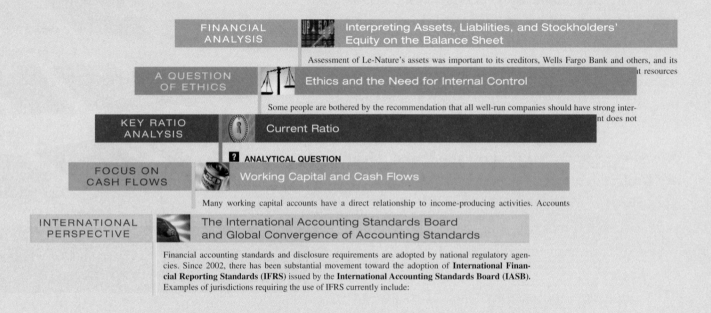

FINANCIAL ANALYSIS — Interpreting Assets, Liabilities, and Stockholders' Equity on the Balance Sheet

Assessment of Le-Nature's assets was important to its creditors, Wells Fargo Bank and others, and its ...nt resources

A QUESTION OF ETHICS — Ethics and the Need for Internal Control

Some people are bothered by the recommendation that all well-run companies should have strong inter-...nt does not

KEY RATIO ANALYSIS — Current Ratio

? ANALYTICAL QUESTION

FOCUS ON CASH FLOWS — Working Capital and Cash Flows

Many working capital accounts have a direct relationship to income-producing activities. Accounts

INTERNATIONAL PERSPECTIVE — The International Accounting Standards Board and Global Convergence of Accounting Standards

Financial accounting standards and disclosure requirements are adopted by national regulatory agencies. Since 2002, there has been substantial movement toward the adoption of **International Financial Reporting Standards (IFRS)** issued by the **International Accounting Standards Board (IASB)**. Examples of jurisdictions requiring the use of IFRS currently include:

FINANCIAL ANALYSIS BOXES—These features tie important chapter concepts to real-world decision-making examples. They also highlight alternative viewpoints and add to the critical-thinking and decision-making focus of the text.

A QUESTION OF ETHICS BOXES—These boxes appear throughout the text, conveying the importance and the consequences of acting responsibly in business practice.

KEY RATIO ANALYSIS BOXES—Each box presents ratio analysis for the focus company in the chapter as well as for comparative companies. Cautions are also provided to help students understand the limitations of certain ratios.

FOCUS ON CASH FLOWS BOXES—Each of the first eleven chapters includes a discussion and analysis of changes in the cash flows of the focus company and explores the decisions that caused those changes.

INTERNATIONAL PERSPECTIVE BOXES—These boxes highlight the emergence of global accounting standards (IFRS) at a level appropriate for the introductory student.

AND CONTENT

Anticipating a greater emphasis on International Financial Reporting Standards (IFRS) in the United States and recognizing its presence in more than 100 countries worldwide, selected IFRS topics are integrated in appropriate chapters at a level suitable for introductory financial accounting so students will be well-prepared to use statements prepared under IFRS in their careers. The coverage in Libby/Libby/Short exceeds the standards suggested by the PricewaterhouseCoopers (PwC) IFRS Ready program (2010) for sophomores and juniors presented below:

- Sophomores interviewing for summer programs and internships and who have had at least one term of accounting should have a pre-awareness of IFRS by being able to define what IFRS stands for and why it could be important to their future careers.

- Juniors and above interviewing for internships or full-time positions should be able to demonstrate an awareness of IFRS by being able to articulate which global organization establishes IFRS, what an example of a difference between U.S. GAAP and IFRS may be, and generally where it is used in the world.

The following table outlines the coverage chapter by chapter.

CHAPTER	TOPIC
1 Financial Statements and Business Decisions, p. 18	The IASB and Global Convergence of Accounting Standards
2 Investing and Financing Decisions and the Accounting System, p. 66	Understanding Foreign Financial Statements
3 Operating Decisions and the Accounting System, p. 104	Income Statement Differences
5 Communicating and Interpreting Accounting Information, p. 243	Differences in Accounting Methods Acceptable under IFRS and U.S. GAAP Treatment of Extraordinary Items
7 Reporting and Interpreting Cost of Goods Sold and Inventory, p. 338	Use of Last-In First-Out Method for Inventory
8 Reporting and Interpreting Property, Plant, and Equipment; Intangibles; and Natural Resources, pp. 399, 408	Component Allocation Differences in Accounting for Tangible and Intangible Assets
9 Reporting and Interpreting Liabilities, pp. 459, 461	Classification of Refinanced Debt Contingent Liabilities
11 Reporting and Interpreting Owners' Equity, p. 560	Stockholders' Equity Terminology
12 Statement of Cash Flows, p. 601	Treatment of Interest Received and Paid

PAUSE FOR FEEDBACK AND SELF-STUDY QUIZ

Research shows that students learn best when they are actively engaged in the learning process. This active learning feature engages the student, provides interactivity, and promotes efficient learning. These quizzes ask students to pause at strategic points throughout each chapter to ensure they understand key points before moving ahead.

"The **Pause for Feedback and Self-Study Quizzes give the student the opportunity to test their understanding of the material before moving forward** and also assist in breaking up the chapter into manageable sections."

—*Betty P. David, Francis Marion University*

GUIDED HELP

NEW! Today's students have a wide variety of time commitments. And research shows that when they have difficulty understanding a key concept, they benefit most when help is available immediately. **Our unique Guided Help feature provides a narrated, animated, step-by-step walk-through of select topics covered in the Self-Study Quiz that can be viewed any time through their mobile device or online.** Students will simply need to scan the QR code to view directly on their mobile device or go to the text website at www.mhhe.com/libby8e to view online. It also saves office hour time!

CHAPTER TAKE-AWAYS

Bulleted end-of-chapter summaries complement the learning objectives outlined at the beginning of the chapter.

COMPREHENSIVE PROBLEMS

Selected chapters include problems that cover topics from earlier chapters to refresh, reinforce, and build an integrative understanding of the course material.

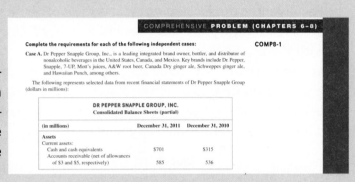

CASES AND PROJECTS

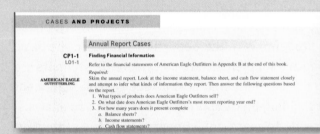

This section includes annual report cases, financial reporting and analysis cases, critical thinking cases, and financial reporting and analysis team projects.

CONTINUING CASE

NEW! The continuing case revolves around Penny's Pool Service & Supply, Inc. and its largest supplier, Pool Corporation, Inc. In the first five chapters, the continuing case follows the establishment, operations, and financial reporting for Penny's. In Chapter 5, Pool Corporation, a real publicly traded corporation, is also introduced in more detail. The Pool Corporation example is then extended to encompass each new topic in the remaining chapters.

"This is an excellent book that can be used for both an introductory course as well as an MBA class. The book has a simple, conversational and easy-to-understand writing style. The book is also very well organized and has a lot of end-of-chapter material. **This is one of the best financial accounting books that I have come across.** It is a must for a financial accounting course."

—*Syed Hasan, George Mason University*

A PROVEN TEACHING AND

Faculty agree the accounting cycle is the most critical concept to learn and master for students studying financial accounting. Libby/Libby/Short believes students struggle with the accounting cycle when transaction analysis is covered in one chapter. If students are exposed to the accounting equation, journal entries, and T-accounts for both balance sheet and income statement accounts in a single chapter, many are left behind and are unable to grasp material in the next chapter, which typically covers adjustments and financial statement preparation.

The market-leading Libby/Libby/Short approach spreads transaction analysis coverage over two chapters so that students have the time to master the material. In Chapter 2 of *Financial Accounting,* students are exposed to the accounting equation and transaction analysis for investing and financing transactions that only affect balance sheet accounts. This provides students with the opportunity to learn the basic structure and tools used in accounting in a simpler setting. In Chapter 3, students are exposed to more complex operating transactions that also affect income statement accounts. As a result of this slower building-block approach to transaction analysis, students are better prepared and ready to learn adjustments, financial statement preparation, and more advanced topics. After the students have developed an understanding of the complete accounting cycle and the resulting statements, Chapter 5 takes students through the corporate reporting and analysis process.

LEARNING METHODOLOGY

Accounting Cycle

Start Early	Compress Coverage	Extend Coverage (Libby/Libby/Short approach)
Overview of F/S and Users, B/S and I/S Transactions with Accounting Equation	Overview of F/S and Users	Overview of F/S and Users
	F/S, Ratios, and Conceptual Framework	**B/S** Transactions with Accounting Equation, Journal Entries, and T-accounts
B/S and I/S Transactions with Journal Entries and T-accounts	B/S and I/S Transactions with Accounting Equation, Journal Entries, and T-accounts	B/S and **I/S** Transactions with Accounting Equation, Journal Entries, and T-accounts
Adjustments, Closing Entries, F/S Preparation	Adjustments, Closing Entries, F/S Preparation	Adjustments, Closing Entries, F/S Preparation

This graphic shows a detailed comparison of the Libby/Libby/Short approach to the accounting cycle chapters compared to the approach taken by other financial accounting texts.

The authors' approach to introducing the accounting cycle has been tested in peer-reviewed, published research studies. One of these award-winning studies has shown that the accounting cycle approach used in this textbook yields learning gains that out-pace approaches used in other textbooks by a significant margin.

> "I really like the way the Balance Sheet accounts are introduced with the accounting equation, then you go directly to Debit and Credit entries. I have not seen a text use this approach. I feel it would break the material down to make it easier to grasp for the first-time accounting student. I LOVE that the journal entries are introduced right in the same chapter as the accounting equation. Most texts introduce the accounting equation in chapter 1, then debits and credits in chapter 2. I like the approach the Libby text is using! Love the illustrations . . . This shows BOTH the accounting equation AND Journal Entries."
>
> —Christy Land, Catawba Valley Community College

WHAT'S NEW IN THE 8th EDITION?

One reason Libby/Libby/Short's *Financial Accounting is a best-selling* textbook is because instructors can trust the flexibility in key topical coverage, the simplified explanations of complex topics, and end-of-chapter material that relates directly to the chapter's text and engages the students with concepts and decision making using details from the chapter.

Chapter 1

Focus Company: Le-Nature's Inc.

- *New* focus company and coverage of an exciting, but simple, recent accounting fraud. Students are introduced to the structure, content, and use of the four basic financial statements through the story of two brothers who founded Le-Nature's Inc., a natural beverage company. Le-Nature's financial statements are used to support increases in borrowing for expansion. When actual sales do not live up to expectations, the brothers turn to financial statement fraud to cover up their failure. The fact that banks and other parties involved lost upwards of $700 million and the perpetrators are now spending a total of 70 years in federal prison emphasizes the importance of controls, responsible ethical conduct, and accurate financial reporting.
- The simple statement of stockholders' equity replaces the statement of retained earnings to match current practice.
- *New* **GUIDED HELP** feature provides all users of the text with free access to step-by-step video instruction on preparing a simple balance sheet, income statement, and statement of stockholders' equity for LaCrosse Footwear, a leading outdoor footwear company.
- *New* **CONTINUING CASE** added to the end-of-chapter problems based on the activities of Penny's Pool Service & Supply, Inc. and its supplier, Pool Corporation. These cases summarize key points emphasized in each chapter in a consistent context throughout the text. In Chapter 1, students prepare a basic income statement, statement of stockholders' equity, and balance sheet based on Penny's estimates for the first year.
- New and updated real companies, as well as modified accounts, names, and amounts for fictional companies in end-of-chapter exercises, problems, and cases.

Chapter 2

Focus Company: Chipotle Mexican Grill

- *New* focus company **Chipotle Mexican Grill** (replacing Papa John's International in 7e), with integration of financial information for the first quarter of 2012 (not for a month as in 7e).
  - Use of Chipotle Mexican Grill eliminates complications of franchise accounting involved in the Papa John's example in the 7e.
  - Chipotle's business strategy is based on sustainable practices that are of growing interest to businesses and society.
- Cash flow statement coverage limited to identifying transactions as operating, investing, or financing.
- Discussion and illustration of issuing common stock using accounts students will likely see in real statements—Common Stock and Additional Paid-in Capital (not Contributed Capital, which was used in 7e). The demonstration case and EOC material have been changed to reflect coverage of these new accounts.
- Update of the conceptual framework to reflect the new definitions from the FASB.
- Trial balance introduced (moved from Chapter 4 in 7e) and updated as needed as part of the continuing illustration of Chipotle Mexican Grill's quarterly transactions.
- T-accounts added after each transaction to illustrate posting the effects.
- *New* **GUIDED HELP** feature provides free access to step-by-step video instruction on transaction analysis and recording, posting, and classifying accounts for investing and financing activities
- *New* **CONTINUING CASE** added to the end-of-chapter problems. In this case, students prepare journal entries, post to T-accounts, prepare a trial balance and classified balance sheet, identify investing and financing activities affecting cash flows, and compute

and interpret the current ratio based on the balance sheet for Penny's Pool Service.

- New and updated real companies, as well as modified accounts, names, and amounts for fictional companies in end-of-chapter exercises, problems, and cases with requirements reflecting the changes in topics emphasized in each chapter.

Chapter 3

Focus Company: Chipotle Mexican Grill

- *New* focus company **Chipotle Mexican Grill**
- Update of the conceptual framework to reflect the new definitions from the FASB.
- The key ratio in this chapter was changed to the Net Profit Margin ratio (replacing coverage of the Total Asset Turnover ratio in the 7e).
- Trial balance updated as needed as part of the continuing illustration of Chipotle Mexican Grill's quarterly transactions.
- T-accounts added after each transaction to illustrate posting the effects.
- *New* **GUIDED HELP** feature provides free access to step-by-step video instruction on transaction analysis and recording, posting, and classifying accounts for operating activities.
- *New* **CONTINUING CASE** where students prepare journal entries for operating activities, prepare a classified income statement, and compute and analyze the net profit margin based on the income statement for Penny's Pool Service.
- New and updated real companies, as well as modified accounts, names, and amounts for fictional companies in end-of-chapter exercises, problems, and cases with requirements reflecting the changes in topics emphasized in each chapter.

Chapter 4

Focus Company: Chipotle Mexican Grill

- *New* focus company **Chipotle Mexican Grill**
  - The March 31, 2012, statements in Chapter 4 are quite similar to the actual quarterly statements of Chipotle, except for a few simplifications.
- The key ratio in this chapter was changed from Net Profit Margin ratio to the Total Asset Turnover ratio.
- *New* **GUIDED HELP** feature provides free access to step-by-step video instruction on recording adjusting entries.

- *New* **CONTINUING CASE** added where students prepare adjusting entries for Penny's Pool Service.
- New and updated real companies, as well as modified accounts, names, and amounts for fictional companies in end-of-chapter exercises, problems, and cases with requirements reflecting the changes in topics emphasized in each chapter.

Chapter 5

Focus Company: Apple Inc.

- *New* focus company **Apple Inc.,** with integration of the financial statements and corporate governance and disclosure processes of students' favorite technology company.
- *New* simplified exhibit explaining the role of management, auditors, boards of directors, and regulators in ensuring the integrity of financial reporting.
- Focus narrowed to three topics: details of the corporate governance and disclosure process; financial statement formats and important subtotals, totals, and additional disclosures; and the analysis of financial statements through gross profit, net profit, total asset turnover, and return on assets analyses.
- Fraud triangle added to corporate governance discussion.
- Issuance of par value stock moved to the discussion of financing activities in Chapter 2.
- *New* section on the effects of transactions on key ratios added to tie the material in this chapter to coverage in Chapters 2, 3, and 4.
- *New* **GUIDED HELP** feature provides free access to step-by-step video instruction on preparing a detailed classified income statement and balance sheet from a trial balance for amazon.com, the world's largest online retailer.
- *Two New* **CONTINUING CASES** added to the end-of-chapter problems. The first asks students to evaluate the effects of key transactions on important statement subtotals and financial ratios for Penny's Pool Service & Supply. The second introduces Penny's supplier, Pool Corporation, a public company, and asks students to prepare a detailed classified income statement and balance sheet and compute the gross profit percentage and return on assets ratios.

- New and updated real companies, as well as modified accounts, names, and amounts for fictional companies in end-of-chapter exercises, problems, and cases.

Chapter 6

Focus Company: Deckers Outdoor Corporation

- Focus and contrast company data updated.
- Content narrowed to three related topics: computing and reporting net sales, receivables valuation, and control of cash.
- Coverage of gross profit percentage moved to Chapter 5.
- Exhibits reorganized to better reflect the chapter flow.
- Coverage of bad debt recoveries increased.
- Coverage of electronic banking increased.
- *New* **GUIDED HELP** feature provides free access to step-by-step video instruction on preparing entries related to bad debts and determining their financial statement effects.
- *New* **CONTINUING CASE** added to the end-of-chapter problems. Students are asked to make summary entries for bad debts and compute the amount to be reported as net sales for Pool Corporation, a public company.
- New and updated real companies, as well as modified accounts, names, and amounts for fictional companies in end-of-chapter exercises, problems, and cases.

Chapter 7

Focus Company: Harley-Davidson, Inc.

- Focus and contrast company data updated.
- Coverage of perpetual versus periodic inventory systems moved to section on cost of goods sold, near the beginning of the chapter.
- *New* **GUIDED HELP** feature provides free access to step-by-step video instruction on computation of goods available for sale and cost of goods sold.
- Exhibits 7.4 and 7.5 revised to make it easier to see the effects of FIFO, LIFO, and average costing methods on the financial statements.
- *New* **GUIDED HELP** feature provides free access to step-by-step video instruction on computing cost of goods sold and ending inventory under FIFO and LIFO costing methods.
- *New* Appendix B added demonstrating the effects of determining FIFO and LIFO cost of goods sold under periodic versus perpetual inventory systems.

- *New* **CONTINUING CASE** added to the end-of-chapter problems. Students are asked to determine the financial statement effects of the choice between FIFO and LIFO when inventory costs are increasing and when they are decreasing for Pool Corporation.
- New and updated real companies, as well as modified accounts, names, and amounts for fictional companies in end-of-chapter exercises, problems, and cases.

Chapter 8

Focus Company: Southwest Airlines

- Focus and contrast company data updated.
- *New* **GUIDED HELP** feature provides free access to step-by-step video instruction on the three cost allocation methods—straight-line method, units-of-production method, and double-declining balance method.
- *New* International Perspective box on component allocation, replacing the International Perspective box on measurement basis for property, plant, and equipment in the previous edition.
- Coverage of intangible assets moved to precede the discussion of natural resources.
- *New* International Perspective box on the differences in accounting for tangible and intangible assets, replacing the International Perspective box on standards in process in the previous edition.
- *New* **CONTINUING CASE** added to the end-of-chapter problems. Students are asked to record the acquisition, depreciation, and disposal of equipment for Pool Corporation, a public company.
- Two demonstration cases: One on accounting for and reporting of property, plant, equipment, and intangible assets; and one on accounting for natural resources.
- New and updated real companies, as well as modified accounts, names, and amounts for fictional companies in end-of-chapter exercises, problems, and cases.

Chapter 9

Focus Company: Starbucks

- Focus and contrast company data updated.
- Quick ratio coverage removed.
- *New* **GUIDED HELP** feature provides free access to step-by-step video instruction on present value.

- *New* **CONTINUING CASE** added to the end-of-chapter problems. Students are asked to record and report liabilities for Pool Corporation, a public company.
- New and updated real companies, as well as modified accounts, names, and amounts for fictional companies in end-of-chapter exercises, problems, and cases.

Chapter 10

Focus Company: AT&T

- *New* focus company **AT&T** and revised coverage related to reporting and interpreting the bonds of **AT&T**.
- *New* **GUIDED HELP** feature provides free access to step-by-step video instruction on calculating the issue price of a bond.
- *New* **CONTINUING CASE** added to the end-of-chapter problems. Students are asked to compute the issue price, interest expense, interest paid, and book value of the bonds for Pool Corporation, a public company.
- New and updated real companies, as well as modified accounts, names, and amounts for fictional companies in end-of-chapter exercises, problems, and cases.

Chapter 11

Focus Company: The Kroger Company

- Focus and contrast company data updated.
- *New* **GUIDED HELP** feature provides free access to step-by-step video instruction on recording transactions related to stock dividends and stock splits.
- New section on the statement of changes in stockholders' equity.
- *New* **CONTINUING CASE** added to the end-of-chapter problems. Students are asked to record the repurchase of shares by Pool Corporation, a public company, as well as all necessary entries related to its dividends.
- New and updated real companies, as well as modified accounts, names, and amounts for fictional companies in end-of-chapter exercises, problems, and cases.

Chapter 12

Focus Company: National Beverage Corporation

- Statement of cash flows coverage moved to Chapter 12.
- Focus and contrast company data updated.
- *New* **GUIDED HELP** feature provides free access to step-by-step video instruction on

preparing the operating section of the statement of cash flows using the indirect method.
- *New* Demonstration Case illustrating preparation of the complete statement of cash flows based on the comparative balance sheet and other related information.
- *New* Chapter Supplement C (and related problem material) illustrates preparation of the statement of cash flows using the complete T-account approach.
- *New* **CONTINUING CASE** involving preparation of the complete statement of cash flows for Pool Corporation, a public company.
- New and updated real companies, as well as modified accounts, names, and amounts for fictional companies in end-of-chapter exercises, problems, and cases.

Chapter 13

Focus Company: The Home Depot

- Financial statement analysis coverage moved to Chapter 13.
- Focus and contrast company data updated.
- *New* **GUIDED HELP** feature provides free access to step-by-step video instruction on the computation of the current ratio, inventory turnover ratio, and price/earnings ratio.
- *New* **CONTINUING CASE** added to the end-of-chapter problems. Students are asked to compute ratios for Pool Corporation, a public company.

Appendix E

Focus Company: The Washington Post Company

- Reporting and interpreting investments in other corporations coverage moved to Appendix E.
- Material organized so that instructors can easily choose which (if any) investments topics they wish to cover.
- Focus and contrast company data updated.
- *New* **GUIDED HELP** feature provides free access to step-by-step video instruction on passive investments accounting.
- *New* Chapter Supplement A on held-to-maturity bonds purchased at other than par value using the amortized cost method.
- *New* **CONTINUING CASE** added to the end-of-chapter problems. Students are asked to prepare journal entries for Pool Corporation, a public company, assuming that it has purchased shares for the trading securities portfolio and the available-for-sale securities portfolio.

LEARN WITH ADAPTIVE

▓▓SMARTBOOK™

Fueled by LearnSmart—the most widely used and intelligent adaptive learning resource—SmartBook is the first and only adaptive reading experience available today.

Distinguishing what a student knows from what they don't, and honing in on concepts they are most likely to forget, SmartBook personalizes content for each student in a continuously adapting reading experience. Reading is no 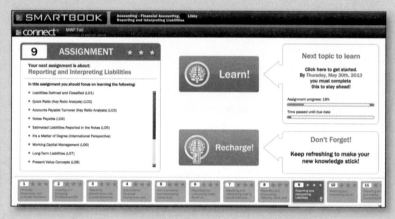 longer a passive and linear experience, but an engaging and dynamic one where students are more likely to master and retain important concepts, coming to class better prepared. Valuable reports provide instructors insight as to how students are progressing through textbook content, and are useful for shaping in-class time or assessment. As a result of the adaptive reading experience found in SmartBook, students are more likely to retain knowledge, stay in class, and get better grades.

This revolutionary technology is available only from McGraw-Hill Education and for hundreds of course areas as part of the LearnSmart Advantage series.

How Does SmartBook Work?

Each SmartBook contains four components: Preview, Read, Practice, and Recharge. Starting with an initial preview of each chapter and key learning objectives, students read the material and are guided to topics that need the most practice based on their responses to a continuously adapting diagnostic. Read and practice continue until SmartBook directs students to recharge important material they are most likely to forget to ensure concept mastery and retention.

TECHNOLOGY

LEARNSMART

LearnSmart is one of the most effective and successful adaptive learning resources available on the market today. More than 2 million students have answered more than 1.3 billion questions in LearnSmart since 2009, making it the most widely used and intelligent adaptive study tool that's proven to strengthen memory recall, keep students in class, and boost grades. Students using LearnSmart are 13% more likely to pass their classes and 35% less likely to dropout.

Distinguishing what students know from what they don't, and honing in on concepts they are most likely to forget, LearnSmart continuously adapts to each student's needs by building an individual learning path so students study smarter and retain more knowledge. Turnkey reports provide valuable insight to instructors, so precious class time can be spent on higher-level concepts and discussion.

This revolutionary learning resource is available only from McGraw-Hill Education, and because LearnSmart is available for most course areas, instructors can recommend it to students in almost every class they teach.

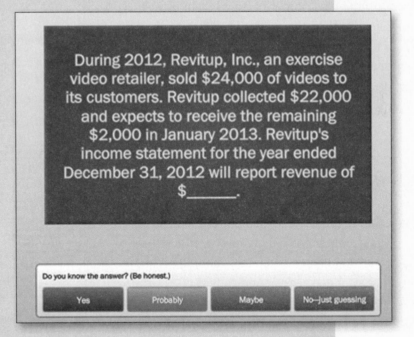

LEADING TECHNOLOGY EXTENDS LEARNING

MCGRAW-HILL *CONNECT ACCOUNTING*

Get *Connect Accounting*. Get Results.

McGraw-Hill *Connect Accounting* is a digital teaching and learning environment that gives students the means to better connect with their coursework, with their instructors, and with the important concepts that they will need to know for success now and in the future. With *Connect Accounting*, instructors can deliver assignments, quizzes, and tests easily online. Students can practice important skills at their own pace and on their own schedule.

Online Assignments

Connect Accounting helps students learn more efficiently by providing feedback and practice material when they need it, where they need it. *Connect Accounting* grades homework automatically and gives immediate feedback on any questions students may have missed.

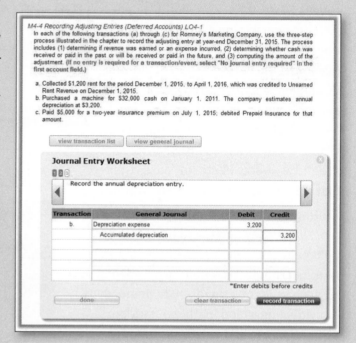

Intelligent Response Technology (IRT)

IRT is a redesigned student interface for our end-of-chapter assessment content. The benefits include improved answer acceptance to reduce students' frustration with formatting issues (such as rounding). Also, select questions have been redesigned to test students' knowledge more fully. They now include tables for students to work through rather than requiring that all calculations be done offline.

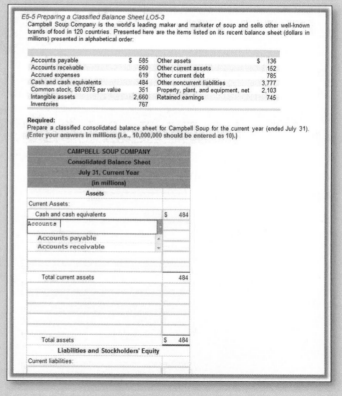

BEYOND THE CLASSROOM

Guided Examples

The Guided Examples in *Connect Accounting* provide a narrated, animated, step-by-step walk-through of select exercises similar to those assigned. These short presentations provide reinforcement when students need it most.

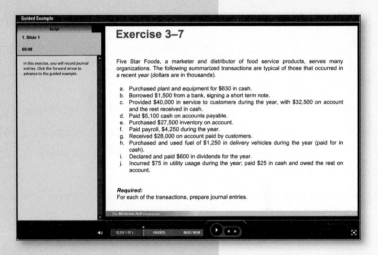

> *As a student I need to interact with course material in order to retain it, and Connect offers a perfect platform for this kind of learning. Rather than just reading through textbooks, Connect has given me the tools to feel engaged in the learning process.*
>
> —Jennah Epstein Kraus, Student, Bunker Hill Community College

Student Library

The *Connect Accounting* Student Library gives students access to additional resources such as recorded lectures, online practice materials, an eBook, and more.

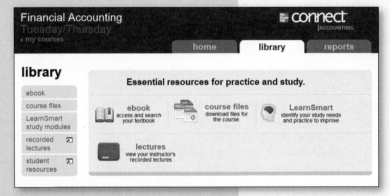

MCGRAW-HILL *CONNECT ACCOUNTING* FEATURES

Connect Accounting offers a number of powerful tools and features to make managing assignments easier, so faculty can spend more time teaching.

Simple Assignment Management and Smart Grading

With *Connect Accounting*, creating assignments is easier than ever, so instructors can spend more time teaching and less time managing.

- Create and deliver assignments easily with selectable end-of-chapter questions and Test Bank items.
- Go paperless with the eBook and online submission and grading of student assignments.
- Have assignments scored automatically, giving students immediate feedback on their work and side-by-side comparisons with correct answers.
- Access and review each response; manually change grades or leave comments for students to review.
- Reinforce classroom concepts with practice tests and instant quizzes.

Student Reporting

Connect Accounting keeps instructors informed about how each student, section, and class is performing, allowing for more productive use of lecture and office hours. The progress-tracking function enables you to:

- View scored work immediately and track individual or group performance with assignment and grade reports.
- Access an instant view of student or class performance relative to learning objectives.
- Collect data and generate reports required by many accreditation organizations, such as AACSB and AICPA.

Instructor Library

The *Connect Accounting* Instructor Library is a repository for additional resources to improve student engagement in and out of class. You can select and use any asset that enhances your lecture. The *Connect Accounting* Instructor Library includes access to the eBook version of the text, videos, slide presentations, Solutions Manual, Instructor's Manual, and Test Bank. The *Connect Accounting* Instructor Library also allows you to upload your own files.

MCGRAW-HILL *CONNECT PLUS ACCOUNTING*

 McGraw-Hill reinvents the text-book learning experience for the modern student with *Connect Plus Accounting*. A seamless integration of an eBook and *Connect Accounting*, *Connect Plus Accounting* provides all of the *Connect Accounting* features plus the following:

- An integrated, media-rich eBook, allowing for anytime, anywhere access to the textbook.
- Media-rich capabilities like embedded audio/visual presentations, highlighting, and sharing notes.
- Dynamic links between the problems or questions you assign to your students and the location in the eBook where that concept is covered.
- A powerful search function to pinpoint key concepts for review.

In short, *Connect Plus Accounting* offers students powerful tools and features that optimize their time and energy, enabling them to focus on learning.

For more information about *Connect Plus Accounting*, go to www.mcgrawhillconnect.com, or contact your local McGraw-Hill sales representative.

TEGRITY CAMPUS: LECTURES 24/7

Tegrity Campus is a service that makes class time available 24/7 by automatically capturing every lecture. With a simple one-click start-and-stop process, you capture all computer screens and corresponding audio in a format that is easily searchable, frame by frame. Students can replay any part of any class with easy-to-use browser-based viewing on a PC, Mac, iPod, or other mobile device.

Educators know that the more students can see, hear, and experience class resources, the better they learn. In fact, studies prove it. Tegrity Campus's unique search feature helps students efficiently find what they need, when they need it, across an entire semester of class recordings. Help turn your students' study time into learning moments immediately supported by your lecture. With Tegrity Campus, you also increase intent listening and class participation by easing students' concerns about note-taking. Tegrity Campus will make it more likely you will see students' faces, not the tops of their heads.

To learn more about Tegrity, watch a 2-minute Flash demo at http://tegritycampus.mhhe.com.

> *Students like the flexibility that Connect offers . . . They can complete their work and catch up on lectures anytime and anywhere.*
>
> —Professor Lisa McKinney, M.T.A., CPA, University of Alabama

MCGRAW-HILL CAMPUS

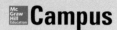 McGraw-Hill Campus™ is a new one-stop teaching and learning experience available to users of any learning management system. This institutional service allows faculty and students to enjoy single sign-on (SSO) access to all McGraw-Hill Higher Education materials, including the award-winning McGraw-Hill *Connect* platform, directly from within the institution's website. McGraw-Hill Campus provides faculty with instant access to teaching materials (e.g., eTextbooks, Test Banks, PowerPoint slides, animations, and learning objects), allowing them to browse, search, and use any ancillary content in our vast library. Students enjoy SSO access to a variety of free products (e.g., quizzes, flash cards, and presentations) and subscription-based products (e.g., McGraw-Hill *Connect*). With McGraw-Hill Campus, faculty and students will never need to create another account to access McGraw-Hill products and services.

Custom Publishing through Create

McGraw-Hill Create™ is a new, self-service website that allows instructors to create custom course materials by drawing upon McGraw-Hill's comprehensive, cross-disciplinary content. Instructors can add their own content quickly and easily and tap into other rights-secured third party sources as well, then arrange the content in a way that makes the most sense for their course. Instructors can even personalize their book with the course name and information and choose the best format for their students—color print, black-and-white print, or an eBook.

Through Create, instructors can

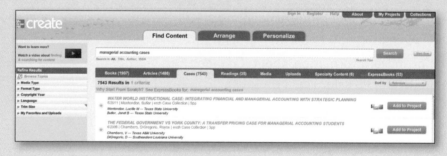

- Select and arrange the content in a way that makes the most sense for their course.
- Combine material from different sources and even upload their own content.
- Choose the best format for their students—print or eBook.
- Edit and update their course materials as often as they'd like.

Begin creating now at www.mcgrawhillcreate.com.

COURSESMART

 ### Learn Smart. Choose Smart.
CourseSmart is a way for faculty to find and review eTextbooks. It's also a great option for students who are interested in accessing their course materials digitally and saving money.

CourseSmart offers thousands of the most commonly adopted textbooks across hundreds of courses from a wide variety of higher education publishers. It is the only place for faculty to review and compare the full text of a textbook online, providing immediate access without the environmental impact of requesting a print exam copy.

With the CourseSmart eTextbook, students can save up to 45 percent off the cost of a print book, reduce their impact on the environment, and access powerful web tools for learning. CourseSmart is an online eTextbook, which means users access and view their textbook online when connected to the Internet. Students can also print sections of the book for maximum portability. CourseSmart eTextbooks are available in one standard online reader with full text search, notes and highlighting, and e-mail tools for sharing notes between classmates. For more information on CourseSmart, go to www.coursesmart.com.

Access to the instructor's key text ancillary materials is at your fingertips. You can find all of the instructor ancillaries on McGraw-Hill *Connect Accounting* and on the password-protected instructor website, including: Presentation Slides, Solutions Manual, Test Bank and Computerized Test Bank, Instructor's Resource Manual, Solutions to Excel Templates, and text exhibits.

☑ **Presentation Slides**

Prepared by Susan Galbreath at David Lipscomb University, Jon Booker and Charles Caldwell at Tennessee Technological University, and Cynthia Rooney, University of New Mexico–Los Alamos. Completely customized PowerPoint presentations for use in your classroom.

☑ **Solutions Manual**

Prepared by Robert Libby, Patricia Libby, and Daniel Short. Provides solutions to end-of-chapter questions, mini-exercises, exercises, problems, alternate problems, and cases.

☑ **Test Bank**

Prepared by Gina Lord at Santa Rosa College. This comprehensive test bank includes more than 1,500 true/false, multiple-choice, and matching questions and problems, each tagged by learning objective, topic area, difficulty level, and AACSB, Bloom's, and AICPA categories.

☑ **Instructor's Resource Manual**

Prepared by Jeannie Folk at College of DuPage. Includes overviews of chapter topics and resources to help you prepare for class. It describes the ready-to-use resources that support the text and presents other enrichment resources, including innovative active learning exercises that you can use in class. This manual is a must-read for any instructor interested in improving teaching evaluations.

☑ **MBA Companion to Financial Accounting**

Available in Create. Prepared by Frank Hodge of University of Washington, the MBA Companion mirrors the format of the text to further explore three important long-term liabilities: leases, taxes, and pensions. It uses UNDER ARMOUR's current disclosures in discussing these topics and provides enough detail to allow MBA students to read, discuss, and actively make decisions related to these topics. The accompanying exercises, problems, and cases allow students to test their understanding of the material.

✓ Instructor Excel Templates

Solutions to the student Excel Templates used to solve selected end-of-chapter exercises and problems. These assignments are designated by the Excel icon.

✓ EZ Test Online

McGraw-Hill's EZ Test Online is a flexible and easy-to-use electronic testing program that allows instructors to create tests from book-specific items. EZ Test Online accommodates a wide range of question types and allows instructors to add their own questions. Multiple versions of the test can be created and any test can be exported for use with course management systems such as BlackBoard/WebCT. EZ Test Online gives instructors a place to easily administer EZ Test–created exams and quizzes online. The program is available for Windows and Macintosh environments.

ASSURANCE OF LEARNING READY

Many educational institutions today are focused on the notion of *assurance of learning*, an important element of some accreditation standards. *Financial Accounting* is designed specifically to support your assurance of learning initiatives with a simple, yet powerful solution.

Each test bank question for *Financial Accounting* maps to a specific chapter learning outcome/objective listed in the text. You can use our test bank software, EZ Test and EZ Test Online, or *Connect Accounting* to easily query for learning outcomes/objectives that directly relate to the learning objectives for your course. You can then use the reporting features of EZ Test or *Connect Accounting* to aggregate student results in similar fashion, making the collection and presentation of assurance of learning data simple and easy.

AACSB STATEMENT

The McGraw-Hill Companies is a proud corporate member of AACSB International. Understanding the importance and value of AACSB accreditation, *Financial Accounting* recognizes the curricula guidelines detailed in the AACSB standards for business accreditation by connecting selected questions in the test bank to the six general knowledge and skill guidelines in the AACSB standards.

The statements contained in *Financial Accounting* are provided only as a guide for the users of this textbook. The AACSB leaves content coverage and assessment within the purview of individual schools, the mission of the school, and the faculty. While *Financial Accounting* and the teaching package make no claim of any specific AACSB qualification or evaluation, we have labeled selected questions within the Test Bank to accompany *Financial Accounting* according to the six general knowledge and skill areas.

☑ Online Learning Center

www.mhhe.com/libby8e

Financial Accounting's Online Learning Center offers students additional study resources, including Self-Study quizzes, B set exercises, PowerPoint slides, and Excel templates tied to the end-of-chapter material, all organized by chapter.

☑ Student PowerPoint Presentations

Selected presentation slides reproduced in student version. Presentation slides are located on the text's website.

☑ Check Figures

Prepared by LuAnn Bean at Florida Institute of Technology. This resource provides answers to select problems and cases. Check Figures are located on the text's Online Learning Center.

☑ Study Guide Available in Create

An outstanding learning tool, this guide gives students a deeper understanding of the course material and reinforces, step by step, what they are learning in the main text.

☑ Working Papers Available in Create

Working Papers are provided to assist students in solving complex text assignments. The Working Papers are available both in print and as Excel spreadsheets.

☑ Excel Templates

Available on the text website www.mhhe.com/libby8e. These templates are tied to selected end-of-chapter material and are available on the text website. These assignments are designated by the Excel icon.

☑ *Understanding Corporate Annual Reports,* by William R. Pasewark

Available in Create

This financial analysis project emphasizes the interpretation and analysis of financial statements. It contains extensive instructions for obtaining an annual report from a publicly traded corporation. Students gain hands-on experience working with annual reports and are then better prepared to understand financial accounting concepts and their use in the business world.

☑ McGraw-Hill Customer Experience Group Contact Information

At McGraw-Hill, we understand that getting the most from new technology can be challenging. That's why our services don't stop after you purchase our products. You can contact our Product Specialists 24 hours a day to get product training online. Or you can search our knowledge bank of Frequently Asked Questions on our support website. For Customer Support, call 800-331-5094, or visit www.mhhe.com/support. One of our Technical Support Analysts will be able to assist you in a timely fashion.

ACKNOWLEDGMENTS

Many dedicated instructors have devoted their time and effort to help us make each edition better. We would like to acknowledge and thank all of our colleagues who have helped guide our development decisions for this and previous editions. This text would not be the success it is without the help of all of you.

Board of Reviewers

Dawn Addington, *Central New Mexico Community College*
Ajay Adhikari, *American University*
Gary Adna Ames, *Brigham Young University*
Peter Aghimien, *Indiana University—South Bend*
Nas Ahadiat, *California Polytechnic University*
John Ahern, *DePaul University*
Pervaiz Alam, *Kent State University*
Robert Allen, *University of Utah—Salt Lake City*
Vern Allen, *Central Florida Community College*
Bridget Anakwe, *Plattsburgh State University of New York*
Brenda Anderson, *Boston University*
Joseph Antenucci, *Youngstown State University*
Frank Aquilino, *Montclair State University*
Liz Arnold, *The Citadel*
Florence Atiase, *University of Texas—Austin*
Jane Baird, *Minnesota State University Mankato*
Kashi R. Balachandran, *New York University*
Laurel Barfitt, *Delta State University*
Melody Barta, *Evergreen College*
Ira W. Bates, *Florida A&M University*
Deborah Beard, *Southeast Missouri State University*
Daisy Beck, *Louisiana State University*
John Bedient, *Albion College*
S. Douglas Beets, *Wake Forest University*
Michael Bitter, *Stetson University*
Eric Blazer, *Millersville University*
Michael G. Booth, *Cabrillo College*
Scott Boylan, *Washington & Lee University*
Mark Bradshaw, *Harvard Business School*
Christopher Brandon, *Indiana University—Purdue University Columbus*
Rodger Brannan, *University of Minnesota Duluth*
Allison Brock, *Imperial Valley College*
Rada Brooks, *University of California at Berkeley*
Nina Brown, *Tarrant County College*
Amy Browning, *Ivy Technical Community College*
Helen Brubeck, *San Jose State University*
Terri Brunsdon, *The University of Akron*
Marci Butterfield, *University of Utah*
Kay Carnes, *Gonzaga University*
Nancy Cassidy, *Texas A&M University*
Michael Cathey, *The George Washington University*
Kam Chan, *Pace University*
Chiaho Chang, *Montclair State University*
Gretchen Charrier, *University of Texas—Austin*
Agnes Cheng, *University of Houston*
Antoinette Clegg, *Palm Beach Community College*
Anne Clem, *Iowa State University*

Judy Colwell, *Northern Oklahoma College*
Elizabeth Conner, *University of Colorado—Denver*
Teresa Conover, *University of North Texas*
Scott Creech, *Johnston Community College*
Marcia Croteau, *University of Maryland—Baltimore*
Sue Cullers, *Tarleton State University*
Dori Danko, *Grand Valley State University*
Betty David, *Francis Marion University*
Harold Davis, *Southeastern Louisiana University*
Paquita Davis-Friday, *Bernard M. Baruch College*
Marinus DeBruine, *Grand Valley State University*
Mark DeFond, *University of Southern California*
Elizabeth Demers, *University of Rochester*
Bettye Desselle, *Prairie View A&M University*
Allan Drebin, *Northwestern University*
Carolyn Dreher, *Southern Methodist University*
Sheri Erickson, *Minnesota State University Moorehead*
Harlan Etheridge, *University of Louisiana—Lafayette*
Thomas Finnegan, *University of Illinois at Urbana—Champaign*
Richard Fleischman, *John Carroll University*
Virginia Fullwood, *Texas A&M University—Commerce*
Cheryl Furbee, *Cabrillo College*
Mohamed Gaber, *SUNY Plattsburgh*
Joseph Galante, *Millersville University of Pennsylvania*
Carolyn Galantine, *Pepperdine University*
Andy Garcia, *Bowling Green State University*
David Gelb, *Seton Hall University*
Lisa Gillespie, *Loyola University, Chicago*
Giorgio Gotti, *University of Massachusetts—Boston*
Anthony Greig, *Purdue University*
A. Kay Guess, *St. Edward's University*
Jeffrey Haber, *Iona College*
Leon Hanouille, *Syracuse University*
Russell Hardin, *Pittsburgh State University*
Sheila Hardy, *Lafayette College*
Betty Harper, *Middle Tennessee State*
Bob Hartman, *University of Iowa*
Syed Hasan, *George Mason University*
Carla Hayn, *University of California—Los Angeles*
Haihong He, *California State University—Los Angeles*
Kenneth R. Henry, *Florida International University*
Siriyama Kanthi Herath, *Clark Atlanta University*
Ann Ownby Hicks, *North Park University*
Lori Holder-Webb, *University of Wisconsin*
Pamela Hopcroft, *Florida Community College*
Merle W. Hopkins, *University of Southern California*
Paul Hribar, *University of Iowa*

Courtland Huber, *University of Texas—Austin*
Dawn Hukai, *University of Wisconsin—River Falls*
Bob Hurt, *California State Polytechnic University Pomona*
Carol Hutchinson, *AB Tech*
Constance M. Hylton, *George Mason University*
Marc Hyman, *University of California—Berkeley*
Laura Ilcisin, *University of Nebraska—Omaha*
Norma Jacobs, *Austin Community College*
Scott Jerris, *San Francisco State University*
Carol Johnson, *Oklahoma State University*
Eric Johnson, *Indiana University—Purdue University Columbus*
Shondra Johnson, *Bradley University*
Christopher Jones, *The George Washington University*
Matthew Josefy, *Texas A&M University*
John Karayan, *California State Polytechnic University Pomona*
Robert Kasmir, *The George Washington University*
Beth Kern, *Indiana University—South Bend*
Irene Kim, *George Washington University*
Janet Kimbrell, *Oklahoma State University*
Janice Klimek, *University of Central Missouri*
Trevor Knox, *Muhlenberg College*
Dennis Lee Kovach, *Community College of Allegheny*
Tammy Kowalczyk, *Western Washington University*
Charles Ladd, *University of St. Thomas*
Steven J. LaFave, *Augsburg College*
Christy Land, *Catawba Valley Community College*
Maria Leach, *Auburn University at Montgomery*
Terry Lease, *Sonoma State*
Marc Lebow, *Christopher Newport University*
Deborah Lee, *Northeastern State University*
Patsy Lee, *University of North Texas*
Christy Lefevers-Land, *Catawba Valley Community College*
Seth Levine, *University of Miami*
Elliott Levy, *Bentley University*
Phil Lewis, *Eastern Michigan University*
June Li, *University of Wisconsin—River Falls*
Ling Lin, *University of Massachusetts—Dartmouth*
Daniel Litt, *University of California—Los Angeles*
Chao-Shin Liu, *University of Notre Dame*
Joshua Livnat, *New York University*
Lawrence Logan, *University of Massachusetts—Dartmouth*
Patricia Lopez, *Valencia Community College*
Barbara Lougee, *University of San Diego*

Joseph Lupino, *St. Mary's College of California*
Luann Lynch, *University of Virginia*
Lori Mason-Olson, *University of Northern Iowa*
Josephine Mathias, *Mercer County Community College*
Larry McCabe, *Muhlenberg College*
Nick McGaughey, *San Jose State University*
Florence McGovern, *Bergen Community College*
Noel McKeon, *Florida Community College—Jacksonville*
Allison McLeod, *University of North Texas*
Michael G. McMillan, *Johns Hopkins University*
L. Kevin McNelis, *New Mexico State University*
Tammy Metzke, *Milwaukee Area Technical College*
Michael J. Meyer, *University of Notre Dame*
Paulette Miller, *Collin County Community College*
Tim Mills, *Eastern Illinois University*
Marilyn Misch, *Pepperdine University*
Birendra Mishra, *University of California at Riverside*
Earl Mitchell, *Santa Ana College*
Dennis P. Moore, *Worcester State College*
Haim Mozes, *Fordham University*
Brian Nagle, *Duquesne University*
Ramesh Narasimhan, *Montclair State University*
Presha Neidermeyer, *Union College*
Samir Nissan, *California Sate University Chico*
Tom Nunamaker, *Washington State University*
Peggy O'Kelly, *Northeastern University*
John O'Shaughnessy, *San Francisco State University*
Janet L. O'Tousa, *University of Notre Dame*
Olga Quintanta, *University of Miami*
Donald Pagach, *North Carolina State—Raleigh*
Sharon Parrish, *Kentucky State University*
Catherine Plante, *University of New Hampshire*
Kay Poston, *University of Indianapolis*
Grace Pownall, *Emory University*
Rama Ramamurthy, *College of William & Mary*
Charles Ransom, *Oklahoma State University*
Keith Richardson, *Bellarmine University*
Laura Rickett, *Kent State University*
Brandi Roberts, *Southeastern Louisiana University*
Joanne Rockness, *University of North Carolina—Wilmington*
Lawrence Roman, *Cuyahoga Community College*
John Rossi III, *Moravian College*
John Rude, *Bloomsburg University*
Joan Ryan, *Clackamas Community College*
Karen Salmela, *University of Minnesota—Duluth*
Angela Sandberg, *Jacksonville State University*
Amy Santos, *Manatee Community College*
Andrew Schmidt, *Columbia University*
Richard Schroeder, *University of North Carolina—Charlotte*

Joann Segovia, *Minnesota State University Moorhead*
Cindy Seipel, *New Mexico State University*
Ann Selk, *University of Wisconsin—Green Bay*
Kathleen Sevigny, *Bridgewater State College*
Howard Shapiro, *Eastern Washington University*
Warren Smock, *Ivy Technical Community College—Lafayette*
Billy Soo, *Boston College*
Sri Sridhanen, *Northwestern University*
David Stein, *Metropolitan State University*
Phillip Stocken, *Dartmouth College*
Dennis Stovall, *Grand Valley State University*
Joel Strong, *St. Cloud State University*
Gina Sturgill, *Concord College*
Susan Sullivan, *University of Massachusetts—Dartmouth*
Martin Taylor, *University of Texas—Arlington*
Mack Tennyson, *College of Charleston*
Peter Theuri, *Northern Kentucky University*
W. Stewart Thomas, *University of North Carolina—Pembroke*
Lynda Thompson, *Massasoit Community College*
Theresa Tiggeman, *University of the Incarnate Word*
Theodore Tully, *DeVry University*
Lana Tuss, *Chemeketa Community College*
Michael Ulinski, *Pace University*
Ingrid Ulstad, *University of Wisconsin—Eau Claire*
Marcia Veit, *University of Central Florida*
Charles Wain, *Babson College*
Charles Wasley, *University of Rochester*
Daniel Weddington, *Ohio University—Zanesville*
David Weiner, *University of San Francisco*
Patti Weiss, *John Carroll University*
Cheryl Westen, *Western Illinois University*
David Wiest, *Washington and Lee University*
Patrick Wilkie, *University of Virginia*
Jefferson Williams, *University of Michigan*
Wendy Wilson, *Southern Methodist University*
Peter Woodlock, *Youngstown State University*
Ron Woods, *North Seattle Community College*
Darryl Woolley, *University of Idaho*
Michael Yampuler, *University of Houston*
Kathryn Yarbrough, *University of North Carolina—Charlotte*
Zhang (May) Yue, *Northeastern University*
Xiao-Jun Zhang, *University of California at Berkeley*

We are grateful to the following individuals who helped develop, critique, and shape the extensive ancillary package: Jeannie Folk, College of DuPage; LuAnn Bean, Florida Institute of Technology; Susan Galbreath, David Lipscomb University; Jon Booker, Tennessee Technological University; Charles Caldwell, Tennessee Technological University; Cynthia Rooney, University of New Mexico—Los Alamos; Helen Roybark, Radford University; Catherine Plante, University of New Hampshire; Sandra Callaghan, Texas Christian University; Nancy Lynch, West Virginia University; Gina Lord, Santa Rosa College; Ilene Leopold Persoff, CW Post Campus–Long Island University; Mark McCarthy, East Carolina University; Kathrine Glass, Indiana University; Kevin Smith, Utah Valley University; Debbie Luna, El Paso Community College; Frank Hodge, University of Washington; and Jack Terry, ComSource Associates, Inc.

We also have received invaluable input and support through the years from present and former colleagues and students. We also appreciate the additional comments, suggestions, and support of our students and our colleagues at Cornell University, Ithaca College, and Texas Christian University.

Last, we applaud the extraordinary efforts of a talented group of individuals at McGraw-Hill who made all of this come together. We would especially like to thank Tim Vertovec, our director; James Heine, our executive brand manager; Rebecca Mann, our development editor; Christina Sanders, our managing development editor; Julie Hankins, our digital development editor; Kathleen Klehr, our senior marketing manager; Diane Nowacyzk, our senior project manager; Cara Hawthorne, Pam Verros, and Keith McPherson, our designers; Michael McCormick, our buyer; Daryl Horrocks, our lead media product manager; Jeremy Cheshareck, our senior content licensing specialist; and David Tietz, our photo researcher.

Robert Libby
Patricia A. Libby
Daniel G. Short

TO OUR STUDENT READERS

THIS BOOK IS AIMED AT TWO GROUPS OF READERS:

Future managers, who will need to interpret and use financial statement information in business decisions.

Future accountants, who will prepare financial statements for those managers.

Future managers need a firm basis for using financial statement information in their careers in marketing, finance, banking, manufacturing, human resources, sales, information systems, or other areas of management. Future accountants need a solid foundation for further professional study.

Both managers and accountants must understand how to *use financial statements in real business decisions* to perform their duties successfully. The best way to learn to do this is to study accounting in real business contexts. This is the key idea behind our *focus company approach,* which we introduce in the first chapter and which integrates each chapter's material around a focus company, its decisions, and its financial statements. The focus companies are drawn from 12 different industries, providing you with a broad range of experience with realistic business and financial accounting practices. In each chapter, *you will actually work with these real companies' statements* and those of additional contrast companies.

When you complete this book, you will be able to read and understand financial statements of real companies. We help you achieve this goal by:

- Selecting learning objectives and content based on the way that seasoned managers use financial statements in modern businesses. *We emphasize the topics that count.*

- Recognizing that students using this book have no previous exposure to accounting and financial statements and often little exposure to the business world. We take you through the financial statements three times at increasing levels of detail (in Chapter 1, Chapters 2 through 5, and Chapters 6 through 13). This is the secret to our "*building block approach.*"

- Helping you "*learn how to learn*" by teaching efficient and effective approaches for learning the material. Keep these learning hints in mind as you work your way through each chapter.

- Providing regular feedback in Self-Study Quizzes, which occur throughout each chapter. *Complete the quizzes before you move on.* Then check your answers against the solution provided in the footnote. If you are still unclear about any of the answers, you should refer back to the chapter material preceding the quiz before moving on.

- Highlighting the *Key Terms* in **bold print** and repeating their definitions in the margins. You should pay special attention to the definitions of these terms and review them at the end of the chapter. A handy glossary is provided at the end of the book; consult it if you forget the meaning of an important term.

- Introducing the *Key Financial Ratios* used to assess different elements of financial performance at the same time you are learning how to measure and report those elements. These will show you what kinds of accounting information managers use and how they interpret it.

At the end of each chapter you can test what you have learned by working the Demonstration Cases. *Working problems is one of the keys to learning accounting.* Good luck in your first accounting course.

Bob Libby

Pat Libby

Daniel G. Short

CONTENTS **IN BRIEF**

Chapter 3

Operating Decisions and the Accounting System   98

Chapter 4

Adjustments, Financial Statements, and the Quality of Earnings   160

Chapter 6

Reporting and Interpreting Sales Revenue, Receivables, and Cash   276

Chapter 7

Reporting and Interpreting Cost of Goods Sold and Inventory   326

Chapter 8

Reporting and Interpreting Property, Plant, and Equipment; Intangibles; and Natural Resources   380

Chapter 9

Reporting and Interpreting Liabilities   450

Chapter 10

Reporting and Interpreting Bonds   498

Chapter 11

Reporting and Interpreting Owners' Equity   544

Chapter 12

Statement of Cash Flows   588

Chapter 13

Analyzing Financial Statements   642

EIGHTH EDITION

Financial Accounting

Financial Statements and Business Decisions

L e-Nature's Inc. designed its business strategy to ride the growing wave of interest in non-carbonated beverages. And its financial statements reported growth in sales from $156 to $275 million in just three years. How did this small family-run business compete with the likes of Coke and Pepsi in this growing market? The business press suggested the first key to its success was manufacturing a broad range of products that fit into the fastest growing "healthy" segments: flavored waters, teas, and fruit drinks. Founder and CEO Gregory Podlucky said that an obsessive drive for quality and efficiency was just as critical. Matching customers' concerns for the environment and healthy living, Le-Nature's was praised as one of the first companies to switch to environmentally friendlier PET plastic bottles and to employ safe in-bottle pasteurization. Its 21st-century manufacturing operation in Latrobe, Pennsylvania, produced everything that goes into its products, from the injection-molded PET bottles to the final packaging. Complete control over the whole process assures quality and provides the flexibility to respond quickly to changes in customers' demands. When convenience stores moved to larger-sized drinks or school cafeterias switched from carbonated beverages to healthier drinks, Le-Nature's could change its production to meet the customers' needs. In August, the company opened a second new state-of-the-art manufacturing facility in Arizona to meet the apparent growing demand.

But here is the twist: Just three short months later, investigators discovered that Le-Nature's phenomenal sales growth was more fiction than fact. How could this seeming success story portrayed in the financial statements really be one of the most remarkable frauds in history?

Chapter 1 concentrates on the key financial statements that businesspeople rely upon when they evaluate a company's performance, and the importance of the accuracy of financial statements in making our economic system work. We will discuss these issues in the context of Le-Nature's rise and fall.

Accounting knowledge will be valuable to you only if you can apply it in the real world. Learning is also easier when it takes place in real contexts. So at the beginning of each chapter we always provide some background about the business that will provide the context for the chapter discussion.

Learning Objectives

After studying this chapter, you should be able to:

1-1 Recognize the information conveyed in each of the four basic financial statements and the way that it is used by different decision makers (investors, creditors, and managers). p. 4

1-2 Identify the role of generally accepted accounting principles (GAAP) in determining financial statement content and how companies ensure the accuracy of their financial statements. p. 16

UNDERSTANDING THE BUSINESS

Le-Nature's Inc., our focus company for this chapter, was founded by Gregory Podlucky and his brother Jonathan, who initially were the sole owners or **stockholders** of the company. They were also the managers of the company. Using expertise gained working at their parents' brewery (Stoney's Beer), the brothers were early believers in the trend toward healthier noncarbonated beverages. Like most entrepreneurs, their growth ambitions quickly outpaced their own financial resources. So they turned to banks, including Wells Fargo Bank and other lenders, to finance additional manufacturing facilities and equipment. Different units of Wells Fargo continued to arrange lending to Le-Nature's as the need arose, becoming its largest lender or **creditor.** Creditors make money on the loans by charging **interest.** The Podluckys also convinced others to buy stock in Le-Nature's. These individuals became part owners or stockholders along with the Podluckys. They hoped to receive a portion of what the company earned in the form of cash payments called **dividends** and to eventually sell their share of the company at a higher price than they paid. Creditors are more willing to lend and stock prices usually rise when creditors and investors expect the company to do well in the future. Both groups often judge future performance based on information in the company's financial statements.

The Accounting System

Managers (often called **internal decision makers**) need information about the company's business activities to manage the operating, investing, and financing activities of the firm. Stockholders and creditors (often called **external decision makers**) need information about these same business activities to assess whether

The Accounting System
and Decision Makers

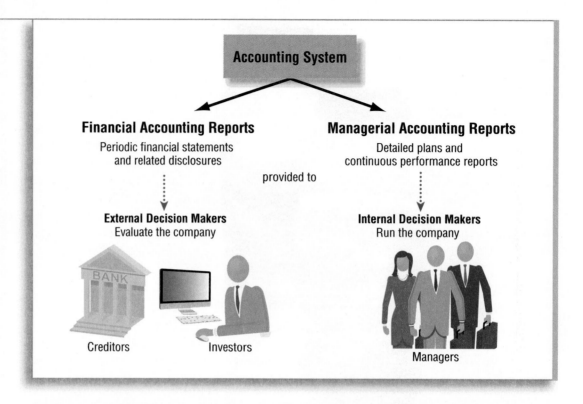

ACCOUNTING is a system that
collects and processes (analyzes,
measures, and records) financial
information about an organization
and reports that information to
decision makers.

LEARNING OBJECTIVE 1-1

Recognize the information
conveyed in each of the four
basic financial statements
and the way that it is used
by different decision makers
(investors, creditors, and
managers).

the company will be able to pay back its debts with interest and pay dividends. All businesses
must have an **accounting system** that collects and processes financial information about an
organization's business activities and reports that information to decision makers. Le-Nature's
business activities included:

- **Financing Activities:** borrowing or paying back money to lenders and receiving additional
  funds from stockholders or paying them dividends.
- **Investing Activities:** buying or selling items such as plant and equipment used in the production of beverages.
- **Operating Activities:** the day-to-day process of purchasing raw tea and other ingredients
  from suppliers, manufacturing beverages, delivering them to customers, collecting cash
  from customers, and paying suppliers.

Exhibit 1.1 outlines the two parts of the accounting system. Internal managers typically
require continuous, detailed information because they must plan and manage the day-to-day
operations of the organization. Developing accounting information for internal decision makers, called managerial or **management accounting,** is the subject of a separate accounting
course. The focus of this text is accounting for external decision makers, called **financial
accounting,** and the four basic financial statements and related disclosures that are periodically produced by that system.

Why Study Financial Accounting?

No matter what your business career goals, you can't get away from financial accounting. You
may want to work for an investment firm, a bank, or an accounting firm that would be involved
in the financing of companies like Le-Nature's. We will focus much of our discussion on the
perspectives of **investors, creditors,** and **preparers** of financial statements. However, you
might not be aware that managers within the firm also make direct use of financial statements. For example, **marketing managers** and **credit managers** use customers' financial
statements to decide whether to extend credit to their customers. **Supply chain managers**

analyze suppliers' financial statements to see whether the suppliers have the resources to meet demand and invest in future development. Both the employees' unions and company **human resource managers** use financial statements as a basis for contract negotiations over pay rates. Financial statement figures even serve as a basis for calculating employee bonuses. Regardless of the functional area of management in which you are employed, you will use financial statement data.

We begin with a brief but comprehensive overview of the information reported in the four basic financial statements and the people and organizations involved in their preparation and use. This overview provides a context in which you can learn the more detailed material presented in the chapters that follow. Then we will discuss the parties that are responsible for the accuracy of financial statements as well as the consequences of misstated financial statements. Le-Nature's stockholders and creditors used its financial statements to learn more about the company before making their investment and lending decisions. In doing so, they assumed that the statements accurately represented Le-Nature's financial condition.

Your Goals for Chapter 1

To understand the way in which creditors and stockholders used Le-Nature's financial statements, we must first understand what specific information is presented in the four basic financial statements for a company such as Le-Nature's. **PLEASE NOTE: Rather than trying to memorize the definitions of every term used in this chapter, try to focus your attention on learning the general content, structure, and use of the statements. Specifically:**

- **Content:** the categories of items (often called **elements**) reported on each of the four statements.
- **Structure:** the equation that shows how the elements within the statement are organized and related.
- **Use:** how the information is used in stockholders' or creditors' decisions.

The Pause for Feedback–Self-Study Quizzes at key points in the chapter will help you assess whether you have reached these goals. Remember that since this chapter is an overview, each concept discussed here will be discussed again in Chapters 2 through 5.

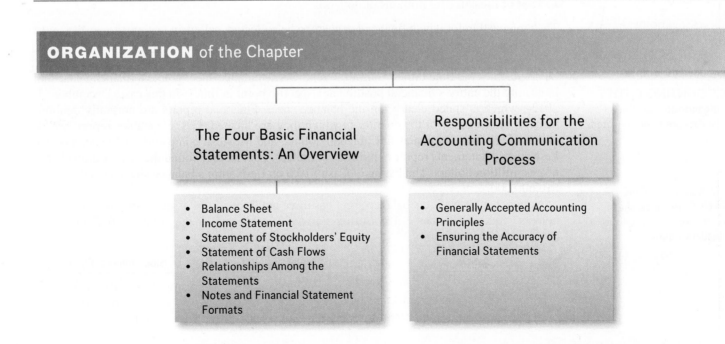

ORGANIZATION of the Chapter

The Four Basic Financial Statements: An Overview

- Balance Sheet
- Income Statement
- Statement of Stockholders' Equity
- Statement of Cash Flows
- Relationships Among the Statements
- Notes and Financial Statement Formats

Responsibilities for the Accounting Communication Process

- Generally Accepted Accounting Principles
- Ensuring the Accuracy of Financial Statements

THE FOUR BASIC FINANCIAL STATEMENTS: AN OVERVIEW

Four financial statements are normally prepared by profit-making organizations for use by investors, creditors, and other external decision makers.

1. On its **balance sheet,** Le-Nature's reports the economic resources it owns and the sources of financing for those resources.

2. On its **income statement,** Le-Nature's reports its ability to sell goods for more than their cost to produce and sell.

3. On its **statement of stockholders' equity,** Le-Nature's reports additional contributions or payments to investors and the amount of income the company reinvested for future growth.

4. On its **statement of cash flows,** Le-Nature's reports its ability to generate cash and how it was used.

The four basic statements can be prepared at any point in time (such as the end of the year, quarter, or month) and can apply to any time span (such as one year, one quarter, or one month). Like most companies, Le-Nature's prepared financial statements for external users (investors and creditors) at the end of each quarter (known as **quarterly reports**) and at the end of the year (known as **annual reports**).

The Balance Sheet

The purpose of the balance sheet is to report the financial position (amount of assets, liabilities, and stockholders' equity) of an accounting entity at a particular point in time. We can learn a great deal about what the balance sheet reports just by reading the statement from the top. The balance sheet Le-Nature's Inc. presented to creditors and stockholders is shown in Exhibit 1.2.

Structure

Notice that the **heading** specifically identifies four significant items related to the statement:

1. **Name of the entity,** Le-Nature's Inc.

2. **Title of the statement,** Balance Sheet.

3. **Specific date of the statement,** At December 31, 2012.

4. **Unit of measure** (in millions of dollars).

The organization for which financial data are to be collected, called an accounting entity, must be precisely defined. On the balance sheet, the business entity itself, not the business owners, is viewed as owning the resources it uses and as owing its debts. The heading of each statement indicates the time dimension of the report. The balance sheet is like a financial snapshot indicating the entity's financial position at a specific point in time—in this case, December 31, 2012—which is stated clearly on the balance sheet. Financial reports are normally denominated in the currency of the country in which they are located. U.S. companies report in U.S. dollars, Canadian companies in Canadian dollars, and Mexican companies in Mexican pesos. Le-Nature's statements report in millions of dollars. That is, they round the last six digits to the nearest **million** dollars. The listing of Cash $10.6 on Le-Nature's balance sheet actually means $10,600,000.

Notice that Le-Nature's balance sheet has three major captions: assets, liabilities, and stockholders' equity. The basic accounting equation, often called the balance sheet equation, explains their relationship:

Assets	=	**Liabilities**	+	**Stockholders' Equity**
Economic resources (e.g., cash, inventory, buildings)		Financing from creditors (e.g., amounts owed to suppliers, employees, banks)		Financing from stockholders (e.g., common stock, retained earnings)

A BALANCE SHEET (Statement of Financial Position) reports the amount of assets, liabilities, and stockholders' equity of an accounting entity at a point in time.

Balance Sheet
Assets
=
Liabilities
+
Stockholders' Equity

An ACCOUNTING ENTITY is the organization for which financial data are to be collected.

BASIC ACCOUNTING EQUATION (Balance Sheet Equation): Assets = Liabilities + Stockholders' Equity

EXHIBIT 1.2

Balance Sheet*

LE-NATURE'S

LE-NATURE'S INC. **Balance Sheet** **At December 31, 2012** **(in millions of dollars)**		EXPLANATION
		Name of the entity
		Title of the statement
		Specific date of the statement
		Unit of measure
Assets:		*Resources controlled by the company*
Cash	$ 10.6	*Amount of cash in the company's bank accounts*
Accounts receivable	6.6	*Amounts owed by customers from prior sales*
Inventories	51.2	*Ingredients and beverages ready for sale*
Property, plant, and equipment	459.0	*Factories, production equipment, and land*
Total assets	**$527.4**	*Total amount of company's resources*
Liabilities and stockholders' equity:		*Sources of financing for company's resources*
Liabilities		*Financing supplied by creditors*
Accounts payable	$ 26.0	*Amounts owed to suppliers for prior purchases*
Notes payable to banks	381.7	*Amounts owed to banks on written debt contracts*
Total liabilities	407.7	
Stockholders' equity		*Financing provided by stockholders*
Common stock	55.7	*Amounts invested in the business by stockholders*
Retained earnings	64.0	*Past earnings not distributed to stockholders*
Total stockholders' equity	119.7	
Total liabilities and stockholders' equity	**$527.4**	*Total sources of financing for company's resources*

The notes are an integral part of these financial statements.

The basic accounting equation shows what we mean when we refer to a company's **financial position:** the economic resources that the company owns and the sources of financing for those resources.

Elements

Assets are the economic resources owned by the entity. Le-Nature's lists four items under the category Assets. The exact items listed as assets on a company's balance sheet depend on the nature of its operations. But these are common names used by many companies. The four items listed by Le-Nature's are the economic resources needed to manufacture and sell beverages to retailers and vending companies. Each of these economic resources is expected to provide future benefits to the firm. To prepare to manufacture the beverages, Le-Nature's first needed cash to purchase land on which to build factories and install production machinery (property, plant, and equipment). Le-Nature's then began purchasing ingredients and producing beverages, which led to the balance assigned to inventories. When Le-Nature's sells its beverages to grocery stores and others, it sells them on credit and receives promises to pay called accounts receivable, which are collected in cash later.

Every asset on the balance sheet is initially measured at the total cost incurred to acquire it. Balance sheets do not generally show the amounts for which the assets could currently be sold.

Liabilities and stockholders' equity are the sources of financing for the company's economic resources. **Liabilities** indicate the amount of financing provided by creditors. They are the company's debts or obligations. Under the category Liabilities, Le-Nature's lists two items. The accounts payable arise from the purchase of goods

*Simplifications have been made in the statements and the dates have been changed for the purpose of our discussions.

or services from suppliers on credit without a formal written contract (or a note). The notes payable to banks result from cash borrowings based on a formal written debt contract with banks.

Stockholders' equity indicates the amount of financing provided by owners of the business and reinvested earnings.[1] The investment of cash and other assets in the business by the stockholders is called common stock. The amount of earnings (profits) reinvested in the business (and thus not distributed to stockholders in the form of dividends) is called retained earnings.

In Exhibit 1.2, the Stockholders' Equity section reports two items. The founders and other stockholders' investment of $55.7 million is reported as common stock. Le-Nature's total earnings (or losses incurred) less all dividends paid to the stockholders since formation of the corporation equals $64 million and is reported as retained earnings. Total stockholders' equity is the sum of the common stock plus the retained earnings.

| FINANCIAL ANALYSIS | Interpreting Assets, Liabilities, and Stockholders' Equity on the Balance Sheet |

Assessment of Le-Nature's assets was important to its creditors, Wells Fargo Bank and others, and its stockholders because assets provide a basis for judging whether the company has sufficient resources available to operate. Assets are also important because they could be sold for cash in the event that Le-Nature's went out of business.

Le-Nature's debts are important because creditors and stockholders are concerned about whether the company has sufficient sources of cash to pay its debts. Le-Nature's debts were also relevant to Wells Fargo Bank's decision to lend money to the company because existing creditors share its claim against Le-Nature's assets. If a business does not pay its creditors, the creditors may force the sale of assets sufficient to meet their claims. The sale of assets often fails to cover all of a company's debts, and some creditors may take a loss.

Le-Nature's stockholders' equity is important to Wells Fargo Bank because creditors' claims legally come before those of owners. If Le-Nature's goes out of business and its assets are sold, the proceeds of that sale must be used to pay back creditors before the stockholders receive any money. Thus, creditors consider stockholders' equity a protective "cushion."

 PAUSE FOR **FEEDBACK**

We just learned the **balance sheet** is a statement of financial position that reports dollar amounts for a company's assets, liabilities, and stockholders' equity at a specific point in time. These elements are related in the basic accounting equation: **Assets = Liabilities + Stockholders' Equity.** Before you move on, complete the following questions to test your understanding of these concepts.

SELF-STUDY **QUIZ**

1. Le-Nature's **assets** are listed in one section and **liabilities** and **stockholders' equity** in another. Notice that the two sections balance in conformity with the basic accounting

---

[1]A corporation is a business that is incorporated under the laws of a particular state. The owners are called **stockholders** or **shareholders.** Ownership is represented by shares of capital stock that usually can be bought and sold freely. The corporation operates as a separate legal entity, separate and apart from its owners. The stockholders enjoy limited liability; they are liable for the debts of the corporation only to the extent of their investments. Chapter Supplement A discusses forms of ownership in more detail.

equation. In the following chapters, you will learn that the basic accounting equation is the basic building block for the entire accounting process. Your task here is to verify that total assets ($527.4 million) is correct using the numbers for liabilities and stockholders' equity presented in Exhibit 1.2.

2. Learning which items belong in each of the balance sheet categories is an important first step in understanding their meaning. Without referring to Exhibit 1.2, mark each balance sheet item in the following list as an asset (A), liability (L), or stockholders' equity (SE).

_L_ Accounts payable   _A_ Inventories
_A_ Accounts receivable   _L_ Notes payable
_A_ Cash   _SE_ Retained earnings
_SE_ Common stock
_A_ Property, plant, and equipment

After you have completed your answers, check them with the solutions at the bottom of the page.

The Income Statement

Structure

The **income statement** (statement of income, statement of earnings, statement of operations, statement of comprehensive income[2]) reports the accountant's primary measure of performance of a business, revenues less expenses during the accounting period. While the term profit is used widely for this measure of performance, accountants prefer to use the technical terms **net income** or net earnings. Le-Nature's net income measures its success in selling beverages for more than the cost to generate those sales.

A quick reading of Le-Nature's income statement (Exhibit 1.3) indicates a great deal about its purpose and content. The heading identifies the name of the entity, the title of the report, and the unit of measure used in the statement. Unlike the balance sheet, however, which reports as of a certain date, the income statement reports for a specified period of time (for the year ended December 31, 2012). The time period covered by the financial statements (one year in this case) is called an **accounting period.** Notice that Le-Nature's income statement has three major captions: revenues, expenses, and net income. The income statement equation that describes their relationship is:

The INCOME STATEMENT (Statement of Income, Statement of Earnings, Statement of Operations, Statement of Comprehensive Income) reports the revenues less the expenses of the accounting period.

The ACCOUNTING PERIOD is the time period covered by the financial statements.

Revenues	−	**Expenses**	=	**Net Income**
(Cash and promises received from delivery of goods and services)		(Resources used to earn period's revenues)		(Revenues earned minus expenses incurred)

Elements

Companies earn **revenues** from the sale of goods or services to customers (in Le-Nature's case, from the sale of beverages). Revenues normally are amounts expected to be received for goods or services that have been delivered to a customer, **whether or not the customer has paid for the goods or services.** Retail stores such as Walmart and McDonald's often receive cash from consumers at the time of sale. However, when Le-Nature's delivers its beverages to retail stores, it receives a promise of future payment called an account receivable, which later is

---

1. Assets ($527.4) = Liabilities ($407.7) + Stockholders' Equity ($119.7) (in millions).
2. L, A, A, SE, A, A, L, SE (reading down the columns).

Solutions to
SELF-STUDY QUIZ

---

[2]Comprehensive income is sometimes presented in a separate statement. This advanced topic is discussed in Chapter 5.

<table>
<tr><td>EXHIBIT 1.3</td></tr>
<tr><td>Income Statement</td></tr>
<tr><td>LE-NATURE'S</td></tr>
</table>

EXHIBIT 1.3		EXPLANATION

LE-NATURE'S INC.
Income Statement
For the Year Ended December 31, 2012
(in millions of dollars)

		EXPLANATION
		Name of the entity
		Title of the statement
		Accounting period
		Unit of measure
Revenues		
Sales revenue	$275.1	*Cash and promises received from sale of beverages*
Expenses		
Cost of goods sold	140.8	*Cost to produce beverages sold*
Selling, general, and administrative		*Other operating expenses (utilities, delivery*
expenses	77.1	*costs, etc.)*
Interest expense	17.2	*Cost of using borrowed funds*
Income before income taxes	40.0	
Income tax expense	17.1	*Income taxes on period's income before income taxes*
Net income	$ 22.9	*Revenues earned minus expenses incurred*

The notes are an integral part of these financial statements.

collected in cash. In either case, the business recognizes total sales (cash and credit) as revenue for the period. Various terms are used in income statements to describe different sources of revenue (e.g., provision of services, sale of goods, rental of property). Le-Nature's lists only one, sales revenue, in its income statement.

Expenses represent the dollar amount of resources the entity used to earn revenues during the period. Expenses reported in one accounting period may actually be paid for in another accounting period. Some expenses require the payment of cash immediately while others require payment at a later date. Some may also require the use of another resource, such as an inventory item, which may have been paid for in a prior period. Le-Nature's lists four types of expenses on its income statement, which are described in Exhibit 1.3. These expenses include income tax expense, which, as a corporation, Le-Nature's must pay on the subtotal income before income taxes.

Net income or net earnings (often called "the bottom line") is the excess of total revenues over total expenses. If total expenses exceed total revenues, a net loss is reported.[3] We noted earlier that revenues are not necessarily the same as collections from customers and expenses are not necessarily the same as payments to suppliers. As a result, net income normally **does not equal** the net cash generated by operations. This latter amount is reported on the cash flow statement discussed later in this chapter.

FINANCIAL ANALYSIS	Analyzing the Income Statement: Beyond the Bottom Line

Investors and creditors such as Wells Fargo Bank closely monitor a firm's net income because it indicates the firm's ability to sell goods and services for more than they cost to produce and deliver. Investors buy stock when they believe that future earnings will improve and lead to dividends and the ability to sell their stock for more than they paid. Lenders also rely on future earnings to provide the resources to repay loans. The details of the statement also are important. For example, Le-Nature's had to sell more than $275 million worth of beverages to make just under $23 million. If a competitor were to lower prices just 10 percent, forcing Le-Nature's to do the same, its net income could easily turn into a net loss. These factors and others help investors and creditors estimate the company's future earnings.

[3]Net losses are normally noted by parentheses around the income figure.

PAUSE FOR **FEEDBACK**

As noted above, the **income statement** is a statement of operations that reports revenues, expenses, and net income for a stated period of time. To practice your understanding of these concepts, complete the following questions.

SELF-STUDY **QUIZ**

1. Learning which items belong in each of the income statement categories is an important first step in understanding their meaning. Without referring to Exhibit 1.3, mark each income statement item in the following list as a revenue (R) or an expense (E).

    _E_ Cost of goods sold   _R_ Sales revenue
    _E_ Income tax   _E_ Selling, general, and administrative

2. During the period 2012, Le-Nature's delivered beverages for which customers paid or promised to pay amounts totaling $275.1 million. During the same period, it collected $250.0 million in cash from its customers. Without referring to Exhibit 1.3, indicate which of these two amounts will be shown on Le-Nature's income statement as **sales revenue** for 2012. Why did you select your answer?

3. During the period 2012, Le-Nature's **produced** beverages with a total cost of production of $142.1 million. During the same period, it **delivered** to customers beverages that cost a total of $140.8 million to produce. Without referring to Exhibit 1.3, indicate which of the two numbers will be shown on Le-Nature's income statement as **cost of goods sold expense** for 2012. Why did you select your answer?

After you have completed your answers, check them with the solutions at the bottom of the page.

Statement of Stockholders' Equity

Structure

Le-Nature's prepares a separate **statement of stockholders' equity,** shown in Exhibit 1.4. The heading identifies the name of the entity, the title of the report, and the unit of measure used in the statement. Like the income statement, the statement of stockholders' equity covers a specified period of time (the accounting period), which in this case is one year. The statement reports the changes in each of the company's stockholders' equity accounts during that period.

Le-Natures' had no changes in common stock during the period. Had it issued or repurchased common stock during the year, the transactions would be reported on separate lines. The retained earnings column reports the way that net income and the distribution of dividends affected the company's financial position during the accounting period. Net income earned during the year increases the balance of retained earnings, showing the relationship

The STATEMENT OF STOCKHOLDERS' EQUITY reports the way that net income and the distribution of dividends affected the financial position of the company during the accounting period.

Solutions to
SELF-STUDY QUIZ

1. E, E, R, E (reading down the columns).

2. Sales revenue in the amount of $275.1 million is recognized. Sales revenue is normally reported on the income statement when goods or services have been delivered to customers who have either paid or promised to pay for them in the future.

3. Cost of goods sold expense is $140.8. Expenses are the dollar amount of resources used up to earn revenues during the period. Only those beverages that have been delivered to customers have been used up.

EXHIBIT 1.4

Statement of Stockholders' Equity

LE-NATURE'S

		EXPLANATION
LE-NATURE'S INC.		*Name of the entity*
Statement of Stockholders' Equity		*Title of the statement*
For the Year Ended December 31, 2012		*Accounting period*
(in millions of dollars)		*Unit of measure*

	Common Stock	Retained Earnings	
Balance December 31, 2011	$55.7	$43.1	*Last period's ending balances*
Net income for 2012		22.9	*Net income reported on the income statement*
Dividends for 2012		(2.0)	*Dividends declared during the period*
Balance December 31, 2012	$55.7	$64.0	*Ending balances on the balance sheet*

The notes are an integral part of these financial statements.

Statement of Stockholders' Equity
Beginning balance
+ Increases
– Decreases
Ending balance

of the income statement to the balance sheet.[4] Declaring dividends to the stockholders decreases retained earnings.

The retained earnings equation that describes these relationships is:

$$\text{Beginning Retained Earnings} + \text{Net Income} - \text{Dividends} = \text{Ending Retained Earnings}$$

Elements

The statement starts with the beginning balances in the stockholders' equity accounts, lists the increases and decreases, and reports the resulting ending balances. The retained earnings portion of the statement in Exhibit 1.4 begins with Le-Nature's **beginning-of-the-year retained earnings.** The current year's **net income** reported on the income statement is added and the current year's **dividends** are subtracted from this amount. During 2012, Le-Nature earned $22.9 million, as shown on the income statement (Exhibit 1.3). This amount was added to the beginning-of-the-year retained earnings. Also, during 2012, Le-Nature's declared and paid a total of $2.0 million in dividends to its stockholders. This amount was subtracted in computing **end-of-the-year retained earnings** on the balance sheet. Note that retained earnings increased by the portion of income reinvested in the business ($22.9 million − $2.0 million = $20.9 million). The ending retained earnings amount of $64.0 million is the same as that reported in Exhibit 1.2 on Le-Nature's balance sheet. Thus, the retained earnings portion of the statement indicates the relationship of the income statement to the balance sheet.

FINANCIAL ANALYSIS

Interpreting Retained Earnings

Reinvestment of earnings, or retained earnings, is an important source of financing for Le-Nature's, representing more than 12% of its financing. Creditors such as Wells Fargo Bank closely monitor a firm's statement of stockholders' equity because the firm's policy on dividend payments to the stockholders affects its ability to repay its debts. Every dollar Le-Nature's pays to stockholders as a dividend is not available for use in paying back its debt to Wells Fargo. Investors examine retained earnings to determine whether the company is reinvesting a sufficient portion of earnings to support future growth.

---

[4]Net losses are subtracted.

The **statement of stockholders' equity** explains changes in stockholders' equity accounts, including the change in the retained earnings balance caused by net income and dividends during the reporting period. Check your understanding of these relationships by completing the following question.

SELF-STUDY **QUIZ**

1. Assume that a company's financial statements reported the following amounts: beginning retained earnings, $5,510; total assets, $20,450; dividends, $900; cost of goods sold expense, $19,475; and net income, $1,780. Without referring to Exhibit 1.4, compute ending retained earnings.

After you have completed your answer, check it with the solution at the bottom of the page.

GUIDED **HELP**

For additional step-by-step video instruction on preparing the balance sheet, income statement, and statement of stockholders' equity, go to the following URL or scan the QR code in the margin with your smartphone or iPad.

www.mhhe.com/libby8e

Statement of Cash Flows

Structure

Le-Nature's statement of cash flows is presented in Exhibit 1.5. The **statement of cash flows** (cash flow statement) divides Le-Nature's cash inflows and outflows (receipts and payments) into the three primary categories of cash flows in a typical business: cash flows from operating, investing, and financing activities. The heading identifies the name of the entity, the title of the report, and the unit of measure used in the statement. Like the income statement, the cash flow statement covers a specified period of time (the accounting period), which in this case is one year.

As discussed earlier in this chapter, reported revenues do not always equal cash collected from customers because some sales may be on credit. Also, expenses reported on the income statement may not be equal to the cash paid out during the period because expenses may be incurred in one period and paid for in another. Because the income statement does not provide information concerning cash flows, accountants prepare the statement of cash flows to report inflows and outflows of cash. The cash flow statement equation describes the causes of the change in cash reported on the balance sheet from the end of last period to the end of the current period:

> The STATEMENT OF CASH FLOWS (Cash Flow Statement) reports inflows and outflows of cash during the accounting period in the categories of operating, investing, and financing.

$$+/- \text{ Cash Flows from Operating Activities (CFO)}$$
$$+/- \text{ Cash Flows from Investing Activities (CFI)}$$
$$+/- \text{ Cash Flows from Financing Activities (CFF)}$$
$$\overline{\text{Change in Cash}}$$
$$+ \text{ Beginning Cash Balance}$$
$$\overline{\text{Ending Cash Balance}}$$

Note that each of the three cash flow sources can be positive or negative.

---

1. Beginning Retained Earnings ($5,510) + Net Income ($1,780) − Dividends ($900) = Ending Retained Earnings ($6,390).

Solution to
SELF-STUDY QUIZ

EXHIBIT 1.5

Statement of Cash Flows

LE-NATURE'S

LE-NATURE'S INC. Statement of Cash Flows (Summary) For the Year Ended December 31, 2012 (in millions of dollars)	
Cash flows from operating activities	$ 87.5
Cash flows from investing activities	(125.5)
Cash flows from financing activities	47.0
Net increase (decrease) in cash	9.0
Cash balance December 31, 2011	1.6
Cash balance December 31, 2012	$ 10.6

The notes are an integral part of these financial statements.

EXPLANATION

Name of the entity
Title of the statement
Accounting period
Unit of measure

Cash flows directly related to earning income
Cash flows from purchase/sale of plant, equipment, & investments
Cash flows from investors and creditors

Change in cash during the period
Last period's cash on the balance sheet

Ending cash on the balance sheet

Elements

Cash flows from operating activities are cash flows that are directly related to earning income. For example, when customers pay Le-Nature's for the beverages it has delivered to them, it lists the amounts collected as cash collected from customers. When Le-Nature's pays salaries to its production employees or pays bills received from its tea suppliers, it includes the amounts in cash paid to suppliers and employees.

   Cash flows from investing activities include those related to the acquisition or sale of the company's plant and equipment and investments. This year, Le-Nature's had only one cash outflow from investing activities, the purchase of additional manufacturing equipment to meet growing demand for its products.

   Cash flows from financing activities are directly related to the financing of the enterprise itself. They involve the receipt or payment of money to investors and creditors (except for suppliers). This year, Le-Nature's borrowed additional money from the bank to purchase most of the new manufacturing equipment. It also paid out dividends to the stockholders.[5]

FINANCIAL ANALYSIS   Interpreting the Cash Flow Statement

Bankers often consider the Operating Activities section to be most important because it indicates the company's ability to generate cash from sales to meet its current cash needs. Any amount left over can be used to pay back the bank debt or expand the company. Stockholders will invest in a company only if they believe that it will eventually generate more cash from operations than it uses so that cash will become available to pay dividends and expand.

 PAUSE FOR **FEEDBACK**

The **statement of cash flows** reports inflows and outflows of cash for a stated period of time classified into three categories: operating, investing, and financing activities. Answer the following questions to test your understanding of the concepts involved.

---

[5]The complete statement of cash flows is discussed in Chapter 13.

1. During the period 2012, Le-Nature's delivered beverages to customers who paid or promised to pay a total of $275.1 million. During the same period, it collected $250.0 million in
   cash from customers. Which of the two amounts will be shown on Le-Nature's cash flow
   statement for 2012?

2. Your task here is to verify that Le-Nature's cash balance increased by $9.0 million during
   the year using the totals for cash flows from operating, investing, and financing activities
   presented in Exhibit 1.5. Recall the cash flow statement equation:

   $$+/-\ \text{Cash Flows from Operating Activities (CFO)}$$
   $$+/-\ \text{Cash Flows from Investing Activities (CFI)}$$
   $$\underline{+/-\ \text{Cash Flows from Financing Activities (CFF)}}$$

   $$\text{Change in Cash}$$

After you have completed your answers, check them with the solutions at the bottom of the page.

Relationships Among the Statements

Our discussion of the four basic financial statements has focused on what elements are reported
in each statement, how the elements are related by the equation for each statement, and how
the information is important to the decisions of investors, creditors, and others. We have also
discovered how the statements, all of which are outputs from the same system, are related to
one another. In particular, we learned:

❶ Net income from the income statement results in an increase in ending retained earnings on
the statement of stockholders' equity.

❷ Ending retained earnings from the statement of stockholders' equity is one of the two components of stockholders' equity on the balance sheet.

❸ The change in cash on the cash flow statement added to the beginning-of-the-year balance
in cash equals the end-of-year balance in cash on the balance sheet.

Thus, we can think of the income statement as explaining, through the statement of stockholders' equity, how the operations of the company improved or harmed the financial position of the company during the year. The cash flow statement explains how the operating,
investing, and financing activities of the company affected the cash balance on the balance
sheet during the year. These relationships are illustrated in Exhibit 1.6 for Le-Nature's financial statements.

Notes and Statement Formats

At the bottom of each of Le-Nature's four basic financial statements is this statement: **"The
notes are an integral part of these financial statements."** This is the accounting equivalent
of the Surgeon General's warning on a package of cigarettes. It warns users that failure to

---

1. The firm recognizes $250.0 million on the cash flow statement because this number represents the actual
cash collected from customers related to current and prior years' sales.

2.	+/- Cash Flows from Operating Activities (CFO)	$ 87.5
	+/- Cash Flows from Investing Activities (CFI)	(125.5)
	+/- Cash Flows from Financing Activities (CFF)	47.0
	Change in Cash	$ 9.0

Solutions to
SELF-STUDY QUIZ

Relationships Among
Le-Nature's Statements

LE-NATURE'S

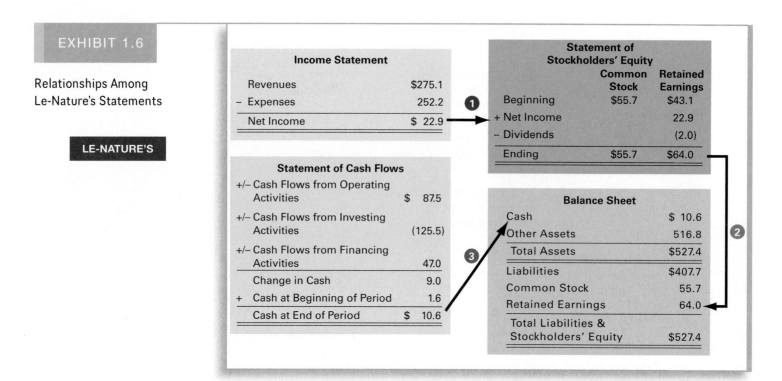

NOTES (Footnotes) provide
supplemental information about
the financial condition of a
company, without which the
financial statements cannot be
fully understood.

read the notes (or footnotes) to the financial statements will result in an incomplete picture of
the company's financial health. Throughout this book, we will discuss many note disclosures
because understanding their content is critical to understanding the company.

A few additional formatting conventions are worth noting here. Assets are listed on the
balance sheet by ease of conversion to cash. Liabilities are listed by their maturity (due date).
Most financial statements include the monetary unit sign (in the United States, the $) beside the
first dollar amount in a group of items (e.g., the cash amount in the assets). Also, it is common
to place a single underline below the last item in a group before a total or subtotal (e.g., land).
A dollar sign is also placed beside group totals (e.g., total assets) and a double underline below.
The same conventions are followed in all four basic financial statements.

Summary of the Four Basic Financial Statements

We have learned a great deal about the content of the four basic financial statements. Exhibit 1.7
summarizes this information. Take a few minutes to review the information in the exhibit before
you move on to the next section of the chapter.

LEARNING OBJECTIVE 1-2

Identify the role of generally
accepted accounting principles
(GAAP) in determining financial
statement content and how
companies ensure the accuracy
of their financial statements.

RESPONSIBILITIES FOR THE ACCOUNTING COMMUNICATION PROCESS

For decision makers to use the information in Le-Nature's financial statements effectively,
they have to know: (1) the information conveyed by the statements and the measurement rules
applied in computing the numbers on the statements and (2) that the numbers on the statements
are correct. The rules that determine the content and measurement rules of the statements are
called generally accepted accounting principles, or GAAP.

GENERALLY ACCEPTED
ACCOUNTING PRINCIPLES
(GAAP) are the measurement and
disclosure rules used to develop
the information in financial
statements.

Generally Accepted Accounting Principles

How Are Generally Accepted Accounting Principles Determined?

The accounting system in use today has a long history. Its foundations are normally traced
back to the works of an Italian monk and mathematician, Fr. Luca Pacioli, published in 1494.

Financial Statement	Purpose	Structure	Examples of Content
Balance Sheet (Statement of Financial Position)	Reports the financial position (economic resources and sources of financing) of an accounting entity *at a point in time.*	**Balance Sheet** Assets = Liabilities + Stockholders' Equity	Cash, accounts receivable, plant and equipment, long-term debt, common stock
Income Statement (Statement of Income, Statement of Earnings, Statement of Operations)	Reports the accountant's primary measure of economic performance *during the accounting period.*	**Income Statement** Revenues − Expenses ───── Net Income	Sales revenue, cost of goods sold, selling expense, interest expense
Statement of Stockholders' Equity	Reports changes in the company's common stock and retained earnings *during the accounting period.*	**Statement of Stockholders' Equity** Beginning balance + Increases − Decreases ───── Ending balance	Beginning and ending stockholders' equity balances, stock issuances, net income, dividends
Statement of Cash Flows (Cash Flow Statement)	Reports inflows (receipts) and outflows (payments) of cash *during the accounting period* in the categories operating, investing, and financing.	**Statement of Cash Flows** +/− CFO +/− CFI +/− CFF ───── Change in Cash	Cash collected from customers, cash paid to suppliers, cash paid to purchase equipment, cash borrowed from banks

EXHIBIT 1.7

Summary of the Four Basic Financial Statements

However, prior to 1933, each company's management largely determined its financial reporting practices. Thus, little uniformity in practice existed among companies.

In the United States, Congress created the **Securities and Exchange Commission (SEC)** and gave it broad powers to determine the measurement rules for financial statements that companies issuing stock to the public (publicly traded companies) must provide to stockholders.[6] The SEC has worked with organizations of professional accountants and other interested parties to establish groups that are given the primary responsibilities to work out the detailed rules that become generally accepted accounting principles. Today, the **Financial Accounting Standards Board** (FASB) has this responsibility. The official pronouncements of the FASB are called the FASB **Accounting Standards Codification.**

Why Is GAAP Important to Managers and External Users?

Generally accepted accounting principles (GAAP) are of great interest to the companies that must prepare financial statements, their auditors, and the readers of the statements. Companies and their managers and owners are most directly affected by the information presented in

---

[6]Contrary to popular belief, these rules are different from those that companies follow when filing their income tax returns. We discuss these differences further in later chapters.

financial statements. Companies incur the cost of preparing the statements and bear the major economic consequences of their publication, which include, among others,

1. Effects on the selling price of a company's stock.

2. Effects on the amount of bonuses received by management and employees.

3. Loss of competitive information to other companies.

As a consequence of these and other concerns, changes in GAAP are actively debated, political lobbying often takes place, and final rules are a compromise among the wishes of interested parties. Most managers do not need to learn all the details included in these standards. Our approach is to focus on those details that have the greatest impact on the numbers presented in financial statements and are appropriate for an introductory course.

INTERNATIONAL PERSPECTIVE	The International Accounting Standards Board and Global Convergence of Accounting Standards

Financial accounting standards and disclosure requirements are adopted by national regulatory agencies. Since 2002, there has been substantial movement toward the adoption of **International Financial Reporting Standards (IFRS)** issued by the **International Accounting Standards Board (IASB).** Examples of jurisdictions requiring the use of IFRS currently include:

- **European Union (United Kingdom, Germany, France, Netherlands, Belgium, Bulgaria, Poland, etc.)**
- **Australia and New Zealand**
- **Hong Kong (S.A.R. of China), Malaysia, and Republic of Korea**
- **Israel and Turkey**
- **Brazil and Chile**
- **Canada and Mexico**

In the United States, the Securities and Exchange Commission now allows foreign companies whose stock is traded in the United States to use IFRS and is considering requiring the use of IFRS for U.S. domestic companies by 2015. To prepare you for this eventuality, we will point out key differences between IFRS and U.S. GAAP starting in Chapter 5. The basic principles and practices we discuss in Chapters 1 through 4 apply equally to both sets of standards.

Source: IFRS Foundation 2012.

Ensuring the Accuracy of Financial Statements

What If the Numbers Are Wrong?

Shortly after the issuance of the statements presented in this chapter, Le-Nature's worked with the Wachovia Capital Markets group from Wells Fargo Bank to borrow an additional $285 million from various lenders. Why would lenders agree to risk such a large amount? Le-Nature's financial statements played a major role in the lenders' decisions to back the loan. The statements presented a picture of a growth company with amazing future prospects. Reported revenues grew from $40 to $275 million (or nearly 600%) in just six years! Reported income rose by 2,400% in the same period! Clearly, Le-Nature's looked like a good bet. But if the numbers are wrong, all bets are off.

The truth about Le-Nature's was revealed when several non-family-member stockholders suspected that all was not right and filed a lawsuit seeking an independent trustee to examine the company. Court records reveal an amazing story. According to the bankruptcy custodian, reported annual sales of $274 million were really about $32 million. Podlucky and his co-conspirators forged checks, invoices, and revenue and expense records to massively overstate revenues and profits. The $10.6 million its balance sheet claimed for cash turned out to be $1.8 million and the company had written checks totaling $2.9 million against that balance. The balance sheet also understated liabilities by $200 million. The company was never a real success—**it was all fake.**

Le Nature's—Reported Versus Actual Sales

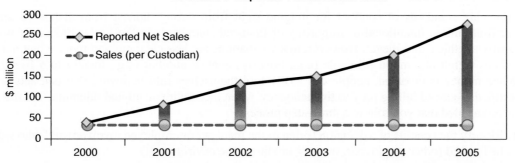

Podlucky was borrowing more and more money and using it to pay off his earlier creditors (this is called a **Ponzi scheme**). At the same time, he was stealing cash to support a lavish lifestyle. When the trustee arrived, Podlucky and his bodyguard were feverishly shredding documents. Federal agents found $20 million in gems, diamond-encrusted watches, and gold, silver, and platinum jewelry in safes in a secret room at the Latrobe plant. Podlucky had also spent more than $10 million of company money on his 25,000-square-foot mansion that was under construction. A sample of the resulting newspaper headlines follows:

LE-NATURE'S

Market Predicts Le-Nature's Is All Washed Up

Grand jury hears LeNature's ex-accountant's testimony

Debt holders sue Wachovia over Le Nature's Loan

Ex-LeNature's exec found guilty of fraud

Le-Nature's Fraud: 2 More Sentenced In $800M Fraud

Ex-Pa. soft-drink CEO gets 20 years in prison

Accountant Guilty of helping CEO Commit Fraud

While this crime may read like a fantastic novel, the consequences for many were severe. This was the largest fraud ever heard in the Federal District Court of Western Pennsylvania. The final prison tally is listed below.

The Prison Tally	
Defendant	**Sentence**
Gregory Podlucky, CEO	20 years in federal prison
Robert Lynn, President	15 years in federal prison
Andrew Murin, Consultant	10 years in federal prison
Jonathan Podlucky, COO	5 years in federal prison
Karla Podlucky (CEO's wife)	4¼ years in federal prison
G. Jesse Podlucky (CEO's son)	9 years in federal prison
Donald Pollinger, Businessman	5 years in federal prison
Tammy Jo Andreycak, Bookkeeper	5 years in federal prison

Crime clearly did not pay for Podlucky and his co-conspirators.

Ethical Conduct

Ethics are standards of conduct for judging right from wrong, honest from dishonest, and fair from unfair. Intentional misreporting of financial statements in the Le-Nature's case was clearly unethical and illegal. However, many situations are less clear cut and require that individuals weigh one moral principle (e.g., honesty) against another (e.g., loyalty to a friend). When money is involved, people can easily fool themselves into believing that bad acts are justified. To avoid falling prey to this tendency, when faced with an ethical dilemma, it is often recommended that you follow a three-step process:

1. Identify the benefits of a decision (often to the manager or employee involved) and who will be harmed (other employees, owners, creditors, the environment).

2. Identify alternative courses of action.

3. Choose the one you would like your family and friends to see reported on your local news. That is usually the ethical choice.

In the Le-Nature's case, Podlucky and his co-conspirators clearly did not follow this process. Little besides the jewelry and the Latrobe plant were left to satisfy Le-Nature's over $800 million in debts. The nonfamily stockholders lost all of their money. Over 240 plant workers lost their jobs. And the town of Latrobe, Pennsylvania, suffered a severe economic blow.

Responsibility and the Need for Controls

As a manager in a business, you are responsible for setting up systems to prevent and detect unethical behavior. Primary responsibility for the information in the financial statements lies with management, represented by the highest officer of the company and the highest financial officer. Companies should take three important steps to assure investors that the company's records are accurate: (1) they should maintain a system of controls over both the records and the assets of the company, (2) they should hire outside independent auditors to **audit** the fairness of the financial statements, and (3) they should form a committee of the board of directors to oversee the integrity of these other safeguards. These safeguards failed in Le-Nature's case. The company had no controls, the independent auditors were duped by management, and the board included only Podlucky's cronies. We will discuss the roles of management, auditors, and directors in more detail in Chapter 5.

An AUDIT is an examination of the financial reports to ensure that they represent what they claim and conform with GAAP.

Three steps to ensure the accuracy of records:

System of Controls   External Auditors   Board of Directors

Those responsible for fraudulent financial statements are subject to criminal and civil penalties. As noted above, those criminally liable at Le-Nature's are serving a total of more than 70 years in prison and have been forced to forfeit all of their assets to be paid to creditors who suffered losses. The auditors who missed the fraud agreed to pay $50 million to the creditors and Wachovia Capital Markets, which marketed the loans, agreed to pay $80 million. The bottling equipment company that provided false documents to support Le-Nature's loans has paid a $15 million fine and $110 million in restitution. Other civil suits are still in process.

Although financial statement fraud is a fairly rare event, the misrepresentations in Le-Nature's statements aptly illustrate the importance of fairly presented financial statements to investors and creditors. Although most managers and owners act in an honest and responsible fashion, this incident, and the much larger frauds at Enron and WorldCom, are stark reminders of the economic consequences of lack of fair presentation in financial reports. All three companies were forced into bankruptcy when their fraudulent financial reporting practices were brought to light. Penalties against Enron and WorldCom's audit firm, Arthur Andersen, also led to its bankruptcy and dissolution. Thousands lost their jobs.

DEMONSTRATION **CASE**

Pier 1 Imports, Inc.

At the end of most chapters, one or more demonstration cases are presented. These cases provide an overview of the primary issues discussed in the chapter. Each demonstration case is followed by a recommended solution. You should read the case carefully and then prepare your own solution before you study the recommended solution. This self-evaluation is highly recommended. The introductory case presented here reviews the elements reported on the income statement, statement of stockholders' equity, and balance sheet and how the elements within the statements are related.

Pier 1 Imports, Inc., sells a wide variety of furniture, decorative home furnishings, dining and kitchen goods, bath and bedding accessories, candles, gifts, and other specialty items for the home through over 1,000 retail stores in North America. Its merchandise largely consists of items that feature a significant degree of handcraftsmanship and are mostly imported directly from foreign suppliers. Following is a list of the financial statement items and amounts adapted from a recent Pier 1 income statement and balance sheet. The numbers are presented in millions of dollars for the year ended February 26, 2011. Assume that the company did not pay dividends, issue stock, or retire stock during the year. Retained earnings at the beginning of the year was $193.

Accounts payable	$237	Long-term debt	94
Accounts receivable	15	Net income	100
Cash	301	Net sales	1,401
Common stock	120	Properties, net	92
Cost of sales	861	Retained earnings	293
Income before income taxes	103	Selling, general and administrative expenses	432
Income tax expense	3	Total assets	744
Interest expense	5	Total liabilities	331
Inventories	336	Total liabilities and shareholders' equity	744
		Total shareholders' equity	413

Required:

1. Prepare a balance sheet, income statement, and a statement of stockholders' equity for the year following the formats in Exhibits 1.2, 1.3, and 1.4.

2. Specify what information these three statements provide.

3. Indicate the other statement that would be included in Pier 1's annual report.

4. Securities regulations require that Pier 1's statements be subject to an independent audit. Suggest why Pier 1 might voluntarily subject its statements to an independent audit if there were no such requirement.

SUGGESTED SOLUTION

1.

PIER 1 IMPORTS, INC.		
Balance Sheet		
At February 28, 2011		
(in millions of dollars)		
Assets		
Cash		$301
Accounts receivable		15
Inventories		336
Properties, net		92
Total assets		$744
Liabilities and shareholders' equity		
Liabilities:		
Accounts payable		$237
Long-term debt		94
Total liabilities		331
Shareholders' equity:		
Common stock		120
Retained earnings		293
Total shareholders' equity		413
Total liabilities and		
shareholders' equity		$744

PIER 1 IMPORTS, INC.	
Income Statement	
For the Year Ended February 28, 2011	
(in millions of dollars)	
Net sales	$1,401
Cost of sales	861
Selling, general and	
administrative expense	432
Interest expense	5
Income before income taxes	103
Income tax expense	3
Net income	$ 100

PIER 1 IMPORTS, INC.		
Statement of Stockholders' Equity		
For the Year Ended February 28, 2011		
(in millions of dollars)		
	Common Stock	Retained Earnings
Balance February 28, 2010	$120	$193
+ Net income	—	100
− Dividends	—	—
Balance February 28, 2011	$120	$293

2. The balance sheet reports the amount of assets, liabilities, and stockholders' equity of an accounting entity at a point in time. The income statement reports the accountant's primary measure of performance of a business, revenues less expenses, during the accounting period. The statement of stockholders' equity reports on changes in the stockholders' equity accounts during the accounting period.

3. Pier 1 would also present a statement of cash flows.

4. Users will have greater confidence in the accuracy of financial statement information if they know that the people who audited the statements were required to meet professional standards of ethics and competence.

Chapter Supplement A

Types of Business Entities

This textbook emphasizes **accounting for profit-making business entities.** The three main types of business entities are sole proprietorship, partnership, and corporation. A **sole proprietorship** is an unincorporated business owned by one person; it usually is small in size and is common in the service, retailing, and farming industries. Often the owner is the manager. Legally, the business and the owner are not separate entities. Accounting views the business as a separate entity, however, that must be accounted for separately from its owner.

A **partnership** is an unincorporated business owned by two or more persons known as **partners.** The agreements between the owners are specified in a partnership contract. This contract deals with matters such as division of income each reporting period and distribution of resources of the business on termination of its operations. A partnership is not legally separate from its owners. Legally, each partner in a general partnership is responsible for the debts of the business (each general partner has **unlimited liability**). The partnership, however, is a separate business entity to be accounted for separately from its several owners.

A **corporation** is a business incorporated under the laws of a particular state. The owners are called **stockholders** or **shareholders.** Ownership is represented by shares of capital stock that usually can be bought and sold freely. When the organizers file an approved application for incorporation, the state issues a charter. This charter gives the corporation the right to operate as a separate legal entity, separate and apart from its owners. The stockholders enjoy **limited liability.** Stockholders are liable for the corporation's debts only to the extent of their investments. The corporate charter specifies the types and amounts of capital stock that can be issued. Most states require a minimum of two or three stockholders and a minimum amount of resources to be contributed at the time of organization. The stockholders elect a governing board of directors, which in turn employs managers and exercises general supervision of the corporation. Accounting also views the corporation as a separate business entity that must be accounted for separately from its owners. Limited liability companies **(LLCs)** and limited liability partnerships **(LLPs)** have many characteristics similar to corporations.

In terms of economic importance, the corporation is the dominant form of business organization in the United States. This dominance is caused by the many advantages of the corporate form: (1) limited liability for the stockholders, (2) continuity of life, (3) ease in transferring ownership (stock), and (4) opportunities to raise large amounts of money by selling shares to a large number of people. The primary disadvantage of a corporation is that its income may be subject to double taxation (income is taxed when it is earned and again when it is distributed to stockholders as dividends). In this textbook, we emphasize the corporate form of business. Nevertheless, the accounting concepts and procedures that we discuss also apply to other types of businesses.

Chapter Supplement B

Employment in the Accounting Profession Today

Since 1900, accounting has attained the stature of professions such as law, medicine, engineering, and architecture. As with all recognized professions, accounting is subject to professional competence requirements, is dedicated to service to the public, requires a high level of academic study, and rests on a common body of knowledge. An accountant may be licensed as a certified public accountant, or CPA. This designation is granted only on completion of requirements specified by the state that issues the license. Although CPA requirements vary among states, they include a college degree with a specified number of accounting courses, good character, professional experience, and successful completion of a professional examination. The CPA examination is prepared by the American Institute of Certified Public Accountants.

Accountants (including CPAs) commonly are engaged in professional practice or are employed by businesses, government entities, nonprofit organizations, and so on. Accountants employed in these activities may take and pass a professional examination to become a certified management accountant, or CMA (the CMA examination is administered by the Institute of Management Accountants), or a certified internal auditor, or CIA (the CIA examination is administered by the Institute of Internal Auditors).

Practice of Public Accounting

Although an individual may practice public accounting, usually two or more individuals organize an accounting firm in the form of a partnership (in many cases, a limited liability partnership, or LLP). Accounting firms vary in size from a one-person office, to regional firms, to the Big Four firms (Deloitte & Touche, Ernst & Young, KPMG, and PricewaterhouseCoopers), which have hundreds of offices located worldwide. Accounting firms usually render three types of services: audit or assurance services, management consulting services, and tax services.

Audit or Assurance Services

Audit or assurance services are independent professional services that improve the quality of information, or its context, for decision makers. The most important assurance service performed by the CPA in public practice is financial statement auditing. The purpose of an audit is to lend credibility to the financial reports, that is, to ensure that they fairly represent what they claim. An audit involves an examination of the financial reports (prepared by the management of the entity) to ensure that they conform with GAAP. Other areas of assurance services include electronic commerce integrity and security and information systems reliability.

Management Consulting Services

Many independent CPA firms offer management consulting services. These services usually are accounting based and encompass such activities as the design and installation of accounting, data processing, and profit-planning and control (budget) systems; financial advice; forecasting; inventory controls; cost-effectiveness studies; and operational analysis. To maintain their independence, CPAs are prohibited from performing certain consulting services for the public companies that they audit.

Tax Services

CPAs in public practice usually provide income tax services to their clients. These services include both tax planning as a part of the decision-making process and the determination of the income tax liability (reported on the annual income tax return). Because of the increasing complexity of state and federal tax laws, a high level of competence is required, which CPAs specializing in taxation can provide. The CPA's involvement in tax planning often is quite significant. Most major business decisions have significant tax impacts; in fact, tax-planning considerations often govern certain business decisions.

Employment by Organizations

Many accountants, including CPAs, CMAs, and CIAs, are employed by profit-making and nonprofit organizations. An organization, depending on its size and complexity, may employ from a few to hundreds of accountants. In a business enterprise, the chief financial officer (usually a vice president or controller) is a member of the management team. This responsibility usually entails a wide range of management, financial, and accounting duties.

In a business entity, accountants typically are engaged in a wide variety of activities, such as general management, general accounting, cost accounting, profit planning and control (budgeting), internal auditing, and data processing. A primary function of the accountants in organizations is to provide data that are useful for internal managerial decision making and for controlling operations. The functions of external reporting, tax planning, control of assets, and a host of related responsibilities normally are also performed by accountants in industry.

Employment in the Public and Not-for-Profit Sector

The vast and complex operations of governmental units, from the local to the international level, create a need for accountants. The same holds true for other not-for-profit organizations such as hospitals and universities. Accountants employed in the public and not-for-profit sector perform functions similar to those performed by their counterparts in private organizations. The Government Accountability Office (GAO) and the regulatory agencies, such as the SEC and Federal Communications Commission (FCC), also use the services of accountants in carrying out their regulatory duties.

CHAPTER **TAKE-AWAYS**

1-1. Recognize the information conveyed in each of the four basic financial statements and the way that it is used by different decision makers (investors, creditors, and managers).   p. 4

The **balance sheet** is a statement of financial position that reports dollar amounts for the assets, liabilities, and stockholders' equity at a specific point in time.

The **income statement** is a statement of operations that reports revenues, expenses, and net income for a stated period of time.

The **statement of stockholders' equity** explains changes in stockholders' equity accounts (common stock and retained earnings) that occurred during the reporting period.

The **statement of cash flows** reports inflows and outflows of cash for a stated period of time.

The statements are used by investors and creditors to evaluate different aspects of the firm's financial position and performance.

1-2. Identify the role of generally accepted accounting principles (GAAP) in determining financial statement content and how companies ensure the accuracy of their financial statements.   p. 16

GAAP are the measurement rules used to develop the information in financial statements. Knowledge of GAAP is necessary for accurate interpretation of the numbers in financial statements.

Management has primary responsibility for the accuracy of a company's financial information. Auditors are responsible for expressing an opinion on the fairness of the financial statement presentations based on their examination of the reports and records of the company.

Users will have confidence in the accuracy of financial statement numbers only if the people associated with their preparation and audit have reputations for ethical behavior and competence. Management and auditors can also be held legally liable for fraudulent financial statements.

In this chapter, we studied the basic financial statements that communicate financial information to external users. Chapters 2, 3, and 4 provide a more detailed look at financial statements and examine how to translate data about business transactions into these statements. Learning how to translate back and forth between business transactions and financial statements is the key to using financial statements in planning and decision making. Chapter 2 begins our discussion of the way that the accounting function collects data about business transactions and processes the data to provide periodic financial statements, with emphasis on the balance sheet. To accomplish this purpose, Chapter 2 discusses key accounting concepts, the accounting model, transaction analysis, and analytical tools. We examine the typical business activities of an actual service-oriented company to demonstrate the concepts in Chapters 2, 3, and 4.

FINDING **FINANCIAL INFORMATION**

Balance Sheet

Assets = Liabilities + Stockholders' Equity

Income Statement

Revenues
− Expenses
Net Income

Statement of Stockholders' Equity

Beginning balance
+ Increases
− Decreases
Ending balance

Statement of Cash Flows

+/− Cash Flows from Operating Activities
+/− Cash Flows from Investing Activities
+/− Cash Flows from Financing Activities
Net Change in Cash

KEY **TERMS**

Accounting   p. 4
Accounting Entity   p. 6
Accounting Period   p. 9
Audit   p. 20
Balance Sheet (Statement of
   Financial Position)   p. 6

Basic Accounting Equation
   (Balance Sheet Equation)   p. 6
Generally Accepted Accounting
   Principles (GAAP)   p. 16
Income Statement (Statement of Income,
   Statement of Earnings, Statement

of Operations, or Statement
   of Comprehensive Income)   p. 9
Notes (Footnotes)   p. 16
Statement of Cash Flows (Cash Flow
   Statement)   p. 13
Statement of Stockholders' Equity   p. 11

QUESTIONS

1. Define **accounting.**
2. Briefly distinguish financial accounting from managerial accounting.
3. The accounting process generates financial reports for both internal and external users. Identify some of the groups of users.
4. Briefly distinguish investors from creditors.
5. What is an accounting entity? Why is a business treated as a separate entity for accounting purposes?
6. Complete the following:

Name of Statement	Alternative Title
a. Income statement	a. _____
b. Balance sheet	b. _____
c. Audit report	c. _____

7. What information should be included in the heading of each of the four primary financial statements?
8. What are the purposes of (a) the income statement, (b) the balance sheet, (c) the statement of cash flows, and (d) the statement of stockholders' equity?

9. Explain why the income statement and the statement of cash flows are dated "For the Year Ended December 31, 2013," whereas the balance sheet is dated "At December 31, 2013."
10. Briefly explain the importance of assets and liabilities to the decisions of investors and creditors.
11. Briefly define **net income** and **net loss.**
12. Explain the equation for the income statement. What are the three major items reported on the income statement?
13. Explain the equation for the balance sheet. Define the three major components reported on the balance sheet.
14. Explain the equation for the statement of cash flows. Explain the three major components reported on the statement of cash flows.
15. Explain the equation for retained earnings. Explain the four major items reported on the statement of stockholders' equity related to retained earnings.
16. Financial statements discussed in this chapter are aimed at **external** users. Briefly explain how a company's **internal** managers in different functional areas (e.g., marketing, purchasing, human resources) might use financial statement information from their own and other companies.
17. Briefly describe the way that accounting measurement rules (generally accepted accounting principles) are determined in the United States.
18. Briefly explain the responsibility of company management and the independent auditors in the accounting communication process.
19. (Supplement A) Briefly differentiate between a sole proprietorship, a partnership, and a corporation.
20. (Supplement B) List and briefly explain the three primary services that CPAs in public practice provide.

MULTIPLE-CHOICE QUESTIONS

1. Which of the following is **not** one of the four basic financial statements?
   a. Balance sheet
   b. Audit report
   c. Income statement
   d. Statement of cash flows
2. As stated in the audit report, or **Report of Independent Accountants,** the primary responsibility for a company's financial statements lies with
   a. The owners of the company.
   b. Independent financial analysts.
   c. The auditors.
   d. The company's management.
3. Which of the following is true?
   a. FASB creates SEC.
   b. GAAP creates FASB.
   c. SEC creates AICPA.
   d. FASB creates GAAP.
4. Which of the following regarding retained earnings is false?
   a. Retained earnings is increased by net income and decreased by a net loss.
   b. Retained earnings is a component of stockholders' equity on the balance sheet.
   c. Retained earnings is an asset on the balance sheet.
   d. Retained earnings represents earnings not distributed to stockholders in the form of dividends.
5. Which of the following is **not** one of the four items required to be shown in the heading of a financial statement?
   a. The financial statement preparer's name.
   b. The title of the financial statement.
   c. The unit of measure in the financial statement.
   d. The name of the business entity.
6. Which of the following statements regarding the statement of cash flows is true?
   a. The statement of cash flows separates cash inflows and outflows into three major categories: operating, investing, and financing.
   b. The ending cash balance shown on the statement of cash flows must agree with the amount shown on the balance sheet for the same fiscal period.
   c. The total increase or decrease in cash shown on the statement of cash flows must agree with the "bottom line" (net income or net loss) reported on the income statement.
   d. "a" and "b."
   e. All of the above.

7. Which of the following is **not** a typical note included in an annual report?
   a. A note describing the auditor's opinion of the management's past and future financial planning for the business.
   b. A note providing more detail about a specific item shown in the financial statements.
   c. A note describing the accounting rules applied in the financial statements.
   d. A note describing financial disclosures about items not appearing in the financial statements.
8. Which of the following is true regarding the income statement?
   a. The income statement is sometimes called the **statement of operations.**
   b. The income statement reports revenues, expenses, and liabilities.
   c. The income statement reports only revenue for which cash was received at the point of sale.
   d. The income statement reports the financial position of a business at a particular point in time.
9. Which of the following is false regarding the balance sheet?
   a. The accounts shown on a balance sheet represent the basic accounting equation for a particular business entity.
   b. The retained earnings balance shown on the balance sheet must agree with the ending retained earnings balance shown on the statement of stockholders' equity.
   c. The balance sheet reports the changes in specific account balances over a period of time.
   d. The balance sheet reports the amount of assets, liabilities, and stockholders' equity of an accounting entity at a point in time.
10. Which of the following regarding GAAP is true?
   a. U.S. GAAP is the body of accounting knowledge followed by all countries in the world.
   b. Changes in GAAP can affect the interests of managers and stockholders.
   c. GAAP is the abbreviation for generally accepted auditing procedures.
   d. Changes to GAAP must be approved by the Senate Finance Committee.

For more practice with multiple-choice questions, go to the text website at **www.mhhe.com/libby8e**.

McGraw Hill **connect**
|ACCOUNTING

MINI-**EXERCISES**

Matching Elements with Financial Statements

M1-1
LO1-1

Match each element with its financial statement by entering the appropriate letter in the space provided.

Element	Financial Statement
___ (1) Expenses	A. Balance sheet
___ (2) Cash flow from investing activities	B. Income statement
___ (3) Assets	C. Statement of stockholders' equity
___ (4) Dividends	D. Statement of cash flows
___ (5) Revenues	
___ (6) Cash flow from operating activities	
___ (7) Liabilities	
___ (8) Cash flow from financing activities	

Matching Financial Statement Items to Financial Statement Categories

M1-2
LO1-1

Mark each item in the following list as an asset (A), liability (L), or stockholders' equity (SE) item that would appear on the balance sheet or a revenue (R) or expense (E) that would appear on the income statement.

___ (1) Retained earnings   ___ (6) Inventories
___ (2) Accounts receivable   ___ (7) Interest expense
___ (3) Sales revenue   ___ (8) Accounts payable
___ (4) Property, plant, and equipment   ___ (9) Land
___ (5) Cost of goods sold expense

M1-3

LO1-2

Identifying Important Accounting Abbreviations

The following is a list of important abbreviations used in the chapter. These abbreviations also are used widely in business. For each abbreviation, give the full designation. The first one is an example.

Abbreviation	Full Designation
(1) CPA	Certified Public Accountant
(2) GAAP	_____
(3) SEC	_____
(4) FASB	_____

EXERCISES

E1-1

LO1-1, 1-2

Matching Definitions with Terms or Abbreviations

Match each definition with its related term or abbreviation by entering the appropriate letter in the space provided.

Term or Abbreviation	Definition
____ (1) SEC	A. A system that collects and processes financial information about an organization and reports that information to decision makers.
____ (2) Audit	
____ (3) Sole proprietorship	
____ (4) Corporation	B. Measurement of information about an entity in terms of the dollar or other national monetary unit.
____ (5) Accounting	
____ (6) Accounting entity	C. An unincorporated business owned by two or more persons.
____ (7) Audit report	D. The organization for which financial data are to be collected (separate and distinct from its owners).
____ (8) Publicly traded	
____ (9) Partnership	E. An incorporated entity that issues shares of stock as evidence of ownership.
____ (10) FASB	
____ (11) CPA	F. An examination of the financial reports to ensure that they represent what they claim and conform with generally accepted accounting principles.
____ (12) Unit of measure	
____ (13) GAAP	
	G. Certified public accountant.
	H. An unincorporated business owned by one person.
	I. A report that describes the auditor's opinion of the fairness of the financial statement presentations and the evidence gathered to support that opinion.
	J. Securities and Exchange Commission.
	K. Financial Accounting Standards Board.
	L. A company with stock that can be bought and sold by investors on established stock exchanges.
	M. Generally accepted accounting principles.

E1-2

LO1-1

Matching Financial Statement Items to Financial Statement Categories

According to its annual report, "P&G's more than 250 brands include Pampers, Tide, Ariel, Always, Whisper, Pantene, Bounty, Pringles, Folgers, Charmin, Downy, Lenor, Iams, Olay, Crest, Vicks and Actonel." The following are items taken from its recent balance sheet and income statement. Note that different companies use slightly different titles for the same item. Mark each item in the following list as an asset (A), liability (L), or stockholders' equity (SE) item that would appear on the balance sheet, or a revenue (R) or expense (E) that would appear on the income statement.

___ (1) Accounts receivable
___ (2) Cash and cash equivalents
___ (3) Net sales
___ (4) Notes payable
___ (5) Taxes payable
___ (6) Retained earnings
___ (7) Cost of products sold
___ (8) Marketing, administrative, and other operating
      expenses

___ (9)   Income taxes
___ (10) Accounts payable
___ (11) Land
___ (12) Property, plant, and equipment
___ (13) Long-term debt
___ (14) Inventories
___ (15) Interest expense

Matching Financial Statement Items to Financial Statement Categories

E1-3

LO1-1

Tootsie Roll Industries

Tootsie Roll Industries is engaged in the manufacture and sale of candy. Major products include Tootsie Roll, Tootsie Roll Pops, Tootsie Pop Drops, Tootsie Flavor Rolls, Charms, and Blow-Pop lollipops. The following items were listed on Tootsie Roll's recent income statement and balance sheet. Mark each item from the balance sheet as an asset (A), liability (L), or shareholders' equity (SE) item and mark each item from the income statement as a revenue (R) or expense (E).

___ (1) Notes payable to banks
___ (2) General and administrative
___ (3) Accounts payable
___ (4) Dividends payable
___ (5) Retained earnings
___ (6) Cash and cash equivalents
___ (7) Accounts receivable
___ (8) Provision for income taxes*
___ (9) Cost of goods sold

___ (10) Machinery and equipment
___ (11) Net sales
___ (12) Inventories
___ (13) Marketing, selling, and advertising
___ (14) Buildings
___ (15) Land
___ (16) Income taxes payable
___ (17) Distribution and warehousing costs
___ (18) Investments (in other companies)

Preparing a Balance Sheet

E1-4

LO1-1

Honda Motor Co.

Honda Motor Corporation of Japan is a leading international manufacturer of automobiles, motorcycles, all-terrain vehicles, and personal watercraft. As a Japanese company, it follows Japanese GAAP and reports its financial statements in billions of yen (the sign for yen is ¥). Its recent balance sheet contained the following items (in billions). Prepare a balance sheet as of March 31, 2011, solving for the missing amount. (**Hint:** Exhibit 1.2 in the chapter provides a good model for completing this exercise.)

Cash and cash equivalents	¥ 1,279
Common stock	259
Accounts payable and other current liabilities	3,568
Inventories	900
Investments	640
Long-term debt	2,043
Net property, plant, and equipment	1,939
Other assets	6,025
Other liabilities	1,377
Retained earnings	4,324
Total assets	11,571
Total liabilities and stockholders' equity	?
Trade accounts, notes, and other receivables	788

Completing a Balance Sheet and Inferring Net Income

E1-5

LO1-1

Carlos Ramirez and Camila Garza organized New World Book Store as a corporation; each contributed $80,000 cash to start the business and received 4,000 shares of common stock. The store completed its first year of operations on December 31, 2014. On that date, the following financial items for the year were determined: December 31, 2014, cash on hand and in the bank, $75,600; December 31, 2014, amounts due from customers from sales of books, $39,000; unused portion of store and office equipment, $73,000; December 31, 2014, amounts owed to publishers for books purchased, $12,000; one-year note payable to a local bank for $3,000. No dividends were declared or paid to the stockholders during the year.

---

*In the United States, "provision for income taxes" is most often used as a synonym for "income tax expense."

Required:

1. Complete the following balance sheet as of the end of 2014.
2. What was the amount of net income for the year? (**Hint:** Use the retained earnings equation [Beginning Retained Earnings + Net Income − Dividends = Ending Retained Earnings] to solve for net income.)

Assets		Liabilities	
Cash	$ ___	Accounts payable	$ ___
Accounts receivable	___	Note payable	___
Store and office equipment	___	Interest payable	300
		Total liabilities	$ ___
		Stockholders' Equity	
		Common stock	___
		Retained earnings	12,300
		Total stockholders' equity	___
Total assets	$ ___	Total liabilities and stockholders' equity	$ ___

E1-6
LO1-1
Analyzing Revenues and Expenses and Preparing an Income Statement

Assume that you are the owner of Campus Connection, which specializes in items that interest students. At the end of January 2014, you find (for January only) this information:

a. Sales, per the cash register tapes, of $150,000, plus one sale on credit (a special situation) of $2,500.
b. With the help of a friend (who majored in accounting), you determine that all of the goods sold during January cost $70,000 to purchase.
c. During the month, according to the checkbook, you paid $37,000 for salaries, rent, supplies, advertising, and other expenses; however, you have not yet paid the $900 monthly utilities for January on the store and fixtures.

Required:
On the basis of the data given (disregard income taxes), what was the amount of net income for January? Show computations. (**Hint:** A convenient form to use has the following major side captions: Revenue from Sales, Expenses, and the difference—Net Income.)

E1-7
LO1-1
Preparing an Income Statement and Inferring Missing Values

Walgreens

Walgreen Co. is one of the nation's leading drugstore chains. Its recent income statement contained the following items (in millions). Prepare an income statement for the year ended August 31, 2011. (**Hint:** First order the items as they would appear on the income statement and then confirm the values of the subtotals and totals. Exhibit 1.3 in the chapter provides a good model for completing this exercise.)

Cost of sales	$51,692
Provision for income taxes*	1,580
Interest expense	71
Net earnings	2,714
Net sales	72,184
Pretax income	4,294
Selling, general, and administration expense	16,561
Other income	434
Total expenses	68,324
Total revenues/income	72,618

E1-8
LO1-1
Analyzing Revenues and Expenses and Completing an Income Statement

Neighborhood Realty, Incorporated, has been operating for three years and is owned by three investors. S. Bhojraj owns 60 percent of the total outstanding stock of 9,000 shares and is the managing executive in

---

*In the United States, "provision for income taxes" is a common synonym for "income tax expense."

charge. On December 31, 2015, the following financial items for the entire year were determined: commissions earned and collected in cash, $150,900, plus $16,800 uncollected; rental service fees earned and collected, $20,000; salaries expense paid, $62,740; commissions expense paid, $35,330; payroll taxes paid, $2,500; rent paid, $2,475 (not including December rent yet to be paid); utilities expense paid, $1,600; promotion and advertising paid, $7,750; income taxes paid, $24,400; and miscellaneous expenses paid, $500. There were no other unpaid expenses at December 31. Also during the year, the company paid the owners "out-of-profit" cash dividends amounting to $12,000. Complete the following income statement:

_____
_____
_____

Revenues
    Commissions earned $ _____
    Rental service fees   _____
       Total revenues $ _____
Expenses
    Salaries expense   _____
    Commission expense   _____
    Payroll tax expense   _____
    Rent expense   _____
    Utilities expense   _____
    Promotion and advertising expense   _____
    Miscellaneous expenses   _____
       Total expenses (excluding income taxes) _____
Pretax income   _____
    Income tax expense   _____
Net income $50,180

Inferring Values Using the Income Statement and Balance Sheet Equations

E1-9
LO1-1

Review the chapter explanations of the income statement and the balance sheet equations. Apply these equations in each independent case to compute the two missing amounts for each case. Assume that it is the end of 2015, the first full year of operations for the company. (**Hint:** Organize the listed items as they are presented in the balance sheet and income statement equations and then compute the missing amounts.)

Independent Cases	Total Revenues	Total Expenses	Net Income (Loss)	Total Assets	Total Liabilities	Stockholders' Equity
A	$93,500	$76,940	$	$140,200	$66,500	$
B		75,834	14,740	107,880		77,500
C	68,120	76,430		98,200	69,850	
D	55,804		21,770		20,300	78,680
E	84,840	75,320			25,520	80,000

Inferring Values Using the Income Statement and Balance Sheet Equations

E1-10
LO1-1

Review the chapter explanations of the income statement and the balance sheet equations. Apply these equations in each independent case to compute the two missing amounts for each case. Assume that it is the end of 2015, the first full year of operations for the company. (**Hint:** Organize the listed items as they are presented in the balance sheet and income statement equations and then compute the missing amounts.)

Independent Cases	Total Revenues	Total Expenses	Net Income (Loss)	Total Assets	Total Liabilities	Stockholders' Equity
A	$242,300	$196,700	$	$253,500	$ 75,000	$
B		176,500	29,920	590,000		350,600
C	73,500	91,890		260,400	190,760	
D	35,840		9,840		190,430	97,525
E	224,130	209,500			173,850	360,100

E1-11

LO1-1

Preparing an Income Statement and Balance Sheet

Painter Corporation was organized by five individuals on January 1, 2013. At the end of January 2013, the following monthly financial data are available:

Total revenues	$305,000
Total expenses (excluding income taxes)	189,000
Income tax expense (all unpaid as of January 31)	35,000
Cash balance, January 31, 2013	65,150
Receivables from customers (all considered collectible)	44,700
Merchandise inventory (by inventory count at cost)	94,500
Payables to suppliers for merchandise purchased from them (will be paid during February 2013)	25,950
Common stock (2,600 shares)	62,400

No dividends were declared or paid during 2013.

Required:
Complete the following two statements:

PAINTER CORPORATION
Income Statement
For the Month of January 2013

Total revenues	$
Less: Total expenses (excluding income tax)	
Pretax income	116
Less: Income tax expense	
Net income	$ 81

PAINTER CORPORATION
Balance Sheet
At January 31, 2013

Assets	
Cash	$ 65 150
Receivables from customers	44700
Merchandise inventory	94 500
Total assets	$ 204 350
Liabilities	
Payables to suppliers	$ 25 950
Income taxes payable	35
Total liabilities	60 950
Stockholders' Equity	
Common stock	62 400
Retained earnings	
Total stockholders' equity	
Total liabilities and stockholders' equity	$

E1-12

LO1-1

Preparing a Statement of Stockholders' Equity

Clint's Stonework Corporation was organized on January 1, 2013. For its first two years of operations, it reported the following:

Net income for 2013	$ 31,000
Net income for 2014	42,000
Dividends for 2013	14,200
Dividends for 2014	18,700
Total assets at the end of 2013	130,000
Total assets at the end of 2014	250,000
Common stock at the end of 2013	100,000
Common stock at the end of 2014	100,000

Required:
On the basis of the data given, prepare a statement of stockholders' equity for 2014. Show computations.

Focus on Cash Flows: Matching Cash Flow Statement Items to Categories

E1-13
LO1-1

The following items were taken from a recent cash flow statement. Note that different companies use slightly different titles for the same item. Without referring to Exhibit 1.5, mark each item in the list as a cash flow from operating activities (O), investing activities (I), or financing activities (F). Also place parentheses around the letter only if it is a cash outflow.

____ (1) Purchases of property, plant, and equipment
____ (2) Cash received from customers
____ (3) Cash paid for dividends to stockholders
____ (4) Cash paid to suppliers
____ (5) Income taxes paid
____ (6) Cash paid to employees
____ (7) Cash proceeds received from sale of investment in another company
____ (8) Repayment of borrowings

To practice with more exercises, go to the text website at **www.mhhe.com/libby8e**.

PROBLEMS

Preparing an Income Statement, Statement of Stockholders' Equity, and Balance Sheet (AP1-1)

P1-1
LO1-1

www.mhhe.com/libby8e

Assume that you are the president of Highlight Construction Company. At the end of the first year (December 31, 2014) of operations, the following financial data for the company are available:

Cash	$ 25,600
Receivables from customers (all considered collectible)	10,800
Inventory of merchandise (based on physical count and priced at cost)	81,000
Equipment owned, at cost less used portion	42,000
Accounts payable owed to suppliers	46,140
Salary payable for 2014 (on December 31, 2014, this was owed to an employee who was away because of an emergency; will return around January 10, 2015, at which time the payment will be made)	2,520
Total sales revenue	128,400
Expenses, including the cost of the merchandise sold (excluding income taxes)	80,200
Income taxes expense at 30% × pretax income; all paid during 2014	?
Common stock (December 31, 2014)	87,000
Dividends declared and paid during 2014	10,000

(Note: The beginning balances in Common stock and Retained earnings are zero because it is the first year of operations.)

Required:
Using the financial statement exhibits in the chapter as models and showing computations:
1. Prepare a summarized income statement for the year 2014.
2. Prepare a statement of stockholders' equity for the year 2014.
3. Prepare a balance sheet at December 31, 2014.

Analyzing a Student's Business and Preparing an Income Statement (AP1-2)

P1-2
LO1-1

During the summer between his junior and senior years, James Cook needed to earn sufficient money for the coming academic year. Unable to obtain a job with a reasonable salary, he decided to try the lawn care business for three months. After a survey of the market potential, James bought a used pickup truck on June 1 for $1,800. On each door he painted "James Cook Lawn Service, Phone 471-4487." He also spent $900 for mowers, trimmers, and tools. To acquire these items, he borrowed $3,000 cash by signing a note payable promising to pay the $3,000 plus interest of $78 at the end of the three months (ending August 31).

At the end of the summer, James realized that he had done a lot of work, and his bank account looked good. This fact prompted him to become concerned about how much profit the business had earned.

A review of the check stubs showed the following: Bank deposits of collections from customers totaled $15,000. The following checks had been written: gas, oil, and lubrication, $1,050; pickup repairs, $250; mower repair, $110; miscellaneous supplies used, $80; helpers, $5,400; payroll taxes, $190; payment for assistance in preparing payroll tax forms, $25; insurance, $125; telephone, $110; and $3,078 to pay off the note including interest (on August 31). A notebook kept in the pickup, plus some unpaid bills, reflected that customers still owed him $700 for lawn services rendered and that he owed $180 for gas and oil (credit card charges). He estimated that the cost for use of the truck and the other equipment (called **depreciation**) for three months amounted to $600.

Required:

1. Prepare a quarterly income statement for James Cook Lawn Service for the months June, July, and August 2014. Use the following main captions: Revenues from Services, Expenses, and Net Income. Assume that the company will not be subject to income tax.
2. Do you see a need for one or more additional financial reports for this company for 2014 and thereafter? Explain.

P1-3

LO1-1

Comparing Income with Cash Flow (A Challenging Problem) (AP1-3)

Huang Trucking Company was organized on January 1, 2014. At the end of the first quarter (three months) of operations, the owner prepared a summary of its activities as shown in the first row of the following tabulation:

Summary of Transactions	Computation of	
	Income	Cash
a. Services performed for customers, $66,000, of which $11,000 remained uncollected at the end of the quarter.	+$66,000	+$55,000
b. Cash borrowed from the local bank, $56,000 (one-year note).		
c. Small service truck purchased at the end of the quarter to be used in the business for two years starting the next quarter: cost, $12,500 cash.		
d. Wages earned by employees, $25,000, of which one-half remained unpaid at the end of the quarter.		
e. Service supplies purchased for use in the business, $3,800 cash, of which $900 were unused (still on hand) at the end of the quarter.		
f. Other operating expenses, $38,000, of which $6,500 remained unpaid at the end of the quarter.		
Based only on these transactions, compute the following for the quarter: Income (or loss) Cash inflow (or outflow)		

Required:

1. For each of the six transactions given in this tabulation, enter what you consider the correct amounts. Enter a zero when appropriate. The first transaction is illustrated.
2. For each transaction, explain the basis for your dollar responses.

P1-4

LO1-1

Evaluating Data to Support a Loan Application (A Challenging Problem)

On January 1, 2014, three individuals organized Northwest Company as a corporation. Each individual invested $10,000 cash in the business. On December 31, 2014, they prepared a list of resources owned (assets) and a list of the debts (liabilities) to support a company loan request for $70,000 submitted to a local bank. None of the three investors had studied accounting. The two lists prepared were as follows:

Company resources

Cash	$ 12,000
Service supplies inventory (on hand)	7,000
Service trucks (four, practically new)	57,000
Personal residences of organizers (three houses)	190,000
Service equipment used in the business (practically new)	30,000
Bills due from customers (for services already completed)	15,000
Total	$311,000

Company obligations

Unpaid wages to employees	$ 19,000
Unpaid taxes	8,000
Owed to suppliers	10,000
Owed on service trucks and equipment (to a finance company)	45,000
Loan from organizer	10,000
Total	$ 92,000

Required:
Prepare a short memo indicating:
1. Which of these items do not belong on the balance sheet? (Bear in mind that the company is considered to be separate from the owners.)
2. What additional questions would you raise about the measurement of items on the list? Explain the basis for each question.
3. If you were advising the local bank on its loan decision, which amounts on the list would create special concerns? Explain the basis for each concern and include any recommendations that you have.
4. In view of your responses to (1) and (2), what do you think the amount of stockholders' equity (i.e., assets minus liabilities) of the company would be? Show your computations.

ALTERNATE PROBLEMS

Preparing an Income Statement, Statement of Stockholders' Equity, and Balance Sheet (P1-1)

AP1-1
LO1-1

Assume that you are the president of Influence Corporation. At the end of the first year (June 30, 2014) of operations, the following financial data for the company are available:

Cash	$13,150
Receivables from customers (all considered collectible)	10,900
Inventory of merchandise (based on physical count and priced at cost)	27,000
Equipment owned, at cost less used portion	66,000
Accounts payable owed to suppliers	31,500
Salary payable for 2014 (on June 30, 2014, this was owed to an employee who was away because of an emergency; will return around July 7, 2014, at which time the payment will be made)	1,500
Total sales revenue	100,000
Expenses, including the cost of the merchandise sold (excluding income taxes)	68,500
Income taxes expense at 30% × pretax income; all paid during June of 2014	?
Common stock (July 1, 2013, and June 30, 2014)	62,000

No dividends were declared or paid during 2014. The beginning balance in Retained earnings is zero because it is the first year of operations.

Required:
Using the financial statement exhibits in the chapter as models and showing computations:
1. Prepare a summarized income statement for the year ended June 30, 2014.
2. Prepare a statement of stockholders' equity for the year ended June 30, 2014.
3. Prepare a balance sheet at June 30, 2014.

Analyzing a Student's Business and Preparing an Income Statement (P1-2)

AP1-2
LO1-1

Upon graduation from high school, Sam List immediately accepted a job as an electrician's assistant for a large local electrical repair company. After three years of hard work, Sam received an electrician's license and decided to start his own business. He had saved $12,000, which he invested in the business. First, he transferred this amount from his savings account to a business bank account for List Electric Repair Company, Incorporated. His lawyer had advised him to start as a corporation. He then purchased a used panel truck for $9,000 cash and secondhand tools for $1,500; rented space in a small building; inserted an ad in the local paper; and opened the doors on October 1, 2014. Immediately, Sam was very busy; after one month, he employed an assistant.

Although Sam knew practically nothing about the financial side of the business, he realized that a number of reports were required and that costs and collections had to be controlled carefully. At the end of the year, prompted in part by concern about his income tax situation (previously he had to report only salary), Sam recognized the need for financial statements. His wife Janet developed some financial statements for the business. On December 31, 2014, with the help of a friend, she gathered the following data for the three months just ended. Bank account deposits of collections for electric repair services totaled $32,000. The following checks had been written: electrician's assistant, $7,500; payroll taxes, $175; supplies purchased and used on jobs, $9,500; oil, gas, and maintenance on truck, $1,200; insurance, $700; rent, $500; utilities and telephone, $825; and miscellaneous expenses (including advertising), $600. Also, uncollected bills to customers for electric repair services amounted to $3,500. The $250 rent for December had not been paid. Sam estimated the cost of using the truck and tools (depreciation) during the three months to be $1,200. Income taxes for the three-month period were $3,930.

Required:

1. Prepare a quarterly income statement for List Electric Repair for the three months October through December 2014. Use the following main captions: Revenues from Services, Expenses, Pretax Income, and Net Income.
2. Do you think that Sam may need one or more additional financial reports for 2014 and thereafter? Explain.

AP1-3
LO1-1

Comparing Income with Cash Flow (A Challenging Problem) (P1-3)

Choice Chicken Company was organized on January 1, 2014. At the end of the first quarter (three months) of operations, the owner prepared a summary of its activities as shown in the first row of the following tabulation:

Summary of Transactions	Computation of	
	Income	Cash
a. Services performed for customers, $85,000, of which $15,000 remained uncollected at the end of the quarter.	+$85,000	+$70,000
b. Cash borrowed from the local bank, $25,000 (one-year note).		
c. Small service truck purchased at the end of the quarter to be used in the business for two years starting the next quarter: cost, $8,000 cash.		
d. Wages earned by employees, $36,000, of which one-sixth remained unpaid at the end of the quarter.		
e. Service supplies purchased for use in the business, $4,000 cash, of which $1,000 were unused (still on hand) at the end of the quarter.		
f. Other operating expenses, $31,000, of which one-half remained unpaid at the end of the quarter.		
Based only on these transactions, compute the following for the quarter: Income (or loss) Cash inflow (or outflow)		

Required:

1. For each of the six transactions given in this tabulation, enter what you consider the correct amounts. Enter a zero when appropriate. The first transaction is illustrated.
2. For each transaction, explain the basis for your dollar responses.

CASES **AND** PROJECTS

Annual Report Cases

CP1-1
LO1-1

AMERICAN EAGLE
OUTFITTERS, INC.

Finding Financial Information

Refer to the financial statements of American Eagle Outfitters in Appendix B at the end of this book.

Required:

Skim the annual report. Look at the income statement, balance sheet, and cash flow statement closely and attempt to infer what kinds of information they report. Then answer the following questions based on the report.

1. What types of products does American Eagle Outfitters sell?
2. On what date does American Eagle Outfitters's most recent reporting year end?
3. For how many years does it present complete
    a. Balance sheets?
    b. Income statements?
    c. Cash flow statements?

4. Are its financial statements audited by independent CPAs? How do you know?
5. Did its total assets increase or decrease over the last year?
6. How much inventory (in dollars) did the company have as of January 28, 2012 (accountants would call this the ending balance)?
7. Write out the basic accounting (balance sheet) equation and provide the values in dollars reported by the company as of January 28, 2012.

Finding Financial Information

Refer to the financial statements of Urban Outfitters in Appendix C at the end of this book.

Required:
1. What is the amount of net income for the most recent year?
2. What amount of revenue was earned in the most recent year?
3. How much inventory (in dollars) does the company have as of January 31, 2012?
4. By what amount did cash and cash equivalents* change during the most recent year?
5. Who is the auditor for the company?

CP1-2
LO1-1

Comparing Companies within an Industry

Refer to the financial statements of American Eagle Outfitters in Appendix B and Urban Outfitters in Appendix C.

Required:
1. Total assets is a common measure of the size of a company. Which company had the higher total assets at the end of the most recent year? **(Note: Some companies will label a year that has a January year-end as having a fiscal year-end dated one year earlier. For example, a January 2012 year-end may be labeled as Fiscal 2011 since the year actually has more months that fall in the 2011 calendar year than in the 2012 calendar year.)**
2. Net sales is also a common measure of the size of a company. Which company had the higher net sales for the most recent year?
3. Growth during a period is calculated as:

$$\frac{\text{Ending amount} - \text{Beginning amount}}{\text{Beginning amount}} \times 100 = \text{Growth rate}$$

Which company had the highest growth in total assets during the most recent year? Which company had the highest growth in net sales during the most recent year?

CP1-3
LO1-1

**AMERICAN EAGLE
OUTFITTERS, INC.**

www.mhhe.com/libby8e

Financial Reporting and Analysis Cases

Using Financial Reports: Identifying and Correcting Deficiencies in an Income Statement and Balance Sheet

CP1-4
LO1-1

Performance Corporation was organized on January 1, 2012. At the end of 2012, the company had not yet employed an accountant; however, an employee who was "good with numbers" prepared the following statements at that date:

PERFORMANCE CORPORATION December 31, 2012	
Income from sales of merchandise	$180,000
Total amount paid for goods sold during 2012	(90,000)
Selling costs	(25,000)
Depreciation (on service vehicles used)	(12,000)
Income from services rendered	52,000
Salaries and wages paid	(62,000)

****Cash equivalents** are short-term investments readily convertible to cash whose value is unlikely to change.

PERFORMANCE CORPORATION December 31, 2012		
Resources		
Cash		$ 32,000
Merchandise inventory (held for resale)		42,000
Service vehicles		50,000
Retained earnings (profit earned in 2012)		32,250
Grand total		$156,250
Debts		
Payables to suppliers		$ 17,750
Note owed to bank		25,000
Due from customers		13,000
Total		$ 55,750
Supplies on hand (to be used in rendering services)	$15,000	
Accumulated depreciation* (on service vehicles)	12,000	
Common stock, 6,500 shares	65,000	
Total		92,000
Grand total		$147,750

Required:
1. List all deficiencies that you can identify in these statements. Give a brief explanation of each one.
2. Prepare a proper income statement (correct net income is $32,250 and income tax expense is $10,750) and balance sheet (correct total assets are $140,000).

Critical Thinking Cases

CP1-5

LO1-2

Making Decisions as an Owner: Deciding about a Proposed Audit

You are one of three partners who own and operate Mary's Maid Service. The company has been operating for seven years. One of the other partners has always prepared the company's annual financial statements. Recently you proposed that the statements be audited each year because it would benefit the partners and preclude possible disagreements about the division of profits. The partner who prepares the statements proposed that his Uncle Ray, who has a lot of financial experience, can do the job and at little cost. Your other partner remained silent.

Required:
1. What position would you take on the proposal? Justify your response.
2. What would you strongly recommend? Give the basis for your recommendation.

CP1-6

LO1-2

Evaluating an Ethical Dilemma: Ethics and Auditor Responsibilities

A key factor that an auditor provides is independence. The **AICPA Code of Professional Conduct** states that "a member in public practice should be independent in fact and appearance when providing auditing and other attestation services."

Required:
Do you consider the following circumstances to suggest a lack of independence? Justify your position. (Use your imagination. Specific answers are not provided in the chapter.)
1. Jack Jones is a partner with a large audit firm and is assigned to the Ford audit. Jack owns 10 shares of Ford.
2. Melissa Chee has invested in a mutual fund company that owns 500,000 shares of Sears stock. She is the auditor of Sears.

---

*Accumulated depreciation represents the used portion of the asset and should be subtracted from the asset's balance.

3. Bob Franklin is a clerk/typist who works on the audit of AT&T. He has just inherited 50,000 shares of AT&T stock. (Bob enjoys his work and plans to continue despite his new wealth.)

4. Nancy Sodoma worked on weekends as the controller for a small business that a friend started. Nancy quit the job in midyear and now has no association with the company. She works full-time for a large CPA firm and has been assigned to do the audit of her friend's business.

5. Mark Jacobs borrowed $100,000 for a home mortgage from First City National Bank. The mortgage was granted on normal credit terms. Mark is the partner in charge of the First City audit.

Financial Reporting and Analysis Team Project

Team Project: Examining an Annual Report   **CP1-7**

As a team, select an industry to analyze. *Yahoo!Finance* provides lists of industries at <u>biz.yahoo</u> <u>.com/p/industries.html</u>. Click on an industry for a list of companies in that industry. Alternatively, go to Google Finance at <u>www.google.com/finance</u>, search for a company you are interested in, and you will be presented with a list including that company and its competitors. Each team member should acquire the annual report or 10-K for one publicly traded company in the industry, with each member selecting a different company (the SEC EDGAR service at <u>www.sec.gov</u> or the company's investor relations website itself are good sources).

Required:
On an individual basis, each team member should write a short report answering the following questions about the selected company. Discuss any patterns across the companies that you as a team observe. Then, as a team, write a short report comparing and contrasting your companies.

1. What types of products or services does it sell?
2. On what day of the year does its fiscal year end?
3. For how many years does it present complete
   a. Balance sheets?
   b. Income statements?
   c. Cash flow statements?
4. Are its financial statements audited by independent CPAs? If so, by whom?
5. Did its total assets increase or decrease over last year? By what percentage? [Percentage change is calculated as (Current year − Last year) ÷ Last year. Show supporting computations.]
6. Did its net income increase or decrease over last year? By what percentage?

CONTINUING **CASE**

Financial Statements for a New Business Plan   **CC1-1**

Penny Cassidy is considering forming her own pool service and supply company, Penny's Pool Service & Supply, Inc. (PPSS). She has decided to incorporate the business to limit her legal liability. She expects to invest $20,000 of her own savings and receive 1,000 shares of common stock. Her plan for the first year of operations forecasts the following amounts at the end of the year December 31, 2014: Cash in bank, $2,900; amounts due from customers for services rendered, $2,300; pool supplies inventory, $4,600; equipment, $28,000; amounts owed to Pool Corporation, Inc., a pool supply wholesaler, $3,500; note payable to the bank, $5,000. Penny forecasts first year sales of $60,000, wages of $24,000, cost of supplies used $8,200, other administrative expenses $4,500, and income tax expense of $4,000. She expects to pay herself a $10,000 dividend as the sole stockholder of the company.

Required:
If Penny's estimates are correct, what would the following first year financial statements look like for Penny's Pool Service & Supply (use Exhibits 1.2, 1.3, and 1.4 as models).
1. Income statement
2. Statement of stockholders' equity
3. Balance sheet

Investing and Financing Decisions and the Accounting System

S teve Ells is a classically trained chef who is often called one of the most innovative men in the world of food. He is the founder, chairman of the board, and co-chief executive officer of Chipotle Mexican Grill, a leader in the fastest-growing segment of the restaurant industry, now called "fast-casual." In 1993, this entrepreneur opened his first restaurant in a former Dolly Madison ice cream store in Denver, Colorado. His vision was a restaurant that serves food fast but uses higher-quality fresh ingredients and cooking techniques found in finer restaurants. As of December 31, 2011, the Chipotle chain had over 1,230 restaurants in the United States, two in Toronto, Canada, and two in London, England. It plans to open about 160 additional restaurants in 2012.

How did Chipotle grow so fast? It did so in two stages. First, in 1999, McDonald's Corporation became the majority stockholder by investing about $360 million in Chipotle. This provided funding for its tremendous early growth from 19 stores to nearly 490 restaurants

Learning Objectives

After studying this chapter, you should be able to:

2-1 Define the objective of financial reporting, the elements of the balance sheet, and the related key accounting assumptions and principles. p. 43

2-2 Identify what constitutes a business transaction and recognize common balance sheet account titles used in business. p. 47

2-3 Apply transaction analysis to simple business transactions in terms of the accounting model: Assets = Liabilities + Stockholders' Equity. p. 49

2-4 Determine the impact of business transactions on the balance sheet using two basic tools: Journal entries and T-accounts. p. 54

2-5 Prepare a trial balance and simple classified balance sheet, and analyze the company using the current ratio. p. 64

2-6 Identify investing and financing transactions and demonstrate how they impact cash flows. p. 68

by the end of 2005. Then, in January 2006, Chipotle "went public." In its IPO or initial public offering, it issued stock to the public for the first time. That stock is listed on the New York Stock Exchange as CMG. McDonald's also sold its ownership in Chipotle for nearly $1.4 billion—a handsome profit of over $1 billion. Comparing its balance sheet from 2005 to 2011 highlights the company's amazing 264 percent growth since becoming a public company:

	(in millions of dollars)		
	Assets =	Liabilities +	Stockholders' Equity
End of 2011	$1,425	$381	$1,044
End of 2005	392	83	309
Change	+ $1,033	+ $298	+ $ 735

This growth was stimulated in part by Ells's evolving vision that "fresh is not enough anymore." He has committed Chipotle to serving naturally raised pork, chicken, and beef; using no-trans-fat cooking oil; serving cheese and sour cream products that are free of synthetic bovine growth hormones; using certified organic beans and locally grown organic produce when in season; and serving preservative-free corn and flour tortillas. In an even more dramatic show of commitment to sustainability, in 2009, Chipotle built the first-ever free-standing restaurant to receive the highest rating (LEED Platinum) from the U.S. Green Building Council,[1] a start toward other sustainable renovations and projects. In 2011, the company created the Chipotle Cultivate Foundation to expand philanthropic work surrounding sustainable agriculture.

As it continues to evolve, Chipotle's recent annual report states its vision is now "to change the way people think about and eat fast food." The belief is that providing good food and service is good business.

UNDERSTANDING THE BUSINESS

The "fast-casual" segment of the $1.7 trillion restaurant industry generates more than $23 billion in sales annually.[2] What identifies a restaurant as fast-casual? Typically, customers still order at the register as in a fast-food restaurant, but there are usually no drive-thru options and the food is made to order and served in modern and upscale surroundings. Checks typically range between $8 and $16. The largest fast-casual restaurant chain is Chipotle Mexican Grill, followed by Panera Bread Company.

Franchising is common in chain restaurants. The largest restaurant to use franchising is Subway, with over 39,000 restaurants—all franchised. Franchising involves selling the right to use or sell a product or service to another. This is an easy way for someone to start his or her own business because the franchisor (the seller, such as Panera Bread) often provides site location, design, marketing, and management training support in exchange for initial franchise fees and ongoing royalty fees usually based on weekly sales. At Panera Bread, for example, only 48 percent of the stores are company-owned.

Unlike most restaurant chains, however, Chipotle does not franchise the business. All restaurants are company-owned. Developing a new site, usually on rented property, costs about $800,000. In 2011, Chipotle spent over $140 million on new and renovated property and equipment. The creation of new restaurants to meet consumer demand for healthier food options explains most of the changes in Chipotle's assets and liabilities from year to year. To understand how the result of Chipotle Mexican Grill's growth strategy is communicated in the balance sheet, we must answer the following questions:

- What business activities cause changes in the balance sheet amounts from one period to the next?
- How do specific business activities affect each of the balance sheet amounts?
- How do companies keep track of the balance sheet amounts?

In this chapter, we focus on some typical asset acquisition activities (often called **investing activities**), along with related **financing activities,** such as borrowing funds from creditors or selling stock to investors to provide the cash necessary to acquire the assets. We examine those activities that affect only balance sheet amounts. Operating activities that affect both the income statement and the balance sheet are covered in Chapters 3 and 4. To begin, let's return to the basic concepts introduced in Chapter 1.

---

[1]See http://www.greenbeanchicago.com/wind-turbine-green-flyash-restaurant-chipotle/ and https://www.usgbc.org/ShowFile.aspx?DocumentID=6953 for more information.
[2]Sources: http://mexican-taco-fast-food-restaurant.franchise-business-tips.com/industry and http://www.fastcasual.com/infographic.php?id=4.

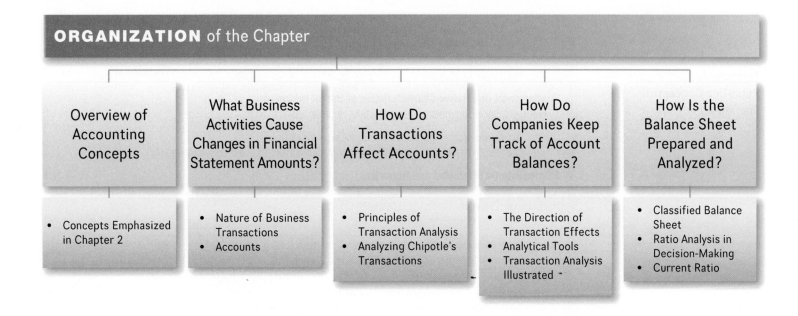

ORGANIZATION of the Chapter

Overview of Accounting Concepts	What Business Activities Cause Changes in Financial Statement Amounts?	How Do Transactions Affect Accounts?	How Do Companies Keep Track of Account Balances?	How Is the Balance Sheet Prepared and Analyzed?
• Concepts Emphasized in Chapter 2	• Nature of Business Transactions • Accounts	• Principles of Transaction Analysis • Analyzing Chipotle's Transactions	• The Direction of Transaction Effects • Analytical Tools • Transaction Analysis Illustrated	• Classified Balance Sheet • Ratio Analysis in Decision-Making • Current Ratio

OVERVIEW OF ACCOUNTING CONCEPTS

Because learning and remembering **how** the accounting process works is much easier if you know **why** it works a certain way, we begin by discussing key accounting terms and concepts. They are part of a **conceptual framework** developed over many years and synthesized by the Financial Accounting Standards Board (FASB) to provide a structure for developing accounting standards. Exhibit 2.1 provides an overview of the key concepts in the framework that will be discussed in each of the next four chapters. A clear understanding of these accounting concepts will be helpful as you study, and they will also help you in future chapters as we examine more complex business activities.

Concepts Emphasized in Chapter 2

Objective of Financial Reporting

The **primary objective of financial reporting to external users** is to provide financial information about the reporting entity that is useful to existing and potential investors, lenders, and other creditors in making decisions about providing resources to the entity. The users of accounting information are all expected to have a reasonable understanding of accounting concepts and procedures—which may be one of the reasons you are studying accounting. Of course, as we discussed in Chapter 1, many other groups, such as suppliers and customers, also use external financial statements.

Most users are interested in information to help them **assess the amount, timing, and uncertainty of a business's future cash inflows and outflows.** For example, creditors and potential creditors need to assess an entity's ability to (1) pay interest on a loan over time and also (2) pay back the principal on the loan when it is due. Investors and potential investors want to assess the entity's ability to (1) pay dividends in the future and (2) be successful so that the stock price rises, enabling investors to sell their stock for more than they paid. Information about a company's economic resources, claims against its resources, and activities that change these items provides insight into cash flows and a company's financial strengths and weaknesses.

LEARNING OBJECTIVE 2-1
Define the objective of financial reporting, the elements of the balance sheet, and the related key accounting assumptions and principles.

PRIMARY OBJECTIVE OF FINANCIAL REPORTING TO EXTERNAL USERS
is to provide financial information about the reporting entity that is useful to existing and potential investors, lenders, and other creditors in making decisions about providing resources to the entity.

EXHIBIT 2.1

Financial Accounting and Reporting Conceptual Framework

Objective of Financial Reporting to External Users: (in Ch. 2)
To provide financial information about the reporting entity that is useful to existing and potential investors, lenders, and other creditors in making decisions about providing resources to the entity
➤ **Pervasive Cost-Benefit Constraint:** Benefits of providing information should outweigh its costs.

Fundamental Qualitative Characteristics of Useful Information: (in Ch. 2)
Relevance (including materiality) and Faithful Representation

　　　　Attributes that Enhance Qualitative Characteristics:
　　　　Comparability (including consistency), Verifiability, Timeliness, and Understandability

Elements to Be Measured and Reported:
Assets, Liabilities, Stockholders' Equity, Investments by Owners, and Distributions to Owners (in Ch. 2)
Revenues, Expenses, Gains, and Losses (in Ch. 3)
Comprehensive Income (in Ch. 5)

Recognition, Measurement, and Disclosure Concepts:
Assumptions: Separate Entity, Continuity (Going Concern), and Stable Monetary Unit (in Ch. 2)
　　　　　　　Time Period (in Ch. 3)
Principles: Mixed-Attribute Measurement (in Ch. 2)
　　　　　Revenue Realization and Expense Matching (in Ch. 3)
　　　　　Full Disclosure (in Ch. 5)

Qualitative Characteristics of Useful Information

RELEVANT INFORMATION can influence a decision; it is timely and has predictive and/or feedback value.

FAITHFUL REPRESENTATION requires that the information be complete, neutral, and free from error.

SEPARATE-ENTITY ASSUMPTION states that a business's activities are accounted for separately from those of its owners.

CONTINUITY (GOING-CONCERN) ASSUMPTION states that businesses are assumed to continue into the foreseeable future.

STABLE MONETARY UNIT ASSUMPTION states that accounting information should be measured and reported in the national monetary unit without any adjustment for changes in purchasing power.

MIXED-ATTRIBUTE MEASUREMENT MODEL is applied to measuring different assets and liabilities.

For accounting information to be useful, it must be relevant and be a faithful representation. **Relevant information** is capable of influencing decisions by allowing users to assess past activities and/or predict future activities. To be reported, the information should also be material in amount depending on the nature of the item and company. **Faithful representation** requires that the information be complete, neutral, and free from error. Comparability, verifiability, timeliness, and understandability are qualitative characteristics that enhance the usefulness of information that is relevant and faithfully represented. For example, our discussions of ratio analysis will emphasize the importance of comparing ratios for the same company over time, as well as with those of competitors. Such comparisons are valid only if the information is prepared on a consistent and comparable basis. These characteristics of useful information guide the FASB in deciding what financial information should be reported.

Recognition and Measurement Concepts

Before we discuss accountants' precise definitions for the elements of the balance sheet, we should consider three assumptions and a measurement concept that underlie much of our application of these definitions. First we make the **separate-entity assumption,** which states that each business's activities must be accounted for separately from the activities of its owners, all other persons, and other entities. This means, for example, that, when an owner purchases property for personal use, the property is not an asset of the business. Second, under the **continuity assumption** (sometimes called the **going-concern assumption**), unless there is evidence to the contrary, we assume that the business will continue operating into the foreseeable future, long enough to meet its contractual commitments and plans. This means, for example, that if there was a high likelihood of bankruptcy, then its assets should be valued and reported on the balance sheet as if the company were to be liquidated (that is, discontinued, with all of its assets sold and all debts paid). Under the **stable monetary unit assumption,** each business entity accounts for and reports its financial results primarily in terms of the national monetary unit (e.g., dollars in the United States, yen in Japan, and euros in Germany), without any adjustment for changes in purchasing power (e.g., inflation).

　　Finally, accountants measure the elements of the balance sheet using what is called a **mixed-attribute measurement model.** Most balance sheet elements are recorded at their cash-equivalent value on the date of the transaction. This is called the **historical cost principle** or **cost principle.** For example, assets are initially recorded at the cash paid plus the dollar value of all noncash considerations on the exchange date. We will discuss the conditions under which these values are adjusted to other amounts, such as their market value, starting in Chapter 6 of this text. With these assumptions in mind, we are now ready to discuss accountants' precise definitions of the elements of the balance sheet.

Elements of the Balance Sheet

The four financial statements—balance sheet, income statement, statement of stockholders' (shareholders' or owners') equity, and statement of cash flows—along with the notes to the statements provide the structure for the information communicated to users. As we learned in Chapter 1, assets, liabilities, and stockholders' equity are the elements of a corporation's balance sheet. The conceptual framework defines them as follows.

Assets are probable future economic benefits owned or controlled by an entity as a result of past transactions or events. In other words, they are the economic resources the entity acquired to use in operating the company in the future. As shown in Chipotle's balance sheet presented in Exhibit 2.2, most companies list assets **in order of liquidity,** or how soon an asset is expected by management to be turned into cash or used. Notice that several of Chipotle's assets are categorized as current assets. Current assets are those resources that Chipotle will use or turn into cash within one year (the next 12 months). Chipotle's current assets include Cash, Short-Term Investments, Accounts Receivable (due from customers and others), Supplies (to make the food), and Prepaid Expenses (for rent, insurance, and advertising paid in advance of use). For manufacturers that produce and sell goods and merchandisers who sell already completed goods, Inventory (for goods to be sold) would also be listed after Accounts Receivable. Inventory is always considered a current asset, regardless of how long it takes to produce and sell the inventory. These are typical titles used by most entities.

All other assets are considered long term (or noncurrent). That is, they are to be used or turned into cash after the coming year. For Chipotle, that includes Property and Equipment (land, buildings, and equipment) and Investments (in other companies). Intangibles (nonphysical assets such as trademarks and patents) may also be listed. Although Chipotle has intangibles, for simplicity in this chapter, intangible assets have been combined with Property and Equipment. Intangibles are discussed in detail in Chapter 8.

Liabilities are defined as probable future sacrifices of economic benefits arising from present obligations of a business as a result of past transactions or events. In other words, they are probable obligations to pay cash or provide goods or services arising from past transactions. Entities that a company owes money to are called **creditors.** Chipotle's balance sheet includes four liabilities: Accounts Payable (to suppliers), Accrued Expenses Payable (for wages, utilities, taxes, and interest on debt), Unearned Revenue (for unredeemed gift cards that have been purchased by customers), and Notes Payable (to banks and other creditors). These and other liabilities will be discussed in more detail in subsequent chapters.

Similar to how assets are reported in order of liquidity, liabilities are usually listed on the balance sheet **in order of maturity** (how soon an obligation is to be paid). Liabilities that Chipotle will need to pay or settle within the coming year (with cash, goods, other current assets, or services) are classified as current liabilities. Distinguishing current assets and current liabilities assists external users of the financial statements in assessing the amounts and timing of future cash flows.

Stockholders' equity (also called **shareholders' equity** or **owners' equity**) is the residual interest in the assets of the entity after subtracting liabilities. It is a combination of the financing provided by the owners and by business operations.

- **Financing Provided by Owners** is referred to as **contributed capital.** Owners invest in the business by providing cash and sometimes other assets and receive in exchange shares of stock as evidence of ownership. The largest investors in Chipotle Mexican Grill are financial institutions (mutual funds, pension funds, etc.). The directors and executive officers also own stock as do other corporate employees and the general public.

ASSETS are probable future economic benefits owned or controlled by an entity as a result of past transactions or events.

CURRENT ASSETS are assets that will be used or turned into cash within one year. Inventory is always considered a current asset regardless of the time needed to produce and sell it.

LIABILITIES are probable future sacrifices of economic benefits arising from present obligations of a business as a result of past transactions or events.

CURRENT LIABILITIES are obligations that will be settled by providing cash, goods, other current assets, or services within the coming year.

STOCKHOLDERS' EQUITY (SHAREHOLDERS' OR OWNERS' EQUITY) is the residual interest in assets of the entity after subtracting liabilities.

EXHIBIT 2.2

Chipotle Mexican Grill, Inc.,
Balance Sheet

CHIPOTLE MEXICAN GRILL, INC. **Consolidated Balance Sheet*** **December 31, 2011** **(in thousands of dollars, except per share data)**		**EXPLANATIONS** *"Consolidated" means all subsidiaries are combined* *Point in time for which the balance sheet was prepared*
ASSETS		
Current Assets:		
Cash	$ 401,200	
Short-term investments	55,000	*Ownership of other companies' stocks and bonds*
Accounts receivable	8,400	*Payments due from customers and others*
Supplies	8,900	*Food, beverage, and packaging supplies on hand*
Prepaid expenses	27,700	*Rent, advertising, and insurance paid in advance*
Total current assets	501,200	
Property and equipment (net)	795,900	*Cost of land, buildings, and equipment to be used*
Long-term investments	128,200	*Ownership of other companies' stocks and bonds*
Total assets	$1,425,300	
LIABILITIES AND STOCKHOLDERS' EQUITY		
Current Liabilities:		
Accounts payable	$ 46,400	*Payments due to suppliers*
Accrued expenses payable	93,100	*Utilities, interest, taxes, and wages due to employees*
Unearned revenue	18,000	*Unredeemed gift cards*
Total current liabilities	157,500	
Notes payable	223,600	*Written obligations due beyond the next 12 months*
Total liabilities	381,100	
Stockholders' Equity:		
Common stock ($0.01 par per share)	300	*Total par value of stock issued by company to investors*
Additional paid-in capital	372,400	*Excess of amount received over par value of stock issued*
Retained earnings	671,500	*Undistributed earnings reinvested in the company*
Total stockholders' equity	1,044,200	
Total liabilities and stockholders' equity	$1,425,300	

Current assets: Cash, Short-term investments, Accounts receivable, Supplies, Prepaid expenses

Noncurrent assets: Property and equipment (net), Long-term investments

Current liabilities: Accounts payable, Accrued expenses payable, Unearned revenue

Noncurrent liabilities: Notes payable

The information has been adapted from actual statements and simplified for this chapter.

RETAINED EARNINGS
are the cumulative earnings of a company that have not been distributed to the owners and are reinvested in the business.

- **Financing Provided by Operations** is referred to as **earned capital** or <u>retained earnings</u>.[3] When companies earn profits, they can be distributed to owners as dividends or reinvested in the business. The <u>portion of profits reinvested in the business is called retained earnings</u>. Companies with a growth strategy often pay little or no dividends to retain funds for expansion. A look at Chipotle's balance sheet (Exhibit 2.2) indicates that its growth has been financed by substantial reinvestment of earnings ($671.5 million).

PAUSE FOR FEEDBACK

We just learned the elements of the balance sheet (assets, liabilities, and stockholders' equity) and how assets and liabilities are usually classified (current or noncurrent). Current assets (including inventory) are expected to be used or turned into cash within the next 12 months and current liabilities are expected to be paid or satisfied within the next 12 months with cash, services, or other current assets.

---

[3]Retained earnings can increase only from profitable operations, but they decrease when a firm has a loss or pays dividends.

The following is a list of items from a recent balance sheet of The Wendy's Company. Indicate on the line provided whether each of the following is usually categorized on the balance sheet as a current asset (CA), noncurrent asset (NCA), current liability CL), noncurrent liability (NCL), or stockholders' equity (SE).

SE a. Retained Earnings   *CA* d. Inventories   *NCA* g. Accounts Receivable

CA EC b. Prepaid Expenses   *SE NCA* e. Additional Paid-in Capital   *NCL* h. Long-Term Debt

NCL c. Accounts Payable   *NCA* f. Properties (buildings and equipment) *NCL* i. Accrued Expenses Payable

After you have completed your answers, check them with the solutions at the bottom of the page.

| Unrecorded but Valuable Assets and Liabilities | FINANCIAL ANALYSIS |

Many very valuable intangible **assets,** such as trademarks, patents, and copyrights that are developed inside a company (not purchased), are **not reported** on the balance sheet. For example, General Electric's balance sheet reveals no listing for the GE trademark because it was developed internally over time through research, development, and advertising (it was not purchased). Likewise, the Coca-Cola Company does not report any asset for its patented Coke formula, although it does report more than $2 billion in various trademarks that it has purchased.

Nearly all companies have some form of off-balance-sheet financing—obligations **not reported** as **liabilities** on the balance sheet. For many companies, renting facilities or equipment can fall into this category, and can be quite significant. For example, Delta Air Lines included in a note to the financial statements in a recent annual report that over $10.8 billion in future cash flows of aircraft rental leases were not reported on the balance sheet as debt, an amount equal to 24 percent of its total liabilities that were reported on the balance sheet. This also illustrates the importance of reading the notes, not just the financial statements, when analyzing a company's financial information and predicting future cash flows.

Now that we have reviewed the basic elements of the balance sheet and related recognition and measurement concepts as part of the conceptual framework, let's see what economic activities cause changes in the amounts reported on the balance sheet.

WHAT BUSINESS ACTIVITIES CAUSE CHANGES IN FINANCIAL STATEMENT AMOUNTS?

Nature of Business Transactions

Accounting focuses on certain events that have an economic impact on the entity. Those events that are recorded as part of the accounting process are called transactions. The first step in translating the results of business events to financial statement numbers is determining which events to include. As the definitions of assets and liabilities indicate, only economic resources and debts **resulting from past transactions** are recorded on the balance sheet. Transactions include two types of events:

1. **External events:** These are **exchanges** of assets, goods, or services by one party for assets, services, or promises to pay (liabilities) from one or more other parties. Examples include the purchase of a machine from a supplier, sale of merchandise to customers, borrowing cash from a bank, and investment of cash in the business by the owners.

LEARNING OBJECTIVE 2-2
Identify what constitutes a business transaction and recognize common balance sheet account titles used in business.

A TRANSACTION is (1) an exchange of assets or services for assets, services, or promises to pay between a business and one or more external parties to a business or (2) a measurable internal event such as adjustments for the use of assets in operations.

---

a. SE; *b.* CA; *c.* CL; *d.* CA; *e.* SE; *f.* NCA; *g.* CA; *h.* NCL; *i.* CL

Solution to
SELF-STUDY QUIZ

2. **Internal events:** These include certain events that are not exchanges between the business and other parties but nevertheless have a direct and measurable effect on the entity. Examples include using up insurance paid in advance and using buildings and equipment over several years.

Throughout this textbook, the word *transaction* is used in the broad sense to include both types of events.

Some important events that have a future economic impact on a company, however, are **not reflected in the financial statements.** In most cases, signing a contract is not considered to be an accounting transaction because it involves **only the exchange of promises,** not of assets such as cash, goods, services, or property. For example, assume that Chipotle signs an employment contract with a new regional manager. From an accounting perspective, no transaction has occurred because no exchange of assets, goods, or services has been made. Each party to the contract has exchanged promises—the manager agrees to work; Chipotle agrees to pay the manager for the work. For each day the new manager works, however, the exchange of services for pay results in a transaction that Chipotle must record. Because of their importance, long-term employment contracts, leases, and other commitments may need to be disclosed in notes to the financial statements.

Accounts

An ACCOUNT is a standardized format that organizations use to accumulate the dollar effect of transactions on each financial statement item.

To accumulate the dollar effect of transactions on each financial statement item, organizations use a standardized format called an **account.** The resulting balances are kept separate for financial statement purposes. To facilitate the recording of transactions, each company establishes a **chart of accounts,** a list of all account titles and their unique numbers. The accounts are usually organized by financial statement element, with asset accounts listed first, followed by liability, stockholders' equity, revenue, and expense accounts in that order. Exhibit 2.3 lists various account titles that are quite common and are used by most companies. The exhibit also provides special notes to help you in learning account titles. When you are completing assignments and are unsure of an account title, refer to this listing for help.

Every company creates its own chart of accounts to fit the nature of its business activities. For example, a small lawn care service may have an asset account titled Lawn Mowing

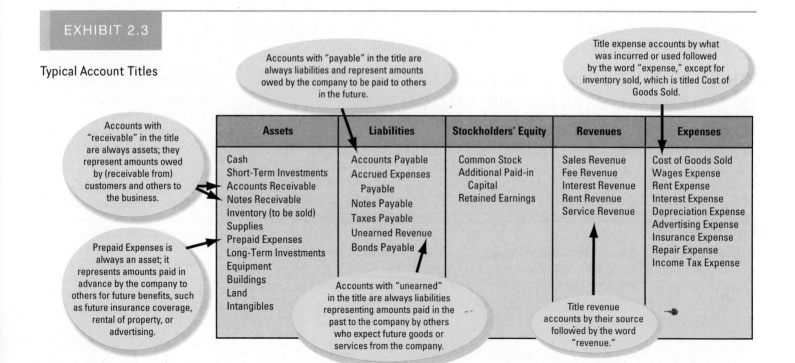

EXHIBIT 2.3

Typical Account Titles

Accounts with "receivable" in the title are always assets; they represent amounts owed by (receivable from) customers and others to the business.

Prepaid Expenses is always an asset; it represents amounts paid in advance by the company to others for future benefits, such as future insurance coverage, rental of property, or advertising.

Accounts with "payable" in the title are always liabilities and represent amounts owed by the company to be paid to others in the future.

Accounts with "unearned" in the title are always liabilities representing amounts paid in the past to the company by others who expect future goods or services from the company.

Title revenue accounts by their source followed by the word "revenue."

Title expense accounts by what was incurred or used followed by the word "expense," except for inventory sold, which is titled Cost of Goods Sold.

Assets	Liabilities	Stockholders' Equity	Revenues	Expenses
Cash	Accounts Payable	Common Stock	Sales Revenue	Cost of Goods Sold
Short-Term Investments	Accrued Expenses Payable	Additional Paid-in Capital	Fee Revenue	Wages Expense
Accounts Receivable	Notes Payable	Retained Earnings	Interest Revenue	Rent Expense
Notes Receivable	Taxes Payable		Rent Revenue	Interest Expense
Inventory (to be sold)	Unearned Revenue		Service Revenue	Depreciation Expense
Supplies	Bonds Payable			Advertising Expense
Prepaid Expenses				Insurance Expense
Long-Term Investments				Repair Expense
Equipment				Income Tax Expense
Buildings				
Land				
Intangibles				

Equipment, but a large corporation such as Dell is unlikely to report such an account. These differences in accounts will become more apparent as we examine the balance sheets of various companies. Because each company has its own chart of accounts, you should **not** try to memorize a typical chart of accounts, but understand the nature of each typical account. Then when you see a company that uses a slightly different title, you will understand what it means. For example, some companies use the terms Trade Accounts Receivable (same as Accounts Receivable) or Merchandise Inventory (same as Inventory). In homework problems, you will either be given the account names or be expected to select appropriate names, similar to the ones in Exhibit 2.3. Once you select a name for an account, you must use that exact name in all transactions affecting that account.

The accounts you see in the financial statements of most large corporations are actually summations (or aggregations) of a number of specific accounts in their recordkeeping system. For example, Chipotle keeps separate accounts for food, beverage, and packaging supplies, but combines them under **Supplies** on the balance sheet. Equipment, buildings, and land are also combined into an account called **Property and Equipment.** Since our aim is to understand financial statements reported by actual entities, we will focus on aggregated accounts.

HOW DO TRANSACTIONS AFFECT ACCOUNTS?

Managers' business decisions often result in transactions that affect the financial statements. For example, decisions to expand the number of stores, advertise a new product, change an employee benefit package, and invest excess cash would all affect the financial statements. Sometimes these decisions have unintended consequences as well. The decision to purchase additional inventory for cash in anticipation of a major sales initiative, for example, will increase inventory and decrease cash. But if there is no demand for the additional inventory, the lower cash balance will also reduce the company's ability to pay its other obligations.

Because business decisions often involve an element of risk, managers should understand exactly how transactions impact the financial statements. The process for determining the effects of transactions is called **transaction analysis.**

> **LEARNING OBJECTIVE 2-3**
> Apply transaction analysis to simple business transactions in terms of the accounting model: Assets = Liabilities + Stockholders' Equity.

Principles of Transaction Analysis

Transaction analysis is the process of studying a transaction to determine its economic effect on the entity in terms of the accounting equation (also known as the **fundamental accounting model**). We outline the process in this section of the chapter and create a visual tool representing the process (the transaction analysis model). The basic accounting equation and two principles are the foundation for this model. Recall from Chapter 1 that the basic accounting equation for a business that is organized as a corporation is as follows:

TRANSACTION ANALYSIS is the process of studying a transaction to determine its economic effect on the fundamental accounting model.

$$\text{Assets (A) = Liabilities (L) + Stockholders' Equity (SE)}$$

The two principles underlying the transaction analysis process follow:

- Every transaction affects at least two accounts; correctly identifying those accounts and the direction of the effect (whether an increase or a decrease) is critical.

- The accounting equation must remain in balance after each transaction.

Success in performing transaction analysis depends on a clear understanding of these principles. Study the following material well.

Dual Effects

The idea that every transaction has **at least two effects** on the basic accounting equation is known as the **dual effects** concept.[4] Most transactions with external parties involve an

---

[4]From this concept, accountants have developed what is known as the *double-entry system* of recordkeeping.

exchange by which the business **entity both receives something and gives up something in return.** For example, suppose Chipotle purchased tomatoes for cash. In this exchange, Chipotle would receive food supplies (an increase in an asset) and in return would give up cash (a decrease in an asset).

$$
\begin{array}{ccc}
A & = L + & SE \\
\hline
+/- & & \\
\end{array}
$$

Transaction	Chipotle Received	Chiptole Gave
Purchased tomatoes for cash	**Supplies** (asset account increased)	**Cash** (asset account decreased)

In analyzing this transaction, we determined that the accounts affected were Supplies and Cash. However, most supplies are purchased on credit (that is, money is owed to suppliers). In that case, Chipotle would engage in *two* separate transactions at different points in time:

$$
\begin{array}{ccc}
A & = L + & SE \\
\hline
+ & + & \\
\end{array}
$$

Transaction	Chipotle Received	Chipotle Gave
Purchased tomatoes on credit	**Supplies** (asset account increased)	**Accounts Payable** A promise to pay later (liability account increased)

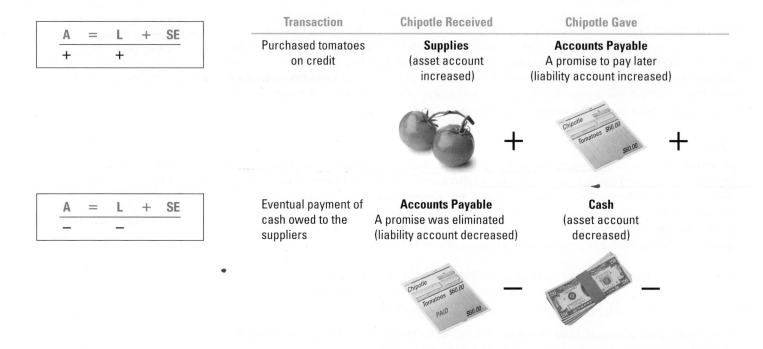

$$
\begin{array}{ccc}
A & = L + & SE \\
\hline
- & - & \\
\end{array}
$$

Eventual payment of cash owed to the suppliers	**Accounts Payable** A promise was eliminated (liability account decreased)	**Cash** (asset account decreased)

Not all important business activities result in a transaction that affects the financial statements. Most importantly, signing a contract involving **the exchange of two promises to perform** (e.g., you promise to work and I promise to pay you) **does not result in an accounting transaction** that is recorded. For example, if Chipotle sent an order for more tomatoes to its food supplier and the supplier accepted the order but did not fill it immediately, no transaction took place. As soon as the food is delivered to Chipotle, however, the supplier has given up its inventory in exchange for a promise from Chipotle to pay for the items in the near future, and Chipotle has exchanged its promise to pay for the supplies it receives. Because a **promise** has been exchanged for **goods,** a transaction has taken place. Both Chipotle and the supplier's statements will be affected.

Balancing the Accounting Equation

Notice in the tomato purchase illustrations on the previous page that the accounting equation next to each transaction remained in balance. The accounting equation must remain in balance after each transaction. That is, total assets (resources) must equal total liabilities and stockholders' equity (claims to resources). If all correct accounts have been identified and the appropriate direction of the effect on each account has been determined, the equation should remain in balance.

Systematic transaction analysis for investing and financing activities includes the following steps:

Step 1: **Ask** → *What was received and what was given?*

- **Identify the account affected by title** (e.g., Cash and Notes Payable).
  Remember: *Make sure that at least two accounts change.*
- **Classify them by type of account:** Asset (A), Liability (L), or Stockholders' Equity (SE) (e.g., Cash is an asset).
- **Determine the direction of the effect:** Did the account increase (+) or decrease (−)?

Step 2: **Verify** → *Is the accounting equation in balance?* **(A = L + SE)**

Analyzing Chipotle's Transactions

To illustrate the use of the transaction analysis process, let's consider transactions of Chipotle that are also common to most businesses. Remember that this chapter presents transactions that affect only the balance sheet accounts. Assume that Chipotle engages in the **following events during the first quarter of 2012,** the first three months following the balance sheet in Exhibit 2.2. Account titles are from that balance sheet, and remember that, for simplicity, all amounts are in **thousands:**

(a) **Chipotle issued 10,000 additional shares of common stock, receiving $62,300 in cash from investors.** Each share of common stock usually has a nominal (low) **par value** printed on the face of the certificate. Par value is a legal amount per share established by the board of directors; it has no relationship to the market price of the stock. Its significance is that it establishes the minimum amount that a stockholder must contribute. Chipotle's common stock has a par value of $.01 per share. When a corporation issues common (capital) stock, the amount received affects two separate accounts: The Common Stock account for the number of shares times the par value per share, and Additional Paid-in Capital (also called Paid-in Capital or Contributed Capital in Excess of Par) for the excess received above par.

PAR VALUE is a legal amount per share established by the board of directors; it represents the minimum amount a stockholder must contribute and has no relationship to the market price of the stock.

COMMON STOCK is the account that is equal to the number of shares issued by a corporation times the par value per share.

ADDITIONAL PAID-IN CAPITAL (Paid-in Capital, Contributed Capital in Excess of Par) is the amount of capital contributed by the shareholders less the par value of the stock.

Step 1: *What was received and what was given* **(account name, type of account, amount, and direction of effect)?**

Received: Cash (+A) $62,300

Given: Additional stock shares:
Common Stock (+SE) $100 *(10,000 shares × $.01 per share)*
Additional Paid-in Capital (+SE) $62,200 *($62,300 − $100)*

	Assets			=	Liabilities		+	Stockholders' Equity		
Cash	Short-term Investments	Property & Equipment	Long-term Investments		Dividends Payable	Notes Payable		Common Stock	Additional Paid-in Capital	Retained Earnings
(a) +62,300				=				+100	+62,200	

Step 2: *Is the accounting equation in balance?* **Assets $62,300 = Liabilities $0 + Stockholders' Equity $62,300**

2000   *A ∞*

(b) **Chipotle borrowed $2,000 from its local bank, signing a note to be paid in three years.**

Step 1: What was received and what was given **(account name, type of account, amount, and direction of effect)?**

    Received: Cash (+A) $2,000   **Given:** A written promise to repay the loan:
                                               Notes Payable (+L) $2,000

	Assets			=	Liabilities		+	Stockholders' Equity		
Cash	Short-term Investments	Property & Equipment	Long-term Investments		Dividends Payable	Notes Payable		Common Stock	Additional Paid-in Capital	Retained Earnings
(a) +62,300				=				+100	+62,200	
(b) +2,000				=		+2,000				

Step 2: Is the accounting equation in balance? **Assets $2,000 = Liabilities $2,000 + Stockholders' Equity $0**

Companies that need cash to buy or build additional facilities often seek funds by selling stock to investors as in transaction *(a)* or by borrowing from creditors as in transaction *(b)*. Any transactions with stockholders (usually issuing additional stock and paying dividends) and transactions with banks (borrowing and repaying loans) are **financing** activities.

(c) **Chipotle purchased new ovens, counters, refrigerators, and other equipment costing $63,100; paid $55,100 in cash and signed a note for the rest.**

Step 1: What was received and what was given **(account name, type of account, amount, and direction of effect)?**

    Received: Property & Equipment (+A) $63,100   **Given:** Cash (−A) $55,100
                                                 Notes Payable (+L) $8,000

	Assets			=	Liabilities		+	Stockholders' Equity		
Cash	Short-term Investments	Property & Equipment	Long-term Investments		Dividends Payable	Notes Payable		Common Stock	Additional Paid-in Capital	Retained Earnings
(a) +62,300				=				+100	+62,200	
(b) +2,000				=		+2,000				
(c) −55,100		+63,100		=		+8,000				

Step 2: Is the accounting equation in balance? **Assets $8,000 = Liabilities $8,000 + Stockholders' Equity $0**

Purchasing and selling property and equipment and investments in the stock of other companies are **investing** activities. In the investing transaction *(c)*, notice that more than two accounts were affected.

(d) **Chipotle paid $400 to the local bank on the amount borrowed in *(b)* above (ignore interest).**

Step 1: What was received and what was given **(account name, type of account, amount, and direction of effect)?**

    Received: Reduction in bank loan: **Given:** Cash (−A) $400
                Notes Payable (−L) $400

	Assets			=	Liabilities		+	Stockholders' Equity		
Cash	Short-term Investments	Property & Equipment	Long-term Investments		Dividends Payable	Notes Payable		Common Stock	Additional Paid-in Capital	Retained Earnings
(a) +62,300				=				+100	+62,200	
(b) +2,000				=		+2,000				
(c) −55,100		+63,100		=		+8,000				
(d) −400				=		−400				

Step 2: Is the accounting equation in balance? **Assets −$400 = Liabilities −$400 + Stockholders' Equity $0**

(e) **Chipotle purchased the stock of other companies, paying $60,400 in cash.** The company intends to hold $20,900 of the stock as long-term investments and the rest as short-term investments.

Step 1: What was received and what was given (**account name, type of account, amount, and direction of effect**)?

Received: Short-term investments (+A) $39,500   **Given:** Cash (−A) $60,400
Long-term investments (+A) $20,900

	Assets			=	Liabilities		+	Stockholders' Equity		
Cash	Short-term Investments	Property & Equipment	Long-term Investments		Dividends Payable	Notes Payable		Common Stock	Additional Paid-in Capital	Retained Earnings
(a) +62,300				=				+100	+62,200	
(b) +2,000				=		+2,000				
(c) −55,100		+63,100		=		+8,000				
(d) −400				=		−400				
(e) −60,400	+39,500		+20,900	=						

Step 2: Is the accounting equation in balance? **Assets $0 = Liabilities $0 + Stockholders' Equity $0**

(f) Chipotle does not pay dividends, but instead reinvests profits into growing the business. However, for illustration purposes, **assume Chipotle's board of directors declared that the Company will pay $3,000 in cash as dividends to shareholders next quarter.**

Step 1: What was received and what was given (**account name, type of account, amount, and direction of effect**)?

Received: Lower claim from stockholders   **Given:** Dividends Payable (+L) $3,000
Retained Earnings (−SE) $3,000

	Assets			=	Liabilities		+	Stockholders' Equity		
Cash	Short-term Investments	Property & Equipment	Long-term Investments		Dividends Payable	Notes Payable		Common Stock	Additional Paid-in Capital	Retained Earnings
(a) +62,300				=				+100	+62,200	
(b) +2,000				=		+2,000				
(c) −55,100		+63,100		=		+8,000				
(d) −400				=		−400				
(e) −60,400	+39,500		+20,900	=						
(f)				=	+3,000					−3,000
−51,600	+39,500	+63,100	+20,900		+3,000	+9,600		+100	+62,200	−3,000

Step 2: Is the accounting equation in balance? **Assets $0 = Liabilities $3,000 + Stockholders' Equity −$3,000**
Overall effects of *(a)–(f)*: Assets $71,900 = Liabilities $12,600 + Stockholders' Equity $59,300
$71,900 = $71,900

PAUSE FOR **FEEDBACK**

Transaction analysis involves identifying accounts (by title) affected in a transaction, recognizing that at least two accounts are affected, classifying the accounts (asset, liability, or stockholders' equity), and determining the direction of the effect on the account (increase or decrease). If all accounts and effects are correct, then the fundamental accounting equation (A = L + SE) will remain in balance. **Practice is the most effective way to develop your transaction analysis skills.**

SELF-STUDY QUIZ

Review the analysis in events (*a*) through (*f*) above, complete the analysis of the following transactions, and indicate the effects in the chart below. Answer from the standpoint of the business.

(*a*) **Paul Knepper contributes $50,000 cash to establish Florida Flippers, Inc., a new scuba business organized as a corporation; in exchange, he receives 25,000 shares of stock with a par value of $0.10 per share.**

Step 1: Identify and classify accounts and effects.
Received: ~~25,000 shares stock~~ *Cash (+A) = 50,000*
Given: *Stock (SE) $2,500   Add. Paid-in Capital (+SE) $47,500*

Step 2: Is the accounting equation in balance?   Yes or No? *yes*

(*b*) **Florida Flippers buys a small building near the ocean for $250,000, paying $25,000 cash and signing a 10-year note payable for the rest.**

Step 1: Identify and classify accounts and effects.
Received: *Property (+A) $250,000   Cash (−) 25,000*
Given: *notes payable (L) $225,000*

Step 2: Is the accounting equation in balance?   Yes or No? *yes*

Assets		=	Liabilities	+	Stockholders' Equity	
Cash	Building		Notes Payable		Common Stock	Additional Paid-in Capital
					$2500	*47,500*
(a) +50,000		=				
(b) − 25,000	+250,000	=	225,000			

275,000 = 275,000

After you have completed your answers, check them with the solutions at the bottom of the page. If your answers did not agree with ours, we recommend that you go back to each event to make sure that you have completed each of the steps of transaction analysis.

LEARNING OBJECTIVE 2-4

Determine the impact of business transactions on the balance sheet using two basic tools: Journal entries and T-accounts.

HOW DO COMPANIES KEEP TRACK OF ACCOUNT BALANCES?

For most organizations, recording transaction effects and keeping track of account balances in the manner just presented is impractical. To handle the multitude of daily transactions that a business generates, companies establish accounting systems, usually computerized, that follow a cycle. Exhibit 2.4 presents the primary activities of the **accounting cycle** performed **during the accounting period** separately from those that occur at the **end of the accounting period.** In Chapters 2 and 3, we will illustrate transactions during Chipotle's first quarter of 2012. In

---

Solution to
SELF-STUDY QUIZ

(*a*) Step 1: Received: Cash (+A) $50,000;   Given: Common Stock (+SE) $2,500 and Additional Paid-in Capital (+SE) $47,500.

Step 2: Yes. The equation remains in balance; Assets (on the left) and Stockholders' Equity (on the right) increase by the same amount, $50,000.

(*b*) Step 1: Received: Building (+A) $250,000;   Given: Cash (−A) $25,000 and Notes Payable (+L) $225,000.

Step 2: Yes. Assets (on the left) increase by $225,000 and Liabilities (on the right) increase by $225,000.

Assets		=	Liabilities	+	Stockholders' Equity	
Cash	Building		Notes Payable		Common Stock	Additional Paid-in Capital
(a) +50,000		=			+2,500	+47,500
(b) −25,000	+250,000	=	+225,000			

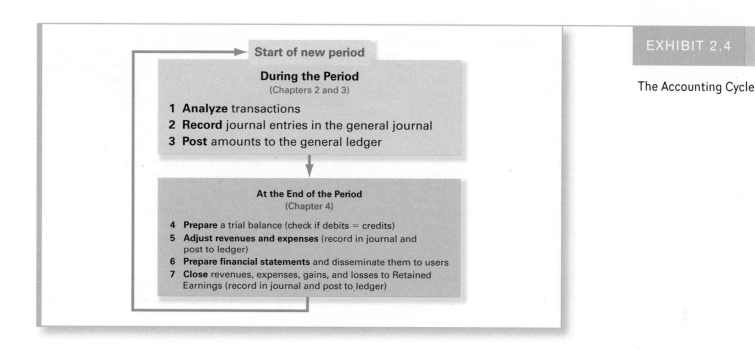

EXHIBIT 2.4

The Accounting Cycle

Chapter 4, we will complete the accounting cycle by discussing and illustrating activities at the end of the period to adjust the records, prepare financial statements, and finally close the accounting records.

During the accounting period, transactions that result in exchanges between the company and other external parties are analyzed to determine the accounts and effects. The effects are recorded first in the **general journal**, a listing in chronological order of each transaction's effects. To determine account balances, the accounts are updated by posting the effects listed in the general journal to the respective accounts in the **general ledger**, a record of effects to and balances of each account.

These formal records are based on two very important tools used by accountants: journal entries and T-accounts. From the standpoint of accounting systems design, these analytical tools are a more efficient way to reflect the effects of transactions, determine account balances, and prepare financial statements. As future business managers, you should develop your understanding and use of these tools in financial analysis. For those studying accounting, this knowledge is the foundation for an understanding of the accounting system and future accounting coursework. After we explain how to perform transaction analysis using these tools, we illustrate their use in financial analysis.

The **ACCOUNTING CYCLE** is the process followed by entities to analyze and record transactions, adjust the records at the end of the period, prepare financial statements, and prepare the records for the next cycle.

The Direction of Transaction Effects

As we saw earlier in this chapter, transaction effects increase and decrease assets, liabilities, and stockholders' equity accounts. To reflect these effects efficiently, we need to structure the transaction analysis model in a manner that shows the **direction** of the effects. As shown in Exhibit 2.5, each account is set up as a "T" with the following structure:

- **Increases in asset accounts are on the left** because assets are on the left side of the accounting equation (A = L + SE).

- **Increases in liability and stockholders' equity accounts are on the right** because they are on the right side of the accounting equation (A = L + SE).

Also notice that:

- The term **debit** (dr for short) always refers to the **left** side of the T.
- The term **credit** (cr for short) always refers to the **right** side of the T.

DEBIT (dr) refers to the left side of a T-account.

CREDIT (cr) refers to the right side of a T-account.

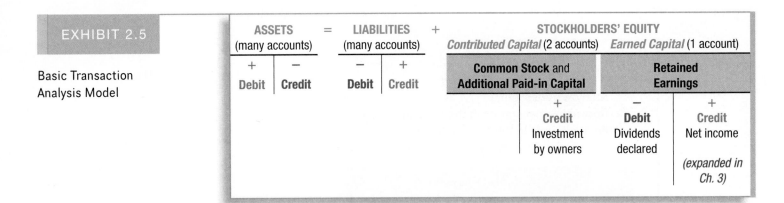

EXHIBIT 2.5

Basic Transaction
Analysis Model

As a consequence:

- Asset accounts increase on the left (debit) side and they normally have debit balances. (It would be highly unusual for an asset account, such as Inventory, to have a negative (credit) balance.)
- Liability and stockholders' equity accounts increase on the right (credit) side and they normally have credit balances.

In summary:

In Chapter 3, we will add revenue and expense account effects to Retained Earnings in our model. Until then, as you are learning to perform transaction analysis, **you should refer to the transaction analysis model in Exhibit 2.5 often until you can construct it on your own without assistance.**

Many students have trouble with accounting because they forget that the term **debit** is simply the **left** side of an account and the term **credit** is simply the **right** side of an account. Perhaps someone once told you that you were a credit to your school or your family. As a result, you may think that credits are good and debits are bad. Such is not the case. Just remember that **debit is on the left** and **credit is on the right.**

If you have identified the correct accounts and effects through transaction analysis, the accounting equation will remain in balance. **The total dollar value of all debits will equal the total dollar value of all credits** in a transaction. For an extra measure of assurance, add this equality check (Debits = Credits) to the transaction analysis process.

PAUSE FOR FEEDBACK

From Exhibit 2.5, we learned that each account can increase and decrease. In the transaction analysis model, the effect of a transaction on each element can be represented with a T with one side increasing and the other side decreasing. Asset accounts on the left side of the fundamental accounting equation increase their balances on the left side of the T. Liability and stockholders' equity accounts are on the right side of the fundamental accounting equation and increase their balance on the right side of the T. In accounting, the left side of the T is called the debit side and the right is called the credit side. Most accounts have a balance on the positive side.

SELF-STUDY **QUIZ**

The following is a list of accounts from a balance sheet of The Wendy's Company. Indicate on the line provided whether each of the following usually has a debit (DR) or credit (CR) balance.

CR Accounts Payable   DR Properties (land, buildings, and equipment)   DR Cash

CR Retained Earnings   DR Inventories   CR Long-Term Debt

CR Accrued Expenses Payable DR Notes Receivable (due in five years)   DR Accounts Receivable

After you have completed your answers, check them with the solutions at the bottom of the page.

Analytical Tools

The Journal Entry

In a bookkeeping system, transactions are <u>recorded in chronological order</u> in a **general journal** (or simply, journal). After analyzing the business documents (such as purchase invoices, receipts, and cash register tapes) that describe a transaction, the bookkeeper enters the effects on the accounts in the journal using debits and credits. The **journal entry,** then, is an accounting method for expressing the effects of a transaction on accounts. It is written in a debits-equal-credits format. To illustrate, we refer back to event (*a*) in Chipotle's transaction analyis on page 51.

A JOURNAL ENTRY is an accounting method for expressing the effects of a transaction on accounts in a debits-equal-credits format.

(*a*) Chipotle issued 10,000 additional shares of common stock, receiving $62,300 in cash from investors. Par value of the stock is $0.01 per share.

The journal entry for event (*a*) in the Chipotle's illustration is as follows:

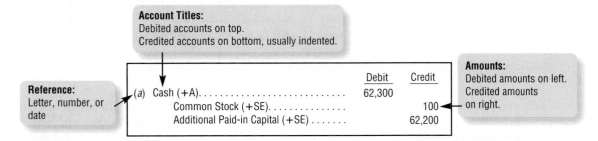

Notice the following:

- It is useful to include a date or some form of reference for each transaction. The debited accounts are written first (on top) with the amounts recorded in the left column. The credited accounts are written below the debits and are usually indented in manual records; the credited amounts are written in the right column. The order of the debited accounts or credited accounts does not matter, as long as the debits are on top and the credits are on the bottom and indented to the right.

- Total debits ($62,300) equal total credits ($100 + $62,200 = $62,300).

- Three accounts are affected by this transaction. Any journal entry that affects more than two accounts is called a **compound entry.** Many transactions in this and subsequent chapters require a compound journal entry.

- As you can see in the illustration of a formal bookkeeping system in Exhibit 2.6, an additional line is written below the journal entry as an explanation of the transaction. For simplicity, explanations will not be included in this text.

While you are learning to perform transaction analysis, use the symbols A, L, and SE next to each account title, as in the preceding journal entry. Specifically identifying accounts as assets (A), liabilities (L), or stockholders' equity (SE) clarifies the transaction analysis and makes journal entries easier to write. For example, if Cash is to be increased, we write Cash (+A). Throughout subsequent chapters, we include the direction of the effect along with the symbol to

Column 1: CR; CR; CR   Column 2: DR; DR; DR   Column 3: DR; CR; DR

EXHIBIT 2.6

Posting Transaction Effects
from the Journal to the
Ledger

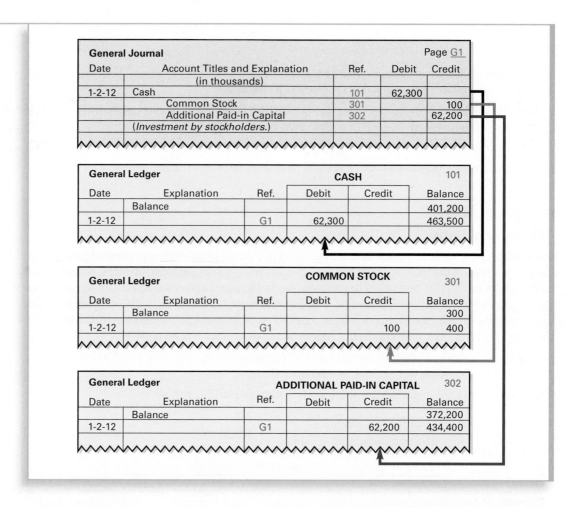

help you understand the effects of each transaction on the financial statements. In transaction (*a*)
on the previous page, we can see that assets are affected by +$62,300 and stockholders' equity
accounts are affected by +$62,300. The accounting equation A = L + SE remains in balance.

A note of caution: Many students try to memorize journal entries without understanding or
using the transaction analysis model. As more detailed transactions are presented in subsequent
chapters, the task becomes increasingly more difficult. In the long run, **memorizing, understanding, and using the transaction analysis model** presented here will save you time and
prevent confusion.

The T-Account

By themselves, journal entries do not provide the balances in accounts. After the journal entries
have been recorded, the bookkeeper **posts** (transfers) the dollar amounts to each account
affected by the transaction to determine the new account balances. (In most computerized
accounting systems, this happens automatically.)

As a group, the accounts are called a **general ledger.** In the manual accounting system used
by some small organizations, the ledger is often a three-ring binder with a separate page for
each account. In a computerized system, accounts are stored on a disk. See Exhibit 2.6 for an
illustration of a journal page and the related ledger pages. Note that the cash effects from the
journal entry have been posted to the Cash ledger page.

One very useful tool for summarizing the transaction effects and determining the balances for individual accounts is a **T-account,** a simplified representation of a ledger account.
Exhibit 2.7 shows the T-accounts for Chipotle's Cash and Common Stock accounts based on
Event (*a*). Notice that, for Cash, which is classified as an asset, increases are shown on the left
and decreases appear on the right side of the T-account. For Common Stock, however, increases
are shown on the right and decreases on the left since Common Stock is a stockholders' equity

The T-ACCOUNT is a tool for
summarizing transaction effects
for each account, determining
balances, and drawing inferences
about a company's activities.

EXHIBIT 2.7

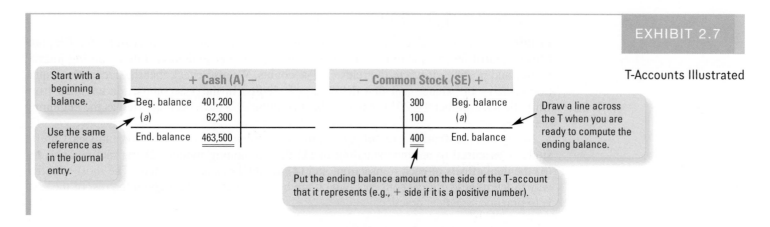

T-Accounts Illustrated

account. Many small businesses still use handwritten or manually maintained accounts in this T-account format. Computerized systems retain the concept but not the format of the T-account.

In Exhibit 2.7, notice that the ending balance is indicated on the positive side with a double underline. To find the account balances, we can express the T-accounts as equations:

	Cash	Common Stock
Beginning balance	$401,200	$ 300
+ "+" side	+ 62,300	+100
− "−" side	− 0	− 0
Ending balance	$463,500	$ 400

A word on terminology: The words **debit** and **credit** may be used as verbs, nouns, and adjectives. For example, we can say that Chipotle's Cash account was debited (verb) when stock was issued to investors, meaning that the amount was entered on the left side of the T-account. Or we can say that a credit (noun) was entered on the right side of an account. Common Stock may be described as a credit account (adjective). These terms will be used instead of **left** and **right** throughout the rest of this textbook. The next section illustrates the steps to follow in analyzing the effects of transactions, recording the effects in journal entries, and determining account balances using T-accounts.

Inferring Business Activities from T-Accounts

FINANCIAL ANALYSIS

T-accounts are useful primarily for instructional and analytical purposes. In many cases, we will use T-accounts to determine what transactions a company engaged in during a period. For example, the primary transactions affecting Accounts Payable for a period are purchases of assets on account from suppliers and cash payments to suppliers. If we know the beginning and ending balances of Accounts Payable and all the amounts that were purchased on credit during a period, we can determine the amount of cash paid. A T-account analysis would include the following:

− Accounts Payable (L) +		
	600	Beg. bal.
Cash payments to suppliers ?	1,500	Purchases on account
	300	End. bal.

Solution:								
Beginning Balance	**+**	**Purchases on Account**	**−**	**Cash Payments to Suppliers**	**=**	**Ending Balance**		
$600	+	$1,500	−	?	=	$ 300		
		$2,100	−	?	=	$ 300		
				?	=	$1,800		

Transaction Analysis Illustrated

In this section, we will use the quarterly investing and financing transactions for Chipotle Mexican Grill (events [a] to [f]) that were analyzed earlier to demonstrate recording journal entries and posting effects to the relevant T-accounts. We also check that the accounting equation remains in balance and that debits equal credits. In the T-accounts, the amounts from Chipotle's December 31, 2011, balance sheet (Exhibit 2.2) have been inserted as the beginning balances.

Study this illustration carefully, including the explanations of transaction analysis. Careful study is **essential** to an understanding of (1) the accounting model, (2) transaction analysis, (3) the dual effects of each transaction, and (4) the dual-balancing system. The most effective way to learn these critical concepts, which are basic to material throughout the rest of the text, is to practice, practice, practice.

(a) **Chipotle issued 10,000 additional shares of common stock ($0.01 par value per share), receiving $62,300 in cash from investors.**

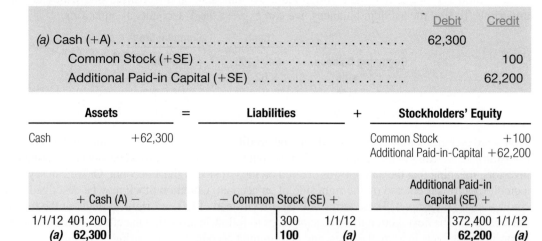

Debits = Credits

	Debit	Credit
(a) Cash (+A)	62,300	
Common Stock (+SE)		100
Additional Paid-in Capital (+SE)		62,200

Equation in balance

Assets	=	Liabilities	+	Stockholders' Equity
Cash +62,300				Common Stock +100 Additional Paid-in-Capital +62,200

Effects posted

+ Cash (A) −	− Common Stock (SE) +	Additional Paid-in − Capital (SE) +
1/1/12 401,200 *(a)* 62,300	300 1/1/12 100 *(a)*	372,400 1/1/12 62,200 *(a)*

The effects reflected in the journal entry have been posted to the appropriate T-accounts. Notice that if an account was debited such as Cash, that effect was written in the debit column of the Cash T-account. Similarly, if an account was credited such as Common Stock, that effect was written in the credit column of the T-account. Also notice that the beginning balances for the first quarter of 2012 are taken from the December 31, 2011, balance sheet (Exhibit 2.2) and are indicated on the positive side of the account—assets have debit balances and liabilities and stockholders' equity accounts have credit balances.

(b) **Chipotle borrowed $2,000 from its local bank, signing a note to be paid in three years.**

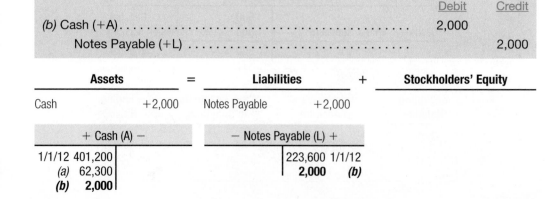

Debits = Credits

	Debit	Credit
(b) Cash (+A)	2,000	
Notes Payable (+L)		2,000

Equation in balance

Assets	=	Liabilities	+	Stockholders' Equity
Cash +2,000		Notes Payable +2,000		

Effects posted

+ Cash (A) −	− Notes Payable (L) +
1/1/12 401,200 *(a)* 62,300 *(b)* 2,000	223,600 1/1/12 2,000 *(b)*

(c) **Chipotle purchased new ovens, counters, refrigerators, and other equipment costing $63,100; paid $55,100 in cash and signed a note for the rest.**

	Debit	Credit
(c) Property and Equipment (+A)	63,100	
Cash (−A)...		55,100
Notes Payable (+L)		8,000

Debits = Credits

Assets	=	Liabilities	+	Stockholders' Equity
Property and Equipment +63,100		Notes Payable +8,000		
Cash −55,100				

Equation in balance

+ Cash (A) −		Property and + Equipment (net) (A) −		− Notes Payable (L) +	
1/1/12 401,200		1/1/12 795,900			223,600 1/1/12
(a) 62,300	**55,100** *(c)*	*(c)* **63,100**			2,000 *(b)*
(b) 2,000					**8,000** *(c)*

Effects posted

(d) **Chipotle paid $400 to the local bank on the amount borrowed in *(b)* above (ignore interest).**

	Debit	Credit
(d) Notes Payable (−L)	400	
Cash (−A).......................................		400

Debits = Credits

Assets	=	Liabilities	+	Stockholders' Equity
Cash −400		Notes Payable −400		

Equation in balance

+ Cash (A) −		− Notes Payable (L) +	
1/1/12 401,200			223,600 1/1/12
(a) 62,300	55,100 *(c)*	*(d)* **400**	2,000 *(b)*
(b) 2,000	**400** *(d)*		8,000 *(c)*

Effects posted

(e) **Chipotle purchased the stock of other companies, paying $60,400 in cash.** The company intends to hold $20,900 of the stock as long-term investments and the rest as short-term investments.

	Debit	Credit
(e) Short-term Investments (+A)	39,500	
Long-term Investments (+A)	20,900	
Cash (−A).......................................		60,400

Debits = Credits

Assets	=	Liabilities	+	Stockholders' Equity
Short-term Investments +39,500				
Long-term Investments +20,900				
Cash −60,400				

Equation in balance

+ Cash (A) −		Short-term + Investments (A) −		Long-term + Investments (A) −	
1/1/12 401,200		1/1/12 55,000		1/1/12 128,200	
(a) 62,300	55,100 *(c)*	*(e)* **39,500**		*(e)* **20,900**	
(b) 2,000	400 *(d)*				
	60,400 *(e)*				

Effects posted

(f) Chipotle does not pay dividends, but instead reinvests profits into growing the business. However, for illustration purposes, **assume Chipotle's board of directors declared that the Company will pay $3,000 in cash as dividends to shareholders next quarter.**

Debits = Credits

	Debit	Credit
(f) Retained Earnings (−SE).	3,000	
Dividends Payable (+L)		3,000

Equation in balance

Assets	=	Liabilities	+	Stockholders' Equity
		Dividends Payable +3,000		Retained Earnings −3,000

Effects posted

− Dividends Payable (L) +		− Retained Earnings (SE) +	
	0 1/1/12		671,500 1/1/12
3,000 **(f)**		**(f)** **3,000**	

Now we determine the balances in the T-accounts that changed during the quarter:

+ Cash (A) −			+ Short-term Investments (A) −			Property and Equipment (net) (A) −			+ Long-term Investments (A) −	
1/1/12 401,200			1/1/12 55,000			1/1/12 795,900			1/1/12 128,200	
(a) 62,300	55,100	(c)	(e) 39,500			(c) 63,100			(e) 20,900	
(b) 2,000	400	(d)	94,500			859,000			149,100	
	60,400	(e)								
349,600										

− Notes Payable (L) +			− Dividends Payable (L) +		
	223,600	1/1/12		0	1/1/12
(c) 400	2,000	(b)		3,000	(f)
	8,000	(c)		3,000	
	233,200				

− Common Stock (SE) +			− Additional Paid-in Capital (SE) +			− Retained Earnings (SE) +		
	300	1/1/12		372,400	1/1/12		671,500	1/1/12
	100	(a)		62,200	(a)	(f) 3,000		
	400			434,600			668,500	

PAUSE FOR FEEDBACK

Accountants analyze and then record transactions in the general journal in chronological order in journal entry form. Debited accounts are written on top with amounts in the left column and credited accounts are written on the bottom with amounts in the right column. Then the effects are posted in the general ledger (similar to a T-account). Each page of the ledger represents a different account that has a debit (left) side and a credit (right) side. To post transaction effects, the amount for each account in a journal entry is written in the appropriate debit or credit column on the ledger page to obtain account balances. Refer to Exhibit 2.5 for the transaction analysis model.

SELF-STUDY **QUIZ**

Record the following transactions and post the effects to the T-accounts. Because this is a new company, all T-accounts start with a beginning balance of $0.

(a) **Paul Knepper contributes $50,000 cash to establish Florida Flippers, Inc., a new scuba business organized as a corporation; he receives in exchange 25,000 shares of stock with a $0.10 per share par value.**

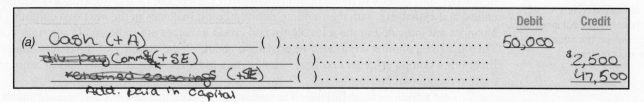

(b) **Florida Flippers buys a small building near the ocean for $250,000, paying $25,000 in cash and signing a 10-year note payable for the rest.**

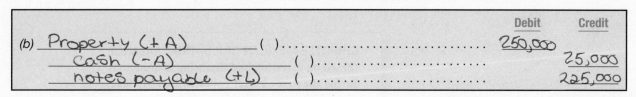

Cash		Property and Equipment		Notes Payable		Common Stock		Additional Paid-in Capital	
Beg. 0		Beg. 0			0 Beg.		0 Beg.		0 Beg.
a) 50,000							2500		47500
b) 250,000 25,000		250,000			225,000				
25,000		250,000			225,000		2,500		47,500

After you have completed your answers, check them with the solutions at the bottom of the page.

$275,000 = 275,000 ✓

GUIDED **HELP**

For additional step-by-step video instruction on analyzing, recording, and posting transaction effects and classifying accounts, go to the URL or scan the QR code in the margin with your smartphone or iPad.

www.mhhe.com/libby8e

Solutions to
SELF-STUDY QUIZ

(a) Cash (+A) 50,000
    Common Stock (+SE)   2,500   [25,000 shares × $0.10 par]
    Additional Paid-in Capital (+SE).   47,500

(b) Property and Equipment (+A). 250,000
    Cash (−A).   25,000
    Notes Payable (+L).   225,000

+ Cash −				+ Property and Equipment −				− Notes Payable +				− Common Stock +				− Additional Paid-in Capital +			
Beg.	0			Beg.	0					0	Beg.			0	Beg.			0	Beg.
(a)	50,000	25,000	*(b)*	*(b)*	250,000					225,000	*(b)*			2,500	*(a)*			47,500	*(a)*
	25,000				250,000					225,000				2,500				47,500	

A TRIAL BALANCE is a list of all accounts with their balances to provide a check on the equality of the debits and credits.

HOW IS THE BALANCE SHEET PREPARED AND ANALYZED?

Although no operating activities occurred yet (they will be illustrated in Chapter 3), it is possible to create a balance sheet based solely on the investing and financing activities recorded above. Usually, businesses will create a **trial balance** spreadsheet first for internal purposes before preparing statements for external users. A trial balance lists the names of the T-accounts in one column, usually in financial statement order (assets, liabilities, stockholders' equity, revenues, and expenses), with their ending debit or credit balances in the next two columns. Debit balances are indicated in the left column and credit balances are indicated in the right column. Then the two columns are totaled to provide a check on the equality of the debits and credits. Errors in a computer-generated trial balance may exist if wrong accounts and/or amounts are used in the journal entries.[5]

Chipotle's trial balance follows. The account balances that did not change are taken from the December 31, 2011, balance sheet in Exhibit 2.2. The accounts that did change due to the investing and financing transactions illustrated in this chapter are shaded; their balances are taken from the T-accounts summarized on page 62.

CHIPOTLE MEXICAN GRILL—TRIAL BALANCE (based on investing and financing transactions during the first quarter ended March 31, 2012)		
(in thousands)	**Debit**	**Credit**
Cash	349,600	
Short-term investments	94,500	
Accounts receivable	8,400	
Supplies	8,900	
Prepaid expenses	27,700	
Property and equipment (net)	859,000	
Long-term investments	149,100	
Accounts payable		46,400
Accrued expenses payable		93,100
Dividends payable		3,000
Unearned revenue		18,000
Notes payable		233,200
Common stock		400
Additional paid-in capital		434,600
Retained earnings		668,500
Total	**1,497,200**	**1,497,200**

---

[5]In homework assignments, if you have an error in your trial balance (the two column totals are not equal), errors can be traced and should be corrected before adjusting the records. To find errors, reverse your steps. Check that:
- You copied the ending balances in all of the T-accounts (both amount and whether a debit or credit) correctly to the trial balance.
- You computed the ending balances in the T-accounts correctly.
- You posted the transaction effects correctly from the journal entries to the T-accounts (amount, account, and whether a debit or credit).
- You prepared the journal entries correctly (amount, account, and whether a debit or credit).

EXHIBIT 2.8

Chipotle Mexican Grill's
First Quarter 2012 Balance
Sheet (based on investing and
financing activities only)

CHIPOTLE MEXICAN GRILL, INC.
Consolidated Balance Sheets
(in thousands of dollars, except per share data)

	March 31, 2012	December 31, 2011
ASSETS		
Current Assets:		
Cash	$ 349,600	$ 401,200
Short-term investments	94,500	55,000
Accounts receivable	8,400	8,400
Supplies	8,900	8,900
Prepaid expenses	27,700	27,700
Total current assets	489,100	501,200
Property and equipment (net)	859,000	795,900
Long-term investments	149,100	128,200
Total assets	**$1,497,200**	**$1,425,300**
LIABILITIES AND STOCKHOLDERS' EQUITY		
Current Liabilities:		
Accounts payable	$ 46,400	$ 46,400
Accrued expenses payable	93,100	93,100
Dividends payable	3,000	—
Unearned revenue	18,000	18,000
Total current liabilities	160,500	157,500
Notes payable	233,200	223,600
Total liabilities	393,700	381,100
Stockholders' Equity:		
Common stock ($0.01 par)	400	300
Additional paid-in capital	434,600	372,400
Retained earnings	668,500	671,500
Total stockholders' equity	1,103,500	1,044,200
Total liabilities and stockholders' equity	**$1,497,200**	**$1,425,300**

Classified Balance Sheet

The balance sheet in Exhibit 2.8 was prepared from the trial balance on page 64. As a formal statement for external users, it needs a good heading (name of the company, title of the statement, date, and if the dollars are in thousands or millions). Notice in Exhibit 2.8 several additional features:

- The assets and liabilities are **classified** into two categories: **current** and **noncurrent.** Current assets are those to be used or turned into cash within the upcoming year, whereas noncurrent assets are those that will last longer than one year. Current liabilities are those obligations to be paid or settled within the next 12 months with current assets.

- Dollar signs are indicated at the top and bottom of the asset section and top and bottom of the liabilities and shareholders' equity section. More than that tends to look messy.

- The statement includes **comparative data.** That is, it compares the account balances at December 31, 2011, with those at March 31, 2012. When multiple periods are presented, the most recent balance sheet amounts are usually listed on the left.

- Unlike Chipotle, most companies do not provide a total liabilities line on the balance sheet. To determine total liabilities on those statements, add total current liabilities and each of the noncurrent liabilities.

INTERNATIONAL PERSPECTIVE

Understanding Foreign Financial Statements

Although IFRS differ from GAAP, they use the same system of analyzing, recording, and summarizing the results of business activities that you have learned in this chapter. One place where IFRS differ from GAAP is in the formatting of financial statements.

Financial statements prepared using GAAP and IFRS include the same elements (assets, liabilities, revenues, expenses, etc.). However, a single, consistent format has not been mandated. Consequently, various formats have evolved over time, with those in the U.S. differing from those typically used internationally. The formatting differences include:

	GAAP	IFRS
Balance Sheet Order	**Assets:**	**Assets:**
	Current	Noncurrent
Similar accounts are shown,	Noncurrent	Current
but the order of liquidity	**Liabilities:**	**Stockholders' Equity**
(for assets) and the order of	Current	**Liabilities:**
maturity (for liabilities) differ	Noncurrent	Noncurrent
	Stockholders' Equity	Current

On the balance sheet, GAAP begins with current items whereas IFRS begins with noncurrent items. Consistent with this, **assets are listed in decreasing order of liquidity under GAAP, but internationally are usually listed in increasing order of liquidity.** IFRS similarly emphasize longer-term financing sources by listing equity before liabilities and, within liabilities, by listing noncurrent liabilities before current liabilities (**decreasing time to maturity**). The key to avoiding confusion is to be sure to **pay attention to the subheadings** in the statement. Any account under the heading "liabilities" must be a liability.

Ratio Analysis in Decision-Making

Why do the classifications of current and noncurrent on the balance sheet matter? Users of financial information compute a number of ratios in analyzing a company's past performance and financial condition as input in predicting its future potential. How ratios change over time and how they compare to the ratios of the company's competitors or industry averages provide valuable information about a company's strategies for its operating, investing, and financing activities. We introduce here the first of many ratios that will be presented throughout the rest of this textbook, with a final summary of ratio analysis in Chapter 13.

KEY RATIO ANALYSIS

Current Ratio

? ANALYTICAL QUESTION

Does the company have the short-term resources to pay its short-term debt?

% RATIO AND COMPARISONS

$$\text{Current Ratio} = \frac{\text{Current Assets}}{\text{Current Liabilities}}$$

The 2011 ratio for Chipotle is (dollars in thousands):

$$\frac{\$501,200}{\$157,500} = 3.182$$

COMPARISONS OVER TIME Chipotle Mexican Grill, Inc.		
2011	**2010**	**2009**
3.182	3.301	2.912

COMPARISONS WITH COMPETITORS Panera Bread, Inc. Fiesta Restaurant Group, Inc.	
2011	**2011**
1.482	0.691
Vies for top fast-casual restaurant	Owns Pollo Tropical and Taco Cabana

💡 INTERPRETATIONS

In General   The current ratio is a very common ratio. Creditors and security analysts use the current ratio to measure the ability of the company to pay its short-term obligations with short-term assets. Generally, the higher the ratio, the more cushion a company has to pay its current obligations if future economic conditions take a downturn. While a ratio above 1.0 normally suggests good liquidity, today, many strong companies use sophisticated management techniques to minimize funds invested in current assets and, as a result, have current ratios below 1.0. Likewise, when compared to others in the industry, too high of a ratio may suggest inefficient use of resources.

Focus Company Analysis   Over time, the current ratio for Chipotle shows a high level of liquidity, well above 1.0, and the ratio has varied slightly around the 3.1 level since 2009. Chipotle has high growth strategies requiring cash to fund expansion.

Compared with competitors, Panera Bread, vying with Chipotle as the top fast-casual restaurant, also maintains a current ratio above 1.0, and both companies report cash as the largest current asset. The ratio for Chipotle is much higher than for Fiesta Restaurant Group, which reports a current ratio below 1.0. Fiesta Restaurant Group owns and franchises two quick-service brands: Pollo Tropical, featuring a tropical and Caribbean-style menu, and Taco Cabana, offering Mexican fast-food. Fiesta expects growth, but franchising (that is, selling rights to others to operate restaurants under the company brands) does not require the cash flow levels needed for company-owned facilities. It is also likely that all of these companies have sophisticated cash management systems that enable them to maintain lower cash balances.

Reuters reports that the restaurant industry has an average current ratio of 1.19. Compared to the industry average, Chipotle and Panera Bread have sufficient current assets to pay short-term obligations (adequate liquidity), while Fiesta Restaurant Group has a ratio below 1.0, suggesting the company will rely on sufficient cash flows generated during the year to meet current obligations.

A Few Cautions   The current ratio may be a misleading measure of liquidity if significant funds are tied up in assets that cannot be easily converted into cash. A company with a high current ratio might still have liquidity problems if the majority of its current assets consists of slow-moving inventory. Analysts also recognize that managers can manipulate the current ratio by engaging in certain transactions just before the close of the fiscal year. In most cases, for example, the current ratio can be improved by paying creditors immediately prior to the preparation of financial statements.

Selected Focus Companies' Current Ratios

Deckers   3.52

Harley-Davidson 1.68

Starbucks   1.83

PAUSE FOR **FEEDBACK**

We just learned that the current ratio measures a company's ability to pay short-term obligations with short-term assets—a liquidity measure. It is computed by dividing current assets by current liabilities. A ratio above 1.0 is normally considered good, although some may need a higher ratio and others with good cash management systems can have a ratio below 1.0 (i.e., more current liabilities than current assets).

Yum! Brands

SELF-STUDY **QUIZ**

Yum! Brands, Inc., is the world's largest quick-service restaurant company that develops, franchises, and operates 37,000 units in more than 120 countries and territories through three restaurant concepts (KFC, Pizza Hut, and Taco Bell). The company reported the following balances on its recent balance sheets (in millions). Compute Yum! Brands's current ratio for the three years.

	Current Assets	Current Liabilities	Current Ratio
	(dollars in millions)		
December 31, 2011	$2,321	$2,450	_____
December 31, 2010	2,313	2,448	_____
December 31, 2009	1,208	1,653	_____

What do these results suggest about Yum! Brands's liquidity in the current year and over time?

After you have completed your answers, check them with the solutions at the bottom of the page.

FOCUS ON CASH FLOWS	Investing and Financing Activities

LEARNING OBJECTIVE 2-6

Identify investing and financing transactions and demonstrate how they impact cash flows.

As discussed in Chapter 1, companies report cash inflows and outflows over a period in their **statement of cash flows,** which is divided into three categories: operating, investing, and financing activities:

- Operating activities are covered in Chapter 3.
- Investing activities include buying and selling noncurrent assets and investments.
- Financing activities include borrowing and repaying debt, including short-term bank loans, issuing and repurchasing stock, and paying dividends.

Only transactions affecting cash are reported on the statement. An important step in constructing and analyzing the statement of cash flows is identifying the various transactions as operating (**O**), investing (**I**), or financing (**F**). Let's analyze the Cash T-account for Chipotle's transactions in this chapter. Refer to transactions *(a)–(f)* illustrated on pages 60 to 62, and remember, **you must see cash in the transaction for it to affect the statement of cash flows.**

		+ Cash (A) −			
		1/1/12 401,200			
From investors	+F	*(a)* 62,300	55,100	*(c)* −I	**For noncurrent assets**
From bank	+F	*(b)* 2,000	400	*(d)* −F	**To bank**
			60,400	*(e)* −I	**For investments in other companies**
		349,600			

Solutions to SELF-STUDY QUIZ

Current Ratio:					
December 31, 2011	$2,321	÷	$2,450	=	0.947
December 31, 2010	2,313	÷	2,448	=	0.945
December 31, 2009	1,208	÷	1,653	=	0.731

Yum! Brands's current ratio is below 1.0 over the three years, suggesting the company has a low level of liquidity—insufficient current assets to settle short-term obligations. However, as a cash-oriented business and with a strong cash management system, Yum! Brands's current ratio below 1.0 is not a concern.

PAUSE FOR **FEEDBACK**

As we discussed, every transaction affecting cash can be classified either as an operating (discussed in Chapter 3), investing, or financing effect. Investing effects relate to purchasing/selling investments or property and equipment or lending funds to/receiving repayment from others. Financing effects relate to borrowing or repaying banks, issuing stock to investors, repurchasing stock from investors, or paying dividends to investors.

Apple, Inc.

SELF-STUDY **QUIZ**

Indicate whether the following transactions from a recent annual statement of cash flows for Apple, Inc., were investing (I) or financing (F) activities and the direction of their effects on cash (+ for increases; − for decreases):

Transactions	Type of Activity (I or F)	Effect on Cash Flows (+ or −)
1. Purchased investments	_____	_____
2. Issued common stock	_____	_____
3. Acquired property, plant, and equipment	_____	_____
4. Sold investments	_____	_____
5. Purchased intangible assets (e.g., patents)	_____	_____

After you have completed your answers, check them with the solutions at the bottom of this page.

DEMONSTRATION **CASE**

On April 1, 2014, three ambitious college students started Terrific Lawn Maintenance Corporation. A summary of transactions completed through April 7, 2014, for Terrific Lawn Maintenance Corporation follows:

a. Issued 500 shares of stock (1,500 shares in total) with a par value of $0.10 per share to each of the three investors in exchange for $9,000 cash.

b. Acquired rakes and other hand tools (equipment) with a list price of $690 for $600; paid the hardware store $200 cash and signed a three-month note for the balance.

c. Ordered three lawn mowers and two edgers from XYZ Lawn Supply, Inc., for $4,000.

d. Purchased four acres of land for the future site of a storage garage; paid cash, $5,000.

e. Received the mowers and edgers that had been ordered, signing a note to pay XYZ Lawn Supply in full in 18 months.

f. Sold for $1,250 one acre of land to the city for a park. Accepted a note from the city for payment by the end of the month.

g. One of the owners borrowed $3,000 from a local bank for personal use.

Required:

1. Set up T-accounts for Cash, Notes Receivable (from the city), Equipment (hand tools and mowing equipment), Land, Short-term Notes Payable (to the hardware store), Long-term Notes Payable, (to the equipment supply company), Common Stock, and Additional Paid-in Capital. Beginning balances are $0; indicate these beginning balances in the T-accounts. Analyze each transaction using the process outlined in the chapter with the transaction analysis model, and prepare journal entries in chronological order. Enter the effects of the transactions in the appropriate T-accounts; identify each amount with its letter in the preceding list. Compute ending balances for each T-account.

Assets (many accounts)		=	Liabilities (many accounts)		+	Stockholders' Equity	
						Contributed Capital (2 accounts)	*Earned Capital* (1 account)
+	−		−	+		**Common Stock** and	**Retained**
Debit	Credit		Debit	Credit		**Additional Paid-in Capital**	**Earnings**

	Retained Earnings		
	+	−	+
	Credit	Debit	Credit
	Investment	Dividends	Net
	by owners	declared	income

2. Use the balances in the T-accounts developed in the previous requirement to prepare a classified balance sheet for Terrific Lawn Maintenance Corporation at April 7, 2014.

3. Identify transactions (*a*)–(*g*) as investing or financing activities affecting cash flows and the direction of each effect. Use +I for investing inflow, −I for investing outflow, +F for financing inflow, and −F for financing outflow.

Check your answers with the solution in the following section.

SUGGESTED SOLUTION

1. **Transaction Analysis:**

Received:	Given:
a. Cash (+A) $9,000	Common Stock (+SE) $150
	(1,500 shares × $0.10 par value per share)
	Additional Paid-in Capital (+SE) $8,850 *($9,000 − $150)*
b. Equipment (+A) $600	Cash (−A) $200
	Short-term Notes Payable (+L) $400
c. Not a transaction—a promise to pay for a promise to deliver from the supplier	
d. Land (+A) $5,000	Cash (−A) $5,000
e. Equipment (+A) $4,000	Long-term Notes Payable (+L) $4,000
f. Notes Receivable (+A) $1,250 Land (−A) $1,250 *(1/4 of the $5,000 cost of the land)*	
g. Not a transaction of the business—separate-entity assumption	

Journal Entries	Debit	Credit
(a) Cash (+A)	9,000	
Common Stock (+SE).		150
Additional Paid-in Capital (+SE).		8,850
(b) Equipment (+A)	600	
Cash (−A)		200
Short-term Notes Payable (+L).		400
(c) No transaction		
(d) Land (+A).	5,000	
Cash (−A)		5,000
(e) Equipment (+A)	4,000	
Long-term Notes Payable (+L).		4,000
(f) Notes Receivable (+A)	1,250	
Land (−A)		1,250
(g) No transaction		

Equality Checks for All
Debits = Credits
Equation balances

A	=	L	+	SE
+ 9,000				+ 9,000

A	=	L	+	SE
+ 400		+ 400		

A	=	L	+	SE
+/− 5,000				

A	=	L	+	SE
+ 4,000		+ 4,000		

A	=	L	+	SE
+/− 1,250				

T-Accounts:

+ Cash (A) −			
4/1/14	0		
(a)	9,000	200	(b)
		5,000	(d)
	3,800		

+ Notes Receivable (A) −		
4/1/14	0	
(f)	1,250	
	1,250	

+ Equipment (A) −		
4/1/14	0	
(b)	600	
(e)	4,000	
	4,600	

+ Land (A) −			
4/1/14	0		
(d)	5,000	1,250	(f)
	3,750		

Short-term − Notes Payable (L) +			
		0	4/1/14
		400	(b)
		400	

Long-term − Notes Payable (L) +			
		0	4/1/14
		4,000	(c)
		4,000	

− Common Stock (SE) +			
		0	4/1/14
		150	(a)
		150	

Additional Paid-in − Capital (SE) +			
		0	4/1/14
		8,850	(a)
		8,850	

2. **Classified Balance Sheet:**

TERRIFIC LAWN MAINTENANCE CORPORATION
Balance Sheet
April 7, 2014

Assets

Current Assets:

Cash	$ 3,800
Notes receivable	1,250
Total current assets	5,050
Equipment	4,600
Land	3,750
Total assets	**$13,400**

Liabilities and Stockholders' Equity

Current Liabilities:

Short-term notes payable	$ 400
Total current liabilities	400
Long-term notes payable	4,000
Total liabilities	4,400

Stockholders' Equity:

Common stock ($0.10 par)	150
Additional paid-in capital	8,850
Total stockholders' equity	9,000
Total liabilities and stockholders' equity	**$13,400**

3. Cash Flows:

+ Cash (A) −			
4/1/14	0		
(a)	9,000	200	(b)
		5,000	(d)
	3,800		

Only transactions *(a)*, *(b)*, and *(d)* affect cash flows (as shown in the Cash T-account).

(a) +F for $9,000

(b) −I for $200

(d) −I for $5,000

CHAPTER **TAKE-AWAYS**

2-1. Define the objective of financial reporting, the elements of the balance sheet, and the related key accounting assumptions and principles.   p. 43

Objective:

- The primary objective of financial reporting to external users is to provide financial information about the reporting entity that is useful to existing and potential investors, lenders, and other creditors in making decisions about providing resources to the entity.

Qualitative characteristics of useful financial information:

- Relevance (including materiality) that allows users to assess past activities and/or predict future activities.
- Faithful representation requires information to be complete, neutral, and free from error.
  - To enhance the qualitative characteristics, information should also be comparable (to other companies and over time), verifiable, timely, and understandable.

Key recognition, measurement, and disclosure concepts:

Assumptions—

- Separate-entity assumption—transactions of the business are accounted for separately from transactions of the owner.
- Continuity (going-concern) assumption—a business is expected to continue to operate into the foreseeable future.
- Stable monetary unit assumption—financial information is reported in the national monetary unit without adjustment for changes in purchasing power.

Principles—

- Mixed-attribute measurement model—most balance sheet elements are recorded following the historical cost (or cost) principle—financial statement elements should be recorded at the cash-equivalent cost on the date of the transaction; however, these values may be adjusted to other amounts such as market value depending on certain conditions.

Elements of the balance sheet:

- Assets—probable future economic benefits owned or controlled by the entity as a result of past transactions.
- Liabilities—probable future sacrifices of economic benefits arising from present obligations of a business as a result of past transactions.

- Stockholders' equity—residual interest of owners in the assets of the entity after settling liabilities; the financing provided by the owners (contributed capital) and by business operations (earned capital).

2-2. **Identify what constitutes a business transaction and recognize common balance sheet account titles used in business.   p. 47**

- An exchange of cash, goods, or services for cash, goods, services, or promises between a business and one or more external parties to a business (not the exchange of a promise for a promise),

or

- A measurable internal event, such as adjustments for the use of assets in operations.

An account is a standardized format that organizations use to accumulate the dollar effects of transactions related to each financial statement item. Typical balance sheet account titles include the following:

- *Assets:* Cash, Accounts Receivable, Inventory, Prepaid Expenses, Investments, Property (buildings and land) and Equipment, and Intangibles (rights without physical substance).
- *Liabilities:* Accounts Payable, Notes Payable, Accrued Expenses Payable, Unearned Revenues, and Taxes Payable.
- *Stockholders' Equity:* Common Stock, Additional Paid-in Capital, and Retained Earnings.

2-3. **Apply transaction analysis to simple business transactions in terms of the accounting model: Assets = Liabilities + Stockholders' Equity. p. 49**

To determine the economic effect of a transaction on an entity in terms of the accounting equation, each transaction must be analyzed to determine the accounts (at least two) that are affected. In an exchange, the company receives something and gives up something. If the accounts, direction of the effects, and amounts are correctly analyzed, the accounting equation will stay in balance. The transaction analysis model is:

Assets	=	Liabilities	+	Stockholders' Equity			
(many accounts)		(many accounts)		*Contributed Capital* (2 accounts)		*Earned Capital* (1 account)	
+	−	−	+	**Common Stock** and		**Retained**	
Debit	Credit	Debit	Credit	**Additional Paid-in Capital**		**Earnings**	
				+	−		+
				Credit	Debit		Credit
				Investment	Dividends		Net
				by owners	declared		income
							(expanded in Ch. 3)

Systematic transaction analysis includes (1) determining the accounts that were received and were given in the exchange, including the type of each account (A, L, or SE), amounts, and direction of the effect, and (2) determining that the accounting equation remains in balance.

2-4. **Determine the impact of business transactions on the balance sheet using two basic tools: Journal entries and T-accounts.   p. 54**

- Journal entries express the effects of a transaction on accounts in a debits-equal-credits format. The accounts and amounts to be debited are listed first. Then the accounts and amounts to be credited are listed below the debits and indented, resulting in debit amounts on the left and credit amounts on the right. Each entry needs a reference (date, number, or letter).

	Debit	Credit
(a) Cash (+A)	62,300	
Common Stock (+SE)		100
Additional Paid-in Capital (+SE)		62,200

- T-accounts summarize the transaction effects for each account. These tools can be used to determine balances and draw inferences about a company's activities.

+ (dr)	Assets	(cr) −	− (dr)	Liabilities and Stockholders' Equity	(cr) +
Beginning balance Increases		Decreases	Decreases		Beginning balance Increases
Ending balance					Ending balance

2-5. **Prepare a trial balance and simple classified balance sheet, and analyze the company using the current ratio.   p. 64**

Classified balance sheets are structured as follows:

- Assets are categorized as current assets (those to be used or turned into cash within the year, with inventory always considered a current asset) and noncurrent assets, such as long-term investments, property and equipment, and intangible assets.

- Liabilities are categorized as current liabilities (those that will be paid with current assets) and long-term liabilities.

- Stockholders' equity accounts are listed as Common Stock (number of shares × par value per share) and Additional Paid-in Capital (amount received minus par value) first, followed by Retained Earnings (earnings reinvested in the business).

The current ratio (Current Assets ÷ Current Liabilities) measures a company's liquidity, that is, the ability of the company to pay its short-term obligations with current assets.

2-6. **Identify investing and financing transactions and demonstrate how they impact cash flows.   p. 68**

A statement of cash flows reports the sources and uses of cash for the period by the type of activity that generated the cash flow: operating, investing, and financing. Investing activities include purchasing and selling long-term assets and making loans and receiving principal repayments from others. Financing activities are borrowing and repaying to banks the principal on loans, issuing and repurchasing stock, and paying dividends.

In this chapter, we discussed the fundamental accounting model and transaction analysis. Journal entries and T-accounts were used to record the results of transaction analysis for investing and financing decisions that affect balance sheet accounts. In Chapter 3, we continue our detailed look at the financial statements, in particular the income statement. The purpose of Chapter 3 is to build on your knowledge by discussing the measurement of revenues and expenses and illustrating the transaction analysis of operating decisions.

KEY **RATIO**

Current ratio measures the ability of the company to pay its short-term obligations with current assets. Although a ratio above 1.0 indicates sufficient current assets to meet obligations when they come due, many companies with sophisticated cash management systems have ratios below 1.0. (p. 66):

$$\text{Current Ratio} = \frac{\text{Current Assets}}{\text{Current Liabilities}}$$

FINDING **FINANCIAL INFORMATION**

Balance Sheet

Current Assets	Current Liabilities
Cash	Accounts payable
Short-term investments	Accrued expenses payable
Accounts receivable	Short-term notes payable
Notes receivable	Unearned revenue
Inventory	**Noncurrent Liabilities**
Prepaid expenses	Long-term debt (notes payable)
Noncurrent Assets	**Stockholders' Equity**
Long-term investments	Common Stock
Property and equipment	Additional paid-in capital
Intangibles	Retained earnings

Income Statement
To be presented in Chapter 3

Statement of Cash Flows

Operating Activities
  To be presented in Chapter 3

Investing Activities
  + Sales of noncurrent assets and investments for cash
  − Purchases of noncurrent assets and investments for cash
  − Loans to others
  + Receipt of loan principal payments from others

Financing Activities
  + Borrowing from banks
  − Repayment of loan principal to banks
  + Issuance of stock
  − Repurchasing stock
  − Dividends paid

Notes
To be discussed in future chapters

KEY **TERMS**

Account p. 48
Accounting Cycle p. 54
Additional Paid-in Capital
  (Paid-in Capital, Contributed
  Capital in Excess of Par) p. 51
Assets p. 45
Common Stock p. 51
Continuity (Going-Concern)
  Assumption p. 44
Credit p. 55

Current Assets p. 45
Current Liabilities p. 45
Debit p. 55
Faithful Representation p. 44
Journal Entry p. 57
Liabilities p. 45
Mixed-Attribute Measurement Model p. 44
Par Value p. 51
Primary Objective of Financial Reporting
  to External Users p. 43

Relevant Information p. 44
Retained Earnings p. 46
Separate-Entity Assumption p. 44
Stable Monetary Unit Assumption p. 44
Stockholders' Equity (Shareholders'
  or Owners' Equity) p. 45
T-account p. 58
Transaction p. 47
Transaction Analysis p. 49
Trial Balance p. 64

QUESTIONS

1. What is the primary objective of financial reporting for external users?
2. Define the following:
   a. Asset
   b. Current asset
   c. Liability
   d. Current liability
   e. Additional paid-in capital
   f. Retained earnings

3. Explain what the following accounting terms mean:
   a. Separate-entity assumption
   c. Continuity assumption
   b. Stable monetary unit assumption
   d. Historical cost principle
4. Why are accounting assumptions necessary?
5. For accounting purposes, what is an account? Explain why accounts are used in an accounting system.
6. What is the fundamental accounting model?
7. Define a business transaction in the broad sense, and give an example of two different kinds of transactions.
8. Explain what *debit* and *credit* mean.
9. Briefly explain what is meant by *transaction analysis*. What are the two steps in transaction analysis?
10. What two accounting equalities must be maintained in transaction analysis?
11. What is a journal entry?
12. What is a T-account? What is its purpose?
13. How is the current ratio computed and interpreted?
14. What transactions are classified as investing activities in a statement of cash flows? What transactions are classified as financing activities?

MULTIPLE-CHOICE QUESTIONS

1. If a publicly traded company is trying to maximize its perceived value to decision makers external to the corporation, the company is most likely to understate which of the following on its balance sheet?
   a. Assets
   c. Retained Earnings
   b. Common Stock
   d. Liabilities
2. Which of the following is not an asset?
   a. Investments
   c. Prepaid Expense
   b. Land
   d. Additional Paid-in Capital
3. Total liabilities on a balance sheet at the end of the year are $150,000, retained earnings at the end of the year is $80,000, net income for the year is $60,000, common stock is $40,000, and additional paid-in capital is $20,000. What amount of total assets would be reported on the balance sheet at the end of the year?
   a. $290,000
   c. $205,000
   b. $270,000
   d. $15,000
4. The dual effects concept can best be described as follows:
   a. When one records a transaction in the accounting system, at least two effects on the basic accounting equation will result.
   b. When an exchange takes place between two parties, both parties must record the transaction.
   c. When a transaction is recorded, both the balance sheet and the income statement must be impacted.
   d. When a transaction is recorded, one account will always increase and one account will always decrease.
5. The T-account is a tool commonly used for analyzing which of the following?
   a. Increases and decreases to a single account in the accounting system.
   b. Debits and credits to a single account in the accounting system.
   c. Changes in specific account balances over a time period.
   d. All of the above describe how T-accounts are used by accountants.
6. Which of the following describes how assets are listed on the balance sheet?
   a. In alphabetical order
   b. In order of magnitude, lowest value to highest value
   c. From most liquid to least liquid
   d. From least liquid to most liquid

7. The Cash T-account has a beginning balance of $21,000. During the year, $100,000 was debited and $110,000 was credited to the account. What is the ending balance of Cash?
   a. $11,000 debit balance
   b. $11,000 credit balance
   c. $31,000 credit balance
   d. $31,000 debit balance

8. Which of the following statements are true regarding the balance sheet?
   1. One cannot determine the true fair market value of a company by reviewing its balance sheet.
   2. Certain internally generated assets, such as a trademark, are not reported on a company's balance sheet.
   3. A balance sheet shows only the ending balances, in a summarized format, of all balance sheet accounts in the accounting system as of a particular date.
   a. None are true.
   b. Statements 1 and 2 only are true.
   c. Statements 2 and 3 only are true.
   d. All statements are true.

9. At the end of a recent year, The Gap, Inc., reported total assets of $7,422 million, current assets of $4,309 million, total liabilities of $4,667, current liabilities of $2,128 million, and stockholders' equity of $2,755 million. What is its current ratio and what does this suggest about the company?
   a. The ratio of 1.59 suggests that The Gap has liquidity problems.
   b. The ratio of 2.02 suggests that The Gap has sufficient liquidity.
   c. The ratio of 1.59 suggests that The Gap has greater current assets than current liabilities.
   d. The ratio of 2.02 suggests that The Gap is not able to pay its short-term obligations with current assets.

10. Which of the following is *not* a financing activity on the statement of cash flows?
    a. When the company lends money.
    b. When the company borrows money.
    c. When the company pays dividends.
    d. When the company issues stock to shareholders.

For more practice with multiple-choice questions, go to the text website at **www.mhhe.com/libby8e**.

 |ACCOUNTING

MINI-**EXERCISES**

Matching Definitions with Terms

M2-1
LO2-1, 2-4

Match each definition with its related term by entering the appropriate letter in the space provided. There should be only one definition per term (that is, there are more definitions than terms).

Term	Definition
___ (1) Continuity assumption	A. = Liabilities + Stockholders' Equity.
___ (2) Historical cost principle	B. Reports assets, liabilities, and stockholders' equity.
___ (3) Credits	C. Accounts for a business separate from its owners.
___ (4) Assets	D. Increase assets; decrease liabilities and stockholders' equity.
___ (5) Account	E. An exchange between an entity and other parties.
	F. The concept that businesses will operate into the foreseeable future.
	G. Decrease assets; increase liabilities and stockholders' equity.
	H. The concept that assets should be recorded at the amount paid on the date of the transaction.
	I. A standardized format used to accumulate data about each item reported on financial statements.

M2-2
LO2-1, 2-2, 2-3, 2-4

Matching Definitions with Terms

Match each definition with its related term by entering the appropriate letter in the space provided. There should be only one definition per term (that is, there are more definitions than terms).

Term	Definition
___ (1) Journal entry	A. Accounting model.
___ (2) A = L + SE, and	B. Four periodic financial statements.
Debits = Credits	C. The two equalities in accounting that aid in providing
___ (3) Assets = Liabilities +	accuracy.
Stockholders' Equity	D. The results of transaction analysis in accounting
___ (4) Liabilities	format.
___ (5) Income statement, balance sheet,	E. The account that is debited when money is borrowed
statement of stockholders' equity,	from a bank.
and statement of cash flows	F. Probable future economic benefits owned by an entity.
	G. Cumulative earnings of a company that are not
	distributed to the owners.
	H. Every transaction has at least two effects.
	I. Probable debts or obligations to be paid with assets
	or services.

M2-3
LO2-2

Identifying Events as Accounting Transactions

For each of the following events, which ones result in an exchange transaction for Dittman Company (Y for yes and N for no)?

____ (1) Six investors in Dittman Company sold their stock to another investor.
____ (2) The founding owner, Megan Dittman, purchased additional stock in another company.
____ (3) The company borrowed $2,500,000 from a local bank.
____ (4) Dittman Company purchased a machine that it paid for by signing a note payable.
____ (5) The company lent $300,000 to a supplier.
____ (6) Dittman Company ordered supplies from Staples to be delivered next week.

M2-4
LO2-2

Classifying Accounts on a Balance Sheet

The following are accounts of Rosa-Perez Company:

___ (1) Accounts Payable	___ (9) Long-Term Investments
___ (2) Accounts Receivable	___ (10) Notes Payable (due in three years)
___ (3) Buildings	___ (11) Notes Receivable (due in six months)
___ (4) Cash	___ (12) Prepaid Rent
___ (5) Common Stock	___ (13) Retained Earnings
___ (6) Land	___ (14) Supplies
___ (7) Merchandise Inventory	___ (15) Utilities Payable
___ (8) Income Taxes Payable	___ (16) Wages Payable

In the space provided, classify each as it would be reported on a balance sheet. Use:

CA for current asset   CL for current liability   SE for stockholders' equity
NCA for noncurrent asset   NCL for noncurrent liability

M2-5
LO2-3

Determining Financial Statement Effects of Several Transactions

For each of the following transactions of Dennen, Inc., for the month of January 2015, indicate the accounts, amounts, and direction of the effects on the accounting equation. A sample is provided.

a. *(Sample)* Borrowed $30,000 from a local bank.
b. Lent $10,000 to an affiliate; accepted a note due in one year.
c. Sold 100 additional shares of stock with a par value of $0.10 per share to investors for $500 cash.
d. Purchased $15,000 of equipment, paying $5,000 cash and signing a note for the rest due in one year.
e. Declared and paid $2,000 in dividends to stockholders.

Assets		=	Liabilities		+	Stockholders' Equity
a. *Sample:* Cash	+30,000		Notes Payable	+30,000		

Identifying Increase and Decrease Effects on Balance Sheet Elements

Complete the following table by entering either the word *increases* or *decreases* in each column.

	Debit	Credit
Assets	_____	_____
Liabilities	_____	_____
Stockholders' equity	_____	_____

M2-6
LO2-4

Identifying Debit and Credit Effects on Balance Sheet Elements

Complete the following table by entering either the word *debit* or *credit* in each column.

	Increase	Decrease
Assets	_____	_____
Liabilities	_____	_____
Stockholders' equity	_____	_____

M2-7
LO2-4

Recording Simple Transactions

For each transaction in M2-5 (including the sample), write the journal entry in the proper form.

M2-8
LO2-4

Completing T-Accounts

For each transaction in M2-5 (including the sample), post the effects to the appropriate T-accounts and determine ending account balances. Beginning balances are provided.

M2-9
LO2-4

Cash		Notes Receivable		Equipment	
Beg. bal. 900		Beg. bal. 1,000		Beg. bal. 15,100	

Notes Payable		Common Stock		Additional Paid-in Capital	
	Beg. bal. 3,000		Beg. bal. 1,000		Beg. bal. 3,000

Retained Earnings	
	Beg. bal. 10,000

Preparing a Trial Balance

Complete M2-9, and then prepare a trial balance for Dennen, Inc., as of January 31, 2015.

M2-10
LO2-5

Preparing a Simple Classified Balance Sheet

Starting with the beginning balances in M2-9 and given the transactions in M2-5 (including the sample), prepare a balance sheet for Dennen, Inc., as of January 31, 2015, classified into current and noncurrent assets and liabilities.

M2-11
LO2-5

Computing and Interpreting the Current Ratio

Calculate the current ratio for Sal's Taco Company at the end of 2011 and 2012, based on the following data:

M2-12
LO2-5

	Current Assets	Current Liabilities
End of 2011	$280,000	$155,000
End of 2012	$270,000	$250,000

What does the result suggest about the company over time? What can you say about Sal's Taco Company's ratio when compared to Chipotle's 2011 ratio?

M2-13
LO2-6

Identifying Transactions as Investing or Financing Activities on the Statement of Cash Flows

For the transactions in M2-5 (including the sample), identify each as an investing (I) activity or financing (F) activity on the statement of cash flows.

EXERCISES

E2-1
LO2-1, 2-2, 2-3, 2-4

Matching Definitions with Terms

Match each definition with its related term by entering the appropriate letter in the space provided. There should be only one definition per term (that is, there are more definitions than terms).

Term	Definition
___ (1) Transaction	A. Economic resources to be used or turned into cash within one year.
___ (2) Continuity assumption	
___ (3) Balance sheet	B. Reports assets, liabilities, and stockholders' equity.
___ (4) Liabilities	C. Business transactions are accounted for separately from the transactions of the owners.
___ (5) Assets = Liabilities + Stockholders' Equity	
___ (6) Notes payable	D. Increase assets; decrease liabilities and stockholders' equity.
___ (7) Common stock	E. An exchange between an entity and other parties.
___ (8) Historical cost principle	F. The concept that businesses will operate into the foreseeable future.
___ (9) Account	G. Decrease assets; increase liabilities and stockholders' equity.
___ (10) Dual effects	H. The concept that assets should be recorded at the amount paid on the exchange date.
___ (11) Retained earnings	
___ (12) Current assets	I. A standardized format used to accumulate data about each item reported on financial statements.
___ (13) Separate-entity assumption	
___ (14) Par value	J. Amounts owed from customers.
___ (15) Debits	K. The fundamental accounting model.
___ (16) Accounts receivable	L. Represents the shares issued at par value.
___ (17) Stable monetary unit assumption	M. The account that is credited when money is borrowed from a bank.
___ (18) Faithful representation	N. The concept that states that accounting information should be measured and reported in the national monetary unit without adjustment for changes in purchasing power.
___ (19) Relevance	
___ (20) Stockholders' equity	
	O. Cumulative earnings of a company that are not distributed to the owners.
	P. Probable debts or obligations to be settled with assets or services.
	Q. Every transaction has at least two effects on the accounting equation.
	R. Financing provided by owners and by business operations.
	S. The concept to exercise care not to overstate assets and revenues or understate liabilities and expenses.
	T. Useful information has predictive and feedback value.
	U. Relatively small amounts not likely to influence users' decisions are to be recorded in the most cost-beneficial way.
	V. Probable economic resources expected to be used or turned into cash beyond the next 12 months.
	W. Useful information should be complete, neutral, and free from error.
	X. A legal amount per share.

Identifying Account Titles

The following are independent situations.

a. A new company is formed and sells 100 shares of $1 per value stock for $12 per share to investors.
b. A company purchases for $18,000 cash a new delivery truck that has a list, or sticker, price of $21,000.
c. A women's clothing retailer orders 30 new display stands for $300 each for future delivery.
d. A company orders and receives 10 personal computers for office use for which it signs a note promising to pay $25,000 within three months.
e. A construction company signs a contract to build a new $500,000 warehouse for a corporate customer. At the signing, the corporation writes a check for $50,000 to the construction company as the initial payment for the construction (receiving construction in progress). Answer from the standpoint of the corporation (not the construction company).
f. A publishing firm purchases for $40,000 cash the copyright (an intangible asset) to a manuscript for an introductory accounting text.
g. A manufacturing firm pays stockholders a $100,000 cash dividend.
h. A company purchases a piece of land for $50,000 cash. An appraiser for the buyer values the land at $52,500.
i. A manufacturing company acquires the patent (an intangible asset) on a new digital satellite system for television reception, paying $500,000 cash and signing a $400,000 note payable due in one year.
j. A local company is a sole proprietorship (one owner); its owner buys a car for $10,000 for personal use. Answer from the local company's point of view.
k. A company purchases 100 shares of Apple Inc. common stock as an investment for $5,000 cash.
l. A company borrows $1,000 from a local bank and signs a six-month note for the loan.
m. A company pays $1,500 principal on its note payable (ignore interest).

Required:
1. Indicate the appropriate account titles, if any, affected in each of the preceding events. Consider what is received and what is given.
2. At what amount would you record the truck in (*b*)? The land in (*h*)? What measurement principle are you applying?
3. For (*c*), what accounting concept did you apply? For (*j*), what accounting concept did you apply?

E2-2
LO2-2

Classifying Accounts and Their Usual Balances

As described in a recent annual report, Verizon Wireless provides wireless voice and data services across one of the most extensive wireless networks in the United States. Verizon now serves more than 80 million customers, making it the largest wireless service provider in the United States in terms of the total number of customers. The following are accounts from a recent balance sheet for Verizon.

(1) Accounts Receivable	(6) Long-Term Investments
(2) Retained Earnings	(7) Plant, Property, and Equipment
(3) Taxes Payable	(8) Accounts Payable
(4) Prepaid Expenses	(9) Short-Term Investments
(5) Common Stock	(10) Long-Term Debt

Required:
For each account, indicate whether the account is usually classified as a current asset (CA), noncurrent asset (NCA), current liability (CL), noncurrent liability (NCL), or stockholders' equity (SE), and whether the account usually has a debit or credit balance.

E2-3
LO2-2, 2-4

Verizon Communications, Inc.

Determining Financial Statement Effects of Several Transactions

The following events occurred for Johnson Company:

a. Received investment of $40,000 cash by organizers and distributed 1,000 shares of $1 par value common stock to them.
b. Purchased $15,000 of equipment, paying $3,000 in cash and signing a note for the rest.
c. Borrowed $10,000 cash from a bank.
d. Loaned $800 to an employee who signed a note.
e. Purchased $13,000 of land; paid $4,000 in cash and signed a mortgage note for the balance.

E2-4
LO2-3

Required:

For each of the events *(a)* through *(e),* perform transaction analysis and indicate the account, amount, and direction of the effect (+ for increase and − for decrease) on the accounting equation. Check that the accounting equation remains in balance after each transaction. Use the following headings:

Event	Assets	=	Liabilities	+	Stockholders' Equity

E2-5

LO2-3

Determining Financial Statement Effects of Several Transactions

Nike, Inc., with headquarters in Beaverton, Oregon, is one of the world's leading manufacturers of athletic shoes and sports apparel. The following activities occurred during a recent year. The amounts are rounded to millions.

a. Purchased additional buildings for $172 and equipment for $270; paid $432 in cash and signed a long-term note for the rest.

b. Issued 100 shares of $2 par value common stock for $345 cash.

c. Declared $145 in dividends to be paid in the following year.

d. Purchased additional short-term investments for $7,616 cash.

e. Several Nike investors sold their own stock to other investors on the stock exchange for $84.

f. Sold $4,313 in short-term investments for $4,313 in cash.

Required:

1. For each of the events *(a)* through *(f),* perform transaction analysis and indicate the account, amount, and direction of the effect on the accounting equation. Check that the accounting equation remains in balance after each transaction. Use the following headings:

Event	Assets	=	Liabilities	+	Stockholders' Equity

2. Explain your response to event *(e).*

E2-6

LO2-4

Recording Investing and Financing Activities

Refer to E2-4.

Required:

For each of the events *(a)* through *(e)* in E2-4, prepare journal entries, checking that debits equal credits.

E2-7

LO2-4

Recording Investing and Financing Activities

Refer to E2-5.

Required:

1. For each of the events *(a)* through *(f)* in E2-5, prepare journal entries, checking that debits equal credits.

2. Explain your response to event *(e).*

E2-8

LO2-4

Analyzing the Effects of Transactions in T-Accounts

Granger Service Company, Inc., was organized by Ted Granger and five other investors. The following activities occurred during the year:

a. Received $70,000 cash from the investors; each was issued 8,400 shares of capital stock with a par value of $0.10 per share.

b. Purchased equipment for use in the business at a cost of $18,000; one-fourth was paid in cash and the company signed a note for the balance (due in six months).

c. Signed an agreement with a cleaning service to pay $120 per week for cleaning the corporate offices next year.

d. Received an additional contribution from investors who provided $3,000 in cash and land valued at $15,000 in exchange for 1,000 shares of stock in the company.

e. Lent $2,500 to one of the investors who signed a note due in six months.

f. Ted Granger borrowed $7,000 for personal use from a local bank, signing a one-year note.

Required:

1. Create T-accounts for the following accounts: Cash, Notes Receivable, Equipment, Land, Notes Payable, Common Stock, and Additional Paid-in Capital. Beginning balances are $0. For each of the preceding transactions, record the effects of the transaction in the appropriate T-accounts. Include good referencing and totals for each T-account.

2. Using the balances in the T-accounts, fill in the following amounts for the accounting equation:

   Assets $_____   =   Liabilities $_____   +   Stockholders' Equity $_____

3. Explain your response to events (c) and (f).

Inferring Investing and Financing Transactions and Preparing a Balance Sheet

E2-9
LO2-4, 2-5

During its first week of operations ending January 7, 2014, FastTrack Sports Inc. completed six transactions with the dollar effects indicated in the following schedule:

Accounts	Dollar Effect of Each of the Six Transactions						Ending Balance
	1	2	3	4	5	6	
Cash	$15,000	$75,000	$(5,000)	$(4,000)	$(9,500)		
Notes receivable (short-term)				4,000			
Store fixtures					9,500		
Land			16,000			$4,000	
Notes payable (due in three months)		75,000	11,000			4,000	
Common stock (15,000 shares)	1,500						
Additional paid-in capital	13,500						

Required:

1. Write a brief explanation of transactions (1) through (6). Explain any assumptions that you made.
2. Compute the ending balance in each account and prepare a classified balance sheet for FastTrack Sports Inc. on January 7, 2014.

Inferring Investing and Financing Transactions and Preparing a Balance Sheet

E2-10
LO2-4, 2-5

During its first month of operations in March 2014, Volz Cleaning, Inc., completed six transactions with the dollar effects indicated in the following schedule:

Accounts	Dollar Effect of Each of the Six Transactions						Ending Balance
	1	2	3	4	5	6	
Cash	$45,000	$(8,000)	$(2,000)	$(7,000)	$3,000	$(4,000)	
Investments (short-term)				7,000	(3,000)		
Notes receivable (due in six months)			2,000				
Computer equipment						$4,000	
Delivery truck		35,000					
Notes payable (due in 10 years)		27,000					
Common stock (3,000 shares)	6,000						
Additional paid-in capital	39,000						

Required:

1. Write a brief explanation of transactions (1) through (6). Explain any assumptions that you made.
2. Compute the ending balance in each account and prepare a classified balance sheet for Volz Cleaning, Inc., at the end of March 2014.

Recording Journal Entries

E2-11
LO2-4

Nathanson Corporation was organized on May 1, 2014. The following events occurred during the first month.

a. Received $70,000 cash from the five investors who organized Nathanson Corporation. Each investor received 100 shares of $10 par value common stock.
b. Ordered store fixtures costing $15,000.

c. Borrowed $18,000 cash and signed a note due in two years.
d. Purchased $11,000 of equipment, paying $1,500 in cash and signing a six-month note for the balance.
e. Lent $2,000 to an employee who signed a note to repay the loan in three months.
f. Received and paid for the store fixtures ordered in (b).

Required:
Prepare journal entries for each transaction. (Remember that debits go on top and credits go on the bottom, indented.) Be sure to use good referencing and categorize each account as an asset (A), liability (L), or stockholders' equity (SE). If a transaction does not require a journal entry, explain the reason.

E2-12
LO2-4

Recording Journal Entries

BMW Group, headquartered in Munich, Germany, manufactures several automotive brands including BMW Group, MINI, and Rolls-Royce. Financial information is reported in the euro (€) monetary unit using International Financial Reporting Standards (IFRS) as applicable to the European Union. The following activities were adapted from the annual report of the BMW Group; amounts are in millions of euros.

a. Declared €1,508 in dividends to be paid next month.
b. Ordered €2,598 of equipment.
c. Paid €852 in dividends declared in prior months.
d. Borrowed €5,899 in cash from banks.
e. Sold equipment at its cost of €53 for cash.
f. Received the equipment ordered in event (b), paying €2,250 in cash and signing a note for the balance.
g. Purchased investments for €2,616 cash.

Required:
Prepare journal entries for each transaction. Be sure to use good referencing and categorize each account as an asset (A), liability (L), or stockholders' equity (SE). If a transaction does not require a journal entry, explain the reason.

E2-13
LO2-4, 2-5

Analyzing the Effects of Transactions Using T-Accounts and Interpreting the Current Ratio as a Manager of the Company

Higgins Company has been operating for one year (2014). You are a member of the management team investigating expansion ideas that will require borrowing funds from banks. At the start of 2015, Higgins's T-account balances were as follows:

Assets:

Cash		Short-Term Investments		Property and Equipment	
5,000		2,500		3,000	

Liabilities:

Short-Term Notes Payable		Long-Term Notes Payable	
	2,200		800

Stockholders' Equity:

Common Stock		Additional Paid-in Capital		Retained Earnings	
	500		4,000		3,000

Required:
1. Using the data from these T-accounts, determine the amounts for the following on January 1, 2015:

   Assets $_____ = Liabilities $_____ + Stockholders' Equity $_____

2. Enter the following 2015 transactions in the T-accounts:
   (a) Borrowed $4,000 from a local bank, signing a note due in three years.
   (b) Sold $1,500 of the investments for $1,500 cash.
   (c) Sold one-half of the property and equipment for $1,500 in cash.
   (d) Declared and paid $800 in cash dividends to stockholders.

3. Compute ending balances in the T-accounts to determine amounts for the following on December 31, 2015:

Assets $_____   =   Liabilities $_____   +   Stockholders' Equity $_____

4. Calculate the current ratio at December 31, 2015. If the industry average for the current ratio is 1.50, what does your computation suggest to you about Higgins Company? Would you suggest that Higgins Company increase its short-term liabilities? Why or why not?

Preparing a Balance Sheet

Refer to E2-13.

Required:
From the ending balances in the T-accounts in E2-13, prepare a classified balance sheet at December 31, 2015, in good form.

E2-14
LO2-5

Analyzing the Effects of Transactions Using T-Accounts, Preparing a Balance Sheet, and Evaluating the Current Ratio over Time as a Bank Loan Officer

E2-15
LO2-4, 2-5

Strauderman Delivery Company, Inc., was organized in 2014 in Wisconsin. The following transactions occurred during year 2014:

a. Received $40,000 cash from organizers in exchange for 10,000 shares of stock (par value of $1.00 per share) in the new company.
b. Purchased land in Wisconsin for $16,000, signing a one-year note (ignore interest).
c. Bought two used delivery trucks for operating purposes at the start of the year at a cost of $10,000 each; paid $4,000 cash and signed a note due in three years for the rest (ignore interest).
d. Paid $1,000 cash to a truck repair shop for a new motor for one of the trucks. (*Hint:* Increase the account you used to record the purchase of the trucks since the productive life of the truck has been improved.)
e. Sold one-fourth of the land for $4,000 to Pablo Development Corporation, which signed a six-month note.
f. Stockholder Melissa Strauderman paid $27,600 cash for a vacant lot (land) in Canada for her personal use.

Required:
1. Set up appropriate T-accounts with beginning balances of zero for Cash, Short-Term Notes Receivable, Land, Equipment, Short-Term Notes Payable, Long-Term Notes Payable, Common Stock, and Additional Paid-in Capital. Using the T-accounts, record the effects of transactions (*a*) through (*f*) by Strauderman Delivery Company.
2. Prepare a trial balance at December 31, 2014.
3. Prepare a classified balance sheet for Strauderman Delivery Company at December 31, 2014.
4. At the end of the next two years, Strauderman Delivery Company reported the following amounts on its balance sheets:

	December 31, 2015	December 31, 2016
Current Assets	$52,000	$ 47,000
Long-Term Assets	38,000	73,000
Total Assets	**90,000**	**120,000**
Short-Term Notes Payable	23,000	40,000
Long-Term Notes Payable	17,000	20,000
Total Liabilities	**40,000**	**60,000**
Stockholders' Equity	**50,000**	**60,000**

Compute the company's current ratio for 2014, 2015, and 2016. What is the trend and what does this suggest about the company?
5. At the beginning of year 2017, Strauderman Delivery Company applied to your bank for a $50,000 short-term loan to expand the business. The vice president of the bank asked you to review the information and make a recommendation on lending the funds based solely on the results of the current ratio. What recommendation would you make to the bank's vice president about lending the money to Strauderman Delivery Company?

Explaining the Effects of Transactions on Balance Sheet Accounts Using T-Accounts

E2-16
LO2-4

Waltman Furniture Repair Service, a company with two stockholders, began operations on June 1, 2014. The following T-accounts indicate the activities for the month of June.

Cash (A)			
6/1/14	0		
a.	20,000	c.	10,000
d.	900	b.	1,800

Notes Receivable (A)		
6/1/14	0	
b.	1,800	

Tools and Equipment (A)			
6/1/14	0		
a.	5,000	d.	900

Building (A)		
6/1/14	0	
c.	40,000	

Notes Payable (L)		
	6/1/14	0
	c.	30,000

Common Stock (100,000 shares) (SE)		
	6/1/14	0
	a.	2,000

Additional Paid-in Capital (SE)		
	6/1/14	0
	a.	23,000

Required:

Explain events (*a*) through (*d*) that resulted in the entries in the T-accounts. That is, for each account, what transactions made it increase and/or decrease?

E2-17

LO2-4

Inferring Typical Investing and Financing Activities in Accounts

The following T-accounts indicate the effects of normal business transactions:

Equipment			
1/1	500		
	250	?	
12/31	100		

Notes Receivable			
1/1	150		
	?	225	
12/31	170		

Notes Payable			
		100	1/1
?		170	
		160	12/31

Required:

1. Describe the typical investing and financing transactions that affect each T-account. That is, what economic events occur to make each of these accounts increase and decrease?
2. For each T-account, compute the missing amounts.

E2-18

LO2-6

Foot Locker, Inc.

Identifying Investing and Financing Activities Affecting Cash Flows

Foot Locker, Inc., is a large global retailer of athletic footwear and apparel selling directly to customers and through the Internet. It includes the Foot Locker family of stores, Champs Sports, Footaction, CCS, and Eastbay. The following are several of Foot Locker's investing and financing activities as reflected in a recent annual statement of cash flows.

a. Reduction of long-term debt.
b. Sale of short-term investments.
c. Issuance of common stock.
d. Capital expenditures (for property, plant, and equipment).
e. Dividends paid on common stock.

Required:

For each of these, indicate whether the activity is investing (I) or financing (F) and the direction of the effect on cash flows (+ for increases cash; − for decreases cash).

E2-19

LO2-6

Starwood Hotels & Resorts Worldwide, Inc.

Identifying the Investing and Financing Activities Affecting Cash Flows

Starwood Hotels & Resorts Worldwide, Inc., is one of the world's largest hotel and leisure companies. It conducts business both directly and through its subsidiaries, including the following hotel brands: Sheraton, Four Points, W, Aloft, The Luxury Collection, Le Meridien, Element, Westin, and St. Regis.* Information adapted from the company's recent annual statement of cash flows indicates the following investing and financing activities during that year (simplified, in millions of dollars):

*Sheraton, Four Points, W, Aloft, The Luxury Collection, Le Meridien, Element, Westin, St. Regis and their respective logos are the trademarks of Starwood Hotels & Resorts Worldwide, Inc., or its affiliates.

a.	Additional borrowing from banks	$ 47
b.	Purchase of investments	8
c.	Sale of assets and investments (assume sold at cost)	294
d.	Issuance of stock	70
e.	Purchase and renovation of properties	385
f.	Payment of debt principal	650
g.	Receipt of principal payment on a note receivable	5

Required:

For each of these indicate whether the activity is investing (I) or financing (F) and the direction of the effects on cash flows (+ for increases cash; − for decreases cash).

Finding Financial Information as a Potential Investor

E2-20
LO2-2, 2-5, 2-6

You are considering investing the cash you inherited from your grandfather in various stocks. You have received the annual reports of several major companies.

Required:

For each of the following, indicate where you would locate the information in an annual report. The information may be in more than one location.

1. Total current assets.
2. Amount of debt principal repaid during the year.
3. Summary of significant accounting policies.
4. Cash received from sales of noncurrent assets.
5. Amount of dividends paid during the year.
6. Short-term obligations.
7. Date of the statement of financial position.

To practice with more exercises, go to the text website at **www.mhhe.com/libby8e**.

PROBLEMS

Identifying Accounts on a Classified Balance Sheet and Their Normal Debit or Credit Balances (AP2-1)

P2-1
LO2-1, 2-2, 2-4

ExxonMobil.

Exxon Mobil Corporation explores, produces, refines, markets, and supplies crude oil, natural gas, and petroleum products in the United States and around the world. The following are accounts from a recent balance sheet of Exxon Mobil Corporation:

	Balance Sheet Classification	Debit or Credit Balance
(1) Notes and Loans Payable (short-term)	_____	_____
(2) Materials and Supplies	_____	_____
(3) Common Stock	_____	_____
(4) Patents (an intangible asset)	_____	_____
(5) Income Taxes Payable	_____	_____
(6) Long-Term Debt	_____	_____
(7) Marketable Securities (short-term investments)	_____	_____
(8) Property, Plant, and Equipment	_____	_____
(9) Retained Earnings	_____	_____
(10) Notes and Accounts Receivable (short-term)	_____	_____
(11) Investments (long-term)	_____	_____
(12) Cash and Cash Equivalents	_____	_____
(13) Accounts Payable	_____	_____
(14) Crude Oil Products and Merchandise	_____	_____
(15) Additional Paid-in Capital	_____	_____

Required:

For each account, indicate how it normally should be categorized on a classified balance sheet. Use CA for current asset, NCA for noncurrent asset, CL for current liability, NCL for noncurrent liability, and SE for stockholders' equity. Also indicate whether the account normally has a debit or credit balance.

P2-2

LO2-2, 2-3, 2-5

Determining Financial Statement Effects of Various Transactions (AP2–2)

East Hill Home Healthcare Services was organized on January 1, 2014, by four friends. Each organizer invested $10,000 in the company and, in turn, was issued 8,000 shares of $1.00 par value stock. To date, they are the only stockholders. At the end of 2015, the accounting records reflected total assets of $700,000 ($50,000 cash; $500,000 land; $50,000 equipment; and $100,000 buildings), total liabilities of $200,000 (short-term notes payable $100,000 and long-term notes payable $100,000), and stockholders' equity of $500,000 ($20,000 common stock, $80,000 additional paid-in capital, and $400,000 retained earnings). During the current year, 2016, the following summarized events occurred:

a. Sold 9,000 additional shares of stock to the original organizers for a total of $90,000 cash.
b. Purchased a building for $60,000, equipment for $15,000, and four acres of land for $14,000; paid $9,000 in cash and signed a note for the balance (due in 15 years). (*Hint:* Five different accounts are affected.)
c. Sold one acre of land acquired in (b) for $3,500 cash to another company.
d. Purchased short-term investments for $18,000 cash.
e. One stockholder reported to the company that 300 shares of his East Hill stock had been sold and transferred to another stockholder for $3,000 cash.
f. Lent one of the shareholders $5,000 for moving costs, receiving a signed six-month note from the shareholder.

Required:

1. Was East Hill Home Healthcare Services organized as a sole proprietorship, a partnership, or a corporation? Explain the basis for your answer.
2. During 2016, the records of the company were inadequate. You were asked to prepare the summary of the preceding transactions. To develop a quick assessment of their economic effects on East Hill Home Healthcare Services, you have decided to complete the tabulation that follows and to use plus (+) for increases and minus (−) for decreases for each account. The first event is used as an example.

	ASSETS						=	LIABILITIES		+	STOCKHOLDERS' EQUITY		
Cash	Short-Term Investments	Notes Receivable	Land	Buildings	Equipment			Short-Term Notes Payable	Long-Term Notes Payable		Common Stock	Additional Paid-in Capital	Retained Earnings
Beg. 50,000			500,000	100,000	50,000		=	100,000	100,000		20,000	80,000	400,000
(a) +90,000							=				+9,000	+81,000	

3. Did you include the transaction between the two stockholders—event (e)—in the tabulation? Why?
4. Based only on the completed tabulation, provide the following amounts (show computations):
    a. Total assets at the end of the year.
    b. Total liabilities at the end of the year.
    c. Total stockholders' equity at the end of the year.
    d. Cash balance at the end of the year.
    e. Total current assets at the end of the year.
5. Compute the current ratio for 2016. What does this suggest about the company?

P2-3

LO2-2, 2-4, 2-5

Recording Transactions in T-Accounts, Preparing the Balance Sheet from a Trial Balance, and Evaluating the Current Ratio (AP2-3)

Cougar Plastics Company has been operating for three years. At December 31, 2014, the accounting records reflected the following:

Cash	$22,000	Accounts payable	$15,000
Investments (short-term)	3,000	Accrued liabilities payable	4,000
Accounts receivable	3,000	Notes payable (short-term)	7,000
Inventory	20,000	Long-term notes payable	47,000
Notes receivable (long-term)	1,000	Common stock	10,000
Equipment	50,000	Additional paid-in capital	80,000
Factory building	90,000	Retained earnings	31,000
Intangibles	5,000		

During the year 2015, the company had the following summarized activities:

a. Purchased short-term investments for $10,000 cash.
b. Lent $5,000 to a supplier who signed a two-year note.
c. Purchased equipment that cost $18,000; paid $5,000 cash and signed a one-year note for the balance.
d. Hired a new president at the end of the year. The contract was for $85,000 per year plus options to purchase company stock at a set price based on company performance.

e. Issued an additional 2,000 shares of $0.50 par value common stock for $11,000 cash.

f. Borrowed $9,000 cash from a local bank, payable in three months.

g. Purchased a patent (an intangible asset) for $3,000 cash.

h. Built an addition to the factory for $24,000; paid $8,000 in cash and signed a three-year note for the balance.

i. Returned defective equipment to the manufacturer, receiving a cash refund of $1,000.

Required:

1. Create T-accounts for each of the accounts on the balance sheet and enter the balances at the end of 2014 as beginning balances for 2015.
2. Record each of the events for 2015 in T-accounts (including referencing) and determine the ending balances.
3. Explain your response to event (*d*).
4. Prepare a trial balance at December 31, 2015.
5. Prepare a classified balance sheet at December 31, 2015.
6. Compute the current ratio for 2015. What does this suggest about Cougar Plastics?

Identifying Effects of Transactions on the Statement of Cash Flows (AP2-4)

Refer to P2-3.

Required:

Using the events (*a*) through (*i*) in P2-3, indicate whether each is an investing (I) or financing (F) activity for the year and the direction of the effect on cash flows (+ for increase and − for decrease). If there is no effect on cash flows, write NE.

Recording Transactions, Preparing Journal Entries, Posting to T-Accounts, Preparing the Balance Sheet, and Evaluating the Current Ratio

Dell Inc., headquartered in Austin, Texas, is the global leader in selling computer products and services. The following is Dell's (simplified) balance sheet from a recent year (fiscal year ending on Friday nearest January 31).

P2-4
LO2-6

P2-5
LO2-2, 2-4, 2-5

Dell

www.mhhe.com/libby8e

DELL INC. Balance Sheet at February 3, 2012 (dollars in millions)	
ASSETS	
Current assets:	
Cash	$13,852
Short-term investments	966
Receivables and other assets	9,803
Inventories	1,404
Other	3,423
Total current assets	**29,448**
Property, plant, and equipment	2,124
Long-term investments	3,404
Other noncurrent assets	9,557
Total assets	**$44,533**
LIABILITIES AND STOCKHOLDERS' EQUITY	
Current Liabilities:	
Accounts payable	$11,656
Other short-term obligations	10,345
Total current liabilities	**22,001**
Long-term liabilities	13,615
Total liabilities	**35,616**
Stockholders' equity:	
Common stock ($0.01 par value)	34
Additional paid-in capital	12,153
Retained earnings	28,236
Other stockholders' equity items	(31,506)
Total stockholders' equity	**8,917**
Total stockholders' equity and liabilities	**$44,533**

Assume that the following transactions (in millions) occurred during the remainder of 2012 (ending on February 1, 2013):

a. Borrowed $50 from banks due in two years.
b. Lent $300 to affiliates, who signed a six-month note.
c. Purchased additional investments for $13,000 cash; one-fifth were long term and the rest were short term.
d. Purchased property, plant, and equipment; paid $875 in cash and $1,410 with additional long-term bank loans.
e. Issued 1,000 additional shares of stock for $400 in cash.
f. Sold short-term investments costing $11,000 for $11,000 cash.
g. Dell does not actually pay dividends; it reinvests its earnings into the company for growth purposes. Assume instead for this problem that Dell declared and paid $60 in dividends during 2012.

Required:
1. Prepare a journal entry for each transaction. Use the account titles in the Dell balance sheet.
2. Create T-accounts for each balance sheet account and include the February 3, 2012, balances. Post each journal entry to the appropriate T-accounts.
3. Prepare a balance sheet from the T-account ending balances for Dell at February 1, 2013, based on these transactions.
4. Compute Dell's current ratio for 2012 (year ending on February 1, 2013). What does this suggest about the company?

P2-6
LO2-6
Dell

Identifying the Investing and Financing Activities Affecting the Statement of Cash Flows

Refer to P2-5.

Required:
For each of the activities (*a*)–(*g*), indicate whether the activity is investing (I) or financing (F) and the direction and amount of the effect on cash flows (+ for increases; − for decreases).

ALTERNATE PROBLEMS

AP2-1
LO2-1, 2-2, 2-4

Identifying Accounts on a Classified Balance Sheet and Their Normal Debit or Credit Balances (P2-1)

According to a recent Form 10-K report of Mattel, Inc., the company "designs, manufactures, and markets a broad variety of toy products worldwide." Mattel's brands include Barbie, Hot Wheels, Fisher-Price toys, and American Girl brand dolls and accessories. The following are several of the accounts from a recent balance sheet:

	Balance Sheet Classification	Debit or Credit Balance
(1) Prepaid Expenses	_____	_____
(2) Inventories	_____	_____
(3) Accounts Receivable	_____	_____
(4) Long-Term Debt	_____	_____
(5) Cash and Equivalents	_____	_____
(6) Goodwill (an intangible asset)	_____	_____
(7) Accounts Payable	_____	_____
(8) Income Taxes Payable	_____	_____
(9) Property, Plant, and Equipment	_____	_____
(10) Retained Earnings	_____	_____
(11) Additional Paid-in Capital	_____	_____
(12) Short-Term Borrowings	_____	_____
(13) Accrued Liabilities	_____	_____
(14) Common Stock	_____	_____

Required:

Indicate how each account normally should be categorized on a classified balance sheet. Use CA for current asset, NCA for noncurrent asset, CL for current liability, NCL for noncurrent liability, and SE for stockholders' equity. Also indicate whether the account normally has a debit or credit balance.

Determining Financial Statement Effects of Various Transactions (P2-2)

Adamson Incorporated is a small manufacturing company that makes model trains to sell to toy stores. It has a small service department that repairs customers' trains for a fee. The company has been in business for five years. At December 31, 2014 (the company's fiscal year-end), the accounting records reflected total assets of $500,000 (cash, $120,000; equipment, $70,000; buildings, $310,000), total liabilities of $200,000 (short-term notes payable, $140,000; long-term notes payable, $60,000), and total stockholders' equity of $300,000 [common stock (par value $1.00 per share), $20,000: additional paid-in capital, $200,000; retained earnings, $80,000]. During the current year, 2015, the following summarized events occurred:

a. Borrowed $110,000 cash from the bank and signed a 10-year note.

b. Purchased equipment for $30,000, paying $3,000 in cash and signing a note due in six months for the balance.

c. Issued an additional 10,000 shares of capital stock for $100,000 cash.

d. Purchased a delivery truck (equipment) for $10,000; paid $5,000 cash and signed a short-term note payable for the remainder.

e. Lent $2,000 cash to the company president, Clark Adamson, who signed a note with terms showing the principal plus interest due in one year.

f. Built an addition on the factory for $200,000 and paid cash to the contractor.

g. Purchased $85,000 in long-term investments.

h. Returned a $3,000 piece of equipment purchased in (*b*) because it proved to be defective; received a reduction of its short-term note payable.

i. A stockholder sold $5,000 of his capital stock in Adamson Incorporated to his neighbor.

Required:

1. Was Adamson Incorporated organized as a sole proprietorship, a partnership, or a corporation? Explain the basis for your answer.
2. During 2015, the records of the company were inadequate. You were asked to prepare the summary of the preceding transactions. To develop a quick assessment of their economic effects on Adamson Incorporated, you have decided to complete the tabulation that follows and to use plus (+) for increases and minus (−) for decreases for each account. The first transaction is used as an example.

	ASSETS					=	LIABILITIES		+	STOCKHOLDERS' EQUITY		
	Cash	Notes Receivable	Long-Term Investments	Equipment	Buildings		Short-Term Notes Payable	Long-Term Notes Payable		Common Stock	Additional Paid-in Capital	Retained Earnings
Beg.	120,000			70,000	310,000	=	140,000	60,000		20,000	200,000	80,000
(*a*)	+110,000					=		+110,000				

3. Did you include event (*i*) in the tabulation? Why?
4. Based on beginning balances plus the completed tabulation, provide the following amounts (show computations):
   a. Total assets at the end of the year.
   b. Total liabilities at the end of the year.
   c. Total stockholders' equity at the end of the year.
   d. Cash balance at the end of the year.
   e. Total current assets at the end of the year.
5. Compute the current ratio for 2015. What does this suggest about the company?

Recording Transactions in T-Accounts, Preparing the Balance Sheet, and Evaluating the Current Ratio (P2-3)

Ethan Allen Interiors, Inc., is a leading manufacturer and retailer of home furnishings in the United States and abroad. The following is adapted from Ethan Allen's June 30, 2011, annual financial report. Amounts are in thousands.

AP2-2
LO2-2, 2-3, 2-5

AP2-3
LO2-2, 2-4, 2-5

ETHAN
ALLEN

Cash and cash equivalents	$ 78,519	Accounts payable	$ 26,958
Short-term investments	12,909	Accrued expenses payable	127,639
Accounts receivable	15,036	Long-term debt (includes the	
Inventories	141,692	current portion of $19)	165,032
Prepaid expenses and		Other long-term liabilities	27,009
other current assets	20,372	Common stock ($0.01 par value)	484
Property, plant, and equipment	294,853	Additional paid-in capital	359,728
Intangibles	45,128	Retained earnings	501,908
Other assets	19,816	Other stockholders' equity items	(580,433)

Assume that the following events occurred in the first quarter ended September 30, 2011:

a. Issued 1,600 additional shares of stock for $1,020 in cash.
b. Purchased $3,400 in additional intangibles for cash.
c. Ordered $43,500 in wood and other raw materials for the manufacturing plants.
d. Sold equipment at its cost for $4,020 cash.
e. Purchased $2,980 in short-term investments for cash.
f. Purchased property, plant, and equipment; paid $1,830 in cash and signed additional long-term notes for $9,400.
g. Sold at cost other assets for $310 cash.
h. Declared and paid $300 in dividends.

Required:
1. Create T-accounts for each of the accounts on the balance sheet; enter the balances at June 30, 2011.
2. Record each of the transactions for the first quarter ended September 30, 2011, in the T-accounts (including referencing) and determine the ending balances.
3. Explain your response to event (c).
4. Prepare a trial balance at September 30, 2011.
5. Prepare a classified balance sheet at September 30, 2011.
6. Compute the current ratio for the quarter ended September 30, 2011. What does this suggest about Ethan Allen Interiors, Inc.?

AP2-4
LO2-6

Identifying Effects of Transactions on the Statement of Cash Flows (P2-4)

Refer to AP2-3.

ETHAN
ALLEN

Required:
Using the events (a) through (h) in AP2-3, indicate whether each transaction is an investing (I) or financing (F) activity for the quarter and the direction and amount of the effect on cash flows (+ for increase and − for decrease). If there is no effect on cash flows, write NE.

CASES **AND PROJECTS**

Annual Report Cases

CP2-1
LO2-1, 2-2, 2-5, 2-6

AMERICAN EAGLE
OUTFITTERS, INC.

Finding Financial Information

Refer to the financial statements of American Eagle Outfitters in Appendix B at the end of this book.

Required:
1. Is the company a corporation, a partnership, or a sole proprietorship? How do you know?
2. The company shows on the balance sheet that inventories are worth $378,426,000. Does this amount represent the expected selling price? Why or why not?

3. List the types of current obligations this company has. You need not provide the amounts.
4. Compute the company's current ratio and explain its meaning.
5. How much cash did the company spend on purchasing property and equipment each year (capital expenditures)? Where did you find the information?

Finding Financial Information

Refer to the financial statements of Urban Outfitters in Appendix C at the end of this book.

CP2-2
LO2-1, 2-2, 2-5, 2-6

URBAN OUTFITTERS INC.

Required:
1. Use the company's balance sheet to determine the amounts in the accounting equation (A = L + SE) as of January 31, 2012.
2. If the company were liquidated at the end of the current year (January 31, 2012), are the shareholders guaranteed to receive $1,066,268,000?
3. What are the company's noncurrent liabilities?
4. What is the company's current ratio?
5. Did the company have a cash inflow or outflow from investing activities? Of how much?

Comparing Companies within an Industry

Refer to the financial statements of American Eagle Outfitters in Appendix B, Urban Outfitters in Appendix C, and the Industry Ratio Report in Appendix D at the end of this book.

CP2-3
LO2-2, 2-5, 2-6

AMERICAN EAGLE OUTFITTERS, INC.

URBAN OUTFITTERS INC.

Required:
1. Compute the current ratio for both companies. Compared to the industry average (from the Industry Ratio Report), are these two companies more or less able to satisfy short-term obligations with current assets? How is the current ratio influenced by these companies' choice to rent space instead of buying it?
2. In the most recent year, how much cash, if any, was spent buying back (repurchasing) each company's own common stock?
3. How much, if any, did each company pay in dividends for the most recent year?
4. What account title or titles does each company use to report any land, buildings, and equipment it may have?

www.mhhe.com/libby8e

Financial Reporting and Analysis Cases

Broadening Financial Research Skills: Locating Financial Information on the SEC's Database

CP2-4
LO2-2, 2-5, 2-6

The Securities and Exchange Commission (SEC) regulates companies that issue stock on the stock market. It receives financial reports from public companies electronically under a system called EDGAR (Electronic Data Gathering and Retrieval Service). Using the Internet, anyone may search the database for the reports that have been filed.

Using your Web browser, access the EDGAR database at www.sec.gov. To search the database, type in "chipotle" for the company name in the search window at the top of the page, and press enter.

Required:
To look at SEC filings, type in "10-Q" in the space indicating "Filing Type" and press enter. Skim down the left side until you locate the Form 10-Q (quarterly report) filed July 20, 2012. Click on the "Documents" for that report, click on the 10-Q document (first item), and skim to the Table of Contents.
1. Click on "Financial Statements" and skim to the "Condensed Consolidated Balance Sheets."
   a. What was the amount of Chipotle's total assets for the most recent quarter reported?
   b. Did current liabilities increase or decrease since December 31, 2011?
   c. Compute the current ratio. How does it compare to the ratio indicated for Chipotle Mexican Grill in the chapter? What does this suggest about the company?

2. Skim to the Chipotle "Consolidated Statements of Cash Flow."
   a. What amount did Chipotle spend on property and equipment for the quarter ended June 30, 2012?
   b. What was the total amount of cash flows from financing activities?

CP2-5

LO2-1, 2-5

Using Financial Reports: Evaluating the Reliability of a Balance Sheet

Frances Sabatier asked a local bank for a $50,000 loan to expand her small company. The bank asked Frances to submit a financial statement of the business to supplement the loan application. Frances prepared the following balance sheet.

FS COMPUTING	
Balance Sheet	
June 30, 2015	
Assets	
Cash and investments	$ 9,000
Inventory	30,000
Equipment	46,000
Personal residence (monthly payments, $2,800)	300,000
Remaining assets	20,000
Total assets	$405,000
Liabilities	
Short-term debt to suppliers	$ 62,000
Long-term debt on equipment	38,000
Total debt	100,000
Stockholders' Equity	305,000
Total liabilities and stockholders' equity	$405,000

Required:
The balance sheet has several flaws. However, there is at least one major deficiency. Identify it and explain its significance.

CP2-6

LO2-2, 2-4, 2-5

Dell

Using Financial Reports: Analyzing the Balance Sheet

Recent balance sheets are provided for Dell, Inc., a leading producer and marketer of a broad range of personal computers, mobility products, software, and related tools and services.

Required:
1. Is Dell a corporation, sole proprietorship, or partnership? Explain the basis of your answer.
2. Use the company's balance sheet (consolidated statement of financial position) to determine the amounts in the accounting equation (A = L + SE) at the end of the most recent year.
3. Calculate the company's current ratio on February 3, 2012. Interpret the ratio that you calculated. What other information would make your interpretation more useful?
4. Prepare the journal entry the company will make in 2012 when it pays its fiscal year 2011 accounts payable (fiscal year 2011 ends on February 3, 2012).
5. Does the company appear to have been profitable over its years in business? On what account are you basing your answer? Assuming no dividends were paid, how much was net income (or net loss) in the most recent year? If it is impossible to determine without an income statement, state so.

DELL INC.
Consolidated Statements of Financial Position
(dollars in millions)

	February 3, 2012	January 28, 2011
ASSETS		
Current assets		
Cash and cash equivalents	$ 13,852	$ 13,913
Short-term investments	966	452
Accounts receivable	9,803	10,136
Inventories	1,404	1,301
Other	3,423	3,219
Total current assets	29,448	29,021
Property, plant and equipment, net	2,124	1,953
Investments	3,404	704
Intangibles	7,695	5,860
Other noncurrent assets	1,862	1,061
	$ 44,533	$ 38,599
LIABILITIES AND STOCKHOLDERS' EQUITY		
Current liabilities		
Short-term debt	$ 2,867	$ 851
Accounts payable	11,656	11,293
Accrued and other liabilities	3,934	4,181
Deferred service revenue	3,544	3,158
Total current liabilities	22,001	19,483
Long-term debt	6,387	5,146
Long-term deferred service revenue	3,836	3,518
Other noncurrent liabilities	3,392	2,686
Total liabilities	35,616	30,833
Stockholders' equity		
Contributed capital	12,187	11,797
Retained earnings	28,236	24,744
Other	(31,506)	(28,775)
Total stockholders' equity	8,917	7,766
	$ 44,533	$ 38,599

Critical Thinking Cases

Making a Decision as a Financial Analyst: Preparing and Analyzing a Balance Sheet

CP2-7
LO2-1, 2-5

Your best friend from home writes you a letter about an investment opportunity that has come her way. A company is raising money by issuing shares of stock and wants her to invest $20,000 (her recent inheritance from her great-aunt's estate). Your friend has never invested in a company before and, knowing that you are a financial analyst, asks that you look over the balance sheet and send her some advice. An **unaudited** balance sheet, in only moderately good form, is enclosed with the letter.

DEWEY, CHEETUM, AND HOWE, INC.
Balance Sheet
For the Year Ending December 31, 2015

Accounts receivable	$ 8,000
Cash	1,000
Inventory	8,000
Furniture and fixtures	52,000
Delivery truck	12,000
Buildings (estimated market value)	98,000
Total assets	**$179,000**
Accounts payable	$ 16,000
Payroll taxes payable	13,000
Notes payable (due in three years)	15,000
Mortgage payable	50,000
Total liabilities	**$ 94,000**
Contributed capital	$ 80,000
Retained earnings	5,000
Total stockholders' equity	**$ 85,000**

There is only one disclosure note, and it states that the building was purchased for $65,000, has been depreciated by $5,000 on the books, and still carries a mortgage (shown in the liability section). The note also states that, in the opinion of the company president, the building is "easily worth $98,000."

Required:
1. Draft a new balance sheet for your friend, correcting any errors you note. (If any of the account balances need to be corrected, you may need to adjust the retained earnings balance correspondingly.) If there are no errors or omissions, so state.
2. Write a letter to your friend explaining the changes you made to the balance sheet, if any, and offer your comments on the company's apparent financial condition based only on this information. Suggest other information your friend might want to review before coming to a final decision on whether to invest.

CP2-8

Evaluating an Ethical Dilemma: Analyzing Management Incentives

U.S. Foodservice, Inc.

In July 2004, the U.S. government filed civil and criminal charges against four former executives of Netherlands-based Ahold's subsidiary U.S. Foodservice, Inc., an operator of supermarkets such as Bi-Lo and Giant Food Stores. Two of the four executives have pleaded guilty, and the other two were indicted. The alleged widespread fraud included recording completely fictitious revenues for false promotions and persuading vendors to confirm to auditors the false promotional payments. U.S. Attorney David Kelley suggested the fraud was motivated by the greed of the executives to reap fat bonuses if the company met certain financial goals. The auditors did not uncover the fraud.

Required:
1. Describe the parties who were harmed or helped by this fraud.
2. Explain how greed may have contributed to the fraud.
3. Why do you think the independent auditors failed to catch the fraud?

Financial Reporting and Analysis Team Project

CP2-9

LO2-2, 2-5, 2-6

Team Project: Analysis of Balance Sheets and Ratios

As a team, select an industry to analyze. *Yahoo!Finance* provides lists of industries at biz.yahoo.com/p/industries.html. Click on an industry for a list of companies in that industry. Alternatively, go to Google Finance at www.google.com/finance, search for a company you are interested in, and you will be presented with a list including that company and its competitors. Each team member should acquire the annual report or 10-K for one publicly traded company in the industry, with each member selecting a different company (the SEC EDGAR service at www.sec.gov or the company's investor relations website itself are good sources).

Required:

On an individual basis, each team member should write a short report answering the following questions about the selected company. Discuss any patterns across the companies that you as a team observe. Then, as a team, write a short report comparing and contrasting your companies.

1. For the most recent year, what are the top three asset accounts by size? What percentage is each of total assets? (Calculated as Asset A ÷ Total Assets)
2. What are the major investing and financing activities (by dollar size) for the most recent year? (Look at the Statement of Cash Flows.)
3. Ratio Analysis:
   a. What does the current ratio measure in general?
   b. Compute the current ratio for each of the last three years. (You may find prior years' information in the section of the annual report or 10-K called "Selected Financial Information," or you may search for prior years' annual reports.)
   c. What do your results suggest about the company?
   d. If available, find the industry ratio for the most recent year, compare it to your results, and discuss why you believe your company differs or is similar to the industry ratio.

CONTINUING **CASE**

Accounting for the Establishment of a New Business (the Accounting Cycle)

CC2-1
LO2-4, 2-5, 2-6

Penny Cassidy has decided to start her business, Penny's Pool Service & Supply, Inc. (PPSS). There is much to do when starting a new business. Here are some transactions that have occurred in the business in March 2013.

a. Received $25,000 cash and a large delivery van with a value of $36,000 from Penny, who was given 4,000 shares of $0.05 par value common stock in exchange.
b. Purchased land with a small office and warehouse by paying $10,000 cash and signing a 10-year mortgage note payable to the local bank for $80,000. The land has a value of $18,000 and the building's value is $72,000. Use separate accounts for land and buildings.
c. Purchased a new computer from Dell for $2,500 cash and office furniture for $4,000, signing a short-term note payable in six months.
d. Hired a receptionist for the office at a salary of $1,500 per month, starting in April 2013.
e. Paid $1,000 on the note payable to the bank at the end of March 2013 (ignore interest).
f. Purchased short-term investments in the stock of other companies for $5,000 cash.
g. Ordered $10,000 in inventory from Pool Corporation, Inc., a pool supply wholesaler, to be received in April 2013.

Required:

1. For each of the events, prepare journal entries if a transaction of the business exists, checking that debits equal credits. If a transaction does not exist, explain why there is no transaction for the business.
2. Create T-accounts, and post each of the transactions to determine balances at March 31, 2013. Because this is a new business, beginning balances are $0.
3. Prepare a trial balance on March 31, 2013, to check that debits equal credits after the transactions are posted to the T-accounts.
4. From the trial balance, prepare a classified balance sheet (with current assets and current liabilities sections) at March 31, 2013 (before the beginning of operations in April).
5. For each of the events, indicate if it is an investing activity (I) or financing activity (F), and the direction (+ for increases; − for decreases) and amount of the effect on cash flows using the following structure. Write NE if there is no effect on cash flows.

	Type of Activity (I, F, or NE)	Effect on Cash Flows (+ or − and amount)
(a)	_____	_____
(b) etc.	_____	_____

6. Calculate the current ratio at March 31, 2013. What does this ratio indicate about the ability of PPSS to pay its current liabilities?

Operating Decisions and the Accounting System

Chipotle Mexican Grill's philosophy of "Food with Integrity" guides its operating decisions. "Food with Integrity" entails finding and serving high-quality sustainably and organically raised food. It also includes showing respect for animals, the environment, and people involved in the operations. The company keeps operations simple, offering a few menu items (burritos, burrito bowls, tacos, and salads). Within these items, customers can choose from four meats, two types of beans and rice, and a variety of additional items such as salsa, guacamole, cheese, and lettuce—creating hundreds of options. The focused menu allows Chipotle to concentrate on the source of the food items, a challenging activity given the smaller and often costlier market for organic meats, produce, and dairy products. Anticipating changes in these food costs and sources is critical to determining menu prices and controlling costs.

To control quality and increase efficiency, the company purchases key ingredients such as meat, beans, and tortillas from a small number of suppliers and other raw materials from approved sources. Twenty-two independently owned and operated regional distribution centers purchase from these suppliers and then deliver the items as needed to the Chipotle restaurants in each region.

Learning Objectives

After studying this chapter, you should be able to:

3-1 Describe a typical business operating cycle and explain the necessity for the time period assumption. p. 100

3-2 Explain how business activities affect the elements of the income statement. p. 102

3-3 Explain the accrual basis of accounting and apply the revenue realization and expense matching principles to measure income. p. 105

3-4 Apply transaction analysis to examine and record the effects of operating activities on the financial statements. p. 111

3-5 Prepare a classified income statement. p. 121

3-6 Compute and interpret the net profit margin ratio. p. 122

The second highest cost for Chipotle, as with most restaurants, is hiring and developing employees. The food is prepared from scratch on stoves and grills, not with microwaves and other automated cooking techniques. Each employee is trained in all aspects of food preparation—from grilling, to making fresh salsa, to cooking rice—and creating a positive interactive experience for customers. The company has numerous incentives to develop strong leadership, with nearly 98 percent of managers promoted from within the company.

Chipotle also competes using marketing strategies. Chipotle spends less on expensive national advertising campaigns than larger restaurant chains and much more on strategic promotional activities to make connections with neighborhoods to explain how Chipotle is different. Most activities are innovative, such as the award-winning two-minute animated video "Back to the Start" that aired during the 2012 Grammy Awards; the Cultivate Chicago festival featuring indie bands, artisanal food, wine producers, and high-profile chefs; and the Chipotle Truck, which travels to various locations, including new store openings, and sells almost a full menu of Chipotle items from the food trailer. As stated in its 2011 annual report:

> Collectively, these efforts and our excellent restaurant teams have helped us create considerable word-of-mouth publicity, with our customers learning about us and telling others, allowing us to build awareness with relatively low advertising expenditures, even in a competitive category, and to differentiate Chipotle as a company that is committed to doing the right things in every facet of our business.

UNDERSTANDING THE BUSINESS

The restaurant industry is extremely competitive. For example, in February 2012, McDonald's Corporation announced a requirement that suppliers need to phase out stalls that restrict the movement of pregnant pigs, a change made in direct response to Chipotle's TV video on its ethical stance aired at the Grammy Awards. Taco Bell announced in July 2012 the creation of a Cantina Bell™ menu featuring "gourmet" food items such as the Cantina Burrito and Cantina Bowl. Jack in the Box, Inc., is expanding its Qdoba Mexican Grill chain to compete in the fast-casual segment of the industry that is dominated by Mexican restaurants.

Restaurants have to manage economic downturns and shifts in consumer tastes for healthier food choices while facing the competition. Based on their projections of these forces, companies set goals for their performance. Published income statements provide the primary basis for comparing projections to the actual results of operations. To understand how business plans and the results of operations are reflected on the income statement, we need to answer the following questions:

1. How do business activities affect the income statement?
2. How are business activities measured?
3. How are business activities reported on the income statement?

In this chapter we focus on Chipotle's operating activities that involve the sale of food to the public. The results of these activities are reported on the income statement.

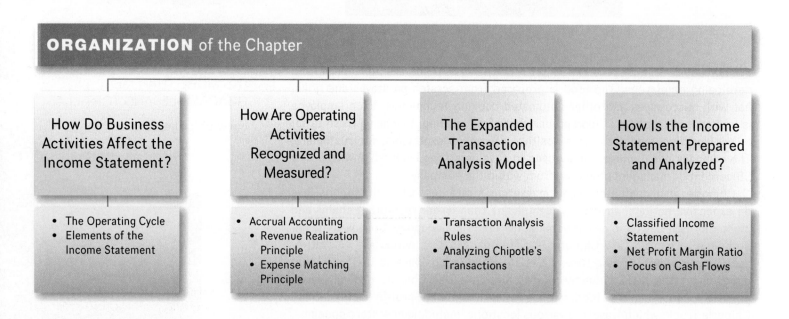

ORGANIZATION of the Chapter

How Do Business Activities Affect the Income Statement?	How Are Operating Activities Recognized and Measured?	The Expanded Transaction Analysis Model	How Is the Income Statement Prepared and Analyzed?

• The Operating Cycle
• Elements of the Income Statement
	• Accrual Accounting
	  • Revenue Realization Principle
	  • Expense Matching Principle
		• Transaction Analysis Rules
		• Analyzing Chipotle's Transactions
			• Classified Income Statement
			• Net Profit Margin Ratio
			• Focus on Cash Flows

LEARNING OBJECTIVE 3-1

Describe a typical business operating cycle and explain the necessity for the time period assumption.

HOW DO BUSINESS ACTIVITIES AFFECT THE INCOME STATEMENT?

The Operating Cycle

The long-term objective for any business is to **turn cash into more cash.** If a company is to stay in business, this excess cash must be generated from operations (that is, from the activities for which the business was established), not from borrowing money or selling long-lived assets.

Companies (1) acquire inventory and the services of employees and (2) sell inventory or services to customers. The operating (cash-to-cash) cycle begins when a company receives goods to sell (or, in the case of a service company, has employees work), pays for them, and sells to customers; it ends when customers pay cash to the company. The length of time for completion of the operating cycle depends on the nature of the business.

The OPERATING (CASH-TO-CASH) CYCLE is the time it takes for a company to pay cash to suppliers, sell goods and services to customers, and collect cash from customers.

BEGIN OPERATING (CASH-TO-CASH) CYCLE

Purchase goods and services on credit

Receive cash from customers

Typical Operating Cycle

Pay cash to suppliers

Sell goods and services to customers

The operating cycle for Chipotle is relatively short. It spends cash to purchase fresh ingredients, prepares the food, and sells it to customers for cash. In some companies, inventory is paid for well before it is sold. Toys R Us, for example, builds its inventory for months preceding the year-end holiday season. It borrows funds from banks to pay for the inventory and repays the loans with interest when it receives cash from customers. In other companies, cash is received from customers well after a sale takes place. For example, furniture retailers often allow customers to make monthly payments over several years. Shortening the operating cycle by creating incentives that encourage customers to buy sooner and/or pay faster improves a company's cash flows.

Until a company ceases its activities, the operating cycle is repeated continuously. However, decision makers require information periodically about the company's financial condition and performance. As indicated in the conceptual framework in Exhibit 2.1, to measure income for a specific period of time, accountants follow the **time period assumption,** which assumes that the long life of a company can be reported in shorter time periods, such as months, quarters, and years.[1] Two types of issues arise in reporting periodic income to users:

The TIME PERIOD ASSUMPTION indicates that the long life of a company can be reported in shorter time periods.

1. Recognition issues: **When** should the effects of operating activities be recognized (recorded)?

2. Measurement issues: **What amounts** should be recognized?

Before we examine the rules accountants follow in resolving these issues, however, let's examine the elements of the income statement that are affected by operating activities.

---

[1]In addition to the audited annual statements, most businesses prepare quarterly financial statements (also known as **interim reports** covering a three-month period) for external users. The Securities and Exchange Commission requires public companies to do so.

EXHIBIT 3.1		
Chipotle Mexican Grill's Income Statement	**CHIPOTLE MEXICAN GRILL, INC.** **Consolidated Statement of Income*** **For the Year ended December 31, 2011** **(in thousands of dollars, except per share data)**	**EXPLANATIONS**

Restaurant sales revenue	$2,269,500	
Restaurant operating expenses:		
Food, beverage, and packaging	738,700	*Includes used supplies*
Salaries and wages	543,100	
Occupancy	147,300	*Includes rent, insurance, and utilities*
Other operating expenses	259,700	*Includes advertising and maintenance*
General and administrative expenses	149,400	*Includes management training*
Depreciation expense	74,900	
Total operating expenses	1,913,100	
Income from operations	356,400	
Other items:		
Investment income	2,100	
Interest expense	(2,900)	
Gain (loss) on disposal of assets	(5,800)	
Income before income taxes	349,800	
Income tax expense	134,800	*Also called Provision for Income Taxes*
Net income	$ 215,000	
Earnings per share	$ 6.89	= *$215,000,000 Net Income ÷ 31,217,000 weighted average number of common stock shares outstanding*

Operating activities (central focus of business) — Restaurant sales revenue through Depreciation expense

Peripheral activities (not central focus of business) — Other items

*The information has been adapted from actual statements and simplified for this chapter.

Elements of the Income Statement

LEARNING OBJECTIVE 3-2
Explain how business activities affect the elements of the income statement.

Exhibit 3.1 shows a recent income statement for Chipotle, simplified for the purposes of this chapter. It has multiple subtotals, such as **operating income** and **income before income taxes.** This format is known as **multiple step** and is very common.[2] In fact, you can tell if a company uses the multiple-step format if you see the Operating Income (also called Income from Operations) subtotal. As we discuss the elements of the income statement, also refer to the conceptual framework outlined in Exhibit 2.1.

Operating Revenues

REVENUES are increases in assets or settlements of liabilities from ongoing operations.

Revenues are defined as increases in assets or settlements of liabilities from **ongoing operations** of the business. Operating revenues result from the sale of goods or services. When Chipotle sells tacos to consumers, it has **earned** revenue. When revenue is earned, assets, usually Cash or Accounts Receivable, often increase. Sometimes if a customer pays for goods or services in advance, a liability account, usually Unearned (or Deferred) Revenue, is created. At this point, no revenue has been earned. There is simply a receipt of cash in exchange for a promise to provide a good or service in the future. When the company provides the promised goods or services to the customer, then the revenue is recognized and the liability eliminated.

Many companies generate revenues from a variety of sources. For example, General Motors reports revenues from its automotive sales as well as from providing financing to customers. In the restaurant industry, many companies, such as McDonald's Corporation, have company-owned stores but also sell franchise rights. The franchisor (seller) reports revenues from both

[2]Another common format, **single step,** reorganizes all accounts from the multiple-step format. All revenues and gains are listed together and all expenses and losses except taxes are listed together. The expense subtotal is then subtracted from the revenue subtotal to arrive at income before income taxes, the same subtotal as on the multiple-step statement.

the sales of food in company-owned stores and the fees from franchisees. Chipotle does not sell franchises. Therefore, the company generates revenue from one source—sales of food orders to customers—that is reported in the **Restaurant Sales Revenue** account.

Operating Expenses

Some students confuse the terms **expenditures** and **expenses.** An expenditure is any outflow of cash for any purpose, whether to buy equipment, pay off a bank loan, or pay employees their wages. Expenses are outflows or the using up of assets or increases in liabilities from **ongoing operations** incurred to generate revenues during the period. Therefore, **not all cash expenditures are expenses, but expenses are necessary to generate revenues.**

Chipotle's employees make and serve food. The company uses electricity to operate equipment and light its facilities, and it uses food and paper supplies. Without incurring these expenses, Chipotle could not generate revenues. Expenses may be incurred before, after, or at the same time as cash is paid. When an expense is incurred, assets such as Supplies decrease (are used up) **or** liabilities such as Wages Payable or Utilities Payable increase. The following are Chipotle's primary operating expenses:

EXPENSES are outflows or the using up of assets or increases in liabilities from ongoing operations incurred to generate revenues during the period.

Restaurant Operating Expenses:

- **Food, Beverage, and Packaging Expense.** In Chipotle's restaurant operations, any food ingredients or beverage and packaging supplies that are used to produce and sell meals are expensed as they are used. For Chipotle, this is its largest expense at $738,700,000 in 2011. In companies with a manufacturing or merchandising focus, Cost of Goods Sold (or Cost of Sales) representing the cost of inventory used in generating sales is usually the most significant expense.

- **Salaries and Wages Expense.** When employees work and generate sales for Chipotle, the company incurs an expense, although wages and salaries will be paid later. Salaries and Wages Expense of $543,100,000 is Chipotle's second largest expense. In purely service-oriented companies in which no products are produced or sold, the cost of having employees generate revenues is usually the largest expense. For example, Federal Express reported $9.365 billion in salaries expense for the year ended May 31, 2012.

- **Occupancy Expense.** Renting facilities, insuring property and equipment at the stores, and using utilities are typical expenses related to occupying facilities. Usually, rent and insurance are paid before occupying the facilities, but utilities are paid after occupying the facilities.

- **Other Operating Expenses.** These expenses include advertising and marketing costs and repair and maintenance of store facilities.

General and Administrative Expenses: General and Administrative Expenses include costs of renting headquarters facilities, executive salaries, and training managers. These are typically expenses that are not directly related to operating stores.

Depreciation Expense: When a company uses buildings and equipment to generate revenues, a part of the cost of these assets is reported as an expense called Depreciation Expense. Chapter 8 discusses methods for estimating the amount of depreciation expense.

Operating revenues less operating expenses equals **Operating Income** (also called Income from Operations)—a measure of the profit from central ongoing operations.

Other Items

Not all activities affecting an income statement are central to ongoing operations. Any revenues, expenses, gains, or losses that result from these other activities are not included as part of operating income, but are instead categorized as Other Items. Typically, these include the following:

- **Investment Income** (or **Investment Revenue, Interest Revenue,** or **Dividend Revenue**). Using excess cash to purchase stocks or bonds in other companies is an investing activity for Chipotle, not the central operation of making and selling fresh Mexican food. Therefore, any interest or dividends earned on investments in other companies are not included as operating revenue.

- **Interest Expense.** Likewise, since borrowing money is a financing activity, any cost of using that money (called interest) is not an operating expense. Except for financial institutions, incurring interest expense and earning investment income are **not** the central operations of most businesses, including Chipotle. We say these are peripheral (normal but not central) transactions.

GAINS are increases in assets or decreases in liabilities from peripheral transactions.

LOSSES are decreases in assets or increases in liabilities from peripheral transactions.

- **Gain (Loss) on Disposal of Assets.** Companies sell property, plant, and equipment from time to time to maintain modern facilities. They also sell investments as needed. Selling these assets for more than the original purchase price does not result in earning revenue because the transaction is not the central operating focus for the business. Gains result in an increase in assets or decrease in liabilities from a **peripheral** transaction. Losses are decreases in assets or increases in liabilities from **peripheral** transactions. In 2011, Chipotle reported a loss of $5,800,000.

Income Tax Expense

Adding and subtracting other items to operating income gives a subtotal of **Income before Income Taxes** (or pretax income). Income Tax Expense (also called **Provision for Income Taxes**) is the last expense listed on the income statement before determining net income. All profit-making corporations are required to compute income taxes owed to federal, state, and foreign governments. Income tax expense is calculated as a percentage of pretax income determined by applying the tax rates of the federal, state, local, and foreign taxing authorities. Chipotle's effective tax rate in 2011 was 38.5 percent ($134,800,000 in income tax expense divided by $349,800,000 in income before income taxes). This indicates that, for every dollar of income before taxes that Chipotle made in 2011, the company paid nearly $0.39 to taxing authorities.

Earnings per Share

Corporations are required to disclose earnings per share on the income statement or in the notes to the financial statements. This ratio is widely used in evaluating the operating performance and profitability of a company. At this introductory level, we can compute earnings per share simply as net income divided by the weighted average number of shares of stock outstanding (Net Income ÷ Weighted Average Number of Shares of Stock Outstanding). Please note, however, that the calculation of the ratio is actually much more complex and beyond the scope of this course. Instead, we used the actual number computed by Chipotle. For 2011, Chipotle reported $6.89 in earnings for each share of stock owned by investors.

INTERNATIONAL PERSPECTIVE

Income Statement Differences

GlaxoSmithKline
Parmalat

Unilever

Reproduced with kind permission of Unilever PLC and group companies.

Under IFRS, the income statement is usually titled the Statement of Operations. There is also a difference in how expenses may be reported:

	GAAP	IFRS
Presentation of Expenses		
• Similar expenses are reported, but they may be grouped in different ways.	Public companies categorize expenses by business **function** (e.g., production, research, marketing, general operations).	Companies can categorize expenses by either **function or nature** (e.g., salaries, rent, supplies, electricity).

In addition, foreign companies often use account titles that differ from those used by U.S. companies. For example, GlaxoSmithKline (a U.K. pharmaceutical company), Parmalat (an Italian food producer of milk, dairy products, and fruit-based beverages), and Unilever (a U.K. and Netherlands-based company supplying food, home, and personal care products such as Hellman's mayonnaise, Dove soap, and

Popsicle treats) use the term *turnover* to refer to sales revenue, *finance income* for income from investments, and *finance cost* for interest expense. BMW Group, on the other hand, reports *revenues* and uses *financial result* for the difference between income from investments and interest expense. All four companies follow IFRS.

HOW ARE OPERATING ACTIVITIES RECOGNIZED AND MEASURED?

You probably determine your personal financial position by the cash balance in your bank account. Your financial performance is measured as the difference between your cash balance at the beginning of the period and the cash balance at the end of the period (that is, whether you end up with more or less cash). If you have a higher cash balance, cash receipts exceeded cash disbursements for the period. Many local retailers, medical offices, and other small businesses use **cash basis accounting**, in which revenues are recorded when cash is received and expenses are recorded when cash is paid, regardless of when the revenues are earned or the expenses incurred. This basis produces net operating cash flow information which is often quite adequate for organizations that do not need to report to external users. The following table illustrates the application of cash basis accounting for the first three years of a new business, Cade Company:

Cade Company Income Statements	Year 1	Year 2	Year 3	Total
Sales on credit	$ 60,000	$60,000	$60,000	$180,000
Cash receipts from customers	$ 20,000	$70,000	$90,000	$180,000
Cash disbursements for:				
Salaries to employees	(30,000)	(30,000)	(30,000)	(90,000)
Insurance for 3 years	(12,000)	(0)	(0)	(12,000)
Supplies	(3,000)	(7,000)	(5,000)	(15,000)
Net operating cash flows	**$(25,000)**	**$33,000**	**$55,000**	**$ 63,000**

In this illustration, $60,000 in sales was earned each year by Cade Company. However, because the sales were on account, customers spread out their payments over three years. Salaries to employees were paid in full each year. Insurance was prepaid at the beginning of the first year for equal coverage over the three years. Supplies were purchased on credit and used evenly over the three years. However, the company paid part of the first year purchases in the second year.

Using cash basis accounting may lead to an incorrect interpretation of future company performance. Simply looking at the first year, investors and creditors might interpret the negative cash flows as a problem with the company's ability to generate cash flows in the future. However, the other two years show positive cash flows. Likewise, performance over time appears uneven, when in actuality it is not. Sales were earned evenly each year, although collections from customers were not. The years in which insurance and supplies were paid for are not the same as the years in which these resources were used.

Accrual Accounting

Financial statements created under cash basis accounting normally postpone or accelerate recognition of revenues and expenses long before or after goods and services are produced and delivered (when cash is received or paid). They also do not necessarily reflect all assets or liabilities of a company on a particular date. For these reasons, cash basis financial statements are not very useful to external decision makers. Therefore, generally accepted accounting principles require **accrual basis accounting** for financial reporting.

In accrual basis accounting, revenues and expenses are recognized when the transaction that causes them occurs, not necessarily when cash is received or paid. That is, **revenues are recognized when they are earned and expenses when they are incurred.**

CASH BASIS
Income Measurement
Revenues (= cash receipts)
−Expenses (= cash payments)
Net Income (cash basis)

CASH BASIS ACCOUNTING records revenues when cash is received and expenses when cash is paid.

LEARNING OBJECTIVE 3-3
Explain the accrual basis of accounting and apply the revenue realization and expense matching principles to measure income.

ACCRUAL BASIS ACCOUNTING records revenues when earned and expenses when incurred, regardless of the timing of cash receipts or payments.

Using the same information for Cade Company, we can apply the accrual basis of accounting.

<table>
<tr><td>Cade Company Income Statements</td><td>Year 1</td><td>Year 2</td><td>Year 3</td><td>Total</td></tr>
<tr><td>Sales revenue (earned)</td><td>$60,000</td><td>$60,000</td><td>$60,000</td><td>$180,000</td></tr>
<tr><td>Expenses (resources used or incurred):</td><td></td><td></td><td></td><td></td></tr>
<tr><td>Salaries expense</td><td>(30,000)</td><td>(30,000)</td><td>(30,000)</td><td>(90,000)</td></tr>
<tr><td>Insurance expense</td><td>(4,000)</td><td>(4,000)</td><td>(4,000)</td><td>(12,000)</td></tr>
<tr><td>Supplies expense</td><td>(5,000)</td><td>(5,000)</td><td>(5,000)</td><td>(15,000)</td></tr>
<tr><td>Net income</td><td>$21,000</td><td>$21,000</td><td>$21,000</strong></td><td><strong>$ 63,000</td></tr>
</table>

ACCRUAL BASIS
Income Measurement
Revenues (= when earned)
−Expenses (= when incurred)
Net Income (accrual basis)

Regardless of when cash is received, Cade Company reported revenues when earned. Likewise, the company used insurance coverage and supplies evenly over the three years, despite prepaying the entire amount of insurance at the beginning of the first year and paying part of the first year's purchases in the second year. The $21,000 net income in the first year is a better predictor of future cash flows and performance than net operating cash flows reported under cash basis accounting. The two basic accounting principles that determine when revenues and expenses are recorded under accrual basis accounting are the **revenue realization principle** and the **expense matching principle.**

Revenue Realization Principle

The REVENUE REALIZATION PRINCIPLE states that revenues are recognized when (1) goods or services are delivered, (2) there is persuasive evidence of an arrangement for customer payment, (3) the price is fixed or determinable, and (4) collection is reasonably assured.

Under the **revenue realization principle,** four criteria or conditions must normally be met for revenue to be recognized. If **any** of the following criteria are **not** met, revenue normally is **not** recognized and cannot be recorded.

1. **Delivery has occurred or services have been rendered.** The company has performed or substantially performed the acts promised to the customer by providing goods or services.

2. **There is persuasive evidence of an arrangement for customer payment.** In exchange for the company's performance, the customer has provided cash or a promise to pay cash (a receivable).

3. **The price is fixed or determinable.** There are no uncertainties as to the amount to be collected.

4. **Collection is reasonably assured.** For cash sales, collection is not an issue since it is received on the date of the exchange. For sales on credit, the company reviews the customer's ability to pay. If the customer is considered creditworthy, collecting cash from the customer is reasonably likely.

These conditions normally occur when the title, risks, and rewards of ownership have transferred to the customers. For most businesses, these conditions are met at the point of delivery of goods or services, **regardless of when cash is received.**

Although businesses expect to receive cash in exchange for their goods and services at the time of delivery, the timing of cash receipts from customers does not dictate when businesses report revenues. Instead, the key to determining when to report revenue is whether the business has done what it promised to do. Exhibit 3.2 illustrates that revenue is earned when the business delivers goods or services, although cash can be received from customers (1) in a period **before** delivery, (2) in the **same** period as delivery, or (3) in a period **after** delivery. Let's see how to handle each of these cases.

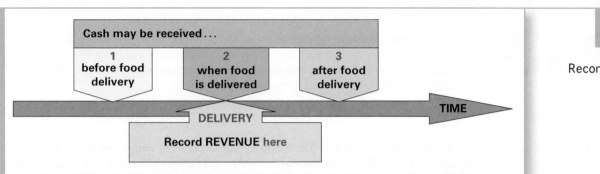

EXHIBIT 3.2

Recording Revenues versus
Cash Receipts

1 **Cash is received *before* the goods or services are delivered.** Chipotle sells gift cards to customers for cash in exchange for the promise to provide future food orders. Since Chipotle has not at that point delivered food, it records **no revenue.** Instead it creates a liability account (Unearned Revenue) representing the amount of food service owed to the customers. Later, when customers redeem their gift cards and Chipotle delivers the food, it earns and records the revenue while reducing the liability account since it has satisfied its promise to deliver.

2 **Cash is received *in the same period as* the goods or services are delivered.** As is a typical timing of cash receipts and revenue recognition in the restaurant industry, Chipotle receives cash from most customers within a few minutes of them receiving their food. Chipotle delivers the food to the customer as ordered in exchange for cash, **earning revenue** in the process.

3 **Cash is received *after* the goods or services are delivered.** When a business sells goods or services on account, the revenue is earned when the goods or services are delivered, not when cash is received at a later date. Let's assume to boost business, Chipotle delivers food when ordered by select customers, such as departments at area colleges or businesses, that pay for the food order when Chipotle bills them at the end of the month, not when the customers receive the food. When delivered, Chipotle records both Restaurant Sales Revenue and the asset Accounts Receivable, representing the customer's promise to pay in the future for past food deliveries. When the customer pays its monthly bill, Chipotle will increase its Cash account and decrease Accounts Receivable.

On receipt of a $100 cash deposit:

Cash (+A)   100
   Unearned Revenue (+L)   100

On delivery of ordered food:

Unearned Revenue (−L)   100
   Restaurant Sales Revenue (+R, +SE) . . .   100

On delivery of ordered food for $12 cash:

Cash (+A)   12
   Restaurant Sales Revenue (+R, +SE) . . .   12

On delivery of ordered food for $50 on account:

Accounts Receivable (+A)   50
   Restaurant Sales Revenue (+R, +SE) . . .   50

On receipt of cash after delivery:

Cash (+A)   50
   Accounts Receivable (−A)   50

Companies usually disclose their revenue recognition practices in the financial statement note titled Significant Accounting Policies. The following excerpt from Note 1 to recent financial statements describes how Chipotle recognizes its revenue:

1. DESCRIPTION OF BUSINESS AND SUMMARY OF SIGNIFICANT ACCOUNTING POLICIES

Revenue Recognition
Revenue from restaurant sales is recognized when food and beverage products are sold . . . The Company recognizes revenue from gift cards when: (i) the gift card is redeemed by the customer; or (ii) the Company determines the likelihood of the gift card being redeemed by the customer is remote (gift card breakage) . . . The determination of the gift card breakage rate is based upon Company-specific historical redemption patterns.

REAL WORLD EXCERPT
Annual Report

PAUSE FOR **FEEDBACK**

We just learned the **revenue realization principle's** criteria: (1) The company delivers goods or performs services, (2) there is persuasive evidence of an arrangement with the customer, (3) the price is fixed or determinable, and (4) collection is reasonably assured. Regardless of when cash is received, revenue is earned and recorded when these criteria are met.

SELF-STUDY QUIZ

Complete this quiz now to make sure you can apply the principle. The following transactions are samples of typical monthly operating activities of Papa John's International, Inc. (dollars in thousands) that makes and delivers pizza and sells franchises. If revenue is to be recognized in **January,** indicate the title of the revenue account and the amount of revenue to be recognized. For account titles, name the revenue account based on the nature of the transaction. For example, sales to customers are Restaurant Sales Revenue and sales of franchisees are Franchise Fee Revenue.

ACTIVITY	REVENUE ACCOUNT TITLE	AMOUNT OF REVENUE RECOGNIZED IN JANUARY
(a) In January, Papa John's company-owned restaurants sold food to customers for $32,000 cash.	*Rest. Sales Revenue*	*$32,000*
(b) In January, Papa John's sold new franchises for $625 cash, providing $400 in services to these new franchisees during January; the remainder of services will be provided over the next three months.	*Franchise Fee Revenue*	*$400*
(c) In January, Papa John's received $210 in cash from customers as deposits on large orders to be delivered in February. *Recognized in Feb.*		
(d) In January, Papa John's delivered $1,630 to select customers on account; the customers will pay when billed at the end of January.	*Rest Sales Revenue*	*$1,630*
(e) In January, customers paid $1,200 on account to Papa John's from December deliveries of pizza. *Recognized in Dec.*		
(f) In January, Papa John's delivered $385 to customers who provided deposits in December.	*Rest. Sales Revenue*	*$385*

After you have completed your answers, check them with the solutions at the bottom of the page.

Solutions to
SELF-STUDY QUIZ

Revenue Account Title	Amount of Revenue Recognized in January
(a) Restaurant Sales Revenue	$32,000
(b) Franchise Fee Revenue	$ 400
(c) No revenue earned in January	—
(d) Restaurant Sales Revenue	$ 1,630
(e) No revenue earned in January	—
(f) Restaurant Sales Revenue	$ 385

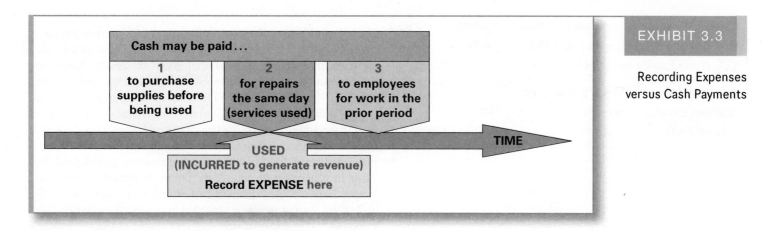

EXHIBIT 3.3

Recording Expenses versus Cash Payments

Expense Matching Principle

The expense matching principle requires that costs incurred to generate revenues be recognized in the same period—a matching of costs with benefits. For example, when Chipotle's restaurants provide food service to customers, revenue is earned. The costs of generating the revenue include expenses incurred such as these:

The **EXPENSE MATCHING PRINCIPLE** requires that expenses be recorded when incurred in earning revenue.

- Salaries and wages to employees who worked **during the period**
- Utilities for the electricity used **during the period**
- Food, beverage, and packaging products used **during the period**
- Facilities rental **during the period**
- Grills and other equipment used **during the period**

As with revenues and cash receipts, expenses are recorded as incurred, **regardless of when cash is paid.** Cash may be paid (1) **before,** (2) **during,** or (3) **after** an expense is incurred (see Exhibit 3.3). An entry will be made on the date the expense is incurred and another on the date the cash is paid, if they occur at different times. Let's see how to handle each of these cases related to the expense matching principle.

1 **Cash is paid** *before* **the expense is incurred to generate revenue.** Companies purchase many assets that are used to generate revenues in future periods. Examples include buying insurance for future coverage, paying rent for future use of space, and acquiring supplies and equipment for future use. When revenues are generated in the future, the company records an expense for the portion of the cost of the assets used—costs are matched with the benefits. As an example, Chipotle buys paper supplies (napkins, bags, cups, etc.) in one month, but uses them the following month. When acquired, the supplies are recorded as an asset called Supplies because they will benefit future periods. When they are used the following month, Food, Beverage, and Packaging Expense (or Supplies Expense) is recorded for the month and the asset Supplies is reduced to the amount yet to be used. Similarly, rent, insurance, and advertising that are prepaid are often recorded in an asset account called Prepaid Expenses and expensed when used.

On payment of $200 cash for supplies:		
Supplies (+A)	200	
Cash (−A)		200
On subsequent use of half of the supplies:		
Food, Beverage, and Packaging		
Expense (+E, −SE)	100	
Supplies (−A)		100

2 **Cash is paid** *in the same period* **as the expense is incurred to generate revenue.** Expenses are sometimes incurred and paid for in the period in which they arise. An example is paying for repairs on grills the day of the service. If Chipotle spends $275 cash to repair grills so that food can be prepared to sell, an expense is incurred and recorded (Other Operating Expenses or Repairs Expense).

On payment of $275 cash for repair service:		
Other Operating Expenses (+E, −SE) . . .	275	
Cash (−A)		275

On use of $400 in employees' services during the period:		
Salaries and Wages Expense (+E, −SE) . .	400	
Accrued Expenses Payable (+L)		400
On payment of cash after using employees:		
Accrued Expenses Payable (−L)	400	
Cash (−A)		400

3 **Cash is paid *after* the cost is incurred to generate revenue.** Although rent and supplies are typically purchased before they are used, many costs are paid after goods or services have been received and used. Examples include using electric and gas utilities in the current period that are not paid for until the following period, using borrowed funds and incurring Interest Expense to be paid in the future, and owing wages to employees who worked in the current period. When Chipotle's restaurants use employees to make and serve food in the current accounting period (and thus assist in generating revenues), the company records Salaries and Wages Expense. Any amount that is owed to employees at the end of the current period is recorded as a liability called Accrued Expenses Payable (also called Salaries Payable or Wages Payable).

 PAUSE FOR FEEDBACK

The **expense matching principle** requires that costs incurred to generate revenues be recognized in the same period—that costs are matched with revenues they generate. Regardless of when cash is paid, expense is recorded when incurred.

SELF-STUDY QUIZ

Complete this quiz now to make sure you can apply the principle. The following transactions are samples of typical monthly operating activities of Papa John's (dollars in thousands). If an expense is to be recognized in **January,** indicate the title of the expense account and the amount of expense to be recognized.

ACTIVITY	EXPENSE ACCOUNT TITLE	AMOUNT OF EXPENSE RECOGNIZED IN JANUARY
(a) At the beginning of January, Papa John's restaurants paid $3,000 in rent for the months of January, February, and March.	Rent Expense	$1000
(b) In January, Papa John's paid suppliers $10,000 on account for supplies received in December.	~~Supply Expense~~ no Expense - supplies not used	~~$10,000~~
(c) In January, the food and paper products supplies used in making and selling pizza products to customers was $9,500. The supplies were purchased in December on account.	Supply Expense	$9,500
(d) In late January, Papa John's received a $400 utility bill for electricity used in January. The bill will be paid in February.	Utilities Expense	$400

After you have completed your answers, check them with the solutions at the bottom of the page.

Solutions to
SELF-STUDY QUIZ

Expense Account Title	Amount of Expense Recognized in January
(a) Rent Expense	$1,000 ($3,000 ÷ 3 months)
(b) No expense in January	Supplies will be expensed when used.
(c) Supplies Expense	$9,500
(d) Utilities Expense	$400

Investors in the stock market base their decisions on their expectations of a company's future earnings. When companies announce quarterly and annual earnings information, investors evaluate how well the companies have met expectations and adjust their investing decisions accordingly. Companies that fail to meet expectations often experience a decline in stock price. Thus, managers are motivated to produce earnings results that meet or exceed investors' expectations to bolster stock prices. Greed may lead some managers to make unethical accounting and reporting decisions, often involving falsifying revenues and expenses. While this sometimes fools people for a short time, it rarely works in the long run and often leads to very bad consequences.

Fraud is a criminal offense for which managers may be sentenced to jail. Samples of fraud cases, a few involving faulty revenue and expense accounting, are shown below. Just imagine what it must have been like to be 65-year-old Bernie Ebbers or 21-year-old Barry Minkow, both sentenced to 25 years in prison for accounting fraud.

The CEO	The Fraud	Conviction/Plea	The Outcome
Bernard Madoff, 71 Madoff Investment Securities	Scammed $50 billion from investors in a Ponzi scheme (in which investors receive "returns" from money paid by subsequent investors).	Confessed, December 2008	Sentenced to 150 years
Bernie Ebbers, 65 Worldcom	Recorded $11 billion in operating expenses as if they were assets.	Convicted, July 2005	Sentenced to 25 years
Sanjay Kumar, 44 Computer Associates	Recorded sales in the wrong accounting period.	Pleaded guilty, April 2006	Sentenced to 12 years
Martin Grass, 49 Rite Aid Corporation	Recorded rebates from drug companies before they were earned.	Pleaded guilty, June 2003	Sentenced to 8 years
Barry Minkow, 21 ZZZZ Best	Made up customers and sales to show profits when, in reality, the company was a sham.	Convicted, December 1988	Sentenced to 25 years

Many others are affected by accounting fraud. Shareholders lose stock value, employees may lose their jobs (and pension funds, as in the case of Enron), and customers and suppliers may become wary of dealing with a company operating under the cloud of fraud. As a manager, you may face an ethical dilemma in the workplace. The ethical decision is the one you will be proud of 20 years later.

THE EXPANDED TRANSACTION ANALYSIS MODEL

We have discussed the variety of business activities affecting the income statement and how they are measured. Now we need to determine how these business activities are recorded in the accounting system and reflected in the financial statements. Chapter 2 covered investing and financing activities that affect assets, liabilities, and contributed capital. We now expand the transaction analysis model to include operating activities.

LEARNING OBJECTIVE 3-4
Apply transaction analysis to examine and record the effects of operating activities on the financial statements.

Transaction Analysis Rules

The complete transaction analysis model presented in Exhibit 3.4 includes **all five elements:** assets, liabilities, stockholders' equity, revenues, and expenses. Recall that the Retained Earnings account is the accumulation of all past revenues and expenses minus any income distributed to stockholders as dividends (that is, earnings not retained in the business).[3] When net income is positive, Retained Earnings increase; a net loss decreases Retained Earnings.

[3]Instead of reducing Retained Earnings directly when dividends are declared, companies may use the account Dividends Declared, which has a debit balance.

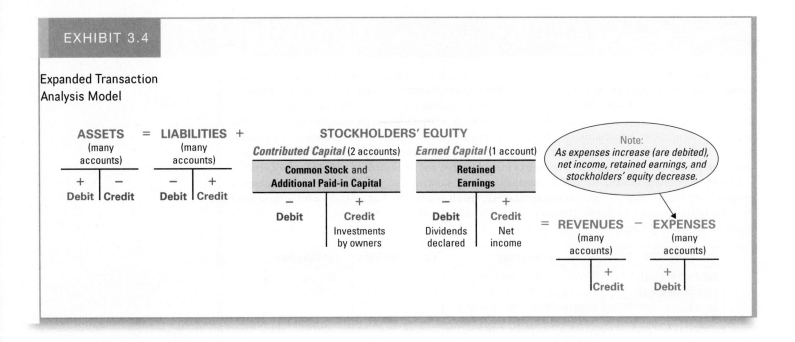

EXHIBIT 3.4

Expanded Transaction
Analysis Model

Some students attempt to memorize journal entries in the introductory accounting course. However, they are often overwhelmed by the number and complexity of transactions as the course progresses. To avoid this pitfall, you should instead be able to construct the transaction analysis model in Exhibit 3.4 on your own without assistance and use it to analyze transactions. It will be very beneficial in completing assignments and analyzing more complex transactions in future chapters. Now let's study Exhibit 3.4 carefully to remember how the model is constructed and to understand the impact of operating activities on both the balance sheet and income statement:

- All accounts can increase or decrease, although revenues and expenses tend to increase throughout a period. For accounts on the left side of the accounting equation, the increase symbol + is written on the left side of the T-account. For accounts on the right side of the accounting equation, the increase symbol + is written on the right side of the T-account, **except for expenses, which increase on the left side of the T-account.**

- Debits (dr) are written on the left of each T-account and credits (cr) are written on the right.

- Every transaction affects at least two accounts.

- Revenues increase stockholders' equity through the account Retained Earnings and therefore have **credit** balances. Recording revenue results in either increasing an asset (such as Cash or Accounts Receivable) or decreasing a liability (such as Unearned Subscriptions Revenue).

- Expenses decrease net income, thus decreasing Retained Earnings and stockholders' equity. Therefore, they have **debit** balances (opposite of the balance in Retained Earnings). That is, to increase an expense, you debit it, thereby decreasing net income and Retained Earnings. Recording an expense results in either decreasing an asset (such as Supplies when used) or increasing a liability (such as Wages Payable when money is owed to employees).

- When revenues exceed expenses, the company reports net income, increasing Retained Earnings and stockholders' equity. However, when expenses exceed revenues, a net loss results that decreases Retained Earnings and thus stockholders' equity.

In summary:

REVENUES	EXPENSES
• Increase net income and stockholders' equity	• Decrease net income and stockholders' equity
• ↑ with Credits	• ↑ with Debits
• Accounts have credit balances	• Accounts have debit balances

The steps to follow in analyzing transactions presented in Chapter 2 are now modified to determine the effects of earning revenues and incurring expenses. Now, as shown below, when a transaction occurs, the questions to ask are:

Transaction Analysis Steps:

Step 1: Ask → **Was a revenue earned by delivering goods or services?**
If so, credit the revenue account and debit the accounts for what was received.

or **Ask →** **Was an expense incurred to generate a revenue in the current period?**
If so, debit the expense account and credit the accounts for what was given.

or **Ask →** **If no revenue was earned or expense incurred, what was received and given?**

- **Identify the accounts affected by title** (e.g., Cash and Notes Payable).
  Remember: *Make sure that at least two accounts change.*
- **Classify them by type of account:** asset (A), liability (L), stockholders' equity (SE), revenue/gain (R), or expense/loss (E).
- **Determine the direction of the effect.** Did the account increase (+) or decrease (−)?

Step 2: Verify → **Is the accounting equation in balance?** (A = L + SE)

Analyzing Chipotle's Transactions

Now we continue activities for Chipotle Mexican Grill, building on the company's trial balance presented at the end of Chapter 2. It included only investing and financing transactions occurring during the first quarter of 2012.

CHIPOTLE MEXICAN GRILL **Trial Balance** (based on investing and financing transactions during the first quarter ended March 31, 2012)		
(in thousands)	**Debit**	**Credit**
Cash	349,600	
Short-term investments	94,500	
Accounts receivable	8,400	
Supplies	8,900	
Prepaid expenses	27,700	
Property and equipment (net)	859,000	
Long-term investments	149,100	
Accounts payable		46,400
Accrued expenses payable		93,100
Dividends payable		3,000
Unearned revenue		18,000
Notes payable		233,200
Common stock		400
Additional paid-in capital		434,600
Retained earnings		668,500
Total	**1,497,200**	**1,497,200**

Using the transaction analysis steps, we analyze, record, and post to the T-accounts the effects of this chapter's operating activities that also occurred during the first quarter. The T-accounts begin with the trial balance amounts on the previous page. All amounts are in thousands of dollars. Because we illustrated six investing and financing transactions in Chapter 2 using referencing of (*a*) to (*f*), we start with transaction (*g*) in this chapter. You should notice that in each journal entry in which a revenue or expense is recorded, we insert (+R, +SE) for revenues and (+E, −SE) for expenses to emphasize the effect of the transaction on the accounting equation and to help you see that the equation remains in balance. In Chapter 4, we complete the accounting cycle with the activities at the end of the quarter (on March 31).

(*g*) **Chipotle purchased food, beverage, and packaging supplies costing $207,700, paying $167,700 in cash and owing the rest on account.**

Debits = Credits

	Debit	Credit
(*g*) Supplies (+A)	207,700	
Cash (−A)		167,700
Accounts Payable (+L)		40,000

Equation in balance

Assets		=	Liabilities		+	Stockholders' Equity
Supplies	+207,700		Accounts payable	+40,000		
Cash	−167,700					

Effects posted

+ Cash (A) −			+ Supplies (A) −			− Accounts Payable (L) +	
Bal. 349,600			Bal. 8,900				46,400 Bal.
	167,700 (*g*)		(*g*) 207,700				40,000 (*g*)

(*h*) **At the beginning of January, Chipotle paid in advance $36,000 for six months of rent, $32,000 for insurance coverage for all of 2012, and $18,000 for advertising over several upcoming months.** All of these are Prepaid Expenses.

Debits = Credits

	Debit	Credit
(*h*) Prepaid Expenses (+A)	86,000	
Cash (−A)		86,000

Equation in balance

Assets		=	Liabilities	+	Stockholders' Equity
Prepaid expenses	+86,000				
Cash	−86,000				

Effects posted

+ Cash (A) −			+ Prepaid Expenses (A) −	
Bal. 349,600	167,700 (*g*)		Bal. 27,700	
	86,000 (*h*)		(*h*) 86,000	

(*i*) **During the first quarter, Chipotle sold food to customers for $619,300; $4,000 was sold to universities on account (to be paid next quarter) and the rest was received in cash in the stores. NOTE:** To measure revenues and expenses in a period, these accounts begin with a $0 balance; notice they are not listed on the trial balance on page 113 because they have no balance yet.

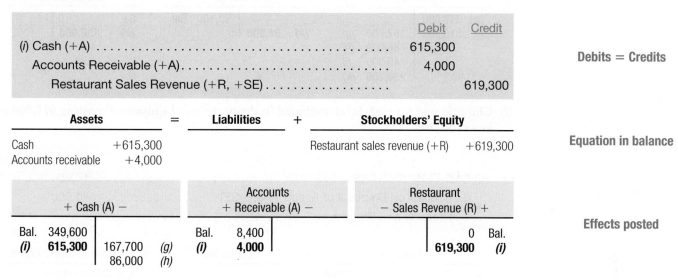

	Debit	Credit
(i) Cash (+A)	615,300	
Accounts Receivable (+A)	4,000	
Restaurant Sales Revenue (+R, +SE)		619,300

Debits = Credits

Assets	=	Liabilities	+	Stockholders' Equity
Cash +615,300				Restaurant sales revenue (+R) +619,300
Accounts receivable +4,000				

Equation in balance

+ Cash (A) −			+ Receivable (A) −		Accounts	− Sales Revenue (R) +		Restaurant
Bal. 349,600			Bal. 8,400				0 Bal.	
(i) 615,300	167,700	(g)	(i) 4,000				619,300	(i)
	86,000	(h)						

Effects posted

(j) **Chipotle paid $49,300 for management training expenses** (part of General and Administrative Expenses).

	Debit	Credit
(j) General and Administrative Expenses (+E, −SE)	49,300	
Cash (−A)		49,300

Debits = Credits

Assets	=	Liabilities	+	Stockholders' Equity
Cash −49,300				General and administrative
				expenses (+E) −49,300

Equation in balance

+ Cash (A) −			General and Administrative + Expenses (E) −	
Bal. 349,600			Bal. 0	
(i) 615,300	167,700	(g)	(j) 49,300	
	86,000	(h)		
	49,300	(j)		

Effects posted

(k) **Chipotle paid employees who worked this quarter for $138,600 and last quarter for $91,500** (recorded last quarter as a liability in Accrued Expenses Payable).

	Debit	Credit
(k) Salaries and Wages Expense (+E, −SE)	138,600	
Accrued Expenses Payable (−L)	91,500	
Cash (−A)		230,100

Debits = Credits

Assets	=	Liabilities	+	Stockholders' Equity
Cash −230,100		Accrued expenses		Salaries and wages
		payable −91,500		expense (+E) −138,600

Equation in balance

Effects posted

+ Cash (A) −				Accrued Expenses − Payable (L) +			Salaries and Wages + Expense (E) −	
Bal. 349,600					93,100	Bal.	Bal. 0	
(i) 615,300	167,700	(g)	**(k) 91,500**				**(k) 138,600**	
	86,000	(h)						
	49,300	(j)						
	230,100	**(k)**						

(l) Chipotle sold for cash land (included in Property and Equipment) costing $11,900 at a loss of $1,300.[4]

Debits = Credits

	Debit	Credit
(l) Cash (+A)	10,600	
Gain (Loss) on Disposal of Assets (+E, −SE)	1,300	
Property and Equipment (−A)		11,900

Equation in balance

Assets		=	Liabilities	+	Stockholders' Equity	
Cash	+10,600				Gain (loss) on disposal	
Property and equipment	−11,900				of assets (+E)	−1,300

Effects posted

+ Cash (A) −				Property and + Equipment (net) (A) −			Gain (loss) on Disposal + of Assets (E) −	
Bal. 349,600				Bal. 859,000			Bal. 0	
(i) 615,300	167,700	(g)			**11,900**	**(l)**	**(l) 1,300**	
(l) 10,600	86,000	(h)						
	49,300	(j)						
	230,100	(k)						

(m) Chipotle received $3,300 cash from customers paying on their accounts.

Debits = Credits

	Debit	Credit
(m) Cash (+A)	3,300	
Accounts Receivable (−A)		3,300

Equation in balance

Assets		=	Liabilities	+	Stockholders' Equity
Cash	+3,300				
Accounts receivable	−3,300				

Effects posted

+ Cash (A) −				+ Accounts Receivable (A) −			
Bal. 349,600				Bal. 8,400			
(i) 615,300	167,700	(g)		(i) 4,000	**3,300**	**(m)**	
(l) 10,600	86,000	(h)					
(m) 3,300	49,300	(j)					
	230,100	(k)					

(n) During the quarter, Chipotle paid suppliers $37,200 on account.

Debits = Credits

	Debit	Credit
(n) Accounts Payable (−L)	37,200	
Cash (−A).		37,200

---

[4]This is an example of a peripheral activity; it will be covered in more depth in Chapter 8.

Assets	=	Liabilities	+	Stockholders' Equity		Equation in balance
Cash	−37,200	Accounts payable	−37,200			

+ Cash (A) −				Accounts − Payable (L) +				Effects posted
Bal. 349,600					46,400	Bal.		
(i) 615,300	167,700	(g)	(n) 37,200	40,000	(g)			
(l) 10,600	86,000	(h)						
(m) 3,300	49,300	(j)						
	230,100	(k)						
	37,200	(n)						

(o) **During the quarter, Chipotle incurred and paid $10,000 for utilities** (part of Occupancy Expense) **and $48,600 in the maintenance of its facilities** (part of Other Operating Expenses).

	Debit	Credit	
(o) Occupancy Expense (+E, −SE).	10,000		**Debits = Credits**
Other Operating Expenses (+E, −SE)	48,600		
Cash (−A).		58,600	

Assets	=	Liabilities	+	Stockholders' Equity		Equation in balance
Cash	−58,600			Occupancy expense (+E)	−10,000	
				Other operating expenses (+E)	−48,600	

+ Cash (A) −				Occupancy + Expense (E) −		Other Operating + Expenses (E) −		Effects posted
Bal. 349,600				Bal. 0		Bal. 0		
(i) 615,300	167,700	(g)		(o) 10,000		(o) 48,600		
(l) 10,600	86,000	(h)						
(m) 3,300	49,300	(j)						
	230,100	(k)						
	37,200	(n)						
	58,600	(o)						

(p) **Chipotle received $4,700 cash as investment income earned during the quarter.**

	Debit	Credit	
(p) Cash (+A).	4,700		**Debits = Credits**
Investment Income (+R, +SE)		4,700	

Assets	=	Liabilities	+	Stockholders' Equity		Equation in balance
Cash	+4,700			Investment income (+R)	+4,700	

+ Cash (A) −				− Investment Income (R) +			Effects posted
Bal. 349,600					0	Bal.	
(i) 615,300	167,700	(g)		4,700		(p)	
(l) 10,600	86,000	(h)					
(m) 3,300	49,300	(j)					
(p) 4,700	230,100	(k)					
	37,200	(n)					
	58,600	(o)					

(q) During the quarter, Chipotle sold gift cards to customers for $15,400 in cash (expected to be redeemed for food next quarter).

Debits = Credits

	Debit	Credit
(q) Cash (+A)...	15,400	
Unearned Revenue (+L)		15,400

Equation in balance

Assets		=	Liabilities		+	Stockholders' Equity
Cash	+15,400		Unearned revenue	+15,400		

Effects posted

+ Cash (A) −				− Unearned Revenue (L) +		
Bal.	349,600				18,000	Bal.
(i)	615,300	167,700	(g)		**15,400**	**(q)**
(l)	10,600	86,000	(h)			
(m)	3,300	49,300	(j)			
(p)	4,700	230,100	(k)			
(q)	**15,400**	37,200	(n)			
		58,600	(o)			

Now we determine the balances in the T-accounts:

Balance Sheet Accounts:

+ Cash (A) −				+ Short-term Investments (A) −			+ Accounts Receivable (A) −				+ Supplies (A) −		
Bal.	349,600			Bal.	94,500		Bal.	8,400			Bal.	8,900	
(i)	615,300	167,700	(g)		94,500		(i)	4,000	3,300	(m)	(g)	207,700	
(l)	10,600	86,000	(h)					9,100				216,600	
(m)	3,300	49,300	(j)										
(p)	4,700	230,100	(k)										
(q)	15,400	37,200	(n)										
		58,600	(o)										
	370,000				113,700			847,100				149,100	

Prepaid + Expenses (A) −			Property and + Equipment (net) (A) −			Long-term + Investments (A) −		
Bal.	27,700		Bal.	859,000		Bal.	149,100	
(h)	86,000				11,900	(l)		
	113,700			847,100			149,100	

Accounts − Payable (L) +				Accrued Expenses − Payable (L) +			Dividends − Payable (L) +		
		46,400	Bal.			93,100	Bal.	3,000	Bal.
(n)	37,200	40,000	(g)	(k)	91,500				
		49,200				1,600		3,000	

− Unearned Revenue (L) +			− Notes Payable (L) +		
		18,000	Bal.	233,200	Bal.
		15,400	(q)		
		33,400		233,200	

− Common Stock (SE) +			− Additional Paid-in Capital (SE) +			− Retained Earnings (SE) +		
		400	Bal.		434,600	Bal.	668,500	Bal.
		400			434,600		668,500	

Income Statement Accounts:

− Restaurant Sales Revenue (R) +	
	0 Bal.
	619,300 (i)
	619,300

− Investment Income (R) +	
	0 Bal.
	4,700 (p)
	4,700

Salaries and Wages + Expense (E) −	
Bal. 0	
(k) 138,600	
138,600	

Occupancy + Expense (E) −	
Bal. 0	
(o) 10,000	
10,000	

Other Operating + Expenses (E) −	
Bal. 0	
(o) 48,600	
48,600	

General and Administrative + Expenses (E) −	
Bal. 0	
(j) 49,300	
49,300	

Gain (Loss) on Disposal + of Assets (E) −	
Bal. 0	
(l) 1,300	
1,300	

PAUSE FOR **FEEDBACK**

We just illustrated the steps in analyzing and recording transactions, including those involving earning revenue and incurring expenses.

Transaction Analysis Steps:

Step 1:   Ask → Was a revenue earned by delivering goods or services?
        If so, credit the revenue account and debit the accounts for what was received.

    Ask → Was an expense incurred to generate a revenue in the current period?
        If so, debit the expense account and credit the accounts for what was given.

    Ask → If no revenue was earned or expense incurred, what was received and given?

• **Identify the accounts affected by title** (e.g., Cash and Notes Payable).
    Remember: *Make sure that at least two accounts change.*
• **Classify them by type of account:** asset (A), liability (L), stockholders' equity (SE), revenue/gain (R), or expense/loss (E).
• **Determine the direction of the effect.** Did the account increase (+) or decrease (−)?

Step 2: Verify → Is the accounting equation in balance? (A = L + SE)

SELF-STUDY **QUIZ**

Now it's your turn. Analyze and record the journal entries for each of the selected **June** transactions for Florida Flippers, Inc., a scuba diving and instruction business. Then post the effects to the T-accounts. Account titles and beginning balances are provided in the T-accounts on the next page. Be sure to check that debits equal credits in each journal entry and that the accounting equation remains in balance.

a. In June, new customers paid Florida Flippers $8,200 in cash for diving trips; $5,200 was for trips made in June, and the rest is for trips that will be provided in July.
b. In June, customers paid $3,900 in cash for instruction they received in May.
c. At the beginning of June, Florida Flippers paid a total of $6,000 cash for insurance to cover the months of June, July, and August.

d. In June, Florida Flippers paid $4,000 in wages to employees who worked in June.

	ACCOUNT TITLES	DEBIT	CREDIT
a.	Cash (A+)	8,200	
	Diving trip revenue (R)		5200
	unearned revenue (L)		3000
b.	Cash (A+)	3900	
	accounts receivable		3900
c.	~~Prepaid Insurance~~ Cash (A-)		6000
	prepaid insurance (A+)	6000	
d.	~~Unknown~~ wage expense	4000	~~4000~~
	~~Unknown~~ cash		4000

+ Cash (A) −			+ Accounts Receivable (A) −			+ Prepaid Insurance (A) −	
Beg. 25,000	6000		Beg. 4,500	3900		Beg. 0	~~6000~~
8200	4000					6000	
End. 3700			End. 600			End. 6000	
27100							

− Unearned Revenue (L) +			− Diving Trip Revenue (R) +			+ Wages Expense (E) −	
	0	Beg.		0	Beg.	Beg. 0	
	3000			5200		4000	
	3000	End.		5200	End.	End. 4000	

After you have completed your answers, check them with the solutions at the bottom of the page.

Solutions to
SELF-STUDY QUIZ

	Account Titles	Debit	Credit
a.	Cash (+A)	8,200	
	Diving Trip Revenue (+R, +SE)		5,200
	Unearned Revenue (+L)		3,000
b.	Cash (+A)	3,900	
	Accounts Receivable (−A)		3,900
c.	Prepaid Insurance (+A)	6,000	
	Cash (−A)		6,000
d.	Wages Expense (+E, −SE)	4,000	
	Cash (−A)		4,000

+ Cash (A) −				+ Accounts Receivable (A) −				+ Prepaid Insurance (A) −		
Beg.	25,000			Beg.	4,500			Beg.	0	
(a)	8,200	6,000	(c)			3,900	(b)	(c)	6,000	
(b)	3,900	4,000	(d)							
End.	27,100			End.	600			End.	6,000	

− Unearned Revenue (L) +				− Diving Trip Revenue (R) +				+ Wages Expense (E) −		
		0	Beg.			0	Beg.	Beg.	0	
		3,000	(a)			5,200	(a)	(d)	4,000	
		3,000	End.			5,200	End.	End.	4,000	

GUIDED **HELP**

For additional step-by-step video instruction on analyzing, recording, and posting transaction effects, go to the URL or scan the QR code in the margin with your smartphone or iPad.

www.mhhe.com/libby8e

HOW IS THE INCOME STATEMENT PREPARED AND ANALYZED?

As we discussed in Chapter 2, companies can prepare financial statements at any point in time. Before we consider creating any statements for Chipotle, however, we must first determine that the debits equal credits after all of the transactions illustrated above by generating a trial balance. Accounts are listed in financial statement order: assets, liabilities, stockholders' equity, revenues/gains, and expenses/losses.

LEARNING OBJECTIVE 3-5
Prepare a classified income statement.

CHIPOTLE MEXICAN GRILL **Unadjusted Trial Balance** **For the first quarter ended March 31, 2012**		
(in thousands)	**Debit**	**Credit**
Cash	370,000	
Short-term investments	94,500	
Accounts receivable	9,100	
Supplies	216,600	
Prepaid expenses	113,700	
Property and equipment (net)	847,100	
Long-term investments	149,100	
Accounts payable		49,200
Accrued expenses payable		1,600
Dividends payable		3,000
Unearned revenue		33,400
Notes payable		233,200
Common stock		400
Additional paid-in capital		434,600
Retained earnings		668,500
Restaurant sales revenue		619,300
Investment income		4,700
Salaries and wages expense	138,600	
Occupancy expense	10,000	
Other operating expenses	48,600	
General and administrative expenses	49,300	
Gain (loss) on disposal of assets	1,300	
Total	**2,047,900**	**2,047,900**

Although debits do equal credits, why is the trial balance labeled "unadjusted"? Does it make sense that supplies were purchased during the quarter, but no Supplies Expense was recorded to show the amount of supplies used? How likely is it that gift cards were sold, but none were redeemed by customers during the quarter? And didn't Chipotle use property and equipment during the quarter to generate revenues? The answer to all of these questions is that no end-of-period adjustments have been made yet to reflect all revenues earned and expenses incurred during the quarter. Therefore, the trial balance is **unadjusted** until adjustments are made, as we discuss in Chapter 4.

CLASSIFIED INCOME STATEMENT

The following classified income statement is presented to highlight the structure **but note that, because it is based on unadjusted balances, it would not be presented to external users.**

CHIPOTLE MEXICAN GRILL, INC.
Consolidated Statement of Income
UNADJUSTED
For the Quarter ended March 31, 2012
(in thousands of dollars)

Restaurant sales revenue	$619,300
Restaurant operating expenses:	
Food, beverage, and packaging	0
Salaries and wages	138,600
Occupancy	10,000
Other operating expenses	48,600
General and administrative expenses	49,300
Depreciation expense	0
Total operating expenses	246,500
Income from operations	372,800
Other items:	
Investment income	4,700
Interest expense	(0)
Gain (loss) on disposal of assets	(1,300)
Income before income taxes	376,200
Income tax expense	0
Net income	$376,200

When comparing this statement with Chipotle's 2011 income statement in Exhibit 3.1, we notice that the income from operations above ($372,800) is higher for just the first quarter of 2012 than for all of 2011 ($356,400). Obviously, numerous adjustments are necessary to revenues and expenses. We would not want to use the information for analysis until it has been adjusted. However, we can analyze the 2011 financial statements using the net profit margin ratio to determine how effective Chipotle's management is at generating profit.

KEY RATIO ANALYSIS   Net Profit Margin

? ANALYTICAL QUESTION

How effective is management in generating profit on every dollar of sales?

% RATIO AND COMPARISONS

LEARNING OBJECTIVE 3-6
Compute and interpret the net profit margin ratio.

$$\text{Net Profit Margin} = \frac{\text{Net Income}}{\text{Net Sales (or Operating Revenues)*}}$$

*Net sales is sales revenue less any returns from customers and other reductions. For companies in the service industry, total operating revenues is equivalent to net sales.

The 2011 ratio for Chipotle using actual reported amounts (in Exhibit 3.1) is (dollars in thousands):

$$\frac{\$215,000}{\$2,269,500} = 0.0947 \text{ or } 9.47\%$$

COMPARISONS OVER TIME Chipotle Mexican Grill, Inc.			COMPARISONS WITH COMPETITORS Panera Bread, Inc. Fiesta Restaurant Group, Inc.	
2011	**2010**	**2009**	**2011**	**2011**
0.0947	0.0975	0.0835	0.0746	0.0201

Selected Focus Companies' Net Profit Margin Ratios for 2011

Washington Post	4.7%
Harley-Davidson	11.3%
Home Depot	5.5%

💡 INTERPRETATIONS

In General   Net profit margin measures how much of every sales dollar generated during the period is profit. A rising net profit margin signals more efficient management of sales and expenses. Differences among industries results from the nature of the products or services provided and the intensity of competition. Differences among competitors in the same industry reflect how each company responds to changes in competition (and demand for the product or service) and changes in managing sales volume, sales price, and costs. Financial analysts expect well-run businesses to maintain or improve their net profit margin over time.

Focus Company Analysis   Chipotle's net profit margin decreased slightly between 2010 and 2011 to 9.47 percent, but increased over the three-year period of 2009 to 2011. As indicated by management in the annual report, the primary changes were in higher food costs, primarily avocados, beef, chicken, and dairy, which grew at a rate (32 percent) higher than the growth in sales revenue (24 percent). Acquiring "Food with Integrity" (naturally raised, free of preservatives and growth hormones) is challenging and costlier than using traditional food products and sources. On the other hand, labor and occupancy costs grew at a lower rate than sales due to higher average sales per restaurant. Chipotle's management did a better job of generating revenues and controlling labor and occupancy costs in 2011.

Panera Bread and Fiesta Restaurant Group each had a lower net profit margin than Chipotle. Chipotle's is nearly 27 percent higher than Panera Bread's. This may suggest that Chipotle has greater effectiveness in generating sales, mostly by a high growth in establishing 150 new restaurants and higher menu prices while controlling costs. Panera, on the other hand, opened about 78 new company-owned restaurants and sold 10 additional franchises. Differences in business strategies explain some of the wide variation in the ratio analysis.

A Few Cautions   The decisions that management makes to maintain the company's net profit margin in the current period may have negative long-run implications. Analysts should perform additional analysis of the ratio to identify trends in each component of revenues and expenses. This involves dividing each line on the income statement by net sales. Statements presented with these percentages are called **common-sized income statements.** Changes in the percentages of the individual components of net income provide information on shifts in management's strategies.

New Revenue Recognition Standard	FINANCIAL ANALYSIS

The FASB and IASB are collaborating on a new revenue recognition accounting standard. By the time you read this, a new standard should be in place. The good news is that the core revenue recognition principle that we discuss in this chapter will not change. **Companies will recognize revenue when goods and services are transferred to customers in an amount they expect to receive.** The major changes we will see relate to complex contracts that require transfer of multiple goods or services, such as when Dell sells computers and a one-year warranty together in a single sale. For these types of sales contracts, companies will determine the separate obligations and split the sales price among them. They will then recognize each part of the revenue when they have provided each promised good or service. Accounting for complex sales transactions will be covered in your intermediate accounting course.

FOCUS ON CASH FLOWS   Operating Activities

In this chapter, we focus on cash flows from operating activities: **cash from** operating sources, primarily customers, and **cash to** suppliers and others involved in operations. The accounts most often associated with operating activities are current assets, such as Accounts Receivable, Inventories, and Prepaid Expenses, and current liabilities, such as Accounts Payable, Wages Payable, and Unearned Revenue.

As discussed in Chapter 2, companies report cash inflows and outflows over a period of time in their **statement of cash flows** that is divided into three categories:

- **O** - Operating activities primarily with customers and suppliers, and interest payments and earnings on investments.
- **I** - Investing activities include buying and selling noncurrent assets and investments.
- **F** - Financing activities include borrowing and repaying debt, including short-term bank loans, issuing and repurchasing stock, and paying dividends.

Only transactions affecting cash are reported on the statement. An important step in constructing and analyzing the statement of cash flows is identifying the various transactions as operating, investing, or financing. Let's analyze the Cash T-account for Chipotle's transactions in this chapter, adding to transactions *(a)—(f)* from Chapter 2. Refer to transactions *(g)—(q)* illustrated earlier in the chapter, and remember, **if you see Cash in a transaction, it will be reflected on the statement of cash flows.**

			+ Cash (A) −				
		1/1/12	401,200				
From investors	+ F	*(a)*	62,300	55,100	*(c)*	− I	**For noncurrent assets**
From bank	+ F	*(b)*	2,000	400	*(d)*	− F	**To bank**
				60,400	*(e)*	− I	**For investment in other companies**
From customers	+ O	*(i)*	615,300	167,700	*(g)*	− O	**For supplies**
From asset disposal	+ I	*(l)*	10,600	86,000	*(h)*	− O	**For prepaid assets**
From customers	+ O	*(m)*	3,300	49,300	*(j)*	− O	**For training**
From investments	+ O	*(p)*	4,700	230,100	*(k)*	− O	**To employees**
From customers	+ O	*(q)*	15,400	37,200	*(n)*	− O	**To suppliers**
				58,600	*(o)*	− O	**For utilities and maintenance**
			370,000				

PAUSE FOR FEEDBACK

As we discussed, every transaction affecting cash can be classified either as an operating, investing, or financing effect.

Operating effects relate to receipts of cash from customers, payments to suppliers (employees, utilities, and other suppliers of goods and services for operating the business), and any interest paid or investment income received.

Investing effects relate to purchasing/selling investments or property and equipment or lending funds to/receiving repayment from others.

Financing effects relate to borrowing or repaying banks, issuing stock to investors, repurchasing stock from investors, or paying dividends to investors.

Mattel, Inc., designs, manufactures, and markets a broad variety of toys (e.g., Barbie, Hot Wheels, Fisher-Price brands, and American Girl dolls) worldwide. Indicate whether these transactions from a recent statement of cash flows were operating (O), investing (I), or financing (F) activities and the direction of their effects on cash (+ for increases in cash; − for decreases in cash):

TRANSACTIONS	TYPE OF ACTIVITY (O, I, OR F)	EFFECT ON CASH FLOWS (1 OR 2)
1. Purchases of property, plant, and equipment	I	−
2. Receipts from customers	O	+
3. Payments of dividends	F	±
4. Payments to employees	O	−
5. Receipts of investment income	O	+

After you have completed your answers, check them with the solutions at the bottom of the next page.

DEMONSTRATION CASE

This case is a continuation of the Terrific Lawn Maintenance Corporation case introduced in Chapter 2. In that chapter, the company was established and supplies, property, and equipment were purchased. Terrific Lawn is now ready for business. The balance sheet at April 7, 2014, based on the first week of investing and financing activities (from Chapter 2) is as follows:

TERRIFIC LAWN MAINTENANCE CORPORATION
Balance Sheet
April 7, 2014

Assets
Current Assets:

Cash	$ 3,800
Notes receivable	1,250
Total current assets	5,050
Equipment	4,600
Land	3,750
Total assets	**$13,400**

Liabilities and Stockholders' Equity
Current Liabilities:

Short-term notes payable	$ 400
Total current liabilities	400
Long-term notes payable	4,000
Total liabilities	4,400

Stockholders' Equity:

Common stock ($0.10 par)	150
Additional paid-in capital	8,850
Total stockholders' equity	9,000
Total liabilities and stockholders' equity	**$13,400**

The additional following activities occurred during the rest of April 2014:

a. Purchased and used gasoline for mowers and edgers, paying $90 in cash at a local gas station.

b. In early April, received from the city $1,600 cash in advance for lawn maintenance service for April through July ($400 each month). The entire amount was recorded as Unearned Revenue.

c. In early April, purchased $300 of insurance covering six months, April through September. The entire payment was recorded as Prepaid Expenses.

d. Mowed lawns for residential customers who are billed every two weeks. A total of $5,200 of service was billed in April.

e. Residential customers paid $3,500 on their accounts.

f. Paid wages every two weeks. Total cash paid in April was $3,900.

g. Received a bill for $320 from the local gas station for additional gasoline purchased on account and used in April. The bill will be paid in May.

h. Paid $700 principal and $40 interest on notes owed to XYZ Lawn Supply.

i. Paid $100 on accounts payable.

j. Collected $1,250 principal and $12 interest on the note owed by the city to Terrific Lawn Maintenance Corporation.

Required:

1. a. On a separate sheet of paper, set up T-accounts for Cash, Accounts Receivable, Notes Receivable, Prepaid Expenses, Equipment, Land, Accounts Payable, Short-term Notes Payable, Long-term Notes Payable, Unearned Revenue (same as deferred revenue), Common Stock, Additional Paid-in Capital, Retained Earnings, Mowing Revenue, Interest Revenue, Wages Expense, Fuel Expense, and Interest Expense. Beginning balances for the balance sheet accounts should be taken from the preceding balance sheet. Beginning balances for operating accounts are $0. Indicate these balances on the T-accounts.

   b. Analyze each transaction, referring to the expanded transaction analysis model presented in this chapter.

   c. On a separate sheet of paper, prepare journal entries in chronological order and indicate their effects on the accounting model (Assets = Liabilities + Stockholders' Equity). Include the equality checks: (1) Debits = Credits, and (2) the accounting equation is in balance.

   d. Enter the effects of each transaction in the appropriate T-accounts. Identify each amount with its letter in the preceding list of activities.

   e. Compute balances in each of the T-accounts.

2. On the Cash T-account, identify each transaction as O for operating activity, I for investing activity, or F for financing activity.

3. Use the amounts in the T-accounts to prepare an unadjusted classified income statement for Terrific Lawn Maintenance Corporation for the month ended April 30, 2014. (Adjustments to accounts will be presented in Chapter 4.)

Now check your answers with the following suggested solution.

SUGGESTED SOLUTION

1. *b.* **and** *c.* Transaction analysis and journal entries:

Journal Entries	Debits	Credits
(a) Fuel Expense (+E, −SE)...............	90	
Cash (−A)...........................		90
(b) Cash (+A)...........................	1,600	
Unearned Revenue (+L)...............		1,600
(c) Prepaid Expenses (+A)...............	300	
Cash (−A)...........................		300
(d) Accounts Receivable (+A).............	5,200	
Mowing Revenue (+R, +SE)...........		5,200
(e) Cash (+A)..........................	3,500	
Accounts Receivable (−A)............		3,500
(f) Wages Expense (+E, −SE).............	3,900	
Cash (−A)...........................		3,900
(g) Fuel Expense (+E, −SE)	320	
Accounts Payable (+L)		320
(h) Interest Expense (+E, −SE)...........	40	
Long-term Notes Payable (−L)...........	700	
Cash (−A)...........................		740
(i) Accounts Payable (−L)	100	
Cash (−A)...........................		100
(j) Cash (+A)	1,262	
Notes Receivable (−A)...............		1,250
Interest Revenue (+R, +SE)		12

Assets	=	Liabilities	+	Stockholders' Equity	
−90				+E	−90
+1,600		+1,600			
+300 −300					
+5,200				+R	+5,200
+3,500 −3,500					
−3,900				+E	−3,900
		+320		+E	−320
−740		−700		+E	−40
−100		−100			
+1,262 −1,250				+R	+12

Equality Checks

For each journal entry: Debits = Credits   For each transaction analysis: Equation balances

1. *a.,* *d.,* **and** *e.* **T-Accounts:**

Assets

+ Cash (A) −			
Beg.	3,800		
(b)	1,600	90	(a)
(e)	3,500	300	(c)
(j)	1,262	3,900	(f)
		740	(h)
		100	(i)
	5,032		

+ Accounts Receivable (A) −			
Beg.	0		
(d)	5,200	3,500	(e)
	1,700		

+ Notes Receivable (A) −			
Beg.	1,250		
		1,250	(j)
	0		

+ Prepaid Expenses (A) −	
Beg. 0	
(c) 300	
300	

+ Equipment (A) −	
Beg. 4,600	
4,600	

+ Land (A) −	
Beg. 3,750	
3,750	

Liabilities

− Accounts Payable (L) +	
	0 Beg.
(i) 100	320 (g)
	220

− Short-term Notes Payable (L) +	
	700 Beg.
	700

− Unearned Revenue (L) +	
	0 Beg.
	1,600 (b)
	1,600

− Long-term Notes Payable (L) +	
	4,000 Beg.
(h) 700	
	3,300

Stockholders' Equity

− Common Stock (SE) +	
	150 Beg.
	150

− Additional Paid-in Capital (SE) +	
	8,850 Beg.
	8,850

− Retained Earnings (SE) +	
	0 Beg.
	0

Revenues

− Mowing Revenue (R) +	
	0 Beg.
	5,200 (d)
	5,200

− Interest Revenue (R) +	
	0 Beg.
	12 (j)
	12

Expenses

+ Wages Expense (E) −	
Beg. 0	
(f) 3,900	
3,900	

+ Fuel Expense (E) −	
Beg. 0	
(a) 90	
(g) 320	
410	

+ Interest Expense (E) −	
Beg. 0	
(h) 40	
40	

2. Cash flow activities identified (O = operating, I = investing, and F = financing):

		+ Cash (A) −			
		Beg. 3,800			
From customers +O	(b)	1,600	90	(a)	−O For fuel
From customers +O	(e)	3,500	300	(c)	−O For insurance
$12 for interest +O; $1,250 for principal +I	(j)	1,262	3,900	(f)	−O To employees
			740	(h)	−O $40 for interest; −F $700 for principal
			100	(i)	−O To suppliers
		5,032			

3. Income Statement:

TERRIFIC LAWN MAINTENANCE CORPORATION
Unadjusted Income Statement
For the Month Ended April 30, 2014

Mowing revenue	$5,200
Operating expenses:	
Wages expense	3,900
Fuel expense	410
Total operating expenses	4,310
Income from operations	890
Other items:	
Interest revenue	12
Interest expense	(40)
Income before taxes	862
Income tax expense	0
Net income	$ 862

To be computed and recorded after adjustments are made to revenue and expense accounts (Chapter 4)

CHAPTER TAKE-AWAYS

3-1. Describe a typical business operating cycle and explain the necessity for the time period assumption. p. 100

- The operating cycle, or cash-to-cash cycle, is the time needed to purchase goods or services from suppliers, sell the goods or services to customers, and collect cash from customers.
- Time period assumption—to measure and report financial information periodically, we assume the long life of a company can be cut into shorter periods.

3-2. Explain how business activities affect the elements of the income statement. p. 102

- Elements of the income statement:
  a. Revenues—increases in assets or settlements of liabilities from ongoing operations.
  b. Expenses—decreases in assets or increases in liabilities from ongoing operations.
  c. Gains—increases in assets or settlements of liabilities from peripheral activities.
  d. Losses—decreases in assets or increases in liabilities from peripheral activities.

3-3. Explain the accrual basis of accounting and apply the revenue realization and expense matching principles to measure income. p. 105

In accrual basis accounting, revenues are recognized when earned and expenses are recognized when incurred.

- Revenue realization principle—recognize revenues when (1) delivery has occurred, (2) there is persuasive evidence of an arrangement for customer payment, (3) the price is fixed or determinable, and (4) collection is reasonably assured.
- Expense matching principle—recognize expenses when they are incurred in generating revenue.

3-4. Apply transaction analysis to examine and record the effects of operating activities on the financial statements. p. 111

The expanded transaction analysis model includes revenues and expenses:

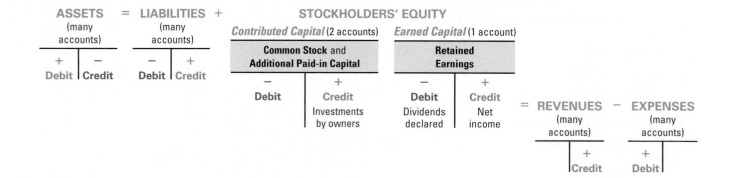

3-5. Prepare a classified income statement. p. 121

Until the accounts have been updated to include all revenues earned and expenses incurred in the period (due to a difference in the time when cash is received or paid), the financial statements are unadjusted:

- Classified income statement—net income is needed to determine ending Retained Earnings; classifications include Operating Revenues, Operating Expenses (to determine Operating Income), Other Items (to determine Pretax Income), Income Tax Expense, Net Income, and Earnings per Share.

3-6. Compute and interpret the net profit margin ratio. p. 122

The net profit margin ratio (Net Income ÷ Net Sales [or Operating Revenues]) measures the profit generated per dollar of sales (operating revenues). The higher the ratio, the more effective the company is at generating revenues and/or controlling costs.

In this chapter, we discussed the operating cycle and accounting concepts relevant to income determination: the time period assumption, definitions of the income statement elements (revenues, expenses, gains, and losses), the revenue realization principle, and the expense matching principle. The accounting principles are defined in accordance with the accrual basis of accounting, which requires revenues to be recorded when earned and expenses to be recorded when incurred in the process of generating revenues. We expanded the transaction analysis model introduced in Chapter 2 by adding revenues and expenses and prepared an unadjusted classified income statement. In Chapter 4, we discuss the activities that occur at the end of the accounting period: the adjustment process, the preparation of adjusted financial statements, and the closing process.

KEY **RATIO**

Net profit margin ratio measures the profit generated per dollar of sales (operating revenues). A high ratio suggests that a company is generating revenues and/or controlling expenses effectively. The ratio is computed as follows (p. 122):

$$\text{Net Profit Margin Ratio} = \frac{\text{Net Income}}{\text{Net Sales (or Operating Revenues)}}$$

FINDING **FINANCIAL INFORMATION**

Balance Sheet

Current Assets
  Cash
  Short-term investments
  Accounts and notes receivable
  Inventory (goods to be sold)
  Supplies
  Prepaid expenses

Noncurrent Assets
  Long-term investments
  Property and equipment
  Intangibles

Current Liabilities
  Accounts payable
  Notes payable
  Accrued expenses payable
  Unearned revenue

Noncurrent Liabilities
  Long-term debt

Stockholders' Equity
  Common Stock
  Additional paid-in capital
  Retained earnings

Income Statement

Revenues (operating)
  Sales (from various operating activities)

Expenses (operating)
  Cost of goods sold (used inventory)
  Rent, wages, depreciation, insurance, etc.

Operating Income
  Other Items
  Interest expense
  Investment income
  Gains on sale of assets
  Losses on sale of assets

Pretax Income
  Income tax expense

Net Income
Earnings per Share

Statement of Cash Flows

Operating Activities
  + Cash from customers
  + Cash from interest and dividends
  − Cash to suppliers
  − Cash to employees
  − Interest paid
  − Income taxes paid

Notes

Under Summary of Significant Accounting Policies
  Description of the company's revenue recognition policy.

KEY **TERMS**

Accrual Basis Accounting   p. 105
Cash Basis Accounting   p. 105
Expense Matching Principle   p. 109
Expenses   p. 103

Gains   p. 104
Losses   p. 104
Operating (Cash-to-Cash) Cycle   p. 101
Revenue Realization Principle   p. 106

Revenues   p. 102
Time Period Assumption   p. 101

QUESTIONS

1. Describe a typical business operating cycle.
2. Explain what the time period assumption means.
3. Write the income statement equation and define each element.
4. Explain the difference between
  a. Revenues and gains.
  b. Expenses and losses.
5. Define **accrual accounting** and contrast it with cash basis accounting.
6. What four criteria must normally be met for revenue to be recognized under accrual basis accounting?
7. Explain the expense matching principle.
8. Explain why stockholders' equity is increased by revenues and decreased by expenses.

9. Explain why revenues are recorded as credits and expenses as debits.

10. Complete the following matrix by entering either **debit** or **credit** in each cell:

Item	Increase	Decrease
Revenues		
Losses		
Gains		
Expenses		

11. Complete the following matrix by entering either **increase** or **decrease** in each cell:

Item	Debit	Credit
Revenues		
Losses		
Gains		
Expenses		

12. Identify whether the following transactions affect cash flow from operating, investing, or financing activities, and indicate the effect of each on cash (+ for increase and − for decrease). If there is no cash flow effect, write "None."

Transaction	Operating, Investing, or Financing Effect on Cash	Direction of the Effect on Cash
Cash paid to suppliers		
Sale of goods on account		
Cash received from customers		
Purchase of investments		
Cash paid for interest		
Issuance of stock for cash		

13. State the equation for the net profit margin ratio and explain how it is interpreted.

MULTIPLE-CHOICE **QUESTIONS**

1. Which of the following is **not** a specific account in a company's chart of accounts?
   a. Gains
   b. Revenue
   c. Net Income
   d. Unearned Revenue
2. Which of the following is **not** one of the four criteria that normally must be met for revenue to be recognized according to the revenue realization principle for accrual basis accounting?
   a. Cash has been collected.
   b. Services have been performed.
   c. The price is determinable.
   d. Evidence of an arrangement exists.
3. The expense matching principle controls
   a. Where on the income statement expenses should be presented.
   b. When costs are recognized as expenses on the income statement.
   c. The ordering of current assets and current liabilities on the balance sheet.
   d. How costs are allocated between Cost of Sales (sometimes called Cost of Goods Sold) and general and administrative expenses.

4. When expenses exceed revenues in a given period,
   a. Retained earnings are not impacted.
   b. Retained earnings are decreased.
   c. Retained earnings are increased.
   d. One cannot determine the impact on retained earnings without additional information.
5. On January 1, 2014, Anson Company started the year with a $300,000 credit balance in Retained Earnings, a $50,000 balance in Common Stock, and a $300,000 balance in Additional Paid-in Capital. During 2014, the company earned net income of $45,000, declared a dividend of $15,000, and issued 900 additional shares of stock (par value of $1 per share) for $10,000. What is total stockholders' equity on December 31, 2014?
   a. $692,500.
   b. $695,000.
   c. $690,000.
   d. None of the above.
6. During 2014, CliffCo Inc. incurred operating expenses of $250,000, of which $150,000 was paid in cash; the balance will be paid in January 2015. Transaction analysis of operating expenses for 2014 should reflect only the following:
   a. Decrease stockholders' equity, $150,000; decrease assets, $150,000.
   b. Decrease assets, $250,000; decrease stockholders' equity, $250,000.
   c. Decrease stockholders' equity, $250,000; decrease assets, $150,000; increase liabilities, $100,000.
   d. Decrease assets, $250,000; increase liabilities, $100,000; decrease stockholders' equity, $150,000.
   e. None of the above is correct.
7. Which of the following is the entry to be recorded by a law firm when it receives a $2,000 retainer from a new client at the initial client meeting?
   a. Debit to Cash, $2,000; credit to Legal Fees Revenue, $2,000.
   b. Debit to Accounts Receivable, $2,000; credit to Legal Fees Revenue, $2,000.
   c. Debit to Unearned Revenue, $2,000; credit to Legal Fees Revenue, $2,000.
   d. Debit to Cash, $2,000; credit to Unearned Revenue, $2,000.
   e. Debit to Unearned Revenue, $2,000; credit to Cash, $2,000.
8. You have observed that the net profit margin ratio for a retail chain has increased steadily over the last three years. The **most** likely explanation is which of the following?
   a. Salaries for upper management as a percentage of total expenses have decreased over the last three years.
   b. A successful advertising campaign increased sales companywide, but with no increases in operating expenses.
   c. New stores were added throughout the last three years, and sales increased as a result of the additional new locations.
   d. The company began construction of a new, larger main office location three years ago that was put into use at the end of the second year.
9. Cash payments for salaries are reported in what section of the Statement of Cash Flows?
   a. Operating.
   b. Investing.
   c. Financing.
   d. None of the above.
10. This period a company collects $100 cash on an account receivable from a customer for a sale last period. How would the receipt of cash impact the following two financial statements this period?

	Income Statement	Statement of Cash Flows
a.	Revenue + $100	Inflow from investing
b.	No impact	Inflow from operations
c.	Revenue − $100	Inflow from operations
d.	No impact	Inflow from financing

For more practice with multiple-choice questions, go to the text website at **www.mhhe.com/libby8e**.

MINI-EXERCISES

M3-1
LO3-1, 3-2, 3-3

Matching Definitions with Terms

Match each definition with its related term by entering the appropriate letter in the space provided. There should be only one definition per term (that is, there are more definitions than terms).

Term	Definition
___ (1) Losses	A. Record revenues when earned and measurable (delivery of goods or services has been performed, there is persuasive evidence of an arrangement, the price is fixed or determinable, and collection is reasonably assured).
___ (2) Expense matching principle	
___ (3) Revenues	
___ (4) Time period assumption	
___ (5) Operating cycle	B. The time it takes to purchase goods or services from suppliers, sell goods or services to customers, and collect cash from customers.
	C. Record expenses when incurred in earning revenue.
	D. Decreases in assets or increases in liabilities from ongoing operations.
	E. Report the long life of a company in shorter time periods.
	F. Increases in assets or decreases in liabilities from ongoing operations.
	G. Decreases in assets or increases in liabilities from peripheral transactions.

M3-2
LO3-3

Reporting Cash Basis versus Accrual Basis Income

Skidmore Music Company had the following transactions in March:

a. Sold instruments to customers for $18,000; received $8,000 in cash and the rest on account. The cost of the instruments was $9,000.

b. Purchased $4,000 of new instruments inventory; paid $1,000 in cash and owed the rest on account.

c. Paid $900 in wages for the month.

d. Received $5,000 from customers as deposits on orders of new instruments to be sold to the customers in April.

e. Received a $300 bill for March utilities that will be paid in April.

Complete the following statements:

Cash Basis Income Statement		Accrual Basis Income Statement	
Revenues		Revenues	
Cash sales		Sales to customers	
Customer deposits			
Expenses		Expenses	
Inventory purchases		Cost of sales	
Wages paid		Wages expense	
		Utilities expense	
Net income	_____	Net income	_____

M3-3
LO3-2, 3-3

Identifying Revenues

The following transactions are July 2014 activities of Craig's Bowling, Inc., which operates several bowling centers (for games and equipment sales). If revenue is to be recognized in **July,** indicate the revenue account title and amount. If revenue is not to be recognized in July, explain why.

Activity	Revenue Account Title and Amount
a. Craig's collected $15,000 from customers for games played in July.	
b. Craig's sold bowling equipment inventory for $8,000; received $3,000 in cash and the rest on account. [The cost of goods sold (expense) related to these sales is in M3-4e.]	
c. Craig's received $4,000 from customers on account who purchased merchandise in June.	
d. The men's and ladies' bowling leagues gave Craig's a deposit of $2,500 for the upcoming fall season.	

Identifying Expenses

M3-4

LO3-2, 3-3

The following transactions are July 2014 activities of Craig's Bowling, Inc., which operates several bowling centers (for games and equipment sales). If expense is to be recognized in **July,** indicate the expense account title and amount. If expense is not to be recognized in July, explain why.

Activity	Expense Account Title and Amount
e. Craig's sold bowling merchandise costing $6,800. [The sale related to the use of this merchandise is in M3-3b.]	
f. Craig's paid $800 on the electricity bill for June (recorded as expense in June).	
g. Craig's paid $3,500 to employees for work in July.	
h. Craig's purchased $1,500 in insurance for coverage from July 1 to October 1.	
i. Craig's paid $700 to plumbers for repairing a broken pipe in the restrooms.	
j. Craig's received the July electricity bill for $900 to be paid in August.	

Recording Revenues

M3-5

LO3-4

For each of the transactions in M3-3, write the journal entry in good form.

Recording Expenses

M3-6

LO3-4

For each of the transactions in M3-4, write the journal entry in good form.

Determining the Financial Statement Effects of Operating Activities Involving Revenues

M3-7

LO3-4

The following transactions are July 2014 activities of Craig's Bowling, Inc., which operates several bowling centers (for games and equipment sales). For each of the following transactions, complete the tabulation, indicating the amount and effect (+ for increase and − for decrease) of each transaction. (Remember that A = L + SE, R − E = NI, and NI affects SE through Retained Earnings.) Write NE if there is no effect. The first transaction is provided as an example.

	BALANCE SHEET			INCOME STATEMENT		
Transaction	Assets	Liabilities	Stockholders' Equity	Revenues	Expenses	Net Income
a. Craig's collected $15,000 from customers for games played in July.	+15,000	NE	+15,000	+15,000	NE	+15,000
b. Craig's sold bowling equipment inventory for $8,000; received $3,000 in cash and the rest on account. [The cost of goods sold (expense) related to these sales is in M3-8e.]						
c. Craig's received $4,000 from customers on account who purchased merchandise in June.						
d. The men's and ladies' bowling leagues gave Craig's a deposit of $2,500 for the upcoming fall season.						

M3-8

LO3-4

Determining the Financial Statement Effects of Operating Activities Involving Expenses

The following transactions are July 2014 activities of Craig's Bowling, Inc., which operates several bowling centers (for games and equipment sales). For each of the following transactions, complete the tabulation, indicating the amount and effect (+ for increase and − for decrease) of each transaction. (Remember that A = L + SE, R − E = NI, and NI affects SE through Retained Earnings.) Write NE if there is no effect. The first transaction is provided as an example.

	BALANCE SHEET			INCOME STATEMENT		
Transaction	Assets	Liabilities	Stockholders' Equity	Revenues	Expenses	Net Income
e. Craig's sold bowling merchandise costing $6,800. [The sale related to the use of this merchandise is in M3-3b.]	−6,800	NE	−6,800	NE	+6,800	−6,800
f. Craig's paid $800 on the electricity bill for June (recorded as expense in June).						
g. Craig's paid $3,500 to employees for work in July.						
h. Craig's purchased $1,500 in insurance for coverage from July 1 to October 1.						
i. Craig's paid $700 to plumbers for repairing a broken pipe in the restrooms.						
j. Craig's received the July electricity bill for $900 to be paid in August.						

M3-9

LO3-5

Preparing a Simple Income Statement

Given the transactions in M3-7 and M3-8 (including the examples), prepare an income statement for Craig's Bowling, Inc., for the month of July 2014.

M3-10

LO3-5

Identifying the Operating Activities in a Statement of Cash Flows

Given the transactions in M3-7 and M3-8 (including the examples), indicate how the transactions will affect the statement of cash flows for Craig's Bowling, Inc., for the month of July 2014. Create a table similar to below for transactions a. through j. Use O for operating, I for investing, and F for financing activities and indicate the direction of their effects on cash (+ for increases in cash; − for decreases in cash). Also include the amount of cash to be reported on the statement. If there is no effect on the statement of cash flows, write NE.

Transaction	Type of Activity (O, I, or F)	Effect on Cash Flows (+ or − and amount)
a.		
b.		
etc.		

Computing and Explaining the Net Profit Margin Ratio

The following data are from annual reports of Jen's Jewelry Company:

	2015	2014	2013
Total assets	$ 60,000	$ 53,000	$ 41,000
Total liabilities	14,000	11,000	6,000
Total stockholders' equity	46,000	42,000	35,000
Sales revenue	163,000	151,000	132,000
Net income	51,000	40,000	25,000

Compute Jen's net profit margin ratio for each year. What do these results suggest to you about Jen's Jewelry Company?

M3-11

LO3-6

---

connect |ACCOUNTING

EXERCISES

Matching Definitions with Terms

Match each definition with its related term by entering the appropriate letter in the space provided. There should be only one definition per term (that is, there are more definitions than terms).

E3-1

LO3-1, 3-2, 3-3

Term	Definition
___ (1) Expenses	A. Report the long life of a company in shorter periods.
___ (2) Gains	B. Record expenses when incurred in earning revenue.
___ (3) Revenue realization principle	C. The time it takes to purchase goods or services from suppliers, sell goods or services to customers, and collect cash from customers.
___ (4) Cash basis accounting	
___ (5) Unearned revenue	
___ (6) Operating cycle	D. Record revenues when earned and expenses when incurred.
___ (7) Accrual basis accounting	E. Increases in assets or decreases in liabilities from peripheral transactions.
___ (8) Prepaid expenses	
___ (9) Revenues − Expenses = Net Income	F. An asset account used to record cash paid before expenses have been incurred.
___ (10) Ending Retained Earnings = Beginning Retained Earnings + Net Income − Dividends Declared	G. Record revenues when earned and measurable (delivery of goods or services has occurred, there is persuasive evidence of an arrangement for customer payment, the price is fixed or determinable, and collection is reasonably assured).
	H. Decreases in assets or increases in liabilities from peripheral transactions.
	I. Record revenues when received and expenses when paid.
	J. The income statement equation.
	K. Decreases in assets or increases in liabilities from ongoing operations.
	L. The retained earnings equation.
	M. A liability account used to record cash received before revenues have been earned.

E3-2

LO3-3

Reporting Cash Basis versus Accrual Basis Income

Payson Sports, Inc., sells sports equipment to customers. Its fiscal year ends on December 31. The following transactions occurred in 2015:

a. Purchased $250,000 of new sports equipment inventory; paid $90,000 in cash and owed the rest on account.
b. Paid employees $180,300 in wages for work during the year; an additional $3,700 for 2015 wages will be paid in January 2016.
c. Sold sports equipment to customers for $750,000; received $500,000 in cash and the rest on account. The cost of the equipment was $485,000.
d. Paid $17,200 cash for utilities for the year.
e. Received $70,000 from customers as deposits on orders of new winter sports equipment to be sold to the customers in January 2016.
f. Received a $1,930 bill for December 2015 utilities that will be paid in January 2016.

Required:
1. Complete the following statements:

Cash Basis Income Statement		Accrual Basis Income Statement	
Revenues		Revenues	
Cash sales		Sales to customers	
Customer deposits			
Expenses		Expenses	
Inventory purchases		Cost of sales	
Wages paid		Wages expense	
Utilities paid	_____	Utilities expense	_____
Net income	_____	Net income	_____

2. Which basis of accounting (cash or accrual) provides more useful information to investors, creditors, and other users? Why?

E3-3

LO3-2, 3-3

Identifying Revenues

Revenues are normally recognized when the delivery of goods or services has occurred, there is persuasive evidence of an arrangement for customer payment, the price is fixed or determinable, and collection is reasonably assured. The amount recorded is the cash-equivalent sales price. The following transactions occurred in **September** 2016:

a. A popular ski magazine company receives a total of $12,345 today from subscribers. The subscriptions begin in the next fiscal year. Answer from the magazine company's standpoint.
b. On September 1, 2016, a bank lends $1,500 to a company; the note principal and $150 ($1,500 × 10 percent) annual interest are due in one year. Answer from the bank's standpoint.
c. Fucillo Hyundai, Inc., sells a truck with a list, or "sticker," price of $20,050 for $19,500 cash.
d. Macy's department store orders 1,000 men's shirts for $15 each for future delivery from Phillips-Van Heusen Corporation, manufacturer of Izod, Arrow, Van Heusen, and Calvin Klein shirts. The terms require payment in full within 30 days of delivery. Answer from Phillips-Van Heusen's standpoint.
e. Phillips-Van Heusen Corporation completes production of the shirts described in (d) and delivers the order. Answer from Phillips-Van Heusen's standpoint.
f. Phillips-Van Heusen receives payment from Macy's for the events described in (d) and (e). Answer from Phillips-Van Heusen's standpoint.
g. A customer purchases a ticket from American Airlines for $780 cash to travel the following January. Answer from American Airlines's standpoint.
h. Ford Motor Company issues $15 million in new common stock.
i. Michigan State University receives $19,500,000 cash for 80,000 five-game season football tickets.
j. Michigan State plays the first football game referred to in (i).

k. Precision Builders signs a contract with a customer for the construction of a new $1,500,000 ware-house. At the signing, Precision receives a check for $200,000 as a deposit on the future construction. Answer from Precision's standpoint.

l. A customer orders and receives 10 personal computers from Dell; the customer promises to pay $9,600 within three months. Answer from Dell's standpoint.

m. Sears, a retail store, sells a $300 lamp to a customer who charges the sale on his store credit card. Answer from Sears's standpoint.

Required:
For each of the transactions, if revenue is to be recognized in September, indicate the revenue account title and amount. If revenue is not to be recognized in September, explain why.

Identifying Expenses

Revenues are normally recognized when goods or services have been provided and payment or promise of payment has been received. Expense recognition is guided by an attempt to match the costs associated with the generation of those revenues to the same time period. The following transactions occurred in **January** 2016:

E3-4
LO3-2, 3-3

a. McGraw-Hill Education uses $3,800 worth of electricity and natural gas in its headquarters building for which it has not yet been billed.

b. At the beginning of January, Turner Construction Company pays $963 for magazine advertising to run in monthly publications each of the first three months of the year.

c. Dell pays its computer service technicians $403,000 in salaries for the two weeks ended January 7. Answer from Dell's standpoint.

d. The University of Florida orders 60,000 season football tickets from its printer and pays $8,340 in advance for the custom printing. The first game will be played in September. Answer from the university's standpoint.

e. The campus bookstore receives 500 accounting texts at a cost of $95 each. The terms indicate that payment is due within 30 days of delivery.

f. During the last week of January, the campus bookstore sold 500 accounting texts received in (e) at a sales price of $130 each.

g. Fucillo Hyundai, Inc., pays its salespersons $13,800 in commissions related to December automobile sales. Answer from Fucillo's standpoint.

h. On January 31, Fucillo Hyundai, Inc., determines that it will pay its salespersons $15,560 in commissions related to January sales. The payment will be made in early February. Answer from Fucillo's standpoint.

i. A new grill is purchased and installed at a Wendy's restaurant at the end of the day on January 31; a $12,750 cash payment is made on that day.

j. Carousel Center Mall had janitorial supplies costing $3,500 in storage. An additional $2,600 worth of supplies was purchased during January. At the end of January, $1,400 worth of janitorial supplies remained in storage.

k. An Iowa State University employee works eight hours, at $15 per hour, on January 31; however, pay-day is not until February 3. Answer from the university's point of view.

l. Wang Company paid $4,800 for a fire insurance policy on January 1. The policy covers 12 months beginning on January 1. Answer from Wang's point of view.

m. Derek Incorporated has its delivery van repaired in January for $600 and charges the amount on account.

n. Hass Company, a farm equipment company, receives its phone bill at the end of January for $154 for January calls. The bill has not been paid to date.

o. Martin Company receives and pays in January a $2,034 invoice (bill) from a consulting firm for services received in January. Answer from Martin's standpoint.

p. Parillo's Taxi Company pays a $595 invoice from a consulting firm for services received and recorded in December.

q. Phillips-Van Heusen Corporation, manufacturer of Izod, Arrow, Van Heusen, and Calvin Klein shirts, completes production of 450 men's shirts ordered by Macy's department stores at a cost of $10 each and delivers the order. Answer from Phillips-Van Heusen's standpoint.

Required:

For each of the transactions, if an expense is to be recognized in January, indicate the expense account title and the amount. If an expense is not to be recognized in January, indicate why.

E3-5

LO3-4

Determining Financial Statement Effects of Various Transactions

The following transactions occurred during a recent year:

a. Issued stock to organizers for cash (example).
b. Purchased equipment on credit.
c. Declared and paid cash dividends.
d. Earned revenue, collected cash.
e. Incurred expenses, on credit.
f. Earned revenue, on credit.
g. Paid cash on account.
h. Incurred expenses; paid cash.

i. Earned revenue; collected three-fourths in cash, balance on credit.
j. Borrowed cash from local bank.
k. Collected cash from customers on account.
l. Experienced theft (a loss) of $100 cash.
m. Incurred expenses; paid four-fifths in cash, balance on credit.
n. Paid income tax expense for the period.

Required:

For each of the transactions, complete the tabulation, indicating the effect (+ for increase and − for decrease) of each transaction. (Remember that A = L + SE, R − E = NI, and NI affects SE through Retained Earnings.) Write NE if there is no effect. The first transaction is provided as an example.

	BALANCE SHEET			INCOME STATEMENT		
Transaction	Assets	Liabilities	Stockholders' Equity	Revenues	Expenses	Net Income
(a) (example)	+	NE	+	NE	NE	NE

E3-6

LO3-4

Wolverine World Wide, Inc.

Determining Financial Statement Effects of Various Transactions

Wolverine World Wide, Inc., manufactures military, work, sport, and casual footwear and leather accessories under a variety of brand names, such as Hush Puppies, Wolverine, and Bates, to a global market. The following transactions occurred during a recent year. Dollars are in thousands.

a. Issued common stock to investors for $14,083 cash (example).
b. Purchased $878,418 of additional inventory on account.
c. Borrowed $11,000.
d. Sold $1,409,068 of products to customers on account; cost of the products sold was $852,316.
e. Paid cash dividends of $22,737.
f. Purchased for cash $19,397 in additional property, plant, and equipment.
g. Incurred $386,534 in selling expenses, paying three-fourths in cash and owing the rest on account.
h. Earned $370 interest on investments, receiving 90 percent in cash.
i. Incurred $1,395 in interest expense to be paid at the beginning of next year.

Required:

For each of the transactions, complete the tabulation, indicating the effect (+ for increase and − for decrease) of each transaction. (Remember that A = L + SE, R − E = NI, and NI affects SE through Retained Earnings.) Write NE if there is no effect. The first transaction is provided as an example.

	BALANCE SHEET			INCOME STATEMENT		
Transaction	Assets	Liabilities	Stockholders' Equity	Revenues	Expenses	Net Income
(a) (example)	+14,083	NE	+14,083	NE	NE	NE

Recording Journal Entries

E3-7
LO3-4

Sysco Corporation

Sysco, formed in 1969, is North America's largest marketer and distributor of food service products, serving approximately 400,000 restaurants, hotels, schools, hospitals, and other institutions. The following summarized transactions are typical of those that occurred in a recent year (dollars are in millions).

a. Purchased plant and equipment for $636 in cash.
b. Borrowed $181 from a bank, signing a short-term note.
c. Provided $39,323 in service to customers during the year, with $28,558 on account and the rest received in cash.
d. Paid $32,074 cash on accounts payable.
e. Purchased $32,305 inventory on account.
f. Paid payroll, $3,500 during the year.
g. Received $39,043 on account paid by customers.
h. Purchased and used fuel of $750 in delivery vehicles during the year (paid for in cash).
i. Declared and paid $597 in dividends for the year.
j. Incurred $68 in utility usage during the year; paid $55 in cash and owed the rest on account.

Required:
For each of the transactions, prepare journal entries. Determine whether the accounting equation remains in balance and debits equal credits after each entry.

Recording Journal Entries

E3-8
LO3-4

Vail Resorts, Inc.

Vail Resorts, Inc., owns and operates five premier year-round ski resort properties (Vail Mountain, Beaver Creek Resort, Breckenridge Mountain, and Keystone Resort, all located in the Colorado Rocky Mountains, and Heavenly Valley Mountain Resort, located in the Lake Tahoe area of California/Nevada). The company also owns a collection of luxury hotels, resorts, and lodging properties. The company sells lift tickets, ski lessons, and ski equipment. The following hypothetical **December** transactions are typical of those that occur at the resorts.

a. Borrowed $2,300,000 from the bank on December 1, signing a note payable due in six months.
b. Purchased a new snowplow for $98,000 cash on December 31.
c. Purchased ski equipment inventory for $35,000 on account to sell in the ski shops.
d. Incurred $62,000 in routine maintenance expenses for the chairlifts; paid cash.
e. Sold $390,000 of January through March season passes and received cash.
f. Sold a pair of skis from a ski shop to a customer for $800 on account. (The cost of the skis was $500).
   Hint: Record two entries.
g. Sold daily lift passes in December for a total of $320,000 in cash.
h. Received a $3,500 deposit on a townhouse to be rented for five days in January.
i. Paid half the charges incurred on account in (c).
j. Received $400 on account from the customer in (f).
k. Paid $245,000 in wages to employees for the month of December.

Required:
1. Prepare journal entries for each transaction. (Remember to check that debits equal credits and that the accounting equation is in balance after each transaction.)
2. Assume that Vail Resorts had a $1,000 balance in Accounts Receivable at the beginning of December. Determine the ending balance in the Accounts Receivable account at the end of December based on transactions (a) through (k). Show your work in T-account format.

Recording Journal Entries

E3-9
LO3-4

Blaine Air Transport Service, Inc., has been in operation for three years. The following transactions occurred in February:

February 1   Paid $275 for rent of hangar space in February.
February 2   Purchased fuel costing $490 on account for the next flight to Dallas.
February 4   Received customer payment of $820 to ship several items to Philadelphia next month.

February 7	Flew cargo from Denver to Dallas; the customer paid $910 for the air transport.
February 10	Paid $175 for an advertisement in the local paper to run on February 19.
February 14	Paid pilot $2,300 in wages for flying in January (recorded as expense in January).
February 18	Flew cargo for two customers from Dallas to Albuquerque for $3,800; one customer paid $1,600 cash and the other asked to be billed.
February 25	Purchased on account $2,550 in spare parts for the planes.
February 27	Declared a $200 cash dividend to be paid in March.

Required:

Prepare journal entries for each transaction. Be sure to categorize each account as an asset (A), liability (L), stockholders' equity (SE), revenue (R), or expense (E).

E3-10

LO3-3, 3-4

Analyzing the Effects of Transactions in T-Accounts and Computing Cash Basis versus Accrual Basis Net Income

Stacey's Piano Rebuilding Company has been operating for one year (2013). At the start of 2014, its income statement accounts had zero balances and its balance sheet account balances were as follows:

Cash	$ 6,400	Accounts payable	$ 9,600
Accounts receivable	32,000	Unearned fee revenue (deposits)	3,840
Supplies	1,500	Note payable (long-term)	48,500
Equipment	9,500	Common stock	1,600
Land	7,400	Additional paid-in capital	7,000
Building	25,300	Retained earnings	11,560

Required:

1. Create T-accounts for the balance sheet accounts and for these additional accounts: Rebuilding Fees Revenue, Rent Revenue, Wages Expense, and Utilities Expense. Enter the beginning balances.
2. Enter the following January 2014 transactions in the T-accounts, using the letter of each transaction as the reference:
   a. Rebuilt and delivered five pianos in January to customers who paid $19,000 in cash.
   b. Received a $600 deposit from a customer who wanted her piano rebuilt.
   c. Rented a part of the building to a bicycle repair shop; received $850 for rent in January.
   d. Received $7,200 from customers as payment on their accounts.
   e. Received an electric and gas utility bill for $400 to be paid in February.
   f. Ordered $960 in supplies.
   g. Paid $2,300 on account in January.
   h. Received from the home of Stacey Eddy, the major shareholder, a $920 tool (equipment) to use in the business in exchange for 100 shares of $1 par value stock.
   i. Paid $16,500 in wages to employees who worked in January.
   j. Declared and paid a $2,200 dividend.
   k. Received and paid cash for the supplies in (*f*).
3. Using the data from the T-accounts, amounts for the following on January 31, 2014, were

   Revenues $ _____ − Expenses $ _____ = Net Income $ _____
   Assets $ _____ = Liabilities $ _____ + Stockholders' Equity $ _____

4. What is net income if Stacey's used the cash basis of accounting? Why does this differ from accrual basis net income (in requirement 3)?

E3-11

LO3-5

Preparing an Income Statement

Refer to E3-10.

Required:

Use the ending balances in the T-accounts in E3-10 to prepare an income statement for January 2014 in good form (ignore income taxes).

Identifying Activities Affecting the Statement of Cash Flows

E3-12

LO3-5

Refer to E3-10.

Required:
Use the transactions in E3-10 to identify the operating (O), investing (I), and financing (F) activities and the direction (+ for increase, − for decrease) and amount of the effect. If there is no effect, use NE.

Analyzing the Effects of Transactions in T-Accounts

E3-13

LO3-4

Lisa Frees and Amelia Ellinger had been operating a catering business for several years. In March 2014, the partners were planning to expand by opening a retail sales shop and decided to form the business as a corporation called Traveling Gourmet, Inc. The following transactions occurred in March 2014:

a. Received $80,000 cash from each of the two shareholders to form the corporation, in addition to $2,000 in accounts receivable, $5,300 in equipment, a van (equipment) appraised at a fair value of $13,000, and $1,200 in supplies. Gave the two owners each 500 shares of common stock with a par value of $1 per share.
b. Purchased a vacant store for sale in a good location for $360,000, making a $72,000 cash down payment and signing a 10-year mortgage from a local bank for the rest.
c. Borrowed $50,000 from the local bank on a 10 percent, one-year note.
d. Purchased and used food and paper supplies costing $10,830 in March; paid cash.
e. Catered four parties in March for $4,200; $1,600 was billed, and the rest was received in cash.
f. Made and sold food at the retail store for $11,900 cash.
g. Received a $420 telephone bill for March to be paid in April.
h. Paid $363 in gas for the van in March.
i. Paid $6,280 in wages to employees who worked in March.
j. Paid a $300 dividend from the corporation to each owner.
k. Purchased $50,000 of equipment (refrigerated display cases, cabinets, tables, and chairs) and renovated and decorated the new store for $20,000 (added to the cost of the building); paid cash.

Required:
1. Set up appropriate T-accounts for Cash, Accounts Receivable, Supplies, Equipment, Building, Accounts Payable, Note Payable, Mortgage Payable, Common Stock, Additional Paid-in Capital, Retained Earnings, Food Sales Revenue, Catering Sales Revenue, Supplies Expense, Utilities Expense, Wages Expense, and Fuel Expense.
2. Record in the T-accounts the effects of each transaction for Traveling Gourmet, Inc., in March. Identify the amounts with the letters starting with (*a*). Compute ending balances.

Preparing an Income Statement, Identifying Cash Flow Effects, and Analyzing Results

E3-14

LO3-5

Refer to E3-13.

Required:
Use the balances in the completed T-accounts in E3-13 to respond to the following:
1. Prepare an income statement in good form for the month of March 2014.
2. Identify operating (O), investing (I), and financing (F) activities affecting cash flows. Include the direction and amount of the effect. If there is no effect on cash flows, use NE.
3. What do you think about the success of this company based on the results of the first month of operations? **Hint:** Compare net income to cash flows from operations.

Inferring Operating Transactions and Preparing an Income Statement and Balance Sheet

E3-15

LO3-2, 3-3, 3-4, 3-5

Kate's Kite Company (a corporation) sells and repairs kites from manufacturers around the world. Its stores are located in rented space in malls and shopping centers. During its first month of operations ended April 30, 2014, Kate's Kite Company completed eight transactions with the dollar effects indicated in the following schedule:

| Accounts | DOLLAR EFFECT OF EACH OF THE EIGHT TRANSACTIONS | | | | | | | | Ending Balance |
	(a)	(b)	(c)	(d)	(e)	(f)	(g)	(h)	
Cash	$82,000	$(15,400)	$(6,200)	$9,820		$(1,300)	$(2,480)	$3,960	
Accounts Receivable				4,180					
Inventory			24,800	(7,000)					
Prepaid Expenses							1,860		
Store Fixtures		15,400							
Accounts Payable			18,600		$1,480				
Unearned Revenue								2,510	
Common Stock ($1 par value)	10,000								
Additional Paid-in Capital	72,000								
Sales Revenue				14,000				1,450	
Cost of Sales				7,000					
Wages Expense						1,300			
Rent Expense							620		
Utilities Expense					1,480				

Required:

1. Write a brief explanation of transactions (*a*) through (*h*). Include any assumptions that you made.
2. Compute the ending balance in each account and prepare an income statement and a classified balance sheet for Kate's Kite Company on April 30, 2014.

E3-16
LO3-4, 3-6

Analyzing the Effects of Transactions Using T-Accounts and Interpreting the Net Profit Margin Ratio as a Financial Analyst

Massa Company, which has been operating for three years, provides marketing consulting services worldwide for dot-com companies. You are a financial analyst assigned to report on the Massa management team's effectiveness at managing its assets efficiently. At the start of 2015 (its fourth year), Massa's T-account balances were as follows. Dollars are in thousands.

Assets

Cash		Accounts Receivable		Long-Term Investments
3,200		8,000		6,400

Liabilities

Accounts Payable		Unearned Revenue		Long-Term Notes Payable
2,400		5,600		1,600

Stockholders' Equity

Common Stock ($.10 par value)	Additional Paid-in Capital	Retained Earnings
800	4,000	3,200

Revenues

Consulting Fee Revenue	Investment Income

Expenses

Wages Expense	Travel Expense	Utilities Expense

Rent Expense

Required:

1. Using the data from these T-accounts, amounts for the following on January 1, 2015, were

    Assets $ _____ = Liabilities $ _____ + Stockholders' Equity $ _____

2. Enter the following 2015 transactions in the T-accounts:
    a. Provided $58,000 in services to clients who paid $48,000 in cash and owed the rest on account.
    b. Received $5,600 cash from clients on account.
    c. Received $400 in cash as income on investments.
    d. Paid $36,000 in wages, $12,000 in travel, $7,600 in rent, and $1,600 on accounts payable.
    e. Received $1,600 in cash from clients in advance of services Massa will provide next year.
    f. Received a utility bill for $800 for 2015 services.
    g. Paid $480 in dividends to stockholders.
3. Compute ending balances in the T-accounts to determine amounts for the following on December 31, 2015:

    Revenues $ _____ − Expenses $ _____ = Net Income $ _____
    Assets $ _____ = Liabilities $ _____ + Stockholders' Equity $ _____

4. Calculate the net profit margin ratio for 2015. If the company had a net profit margin ratio of 2.9 percent in 2014 and 2.5 percent in 2013, what does your computation suggest to you about Massa Company? What would you say in your report?

Inferring Transactions and Computing Effects Using T-Accounts

A recent annual report of Gannett Company, Inc., a diversified media and marketing solutions company that currently includes newspapers (including *USA Today*) and Internet businesses (including Career-Builder), included the following accounts. Dollars are in millions:

E3-17

LO3-4

Gannett Company, Inc.

Trade Accounts Receivable		Prepaid Expenses		Unearned Subscriptions	
1/1 717		1/1 95			224 1/1
5,240	?	203	?	?	2,690
12/31 693		12/31 107			231 12/31

Required:
1. For each T-account, describe the typical transactions that affect each account (that is, the economic events that occur to make these accounts increase and decrease).
2. For each T-account, compute the missing amounts.

E3-18
LO3-5, 3-6

Finding Financial Information as an Investor

You are evaluating your current portfolio of investments to determine those that are not performing to your expectations. You have all of the companies' most recent annual reports.

Required:
For each of the following, indicate where you would locate the information in an annual report. (**Hint:** The information may be in more than one location.)
1. Description of a company's primary business(es).
2. Income taxes paid.
3. Accounts receivable.
4. Cash flow from operating activities.
5. Description of a company's revenue recognition policy.
6. The inventory sold during the year.
7. The data needed to compute the total net profit margin ratio.

To practice with more exercises, go to the text website at **www.mhhe.com/libby8e**.

PROBLEMS

P3-1
LO3-4

Recording Nonquantitative Journal Entries (AP3-1)

The following list includes a series of accounts for Sanjeev Corporation, which has been operating for three years. These accounts are listed and numbered for identification. Following the accounts is a series of transactions. For each transaction, indicate the account(s) that should be debited and credited by entering the appropriate account number(s) to the right of each transaction. If no journal entry is needed, write **none** after the transaction. The first transaction is used as an example.

Account No.	Account Title	Account No.	Account Title
1	Cash	10	Income Taxes Payable
2	Accounts Receivable	11	Common Stock
3	Supplies	12	Additional Paid-in Capital
4	Prepaid Expenses	13	Retained Earnings
5	Equipment	14	Service Revenue
6	Patents	15	Operating Expenses (wages, supplies)
7	Accounts Payable	16	Income Tax Expense
8	Note Payable	17	Interest Expense
9	Wages Payable		

Transactions	Debit	Credit
a. Example: Purchased equipment for use in the business; paid one-third cash and signed a note payable for the balance.	5	1, 8
b. Paid cash for salaries and wages earned by employees this period.	_____	_____
c. Paid cash on accounts payable for expenses incurred last period.	_____	_____
d. Purchased supplies to be used later; paid cash.	_____	_____
e. Performed services this period on credit.	_____	_____
f. Collected cash on accounts receivable for services performed last period.	_____	_____

Transactions	Debit	Credit
g. Issued stock to new investors.	————	————
h. Paid operating expenses incurred this period.	————	————
i. Incurred operating expenses this period to be paid next period.	————	————
j. Purchased a patent (an intangible asset); paid cash.	————	————
k. Collected cash for services performed this period.	————	————
l. Used some of the supplies on hand for operations.	————	————
m. Paid three-fourths of the income tax expense incurred for the year; the balance will be paid next year.	————	————
n. Made a payment on the equipment note in (a); the payment was part principal and part interest expense.	————	————
o. On the last day of the current period, paid cash for an insurance policy covering the next two years.	————	————

Recording Journal Entries (AP3-2)

P3-2
LO3-4

Ryan Terlecki organized a new Internet company, CapUniverse, Inc. The company specializes in baseball-type caps with logos printed on them. Ryan, who is never without a cap, believes that his target market is college and high school students. You have been hired to record the transactions occurring in the first two weeks of operations.

a. Issued 2,000 shares of $.01 par value common stock to investors for cash at $20 per share.
b. Borrowed $60,000 from the bank to provide additional funding to begin operations; the note is due in two years.
c. Paid $1,500 for the current month's rent of a warehouse and another $1,500 for next month's rent.
d. Paid $2,400 for a one-year fire insurance policy on the warehouse (recorded as a prepaid expense).
e. Purchased furniture and fixtures for the warehouse for $15,000, paying $3,000 cash and the rest on account. The amount is due within 30 days.
f. Purchased for $2,800 cash The University of Florida, UCLA, Texas A&M, and Michigan State University baseball caps as inventory to sell online.
g. Placed advertisements on Google for a total of $350 cash.
h. Sold caps totaling $1,700, half of which was charged on account. The cost of the caps sold was $900.
i. Made full payment for the furniture and fixtures purchased on account in (e).
j. Received $210 from a customer on account.

Required:
For each of the transactions, prepare journal entries. Be sure to categorize each account as an asset (A), liability (L), stockholders' equity (SE), revenue (R), or expense (E). Note that transaction (h) will require two entries, one for revenue and one for the related expense.

Determining Financial Statement Effects of Various Transactions and Identifying Cash Flow Effects (AP3-3)

P3-3
LO3-4

According to its annual report, The Wendy's Company serves "the best hamburgers in the business" and other fresh food including salads, chicken sandwiches, and baked potatoes in more than 6,500 restaurants worldwide. The company operates its own restaurants and sells franchises to others. The following activities were inferred from a recent annual report.

a. Purchased food and paper products; paid part in cash and the rest on account.
b. Purchased additional investments.
c. Incurred restaurant operating costs in company-owned facilities; paid part in cash and the rest on account.
d. Served food to customers for cash.
e. Used food and paper products.
f. Paid cash dividends.
g. Sold franchises, receiving part in cash and the rest in notes due from franchisees.
h. Paid interest on debt incurred and due during the period.

Required:

1. For each of the transactions, complete the tabulation, indicating the effect (+ for increase and − for decrease) of each transaction. (Remember that A = L + SE, R − E = NI, and NI affects SE through Retained Earnings.) Write NE if there is no effect. The first transaction is provided as an example.

	BALANCE SHEET			INCOME STATEMENT		
Transaction	**Assets**	**Liabilities**	**Stockholders' Equity**	**Revenues**	**Expenses**	**Net Income**
(*a*) (example)	+/−	+	NE	NE	NE	NE

2. Where, if at all, would each transaction be reported on the statement of cash flows? Use O for operating activities, I for investing activities, F for financing activities, and NE if the transaction would not be included on the statement.

P3-4

LO3-4, 3-5, 3-6

www.mhhe.com/libby8e

Analyzing the Effects of Transactions Using T-Accounts, Preparing an Income Statement, and Evaluating the Net Profit Margin Ratio as a Manager (AP3-4)

Kaylee James, a connoisseur of fine chocolate, opened Kaylee's Sweets in Collegetown on February 1, 2014. The shop specializes in a selection of gourmet chocolate candies and a line of gourmet ice cream. You have been hired as manager. Your duties include maintaining the store's financial records. The following transactions occurred in February 2014, the first month of operations.

a. Received four shareholders' contributions totaling $30,200 cash to form the corporation; issued 400 shares of $.10 par value common stock.
b. Paid three months' rent for the store at $1,750 per month (recorded as prepaid expenses).
c. Purchased and received candy for $6,000 on account, due in 60 days.
d. Purchased supplies for $1,560 cash.
e. Negotiated and signed a two-year $11,000 loan at the bank, receiving cash at the time.
f. Used the money from (e) to purchase a computer for $2,750 (for recordkeeping and inventory tracking); used the balance for furniture and fixtures for the store.
g. Placed a grand opening advertisement in the local paper for $400 cash; the ad ran in the current month.
h. Made sales on Valentine's Day totaling $3,500; $2,675 was in cash and the rest on accounts receivable. The cost of the candy sold was $1,600.
i. Made a $550 payment on accounts payable.
j. Incurred and paid employee wages of $1,300.
k. Collected accounts receivable of $600 from customers.
l. Made a repair to one of the display cases for $400 cash.
m. Made cash sales of $1,200 during the rest of the month. The cost of the candy sold was $600.

Required:

1. Set up appropriate T-accounts for Cash, Accounts Receivable, Supplies, Inventory, Prepaid Expenses, Equipment, Furniture and Fixtures, Accounts Payable, Notes Payable, Common Stock, Additional Paid-in Capital, Sales Revenue, Cost of Goods Sold (expense), Advertising Expense, Wage Expense, and Repair Expense. All accounts begin with zero balances.
2. Record in the T-accounts the effects of each transaction for Kaylee's Sweets in February, referencing each transaction in the accounts with the transaction letter. Show the ending balances in the T-accounts. Note that transactions (*h*) and (*m*) require two types of entries, one for revenue recognition and one for the expense.
3. Prepare an income statement at the end of the month ended February 28, 2014.
4. Write a short memo to Kaylee offering your opinion on the results of operations during the first month of business.

5. After three years in business, you are being evaluated for a promotion. One measure is how effectively you managed the sales and expenses of the business. The following data are available:

	2016*	2015	2014
Total assets	$88,000	$58,500	$52,500
Total liabilities	49,500	22,000	18,500
Total stockholders' equity	38,500	36,500	34,000
Net sales revenue	93,500	82,500	55,000
Net income	22,000	11,000	4,400

At the end of 2016, Kaylee decided to open a second store, requiring loans and inventory purchases prior to the store's opening in early 2017.

Compute the net profit margin ratio for each year and evaluate the results. Do you think you should be promoted? Why?

Identifying Cash Flow Effects (AP3-5)

Refer to P3-4.

Required:
For the transactions listed in P3-4, indicate the type of effect on cash flows (O for operating, I for investing, and F for financing) and the direction (+ for increase and − for decrease) and amount of the effect. If there is no effect, write NE.

Analyzing the Effects of Transactions Using T-Accounts, Preparing an Income Statement, and Evaluating the Net Profit Margin Ratio (AP3-6)

Following are account balances (in millions of dollars) from a recent FedEx annual report, followed by several typical transactions. Assume that the following are account balances on May 31, 2014:

Account	Balance	Account	Balance
Property and equipment (net)	$15,543	Receivables	$4,581
Retained earnings	12,716	Other current assets	610
Accounts payable	1,702	Cash	2,328
Prepaid expenses	329	Spare parts, supplies, and fuel	437
Accrued expenses payable	1,894	Other noncurrent liabilities	5,616
Long-term notes payable	1,667	Other current liabilities	1.286
Other noncurrent assets	3,557	Additional paid-in capital	2,472
Common stock ($0.10 par value)	32		

These accounts are not necessarily in good order and have normal debit or credit balances. Assume the following transactions (in millions) occurred the next year ending May 31, 2015:

a. Provided delivery service to customers, receiving $21,704 in accounts receivable and $17,600 in cash.
b. Purchased new equipment costing $3,434; signed a long-term note.
c. Paid $13,864 cash to rent equipment and aircraft, with $10,136 for rental this year and the rest for rent next year.
d. Spent $3,864 cash to maintain and repair facilities and equipment during the year.
e. Collected $24,285 from customers on account.
f. Repaid $350 on a long-term note (ignore interest).
g. Issued 20 shares of additional stock for $16.
h. Paid employees $15,276 during the year.

P3-5
LO3-5

www.mhhe.com/libby8e

P3-6
LO3-4, 3-5, 3-6

FedEx

www.mhhe.com/libby8e

i. Purchased for cash and used $8,564 in fuel for the aircraft and equipment during the year.
j. Paid $784 on accounts payable.
k. Ordered $88 in spare parts and supplies.

Required:

1. Prepare T-accounts for May 31, 2014, from the preceding list; enter the respective beginning balances. You will need additional T-accounts for income statement accounts; enter zero for beginning balances.
2. For each transaction, record the 2015 effects in the T-accounts. Label each using the letter of the transaction. Compute ending balances.
3. Prepare an income statement for the period ended May 31, 2015.
4. Compute the company's net profit margin ratio for the year ended May 31, 2015. What does it suggest to you about FedEx?

P3-7

LO3-4

Cedar Fair. L.P.

www.mhhe.com/libby8e

Recording Journal Entries and Identifying Cash Flow Effects

Cedar Fair, L.P. (Limited Partnership) is one of the largest regional amusement park operators in the world, owning 11 amusement parks, four outdoor water parks, one indoor water park, and five hotels. The parks include Cedar Point in Ohio, Valleyfair near Minneapolis/St. Paul, Dorney Park and Wildwater Kingdom near Allentown, Pennsylvania, Worlds of Fun/Oceans of Fun in Kansas City, Great America in Santa Clara, California, and Canada's Wonderland near Toronto, Canada, among others. The following are summarized transactions similar to those that occurred in a recent year (assume 2014). Dollars are in thousands:

a. Guests at the parks paid $596,042 cash in admissions.
b. The primary operating expenses (such as employee wages, utilities, and repairs and maintenance on buildings and equipment) for the year were $433,416, with $401,630 paid in cash and the rest on account.
c. Cedar Fair paid $47,100 principal on notes payable.
d. The parks sell food and merchandise and operate games. The cash received during the year for these combined activities was $365,693. The cost of merchandise sold during the year was $92,057.
e. Cedar Fair purchased and built additional buildings, rides, and equipment during the year, paying $90,190 in cash.
f. Guests may stay in the parks at accommodations owned by the company. During the year, accommodations revenue was $82,994; $81,855 was paid by the guests in cash and the rest was owed on account.
g. Interest incurred and paid on long-term debt was $153,326.
h. The company purchased $147,531 in food and merchandise inventory for the year, paying $119,431 in cash and owing the rest on account.
i. The selling, general, and administrative expenses, such as the president's salary and advertising for the parks, were $140,426 for the year and were classified as operating expenses; $134,044 was paid in cash, and the rest was owed on account.
j. Cedar Fair paid $11,600 on accounts payable during the year.

Required:

1. For each of these transactions, record journal entries. Use the letter of each transaction as its reference. Note that transaction (*d*) will require two entries, one for revenue recognition and one for the related expense.
2. Use the following chart to identify whether each transaction results in a cash flow effect from operating (O), investing (I), or financing (F) activities, and indicate the direction and amount of the effect on cash (+ for increase and − for decrease). If there is no cash flow effect, write **none.** The first transaction is provided as an example.

Transaction	Operating, Investing, or Financing Effect	Direction and Amount of the Effect (in thousands)
(a)	O	+596,042

Recording Nonquantitative Journal Entries (P3-1)

AP3-1
LO3-4

The following is a series of accounts for Kruger & Laurenzo, Incorporated, which has been operating for two years. The accounts are listed and numbered for identification. Following the accounts is a series of transactions. For each transaction, indicate the account(s) that should be debited and credited by entering the appropriate account number(s) to the right of each transaction. If no journal entry is needed, write **none** after the transaction. The first transaction is given as an example.

Account No.	Account Title	Account No.	Account Title
1	Cash	9	Wages Payable
2	Accounts Receivable	10	Income Taxes Payable
3	Supplies	11	Common Stock
4	Prepaid Expenses	12	Additional Paid-in Capital
5	Buildings	13	Retained Earnings
6	Land	14	Service Revenue
7	Accounts Payable	15	Other Expenses (wages, supplies, interest)
8	Mortgage Payable	16	Income Tax Expense

Transactions	Debit	Credit
a. *Example:* Issued stock to new investors.	1	11, 12
b. Incurred and recorded operating expenses on credit to be paid next period.	___	___
c. Purchased on credit but did not use supplies this period.	___	___
d. Performed services for customers this period on credit.	___	___
e. Prepaid a fire insurance policy this period to cover the next 12 months.	___	___
f. Purchased a building this period by making a 20 percent cash down payment and signing a mortgage loan for the balance.	___	___
g. Collected cash this year for services rendered and recorded in the prior year.	___	___
h. Collected cash for services rendered this period.	___	___
i. Paid cash this period for wages earned and recorded last period.	___	___
j. Paid cash for operating expenses charged on accounts payable in the prior period.	___	___
k. Paid cash for operating expenses incurred in the current period.	___	___
l. Made a payment on the mortgage loan, which was part principal repayment and part interest.	___	___
m. This period a shareholder sold some shares of her stock to another person for an amount above the original issuance price.	___	___
n. Used supplies on hand to clean the offices.	___	___
o. Recorded income taxes for this period to be paid at the beginning of the next period.	___	___
p. Declared and paid a cash dividend this period.	___	___

Recording Journal Entries (P3-2)

AP3-2
LO3-4

Jimmy Langenberger is the president of TemPro, Inc., a company that provides temporary employees for not-for-profit companies. TemPro has been operating for five years; its revenues are increasing with each passing year. You have been hired to help Jimmy analyze the following transactions for the first two weeks of April:

a. Billed the local United Way office $23,500 for temporary services provided.
b. Paid $3,005 for supplies purchased and recorded on account last period.

c. Purchased office supplies for $2,600 on account.

d. Purchased a new computer for the office costing $3,800 cash.

e. Placed an advertisement in the local paper for $1,400 cash.

f. Paid employee wages of $11,900. Of this amount, $3,800 had been earned by employees and recorded in the Wages Payable account in the prior period.

g. Issued 3,000 additional shares of common stock for cash at $45 per share in anticipation of building a new office. The common stock had a par value of $0.50 per share.

h. Received $12,500 on account from the local United Way office from the services provided in (a).

i. Billed Family & Children's Service $14,500 for services rendered.

j. Purchased land as the site of a future office for $10,000. Paid $3,000 cash as a down payment and signed a note payable for the balance.

k. Received the April telephone bill for $1,950 to be paid next month.

Required:

For each of the transactions, prepare journal entries. Be sure to categorize each account as an asset (A), liability (L), stockholders' equity (SE), revenue (R), or expense (E).

AP3-3
LO3-4

Big Dog Holdings, Inc.

Determining Financial Statement Effects of Various Transactions and Identifying Cash Flow Effects (P3-3)

Big Dog Holdings, Inc., is the parent company of Big Dog USA, a company that develops, markets, and retails a collection of consumer products centered around the signature BIG DOGS name, logo, and "Big Dog" characters. The following activities were inferred from a recent annual report.

a. *Example:* Incurred expenses; paid part in cash and part on credit.

b. Paid interest on long-term debt.

c. Sold merchandise to customers on account. (**Hint:** Indicate the effects of the sale; then reduce inventory for the amount sold—two transactions.)

d. Sold investments for cash for more than their cost.

e. Collected cash on account.

f. Used supplies.

g. Repaid long-term debt principal.

h. Received dividends and interest on investments.

i. Purchased equipment; paid part in cash and part on credit.

j. Paid cash on account.

k. Issued additional stock.

l. Paid rent to outlet mall owners.

Required:

1. For each of the transactions, complete the tabulation, indicating the effect (+ for increase and − for decrease) of each transaction. (Remember that A = L + SE, R − E = NI, and NI affects SE through Retained Earnings.) Write NE if there is no effect. The first transaction is provided as an example.

| Transaction | BALANCE SHEET | | | INCOME STATEMENT | | |
	Assets	Liabilities	Stockholders' Equity	Revenues	Expenses	Net Income
(a) (example)	−	+	−	NE	+	−

2. For each transaction, indicate where, if at all, it would be reported on the statement of cash flows. Use O for operating activities, I for investing activities, F for financing activities, and NE if the transaction would not be included on the statement.

Analyzing the Effects of Transactions Using T-Accounts, Preparing an Income Statement, and Evaluating the Net Profit Margin Ratio as a Manager (P3-4)

Alpine Stables, Inc., was established in Denver, Colorado, on April 1, 2014. The company provides stables, care for animals, and grounds for riding and showing horses. You have been hired as the new assistant controller. The following transactions for April 2014 are provided for your review.

a. Received contributions from five investors of $60,000 in cash ($12,000 each), a barn valued at $100,000, land valued at $90,000, and supplies valued at $12,000. Each investor received 3,000 shares of stock with a par value of $0.01 per share.

b. Built a small barn for $62,000. The company paid half the amount in cash on April 1, 2014, and signed a three-year note payable for the balance.

c. Provided $35,260 in animal care services for customers, all on credit.

d. Rented stables to customers who cared for their own animals; received cash of $13,200.

e. Received from a customer $2,400 to board her horse in May, June, and July (record as unearned revenue).

f. Purchased hay and feed supplies on account for $3,810 to be used in the summer.

g. Paid $1,240 in cash for water utilities incurred in the month.

h. Paid $2,700 on accounts payable for previous purchases.

i. Received $10,000 from customers on accounts receivable.

j. Paid $6,000 in wages to employees who worked during the month.

k. At the end of the month, purchased a two-year insurance policy for $3,600.

l. Received an electric utility bill for $1,800 for usage in April; the bill will be paid next month.

m. Paid $100 cash dividend to each of the five investors at the end of the month.

Required:

1. Set up appropriate T-accounts. All accounts begin with zero balances.

2. Record in the T-accounts the effects of each transaction for Alpine Stables in April, referencing each transaction in the accounts with the transaction letter. Show the ending balances in the T-accounts.

3. Prepare an income statement for April.

4. Write a short memo to the five owners offering your opinion on the results of operations during the first month of business.

5. After three years in business, you are being evaluated for a promotion to chief financial officer. One measure is how effectively you have managed the revenues and expenses of the business. The following annual data are available:

	2016*	2015	2014
Total assets	$480,000	$320,000	$300,000
Total liabilities	125,000	28,000	30,000
Total stockholders' equity	355,000	292,000	270,000
Operating revenue	450,000	400,000	360,000
Net income	50,000	30,000	(10,000)

At the end of 2016, Alpine Stables decided to build an indoor riding arena for giving lessons year-round. The company borrowed construction funds from a local bank in 2016, and the arena was opened in early 2017.

Compute the net profit margin ratio for each year and evaluate the results. Do you think you should be promoted? Why?

Identifiying Cash Flow Effects (P3-5)

Refer to AP3-4.

Required:

For the transactions listed in AP3-4, indicate the type of activity (O for operating, I for investing, and F for financing) and the direction (+ for increase, − for decrease) and amount of the effect. If the transaction had no effect on cash flows, write NE.

AP3-6

LO3-4, 3-5, 3-6

Analyzing the Effects of Transactions Using T-Accounts, Preparing an Income Statement, and Evaluating the Net Profit Margin Ratio (P3-6)

The following are the summary account balances from a recent balance sheet of Exxon Mobil Corporation. The accounts have normal debit or credit balances, but they are not necessarily listed in good order. The amounts are shown in millions of dollars. Assume the year-end is December 31, 2013.

Cash	$ 12,664	Marketable securities	
Notes payable (long-term)	7,711	(short-term investments)	$ 404
Accounts receivable	38,642	Accounts payable	57,067
Inventories	11,665	Income tax payable	12,727
Other long-term debt	83,481	Prepaid expenses	3,359
Property and equipment, net	214,664	Investments	34,333
Contributed capital	9,512	Other assets and intangibles, net	9,092
Other current assets	6,229	Notes payable (short-term)	9,322
Retained earnings	151,232		

The following is a list of hypothetical transactions for January 2014 (in millions of dollars):

a. Purchased on account $1,610 of new equipment.
b. Received $3,100 on accounts receivable.
c. Received and paid $3 for utility bills.
d. Earned $39,780 in sales on account with customers; cost of sales was $5,984.
e. Paid employees $1,238 for wages earned during the month.
f. Paid three-fourths of the income taxes payable.
g. Purchased $23 in supplies on account (include in Inventories).
h. Prepaid $82 to rent a warehouse next month.
i. Paid $10 of other long-term debt principal and $1 in interest expense on the debt.
j. Purchased a patent (an intangible asset) for $6 cash.

Required:

1. Prepare T-accounts for December 31, 2013, from the preceding list; enter the beginning balances. You will need additional T-accounts for income statement accounts; enter zero for beginning balances.
2. For each transaction, record the effects in the T-accounts. Label each using the letter of the transaction. Compute ending balances. (**Note:** Record two transactions in (*d*), one for revenue recognition and one for the expense.)
3. Prepare an income statement for January 2014.
4. Compute the company's net profit margin ratio for the month ended January 31, 2014. What does it suggest to you about Exxon Mobil?

CASES **AND PROJECTS**

Annual Report Cases

CP3-1

LO3-2, 3-4, 3-6

AMERICAN EAGLE
OUTFITTERS, INC.

Finding Financial Information

Refer to the financial statements of American Eagle Outfitters in Appendix B at the end of the book.

Required:

1. State the amount of the largest expense on the income statement for the year ended January 28, 2012, and describe the transaction represented by the expense.
2. Assuming that all net sales are on credit, how much cash did American Eagle Outfitters collect from customers?* (**Hint:** Use a T-account of accounts receivable to infer collection.)
3. A shareholder has complained that "more dividends should be paid because the company had net earnings of $151,705,000. Since this amount is all cash, more of it should go to the owners." Explain why the shareholder's assumption that earnings equal net cash inflow is valid. If you believe that the assumption is **not** valid, state so and support your position concisely.
4. Describe and contrast the purpose of an income statement versus a balance sheet.
5. Compute the company's net profit margin for each year presented. Explain its meaning.

Finding Financial Information

Refer to the financial statements of Urban Outfitters in Appendix C at the end of the book.

Required:

1. What is the company's revenue recognition policy? (**Hint:** Look in the notes to the financial statements.)
2. Assuming that $50 million of cost of sales was due to noninventory purchase expenses (distribution and occupancy costs), how much inventory did the company buy during the year? (**Hint:** Use a T-account of inventory to infer how much was purchased.)
3. Calculate selling, general, and administrative expenses as a percent of sales for each year presented. By what percent did these expenses increase or decrease from fiscal years ended 2011 and 2012 and between 2010 and 2011? (**Hint:** Percentage Change = [Current Year Amount − Prior Year Amount]/Prior Year Amount.)
4. Compute the company's net profit margin for each year presented and explain its meaning.

CP3-2
LO3-2, 3-4, 3-6

URBAN OUTFITTERS INC.

Comparing Companies within an Industry

Refer to the financial statements of American Eagle Outfitters in Appendix B, Urban Outfitters in Appendix C, and the Industry Ratio Report in Appendix D at the end of this book.

Required:

1. By what title does each company call its income statement? Explain what "Consolidated" means.
2. Which company had higher net income for the fiscal year?
3. Compute the net profit margin ratio for both companies for the year. Which company is managing revenues and expenses more effectively?
4. Compare the net profit margin ratio for both companies for the most recent year presented to the industry average. On average, are these two companies managing sales and expenses better or worse than their competitors?
5. How much cash was provided by operating activities for each year by each company? What was the percentage change in operating cash flows (1) from fiscal year ended 2010 to 2011 and (2) from fiscal year ended 2011 to 2012? (**Hint:** Percentage Change = [Current Year Amount − Prior Year Amount]/Prior Year Amount.)

CP3-3
LO3-2, 3-4, 3-6

AMERICAN EAGLE
OUTFITTERS, INC.

URBAN OUTFITTERS INC.

www.mhhe.com/libby8e

Financial Reporting and Analysis Cases

Analyzing a Company over Time

Refer to the annual report for American Eagle Outfitters in Appendix B.

CP3-4
LO3-6

AMERICAN EAGLE
OUTFITTERS, INC.

---

*Note that most retailers settle sales in cash at the register and would not have accounts receivable related to sales unless they had layaway or private credit. For American Eagle, the accounts receivable on the balance sheet primarily relates to amounts owed from landlords for their construction allowances for building new American Eagle stores in malls.

Required:

1. The annual report or 10-K report for American Eagle Outfitters provides selected financial data for the last five years. Compute the net profit margin ratio for each of the years presented. Use income from continuing operations in place of net income. (**Hint:** See Item 6 from the 10-K, which is disclosed within the annual report for the data. **Note:** Some companies will label a year that has a January year-end as having a fiscal year-end dated one year earlier. For example, a January 2012 year-end may be labeled as Fiscal 2011 since the year actually has more months that fall in the 2011 calendar year than in the 2012 calendar year.)
2. In Chapter 2, we discussed the current ratio. This ratio is computed in Item 6. Observe the trends over time for both the net profit margin and the current ratio. What do they suggest about American Eagle Outfitters?

CP3-5
LO3-3

Interpreting the Financial Press

The October 4, 2004, edition of *BusinessWeek* presented an article titled "Fuzzy Numbers" on issues related to accrual accounting and its weaknesses that have led some corporate executives to manipulate estimates in their favor, sometimes fraudulently. You can access the article on the text's website at www .mhhe.com/libby8e.

Required:
Read the article and then answer the following questions:
1. What is accrual accounting?
2. What does the article's title "Fuzzy Numbers" mean?
3. What does the article suggest about the reforms adopted by Congress and the SEC?

Critical Thinking Cases

CP3-6
LO3-3, 3-4, 3-5

Making a Decision as a Bank Loan Officer: Analyzing and Restating Financial Statements That Have Major Deficiencies (A Challenging Case)

Julio Estela started and operated a small boat repair service company during 2015. He is interested in obtaining a $100,000 loan from your bank to build a dry dock to store boats for customers in the winter months. At the end of the year, he prepared the following statements based on information stored in a large filing cabinet:

ESTELA COMPANY Profit for 2015		
Service fees collected during 2015		$ 55,000
Cash dividends received		10,000
Total		65,000
Expense for operations paid during 2015	$22,000	
Cash stolen	500	
New tools purchased during 2015 (cash paid)	1,000	
Supplies purchased for use on service jobs (cash paid)	3,200	
Total		26,700
Profit		$ 38,300
Assets Owned at the End of 2015		
Cash in checking account		$ 29,300
Building (at current market value)		32,000
Tools and equipment		18,000
Land (at current market value)		30,000
Stock in ABC Industrial		130,000
Total		$239,300

The following is a summary of completed transactions:

a. Received the following contributions (at fair value) to the business from the owner when it was started in exchange for 1,000 shares of $1 par value common stock in the new company:

Building	$21,000	Land	$20,000
Tools and equipment	17,000	Cash	1,000

b. Earned service fees during 2015 of $87,000; of the cash collected, $20,000 was for deposits from customers on work to be done by Julio in the next year.

c. Received the cash dividends on shares of ABC Industrial stock purchased by Julio Estela six years earlier (the stock was not owned by the company).

d. Incurred expenses during 2015 of $61,000.

e. Determined amount of supplies on hand (unused) at the end of 2015 as $700.

Required:

1. Did Julio prepare the income statement on a cash basis or an accrual basis? Explain how you can tell. Which basis should be used? Explain why.

2. Reconstruct the correct entries under accrual accounting principles and post the effects to T-accounts.

3. Prepare an accrual-based income statement. Explain (using footnotes) the reason for each change that you make to the income statement.

4. What additional information would assist you in formulating your decision regarding the loan to Julio?

5. Based on the revised statements and additional information needed, write a letter to Julio explaining your decision at this time regarding the loan.

Evaluating an Ethical Dilemma

Mike Lynch is the manager of an upstate New York regional office for an insurance company. As the regional manager, his compensation package comprises a base salary, commissions, and a bonus when the region sells new policies in excess of its quota. Mike has been under enormous pressure lately, stemming largely from two factors. First, he is experiencing a mounting personal debt due to a family member's illness. Second, compounding his worries, the region's sales of new policies have dipped below the normal quota for the first time in years.

You have been working for Mike for two years, and like everyone else in the office, you consider yourself lucky to work for such a supportive boss. You also feel great sympathy for his personal problems over the last few months. In your position as accountant for the regional office, you are only too aware of the drop in new policy sales and the impact this will have on the manager's bonus. While you are working late at year-end, Mike stops by your office.

Mike asks you to change the manner in which you have accounted for a new property insurance policy for a large local business. A substantial check for the premium came in the mail on December 31, the last day of the reporting year. The premium covers a period beginning on January 5. You deposited the check and correctly debited Cash and credited an **unearned revenue** account. Mike says, "Hey, we have the money this year, so why not count the revenue this year? I never did understand why you accountants are so picky about these things anyway. I'd like you to change the way you have recorded the transaction. I want you to credit a *revenue* account. And anyway, I've done favors for you in the past, and I am asking for such a small thing in return." With that, he leaves for the day.

Required:

1. How should you handle this situation?
2. What are the ethical implications of Mike's request?
3. Who are the parties who would be helped or harmed if you complied with the request?
4. If you fail to comply with his request, how will you explain your position to him in the morning?

CP3-7
LO3-3

Financial Reporting and Analysis Team Project

CP3-8
LO3-2, 3-3, 3-6

Team Project: Analysis of Income Statements and Ratios

As a team, select an industry to analyze. *Yahoo!Finance* provides lists of industries at <u>biz.yahoo.com/p/industries.html</u>. Click on an industry for a list of companies in that industry. Alternatively, go to Google Finance at <u>www.google.com/finance</u>, search for a company you are interested in, and you will be presented with a list including that company and its competitors. Each team member should acquire the annual report or 10-K for one publicly traded company in the industry, with each member selecting a different company (the SEC EDGAR service at <u>www.sec.gov</u> or the company's investor relations website itself are good sources).

Required:

On an individual basis, each team member should write a short report answering the following questions about the selected company. Discuss any patterns across the companies that you as a team observe. Then, as a team, write a short report comparing and contrasting your companies.

1. For the most recent year, what is (are) the major revenue account(s)? What percentage is each to total operating revenues? (Calculated as Revenue A ÷ Total revenues.)
2. For the most recent year, what is (are) the major expense account(s)? What percentage is each to total operating expenses? (Calculated as Expense A ÷ Total expenses.)
3. Ratio Analysis:
   a. What does the total asset turnover ratio measure in general?
   b. Compute the ratio for the last three years.
   c. What do your results suggest about the company?
   d. If available, find the industry ratio for the most recent year, compare it to your results, and discuss why you believe your company differs or is similar to the industry ratio.
4. Describe the company's revenue recognition policy, if reported. (Usually in the Significant Accounting Policies footnote.)
5. The ratio of Cash from Operating Activities divided by Net Income measures how liberal (that is, speeding up revenue recognition or delaying expense recognition) or conservative (that is, taking care not to record revenues too early or expenses too late) management is in choosing among various revenue and expense recognition policies. A ratio above 1.0 suggests more conservative policies and below 1.0, more liberal policies. Compute the ratio for each of the last three years. What do your results suggest about the company's choice in accounting policies?

CONTINUING CASE

CC3-1
LO3-4, 3-5, 3-6

Accounting for Operating Activities in a New Business (the Accounting Cycle)

Penny's Pool Service & Supply, Inc. (PPSS) had the following transactions related to operating the business in its first year's busiest quarter ended September 30, 2013:

a. Placed and paid for $2,600 in advertisements with several area newspapers (including the online versions), all of which ran in the newspapers during the quarter.
b. Cleaned pools for customers for $19,200, receiving $16,000 in cash with the rest owed by customers who will pay when billed in October.
c. Paid Pool Corporation, Inc., a pool supply wholesaler, $10,600 for inventory received by PPSS in May.
d. As an incentive to maintain customer loyalty, PPSS offered customers a discount for prepaying next year's pool cleaning service. PPSS received $10,000 from customers who took advantage of the discount.
e. Paid the office receptionist $4,500, with $1,500 owed from work in the prior quarter and the rest from work in the current quarter. Last quarter's amount was recorded as an expense and a liability Wages Payable.

f. Had the company van repaired, paying $310 to the mechanic.

g. Paid $220 for phone, water, and electric utilities used during the quarter.

h. Received $75 cash in interest earned during the current quarter on short-term investments.

i. Received a property tax bill for $600 for use of the land and building in the quarter; the bill will be paid next quarter.

j. Paid $2,400 for the next quarter's insurance coverage.

Required:

1. For each of the events, prepare journal entries, checking that debits equal credits.
2. Based only on these quarterly transactions, prepare a classified income statement (with income from operations determined separately from other items) for the quarter ended September 30, 2013.
3. Calculate the net profit margin ratio at September 30, 2013 (using income before taxes in place of net income). What does this ratio indicate about the ability of PPSS to control operations?

Adjustments, Financial Statements, and the Quality of Earnings

The end of the accounting period is a very busy time for Chipotle Mexican Grill. Although the last day of the fiscal year for Chipotle falls on the last day of December each year, the financial statements are not distributed to users until management and the external auditors (independent CPAs) make many critical evaluations.

- Management must ensure that the correct amounts are reported on the balance sheet and income statement. This often requires estimations, assumptions, and judgments about the timing of revenue and expense recognition and values for assets and liabilities.

- The auditors have to (1) assess the strength of the controls established by management to safeguard the company's assets and ensure the accuracy of the financial records, and (2) evaluate the appropriateness of estimates and accounting principles used by management in determining revenues and expenses.

Managers of most companies understand the need to present financial information fairly so as not to mislead users. However, since end-of-period adjustments are the most complex portion of the annual recordkeeping process, they are prone to error. External auditors examine the company's records on a test, or sample, basis. To maximize the chance of detecting any errors significant enough to affect users' decisions, CPAs allocate more of their testing to transactions most likely to be in error.

Several accounting research studies have documented the most error-prone transactions for medium-size manufacturing companies. End-of-period adjustment errors, such as failure to provide adequate product warranty liability, failure to include items that should be

Learning Objectives

After studying this chapter, you should be able to:

4-1 Explain the purpose of adjustments and analyze the adjustments necessary at the end of the period to update balance sheet and income statement accounts. p. 162

4-2 Present an income statement with earnings per share, statement of stockholders' equity, and balance sheet. p. 175

4-3 Compute and interpret the total asset turnover ratio. p. 180

4-4 Explain the closing process. p. 181

expensed, and end-of-period transactions recorded in the wrong period (called cut-off errors), are in the top category and thus receive a great deal of attention from auditors.

For 2011, Chipotle's year-end estimation and auditing process took until February 10, 2012, the date on which the auditor Ernst & Young LLP completed the audit work and signed its audit opinion. At that point, the financial statements were made available to the public.

UNDERSTANDING THE BUSINESS

Managers are responsible for preparing financial statements that will be useful to investors, creditors, and others. Financial information is most useful for analyzing the past and predicting the future when it is considered by users to be of **high quality.** High-quality information is information that is relevant (that is, material and able to influence users' decisions) and a faithful representation of what is being reported (that is, complete, free from error, and unbiased in portraying economic reality).

Users expect revenues and expenses to be reported in the proper period based on the revenue realization and expense matching principles discussed in Chapter 3. Revenues are to be recorded when earned, and expenses are to be recorded when incurred regardless of when cash receipts or payments occur. Many operating activities take place over a period of time or over several periods, such as using insurance that has been prepaid or owing wages to employees for past work. Because recording these and similar activities daily is often very costly, most companies wait until the end of the period (usually monthly, quarterly, or annually) to make **adjustments** to record related revenues and expenses in the correct period. These entries update the records and are the focus of this chapter.

In this chapter, we emphasize the use of the same analytical tools illustrated in Chapters 2 and 3 (T-accounts and journal entries) to understand how common adjustments are analyzed and recorded at the end of the accounting period. These tools provide the foundation for understanding adjustments that require additional estimation and judgments by management, which we discuss in future chapters. Then, in this chapter, we prepare financial statements using adjusted accounts, and finally, we illustrate how to prepare the accounting records for the next period by performing a process called **closing the books.**

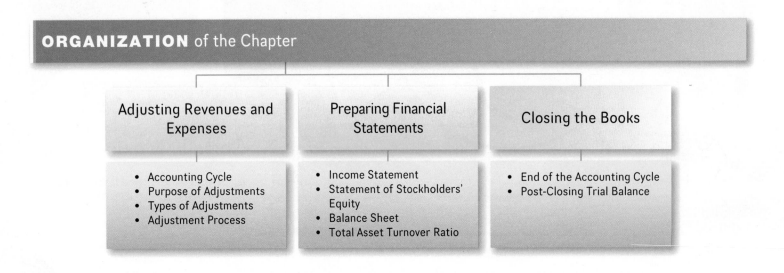

ORGANIZATION of the Chapter

Adjusting Revenues and Expenses	Preparing Financial Statements	Closing the Books
• Accounting Cycle • Purpose of Adjustments • Types of Adjustments • Adjustment Process	• Income Statement • Statement of Stockholders' Equity • Balance Sheet • Total Asset Turnover Ratio	• End of the Accounting Cycle • Post-Closing Trial Balance

ADJUSTING REVENUES AND EXPENSES

Accounting Cycle

LEARNING OBJECTIVE 4-1

Explain the purpose of adjustments and analyze the adjustments necessary at the end of the period to update balance sheet and income statement accounts.

Exhibit 4.1 presents the basic steps in the **accounting cycle.** As initially discussed in Chapter 2, the accounting cycle is the process followed by entities to analyze and record transactions, adjust the records at the end of the period, prepare financial statements, and prepare the records for the next cycle. **During** the accounting period, transactions that result in exchanges between the company and other external parties are analyzed and recorded in the general journal in chronological order (journal entries), and the related accounts are updated in the general ledger (T-accounts), similar to our Chipotle illustrations in Chapters 2 and 3. In this chapter, we examine the **end-of-period** steps that focus primarily on adjustments to record revenues and expenses in the proper period and to update the balance sheet accounts for reporting purposes.

Purpose of Adjustments

Accounting systems are designed to record most recurring daily transactions, particularly those involving cash. As cash is received or paid, it is recorded in the accounting system. In general, this focus on cash works well, especially when cash receipts and payments occur in the

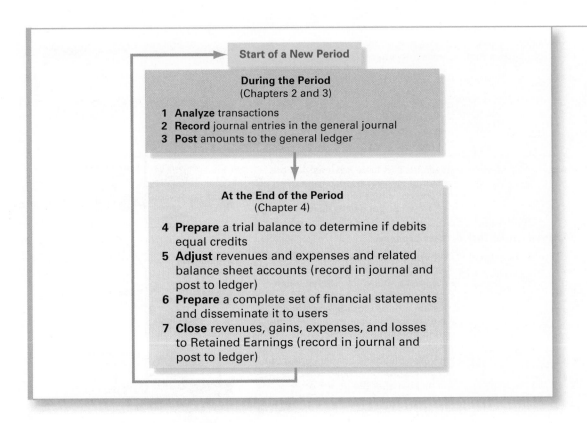

EXHIBIT 4.1

The Accounting Cycle

same period as the activities that produce revenues and expenses. However, cash is not always received in the period in which the company earns revenue; likewise, cash is not always paid in the period in which the company incurs an expense.

How does the accounting system record revenues and expenses when one transaction is needed to record a cash receipt or payment and another transaction is needed to record revenue when it is earned or an expense when it is incurred? The solution to the problem created by such differences in timing is to record **adjusting entries** at the end of every accounting period, so that

- Revenues are recorded when they are earned (the **revenue realization principle**),
- Expenses are recorded when they are incurred to generate revenue (the **expense matching principle**),
- **Assets** are reported at amounts that represent the probable future benefits remaining at the end of the period, and
- **Liabilities** are reported at amounts that represent the probable future sacrifices of assets or services owed at the end of the period.

Companies wait until the **end of the accounting period** to adjust their accounts in this way because adjusting the records daily would be very costly and time-consuming. Adjusting entries are required every time a company wants to prepare financial statements for external users.

ADJUSTING ENTRIES are entries necessary at the end of the accounting period to measure all revenues and expenses of that period.

Types of Adjustments

Exhibit 4.2 describes the four types of adjustments (two in which cash was already received or paid and two in which cash will be received or paid). Because of the timing of the cash receipts or payments, each of these types of adjustments involves two entries:

- One for the cash receipt or payment either before or after the end of the period.
- One for the adjustment to record the revenue or expense in the proper period (the adjusting entry).

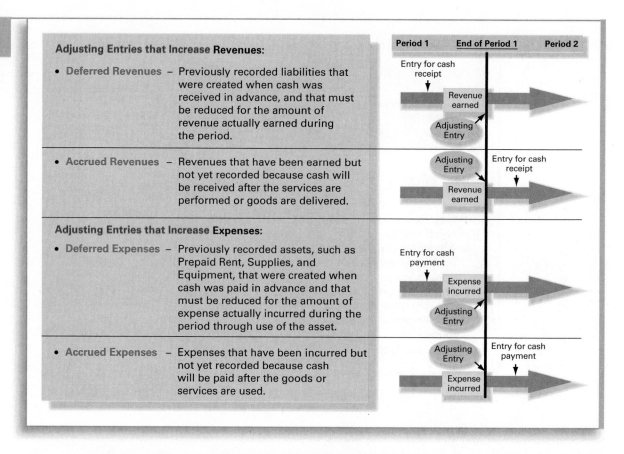

EXHIBIT 4.2

Four Types of
Adjustments

In practice, almost every account, **except Cash,** could require an adjustment. Rather than trying to memorize an endless list of specific examples, you should focus instead on learning the general types of adjustments that are needed and the process that is used to determine how to adjust the accounts. We will illustrate the process involved in analyzing and adjusting the accounts by reviewing all the adjustments needed for Chipotle Mexican Grill before preparing the financial statements for the first quarter of 2012 based on adjusted balances.

Adjustment Process

In analyzing adjustments at the end of the period, there are three steps:

Step 1: Ask: **Was revenue earned or an expense incurred that is not yet recorded?**

If the answer is YES, credit the revenue account or debit the expense account in the adjusting entry.

Step 2: Ask: **Was the related cash received or paid in the past or will it be received or paid in the future?**

If cash **was received** in the past, a deferred revenue (liability) account was recorded in the past → Now, reduce the liability account (usually Unearned Revenue) that was recorded when cash was received, because some or all of the liability has been earned since then.

If cash **will be received** in the future → Increase the receivable account (such as Interest Receivable or Rent Receivable) to record what is owed by others to the company (creating an accrued revenue).

If cash **was paid** in the past, a deferred expense account (asset) was created in the past → Now reduce the asset account (such as Supplies or Prepaid Expenses) that was recorded in the past, because some of or the entire asset has been used since then.

If cash **will be paid** in the future → Increase the payable account (such as Interest Payable or Wages Payable) to record what is owed by the company to others (creating an accrued expense).

NOTE: Cash is never included in the adjusting entry, because it was recorded already in the past or will be recorded in the future.

Step 3: Compute the amount of revenue earned or expense incurred. Sometimes the amount is given or known, sometimes it must be computed, and sometimes it must be estimated.

In summary, the pattern that results when the adjusting entry is recorded is as follows:

When revenue is earned, the adjusting entry is:
DEFERRED REVENUE if cash was received and previously recorded ↓
Unearned Revenue (−L) xx   Revenue (+R, +SE) xx
OR
ACCRUED REVENUE if cash will be received ↓
Receivable (+A) xx   Revenue (+R, +SE) xx

When expense is incurred, the adjusting entry is:
Expense (+E, −SE) xx   Prepaid Expense (−A) xx
↑ **DEFERRED EXPENSE** if cash was paid and previously recorded OR
Expense (+E, −SE) xx   Payable (+L) xx
↑ **ACCRUED EXPENSE** if cash will be paid

Now let's illustrate the adjustment process for Chipotle at the end of the first quarter of 2012. We start by reviewing the unadjusted trial balance from Chapter 3 with one modification (highlighted):

CHIPOTLE MEXICAN GRILL
Unadjusted Trial Balance
For the first quarter ended March 31, 2012

(in thousands)	Debit	Credit
Cash	370,000	
Short-term investments	94,500	
Accounts receivable	9,100	
Supplies	216,600	
Prepaid expenses	113,700	
Property and equipment (*cost*)	1,217,100	
Accumulated depreciation (*used cost*)		370,000
Long-term investments	149,100	
Accounts payable		49,200
Accrued expenses payable		1,600
Dividends payable		3,000
Unearned revenue		33,400
Notes payable		233,200
Common stock		400
Additional paid-in capital		434,600
Retained earnings		668,500
Restaurant sales revenue		619,300
Investment income		4,700
Salaries and wages expense	138,600	
Occupancy expense	10,000	
Other operating expenses	48,600	
General and administrative expenses	49,300	
Gain (loss) on disposal of assets	1,300	
Total	**2,417,900**	**2,417,900**

— *This represents the historical cost of the property and equipment.*

— *This represents the total amount of cost used in prior periods to generate revenues.*

Cost $1,217,100
− Used cost   370,000
* $ 847,100 Property and Equipment (net)*
as presented in the prior
chapters for reporting purposes.

} *Total unadjusted revenues = $624,000*

} *Total unadjusted expenses and losses = $247,800*

From a review of the unadjusted trial balance on the previous page, we identify several accounts that may need an adjustment:

- One deferred revenue account:
    Unearned Revenue representing the amount received from customers on gift cards. A portion may have been earned during the quarter.

- One accrued revenue:
    Interest on investments may have been earned but not yet received by the end of the quarter.

- Three deferred expense accounts:
    Supplies of food, beverage, and packaging were used during the period.
    Prepaid Expenses relating to rent, insurance, and advertising paid in the past were partially used during the period.
    Property and Equipment was used during the period to generate revenue. As explained in the margin of the unadjusted trial balance, the cost of property and equipment is maintained in a separate account from the accumulated amount of cost used to generate revenue in prior periods. Because property and equipment was used during the quarter, we must make an adjustment to reflect that in the Accumulated Depreciation account.

- Four accrued expenses:
    Salaries and wages, utilities, interest on notes payable, and income taxes may need to be adjusted for amounts incurred during the quarter but not yet paid. These would be included in Accrued Expenses Payable.

For each of the following adjustments, we shorten the term **adjusting journal entry** to AJE for ease of labeling. Also, as you learned in Chapters 2 and 3, it is important to continue to check that debits equal credits in each entry and that the accounting equation remains in balance. In the following adjustments, all entries and the accounting equation are in balance.

Deferred Revenues

When a customer pays for goods or services before the company delivers them, the company records the amount of cash received in a deferred (unearned) revenue account. This unearned revenue is a liability representing the company's promise to perform or deliver the goods or services in the future. Recognition of (recording) the revenue is postponed (deferred) until the company meets its obligation.

DEFERRED (UNEARNED) REVENUES are previously recorded liabilities that need to be adjusted at the end of the accounting period to reflect the amount of revenue earned.

AJE 1   **Unearned Revenue** Chipotle received cash last period from customers purchasing gift cards and recorded an increase in Cash and an increase in Unearned Revenues, a liability, to recognize the business's obligation to provide future services to customers. During the first quarter of 2012, customers redeemed the gift cards for $21,300 in food service.

Step 1: Was revenue earned that is not yet recorded? **Yes.** When customers redeemed their gift cards, Chipotle provided food service. Therefore, Chipotle has earned $21,300 in Restaurant Sales Revenue that is not yet recorded. Record an increase in the revenue account.

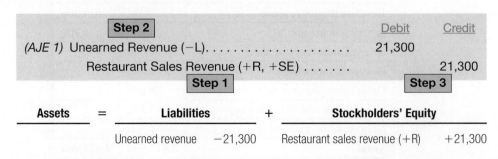

	Step 2	Debit	Credit
(AJE 1) Unearned Revenue (−L).		21,300	
Restaurant Sales Revenue (+R, +SE)			21,300
	Step 1	**Step 3**	

Assets	=	Liabilities	+	Stockholders' Equity
		Unearned revenue −21,300		Restaurant sales revenue (+R) +21,300

Step 2: Was the related cash received in the past or will it be received in the future? **In the past.** The Unearned Revenue account was created when cash was received in the past. At the end of the quarter, there is a $33,400 balance in the account. However, it is too large because a portion of it has been earned. Therefore, reduce the unearned revenue account for the amount earned.

Step 3: Compute the amount of revenue earned. The amount of the revenue that was earned is given as $21,300. Record this amount in the adjusting journal entry.

Additional examples of deferred revenues include magazine subscription sales by publishing companies; season tickets sold in advance to sporting events, plays, and concerts by these types of organizations; air flight tickets sold in advance by airlines; and rent received in advance by landlords. Each of these requires an adjusting entry at the end of the accounting period to report the amount of revenue earned during the period.

Accrued Revenues

Sometimes companies perform services or provide goods (that is, earn revenue) before customers pay. Because the cash that is owed for these goods and services has not yet been received and the customers have not yet been billed, the revenue that was earned may not have been recorded. Revenues that have been earned but have not yet been recorded at the end of the accounting period are called **accrued revenues.**

AJE 2 **Interest on Investments** Investments owned by Chipotle earned $200 in additional investment income for the quarter, but the cash has not yet been received.

Step 1: Was revenue earned that is not yet recorded? **Yes.** Investments earned an additional amount during the quarter, but no Investment Income has yet been recorded. Revenue is understated. Record an increase in the revenue account.

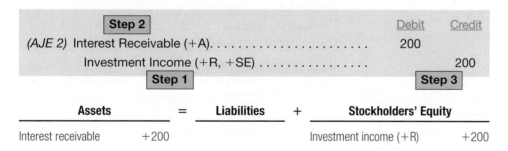

Step 2: Was the related cash received in the past or will it be received in the future? **In the future.** Chipotle will receive the cash from the investment income in the next quarter. Because cash will be received, a receivable needs to be increased. Increase Interest Receivable.

Step 3: Compute the amount of revenue earned. The amount of the revenue that was earned is given as $200. Record this amount in the adjusting journal entry

Deferred Expenses

Assets represent resources with probable future benefits to the company. Many assets are used over time to generate revenues, including supplies, buildings, equipment, prepaid insurance, prepaid advertising, and prepaid rent. These assets are deferred expenses. At the end of every period, an adjustment must be made to record the amount of the asset that was used during the period.

AJE 3 **Supplies** Supplies include food, beverage, and paper products for Chipotle. At the end of the quarter, Chipotle counted $10,000 in supplies on hand, but the Supplies account indicated a balance of $216,600 (from the unadjusted trial balance on page 165).

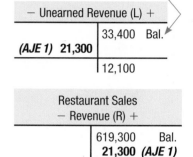

NOTE: The beginning balance for each T-account is from the 3/31/12 unadjusted trial balance on page 165.

− Unearned Revenue (L) +	
	33,400 Bal.
(AJE 1) **21,300**	
	12,100

Restaurant Sales − Revenue (R) +	
	619,300 Bal.
	21,300 *(AJE 1)*
	640,600

ACCRUED REVENUES are previously unrecorded revenues that need to be adjusted at the end of the accounting period to reflect the amount earned and the related receivable account.

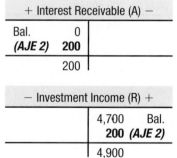

+ Interest Receivable (A) −	
Bal. 0	
(AJE 2) **200**	
200	

− Investment Income (R) +	
	4,700 Bal.
	200 *(AJE 2)*
	4,900

DEFERRED EXPENSES are previously acquired assets that need to be adjusted at the end of the accounting period to reflect the amount of expense incurred in using the assets to generate revenue.

Step 1: Was expense incurred that is not yet recorded? Yes. Supplies were used during the quarter to generate revenue, but no entry has been made to record the amount used. Expenses are understated. Record an increase in the Food, Beverage, and Packaging Expense account (also called Supplies Expense by many companies).

		Debit	Credit
Step 1			
(AJE 3) Food, Beverage, and Packaging Expense (+E, −SE).		206,600	
Supplies (−A)			206,600
Step 2		**Step 3**	

Assets	=	Liabilities	+	Stockholders' Equity	
Supplies −206,600				Food, beverage, and packaging expense (+E)	−206,600

Step 2: Was the related cash paid in the past or will it be paid in the future? In the past. Chipotle purchased supplies during the quarter and recorded the acquisition in the Supplies account. Some of these supplies have been used during the quarter, but no entry has been made yet to reduce the account. Assets are overstated. Record a decrease in the Supplies account.

Step 3: Compute the amount of expense incurred. The easiest way to determine the dollar amount of supplies used is to add the dollar amount of supplies available at the beginning of the period plus any purchases made during the period, and then subtract the dollar amount of supplies remaining on hand at the end of the period.

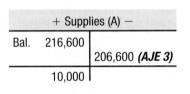

+ Supplies (A) −	
Bal. 216,600	
	206,600 *(AJE 3)*
10,000	

Food, Beverage, and + Packaging Expense (E) −	
Bal. 0	
(AJE 3) 206,600	
206,600	

Computation of Supplies Expense	
Beginning balance—Supplies	$ 8,900
+ Purchases during quarter	207,700
Unadjusted balance	216,600
− Amount on hand at end of quarter	(10,000)
Supplies used during quarter	$206,600

The balance of Supplies on the unadjusted trial balance is $216,600 which includes the beginning balance for the quarter ($8,900) and the purchases during the quarter ($207,700). With $10,000 remaining on hand, the amount of supplies used during the period is $206,600. Add this amount in the adjusting entry.

AJE 4 **Prepaid Expenses** The Prepaid Expenses account includes:

- $36,000 paid at the beginning of the quarter for rental of facilities at $6,000 per month,
- $32,000 for insurance coverage for one year beginning January 2012, and
- $20,000 for advertising paid at the beginning of the quarter for advertisements to be placed during the quarter.

Step 1: Was expense incurred that is not yet recorded? Yes. A portion of the rent and insurance and all of the advertising have been used during the quarter to generate revenue, but no entry has been made to record the amount used. Expenses are understated. Since rent, insurance, and advertising are categorized as occupancy expenses, record an increase in the Occupancy Expense account. (Some companies would record these separately as Rent Expense, Insurance Expense, and Advertising Expense, as you may use in several assignments.)

		Debit	Credit
Step 1			
(AJE 4) Occupancy Expense (+E, −SE).		46,000	
Prepaid Expenses (−A)			46,000
Step 2		**Step 3**	

Assets	=	Liabilities	+	Stockholders' Equity	
Prepaid expenses −46,000				Occupancy expense (+E) −46,000	

Step 2: **Was the related cash paid in the past or will it be paid in the future? In the past.** Chipotle prepaid rent, insurance, and advertising at the beginning of the quarter. These provided probable future benefits and were recorded as an asset Prepaid Expenses. Because a portion of these prepaid expenses have been used during the quarter, but no entry has been made yet to reflect that, Prepaid Expenses are overstated. Record a decrease in the Prepaid Expenses account.

Step 3: **Compute the amount of expense incurred.** The computations for each are as follows:

- Rent: $36,000 × (3 months in the quarter / 6 months prepaid) = **$18,000** rent used.
- Insurance: $32,000 prepaid × (3 months in the quarter / 12 months coverage) = **$8,000** insurance used.
- Advertising: **$20,000** all used during the quarter.

   Total expense = $18,000 + $8,000 + $20,000 = **$46,000**

+ Prepaid Expenses (A) −	
Bal. 113,700	
	46,000 **(AJE 4)**
67,700	

+ Occupancy Expense (E) −	
Bal. 10,000	
(AJE 4) 46,000	
56,000	

AJE 5 **Property and Equipment** Before illustrating the adjustment process for buildings and equipment, notice that the Property and Equipment account is stated at the original cost of $1,217,100 in the unadjusted trial balance but was shown at a lower **net** amount in previous chapters. Unlike supplies, which are purchased and then used over a relatively short period, buildings and equipment represent deferred expenses that will be used over many years. Buildings and equipment accounts increase by the cost of the assets when they are **acquired** and decrease by the cost of the assets when they are **sold.** However, these assets are also **used** over time to generate revenue. Thus, a part of their cost should be expensed in the same period (the expense matching principle). Accountants say that buildings and equipment **depreciate** over time as they are used. In accounting, **depreciation is an allocation of an asset's cost over its estimated useful life to the organization.**

To keep track of the asset's historical cost, the amount that has been used is not subtracted directly from the asset account. Instead, it is accumulated in a new kind of account called a **contra-account.** Contra-accounts are accounts that are **directly linked to another account, but with an opposite balance.** For Property and Equipment, the contra-account for the total cost used to date is called **Accumulated Depreciation.** This is the first of several contra-accounts you will learn throughout the text. We will designate contra-accounts with an X in front of the type of account to which it is related. For example, this first contra-account will be shown as Accumulated Depreciation (XA).

Since assets have debit balances, Accumulated Depreciation has a credit balance. On the balance sheet, the amount that is reported for Property and Equipment is its **net book value** (also called the **book value** or **carrying value**), which equals the ending balance in the Property and Equipment account (cost) minus the ending balance in the Accumulated Depreciation account (used cost).

A CONTRA-ACCOUNT is an account that is an offset to, or reduction of, the primary account.

The NET BOOK VALUE (BOOK VALUE, CARRYING VALUE) of an asset is the difference between its acquisition cost and accumulated depreciation, its related contra-account.

+ Property and Equipment (A) −		− Accumulated Depreciation (XA) +		Amount reported on the balance sheet
		Accumulated portion of asset cost used when sold	Beginning bal. Portion of asset cost used during period	
Beginning bal. Buy (cost)	Sell (cost)			
Ending bal.		—	Ending bal.	= Net book value

For Chipotle, Accumulated Depreciation has a credit balance of $370,000.

On the balance sheet (based on unadjusted balances):
   Property and equipment (net of accumulated depreciation of $370,000) $847,100

Depreciation is discussed in much greater detail in Chapter 8. Until then, we will give you the amount of depreciation estimated by the company for the period. Chipotle estimates depreciation to be $80,400 per year.

Step 1: **Was expense incurred that is not yet recorded? Yes.** The company used buildings and equipment during the first quarter of 2012. However, no expense has yet been recorded, so expenses are understated. Record an increase in the expense account, Depreciation Expense.

Step 1	Debit	Credit
(AJE 5) Depreciation Expense (+E, −SE).	20,100	
Accumulated Depreciation (+XA, −A)		20,100

Step 2   **Step 3**

Assets	=	Liabilities	+	Stockholders' Equity
Accumulated depreciation (+XA) −20,100				Depreciation expense (+E) −20,100

Accumulated	
− Depreciation (XA, −A) +	
	370,000 Bal.
	20,100 *(AJE 5)*
	390,100

+ Depreciation Expense (E) −	
Bal. 0	
(AJE 5) 20,100	
20,100	

Step 2: **Was the related cash paid in the past or will it be paid in the future? In the past.** Chipotle purchased property and equipment in the past to be used over several years. The acquisitions were recorded in the asset account Property and Equipment, which maintains the historical cost of the assets. The amount to be used in the future (net book value) must now be reduced for the depreciation for the first quarter of 2012. Reduce the net book value by increasing the contra-account Accumulated Depreciation.

Step 3: **Compute the amount of expense incurred.** The property and equipment has been used to generate revenue for the quarter. Thus, we need to calculate one quarter of Depreciation Expense:

$$\text{Depreciation for the quarter} = \$80,400 \text{ annual depreciation (given)} \times \tfrac{1}{4} \text{ of the year}$$
$$= \$20,100 \text{ depreciation for the quarter}$$

Accrued Expenses

Numerous expenses are incurred in the current period without being paid for until the next period. Common examples include Salaries Expense for the wages owed to employees, Utilities Expense for the water, gas, and electricity used during the period, and the Interest Expense incurred on debt. These accrued expenses accumulate (accrue) over time but are not recognized until the end of the period in an adjusting entry.

ACCRUED EXPENSES are previously unrecorded expenses that need to be adjusted at the end of the accounting period to reflect the amount incurred and the related payable account.

AJE 6 **Salaries and Wages** Chipotle's employees earned $13,400 in salaries and wages for working two days at the end of the quarter. They will be paid in the next quarter.

Step 1: **Was expense incurred that is not yet recorded? Yes.** The company used employee labor near the end of the first quarter of 2012. However, no expense has yet been recorded, so expenses are understated. Record an increase in the expense account, Salaries and Wages Expense.

Step 1	Debit	Credit
(AJE 6) Salaries and Wages Expense (+E, −SE).	13,400	
Accrued Expenses Payable (+L).		13,400

Step 2   **Step 3**

Assets	=	Liabilities	+	Stockholders' Equity
		Accrued expenses payable +13,400		Salaries and wages expense (+E) −13,400

Accrued Expenses	
− Payable (L) +	
	1,600 Bal.
	13,400 *(AJE 6)*
	15,000

Salaries and Wages	
+ Expense (E) −	
Bal. 138,600	
(AJE 6) 13,400	
152,000	

Step 2: **Was the related cash paid in the past or will it be paid in the future? In the future.** Chipotle will pay the employees in the next quarter, but no liability has yet been recorded. Because liabilities are understated, record an increase in Accrued Expenses Payable.

Step 3: Compute the amount of expense incurred. The amount of the salaries and wages owed to employees is given at $13,400.

AJE 7   **Interest on Debt** Chipotle owed $233,200 in notes payable during the quarter. There are two components when borrowing (or lending) money: **principal** (the amount borrowed or loaned) and **interest** (the cost of borrowing or lending). The average interest rate on Chipotle's borrowings is 7.7 percent. Notes Payable (the principal) was recorded properly when the money was borrowed. Its balance does not need to be adjusted. However, interest expense is incurred by Chipotle over time as the money is used.

Step 1: Was expense incurred that is not yet recorded? **Yes.** Chipotle used borrowed funds during the quarter, but the expense has not yet been recognized. Expenses are understated. Record an increase in the Interest Expense account.

	Step 1	Debit	Credit
(AJE 7)	Interest Expense (+E, −SE).	4,500	
	Accrued Expenses Payable (+L).		4,500
	Step 2	Step 3	

Assets	=	Liabilities		+	Stockholders' Equity	
		Accrued expenses payable	+4,500		Interest expense (+E)	−4,500

Step 2: Was the related cash paid in the past or will it be paid in the future? **In the future.** Chipotle will pay interest on the debt in the future. Because cash is owed, a payable account needs to be increased. Increase Accrued Expenses Payable.

Step 3: Compute the amount of expense incurred. **NOTE: Unless told otherwise, the interest rate on loans to others and borrowings is always given as an annual percentage.** To compute interest expense on notes payable for less than a full year, the number of months needed in the calculation is divided by 12. Because the borrowings were outstanding for most of the quarter, the formula to compute interest expense is:

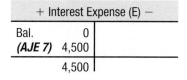

Principal	×	Rate per year	×	Number of Months (since last computation) / 12	=	Interest for the Period
$233,200	×	.077	×	3 months / 12 months	=	$4,500 (rounded to the nearest hundred)

AJE 8   **Utilities** Most organizations receive utility bills after using utility services such as electricity, natural gas, and telephone. Chipotle received a utility bill for $4,400 for usage during the quarter. The bill will be paid next quarter.

Step 1: Was expense incurred that is not yet recorded? **Yes.** Chipotle used the utilities during the first quarter, but has not yet recorded the expense. Since expenses are understated, increase Occupancy Expense.

	Step 1	Debit	Credit
(AJE 8)	Occupancy Expense (+E, −SE).	4,400	
	Accrued Expenses Payable (+L).		4,400
	Step 2	Step 3	

Assets	=	Liabilities		+	Stockholders' Equity	
		Accrued expenses payable	+4,400		Occupancy expense (+E)	−4,400

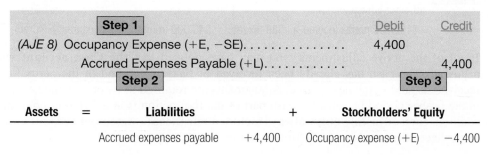

Accrued Expenses – Payable (L) +

	1,600	Bal.
	13,400	(AJE 6)
	4,500	(AJE 7)
	4,400	**(AJE 8)**
	23,900	

+ Occupancy Expense (E) –

Bal.	10,000	
(AJE 4)	46,000	
(AJE 8)	4,400	
	60,400	

Step 2: Was the related cash paid in the past or will it be paid in the future? **In the future.** Chipotle will pay next quarter the utility bill owed for usage in the first quarter. The liability is understated. Increase the Accrued Expenses Payable account.

Step 3: Compute the amount of expense incurred. The amount of the utilities incurred in the first quarter is given as $4,400.

AJE 9 **Income Taxes** The final adjusting entry is to record the accrual of income taxes that will be paid in the next quarter. This requires computing adjusted pretax income—the balances in the revenue and expense accounts from the unadjusted trial balance plus the effect of all of the other adjustments:

	Revenues and Gains	–	Expenses and Losses	
On unadjusted trial balance	$624,000		$247,800	
AJE 1	21,300			
AJE 2	200			
AJE 3			206,600	
AJE 4			46,000	
AJE 5			20,100	
AJE 6			13,400	
AJE 7			4,500	
AJE 8			4,400	
	$645,500	–	$542,800	= **$102,700 Pretax Income**

Chipotle estimated a tax rate of 38.9 percent for the quarter, with the taxes due to be paid next quarter.

Step 1: Was expense incurred that is not yet recorded? **Yes.** Chipotle incurred taxes on its quarterly income. Until an adjusting entry is recorded at the end of the period based on all adjusted revenues, gains, expenses, and losses, expenses on the income statement are understated. Record an increase in Income Tax Expense.

Step 1		Debit	Credit
(AJE 9) Income Tax Expense (+E, −SE).		40,000	
Accrued Expenses Payable (+L).			40,000
	Step 2	Step 3	

Assets	=	Liabilities	+	Stockholders' Equity
		Accrued expenses payable +40,000		Income tax expense (+E) −40,000

Accrued Expenses – Payable (L) +

	1,600	Bal.
	13,400	(AJE 6)
	4,500	(AJE 7)
	4,400	(AJE 8)
	40,000	**(AJE 9)**
	63,900	

+ Income Tax Expense (E) –

Bal.	0	
(AJE 9)	40,000	
	40,000	

Step 2: Was the related cash paid in the past or will it be paid in the future? **In the future.** Income taxes from the first quarter are due by the end of the second quarter. So the liabilities on the balance sheet must be increased. Increase Accrued Expenses Payable.

Step 3: Compute the amount of expense incurred. Income taxes are computed on the pretax income after all other adjustments:

$102,700 pretax income × .389 tax rate = $40,000 (rounded to the nearest hundred)

In all of the above adjustments, you may have noticed that **the Cash account was never adjusted.** The cash has already been received or paid by the end of the period, or will be received or paid in the next period. Adjustments are required to record revenues and expenses in the proper period because the cash part of the transaction is at a different point in time. In addition, **each adjusting entry always included one income statement account and one balance sheet account.** Now it's your turn to practice the adjustment process.

Adjustments are necessary at the end of the accounting cycle to record all revenues and expenses in the proper period and to reflect the proper valuation for assets and liabilities.

- **Deferred revenues** (liabilities) have balances at the end of the period because cash was received before it was earned. If all or part of the liability has been satisfied by the end of the period, revenue needs to be recorded and the liability reduced.

- **Accrued revenue** adjustments are necessary when the company has earned revenue, but the cash will be received in the next period. Since nothing has yet been recorded, revenue needs to be recognized and an asset (a receivable) increased.

- **Deferred expenses** (assets) have balances at the end of the period because cash was paid in the past by the company for the assets. If all or part of the asset has been used to generate revenues in the period, an expense needs to be recorded and the asset reduced.

- **Accrued expense** adjustments are necessary when the company has incurred an expense but the cash will be paid in the next period. Since nothing has yet been recorded, an expense needs to be recognized and a liability (a payable) increased.

SELF-STUDY QUIZ

For practice, complete the following adjustments using the three-step process outlined in the chapter: (1) Determine if revenue was earned or an expense incurred; (2) determine if cash was received or paid in the past or will be received or paid in the future; and (3) compute the amount.

Florida Flippers, a scuba diving and instruction business, completed its first year of operations on December 31, 2014.

AJE 1: Florida Flippers received $6,000 from customers on November 15, 2014, for diving trips to the Bahamas in December and January. The $6,000 was recorded in Unearned Revenue on that date. By the end of December, one-third of the diving trips had been completed.

AJE 2: On December 31, 2014, Florida Flippers provided advanced diving instruction to 10 customers who will pay the business $800 in January. No entry was made when the instruction was provided.

AJE 3: On September 1, 2014, Florida Flippers paid $24,000 for insurance for the 12 months beginning on September 1. The amount was recorded as Prepaid Insurance on September 1.

AJE 4: On March 1, 2014, Florida Flippers borrowed $300,000 at 12 percent. Interest is payable each March 1 for three years.

	(1) Revenue earned or expense incurred?	(2) Cash received/paid in the past or cash to be received/paid in the future?	(3) Amount	Adjusting Journal Entry		
				Accounts	Debit	Credit
AJE 1	yes rev. earned	received in past	2000	unearned revenue / diving trip rev.	2000	2000
AJE 2	yes rev. earn	cash received in future	800	acct. receivable / instruct. rev.	800	800
AJE 3	expense incurred	cash paid past deferred exp.	8000	Insurance Expense / Prepaid Ins.	8000	8000
AJE 4	expense incured	cash paid in future	30,000	Intrest Expense / Intrest Pay.	30,000	30,000

After you have completed your answers, check them with the solutions at the bottom of the next page.

GUIDED HELP

For additional step-by-step video instruction on recording adjusting entries, go to the URL or scan the QR code in the margin with your smartphone or iPad.

A QUESTION OF ETHICS   Adjustments and Incentives

Owners and managers of companies are most directly affected by the information presented in financial statements. If the financial performance and condition of the company appear strong, the company's stock price rises. Shareholders usually receive dividends and increase their investment value. Managers often receive bonuses based on the strength of a company's financial performance, and many in top management are compensated with options to buy their company's stock at prices below market value. The higher the market value, the more compensation they earn. When actual performance lags behind expectations, managers and owners may be tempted to manipulate accruals and deferrals to make up part of the difference. For example, managers may record cash received in advance of being earned as revenue in the current period or may fail to accrue certain expenses at year-end.

Evidence from studies of large samples of companies indicates that some managers do engage in such behavior. This research is borne out by enforcement actions of the Securities and Exchange Commission against companies and sometimes against their auditors. In January 2003, an SEC study reported that, in a five-year period, there were 227 enforcement investigations. Of these, "126 involved improper revenue recognition and 101 involved improper expense recognition. . . . Of the 227 enforcement matters during the Study period, 157 resulted in charges against at least one senior manager. . . . Furthermore, the Study found that 57 enforcement matters resulted in charges for auditing violations. . . ." (p. 47).*

In many of these cases, the firms involved, their managers, and their auditors are penalized for such actions. Furthermore, owners suffer because news of an SEC investigation negatively affects the company's stock price.

*These statistics are reported in the Securities and Exchange Commission's study, "Report Pursuant to Section 704 of the Sarbanes-Oxley Act of 2002," January 27, 2003.

Solutions to SELF-STUDY QUIZ

	(1) Revenue earned or expense incurred?	(2) Cash received/paid in the past or cash to be received/paid in the future?	(3) Amount	Adjusting Journal Entry		
				Accounts	Debit	Credit
AJE 1	Diving Trip Revenue earned	Received in past: *Unearned Revenue*	$6,000 × 1/3 = $2,000 earned	Unearned Revenue (−L) Diving Trip Revenue (+R, +SE)	2,000	2,000
AJE 2	Instruction Revenue earned	To be received: *Accrued Revenue*	$800 earned (given)	Accounts Receivable (+A) Instruction Revenue (+R, +SE)	800	800
AJE 3	Insurance Expense incurred	Paid in past: *Prepaid Expense*	$24,000 × 4 months/ 12 = $8,000 used	Insurance Expense (+E, −SE) Prepaid Insurance (−A)	8,000	8,000
AJE 4	Interest Expense incurred	To be paid: *Accrued Expense*	$300,000 × .12 × 10/12 = $30,000 incurred and owed	Interest Expense (+E, −SE) Interest Payable (+L)	30,000	30,000

PREPARING FINANCIAL STATEMENTS

As you learned in Chapter 1, the financial statements are interrelated—that is, the numbers from one statement flow into the next statement. The following illustration highlights the interconnections among the statements using the fundamental accounting equation.

Also notice special labels for the accounts. Balance sheet accounts are considered **permanent,** indicating that they retain their balances from the end of one period to the beginning of the next. Revenue, expense, gain, and loss accounts are **temporary** accounts because their balances accumulate for a period but start with a zero balance at the beginning of the next period. These labels will be discussed in the section on closing the books, which follows our presentation of Chipotle's financial statements.

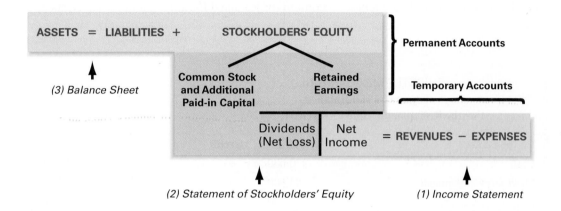

Starting on the bottom right, notice that

- Revenues minus expenses yields net income on the **Income Statement.**
- Net income (or net loss) and dividends to stockholders affect Retained Earnings and any additional issuances of stock during the period affect the balance in Common Stock and Additional Paid-in Capital, all of which appear on the **Statement of Stockholders' Equity.**
- Stockholders' Equity is a component of the **Balance Sheet.**

Thus, if a number on the income statement changes or is in error, it will impact the other statements.

Another way of presenting the relationships among the statements is illustrated below.

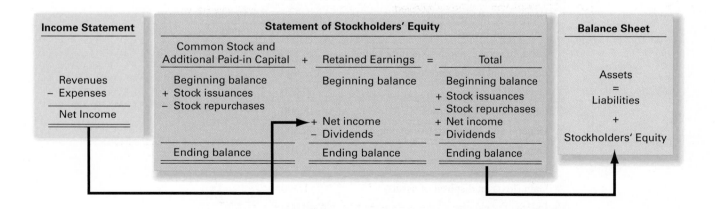

Before we prepare a complete set of financial statements, let's update the trial balance to reflect the adjustments and the adjusted balances for the statements. Any account that changed due to adjustments is highlighted. The balances are taken from the T-accounts in the margin next to each adjustment. For example, in the case of Accrued Expenses Payable, the balance is from the last adjustment (AJE 9) made to the account. Again, we note that the total debits equal the total credits in each of the columns. Also notice that nearly every revenue and expense account was adjusted, and several new accounts were created during the adjustment process at the end of the period (e.g., Interest Receivable and Depreciation Expense).

It is from these adjusted balances that we will prepare an income statement, a statement of stockholders' equity (which includes a column for Retained Earnings), and a balance sheet.

CHIPOTLE MEXICAN GRILL
Adjusted Trial Balance
For the first quarter ended March 31, 2012

(in thousands)	Debit	Credit
Cash	370,000	
Short-term investments	94,500	
Accounts receivable	9,100	
Interest receivable	200	
Supplies	10,000	
Prepaid expenses	67,700	
Property and equipment (*cost*)	1,217,100	
Accumulated depreciation (*used cost*)		390,100
Long-term investments	149,100	
Accounts payable		49,200
Accrued expenses payable		63,900
Dividends payable		3,000
Unearned revenue		12,100
Notes payable		233,200
Common stock		400
Additional paid-in capital		434,600
Retained earnings		668,500
Restaurant sales revenue		640,600
Investment income		4,900
Food, beverage, and packaging expense	206,600	
Salaries and wages expense	152,000	
Occupancy expense	60,400	
Other operating expenses	48,600	
General and administrative expenses	49,300	
Depreciation expense	20,100	
Interest expense	4,500	
Gain (loss) on disposal of assets	1,300	
Income tax expense	40,000	
Total	**2,500,500**	**2,500,500**

new

NOTE: Cash did not change because cash is never adjusted.

Income Statement

The income statement is prepared first because net income is a component of Retained Earnings. The first quarter 2012 income statement for Chipotle based on the adjusted trial balance follows.

CHIPOTLE MEXICAN GRILL, INC. Consolidated Statement of Income For the Quarter ended March 31, 2012 (in thousands of dollars, except per share data)	
Restaurant sales revenue	$640,600
Restaurant operating expenses:	
Food, beverage, and packaging	206,600
Salaries and wages	152,000
Occupancy	60,400
Other operating expenses	48,600
General and administrative expenses	49,300
Depreciation expense	20,100
Total operating expenses	537,000
Income from operations	103,600
Other items:	
Investment income	4,900
Interest expense	(4,500)
Gain (loss) on disposal of assets	(1,300)
Income before income taxes	102,700
Income tax expense	40,000
Net income	$ 62,700
Earnings per share (for the quarter)	$1.73

You will note that the earnings per share (EPS) ratio is reported on the income statement. It is widely used in evaluating the operating performance and profitability of a company, and it is the only ratio required to be disclosed on the statement or in the notes to the statements. The actual computation of the ratio is quite complex and appropriate for more advanced accounting courses. In this text, we simplify the earnings per share computation as:

$$\text{Earnings per Share*} = \frac{\text{Net income}}{\text{Average number of shares of common stock outstanding** during the period}}$$

---

*If there are preferred dividends (discussed in Chapter 11), the amount is subtracted from net income in the numerator. In addition, the denominator is the weighted average of shares outstanding, a complex computation.

**Outstanding shares are those that are currently held by the shareholders.

The denominator in the EPS ratio is the average number of shares outstanding (the number at the beginning of the period plus the number at the end of the period, divided by 2). For Chipotle Mexican Grill, the number of shares at the end of 2011 was 31,217,000 (from the annual report) and we recorded an additional issuance of 10,000,000 shares at the end of the quarter.

$$\text{Average number of shares outstanding} = (31{,}217{,}000 \text{ at beginning} + 41{,}217{,}000 \text{ at ending}) \div 2$$
$$= 36{,}217{,}000 \text{ shares}$$

$$\text{EPS} = \frac{\$62{,}700{,}000 \text{ Net income for the quarter}}{36{,}217{,}000 \text{ average number of shares outstanding}} = \$1.73 \text{ for the quarter}$$

If this quarterly EPS is repeated in the next three quarters, an annual EPS of $6.92 is expected. This would be higher than the 2011 EPS of $6.89, suggesting continued growth.

Statement of Stockholders' Equity

The final total from the income statement, net income, is carried forward to the Retained Earnings column of the statement of stockholders' equity. To this, the additional elements of the statement are added. Dividends declared and an additional stock issuance (from prior chapters) are also included in the statement:

CHIPOTLE MEXICAN GRILL, INC.
Consolidated Statement of Stockholders' Equity
For the Quarter ended March 31, 2012
(in thousands of dollars)

	Common Stock	Additional Paid-in Capital	Retained Earnings	Total Stockholders' Equity
Balance at December 31, 2011	$300	$372,400	$671,500	$1,044,200
Additional stock issuance	100	62,200		62,300
Net income			62,700	62,700
Dividends declared			(3,000)	(3,000)
Balance at March 31, 2012	$400	$434,600	$731,200	$1,166,200

From transaction (a) in Ch. 2 → Additional stock issuance
From the income statement → Net income
From transaction (f) in Ch. 2 → Dividends declared
On the balance sheet → Balance at March 31, 2012

Balance Sheet

The ending balances for Common Stock, Additional Paid-in Capital, and Retained Earnings from the statement of stockholders' equity are included on the balance sheet that follows. You will notice that the contra-asset account, Accumulated Depreciation, has been subtracted from the Property and Equipment account to reflect **net book value** (or carrying value) at month-end for balance sheet purposes. Also recall that assets are listed in order of liquidity, and liabilities are listed in order of due dates. Current assets are those used or turned into cash within one year (as well as inventory). Current liabilities are obligations to be paid with current assets within one year. We present the balances at the end of 2011 and the balances at the end of the first quarter of 2012.

CHIPOTLE MEXICAN GRILL, INC.
Consolidated Balance Sheets
(in thousands of dollars, except per share data)

	March 31, 2012	December 31, 2011
ASSETS		
Current Assets:		
Cash	$ 370,000	$ 401,200
Short-term investments	94,500	55,000
Accounts receivable	9,100	8,400
Interest receivable	200	
Supplies	10,000	8,900
Prepaid expenses	67,700	27,700
Total current assets	551,500	501,200
Property and equipment (net)	827,000	795,900
Long-term investments	149,100	128,200
Total assets	$1,527,600	$1,425,300
LIABILITIES AND STOCKHOLDERS' EQUITY		
Current Liabilities:		
Accounts payable	$ 49,200	$ 46,400
Accrued expenses payable	63,900	93,100
Dividends payable	3,000	
Unearned revenue	12,100	18,000
Total current liabilities	128,200	157,500
Notes payable	233,200	223,600
Total liabilities	361,400	381,100
Stockholders' Equity:		
Common stock ($0.10 par per share)	400	300
Additional paid-in capital	434,600	372,400
Retained earnings	731,200	671,500
Total stockholders' equity	1,166,200	1,044,200
Total liabilities and stockholders' equity	$1,527,600	$1,425,300

Cash Flows from Operations, Net Income, and the Quality of Earnings

FOCUS ON CASH FLOWS

As presented in the previous chapters, the statement of cash flows explains the difference between the ending and beginning balances in the Cash account on the balance sheet during the accounting period. Put simply, the cash flow statement is a categorized list of all transactions of the period that affected the Cash account. The three categories are operating, investing, and financing activities. **Since no adjustments made in this chapter affected cash, the cash flow categories identified on the Cash T-account at the end of Chapter 3 remain the same.**

Many standard financial analysis texts warn analysts to look for unusual deferrals and accruals when they attempt to predict future periods' earnings. They often suggest that wide disparities between net

(*continued*)

income and cash flow from operations are a useful warning sign. For example, Subramanyan suggests the following:

> Accounting accruals determining net income rely on estimates, deferrals, allocations, and valuations. These considerations sometimes allow more subjectivity than do the factors determining cash flows. For this reason we often relate cash flows from operations to net income in assessing its quality. **Some users consider earnings of higher quality when the ratio of cash flows from operations divided by net income is greater.** This derives from a concern with revenue recognition or expense accrual criteria yielding high net income but low cash flows (emphasis added).*

The cash flows from operations to net income ratio is illustrated and discussed in more depth in Chapter 13.

*K. Subramanyan, *Financial Statement Analysis* (New York, McGraw-Hill/Irwin, 2009), p. 412.

KEY RATIO ANALYSIS

 Total Asset Turnover Ratio

? ANALYTICAL QUESTION

How efficient is management in using assets (its resources) to generate sales?

% RATIO AND COMPARISONS

LEARNING OBJECTIVE 4-3
Compute and interpret the total asset turnover ratio.

$$\text{Total Asset Turnover Ratio} = \frac{\text{Net Sales (or Operating Revenues)}}{\text{Average Total Assets*}}$$

*To compute "average": (Beginning balance + Ending balance)/2

The 2011 ratio for Chipotle is (dollars in thousands):

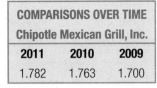

$$\frac{\$2,269,500 \text{ (from Exhibit 3.1)}}{\$1,273,450*} = 1.782$$

*($1,121,600 + $1,425,300)/2 (from 2011 10-K)

**Selected Focus Companies'
Total Asset Turnover Ratios
for 2011**

Southwest Airlines   .934

Harley-Davidson   .556

Home Depot   1.746

COMPARISONS OVER TIME			COMPARISONS WITH COMPETITORS	
Chipotle Mexican Grill, Inc.			Panera Bread, Inc.	Fiesta Restaurant Group, Inc.
2011	2010	2009	2011	2011
1.782	1.763	1.700	1.867	1.305

💡 INTERPRETATIONS

In General   The total asset turnover ratio measures the sales generated per dollar of assets. A high asset turnover ratio signifies efficient management of assets; a low asset turnover ratio signifies less efficient management. A company's products or services and business strategy contribute significantly to its asset turnover ratio. However, when competitors are similar, management's ability to control the firm's assets is vital in determining its success. Stronger financial performance improves the asset turnover ratio.

Creditors and security analysts use this ratio to assess a company's effectiveness at controlling both current and noncurrent assets. In a well-run business, creditors expect the ratio on a quarterly basis to fluctuate due to seasonal upswings and downturns. For example, as inventory is built up prior to a heavy sales season, companies need to borrow funds. The asset turnover ratio declines with this increase in assets. Eventually, the season's high sales provide the cash needed to repay the loans. The asset turnover ratio then rises with the increased sales.

Focus Company Analysis   Chipotle's total asset turnover ratio has increased slightly since 2009, suggesting an increase in management efficiency in using assets to generate sales. Compared to its competitors, Chipotle's total asset turnover ratio is slightly lower than Panera Bread, but higher than Fiesta Restaurant Group. This is due in part to differences in business strategies. Chipotle and Panera are the two largest fast casual restaurant chains. Chipotle's recent growth strategy is to open a higher percentage of new stores annually than Panera. Adding new restaurants increases total assets, but the increase in sales may lag behind until the stores are more well-established. In fact, Chipotle's total asset turnover ratio has remained about the same over five years of continued growth, whereas Panera Bread's ratio has fallen slightly and the ratio for Fiesta Restaurant Group, which is much smaller, has increased.

A Few Cautions   While the total asset turnover ratio may decrease due to seasonal fluctuations, a declining ratio may also be caused by changes in corporate policies leading to a rising level of assets. Examples include relaxing credit policies for new customers or reducing collection efforts in accounts receivable. A detailed analysis of the changes in the key components of assets is needed to determine the causes of a change in the asset turnover ratio and thus management's decisions.

CLOSING THE BOOKS
End of the Accounting Cycle

The ending balance in each of the asset, liability, and stockholders' equity accounts becomes the beginning account balance for the next period. These accounts, called **permanent (real) accounts,** are not reduced to a zero balance at the end of the accounting period. For example, the ending Cash balance of the prior accounting period is the beginning Cash balance of the next accounting period. The only time a permanent account has a zero balance is when the item it represents is no longer owned or owed.

On the other hand, revenue, expense, gain, and loss accounts are used to accumulate data for the **current accounting period only;** they are called **temporary (nominal) accounts.** The final step in the accounting cycle, closing the books, is done to prepare income statement accounts for the next accounting cycle. Therefore, at the end of each period, the balances in the temporary accounts are transferred, or **closed,** to the Retained Earnings account by recording a closing entry.

The **closing entry** has two purposes:

1. To transfer the balances in the temporary accounts (income statement accounts) to Retained Earnings.[1]

2. To establish a zero balance in each of the temporary accounts to start the accumulation in the next accounting period.

In this way, the income statement accounts are again ready for their temporary accumulation function for the next period. The closing entry is dated the last day of the accounting period, entered in the usual debits-equal-credits format (in the journal), and immediately posted to the ledger (or T-accounts). **Temporary accounts with debit balances are credited and temporary accounts with credit balances are debited.** The net amount, equal to net income, affects Retained Earnings.

LEARNING OBJECTIVE 4-4
Explain the closing process.

PERMANENT (REAL) ACCOUNTS are the balance sheet accounts that carry their ending balances into the next accounting period.

TEMPORARY (NOMINAL) ACCOUNTS are income statement accounts that are closed to Retained Earnings at the end of the accounting period.

A CLOSING ENTRY transfers balances in temporary accounts to Retained Earnings and establishes zero balances in temporary accounts.

---

[1]Companies may close income statement accounts to a special temporary summary account, called **Income Summary,** which is then closed to Retained Earnings.

To illustrate the process, we create an example using just a few accounts. The journal entry amounts are taken from the adjusted balances in the T-accounts:

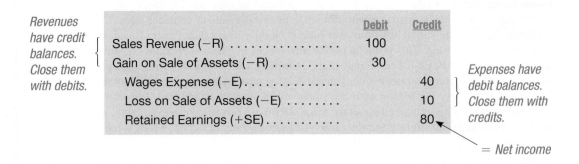

	Debit	Credit
Sales Revenue (−R)	100	
Gain on Sale of Assets (−R)	30	
Wages Expense (−E)...............		40
Loss on Sale of Assets (−E)		10
Retained Earnings (+SE)...........		80

Revenues have credit balances. Close them with debits.

Expenses have debit balances. Close them with credits.

= Net income

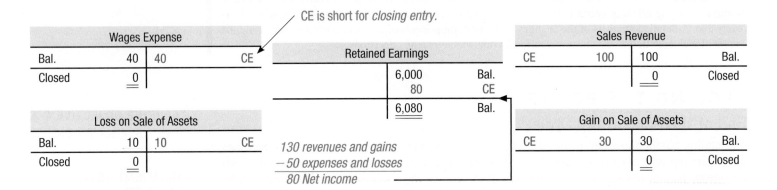

CE is short for *closing entry.*

Wages Expense			
Bal.	40	40	CE
Closed	0		

Retained Earnings			
		6,000	Bal.
		80	CE
		6,080	Bal.

Sales Revenue			
CE	100	100	Bal.
		0	Closed

Loss on Sale of Assets			
Bal.	10	10	CE
Closed	0		

130 revenues and gains
−50 expenses and losses
80 Net income

Gain on Sale of Assets			
CE	30	30	Bal.
		0	Closed

We will now prepare the closing entry (CE) for Chipotle at March 31, 2012, although companies close their records only at the end of the fiscal year.[2] These amounts are taken from the adjusted trial balance on page 176.

(CE)	Debit	Credit
Restaurant Sales Revenue (−R)	640,600	
Investment Income (−R)	4,900	
Food, Beverage, and Packaging Expense (−E) ...		206,600
Salaries and Wages Expense (−E)		152,000
Occupancy Expense (−E)		60,400
Other Operating Expenses (−E)		48,600
General and Administrative Expenses (−E).......		49,300
Depreciation Expense (−E)		20,100
Interest Expense (−E)		4,500
Gain (loss) on Disposal of Assets (−E)		1,300
Income Tax Expense (−E)		40,000
Retained Earnings (+SE)		62,700

[2]Most companies use computerized accounting software to record journal entries, produce trial balances and financial statements, and close the books.

The process of closing the books (after adjustments) includes making all temporary account balances (from the income statement) zero and transferring the difference to Retained Earnings. The following is an adjusted trial balance from a recent year for Toys R Us. Dollars are in millions. Record the journal entry at the end of the accounting cycle to close the books.

SELF-STUDY QUIZ

	DEBIT	CREDIT
Cash	783	
Accounts receivable	251	
Merchandise inventories	1,781	
Buildings	7,226	
Accumulated depreciation		3,039
Other assets	1,409	
Accounts payable		1,412
Accrued expenses payable		847
Long-term debt		5,447
Other liabilities		979
Contributed capital		19
Retained earnings (accumulated deficit)	399	
Sales revenue		13,724
Interest income		16
Gain on sale of business		5
Other income		130
Cost of sales	8,976	
Selling, general, and administrative expenses	3,968	
Depreciation expense	399	
Interest expense	419	
Income tax expense	7	
Totals	25,618	25,618

Closing entry:

Sales Rev

13875 debits — rev + gain

14168 credits — loss + expenses

= -293 net income

399 − 293 = 106

Switch debits and credits

retained earnings

After you have completed your answers, check them with the solutions at the bottom of the page.

	Debit	Credit
Sales revenue (−R)	13,724	
Interest income (−R)	16	
Gain on sale of business (−R)	5	
Other income (−R)	130	
Cost of sales (−E)		8,976
Selling, general, and administrative expenses (−E)		3,968
Depreciation expense (−E)		399
Interest expense (−E)		419
Income tax expense (−E)		7
Retained earnings (+SE)		106

Solutions to
SELF-STUDY QUIZ

Post-Closing Trial Balance

A POST-CLOSING TRIAL BALANCE should be prepared as an additional step of the accounting cycle to check that debits equal credits and all temporary accounts have been closed.

After the closing process is complete, all income statement accounts have a zero balance. These accounts are then ready for recording revenues and expenses in the new accounting period. The ending balance in Retained Earnings now is up-to-date (matches the amount on the balance sheet) and is carried forward as the beginning balance for the next period. As an additional step of the accounting information processing cycle, a post-closing trial balance should be prepared as a check that debits still equal credits and that all temporary accounts have been closed. The accounting cycle for the period is now complete.

DEMONSTRATION CASE

We take our final look at the accounting activities of Terrific Lawn Maintenance Corporation by illustrating the activities at the end of the accounting cycle: the adjustment process, financial statement preparation, and the closing process. No adjustments had been made to the accounts to reflect all revenues earned and expenses incurred in April. The trial balance for Terrific Lawn on April 30, 2014, based on the unadjusted balances in Chapter 3, is as follows:

TERRIFIC LAWN MAINTENANCE CORPORATION
Unadjusted Trial Balance at April 30, 2014

	Debit	Credit
Cash	5,032	
Accounts receivable	1,700	
Prepaid expenses	300	
Equipment *(cost)*	4,600	
Accumulated depreciation *(used cost)*		0
Land	3,750	
Accounts payable		220
Wages payable		0
Utilities payable		0
Short-term notes payable		400
Interest payable		0
Income tax payable		0
Unearned revenue		1,600
Long-term notes payable		3,300
Common stock		150
Additional paid-in capital		8,850
Retained earnings		0
Mowing revenue		5,200
Interest revenue		12
Wages expense	3,900	
Fuel expense	410	
Insurance expense	0	
Utilities expense	0	
Depreciation expense	0	
Interest expense	40	
Income tax expense	0	
Total	**19,732**	**19,732**

Additional information follows:

a. The $1,600 in Unearned Revenues represents four months of service from April through July.

b. Prepaid Expenses includes insurance costing $300 for coverage for six months (April through September).

c. Mowers, edgers, rakes, and hand tools (equipment) have been used in April to generate revenues. The company estimates $300 in depreciation each year.

d. Wages have been paid through April 28. Employees worked the last two days of April and will be paid in May. Wages accrue at $200 per day.

e. An extra telephone line was installed in April at an estimated cost of $52, including hookup and usage charges. No entry has yet been recorded. The bill will be received and paid in May.

f. Interest accrues on the outstanding short-term and long-term notes payable at an annual rate of 12 percent. The $3,700 total in principal has been outstanding all month.

g. The estimated income tax rate for Terrific Lawn is 35 percent.

Required:

1. Prepare the adjusting journal entries for April, using the account titles shown in the trial balance. In your analysis, be sure to use the three-step process outlined in this chapter: (1) Determine if a revenue was earned or an expense incurred that needs to be recorded for the period, (2) determine whether cash was or will be received or paid, and (3) compute the amount.

2. Prepare an adjusted trial balance.

3. Prepare an income statement, statement of stockholders' equity, and balance sheet from the amounts in the adjusted trial balance. Include earnings per share on the income statement. The company issued 1,500 shares.

4. Prepare the closing entry for April 30, 2014.

5. Compute the following ratios for the month:

    a. Current ratio

    b. Net profit margin

    c. Total asset turnover

Now you can check your answers with the following solutions.

SUGGESTED SOLUTION

1. Adjusting Entries

AJE	Debit	Credit
a. Unearned Revenue (−L)	400	
Mowing Revenue (+R, +SE)		400
$1,600 × 1/4 = $400 earned in April		
b. Insurance Expense (+E, −SE)	50	
Prepaid Expenses (−A)		50
$300 × 1/6 = $50 insurance used in April		

AJE	Debit	Credit
c. Depreciation Expense (+E, −SE)	25	
Accumulated Depreciation (+XA, −A)		25
$300 × 1/12 = $25 depreciation in April		
d. Wages Expense (+E, −SE)	400	
Wages Payable (+L)		400
$200 per day × 2 days = $400 incurred in April		
e. Utilities Expense (+E, −SE)	52	
Utilities Payable (+L)		52
$52 is estimated as incurred in April		
f. Interest Expense (+E, −SE)	37	
Interest Payable (+L)		37
$3,700 principal × .12 annual rate × 1/12 = $37 interest incurred in April		
g. Income Tax Expense (+E, −SE)	244	
Income Tax Payable (+L)		244

	Revenues	*Expenses*
Unadjusted balances	*$5,212*	*$4,350*
AJE (a)	*400*	
AJE (b)		*50*
AJE (c)		*25*
AJE (d)		*400*
AJE (e)		*52*
AJE (f)		*37*
Adjusted balances	*$5,612 −*	*$4,914 =*

$698 Pretax Income
× .35 tax rate
$244 (rounded)

2. Adjusted Trial Balance

TERRIFIC LAWN MAINTENANCE CORPORATION
Adjusted Trial Balance at April 30, 2014

	Debit	Credit
Cash	5,032	
Accounts receivable	1,700	
Prepaid expenses	250	
Equipment (*cost*)	4,600	
Accumulated depreciation (*used cost*)		25
Land	3,750	
Accounts payable		220
Wages payable		400
Utilities payable		52
Short-term notes payable		400
Interest payable		37
Income tax payable		244
Unearned revenue		1,200
Long-term notes payable		3,300
Common stock		150
Additional paid-in capital		8,850
Retained earnings		0
Mowing revenue		5,600
Interest revenue		12
Wages expense	4,300	
Fuel expense	410	
Insurance expense	50	
Utilities expense	52	
Depreciation expense	25	
Interest expense	77	
Income tax expense	244	
Total	**20,490**	**20,490**

3. Financial statements:

TERRIFIC LAWN MAINTENANCE CORPORATION
Income Statement
For the Month Ended April 30, 2014

Operating revenues:	
Mowing revenue	$5,600
Operating expenses:	
Wages expense	4,300
Fuel expense	410
Insurance expense	50
Utilities expense	52
Depreciation expense	25
	4,837
Operating income	763
Other items:	
Interest revenue	12
Interest expense	(77)
Pretax income	698
Income tax expense	244
Net Income	**$ 454**
Earnings per share (for the month) ($454 ÷ 1,500 shares)	$ .30

TERRIFIC LAWN MAINTENANCE CORPORATION
Statement of Stockholders' Equity
For the Month Ended April 30, 2014

	Common Stock	Additional Paid-in Capital	Retained Earnings	Total
Beginning April 1, 2014	$ 0	$ 0	$ 0	$ 0
Stock issuance	150	8,850		9,000
Net income			454	454
Dividends declared			0	0
Balance, April 30, 2014	$150	$8,850	$454	$9,454

TERRIFIC LAWN MAINTENANCE CORPORATION
Balance Sheet
April 30, 2014

Assets		**Liabilities**	
Current Assets:		Current Liabilities:	
Cash	$ 5,032	Accounts payable	$ 220
Accounts receivable	1,700	Wages payable	400
Prepaid expenses	250	Utilities payable	52
Total current assets	6,982	Short-term notes payable	400
		Interest payable	37
		Income tax payable	244
		Unearned revenue	1,200
		Total current liabilities	2,553
Equipment (net of $25		Long-term notes payable	3,300
accumulated depreciation)	4,575	**Stockholders' Equity**	
Land	3,750	Common stock	150
		Additional paid-in capital	8,850
		Retained earnings	454
		Total stockholders' equity	9,454
		Total liabilities and	
Total assets	**$15,307**	**stockholders' equity**	**$15,307**

4. Closing entry:

Mowing Revenue (−R)	5,600	
Interest Revenue (−R)	12	
Wages Expense (−E)		4,300
Fuel Expense (−E)		410
Insurance Expense (−E)		50
Utilities Expense (−E)		52
Depreciation Expense (−E)		25
Interest Expense (−E)		77
Income Tax Expense (−E)		244
Retained Earnings (+SE)		454

5. Ratios:

a. $\text{Current Ratio} = \dfrac{\text{Current Assets}}{\text{Current Liabilities}} = \dfrac{\$6,982}{\$2,553} = 2.735$

b. $\text{Net Profit Margin for April} = \dfrac{\text{Net Income}}{\text{Net Sales (or Operating Revenues)}} = \dfrac{\$454}{\$5,600} = 0.081 \text{ or } 8.1\%$

c. $\text{Total Asset Turnover for April} = \dfrac{\text{Net Sales (or Operating Revenues)}}{\text{Average Total Assets}} = \dfrac{\$5,600}{\$7,653.50^*} = 0.732$

*(Beginning \$0 + Ending \$15,307)/2 = \$7,653.50

CHAPTER **TAKE-AWAYS**

4-1. Explain the purpose of adjustments and analyze the adjustments necessary at the end of the period to update balance sheet and income statement accounts.   p. 162

- Adjusting entries are necessary at the end of the accounting period to measure income properly, correct errors, and provide for adequate valuation of balance sheet accounts. There are four types:
  a. Deferred revenues—previously recorded liabilities created when cash was received before being earned that must be adjusted for the amount of revenue earned during the period.
  b. Accrued revenues—revenues that were earned during the period but have not yet been recorded (cash will be received in the future).
  c. Deferred expenses—previously recorded assets (Prepaid Rent, Supplies, and Equipment) that must be adjusted for the amount of expense incurred during the period.
  d. Accrued expenses—expenses that were incurred during the period but have not yet been recorded (cash will be paid in the future).

The analysis involves:

Step 1:   Determining if revenue was earned or an expense was incurred. Record an increase in the revenue or expense account.

Step 2:   Determining whether cash was received or paid in the past or will be received or paid in the future. If in the past, the existing asset or liability is overstated and needs to be reduced. If in the future, the related receivable or payable account needs to be increased.

Step 3:   Computing the amount of revenue earned or expense incurred in the period.

- Recording adjusting entries has no effect on the Cash account.

4-2. **Present an income statement with earnings per share, statement of stockholders' equity, and balance sheet.   p. 175**

Adjusted account balances are used in preparing the following financial statements:

- Income Statement: Revenues − Expenses = Net Income (including earnings per share, computed as net income divided by the average number of shares of common stock outstanding during the period).

- Statement of Stockholders' Equity: (Beginning Contributed Capital + Stock Issuances − Stock Repurchases) + (Beginning Retained Earnings + Net Income − Dividends Declared) = Ending Total Stockholders' Equity.

- Balance Sheet: Assets = Liabilities + Stockholders' Equity.

4-3. **Compute and interpret the total asset turnover ratio.   p. 180**

The total asset turnover ratio (Net Sales (or Operating Revenues) ÷ Average Total Assets) measures sales generated per dollar of assets. A rising total asset turnover signals more efficient management of assets.

4-4. **Explain the closing process.   p. 181**

Closing Entry:		
Each revenue..............................	xx	
Each gain	xx	
Each expense		xx
Each loss................................		xx
Retained earnings		xx
(assumes net income is positive)		

Temporary accounts (revenues, expenses, gains, and losses) are closed to a zero balance at the end of the accounting period to allow for the accumulation of income items in the following period and to update Retained Earnings for the period's net income. To close these accounts, debit each revenue and gain account, credit each expense and loss account, and record the difference (equal to net income) to Retained Earnings.

This chapter discussed the important steps in the accounting cycle that take place at year-end. These include the adjustment process, the preparation of the basic financial statements, and the closing process that prepares the records for the next accounting period. This end to the internal portions of the accounting cycle, however, is just the beginning of the process of communicating accounting information to external users.

In the next chapter we take a closer look at more sophisticated financial statements and related disclosures. We also examine the process by which financial information is disseminated to professional analysts, investors, the Securities and Exchange Commission, and the public, and the role each plays in analyzing and interpreting the information. These discussions will help you consolidate much of what you have learned about the financial reporting process from previous chapters. It will also preview many of the important issues we address in later chapters. These later chapters include many other adjustments that involve difficult and complex estimates about the future, such as estimates of customers' ability to make payments to the company for purchases on account, the useful lives of new machines, and future amounts that a company may owe on warranties of products sold in the past. Each of these estimates and many others can have significant effects on the stream of net earnings that companies report over time.

KEY **RATIO**

Total asset turnover measures the sales generated per dollar of assets. A high or rising ratio suggests that the company is managing its assets more efficiently. It is computed as follows (p. 180):

$$\text{Total Asset Turnover} = \frac{\text{Net Sales (or Operating Revenues)}}{\text{Average Total Assets}}$$

FINDING **FINANCIAL INFORMATION**

Balance Sheet

Current Assets

Accrued revenues include:
   Interest receivable
   Rent receivable
Deferred expenses include:
   Supplies
   Prepaid insurance

Noncurrent Assets

Deferred expenses include:
   Property and equipment
   Intangibles

Statement of Cash Flows

Adjusting Entries Do Not Affect Cash

Current Liabilities

Accrued expenses include:
   Interest payable
   Wages payable
   Utilities payable
   Income tax payable
Deferred revenues include:
   Unearned revenue

Income Statement

Revenues
Increased by adjusting entries

Expenses
Increased by adjusting entries

Pretax Income
Income tax expense

Net Income

Notes

In Various Notes (if not on the balance sheet)
Details of accrued expenses payable
Interest paid and income taxes paid

KEY **TERMS**

Accrued Expenses   p. 167
Accrued Revenues   p. 170
Adjusting Entries   p. 163
Closing Entry   p. 181

Contra-Account   p. 169
Deferred Expenses   p. 167
Deferred (Unearned) Revenues   p. 166
Net Book Value (Book Value,
   Carrying Value)   p. 169

Permanent (Real) Accounts   p. 181
Post-Closing Trial Balance   p. 184
Temporary (Nominal)
   Accounts   p. 181

QUESTIONS

1. What is the purpose of recording adjusting entries?
2. List the four types of adjusting entries, and give an example of each type.
3. What is a contra-asset? Give an example of one.
4. Explain how the financial statements relate to each other.
5. What is the equation for each of the following statements: (*a*) income statement, (*b*) balance sheet, and (*c*) statement of stockholders' equity?
6. Explain the effect of adjusting entries on cash.
7. How is earnings per share computed and interpreted?
8. How is the total asset turnover ratio computed and interpreted?
9. What are the purposes for closing the books?
10. Differentiate among (*a*) permanent, (*b*) temporary, (*c*) real, and (*d*) nominal accounts.
11. Explain why the income statement accounts are closed but the balance sheet accounts are not.
12. What is a post-closing trial balance? Is it a useful part of the accounting information processing cycle? Explain.

MULTIPLE-CHOICE **QUESTIONS**

1. Which of the following accounts would not appear in a closing entry?
   - a. Salary Expense
   - b. Interest Income
   - c. Accumulated Depreciation
   - d. Retained Earnings

2. Which account is least likely to appear in an adjusting journal entry?
   - a. Interest Receivable
   - b. Cash
   - c. Property Tax Expense
   - d. Salaries Payable

3. On October 1, 2014, the $12,000 premium on a one-year insurance policy for the building was paid and recorded as Prepaid Insurance. On December 31, 2014 (end of the accounting period), what adjusting entry is needed?

a. Insurance Expense (+E)	2,000	
Prepaid Insurance (−A)		2,000
b. Insurance Expense (+E)	3,000	
Prepaid Insurance (−A)		3,000
c. Prepaid Insurance (+A)	3,000	
Insurance Expense (−E)		3,000
d. Prepaid Insurance (+A)	9,000	
Insurance Expense (−E)		9,000

4. On June 1, 2013, Oakcrest Company signed a three-year $110,000 note payable with 9 percent interest. Interest is due on June 1 of each year beginning in 2014. What amount of interest expense should be reported on the income statement for the year ended December 31, 2013?
   - a. $5,250
   - b. $5,775
   - c. $4,950
   - d. $9,900

5. Failure to make an adjusting entry to recognize accrued salaries payable would cause which of the following?
   - a. An understatement of expenses, liabilities, and stockholders' equity.
   - b. An understatement of expenses and liabilities and an overstatement of stockholders' equity.
   - c. An overstatement of assets and stockholders' equity.
   - d. An overstatement of assets and liabilities.

6. An adjusted trial balance
   - a. Shows the ending account balances in a "debit" and "credit" format before posting the adjusting journal entries.
   - b. Is prepared after closing entries have been posted.
   - c. Shows the ending account balances resulting from the adjusting journal entries in a "debit" and "credit" format.
   - d. Is a tool used by financial analysts to review the performance of publicly traded companies.

7. JJ Company owns a building. Which of the following statements regarding depreciation as used by accountants is false?
   - a. As depreciation is recorded, stockholders' equity is reduced.
   - b. As depreciation is recorded, the net book value of the asset is reduced.
   - c. As the value of the building decreases over time, it "depreciates."
   - d. Depreciation is an estimated expense to be recorded over the building's estimated useful life.

8. At the beginning of 2014, Donna Company had $1,000 of supplies on hand. During 2014, the company purchased supplies amounting to $6,400 (paid for in cash and debited to Supplies). At December 31, 2014, a count of supplies reflected $2,000. The adjusting entry Donna Company would record on December 31, 2014, to adjust the Supplies account would include a
   - a. Debit to Supplies for $2,000.
   - b. Credit to Supplies Expense for $5,400.
   - c. Credit to Supplies for $5,400.
   - d. Debit to Supplies Expense for $4,400.

9. What ratio is required by GAAP to be reported on the financial statements or in the notes to the statements?
   - a. Return on equity ratio.
   - b. Net profit margin ratio.
   - c. Earnings per share ratio.
   - d. Current ratio.

10. If a company is successful in acquiring several large buildings at the end of the year, what is the effect on the total asset turnover ratio?
   a. The ratio will increase.
   c. The ratio will decrease.
   b. The ratio will not change.
   d. Either (a) or (c).

For more practice with multiple-choice questions, go to the text website at **www.mhhe.com/libby8e.**

|ACCOUNTING

MINI-EXERCISES

Preparing a Trial Balance

M4-1
LO4-1

Hagadorn Company has the following adjusted accounts and balances at year-end (June 30, 2014):

Accounts Payable	$ 250	Interest Expense	$ 70
Accounts Receivable	420	Interest Income	60
Accrued Expenses Payable	160	Inventories	710
Accumulated Depreciation	250	Land	300
Additional Paid-in Capital	300	Long-Term Debt	1,460
Buildings and Equipment	1,400	Prepaid Expenses	30
Cash	175	Salaries Expense	640
Common Stock	100	Sales Revenue	2,400
Cost of Sales	780	Rent Expense	460
Depreciation Expense	150	Retained Earnings	150
Income Taxes Expense	135	Unearned Fees	90
Income Taxes Payable	50		

Prepare an adjusted trial balance in good form for the Hagadorn Company at June 30, 2014.

Matching Definitions with Terms

M4-2
LO4-1

Match each definition with its related term by entering the appropriate letter in the space provided.

Definition	Term
___ (1) A revenue not yet earned; collected in advance.	A. Accrued expense
___ (2) Rent not yet collected; already earned.	B. Deferred expense
___ (3) Property taxes incurred; not yet paid.	C. Accrued revenue
___ (4) Rent revenue collected; not yet earned.	D. Deferred revenue
___ (5) An expense incurred; not yet paid or recorded.	
___ (6) Office supplies on hand to be used next accounting period.	
___ (7) An expense not yet incurred; paid in advance.	
___ (8) A revenue earned; not yet collected.	

Matching Definitions with Terms

M4-3
LO4-1

Match each definition with its related term by entering the appropriate letter in the space provided.

Definition	Term
___ (1) At year-end, service revenue of $1,000 was collected in cash but was not yet earned.	A. Accrued expense
	B. Deferred expense
___ (2) Interest of $550 on a note receivable was earned at year-end, although collection of the interest is not due until the following year.	C. Accrued revenue
	D. Deferred revenue
___ (3) At year-end, wages payable of $5,600 had not been recorded or paid.	
___ (4) Office supplies were purchased during the year for $700, and $100 of them remained on hand (unused) at year-end.	

M4-4

LO4-1

Recording Adjusting Entries (Deferred Accounts)

In each of the following transactions (*a*) through (*c*) for Romney's Marketing Company, use the three-step process illustrated in the chapter to record the adjusting entry at year-end December 31, 2015. The process includes (1) determining if revenue was earned or an expense incurred, (2) determining whether cash was received or paid in the past or will be received or paid in the future, and (3) computing the amount of the adjustment.

a. Collected $1,200 rent for the period December 1, 2015, to April 1, 2016, which was credited to Unearned Rent Revenue on December 1, 2015.

b. Purchased a machine for $32,000 cash on January 1, 2011. The company estimates annual depreciation at $3,200.

c. Paid $5,000 for a two-year insurance premium on July 1, 2015; debited Prepaid Insurance for that amount.

M4-5

LO4-1

Determining Financial Statement Effects of Adjusting Entries (Deferred Accounts)

For each of the transactions in M4-4, indicate the amounts and direction of effects of the adjusting entry on the elements of the balance sheet and income statement. Using the following format, indicate + for increase, − for decrease, and NE for no effect.

	BALANCE SHEET			INCOME STATEMENT		
Transaction	Assets	Liabilities	Stockholders' Equity	Revenues	Expenses	Net Income
a.						
b.						
c.						

M4-6

LO4-1

Recording Adjusting Entries (Accrued Accounts)

In each of the following transactions (*a*) through (*c*) for Romney's Marketing Company, use the three-step process illustrated in the chapter to record the adjusting entry at year-end December 31, 2015. The process includes (1) determining if revenue was earned or an expense incurred, (2) determining whether cash was received or paid in the past or will be received or paid in the future, and (3) computing the amount of the adjustment.

a. Estimated electricity usage at $450 for December; to be paid in January 2016.

b. On September 1, 2015, loaned $6,000 to an officer who will repay the loan principal and interest in one year at an annual interest rate of 14 percent.

c. Owed wages to 10 employees who worked four days at $200 each per day at the end of December. The company will pay employees at the end of the first week of January 2016.

M4-7

LO4-1

Determining Financial Statement Effects of Adjusting Entries (Accrued Accounts)

For each of the transactions in M4-6, indicate the amounts and direction of effects of the adjusting entry on the elements of the balance sheet and income statement. Using the following format, indicate + for increase, − for decrease, and NE for no effect.

	BALANCE SHEET			INCOME STATEMENT		
Transaction	Assets	Liabilities	Stockholders' Equity	Revenues	Expenses	Net Income
a.						
b.						
c.						

Reporting an Income Statement with Earnings per Share

M4-8
LO4-2

Romney's Marketing Company has the following adjusted trial balance at December 31, 2015. No dividends were declared. However, 500 shares ($0.10 par value per share) issued at the end of the year for $3,000 are included below:

	Debit	Credit
Cash	1,500	
Accounts receivable	2,200	
Interest receivable	100	
Prepaid insurance	1,600	
Notes receivable (long-term)	2,800	
Equipment	15,290	
Accumulated depreciation		3,000
Accounts payable		2,400
Accrued expenses payable		3,920
Income taxes payable		2,700
Unearned rent revenue		500
Common Stock (800 shares)		80
Additional paid-in capital		3,620
Retained earnings		2,000
Sales revenue		38,500
Interest revenue		100
Rent revenue		800
Wages expense	19,500	
Depreciation expense	1,800	
Utilities expense	380	
Insurance expense	750	
Rent expense	9,000	
Income tax expense	2,700	
Total	57,620	57,620

Prepare a multi-step income statement in good form for 2015. Include earnings per share.

Reporting a Statement of Stockholders' Equity

M4-9
LO4-2

Refer to M4-8. Prepare a statement of stockholders' equity in good form for 2015.

Reporting a Balance Sheet and Explaining the Effects of Adjustments on the Statement of Cash Flows

M4-10
LO4-2

1. Prepare a classified balance sheet in good form at December 31, 2015, from the information in M4-8.
2. Explain how the adjustments in M4-4 and M4-6 affected the operating, investing, and financing activities on the statement of cash flows.

Analyzing Total Asset Turnover

M4-11
LO4-3

Compute total assets based on the adjusted trial balance in M4-8. Then compute Romney's Marketing Company's total asset turnover for 2015, assuming total assets at December 31, 2014, were $16,050.

Recording Closing Entries

M4-12
LO4-4

Refer to the adjusted trial balance in M4-8. Prepare the closing entry on December 31, 2015.

EXERCISES

E4-1
LO4-1

Preparing a Trial Balance

Paige Consultants, Inc., provides marketing research for clients in the retail industry. The company had the following unadjusted balances at September 30, 2015:

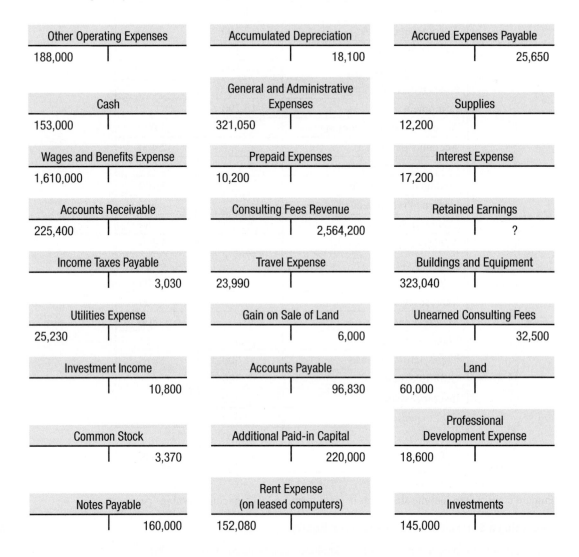

Other Operating Expenses	Accumulated Depreciation	Accrued Expenses Payable
188,000	18,100	25,650

Cash	General and Administrative Expenses	Supplies
153,000	321,050	12,200

Wages and Benefits Expense	Prepaid Expenses	Interest Expense
1,610,000	10,200	17,200

Accounts Receivable	Consulting Fees Revenue	Retained Earnings
225,400	2,564,200	?

Income Taxes Payable	Travel Expense	Buildings and Equipment
3,030	23,990	323,040

Utilities Expense	Gain on Sale of Land	Unearned Consulting Fees
25,230	6,000	32,500

Investment Income	Accounts Payable	Land
10,800	96,830	60,000

Common Stock	Additional Paid-in Capital	Professional Development Expense
3,370	220,000	18,600

Notes Payable	Rent Expense (on leased computers)	Investments
160,000	152,080	145,000

Required:
Prepare in good form an unadjusted trial balance for Paige Consultants, Inc., at September 30, 2015.

E4-2
LO4-1, 4-4

Hewlett-Packard Company

Identifying Adjusting Entries from Unadjusted Trial Balance

In its annual report, Hewlett-Packard Company states, "We are a leading global provider of products, technologies, solutions and services to individual consumers, small- and medium-sized businesses, and large enterprises, including customers in the government, health, and education sectors." Its offerings span personal computing and other access drivers, imaging and printing-related products and services, enterprise information technology infrastructure, and multi-vendor customer services. Following is a trial balance listing accounts that Hewlett-Packard uses. Assume that the balances are unadjusted at the end of a recent fiscal year ended October 31.

HEWLETT-PACKARD COMPANY Unadjusted Trial Balance (dollars in millions) For the year ended October 31		
	Debit	**Credit**
Cash	8,000	
Accounts receivable	21,400	
Inventory	7,500	
Other current assets	14,100	
Property, plant, and equipment	25,500	
Accumulated depreciation		13,200
Other assets	66,200	
Short-term note payable		8,100
Accounts payable		14,800
Accrued liabilities		19,100
Deferred revenue		7,400
Income tax payable		1,000
Long-term debt		22,600
Other liabilities		17,500
Common stock		200
Additional paid-in capital		7,000
Retained earnings		24,700
Product revenue		84,800
Service revenue		42,000
Interest revenue		400
Cost of products	65,200	
Cost of services	32,100	
Interest expense	1,000	
Research and development expense	3,300	
Selling, general, and administrative expense	13,500	
Other expenses	3,100	
Income tax expense	1,900	
Total	262,800	262,800

Required:

1. Based on the information in the unadjusted trial balance, list types of adjustments on the balance sheet that may need to be adjusted at October 31 and the related income statement account for each (no computations are necessary). You may need to make assumptions.
2. Which accounts should be closed at the end of the year? Why?

Recording Adjusting Entries

E4-3

LO4-1

Diane Company completed its first year of operations on December 31, 2014. All of the 2014 entries have been recorded except for the following:

a. At year-end, employees earned wages of $4,000, which will be paid on the next payroll date, January 6, 2015.
b. At year-end, the company had earned interest revenue of $1,500. The cash will be collected March 1, 2015.

Required:

1. What is the annual reporting period for this company?
2. Identify whether each transaction results in adjusting a deferred or an accrued account. Using the process illustrated in the chapter, prepare the required adjusting entry for transactions (*a*) and (*b*). Include appropriate dates and write a brief explanation of each entry.
3. Why are these adjustments made?

E4-4

LO4-1, 4-2

Recording Adjusting Entries and Reporting Balances in Financial Statements

Aubrae Company is making adjusting entries for the year ended December 31, 2014. In developing information for the adjusting entries, the accountant learned the following:

a. A two-year insurance premium of $4,800 was paid on October 1, 2014, for coverage beginning on that date.
b. At December 31, 2014, the following data relating to Shipping Supplies were obtained from the records and supporting documents.

Shipping supplies on hand, January 1, 2014	$13,000
Purchases of shipping supplies during 2014	75,000
Shipping supplies on hand, counted on December 31, 2014	20,000

Required:

1. Using the process illustrated in the chapter, record the adjusting entry for insurance at December 31, 2014, assuming that the premium was paid on October 1, 2014, and the bookkeeper debited the full amount to Prepaid Insurance.
2. Using the process illustrated in the chapter, record the adjusting entry for supplies at December 31, 2014, assuming that the purchases of shipping supplies were debited in full to Shipping Supplies.
3. What amount should be reported on the 2014 income statement for Insurance Expense? For Shipping Supplies Expense?
4. What amount should be reported on the December 31, 2014, balance sheet for Prepaid Insurance? For Shipping Supplies?

E4-5

LO4-1

Determining Financial Statement Effects of Adjusting Entries

Refer to E4-3 and E4-4.

Required:

For each of the transactions in E4-3 and E4-4, indicate the amount and direction of effects of the adjusting entry on the elements of the balance sheet and income statement. Using the following format, indicate + for increase, − for decrease, and NE for no effect.

	BALANCE SHEET			INCOME STATEMENT		
Transaction	Assets	Liabilities	Stockholders' Equity	Revenues	Expenses	Net Income
E4-3 (*a*)						
E4-3 (*b*)						
E4-4 (*a*)						
E4-4 (*b*)						

E4-6

LO4-1

Recording Seven Typical Adjusting Entries

Dittman's Variety Store is completing the accounting process for the year just ended, December 31, 2014. The transactions during 2014 have been journalized and posted. The following data with respect to adjusting entries are available:

a. Wages earned by employees during December 2014, unpaid and unrecorded at December 31, 2014, amounted to $2,700. The last payroll was December 28; the next payroll will be January 6, 2015.

b. Office supplies on hand at January 1, 2014, totaled $450. Office supplies purchased and debited to Office Supplies during the year amounted to $500. The year-end count showed $275 of supplies on hand.

c. One-fourth of the basement space is rented to Heald's Specialty Shop for $560 per month, payable monthly. On December 31, 2014, the rent for November and December 2014 had not been collected or recorded. Collection is expected January 10, 2015.

d. The store used delivery equipment that cost $60,500; $12,100 was the estimated depreciation for 2014.

e. On July 1, 2014, a two-year insurance premium amounting to $2,400 was paid in cash and debited in full to Prepaid Insurance. Coverage began on July 1, 2014.

f. The remaining basement of the store is rented for $1,600 per month to another merchant, M. Carlos, Inc. Carlos sells compatible, but not competitive, merchandise. On November 1, 2014, the store collected six months' rent in the amount of $9,600 in advance from Carlos; it was credited in full to Unearned Rent Revenue when collected.

g. Dittman's Variety Store operates a repair shop to meet its own needs. The shop also does repairs for M. Carlos. At the end of December 31, 2014, Carlos had not paid $800 for completed repairs. This amount has not yet been recorded as Repair Shop Revenue. Collection is expected during January 2015.

Required:

1. Identify each of these transactions as a deferred revenue, deferred expense, accrued revenue, or accrued expense.
2. Prepare the adjusting entries that should be recorded for Dittman's Variety Store at December 31, 2014.

Recording Seven Typical Adjusting Entries

E4-7
LO4-1

John's Boat Yard, Inc., repairs, stores, and cleans boats for customers. It is completing the accounting process for the year just ended, November 30, 2015. The transactions for the past year have been journalized and posted. The following data with respect to adjusting entries at year-end are available:

a. John's winterized (cleaned and covered) three boats for customers at the end of November, but did not record the service for $3,300.

b. On October 1, 2015, John's paid $2,200 to the local newspaper for an advertisement to run every Thursday for 12 weeks. All ads have been run except for three Thursdays in December to complete the 12-week contract.

c. John's borrowed $300,000 at an 11 percent annual interest rate on April 1, 2015, to expand its boat storage facility. The loan requires John's to pay the interest quarterly until the note is repaid in three years. John's paid quarterly interest on July 1 and October 1.

d. The Johnson family paid John's $4,500 on November 1, 2015, to store its sailboat for the winter until May 1, 2016. John's credited the full amount to Unearned Storage Revenue on November 1.

e. John's used boat-lifting equipment that cost $180,000; $18,000 was the estimated depreciation for 2015.

f. Boat repair supplies on hand at December 1, 2014, totaled $18,900. Repair supplies purchased and debited to Supplies during the year amounted to $45,200. The year-end count showed $15,600 of the supplies on hand.

g. Wages earned by employees during November 2015, unpaid and unrecorded at November 30, 2015, amounted to $5,600. The next payroll date will be December 5, 2015.

Required:

1. Identify each of these transactions as a deferred revenue, deferred expense, accrued revenue, or accrued expense.
2. Prepare the adjusting entries that should be recorded for John's at November 30, 2015.

E4-8

LO4-1

Determining Financial Statement Effects of Seven Typical Adjusting Entries

Refer to E4-6.

Required:

For each of the transactions in E4-6, indicate the amount and direction of effects of the adjusting entry on the elements of the balance sheet and income statement. Using the following format, indicate + for increase, − for decrease, and NE for no effect.

	BALANCE SHEET			INCOME STATEMENT		
Transaction	Assets	Liabilities	Stockholders' Equity	Revenues	Expenses	Net Income
a.						
b.						
c.						
(etc.)						

E4-9

LO4-1

Determining Financial Statement Effects of Seven Typical Adjusting Entries

Refer to E4-7.

Required:

For each of the transactions in E4-7, indicate the amount and direction of effects of the adjusting entry on the elements of the balance sheet and income statement. Using the following format, indicate + for increase, − for decrease, and NE for no effect.

	BALANCE SHEET			INCOME STATEMENT		
Transaction	Assets	Liabilities	Stockholders' Equity	Revenues	Expenses	Net Income
a.						
b.						
c.						
(etc.)						

E4-10

LO4-1, 4-4

Recording Transactions Including Adjusting and Closing Entries (Nonquantitative)

The following accounts are used by Britt's Knits, Inc.

Codes	Accounts	Codes	Accounts
A	Cash	J	Common Stock and Additional Paid-in Capital
B	Office Supplies	K	Retained Earnings
C	Accounts Receivable	L	Service Revenue
D	Office Equipment	M	Interest Revenue
E	Accumulated Depreciation	N	Wage Expense
F	Note Payable	O	Depreciation Expense
G	Wages Payable	P	Interest Expense
H	Interest Payable	Q	Supplies Expense
I	Unearned Service Revenue	R	None of the above

Required:

For each of the following nine independent situations, prepare the journal entry by entering the appropriate code(s) and amount(s). The first transaction is used as an example.

Independent Situations	DEBIT		CREDIT	
	Code	Amount	Code	Amount
a. Accrued wages, unrecorded and unpaid at year-end, $400 (example).	N	400	G	400
b. Service revenue earned but not yet collected at year-end, $600.				
c. Dividends declared and paid during the year, $900.				
d. Office supplies on hand during the year, $400; supplies on hand at year-end, $160.				
e. Service revenue collected in advance and not yet earned, $800.				
f. Depreciation expense for the year, $1,000.				
g. At year-end, interest on note payable not yet recorded or paid, $220.				
h. Balance at year-end in Service Revenue account, $56,000. Prepare the closing entry at year-end.				
i. Balance at year-end in Interest Expense account, $460. Prepare the closing entry at year-end.				

Determining Financial Statement Effects of Three Adjusting Entries

E4-11

LO4-1, 4-2

Daniel Company started operations on January 1, 2015. It is now December 31, 2015, the end of the annual accounting period. The part-time bookkeeper needs your help to analyze the following three transactions:

a. During 2015, the company purchased office supplies that cost $3,000. At the end of 2015, office supplies of $800 remained on hand.
b. On January 1, 2015, the company purchased a special machine for cash at a cost of $25,000. The machine's cost is estimated to depreciate at $2,500 per year.
c. On July 1, 2015, the company paid cash of $1,000 for a two-year premium on an insurance policy on the machine; coverage begins on July 1, 2015.

Required:
Complete the following schedule with the amounts that should be reported for 2015:

Selected Balance Sheet Accounts at December 31, 2015	Amount to Be Reported
Assets	
Equipment	$ _____
Accumulated depreciation	_____
Net book value of equipment	_____
Office supplies	_____
Prepaid insurance	_____
Selected Income Statement Accounts for the Year Ended December 31, 2015	
Expenses	
Depreciation expense	$ _____
Office supplies expense	_____
Insurance expense	_____

Determining Financial Statement Effects of Adjustments for Interest on Two Notes

E4-12

LO4-1

Note 1: On April 1, 2014, Warren Corporation received a $30,000, 10 percent note from a customer in settlement of a $30,000 open account receivable. According to the terms, the principal of the note and interest are payable at the end of 12 months. The annual accounting period for Warren ends on December 31, 2014.

Note 2: On August 1, 2014, to meet a cash shortage, Warren Corporation obtained a $30,000, 12 percent loan from a local bank. The principal of the note and interest expense are payable at the end of six months.

Required:

For the relevant transaction dates of each note, indicate the amounts and direction of effects on the elements of the balance sheet and income statement. Using the following format, indicate + for increase, − for decrease, and NE for no effect. (**Reminder:** Assets = Liabilities + Stockholders' Equity; Revenues − Expenses = Net Income; and Net Income accounts are closed to Retained Earnings, a part of Stockholders' Equity.)

	BALANCE SHEET			INCOME STATEMENT		
Date	Assets	Liabilities	Stockholders' Equity	Revenues	Expenses	Net Income
Note 1						
April 1, 2014						
December 31, 2014						
March 31, 2015						
Note 2						
August 1, 2014						
December 31, 2014						
January 31, 2015						

E4-13

LO4-1

Deere & Company

Inferring Transactions

Deere & Company is the world's leading producer of agricultural equipment; a leading supplier of a broad range of industrial equipment for construction, forestry, and public works; a producer and marketer of a broad line of lawn and grounds care equipment; and a provider of credit, managed health care plans, and insurance products for businesses and the general public. The following information is from a recent annual report (in millions of dollars):

Income Taxes Payable				Dividends Payable				Interest Payable		
		Beg. bal.	154			Beg. bal.	127		Beg. bal.	190
(a)	?	(b)	1,424	(c)	?	(d)	634	(e) 759	(f)	?
		End. bal.	166			End. bal.	168		End. bal.	191

Required:
1. Identify the nature of each of the transactions (*a*) through (*f*). Specifically, what activities cause the accounts to increase and decrease?
2. For transactions (*a*), (*c*), and (*f*), compute the amount.

E4-14

LO4-1

Analyzing the Effects of Errors on Financial Statement Items

Cohen & Boyd, Inc., publishers of movie and song trivia books, made the following errors in adjusting the accounts at year-end (December 31):

a. Did not accrue $1,400 owed to the company by another company renting part of the building as a storage facility.
b. Did not record $15,000 depreciation on the equipment costing $115,000.
c. Failed to adjust the Unearned Fee Revenue account to reflect that $1,500 was earned by the end of the year.
d. Recorded a full year of accrued interest expense on a $17,000, 9 percent note payable that has been outstanding only since November 1.
e. Failed to adjust Prepaid Insurance to reflect that $650 of insurance coverage has been used.

Required:

1. For each error, prepare (*a*) the adjusting journal entry that was made, if any, and (*b*) the adjusting journal entry that should have been made at year-end.
2. Using the following headings, indicate the effect of each error and the amount of the effect (that is, the difference between the entry that was or was not made and the entry that should have been made). Use O if the effect overstates the item, U if the effect understates the item, and NE if there is no effect. (**Reminder:** Assets = Liabilities + Stockholders' Equity; Revenues − Expenses = Net Income; and Net Income accounts are closed to Retained Earnings, a part of Stockholders' Equity.)

	BALANCE SHEET			INCOME STATEMENT		
Transaction	Assets	Liabilities	Stockholders' Equity	Revenues	Expenses	Net Income
a.						
b.						
c.						
(etc.)						

Analyzing the Effects of Adjusting Entries on the Income Statement and Balance Sheet

E4-15
LO4-1, 4-2

On December 31, 2014, Fawzi Company prepared an income statement and balance sheet and failed to take into account four adjusting entries. The income statement, prepared on this incorrect basis, reflected pretax income of $65,000. The balance sheet (before the effect of income taxes) reflected total assets, $185,000; total liabilities, $90,000; and stockholders' equity, $95,000. The data for the four adjusting entries follow:

a. Wages amounting to $37,000 for the last three days of December 2014 were not paid and not recorded (the next payroll will be on January 10, 2015).
b. Depreciation of $19,000 for the year on equipment that cost $190,000 was not recorded.
c. Rent revenue of $10,500 was collected on December 1, 2014, for office space for the period December 1, 2014, to February 28, 2015. The $10,500 was credited in full to Unearned Rent Revenue when collected.
d. Income taxes were not recorded. The income tax rate for the company is 30 percent.

Required:
Complete the following tabulation to correct the financial statements for the effects of the four errors (indicate deductions with parentheses):

Items	Net Income	Total Assets	Total Liabilities	Stockholders' Equity
Balances reported	$65,000	$185,000	$90,000	$95,000
Additional adjustments:				
a. Wages				
b. Depreciation				
c. Rent revenue				
Adjusted balances				
d. Income taxes				
Correct balances				

Recording the Effects of Adjusting Entries and Reporting a Corrected Income Statement and Balance Sheet

E4-16
LO4-1, 4-2

On December 31, 2014, the bookkeeper for Grillo Company prepared the following income statement and balance sheet summarized here but neglected to consider three adjusting entries.

	As Prepared	Effects of Adjusting Entries	Corrected Amounts
Income Statement			
Revenues	$ 97,000	_____	_____
Expenses	(73,000)	_____	_____
Income tax expense	_____	_____	_____
Net income	$ 24,000		_____
Balance Sheet			
Assets			
Cash	$ 20,000	_____	_____
Accounts receivable	22,000	_____	_____
Rent receivable		_____	_____
Equipment	50,000	_____	_____
Accumulated depreciation	(10,000)	_____	_____
	$ 82,000		_____
Liabilities			
Accounts payable	$ 10,000	_____	_____
Income taxes payable		_____	_____
Stockholders' Equity			
Common stock	10,000	_____	_____
Additional paid-in capital	30,000	_____	_____
Retained earnings	32,000	_____	_____
	$ 82,000		_____

Data on the three adjusting entries follow:

a. Rent revenue of $2,500 earned for December 2014 was neither collected nor recorded.
b. Depreciation of $4,500 on the equipment for 2014 was not recorded.
c. Income tax expense of $5,100 for 2014 was neither paid nor recorded.

Required:
1. Prepare the three adjusting entries that were omitted. Use the account titles shown in the income statement and balance sheet data.
2. Complete the two columns to the right in the preceding tabulation to show the correct amounts on the income statement and balance sheet.

E4-17
LO4-1, 4-2, 4-3

Reporting a Correct Income Statement with Earnings per Share to Include the Effects of Adjusting Entries and Evaluating Total Asset Turnover as an Auditor

Jay, Inc., a party rental business, completed its first year of operations on December 31, 2014. Because this is the end of the annual accounting period, the company bookkeeper prepared the following tentative income statement:

Income Statement, 2014	
Rental revenue	$109,000
Expenses:	
Salaries and wages expense	26,500
Maintenance expense	12,000
Rent expense	8,800
Utilities expense	4,300
Gas and oil expense	3,000
Miscellaneous expenses (items not listed elsewhere)	1,000
Total expenses	55,600
Income	$ 53,400

You are an independent CPA hired by the company to audit the company's accounting systems and review the financial statements. In your audit, you developed additional data as follows:

a. Wages for the last three days of December amounting to $730 were not recorded or paid.
b. Jay estimated telephone usage at $440 for December 2014, but nothing has been recorded or paid.
c. Depreciation on rental autos, amounting to $24,000 for 2014, was not recorded.
d. Interest on a $15,000, one-year, 8 percent note payable dated October 1, 2014, was not recorded. The 8 percent interest is payable on the maturity date of the note.
e. Maintenance expense excludes $1,100 representing the cost of maintenance supplies used during 2014.
f. The Unearned Rental Revenue account includes $4,100 of revenue to be earned in January 2015.
g. The income tax expense is $5,800. Payment of income tax will be made in 2015.

Required:
1. What adjusting entry for each item (*a*) through (*g*) should Jay record at December 31, 2014? If none is required, explain why.
2. Prepare a corrected income statement for 2014 in good form, including earnings per share, assuming that 7,000 shares of stock are outstanding all year. Show computations.
3. Compute the total asset turnover ratio based on the corrected information. Assume Jay's December 31, 2013, total assets were $58,020 and its December 31, 2014, total assets were $65,180. What does this ratio suggest? If the average total asset turnover ratio for the industry is 2.31, what might you infer about Jay, Inc.?

Recording Four Adjusting Entries and Completing the Trial Balance Worksheet

E4-18
LO4-1

Green Valley Company prepared the following trial balance at the end of its first year of operations ending December 31, 2014. To simplify the case, the amounts given are in thousands of dollars.

Account Titles	UNADJUSTED Debit	UNADJUSTED Credit	ADJUSTMENTS Debit	ADJUSTMENTS Credit	ADJUSTED Debit	ADJUSTED Credit
Cash	20					
Accounts receivable	13					
Prepaid insurance	8					
Machinery	85					
Accumulated depreciation						
Accounts payable		11				
Wages payable						
Income taxes payable						
Common stock (4,000 shares)		4				
Additional paid-in capital		67				
Retained earnings	6					
Revenues (not detailed)		82				
Expenses (not detailed)	32					
Totals	164	164				

Other data not yet recorded at December 31, 2014, include:

a. Insurance expired during 2014, $7.
b. Wages payable, $4.
c. Depreciation expense for 2014, $9.
d. Income tax expense, $11.

Required:
1. Prepare the adjusting entries for 2014.
2. Complete the trial balance Adjustments and Adjusted columns.

E4-19

LO4-2

Reporting an Income Statement, Statement of Stockholders' Equity, and Balance Sheet

Refer to E4-18.

Required:

Using the adjusted balances in E4-18, prepare an income statement, statement of stockholders' equity, and balance sheet for 2014.

E4-20

LO4-4

Recording Closing Entries

Refer to E4-18.

Required:

1. What are the purposes of "closing the books" at the end of the accounting period?
2. Using the adjusted balances in E4-18, prepare the closing entry for 2014.

For more practice with exercises, go to the text website at **www.mhhe.com/libby8e**.

PROBLEMS
                                          |ACCOUNTING

P4-1

LO4-1

Dell

Preparing a Trial Balance (AP4-1)

Dell Inc. is the world's largest computer systems company selling directly to customers. Products include desktop computer systems, notebook computers, workstations, network server and storage products, and peripheral hardware and software. The following is a list of accounts and amounts reported in a recent year. The accounts have normal debit or credit balances and the dollars are rounded to the nearest million. Assume the company's year ended on January 31, 2015.

Accounts Payable	$11,656	Marketable Securities (investments)	$ 966
Accounts Receivable	9,803	Other Assets	16,384
Accrued Expenses Payable	3,934	Other Expenses	191
Accumulated Depreciation	2,810	Other Liabilities	13,639
Cash	13,852	Property, Plant, and Equipment	4,934
Common Stock and Additional Paid-in Capital	187	Research and Development Expense	856
Cost of Sales	48,260	Retained Earnings	?
Income Tax Expense	748	Sales Revenue	62,071
Inventories	1,404	Selling, General,	
Long-Term Debt	6,387	and Administrative Expenses	8,524

Required:

1. Prepare an adjusted trial balance at January 31, 2015.
2. How did you determine the amount for retained earnings?

P4-2

LO4-1

Recording Adjusting Entries (AP4-2)

Zimmerman Company's annual accounting year ends on December 31. It is December 31, 2014, and all of the 2014 entries except the following adjusting entries have been made:

a. On September 1, 2014, Zimmerman collected six months' rent of $8,400 on storage space. At that date, Zimmerman debited Cash and credited Unearned Rent Revenue for $8,400.

b. On October 1, 2014, the company borrowed $18,000 from a local bank and signed a 12 percent note for that amount. The principal and interest are payable on the maturity date, September 30, 2015.

c. Depreciation of $2,500 must be recognized on a service truck purchased on July 1, 2014, at a cost of $15,000.

d. Cash of $3,000 was collected on November 1, 2014, for services to be rendered evenly over the next year beginning on November 1, 2014. Unearned Service Revenue was credited when the cash was received.

e. On November 1, 2014, Zimmerman paid a one-year premium for property insurance, $9,000, for coverage starting on that date. Cash was credited and Prepaid Insurance was debited for this amount.

f. The company earned service revenue of $4,000 on a special job that was completed December 29, 2014. Collection will be made during January 2015. No entry has been recorded.

g. At December 31, 2014, wages earned by employees totaled $14,000. The employees will be paid on the next payroll date, January 15, 2015.

h. On December 31, 2014, the company estimated it owed $500 for 2014 property taxes on land. The tax will be paid when the bill is received in January 2015.

Required:

1. Indicate whether each transaction relates to a deferred revenue, deferred expense, accrued revenue, or accrued expense.
2. Give the adjusting entry required for each transaction at December 31, 2014.

Recording Adjusting Entries (AP4-3)

P4-3
LO4-1

Martin Towing Company is at the end of its accounting year, December 31, 2014. The following data that must be considered were developed from the company's records and related documents:

a. On January 1, 2014, the company purchased a new hauling van at a cash cost of $28,000. Depreciation estimated at $3,500 for the year has not been recorded for 2014.

b. During 2014, office supplies amounting to $1,000 were purchased for cash and debited in full to Supplies. At the end of 2013, the count of supplies remaining on hand was $500. The inventory of supplies counted on hand at December 31, 2014, was $150.

c. On December 31, 2014, Lanie's Garage completed repairs on one of the company's trucks at a cost of $2,600; the amount is not yet recorded by Martin and by agreement will be paid during January 2015.

d. On December 31, 2014, property taxes on land owned during 2014 were estimated at $1,800. The taxes have not been recorded, and will be paid in 2015 when billed.

e. On December 31, 2014, the company completed towing service for an out-of-state company for $4,000 payable by the customer within 30 days. No cash has been collected, and no journal entry has been made for this transaction.

f. On July 1, 2014, a three-year insurance premium on equipment in the amount of $900 was paid and debited in full to Prepaid Insurance on that date. Coverage began on July 1.

g. On October 1, 2014, the company borrowed $13,000 from the local bank on a one-year, 12 percent note payable. The principal plus interest is payable at the end of 12 months.

h. The income before any of the adjustments or income taxes was $30,000. The company's federal income tax rate is 30 percent. (**Hint:** Compute adjusted pre-tax income based on (*a*) through (*g*) to determine income tax expense.)

Required:

1. Indicate whether each transaction relates to a deferred revenue, deferred expense, accrued revenue, or accrued expense.
2. Prepare the adjusting entry required for each transaction at December 31, 2014.

Determining Financial Statement Effects of Adjusting Entries (AP4-4)

P4-4
LO4-1

Refer to P4-2.

Required:

1. Indicate whether each transaction relates to a deferred revenue, deferred expense, accrued revenue, or accrued expense.
2. Using the following headings, indicate the effect of each adjusting entry and the amount of the effect. Use + for increase, − for decrease, and NE for no effect. (**Reminder:** Assets = Liabilities + Stockholders' Equity; Revenues − Expenses = Net Income; and Net Income accounts are closed to Retained Earnings, a part of Stockholders' Equity.)

www.mhhe.com/libby8e

	BALANCE SHEET			INCOME STATEMENT		
Transaction	Assets	Liabilities	Stockholders' Equity	Revenues	Expenses	Net Income
a.						
b.						
(etc.)						

P4-5

LO4-1

www.mhhe.com/libby8e

Determining Financial Statement Effects of Adjusting Entries (AP4-5)

Refer to P4-3.

Required:

1. Indicate whether each transaction relates to a deferred revenue, deferred expense, accrued revenue, or accrued expense.
2. Using the following headings, indicate the effect of each adjusting entry and the amount of each. Use + for increase, − for decrease, and NE for no effect. (**Reminder :** Assets = Liabilities + Stockholders' Equity; Revenues − Expenses = Net Income; and Net Income accounts are closed to Retained Earnings, a part of Stockholders' Equity.)

	BALANCE SHEET			INCOME STATEMENT		
Transaction	Assets	Liabilities	Stockholders' Equity	Revenues	Expenses	Net Income
a.						
b.						
(etc.)						

P4-6

LO4-1, 4-3, 4-4

Inferring Year-End Adjustments, Computing Earnings per Share and Total Asset Turnover, and Recording Closing Entries (AP4-6)

Ramirez Company is completing the information processing cycle at its fiscal year-end, December 31, 2015. Following are the correct balances at December 31, 2015, for the accounts both before and after the adjusting entries for 2015.

Trial Balance, December 31, 2015						
	Before Adjusting Entries		Adjustments		After Adjusting Entries	
Items	Debit	Credit	Debit	Credit	Debit	Credit
a. Cash	13,500				13,500	
b. Accounts receivable					1,820	
c. Prepaid insurance	850				720	
d. Equipment	168,280				168,280	
e. Accumulated depreciation, equipment		42,100				48,100
f. Income taxes payable						1,380
g. Common stock and additional paid-in capital		112,000				112,000
h. Retained earnings, January 1, 2015		19,600				19,600
i. Service revenue		64,400				66,220
j. Salary expense	55,470				55,470	
k. Depreciation expense					6,000	
l. Insurance expense					130	
m. Income tax expense					1,380	
	238,100	238,100			247,300	247,300

Required:

1. Compare the amounts in the columns before and after the adjusting entries to reconstruct the adjusting entries made in 2015. Provide an explanation of each.
2. Compute the amount of net income assuming that it is based on the amounts (*a*) before adjusting entries and (*b*) after adjusting entries. Which net income amount is correct? Explain why.
3. Compute earnings per share, assuming that 3,000 shares of stock are outstanding all year.
4. Compute the total asset turnover ratio, assuming total assets at December 31, 2014, were $110,000. If the industry average is 0.49, what does this suggest to you about the company?
5. Record the closing entry at December 31, 2015.

Recording Adjusting and Closing Entries and Preparing a Balance Sheet and Income Statement Including Earnings per Share (AP4-7)

P4-7
LO4-1, 4-2, 4-4

Tunstall, Inc., a small service company, keeps its records without the help of an accountant. After much effort, an outside accountant prepared the following unadjusted trial balance as of the end of the annual accounting period, December 31, 2014:

Account Titles	Debit	Credit
Cash	42,000	
Accounts receivable	11,600	
Supplies	900	
Prepaid insurance	800	
Service trucks	19,000	
Accumulated depreciation		9,200
Other assets	8,300	
Accounts payable		3,000
Wages payable		
Income taxes payable		
Note payable (3 years; 10% interest due each December 31)		17,000
Common stock (5,000 shares outstanding)		400
Additional paid-in capital		19,000
Retained earnings		6,000
Service revenue		61,360
Remaining expenses (not detailed; excludes income tax)	33,360	
Income tax expense		
Totals	115,960	115,960

Data not yet recorded at December 31, 2014, included:

a. The supplies count on December 31, 2014, reflected $300 remaining supplies on hand to be used in 2015.
b. Insurance expired during 2014, $800.
c. Depreciation expense for 2014, $3,700.
d. Wages earned by employees not yet paid on December 31, 2014, $640.
e. Income tax expense, $5,540.

Required:

1. Record the 2014 adjusting entries.
2. Prepare an income statement and a classified balance sheet that include the effects of the preceding five transactions.
3. Record the 2014 closing entry.

ALTERNATE PROBLEMS

AP4-1

LO4-1

Starbucks Corporation

Preparing a Trial Balance (P4-1)

Starbucks Corporation purchases and roasts high-quality whole bean coffees and sells them along with fresh-brewed coffees, Italian-style espresso beverages, a variety of pastries and confections, coffee-related accessories and equipment, and a line of premium teas. In addition to sales through its company-operated retail stores, Starbucks also sells coffee and tea products through other channels of distribution. The following is a simplified list of accounts and amounts reported in recent financial statements. The accounts have normal debit or credit balances, and the dollars are rounded to the nearest million. Assume that the year ended on September 30, 2015.

Accounts Payable	$ 540	Inventories	$ 966
Accounts Receivable	387	Long-Term Investments	479
Accrued Liabilities	1,536	Long-Term Liabilities	897
Accumulated Depreciation	3,808	Net Revenues	11,903
Additional Paid-in Capital	39	Other Current Assets	230
Cash	1,148	Other Long-Lived Assets	730
Common Stock	2	Other Operating Expenses	402
Cost of Sales	4,949	Prepaid Expenses	162
Depreciation Expense	523	Property, Plant, and	
General and Administrative Expense	636	Equipment	6,163
Income Tax Expense	563	Retained Earnings	?
Interest Expense	33	Short-Term Investments	903
Interest Income	116	Store Operating Expenses	3,665

Required:

1. Prepare an adjusted trial balance at September 30, 2015.
2. How did you determine the amount for retained earnings?

AP4-2

LO4-1

Recording Adjusting Entries (P4-2)

Hannah Company's annual accounting year ends on June 30. It is June 30, 2015, and all of the entries for the current year have been made except the following adjusting entries:

a. On March 30, 2015, Hannah paid a six-month premium for property insurance, $3,200, for coverage starting on that date. Cash was credited and Prepaid Insurance was debited for this amount.

b. On June 1, 2015, Hannah collected two months' maintenance revenue of $450. At that date, Hannah debited Cash and credited Unearned Maintenance Revenue for $450.

c. At June 30, 2015, wages of $900 were earned by employees but not yet paid. The employees will be paid on the next payroll date, July 15, 2015.

d. Depreciation of $3,000 must be recognized on a service truck that cost $15,000 when purchased on July 1, 2014.

e. Cash of $4,200 was collected on May 1, 2015, for services to be rendered evenly over the next year beginning on May 1, 2015. Unearned Service Revenue was credited when the cash was received.

f. On February 1, 2015, the company borrowed $18,000 from a local bank and signed a 9 percent note for that amount. The principal and interest are payable on the maturity date, January 31, 2016.

g. On June 30, 2015, the company estimated that it owed $500 in property taxes on land it owned in the first half of 2015. The taxes will be paid when billed in August 2015.

h. The company earned service revenue of $2,000 on a special job that was completed June 29, 2015. Collection will be made during July 2015; no entry has been recorded.

Required:

1. Indicate whether each transaction relates to a deferred revenue, deferred expense, accrued revenue, or accrued expense.
2. Prepare the adjusting entry required for each transaction at June 30, 2015.

Recording Adjusting Entries (P4-3)

AP4-3
LO4-1

Bill's Catering Company is at its accounting year-end, December 31, 2014. The following data that must be considered were developed from the company's records and related documents:

a. During 2014, office supplies amounting to $1,200 were purchased for cash and debited in full to Supplies. At the beginning of 2014, the count of supplies on hand was $450; at December 31, 2014, the count of supplies on hand was $400.

b. On December 31, 2014, the company catered an evening gala for a local celebrity. The $7,500 bill was due from the customer by the end of January 2015. No cash has been collected, and no journal entry has been made for this transaction.

c. On October 1, 2014, a one-year insurance premium on equipment in the amount of $1,200 was paid and debited in full to Prepaid Insurance on that date. Coverage began on November 1, 2014.

d. On December 31, 2014, repairs on one of the company's delivery vans were completed at a cost estimate of $600; the amount has not yet been paid or recorded by Bill's. The repair shop will bill Bill's Catering at the beginning of January 2015.

e. In November 2014, Bill's Catering signed a lease for a new retail location, providing a down payment of $2,100 for the first three months' rent that was debited in full to Prepaid Rent. The lease began on December 1, 2014.

f. On July 1, 2014, the company purchased new refrigerated display counters at a cash cost of $18,000. Depreciation of $2,600 has not been recorded for 2014.

g. On November 1, 2014, the company loaned $4,000 to one of its employees on a one-year, 12 percent note. The principal plus interest is payable by the employee at the end of 12 months.

h. The income before any of the adjustments or income taxes was $22,400. The company's federal income tax rate is 30 percent. (**Hint:** Compute adjusted pre-tax income based on (*a*) through (*g*) to determine income tax expense.)

Required:

1. Indicate whether each transaction relates to a deferred revenue, deferred expense, accrued revenue, or accrued expense.
2. Prepare the adjusting entry required for each transaction at December 31, 2014.

Determining Financial Statement Effects of Adjusting Entries (P4-4)

AP4-4
LO4-1

Refer to AP4-2.

Required:

1. Indicate whether each transaction relates to a deferred revenue, deferred expense, accrued revenue, or accrued expense.
2. Using the following headings, indicate the effect of each adjusting entry and the amount of the effect. Use + for increase, − for decrease, and NE for no effect. (**Reminder:** Assets = Liabilities + Stockholders' Equity; Revenues − Expenses = Net Income; and Net Income accounts are closed to Retained Earnings, a part of Stockholders' Equity.)

	BALANCE SHEET			INCOME STATEMENT		
Transaction	Assets	Liabilities	Stockholders' Equity	Revenues	Expenses	Net Income
a.						
b.						
(etc.)						

AP4-5
LO4-1

Determining Financial Statement Effects of Adjusting Entries (P4-5)

Refer to AP4-3.

Required:
1. Indicate whether each transaction relates to a deferred revenue, deferred expense, accrued revenue, or accrued expense.
2. Using the following headings, indicate the effect of each adjusting entry and the amount of each. Use + for increase, − for decrease, and NE for no effect. (**Reminder:** Assets = Liabilities + Stockholders' Equity; Revenues − Expenses = Net Income; and Net Income accounts are closed to Retained Earnings, a part of Stockholders' Equity.)

	BALANCE SHEET			INCOME STATEMENT		
Transaction	Assets	Liabilities	Stockholders' Equity	Revenues	Expenses	Net Income
a.						
b.						
(etc.)						

AP4-6
LO4-1, 4-2, 4-3, 4-4

Inferring Year-End Adjustments, Computing Earnings per Share and Total Asset Turnover, and Recording Closing Entries (P4-6)

Taos Company is completing the information processing cycle at the end of its fiscal year, December 31, 2014. Following are the correct balances at December 31, 2014, for the accounts both before and after the adjusting entries for 2014.

	Trial Balance, December 31, 2014					
	Before Adjusting Entries		Adjustments		After Adjusting Entries	
Items	Debit	Credit	Debit	Credit	Debit	Credit
a. Cash	18,000				18,000	
b. Accounts receivable					1,500	
c. Prepaid rent	1,200				800	
d. Property, plant, and equipment	208,000				208,000	
e. Accumulated depreciation		52,500				70,000
f. Income taxes payable						6,500
g. Unearned revenue		16,000				8,000
h. Common stock and additional paid-in capital		110,000				110,000
i. Retained earnings, January 1, 2014		21,700				21,700
j. Service revenue		83,000				92,500
k. Salary expense	56,000				56,000	
l. Depreciation expense					17,500	
m. Rent expense					400	
n. Income tax expense					6,500	
	283,200	283,200			308,700	308,700

Required:

1. Compare the amounts in the columns before and after the adjusting entries to reconstruct the adjusting entries made in 2014. Provide an explanation of each.
2. Compute the amount of net income, assuming that it is based on the amount (*a*) before adjusting entries and (*b*) after adjusting entries. Which net income amount is correct? Explain why.
3. Compute earnings per share, assuming that 5,000 shares of stock are outstanding.
4. Compute the total asset turnover ratio. Assuming total assets on December 31, 2013, were $136,000, what does this suggest to you about the company?
5. Record the closing entry at December 31, 2014.

Recording Adjusting and Closing Entries and Preparing a Balance Sheet and Income Statement Including Earnings per Share (P4-7)

AP4-7
LO4-1, 4-2, 4-4

South Bend Repair Service Co. keeps its records without the help of an accountant. After much effort, an outside accountant prepared the following unadjusted trial balance as of the end of the annual accounting period, December 31, 2014:

Account Titles	Debit	Credit
Cash	19,600	
Accounts receivable	7,000	
Supplies	1,300	
Prepaid insurance	900	
Equipment	27,000	
Accumulated depreciation		12,000
Other assets	5,100	
Accounts payable		2,500
Wages payable		
Income taxes payable		
Note payable (two years; 12% interest due each December 31)		5,000
Common stock (3,000 shares outstanding all year)		300
Additional paid-in capital		15,700
Retained earnings		10,300
Service revenue		48,000
Remaining expenses (not detailed; excludes income tax)	32,900	
Income tax expense		
Totals	93,800	93,800

Data not yet recorded at December 31, 2014, include:

a. Depreciation expense for 2014, $3,000.
b. Insurance expired during 2014, $450.
c. Wages earned by employees but not yet paid on December 31, 2014, $2,100.
d. The supplies count on December 31, 2014, reflected $800 remaining supplies on hand to be used in 2015.
e. Income tax expense was $3,150.

Required:

1. Record the 2014 adjusting entries.
2. Prepare an income statement and a classified balance sheet for 2014 to include the effects of the preceding five transactions.
3. Record the 2014 closing entry.

COMPREHENSIVE PROBLEMS (CHAPTERS 1–4)

COMP4-1
LO4-1, 4-2, 4-3, 4-4

Recording Transactions (Including Adjusting and Closing Entries), Preparing Financial Statements, and Performing Ratio Analysis

Brothers Mike and Tim Hargen began operations of their tool and die shop (H & H Tool, Inc.) on January 1, 2014. The annual reporting period ends December 31. The trial balance on January 1, 2015, follows:

Account Titles	Debit	Credit
Cash	6,000	
Accounts receivable	5,000	
Supplies	13,000	
Land		
Equipment	78,000	
Accumulated depreciation (on equipment)		8,000
Other assets (not detailed to simplify)	7,000	
Accounts payable		
Wages payable		
Interest payable		
Income taxes payable		
Long-term notes payable		
Common stock (8,000 shares, $0.50 par value)		4,000
Additional paid-in capital		80,000
Retained earnings		17,000
Service revenue		
Depreciation expense		
Supplies expense		
Wages expense		
Interest expense		
Income tax expense		
Remaining expenses (not detailed to simplify)		
Totals	109,000	109,000

Transactions during 2015 follow:

a. Borrowed $15,000 cash on a five-year, 8 percent note payable, dated March 1, 2015.
b. Purchased land for a future building site; paid cash, $13,000.
c. Earned $215,000 in revenues for 2015, including $52,000 on credit and the rest in cash.
d. Sold 4,000 additional shares of capital stock for cash at $1 market value per share on January 1, 2015.
e. Incurred $114,000 in Remaining Expenses for 2015, including $20,000 on credit and the rest paid in cash.
f. Collected accounts receivable, $34,000.
g. Purchased other assets, $15,000 cash.
h. Purchased supplies on account for future use, $27,000.
i. Paid accounts payable, $26,000.
j. Signed a three-year $33,000 service contract to start February 1, 2016.
k. Declared and paid cash dividends, $25,000.

Data for adjusting entries:

l. Supplies counted on December 31, 2015, $18,000.
m. Depreciation for the year on the equipment, $10,000.

n. Interest accrued on notes payable (to be computed).

o. Wages earned by employees since the December 24 payroll but not yet paid, $16,000.

p. Income tax expense, $11,000, payable in ~~2016~~. *2018*

Required:

1. Set up T-accounts for the accounts on the trial balance and enter beginning balances.
2. Prepare journal entries for transactions (*a*) through (*k*) and post them to the T-accounts.
3. Journalize and post the adjusting entries (*l*) through (*p*).
4. Prepare an income statement (including earnings per share), statement of stockholders' equity, and balance sheet.
5. Identify the type of transaction for (*a*) through (*k*) for the statement of cash flows (O for operating, I for investing, F for finacing), and the direction and amount of the effect.
6. Journalize and post the closing entry.
7. Compute the following ratios for 2015 and explain what the results suggest about the company:
   a. Current ratio
   b. Total asset turnover
   c. Net profit margin

Recording Transactions (Including Adjusting and Closing Entries), Preparing Financial Statements, and Performing Ratio Analysis

COMP4-2
LO4-1, 4-2, 4-3, 4-4

Josh and Kelly McKay began operations of their furniture repair shop (Furniture Refinishers, Inc.) on January 1, 2015. The annual reporting period ends December 31. The trial balance on January 1, 2016, was as follows:

Account Titles	Debit	Credit
Cash	5,000	
Accounts receivable	4,000	
Supplies	2,000	
Small tools	6,000	
Equipment		
Accumulated depreciation (on equipment)		
Other assets (not detailed to simplify)	9,000	
Accounts payable		7,000
Notes payable		
Wages payable		
Interest payable		
Income taxes payable		
Unearned revenue		
Common stock (60,000 shares, $0.10 par value)		6,000
Additional paid-in capital		9,000
Retained earnings		4,000
Service revenue		
Depreciation expense		
Wages expense		
Interest expense		
Income tax expense		
Remaining expenses (not detailed to simplify)		
Totals	26,000	26,000

Transactions during 2016 follow:

a. Borrowed $20,000 cash on July 1, 2016, signing a one-year, 10 percent note payable.

b. Purchased equipment for $18,000 cash on July 1, 2016.

c. Sold 10,000 additional shares of capital stock for cash at $0.50 market value per share at the beginning of the year.

d. Earned $70,000 in revenues for 2016, including $14,000 on credit and the rest in cash.

e. Incurred remaining expenses of $35,000 for 2016, including $7,000 on credit and the rest paid with cash.

f. Purchased additional small tools, $3,000 cash.

g. Collected accounts receivable, $8,000.

h. Paid accounts payable, $11,000.

i. Purchased $10,000 of supplies on account.

j. Received a $3,000 deposit on work to start January 15, 2017.

k. Declared and paid a cash dividend, $10,000.

Data for adjusting entries:

l. Supplies of $4,000 and small tools of $8,000 were counted on December 31, 2016 (debit Remaining Expenses).

m. Depreciation for 2016, $2,000.

n. Interest accrued on notes payable (to be computed).

o. Wages earned since the December 24 payroll but not yet paid, $3,000.

p. Income tax expense was $4,000, payable in 2017.

Required:

1. Set up T-accounts for the accounts on the trial balance and enter beginning balances.
2. Prepare journal entries for transactions (*a*) through (*k*) and post them to the T-accounts.
3. Journalize and post the adjusting entries (*l*) through (*p*).
4. Prepare an income statement (including earnings per share), statement of stockholders' equity, and balance sheet.
5. Identify the type of transaction for (*a*) through (*k*) for the statement of cash flows (O for operating, I for investing, F for financing), and the direction and amount of the effect.
6. Journalize and post the closing entry.
7. Compute the following ratios for 2016 and explain what the results suggest about the company:
   a. Current ratio
   b. Total asset turnover
   c. Net profit margin

CASES **AND PROJECTS**

Annual Report Cases

CP4-1

LO4-2, 4-3, 4-4

Finding Financial Information

Refer to the financial statements of American Eagle Outfitters in Appendix B at the end of this book.

AMERICAN EAGLE
OUTFITTERS, INC.

Required:

(**Hint:** The notes to the financial statements may be helpful for many of these questions.)

1. How much cash did the company pay for income taxes in its 2011 fiscal year (for the year ended January 30, 2012)?
2. What was the company's best quarter in terms of sales in its 2011 fiscal year? Where did you find this information?
3. Give the closing entry for the Other Income (net) account.
4. What does Accounts Receivable consist of? Provide the names of the accounts and their balances as of January 30, 2012. Where did you find this information?
5. Compute the company's total asset turnover ratio for the three years reported. What does the trend suggest to you about American Eagle Outfitters?

Finding Financial Information

Refer to the financial statements of Urban Outfitters in Appendix C at the end of this book.

CP4-2
LO4-2, 4-3, 4-4

Required:

1. How much is in the Prepaid Expenses and Other Current Assets account at the end of the most recent year (for the year ended January 31, 2012)? Where did you find this information?
2. What did the company report for Deferred Rent and Other Liabilities at January 31, 2012? Where did you find this information?
3. What is the difference between prepaid rent and deferred rent?
4. Describe in general terms what accrued liabilities are.
5. What would generate the interest income that is reported on the income statement?
6. What company accounts would not have balances on a post-closing trial balance?
7. Prepare the closing entry, if any, for Prepaid Expenses.
8. What is the company's earnings per share (basic only) for the three years reported?
9. Compute the company's total asset turnover ratio for the three years reported. What does the trend suggest to you about Urban Outfitters?

Comparing Companies within an Industry and Over Time

Refer to the financial statements of American Eagle Outfitters in Appendix B, Urban Outfitters in Appendix C, and the Industry Ratio Report in Appendix D at the end of this book.

CP4-3
LO4-2, 4-3

AMERICAN EAGLE
OUTFITTERS, INC.

www.mhhe.com/libby8e

Required:

1. What was Advertising Expense for each company for the most recent year? Where did you find the information?
2. Compute the percentage of Advertising Expense to Net Sales for the most recent year for both companies. Which company incurred the higher percentage? Show computations. Are you able to perform the same comparison for the previous two years? If so, show the computations. If not, explain why not.
3. Compare the Advertising Expense to Net Sales ratio for the most recent year computed in requirement (2) to the industry average found in the Industry Ratio Report (Appendix D). Were these two companies spending more or less than their average competitor on advertising (on a relative basis)? What does this ratio tell you about the general effectiveness of each company's advertising strategy?
4. Both companies include a note to the financial statements explaining the accounting policy for advertising. How do the policies differ, if at all?
5. Compute each company's total asset turnover ratio for the three years reported. What do your results suggest to you about each company over time and in comparison to each other?
6. Compare each company's total asset turnover ratio for the most recent year to the industry average total asset turnover ratio in the Industry Ratio Report. Were these two companies performing better or worse than the average company in the industry?

Financial Reporting and Analysis Cases

Computing Amounts on Financial Statements and Finding Financial Information

The following information was provided by the records of Liberty Circle Apartments (a corporation) at the end of the annual fiscal period, December 31, 2014:

CP4-4
LO4-1, 4-2

Rent

a. Rent revenue collected in cash during 2014 for occupancy in 2014, $500,000.
b. Rent revenue earned for occupancy in December 2014; not collected until 2015, $10,000.
c. In December 2014, rent revenue collected in advance for January 2015, $14,000.

Salaries

d. Cash payment in January 2014 to employees for work in December 2013 (accrued in 2013), $6,000.
e. Salaries incurred and paid during 2014, $70,000.
f. Salaries earned by employees during December 2014 that will be paid in January 2015, $3,000.
g. Cash advances to employees in December 2014 for salaries that will be earned in January 2015, $2,000.

Supplies

h. Maintenance supplies on January 1, 2014 (balance on hand), $7,000.

i. Maintenance supplies purchased for cash during 2014, $8,000.

j. Maintenance supplies counted on December 31, 2014, $2,000.

Required:

For each of the following accounts, compute the balance to be reported in 2014, the statement the account will be reported on, and the effect (direction and amount) on cash flows (+ for increases cash and − for decreases cash). (**Hint:** Create T-accounts to determine balances.)

Account	2014 Balance	Financial Statement	Effect on Cash Flows
1. Rent revenue			
2. Salary expense			
3. Maintenance supplies expense			
4. Rent receivable			
5. Receivables from employees			
6. Maintenance supplies			
7. Unearned rent revenue			
8. Salaries payable			

CP4-5
LO4-1, 4-4

Using Financial Reports: Inferring Adjusting Entries and Information Used in Computations and Recording Closing Entries

The pre-closing balances in the T-accounts of Naim Company at the end of the third year of operations, December 31, 2014, follow. The 2014 adjusting entries are identified by letters.

Cash	
Bal. 25,000	

Note Payable (6%)	
	Bal. 10,000

Common Stock (10,000 shares)	
	Bal. 10,000

Maintenance Supplies	
Bal. 800 | (a) 500	

Interest Payable	
	(b) 600

Retained Earnings	
	Bal. 12,000

Service Equipment	
Bal. 90,000	

Income Taxes Payable	
	(f) 13,020

Service Revenue	
	Bal. 214,000
	(c) 10,000

Accumulated Depreciation, Service Equipment	
	Bal. 21,000
	(d) 9,000

Wages Payable	
	(e) 400

Expenses	
Bal. 160,000	
(a) 500	
(b) 600	
(d) 9,000	
(e) 400	
(f) 13,020	

Remaining Assets	
Bal. 44,800	

Unearned Revenue	
(c) 10,000 | Bal. 13,600	

Additional Paid-in Capital	
	Bal. 40,000

Required:
1. Develop three 2014 trial balances for Naim Company using the following format:

	UNADJUSTED TRIAL BALANCE		ADJUSTED TRIAL BALANCE		POST-CLOSING TRIAL BALANCE	
Account	Debit	Credit	Debit	Credit	Debit	Credit

2. Write an explanation for each adjusting entry for 2014.
3. Record the closing journal entry at the end of 2014.
4. What was the average income tax rate for 2014?
5. What was the average issue (sale) price per share of the capital stock?

Using Financial Reports: Analyzing the Effects of Adjustments

CP4-6
LO4-1, 4-2

Carey Land Company, a closely held corporation, invests in commercial rental properties. Carey's annual accounting period ends on December 31. At the end of each year, numerous adjusting entries must be made because many transactions completed during current and prior years have economic effects on the financial statements of the current and future years. Assume that the current year is 2016.

Required:
This case concerns four transactions that have been selected for your analysis. Answer the questions for each.

Transaction (*a*): On January 1, 2014, the company purchased office equipment costing $14,000 for use in the business. The company estimates that the equipment's cost should be allocated at $1,000 annually.

1. Over how many accounting periods will this transaction directly affect Carey's financial statements? Explain.
2. How much depreciation expense was reported on the 2014 and 2015 income statements?
3. How should the office equipment be reported on the 2016 balance sheet?
4. Would Carey make an adjusting entry at the end of each year during the life of the equipment? Explain your answer.

Transaction (*b*): On September 1, 2016, Carey collected $30,000 rent on office space. This amount represented the monthly rent in advance for the six-month period, September 1, 2016, through February 28, 2017. Unearned Rent Revenue was increased (credited) and Cash was increased (debited) for $30,000.

1. Over how many accounting periods will this transaction affect Carey's financial statements? Explain.
2. How much rent revenue on this office space should Carey report on the 2016 income statement? Explain.
3. Did this transaction create a liability for Carey as of the end of 2016? Explain. If yes, how much?
4. Should Carey make an adjusting entry on December 31, 2017? Explain why. If your answer is yes, prepare the adjusting entry.

Transaction (*c*): On December 31, 2016, Carey owed employees unpaid and unrecorded wages of $7,500 because the employees worked the last three days in December 2016. The next payroll date is January 5, 2017.

1. Over how many accounting periods will this transaction affect Carey's financial statements? Explain.
2. How will this $7,500 affect Carey's 2016 income statement and balance sheet?
3. Should Carey make an adjusting entry on December 31, 2016? Explain why. If your answer is yes, prepare the adjusting entry.

Transaction (*d*): On January 1, 2016, Carey agreed to supervise the planning and subdivision of a large tract of land for a customer, J. Signanini. This service job that Carey will perform involves four separate phases. By December 31, 2016, three phases had been completed to Signanini's satisfaction. The remaining phase will be performed during 2017. The total price for the four phases (agreed on in advance by both parties) was $60,000. Each phase involves about the same amount of services. On December 31, 2016, Carey had collected no cash for the services already performed.

1. Should Carey record any service revenue on this job for 2016? Explain why. If yes, how much?
2. If your answer to part (1) is yes, should Carey make an adjusting entry on December 31, 2016? If yes, prepare the entry. Explain.
3. What entry will Carey make when it completes the last phase, assuming that the full contract price is collected on the completion date, February 15, 2017?

CP4-7
LO4-1, 4-2

www.mhhe.com/libby8e

Using Financial Reports: Analyzing Financial Information in a Sale of a Business (A Challenging Case)

Crystal Mullinex owns and operates Crystal's Day Spa and Salon, Inc. She has decided to sell the business and retire. She has had discussions with a representative from a regional chain of day spas. The discussions are at the complex stage of agreeing on a price. Among the important factors have been the financial statements of the business. Crystal's secretary, Kenya, under Crystal's direction, maintained the records. Each year they developed a statement of profits on a cash basis; no balance sheet was prepared. Upon request, Crystal provided the other company with the following statement for 2015 prepared by Kenya:

CRYSTAL'S DAY SPA AND SALON, INC. Statement of Profits 2015		
Spa fees collected		$1,215,000
Expenses paid:		
Rent for office space	$130,000	
Utilities expense	43,600	
Telephone expense	12,200	
Salaries expense	562,000	
Supplies expense	31,900	
Miscellaneous expenses	12,400	
Total expenses		792,100
Profit for the year		$ 422,900

Upon agreement of the parties, you have been asked to examine the financial figures for 2015. The other company's representative said, "I question the figures because, among other things, they appear to be on a 100 percent cash basis." Your investigations revealed the following additional data at December 31, 2015:

a. Of the $1,215,000 in spa fees collected in 2015, $142,000 was for services performed prior to 2015.
b. At the end of 2015, spa fees of $29,000 for services performed during the year were uncollected.
c. Office equipment owned and used by Crystal cost $205,000. Depreciation was estimated at $20,500 annually.
d. A count of supplies at December 31, 2015, reflected $5,200 worth of items purchased during the year that were still on hand. Also, the records for 2014 indicated that the supplies on hand at the end of that year were $3,125.
e. At the end of 2015, the secretary whose salary is $18,000 per year had not been paid for December because of a long trip that extended to January 15, 2016.
f. The December 2015 telephone bill for $1,400 has not been recorded or paid. In addition, the $12,200 amount on the statement of profits includes payment of the December 2014 bill of $1,800 in January 2015.
g. The $130,000 office rent paid was for 13 months (it included the rent for January 2016).

Required:

1. On the basis of this information, prepare a corrected income statement for 2015 (ignore income taxes). Show your computations for any amounts changed from those in the statement prepared by Crystal's secretary. (**Suggestion:** Format solution with four column headings: Items; Cash Basis per Crystal's Statement, $; Explanation of Changes; and Corrected Basis, $.)
2. Write a memo to support your schedule prepared in requirement (1). The purpose should be to explain the reasons for your changes and to suggest other important items that should be considered in the pricing decision.

Critical Thinking Cases

Using Financial Reports: Evaluating Financial Information as a Bank Loan Officer

CP4-8

LO4-1, 4-2, 4-3

Stoscheck Moving Corporation has been in operation since January 1, 2015. It is now December 31, 2015, the end of the annual accounting period. The company has not done well financially during the first year, although revenue has been fairly good. The three stockholders manage the company, but they have not given much attention to recordkeeping. In view of a serious cash shortage, they have applied to your bank for a $30,000 loan. You requested a complete set of financial statements. The following 2015 annual financial statements were prepared by a clerk and then were given to the bank.

<table>
<tr><td colspan="2" align="center">STOSCHECK MOVING CORP.
Balance Sheet
At December 31, 2015</td></tr>
<tr><td colspan="2" align="center">Assets</td></tr>
<tr><td>Cash</td><td align="right">$ 2,000</td></tr>
<tr><td>Receivables</td><td align="right">3,000</td></tr>
<tr><td>Supplies</td><td align="right">4,000</td></tr>
<tr><td>Equipment</td><td align="right">40,000</td></tr>
<tr><td>Prepaid insurance</td><td align="right">6,000</td></tr>
<tr><td>Remaining assets</td><td align="right">27,000</td></tr>
<tr><td>Total assets</td><td align="right">$82,000</td></tr>
<tr><td colspan="2" align="center">Liabilities</td></tr>
<tr><td>Accounts payable</td><td align="right">$ 9,000</td></tr>
<tr><td colspan="2" align="center">Stockholders' Equity</td></tr>
<tr><td>Common Stock (10,000 shares outstanding)</td><td align="right">35,000</td></tr>
<tr><td>Retained earnings</td><td align="right">38,000</td></tr>
<tr><td>Total liabilities and stockholders' equity</td><td align="right">$82,000</td></tr>
</table>

<table>
<tr><td colspan="2" align="center">STOSCHECK MOVING CORP.
Income Statement
For the Period Ended December 31, 2015</td></tr>
<tr><td>Transportation revenue</td><td align="right">$85,000</td></tr>
<tr><td>Expenses:</td><td></td></tr>
<tr><td>Salaries expense</td><td align="right">17,000</td></tr>
<tr><td>Supplies expense</td><td align="right">12,000</td></tr>
<tr><td>Other expenses</td><td align="right">18,000</td></tr>
<tr><td>Total expenses</td><td align="right">47,000</td></tr>
<tr><td>Net income</td><td align="right">$38,000</td></tr>
</table>

After briefly reviewing the statements and "looking into the situation," you requested that the statements be redone (with some expert help) to "incorporate depreciation, accruals, inventory counts, income taxes, and so on." As a result of a review of the records and supporting documents, the following additional information was developed:

a. The Supplies of $4,000 shown on the balance sheet has not been adjusted for supplies used during 2015. A count of the supplies on hand on December 31, 2015, showed $1,800.
b. The insurance premium paid in 2015 was for years 2015 and 2016. The total insurance premium was debited in full to Prepaid Insurance when paid in 2015 and no adjustment has been made.
c. The equipment cost $40,000 when purchased January 1, 2015. It had an estimated annual depreciation of $8,000. No depreciation has been recorded for 2015.
d. Unpaid (and unrecorded) salaries at December 31, 2015, amounted to $3,200.

e. At December 31, 2015, transportation revenue collected in advance amounted to $7,000. This amount was credited in full to Transportation Revenue when the cash was collected earlier during 2015.

f. The income tax rate is 35 percent.

Required:

1. Record the six adjusting entries required on December 31, 2015, based on the preceding additional information.

2. Recast the preceding statements after taking into account the adjusting entries. You do not need to use classifications on the statements. Suggested form for the solution:

		CHANGES		
Items	Amounts Reported	Debit	Credit	Corrected Amounts
(List here each item from the two statements)				

3. Omission of the adjusting entries caused:
   a. Net income to be overstated or understated (select one) by $ _____.
   b. Total assets on the balance sheet to be overstated or understated (select one) by $ _____.
   c. Total liabilities on the balance sheet to be overstated or understated (select one) by $ _____.

4. For both of the unadjusted and adjusted balances, calculate these ratios for the company: (*a*) earnings per share and (*b*) total asset turnover. There were 10,000 shares outstanding all year. Explain the causes of the differences and the impact of the changes on financial analysis.

5. Write a letter to the company explaining the results of the adjustments, your analysis, and your decision regarding the loan.

CP4-9
LO4-1

Evaluating the Effect of Adjusting Unearned Subscriptions on Cash Flows and Performance as a Manager

You are the regional sales manager for Miga News Company. Miga is making adjusting entries for the year ended March 31, 2016. On September 1, 2015, customers in your region paid $36,000 cash for three-year magazine subscriptions beginning on that date. The magazines are published and mailed to customers monthly. These were the only subscription sales in your region during the year.

Required:

1. What amount should be reported as cash from operations on the statement of cash flows for the year ended March 31, 2016?

2. What amount should be reported on the income statement for subscriptions revenue for the year ended March 31, 2016?

3. What amount should be reported on the March 31, 2016, balance sheet for unearned subscriptions revenue?

4. Prepare the adjusting entry at March 31, 2016, assuming that the subscriptions received on September 1, 2015, were recorded for the full amount in Unearned Subscriptions Revenue.

5. The company expects your region's annual revenue target to be $9,000.
   a. Evaluate your region's performance, assuming that the revenue target is based on cash sales.
   b. Evaluate your region's performance, assuming that the revenue target is based on accrual accounting.

Financial Reporting and Analysis Team Project

CP4-10
LO4-1, 4-2, 4-3

Team Project: Analysis of Accruals, Earnings per Share, and Net Profit Margin

As a team, select an industry to analyze. *Yahoo!Finance* provides lists of industries at biz.yahoo.com/p/industries.html. Click on an industry for a list of companies in that industry. Alternatively, go to Google Finance at www.google.com/finance, search for a company you are interested in, and you will be presented with a list including that company and its competitors. Each team member should acquire the annual report or 10-K for one publicly traded company in the industry, with each member selecting a different company (the SEC EDGAR service at www.sec.gov or the company's investor relations website itself are good sources).

Required:

On an individual basis, each team member should write a short report answering the following questions about the selected company. Discuss any patterns across the companies that you as a team observe. Then, as a team, write a short report comparing and contrasting your companies.

1. From the income statement, what is the company's basic earnings per share for each of the last three years?
2. Ratio analysis:
    a. What does the total asset turnover ratio measure in general?
    b. Compute the total asset turnover ratio for the last three years.
    c. What do your results suggest about the company? (You may refer to the Management Discussion and Analysis section of the 10-K or annual report to read what the company says about the reasons for any change over time.)
    d. If available, find the industry ratio for the most recent year, compare it to your results, and discuss why you believe your company differs or is similar to the industry ratio.
3. List the accounts and amounts of accrued expenses payable on the most recent balance sheet. (You may find the detail in the notes to the statements.) What is the ratio of the total accrued expenses payable to total liabilities?

CONTINUING **CASE**

Adjusting Accounts at Year-End (the Accounting Cycle)

CC4-1

Penny's Pool Service & Supply, Inc. (PPSS) is completing the accounting process for the year just ended, December 31, 2015. The transactions during 2015 have been journalized and posted. The following data with respect to adjusting entries are available:

a. PPSS owed $7,500 wages to the office receptionist and three assistants for working the last 10 days in December. The employees will be paid in January 2016.
b. On October 1, 2015, PPSS received $24,000 from customers who prepaid pool cleaning service for one year beginning on November 1, 2015.
c. The company received a $520 utility bill for December utility usage. It will be paid in January 2016.
d. PPSS borrowed $30,000 from a local bank on May 1, 2015, signing a note with a 10 percent interest rate. The note and interest are due on May 1, 2016.
e. On December 31, 2015, PPSS cleaned and winterized a customer's pool for $800, but the service was not yet recorded on December 31.
f. On August 1, 2015, PPSS purchased a two-year insurance policy for $4,200, with coverage beginning on that date. The amount was recorded as Prepaid Insurance when paid.
g. On December 31, 2015, PPSS had $3,100 of pool cleaning supplies on hand. During 2015, PPSS purchased supplies costing $23,000 from Pool Corporation, Inc., and had $2,400 of supplies on hand on December 31, 2014.
h. PPSS estimated that depreciation on its buildings and equipment was $8,300 for the year.
i. At December 31, 2015, $110 of interest on investments was earned that will be received in 2016.

Required:
Prepare adjusting entries for Penny's Pool Service & Supply, Inc., on December 31, 2015.

Communicating and Interpreting Accounting Information

It is the rare person today who has not been affected by Apple products and services. From the first commercially viable personal computer, the Apple II introduced in 1977, to the raft of mobile communication and media devices, personal computers, software, and iStore content that we all use today, Apple has fundamentally changed the way we work, play, and interact. Apple Inc. the company is a far cry from the startup incorporated by Steve Jobs, Steve Wozniak, and a group of venture capitalists in 1977. Its 1977 sales of $1 million rose to $1 billion by 1982 and exceeded *$100 billion* in 2011. To accomplish this feat, Apple didn't just invent new products, it created whole new product categories such as the personal music player, the smartphone, and the tablet. And its laserlike focus on superior ease-of-use, seamless integration of hardware, software, and content, innovative design, and frequent updating make it very difficult for others to compete.

Apple's financial statements reflect its phenomenal sales and profit growth and convey this information to the stock market. Apple's stock price increased five-fold over the last five years in response to news of its success.

Financial statement information will only affect a company's stock price if the market believes in the integrity of the financial communication process. As a publicly traded company, Apple Inc. is required to provide detailed information in regular filings with the Securities and Exchange Commission. As the certifying officers of the company, current President and CEO Timothy Cook and Peter Oppenheimer, Senior Vice President and Chief Financial Officer, are responsible for the accuracy of the filings. The board of directors and auditors

Learning Objectives

After studying this chapter, you should be able to:

5-1 Recognize the people involved in the accounting communication process (regulators, managers, directors, auditors, information intermediaries, and users), their roles in the process, and the guidance they receive from legal and professional standards. p. 227

5-2 Identify the steps in the accounting communication process, including the issuance of press releases, annual reports, quarterly reports, and SEC filings, as well as the role of electronic information services in this process. p. 232

5-3 Recognize and apply the different financial statement and disclosure formats used by companies in practice and analyze the gross profit percentage. p. 234

5-4 Analyze a company's performance based on return on assets and its components and the effects of transactions on financial ratios. p. 244

chapter 5

FOCUS COMPANY:

Apple Inc.

COMMUNICATING FINANCIAL
INFORMATION AND
CORPORATE STRATEGY

www.apple.com

monitor the integrity of the system that produces the disclosures. Integrity in communication with investors and other users of financial statements is a key to maintaining relationships with suppliers of capital.

UNDERSTANDING THE BUSINESS

Apple Inc.'s best-known products and services are the iPhone®, iPad®, Mac®, iPod®, and the iTunes Store®. The company sells its products and services worldwide through its own Apple Store retail and online stores, as well as through third-party cellphone companies such as AT&T and Verizon and retailers such as Best Buy. Components for its products are produced by outsourcing partners in the United States, Asia, and Europe. Final assembly of the company's products is currently performed in the company's manufacturing facility in Ireland and by outsourcing partners, primarily located in Asia. Apple invests considerable sums in research and development, marketing, and advertising and is known for introducing new and innovative products long before the end of existing products' life cycles.

Apple also invests in **corporate governance:** procedures designed to ensure that the company is managed in the interests of the shareholders. Much of its corporate governance system is aimed at ensuring integrity in the financial reporting process. Good corporate governance eases the company's access to capital, lowering both the costs of borrowing (interest rates) and the perceived riskiness of Apple's stock.

Apple knows that when investors lose faith in the truthfulness of a firm's accounting numbers, they also normally punish the company's stock. Disclosure of an accounting fraud causes, on average, a 20 percent drop in the price of a company's stock.

CORPORATE GOVERNANCE refers to the procedures designed to ensure that the company is managed in the interests of the shareholders.

The SARBANES-OXLEY ACT is a law which strengthens U.S. financial reporting and corporate governance regulations.

The extreme accounting scandals at Le-Nature's (discussed in Chapter 1), Enron, and WorldCom caused their stock to become worthless. In an attempt to restore investor confidence, Congress passed the Public Accounting Reform and Investor Protection Act (the **Sarbanes-Oxley Act**), which strengthens financial reporting and corporate governance for public companies.

A QUESTION OF ETHICS

 The Fraud Triangle

THE FRAUD TRIANGLE

Three conditions are necessary for financial statement fraud to occur. There must be: (1) an incentive to commit fraud, (2) the opportunity to commit fraud, and (3) the ability to rationalize the misdeed. These conditions make up what antifraud experts call the fraud triangle. A good system of corporate governance is designed to address these conditions. Clear lines of responsibility and sure and severe punishment counteract incentives to commit fraud. Strong internal controls and oversight by directors and auditors reduce opportunity to commit fraud. A strong code of ethics, ethical actions by those at the top of the organization, fair dealings with employees, and rewards for whistle-blowing make it more difficult for individuals to rationalize fraud. Financial statement users also have a role to play in preventing fraud. While even the savviest user can still be surprised by fraudulent reports in some cases, accounting knowledge and healthy skepticism are the best protection from such surprises.

Chapters 2 through 4 focused on the mechanics of preparing the income statement, balance sheet, statement of stockholders' equity, and cash flow statement. Based on your better understanding of financial statements, we will next take a closer look at the people involved and the regulations that govern the process that conveys accounting information to statement users in the Internet age. We will also take a more detailed look at statement formats and additional disclosures provided in financial reports to help you learn how to find relevant information. Finally, we will examine a general framework for assessing a company's business strategy and performance based on these reports.

ORGANIZATION of the Chapter

Players in the Accounting Communication Process

- Regulators (SEC, FASB, PCAOB, Stock Exchanges)
- Managers (CEO, CFO, and Accounting Staff)
- Boards of Directors (Audit Committee)
- Auditors
- Information Intermediaries: Information Services and Financial Analysts
- Users: Institutional and Private Investors, Creditors, and Others

The Disclosure Process

- Press Releases
- Annual Reports and Form 10-K
- Quarterly Reports and Form 10-Q
- Other SEC Reports

A Closer Look at Financial Statement Formats and Notes

- Classified Balance Sheet
- Classified Income Statement
- Gross Profit Percentage
- Statement of Stockholders' Equity
- Statement of Cash Flows
- Notes to Financial Statements
- Voluntary Disclosures

ROA Analysis: A Framework for Evaluating Company Performance

- Return on Assets (ROA)
- ROA Profit Driver Analysis and Business Strategy
- How Transactions Affect Ratios

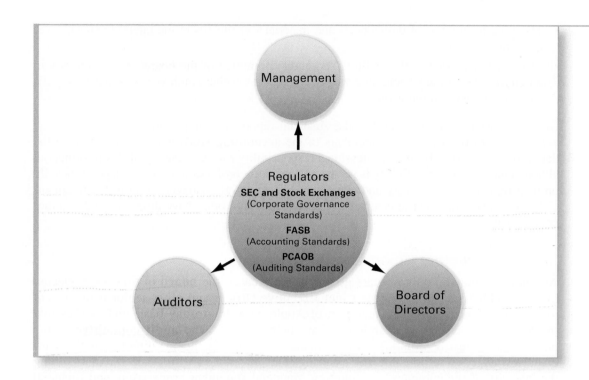

EXHIBIT 5.1

Ensuring the Integrity of Financial Information

PLAYERS IN THE ACCOUNTING COMMUNICATION PROCESS

Exhibit 5.1 summarizes the major actors involved in ensuring the integrity of the financial reporting process.

Regulators (SEC, FASB, PCAOB, Stock Exchanges)

The mission of the U.S. **Securities and Exchange Commission (SEC)** is to protect investors and maintain the integrity of the securities markets. As part of this mission, the SEC oversees the work of the **Financial Accounting Standards Board (FASB),** which sets generally accepted accounting principles (GAAP), and the **Public Company Accounting Oversight Board (PCAOB),** which sets auditing standards for independent auditors (CPAs) of public companies.

The SEC staff also reviews the reports filed with it for compliance with its standards, investigates irregularities, and punishes violators. During 2007 through 2012, the SEC brought 830 enforcement actions related to financial fraud and issuer financial reporting.[1] As a consequence, a number of high profile company officers have recently been fined and sentenced to jail. Consequences to the company can include enormous financial penalties as well as bankruptcy, as in the cases of Le-Nature's, Enron, and WorldCom. You can read about recent SEC enforcement actions at

www.sec.gov/divisions/enforce/friactions.shtml

Managers (CEO, CFO, and Accounting Staff)

The primary responsibility for the information in Apple's financial statements and related disclosures lies with management, specifically the highest officer in the company, often called the **chief executive officer** (CEO), and the highest officer associated with the financial and accounting side of the business, often called the **chief financial officer** (CFO). At Apple and all public companies, these two officers must personally certify that:

- Each report filed with the Securities and Exchange Commission does not contain any untrue material statement or omit a material fact and fairly presents in all material respects the financial condition, results of operations, and cash flows of the company.

[1]Source: www.sec.gov/news/newsroom/images/enfstats.pdf.

LEARNING OBJECTIVE 5-1
Recognize the people involved in the accounting communication process (regulators, managers, directors, auditors, information intermediaries, and users), their roles in the process, and the guidance they receive from legal and professional standards.

The SECURITIES AND EXCHANGE COMMISSION (SEC) is the U.S. government agency that determines the financial statements that public companies must provide to stockholders and the measurement rules that they must use in producing those statements.

The FINANCIAL ACCOUNTING STANDARDS BOARD (FASB) is the private sector body given the primary responsibility to work out the detailed rules that become generally accepted accounting principles.

The PUBLIC COMPANY ACCOUNTING OVERSIGHT BOARD (PCAOB) is the private sector body given the primary responsibility to issue detailed auditing standards.

- There are no significant deficiencies and material weaknesses in the internal controls over financial reporting.
- They have disclosed to the auditors and audit committee of the board any weaknesses in internal controls or any fraud involving management or other employees who have a significant role in financial reporting.

Executives who knowingly certify false financial reports are subject to a fine of $5 million and a 20-year prison term. The members of the **accounting staff,** who actually prepare the details of the reports, also bear professional responsibility for the accuracy of this information, although their legal responsibility is smaller. Their future professional success depends heavily on their reputation for honesty and competence. Accounting managers responsible for financial statements with material errors are routinely fired and often have difficulty finding other employment.

Board of Directors (Audit Committee)

The BOARD OF DIRECTORS is elected by the stockholders to represent their interests; its audit committee is responsible for maintaining the integrity of the company's financial reports.

As Apple's statement on corporate governance indicates, the board of directors (elected by the stockholders) oversees the Chief Executive Officer and other senior management in the competent and ethical operation of Apple on a day-to-day basis and assures that the long-term interests of shareholders are being served. The **audit committee** of the board, which must be composed of nonmanagement (independent) directors with financial knowledge, is responsible for ensuring that processes are in place for maintaining the integrity of the company's accounting, financial statement preparation, and financial reporting. It is responsible for hiring the company's independent auditors. They meet separately with the auditors to discuss management's compliance with their financial reporting responsibilities.

Auditors

An UNQUALIFIED (CLEAN) AUDIT OPINION is an auditor's statement that the financial statements are fair presentations in all material respects in conformity with GAAP.

The SEC requires publicly traded companies to have their statements and their control systems over the financial reporting process audited by an independent registered public accounting firm (independent auditor) following auditing standards established by the PCAOB. Many privately owned companies also have their statements audited. By signing an **unqualified (clean) audit opinion,** a CPA firm assumes part of the financial responsibility for the fairness of the financial statements and related presentations. This opinion, which adds credibility to the statements, is also often required by agreements with lenders and private investors. Subjecting the company's statements to independent verification reduces the risk that the company's financial condition is misrepresented in the statements. As a result, rational investors and lenders should lower the rate of return (interest) they charge for providing capital. Examples of an unqualified audit opinion are presented on pages B10 and C2 of this text.

Ernst & Young is currently Apple's auditor. Ernst & Young, Deloitte, KPMG, and PricewaterhouseCoopers make up what are referred to as the "Big 4" CPA firms. Each of these firms employs thousands of CPAs in offices scattered throughout the world. They audit the great majority of publicly traded companies as well as many that are privately held. Some public companies and most private companies are audited by smaller CPA firms. A list of the auditors for selected focus companies follows.

Focus Company	Industry	Auditor
Starbucks	Coffee	Deloitte & Touche
Deckers Outdoor	Footwear	KPMG
Washington Post	Education & Media	PricewaterhouseCoopers

Information Intermediaries: Information Services and Financial Analysts

Students often view the communication process between companies and financial statement users as a simple process of mailing the report to individual shareholders who read the report and then make investment decisions based on what they have learned. This simple picture is far from today's reality. Now most investors rely on company websites, information services, and financial analysts to gather and analyze information.

Companies actually file their SEC forms electronically through the EDGAR (Electronic Data Gathering and Retrieval) Service, which is sponsored by the SEC. Each fact in the report is now tagged to identify its source and meaning using a language called **XBRL.** Users can retrieve information from EDGAR within 24 hours of its submission, long before it is available through the mail. EDGAR is a free service available on the Web under "Filings & Forms" at

www.sec.gov

Most companies also provide direct access to their financial statements and other information over the Web. You can contact Apple at

investor.apple.com

Information services allow investors to gather their own information about the company and monitor the recommendations of a variety of analysts. Financial analysts and other sophisticated users obtain much of the information they use from the wide variety of commercial online information services. Fee-based services such as Compustat and ThomsonReuters provide broad access to financial statements and news information. A growing number of other resources offering a mixture of free and fee-based information exist on the Web. These include:

| www.google.com/finance | finance.yahoo.com | www.marketwatch.com |
| www.bloomberg.com | www.smartmoney.com | |

Exhibit 5.2 suggests the wide range of information about Apple available on the Google Finance website. It includes stock price and financial statement information, news accounts, and important future events related to Apple. Note that the financial information at the bottom of the exhibit matches the income statement information and ratio calculations for Apple and its two largest competitors presented later in this chapter. To see what has happened to Apple since this chapter was written, go to www.google.com/finance?q=NASDAQ:AAPL. Look at the "Related companies" section to see how Apple has fared compared to its competitors. Click on "Financials" on the top left menu to review the most recent financial statements.

Financial analysts receive accounting reports and other information about the company from electronic information services. They also gather information through conversations with company executives and visits to company facilities and competitors. The results of their analyses are combined into analysts' reports. Analysts' reports normally include forecasts of future quarterly and annual earnings per share and share price; a buy, hold, or sell recommendation for the company's shares; and explanations for these judgments. In making their **earnings forecasts,** the analysts rely heavily on their knowledge of the way the accounting system translates business events into the numbers on a company's financial statements, which is the subject matter of this text. Individual analysts often specialize in particular industries (such as sporting goods or energy companies). Analysts are regularly evaluated based on the accuracy of their forecasts, as well as the

EARNINGS FORECASTS are predictions of earnings for future accounting periods, prepared by financial analysts.

Google Finance Information on Apple

REAL WORLD EXCERPT

Google Finance

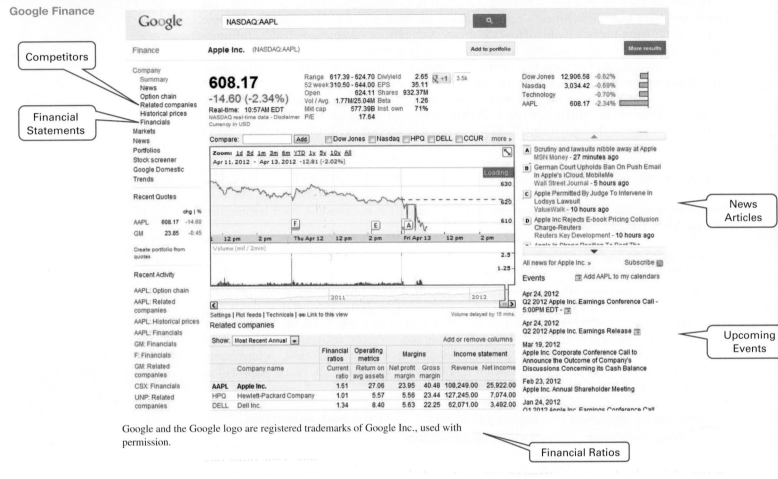

Google and the Google logo are registered trademarks of Google Inc., used with permission.

profitability of their stock picks. A sample of these forecasts and stock recommendations for Apple at the time this chapter was written follow:

Firm	Stock Recommendation	Earnings per Share Forecast for 2012	Earnings per Share Forecast for 2013
Bernstein Research	Overweight	44.19	51.29
Credit Suisse	Overweight	46.40	51.91
Gabelli & Company	Buy	45.00	49.00
Wedbush Securities	Buy	41.95	46.02
Consensus of 49 analysts	Buy	42.92	47.91

Analysts often work in the research departments of brokerage and investment banking houses such as Credit Suisse, mutual fund companies such as Fidelity Investments, and investment advisory services such as Value Line that sell their advice to others. Through their reports and recommendations, analysts are transferring their knowledge of accounting, the company, and the industry to customers who lack this expertise.

Information Services and Your Job Search

Information services have become the primary tool for professional analysts who use them to analyze competing firms. Information services are also an important source of information for job seekers. Potential employers expect job applicants to demonstrate knowledge of their companies during an interview, and electronic information services are an excellent source of company information. The best place to begin learning about potential employers is to visit their websites. Be sure to read the material in the employment section and the investor relations section of the site. To learn more about electronic information services, contact the business or reference librarian at your college or university or explore the websites discussed in this section.

Users: Institutional and Private Investors, Creditors, and Others

Institutional investors include pension funds (associated with companies, unions, or government agencies); mutual funds; and endowment, charitable foundation, and trust funds (such as the endowment of your college or university). These institutional stockholders usually employ their own analysts who also rely on the information intermediaries just discussed. Institutional shareholders control the majority of publicly traded shares of U.S. companies. For example, at the time this chapter is being written, institutional investors owned 70 percent of Apple stock. Apple's three largest institutional investors follow:

Institution	Approximate Ownership
FMR LLC	5.43%
Vanguard Group Inc.	3.99%
State Street Corp.	3.73%

Most small investors own stock in companies such as Apple indirectly through mutual and pension funds.

Private investors include large individual investors such as the venture capitalists who originally invested directly in Apple, as well as small retail investors who buy shares of publicly traded companies through brokers such as Fidelity. Retail investors normally lack the expertise to understand financial statements and the resources to gather data efficiently. They often rely on the advice of information intermediaries or turn their money over to the management of mutual and pension funds (institutional investors).

Lenders, or creditors, include suppliers, banks, commercial credit companies, and other financial institutions that lend money to companies. Lending officers and financial analysts in these organizations use the same public sources of information. They also use additional financial information (e.g., monthly statements) that companies often agree to provide as part of the lending contract. Lenders are the primary external user group for financial statements of private companies. Institutional and private investors also become creditors when they buy a company's publicly traded bonds.

Financial statements also play an important role in the relationships between suppliers and customers. Customers evaluate the financial health of suppliers to determine whether they will be reliable, up-to-date sources of supply. Suppliers evaluate their customers to estimate their future needs and ability to pay debts. Competitors also attempt to learn useful information about a company from its statements. The potential loss of competitive advantage is one of the costs of public financial disclosures. Accounting regulators consider these costs as well as the direct costs of preparation when they consider requiring new disclosures. **Cost effectiveness** requires the benefits of accounting for and reporting information to outweigh the costs. Small amounts do not have to be reported separately or accounted for precisely according to GAAP if they would not influence users' decisions. Accountants usually designate such items and amounts as **immaterial.** Determining **material amounts** is often very subjective.

INSTITUTIONAL INVESTORS are managers of pension, mutual, endowment, and other funds that invest on the behalf of others.

PRIVATE INVESTORS include individuals who purchase shares in companies.

LENDERS (CREDITORS) include suppliers and financial institutions that lend money to companies.

COST EFFECTIVENESS requires that the benefits of accounting for and reporting information outweigh the costs.

MATERIAL AMOUNTS are amounts that are large enough to influence a user's decisions.

PAUSE FOR FEEDBACK

In this section, we learned the roles of different parties in the accounting communication process and the guidance they receive from legal and professional standards. Management of the reporting company decides the appropriate format and level of detail to present in its financial reports. Independent audits increase the credibility of the information. Directors monitor managers' compliance with reporting standards and hire the auditor. The SEC staff reviews public financial reports for compliance with legal and professional standards and punishes violators. Financial statement announcements from public companies usually are first transmitted to users through electronic information services. Analysts play a major role in making financial statement and other information available to average investors through their stock recommendations and earnings forecasts. Before you move on, complete the following exercise to test your understanding of these concepts.

SELF-STUDY **QUIZ**

Match the key terms in the left column with their definitions in the right column.

1. Material amount B C   a. Management primarily responsible for accounting information.
2. CEO and CFO A   b. An independent party who verifies financial statements.
3. Financial analyst E   c. Amount large enough to influence users' decisions.
4. Auditor B   d. Reporting only information that provides benefits in excess of costs.
5. Cost effectiveness X D e. An individual who analyzes financial information and provides advice.

After you have completed your answers, check them with the solutions at the bottom of the page.

THE DISCLOSURE PROCESS

LEARNING OBJECTIVE 5-2

Identify the steps in the accounting communication process, including the issuance of press releases, annual reports, quarterly reports, and SEC filings, as well as the role of electronic information services in this process.

As noted in our discussion of information services and information intermediaries, the accounting communication process includes more steps and participants than one would envision in a world in which annual and quarterly reports are simply mailed to shareholders. SEC regulation FD, for "Fair Disclosure," requires that companies provide all investors equal access to all important company news. Managers and other insiders are also prohibited from trading their company's shares based on nonpublic (insider) information so that no party benefits from early access.

Press Releases

A PRESS RELEASE is a written public news announcement normally distributed to major news services.

To provide timely information to external users and to limit the possibility of selective leakage of information, Apple and other public companies announce quarterly and annual earnings through a **press release** as soon as the verified figures (audited for annual and reviewed for quarterly earnings) are available. Apple normally issues its earnings press releases within four weeks of the end of the accounting period. The announcements are sent electronically to the major print and electronic news services, including *DowJones, Thomson/Reuters,* and *Bloomberg,* which make them immediately available to subscribers. Exhibit 5.3 shows an excerpt from a typical earnings press release for Apple that includes key financial figures. This excerpt is followed by management's discussion of the results and condensed income statements and balance sheets, which will be included in the formal report to shareholders, distributed after the press release.

Many companies, including Apple, follow these press releases with a **conference call** during which senior managers answer analysts' questions about the quarterly results. These calls are open to the investing public. Listening to these recordings is a good way to learn about a company's business strategy and its expectations for the future, as well as key factors that analysts consider when they evaluate a company.

Solutions to
SELF-STUDY QUIZ

1. *c;* 2. *a;* 3. *e;* 4. *b;* 5. *d.*

EXHIBIT 5.3

Earnings Press Release
Excerpt for Apple Inc.

APPLE

REAL WORLD EXCERPT
Press Release

APPLE REPORTS FIRST QUARTER RESULTS

Highest Quarterly Revenue and Earnings Ever

All-Time Record iPhone, iPad and Mac Sales

CUPERTINO, California—January 24, 2012—Apple® today announced financial results for its fiscal 2012 first quarter which spanned 14 weeks and ended December 31, 2011. The Company posted record quarterly revenue of $46.33 billion and record quarterly net profit of $13.06 billion, or $13.87 per diluted share. These results compare to revenue of $26.74 billion and net quarterly profit of $6 billion, or $6.43 per diluted share, in the year-ago quarter. Gross margin was 44.7 percent compared to 38.5 percent in the year-ago quarter. International sales accounted for 58 percent of the quarter's revenue.

The Company sold 37.04 million iPhones in the quarter, representing 128 percent unit growth over the year-ago quarter. Apple sold 15.43 million iPads during the quarter, a 111 percent unit increase over the year-ago quarter. The Company sold 5.2 million Macs during the quarter, a 26 percent unit increase over the year-ago quarter. Apple sold 15.4 million iPods, a 21 percent unit decline from the year-ago quarter.

"We're thrilled with our outstanding results and record-breaking sales of iPhones, iPads and Macs," said Tim Cook, Apple's CEO. "Apple's momentum is incredibly strong, and we have some amazing new products in the pipeline."

How Does the Stock Market React to Earnings Announcements?

FINANCIAL ANALYSIS

For actively traded stocks such as Apple, most of the stock market reaction (stock price increases and decreases from investor trading) to the news in the press release usually occurs quickly. Recall that a number of analysts follow Apple and regularly predict the company's earnings. When the actual earnings are published, the market reacts not to the amount of earnings, but to the difference between expected earnings and actual earnings. This amount is called **unexpected earnings.** In January, analysts expected Apple to report quarterly profit of $10.08 per share. In its press release presented in Exhibit 5.3, Apple's actual earnings per share for the quarter ended up being $13.87 per share. Unexpected earnings (Actual – Expected) were thus $3.79 cents per share ($13.87 – $10.08), and, as a result, the share price jumped $34 or 8 percent on that day.

Companies such as Apple also issue press releases concerning other important events such as new product announcements. Press releases related to annual earnings and quarterly earnings often precede the issuance of the quarterly or annual report by 15 to 45 days. This time is necessary to prepare the additional detail and to distribute those reports.

Annual Reports and Form 10-K

For privately held companies, **annual reports** are relatively simple documents photocopied on white bond paper. They normally include only the following:

1. Four basic financial statements: income statement, balance sheet, stockholders' equity or retained earnings statement, and cash flow statement.
2. Related notes (footnotes).
3. Report of Independent Accountants (Auditor's Opinion) if the statements are audited.

The annual reports of public companies filed on **Form 10-K** are significantly more elaborate mainly because of additional SEC reporting requirements. SEC reports are normally referred

The FORM 10-K is the annual report that publicly traded companies must file with the SEC.

to by number (for example, the "10-K"). The principal components of the financial disclosures in the 10-K include:

Item 1. Business: Description of business operations and company strategy.

Item 6. Selected Financial Data: Summarized financial data for a 5-year period.

Item 7. Management's Discussion and Analysis of Financial Condition and Results of Operations: Management's views on the causes of its successes and failures during the reporting periods and the risks it faces in the future.

Item 8. Financial Statements and Supplemental Data: The four basic financial statements and related notes, the report of management, and the auditor's report (Report of Independent Registered Public Accounting Firm).

Except for the Management's Discussion and Analysis, most of these elements have been covered in earlier chapters. This element includes an explanation of key figures on the financial statements and the risks the company faces in the future. The Form 10-K also provides a more detailed description of the business including its products, product development, sales and marketing, manufacturing, and competitors. It also lists properties owned or leased, any legal proceedings it is involved in, and significant contracts it has signed.

Quarterly Reports and Form 10-Q

The FORM 10-Q is the quarterly report that publicly traded companies must file with the SEC.

Quarterly reports for private companies include condensed financial statements providing fewer details than annual statements and only key notes to the statements. They are not audited and so are marked **unaudited.** Often the cash flow statement, statement of stockholders' equity, and some notes to the financial statements are omitted. Private companies normally prepare quarterly reports for their lenders. Public companies file their quarterly reports on **Form 10-Q** with the SEC. The Form 10-Q contains most of the information items provided in the financial section (PART II) of the 10-K and some additional items.

Other SEC Reports

The FORM 8-K is used by publicly traded companies to disclose any material event not previously reported that is important to investors (e.g., auditor changes, mergers).

Public companies must file other reports with the SEC. These include the current event reports **Form 8-K,** which is used to disclose any material event not previously reported that is important to investors (e.g., auditor changes, mergers). Other filing requirements for public companies are described on the SEC website.

A CLOSER LOOK AT FINANCIAL STATEMENT FORMATS AND NOTES

LEARNING OBJECTIVE 5-3

Recognize and apply the different financial statement and disclosure formats used by companies in practice and analyze the gross profit percentage.

The financial statements shown in previous chapters provide a good introduction to their content and structure. In this section, we will discuss three additional characteristics of financial statements and the related disclosures that are designed to make them more useful to investors, creditors, and analysts:

- **Comparative financial statements.** To allow users to compare performance from period to period, companies report financial statement values for the current period and one or more prior periods. Apple and most U.S. companies present two years' balance sheets and three years' income statements, cash flow statements, and statements of stockholders' equity.

- **Additional subtotals and classifications in financial statements.** You should not be confused when you notice slightly different statement formats used by different companies. In this section, we will focus on similarities and differences in the classifications and line items presented on Apple's and Chipotle's balance sheet, income statement, and cash flow statement.

- **Additional disclosures.** Most companies present voluminous notes that are necessary to understand a company's performance and financial condition. In addition, certain complex transactions require additional statement disclosures. We take a closer look at some of Apple's note disclosures to prepare you for more detailed discussions in the remaining chapters in this text.

Classified Balance Sheet

Exhibit 5.4 shows the September 24, 2011, balance sheet for Apple. This balance sheet looks very similar in structure to the balance sheet for Chipotle presented in Chapter 4, but it is presented for two years to ease comparisons over time. The statement classifications (current vs. noncurrent assets and current vs. noncurrent liabilities) play a major role in our discussions of ratio analysis (e.g., the current ratio in Chapter 2).

Apple's balance sheet contains an item, not included in Chipotle's, that is worthy of additional discussion. **Intangible assets** (discussed in Chapter 8) have no physical existence and a long life. Examples are patents, trademarks, copyrights, franchises, and goodwill from purchasing other companies. Most intangibles (except goodwill, trademarks, and other intangibles

APPLE INC. **Consolidated Balance Sheets*** **(in millions except number of shares which are in thousands)**		
	September 24, 2011	**September 25, 2010**
ASSETS		
Current assets:		
Cash and cash equivalents	$ 9,815	$11,261
Short-term marketable securities	16,137	14,359
Accounts receivable, less allowances of $53 and		
$55, respectively	5,369	5,510
Inventories	776	1,051
Deferred tax assets	2,014	1,636
Vendor non-trade receivables	6,348	4,414
Other current assets	4,529	3,447
Total current assets	44,988	41,678
Long-term marketable securities	55,618	25,391
Property, plant, and equipment, net	7,777	4,768
Goodwill	896	741
Acquired intangible assets, net	3,536	342
Other assets	3,556	2,263
Total assets	**$116,371**	**$75,183**
LIABILITIES AND SHAREHOLDERS' EQUITY		
Current liabilities:		
Accounts payable	$ 14,632	$12,015
Accrued expenses	9,247	5,723
Deferred revenue	4,091	2,984
Total current liabilities	27,970	20,722
Deferred revenue - noncurrent	1,686	1,139
Other noncurrent liabilities	10,100	5,531
Total liabilities	39,756	27,392
Commitments and contingencies		
Shareholders' equity:		
Common stock, no par value; 1,800,000 shares		
authorized; 929,277 and 915,970 shares issued		
and outstanding, respectively	13,774	10,942
Retained earnings	62,841	36,849
Total shareholders' equity	76,615	47,791
Total liabilities and shareholders' equity	**$116,371**	**$75,183**

Apple's statements have been simplified for purposes of our discussion.

with indefinite lives) are amortized as they are used in a manner similar to the depreciation of tangible assets (Amortization Expense is debited and the contra-asset Accumulated Amortization is credited). Just as tangible fixed assets are reported net of accumulated depreciation, **intangible assets are reported net of accumulated amortization** on the balance sheet. **Goodwill** is a more general intangible asset representing the excess of the price paid for another company over the value of its identifiable assets. It is discussed in more detail in Chapter 8.

Also recall our discussion of deferred revenues from Chapter 4. These are liabilities created when customers pay for goods or services before the company delivers them. In Apple's balance sheet, **deferred revenues show up in two places: current liabilities and noncurrent liabilities.** They both relate primarily to product warranties that Apple includes with its products. The deferred revenues related to repairs Apple expects to provide during the next year are classified as current. Those that relate to repairs to be provided in later years are classified as noncurrent.

When you first look at a new set of financial statements, try not to be confused by differences in terminology. When interpreting line items you have never seen before, be sure to consider their description **and their classification.**

Classified Income Statement

Apple's 2011 consolidated income statement is reprinted for you in Exhibit 5.5. It presents the income statement followed by earnings per share for three years as required by the SEC. Apple's income statement includes one subtotal not included in Chipotle's. Like many manufacturing and merchandising (retail and wholesale) companies that sell goods, Apple reports the subtotal **Gross Profit** (gross margin), which is the difference between net sales and cost of goods sold. **It is important to note that regardless of whether a company reports a gross profit subtotal, the income statement presents the same information.** Another subtotal—**Operating Income** (also called Income from Operations)—is computed by subtracting operating expenses from gross profit.

Nonoperating (other) Items are revenues, expenses, gains, and losses that do not relate to the company's primary operations. Examples include interest income, interest expense, and gains and losses on the sale of fixed assets and investments. These nonoperating items are added to or subtracted from income from operations to obtain **Income before Income Taxes,** also called Pretax Earnings. At this point, Provision for Income Taxes (Income Tax Expense) is subtracted to obtain Net Income. Some companies show fewer subtotals on their income statements. No difference exists in the revenue, expense, gain, and loss items reported using the different formats. Only the categories and subtotals differ.

Nonrecurring Items that companies may also report on their income statements are:

1. Discontinued operations

2. Extraordinary items

If one or both of these items exists, an additional subtotal is presented for Income from Continuing Operations (or Income before Nonrecurring Items), after which the nonrecurring items are presented. These two items are presented separately because they are not useful in predicting the future income of the company given their nonrecurring nature.

When a major component of a business is sold or abandoned, income or loss from that component earned before the disposal, as well as any gain or loss on disposal, are included as discontinued operations. Extraordinary Items are gains or losses incurred that are both unusual and infrequent in occurrence. **Companies report extraordinary items very rarely.** For example, only 3 of the 500 companies followed by Accounting Trends and Techniques reported extraordinary items. Apple does not report either item.

Finally, **earnings per share** is reported. Simple computations of earnings per share (EPS) are as follows:

$$\text{Earnings per Share} = \frac{\text{Net Income}^*}{\text{Average Number of Shares of Common Stock Outstanding during the Period}}$$

GROSS PROFIT (GROSS MARGIN) is net sales less cost of goods sold.

OPERATING INCOME (INCOME FROM OPERATIONS) equals net sales less cost of goods sold and other operating expenses.

INCOME BEFORE INCOME TAXES (PRETAX EARNINGS) is revenues minus all expenses except income tax expense.

---

*If there are preferred dividends (discussed in Chapter 11), the amount is subtracted from Net Income in the numerator.

APPLE INC.
Consolidated Statements of Operations*
(in millions except number of shares which are in thousands and per share amounts)

Three years ended September 24, 2011	2011	2010	2009
Net sales	$108,249	$ 65,225	$ 42,905
Cost of sales	64,431	39,541	25,683
Gross profit	43,818	25,684	17,222
Operating expenses:			
Research and development	2,429	1,782	1,333
Selling, general, and administrative	7,599	5,517	4,149
Total operating expenses	10,028	7,299	5,482
Operating income	33,790	18,385	11,740
Other income and expense	415	155	326
Income before provision for income taxes	34,205	18,540	12,066
Provision for income taxes	8,283	4,527	3,831
Net income	$ 25,922	$ 14,013	$ 8,235
Earnings per common share:			
Basic	$ 28.05	$ 15.41	$ 9.22
Shares used in computing earnings per share:			
Basic	924,258	909,461	893,016

Apple's statements have been simplified for purposes of our discussion.

Income Statement of Apple Inc.

APPLE

REAL WORLD EXCERPT
Annual Report

} *Operating activities (central focus of the business)*

} *Peripheral activities (not the main focus of the business)*

} *Income tax expense*

} *= Net Income/Average Number of Shares Outstanding*

Statement of Comprehensive Income

FINANCIAL ANALYSIS

Both the FASB and IASB require an additional statement entitled the Statement of Comprehensive Income which can be presented separately or in combination with the income statement. When presented separately, the statement starts with Net Income, the bottom line of the income statement. Following this total would be the components of other comprehensive income. The Net Income and other comprehensive income items are then combined to create a total called Comprehensive Income (the bottom line for this statement). Apple's competitor Lenovo Group Ltd., maker of ThinkPad computers, presented the following in a recent quarterly report. Other comprehensive income items include fair value changes on certain investment securities, which are discussed in Appendix A, as well as other items discussed in more advanced accounting classes

Lenovo Group Ltd. Consolidated Statement of Comprehensive Income 3 months ended September 30, 2011 (in thousands)	
Net income	$144,671
Other comprehensive (loss)/income	
Fair value change on available-for-sale investments	(35,000)
Fair value change on cash flow hedge	38,882
Actuarial loss from defined benefit pension plans	(318)
Currency translation differences	(31,224)
Comprehensive income	$117,011

PAUSE FOR **FEEDBACK**

As Apple's statements suggest, most statements are classified and include subtotals that are relevant to analysis. On the balance sheet, the most important distinctions are between current and noncurrent assets and liabilities. On the income statement, the subtotals gross profit and income from operations are most important. So the next step in preparing to analyze financial statements is to see if you understand the effects of transactions you have already studied on these subtotals. The following questions will test your ability to do so.

SELF-STUDY **QUIZ**

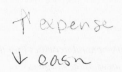

1. Complete the following tabulation, indicating the **direction** (+ for increase, – for decrease, and NE for no effect) **and amount** of the effect of each transaction. Consider each item independently. (Hint: Prepare journal entries for each transaction. Then consider the balance sheet or income statement classification of each account affected to come up with your answers.)

   a. Recorded and paid rent expense of $200.

   b. Recorded the sale of services on account for $400.

Transaction	Current Assets	Gross Profit	Income from Operations
a.	↓ 200	~~↓ 200~~ NE	↓ 200
b.	↑ 400	↑ 400	↑ 400

After you have completed your answers, check them with the solutions at the bottom of the page.

www.mhhe.com/libby8e

GUIDED **HELP**

For additional step-by-step video instruction on preparing the balance sheet and income statement from a trial balance, go to the URL or scan the QR code in the margin with your smartphone or iPad.

KEY RATIO ANALYSIS	Gross Profit Percentage

The key subtotals on the income statement we just discussed also play a major role in financial ratio analysis. As we noted above, net sales less cost of goods sold equals the subtotal **gross profit** or **gross margin.** Analysts often examine gross profit as a percentage of sales (the gross profit or gross margin percentage).

❓ ANALYTICAL QUESTION

How effective is management in selling goods and services for more than the costs to purchase or produce them?

% RATIO AND COMPARISONS

The gross profit percentage ratio is computed as follows:

$$\text{Gross Profit Percentage} = \frac{\text{Gross Profit*}}{\text{Net Sales}}$$

Solutions to
SELF-STUDY QUIZ

1. *a.* Rent expense (+E, −SE) 200	*b.* Accounts receivable (+A) 400	
Cash (−A) 200	Sales revenue (+R, +SE) 400	
−200, NE, −200	+400, +400, +400	

The ratio for 2011 for Apple is:

$$\frac{\$43,818}{\$108,249} = 0.405 \ (40.5\%)$$

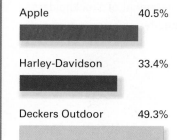

Selected Focus Companies' Gross Profit Percentage Ratios

Apple 40.5%

Harley-Davidson 33.4%

Deckers Outdoor 49.3%

COMPARISONS OVER TIME			COMPARISONS WITH COMPETITORS	
Apple			**Dell**	**HP**
2009	**2010**	**2011**	**2011**	**2011**
40.1%	39.4%	40.5%	22.3%	23.4%

💡 INTERPRETATIONS

In General The gross profit percentage measures a company's ability to charge premium prices and produce goods and services at low cost. All other things equal, a higher gross profit results in higher net income.

Business strategy, as well as competition, affects the gross profit percentage. Companies pursuing a product-differentiation strategy use research and development and product promotion activities to convince customers of the superiority or distinctiveness of the company's products. This allows them to charge premium prices, producing a higher gross profit percentage. Companies following a low-cost strategy rely on more efficient management of production to reduce costs and increase the gross profit percentage. Managers, analysts, and creditors use this ratio to assess the effectiveness of the company's product development, marketing, and production strategy.

Focus Company Analysis Apple's gross profit percentage has remained steady over the past three years and remains well above all of its competitors, including Dell and HP. At the beginning of the chapter, we discussed key elements of Apple's business strategy that focused on introducing new integrated technologies, product lines, and styles, as well as managing production and inventory costs. Each of these elements can have a large effect on gross profit. Its Form 10-K indicates that its various product lines have different gross profit percentages, and that a large increase in iPhone sales increased the overall gross profit percentage. Introducing new products with higher initial cost structures such as the iPad can decrease gross profit percentage.

A Few Cautions To assess the company's ability to sustain its gross profits, you must understand the sources of any change in the gross profit percentage. For example, an increase in margin resulting from increased sales of high-margin new products can be eroded by actions of competitors or increases in component costs for popular products. Also, higher prices must often be sustained with higher R&D and advertising costs, which reduce net income and can offset any increase in gross profit. This has not been the case for Apple in recent years as we will see later in the chapter. Apple's astonishing gross profit results in an industry-leading net profit margin and return on assets.

---

*Gross Profit = Net Sales − Cost of Sales

Statement of Stockholders' Equity

The statement of stockholders' (shareholders') equity reports the changes in each of the company's stockholders' equity accounts during the accounting period. Exhibit 5.6 presents Apple's 2011 consolidated statement of stockholders' equity. The statement has a column for each stockholders' equity account and one for the effect on total stockholders' equity. (Apple does not have an additional paid-in capital account; if it did, this account would have its own column.) The first row of the statement starts with the beginning balances in each account, which correspond to the prior year's ending balances on the balance sheet. Each row that follows lists each event that occurred during the period that affected any stockholders' equity accounts. Apple reported net income of $25,992 for the year, which increases retained earnings. Apple declared no dividends. Had it done so, the amount would have been subtracted from retained earnings. Apple issued 13,307 shares of common stock during the year and received $2,832 million for the issuance. **Note that the number of shares and the dollar amount are both listed. It is important not to confuse them.** If Apple had repurchased and retired shares, the

EXHIBIT 5.6

Statement of Stockholders'
Equity

APPLE INC.
Consolidated Statements of Shareholders' Equity (partial)*
(In millions, except number of shares which are reflected in thousands)

	Common Stock		Retained Earnings	Total Stockholders' Equity
	Shares	**Amount**		
Balances as of September 25, 2010	915,970	$10,942	$36,849	$47,791
Net income			25,992	25,992
Dividends declared			–	–
Stock issued	13,307	2,832		2,832
Stock repurchased		–		–
Balances as of September 24, 2011	**929,277**	**$13,774**	**$62,841**	**$76,615**

Apple's statements have been simplified for purposes of our discussion.

number of shares and dollar amount would have been subtracted from common stock. The final row lists the ending balances in the accounts, which correspond to the ending balances on the balance sheet. Public companies must present information for the prior three years in their statements of stockholders' equity. So Apple's 2009 and 2010 statements would be presented above the information shown in Exhibit 5.6.

Statement of Cash Flows

We introduced the three cash flow statement classifications in prior chapters:

Cash Flows from Operating Activities. This section reports cash flows associated with earning income.

Cash Flows from Investing Activities. Cash flows in this section are associated with the purchase and sale of (1) productive assets (other than inventory) and (2) investments in other companies.

Cash Flows from Financing Activities. These cash flows are related to financing the business through borrowing and repaying loans from financial institutions, stock (equity) issuances and repurchases, and dividend payments.

Exhibit 5.7 presents Apple's 2011 consolidated statement of cash flows. The first section (Cash Flows from Operating Activities) can be reported using either the **direct** or **indirect** method. For Apple, this first section is reported using the indirect method, which presents a reconciliation of net income on an accrual basis to cash flows from operations.

The Operating Activities section prepared using the indirect method helps the analyst understand the **causes of differences** between a company's net income and its cash flows. Net income and cash flows from operating activities can be quite different. Remember that the income statement is prepared under the accrual concept. Revenues are recorded when earned without regard to when the related cash flows occur. Likewise, expenses are matched with revenues and recorded in the same period without regard to when the related cash flows occur.

In the indirect method, the operating activities section starts with net income computed under the accrual concept and then eliminates noncash items, leaving cash flow from operating activities:

> **Net income**
> **+/− Adjustments for noncash items**
> **Cash provided by operating activities**

APPLE INC.
Consolidated Statements of Cash Flows*
(in millions)

Three years ended September 24, 2011	2011	2010	2009
Cash and cash equivalents, beginning of the year	$ 11,261	$ 5,263	$ 11,875
Operating activities:			
Net income	25,922	14,013	8,235
Adjustments to reconcile net income to cash generated by operating activities:			
Depreciation	1,814	1,027	734
Other noncash items	4,036	2,319	1,750
Changes in operating assets and liabilities:	5,757	1,236	(560)
Cash generated by operating activities	37,529	18,595	10,159
Investing activities:			
Purchases of marketable securities	(102,317)	(57,793)	(46,724)
Proceeds from sales/maturities of marketable securities	69,853	46,718	30,678
Payments for acquisition of property, plant, and equipment	(4,504)	(2,643)	(1,144)
Payments for acquisition of intangible assets	(3,192)	(116)	(69)
Other investing activities	(259)	(20)	(175)
Cash used in investing activities	(40,419)	(13,854)	(17,434)
Financing activities:			
Proceeds from issuance of common stock	831	912	475
Other financing activities	613	345	188
Cash generated by financing activities	1,444	1,257	663
(Decrease)/increase in cash and cash equivalents	(1,446)	5,998	(6,612)
Cash and cash equivalents, end of the year	$ 9,815	$ 11,261	$ 5,263
Supplemental cash flow disclosure:			
Cash paid for income taxes, net	$ 3,338	$ 2,697	$ 2,997

Apple's statements have been simplified for purposes of our discussion.

Cash flows associated with earning income computed by eliminating noncash items from net income

Cash flows associated with purchase and sale of productive assets and investments

Cash flows associated with borrowing and repaying loans, issuing and repurchasing stock, and dividends

} *Total change in cash*

} *End of year cash on balance sheet*

The items listed between these two amounts explain the reasons they differ. For example, since no cash is paid during the current period for Apple's depreciation expense reported on the income statement, this amount is added back to net income to eliminate its effect. Similarly, increases and decreases in certain current assets and liabilities also account for some of the difference between net income and cash flow from operations. For example, sales on account increase net income as well as the current asset accounts receivable, but sales on account do not increase cash. As we cover different portions of the income statement and balance sheet in more detail in Chapters 6 through 11, we will also discuss the relevant sections of the cash flow statement. Then we discuss the complete cash flow statement in detail in Chapter 12.

Notes to Financial Statements

While the numbers reported on the various financial statements provide important information, users require additional details to facilitate their analysis. All financial reports include additional information in notes that follow the statements. Apple's 2011 notes include three types of information:

1. Descriptions of the key accounting rules applied to the company's statements.

2. Additional detail supporting reported numbers.

3. Relevant financial information not disclosed on the statements.

Accounting Rules Applied in the Company's Statements

One of the first notes is typically a summary of significant accounting policies. As you will see in your study of subsequent chapters, generally accepted accounting principles (GAAP) permit companies to select from alternative methods for measuring the effects of transactions. The summary of significant accounting policies tells the user which accounting methods the company has adopted. Apple's accounting policy for property, plant, and equipment is as follows:

NOTE 1 – SUMMARY OF SIGNIFICANT ACCOUNTING POLICIES

Property, Plant, and Equipment

Property, plant, and equipment are stated at cost. Depreciation is computed by use of the straight-line method over the estimated useful lives of the assets, which for buildings is the lesser of 30 years or the remaining life of the underlying building, up to five years for equipment, and the shorter of lease terms or ten years for leasehold improvements.

We will discuss alternative depreciation methods in Chapter 8. Without an understanding of the various accounting methods used, it is impossible to analyze a company's financial results effectively.

Additional Detail Supporting Reported Numbers

The second category of notes provides supplemental information concerning the data shown on the financial statements. Among other information, these notes may show revenues broken out by geographic region or business segment, describe unusual transactions, and/or offer expanded detail on a specific classification. For example, in Note 3, Apple indicates the makeup of property, plant, and equipment presented on the balance sheet.

NOTE 3 – CONSOLIDATED FINANCIAL STATEMENT DETAILS

Property, Plant, and Equipment

	2011	2010
Land and buildings	$ 2,059	$ 1,471
Machinery, equipment, and internal-use software	6,926	3,589
Office furniture and equipment	184	144
Leasehold improvements	2,599	2,030
Gross property, plant, and equipment	11,768	7,234
Accumulated depreciation and amortization	(3,991)	(2,466)
Net property, plant, and equipment	$ 7,777	$ 4,768

Relevant Financial Information Not Disclosed on the Statements

The final category includes information that impacts the company financially but is not shown on the statements. Examples include information on legal matters and contractual agreements that do not result in an asset or liability on the balance sheet. In Note 7, Apple disclosed the details of its commitments under supply agreements, which total over $15 billion and are not shown as a liability on the balance sheet.

NOTE 7 – COMMITMENTS AND CONTINGENCIES

Other Commitments

As of September 24, 2011, the Company had outstanding off-balance sheet commitments for outsourced manufacturing and component purchases of $13.9 billion.

Additionally, other outstanding obligations were $2.4 billion as of September 24, 2011, and were comprised mainly of commitments under long-term supply agreements to make additional inventory component prepayments and to acquire capital equipment, commitments to acquire product tooling and manufacturing process equipment, and commitments related to advertising, research and development, Internet and telecommunications services and other obligations.

APPLE

REAL WORLD EXCERPT
Annual Report

Voluntary Disclosures

GAAP and SEC regulations set only the minimum level of required financial disclosures. Many companies provide important disclosures beyond those required. For example, in its annual report, 10-K, and recent earnings press release, Apple discloses sales by major product category, which helps investors track the success of new products.

	2011	Change	2010	Change	2009
Net Sales by Product:					
Desktops (a)	$ 6,439	4%	$ 6,201	43%	$ 4,324
Portables (b)	15,344	36%	11,278	18%	9,535
Total Mac net sales	21,783	25%	17,479	26%	13,859
iPod	7,453	(10)%	8,274	2%	8,091
Other music related products and services (c)	6,314	28%	4,948	23%	4,036
iPhone and related products and services (d)	47,057	87%	25,179	93%	13,033
iPad and related products and services (e)	20,358	311%	4,958	NM	0
Peripherals and other hardware (f)	2,330	28%	1,814	23%	1,475
Software, service and other sales (g)	2,954	15%	2,573	7%	2,411
Total net sales	$108,249	66%	$65,225	52%	$42,905

APPLE

REAL WORLD EXCERPT
Annual Report

Differences in Accounting Methods Acceptable under IFRS and U.S. GAAP

INTERNATIONAL PERSPECTIVE

Financial accounting standards and disclosure requirements are adopted by national regulatory agencies. Many countries, including the members of the European Union, have adopted international financial reporting standards (IFRS) issued by the International Accounting Standards Board (IASB). IFRS are similar to U.S. GAAP, but there are several important differences. A partial list of the differences at the time this chapter is being written is presented below, along with the chapter in which these issues will be addressed:

(continued)

Difference	U.S. GAAP	IFRS	Chapter
Extraordinary items	Permitted	Prohibited	5
Last-in first-out (LIFO) method for inventory	Permitted	Prohibited	7
Reversal of inventory write-downs	Prohibited	Required	7
Basis for property, plant, and equipment	Historical cost	Fair value or historical cost	8
Development costs	Expensed	Capitalized	8
Debt to be refinanced	Current	Noncurrent	9
Recognition of contingent liabilities	Probable	More likely than not	9
Stockholders' equity accounts	Capital stock	Share capital	11
	Paid-in capital	Share premium	
Interest received on cash flow statement	Operating	Operating or investing	12
Interest paid on cash flow statement	Operating	Operating or financing	12

The FASB and IASB are working together to eliminate these and other differences.

RETURN ON ASSETS ANALYSIS: A FRAMEWORK FOR EVALUATING COMPANY PERFORMANCE

LEARNING OBJECTIVE 5-4

Analyze a company's performance based on return on assets and its components and the effects of transactions on financial ratios.

Evaluating company performance is the primary goal of financial statement analysis. Company managers, as well as competitors, use financial statements to better understand and evaluate a company's business strategy. Analysts, investors, and creditors use these same statements to judge company performance when they estimate the value of the company's stock and its creditworthiness. Our discussion of the financial data contained in accounting reports has now reached the point where we can develop an overall framework for using that data to evaluate company performance. The most general framework for evaluating company performance is called return on assets (ROA) analysis.

KEY RATIO ANALYSIS

Return on Assets (ROA)

? ANALYTICAL QUESTION

During the period, how well has management used the company's total investment in assets financed by both debt holders and stockholders?

% RATIO AND COMPARISONS

$$\text{Return on Assets} = \frac{\text{Net Income*}}{\text{Average Total Assets}^\dagger}$$

The 2011 ratio for Apple:

$$\frac{\$25,922}{(\$75,183 + \$116,371) \div 2} = 0.271\ (27.1\%)$$

Selected Focus Companies' Return on Assets Ratios

Chipotle   16.9%

Harley-Davidson   6.3%

Deckers Outdoor   20.6%

COMPARISONS OVER TIME			COMPARISONS WITH COMPETITORS	
Apple			Dell	HP
2009	**2010**	**2011**	**2011**	**2011**
19.7%	22.8%	27.1%	8.4%	5.6%

💡 INTERPRETATIONS

In General   ROA measures how much the firm earned for each dollar of investment in assets. It is the broadest measure of profitability and management effectiveness, independent of financing strategy. Firms with higher ROA are doing a better job of selecting and managing investments, all other things equal. Since it is independent of the source of financing (debt vs. equity), it can be used to evaluate performance at any level within the organization. It is often computed on a division-by-division or product line basis and used to evaluate division or product line managers' relative performance.

Focus Company Analysis   The increase in return on assets between 2009 and 2011 was mainly due to an increase in overall sales and a change in product mix to products with higher gross profit percentages. For example, as disclosed in the voluntary disclosure of product line sales presented above, iPhone sales have nearly doubled each of the last two years. They have a higher gross profit percentage than most other Apple products, and this carries over to higher net income. The company is doing much better than its more traditional rivals Dell and HP.

A Few Cautions   Like all ratios, the key to interpreting change is to dig deeper to understand the reason for each change. Our next topic, ROA Profit Driver Analysis and Business Strategy, is aimed at just that.

---

*In more complex return on assets analyses, interest expense (net of tax) and minority interest are added back to net income in the numerator of the ratio, since the measure assesses return on capital independent of its source.

†Average Total Assets = (Beginning Total Assets + Ending Total Assets) ÷ 2.

ROA Profit Driver Analysis and Business Strategy

Effective analysis of Apple's performance also requires understanding **why** its ROA differs both from prior levels and from those of its competitors. ROA profit driver analysis (also called **ROA decomposition** or **DuPont analysis**) breaks down ROA into the two factors shown in Exhibit 5.8. These factors are often called **profit drivers** or **profit levers** because they describe the two ways that management can improve ROA. They are measured by the key ratios you learned in Chapters 3 and 4.

1. **Net profit margin = Net Income ÷ Net Sales.** It measures how much of every sales dollar is profit. It can be increased by
   a. Increasing sales volume.
   b. Increasing sales price.
   c. Decreasing cost of goods sold and operating expenses.

2. **Total asset turnover = Net Sales ÷ Average Total Assets.** It measures how many sales dollars the company generates with each dollar of assets (efficiency of use of assets). It can be increased by
   a. Centralizing distribution to reduce inventory kept on hand.
   b. Consolidating production facilities in fewer factories to reduce the amount of assets necessary to generate each dollar of sales.

EXHIBIT 5.8

ROA Profit Driver Analysis

These two ratios report on the effectiveness of the company's operating and investing activities, respectively.

Successful manufacturers often follow one of two business strategies. The first is a **high-value** or **product-differentiation** strategy. Companies following this strategy rely on research and development and product promotion to convince customers of the superiority or distinctiveness of their products. This allows the company to charge higher prices and earn a higher net profit margin. The second is a **low-cost strategy,** which relies on efficient management of accounts receivable, inventory, and productive assets to produce high asset turnover.

The ROA profit driver analysis presented in Exhibit 5.9 indicates the sources of Apple's ROA and compares them to the same figures for Dell. **Apple** follows a classic **high-value strategy,** developing a reputation for the most innovative products in its markets. The success of this strategy is evident in its market leading **net profit margin** of .239 or **23.9%.** This means that 23.9 cents of every sales dollar is net profit. This compares with Dell's 5.6% net profit margin, which matches other competitors such as HP.

Dell primarily follows a **low-cost strategy** by offering excellent products and service at competitive prices. The efficiency of Dell's operations is evident in its higher **total asset turnover** of **1.49** compared to Apple's 1.13. Apple has produced a much higher ROA than Dell because its phenomenal net profit margin more than offsets its lower total asset turnover, and its stock price has responded accordingly.

If Apple follows the same strategy it has in the past, the secret to maintaining its ROA must be continued product development to support premium selling prices. In 2011, Apple made major strides in new product development and the success of its new product introductions bodes well for a high ROA in the longer term. As the preceding discussion indicates, a company can take many different actions to try to affect its profit drivers. To understand the impact of these actions, financial analysts disaggregate each of the profit drivers into more detailed ratios. For example, the total asset turnover ratio is further disaggregated into turnover ratios for specific assets such as accounts receivable, inventory, and fixed assets. We will develop our understanding of these more specific ratios in the next seven chapters of the book. Then, in Chapter 13, we will combine the ratios in a comprehensive review.

How Transactions Affect Ratios

Apple and other companies know that investors and creditors follow their key financial ratios closely. Changes in ROA and its components can have a major effect on a company's stock price and interest rates that lenders charge. As a consequence, company managers closely follow the effects of their actual and planned transactions on these same key financial ratios. We have already learned how to determine the effects of transactions on key subtotals on the income statement and balance sheet (gross profit, current assets, etc.). So we are only one step away from being able to compute the effects of transactions on ratios. The following three-step process will help you do so:

1. **Journalize the transaction to determine its effects on various accounts,** just as we did in Chapters 2 through 4.

2. **Determine which accounts belong to the financial statement subtotals or totals in the numerator (top) and denominator (bottom) of the ratio and the direction of their effects.**

3. **Evaluate the combined effects from step 2 on the ratio.**

EXHIBIT 5.9	ROA Profit Drivers	Formulas	Apple	Dell
	Net Profit Margin	Net Income/Net Sales	0.239	0.056
Apple vs. Dell ROA Profit Driver Analysis	× Total Asset Turnover	× Net Sales/Average Total Assets	1.13	1.49
	= Return on Assets	= Net Income/Average Total Assets	0.271	0.084

Let's try a few examples to get a feel for the process. What would be the effect of the following transactions on the following ratios (ignoring taxes)? The examples we will consider illustrate that the effect depends on what part of the ratio, numerator (top) and/or denominator (bottom), is affected. We need to consider three cases.

What if only the numerator or denominator is affected?

Example 1: Apple incurred an additional $1,000 in research and development expense paid for in cash (all numbers in millions). What would be the effect on the **net profit margin** ratio? The entry would be:

Research and development expense (+E, −SE).....................	1,000	
Cash (−A)		1,000

Note that the transaction would decrease the numerator Net Income, and have no effect on the denominator Net Sales. The ratio was .239. It would decrease to .230 as follows.

	Net Income	÷	Net Sales	=	Net Profit Margin
As reported:	$25,922	÷	$108,249	=	.239
Transaction effect:	−1,000		−		
After transaction:	$24,922	÷	$108,249	=	.230

This example illustrates a general point about the effect of transactions on ratios. If a transaction **only** affects the numerator **or** denominator of the ratio, it will have the following effects on the ratio:

Ratio Changes Given Changes in Numerator _or_ Denominator	
Numerator	**Ratio**
Increases	Increases
Decreases	Decreases
Denominator	
Increases	Decreases
Decreases	Increases

What if both the numerator and denominator are affected but by different amounts?

Example 2: Consider the same transaction in Example 1. What would be the effect on the **return on assets** ratio? Note that the transaction would decrease the numerator Net Income by $1,000. It would also **decrease the ending** total assets by $1,000, but have **no effect on beginning** total assets. So the denominator, **average** total assets, would only decrease by $500:

$$\text{Avg. Total Assets} = (\$75,183 + \$116,371 - \$1,000) \div 2 = \$95,277$$

The ratio was .271 in Exhibit 5.9. It would decrease as follows:

	Net Income	÷	Avg. Total Assets	=	Return on Assets
As reported:	$25,922	÷	$95,777	=	.271
Transaction effect:	−1,000		−500		
After transaction:	$24,922	÷	$95,277	=	.262

This example illustrates a second general point about the effect of transactions on ratios. If a transaction affects the numerator by more than it affects the denominator, or if it affects the denominator by more than it affects the numerator, **focus only on the larger effect and the effects in the table above still hold.**

What if the numerator and denominator are affected by the same amount?
Example 3: Apple paid $2,000 of accounts payable in cash (all numbers in millions). What would be the effect on the **current ratio?** The entry would be:

Accounts payable (−L)   2,000
    Cash (−A)   2,000

Note that the transaction would decrease the numerator, Current Assets, and the denominator, Current Liabilities, by the same amount. The ratio was 1.61 (using numbers from Exhibit 5.4). It would increase as follows.

	Current Assets	**÷**	**Current Liabilities**	**=**	**Current Ratio**
As reported:	$44,988	÷	$27,970	=	1.61
Transaction effect:	−2,000		−2,000		
After transaction:	$42,998	÷	$25,970	=	1.66

This example illustrates a third general point about the effect of transactions on ratios. **If a transaction affects the numerator and denominator of the ratio by the same amount, the effect will depend on whether the original ratio value was greater or less than 1.00:**

Ratio Changes Given _Same_ Change in Numerator _and_ Denominator		
Numerator and Denominator	**Ratio < 1**	**Ratio > 1**
Increase both	Increases	Decreases
Decrease both	Decreases	Increases

PAUSE FOR **FEEDBACK**

STOP

ROA measures how well management used the company's invested capital during the period. Its two determinants, net profit margin and asset turnover, indicate why ROA differs from prior levels or the ROAs of competitors. They also suggest strategies to improve ROA in future periods. The effect of an individual transaction on a financial ratio depends on its effects on both the numerator and denominator of the ratio.

SELF-STUDY **QUIZ**

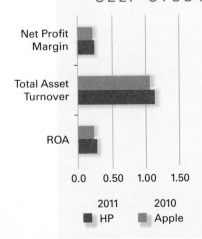

Net Profit Margin

Total Asset Turnover

ROA

0.0   0.50   1.00   1.50

2011   2010
■ HP   ■ Apple

1. We used profit driver analysis in Exhibit 5.9 to explain why a company has an ROA different from its competitors at a single point in time. This type of analysis is called **cross-sectional analysis.** Profit driver analysis can also be used to explain how changes in net profit margin (Net Income/Net Sales) and total asset turnover (Net Sales/Average Total Assets) changed Apple's ROA over time. This type of analysis is often called **time-series analysis.** Following is the recent year's ROA analysis for Apple Inc. Using profit driver analysis, explain how Apple has increased its ROA.

ROA Profit Drivers	2011	2010
Net Income/Net Sales	.239	.215
× Net Sales/Average Total Assets	1.13	1.06
= Net Income/Average Total Assets	.271	.228

2. What would be the **direction** of the effect of the following transactions on the following ratios (+ for increase, − for decrease, and NE for no effect)? Consider each item independently.

a. Recorded and paid rent expense of $200.

b. Recorded the sale of services on account for $400.

Transaction	Gross Profit Margin	Return on Assets	Current Ratio
a.			
b.			

After you have completed your answers, check them with the solutions at the bottom of the page.

DEMONSTRATION CASE

MICROSOFT CORPORATION

Complete the following requirements before proceeding to the suggested solution. Microsoft Corporation is the developer of a broad line of computer software, including the Windows operating systems and Word (word processing) and Excel (spreadsheet) programs. Following is a list of the financial statement items and amounts adapted from a recent Microsoft income statement and balance sheet. These items have normal debit and credit balances and are reported in millions of dollars. For that year, 8,908 million (weighted average) shares of stock were outstanding. The company closed its books on June 30, 2009.

Microsoft Corporation

Accounts payable	$ 3,324	Other income (expense)	$ (542)
Accounts receivable (net)	11,192	Other investments	4,933
Accrued compensation	3,156	Other noncurrent assets	16,140
Cash and short-term investments	31,447	Property, plant, and equipment (net)	7,535
Common stock and paid-in capital	62,382	Provision for income taxes	5,252
Cost of goods sold	12,155	Research and development	9,010
General and administrative	4,030	Retained earnings (deficit)	(22,824)
Income taxes payable	725	Sales and marketing	12,879
Net revenues	58,437	Unearned revenue	13,003
Other current assets	6,641	Long-term liabilities	11,296
Other current liabilities	6,826		

Required:

1. Prepare in good form a classified (multiple-step) income statement (showing gross profit, operating income, income before income taxes, net income, and earnings per share) and a classified balance sheet for the year.

2. Compute the company's ROA. Briefly explain its meaning using ROA profit driver analysis. (Microsoft's total assets at the beginning of the year were $72,793 million.)

3. If Microsoft had additional $1,500 in general and administrative expenses (paid for in cash), what would be the effect on its ROA (increase, decrease, or no effect)?

---

1. Apple's 4.3% increase (27.1% − 22.8%) in ROA resulted from improvements in both its net profit margin and its total asset turnover. Apple's dramatic increase in sales is reflected in its income statement presented in Exhibit 5.5. The management discussion and analysis in its 10-K indicates that most of this increase involved increases in sales volume of high-margin iPhones and iPads.

2. *a.* Rent expense (+E, −SE)   200   *b.* Accounts receivable (+A)   400
        Cash (−A)   200   Sales revenue (+R, +SE)   400
           NE, −, −   +, +, +

SUGGESTED SOLUTION

1.

MICROSOFT CORPORATION **Income Statement** **For the Year Ended June 30, 2009** **(dollars in millions)**	
Net revenues	$58,437
Cost of goods sold	12,155
Gross profit	46,282
Operating expenses:	
Research and development	9,010
Sales and marketing	12,879
General and administrative	4,030
Total operating expenses	25,919
Operating income	20,363
Nonoperating income and expenses:	
Other income (expense)	(542)
Income before income taxes	19,821
Provision for income taxes	5,252
Net income	$14,569
Earnings per share	$ 1.64

MICROSOFT CORPORATION **Balance Sheet** **June 30, 2009** **(dollars in millions)**	
ASSETS	
Current assets	
Cash and short-term investments	$31,447
Accounts receivable (net)	11,192
Other current assets	6,641
Total current assets	49,280
Noncurrent assets	
Property, plant, and equipment (net)	7,535
Other investments	4,933
Other noncurrent assets	16,140
Total assets	$77,888
LIABILITIES	
Current liabilities	
Accounts payable	$ 3,324
Accrued compensation	3,156
Income taxes payable	725
Unearned revenue	13,003
Other current liabilities	6,826
Total current liabilities	27,034
Long-term liabilities	11,296
Stockholders' equity	
Common stock and paid-in capital	62,382
Retained earnings (deficit)	(22,824)
Total stockholders' equity	39,558
Total liabilities and stockholders' equity	$77,888

2.

Fiscal Year Ending June 30, 2009	
Net Income/Net Sales	0.25
$\times$ Net Sales/Average Total Assets	0.78
= Net Income/Average Total Assets	0.19

For the year ended June 30, Microsoft earned an ROA of 19 percent. Microsoft maintains high profit margins, earning $0.25 of net income for every $1 of net sales, but the company has a lower asset efficiency with only $0.78 in sales generated for each $1 of assets. The analysis also indicates Microsoft's dominance of the computer software business, which allows the company to charge premium prices for its products.

3.

General and administrative expenses (+E, −SE)	1,500	
Cash (−A)		1,500

The numerator Net Income would decrease by $1,500 and the denominator Average Total Assets would decrease by $750. As a consequence, ROA would decrease.

5-1. Recognize the people involved in the accounting communication process (regulators, managers, directors, auditors, information intermediaries, and users), their roles in the process, and the guidance they receive from legal and professional standards. p. 227

Management of the reporting company must decide on the appropriate format (categories) and level of detail to present in its financial reports. Independent audits increase the credibility of the information. Directors monitor managers' compliance with reporting standards and hire the auditor. Financial statement announcements from public companies usually are first transmitted to users through electronic information services. The SEC staff reviews public financial reports for compliance with legal and professional standards, investigates irregularities, and punishes violators. Analysts play a major role in making financial statement and other information available to average investors through their stock recommendations and earnings forecasts.

5-2. Identify the steps in the accounting communication process, including the issuance of press releases, annual reports, quarterly reports, and SEC filings, as well as the role of electronic information services in this process. p. 232

Earnings are first made public in press releases. Companies follow these announcements with annual and quarterly reports containing statements, notes, and additional information. Public companies must file additional reports with the SEC, including the 10-K, 10-Q, and 8-K, which contain more details about the company. Electronic information services are the key source of dissemination of this information to sophisticated users.

5-3. Recognize and apply the different financial statement and disclosure formats used by companies in practice and analyze the gross profit percentage. p. 234

Most statements are classified and include subtotals that are relevant to analysis. On the balance sheet, the most important distinctions are between current and noncurrent assets and liabilities. On the income and cash flow statements, the distinction between operating and nonoperating items is most important. The notes to the statements provide descriptions of the accounting rules applied, add more information about items disclosed on the statements, and present information about economic events not included in the statements.

5-4. Analyze a company's performance based on return on assets and its components and the effects of transactions on financial ratios. p. 244

ROA measures how well management used the company's invested capital during the period. Its two determinants, net profit margin and asset turnover, indicate why ROA differs from prior levels or the ROAs of competitors. They also suggest strategies to improve ROA in future periods. The effect of an individual transaction on a financial ratio depends on its effects on both the numerator and denominator of the ratio.

In Chapter 6, we will begin our in-depth discussion of individual items presented in financial statements. We will start with two of the most liquid assets, cash and accounts receivable, and transactions that involve revenues and certain selling expenses. Accuracy in revenue recognition and the related recognition of cost of goods sold (discussed in Chapter 7) are the most important determinants of the accuracy—and, thus, the usefulness—of financial statements. We will also introduce concepts related to the management and control of cash and receivables, a critical business function. A detailed understanding of these topics is crucial to future managers, accountants, and financial analysts.

Gross profit percentage measures the excess of sales prices over the costs to purchase or produce the goods or services sold as a percentage. It is computed as follows (p. 238):

$$\text{Gross Profit Percentage} = \frac{\text{Gross Profit}}{\text{Net Sales}}$$

Return on assets (ROA) measures how much the firm earned for each dollar of investment. It is computed as follows (p. 244):

$$\text{Return on Assets} = \frac{\text{Net Income}}{\text{Average Total Assets}}$$

FINDING **FINANCIAL INFORMATION**

Balance Sheet

Assets (by order of liquidity)
   Current assets (short-term)
   Noncurrent assets
     Total assets

Liabilities (by order of time to maturity)
   Current liabilities (short-term)
   Long-term liabilities
     Total liabilities

Stockholders' equity (by source)
   Common stock and Additional paid-in capital (by owners)
   Retained earnings (accumulated earnings minus accumulated dividends declared)
     Total stockholders' equity
     Total liabilities and stockholders' equity

Income Statement

   Net sales
− Cost of goods sold

   Gross margin
− Operating expenses

   Income from operations
+/− Nonoperating revenues/expenses and gains/losses

   Income before income taxes
− Income tax expense

   Net income

   Earnings per share

Statement of Stockholders' Equity

	Common Stock	Add'l Paid-in Capital	Retained Earnings	Total Stockholders' Equity
Beginning balance	xx	xx	xx	xx
Net income			xx	xx
Dividends declared			(xx)	(xx)
Stock issued	xx	xx		xx
Stock retired	(xx)	(xx)		(xx)
Ending balance	xx	xx	xx	xx

Statement of Cash Flows

Operating activities:
   Net income
    +/−Adjustments for noncash items
    Cash provided by operating activities
Investing activities:
Financing activities:

Notes

Key Classifications
   Descriptions of accounting rules applied in the statements
   Additional detail supporting reported numbers
   Relevant financial information not disclosed on the statements

KEY **TERMS**

QUESTIONS

1. Describe the roles and responsibilities of management and independent auditors in the financial reporting process.
2. Define the following three users of financial accounting disclosures and the relationships among them: (*a*) financial analysts, (*b*) private investors, and (*c*) institutional investors.
3. Briefly describe the role of information services in the communication of financial information.
4. Explain what is a material amount.
5. What basis of accounting (cash or accrual) does GAAP require on the (*a*) income statement, (*b*) balance sheet, and (*c*) statement of cash flows?
6. Briefly explain the normal sequence and form of financial reports produced by private companies in a typical year.
7. Briefly explain the normal sequence and form of financial reports produced by public companies in a typical year.
8. What are the four major subtotals or totals on the income statement?
9. List the six major classifications reported on a balance sheet.
10. For property, plant, and equipment, as reported on the balance sheet, explain (*a*) cost, (*b*) accumulated depreciation, and (*c*) net book value.
11. Briefly explain the major classifications of stockholders' equity for a corporation.
12. What are the three major classifications on a statement of cash flows?
13. What are the three major categories of notes or footnotes presented in annual reports? Cite an example of each.
14. Briefly define return on assets and what it measures.

MULTIPLE-CHOICE QUESTIONS

1. If average total assets increase, but net income, net sales, and average stockholders' equity remain the same, what is the impact on the return on assets ratio?
   a. Increases.
   b. Decreases.
   c. Remains the same.
   d. Cannot be determined without additional information.
2. If a company plans to differentiate its products by offering low prices and discounts for items packaged in bulk (like a discount retailer that requires memberships for its customers), which component in the ROA profit driver analysis is the company attempting to boost?
   a. Net profit margin.
   b. Asset turnover.
   c. Financial leverage.
   d. All of the above.
3. If a company reported the following items on its income statement (cost of goods sold $6,000, income tax expense $2,000, interest expense $500, operating expenses $3,500, sales revenue $14,000), what amount would be reported for the subtotal "income from operations"?
   a. $8,000
   b. $2,000
   c. $4,500
   d. $4,000
4. Which of the following is **not** one of the possible nonrecurring items that must be shown in a separate line item below the Income from Continuing Operations subtotal in the income statement?
   a. Gains and losses from the sale of fixed assets.
   b. Discontinued operations.
   c. Extraordinary items.
   d. Both a and b.
5. Which of the following reports is filed annually with the SEC?
   a. Form 10-Q
   b. Form 10-K
   c. Form 8-K
   d. Press release

6. Which of the following would normally **not** be found in the notes to the financial statements?
   a. Accounting rules applied in the company's financial statements.
   b. Additional detail supporting numbers reported in the company's financial statements.
   c. Relevant financial information not presented in the company's financial statements.
   d. All of the above would be found in the notes to the financial statements.

7. Which of the following is **not** a normal function of a financial analyst?
   a. Issue earnings forecasts.
   b. Examine the records underlying the financial statements to certify their conformance with GAAP.
   c. Make buy, hold, and sell recommendations on companies' stock.
   d. Advise institutional investors on their securities holdings.

8. The classified balance sheet format allows one to ascertain quickly which of the following?
   a. The most valuable asset of the company.
   b. The specific due date for all liabilities of the company.
   c. What liabilities must be paid within the upcoming year.
   d. None of the above.

9. When a company issues stock with a par value, what columns are typically presented in the statement of stockholders' equity?
   a. Common Stock; Additional Paid-In Capital; and Property, Plant, and Equipment, Net.
   b. Cash; and Property, Plant, and Equipment, Net.
   c. Common Stock; Additional Paid-In Capital; and Retained Earnings.
   d. Common Stock; Additional Paid-In Capital; and Cash.

10. Net income was $850,000. Beginning and ending assets were $8,500,000 and $9,600,000, respectively. What was the return on assets (ROA)?
    a. 9.39%   c. 9.94%
    b. 10.59%   d. 10.41%

For more practice with multiple-choice questions, go to the text website at **www.mhhe.com/libby8e**.

MINI-**EXERCISES**

M5-1
LO5-1

Matching Players in the Accounting Communication Process with Their Definitions

Match each player with the related definition by entering the appropriate letter in the space provided.

Players	Definitions
___ (1) Independent auditor	A. Adviser who analyzes financial and other economic information to form forecasts and stock recommendations.
___ (2) CEO and CFO	B. Institutional and private investors and creditors (among others).
___ (3) Users	C. Chief executive officer and chief financial officer who have primary responsibility for the information presented in financial statements.
___ (4) Financial analyst	D. Independent CPA who examines financial statements and attests to their fairness.

M5-2
LO5-2

Identifying the Disclosure Sequence

Indicate the order in which the following disclosures or reports are normally issued by public companies.

No.	Title
_____	Form 10-K
_____	Earnings press release
_____	Annual report

Finding Financial Information: Matching Financial Statements with the Elements of Financial Statements

M5-3
LO5-3

Match each financial statement with the items presented on it by entering the appropriate letter in the space provided.

Elements of Financial Statements	Financial Statements
___ (1) Expenses	A. Income statement
___ (2) Cash from operating activities	B. Balance sheet
___ (3) Losses	C. Cash flow statement
___ (4) Assets	D. None of the above
___ (5) Revenues	
___ (6) Cash from financing activities	
___ (7) Gains	
___ (8) Owners' equity	
___ (9) Liabilities	
___ (10) Assets personally owned by a stockholder	

Determining the Effects of Transactions on Balance Sheet and Income Statement Categories

M5-4
LO5-3

Complete the following tabulation, indicating the sign of the effect (+ for increase, − for decrease, and NE for no effect) of each transaction. Consider each item independently.

a. Recorded sales on account of $300 and related cost of goods sold of $200.
b. Recorded advertising expense of $10 incurred but not paid for.

Transaction	Current Assets	Gross Profit	Current Liabilities
(a)			
(b)			

Determining Financial Statement Effects of Sales and Cost of Goods Sold and Issuance of Par Value Stock

M5-5
LO5-3

Using the following categories, indicate the effects of the following transactions. Use + for increase and − for decrease and indicate the accounts affected and the amounts.

a. Sales on account were $1,800 and related cost of goods sold was $1,200.
b. Issued 5,000 shares of $1 par value stock for $60,000 cash.

Event	Assets	=	Liabilities	+	Stockholders' Equity
(a)					
(b)					

Recording Sales and Cost of Goods Sold and Issuance of Par Value Stock

M5-6
LO5-3

Prepare journal entries for each transaction listed in M5-5.

Computing and Interpreting Return on Assets

M5-7
LO5-4

Saunders, Inc., recently reported the following December 31 amounts in its financial statements (dollars in thousands):

	Current Year	Prior Year
Gross profit	$ 200	$120
Net income	100	40
Total assets	1,000	800
Total shareholders' equity	800	600

Compute return on assets for the current year. What does this ratio measure?

E5-1
LO5-1

Matching Players in the Accounting Communication Process with Their Definitions

Match each player with the related definition by entering the appropriate letter in the space provided.

Players	Definitions
___ (1) Financial analyst	A. Financial institution or supplier that lends money to the company.
___ (2) Creditor	
___ (3) Independent auditor	B. Chief executive officer and chief financial officer who have primary responsibility for the information presented in financial statements.
___ (4) Private investor	
___ (5) SEC	C. Manager of pension, mutual, and endowment funds that invest on the behalf of others.
___ (6) Information service	
___ (7) Institutional investor	D. Securities and Exchange Commission, which regulates financial disclosure requirements.
___ (8) CEO and CFO	
	E. A company that gathers, combines, and transmits (paper and electronic) financial and related information from various sources.
	F. Adviser who analyzes financial and other economic information to form forecasts and stock recommendations.
	G. Individual who purchases shares in companies.
	H. Independent CPA who examines financial statements and attests to their fairness.

E5-2
LO5-2

Matching Definitions with Information Releases Made by Public Companies

Following are the titles of various information releases. Match each definition with the related release by entering the appropriate letter in the space provided.

Information Release	Definitions
___ (1) Form 10-Q	A. Report of special events (e.g., auditor changes, mergers) filed by public companies with the SEC.
___ (2) Quarterly report	
___ (3) Press release	B. Brief unaudited report for quarter normally containing summary income statement and balance sheet.
___ (4) Annual report	
___ (5) Form 10-K	C. Quarterly report filed by public companies with the SEC that contains additional unaudited financial information.
___ (6) Form 8-K	
	D. Written public news announcement that is normally distributed to major news services.
	E. Annual report filed by public companies with the SEC that contains additional detailed financial information.
	F. Report containing the four basic financial statements for the year, related notes, and often statements by management and auditors.

E5-3
LO5-2

Finding Financial Information: Matching Information Items to Financial Reports

Following are information items included in various financial reports. Match each information item with the report(s) where it would most likely be found by entering the appropriate letter(s) in the space provided.

Information Item	Report
____ (1) Summarized financial data for 5-year period.	A. Form 10-Q
____ (2) Notes to financial statements.	B. Annual report
____ (3) The four basic financial statements for the year.	C. Form 8-K
____ (4) Summarized income statement information for the quarter.	D. Press release
____ (5) Detailed discussion of the company's competition.	E. Quarterly report
____ (6) Initial announcement of hiring of new vice president for sales.	F. Form 10-K
____ (7) Initial announcement of quarterly earnings.	G. None of the
____ (8) Description of those responsible for the financial statements.	above
____ (9) Complete quarterly income statement, balance sheet, and cash flow statement.	
____ (10) Announcement of a change in auditors.	

Ordering the Classifications on a Typical Balance Sheet

E5-4
LO5-3

Following is a list of classifications on the balance sheet. Number them in the order in which they normally appear on a balance sheet.

No.	Title
____	Long-term liabilities
____	Current liabilities
____	Long-term investments
____	Intangible assets
____	Contributed capital
____	Current assets
____	Retained earnings
____	Property, plant, and equipment
____	Other noncurrent assets

Preparing a Classified Balance Sheet

E5-5
LO5-3

Campbell Soup Co.

Campbell Soup Company is the world's leading maker and marketer of soup and sells other well-known brands of food in 120 countries. Presented here are the items listed on its recent balance sheet (dollars in millions) presented in alphabetical order:

Accounts payable	$ 585	Other assets	$ 136
Accounts receivable	560	Other current assets	152
Accrued expenses	619	Other current debt	785
Cash and cash equivalents	484	Other noncurrent liabilities	3,777
Common stock, $0.0375 par value	351	Property, plant, and equipment, net	2,103
Intangible assets	2,660	Retained earnings	745
Inventories	767		

Required:

Prepare a classified consolidated balance sheet for Campbell Soup for the current year (ended July 31) using the categories presented in the chapter.

Preparing and Interpreting a Classified Balance Sheet with Discussion of Terminology (Challenging)

E5-6
LO5-3

Snyder's-Lance manufactures, markets, and distributes a variety of snack food products including pretzels, sandwich crackers, kettle chips, cookies, potato chips, tortilla chips, other salty snacks, sugar wafers, nuts, and restaurant style crackers. These items are sold under trade names including Snyder's of

Hanover, Lance, Cape Cod, Krunchers!, Jays, Tom's, Archway, and others. Presented here are the items listed on its recent balance sheet (dollars in millions) in alphabetical order:

Accounts payable	$ 52,930	Other assets (noncurrent)	$ 21,804
Accounts receivable, net	143,238	Other current assets	96,983
Accrued compensation	29,248	Other intangible assets, net	376,062
Additional paid-in capital	730,338	Other long-term liabilities	219,114
Cash and cash equivalents	20,841	Other payables and accrued	
Common stock, 67,820,798 shares		liabilities	68,712
outstanding	56,515	Prepaid expenses and other	20,705
Goodwill	367,853	Property, plant, and equipment, net	313,043
Inventories	106,261	Retained earnings	51,738
Long-term debt	253,939	Short-term debt	4,256

Required:

1. Prepare a classified consolidated balance sheet for Snyder's-Lance for the current year (ended December 31) using the categories presented in the chapter.
2. Three of the items end in the term **net.** Explain what this term means in each case.

E5-7

LO5-3

Matching Definitions with Income Statement-Related Terms

Following are terms related to the income statement. Match each definition with its related term by entering the appropriate letter in the space provided.

Terms	Definitions
___ (1) Net income	A. Revenues + Gains − Expenses − Losses including
___ (2) Income tax expense on	effects of discontinued operations and extraordinary
operations	items (if any).
___ (3) Income before extraordinary	B. Income Tax on (Revenues − Operating Expenses).
items	C. Sales Revenue − Cost of Goods Sold.
___ (4) Cost of goods sold	D. Sales of services for cash or on credit.
___ (5) Operating expenses	E. Amount of resources used to purchase or produce the
___ (6) Gross margin on sales	goods that were sold during the reporting period.
___ (7) EPS	F. Total expenses directly related to operations.
___ (8) Interest expense	G. Income before all income tax and before discontinued
___ (9) Service revenue	operations and extraordinary items (if any).
___ (10) Pretax income from	H. Cost of money (borrowing) over time.
operations	I. Item that is both unusual and infrequent.
	J. Net Income ÷ Average Shares Outstanding.
	K. Income before unusual and infrequent items and the
	related income tax.
	L. None of the above.

E5-8

LO5-3

Preparing a Classified Income Statement and Computing the Gross Profit Percentage

The following data were taken from the records of Township Corporation at December 31, 2015:

Sales revenue	$85,000
Gross profit	30,000
Selling (distribution) expense	7,000
Administrative expense	?
Pretax income	13,000
Income tax rate	35%
Shares of stock outstanding	2,500

Required:

Prepare a complete multiple-step income statement for the company (showing both gross profit and income from operations). Show all computations. (**Hint:** Set up the side captions or rows starting with sales revenue and ending with earnings per share; rely on the amounts and percentages given to infer missing values.) What is the gross profit percentage?

Preparing a Classified Income Statement (Challenging)

Most people know Hewlett Packard Company (HP) as a leading supplier of personal computers, printers and scanners, and storage and networking products for large and small customers alike. However, HP also is a major provider of technology consulting, outsourcing, and services to business, educational, and government organizations. Finally, HP also provides financing for products and services to its larger customers. As a consequence, its income statement shows three sources of operating revenues (goods/services/financing) and three related costs of goods/services/financing provided to customers. Presented below are the items adapted from its recent income statement for the year ended October 31 (in millions, except per share amounts). Net earnings per share was $3.78 and the weighted-average shares used in the computation was 2,319.

E5-9
LO5-3

Hewlett-Packard Company

Acquisition-related charges	$ 293	Product sales	$84,799
Amortization of purchased intangible assets	1,484	Provision for taxes	2,213
Cost of financing	302	Research and development	2,959
Cost of products	65,064	Restructuring charges	1,144
Cost of services	30,590	Selling, general and administrative	12,718
Financing income	418	Service sales	40,816
Interest expense	505		

Required:
1. Recognizing that HP has three sources of operating revenues, prepare a classified income statement for HP following the format and using the subtotals presented in Exhibit 5.5. (**Hint:** The term "charge" is a synonym for "expense.")
2. Which source of operating revenues produces the highest gross profit?

Inferring Income Statement Values

Supply the missing dollar amounts for the 2015 income statement of NexTech Company for each of the following independent cases. (**Hint:** Organize each case in the format of the classified or multiple-step income statement discussed in the chapter. Rely on the amounts given to infer the missing values.)

E5-10
LO5-3

	Case A	Case B	Case C	Case D	Case E
Sales revenue	$800	$600	$500	$?	$?
Selling expense	?	50	80	350	240
Cost of goods sold	?	150	?	500	320
Income tax expense	?	30	20	50	20
Gross margin	375	?	?	?	440
Pretax income	200	300	?	200	?
Administrative expense	125	?	70	120	80
Net income	150	?	50	?	100

Inferring Income Statement Values

Supply the missing dollar amounts for the 2015 income statement of BGT Company for each of the following independent cases. (**Hint:** Organize each case in the format of the classified or multiple-step income statement discussed in the chapter. Rely on the amounts given to infer the missing values.)

E5-11
LO5-3

	Case A	Case B	Case C	Case D	Case E
Sales revenue	$770	$?	$?	$600	$1,050
Pretax income	?	?	150	130	370
Income tax expense	65	210	60	45	?
Cost of goods sold	?	320	125	250	?
Gross margin	?	880	?	?	630
Selling expense	90	275	45	70	?
Net income	115	275	?	?	240
Administrative expense	200	120	80	?	175

E5-12

LO5-3

Coach, Inc.

Stock Issuances and the Statement of Stockholders' Equity

In a recent year, Coach, Inc., a designer and marketer of handbags and other accessories, issued 12,100 shares of its $0.01 par value stock for $344,000 (these numbers are rounded). These additional shares were issued under an employee stock option plan. Prepare the line on the statement of stockholders' equity that would reflect this transaction. The statement has the following columns:

Common Stock		Additional Paid-in Capital	Retained Earnings	Total Stockholders' Equity
Shares	Amount			

E5-13

LO5-3

Inferring Stock Issuances and Cash Dividends from Changes in Stockholders' Equity

The Kroger Co. is one of the largest retailers in the United States and also manufactures and processes some of the food for sale in its supermarkets. Kroger reported the following January 31 balances in its statement of stockholders' equity (dollars in millions):

	Current Year	Prior Year
Common stock	$ 959	$ 958
Paid-in capital	3,427	3,394
Retained earnings	8,571	8,225

During the current year, Kroger reported net income of $602.

Required:
1. How much did Kroger declare in dividends for the year?
2. Assume that the only other transaction that affected stockholders' equity during the current year was a single stock issuance. Recreate the journal entry reflecting the stock issuance.

E5-14

LO5-3

Hasbro, Inc.

Determining the Effects of Transactions on Balance Sheet and Income Statement Categories

Hasbro is one of the world's leading toy manufacturers and maker of such popular board games as Monopoly, Scrabble, and Clue, among others. Listed here are selected aggregate transactions from a recent year (dollars in millions). Complete the following tabulation, indicating the sign (+ for increase, − for decrease, and NE for no effect) and amount of the effect of each transaction. Consider each item independently.

a. Recorded sales on account of $4,285.6 and related cost of goods sold of $1,836.3.
b. Issued debt due in six months with a principal amount of $500.0.
c. Incurred research and development expense of $197.6, which was paid in cash.

Transaction	Current Assets	Gross Profit	Current Liabilities
a.			
b.			
c.			

E5-15

LO5-3

Determining the Effects of Transactions on Balance Sheet, Income Statement, and Statement of Cash Flows Categories

Listed here are selected aggregate transactions for ModernStyle Furniture Company from the first quarter of a recent year (dollars in millions). Complete the following tabulation, indicating the sign (+ for increase, − for decrease, and NE for no effect) and amount of the effect of each additional transaction. Consider each item independently.

a. Recorded collections of cash from customers owed on open account of $40.8.
b. Repaid $5.6 in principal on line of credit with a bank with principal payable within one year.

Transaction	Current Assets	Gross Profit	Current Liabilities	Cash Flow from Operating Activities
a.				
b.				

Preparing a Simple Statement of Cash Flows Using the Indirect Method

E5-16
LO5-3

Avalos Corporation is preparing its annual financial statements at December 31, 2014. Listed here are the items on its statement of cash flows presented in alphabetical order. Parentheses indicate that a listed amount should be subtracted on the cash flow statement. The beginning balance in cash was $25,000 and the ending balance was $50,000.

Cash borrowed on three-year note	$30,000
Decrease in accounts payable	(3,000)
Decrease in inventory	1,000
Increase in accounts receivable	(9,000)
Land purchased	(36,000)
Net income	25,000
New delivery truck purchased for cash	(7,000)
Stock issued for cash	24,000

Required:
Prepare the 2014 statement of cash flows for Avalos Corporation. The section reporting cash flows from operating activities should be prepared using the indirect method discussed in the chapter.

Analyzing and Interpreting Return on Assets

E5-17
LO5-4

Tiffany & Co. is one of the world's premier jewelers and a designer of other fine gifts and housewares. Presented here are selected income statement and balance sheet amounts (dollars in thousands).

TIFFANY & CO.

	Current Year	Prior Year
Net sales	$3,642,937	$3,085,290
Net income	439,190	368,403
Average shareholders' equity	2,263,190	2,030,357
Average total assets	3,947,331	3,612,015

Required:
1. Compute ROA for the current and prior years and explain the meaning of the change.
2. Explain the major cause(s) of the change in ROA using ROA profit driver analysis.

Analyzing and Evaluating Return on Assets from a Security Analyst's Perspective

E5-18
LO5-4

Papa John's is one of the fastest-growing pizza delivery and carry-out restaurant chains in the country. Presented here are selected income statement and balance sheet amounts (dollars in thousands).

	Current Year	Prior Year
Net sales	$1,217,882	$1,126,397
Net income	59,387	55,425
Average shareholders' equity	212,711	246,119
Average total assets	403,162	394,143

Better Ingredients.
Better Pizza.

Required:
1. Compute ROA for the current and prior years and explain the meaning of the change.
2. Would security analysts more likely increase or decrease their estimates of share value on the basis of this change? Explain.

Determining the Effects of Transactions on Ratios

E5-19
LO5-4

What would be the **direction** of the effect of the following transactions on the following ratios (+ for increase, − for decrease, and NE for no effect)? Consider each item independently.

a. Repaid principal of $2,000 on a long-term note payable with the bank.
b. Recorded rent expense of $100 paid for in cash.

Transaction	Net Profit Margin	Return on Assets	Current Ratio
a.			
b.			

PROBLEMS

P5-1
LO5-1, 5-2

Matching Transactions with Concepts

Following are the concepts of accounting covered in Chapters 2 through 5. Match each transaction or definition with its related concept by entering the appropriate letter in the space provided. Use one letter for each blank.

Concepts	Transactions/Definitions

Concepts

_____ (1) Users of financial statements

_____ (2) Objective of financial statements

Qualitative Characteristics

_____ (3) Relevance

_____ (4) Reliability

Assumptions

_____ (5) Separate entity

_____ (6) Continuity

_____ (7) Unit of measure

_____ (8) Time period

Elements of Financial Statements

_____ (9) Revenues

_____ (10) Expenses

_____ (11) Gains

_____ (12) Losses

_____ (13) Assets

_____ (14) Liabilities

_____ (15) Stockholders' equity

Principles

_____ (16) Cost

_____ (17) Revenue

_____ (18) Matching

_____ (19) Full disclosure

Constraints of Accounting

_____ (20) Materiality threshold

_____ (21) Cost effectiveness

_____ (22) Conservatism constraint

_____ (23) Special industry practices

Transactions/Definitions

A. Recorded a $2,000 sale of merchandise on credit.

B. Counted (inventoried) the unsold items at the end of the period and valued them in dollars.

C. Acquired a vehicle for use in operating the business.

D. Reported the amount of depreciation expense because it likely will affect important decisions of statement users.

E. The investors, creditors, and others interested in the business.

F. Used special accounting approaches because of the uniqueness of the industry.

G. Sold and issued bonds payable of $3 million.

H. Used services from outsiders; paid cash for some and put the remainder on credit.

I. Engaged an outside independent CPA to audit the financial statements.

J. Sold an asset at a loss that was a peripheral or incidental transaction.

K. Established an accounting policy that sales revenue shall be recognized only when ownership to the goods sold passes to the customer.

L. To design and prepare the financial statements to assist the users in making decisions.

M. Established a policy not to include in the financial statements the personal financial affairs of the owners of the business.

N. Sold merchandise and services for cash and on credit during the year; then determined the cost of those goods sold and the cost of rendering those services.

O. The user value of a special financial report exceeds the cost of preparing it.

P. Valued an asset, such as inventory, at less than its purchase cost because the replacement cost is less.

Q. Dated the income statement "For the Year Ended December 31, 2014."

R. Paid a contractor for an addition to the building with $15,000 cash and $20,000 market value of the stock of the company ($35,000 was deemed to be the cash-equivalent price).

S. Acquired an asset (a pencil sharpener that will have a useful life of five years) and recorded it as an expense when purchased for $1.99.

T. Disclosed in the financial statements all relevant financial information about the business; necessitated the use of notes to the financial statements.

U. Sold an asset at a gain that was a peripheral or incidental transaction.

V. Assets of $600,000 − Liabilities of $400,000 = ?

W. Accounting and reporting assume a "going concern."

Matching Definitions with Balance Sheet–Related Terms

P5-2
LO5-3

Following are terms related to the balance sheet that were discussed in Chapters 2 through 5. Match each definition with its related term by entering the appropriate letter in the space provided.

Terms	Definitions
____ (1) Capital in excess of par	A. Nearness of assets to cash (in time).
____ (2) Assets	B. Liabilities expected to be paid out of current assets normally within the next year.
____ (3) Retained earnings	
____ (4) Book value	C. All liabilities not classified as current liabilities.
____ (5) Other assets	D. Total assets minus total liabilities.
____ (6) Shares outstanding	E. Probable future economic benefits owned by the entity from past transactions.
____ (7) Shareholders' equity	
____ (8) Liquidity	F. Debts or obligations from past transactions to be paid with assets or services.
____ (9) Normal operating cycle	
____ (10) Current assets	G. Assets expected to be collected in cash within one year or the operating cycle, if longer.
____ (11) Current liabilities	
____ (12) Long-term liabilities	H. Assets that do not have physical substance.
____ (13) Fixed assets	I. Balance of the Common Stock account divided by the par value per share.
____ (14) Liabilities	
____ (15) Contra-asset account	J. A miscellaneous category of assets.
____ (16) Accumulated depreciation	K. Sum of the annual depreciation expense on an asset from its acquisition to the current date.
____ (17) Intangible assets	
	L. Asset offset account (subtracted from asset).
	M. Accumulated earnings minus accumulated dividends.
	N. Property, plant, and equipment.
	O. Same as carrying value; cost less accumulated depreciation to date.
	P. Amount of contributed capital less the par value of the stock.
	Q. The average cash-to-cash time involved in the operations of the business.
	R. None of the above.

Preparing a Balance Sheet and Analyzing Some of Its Parts (AP5-1)

P5-3
LO5-3

www.mhhe.com/libby8e

Exquisite Jewelers is developing its annual financial statements for 2015. The following amounts were correct at December 31, 2015: cash, $58,000; accounts receivable, $71,000; merchandise inventory, $154,000; prepaid insurance, $1,500; investment in stock of Z corporation (long-term), $36,000; store equipment, $67,000; used store equipment held for disposal, $9,000; accumulated depreciation, store equipment, $19,000; accounts payable, $52,500; long-term note payable, $42,000; income taxes payable, $9,000; retained earnings, $164,000; and common stock, 100,000 shares outstanding, par value $1.00 per share (originally sold and issued at $1.10 per share).

Required:
1. Based on these data, prepare a December 31, 2015, balance sheet. Use the following major captions (list the individual items under these captions):
   a. Assets: Current Assets, Long-Term Investments, Fixed Assets, and Other Assets.
   b. Liabilities: Current Liabilities and Long-Term Liabilities.
   c. Stockholders' Equity: Contributed Capital and Retained Earnings.
2. What is the net book value of the store equipment? Explain what this value means.

P5-4

LO5-3

Preparing a Statement of Stockholders' Equity (AP5-2)

At the end of the 2014 annual reporting period, Barnard Corporation's balance sheet showed the following:

BARNARD CORPORATION Balance Sheet At December 31, 2014	
Stockholders' Equity	
Contributed capital	
Common stock (par $15; 5,500 shares)	$ 82,500
Paid-in capital	13,000
Total contributed capital	95,500
Retained earnings	44,000
Total stockholders' equity	$139,500

During 2015, the following selected transactions (summarized) were completed:

a. Sold and issued 1,000 shares of common stock at $35 cash per share (at year-end).
b. Determined net income, $37,000.
c. Declared and paid a cash dividend of $2 per share on the beginning shares outstanding.

Required:
Prepare a statement of stockholders' equity for the year ended December 31, 2015. Be sure to show both the dollar amount and number of shares of common stock.

P5-5

LO5-3

AÉROPOSTALE

Preparing a Multiple-Step Income Statement and Interpreting the Gross Profit Percentage

Aeropostale, Inc., is a mall-based specialty retailer of casual apparel and accessories. The company concept is to provide the customer with a focused selection of high-quality, active-oriented fashions at compelling values. The items reported on its income statement for a recent year (ended March 31) are presented here (dollars in thousands) in alphabetical order:

Cost of goods sold	$1,733,916
Interest expense	417
Net revenue	2,342,260
Other selling, general, and administrative expenses	494,829
Provision for income taxes	43,583
Weighted average shares outstanding	81,208

Required:
Prepare a multiple-step consolidated income statement (showing gross profit, operating income, and income before income taxes). Include a presentation of basic earnings per share. What is the gross profit percentage? Explain its meaning.

P5-6

LO5-3

Preparing Both an Income Statement and a Balance Sheet from a Trial Balance (AP5-3)

Jordan Sales Company (organized as a corporation on April 1, 2014) has completed the accounting cycle for the second year, ended March 31, 2016. Jordan also has completed a correct trial balance as follows:

JORDAN SALES COMPANY
Trial Balance
At March 31, 2016

Account Titles	Debit	Credit
Cash	$ 58,000	
Accounts receivable	49,000	
Office supplies inventory	1,000	
Automobiles (company cars)	34,000	
Accumulated depreciation, automobiles		$ 14,000
Office equipment	3,000	
Accumulated depreciation, office equipment		1,000
Accounts payable		22,000
Income taxes payable		0
Salaries and commissions payable		2,000
Note payable, long-term		33,000
Capital stock (par $1; 33,000 shares)		33,000
Paid-in capital		5,000
Retained earnings (on April 1, 2015)		7,500
Dividends declared and paid during the current year	10,500	
Sales revenue		99,000
Cost of goods sold	33,000	
Operating expenses (detail omitted to conserve time)	19,000	
Depreciation expense (on autos and including $500 on office equipment)	8,000	
Interest expense	1,000	
Income tax expense (not yet computed)		
Totals	$216,500	$216,500

Required:
Complete the financial statements as follows:

a. Classified (multiple-step) income statement for the reporting year ended March 31, 2016. Include income tax expense, assuming a 25 percent tax rate. Use the following subtotals: Gross Profit, Total Operating Expenses, Income from Operations, Income before Income Taxes, and Net Income, and show EPS.

b. Classified balance sheet at the end of the reporting year, March 31, 2016. Include (1) income taxes for the current year in Income Taxes Payable and (2) dividends in Retained Earnings. Use the following captions (list each item under these captions).

Assets	**Stockholders' Equity**
Current assets	Contributed capital
Noncurrent assets	Retained earnings

Liabilities

Current liabilities
Long-term liabilities

Determining and Interpreting the Effects of Transactions on Income Statement Categories and Return on Assets (AP5-4)

P5-7

LO5-3, 5-4

Creative Technology

Creative Technology, a computer hardware company based in Singapore, developed the modern standard for computer sound cards in the early 1990s. Recently, Creative has released a line of portable audio products to directly compete with Apple's popular iPod. Presented here is a recent income statement (dollars in millions).

Net sales	$ 231
Costs and expenses	
Cost of sales	182
Research and development	66
Selling, general, and administrative	62
Operating income (loss)	(79)
Interest and other income (expenses), net	27
Income (loss) before provision (benefit) for income taxes	(52)
Provision (benefit) for income taxes	(5)
Net income (loss)	$ (47)

Its beginning and ending assets were $403 and $342, respectively.

Required:
Listed here are hypothetical **additional** transactions. Assuming that they **also** occurred during the fiscal year, complete the following tabulation, indicating the sign of the effect of each **additional** transaction (+ for increase, − for decrease, and NE for no effect). Consider each item independently and ignore taxes. (**Hint:** Construct the journal entry for each transaction before evaluating its effect.)

a. Recorded sales on account of $400 and related cost of goods sold of $300.
b. Incurred additional research and development expense of $100, which was paid in cash.
c. Issued additional shares of common stock for $260 cash.
d. Declared and paid dividends of $90.

Transaction	Gross Profit	Operating Income	Return on Assets
a.			
b.			
c.			
d.			

P5-8

LO5-4

Determining the Effects of Transactions on Ratios

Mateo Inc. is a retailer of men's and women's clothing aimed at college-age customers. Listed below are additional transactions that Mateo was considering at the end of the accounting period.

Required:
Assuming that each had occurred during the fiscal year, complete the following tabulation, indicating the sign of the effect of each additional transaction (+ for increase, − for decrease, and NE for no effect). Consider each item independently and ignore taxes. (**Hint:** Construct the journal entry for each transaction before evaluating its effect.)

a. Borrowed $3,000 on a line of credit with the bank.
b. Incurred salary expense of $1,000 paid for in cash.
c. Provided $2,000 of services on account.
d. Purchased $700 of inventory on account.
e. Sold $500 of goods on account. The related cost of goods sold was $300. Gross profit margin was 45% before this sale.

Transaction	Total Asset Turnover	Return on Assets	Gross Profit Percentage
a.			
b.			
c.			
d.			
e.			

(Supplement) Preparing a Multiple-Step Income Statement with Discontinued Operations

Newell Rubbermaid Inc. manufactures and markets a broad array of office products, tools and hardware, and home products under a variety of brand names, including Sharpie, Paper Mate, Rolodex, Rubbermaid, Levolor, and others. The items reported on its income statement for the year ended December 31, 2011, are presented here (dollars in thousands) in alphabetical order:

P5-9
LO5-3

Brands That Matter

Cost of Products Sold	$3,659.4
Income Tax Expense	17.9
Interest and Other Non-operating Expense	104.7
Loss on Sale of Discontinued Operations,	
Net of Income Taxes	(9.4)
Net Sales	5,864.6
Other Expense	432.7
Selling, General, and Administrative Expenses	1,515.3

Required:

Using appropriate headings and subtotals, prepare a multiple-step consolidated income statement (showing gross profit, operating income, and any other subheadings you deem appropriate).

ALTERNATE **PROBLEMS**

Preparing a Balance Sheet and Analyzing Some of Its Parts (P5-3)

TangoCo is developing its annual financial statements for 2015. The following amounts were correct at December 31, 2015: cash, $48,800; investment in stock of PIL Corporation (long-term), $36,400; store equipment, $67,200; accounts receivable, $71,820; inventory, $154,000; prepaid rent, $1,120; used store equipment held for disposal, $9,800; accumulated depreciation, store equipment, $13,440; income taxes payable, $9,800; long-term note payable, $32,000; accounts payable, $58,800; retained earnings, $165,100; and common stock, 100,000 shares outstanding, par value $1 per share (originally sold and issued at $1.10 per share).

AP5-1
LO5-3

Required:
1. Based on these data, prepare a 2015 balance sheet. Use the following major captions (list the individual items under these captions):
    a. Assets: Current Assets, Long-Term Investments, Fixed Assets, and Other Assets.
    b. Liabilities: Current Liabilities and Long-Term Liabilities.
    c. Stockholders' Equity: Contributed Capital and Retained Earnings.
2. What is the net book value of the store equipment? Explain what this value means.

Preparing a Statement of Stockholders' Equity (P5-4)

At the end of the 2014 annual reporting period, Mesa Industries's balance sheet showed the following:

AP5-2
LO5-3

MESA INDUSTRIES	
Balance Sheet	
At December 31, 2014	
Stockholders' Equity	
Common stock (par $15; 7,000 shares)	$105,000
Additional paid-in capital	9,000
Retained earnings	48,000
Total stockholders' equity	$162,000

During 2015, the following selected transactions (summarized) were completed:

a. Sold and issued 1,500 shares of common stock at $26 cash per share (at year-end).
b. Determined net income, $46,000.
c. Declared and paid a cash dividend of $1 per share on the beginning shares outstanding.

Required:
Prepare a statement of stockholders' equity for the year ended December 31, 2015. Be sure to show both the dollar amount and number of shares of common stock.

AP5-3
LO5-3

Preparing Both an Income Statement and a Balance Sheet from a Trial Balance (P5-6)

Dynamite Sales (organized as a corporation on September 1, 2013) has completed the accounting cycle for the second year, ended August 31, 2015. Dynamite also has completed a correct trial balance as follows:

DYNAMITE SALES Trial Balance At August 31, 2015		
Account Titles	**Debit**	**Credit**
Cash	$ 47,700	
Accounts receivable	38,320	
Office supplies	270	
Company vehicles (delivery vans)	27,000	
Accumulated depreciation, company vehicles		$ 9,000
Equipment	2,700	
Accumulated depreciation, equipment		900
Accounts payable		16,225
Income taxes payable		0
Salaries payable		1,350
Long-term debt		25,000
Capital stock (par $1; 29,000 shares)		29,000
Paid-in capital		4,500
Retained earnings (on September 1, 2014)		6,615
Dividends declared and paid during the current year	7,200	
Sales revenue		81,000
Cost of goods sold	27,000	
Operating expenses (detail omitted to conserve time)	16,200	
Depreciation expense (on vehicles and including $3,450 on equipment)	4,950	
Interest expense	2,250	
Income tax expense (not yet computed)		
Totals	$173,590	$173,590

Required:
Complete the financial statements, as follows:

a. Classified (multiple-step) income statement for the reporting year ended August 31, 2015. Include income tax expense, assuming a 30 percent tax rate. Use the following subtotals: Gross Profit, Total Operating Expenses, Income from Operations, Income before Income Taxes, and Net Income, and show EPS.

b. Classified balance sheet at the end of the reporting year, August 31, 2015. Include (1) income taxes for the current year in Income Taxes Payable and (2) dividends in Retained Earnings. Use the following captions (list each item under these captions).

Assets	**Stockholders' Equity**
Current assets	Contributed capital
Noncurrent assets	Retained earnings

Liabilities

Current liabilities
Long-term liabilities

Determining and Interpreting the Effects of Transactions on Income Statement Categories and Return on Assets (P5-7)

AP5-4

LO5-3, 5-4

Avon

Avon Products, Inc., is a leading manufacturer and marketer of beauty products and related merchandise. The company sells its products in 110 countries through a combination of direct selling and use of individual sales representatives. Presented here is a recent income statement (dollars in millions).

Net sales	$11,292
Costs and expenses	
Cost of sales	4,149
Selling, general, and administrative	6,288
Operating income (loss)	855
Interest and other income (expenses), net	(125)
Income (loss) before provision (benefit) for income taxes	730
Provision (benefit) for income taxes	216
Net income (loss)	$ 514

Its beginning and ending total assets were $7,874 and $7,735, respectively.

Required:

1. Listed here are hypothetical **additional** transactions. Assuming that they **also** occurred during the fiscal year, complete the following tabulation, indicating the sign of the effect of each **additional** transaction (+ for increase, − for decrease, and NE for no effect). Consider each item independently and ignore taxes.
   a. Recorded and received additional interest income of $7.
   b. Purchased $80 of additional inventory on open account.
   c. Recorded and paid additional advertising expense of $16.
   d. Issued additional shares of common stock for $40 cash.

Transaction	Operating Income (Loss)	Net Income	Return on Assets
a.			
b.			
c.			
d.			

2. Assume that next period, Avon does not pay any dividends, does not issue or retire stock, and earns 20 percent more than during the current period. If total assets increase by 5 percent, will Avon's ROA next period be higher, lower, or the same as in the current period? Why?

CASES **AND PROJECTS**

Annual Report Cases

CP5-1

LO5-2, 5-3, 5-4

AMERICAN EAGLE
OUTFITTERS, INC.

Finding Financial Information

Refer to the financial statements of American Eagle Outfitters given in Appendix B at the end of this book. At the bottom of each statement, the company warns readers to "Refer to Notes to Consolidated Financial Statements." The following questions illustrate the types of information that you can find in the financial statements and accompanying notes. (**Hint:** Use the notes.)

Required:
1. What items were included as noncurrent assets on the balance sheet?
2. How much land did the company own at the end of the most recent reporting year?
3. What portion of current liabilities were "Unredeemed store value cards and gift certificates" during the current year?
4. At what point were website sales recognized as revenue?
5. The company reported cash flows from operating activities of $239,256,000. However, its cash and cash equivalents increased by $51,952,000 for the year. Explain how that happened.
6. What was the highest stock price for the company during fiscal 2011? (**Note:** Some companies will label a year that has a January year-end as having a fiscal year-end dated one year earlier. For example, a January 2012 year-end may be labeled as Fiscal 2011 since the year actually has more months that fall in the 2011 calendar year than in the 2012 calendar year.)
7. Calculate the company's ROA for fiscal 2011 and 2010. Did it increase or decrease? How would you expect the change in ROA to be reflected in the company's share price?

CP5-2

LO5-2, 5-3

URBAN OUTFITTERS INC.

Finding Financial Information

Refer to the financial statements of Urban Outfitters given in Appendix C at the end of this book. At the bottom of each statement, the company warns readers that "The accompanying notes are an integral part of these financial statements." The following questions illustrate the types of information that you can find in the financial statements and accompanying notes. (**Hint:** Use the notes.)

Required:
1. What subtotals does Urban Outfitters report on its income statement?
2. The company spent $190,010,000 on capital expenditures (property, plant, and equipment) and $169,467,000 purchasing investments during the most recent year. Were operating activities or financing activities the major source of cash for these expenditures?
3. What was the company's largest asset (net) at the end of the most recent year?
4. How does the company account for costs associated with developing its websites?
5. Over what useful lives are buildings depreciated?
6. What portion of gross "Property and Equipment" is composed of "Buildings"?
7. Compute the company's gross profit percentage for the most recent two years. Has it risen or fallen? Explain the meaning of the change.

CP5-3

LO5-4

AMERICAN EAGLE
OUTFITTERS, INC.

URBAN OUTFITTERS INC.

Comparing Companies within an Industry

Refer to the financial statements of American Eagle Outfitters (Appendix B) and Urban Outfitters (Appendix C) and the Industry Ratio Report (Appendix D) at the end of this book.

Required:
1. Compute return on assets for the most recent year. Which company provided the highest return on invested capital during the current year?
2. Use ROA profit driver analysis to determine the cause(s) of any differences. How might the ownership versus rental of property, plant, and equipment affect the total asset turnover ratio?
3. Compare the ROA profit driver analysis for American Eagle Outfitters and Urban Outfitters to the ROA profit driver analysis for their industry. Where does American Eagle Outfitters outperform or underperform the industry? Where does Urban Outfitters outperform or underperform the industry?

Financial Reporting and Analysis Case

Using Financial Reports: Financial Statement Inferences

The following amounts were selected from the annual financial statements for Genesis Corporation at December 31, 2015 (end of the third year of operations):

CP5-4
LO5-3

From the 2015 income statement:	
Sales revenue	$275,000
Cost of goods sold	(170,000)
All other expenses (including income tax)	(95,000)
Net income	$ 10,000
From the December 31, 2015, balance sheet:	
Current assets	$ 90,000
All other assets	212,000
Total assets	$302,000
Current liabilities	$ 40,000
Long-term liabilities	66,000
Capital stock (par $10)	100,000
Paid-in capital	16,000
Retained earnings	80,000
Total liabilities and stockholders' equity	$302,000

Required:

Analyze the data on the 2015 financial statements of Genesis by answering the questions that follow. Show computations.

1. What was the gross margin on sales?
2. What was the amount of EPS?
3. If the income tax rate was 25%, what was the amount of pretax income?
4. What was the average sales price per share of the capital stock?
5. Assuming that no dividends were declared or paid during 2015, what was the beginning balance (January 1, 2015) of retained earnings?

Critical Thinking Cases

Making Decisions as a Manager: Evaluating the Effects of Business Strategy on Return on Assets

CP5-5
LO5-4

Sony Corporation

www.mhhe.com/libby8e

Sony is a world leader in the manufacture of consumer and commercial electronics as well as in the entertainment and insurance industries. Its ROA has decreased over the last three years.

Required:

Indicate the most likely effect of each of the changes in business strategy on Sony's ROA for the next period and future periods (+ for increase, − for decrease, and NE for no effect), assuming all other things are unchanged. Explain your answer for each. Treat each item independently.

a. Sony decreases its investment in research and development aimed at products to be brought to market in more than one year.
b. Sony begins a new advertising campaign for a movie to be released during the next year.

Strategy Change	Current Period ROA	Future Periods' ROA
a.		
b.		

CP5-6
LO5-1, 5-3

Making a Decision as an Auditor: Effects of Errors on Income, Assets, and Liabilities

Megan Company (not a corporation) was careless about its financial records during its first year of operations, 2013. It is December 31, 2013, the end of the annual accounting period. An outside CPA has examined the records and discovered numerous errors, all of which are described here. Assume that each error is independent of the others.

Required:

Analyze each error and indicate its effect on 2013 and 2014 net income, assets, and liabilities if not corrected. Do not assume any other errors. Use these codes to indicate the effect of each dollar amount: O = overstated, U = understated, and NE = no effect. Write an explanation of your analysis of each transaction to support your response. The first transaction is used as an example.

| | Effect On | | | | | |
| | Net Income | | Assets | | Liabilities | |
Independent Errors	2013	2014	2013	2014	2013	2014
1. Depreciation expense for 2013, not recorded in 2013, $950.	O $950	NE	O $950	O $950	NE	NE
2. Wages earned by employees during 2013 not recorded or paid in 2013 but recorded and paid in 2014, $500.						
3. Revenue earned during 2013 but not collected or recorded until 2014, $600.						
4. Amount paid in 2013 and recorded as expense in 2013 but not an expense until 2014, $200.						
5. Revenue collected in 2013 and recorded as revenue in 2013 but not earned until 2014, $900.						
6. Sale of services and cash collected in 2013. Recorded as a debit to Cash and as a credit to Accounts Receivable, $300.						
7. On December 31, 2013, bought land on credit for $8,000, not recorded until payment was made on February 1, 2014.						

Following is a sample explanation of the first error:

Failure to record depreciation in 2013 caused depreciation expense to be too low; therefore, income was overstated by $950. Accumulated depreciation also is too low by $950, which causes assets to be overstated by $950 until the error is corrected.

CP5-7
LO5-1, 5-3

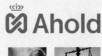

Evaluating an Ethical Dilemma: Management Incentives and Fraudulent Financial Statements

Netherlands-based Royal Ahold ranks among the world's three largest food retailers. In the United States it operates the Stop & Shop and Giant supermarket chains. Dutch and U.S regulators and prosecutors have brought criminal and civil charges against the company and its executives for overstating earnings by more than $1 billion. The nature of the fraud is described in the following excerpt:

Two Former Execs of Ahold Subsidiary Plead Not Guilty to Fraud

28 July 2004 Associated Press Newswires © 2004. The Associated Press.

NEW YORK (AP)—Two former executives pleaded not guilty Wednesday to devising a scheme to inflate the earnings of U.S. Foodservice Inc., a subsidiary of Dutch supermarket giant Royal Ahold NV. Former chief financial officer Michael Resnick and former chief marketing officer Mark Kaiser entered their pleas in a Manhattan federal court, a day after prosecutors announced fraud and conspiracy charges against them.

The government contends they worked together to boost the company's earnings by $800 million from 2000 to 2003 by reporting fake rebates from suppliers—and sweetened their own bonuses in the process. Two other defendants have already pleaded guilty in the alleged scheme: Timothy Lee, a former executive vice president, and William Carter, a former vice president. Both are set for sentencing in January. Netherlands-based Ahold's U.S. properties include the Stop & Shop and Giant supermarket chains. U.S. Foodservice is one of the largest distributors of food products in the country, providing to restaurants and cafeterias.

Ahold said last year it had overstated its earnings by more than $1 billion, mostly because of the fraud at U.S. Foodservice. Its stock lost 60 percent of its value, and about $6 billion in market value evaporated.

Required:

Using more recent news reports (*The Wall Street Journal Index, Factiva,* and *Bloomberg Business News* are good sources), answer the following questions.

1. Whom did the courts and regulatory authorities hold responsible for the misstated financial statements?
2. Did the company cooperate with investigations into the fraud? How did this affect the penalties imposed against the company?
3. How might executive compensation plans that tied bonuses to accounting earnings have motivated unethical conduct in this case?

Financial Reporting and Analysis Team Project

Analyzing the Accounting Communication Process

CP5-8
LO5-1, 5-2, 5-3, 5-4

As a team, select an industry to analyze. *Yahoo!Finance* provides lists of industries at <u>biz.yahoo.com/p/industries.html</u>. Click on an industry for a list of companies in that industry. Alternatively, go to Google Finance at <u>www.google.com/finance</u> and search for a company you are interested in. You will be presented with a list including that company and its competitors. Each team member should acquire the annual report or 10-K for one publicly traded company in the industry, with each member selecting a different company (the SEC EDGAR service at <u>www.sec.gov</u> or the company's investor relations website itself are good sources).

Required:

On an individual basis, each team member should write a short report answering the following questions about the selected company. Discuss any patterns across the companies that you as a team observe. Then, as a team, write a short report comparing and contrasting your companies.

1. What formats are used to present the
   a. Balance Sheets?
   b. Income Statements?
   c. Operating Activities section of the Statement of Cash Flows?
2. Find one footnote for each of the following and describe its contents in brief:
   a. An accounting rule applied in the company's statements.
   b. Additional detail about a reported financial statement number.
   c. Relevant financial information but with no number reported in the financial statements.
3. Using electronic sources, find one article reporting the company's annual earnings announcement. When is it dated and how does that date compare to the balance sheet date?
4. Using electronic sources, find two analysts' reports for your company.
   a. Give the date, name of the analyst, and his or her recommendation from each report.
   b. Discuss why the recommendations are similar or different. Look at the analysts' reasoning for their respective recommendations.
5. Using the SEC EDGAR website (<u>www.sec.gov</u>), what is the most recent document filed by your company with the SEC (e.g., 8-K, S-1) and what did it say in brief?

6. Ratio analysis:
   a. What does the return on total assets ratio measure in general?
   b. Compute the ROA ratio for the last three years.
   c. What do your results suggest about the company?
   d. If available, find the industry ratio for the most recent year, compare it to your results, and discuss why you believe your company differs from or is similar to the industry ratio.
7. Use the ROA profit driver analysis to determine the cause(s) of any differences in the ROA ratio over the last three years. (Remember that you computed the three profit driver ratios in the last three chapters.)

CONTINUING **CASE**

CC5-1   **Evaluating the Impact of Transactions on Statement Categories and Ratios**

After completing her first year of operations, Penny Cassidy used a number of ratios to evaluate the performance of Penny's Pool Service & Supply, Inc. She was particularly interested in the effects of the following transactions from the last quarter:

a. Paid herself a dividend of $10,000 as the sole stockholder.
b. Recorded advance payments from customers of $2,000.
c. Paid the current month's rent in cash, $500.
d. Purchased a new truck for $14,000 and signed a note payable for the whole amount. The truck was not placed in service until January 2015.
e. Recorded depreciation expense on office equipment of $600.
f. Accrued interest expense on the note payable to the bank was $400.

Required:
(**Hint:** Construct the journal entry for each transaction before evaluating its effect.)
1. Complete the following table, indicating the effects of each transaction on each financial statement category listed. Indicate the amount and use + for increase, − for decrease, and NE for no effect.

Transaction	Gross Profit	Operating Income (Loss)	Current Assets
a.			
etc.			

2. Complete the following table, indicating the sign of the effects of each transaction on the financial ratio listed. Use + for increase, − for decrease, and NE for no effect.

Transaction	Net Profit Margin	Total Asset Turnover	Return on Assets
a.			
etc.			

CC5-2   **Preparing an Income Statement and Balance Sheet and Computing Gross Profit Percentage and Return on Assets for a Public Company**

≋POOLCORP   Pool Corporation, Inc., is the world's largest wholesale distributor of swimming pool supplies and equipment. It is a publicly traded corporation that trades on the NASDAQ exchange under the symbol POOL. It sells these products to swimming pool repair and service businesses like Penny's Pool Service & Supply, Inc., swimming pool builders, and retail swimming pool stores. The majority of these customers are small, family-owned businesses like Penny's. Its trial balance and additional information adapted from a recent year ended December 31 are presented below. All numbers are in thousands.

Cash and cash equivalents	$ 17,487	
Receivables, net	110,555	
Product inventories, net	386,924	
Prepaid expenses and other current assets	23,035	
Property and equipment, net	41,394	
Intangible assets	188,841	
Other noncurrent assets, net	30,386	
Accounts payable		$ 177,437
Accrued expenses and other current liabilities		53,398
Current portion of long-term debt		22
Long-term debt		247,300
Other long-term liabilities		40,719
Common stock		47
Additional paid-in capital		173,180
Retained earnings		34,526
Net sales		1,793,318
Cost of sales	1,261,728	
Selling and administrative expenses	406,523	
Interest expense	7,755	
Provision for income taxes	45,319	
	$2,519,947	$2,519,947

Required:

1. Prepare a classified income statement (with earnings per share) and balance sheet for the current year. Number of shares outstanding used in computation of earnings per share was 48,158.

2. Compute gross profit percentage and return on assets. Total assets at the beginning of the year was $728,545.

Reporting and Interpreting Sales Revenue, Receivables, and Cash

Founded by then University of California, Santa Barbara, student Doug Otto, Deckers Outdoor is best known for its Teva sports sandals and UGG sheepskin boots. Deckers has become a major player in the casual, outdoor, and athletic footwear market by building on the needs of hikers, trail runners, kayakers, surfers, and whitewater rafters for comfort, function, and performance. Its growth strategy requires building brand recognition by developing and introducing additional innovative footwear that satisfies the company's high standards. "Building the brands" allows Deckers to maintain a loyal consumer following and penetrate new markets. It also has allowed Deckers to continue to grow during the worst recession in more than 25 years.

There is a second key component to Deckers's successful growth strategy. Success in the ultracompetitive footwear market requires careful matching of production schedules to customers' needs and careful management of customer receivables. Deckers's successful focus on brand development, product innovation, and working capital management has allowed the company to report the highest gross profit and net income in its history.

Learning Objectives

After studying this chapter, you should be able to:

6-1 Apply the revenue realization principle to determine the accepted time to record sales revenue for typical retailers, wholesalers, manufacturers, and service companies. p. 278

6-2 Analyze the impact of credit card sales, sales discounts, and sales returns on the amounts reported as net sales. p. 279

6-3 Estimate, report, and evaluate the effects of uncollectible accounts receivable (bad debts) on financial statements. p. 283

6-4 Analyze and interpret the receivables turnover ratio and the effects of accounts receivable on cash flows. p. 290

6-5 Report, control, and safeguard cash. p. 293

chapter 6

FOCUS COMPANY:

Deckers Outdoor Corporation*

BUILDING BRANDS TO BUILD GROSS PROFIT: MANAGING PRODUCT DEVELOPMENT, PRODUCTION, AND WORKING CAPITAL

www.deckers.com

UNDERSTANDING THE BUSINESS

Planning Deckers's growth strategy requires careful coordination of sales activities, as well as cash collections from customers. Much of this coordination revolves around allowing consumers to use credit cards, providing business customers discounts for early payment, and allowing sales returns and allowances under certain circumstances—strategies that motivate customers to buy its products and make payment for their purchases. These activities affect **net sales** revenue, the top line on the income statement. Coordinating sales and cash collections from customers also involves managing bad debts, which affect selling, general, and administrative expenses on the income statement and **cash** and **accounts receivable** on the balance sheet. Net sales, accounts receivable, and cash are the focus of this chapter. We will also introduce the receivables turnover ratio as a measure of the efficiency of credit-granting and collection activities. Finally, since the cash collected from customers is also a tempting target for fraud and embezzlement, we will discuss how accounting systems commonly include controls to prevent and detect such misdeeds.

ORGANIZATION of the Chapter

Accounting for Net Sales Revenue	Measuring and Reporting Receivables	Reporting and Safeguarding Cash
• Motivating Sales and Collections • Credit Card Sales to Consumers • Sales Discounts to Businesses • Sales Returns and Allowances • Reporting Net Sales	• Classifying Receivables • Accounting for Bad Debts • Reporting Accounts Receivable and Bad Debts • Estimating Bad Debts • Control Over Accounts Receivable • Receivables Turnover Ratio	• Cash and Cash Equivalents Defined • Cash Management • Internal Control of Cash • Reconciliation of the Cash Accounts and the Bank Statements

ACCOUNTING FOR NET SALES REVENUE

LEARNING OBJECTIVE 6-1

Apply the revenue realization principle to determine the accepted time to record sales revenue for typical retailers, wholesalers, manufacturers, and service companies.

As indicated in Chapter 3, the **revenue realization principle** requires that revenues be recorded when they are earned (delivery has occurred or services have been rendered, there is persuasive evidence of an arrangement for customer payment, the price is fixed or determinable, and collection is reasonably assured). For sellers of goods, these criteria are most often met and sales revenue is recorded when title and risks of ownership transfer to the buyer.[1] The point at which title (ownership) changes hands is determined by the shipping terms in the sales contract. When goods are shipped **FOB (free on board) shipping point,** title changes hands at shipment, and the buyer normally pays for shipping. When they are shipped **FOB destination,** title changes hands on delivery, and the seller normally pays for shipping. Revenues from goods shipped FOB shipping point are normally recognized at shipment. Revenues from goods shipped FOB destination are normally recognized at delivery.

Service companies most often record sales revenue when they have provided services to the buyer. Companies disclose the revenue recognition rule they follow in the footnote to the financial statements entitled Summary of Significant Accounting Policies. In that note, Deckers reports the following:

DECKERS
outdoor corporation

REAL WORLD EXCERPT
Annual Report

NOTES TO CONSOLIDATED FINANCIAL STATEMENTS

1. Summary of Significant Accounting Policies
Revenue Recognition

The Company recognizes wholesale, eCommerce, and international distributor revenue when products are shipped and retail revenue at the point of sale. All sales are recognized when the customer takes title and assumes risk of loss, collection of relevant receivable is reasonably assured, persuasive evidence of an arrangement exists, and the sales price is fixed or determinable.

The appropriate **amount** of revenue to record is the **cash equivalent sales price.**

---

[1]See SEC Staff Accounting Bulletin 101, *Revenue Recognition in Financial Statements,* 2000.

Motivating Sales and Collections

Some sales practices differ depending on whether sales are made to businesses or consumers. Deckers sells footwear and apparel to other **businesses** (retailers), including Athlete's Foot and Eastern Mountain Sports, which then sell the goods to consumers. It also operates its own Internet and retail stores that sell footwear directly to **consumers.**

Deckers uses a variety of methods to motivate both groups of customers to buy its products and make payment for their purchases. The principal methods include (1) allowing consumers to use credit cards to pay for purchases, (2) providing business customers direct credit and discounts for early payment, and (3) allowing returns from all customers under certain circumstances. These methods, in turn, affect the way we compute **net sales revenue.**

Credit Card Sales to Consumers

Deckers accepts cash or credit card payment for its retail store and Internet sales. Deckers's managers decided to accept credit cards (mainly Visa, Mastercard, and American Express) for a variety of reasons:

LEARNING OBJECTIVE 6-2
Analyze the impact of credit card sales, sales discounts, and sales returns on the amounts reported as net sales.

1. Increasing customer traffic.

2. Avoiding the costs of providing credit directly to consumers, including recordkeeping and bad debts (discussed later).

3. Lowering losses due to bad checks.

4. Avoiding losses from fraudulent credit card sales. (As long as Deckers follows the credit card company's verification procedure, the credit card company [e.g., Visa] absorbs any losses.)

5. Receiving money faster. (Since credit card receipts can be directly deposited in its bank account, Deckers receives its money faster than it would if it provided credit directly to consumers.)

The credit card company charges a fee for the service it provides. When Deckers deposits its credit card receipts in the bank, it might receive credit for only 97 percent of the sales price. The credit card company is charging a 3 percent fee (the **credit card discount**) for its services. If daily credit card sales were $3,000, Deckers would report the following:

A CREDIT CARD DISCOUNT is the fee charged by the credit card company for its services.

Sales revenue	$3,000
Less: Credit card discounts (0.03 × 3,000)	90
Net sales (reported on the income statement)	$2,910

Sales Discounts to Businesses

Most of Deckers's sales to businesses are credit sales on open account; that is, there is no formal written promissory note or credit card. When Deckers sells footwear to retailers on credit, credit terms are printed on the sales document and invoice (bill) sent to the customer. Often credit terms are abbreviated. For example, if the full price is due within 30 days of the invoice date, the credit terms would be noted as **n/30.** Here, the **n** means the sales amount **net** of, or less, any sales returns.

Early Payment Incentive

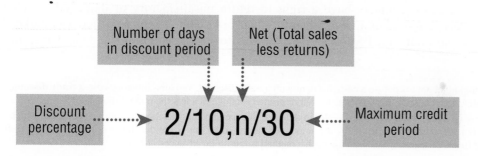

A SALES DISCOUNT (cash discount) is a cash discount offered to encourage prompt payment of an account receivable.

In some cases, a **sales discount** (often called a cash discount) is granted to the purchaser to encourage early payment.[2] For example, Deckers may offer terms of 2/10, n/30, which means that the customer may deduct 2 percent from the invoice price if cash payment is made within 10 days from the date of sale. If cash payment is not made within the 10-day discount period, the full sales price (less any returns) is due within a maximum of 30 days.

Deckers offers this sales discount to encourage customers to pay more quickly. This provides two benefits to Deckers:

1. Prompt receipt of cash from customers reduces the necessity to borrow money to meet operating needs.

2. Since customers tend to pay bills providing discounts first, a sales discount also decreases the chances that the customer will run out of funds before Deckers's bill is paid.

Companies commonly record sales discounts taken by subtracting the discount from sales if payment is made **within** the discount period (the usual case).[3] For example, if credit sales of $1,000 are recorded with terms 2/10, n/30 and payment of $980 ($1,000 × 0.98 = $980) is made within the discount period, net sales of the following amount would be reported:

Sales revenue	$1,000
Less: Sales discounts (0.02 × $1,000)	20
Net sales (reported on the income statement)	$ 980

If payment is made after the discount period, the full $1,000 would be reported as net sales. Accounting for sales discounts is discussed in more detail in the Supplement at the end of this chapter.

FINANCIAL ANALYSIS

To Take or Not to Take the Discount, That Is the Question

Customers usually pay within the discount period because the savings are substantial. With terms 2/10, n/30, customers save 2 percent by paying 20 days early (on the 10th day instead of the 30th). This translates into a 37 percent annual interest rate. To calculate the annual interest rate, first compute the interest rate for the discount period. When the 2 percent discount is taken, the customer pays only 98 percent of the gross sales price. For example, on a $100 sale with terms 2/10, n/30, $2 would be saved and $98 would be paid 20 days early.

The interest rate for the 20-day discount period and the annual interest rate are computed as follows:

$$\frac{\text{Amount Saved}}{\text{Amount Paid}} = \text{Interest Rate for 20 Days} \qquad \text{Interest Rate for 20 Days} \times \frac{365 \text{ days}}{20 \text{ days}} = \text{Annual Interest Rate}$$

$$\frac{\$2}{\$98} = 2.04\% \text{ for 20 Days} \qquad 2.04\% \times \frac{365 \text{ days}}{20 \text{ days}} = 37.23\% \text{ Annual Interest Rate}$$

As long as the bank's interest rate is less than the interest rate associated with failing to take cash discounts, the customer will save by taking the cash discount. For example, even if credit customers had to borrow from that bank at a high rate such as 15 percent, they would save a great deal.

SALES RETURNS AND ALLOWANCES is a reduction of sales revenues for return of or allowances for unsatisfactory goods.

Sales Returns and Allowances

Retailers and consumers have a right to return unsatisfactory or damaged merchandise and receive a refund or an adjustment to their bill. Such returns are often accumulated in a separate account called **Sales Returns and Allowances** and must be deducted from gross

---

[2] It is important not to confuse a cash discount with a trade discount. Vendors sometimes use a **trade discount** for quoting sales prices; the sales price is the list or printed catalog price **less** the trade discount.

[3] We use the gross method in all examples in this text. Some companies use the alternative net method, which records sales revenue after deducting the amount of the cash discount. Since the choice of method has little effect on the financial statements, discussion of this method is left for an advanced course.

sales revenue in determining net sales. This account informs Deckers's managers of the volume of returns and allowances and thus provides an important measure of the quality of customer service. Assume that Fontana Shoes of Ithaca, New York, buys 40 pairs of sandals (at $50 each) from Deckers for $2,000 on account. Before paying for the sandals, Fontana discovers that 10 pairs of sandals are not the color ordered and returns them to Deckers.[4] Deckers computes net sales as follows:

Sales revenue	$2,000
Less: Sales returns and allowances (10 × $50)	500
Net sales (reported on the income statement)	$1,500

Cost of goods sold related to the 10 pairs of sandals would also be reduced.

Reporting Net Sales

On the company's books, credit card discounts, sales discounts, and sales returns and allowances are accounted for separately to allow managers to monitor the costs of credit card use, sales discounts, and returns. Using the numbers in the preceding examples, the amount of net sales reported on the income statement is computed in the following manner:

Sales revenue	$6,000
Less: Credit card discounts (a contra-revenue)	90
Sales discounts (a contra-revenue)	20
Sales returns and allowances (a contra-revenue)	500
Net sales (included on the first line of the income statement)	$5,390

Net sales to all customers is the top line reported on Deckers's income statement, presented in Exhibit 6.1. Deckers indicates in its revenue recognition footnote that the appropriate subtractions are made.

NET SALES is the top line reported on the income statement. It is computed as follows:

Sales revenue	
Less: Credit card discounts	
Sales discounts	
Sales returns and allowances	
Net sales	

EXHIBIT 6.1

Net Sales on the Income Statement

DECKERS outdoor corporation

REAL WORLD EXCERPT
Annual Report

DECKERS OUTDOOR CORPORATION AND SUBSIDIARIES
Consolidated Statements of Operations
Three Years Ended December 31, 2011, 2010, 2009
(amounts in thousands except per share data)

	2011	2010	2009
Net sales	$1,377,283	$1,000,989	$813,177
Cost of sales	698,288	498,051	442,087
Gross profit	678,995	502,938	371,090
Selling, general, and administrative expenses	394,157	253,850	189,843
Income from operations	284,838	249,088	181,247
Interest income (expense)	424	1,021	1,976
Income before income taxes	285,262	250,109	183,223
Income taxes	83,404	89,732	66,304
Net income	$ 201,858	$ 160,377	$116,919

[4]Alternatively, Deckers might offer Fontana a $200 allowance to keep the wrong-color sandals. If Fontana accepts the offer, Deckers reports $200 as sales returns and allowances.

DECKERS outdoor corporation

REAL WORLD EXCERPT
Annual Report

> **NOTES TO CONSOLIDATED FINANCIAL STATEMENTS**
>
> **1. Summary of Significant Accounting Policies**
>
> *Revenue Recognition*
>
> . . . allowances for estimated returns, discounts . . . are provided for when related revenue is recorded.

In 2014, Deckers disclosed that it provided its customers with $24,075,000 in sales discounts based on meeting certain order, shipment, and payment timelines.

PAUSE FOR **FEEDBACK**

DECKERS outdoor corporation

In the last section, we learned to analyze the impact of **credit card sales, sales discounts,** and **sales returns,** all of which reduce the amounts reported as net sales. Both credit card discounts and sales or cash discounts promote faster receipt of cash. Sales returns and allowances include refunds and adjustments to customers' bills for defective or incorrect merchandise.

Before you move on, complete the following questions to test your understanding of these concepts.

SELF-STUDY **QUIZ**

1. Assume that Deckers sold $30,000 worth of footwear to various retailers with terms 1/10, n/30 and half of that amount was paid within the discount period. Gross catalog and Internet sales were $5,000 for the same period; 80 percent of these sales were paid for with credit cards with a 3 percent discount and the rest were paid for with cash. Compute net sales for the period.

   _____

   _____

2. During the first quarter of 2011, Deckers's net sales totaled $204,851, and cost of sales was $102,373. What was Deckers's gross profit for 2011?

   _____

   _____

After you have completed your answers, check them with the solutions at the bottom of the page.

Solutions to
SELF-STUDY QUIZ

1.	Gross Sales		$35,000
	Less: Sales Discounts (0.01 × 1/2 × $30,000)		150
	Credit Card Discounts (0.03 × 0.80 × $5,000)		120
	Net Sales		$34,730

2.	Net Sales	$204,851	
	Cost of Sales	102,373	
	Gross Profit	$102,478	

MEASURING AND REPORTING RECEIVABLES

Classifying Receivables

Receivables may be classified in three common ways. First, they may be classified as either an account receivable or a note receivable. An **account receivable** is created by a credit sale on an open account. For example, an account receivable is created when Deckers sells shoes on open account to Fontana Shoes in Ithaca, New York. A **note receivable** is a promise in writing (a formal document) to pay (1) a specified amount of money, called the **principal,** at a definite future date known as the maturity date and (2) a specified amount of **interest** at one or more future dates. The interest is the amount charged for use of the principal.

Second, receivables may be classified as trade or nontrade receivables. A **trade receivable** is created in the normal course of business when a sale of merchandise or services on credit occurs. A **nontrade receivable** arises from transactions other than the normal sale of merchandise or services. For example, if Deckers loaned money to a new vice president to help finance a home at the new job location, the loan would be classified as a nontrade receivable. Third, in a classified balance sheet, receivables also are classified as either **current** or **noncurrent** (short term or long term), depending on when the cash is expected to be collected. Like many companies, Deckers reports only one type of receivable account, Trade Accounts Receivable, from customers and classifies the asset as a current asset because the accounts receivable are all due to be paid within one year.

ACCOUNTS RECEIVABLE (Trade Receivables, Receivables) are open accounts owed to the business by trade customers.

NOTES RECEIVABLE are written promises that require another party to pay the business under specified conditions (amount, time, interest).

Foreign Currency Receivables

INTERNATIONAL PERSPECTIVE

Export (international) sales are a growing part of the U.S. economy. For example, international sales amounted to 31.4 percent of Deckers's revenues in 2011. Most export sales to businesses are on credit. When a buyer agrees to pay in its local currency, Deckers cannot add the resulting accounts receivable, which are denominated in foreign currency, directly to its U.S. dollar accounts receivable. Deckers's accountants must first convert them to U.S. dollars using the end-of-period exchange rate between the two currencies. For example, if a French department store owed Deckers €20,000 (euros, the common currency of the European Monetary Union) on December 31, 2011, and each euro was worth US$1.29 on that date, it would add US$25,800 to its accounts receivable on the balance sheet.

Selected Foreign Currency Exchange Rates (in US$)

Mexican Peso	$0.08
Singapore Dollar	$0.80
Euro	$1.29

Accounting for Bad Debts

For billing and collection purposes, Deckers keeps a separate accounts receivable account for each retailer that resells its footwear and apparel (called a **subsidiary account**). The accounts receivable amount on the balance sheet represents the total of these individual customer accounts.

When Deckers extends credit to its commercial customers, it knows that some of these customers will not pay their debts. The expense matching principle requires recording of bad debt expense in the **same** accounting period in which the related sales are made. This presents an important accounting problem. Deckers may not learn which particular customers will not pay until the **next** accounting period. So, at the end of the period of sale, it normally does not know which customers' accounts receivable are bad debts.

LEARNING OBJECTIVE 6-3
Estimate, report, and evaluate the effects of uncollectible accounts receivable (bad debts) on financial statements.

The ALLOWANCE METHOD bases bad debt expense on an estimate of uncollectible accounts.

Deckers resolves this problem by using the allowance method to measure bad debt expense. The allowance method is based on **estimates** of the expected amount of bad debts. Two primary steps in employing the allowance method are:

1. Making the end-of-period adjusting entry to record estimated bad debt expense.
2. Writing off specific accounts determined to be uncollectible during the period.

Recording Bad Debt Expense Estimates

BAD DEBT EXPENSE (Doubtful Accounts Expense, Uncollectible Accounts Expense, Provision for Uncollectible Accounts) is the expense associated with estimated uncollectible accounts receivable.

Bad debt expense (doubtful accounts expense, uncollectible accounts expense, provision for uncollectible accounts) is the expense associated with estimated uncollectible accounts receivable. An **adjusting journal entry at the end of the accounting period** records the bad debt estimate. For the year ended December 31, 2011, Deckers estimated bad debt expense to be $75,995 (all numbers in thousands of dollars) and made the following adjusting entry:

Bad debt expense (+E, −SE)	75,995	
Allowance for doubtful accounts (+XA, −A)		75,995

Assets	=	Liabilities	+	Stockholders' Equity
Allowance for doubtful accounts −75,995				Bad debt expense (+E) −75,995

The Bad Debt Expense is included in the category "Selling" expenses on the income statement. It decreases net income and stockholders' equity. Accounts Receivable could not be credited in the journal entry because there is no way to know which customers' accounts receivable are involved. So the credit is made, instead, to a contra-asset account called **Allowance for Doubtful Accounts** (Allowance for Bad Debts or Allowance for Uncollectible Accounts). As a contra-asset, the balance in Allowance for Doubtful Accounts is always subtracted from the balance of the asset Accounts Receivable. Thus, the entry decreases the net book value of Accounts Receivable and total assets.

ALLOWANCE FOR DOUBTFUL ACCOUNTS (Allowance for Bad Debts, Allowance for Uncollectible Accounts) is a contra-asset account containing the estimated uncollectible accounts receivable.

Writing Off Specific Uncollectible Accounts

Throughout the year, when it is determined that a customer will not pay its debts (e.g., due to bankruptcy), the write-off of that individual bad debt is recorded through a journal entry. Now that the specific uncollectible customer account receivable has been identified, it can be removed with a credit. At the same time, we no longer need the related estimate in the contra-asset Allowance for Doubtful Accounts, which is removed by a debit. The journal entry summarizing Deckers's total write-offs of $68,075 during 2011 follows:

Allowance for doubtful accounts (−XA, +A)	68,075	
Accounts receivable (−A)		68,075

Assets	=	Liabilities	+	Stockholders' Equity
Allowance for doubtful accounts +68,075				
Accounts receivable −68,075				

Notice that this journal entry did **not affect any income statement accounts.** It did not record a bad debt expense because the estimated expense was recorded with an adjusting entry in the period of sale. Also, the entry did **not change the net book value of accounts receivable,** since the decrease in the asset account (Accounts Receivable) was offset by the decrease in the contra-asset account (Allowance for Doubtful Accounts). Thus, it also did not affect total assets.

Bad Debt Recoveries

FINANCIAL ANALYSIS

When a company receives a payment on an account that has already been written off, the journal entry to write off the account is reversed to put the receivable back on the books, and the collection of cash is recorded. For example, if the previously written off amount was $677, it would make the following entries:

Accounts receivable (+A)	677	
Allowance for doubtful accounts (+XA, −A)		677
Cash (+A)	677	
Accounts receivable (−A)		677

Note that these entries, like the original write-off, do not affect total assets or net income. Only the estimate of bad debts affects these amounts.

Summary of the Accounting Process

It is important to remember that accounting for bad debts is a two-step process:

Step	Timing	Accounts Affected	Financial Statement Effects	
1. Record estimated bad debts adjustment	End of period in which sales are made	Bad Debt Expense (E) ↑	Net Income ↓	
		Allowance for Doubtful Accounts (XA) ↑	Assets (Accounts Receivable, Net) ↓	
2. Identify and write off actual bad debts	Throughout period as bad debts become known	Accounts Receivable (A) ↓	Net Income	No effect
		Allowance for Doubtful Accounts (XA) ↓	Assets (Accounts Receivable, Net)	

Deckers's complete 2011 accounting process for bad debts can now be summarized in terms of the changes in Accounts Receivable (Gross) and the Allowance for Doubtful Accounts:[5]

Accounts Receivable Dec. 31, 2011

Accounts Receivable (Gross) (A)	$215,067
Allowance for Doubtful Accounts (XA)	21,692
Accounts Receivable (Net) (A)	$193,375

Accounts Receivable (Gross) (A)			
Beginning balance	130,435	Collections on account	1,224,576
Sales on account	1,377,283	Write-offs	68,075
Ending balance	215,067		

Allowance for Doubtful Accounts (XA)			
		Beginning balance	13,772
Write-offs	68,075	Bad debt expense adjustment	75,995
		Ending balance	21,692

---

[5]This assumes that all sales are on account.

Accounts Receivable (Gross) includes the total accounts receivable, both collectible and uncollectible. The balance in the Allowance for Doubtful Accounts is the portion of the accounts receivable balance the company estimates to be uncollectible. Accounts Receivable (Net) reported on the balance sheet is the portion of the accounts the company expects to collect (or its estimated net realizable value).

Reporting Accounts Receivable and Bad Debts

Analysts who want information on Deckers's receivables will find Accounts Receivable, net of allowance for doubtful accounts (the **net book value**), of $193,375 and $116,663 for 2011 and 2010, respectively, reported on the balance sheet (Exhibit 6.2). Deckers reports the balance in the Allowance for Doubtful Accounts ($21,692 in 2011 and $13,772 in 2010) within the account title. Other companies report the balance in the Allowance for Doubtful Accounts in a note. Accounts Receivable (Gross), the total accounts receivable, can be computed by adding the two amounts together.

The amounts of bad debt expense and accounts receivable written off for the period, if material, are reported on a schedule that publicly traded companies must include in their Annual Report Form 10-K filed with the SEC. Exhibit 6.3 presents this schedule from Deckers's 2011 filing.

EXHIBIT 6.2	DECKERS OUTDOOR CORPORATION AND SUBSIDIARIES

Accounts Receivable on the Partial Balance Sheet

DECKERS outdoor corporation

REAL WORLD EXCERPT
Annual Report

DECKERS OUTDOOR CORPORATION AND SUBSIDIARIES
Consolidated Balance Sheets
December 31, 2011 and 2010
(amounts in thousands of dollars except share data)

	2011	2010
Assets		
Current assets:		
Cash and cash equivalents	$263,606	$445,226
Trade accounts receivable, net of allowances of $21,692 and $13,772 in 2011 and 2010, respectively	193,375	116,663
Inventories	253,270	124,995
Prepaid expenses	8,697	7,928
Other current assets	84,540	8,918
Deferred tax assets	14,414	12,002
Total current assets	$817,902	$715,732

EXHIBIT 6.3	DECKERS OUTDOOR CORPORATION AND SUBSIDIARIES

Accounts Receivable Valuation Schedule (Form 10-K)

DECKERS outdoor corporation

REAL WORLD EXCERPT
Annual Report

DECKERS OUTDOOR CORPORATION AND SUBSIDIARIES
Valuation and Qualifying Accounts
Three Years Ended December 31, 2011, 2010, and 2009

Description	Balance at Beginning of Year	Additions	Deductions	Balance at End of Year
Allowance for doubtful account year ended:				
December 31, 2011	$13,772	$75,995	$68,075	$21,692
December 31, 2010	11,790	46,224	44,242	13,772
December 31, 2009	10,706	40,620	39,536	11,790

When receivables are material, companies must employ the allowance method to account for uncollectibles. These are the steps in the process:

a. The end-of-period adjusting entry to record the estimate of bad debt expense and *increase* the allowance for doubtful accounts.

b. Writing off specific accounts determined to be uncollectible during the period to eliminate the specific uncollectible account receivable and *decrease* the allowance for doubtful accounts.

crocs™
© Crocs, Inc.

The adjusting entry reduces net income as well as net accounts receivable. The write-off affects neither. Before you move on, complete the following questions to test your understanding of these concepts.

SELF-STUDY QUIZ

In a recent year, Crocs, Inc., a major Deckers competitor, had a beginning credit balance in the Allowance for Doubtful Accounts of $3,973 (all numbers in thousands of dollars). It wrote off accounts receivable totaling $1,535 during the year and made a bad debt expense adjustment for the year of $2,204.

1. What adjusting journal entry did Crocs make for bad debts at the end of the year? *[handwritten: Deb. bad debt expense, credit XA Acct recivable 2204]*
2. Make the journal entry summarizing Crocs's total write-off of bad debts during the year.
3. Compute the balance in the Allowance for Doubtful Accounts at the end of the year.

After you have completed your answers, check them with the solutions at the bottom of the page.

GUIDED **HELP**

For additional step-by-step video instruction on preparing journal entries related to bad debts, go to the URL or scan the QR code in the margin with your smartphone or iPad.

www.mhhe.com/libby8e

Estimating Bad Debts

The bad debt expense amount recorded in the end-of-period adjusting entry often is estimated based on either (1) a percentage of total credit sales for the period or (2) an aging of accounts receivable. Both methods are acceptable under GAAP and are widely used. The percentage of credit sales method is simpler to apply, but the aging method is generally more accurate. Many companies use the simpler method on a weekly or monthly basis and use the more accurate method on a monthly or quarterly basis to check the accuracy of the earlier estimates. In our example, both methods produce exactly the same estimate, which rarely occurs in practice.

Percentage of Credit Sales Method

The **percentage of credit sales method** bases bad debt expense on the historical percentage of credit sales that result in bad debts. The average percentage of credit sales that result in bad debts can be computed by dividing total bad debt losses by total **credit** sales. A company that has been operating for some years has sufficient experience to project probable future bad debt losses. For

The PERCENTAGE OF CREDIT SALES METHOD bases bad debt expense on the historical percentage of credit sales that result in bad debts.

Solutions to
SELF-STUDY QUIZ

1. Bad debt expense (+E, −SE)   2,204
       Allowance for doubtful accounts (+XA, −A)   2,204
2. Allowance for doubtful accounts (−XA, +A)   1,535
       Accounts receivable (−A)   1,535
3. Beginning Balance + Bad Debt Expense Estimate − Write-Offs = Ending Balance,
   $3,973 + 2,204 − 1,535 = $4,642

example, if we assume that, during the year 2012, Deckers expected bad debt losses of 1.0 percent of credit sales, and its credit sales were $1,500,000, it would estimate the current year's bad debts as:

Credit sales	$1,500,000
× **Bad debt loss rate** (1.0%)	× .01
Bad debt expense	$ 15,000

This amount would be directly recorded as Bad Debt Expense (and an increase in Allowance for Doubtful Accounts) in the current year. Our beginning balance in the Allowance for Doubtful Accounts for 2012 would be the ending balance for 2011. Assuming write-offs during 2012 of $13,692, the ending balance is computed as follows:

Beginning balance	$21,692
+ Bad debt expense	15,000
− Write-offs	13,692
Ending balance	$23,000

Percent of credit sales estimate

Allowance for Doubtful Accounts (XA)

2012 Write-offs	13,692	2012 Beginning balance	21,692
		2012 Bad debt expense adjustment	15,000
		2012 Ending balance	? = 23,000

Aging of Accounts Receivable

The AGING OF ACCOUNTS RECEIVABLE METHOD estimates uncollectible accounts based on the age of each account receivable.

The **aging of accounts receivable method** relies on the fact that, as accounts receivable become older and more overdue, it is less likely that they will be collected. For example, a receivable that was due in 30 days but has not been paid after 120 days is less likely to be collected, on average, than a similar receivable that remains unpaid after 45 days.

If Deckers split its assumed 2012 ending balance in accounts receivable (gross) of $230,000 into three age categories, it would first examine the individual customer accounts receivable and sort them into the three age categories. Based on prior experience, management would then **estimate** the probable bad debt loss rates for each category: for example, not yet due, 2 percent; 1 to 90 days past due, 10 percent; over 90 days, 30 percent.

As illustrated in the aging schedule below, this would result in an estimate of total uncollectible amounts of $23,000, the **estimated ending balance** that **should be** in the Allowance for Doubtful Accounts. From this, the adjustment to record Bad Debt Expense (and an increase in Allowance for Doubtful Accounts) for 2012 would be computed as follows:

Aging Schedule 2012

Aged Accounts Receivable		Estimated Percentage Uncollectible		Estimated Amount Uncollectible
Not yet due	$115,000	× 2%	=	$ 2,300
Up to 90 days past due	69,000	× 10%	=	6,900
Over 90 days past due	46,000	× 30%	=	13,800
Estimated ending balance in Allowance for Doubtful Accounts				$23,000
Less: Balance in Allowance for Doubtful Accounts before adjustment (21,692 − 13,692)				8,000
Bad Debt Expense for the year				$15,000

Allowance for Doubtful Accounts (XA)

2012 Write-offs	13,692	2012 Beginning balance	21,692
		2012 Bad debt expense adjustment	?
		2012 Ending balance	23,000

= 15,000 ◄ Total estimated uncollectible accounts

Comparison of the Two Methods

Students often fail to recognize that the approach to recording bad debt expense using the percentage of credit sales method is different from that for the aging method:

- **Percentage of credit sales.** Directly compute the amount to be recorded as **Bad Debt Expense** on the **income statement** for the period in the adjusting journal entry.

- **Aging of Accounts Receivable.** Compute the **estimated ending balance** we would like to have in the **Allowance for Doubtful Accounts** on the **balance sheet** after we make the necessary adjusting entry. The **difference** between the current balance in the account and the estimated balance is recorded as the adjusting entry for Bad Debt Expense for the period.

In either case, the balance sheet presentation for 2012 would show Accounts Receivable, less Allowance for Doubtful Accounts, of $207,000 ($230,000 − $23,000).

Actual Write-Offs Compared with Estimates

Deckers's Form 10-K provides particularly clear information on its approach to estimating uncollectible accounts and the potential effect of any errors in those estimates:

CRITICAL ACCOUNTING POLICIES

Allowance for Doubtful Accounts

We provide a reserve against trade accounts receivable for estimated losses that may result from customers' inability to pay. We determine the amount of the reserve by analyzing known uncollectible accounts, aged trade accounts receivables, economic conditions and forecasts, historical experience and the customers' credit-worthiness. . . . Our use of different estimates and assumptions could produce different financial results. For example, a 1.0% change in the rate used to estimate the reserve for the accounts we consider to have credit risk and not specifically identified as uncollectible would change the allowance for doubtful accounts by $1,100.

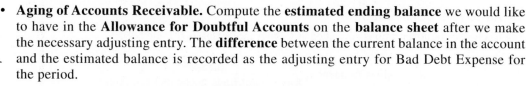

DECKERS outdoor corporation

REAL WORLD EXCERPT
Form 10-K

If uncollectible accounts actually written off differ from the estimated amount previously recorded, a higher or lower amount is recorded in the next period to make up for the previous period's error in estimate. **When estimates are found to be incorrect, financial statement values for prior annual accounting periods are not corrected.**

Control Over Accounts Receivable

Many managers forget that extending credit will increase sales volume, but unless the related receivables are collected, they do not add to the bottom line. Companies that emphasize sales without monitoring the collection of credit sales soon find much of their current assets tied up in accounts receivable. The following practices can help minimize bad debts:

1. Require approval of customers' credit history by a person independent of the sales and collections functions.

2. Age accounts receivable periodically and contact customers with overdue payments.

3. Reward both sales and collections personnel for speedy collections so that they work as a team.

To assess the effectiveness of overall credit-granting and collection activities, managers and analysts often compute the receivables turnover ratio.

KEY RATIO ANALYSIS	Receivables Turnover Ratio

LEARNING OBJECTIVE 6-4
Analyze and interpret the receivables turnover ratio and the effects of accounts receivable on cash flows.

? ANALYTICAL QUESTION

How effective are credit-granting and collection activities?

% RATIO AND COMPARISONS

The receivables turnover ratio is computed as follows (see Exhibits 6.1 and 6.2):

$$\text{Receivables Turnover} = \frac{\text{Net Sales*}}{\text{Average Net Trade Accounts Receivable}^\dagger}$$

The 2011 receivables turnover ratio for Deckers:

$$\frac{\$1,377,283}{(116,663 + 193,375)/2} = 8.9$$

COMPARISONS OVER TIME			COMPARISONS WITH COMPETITORS	
Deckers			Skechers U.S.A.	Crocs
2009	**2010**	**2011**	**2011**	**2011**
8.8	10.4	8.9	7.3	13.4

Selected Industry Comparisons: Receivables Turnover Ratio

Department stores	46.1
Malt beverages	21.4
Forest & wood products	14.7

💡 INTERPRETATIONS

In General   The receivables turnover ratio reflects how many times average trade receivables are recorded and collected during the period. The higher the ratio, the faster the collection of receivables. A higher ratio benefits the company because it can invest the money collected to earn interest income or reduce borrowings to reduce interest expense. Overly generous payment schedules and ineffective collection methods keep the receivables turnover ratio low. Analysts and creditors watch this ratio because a sudden decline may mean that a company is extending payment deadlines in an attempt to prop up lagging sales or is even recording sales that will later be returned by customers. Many managers and analysts compute the related number **average collection period** or **average days sales in receivables,** which is equal to 365 ÷ Receivables Turnover Ratio. It indicates the average time it takes a customer to pay its accounts. For Deckers, the amount would be computed as follows for 2011:

$$\text{Average Collection Period} = \frac{365}{\text{Receivables Turnover}} = \frac{365}{8.9} = 41.0 \text{ days}$$

Focus Company Analysis   Deckers's receivables turnover increased from a 2009 low of 8.8 to 8.9 in 2011. This indicates that the company is taking less time to convert its receivables into cash. Compared to the receivables turnover ratios of its competitors, Deckers's ratio is above that of Skechers and below that of Crocs.

A Few Cautions   Since differences across industries and between firms in the manner in which customer purchases are financed can cause dramatic differences in the ratio, a particular firm's ratio should be compared only with its prior years' figures or with other firms in the same industry following the same financing practices.

---

*Since the amount of net credit sales is normally not reported separately, most analysts use net sales in this equation.
†Average Net Trade Accounts Receivable = (Beginning Net Trade Accounts Receivable + Ending Net Trade Accounts Receivable) ÷ 2.

| Accounts Receivable | FOCUS ON CASH FLOWS |

The change in accounts receivable can be a major determinant of a company's cash flow from operations. While the income statement reflects the revenues of the period, the cash flow from operating activities reflects cash collections from customers. Since sales on account increase the balance in accounts receivable and cash collections from customers decrease the balance in accounts receivable, the change in accounts receivable from the beginning to the end of the period is the difference between sales and collections.

EFFECT ON STATEMENT OF CASH FLOWS

In General   When there is a net **decrease in accounts receivable** for the period, cash collected from customers is more than revenue; thus, the decrease must be **added** in computing cash flows from operations. When a net **increase in accounts receivable** occurs, cash collected from customers is less than revenue; thus, the increase must be **subtracted** in computing cash flows from operations.*

	Effect on Cash Flows
Operating activities (indirect method)	
Net income	$ xxx
Adjusted for	
Add accounts receivable decrease	+
or	
Subtract accounts receivable increase	−

Focus Company Analysis   The excerpt below shows the Operating Activities section of Deckers's statement of cash flows. Sales growth during 2011 has resulted in an increase in Deckers's balance in receivables. This increase is subtracted in reconciling net income to cash flow from operating activities because revenues are higher than cash collected from customers for 2011. When receivables decrease, the amount of the reduction in receivables is added in reconciling net income to cash flow from operating activities because cash collected from customers is higher than revenues.

	2011
Cash flows from operating activities	
Net income	$201,858
Adjustments to reconcile net income to net cash provided by operating activities:	
. . . .	. . .
Changes in operating assets and liabilities:	
Trade accounts receivable, net of provision for doubtful accounts	(76,712)
Inventories	(128,275)
	. . .
	. . . .
Net cash provided by operating activities	$ 30,091

For companies with receivables in foreign currency or business acquisitions/dispositions, the change reported on the cash flow statement will not equal the change in the accounts receivable reported on the balance sheet.

PAUSE FOR FEEDBACK

crocs™

© Crocs, Inc.

When using the **percentage of sales method,** you directly compute the bad debt expense for the period by multiplying the amount of credit sales by the bad debt loss rate. With the **aging method,** you compute the estimated ending balance in the allowance and solve for the bad debt expense. This process involves multiplying the amount in each age category by the estimated percentage uncollectible to produce the estimated ending balance in the allowance for doubtful accounts. The difference between the estimated ending balance and the balance in the allowance before the adjustment becomes the bad debt expense for the year. Before you move on, try an example of the more difficult aging method computations based on Crocs's numbers reported in an earlier year.

SELF-STUDY QUIZ

1. In an earlier year, Deckers's competitor Crocs reported a beginning balance in the Allowance for Doubtful Accounts of $5,262. It also wrote off bad debts amounting to $2,551 during the year. At the end of the year, it computed total estimated uncollectible accounts using the aging method to be $3,973 (all numbers in thousands of dollars). What amount did Crocs record as bad debt expense for the period? (**Solution approach:** Use the Allowance for Doubtful Accounts T-account or the following equation to solve for the missing value.)

Allowance for Doubtful Accounts (XA)	
Write off 2551	5262 – beg. bal
	? — bad debt exp
	3973

Estimated ending balance in Allowance for Doubtful Accounts = 3973
Less: Current balance in Allowance for Doubtful Accounts − 2711
Bad Debt Expense for the year

1262

The accounts receivable turnover ratio measures the effectiveness of credit-granting and collection activities. Faster turnover means faster receipt of cash from your customers. To test whether you understand this concept, answer the following question:

2. Indicate whether **granting later payment deadlines** (e.g., 60 days instead of 30 days) will most likely **increase** or **decrease** the accounts receivable turnover ratio. Explain.

After you have completed your answers, check them with the solutions at the bottom of the page.

Solutions to
SELF-STUDY QUIZ

1.

Allowance for Doubtful Accounts (XA)			
		Beginning balance	5,262
Write-offs	2,551	Bad debt expense (solve)	1,262
		Ending balance	3,973

Estimated ending balance in Allowance for Doubtful Accounts	3,973
Less: Current balance in Allowance for Doubtful Accounts ($5,262 − $2,551)	2,711
Bad Debt Expense for the year	$1,262

2. Granting later payment deadlines will most likely **decrease** the accounts receivable turnover ratio because later collections from customers will increase the average accounts receivable balance (the denominator of the ratio), decreasing the ratio.

REPORTING AND SAFEGUARDING CASH

Cash and Cash Equivalents Defined

Cash is defined as money or any instrument that banks will accept for deposit and immediate credit to a company's account, such as a check, money order, or bank draft. Cash equivalents are investments with original maturities of three months or less that are readily convertible to cash and whose value is unlikely to change (that is, they are not sensitive to interest rate changes). Typical instruments included as cash equivalents are bank certificates of deposit and Treasury bills that the U.S. government issues to finance its activities.

Like most companies, Deckers combines all of its bank accounts and cash equivalents into one amount, Cash and Cash Equivalents, on the balance sheet. It also reports that the book values of cash equivalents on the balance sheet equal their fair market values—which we should expect given the nature of the instruments (investments whose value is unlikely to change).

Cash Management

Many businesses receive a large amount of cash, checks, and credit card receipts from their customers each day. Anyone can spend cash, so management must develop procedures to safeguard the cash it uses in the business. Effective cash management involves more than protecting cash from theft, fraud, or loss through carelessness. Other cash management responsibilities include:

1. Accurate accounting so that reports of cash flows and balances may be prepared.

2. Controls to ensure that enough cash is available to meet (*a*) current operating needs, (*b*) maturing liabilities, and (*c*) unexpected emergencies.

3. Prevention of the accumulation of excess amounts of idle cash. Idle cash earns no revenue. Therefore, it is often invested in securities to earn a return until it is needed for operations.

Internal Control of Cash

The term internal controls refers to the process by which a company safeguards its assets and provides reasonable assurance regarding the reliability of the company's financial reporting, the effectiveness and efficiency of its operations, and its compliance with applicable laws and regulations. Internal control procedures should extend to all assets: cash, receivables, investments, plant and equipment, and so on. Controls that ensure the accuracy of the financial records are designed to prevent inadvertent errors and outright fraud. Because internal control increases the reliability of the financial statements, it is reviewed by the outside independent auditor.

Because cash is the asset most vulnerable to theft and fraud, a significant number of internal control procedures should focus on cash. You have already observed internal control procedures for cash, although you may not have known it at the time. At most movie theaters, one employee sells tickets and another employee collects them. Having one employee do both jobs would be less expensive, but that single employee could easily steal cash and admit a patron without issuing a ticket. If different employees perform the tasks, a successful theft requires the participation of both.

Effective internal control of cash should include the following:

1. Separation of duties.

   a. Complete separation of the jobs of receiving cash and disbursing cash.

   b. Complete separation of the procedures of accounting for cash receipts and cash disbursements.

   c. Complete separation of the physical handling of cash and all phases of the accounting function.

LEARNING OBJECTIVE 6-5
Report, control, and safeguard cash.

CASH is money or any instrument that banks will accept for deposit and immediate credit to a company's account, such as a check, money order, or bank draft.

CASH EQUIVALENTS are short-term investments with original maturities of three months or less that are readily convertible to cash and whose value is unlikely to change.

INTERNAL CONTROLS are the processes by which a company safeguards its assets and provides reasonable assurance regarding the reliability of the company's financial reporting, the effectiveness and efficiency of its operations, and its compliance with applicable laws and regulations.

2. Prescribed policies and procedures.

  a. Require that all cash receipts be deposited in a bank daily. Keep any cash on hand under strict control.

  b. Require separate approval of the purchases and the actual cash payments. Prenumbered checks should be used. Special care must be taken with payments by **electronic funds transfers** since they involve no controlled documents (checks).

  c. Assign the responsibilities for cash payment approval and check-signing or electronic funds transfer transmittal to different individuals.

  d. Require monthly reconciliation of bank accounts with the cash accounts on the company's books (discussed in detail in the next section).

A QUESTION OF ETHICS

Ethics and the Need for Internal Control

Some people are bothered by the recommendation that all well-run companies should have strong internal control procedures. These people believe that control procedures suggest that management does not trust the company's employees. Although the vast majority of employees are trustworthy, employee theft does cost businesses billions of dollars each year. Interviews with convicted felons indicate that in many cases they stole from their employers because they thought that it was easy and that no one cared (there were no internal control procedures).

  Many companies have a formal code of ethics that requires high standards of behavior in dealing with customers, suppliers, fellow employees, and the company's assets. Although each employee is ultimately responsible for his or her own ethical behavior, internal control procedures can be thought of as important value statements from management.

Reconciliation of the Cash Accounts and the Bank Statements

Content of a Bank Statement

A BANK STATEMENT is a monthly report from a bank that shows deposits recorded, checks cleared, other debits and credits, and a running bank balance.

Proper use of the bank accounts can be an important internal cash control procedure. Each month, the bank provides the company (the depositor) with a **bank statement** that lists (1) each paper or electronic deposit recorded by the bank during the period, (2) each paper or electronic check cleared by the bank during the period, and (3) the balance in the company's account. The bank statement also shows the bank charges or deductions (such as service charges) made directly to the company's account by the bank. A typical bank statement for ROW.COM, Inc., is shown in Exhibit 6.4.

  Exhibit 6.4 lists four items that need explanation. Notice the $500 and $100 items listed in the Checks and Debits column and coded **EFT.**[6] This is the code for **electronic funds transfers.** ROW.COM pays its electricity and insurance bills using electronic checking. When it orders the electronic payments, it records these items on the company's books in the same manner as a paper check. So no additional entry is needed.

  Notice that listed in the Checks and Debits column there is a deduction for $18 coded **NSF.** This entry refers to a check for $18 received from a customer and deposited by ROW.COM with its bank. The bank processed the check through banking channels to the customer's bank, but the account did not have sufficient funds to cover the check. The customer's bank therefore returned it to ROW.COM's bank, which then charged it back to ROW.COM's account. This type of check often is called an **NSF check** (not sufficient funds). The NSF check is now a receivable; consequently, ROW.COM must make an entry to debit Receivables and credit Cash for the $18.

---

[6] These codes vary among banks.

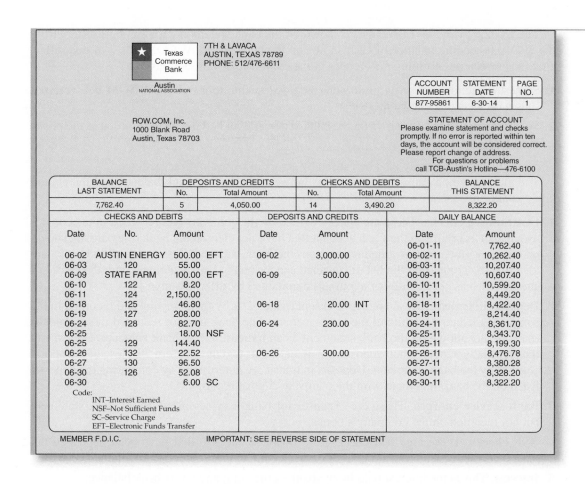

EXHIBIT 6.4

Example of a Bank Statement

Notice the $6 listed on June 30 in the Checks and Debits column and coded **SC.** This is the code for bank service charges. The bank statement included a memo by the bank explaining this service charge (which was not documented by a check). ROW.COM must make an entry to reflect this $6 decrease in the bank balance as a debit to a relevant expense account, such as Bank Service Expense, and a credit to Cash.

Notice the $20 listed on June 18 in the Deposits and Credits column and coded **INT** for interest earned. The bank pays interest on checking account balances, and it increased ROW .COM's account for interest earned during the period. ROW.COM must record the interest by making an entry to debit Cash and credit Interest Income for the $20.

Need for Reconciliation

A **bank reconciliation** is the process of comparing (reconciling) the ending cash balance in the company's records and the ending cash balance reported by the bank on the monthly bank statement. A bank reconciliation should be completed at the end of each month. Usually, the ending cash balance as shown on the bank statement does not agree with the ending cash balance shown by the related Cash ledger account on the books of the company. For example, the Cash ledger account of ROW.COM showed the following at the end of June (ROW.COM has only one checking account):

A BANK RECONCILIATION is the process of verifying the accuracy of both the bank statement and the cash accounts of a business.

Cash (A)			
June 1 balance	7,753.40		
June deposits	5,830.00	June payments	4,543.40
Ending balance	9,040.00		

The $8,322.20 ending cash balance shown on the bank statement (Exhibit 6.4) differs from the $9,040.00 ending balance of cash shown on the books of ROW.COM. Most of this difference exists because of timing differences in the recording of transactions:

1. Some transactions affecting cash were recorded in the books of ROW.COM but were not shown on the bank statement.

2. Some transactions were shown on the bank statement but had not been recorded in the books of ROW.COM.

Some of the difference may also be caused by errors in recording transactions.

The most common causes of differences between the ending bank balance and the ending book balance of cash are as follows:

1. **Outstanding checks.** These are checks written by the company and recorded in the company's ledger as credits to the Cash account that have not cleared the bank (they are not shown on the bank statement as a deduction from the bank balance). The outstanding checks are identified by comparing the list of canceled checks on the bank statement with the record of checks (such as check stubs or a journal) maintained by the company.

2. **Deposits in transit.** These are deposits sent to the bank by the company and recorded in the company's ledger as debits to the Cash account. The bank has not recorded these deposits (they are not shown on the bank statement as an increase in the bank balance). Deposits in transit usually happen when deposits are made one or two days before the close of the period covered by the bank statement. Deposits in transit are determined by comparing the deposits listed on the bank statement with the company deposit records.

3. **Bank service charges.** These are expenses for bank services listed on the bank statement but not recorded on the company's books.

4. **NSF checks.** These are "bad checks" or "bounced checks" that have been deposited but must be deducted from the company's cash account and rerecorded as accounts receivable.

5. **Interest.** This is the interest paid by the bank to the company on its bank balance.

6. **Errors.** Both the bank and the company may make errors, especially when the volume of cash transactions is large.

Bank Reconciliation Illustrated

The company should make a bank reconciliation immediately after receiving each bank statement. The general format for the bank reconciliation follows:

Ending cash balance per books	$xxx	Ending cash balance per bank statement	$xxx
+ Interest paid by bank	xx	+ Deposits in transit	xx
− NSF checks/Service charges	xx	− Outstanding checks	xx
± Company errors	xx	± Bank errors	xx
Ending correct cash balance	$xxx	Ending correct cash balance	$xxx

Exhibit 6.5 shows the bank reconciliation prepared by ROW.COM for the month of June to reconcile the ending bank balance ($8,322.20) with the ending book balance ($9,040.00). On the completed reconciliation, the correct cash balance is $9,045.00. This correct balance is the amount that should be shown in the Cash account after the reconciliation. Since ROW.COM has only one checking account and no cash on hand, it is also the correct amount of cash that should be reported on the balance sheet.[7]

---

[7]In this example, there were no outstanding checks or deposits in transit at the end of May.

ROW.COM INC. Bank Reconciliation For the Month Ending June 30, 2014			
Company's Books		**Bank Statement**	
Ending cash balance per books	$9,040.00	Ending cash balance per bank statement	$ 8,322.20
Additions		Additions	
Interest paid by the bank	20.00	Deposit in transit	1,800.00
Error in recording payment	9.00		
	9,069.00		10,122.20
Deductions		Deductions	
NSF check of R. Smith	18.00	Outstanding checks	1,077.20
Bank service charges	6.00		
Ending correct cash balance	$9,045.00	Ending correct cash balance	$ 9,045.00

EXHIBIT 6.5

Bank Reconciliation Illustrated

ROW.COM followed these steps in preparing the bank reconciliation:

1. **Identify the outstanding checks.** A comparison of the checks and electronic payments listed on the bank statement with the company's record of all checks drawn and electronic payments made showed the following checks were still outstanding (had not cleared the bank) at the end of June:

Check No.	Amount
121	$ 145.00
123	815.00
131	117.20
Total	$1,077.20

This total was entered on the reconciliation as a deduction from the bank account. These checks will be deducted by the bank when they clear the bank.

2. **Identify the deposits in transit.** A comparison of the deposit slips on hand with those listed on the bank statement revealed that a deposit of $1,800 made on June 30 was not listed on the bank statement. This amount was entered on the reconciliation as an addition to the bank account. It will be added by the bank when it records the deposit.

3. **Record bank charges and credits:**
   a. Interest received from the bank, $20—entered on the bank reconciliation as an addition to the book balance; it already has been included in the bank balance.
   b. NSF check of R. Smith, $18—entered on the bank reconciliation as a deduction from the book balance; it has been deducted from the bank statement balance.
   c. Bank service charges, $6—entered on the bank reconciliation as a deduction from the book balance; it has been deducted from the bank balance.

4. **Determine the impact of errors.** At this point, ROW.COM found that the reconciliation did not balance by $9. Upon checking the journal entries made during the month, the electronic payment on 6-09 for $100 to pay an account payable was found. The payment was recorded in the company's accounts as $109. Therefore, $9 (i.e., $109 − $100) must be added to the book cash balance on the reconciliation; the bank cleared the electronic payment for the correct amount, $100.

Note that in Exhibit 6.5 the two sections of the bank reconciliation now agree at a correct cash balance of $9,045.00.

A bank reconciliation as shown in Exhibit 6.5 accomplishes two major objectives:

1. It checks the accuracy of the bank balance and the company cash records, which involves developing the correct cash balance. The correct cash balance (plus cash on hand, if any) is the amount of cash that is reported on the balance sheet.

2. It identifies any previously unrecorded transactions or changes that are necessary to cause the company's Cash account(s) to show the correct cash balance. Any transactions or changes on the **company's books side** of the bank reconciliation need journal entries. Therefore, the following journal entries based on the company's books side of the bank reconciliation (Exhibit 6.5) must be entered into the company's records:

Accounts of ROW.COM

(a) Cash (+A)	20	
Interest income (+R, +SE)		20
To record interest by bank.		
(b) Accounts receivable (+A)	18	
Cash (−A)		18
To record NSF check.		
(c) Bank service expense (+E, −SE)	6	
Cash (−A)		6
To record service fees charged by bank.		
(d) Cash (+A)	9	
Accounts payable (+L)		9
To correct error made in recording a check payable to a creditor.		

Assets		=	Liabilities	+	Stockholders' Equity	
Cash (+20, −18, −6, +9)	+5		Accounts payable +9		Interest income (+R)	+20
Accounts receivable	+18				Bank service expense (+E)	−6

Notice again that all of the additions and deductions on the company's books side of the reconciliation need journal entries to update the Cash account. The additions and deductions on the bank statement side do not need journal entries because they will work out automatically when they clear the bank.

PAUSE FOR FEEDBACK

Cash is the most liquid of all assets, flowing continually into and out of a business. As a result, a number of critical control procedures, including the **reconciliation** of bank accounts, should be applied. Also, management of cash may be critically important to decision makers who must have cash available to meet current needs yet must avoid excess amounts of idle cash that produce no revenue. To see if you understand the basics of a bank reconciliation, answer the following questions:

Indicate which of the following items discovered while preparing a company's bank reconciliation will result in adjustment of the cash balance on the balance sheet.

1. Outstanding checks.
2. Deposits in transit.
3. Bank service charges.
4. NSF checks that were deposited.

After you have completed your answers, check them with the solution at the bottom of the page.

EPILOGUE

As we noted at the beginning of the chapter, Deckers recognized that to turn growth into profits, it had to (1) continually refresh its product lines by introducing new technologies, new styles, and new product categories; (2) become a leaner and more nimble manufacturer, taking advantage of lower-cost, more flexible production locations; and (3) focus attention on inventory management and collections of accounts receivable since an uncollected account is of no value to the company. Each of these efforts is aimed at increasing net sales and/or decreasing cost of goods sold, thereby increasing gross profit. The first quarter of 2012 was a mixed bag for Deckers. Sales increased, but gross profit and net income declined compared to the first quarter of 2011. You can evaluate the further success of the company's strategy by going to the Web at **www.deckers.com** to check Deckers's latest annual and quarterly reports.

DEMONSTRATION **CASE A**

(Complete the requirements before proceeding to the suggested solutions.) Wholesale Warehouse Stores sold $950,000 in merchandise during 2014. Of this amount, $400,000 was on credit with terms 2/10, n/30 (75 percent of these amounts were paid within the discount period), $500,000 was paid with credit cards (there was a 3 percent credit card discount), and the rest was paid in cash. On December 31, 2014, the Accounts Receivable balance was $80,000. The beginning balance in the Allowance for Doubtful Accounts was $9,000 and $6,000 of bad debts was written off during the year.

Required:

1. Compute net sales for 2014, assuming that sales and credit card discounts are treated as contra-revenues.

2. Assume that Wholesale uses the percentage of sales method for estimating bad debt expense and that it estimates that 2 percent of credit sales will produce bad debts. Record bad debt expense for 2014.

3. Assume instead that Wholesale uses the aging of accounts receivable method and that it estimates that $10,000 worth of current accounts is uncollectible. Record bad debt expense for 2014.

3. Bank service charges are deducted from the company's account; thus, cash must be reduced and an expense must be recorded.
4. NSF checks that were deposited were recorded on the books as increases in the cash account; thus, cash must be decreased and the related accounts receivable increased if payment is still expected.

SUGGESTED SOLUTION

1. Both sales discounts and credit card discounts should be subtracted from sales revenues in the computation of net sales.

Sales revenue	$950,000
Less: Sales discounts (0.02 × 0.75 × $400,000)	6,000
Credit card discounts (0.03 × $500,000)	15,000
Net sales	$929,000

2. The percentage estimate of bad debts should be applied to credit sales. Cash sales never produce bad debts.

Bad debt expense (+E, −SE) (0.02 × $400,000)	8,000	
Allowance for doubtful accounts (+XA, −A)		8,000

Assets	=	Liabilities	+	Stockholders' Equity
Allowance for				Bad debt
doubtful accounts	−8,000			expense (+E) −8,000

3. The entry made when using the aging of accounts receivable method is the estimated balance minus the current balance.

Estimated ending balance in Allowance for Doubtful Accounts	$10,000
Less: Current balance in Allowance for Doubtful Accounts ($9,000 − $6,000)	3,000
Bad Debt Expense for the year	$ 7,000

Bad debt expense (+E, −SE)	7,000	
Allowance for doubtful accounts (+XA, −A)		7,000

Assets	=	Liabilities	+	Stockholders' Equity
Allowance for				Bad debt
doubtful accounts	−7,000			expense (+E) −7,000

DEMONSTRATION   CASE B

(Complete the requirements before proceeding to the suggested solution that follows.) Heather Ann Long, a freshman at a large state university, has just received her first checking account statement. This was her first chance to attempt a bank reconciliation. She had the following information to work with:

Bank balance, September 1	$1,150
Deposits during September	650
Checks cleared during September	900
Bank service charge	25
Bank balance, October 1	875

Heather was surprised that the deposit of $50 she made on September 29 had not been posted to her account and was pleased that her rent check of $200 had not cleared her account. Her checkbook balance was $750.

Required:

1. Complete Heather's bank reconciliation.

2. Why is it important for individuals such as Heather and businesses to do a bank reconciliation each month?

SUGGESTED SOLUTION

1. Heather's bank reconciliation:

Heather's Books		Bank Statement	
October 1 cash balance	$750	October 1 cash balance	$875
Additions		Additions	
None		Deposit in transit	50
Deductions		Deductions	
Bank service charge	(25)	Outstanding check	(200)
Correct cash balance	$725	Correct cash balance	$725

2. Bank statements, whether personal or business, should be reconciled each month. This process helps ensure that a correct balance is reflected in the customer's books. Failure to reconcile a bank statement increases the chance that an error will not be discovered and may result in bad checks being written. Businesses must reconcile their bank statements for an additional reason: The correct balance that is calculated during reconciliation is recorded on the balance sheet.

Chapter Supplement

Recording Discounts and Returns

In this chapter, both **credit card discounts** and **cash discounts** have been recorded as contra-revenues. For example, if the credit card company is charging a 3 percent fee for its service and Deckers's Internet credit card sales are $3,000 for January 2, Deckers will record the following:

Cash (+A)	2,910	
Credit card discount (+XR,−R,−SE)	90	
Sales revenue (+R, +SE).		3,000

Assets		=	Liabilities		+	Stockholders' Equity	
Cash	+2,910					Sales revenue (+R)	+3,000
						Credit card discount (+XR)	−90

Similarly, if credit sales of $1,000 are recorded with terms 2/10, n/30 ($1,000 × 0.98 = $980), and payment is made within the discount period, Deckers will record the following:

Accounts receivable (+A)	1,000	
Sales revenue (+R, +SE).		1,000

Assets		=	Liabilities		+	Stockholders' Equity	
Accounts receivable	+1,000					Sales revenue (+R)	+1,000

Cash (+A)	980	
Sales discount (+XR, −R, −SE)	20	
Accounts receivable (−A)		1,000

Assets		=	Liabilities	+	Stockholders' Equity	
Cash	+980				Sales discount (+XR)	−20
Accounts receivable	−1,000					

Sales returns and allowances should always be treated as a contra-revenue. Assume that Fontana Shoes of Ithaca, New York, buys 40 pairs of sandals from Deckers for $2,000 on account. On the date of sale, Deckers makes the following journal entry:

| Accounts receivable (+A) | 2,000 | |
| Sales revenue (+R, +SE) | | 2,000 |

Assets		=	Liabilities	+	Stockholders' Equity	
Accounts receivable	+2,000				Sales revenue (+R)	+2,000

Before paying for the sandals, however, Fontana discovers that 10 pairs of sandals are not the color ordered and returns them to Deckers. On that date Deckers records:

| Sales returns and allowances (+XR, −R, −SE) | 500 | |
| Accounts receivable (−A) | | 500 |

Assets		=	Liabilities	+	Stockholders' Equity	
Accounts receivable	−500				Sales returns and allowances (+XR)	−500

In addition, the related cost of goods sold entry for the 10 pairs of sandals would be reversed.

CHAPTER TAKE-AWAYS

6-1. Apply the revenue realization principle to determine the accepted time to record sales revenue for typical retailers, wholesalers, manufacturers, and service companies.   p. 278

Revenue recognition policies are widely recognized as one of the most important determinants of the fair presentation of financial statements. For most merchandisers and manufacturers, the required revenue recognition point is the time that title changes to the buyer (shipment or delivery of goods). For service companies, it is the time that services are provided.

6-2. Analyze the impact of credit card sales, sales discounts, and sales returns on the amounts reported as net sales.   p. 279

Both **credit card discounts** and **sales** or **cash discounts** can be recorded either as contra-revenues or as expenses. When recorded as contra-revenues, they reduce net sales. **Sales returns and allowances,** which should always be treated as a contra-revenue, also reduce net sales.

6-3. Estimate, report, and evaluate the effects of uncollectible accounts receivable (bad debts) on financial statements.   p. 283

When receivables are material, companies must employ the allowance method to account for uncollectibles. These are the steps in the process:

a. The end-of-period adjusting entry to record bad debt expense estimates.

b. Writing off specific accounts determined to be uncollectible during the period.

The adjusting entry reduces net income as well as net accounts receivable. The write-off affects neither.

6-4. **Analyze and interpret the receivables turnover ratio and the effects of accounts receivable on cash flows.   p. 290**

  a. **Receivables turnover ratio**—This ratio measures the effectiveness of credit-granting and collection activities. It reflects how many times average trade receivables were recorded and collected during the period. Analysts and creditors watch this ratio because a sudden decline in it may mean that a company is extending payment deadlines in an attempt to prop up lagging sales or is recording sales that later will be returned by customers.

  b. **Effects on cash flows**—When a net decrease in accounts receivable for the period occurs, cash collected from customers is always more than revenue, and cash flows from operations increases. When a net increase in accounts receivable occurs, cash collected from customers is always less than revenue. Thus, cash flows from operations declines.

6-5. **Report, control, and safeguard cash.   p. 293**

  Cash is the most liquid of all assets, flowing continually into and out of a business. As a result, a number of critical control procedures, including the reconciliation of bank accounts, should be applied. Also, management of cash may be critically important to decision makers who must have cash available to meet current needs yet must avoid excess amounts of idle cash that produce no revenue.

Closely related to recording revenue is recording the cost of what was sold. Chapter 7 will focus on transactions related to inventory and cost of goods sold. This topic is important because cost of goods sold has a major impact on a company's gross profit and net income, which are watched closely by investors, analysts, and other users of financial statements. Increasing emphasis on quality, productivity, and costs have further focused production managers' attention on cost of goods sold and inventory. Since inventory cost figures play a major role in product introduction and pricing decisions, they also are important to marketing and general managers. Finally, since inventory accounting has a major effect on many companies' tax liabilities, this is an important place to introduce the effect of taxation on management decision making and financial reporting.

KEY **RATIOS**

Receivables turnover ratio measures the effectiveness of credit-granting and collection activities. It is computed as follows (p. 290):

$$\text{Receivables Turnover} = \frac{\text{Net Sales}}{\text{Average Net Trade Accounts Receivable}}$$

FINDING **FINANCIAL INFORMATION**

Balance Sheet

Under Current Assets
   Accounts receivable (net of allowance for doubtful accounts)

Income Statement

Revenues
   Net sales (sales revenue less discounts and sales returns and allowances)

Expenses
   Selling expenses (including bad debt expense)

Statement of Cash Flows

Under Operating Activities (indirect method)
   Net income
   + decreases in accounts receivable (net)
   − increases in accounts receivable (net)

Notes

Under Summary of Significant Accounting Policies
   Revenue recognition policy

Under a Separate Note on Form 10-K
   Bad debt expense and write-offs of bad debts

KEY **TERMS**

Accounts Receivable (Trade Receivables or
   Receivables)   p. 283
Aging of Accounts Receivable
   Method   p. 288
Allowance for Doubtful Accounts
   (Allowance for Bad Debts or Allowance
   for Uncollectible Accounts)   p. 284
Allowance Method   p. 284

Bad Debt Expense (Doubtful Accounts
   Expense, Uncollectible Accounts
   Expense, or Provision for Uncollectible
   Accounts)   p. 284
Bank Reconciliation   p. 295
Bank Statement   p. 294
Cash   p. 293
Cash Equivalents   p. 293

Credit Card Discount   p. 279
Internal Controls   p. 293
Net Sales   p. 281
Notes Receivable   p. 283
Percentage of Credit Sales
   Method   p. 287
Sales (or Cash) Discount   p. 280
Sales Returns and Allowances   p. 280

QUESTIONS

1. Explain the difference between sales revenue and net sales.
2. What is gross profit or gross margin on sales? In your explanation, assume that net sales revenue was $100,000 and cost of goods sold was $60,000.
3. What is a credit card discount? How does it affect amounts reported on the income statement?
4. What is a sales discount? Use 1/10, n/30 in your explanation.
5. What is the distinction between sales allowances and sales discounts?
6. Differentiate accounts receivable from notes receivable.
7. Which basic accounting principle is the allowance method of accounting for bad debts designed to satisfy?
8. Using the allowance method, is bad debt expense recognized in (a) the period in which sales related to the uncollectible account are made or (b) the period in which the seller learns that the customer is unable to pay?
9. What is the effect of the write-off of bad debts (using the allowance method) on (a) net income and (b) accounts receivable, net?
10. Does an increase in the receivables turnover ratio generally indicate faster or slower collection of receivables? Explain.
11. Define cash and cash equivalents in the context of accounting. Indicate the types of items that should be included and excluded.
12. Summarize the primary characteristics of an effective internal control system for cash.
13. Why should cash-handling and cash-recording activities be separated? How is this separation accomplished?
14. What are the purposes of a bank reconciliation? What balances are reconciled?
15. Briefly explain how the total amount of cash reported on the balance sheet is computed.
16. (Chapter Supplement) Under the gross method of recording sales discounts discussed in this chapter, is the amount of sales discount taken recorded (a) at the time the sale is recorded or (b) at the time the collection of the account is recorded?

MULTIPLE-CHOICE **QUESTIONS**

1. Sales discounts with terms 2/10, n/30 mean:
   a. 10 percent discount for payment within 30 days.
   b. 2 percent discount for payment within 10 days, or the full amount (less returns) due within 30 days.
   c. Two-tenths of a percent discount for payment within 30 days.
   d. None of the above.

2. Gross sales total $300,000, one-half of which were credit sales. Sales returns and allowances of $15,000 apply to the credit sales, sales discounts of 2% were taken on all of the net credit sales, and credit card sales of $100,000 were subject to a credit card discount of 3%. What is the dollar amount of net sales?
   a. $227,000
   b. $229,800
   c. $279,300
   d. $240,000

3. A company has been successful in reducing the amount of sales returns and allowances. At the same time, a credit card company reduced the credit card discount from 3% to 2%. What effect will these changes have on the company's net sales, all other things equal?
   a. Net sales will not change.
   b. Net sales will increase.
   c. Net sales will decrease.
   d. Either (b) or (c).

4. When a company using the allowance method writes off a specific customer's $100,000 account receivable from the accounting system, which of the following statements are true?
   1. Total stockholders' equity remains the same.
   2. Total assets remain the same.
   3. Total expenses remain the same.
   a. 2
   b. 1 and 3
   c. 1 and 2
   d. 1, 2, and 3

5. You have determined that Company X estimates bad debt expense with an aging of accounts receivable schedule. Company X's estimate of uncollectible receivables resulting from the aging analysis equals $250. The beginning balance in the allowance for doubtful accounts was $220. Write-offs of bad debts during the period were $180. What amount would be recorded as bad debt expense for the current period?
   a. $180
   b. $250
   c. $210
   d. $220

6. Upon review of the most recent bank statement, you discover that you recently received an "insufficient funds check" from a customer. Which of the following describes the actions to be taken when preparing your bank reconciliation?

	Balance per Books	**Balance per Bank Statement**
a.	No change	Decrease
b.	Decrease	Increase
c.	Decrease	No change
d.	Increase	Decrease

7. Which of the following is **not** a step toward effective internal control over cash?
   a. Require signatures from a manager and one financial officer on all checks.
   b. Require that cash be deposited daily at the bank.
   c. Require that the person responsible for removing the cash from the register have no access to the accounting records.
   d. All of the above are steps toward effective internal control.

8. When using the allowance method, as bad debt expense is recorded,
   a. Total assets remain the same and stockholders' equity remains the same.
   b. Total assets decrease and stockholders' equity decreases.
   c. Total assets increase and stockholders' equity decreases.
   d. Total liabilities increase and stockholders' equity decreases.

9. Which of the following best describes the proper presentation of accounts receivable in the financial statements?
   a. Gross accounts receivable plus the allowance for doubtful accounts in the asset section of the balance sheet.
   b. Gross accounts receivable in the asset section of the balance sheet and the allowance for doubtful accounts in the expense section of the income statement.
   c. Gross accounts receivable less bad debt expense in the asset section of the balance sheet.
   d. Gross accounts receivable less the allowance for doubtful accounts in the asset section of the balance sheet.

10. Which of the following is **not** a component of net sales?
    a. Sales returns and allowances
    b. Sales discounts
    c. Cost of goods sold
    d. Credit card discounts

MINI-**EXERCISES**

M6-1
LO6-1

Interpreting the Revenue Principle

Indicate the most likely time you expect sales revenue to be recorded for each of the listed transactions.

Transaction	Point A	Point B
a. Sale of inventory to a business customer on open account	_____ Shipment	_____ Collection of account
b. Computer sold by mail order company on a credit card	_____ Shipment	_____ Delivery
c. Airline tickets sold by an airline on a credit card	_____ Point of sale	_____ Completion of flight

M6-2
LO6-2

Reporting Net Sales with Sales Discounts

Merchandise invoiced at $9,500 is sold on terms 1/10, n/30. If the buyer pays within the discount period, what amount will be reported on the income statement as net sales?

M6-3
LO6-2

Reporting Net Sales with Sales Discounts, Credit Card Discounts, and Sales Returns

Total gross sales for the period include the following:

Credit card sales (discount 3%)	$ 9,400
Sales on account (2/15, n/60)	$12,000

Sales returns related to sales on account were $650. All returns were made before payment. One-half of the remaining sales on account were paid within the discount period. The company treats all discounts and returns as contra-revenues. What amount will be reported on the income statement as net sales?

M6-4
LO6-3

Recording Bad Debts

Prepare journal entries for each transaction listed.

a. During the period, bad debts are written off in the amount of $14,500.
b. At the end of the period, bad debt expense is estimated to be $16,000.

M6-5
LO6-3

Determining Financial Statement Effects of Bad Debts

Using the following categories, indicate the effects of the following transactions. Use + for increase and − for decrease and indicate the accounts affected and the amounts.

a. At the end of the period, bad debt expense is estimated to be $15,000.
b. During the period, bad debts are written off in the amount of $9,500.

Assets	=	Liabilities	+	Stockholders' Equity

M6-6
LO6-4

Determining the Effects of Credit Policy Changes on Receivables Turnover Ratio

Indicate the most likely effect of the following changes in credit policy on the receivables turnover ratio (+ for increase, − for decrease, and NE for no effect).

a. Granted credit with shorter payment deadlines.
b. Increased effectiveness of collection methods.
c. Granted credit to less creditworthy customers.

Matching Reconciling Items to the Bank Reconciliation

M6-7
LO6-5

Indicate whether the following items would be added (+) or subtracted (−) from the company's books or the bank statement during the construction of a bank reconciliation.

Reconciling Item	Company's Books	Bank Statement
a. Outstanding checks		
b. Bank service charge		
c. Deposit in transit		

(Supplement) Recording Sales Discounts

M6-8

A sale is made for $6,000; terms are 3/10, n/30. At what amount should the sale be recorded under the gross method of recording sales discounts? Give the required entry. Also give the collection entry, assuming that it is during the discount period.

EXERCISES

Reporting Net Sales with Credit Sales and Sales Discounts

E6-1
LO6-2

During the months of January and February, Hancock Corporation sold goods to three customers. The sequence of events was as follows:

Jan.	6	Sold goods for $1,500 to S. Green and billed that amount subject to terms 2/10, n/30.
	6	Sold goods to M. Munoz for $850 and billed that amount subject to terms 2/10, n/30.
	14	Collected cash due from S. Green.
Feb.	2	Collected cash due from M. Munoz.
	28	Sold goods for $500 to R. Reynolds and billed that amount subject to terms 2/10, n/45.

Required:
Assuming that Sales Discounts is treated as a contra-revenue, compute net sales for the two months ended February 28.

Reporting Net Sales with Credit Sales, Sales Discounts, and Credit Card Sales

E6-2
LO6-2

The following transactions were selected from the records of OceanView Company:

July	12	Sold merchandise to Customer R, who charged the $3,000 purchase on his Visa credit card. Visa charges OceanView a 2 percent credit card fee.
	15	Sold merchandise to Customer S at an invoice price of $9,000; terms 3/10, n/30.
	20	Sold merchandise to Customer T at an invoice price of $4,000; terms 3/10, n/30.
	23	Collected payment from Customer S from July 15 sale.
Aug.	25	Collected payment from Customer T from July 20 sale.

Required:
Assuming that Sales Discounts and Credit Card Discounts are treated as contra-revenues, compute net sales for the two months ended August 31.

E6-3

LO6-2

Reporting Net Sales with Credit Sales, Sales Discounts, Sales Returns, and Credit Card Sales

The following transactions were selected from among those completed by Cadence Retailers in 2013:

Nov.	20	Sold 20 items of merchandise to Customer B at an invoice price of $5,500 (total); terms 3/10, n/30.
	25	Sold two items of merchandise to Customer C, who charged the $400 sales price on her Visa credit card. Visa charges Cadence Retailers a 2 percent credit card fee.
	28	Sold 10 identical items of merchandise to Customer D at an invoice price of $9,000 (total); terms 3/10, n/30.
	29	Customer D returned one of the items purchased on the 28th; the item was defective, and credit was given to the customer.
Dec.	6	Customer D paid the account balance in full.
	20	Customer B paid in full for the invoice of November 20, 2013.

Required:

Assume that Sales Returns and Allowances, Sales Discounts, and Credit Card Discounts are treated as contra-revenues; compute net sales for the two months ended December 31, 2013.

E6-4

LO6-2

Determining the Effects of Credit Sales, Sales Discounts, Credit Card Sales, and Sales Returns and Allowances on Income Statement Categories

Brazen Shoe Company records Sales Returns and Allowances, Sales Discounts, and Credit Card Discounts as contra-revenues. Complete the following tabulation, indicating the effect (+ for increase, − for decrease, and NE for no effect) and amount of the effects of each transaction, including related cost of goods sold.

July	12	Sold merchandise to customer at factory store who charged the $300 purchase on her American Express card. American Express charges a 1 percent credit card fee. Cost of goods sold was $175.
July	15	Sold merchandise to Customer T at an invoice price of $5,000; terms 3/10, n/30. Cost of goods sold was $2,500.
July	20	Collected cash due from Customer T.
July	21	Before paying for the order, a customer returned shoes with an invoice price of $1,000, and cost of goods sold was $600.

Transaction	Net Sales	Cost of Goods Sold	Gross Profit
July 12			
July 15			
July 20			
July 21			

E6-5

LO6-2

Evaluating the Annual Interest Rate Implicit in a Sales Discount with Discussion of Management Choice of Financing Strategy

Clark's Landscaping bills customers subject to terms 3/10, n/50.

Required:

1. Compute the annual interest rate implicit in the sales discount. (Round to two decimal places.)
2. If his bank charges 15 percent interest, should the customer borrow from the bank so that he can take advantage of the discount? Explain your recommendation.

E6-6

LO6-3

Recording Bad Debt Expense Estimates and Write-Offs Using the Percentage of Credit Sales Method

During 2014, Adams Assembly, Inc., recorded credit sales of $1,300,000. Based on prior experience, it estimates a 1 percent bad debt rate on credit sales.

Required:
Prepare journal entries for each transaction:
a. The appropriate bad debt expense adjustment was recorded for the year 2014.
b. On December 31, 2014, an account receivable for $4,000 from March of the current year was deter-mined to be uncollectible and was written off.

Recording Bad Debt Expense Estimates and Write-Offs Using the Percentage of Credit Sales Method

E6-7

LO6-3

During 2014, Sun Electronics, Incorporated, recorded credit sales of $5,000,000. Based on prior experi-ence, it estimates a 2 percent bad debt rate on credit sales.

Required:
Prepare journal entries for each transaction:
a. The appropriate bad debt expense adjustment was recorded for the year 2014.
b. On December 31, 2014, an account receivable for $98,000 from a prior year was determined to be uncollectible and was written off.

Determining Financial Statement Effects of Bad Debts Using the Percentage of Credit Sales Method

E6-8

LO6-3

Using the following categories, indicate the effects of the transactions listed in E6-7. Use + for increase and − for decrease and indicate the accounts affected and the amounts.

Assets	=	Liabilities	+	Stockholders' Equity

Recording and Determining the Effects of Bad Debt Transactions on Income Statement Categories Using the Percentage of Credit Sales Method

E6-9

LO6-3

During 2014, Giatras Electronics recorded credit sales of $680,000. Based on prior experience, it esti-mates a 3.5 percent bad debt rate on credit sales.

Required:
1. Prepare journal entries for each of the following transactions.
   a. The appropriate bad debt expense adjustment was recorded for the year 2014.
   b. On December 31, 2014, an account receivable for $2,800 from a prior year was determined to be uncollectible and was written off.
2. Complete the following tabulation, indicating the amount and effect (+ for increase, − for decrease, and NE for no effect) of each transaction.

Transaction	Net Sales	Gross Profit	Income from Operations
a.			
b.			

Computing Bad Debt Expense Using Aging Analysis

E6-10

LO6-3

Lin's Dairy uses the aging approach to estimate bad debt expense. The balance of each account receiv-able is aged on the basis of three time periods as follows: (1) not yet due, $22,000, (2) up to 120 days past due, $6,500, and (3) more than 120 days past due, $2,800. Experience has shown that for each age group, the average loss rate on the amount of the receivables at year-end due to uncollectability is (1) 3 percent, (2) 14 percent, and (3) 34 percent, respectively. At December 31, 2014 (end of the current year), the Allowance for Doubtful Accounts balance is $1,200 (credit) before the end-of-period adjust-ing entry is made.

Required:
What amount should be recorded as Bad Debt Expense for the current year?

E6-11

LO6-3

Recording and Reporting a Bad Debt Estimate Using Aging Analysis

Casilda Company uses the aging approach to estimate bad debt expense. The balance of each account receivable is aged on the basis of three time periods as follows: (1) not yet due, $50,000, (2) up to 180 days past due, $14,000, and (3) more than 180 days past due, $4,000. Experience has shown that for each age group, the average loss rate on the amount of the receivables at year-end due to uncollectability is (1) 3 percent, (2) 12 percent, and (3) 30 percent, respectively. At December 31, 2013 (end of the current year), the Allowance for Doubtful Accounts balance is $200 (credit) before the end-of-period adjusting entry is made.

Required:
1. Prepare the appropriate bad debt expense adjusting entry for the year 2013.
2. Show how the various accounts related to accounts receivable should be shown on the December 31, 2013, balance sheet.

E6-12

LO6-3

Recording and Reporting a Bad Debt Estimate Using Aging Analysis

Chou Company uses the aging approach to estimate bad debt expense. The balance of each account receivable is aged on the basis of three time periods as follows: (1) not yet due, $295,000, (2) up to 120 days past due, $55,000, and (3) more than 120 days past due, $18,000. Experience has shown that for each age group, the average loss rate on the amount of the receivables at year-end due to uncollectability is (1) 2.5 percent, (2) 11 percent, and (3) 30 percent, respectively. At December 31, 2015 (end of the current year), the Allowance for Doubtful Accounts balance is $100 (credit) before the end-of-period adjusting entry is made.

Required:
1. Prepare the appropriate bad debt expense adjusting entry for the year 2015.
2. Show how the various accounts related to accounts receivable should be shown on the December 31, 2015, balance sheet.

E6-13

LO6-3

SIEMENS

Interpreting Bad Debt Disclosures

Siemens is one of the world's largest electrical engineering and electronics companies. Headquartered in Germany, the company has been in business for over 160 years and operates in 190 countries. In a recent annual report, it disclosed the following information concerning its allowance for doubtful accounts (euros in millions denoted as €):

Balance at Beginning of Period	Charged to Costs and Expenses	Amounts Written Off	Balance at End of Period
€993	€213	€(201)	€1,005

Required:
1. Record summary journal entries related to the allowance for doubtful accounts for the current year.
2. If Siemens had written off an additional €10 million of accounts receivable during the period, how would receivables, net, and net income have been affected? Explain why.

E6-14

LO6-3

Inferring Bad Debt Write-Offs and Cash Collections from Customers

On its recent financial statements, Hassell Fine Foods reported the following information about net sales revenue and accounts receivable (amounts in thousands):

	Current Year	Prior Year
Accounts receivable, net of allowances of $153 and $117	$13,589	$11,338
Net revenues	60,420	51,122

According to its Form 10-K, Hassell recorded bad debt expense of $88 and did not reinstate any previously written-off accounts during the current year. (**Hint:** Refer to the summary of the effects of accounting for bad debts on the Accounts Receivable (Gross) and the Allowance for Doubtful Accounts T-accounts. Use the T-accounts to solve for the missing values.)

Required:

1. What amount of bad debts was written off during the current year?
2. Based on your answer to requirement (1), solve for cash collected from customers for the current year, assuming that all of Hassell's sales during the period were on open account.

Inferring Bad Debt Write-Offs and Cash Collections from Customers

Microsoft develops, produces, and markets a wide range of computer software, including the Windows operating system. On its recent financial statements, Microsoft reported the following information about net sales revenue and accounts receivable (amounts in millions).

E6-15
LO6-3
Microsoft

	Current Year	Prior Year
Accounts receivable, net of allowances of $333 and $375	$14,987	$13,014
Net revenues	69,943	62,484

According to its Form 10-K, Microsoft recorded bad debt expense of $14 and did not reinstate any previously written-off accounts during the current year. (**Hint:** Refer to the summary of the effects of accounting for bad debts on the Accounts Receivable (Gross) and the Allowance for Doubtful Accounts T-accounts. Use the T-accounts to solve for the missing values.)

Required:

1. What amount of bad debts was written off during the current year?
2. Based on your answer to requirement (1), solve for cash collected from customers for the current year, assuming that all of Microsoft's sales during the period were on open account.

Inferring Bad Debt Expense and Determining the Impact of Uncollectible Accounts on Income and Working Capital

A recent annual report for Target contained the following information (dollars in thousands) at the end of its fiscal year:

E6-16
LO6-3
Target

	Year 2	Year 1
Accounts receivable	$6,357,000	$6,843,000
Allowance for doubtful accounts	(430,000)	(690,000)
	$5,927,000	$6,153,000

A footnote to the financial statements disclosed that uncollectible accounts amounting to $414,000 and $854,000 were written off as bad debts during year 2 and year 1, respectively. Assume that the tax rate for Target was 30 percent.

Required:

1. Determine the bad debt expense for year 2 based on the preceding facts. (**Hint:** Use the Allowance for Doubtful Accounts T-account to solve for the missing value.)
2. **Working capital** is defined as current assets minus current liabilities. How was Target's working capital affected by the write-off of $414,000 in uncollectible accounts during year 2? What impact did the recording of bad debt expense have on working capital in year 2?
3. How was net income affected by the $414,000 write-off during year 2? What impact did recording bad debt expense have on net income for year 2?

E6-17

LO6-3

Recording, Reporting, and Evaluating a Bad Debt Estimate

During 2014, Robby's Camera Shop had sales revenue of $170,000, of which $75,000 was on credit. At the start of 2014, Accounts Receivable showed a $16,000 debit balance, and the Allowance for Doubtful Accounts showed a $900 credit balance. Collections of accounts receivable during 2014 amounted to $60,000.

Data during 2014 follows:

a. On December 31, 2014, an Account Receivable (J. Doe) of $1,700 from a prior year was determined to be uncollectible; therefore, it was written off immediately as a bad debt.

b. On December 31, 2014, on the basis of experience, a decision was made to continue the accounting policy of basing estimated bad debt losses on 1.5 percent of credit sales for the year.

Required:

1. Give the required journal entries for the two items on December 31, 2014 (end of the accounting period).
2. Show how the amounts related to Accounts Receivable and Bad Debt Expense would be reported on the income statement and balance sheet for 2014. Disregard income tax considerations.
3. On the basis of the data available, does the 1.5 percent rate appear to be reasonable? Explain.

E6-18

LO6-3

Recording, Reporting, and Evaluating a Bad Debt Estimate

During 2014, Bob's Ceramics Shop had sales revenue of $60,000, of which $25,000 was on credit. At the start of 2014, Accounts Receivable showed a $3,500 debit balance, and the Allowance for Doubtful Accounts showed a $300 credit balance. Collections of accounts receivable during 2014 amounted to $18,000.

Data during 2014 follows:

a. On December 31, 2014, an Account Receivable (Toby's Gift Shop) of $550 from a prior year was determined to be uncollectible; therefore, it was written off immediately as a bad debt.

b. On December 31, 2014, on the basis of experience, a decision was made to continue the accounting policy of basing estimated bad debt losses on 2 percent of credit sales for the year.

Required:

1. Give the required journal entries for the two items on December 31, 2014 (end of the accounting period).
2. Show how the amounts related to Accounts Receivable and Bad Debt Expense would be reported on the income statement and balance sheet for 2014. Disregard income tax considerations.
3. On the basis of the data available, does the 2 percent rate appear to be reasonable? Explain.

E6-19

LO6-4

FedEx

Computing and Interpreting the Receivables Turnover Ratio

A recent annual report for FedEx contained the following data:

	(dollars in thousands)	
	Current Year	Previous Year
Accounts receivable	$ 4,763,000	$4,329,000
Less: Allowance for doubtful accounts	182,000	166,000
Net accounts receivable	$ 4,581,000	$4,163,000
Net sales (assume all on credit)	$39,304,000	

Required:

1. Determine the receivables turnover ratio and average days sales in receivables for the current year.
2. Explain the meaning of each number.

Computing and Interpreting the Receivables Turnover Ratio

A recent annual report for Dell, Inc., contained the following data:

	(dollars in thousands)	
	Current Year	Previous Year
Accounts receivable	$ 6,539,000	$6,589,000
Less: Allowance for doubtful accounts	63,000	96,000
Net accounts receivable	$ 6,476,000	$6,493,000
Net sales (assume all on credit)	$62,071,000	

Required:
1. Determine the receivables turnover ratio and average days sales in receivables for the current year.
2. Explain the meaning of each number.

Interpreting the Effects of Sales Declines and Changes in Receivables on Cash Flow from Operations

Stride Rite Corporation manufactures and markets shoes under the brand names Stride Rite, Keds, and Sperry Top-Sider. Three recent years produced a combination of declining sales revenue and net income culminating in a net loss of $8,430,000. Each year, however, Stride Rite was able to report positive cash flows from operations. Contributing to that positive cash flow was the change in accounts receivable. The current and prior year balance sheets reported the following:

	(dollars in thousands)	
	Current Year	Previous Year
Accounts and notes receivable, less allowances	$48,066	$63,403

Required:
1. On the current year's cash flow statement (indirect method), how would the change in accounts receivable affect cash flow from operations? Explain why it would have this effect.
2. Explain how declining sales revenue often leads to (*a*) declining accounts receivable and (*b*) cash collections from customers being higher than sales revenue.

Preparing Bank Reconciliation, Entries, and Reporting Cash

Bentley Company's June 30, 2014, bank statement and June ledger accounts for cash are summarized below:

BANK STATEMENT			
	Checks	Deposits	Balance
Balance, June 1, 2014			$ 6,500
Deposits during June		$16,200	22,700
Checks cleared during June	$16,600		6,100
Bank service charges	40		6,060
Balance, June 30, 2014			6,060

Cash (A)					
June 1	Balance	6,500	June	Checks written	19,000
June	Deposits	18,100			

Required:

1. Reconcile the bank account. A comparison of the checks written with the checks that have cleared the bank shows outstanding checks of $2,400. A deposit of $1,900 is in transit at the end of June.
2. Give any journal entries that should be made as a result of the bank reconciliation.
3. What is the balance in the Cash account after the reconciliation entries?
4. What is the total amount of cash that should be reported on the balance sheet at June 30?

E6-23

LO6-5

Preparing Bank Reconciliation, Entries, and Reporting Cash

The September 30, 2014, bank statement for Bennett Company and the September ledger accounts for cash are summarized here:

BANK STATEMENT			
	Checks	**Deposits**	**Balance**
Balance, September 1, 2014			$ 6,500
Deposits recorded during September		$26,900	33,400
Checks cleared during September	$27,400		6,000
NSF checks—Betty Brown	170		5,830
Bank service charges	60		5,770
Balance, September 30, 2014			5,770

Cash (A)				
Sept. 1	Balance	6,500	Sept. Checks written	28,900
Sept.	Deposits	28,100		

No outstanding checks and no deposits in transit were carried over from August; however, there are deposits in transit and checks outstanding at the end of September.

Required:

1. Reconcile the bank account.
2. Give any journal entries that should be made as the result of the bank reconciliation.
3. What should the balance in the Cash account be after the reconciliation entries?
4. What total amount of cash should the company report on the September 30 balance sheet?

E6-24

(Supplement) Recording Credit Sales, Sales Discounts, Sales Returns, and Credit Card Sales

The following transactions were selected from among those completed by Hailey Retailers in 2013:

Nov.	20	Sold two items of merchandise to Customer B, who charged the $450 sales price on her Visa credit card. Visa charges Hailey a 2 percent credit card fee.
	25	Sold 14 items of merchandise to Customer C at an invoice price of $2,800 (total); terms 2/10, n/30.
	28	Sold 12 identical items of merchandise to Customer D at an invoice price of $7,200 (total); terms 2/10, n/30.
	30	Customer D returned one of the items purchased on the 28th; the item was defective, and credit was given to the customer.
Dec.	6	Customer D paid the account balance in full.
	30	Customer C paid in full for the invoice of November 25, 2013.

Required:

Give the appropriate journal entry for each of these transactions, assuming the company records sales revenue under the gross method. Do not record cost of goods sold. Compute Net Sales.

To practice with more exercises, go to the text website at **www.mhhe.com/libby8e**.

Applying the Revenue Principle

At what point should revenue be recognized in each of the following independent cases?

Case A. For Christmas presents, a Wendy's restaurant sells coupon books for $15. Each of the $1 coupons may be used in the restaurant any time during the following 12 months. The customer must pay cash when purchasing the coupon book.

Case B. Russell Land Development Corporation sold a lot to Upland Builders to construct a new home. The price of the lot was $50,000. Upland made a down payment of $250 and agreed to pay the balance in six months. After making the sale, Russell learned that Upland Builders often entered into these agreements but refused to pay the balance if it did not find a customer who wanted a house built on the lot.

Case C. Davis Corporation has always recorded revenue at the point of sale of its refrigerators. Recently, it has extended its warranties to cover all repairs for a period of seven years. One young accountant with the company now questions whether Davis has completed its earning process when it sells the refrigerators. She suggests that the warranty obligation for seven years means that a significant amount of additional work must be performed in the future.

P6-1

LO6-1

Reporting Net Sales and Expenses with Discounts, Returns, and Bad Debts (AP6-1)

The following data were selected from the records of Sykes Company for the year ended December 31, 2014.

P6-2

LO6-2, 6-3

Balances January 1, 2014	
Accounts receivable (various customers)	$120,000
Allowance for doubtful accounts	8,000

In the following order, except for cash sales, the company sold merchandise and made collections on credit terms 2/10, n/30 (assume a unit sales price of $500 in all transactions and use the gross method to record sales revenue).

Transactions during 2014

a. Sold merchandise for cash, $235,000.
b. Sold merchandise to R. Smith; invoice price, $11,500.
c. Sold merchandise to K. Miller; invoice price, $26,500.
d. Two days after purchase date, R. Smith returned one of the units purchased in (b) and received account credit.
e. Sold merchandise to B. Sears; invoice price, $24,000.
f. R. Smith paid his account in full within the discount period.
g. Collected $98,000 cash from customer sales on credit in prior year, all within the discount periods.
h. K. Miller paid the invoice in (c) within the discount period.
i. Sold merchandise to R. Roy; invoice price, $19,000.
j. Three days after paying the account in full, K. Miller returned seven defective units and received a cash refund.
k. After the discount period, collected $6,000 cash on an account receivable on sales in a prior year.
l. Wrote off a 2013 account of $3,000 after deciding that the amount would never be collected.
m. The estimated bad debt rate used by the company was 1.5 percent of credit sales net of returns.

Required:

1. Using the following categories, indicate the effect of each listed transaction, including the write-off of the uncollectible account and the adjusting entry for estimated bad debts (ignore cost of goods sold). Indicate the sign and amount of the effect or "NE" for "no effect." The first transaction is used as an example.

	Sales Revenue	Sales Discounts (taken)	Sales Returns and Allowances	Bad Debt Expense
(a)	+235,000	NE	NE	NE

2. Show how the accounts related to the preceding sale and collection activities should be reported on the 2014 income statement. (Treat sales discounts as a contra-revenue.)

P6-3

LO6-3

Peet's Coffee & Tea

Recording Bad Debts and Interpreting Disclosure of Allowance for Doubtful Accounts (AP6-2)

Peet's Coffee & Tea, Inc., is a specialty coffee roaster and marketer of branded fresh-roasted whole bean coffee. It recently disclosed the following information concerning the Allowance for Doubtful Accounts on its Form 10-K Annual Report submitted to the Securities and Exchange Commission.

A summary of the Allowance for Doubtful Accounts is as follows (dollars in thousands):

Allowance for Doubtful Accounts	Balance at Beginning of Period	Additions (Charges) to Expense	Write-Offs	Balance at End of Period
Year 1	$128	$?	$ 0	$132
Year 2	132	187	?	283
Year 3	283	42	201	124

Required:
1. Record summary journal entries related to bad debts for year 3.
2. Supply the missing dollar amounts noted by (?) for year 1 and year 2.

P6-4

LO6-3

Determining Bad Debt Expense Based on Aging Analysis (AP6-3)

Blue Skies Equipment Company uses the aging approach to estimate bad debt expense at the end of each accounting year. Credit sales occur frequently on terms n/60. The balance of each account receivable is aged on the basis of three time periods as follows: (1) not yet due, (2) up to one year past due, and (3) more than one year past due. Experience has shown that for each age group, the average loss rate on the amount of the receivable at year-end due to uncollectability is (*a*) 3 percent, (*b*) 9 percent, and (*c*) 28 percent, respectively.

At December 31, 2014 (end of the current accounting year), the Accounts Receivable balance was $48,700, and the Allowance for Doubtful Accounts balance was $920 (credit). In determining which accounts have been paid, the company applies collections to the oldest sales first. To simplify, only five customer accounts are used; the details of each on December 31, 2014, follow:

B. Brown—Account Receivable				
Date	Explanation	Debit	Credit	Balance
3/11/2013	Sale	13,000		13,000
6/30/2013	Collection		3,000	10,000
1/31/2014	Collection		3,800	6,200

D. Donalds—Account Receivable				
2/28/2014	Sale	21,000		21,000
4/15/2014	Collection		8,000	13,000
11/30/2014	Collection		6,000	7,000

N. Napier—Account Receivable				
11/30/2014	Sale	8,000		8,000
12/15/2014	Collection		1,000	7,000

S. Strothers—Account Receivable				
3/2/2012	Sale	4,000		4,000
4/15/2012	Collection		4,000	–0–
9/1/2013	Sale	9,000		9,000
10/15/2013	Collection		4,500	4,500
2/1/2014	Sale	21,000		25,500
3/1/2014	Collection		5,000	20,500
12/31/2014	Sale	4,000		24,500

T. Thomas—Account Receivable				
12/30/2014	Sale	4,000		4,000

Required:

1. Compute the total accounts receivable in each age category.
2. Compute the estimated uncollectible amount for each age category and in total.
3. Give the adjusting entry for bad debt expense at December 31, 2014.
4. Show how the amounts related to accounts receivable should be presented on the 2014 income statement and balance sheet.

Preparing an Income Statement and Computing the Receivables Turnover Ratio with Discounts, Returns, and Bad Debts (AP6-4)

P6-5

LO6-2, 6-3, 6-4

Tungsten Company, Inc., sells heavy construction equipment. There are 10,000 shares of capital stock outstanding. The annual fiscal period ends on December 31. The following condensed trial balance was taken from the general ledger on December 31, 2014:

www.mhhe.com/libby8e

Account Titles	Debit	Credit
Cash	$ 33,600	
Accounts receivable (net)	14,400	
Inventory, ending	52,000	
Operational assets	40,000	
Accumulated depreciation		$ 16,800
Liabilities		24,000
Capital stock		72,000
Retained earnings, January 1, 2014		9,280
Sales revenue		147,100
Sales returns and allowances	5,600	
Cost of goods sold	78,400	
Selling expense	14,100	
Administrative expense	15,400	
Bad debt expense	1,600	
Sales discounts	6,400	
Income tax expense	7,680	
Totals	$269,180	$269,180

Required:

1. Beginning with the amount for net sales, prepare an income statement (showing both gross profit and income from operations). Treat sales discounts and sales returns and allowances as a contra-revenue.
2. The beginning balance in Accounts Receivable (net) was $16,000. Compute the receivables turnover ratio and explain its meaning.

Preparing a Bank Reconciliation and Related Journal Entries

P6-6

LO6-5

The bookkeeper at Jefferson Company has not reconciled the bank statement with the Cash account, saying, "I don't have time." You have been asked to prepare a reconciliation and review the procedures with the bookkeeper.

The April 30, 2014, bank statement and the April ledger accounts for cash showed the following (summarized):

www.mhhe.com/libby8e

BANK STATEMENT			
	Checks	Deposits	Balance
Balance, April 1, 2014			$31,000
Deposits during April		$37,100	68,100
Interest collected		1,180	69,280
Checks cleared during April	$43,000		26,280
NSF check—A. B. Wright	160		26,120
Bank service charges	50		26,070
Balance, April 30, 2014			26,070

Cash (A)				
Apr. 1 Balance	23,500	Apr. Checks written	41,100
Apr. Deposits	41,500		

A comparison of checks written before and during April with the checks cleared through the bank showed outstanding checks at the end of April of $5,600. No deposits in transit were carried over from March, but a deposit was in transit at the end of April.

Required:

1. Prepare a detailed bank reconciliation for April.
2. Give any required journal entries as a result of the reconciliation. Why are they necessary?
3. What was the balance in the cash account in the ledger on May 1, 2014?
4. What total amount of cash should be reported on the balance sheet at the end of April?

P6-7
LO6-5

www.mhhe.com/libby8e

Computing Outstanding Checks and Deposits in Transit and Preparing a Bank Reconciliation and Journal Entries (AP6-5)

The August 2014 bank statement for Allison Company and the August 2014 ledger account for cash follow:

BANK STATEMENT			
Date	Checks and EFTs	Deposits	Balance
Aug. 1			$17,510
2	$ 320		17,190
3		$11,700	28,890
4	430		28,460
5	270		28,190
9	880		27,310
10	250 EFT		27,060
15		4,000	31,060
21	350		30,710
24	20,400		10,310
25		6,500	16,810
30	850 EFT		15,960
30		2,350*	18,310
31	120†		18,190

*$2,350 interest collected.
†Bank service charge.

Cash (A)			
Aug. 1 Balance	16,490	Checks written and electronic funds transfers	
Deposits		Aug. 2	EFT 250
Aug. 2	11,700	4	880
12	4,000	15	280
24	6,500	17	510
31	5,200	18	EFT 850
		20	350
		23	20,400

Outstanding checks at the end of July were for $270, $430, and $320. No deposits were in transit at the end of July.

Required:

1. Compute the deposits in transit at the end of August by comparing the deposits on the bank statement to the deposits listed on the cash ledger account.
2. Compute the outstanding checks at the end of August by comparing the checks listed on the bank statement with those on the cash ledger account and the list of outstanding checks at the end of July.
3. Prepare a bank reconciliation for August.
4. Give any journal entries that the company should make as a result of the bank reconciliation. Why are they necessary?
5. What total amount of cash should be reported on the August 31, 2014, balance sheet?

(Supplement) Recording Sales, Returns, and Bad Debts

P6-8

Use the data presented in P6-2, which were selected from the records of Sykes Company for the year ended December 31, 2014.

Required:

1. Give the journal entries for these transactions, including the write-off of the uncollectible account and the adjusting entry for estimated bad debts. Do not record cost of goods sold. Show computations for each entry.
2. Show how the accounts related to the preceding sale and collection activities should be reported on the 2014 income statement. (Treat sales discounts as a contra-revenue.)

ALTERNATE PROBLEMS

Reporting Net Sales and Expenses with Discounts, Returns, and Bad Debts (P6-2)

AP6-1

LO6-2, 6-3

The following data were selected from the records of Sharkim Company for the year ended December 31, 2014.

Balances January 1, 2014:	
Accounts receivable (various customers)	$116,000
Allowance for doubtful accounts	5,200

In the following order, except for cash sales, the company sold merchandise and made collections on credit terms 2/10, n/30 (assume a unit sales price of $500 in all transactions and use the gross method to record sales revenue).

Transactions during 2014

a. Sold merchandise for cash, $227,000.
b. Sold merchandise to Karen Corp; invoice price, $12,000.
c. Sold merchandise to White Company; invoice price, $23,500.
d. Karen paid the invoice in (b) within the discount period.
e. Sold merchandise to Cavendish Inc.; invoice price, $26,000.
f. Two days after paying the account in full, Karen returned one defective unit and received a cash refund.
g. Collected $88,200 cash from customer sales on credit in prior year, all within the discount periods.
h. Three days after purchase date, White returned seven of the units purchased in (c) and received account credit.
i. White paid its account in full within the discount period.
j. Sold merchandise to Delta Corporation; invoice price, $18,500.
k. Cavendish paid its account in full after the discount period.
l. Wrote off a 2013 account of $2,400 after deciding that the amount would never be collected.
m. The estimated bad debt rate used by the company was 4 percent of credit sales net of returns.

Required:

1. Using the following categories, indicate the effect of each listed transaction, including the write-off of the uncollectible account and the adjusting entry for estimated bad debts (ignore cost of goods sold). Indicate the sign and amount of the effect or use "NE" to indicate "no effect." The first transaction is used as an example.

	Sales Revenue	Sales Discounts (taken)	Sales Returns and Allowances	Bad Debt Expense
(a)	+227,000	NE	NE	NE

2. Show how the accounts related to the preceding sale and collection activities should be reported on the 2014 income statement. (Treat sales discounts as a contra-revenue.)

AP6-2

LO6-3

Saucony, Inc.

Recording Bad Debts and Interpreting Disclosure of Allowance for Doubtful Accounts (P6-3)

Under various registered brand names, Saucony, Inc., and its subsidiaries develop, manufacture, and market bicycles and component parts, athletic apparel, and athletic shoes. It recently disclosed the following information concerning the allowance for doubtful accounts on its Form 10-K Annual Report submitted to the Securities and Exchange Commission.

Schedule II				
Valuation and Qualifying Accounts				
(dollars in thousands)				
Allowances for Doubtful Accounts	Balance at Beginning of Year	Additions Charged to Costs and Expenses	Deductions from Reserve	Balance at End of Year
Year 3	$1,108	$6,014	$5,941	(?)
Year 2	2,406	(?)	5,751	$1,108
Year 1	2,457	4,752	(?)	2,406

Required:

1. Record summary journal entries related to bad debts for year 3.
2. Supply the missing dollar amounts noted by (?) for year 1, year 2, and year 3.

AP6-3

LO6-3

Determining Bad Debt Expense Based on Aging Analysis (P6-4)

Briggs & Stratton Engines Inc. uses the aging approach to estimate bad debt expense at the end of each accounting year. Credit sales occur frequently on terms n/45. The balance of each account receivable is aged on the basis of four time periods as follows: (1) not yet due, (2) up to 6 months past due, (3) 6 to 12 months past due, and (4) more than one year past due. Experience has shown that for each age group, the average loss rate on the amount of the receivable at year-end due to uncollectability is (*a*) 1 percent, (*b*) 5 percent, (*c*) 20 percent, and (*d*) 50 percent, respectively.

At December 31, 2014 (end of the current accounting year), the Accounts Receivable balance was $39,500, and the Allowance for Doubtful Accounts balance was $1,550 (credit). In determining which accounts have been paid, the company applies collections to the oldest sales first. To simplify, only five customer accounts are used; the details of each on December 31, 2014, follow:

Date	Explanation	Debit	Credit	Balance
R. Devens—Account Receivable				
3/13/2014	Sale	19,000		19,000
5/12/2014	Collection		10,000	9,000
9/30/2014	Collection		7,000	2,000
C. Howard—Account Receivable				
11/01/2013	Sale	31,000		31,000
06/01/2014	Collection		20,000	11,000
12/01/2014	Collection		5,000	6,000
D. McClain—Account Receivable				
10/31/2014	Sale	12,000		12,000
12/10/2014	Collection		8,000	4,000
T. Skibinski—Account Receivable				
05/02/2014	Sale	15,000		15,000
06/01/2014	Sale	10,000		25,000
06/15/2014	Collection		15,000	10,000
07/15/2014	Collection		10,000	0
10/01/2014	Sale	26,000		26,000
11/15/2014	Collection		16,000	10,000
12/15/2014	Sale	4,500		14,500
H. Wu—Account Receivable				
12/30/2014	Sale	13,000		13,000

Required:

1. Compute the total accounts receivable in each age category.
2. Compute the estimated uncollectible amount for each age category and in total.
3. Give the adjusting entry for bad debt expense at December 31, 2014.
4. Show how the amounts related to accounts receivable should be presented on the 2014 income statement and balance sheet.

Preparing an Income Statement and Computing the Receivables Turnover Ratio with Discounts, Returns, and Bad Debts (P6-5)

AP6-4
LO6-2, 6-3, 6-4

Perry Corporation is a local grocery store organized seven years ago as a corporation. At that time, a total of 10,000 shares of common stock were issued to the three organizers. The store is in an excellent location, and sales have increased each year. At the end of 2014, the bookkeeper prepared the following statement (assume that all amounts are correct; note the incorrect terminology and format):

	Debit	Credit
PERRY CORPORATION		
Profit and Loss		
December 31, 2014		
Sales		$184,000
Cost of goods sold	$ 98,000	
Sales returns and allowances	9,000	
Selling expense	17,000	
Administrative and general expense	18,000	
Bad debt expense	2,000	
Sales discounts	8,000	
Income tax expense	10,900	
Net profit	21,100	
Totals	$184,000	$184,000

Required:

1. Beginning with the amount of net sales, prepare an income statement (showing both gross profit and income from operations). Treat sales discounts as a contra-revenue.
2. The beginning and ending balances in accounts receivable were $16,000 and $18,000, respectively. Compute the receivables turnover ratio and explain its meaning.

Computing Outstanding Checks and Deposits in Transit and Preparing a Bank Reconciliation and Journal Entries (P6-7)

AP6-5
LO6-5

The December 31, 2014, bank statement for Rivas Company and the December 2014 ledger accounts for cash follow.

BANK STATEMENT			
Date	Checks and EFTs	Deposits	Balance
Dec. 1			$48,000
2	$400; 300	$17,000	64,300
4	7,000; 90		57,210
6	120; 180; 1,600 EFT		55,310
11	500; 1,200; 70	28,000	81,540
13	480; 700; 1,900		78,460
17	12,000; 8,000		58,460
23	60; 23,500	36,000	70,900
26	900; 2,650		67,350
28	2,200; 5,200		59,950
30	17,000; 1,890; 300*	19,000	59,760
31	1,650; 1,350; 150†	5,250‡	61,860

*NSF check, J. Left, a customer.
†Bank service charge.
‡Interest collected.

Cash (A)					
Dec. 1	Balance	64,100	Checks written during December:		
Deposits			60	5,000	2,650
Dec. 11		28,000	17,000	5,200	1,650
23		36,000	700	1,890	2,200
30		19,000	3,500	EFT 1,600	7,000
31		13,000	1,350	120	300
			180	90	480
			12,000	23,500	EFT 8,000
			70	500	1,900
			900	1,200	

The November 2014 bank reconciliation showed the following: correct cash balance at November 30, $64,100; deposits in transit on November 30, $17,000; and outstanding checks on November 30, $400 + $500 = $900.

Required:
1. Compute the deposits in transit December 31, 2014, by comparing the deposits on the bank statement to the deposits listed on the cash ledger account and the list of deposits in transit at the end of November.
2. Compute the outstanding checks at December 31, 2014, by comparing the checks listed on the bank statement with those on the cash ledger account and the list of outstanding checks at the end of November.
3. Prepare a bank reconciliation at December 31, 2014.
4. Give any journal entries that should be made as a result of the bank reconciliation made by the company. Why are they necessary?
5. What total amount of cash should be reported on the December 31, 2014, balance sheet?

CASES **AND PROJECTS**

Annual Report Cases

CP6-1

LO6-3, 6-4, 6-5

AMERICAN EAGLE OUTFITTERS, INC.

Finding Financial Information

Refer to the financial statements of American Eagle Outfitters given in Appendix B at the end of this book.

Required:
1. What does the company include in its category of cash and cash equivalents? How close do you think the disclosed amount is to actual fair market value? (**Hint:** The notes may be helpful in answering this question.)
2. What expenses does American Eagle Outfitters subtract from net sales in the computation of gross profit? How does this differ from Deckers's practice and how might it affect the manner in which you interpret the gross profit?
3. Compute American Eagle Outfitters's receivables turnover ratio for the current year. What characteristics of its business might cause it to be so high?
4. Does the company report an allowance for doubtful accounts on the balance sheet or in the notes? Explain why it does or does not. (**Hint:** Consider the makeup of its receivables.)

CP6-2

LO6-1, 6-3, 6-5

URBN
URBAN OUTFITTERS INC.

Finding Financial Information

Refer to the financial statements of Urban Outfitters given in Appendix C at the end of this book.

Required:
1. How much cash and cash equivalents does the company report at the end of the current year?
2. What was the change in accounts receivable and how did it affect net cash provided by operating activities for the current year?

3. Which types of customers account for most of the company's accounts receivable? Did bad debts expense increase or decrease between 2010 and 2011? How did you know?
4. Where does the company disclose its revenue recognition policy? When does the company record revenues for the "sale" of gift cards?

Comparing Companies within an Industry

Refer to the financial statements of American Eagle Outfitters (Appendix B) and Urban Outfitters (Appendix C) and the Industry Ratio Report (Appendix D) at the end of this book.

Required:
1. Compute the receivables turnover ratio for both companies for the most recent year.
2. What do you think explains the difference in the ratios? Consider to whom the amounts are owed.
3. Compare the receivables turnover ratio for each company for the most recent reporting year to the industry average. Are these two companies doing better or worse than the industry average?

CP6-3
LO6-3, 6-5

AMERICAN EAGLE
OUTFITTERS, INC.

URBAN OUTFITTERS INC.

www.mhhe.com/libby8e

Financial Reporting and Analysis Cases

Making a Decision as a Manager: Choosing among Alternative Recognition Points

When companies involved in long-term construction projects can estimate the percentage of work completed and the total expected costs with reasonable accuracy, GAAP allows them to recognize revenues based on the incurred contract costs to date divided by the estimated total contract costs. This is called the **percentage of completion method.** When total costs cannot be accurately estimated, the companies must wait until the contract is completed to recognize all contract revenue in the period of completion. These revenue recognition points correspond to continuous recognition and the end of the earnings process.

Required:
1. Assume that a construction company works on a single construction project at a time and that each project takes three years to complete. Do you think that the choice between the two revenue recognition policies would materially affect the reported earnings? Why or why not?
2. Given your answers to requirement (1), under what conditions would that answer change?
3. Which revenue recognition rule for financial reporting purposes would you prefer as a manager? Why?

CP6-4
LO6-1

Critical Thinking Cases

Evaluating an Ethical Dilemma: Management Incentives, Revenue Recognition, and Sales with the Right of Return

Symbol Technologies, Inc., was a fast-growing maker of bar-code scanners. According to the federal charges, Tomo Razmilovic, the CEO at Symbol, was obsessed with meeting the stock market's expectation for continued growth. His executive team responded by improperly recording revenue and allowances for returns, as well as a variety of other tricks, to overstate revenues by $230 million and pretax earnings by $530 million. What makes this fraud nearly unique is that virtually the whole senior management team is charged with participating in the six-year fraud. Five have pleaded guilty, another eight are under indictment, and the former CEO has fled the country to avoid prosecution. The exact nature of the fraud is described in the following excerpt dealing with the guilty plea by the former vice president for finance:

CP6-5
LO6-1

Symbol Technologies, Inc.

Ex-Official at Symbol Pleads Guilty

By Kara Scannell
26 March 2003
The Wall Street Journal
(Copyright © 2003, Dow Jones & Company, Inc.)

A former finance executive at Symbol Technologies Inc. pleaded guilty to participating in a vast account-ing fraud that inflated revenue at the maker of bar-code scanners by roughly 10%, or $100 million a year, from 1999 through 2001.

. . .

The criminal information and civil complaint filed yesterday accused Mr. Asti and other high-level exec-utives of stuffing the firm's distribution channel with phony orders at the end of each quarter to meet revenue and earnings targets. Under generally accepted accounting practices, revenue can be booked only when the products are shipped to a customer. Symbol's customers include delivery services and grocery stores.

Investigators alleged that Mr. Asti and others engaged in "candy" deals, where Symbol bribed resellers with a 1% fee to "buy" products from a distributor at the end of a quarter, which Symbol would later buy back. Symbol then allegedly would convince the distributor to order more products from the company to satisfy the newly created inventory void.

The SEC said the inflated revenue figures helped boost Symbol's stock price, as well as enriching Mr. Asti. He allegedly sold thousands of shares of Symbol stock, which he received from exercising stock options, when the stock was trading at inflated levels.

Required:
1. What facts, if any, presented in the article suggest that Symbol violated the revenue realization principle?
2. Assuming that Symbol did recognize revenue when goods were shipped, how could it have prop-erly accounted for the fact that customers had a right to cancel the contracts (make an analogy with accounting for bad debts)?
3. What do you think may have motivated management to falsify the statements? Why was manage-ment concerned with reporting continued growth in net income?
4. Explain who was hurt by management's unethical conduct.
5. Assume that you are the auditor for other firms. After reading about the fraud, what types of transac-tions would you pay special attention to in the audit of your clients in this industry? What ratio might provide warnings about possible channel stuffing?

CP6-6

LO6-5

Evaluating Internal Control

Cripple Creek Company has one trusted employee who, as the owner said, "handles all of the bookkeep-ing and paperwork for the company." This employee is responsible for counting, verifying, and recording cash receipts and payments, making the weekly bank deposit, preparing checks for major expenditures (signed by the owner), making small expenditures from the cash register for daily expenses, and col-lecting accounts receivable. The owners asked the local bank for a $20,000 loan. The bank asked that an audit be performed covering the year just ended. The independent auditor (a local CPA), in a private conference with the owner, presented some evidence of the following activities of the trusted employee during the past year.

a. Cash sales sometimes were not entered in the cash register, and the trusted employee pocketed approximately $50 per month.
b. Cash taken from the cash register (and pocketed by the trusted employee) was replaced with expense memos with fictitious signatures (approximately $12 per day).
c. A $300 collection on an account receivable of a valued out-of-town customer was pocketed by the trusted employee and was covered by making a $300 entry as a debit to Sales Returns and a credit to Accounts Receivable.
d. An $800 collection on an account receivable from a local customer was pocketed by the trusted employee and was covered by making an $800 entry as a debit to Allowance for Doubtful Accounts and a credit to Accounts Receivable.

Required:
1. What was the approximate amount stolen during the past year?
2. What would be your recommendations to the owner?

Financial Reporting and Analysis Team Project

Team Project: Analyzing Revenues and Receivables

As a team, select an industry to analyze. *Yahoo!Finance* provides lists of industries at biz.yahoo.com/p/ industries.html. Click on an industry for a list of companies in that industry. Alternatively, go to Google Finance at www.google.com/finance and search for a company you are interested in. You will be presented with a list including that company and its competitors. Each team member should acquire the annual report or 10-K for one publicly traded company in the industry, with each member selecting a different company (the SEC EDGAR service at www.sec.gov or the company's investor relations website itself are good sources).

Required:
On an individual basis, each team member should write a short report answering the following questions about the selected company. Discuss any patterns across the companies that you as a team observe. Then, as a team, write a short report comparing and contrasting your companies.
1. If your company lists receivables in its balance sheet, what percentage is it of total assets for each of the last three years? If your company does not list receivables, discuss why this is so.
2. Ratio analysis
   a. What does the receivables turnover ratio measure in general?
   b. If your company lists receivables, compute the ratio for the last three years.
   c. What do your results suggest about the company?
   d. If available, find the industry ratio for the most recent year, compare it to your results, and discuss why you believe your company differs or is similar to the industry ratio.
3. If your company lists receivables, use the 10-K to determine what additional disclosure is available concerning the allowance for doubtful accounts. (Usually the information is in a separate schedule, Item 15.)
   a. What is bad debt expense as a percentage of sales for the last three years?
4. What is the effect of the change in receivables on cash flows from operating activities for the most recent year (that is, did the change increase or decrease operating cash flows)? Explain your answer.

CP6-7
LO6-3

CONTINUING CASE

Computing Net Sales and Recording Bad Debt Estimates and Write-offs

CC6-1

POOLCORP

Pool Corporation, Inc., is the world's largest wholesale distributor of swimming pool supplies and equipment.

Required:
1. Pool Corp. reported the following information related to bad debt estimates and write-offs for the current year. Prepare journal entries for the bad debt expense adjustment and total write-offs of bad debts for the current year.

Allowance for doubtful accounts:	
Balance at beginning of year	$ 7,102
Bad debt expense	2,958
Write-offs	(4,160)
Balance at end of year	$ 5,900

2. Pool Corp. reduces net sales by the amount of sales returns and allowances, cash discounts, and credit card fees. Bad debt expense is recorded as part of selling and administrative expense. Assume that gross sales revenue for the month was $137,256, bad debt expense was $146, sales discounts were $1,134, sales returns were $856, and credit card fees were $1,849. What amount would Pool Corp. report for net sales for the month?

Reporting and Interpreting Cost of Goods Sold and Inventory

The Harley-Davidson eagle trademark was once known best as a popular request in tattoo parlors. Now, Harley-Davidson dominates the heavyweight motorcycle market in North America with a 55.7 percent market share. Harley is also the market leader in Canada, Japan, and Australia and is a growing presence in Europe.

But the heavyweight king took a major hit from the worldwide economic downturn that started in 2008. Harley responded with an aggressive plan to enhance profitability through continuous improvement in manufacturing, product development, and business operations. These plans are aimed at shortening product development lead times and implementing flexible manufacturing at its Wisconsin, Missouri, and Pennsylvania facilities, which will reduce costs and allow the company to better respond to the needs of the dealer network.

Controlling inventory quality, quantities, and cost are key to maintaining gross profit margin. Introducing new products to stay ahead of major competitors Honda and BMW

Learning Objectives

After studying this chapter, you should be able to:

7-1 Apply the cost principle to identify the amounts that should be included in inventory and the expense matching principle to determine cost of goods sold for typical retailers, wholesalers, and manufacturers. p. 329

7-2 Report inventory and cost of goods sold using the four inventory costing methods. p. 334

7-3 Decide when the use of different inventory costing methods is beneficial to a company. p. 339

7-4 Report inventory at the lower of cost or market (LCM). p. 342

7-5 Evaluate inventory management using the inventory turnover ratio. p. 343

7-6 Compare companies that use different inventory costing methods. p. 344

7-7 Understand methods for controlling inventory, analyze the effects of inventory errors on financial statements, and analyze the effects of inventory on cash flows. p. 347

FOCUS COMPANY:

Harley-Davidson, Inc.

BUILDING A LEGEND
INTO A WORLD-CLASS
MANUFACTURER

www.harley-davidson.com

and providing a premium dealer experience to all of Harley's customers will also increase gross margin. Finally, selecting appropriate accounting methods for inventory can have a dramatic effect on the amount Harley-Davidson pays in income taxes. Harley produced strong financial results in 2011, but continuous improvement in all of these areas will be necessary for the Harley-Davidson eagle to continue its rise.

UNDERSTANDING THE BUSINESS

The cost and quality of inventory are concerns faced by all modern manufacturers and merchandisers and so we turn our attention to **cost of goods sold** (cost of sales, cost of products sold) on the income statement and **inventory** on the balance sheet. Exhibit 7.1 presents the relevant excerpts from Harley-Davidson's financial statements that include these accounts. Note that Cost of Goods Sold is subtracted from Net Sales to produce Gross Profit on its income statement. On the balance sheet, Inventory is a current asset; it is reported below Cash, Marketable Securities, and Accounts and Finance Receivables because it is less liquid than those assets.

The primary goals of inventory management are to have sufficient quantities of high-quality inventory available to serve customers' needs while minimizing the costs of carrying inventory (production, storage, obsolescence, and financing). Low quality leads to customer dissatisfaction, returns, and a decline in

HARLEY-DAVIDSON, INC.
Consolidated Statements of Income
(dollars in thousands, except per share amounts)

Years Ended December 31,	2011	2010	2009
Net Sales	$4,662,264	$4,176,627	$4,287,130
Cost of Goods Sold	3,106,288	2,749,224	2,900,934
Gross Profit	$1,555,976	$1,427,403	$1,386,196

HARLEY-DAVIDSON, INC.
Consolidated Balance Sheets
(dollars in thousands, except share amounts)

	2011	2010
Assets		
Current Assets		
Cash and cash equivalents	$1,526,950	$1,021,933
Marketable securities	153,380	140,118
Accounts receivable, net	219,039	262,382
Finance receivables, net	1,760,467	1,779,458
Inventories	418,006	326,446
Deferred income taxes	132,331	146,411
Other current assets	332,033	389,878
Total current assets	$4,542,206	$4,066,626

future sales. Also, purchasing or producing too few units of a hot-selling item causes stock-outs that mean lost sales revenue and decreases in customer satisfaction. Conversely, purchasing too many units of a slow-selling item increases storage costs as well as interest costs on short-term borrowings that finance the purchases. It may even lead to losses if the merchandise cannot be sold at normal prices.

The accounting system plays three roles in the inventory management process. First, the system must provide accurate information for preparation of periodic financial statements and tax returns. Second, it must provide up-to-date information on inventory quantities and costs to facilitate ordering and manufacturing decisions. Third, since inventories are subject to theft and other forms of misuse, the system must also provide the information needed to help protect these important assets.

Harley's mix of product lines makes it a particularly good example for this chapter. Although best known as a **manufacturer** of motorcycles, Harley also purchases and resells completed products such as its popular line of Motorclothes apparel. In the second case, it acts as a **wholesaler.** Both the motorcycle and Motorclothes product lines are sold to the company's network of independent dealers. From an accounting standpoint, these independent dealers are Harley-Davidson's customers. The independent dealers are the **retailers** who sell the products to the public.

We begin this chapter with a discussion of the makeup of inventory, the important choices management must make in the financial and tax reporting process, and how these choices affect the financial statements and taxes paid. Then we discuss how managers and analysts evaluate the efficiency of inventory management. Finally, we briefly discuss how accounting systems are organized to keep track of inventory quantities and costs for decision making and control. This topic will be the principal subject matter of your managerial accounting course.

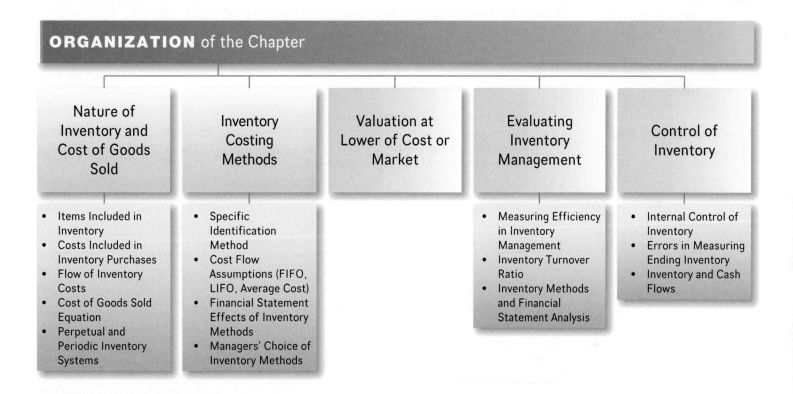

ORGANIZATION of the Chapter

Nature of Inventory and Cost of Goods Sold	Inventory Costing Methods	Valuation at Lower of Cost or Market	Evaluating Inventory Management	Control of Inventory
• Items Included in Inventory • Costs Included in Inventory Purchases • Flow of Inventory Costs • Cost of Goods Sold Equation • Perpetual and Periodic Inventory Systems	• Specific Identification Method • Cost Flow Assumptions (FIFO, LIFO, Average Cost) • Financial Statement Effects of Inventory Methods • Managers' Choice of Inventory Methods		• Measuring Efficiency in Inventory Management • Inventory Turnover Ratio • Inventory Methods and Financial Statement Analysis	• Internal Control of Inventory • Errors in Measuring Ending Inventory • Inventory and Cash Flows

NATURE OF INVENTORY AND COST OF GOODS SOLD

Items Included in Inventory

Inventory is tangible property that is (1) held for sale in the normal course of business or (2) used to produce goods or services for sale. Inventory is reported on the balance sheet as a current asset because it normally is used or converted into cash within one year or the next operating cycle. The types of inventory normally held depend on the characteristics of the business.

Merchandisers (wholesale or retail businesses) hold the following:

Merchandise inventory   Goods (or merchandise) held for resale in the normal course of business. The goods usually are acquired in a finished condition and are ready for sale without further processing.

For Harley-Davidson, merchandise inventory includes the Motorclothes line and the parts and accessories it purchases for sale to its independent dealers.

Manufacturing businesses hold three types of inventory:

Raw materials inventory   Items acquired for processing into finished goods. These items are included in raw materials inventory until they are used, at which point they become part of work in process inventory.

Work in process inventory   Goods in the process of being manufactured but not yet complete. When completed, work in process inventory becomes finished goods inventory.

Finished goods inventory   Manufactured goods that are complete and ready for sale.

Inventories related to Harley-Davidson's motorcycle manufacturing operations are recorded in these accounts.

WORK IN PROCESS INVENTORY includes goods in the process of being manufactured.

FINISHED GOODS INVENTORY includes manufactured goods that are complete and ready for sale.

HARLEY-DAVIDSON, INC.

REAL WORLD EXCERPT
Annual Report

Harley-Davidson's recent inventory note reports the following:

HARLEY-DAVIDSON, INC. Notes to Consolidated Financial Statements		
2. ADDITIONAL BALANCE SHEET AND CASH FLOWS INFORMATION (dollars in thousands)		
	December 31,	
	2011	**2010**
Inventories:		
Components at the lower of FIFO cost or market:		
Raw materials and work in process	$113,932	$100,082
Motorcycle finished goods	226,261	158,425
Parts and accessories and general merchandise	121,340	101,975

Note that Harley-Davidson combines the raw materials and work in process into one number. Other companies separate the two components. The parts and accessories and general merchandise category includes purchased parts and Motorclothes and other accessories that make up merchandise inventory.[1]

Costs Included in Inventory Purchases

Goods in inventory are initially recorded at cost. Inventory cost includes the sum of the costs incurred in bringing an article to usable or salable condition and location. When Harley-Davidson purchases raw materials and merchandise inventory, the amount recorded should include the invoice price to be paid plus other expenditures related to the purchase, such as freight charges to deliver the items to its warehouses (**Freight-in**) and inspection and preparation costs. Any **purchase returns and allowances** or **purchase discounts** taken are subtracted. In general, the company should cease accumulating purchase costs when the raw materials are **ready for use** or when the merchandise inventory is **ready for shipment.** Any additional costs related to selling the inventory to the dealers, such as marketing department salaries and dealer training sessions, are incurred after the inventory is ready for use. So they should be included in selling, general, and administrative expenses in the period in which they are incurred.

FINANCIAL ANALYSIS

Applying the Materiality Constraint in Practice

Incidental costs such as inspection and preparation costs often are not material in amount (see the discussion of the materiality constraint in Chapter 5) and do not have to be assigned to the inventory cost. Thus, for practical reasons, many companies use the invoice price, less returns and discounts, to assign a unit cost to raw materials or merchandise and record other indirect expenditures as a separate cost that is reported as an expense.

Flow of Inventory Costs

The flow of inventory costs for merchandisers (wholesalers and retailers) is relatively simple, as Exhibit 7.2A shows. When merchandise is purchased, the merchandise inventory account is increased. When the goods are sold, cost of goods sold is increased and merchandise inventory is decreased.

---

[1]These do not add up to the balance reported in Exhibit 7.1 because they do not include the LIFO adjustment discussed later.

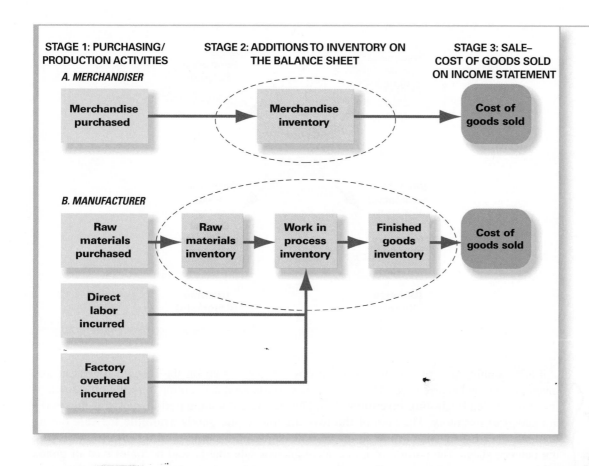

EXHIBIT 7.2

Flow of Inventory Costs

The flow of inventory costs in a manufacturing environment is more complex, as diagrammed in Exhibit 7.2B. First, **raw materials** (also called **direct materials**) must be purchased. For Harley-Davidson, these raw materials include steel and aluminum castings, forgings, sheet, and bars, as well as certain motorcycle component parts produced by its small network of suppliers, including carburetors, batteries, and tires. When they are used, the cost of these materials is removed from the raw materials inventory and added to the work in process inventory.

Two other components of manufacturing cost, direct labor and factory overhead, are also added to the work in process inventory when they are used. **Direct labor** cost represents the earnings of employees who work directly on the products being manufactured. **Factory overhead** costs include all other manufacturing costs. For example, the factory supervisor's salary and the cost of heat, light, and power to operate the factory are included in factory overhead. When the motorcycles are completed and ready for sale, the related amounts in work in process inventory are transferred to finished goods inventory. When the finished goods are sold, cost of goods sold increases, and finished goods inventory decreases.

As Exhibit 7.2 indicates, there are three stages to inventory cost flows for both merchandisers and manufacturers. The first involves purchasing and/or production activities. In the second stage, these activities result in additions to inventory accounts on the balance sheet. In the third stage, the inventory items are sold and the amounts become cost of goods sold expense on the income statement. Since the flow of inventory costs from merchandise inventory and finished goods to cost of goods sold are very similar, we will focus the rest of our discussion on merchandise inventory.

DIRECT LABOR refers to the earnings of employees who work directly on the products being manufactured.

FACTORY OVERHEAD are manufacturing costs that are not raw material or direct labor costs.

Cost of Goods Sold Equation

Cost of goods sold (CGS) expense is directly related to sales revenue. Sales revenue during an accounting period is the number of units sold multiplied by the sales price. Cost of goods sold is the same number of units multiplied by their unit costs.

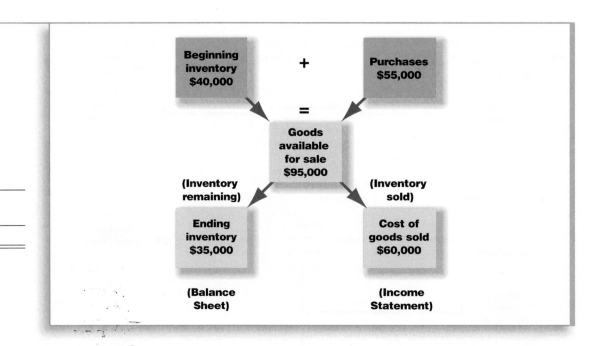

EXHIBIT 7.3

Cost of Goods Sold for
Merchandise Inventory

	Beginning inventory
+	Purchases of merchandise during the year
	Goods available for sale
−	Ending inventory
	Cost of goods sold

**GOODS AVAILABLE FOR
SALE** refers to the sum of
beginning inventory and purchases
(or transfers to finished goods) for
the period.

**COST OF GOODS SOLD
EQUATION:** $BI + P - EI = CGS$

Let's examine the relationship between cost of goods sold on the income statement and inventory on the balance sheet. Harley-Davidson starts each accounting period with a stock of inventory called **beginning inventory** (BI). During the accounting period, new **purchases** (P) are added to inventory. The sum of the two amounts is the goods available for sale during that period. What remains unsold at the end of the period becomes **ending inventory** (EI) on the balance sheet. The portion of goods available for sale that is sold becomes **cost of goods sold** on the income statement. The ending inventory for one accounting period then becomes the beginning inventory for the next period. The relationships between these various inventory amounts are brought together in the cost of goods sold equation:

$$BI + P - EI = CGS$$

To illustrate, assume that Harley-Davidson began the period with $40,000 worth of Motor-clothes in beginning inventory, purchased additional merchandise during the period for $55,000, and had $35,000 left in inventory at the end of the period. These amounts are combined as follows to compute cost of goods sold of $60,000:

Beginning inventory	$40,000
+ Purchases of merchandise during the year	55,000
Goods available for sale	95,000
− Ending inventory	35,000
Cost of goods sold	$60,000

These same relationships are illustrated in Exhibit 7.3 and can be represented in the merchandise inventory T-account as follows:

Merchandise Inventory (A)			
Beginning inventory	40,000		
Add: Purchases of inventory	55,000	Deduct: Cost of goods sold	60,000
Ending inventory	35,000		

If three of these four values are known, either the cost of goods sold equation or the inventory T-account can be used to solve for the fourth value.

Inventory should include all items owned that are held for resale. Costs flow into inventory when goods are purchased or manufactured. They flow out (as an expense) when they are sold or disposed of. The cost of goods sold equation describes these flows.

SELF-STUDY **QUIZ**

1. Assume the following facts for Harley-Davidson's Motorclothes leather baseball jacket product line for the year 2013.

   Beginning inventory: 400 units at unit cost of $75.

   Purchases: 600 units at unit cost of $75.

   Sales: 700 units at a sales price of $100 (cost per unit $75).

   Using the cost of goods sold equation, compute the dollar amount of **goods available for sale, ending inventory,** and **cost of goods sold** of leather baseball jackets for the period.

Beginning inventory	~~400~~ 30,000
+ Purchases of merchandise during the year	45,000
Goods available for sale	75,000
− Ending inventory	~~52,500~~ 22,500
Cost of goods sold	52,500

2. Assume the following facts for Harley-Davidson's Motorclothes leather baseball jacket product line for the year 2014.

   Beginning inventory: 300 units at unit cost of $75.

   Ending inventory: 600 units at unit cost of $75.

   Sales: 1,100 units at a sales price of $100 (cost per unit $75).

   Using the cost of goods sold equation, compute the dollar amount of **purchases** of leather baseball jackets for the period. Remember that if three of these four values are known, the cost of goods sold equation can be used to solve for the fourth value.

Beginning inventory	22500
+ Purchases of merchandise during the year	~~64,500~~ 105,000
− Ending inventory	45,000
Cost of goods sold	82,500

After you have completed your answers, check them with the solutions at the bottom of this page.

GUIDED **HELP**

For additional step-by-step video instruction on using the cost of goods sold equation to compute relevant income statement amounts, go to the URL or scan the QR code in the margin with your smartphone or iPad.

www.mhhe.com/libby8e

1.

Beginning inventory (400 × $75)	$30,000
+ Purchases of merchandise during the year (600 × $75)	45,000
Goods available for sale (1,000 × $75)	75,000
− Ending inventory (300 × $75)	22,500
Cost of goods sold (700 × $75)	$52,500

2. BI = 300 × $75 = $22,500   BI + P − EI = CGS
   EI = 600 × $75 = $45,000   22,500 + P − 45,000 = 82,500
   CGS = 1,100 × $75 = $82,500   P = 105,000

Perpetual and Periodic Inventory Systems

The amount of purchases for the period is always accumulated in the accounting system. The amount of cost of goods sold and ending inventory can be determined by using one of two different inventory systems: perpetual or periodic.

Perpetual Inventory System

In a PERPETUAL INVENTORY SYSTEM, a detailed inventory record is maintained, recording each purchase and sale during the accounting period.

To this point in the text, all journal entries for purchase and sale transactions have been recorded using a perpetual inventory system. In a **perpetual inventory system, purchase transactions are recorded directly in an inventory account**. When each sale is recorded, a companion cost of goods sold entry is made, decreasing inventory and recording cost of goods sold. You have already experienced the starting point for that process when your purchases are scanned at the checkout counter at Walmart or Target. Not only does that process determine how much you must pay the cashier, it also removes the sold items from the store inventory records. As a result, information on cost of goods sold and ending inventory is available on a continuous (perpetual) basis.

In a perpetual inventory system, a detailed record is maintained for each type of merchandise stocked, showing (1) units and cost of the beginning inventory, (2) units and cost of each purchase, (3) units and cost of the goods for each sale, and (4) units and cost of the goods on hand at any point in time. This up-to-date record is maintained on a transaction-by-transaction basis. Most modern companies could not survive without this information. As noted at the beginning of the chapter, cost and quality pressures brought on by increasing competition, combined with dramatic declines in the cost of computers, have made sophisticated perpetual inventory systems a requirement at all but the smallest companies. As a consequence, we will continue to focus on perpetual inventory systems throughout the book.

Periodic Inventory System

In a PERIODIC INVENTORY SYSTEM, ending inventory and cost of goods sold are determined at the end of the accounting period based on a physical count.

Under the **periodic inventory system,** no up-to-date record of inventory is maintained during the year. An actual physical count of the goods remaining on hand is required at the **end of each period.** The number of units of each type of merchandise on hand is multiplied by unit cost to compute the dollar amount of the ending inventory. Cost of goods sold is calculated using the cost of goods sold equation.

Because the amount of inventory is not known until the end of the period when the inventory count is taken, the amount of cost of goods sold cannot be reliably determined until the inventory count is complete. The primary disadvantage of a periodic inventory system is the lack of inventory information. Managers are not informed about low or excess stock situations.

INVENTORY COSTING METHODS

LEARNING OBJECTIVE 7-2

Report inventory and cost of goods sold using the four inventory costing methods.

In the Motorclothes example presented in the Self-Study Quiz, the cost of all units of the leather baseball jackets was the same—$75. If inventory costs normally did not change, this would be the end of our discussion. As we are all aware, however, the prices of most goods do change. In recent years, the costs of many manufactured items such as automobiles and motorcycles have risen gradually. In some industries such as computers, costs of production have dropped dramatically along with retail prices.

When inventory costs have changed, which inventory items are treated as sold or remaining in inventory can turn profits into losses and cause companies to pay or save millions in taxes. A simple example will illustrate these dramatic effects. Do not let the simplicity of our example mislead you. It applies broadly to actual company practices.

Assume that a Harley-Davidson dealer made the following purchases:

Jan. 1   Had beginning inventory of two units of a Model A leather jacket at $70 each.

Jan. 12   Purchased four units of the Model A leather jacket at $80 each.

Jan. 14   Purchased one unit of the Model A leather jacket at $100.

Jan. 15   Sold four units for $120 each.

Note that the **cost of the leather jacket rose** rapidly during January. On January 15, four units are sold for $120 each and revenues of $480 are recorded. What amount is recorded as cost of goods sold? The answer depends on which specific goods we assume are sold. Four generally accepted inventory costing methods are available for determining cost of goods sold:

1. Specific identification.

2. First-in, first-out (FIFO).

3. Last-in, first-out (LIFO).

4. Average cost.

The four inventory costing methods are alternative ways to assign the total dollar amount of goods available for sale between (1) ending inventory and (2) cost of goods sold. The first method identifies individual items that remain in inventory or are sold. The remaining three methods assume that the inventory costs follow a certain flow.

Specific Identification Method

When the **specific identification method** is used, the cost of each item sold is individually identified and recorded as cost of goods sold. This method requires keeping track of the purchase cost of each item. In the leather jacket example, any four of the items could have been sold. If we assume that one of the $70 items, two of the $80 items, and the one $100 item have been sold, the cost of those items ($70 + $80 + $80 + $100) would become cost of goods sold ($330). The cost of the remaining items would be ending inventory.

    The specific identification method is impractical when large quantities of similar items are stocked. On the other hand, when dealing with expensive unique items such as houses or fine jewelry, this method is appropriate. As a consequence, most inventory items are accounted for using one of three cost flow assumptions.

The SPECIFIC IDENTIFICATION METHOD identifies the cost of the specific item that was sold.

Cost Flow Assumptions

The **choice of an inventory costing method is NOT based on the physical flow of goods** on and off the shelves. That is why they are called **cost flow assumptions.** A useful tool for representing inventory cost flow assumptions is a bin, or container. Try visualizing these inventory costing methods as flows of inventory in and out of the bin.

First-In, First-Out Method

The **first-in, first-out method,** frequently called **FIFO,** assumes that the earliest goods purchased (the first ones in) are the first goods sold, and the last goods purchased are left in ending inventory. Under FIFO, cost of goods sold and ending inventory are computed as if the flows in and out of the FIFO inventory bin in Exhibit 7.4A had taken place. First, each purchase is treated as if it were deposited in the bin from the top in sequence (two units of beginning inventory at $70 followed by purchases of four units at $80 and one unit at $100) producing goods available for sale of $560. Each good sold is then removed from the *bottom* in sequence (two units at $70 and two at $80); **first in is first out.** These goods totaling $300 become cost of goods sold (CGS). The remaining units (two units at $80 and one unit at $100 = $260) become ending inventory. FIFO allocates the **oldest** unit costs **to cost of goods sold** and the **newest** unit costs **to ending inventory.**

The FIRST-IN, FIRST-OUT (FIFO) METHOD assumes that the first goods purchased (the first in) are the first goods sold (the first out).

Cost of Goods Sold Calculation (FIFO)		
Beginning inventory	(2 units at $70 each)	$140
+ Purchases	(4 units at $80 each)	320
	(1 unit at $100 each)	100
Goods available for sale		560
− Ending inventory	(2 units at $80 each and 1 unit at $100)	260
Cost of goods sold	(2 units at $70 each and 2 units at $80 each)	$300

FIFO and LIFO
Inventory Flows

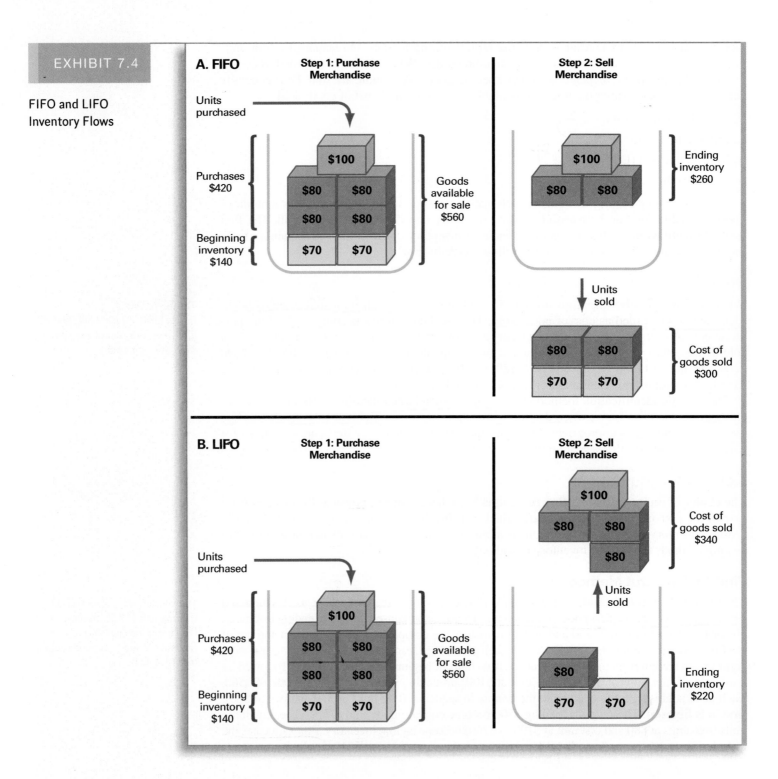

Last-In, First-Out Method

The **last-in, first-out method,** often called **LIFO,** assumes that the most recently purchased goods (the last ones in) are sold first and the oldest units are left in ending inventory. It is illustrated by the LIFO inventory bin in Exhibit 7.4B. As in FIFO, each purchase is treated as if it were deposited in the bin from the top (two units of beginning inventory at $70 followed by purchases of four units at $80 and one unit at $100), resulting in the goods available for sale of $560. Unlike FIFO, however, each good sold is treated as if it were removed from the *top* in sequence (one unit at $100 followed by three units at $80). These goods totaling $340 become cost of goods sold (CGS). The remaining units (one at $80 and two at $70 = $220) become ending inventory. LIFO allocates the **newest** unit costs **to cost of goods sold** and the **oldest** unit costs to ending inventory.

Cost of Goods Sold Calculation (LIFO)		
Beginning inventory	(2 units at $70 each)	$140
+ Purchases	(4 units at $80 each)	320
	(1 unit at $100)	100
Goods available for sale		560
− Ending inventory	(2 units at $70 each and 1 unit at $80)	220
Cost of goods sold	(3 units at $80 each and 1 unit at $100)	$340

The LIFO cost flow assumption is the exact opposite of the FIFO cost flow assumption:

	FIFO	LIFO
Cost of goods sold on income statement	Oldest unit costs	Newest unit costs
Inventory on balance sheet	Newest unit costs	Oldest unit costs

Average Cost Method

The **average cost method** (weighted average cost method) uses the weighted average unit cost of the goods available for sale for both cost of goods sold and ending inventory. The weighted average unit cost of the goods available for sale is computed as follows.

The AVERAGE COST METHOD uses the weighted average unit cost of the goods available for sale for both cost of goods sold and ending inventory.

Number of Units	×	Unit Cost	=	Total Cost
2	×	$ 70	=	$140
4	×	$ 80	=	320
1	×	$100	=	100
7				$560

$$\text{Average cost} = \frac{\text{Cost of Goods Available for Sale}}{\text{Number of Units Available for Sale}}$$

$$\text{Average Cost} = \frac{\$560}{7 \text{ Units}} = \$80 \text{ per Unit}$$

Cost of goods sold and ending inventory are assigned the same weighted average cost per unit of $80.

Cost of Goods Sold Calculation (Average Cost)		
Beginning inventory	(2 units at $70 each)	$140
+ Purchases	(4 units at $80 each)	320
	(1 unit at $100)	100
Goods available for sale	(7 units at $80 average cost each)	560
− Ending inventory	(3 units at $80 average cost each)	240
Cost of goods sold	(4 units at $80 average cost each)	$320

	FIFO	LIFO	Average Cost
Effect on the Income Statement			
Sales	$480	$480	$480
Cost of goods sold	300	340	320
Gross profit	180	140	160
Other expenses	80	80	80
Income before income taxes	100	60	80
Income tax expense (25%)	25	15	20
Net income	$ 75	$ 45	$ 60
Effect on the Balance Sheet			
Inventory	$260	$220	$240

EXHIBIT 7.5

Financial Statement Effects of Inventory Costing Methods

Perpetual Inventory Systems and Cost Flow Assumptions in Practice

You should have noted that, in our example, all inventory units were purchased before a sale was made and cost of goods sold recorded. In reality, most companies make numerous purchases and sales of the same inventory item throughout the accounting period. How can we apply our simple example to these circumstances given that companies normally employ perpetual inventory systems?

First, it is important to know that FIFO inventory and cost of goods sold are the same whether computed on a perpetual or periodic basis. Second, accounting systems that keep track of the costs of individual items normally do so on a FIFO or average cost basis, regardless of the cost flow assumption used for financial reporting. As a consequence, companies that wish to report under LIFO convert the outputs of their perpetual inventory system to LIFO with an adjusting entry at the end of each period. By waiting until the end of the period to calculate this LIFO adjustment, LIFO ending inventory and cost of goods sold are calculated *as if* all purchases during the period were recorded before cost of goods sold is calculated and recorded. In other words, our simple example of how to calculate cost of goods sold applies even though a company actually tracks the number of units bought and sold on a perpetual basis.[2]

INTERNATIONAL PERSPECTIVE

LIFO and International Comparisons

While U.S. GAAP allows companies to choose between FIFO, LIFO, and average cost inventory accounting methods, International Financial Reporting Standards (IFRS) currently prohibit the use of LIFO. U.S. GAAP also allows different inventory accounting methods to be used for different types of inventory items and even for the same item in different locations. IFRS requires that the same method be used for all inventory items that have a similar nature and use. These differences can create comparability problems when one attempts to compare companies across international borders. For example, Ford uses LIFO to value U.S. inventories and average cost or FIFO for non–U.S. inventories, while Honda (of Japan) uses FIFO for all inventories. Each individual country's tax laws determine the acceptability of different inventory methods for tax purposes.

---

[2]We show an example comparing calculation of cost of goods sold under perpetual versus periodic FIFO and LIFO in Chapter Supplement B.

Financial Statement Effects of Inventory Methods

Each of the four alternative inventory costing methods is in conformity with GAAP and the tax law. To understand why managers choose different methods in different circumstances, we must first understand their effects on the income statement and balance sheet. Exhibit 7.5 summarizes the financial statement effects of the FIFO, LIFO, and average cost inventory methods in our example. Remember that the methods differ only in the dollar amount of goods available for sale allocated to cost of goods sold versus ending inventory. For that reason, the method that gives the highest ending inventory amount also gives the lowest cost of goods sold and the highest gross profit, income tax expense, and income amounts, and vice versa. The weighted average cost method generally gives income and inventory amounts that are between the FIFO and LIFO extremes.

In our example, recall that unit costs were increasing. **When unit costs are rising, LIFO produces lower income and a lower inventory valuation than FIFO.** Even in inflationary times, some companies' costs decline. **When unit costs are declining, LIFO produces higher income and higher inventory valuation than FIFO.** These effects, which hold as long as inventory quantities are constant or rising,[3] are summarized in the following table:

Increasing Costs: Normal Financial Statement Effects

	FIFO	LIFO
Cost of goods sold on income statement	Lower	Higher
Net income	Higher	Lower
Income taxes	Higher	Lower
Inventory on balance sheet	Higher	Lower

Decreasing Costs: Normal Financial Statement Effects

	FIFO	LIFO
Cost of goods sold on income statement	Higher	Lower
Net income	Lower	Higher
Income taxes	Lower	Higher
Inventory on balance sheet	Lower	Higher

Managers' Choice of Inventory Methods

What motivates companies to choose different inventory costing methods? Most managers choose accounting methods based on two factors:

1. Net income effects (managers prefer to report higher earnings for their companies).

2. Income tax effects (managers prefer to pay the least amount of taxes allowed by law as late as possible—the **least–latest rule of thumb**).

Any conflict between the two motives is normally resolved by choosing one accounting method for external financial statements and a different method for preparing its tax return. The choice of inventory costing methods is a special case, however, because of what is called the **LIFO conformity rule:** If LIFO is used on the U.S. income tax return, it must also be used to calculate inventory and cost of goods sold for the financial statements.

LEARNING OBJECTIVE 7-3
Decide when the use of different inventory costing methods is beneficial to a company.

Increasing Cost Inventories

- **For inventory with increasing costs, LIFO is used on the tax return because it normally results in lower income taxes.**

---

[3]The impact of a decline in inventory **quantity** on LIFO amounts is discussed in Supplement A to this chapter.

This is illustrated in Exhibit 7.5, where income before income taxes was lowered from $100 under FIFO to $60 under LIFO. On the income tax expense line, this lowers income taxes from $25 under FIFO to $15 under LIFO, generating cash tax savings of $10 under LIFO.[4] The LIFO conformity rule leads companies to adopt LIFO for **both** tax and financial reporting purposes for increasing cost inventories located in the United States. Harley-Davidson is a fairly typical company facing increasing costs. It has saved approximately $15 million in taxes from the date it adopted the LIFO method through 2011.

For inventory located in countries that do not allow LIFO for tax purposes or that do not have a LIFO conformity rule, companies with increasing costs most often use FIFO or average cost to report higher income on the income statement.

Decreasing Cost Inventories

For inventory with decreasing costs, FIFO is most often used for both the tax return and financial statements.

Using this method (along with lower of cost or market valuation, discussed later) produces the lowest tax payments for companies with decreasing cost inventories. Many high-technology companies are facing declining costs. In such circumstances, the FIFO method, in which the oldest, most expensive goods become cost of goods sold, produces the highest cost of goods sold, the lowest pretax earnings, and thus the lowest income tax liability. For example, Apple Inc. and Dell Inc. account for inventories using the FIFO method.

Since most companies in the same industry face similar cost structures, clusters of companies in the same industries often choose the same accounting method.

Consistency in Use of Inventory Methods

It is important to remember that regardless of the physical flow of goods, a company can use any of the inventory costing methods. Also, a company is not required to use the same inventory costing method for all inventory items, and no particular justification is needed for the selection of one or more of the acceptable methods. Harley-Davidson, and most large companies, use different inventory methods for different inventory items. However, accounting rules require companies to apply their accounting methods on a consistent basis over time. A company is not permitted to use LIFO one period, FIFO the next, and then go back to LIFO. A change in method is allowed only if the change will improve the measurement of financial results and financial position.

A QUESTION OF ETHICS	LIFO and Conflicts between Managers' and Owners' Interests

We have seen that the selection of an inventory method can have significant effects on the financial statements. Company managers may have an incentive to select a method that is not consistent with the owners' objectives. For example, during a period of rising prices, using LIFO may be in the best interests of the owners, because LIFO often reduces a company's tax liability. However, if managers' compensation is tied to reported profits, they may prefer FIFO, which typically results in higher profits.

While a well-designed compensation plan should reward managers for acting in the best interests of the owners, that is not always the case. Clearly, a manager who selects an accounting method that is not optimal for the company solely to increase his or her compensation is engaging in questionable ethical behavior.

---

[4]In theory, LIFO cannot provide permanent tax savings because (1) when inventory levels drop or (2) costs drop, the income effect reverses and the income taxes deferred must be paid. The economic advantage of deferring income taxes in such situations is due to the fact that interest can be earned on the money that otherwise would be paid as taxes for the current year.

PAUSE FOR **FEEDBACK**

Four different inventory costing methods may be used to allocate costs between the units remaining in inventory and the units sold, depending on economic circumstances. The methods include specific identification, FIFO, LIFO, and average cost. Each of the inventory costing methods conforms to GAAP. Remember that the cost flow assumption need not match the physical flow of inventory. The following questions test your understanding of the FIFO and LIFO methods.

SELF-STUDY **QUIZ**

1. Compute cost of goods sold and pretax income for **2012** under the FIFO and LIFO accounting methods. Assume that a company's beginning inventory and purchases for 2012 included:

Beginning inventory	10 units @ $ 6 each
Purchases January	5 units @ $10 each
Purchases May	5 units @ $12 each

During 2012, 15 units were sold for $20 each, and other operating expenses totaled $100.

2. Compute cost of goods sold and pretax income for **2013** under the FIFO and LIFO accounting methods. (**Hint:** The 2012 ending inventory amount from Part 1 becomes the 2013 beginning inventory amount.) Assume that the company's purchases for 2013 included:

Purchases March	6 units @ $13 each
Purchases November	5 units @ $14 each

During 2013, 10 units were sold for $24 each, and other operating expenses totaled $70.

3. Which method would you recommend that the company adopt? Why?

After you have completed your answers, check them with the solutions at the bottom of the page.

GUIDED **HELP**

For additional step-by-step video instruction on computing ending inventory and cost of goods sold using different cost flow assumptions, go to the URL or scan the QR code in the margin with your smartphone or iPad.

www.mhhe.com/libby8e

Solutions to
SELF-STUDY QUIZ

1.

2012	FIFO	LIFO		FIFO	LIFO
Beginning inventory	$ 60	$ 60	Sales revenue (15 × $20)	$300	$300
Purchases (5 × $10) + (5 × $12)	110	110	Cost of goods sold	110	140
Goods available for sale	170	170	Gross profit	190	160
Ending inventory*	60	30	Other expenses	100	100
Cost of goods sold	$110	$140	Pretax income	$ 90	$ 60

*FIFO ending inventory = (5 × $12) = $60
Cost of goods sold = (10 × $6) + (5 × $10) = $110
LIFO ending inventory = (5 × $6) = $30
Cost of goods sold = (5 × $12) + (5 × $10) + (5 × $6) = $140

2.

2013	FIFO	LIFO		FIFO	LIFO
Beginning inventory	$ 60	$ 30	Sales revenue (10 × $24)	$240	$240
Purchases (6 × $13) + (5 × $14)	148	148	Cost of goods sold	125	135
Goods available for sale	208	178	Gross profit	115	105
Ending inventory*	83	43	Other expenses	70	70
Cost of goods sold	$125	$135	Pretax income	$ 45	$ 35

*FIFO ending inventory = (5 × $14) + (1 × $13) = $83
Cost of goods sold = (5 × $12) + (5 × $13) = $125
LIFO ending inventory = (5 × $6) + (1 × $13) = $43
Cost of goods sold = (5 × $14) + (5 × $13) = $135

3. LIFO would be recommended because it produces lower pretax income and lower taxes when inventory costs are rising.

VALUATION AT LOWER OF COST OR MARKET

REPLACEMENT COST
is the current purchase price for identical goods.

NET REALIZABLE VALUE
is the expected sales price less selling costs (e.g., repair and disposal costs).

LOWER OF COST OR MARKET (LCM) is a valuation method departing from the cost principle; it serves to recognize a loss when replacement cost or net realizable value drops below cost.

Inventories should be measured initially at their purchase cost in conformity with the cost principle. When the goods remaining in ending inventory can be replaced with identical goods at a lower cost, however, the lower replacement cost should be used as the inventory valuation. Damaged, obsolete, and deteriorated items in inventory should also be assigned a unit cost that represents their current estimated net realizable value (sales price less costs to sell) if that is below cost. This rule is known as measuring inventories at the lower of cost or market (LCM).

This departure from the cost principle is based on the **conservatism** constraint, which requires special care to avoid overstating assets and income. It is particularly important for two types of companies: (1) high-technology companies such as Dell Inc. that manufacture goods for which costs of production and selling price are declining and (2) companies such as American Eagle Outfitters that sell seasonal goods such as clothing, the value of which drops dramatically at the end of each selling season (fall or spring).

Under LCM, companies recognize a "holding" loss in the period in which the replacement cost of an item drops, rather than in the period the item is sold. The holding loss is the difference between the purchase cost and the lower replacement cost. It is added to the cost of goods sold for the period. To illustrate, assume that Dell Inc. had the following in the current period ending inventory:

Item	Quantity	Cost per Item	Replacement Cost (Market) per Item	Lower of Cost or Market per Item	Total Lower of Cost or Market
Intel chips	1,000	$250	$200	$200	1,000 × $200 = $200,000
Disk drives	400	100	110	100	400 × $100 = 40,000

The 1,000 Intel chips should be recorded in the ending inventory at the current market value ($200) because it is **lower** than the cost ($250). Dell makes the following journal entry to record the write-down:

Cost of goods sold (+E, −SE) (1,000 × $50)	50,000	
Inventory (−A)		50,000

Assets	=	Liabilities	+	Stockholders' Equity	
Inventory −50,000				Cost of Goods Sold (+E)	−50,000

Since the market price of the disk drives ($110) is higher than the original cost ($100), no write-down is necessary. The drives remain on the books at their cost of $100 per unit ($40,000 in total). Recognition of holding gains on inventory is not permitted by GAAP.

The write-down of the Intel chips to market produces the following effects on the income statement and balance sheet:

Effects of LCM Write-Down	Current Period	Next Period (if sold)
Cost of goods sold	Increase $50,000	Decrease $50,000
Pretax income	Decrease $50,000	Increase $50,000
Ending inventory on balance sheet	Decrease $50,000	Unaffected

Note that the effects in the period of sale are the opposite of those in the period of the write-down. Lower of cost or market changes only the timing of cost of goods sold. It transfers cost of goods sold from the period of sale to the period of write-down.

Note that in the two examples that follow, both Harley-Davidson, which is a mixed LIFO company, and Dell Inc., which is a FIFO company, report the use of lower of cost or market for financial statement purposes.[5]

---

[5]For tax purposes, lower of cost or market may be applied with all inventory costing methods except LIFO.

HARLEY-DAVIDSON, INC.
Notes to Consolidated Financial Statements
1. SUMMARY OF SIGNIFICANT ACCOUNTING POLICIES

Inventories—Inventories are valued at the lower of cost or market. Substantially all inventories located in the United States are valued using the last-in, first-out (LIFO) method. Other inventories totaling $215.2 million at December 31, 2011, and $153.4 million at December 31, 2010, are valued at the lower of cost or market using the first-in, first-out (FIFO) method.

DELL INC.
Notes to Consolidated Financial Statements
NOTE 1—Description of Business and Summary of Significant Accounting Policies

Inventories—Inventories are stated at the lower of cost or market with cost being determined on a first-in, first-out basis.

EVALUATING INVENTORY MANAGEMENT
Measuring Efficiency in Inventory Management

As noted at the beginning of the chapter, the primary goals of inventory management are to have sufficient quantities of high-quality inventory available to serve customers' needs while minimizing the costs of carrying inventory (production, storage, obsolescence, and financing). The inventory turnover ratio is an important measure of the company's success in balancing these conflicting goals.

LEARNING OBJECTIVE 7-5
Evaluate inventory management using the inventory turnover ratio.

Inventory Turnover   **KEY RATIO ANALYSIS**

? **ANALYTICAL QUESTION**

How efficient are inventory management activities?

% **RATIO AND COMPARISONS**

$$\text{Inventory Turnover} = \frac{\text{Cost of Goods Sold}}{\text{Average Inventory}}$$

The 2011 ratio for Harley-Davidson (see Exhibit 7.1 for the inputs to the equation):

$$\frac{\$3,106,288}{(\$326,446 + 418,006)/2} = 8.3$$

COMPARISONS OVER TIME			COMPARISONS WITH COMPETITORS	
Harley-Davidson			Polaris	Honda Motor
2009	2010	2011	2011	2011
8.3	8.5	8.3	7.2	7.1

💡 **INTERPRETATIONS**

In General   The inventory turnover ratio reflects how many times average inventory was produced and sold during the period. A higher ratio indicates that inventory moves more quickly through the production process to the ultimate customer, reducing storage and obsolescence costs. Because less money is tied

(continued)

Selected Focus Companies' Inventory Turnover

National Beverage	11.20
Home Depot	4.40
Deckers	3.69

up in inventory, the excess can be invested to earn interest income or reduce borrowing, which reduces interest expense. More efficient purchasing and production techniques, such as just-in-time inventory, as well as high product demand cause this ratio to be high. Analysts and creditors also watch the inventory turnover ratio because a sudden decline may mean that a company is facing an unexpected drop in demand for its products or is becoming sloppy in its production management. Many managers and analysts compute the related number average days to sell inventory, which, for Harley-Davidson, is equal to:

$$\text{Average Days to Sell Inventory} = \frac{365}{\text{Inventory Turnover}} = \frac{365}{8.3} = 44.0 \text{ days}$$

It indicates the average time it takes the company to produce and deliver inventory to customers.

Focus Company Analysis   Harley-Davidson's inventory turnover was generally stable from 2009 to 2011, fluctuating around a ratio of 8.3 during those three years. Harley's ratio is higher than that of related company Polaris and also higher than that of giant Japanese auto and motorcycle manufacturer Honda.

A Few Cautions   Differences across industries in purchasing, production, and sales processes cause dramatic differences in this ratio. For example, restaurants such as Papa John's, which must turn over their perishable inventory very quickly, tend to have much higher inventory turnover. A particular firm's ratio should be compared only with its figures from prior years or with figures for other firms in the same industry.

PAUSE FOR **FEEDBACK**

The inventory turnover ratio measures the efficiency of inventory management. It reflects how many times average inventory was produced and sold during the period. Analysts and creditors watch this ratio because a sudden decline may mean that a company is facing an unexpected drop in demand for its products or is becoming sloppy in its production management. When a net **decrease in inventory** for the period occurs, sales are more than purchases; thus, the decrease must be **added** in computing cash flows from operations. When a net **increase in inventory** for the period occurs, the opposite is true. Before you move on, complete the following questions to test your understanding of these concepts.

SELF-STUDY **QUIZ**

1. Refer to the Key Ratio Analysis for Harley-Davidson's inventory turnover. Based on the computations for 2011, answer the following question. If Harley-Davidson had been able to manage its inventory more efficiently and decrease purchases and ending inventory by $10,000 for 2011, would its inventory turnover ratio have increased or decreased? Explain.

After you have completed your answer, check them with the solution at the bottom of the page.

LEARNING OBJECTIVE 7-6

Compare companies that use different inventory costing methods.

Inventory Methods and Financial Statement Analysis

What would analysts do if they wanted to compare two companies that prepared their statements using different inventory accounting methods? Before meaningful comparisons could be made, one company's statements would have to be converted to a comparable basis. Making such a conversion is eased by the requirement that U.S. public companies using LIFO also

Solution to
SELF-STUDY QUIZ

1. Inventory turnover would have increased because the denominator of the ratio (average inventory) would have decreased by $5,000.

$$\frac{\$3,106,288}{(\$326,446 + \$408,006)/2} = 8.5$$

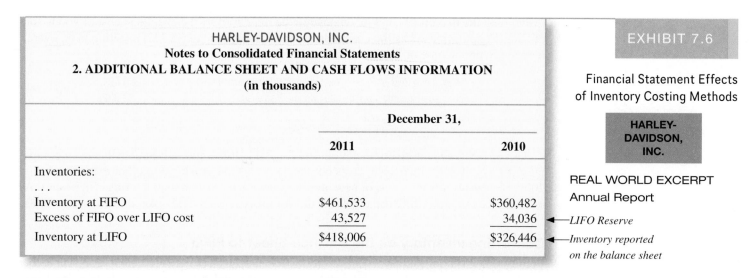

EXHIBIT 7.6

Financial Statement Effects of Inventory Costing Methods

HARLEY-DAVIDSON, INC.

REAL WORLD EXCERPT
Annual Report

LIFO Reserve

Inventory reported on the balance sheet

report beginning and ending inventory on a FIFO basis in the notes if the FIFO values are materially different. We can use this information along with the cost of goods sold equation to convert the balance sheet and income statement to the FIFO basis.

Converting the Income Statement to FIFO

Recall that the choice of a cost flow assumption affects how goods available for sale are allocated to ending inventory and cost of goods sold. It does not affect the recording of purchases. Ending inventory will be different under the alternative methods, and, since last year's ending inventory is this year's beginning inventory, beginning inventory will also be different:

Beginning inventory	**Different**
+ Purchases of merchandise during the year	**Same**
− Ending inventory	**Different**
− Cost of goods sold	**Different**

This equation suggests that if we know the differences between a company's inventory valued at LIFO and FIFO for both beginning and ending inventory, we can compute the difference in cost of goods sold. Exhibit 7.6 shows Harley-Davidson's 2011 disclosure of the differences between LIFO and FIFO values for beginning and ending inventory. These amounts, referred to as the **LIFO reserve** or "Excess of FIFO over LIFO," are disclosed by LIFO users in their inventory footnotes.

Using Harley-Davidson's LIFO reserve values reported in the footnote presented in Exhibit 7.6, we see that cost of goods sold would have been $9,491 **lower** had it used FIFO.

The LIFO RESERVE is a contra-asset for the excess of FIFO over LIFO inventory.

Beginning LIFO Reserve (Excess of FIFO over LIFO)	$34,036
− Less: Ending LIFO Reserve (Excess of FIFO over LIFO)	−43,527
Difference in Cost of Goods Sold under FIFO	($9,491)

Since FIFO cost of goods sold expense is **lower,** income before income taxes would have been $9,491 **higher.** Income taxes would be that amount times its tax rate of 35 percent **higher** had it used FIFO.

Difference in pretax income under FIFO	$9,491
Tax rate	× .35
Difference in taxes under FIFO	$3,322

Combining the two effects, net income would be increased by the change in cost of goods sold of $9,491 and decreased by the change in income tax expense of $3,322, resulting in an overall increase in net income of $6,169.

Decrease in Cost of Goods Sold Expense (*Income increases*)	$ 9,491
Increase in Income Tax Expense (*Income decreases*)	(3,322)
Increase in Net Income	$ 6,169

These Harley-Davidson computations are for 2011. It is important to note that even companies that usually face increasing costs occasionally face decreasing costs. For example, during 2000, Harley-Davidson's costs of new inventory declined due to manufacturing efficiencies. As a result, even though LIFO usually **saves** the company taxes, Harley paid **extra** taxes in 2000.

Converting Inventory on the Balance Sheet to FIFO

You can adjust the inventory amounts on the balance sheet to FIFO by substituting the FIFO values in the note ($461,533 and $360,482 for 2011 and 2010, respectively) for the LIFO values (see Exhibit 7.6). Alternatively, you can add the LIFO reserve to the LIFO value on the balance sheet to arrive at the same numbers.

FINANCIAL ANALYSIS **LIFO and Inventory Turnover Ratio**

For many LIFO companies, the inventory turnover ratio can be deceptive. Remember that, for these companies, the beginning and ending inventory numbers that make up the denominator of the ratio will be artificially small because they reflect old lower costs. Consider Deere & Co., manufacturer of John Deere farm, lawn, and construction equipment. Its inventory note lists the following values:

REAL WORLD EXCERPT

Deere & Company
Annual Report

DEERE & COMPANY Notes to Consolidated Financial Statements (dollars in millions)		
	2011	**2010**
Inventories:		
Total FIFO value	$5,857	$4,461
Adjustment to LIFO basis	1,486	1,398
Inventories	$4,371	$3,063

John Deere's cost of goods sold for 2011 was $21,919.4 million. If the ratio is computed using the reported LIFO inventory values for the ratio, it would be

$$\text{Inventory Turnover Ratio} = \frac{\$21,919.4}{(\$4,371 + \$3,063)/2} = 5.9$$

Converting cost of goods sold (the numerator) to a FIFO basis and using the more current FIFO inventory values in the denominator, it would be

$$\text{Inventory Turnover Ratio} = \frac{\$21,919.4 - 88}{(\$5,857 + \$4,461)/2} = 4.2$$

Note that the major difference between the two ratios is in the denominator. FIFO inventory values are nearly 34 percent higher than the LIFO values. The LIFO beginning and ending inventory numbers are artificially small because they reflect older lower costs.

PAUSE FOR **FEEDBACK**

The selection of an inventory costing method is important because it will affect reported income, income tax expense (and hence cash flow), and the inventory valuation reported on the balance sheet. In a period of rising prices, FIFO normally results in a higher income and higher taxes than LIFO; in a period of falling prices, the opposite occurs. The choice of methods is normally made to minimize taxes. Answer the following question to practice converting cost of goods sold and pretax income from the LIFO to the FIFO method for a company facing increasing prices.

Caterpillar

SELF-STUDY **QUIZ**

In a recent year, Caterpillar Inc., a major manufacturer of farm and construction equipment, reported pretax earnings of $6,725 million. Its inventory note indicated "if the FIFO (first-in, first-out) method had been in use, inventories would have been $2,422 and $2,575 higher than reported at the end of the current and prior year, respectively." (The amounts noted are for the LIFO reserve.) Convert pretax earnings for the current year from a LIFO to a FIFO basis.

Beginning LIFO Reserve (Excess of FIFO over LIFO)	_____
Less: Ending LIFO Reserve (Excess of FIFO over LIFO)	_____
Difference in cost of goods sold under FIFO	_____
Pretax income (LIFO)	_____
Difference in pretax income under FIFO	_____
Pretax income (FIFO)	_____

After you have completed your answers, check them with the solutions at the bottom of the page.

CONTROL OF INVENTORY

Internal Control of Inventory

After cash, inventory is the asset second most vulnerable to theft. Efficient management of inventory to avoid the cost of stock-outs and overstock situations is also crucial to the profitability of most companies. As a consequence, a number of control features focus on safeguarding inventories and providing up-to-date information for management decisions. Key among these are:

> **LEARNING OBJECTIVE 7-7**
> Understand methods for controlling inventory, analyze the effects of inventory errors on financial statements, and analyze the effects of inventory on cash flows.

1. Separation of responsibilities for inventory accounting and physical handling of inventory.
2. Storage of inventory in a manner that protects it from theft and damage.
3. Limiting access to inventory to authorized employees.
4. Maintaining perpetual inventory records (described earlier in this chapter).
5. Comparing perpetual records to periodic physical counts of inventory.

Errors in Measuring Ending Inventory

As the cost of goods sold equation indicates, a direct relationship exists between ending inventory and cost of goods sold because items not in the ending inventory are assumed to have been sold. Thus, the measurement of ending inventory quantities and costs affects both the balance sheet (assets) and the income statement (cost of goods sold, gross profit, and net income). The measurement of ending inventory affects not only the net income for that period but also the net income for the next accounting period. This two-period effect occurs because the ending inventory for one period is the beginning inventory for the next accounting period.

Greeting card maker Gibson Greetings overstated its net income by 20 percent because one division overstated ending inventory for the year. You can compute the effects of the error on both the current year's and the next year's income before taxes using the cost of goods sold

Beginning LIFO Reserve	$2,575	Pretax income (LIFO)	$6,725	Solutions to
Less: Ending LIFO Reserve	2,422	Difference in pretax income	(153)	SELF-STUDY QUIZ
Difference in cost of goods sold	$ 153	Pretax income (FIFO)	$6,572	

equation. Assume that ending inventory was overstated by $10,000 due to a clerical error that was not discovered. This would have the following effects in the current year and next year:

Current Year	
Beginning inventory	
+ Purchases of merchandise during the year	
− Ending inventory	**Overstated $10,000**
Cost of goods sold	**Understated $10,000**

Next Year	
Beginning inventory	**Overstated $10,000**
+ Purchases of merchandise during the year	
− Ending inventory	
Cost of goods sold	**Overstated $10,000**

Because cost of goods sold was understated, **income before taxes would be overstated** by $10,000 in the **current year.** And, since the current year's ending inventory becomes next year's beginning inventory, it would have the following effects: Because cost of goods sold was overstated, **income before taxes would be understated** by $10,000 in the **next year.**

Each of these errors would flow into retained earnings so that at the end of the current year, retained earnings would be overstated by $10,000 (less the related income tax expense). This error would be offset in the next year, and retained earnings and inventory at the end of next year would be correct.

In this example, we assumed that the overstatement of ending inventory was inadvertent, the result of a clerical error. However, inventory fraud is a common form of financial statement fraud.

PAUSE FOR **FEEDBACK**

An error in the measurement of ending inventory affects cost of goods sold on the current period's income statement and ending inventory on the balance sheet. Because this year's ending inventory becomes next year's beginning inventory, it also affects cost of goods sold in the following period by the same amount but in the opposite direction. These relationships can be seen through the cost of goods sold equation (BI + P − EI = CGS).

SELF-STUDY **QUIZ**

Assume that it is now the end of 2013, and for the first time, the company will undergo an audit by an independent CPA. The annual income statement prepared by the company is presented here. Assume further that the independent CPA discovered that the ending inventory for 2013 was understated by $15,000. Correct and reconstruct the income statement in the space provided.

	For the Year Ended December 31		
	2013 Uncorrected		**2013 Corrected**
Sales revenue		$750,000	
Cost of goods sold			
Beginning inventory	$ 45,000		
Add purchases	460,000		
Goods available for sale	505,000		
Less ending inventory	40,000		_____
Cost of goods sold		465,000	_____
Gross margin on sales		285,000	
Operating expenses		275,000	
Pretax income		10,000	_____
Income tax expense (20%)		2,000	_____
Net income		$ 8,000	_____

After you have completed your answers, check them with the solutions at the bottom of the next page.

Inventory and Cash Flows

When companies expand production to meet increases in demand, this increases the amount of inventory reported on the balance sheet. However, when companies overestimate demand for a product, they usually produce too many units of the slow-selling item. This increases storage costs as well as the interest costs on short-term borrowings that finance the inventory. It may even lead to losses if the excess inventory cannot be sold at normal prices. The cash flow statement often provides the first sign of such problems.

Inventory	FOCUS ON CASH FLOWS

As with a change in accounts receivable, a change in inventories can have a major effect on a company's cash flow from operations. Cost of goods sold on the income statement may be more or less than the amount of cash paid to suppliers during the period. Since most inventory is purchased on open credit (borrowing from suppliers is normally called accounts payable), reconciling cost of goods sold with cash paid to suppliers requires consideration of the changes in both the Inventory and Accounts Payable accounts.

The simplest way to think about the effects of changes in inventory is that buying (increasing) inventory eventually decreases cash, while selling (decreasing) inventory eventually increases cash. Similarly, borrowing from suppliers, which increases accounts payable, increases cash. Paying suppliers, which decreases accounts payable, decreases cash.

EFFECT ON STATEMENT OF CASH FLOWS

In General   When a net **decrease in inventory** for the period occurs, sales are greater than purchases; thus, the decrease must be **added** in computing cash flows from operations.

When a net **increase in inventory** for the period occurs, sales are less than purchases; thus, the increase must be **subtracted** in computing cash flows from operations.

When a net **decrease in accounts payable** for the period occurs, payments to suppliers are greater than new purchases; thus, the decrease must be **subtracted** in computing cash flows from operations.

When a net **increase in accounts payable** for the period occurs, payments to suppliers are less than new purchases; thus, the increase must be **added** in computing cash flows from operations.

	Effect on Cash Flows
Operating activities (indirect method)	
Net income	$xxx
Adjusted for	
Add inventory **decrease**	+
or	
Subtract inventory **increase**	−
Add accounts payable **increase**	+
or	
Subtract accounts payable **decrease**	−

(*continued*)

Solutions to
SELF-STUDY QUIZ

Sales revenue		$750,000
Cost of goods sold		
Beginning inventory	$ 45,000	
Add purchases	460,000	
Goods available for sale	505,000	
Less ending inventory	55,000	
Cost of goods sold		450,000
Gross margin on sales		300,000
Operating expenses		275,000
Pretax income		25,000
Income tax expense (20%)		5,000
Net income		$ 20,000

Note: An ending inventory error in one year affects pretax income by the amount of the error and in the next year affects pretax income again by the same amount, but in the opposite direction.

Focus Company Analysis   When the inventory balance increases during the period, as was the case at Harley-Davidson in 2011, the company has purchased or produced more inventory than it has sold. Thus, the increase is subtracted in the computation of cash flow from operations. Conversely, when the inventory balance decreases during the period, the company has sold more inventory than it purchased or produced. Thus, the decrease is added in the computation of cash flow from operations. When the accounts payable balance increases during the period, the company has borrowed more from suppliers than it has paid them (or postponed payments). Thus, the increase is added in the computation of cash flow from operations.*

HARLEY-DAVIDSON, INC.
Consolidated Statement of Cash Flows
Year Ended December 31, 2011
(dollars in thousands)

	2011
Cash flows from operating activities:	
Income from continuing operations	$548,078
Adjustments to reconcile net income to net cash provided by operating activities:	
Depreciation	180,408
. . . .	
Changes in current assets and current liabilities:	
. . . .	
Inventories	(94,957)
Accounts payable and accrued liabilities	120,291
. . . .	
Total Adjustments	$337,213
Net cash (used by) provided by continuing operating activities	$885,291

*For companies with foreign currency or business acquisitions/dispositions, the amount of the change reported on the cash flow statement will not equal the change in the accounts reported on the balance sheet.

DEMONSTRATION   CASE

(Complete the requirements before proceeding to the suggested solution that follows.) This case reviews the application of the FIFO and LIFO inventory costing methods and the inventory turnover ratio.

Balent Appliances distributes a number of household appliances. One product, microwave ovens, has been selected for case purposes. Assume that the following summarized transactions were completed during the year ended December 31, 2013, in the order given (assume that all transactions are cash):

	Units	Unit Cost
a. Beginning inventory	11	$200
b. New inventory purchases	9	220
c. Sales (selling price, $420)	8	?

Required:

1. Compute the following amounts, assuming the application of the FIFO and LIFO inventory costing methods:

	Ending Inventory		Cost of Goods Sold	
	Units	Dollars	Units	Dollars
FIFO				
LIFO				

2. Assuming that inventory cost was expected to follow current trends, which method would you suggest that Balent select to account for these inventory items? Explain your answer.

3. Assuming that other operating expenses were $500 and the income tax rate is 25 percent, prepare the income statement for the period using your selected method.

4. Compute the inventory turnover ratio for the current period using your selected method. What does it indicate?

SUGGESTED SOLUTION

1.

	Ending Inventory		Cost of Goods Sold	
	Units	**Dollars**	**Units**	**Dollars**
FIFO	12	$2,580	8	$1,600
LIFO	12	$2,420	8	$1,760

Computations

Beginning inventory (11 units × $200)	$2,200
+ Purchases (9 units × $220)	1,980
Goods available for sale	$4,180

FIFO inventory (costed at end of period)

Goods available for sale (from above)	$4,180
− Ending inventory (9 units × $220) + (3 units × $200)	2,580
Cost of goods sold (8 units × $200)	$1,600

LIFO inventory (costed at end of period)

Goods available for sale (from above)	$4,180
− Ending inventory (11 units × $200) + (1 unit × $220)	2,420
Cost of goods sold (8 units × $220)	$1,760

2. LIFO should be selected. Because costs are rising, LIFO produces higher cost of goods sold, lower pretax income, and lower income tax payments. It is used on the tax return and income statement because of the LIFO conformity rule.

3.

BALENT APPLIANCES
Statement of Income
Year Ended December 31, 2013

Sales	$3,360
Cost of goods sold	1,760
Gross profit	1,600
Other expenses	500
Income before income taxes	1,100
Income tax expense (25%)	275
Net income	$ 825

Computations

Sales = 8 × $420 = $3,360

4. Inventory turnover ratio = Cost of Goods Sold ÷   Average Inventory

$$= \quad \$1,760 \quad ÷ [(\$2,200 + \$2,420) ÷ 2 = \$2,310]$$
$$= \quad 0.76$$

The inventory turnover ratio reflects how many times average inventory was produced or purchased and sold during the period. Thus, Balent Appliances purchased and sold its average inventory less than one time during the year.

Chapter Supplement A

LIFO Liquidations

A LIFO LIQUIDATION is a sale of a lower-cost inventory item from beginning LIFO inventory.

When a LIFO company sells more inventory than it purchases or manufactures, items from beginning inventory become part of cost of goods sold. This is called a **LIFO liquidation.** When inventory costs are rising, these lower cost items in beginning inventory produce a higher gross profit, higher taxable income, and higher taxes when they are sold. We illustrate this process by continuing our Harley-Davidson Model A leather baseball jacket example into its second year.

Financial Statement Effects of LIFO Liquidations

Recall that, in its first year of operation, the store purchased units for $70, $80, and $100 in sequence. Then, the $100 unit and three of the $80 units were sold under LIFO, leaving one $80 unit and two $70 units in ending inventory. We will continue this illustration into a second year. The ending inventory from year 1 becomes the beginning inventory for year 2.

First, we assume that in year 2, the Harley-Davidson store purchases a total of **three** inventory units at the current $120 price, the sales price has been raised to $140, and **three** units are sold. Using LIFO, the units are allocated to ending inventory and cost of goods sold as follows.

Cost of Goods Sold Calculation (LIFO with three units purchased and three units sold)		
Beginning inventory	(2 units at $70 each and 1 unit at $80)	$220
+ Purchases	(3 units at $120 each)	360
Goods available for sale		580
− Ending inventory	(2 units at $70 each and 1 unit at $80)	220
Cost of goods sold	(3 units at $120 each)	$360

Given that revenue is $140 per unit, the gross profit on the three newly purchased units is 3 units × $20 = $60.

Now assume instead that the store purchases only *two* additional units at $120 each. Using LIFO, these two new $120 units and the old $80 unit would become cost of goods sold.

Cost of Goods Sold Calculation (LIFO with two units purchased and three units sold)		
Beginning inventory	(2 units at $70 each and 1 unit at $80)	$220
+ Purchases	(2 units at $120 each)	240
Goods available for sale		460
− Ending inventory	(2 units at $70 each)	140
Cost of goods sold	(2 units at $120 each and 1 unit at $80)	$320

Given that revenue is $140 per unit, the gross profit on the newly purchased units is 2 units × $20 = $40. Since the cost of the old unit is only $80, the gross profit on this one unit is $60 ($140 − $80) instead of $20, raising total gross profit to $100. The complete income statement effects are reflected below.

	No Liquidation (purchase 3 units)	Liquidation (purchase 2 units)
Effect on the Income Statement		
Sales	$420	$420
Cost of goods sold	360	320
Gross profit	60	100
Other expenses	48	48
Income before income taxes	12	52
Income tax expense (25%)	3	13
Net income	$ 9	$ 39

This $40 change is the **pretax effect of the LIFO liquidation.** Given the assumed tax rate of 25 percent, taxes paid are $10 (0.25 × $40) higher than if no liquidation had taken place.

In practice, LIFO liquidations and extra tax payments can be avoided even if purchases of additional inventory take place **after** the sale of the item it replaces. Tax law allows LIFO to be applied **as if** all purchases during an accounting period took place before any sales and cost of goods sold were recorded. Thus, temporary LIFO liquidations can be eliminated by purchasing additional inventory before year-end. Most companies apply LIFO in this manner.

Chapter Supplement B

FIFO and LIFO Cost of Goods Sold under Periodic versus Perpetual Inventory Systems

The purpose of this supplement is to compare the calculation of FIFO and LIFO cost of goods sold under a periodic versus a perpetual inventory system. As we noted in the chapter, calculations of FIFO cost of goods sold will always be the same under both systems. However, calculations of LIFO cost of goods sold will usually differ in a manner that causes the company to pay higher income taxes when inventory costs are rising if it uses the perpetual computation. Consider the following company purchase and sale data for the month of January. Note in the example, beginning inventory is 2,000 units, purchases are 14,000 units, and sales are 9,000 units.

	Units	Unit Cost
January 1 Beginning inventory	2,000	$20.60
January 5 Sold	1,000	
January 13 Purchased	6,000	22.00
January 17 Sold	3,000	
January 25 Purchased	8,000	25.10
January 27 Sold	5,000	

FIFO (First-in, First-out)

FIFO assumes that the oldest goods are the first ones sold. Using a **periodic inventory** calculation, the **9,000 oldest goods available during the month** would include the 2,000 in beginning inventory, the 6,000 purchased on January 13, and 1,000 of the units purchased January 25. Cost of goods sold would be calculated as follows:

Cost of Goods Sold

Units	Unit Cost	Total Cost
2,000	$20.60	$ 41,200
6,000	22.00	132,000
1,000	25.10	25,100
Total		$198,300

Using a **perpetual inventory** calculation, we would compute the cost of goods sold for each sale separately using the **oldest goods available at the time of each sale.**

Cost of Goods Sold

Date of Sale	Units	Unit Cost	Total Cost
Jan. 5	1,000	$20.60	$ 20,600
Jan. 17	1,000	20.60	20,600
	2,000	22.00	44,000
Jan. 27	4,000	22.00	88,000
	1,000	25.10	25,100
Total			$198,300

Note that cost of goods sold is $198,300 using both computations. This is true because the oldest goods available during the month are the same as the oldest goods available at the time of each sale. This will always be true.

LIFO (Last-in, First-out)

LIFO assumes that the newest goods are the first ones sold. Using a **periodic inventory** calculation, the 9,000 **newest goods available during the month** would include the 8,000 units purchased January 25 and 1,000 of the units purchased on January 13. Cost of goods sold would be calculated as follows:

Cost of Goods Sold		
Units	**Unit Cost**	**Total Cost**
8,000	$25.10	$200,800
1,000	22.00	22,000
Total		$222,800

Using a **perpetual inventory** calculation, we would compute the cost of goods sold for each sale separately using the **newest goods available at the time of each sale.**

Cost of Goods Sold			
Date of Sale	**Units**	**Unit Cost**	**Total Cost**
Jan. 5	1,000	$20.60	$ 20,600
Jan. 17	3,000	22.00	66,000
Jan. 27	5,000	25.10	125,500
Total			$212,100

Note that cost of goods sold is higher using the periodic computation. This is true because the newest goods available during the month are **not** the same as the newest goods available at the time of each sale. **When costs are rising, the periodic calculation will always produce the same or a higher value for cost of goods sold than the perpetual calculation.** In this case, the periodic calculation gives you a $10,700 higher value for cost of goods sold ($222,800 − $212,100). This higher value will result in a $10,700 lower amount for income before taxes. If the tax rate is 35 percent, the company would end up paying $3,745 less in taxes for the current year (.35 × $10,700).

Why You Won't See LIFO Perpetual Calculations in Practice

This added tax savings from the periodic calculation illustrated above is one of the two reasons you will rarely if ever see LIFO perpetual calculations in practice in medium- to large-sized companies. The other reason relates to the complexity and cost of the calculations. Even if a company's perpetual inventory information system is sophisticated enough to instantaneously record the arrival of new inventory, it is unlikely that it will have sufficient information concerning invoice pricing, returns, allowances, and discounts to instantaneously compute a unit cost for those goods. Also, consider the number of calculations of goods available for sale that would have to be made by a company that has numerous sales and purchases of many different inventory items. This makes it very costly or impossible for most companies to apply LIFO using a perpetual calculation. Instead, companies keep perpetual inventory records on a FIFO basis and then make an end-of-period adjusting entry using the periodic calculation to convert both inventory on the balance sheet and cost of goods sold on the income statement to a LIFO basis.

Chapter Supplement C

Additional Issues in Measuring Purchases

Purchase Returns and Allowances

PURCHASE RETURNS AND ALLOWANCES are a reduction in the cost of purchases associated with unsatisfactory goods.

Purchased goods may be returned to the vendor if they do not meet specifications, arrive in damaged condition, or are otherwise unsatisfactory. **Purchase returns and allowances** require a reduction in the cost of inventory purchases and the recording of a cash refund or a reduction in the liability to the vendor. For example, assume that Harley-Davidson returned to a supplier damaged harness boots that cost $1,000. The return would be recorded as follows:

Accounts payable (−L) (or Cash +A)   1,000
    Inventory (−A)   1,000

Assets		=	Liabilities		+	Stockholders' Equity
Inventory	−1,000		Accounts Payable	−1,000		

Purchase Discounts

Cash discounts must be accounted for by both the seller and the buyer (accounting by the seller was discussed in Chapter 6). When merchandise is bought on credit, terms such as 2/10, n/30 are sometimes specified. That is, if payment is made within 10 days from the date of purchase, a 2 percent cash discount known as the **purchase discount** is granted. If payment is not made within the discount period, the full invoice cost is due 30 days after the purchase.

Assume that on January 17, Harley-Davidson bought goods that had a $1,000 invoice price with terms 2/10, n/30. The purchase would be recorded as follows (using what is called the **gross method**):

A PURCHASE DISCOUNT is a cash discount received for prompt payment of an account.

Date of Purchase

Jan. 17   Inventory (+A)   1,000
              Accounts payable (+L)   1,000

Assets		=	Liabilities		+	Stockholders' Equity
Inventory	+1,000		Accounts Payable	+1,000		

Date of Payment, within the Discount Period

Jan. 26   Accounts payable (−L)   1,000
              Inventory (−A)   20
              Cash (−A)   980

Assets		=	Liabilities		+	Stockholders' Equity
Inventory	−20		Accounts Payable	−1,000		
Cash	−980					

If for any reason Harley-Davidson did not pay within the 10-day discount period, the following entry would be needed:

Date of Payment, after the Discount Period

Feb. 1   Accounts payable (−L)   1,000
             Cash (−A).   1,000

Assets		=	Liabilities		+	Stockholders' Equity
Cash	−1,000		Accounts Payable	−1,000		

CHAPTER **TAKE-AWAYS**

7-1. Apply the cost principle to identify the amounts that should be included in inventory and the expense matching principle to determine cost of goods sold for typical retailers, wholesalers, and manufacturers.   p. 329

Inventory should include all items owned that are held for resale. Costs flow into inventory when goods are purchased or manufactured. They flow out (as an expense) when they are sold or disposed of. In conformity with the expense matching principle, the total cost of the goods sold during the period must be matched with the sales revenue earned during the period. A company can keep track of the ending inventory and cost of goods sold for the period using (1) the perpetual inventory system, which is based on the maintenance of detailed and continuous inventory records, and (2) the periodic inventory system, which is based on a physical count of ending inventory and use of the cost of goods sold equation to determine cost of goods sold.

7-2. Report inventory and cost of goods sold using the four inventory costing methods.   p. 334

The chapter discussed four different inventory costing methods used to allocate costs between the units remaining in inventory and the units sold and their applications in different economic circumstances. The methods discussed were specific identification, FIFO, LIFO, and average cost. Each of the inventory costing methods conforms to GAAP. Public companies using LIFO must provide note disclosures that allow conversion of inventory and cost of goods sold to FIFO amounts. Remember that the cost flow assumption need not match the physical flow of inventory.

7-3. Decide when the use of different inventory costing methods is beneficial to a company.   p. 339

The selection of an inventory costing method is important because it will affect reported income, income tax expense (and hence cash flow), and the inventory valuation reported on the balance sheet. In a period of rising prices, FIFO normally results in a higher income and higher taxes than LIFO; in a period of falling prices, the opposite occurs. The choice of methods is normally made to minimize taxes.

7-4. Report inventory at the lower of cost or market (LCM).   p. 342

Ending inventory should be measured based on the lower of actual cost or replacement cost (LCM basis). This practice can have a major effect on the statements of companies facing declining costs. Damaged, obsolete, and out-of-season inventory should also be written down to their current estimated net realizable value if below cost. The LCM adjustment increases cost of goods sold, decreases income, and decreases reported inventory in the year of the write-down.

7-5. Evaluate inventory management using the inventory turnover ratio.   p. 343

The inventory turnover ratio measures the efficiency of inventory management. It reflects how many times average inventory was produced and sold during the period. Analysts and creditors watch this ratio because a sudden decline may mean that a company is facing an unexpected drop in demand for its products or is becoming sloppy in its production management.

7-6. Compare companies that use different inventory costing methods.   p. 344

These comparisons can be made by converting the LIFO company's statements to FIFO. Public companies using LIFO must disclose the differences between LIFO and FIFO values for beginning and ending inventory. These amounts are often called the LIFO reserve. The beginning LIFO reserve minus the ending LIFO reserve equals the difference in cost of goods sold under FIFO. Pretax income is affected by the same amount in the opposite direction. This amount times the tax rate is the tax effect.

7-7. Understand methods for controlling inventory, analyze the effects of inventory errors on financial statements, and analyze the effects of inventory on cash flows.   p. 347

Various control procedures can limit inventory theft or mismanagement. An error in the measurement of ending inventory affects cost of goods sold on the current period's income statement and ending inventory on the balance sheet. Because this year's ending inventory becomes next year's beginning inventory, it also affects cost of goods sold in the following period by the same amount but in the opposite direction. These relationships can be seen through the cost of goods sold equation (BI + P − EI = CGS). When a net **decrease in inventory** for the period occurs, sales are more than purchases; thus, the decrease must be **added** in computing cash flows from operations. When a net **increase in inventory** for the period occurs, sales are less than purchases; thus, the increase must be **subtracted** in computing cash flows from operations.

In this and previous chapters, we discussed the current assets of a business. These assets are critical to operations, but many of them do not directly produce value. In Chapter 8, we will discuss the noncurrent assets property, plant, and equipment; natural resources; and intangibles that are the elements of productive capacity. Many of the noncurrent assets produce value, such as a factory that manufactures cars. These assets present some interesting accounting problems because they benefit a number of accounting periods.

KEY **RATIO**

Inventory turnover ratio measures the efficiency of inventory management. It reflects how many times average inventory was produced and sold during the period (p. 343):

$$\text{Inventory Turnover} = \frac{\text{Cost of Goods Sold}}{\text{Average Inventory}}$$

FINDING **FINANCIAL INFORMATION**

Balance Sheet

Under Current Assets
   Inventories

Income Statement

Expenses
   Cost of goods sold

Statement of Cash Flows

Under Operating Activities (indirect method):
   Net income
     − increases in inventory
     + decreases in inventory
     + increases in accounts payable
     − decreases in accounts payable

Notes

Under Summary of Significant Accounting Policies:
   Description of management's choice of inventory accounting policy (FIFO, LIFO, LCM, etc.)

In Separate Note
   If not listed on balance sheet, components of inventory (merchandise, raw materials, work in progress, finished goods)
   If using LIFO, LIFO reserve (excess of FIFO over LIFO)

KEY **TERMS**

Average Cost Method   p. 337
Cost of Goods Sold Equation   p. 332
Direct Labor   p. 331
Factory Overhead   p. 331
Finished Goods Inventory   p. 329
First-In, First-Out (FIFO)
   Method   p. 335
Goods Available for Sale   p. 332

Inventory   p. 329
Last-In, First-Out (LIFO) Method   p. 336
LIFO Liquidation   p. 352
LIFO Reserve   p. 345
Lower of Cost or Market (LCM)   p. 342
Merchandise Inventory   p. 329
Net Realizable Value   p. 342
Periodic Inventory System   p. 334

Perpetual Inventory System   p. 334
Purchase Discount   p. 355
Purchase Returns and
   Allowances   p. 354
Raw Materials Inventory   p. 329
Replacement Cost   p. 342
Specific Identification Method   p. 335
Work in Process Inventory   p. 329

QUESTIONS

1. Why is inventory an important item to both internal (management) and external users of financial statements?
2. What are the general guidelines for deciding which items should be included in inventory?
3. Explain the application of the cost principle to an item in the ending inventory.
4. Define goods available for sale. How does it differ from cost of goods sold?
5. Define beginning inventory and ending inventory.
6. The chapter discussed four inventory costing methods. List the four methods and briefly explain each.
7. Explain how income can be manipulated when the specific identification inventory costing method is used.
8. Contrast the effects of LIFO versus FIFO on reported assets (i.e., the ending inventory) when (a) prices are rising and (b) prices are falling.
9. Contrast the income statement effect of LIFO versus FIFO (i.e., on pretax income) when (a) prices are rising and (b) prices are falling.
10. Contrast the effects of LIFO versus FIFO on cash outflow and inflow.
11. Explain briefly the application of the LCM concept to the ending inventory and its effect on the income statement and balance sheet when market is lower than cost.
12. When a perpetual inventory system is used, unit costs of the items sold are known at the date of each sale. In contrast, when a periodic inventory system is used, unit costs are known only at the end of the accounting period. Why are these statements correct?

MULTIPLE-CHOICE QUESTIONS

1. Consider the following information: ending inventory, $24,000; sales, $250,000; beginning inventory, $30,000; selling and administrative expenses, $70,000; and purchases, $90,000. What is cost of goods sold?
   a. $86,000   c. $96,000
   b. $94,000   d. $84,000
2. The inventory costing method selected by a company will affect
   a. The balance sheet.   c. The statement of retained earnings.
   b. The income statement.   d. All of the above.
3. Which of the following is **not** a component of the cost of inventory?
   a. Administrative overhead   c. Raw materials
   b. Direct labor   d. Factory overhead
4. Consider the following information: beginning inventory 10 units @ $20 per unit; first purchase 35 units @ $22 per unit; second purchase 40 units @ $24 per unit; 50 units were sold. What is cost of goods sold using the **FIFO** method of inventory costing?
   a. $1,090   c. $1,180
   b. $1,060   d. $1,200
5. Consider the following information: beginning inventory 10 units @ $20 per unit; first purchase 35 units @ $22 per unit; second purchase 40 units @ $24 per unit; 50 units were sold. What is cost of goods sold using the **LIFO** method of inventory costing?
   a. $1,090   c. $1,180
   b. $1,060   d. $1,200
6. An increasing inventory turnover ratio
   a. Indicates a longer time span between the ordering and receiving of inventory.
   b. Indicates a shorter time span between the ordering and receiving of inventory.
   c. Indicates a shorter time span between the purchase and sale of inventory.
   d. Indicates a longer time span between the purchase and sale of inventory.

7. If the ending balance in accounts payable decreases from one period to the next, which of the following is true?
   a. Cash payments to suppliers exceeded current period purchases.
   b. Cash payments to suppliers were less than current period purchases.
   c. Cash receipts from customers exceeded cash payments to suppliers.
   d. Cash receipts from customers exceeded current period purchases.

8. Which of the following regarding the lower of cost or market rule for inventory are true?
   (1) The lower of cost or market rule is an example of the historical cost principle.
   (2) When the replacement cost of inventory drops below the cost shown in the financial records, net income is reduced.
   (3) When the replacement cost of inventory drops below the cost shown in the financial records, total assets are reduced.
   a. (1)   c. (2) and (3)
   b. (2)   d. All three

9. Which inventory method provides a better matching of current costs with sales revenue on the income statement and outdated values for inventory on the balance sheet?
   a. FIFO   c. LIFO
   b. Average cost   d. Specific identification

10. Which of the following is false regarding a perpetual inventory system?
   a. Physical counts are not needed since records are maintained on a transaction-by-transaction basis.
   b. The balance in the inventory account is updated with each inventory purchase and sale transaction.
   c. Cost of goods sold is increased as sales are recorded.
   d. The account Purchases is not used as inventory is acquired.

For more practice with multiple-choice questions, go to the text website at **www.mhhe.com/libby8e**.

MINI-**EXERCISES**

Matching Inventory Items to Type of Business

M7-1
LO7-1

Match the type of inventory with the type of business in the following matrix:

	TYPE OF BUSINESS	
Type of Inventory	Merchandising	Manufacturing
Work in process		
Finished goods		
Merchandise		
Raw materials		

Recording the Cost of Purchases for a Merchandiser

M7-2
LO7-1

Select Apparel purchased 90 new shirts and recorded a total cost of $2,258 determined as follows:

Invoice cost	$1,800
Shipping charges	185
Import taxes and duties	165
Interest (6.0%) on $1,800 borrowed to finance the purchase	108
	$2,258

Required:
Make the needed corrections in this calculation. Give the journal entry(ies) to record this purchase in the correct amount, assuming a perpetual inventory system. Show computations.

M7-3

LO7-1

Identifying the Cost of Inventories for a Manufacturer

Operating costs incurred by a manufacturing company become either (1) part of the cost of inventory to be expensed as cost of goods sold at the time the finished goods are sold or (2) expenses at the time they are incurred. Indicate whether each of the following costs belongs in category (1) or (2).

____   *a.* Wages of factory workers
____   *b.* Costs of raw materials purchased
____   *c.* Sales salaries
____   *d.* Heat, light, and power for the factory building
____   *e.* Heat, light, and power for the headquarters office building

M7-4

LO7-1

JCPenney
Every Day Matters

Inferring Purchases Using the Cost of Goods Sold Equation

JCPenney Company, Inc., is a major retailer with department stores in all 50 states. The dominant portion of the company's business consists of providing merchandise and services to consumers through department stores that include catalog departments. In a recent annual report, JCPenney reported cost of goods sold of $11,042 million, ending inventory for the current year of $2,916 million, and ending inventory for the previous year of $3,213 million.

Required:
Is it possible to develop a reasonable estimate of the merchandise purchases for the year? If so, prepare the estimate; if not, explain why.

M7-5

LO7-2

Matching Financial Statement Effects to Inventory Costing Methods

Indicate whether the FIFO or LIFO inventory costing method normally produces each of the following effects under the listed circumstances.

a. Declining costs
   Highest net income _____
   Highest inventory _____
b. Rising costs
   Highest net income _____
   Highest inventory _____

M7-6

LO7-3

Matching Inventory Costing Method Choices to Company Circumstances

Indicate whether the FIFO or LIFO inventory costing method would normally be selected when inventory costs are rising. Explain why.

M7-7

LO7-4

Reporting Inventory under Lower of Cost or Market

Wood Company had the following inventory items on hand at the end of the year:

	Quantity	Cost per Item	Replacement Cost per Item
Item A	70	$110	$100
Item B	30	60	85

Computing the lower of cost or market on an item-by-item basis, determine what amount would be reported on the balance sheet for inventory.

M7-8

LO5

Determining the Effects of Inventory Management Changes on Inventory Turnover Ratio

Indicate the most likely effect of the following changes in inventory management on the inventory turnover ratio (use + for increase, − for decrease, and NE for no effect).

____   *a.* Have parts inventory delivered daily by suppliers instead of weekly.
____   *b.* Extend payments for inventory purchases from 15 days to 30 days.
____   *c.* Shorten production process from 10 days to 8 days.

Determining the Financial Statement Effects of Inventory Errors   **M7-9**
                                                                               LO7-7

Assume the 2014 ending inventory was understated by $50,000. Explain how this error would affect the 2014 and 2015 pretax income amounts. What would be the effects if the 2014 ending inventory were overstated by $50,000 instead of understated?

EXERCISES

Analyzing Items to Be Included in Inventory   **E7-1**
                                                           LO7-1

Based on its physical count of inventory in its warehouse at year-end, December 31, 2014, Madison Company planned to report inventory of $34,500. During the audit, the independent CPA developed the following additional information:

a. Goods from a supplier costing $700 are in transit with UPS on December 31, 2014. The terms are FOB shipping point (explained in the "Required" section). Because these goods had not yet arrived, they were excluded from the physical inventory count.
b. Madison delivered samples costing $1,800 to a customer on December 27, 2014, with the understanding that they would be returned to Madison on January 15, 2015. Because these goods were not on hand, they were excluded from the inventory count.
c. On December 31, 2014, goods in transit to customers, with terms FOB shipping point, amounted to $6,500 (expected delivery date January 10, 2015). Because the goods had been shipped, they were excluded from the physical inventory count.
d. On December 31, 2014, goods in transit to customers, with terms FOB destination, amounted to $1,500 (expected delivery date January 10, 2015). Because the goods had been shipped, they were excluded from the physical inventory count.

Required:
Madison's accounting policy requires including in inventory all goods for which it has title. Note that the point where title (ownership) changes hands is determined by the shipping terms in the sales contract. When goods are shipped "FOB shipping point," title changes hands at shipment and the buyer normally pays for shipping. When they are shipped "FOB destination," title changes hands on delivery, and the seller normally pays for shipping. Begin with the $34,500 inventory amount and compute the correct amount for the ending inventory. Explain the basis for your treatment of each of the preceding items. (**Hint:** Set up three columns: Item, Amount, and Explanation.)

Inferring Missing Amounts Based on Income Statement Relationships   **E7-2**
                                                                                LO7-1

Supply the missing dollar amounts for the income statement for each of the following independent cases. (**Hint:** In Case B, work from the bottom up.)

	Case A	Case B	Case C
Net sales revenue	$7,500	$?	$5,000
Beginning inventory	$11,200	$ 7,000	$ 4,000
Purchases	4,500	?	9,500
Goods available for sale	?	15,050	13,500
Ending inventory	9,000	11,050	?
Cost of goods sold	?	?	4,200
Gross profit	?	800	?
Expenses	300	?	700
Pretax income (loss)	$ 500	($200)	$ 100

Inferring Missing Amounts Based on Income Statement Relationships   **E7-3**
                                                                                LO7-1

Supply the missing dollar amounts for the income statement for each of the following independent cases:

Cases	Sales Revenue	Beginning Inventory	Purchases	Total Available	Ending Inventory	Cost of Goods Sold	Gross Profit	Expenses	Pretax Income (Loss)
A	$ 650	$100	$700	$?	$500	$?	$?	$200	$?
B	1,100	200	900	?	?	?	?	150	150
C	?	150	?	?	300	200	400	100	?
D	800	?	550	?	300	?	?	200	200
E	1,000	?	900	1,100	?	?	500	?	(50)

E7-4
LO7-1
Abercrombie and Fitch

Inferring Merchandise Purchases

Abercrombie and Fitch is a leading retailer of casual apparel for men, women, and children. Assume that you are employed as a stock analyst and your boss has just completed a review of the new Abercrombie annual report. She provided you with her notes, but they are missing some information that you need. Her notes show that the ending inventory for Abercrombie in the current year was $569,818,000 and in the previous year was $385,857,000. Net sales for the current year were $4,158,058,000. Cost of goods sold was $1,639,188,000. Net income was $127,658,000. For your analysis, you determine that you need to know the amount of purchases for the year.

Required:
Can you develop the information from her notes? Explain and show calculations. (**Hint:** Use the cost of goods sold equation or the inventory T-account to solve for the needed value.)

E7-5
LO7-2

Calculating Ending Inventory and Cost of Goods Sold under FIFO, LIFO, and Average Cost

Penn Company uses a periodic inventory system. At the end of the annual accounting period, December 31, 2015, the accounting records provided the following information for product 1:

	Units	Unit Cost
Inventory, December 31, 2014	2,000	$5
For the year 2015:		
Purchase, March 21	5,000	6
Purchase, August 1	3,000	8
Inventory, December 31, 2015	4,000	

Required:
Compute ending inventory and cost of goods sold under FIFO, LIFO, and average cost inventory costing methods. (**Hint:** Set up adjacent columns for each case.)

E7-6
LO7-2

Calculating Ending Inventory and Cost of Goods Sold under FIFO, LIFO, and Average Cost

Hamilton Company uses a periodic inventory system. At the end of the annual accounting period, December 31, 2015, the accounting records provided the following information for product 1:

	Units	Unit Cost
Inventory, December 31, 2014	2,000	$5
For the year 2015:		
Purchase, March 21	6,000	4
Purchase, August 1	4,000	2
Inventory, December 31, 2015	3,000	

Required:
Compute ending inventory and cost of goods sold under FIFO, LIFO, and average cost inventory costing methods. (**Hint:** Set up adjacent columns for each case.)

Analyzing and Interpreting the Financial Statement Effects of LIFO and FIFO

E7-7

LO7-2, 7-3

Broadhead Company uses a periodic inventory system. At the end of the annual accounting period, December 31, 2015, the accounting records provided the following information for product 2:

	Units	Unit Cost
Inventory, December 31, 2014	3,000	$ 9
For the year 2015:		
Purchase, April 11	9,000	10
Purchase, June 1	7,000	15
Sales ($50 each)	10,000	
Operating expenses (excluding income tax expense) $195,000		

Required:

1. Prepare a separate income statement through pretax income that details cost of goods sold for (*a*) Case A: FIFO and (*b*) Case B: LIFO. For each case, show the computation of the ending inventory and cost of good sold. (**Hint:** Set up adjacent columns for each case.)
2. Compare the pretax income and the ending inventory amounts between the two cases. Explain the similarities and differences.
3. Which inventory costing method may be preferred for income tax purposes? Explain.

Analyzing and Interpreting the Financial Statement Effects of LIFO and FIFO

E7-8

LO7-2, 7-3

Beck Inc. uses a periodic inventory system. At the end of the annual accounting period, December 31, 2015, the accounting records provided the following information for product 2:

	Units	Unit Cost
Inventory, December 31, 2014	7,000	$ 5
For the year 2015:		
Purchase, March 5	19,000	9
Purchase, September 19	10,000	11
Sale ($28 each)	8,000	
Sale ($30 each)	16,000	
Operating expenses (excluding income tax expense) $500,000		

Required:

1. Prepare a separate income statement through pretax income that details cost of goods sold for (*a*) Case A: FIFO and (*b*) Case B: LIFO. For each case, show the computation of the ending inventory and cost of good sold. (**Hint:** Set up adjacent columns for each case.)
2. Compare the pretax income and the ending inventory amounts between the two cases. Explain the similarities and differences.
3. Which inventory costing method may be preferred for income tax purposes? Explain.

Evaluating the Choice among Three Alternative Inventory Methods Based on Income and Cash Flow Effects

E7-9

LO7-2, 7-3

Daniel Company uses a periodic inventory system. Data for 2015: beginning merchandise inventory (December 31, 2014), 2,000 units at $38; purchases, 8,000 units at $40; expenses (excluding income taxes), $194,500; ending inventory per physical count at December 31, 2015, 1,800 units; sales, 8,200 units; sales price per unit, $75; and average income tax rate, 30 percent.

Required:

1. Compute cost of goods sold and prepare income statements under the FIFO, LIFO, and average cost inventory costing methods. Use a format similar to the following:

		INVENTORY COSTING METHOD		
Cost of Goods Sold	Units	FIFO	LIFO	Average Cost
Beginning inventory	_____	$_____	$_____	$_____
Purchases	_____	_____	_____	_____
Goods available for sale	_____	_____	_____	_____
Ending inventory	_____			
Cost of goods sold	_____	$_____	$_____	$_____

Income Statement	FIFO	LIFO	Average Cost
Sales revenue	$_____	$_____	$_____
Cost of goods sold	_____	_____	_____
Gross profit	_____	_____	_____
Expenses	_____	_____	_____
Pretax income	_____	_____	_____
Income tax expense	_____	_____	_____
Net income	$_____	$_____	$_____

2. Between FIFO and LIFO, which method is preferable in terms of (a) net income and (b) income taxes paid (cash flow)? Explain.

3. What would your answer to requirement (2) be, assuming that prices were falling? Explain.

E7-10

LO7-2, 7-3

Evaluating the Choice among Three Alternative Inventory Methods Based on Cash Flow Effects

Following is partial information for the income statement of Audio Solutions Company under three different inventory costing methods, assuming the use of a periodic inventory system:

	FIFO	LIFO	Average Cost
Cost of goods sold			
Beginning inventory (400 units)	$11,200	$11,200	$11,200
Purchases (475 units)	16,625	16,625	16,625
Goods available for sale			
Ending inventory (525 units)			
Cost of goods sold			$

Sales, 350 units; unit sales price, $50

Expenses, $1,700

Required:

1. Compute cost of goods sold under the FIFO, LIFO, and average cost inventory costing methods.

2. Prepare an income statement through pretax income for each method.

3. Rank the three methods in order of income taxes paid (favorable cash flow) and explain the basis for your ranking.

E7-11

LO7-4

Reporting Inventory at Lower of Cost or Market

Jones Company is preparing the annual financial statements dated December 31, 2015. Ending inventory information about the five major items stocked for regular sale follows:

		ENDING INVENTORY, 2015	
Item	Quantity on Hand	Unit Cost When Acquired (FIFO)	Replacement Cost (Market) at Year-End
A	50	$15	$12
B	80	30	40
C	10	48	52
D	70	25	30
E	350	10	5

Required:

Compute the valuation that should be used for the 2015 ending inventory using the LCM rule applied on an item-by-item basis. (**Hint:** Set up columns for Item, Quantity, Total Cost, Total Market, and LCM Valuation.)

Reporting Inventory at Lower of Cost or Market

Parson Company was formed on January 1, 2015, and is preparing the annual financial statements dated December 31, 2015. Ending inventory information about the four major items stocked for regular sale follows:

		ENDING INVENTORY, 2015	
Item	Quantity on Hand	Unit Cost When Acquired (FIFO)	Replacement Cost (Market) at Year-End
A	30	$20	$15
B	55	40	44
C	35	52	55
D	15	27	32

Required:

1. Compute the valuation that should be used for the 2015 ending inventory using the LCM rule applied on an item-by-item basis. (**Hint:** Set up columns for Item, Quantity, Total Cost, Total Market, and LCM Valuation.)
2. What will be the effect of the write-down of inventory to lower of cost or market on cost of goods sold for the year ended December 31, 2015?

Analyzing and Interpreting the Inventory Turnover Ratio

Dell Inc. is the leading manufacturer of personal computers. In a recent year, it reported the following in dollars in millions:

Net sales revenue	$62,071
Cost of sales	48,260
Beginning inventory	1,301
Ending inventory	1,404

Required:

1. Determine the inventory turnover ratio and average days to sell inventory for the current year.
2. Explain the meaning of each number.

Analyzing and Interpreting the Effects of the LIFO/FIFO Choice on Inventory Turnover Ratio

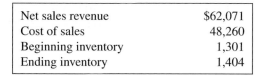

The records at the end of January 2015 for Young Company showed the following for a particular kind of merchandise:

Inventory, December 31, 2014, at FIFO: 19 Units @ $16 = $304
Inventory, December 31, 2014, at LIFO: 19 Units @ $12 = $228

Transactions	Units	Unit Cost	Total Cost
Purchase, January 9, 2015	25	$13	$325
Purchase, January 20, 2015	50	19	950
Sale, January 21, 2015 (at $38 per unit)	40		
Sale, January 27, 2015 (at $39 per unit)	25		

Required:

Compute the inventory turnover ratio under the FIFO and LIFO inventory costing methods (show computations and round to the nearest dollar). Which costing method is the more accurate indicator of the efficiency of inventory management? Explain.

E7-15

LO7-6

Analyzing Notes to Adjust Inventory from LIFO to FIFO

The following note was contained in a recent Ford Motor Company annual report:

NOTE 8. INVENTORIES—AUTOMOTIVE SECTOR		
Inventories at December 31 were as follows (dollars in millions)		
	Current Year	Previous Year
Raw material, work in process, & supplies	$2,847	$2,812
Finished products	3,982	3,970
Total inventories at FIFO	6,829	6,782
Less LIFO adjustment	(928)	(865)
Total	$5,901	$5,917
About one-third of inventories were determined under the last-in, first-out method.		

Required:

1. What amount of ending inventory would have been reported in the current year if Ford had used only FIFO?
2. The cost of goods sold reported by Ford for the current year was $113,345 million. Determine the cost of goods sold that would have been reported if Ford had used only FIFO for both years.
3. Explain why Ford management chose to use LIFO for certain of its inventories.

E7-16

LO7-7

Analyzing the Effects of an Error in Recording Purchases

Zocco Ski Company mistakenly recorded purchases of inventory on account received during the last week of December 2014 as purchases during January of 2015 (this is called a purchases cutoff error). Zocco uses a periodic inventory system, and ending inventory was correctly counted and reported each year.

Required:

Assuming that no correction was made in 2014 or 2015, indicate whether each of the following financial statement amounts will be understated, overstated, or correct.

1. Net Income for 2014.
2. Net Income for 2015.
3. Retained Earnings for December 31, 2014.
4. Retained Earnings for December 31, 2015.

E7-17

LO7-7

Analyzing the Effect of an Inventory Error Disclosed in an Actual Note to a Financial Statement

Several years ago, the financial statements of Gibson Greeting Cards, now part of American Greetings, contained the following note:

> On July 1, the Company announced that it had determined that the inventory . . . had been overstated. . . . The overstatement of inventory . . . was $8,806,000.

Gibson reported an incorrect net income amount of $25,852,000 for the year in which the error occurred and the income tax rate was 39.3 percent.

Required:

1. Compute the amount of net income that Gibson reported after correcting the inventory error. Show computations.
2. Assume that the inventory error was not discovered. Identify the financial statement accounts that would have been incorrect (*a*) for the year the error occurred and (*b*) for the subsequent year. State whether each account was understated or overstated.

Analyzing and Interpreting the Impact of an Inventory Error

Grants Corporation prepared the following two income statements (simplified for illustrative purposes):

E7-18

LO7-7

	First Quarter 2014		Second Quarter 2014	
Sales revenue		$11,000		$18,000
Cost of goods sold				
Beginning inventory	$4,000		$ 3,800	
Purchases	3,000		13,000	
Goods available for sale	7,000		16,800	
Ending inventory	3,800		9,000	
Cost of goods sold		3,200		7,800
Gross profit		7,800		10,200
Expenses		5,000		6,000
Pretax income		$ 2,800		$ 4,200

During the third quarter, it was discovered that the ending inventory for the first quarter should have been $4,400.

Required:
1. What effect did this error have on the combined pretax income of the two quarters? Explain.
2. Did this error affect the EPS amounts for each quarter? (See Chapter 5 for discussion of EPS.) Explain.
3. Prepare corrected income statements for each quarter.
4. Set up a schedule with the following headings to reflect the comparative effects of the correct and incorrect amounts on the income statement:

	1st Quarter			2nd Quarter		
Income Statement Item	Incorrect	Correct	Error	Incorrect	Correct	Error

Interpreting the Effect of Changes in Inventories and Accounts Payable on Cash Flow from Operations

In its recent annual report, PepsiCo included the following information in its balance sheets (dollars in millions):

E7-19

LO7-7

CONSOLIDATED BALANCE SHEETS		
	Current Year	Previous Year
. . .		
Inventories	$ 3,827	$ 3,372
. . .		
Accounts payable	11,757	10,923

Required:
Explain the effects of the changes in inventory and accounts payable on cash flow from operating activities for the current year.

(Supplement A) Analyzing the Effects of a Reduction in the Amount of LIFO Inventory

In its annual report, ConocoPhillips reported that the company decreased its inventory levels during 2011. ConocoPhillips's 2011 financial statements contain the following note:

E7-20

ConocoPhillips

> In 2011, a liquidation of LIFO inventory values increased net income attributable to ConocoPhillips $160 million, of which $155 million was attributable to the R&M segment.

Required:

1. Explain why the reduction in inventory quantity increased net income for ConocoPhillips.
2. If ConocoPhillips had used FIFO, would the reductions in inventory quantity during the two years have increased net income? Explain.

E7-21   **(Supplement B) FIFO and LIFO Cost of Goods Sold under Periodic versus Perpetual Inventory Systems**

Assume that a retailer's beginning inventory and purchases of a popular item during January included: (1) 300 units at $7 in beginning inventory on January 1, (2) 450 units at $8 purchased on January 8, and (3) 750 units at $9 purchased on January 29. The company sold 350 units on January 12 and 550 units on January 30.

Required:

1. Calculate the cost of goods sold for the month of January under (*a*) FIFO (periodic calculation), (b) FIFO (perpetual calculation), (c) LIFO (periodic calculation), and (d) LIFO (perpetual calculation).
2. Which cost flow assumption would you recommend to management and why? Which calculation approach, periodic or perpetual, would you recommend and why?

E7-22   **(Supplement C) Recording Sales and Purchases with Cash Discounts**

Scott's Cycles sells merchandise on credit terms of 2/15, n/30. A sale invoiced at $1,500 (cost of sales $975) was made to Shannon Allen on February 1, 2014. The company uses the gross method of recording sales discounts.

Required:

1. Give the journal entry to record the credit sale. Assume use of the perpetual inventory system.
2. Give the journal entry, assuming that the account was collected in full on February 9, 2014.
3. Give the journal entry, assuming, instead, that the account was collected in full on March 2, 2014.

On March 4, 2014, the company purchased bicycles and accessories from a supplier on credit, invoiced at $9,000; the terms were 3/10, n/30. The company uses the gross method to record purchases.

Required:

4. Give the journal entry to record the purchase on credit. Assume the use of the perpetual inventory system.
5. Give the journal entry, assuming that the account was paid in full on March 12, 2014.
6. Give the journal entry, assuming, instead, that the account was paid in full on March 28, 2014.

To practice with more exercises, go to the text website at **www.mhhe.com/libby8e**.

PROBLEMS

P7-1   **Analyzing Items to Be Included in Inventory**

LO7-1

Travis Company has just completed a physical inventory count at year-end, December 31, 2014. Only the items on the shelves, in storage, and in the receiving area were counted and costed on a FIFO basis. The inventory amounted to $80,000. During the audit, the independent CPA developed the following additional information:

a. Goods costing $900 were being used by a customer on a trial basis and were excluded from the inventory count at December 31, 2014.

b. Goods in transit on December 31, 2014, from a supplier, with terms FOB destination (explained in the "Required" section), cost $900. Because these goods had not yet arrived, they were excluded from the physical inventory count.

c. On December 31, 2014, goods in transit to customers, with terms FOB shipping point, amounted to $1,700 (expected delivery date January 10, 2015). Because the goods had been shipped, they were excluded from the physical inventory count.

d. On December 28, 2014, a customer purchased goods for cash amounting to $2,650 and left them "for pickup on January 3, 2015." Travis Company had paid $1,750 for the goods and, because they were on hand, included the latter amount in the physical inventory count.

e. On the date of the inventory count, the company received notice from a supplier that goods ordered earlier at a cost of $3,550 had been delivered to the transportation company on December 27, 2014; the terms were FOB shipping point. Because the shipment had not arrived by December 31, 2014, it was excluded from the physical inventory count.

f. On December 31, 2014, the company shipped $700 worth of goods to a customer, FOB destination. The goods are expected to arrive at their destination no earlier than January 8, 2015. Because the goods were not on hand, they were not included in the physical inventory count.

g. One of the items sold by the company has such a low volume that management planned to drop it last year. To induce Travis Company to continue carrying the item, the manufacturer-supplier provided the item on a "consignment basis." This means that the manufacturer-supplier retains ownership of the item, and Travis Company (the consignee) has no responsibility to pay for the items until they are sold to a customer. Each month, Travis Company sends a report to the manufacturer on the number sold and remits cash for the cost. At the end of December 2014, Travis Company had six of these items on hand; therefore, they were included in the physical inventory count at $950 each.

Required:

Assume that Travis's accounting policy requires including in inventory all goods for which it has title. Note that the point where title (ownership) changes hands is determined by the shipping terms in the sales contract. When goods are shipped "FOB shipping point," title changes hands at shipment and the buyer normally pays for shipping. When they are shipped "FOB destination," title changes hands on delivery, and the seller normally pays for shipping. Begin with the $80,000 inventory amount and compute the correct amount for the ending inventory. Explain the basis for your treatment of each of the preceding items. (**Hint:** Set up three columns: Item, Amount, and Explanation.)

Analyzing the Effects of Four Alternative Inventory Methods (AP7-1)

P7-2
LO7-2

Kirtland Corporation uses a periodic inventory system. At the end of the annual accounting period, December 31, 2015, the accounting records for the most popular item in inventory showed the following:

Transactions	Units	Unit Cost
Beginning inventory, January 1, 2015	400	$3.00
Transactions during 2015:		
a. Purchase, January 30	300	3.40
b. Purchase, May 1	460	4.00
c. Sale ($5 each)	(160)	
d. Sale ($5 each)	(700)	

Required:

Compute the amount of (a) goods available for sale, (b) ending inventory, and (c) cost of goods sold at December 31, 2015, under each of the following inventory costing methods (show computations and round to the nearest dollar):

1. Average cost (round the average cost per unit to the nearest cent).
2. First-in, first-out.
3. Last-in, first-out.
4. Specific identification, assuming that the first sale was selected two-fifths from the beginning inventory and three-fifths from the purchase of January 30, 2015. Assume that the second sale was selected from the remainder of the beginning inventory, with the balance from the purchase of May 1, 2015.

Evaluating Four Alternative Inventory Methods Based on Income and Cash Flow (AP7-2)

P7-3
LO7-2, 7-3

At the end of January 2014, the records of Donner Company showed the following for a particular item that sold at $16 per unit:

Transactions	Units	Amount
Inventory, January 1, 2014	500	$2,365
Purchase, January 12	600	3,600
Purchase, January 26	160	1,280
Sale	(370)	
Sale	(250)	

Required:

1. Assuming the use of a periodic inventory system, prepare a summarized income statement through gross profit for the month of January under each method of inventory: (*a*) average cost, (*b*) FIFO, (*c*) LIFO, and (*d*) specific identification. For specific identification, assume that the first sale was selected from the beginning inventory and the second sale was selected from the January 12 purchase. Round the average cost per unit to the nearest cent. Show the inventory computations in detail.

2. Of FIFO and LIFO, which method would result in the higher pretax income? Which would result in the higher EPS?

3. Of FIFO and LIFO, which method would result in the lower income tax expense? Explain, assuming a 30 percent average tax rate.

4. Of FIFO and LIFO, which method would produce the more favorable cash flow? Explain.

P7-4

LO7-2, 7-3

Analyzing and Interpreting Income Manipulation under the LIFO Inventory Method

Pacific Company sells electronic test equipment that it acquires from a foreign source. During the year 2014, the inventory records reflected the following:

	Units	Unit Cost	Total Cost
Beginning inventory	20	$12,000	$240,000
Purchases	42	10,000	420,000
Sales (47 units at $24,500 each)			

Inventory is valued at cost using the LIFO inventory method.

Required:

1. Complete the following income statement summary using the LIFO method and the periodic inventory system (show computations):

Sales revenue	$_____
Cost of goods sold	_____
Gross profit	_____
Expenses	300,000
Pretax income	$_____
Ending inventory	$_____

2. The management, for various reasons, is considering buying 20 additional units before December 31, 2014, at $9,000 each. Restate the income statement (and ending inventory), assuming that this purchase is made on December 31, 2014.

3. How much did pretax income change because of the decision on December 31, 2014? Assuming that the unit cost of test equipment is expected to continue to decline in 2015, is there any evidence of income manipulation? Explain.

P7-5

LO7-2, 7-3

www.mhhe.com/libby8e

Evaluating the LIFO and FIFO Choice When Costs Are Rising and Falling (AP7-3)

Income is to be evaluated under four different situations as follows:

a. Prices are rising:
   (1) Situation A: FIFO is used.
   (2) Situation B: LIFO is used.
b. Prices are falling:
   (1) Situation C: FIFO is used.
   (2) Situation D: LIFO is used.

The basic data common to all four situations are: sales, 500 units for $15,000; beginning inventory, 300 units; purchases, 400 units; ending inventory, 200 units; and operating expenses, $4,000. The following tabulated income statements for each situation have been set up for analytical purposes:

	PRICES RISING		PRICES FALLING	
	Situation A FIFO	Situation B LIFO	Situation C FIFO	Situation D LIFO
Sales revenue	$15,000	$15,000	$15,000	$15,000
Cost of goods sold:				
Beginning inventory	3,300	?	?	?
Purchases	4,800	?	?	?
Goods available for sale	8,100	?	?	?
Ending inventory	2,400	?	?	?
Cost of goods sold	5,700	?	?	?
Gross profit	9,300	?	?	?
Expenses	4,000	4,000	4,000	4,000
Pretax income	5,300	?	?	?
Income tax expense (30%)	1,590	?	?	?
Net income	$ 3,710			

Required:

1. Complete the preceding tabulation for each situation. In Situations A and B (prices rising), assume the following: beginning inventory, 300 units at $11 = $3,300; purchases, 400 units at $12 = $4,800. In Situations C and D (prices falling), assume the opposite; that is, beginning inventory, 300 units at $12 = $3,600; purchases, 400 units at $11 = $4,400. Use periodic inventory procedures.
2. Analyze the relative effects on pretax income and on net income as demonstrated by requirement (1) when prices are rising and when prices are falling.
3. Analyze the relative effects on the cash position for each situation.
4. Would you recommend FIFO or LIFO? Explain.

Evaluating the Income Statement and Cash Flow Effects of Lower of Cost or Market

P7-6
LO7-4

Jaffa Company prepared its annual financial statements dated December 31, 2014. The company applies the FIFO inventory costing method; however, the company neglected to apply LCM to the ending inventory. The preliminary 2014 income statement follows:

Sales revenue		$300,000
Cost of goods sold		
Beginning inventory	$ 33,000	
Purchases	184,000	
Goods available for sale	217,000	
Ending inventory (FIFO cost)	50,450	
Cost of goods sold		166,550
Gross profit		133,450
Operating expenses		62,000
Pretax income		71,450
Income tax expense (30%)		21,435
Net income		$ 50,015

Assume that you have been asked to restate the 2014 financial statements to incorporate LCM. You have developed the following data relating to the 2014 ending inventory:

Item	Quantity	Acquisition Cost Unit	Acquisition Cost Total	Current Replacement Unit Cost (Market)
A	3,050	$3	$ 9,150	$4
B	1,500	5.5	8,250	3.5
C	7,100	1.5	10,650	3.5
D	3,200	7	22,400	4
			$50,450	

Required:

1. Restate this income statement to reflect LCM valuation of the 2014 ending inventory. Apply LCM on an item-by-item basis and show computations.
2. Compare and explain the LCM effect on each amount that was changed on the income statement in requirement (1).
3. What is the conceptual basis for applying LCM to merchandise inventories?
4. Thought question: What effect did LCM have on the 2014 cash flow? What will be the long-term effect on cash flow?

P7-7
LO7-5, 7-7

www.mhhe.com/libby8e

Evaluating the Effects of Manufacturing Changes on Inventory Turnover Ratio and Cash Flows from Operating Activities

Mears and Company has been operating for five years as an electronics component manufacturer specializing in cellular phone components. During this period, it has experienced rapid growth in sales revenue and in inventory. Mr. Mears and his associates have hired you as its first corporate controller. You have put into place new purchasing and manufacturing procedures that are expected to reduce inventories by approximately one-third by year-end. You have gathered the following data related to the changes:

(dollars in thousands)	Beginning of Year	End of Year (projected)
Inventory	$582,500	$384,610
		Current Year (projected)
Cost of goods sold		$7,283,566

Required:

1. Compute the inventory turnover ratio based on two different assumptions:
   a. Those presented in the preceding table (a decrease in the balance in inventory).
   b. No change from the beginning-of-the-year inventory balance.
2. Compute the effect of the projected change in the balance in inventory on cash flow from operating activities for the year (the sign and amount of effect).
3. On the basis of the preceding analysis, write a brief memo explaining how an increase in inventory turnover can result in an increase in cash flow from operating activities. Also explain how this increase can benefit the company.

P7-8
LO7-6

Evaluating the Choice between LIFO and FIFO Based on an Inventory Note

An annual report for International Paper Company included the following note:

> The last-in, first-out inventory method is used to value most of International Paper's U.S. inventories . . . If the first-in, first-out method had been used, it would have increased total inventory balances by approximately $350 million and $334 million at December 31, 2011 and 2010, respectively.

For the year 2011, International Paper Company reported net income (after taxes) of $1,341 million. At December 31, 2011, the balance of International Paper Company's retained earnings account was $3,330 million.

Required:
1. Determine the amount of net income that International Paper would have reported in 2011 if it had used the FIFO method (assume a 30 percent tax rate).
2. Determine the amount of retained earnings that International Paper would have reported at the end of 2011 if it always had used the FIFO method (assume a 30 percent tax rate).
3. Use of the LIFO method reduced the amount of taxes that International Paper had to pay in 2011 compared with the amount that would have been paid if International Paper had used FIFO. Calculate the amount of this reduction (assume a 30 percent tax rate).

Analyzing and Interpreting the Effects of Inventory Errors (AP7-4)

The income statement for Pruitt Company summarized for a four-year period shows the following:

	2014	2015	2016	2017
Sales revenue	$2,025,000	$2,450,000	$2,700,000	$2,975,000
Cost of goods sold	1,505,000	1,627,000	1,782,000	2,113,000
Gross profit	520,000	823,000	918,000	862,000
Expenses	490,000	513,000	538,000	542,000
Pretax income	30,000	310,000	380,000	320,000
Income tax expense (30%)	9,000	93,000	114,000	96,000
Net income	$ 21,000	$ 217,000	$ 266,000	$ 224,000

An audit revealed that in determining these amounts, the ending inventory for 2015 was overstated by $18,000. The company uses a periodic inventory system.

Required:
1. Recast the income statements to reflect the correct amounts, taking into consideration the inventory error.
2. Compute the gross profit percentage for each year (*a*) before the correction and (*b*) after the correction.
3. What effect would the error have had on the income tax expense assuming a 30 percent average rate?

(Supplement A) Analyzing LIFO and FIFO When Inventory Quantities Decline Based on an Actual Note

In a recent annual report, General Electric reported the following in its inventory note:

December 31 (dollars in millions)	Current Year	Prior Year
Raw materials and work in progress	$5,603	$5,515
Finished goods	2,863	2,546
Unbilled shipments	246	280
	8,712	8,341
Less revaluation to LIFO	(2,226)	(2,076)
LIFO value of inventories	$6,486	$6,265

It also reported a $23 million change in cost of goods sold due to "lower inventory levels."

Required:
1. Compute the increase or decrease in the pretax operating profit (loss) that would have been reported for the current year had GE employed FIFO accounting for all inventory for both years.
2. Compute the increase or decrease in pretax operating profit that would have been reported had GE employed LIFO but not reduced inventory quantities during the current year.

P7-9
LO7-7

www.mhhe.com/libby8e

P7-10

ALTERNATE PROBLEMS

AP7-1

LO7-2

Analyzing the Effects of Four Alternative Inventory Methods (P7-2)

Dixon Company uses a periodic inventory system. At the end of the annual accounting period, December 31, 2014, the accounting records for the most popular item in inventory showed the following:

Transactions	Units	Unit Cost
Beginning inventory, January 1, 2014	390	$32.00
Transactions during 2014:		
a. Purchase, February 20	700	34.25
b. Purchase, June 30	460	37.00
c. Sale ($50 each)	(70)	
d. Sale ($50 each)	(750)	

Required:

Compute the cost of (a) goods available for sale, (b) ending inventory, and (c) goods sold at December 31, 2014, under each of the following inventory costing methods (show computations and round to the nearest dollar):

1. Average cost (round average cost per unit to the nearest cent).
2. First-in, first-out.
3. Last-in, first-out.
4. Specific identification, assuming that the first sale was selected two-fifths from the beginning inventory and three-fifths from the purchase of February 20, 2014. Assume that the second sale was selected from the remainder of the beginning inventory, with the balance from the purchase of June 30, 2014.

AP7-2

LO7-2, 7-3

Evaluating Four Alternative Inventory Methods Based on Income and Cash Flow (P7-3)

At the end of January 2015, the records of NewRidge Company showed the following for a particular item that sold at $16 per unit:

Transactions	Units	Amount
Inventory, January 1, 2015	120	$ 960
Purchase, January 12	380	3,420
Purchase, January 26	200	2,200
Sale	(100)	
Sale	(140)	

Required:

1. Assuming the use of a periodic inventory system, prepare a summarized income statement through gross profit for January 2015 under each method of inventory: (a) weighted average cost, (b) FIFO, (c) LIFO, and (d) specific identification. For specific identification, assume that the first sale was selected from the beginning inventory and the second sale was selected from the January 12 purchase. Show the inventory computations (including for ending inventory) in detail.
2. Of FIFO and LIFO, which method would result in the higher pretax income? Which would result in the higher EPS?
3. Of FIFO and LIFO, which method would result in the lower income tax expense? Explain, assuming a 30 percent average tax rate.
4. Of FIFO and LIFO, which method would produce the more favorable cash flow? Explain.

AP7-3

LO7-2, 7-3

Evaluating the LIFO and FIFO Choice When Costs Are Rising and Falling (P7-5)

Income is to be evaluated under four different situations as follows:

a. Prices are rising:
(1) Situation A: FIFO is used.
(2) Situation B: LIFO is used.
b. Prices are falling:
(1) Situation C: FIFO is used.
(2) Situation D: LIFO is used.

The basic data common to all four situations are: sales, 510 units for $13,260; beginning inventory, 340 units; purchases, 410 units; ending inventory, 240 units; and operating expenses, $5,000. The following tabulated income statements for each situation have been set up for analytical purposes:

| | PRICES RISING | | PRICES FALLING | |
	Situation A FIFO	Situation B LIFO	Situation C FIFO	Situation D LIFO
Sales revenue	$13,260	$13,260	$13,260	$13,260
Cost of goods sold:				
Beginning inventory	3,060	?	?	?
Purchases	4,100	?	?	?
Goods available for sale	7,160	?	?	?
Ending inventory	2,400	?	?	?
Cost of goods sold	4,760	?	?	?
Gross profit	8,500	?	?	?
Expenses	5,000	5,000	5,000	5,000
Pretax income	3,500	?	?	?
Income tax expense (30%)	1,050	?	?	?
Net income	$ 2,450			

Required:

1. Complete the preceding tabulation for each situation. In Situations A and B (prices rising), assume the following: beginning inventory, 340 units at $9 = $3,060; purchases, 410 units at $10 = $4,100. In Situations C and D (prices falling), assume the opposite; that is, beginning inventory, 340 units at $10 = $3,400; purchases, 410 units at $9 = $3,690. Use periodic inventory procedures.
2. Analyze the relative effects on pretax income and on net income as demonstrated by requirement (1) when prices are rising and when prices are falling.
3. Analyze the relative effects on the cash position for each situation.
4. Would you recommend FIFO or LIFO? Explain.

Analyzing and Interpreting the Effects of Inventory Errors (P7-9)

AP7-4
LO7-7

The income statements for four consecutive years for Colca Company reflected the following summarized amounts:

	2014	2015	2016	2017
Sales revenue	$60,000	$63,000	$65,000	$68,000
Cost of goods sold	39,000	43,000	44,000	46,000
Gross profit	21,000	20,000	21,000	22,000
Expenses	16,000	17,000	17,000	19,000
Pretax income	$ 5,000	$ 3,000	$ 4,000	$ 3,000

Subsequent to development of these amounts, it has been determined that the physical inventory taken on December 31, 2015, was understated by $2,000.

Required:

1. Recast the income statements to reflect the correct amounts, taking into consideration the inventory error.
2. Compute the gross profit percentage for each year (*a*) before the correction and (*b*) after the correction.
3. What effect would the error have had on the income tax expense, assuming a 30 percent average rate?

CASES AND PROJECTS

Annual Report Cases

CP7-1

LO7-1, 7-2, 7-5

AMERICAN EAGLE
OUTFITTERS, INC.

Finding Financial Information

Refer to the financial statements of American Eagle Outfitters given in Appendix B at the end of this book.

Required:
1. How much inventory does the company hold at the end of the most recent year?
2. Estimate the amount of merchandise that the company purchased during the current year. (**Hint:** Use the cost of goods sold equation and ignore "certain buying, occupancy, and warehousing expenses.")
3. What method does the company use to determine the cost of its inventory?
4. Compute the inventory turnover ratio for the current year. What does an inventory turnover ratio tell you?

CP7-2

LO7-2, 7-4, 7-5, 7-7

URBAN OUTFITTERS INC.

Finding Financial Information

Refer to the financial statements of Urban Outfitters given in Appendix C at the end of this book.

Required:
1. The company uses lower of cost or market to account for its inventory. At the end of the year, do you expect the company to write its inventory down to replacement cost or net realizable value? Explain your answer.
2. What method does the company use to determine the cost of its inventory?
3. If the company overstated ending inventory by $10 million for the year ended January 31, 2012, what would be the corrected value for Income before Income Taxes?
4. Compute the inventory turnover ratio for the current year. What does an inventory turnover ratio tell you?

CP7-3

LO7-5

AMERICAN EAGLE
OUTFITTERS, INC.

URBAN OUTFITTERS INC.

www.mhhe.com/libby8e

Comparing Companies within an Industry

Refer to the financial statements of American Eagle Outfitters (Appendix B) and Urban Outfitters (Appendix C) and the Industry Ratio Report (Appendix D) at the end of this book.

Required:
1. Compute the inventory turnover ratio for both companies for the current year. What do you infer from the difference?
2. Compare the inventory turnover ratio for both companies to the industry average. Are these two companies doing better or worse than the industry average in turning over their inventory?

Financial Reporting and Analysis Cases

Using Financial Reports: Interpreting the Effect of Charging Costs to Inventory as Opposed to Current Operating Expenses

CP7-4

LO7-1

Dana Holding Corporation designs and manufactures component parts for the vehicular, industrial, and mobile off-highway original equipment markets. In a recent annual report, Dana's inventory note indicated the following:

> Dana changed its method of accounting for inventories effective January 1 . . . to include in inventory certain production-related costs previously charged to expense. This change in accounting principle resulted in a better matching of costs against related revenues. The effect of this change in accounting increased inventories by $23.0 and net income by $12.9.

Required:

1. Under Dana's previous accounting method, certain production costs were recognized as expenses on the income statement in the period they were incurred. When will they be recognized under the new accounting method?
2. Explain how including these costs in inventory increased both inventories and net income for the year.

Using Financial Reports: Interpreting Effects of the LIFO/FIFO Choice on Inventory Turnover

CP7-5

LO7-5, 7-6

Caterpillar

In its annual report, Caterpillar, Inc., a major manufacturer of farm and construction equipment, reported the following information concerning its inventories:

> Inventories are stated at the lower of cost or market. Cost is principally determined using the last-in, first-out (LIFO) method. The value of inventories on the LIFO basis represented about 65% of total inventories at December 31, 2011, and about 70% of total inventories at December 31, 2010 and 2009.
>
> If the FIFO (first-in, first-out) method had been in use, inventories would have been $2,422 million, $2,575 million, and $3,022 million higher than reported at December 31, 2011, 2010, and 2009, respectively.

On its balance sheet, Caterpillar reported:

	2011	2010	2009
Inventories	$14,544	$9,587	$6,360

	2011	2010	2009
Cost of goods sold	$43,578	$30,367	$23,886

Required:

As a recently hired financial analyst, you have been asked to analyze the efficiency with which Caterpillar has been managing its inventory and to write a short report. Specifically, you have been asked to compute inventory turnover for 2011 based on FIFO and LIFO and to compare the two ratios with two standards: (1) Caterpillar for the prior year 2010 and (2) its chief competitor, John Deere. For 2011, John Deere's inventory turnover was 4.2 based on FIFO and 5.9 based on LIFO. In your report, include:

1. The appropriate ratios computed based on FIFO and LIFO.
2. An explanation of the differences in the ratios across the FIFO and LIFO methods.
3. An explanation of whether the FIFO or LIFO ratios provide a more accurate representation of the companies' efficiency in use of inventory.

Critical Thinking Cases

Making a Decision as a Financial Analyst: Analysis of the Effect of a Change to LIFO

CP7-6

LO7-6

Seneca Foods

A press release for Seneca Foods (licensee of the Libby's brand of canned fruits and vegetables) included the following information:

> The current year's net earnings were $8,019,000 or $0.65 per diluted share, compared with $32,067,000 or $2.63 per diluted share, last year. These results reflect the Company's decision to implement the LIFO (last-in, first-out) inventory valuation method effective December 30, 2007 (fourth quarter). The effect of this change was to reduce annual pre-tax earnings by $28,165,000 and net earnings by $18,307,000 or $1.50 per share ($1.49 diluted) below that which would have been reported using the Company's previous inventory method. The Company believes that in this period of significant inflation, the use of the LIFO method better matches current costs with current revenues. This change also results in cash savings of $9,858,000 by reducing the Company's income taxes, based on

statutory rates. If the Company had remained on the FIFO (first-in, first-out) inventory valuation method, the pretax results, less non-operating gains and losses, would have been an all-time record of $42,644,000, up from $40,009,000 in the prior year.

Required:

As a new financial analyst at a leading Wall Street investment banking firm, you are assigned to write a memo outlining the effects of the accounting change on Seneca's financial statements. Assume a 35 percent tax rate. In your report, be sure to include the following:

1. Why did management adopt LIFO?
2. By how much did the change affect pretax earnings and ending inventory? Verify that the amount of the tax savings listed in the press release is correct.
3. As an analyst, how would you react to the decrease in income caused by the adoption of LIFO? Consider all of the information in the press release.

CP7-7

Micro Warehouse

Evaluating an Ethical Dilemma: Earnings, Inventory Purchases, and Management Bonuses

Micro Warehouse was a computer software and hardware online and catalog sales company.* A *Wall Street Journal* article disclosed the following:

MICRO WAREHOUSE IS REORGANIZING TOP MANAGEMENT

Micro Warehouse Inc. announced a "significant reorganization" of its management, including the resignation of three senior executives. The move comes just a few weeks after the Norwalk, Conn., computer catalogue sales company said it overstated earnings by $28 million since 1992 as a result of accounting irregularities. That previous disclosure prompted a flurry of shareholder lawsuits against the company. In addition, Micro Warehouse said it is cooperating with an "informal inquiry" by the Securities and Exchange Commission.

Source: Stephan E. Frank, *The Wall Street Journal*, November 21, 1996, p. B2.

Its Form 10-Q quarterly report filed with the Securities and Exchange Commission two days before indicated that inaccuracies involving understatement of purchases and accounts payable in current and prior periods amounted to $47.3 million. It also indicated that, as a result, $2.2 million of executive bonuses for 1995 would be rescinded. Micro Warehouse's total tax rate is approximately 40.4 percent. Both cost of goods sold and executive bonuses are fully deductible for tax purposes.

Required:

As a new staff member at Micro Warehouse's auditing firm, you are assigned to write a memo outlining the effects of the understatement of purchases and the rescinding of the bonuses. In your report, be sure to include the following:

1. The total effect on pretax and after-tax earnings of the understatement of purchases.
2. The total effect on pretax and after-tax earnings of the rescinding of the bonuses.
3. An estimate of the percentage of after-tax earnings management is receiving in bonuses.
4. A discussion of why Micro Warehouse's board of directors may have decided to tie managers' compensation to reported earnings and the possible relation between this type of bonus scheme and the accounting errors.

*Micro Warehouse declared bankruptcy in 2003.

Financial Reporting and Analysis Team Project

CP7-8

LO7-2, 7-3, 7-5, 7-7

Team Project: Analyzing Inventories

As a team, select an industry to analyze. *Yahoo!Finance* provides lists of industries at biz.yahoo.com/p/industries.html. Click on an industry for a list of companies in that industry. Alternatively, go to Google Finance at www.google.com/finance and search for a company you are interested in. You will be presented with a list including that company and its competitors. Each team member should acquire the annual report or 10-K for one publicly traded company in the industry, with each member selecting a different company (the SEC EDGAR service at www.sec.gov or the company's investor relations website itself are good sources).

Required:

On an individual basis, each team member should write a short report answering the following questions about the selected company. Discuss any patterns across the companies that you as a team observe. Then, as a team, write a short report comparing and contrasting your companies.

1. If your company lists inventories in its balance sheet, what percentage is it of total assets for each of the last three years? If your company does not list inventories, discuss why this is so.
2. If your company lists inventories, what inventory costing method is applied to U.S. inventories?
   a. What do you think motivated this choice?
   b. If the company uses LIFO, how much higher or lower would net income before taxes be if it had used FIFO or a similar method instead?
3. Ratio Analysis:
   a. What does the inventory turnover ratio measure in general?
   b. If your company reports inventories, compute the ratio for the last three years.
   c. What do your results suggest about the company?
   d. If available, find the industry ratio for the most recent year, compare it to your results, and discuss why you believe your company differs or is similar to the industry ratio.
4. What is the effect of the change in inventories on cash flows from operating activities for the most recent year (that is, did the change increase or decrease operating cash flows)? Explain your answer.

Evaluating the Choice of Inventory Method When Costs Are Rising and Falling

CC7-1

≋POOLCORP

Pool Corporation, Inc., reported in its recent annual report that "In 2010, our industry experienced some price deflation. . . . In 2011, our industry experienced more normalized price inflation of approximately 2% overall despite price deflation for certain chemical products." This suggests that in some years Pool's overall inventory costs rise, and in some years they fall. Furthermore, in many years, the costs of some inventory items rise while others fall. Assume that Pool has only two product items in its inventory this year. Purchase and sale data are presented below.

Transaction	Inventory Item A		Inventory Item B	
	Units	Unit Cost	Units	Unit Cost
Beginning inventory	40	$6	40	$6
Purchases, February 7	80	8	80	5
Purchases, March 16	100	9	100	3
Sales, April 28	160		160	

Required:

1. Compute cost of goods sold for each of the two items separately using the FIFO and LIFO inventory costing methods.
2. Between FIFO and LIFO, which method is preferable in terms of (*a*) net income and (*b*) income taxes paid (cash flow)? Answer the question for each item separately. Explain.

Reporting and Interpreting Property, Plant, and Equipment; Intangibles; and Natural Resources

As of December 31, 2011, Southwest Airlines operated 610 Boeing 737 aircraft and 88 Boeing 717 aircraft, providing service to 73 domestic cities in 38 states, and was the largest U.S. air carrier in number of originating passengers boarded and number of scheduled domestic departures. Southwest is a capital-intensive company with more than $12 billion in property, plant, and equipment reported on its balance sheet. In fiscal year 2011, Southwest spent $968 million on aircraft and other flight equipment as well as ground equipment. Since the demand for air travel is seasonal, with peak demand occurring during the summer months, planning for optimal productive capacity in the airline industry is very

Learning Objectives

After studying this chapter, you should be able to:

8-1 Define, classify, and explain the nature of long-lived productive assets and interpret the fixed asset turnover ratio. p. 383

8-2 Apply the cost principle to measure the acquisition and maintenance of property, plant, and equipment. p. 384

8-3 Apply various cost allocation methods as assets are held and used over time. p. 390

8-4 Explain the effect of asset impairment on the financial statements. p. 401

8-5 Analyze the disposal of property, plant, and equipment. p. 402

8-6 Apply measurement and reporting concepts for intangible assets and natural resources. p. 404

8-7 Explain how the acquisition, use, and disposal of long-lived assets impact cash flows. p. 410

difficult. Southwest's managers must determine how many aircraft are needed in which cities at what points in time to fill all seats demanded. Otherwise, the company loses revenue (not enough seats) or incurs higher costs (too many seats).

Demand is also highly sensitive to general economic conditions and other events beyond the control of the company. Even the best corporate planners could not have predicted the September 11, 2001, terrorist attacks against the United States that rocked the airline industry. The war in Iraq led to further declines in the demand for air travel. In response to the precipitous drop in demand, many airlines accelerated retirement of various aircraft, temporarily grounded aircraft, and considered delaying the purchase of new aircraft. Then, a worsening global economic environment provided more challenges for the airline industry. With fuel prices more than tripling between 2000 and 2011, many carriers were forced to reduce capacity.

UNDERSTANDING THE BUSINESS

One of the major challenges managers of most businesses face is forecasting the company's long-term productive capacity—that is, predicting the amount of plant and equipment it will need. If managers underestimate the need, the company will not be able to produce enough goods or services to meet demand and will miss an opportunity to earn revenue. On the other hand, if they overestimate the need, the company will incur excessive costs that will reduce its profitability.

The airline industry provides an outstanding example of the difficulty of planning for and analyzing productive capacity. If an airplane takes off from Kansas City, Missouri, en route to New York City with empty seats, the economic value associated with those seats is lost for that flight. There is obviously no way to sell the seat to a customer after the airplane has left the gate. Unlike a manufacturer, an airline cannot "inventory" seats for the future.

Likewise, if an unexpectedly large number of people want to board a flight, the airline must turn away some customers. You might be willing to buy a television set from Sears even if you had to wait one week for delivery, but you probably wouldn't book a flight home on Thanksgiving weekend on an airline that told you no seats were available. You would simply pick another airline or use a different mode of transportation.

Southwest has a number of large competitors with familiar names such as American, United Continental, JetBlue, and Delta. Southwest's 10-K report mentions that the company "currently competes with other airlines on almost all of its routes . . . Some of these airlines have larger fleets than Southwest and some may have wider name recognition in certain markets."

Much of the battle for passengers in the airline industry is fought in terms of property, plant, and equipment. Passengers want convenient schedules (which requires a large number of aircraft), and they want to fly on new, modern airplanes. Because airlines have such a large investment in equipment but no opportunity to inventory unused seats, they work very hard to fill their aircraft to capacity for each flight. Southwest's Annual Report for 2011 describes the keys to its ability to offer low fares and generous frequent flyer benefits.

SOUTHWEST.COM®

REAL WORLD EXCERPT
Annual Report

> A key component of the Company's business strategy has been its low-cost structure, which was designed to allow it to profitably charge low Southwest fares. Adjusted for stage length, Southwest and AirTran have lower unit costs, on average, than most major carriers. The Company's low-cost structure has historically been facilitated by Southwest's use of a single aircraft type, the Boeing 737, an operationally efficient point-to-point route structure, and highly productive Employees.

As you can see from this discussion, issues surrounding property, plant, and equipment have a pervasive impact on a company in terms of strategy, pricing decisions, and profitability. Managers devote considerable time to planning optimal levels of productive capacity, and financial analysts closely review a company's statements to determine the impact of management's decisions.

This chapter is organized according to the life cycle of long-lived assets—acquisition, use, and disposal. First we will discuss the measuring and reporting issues related to land, buildings, and equipment. Then we will discuss the measurement and reporting issues for intangible assets and natural resources. Among the issues we will discuss are the maintenance, use, and disposal of property and equipment over time and the measurement and reporting of assets considered impaired in their ability to generate future cash flows.

ORGANIZATION of the Chapter

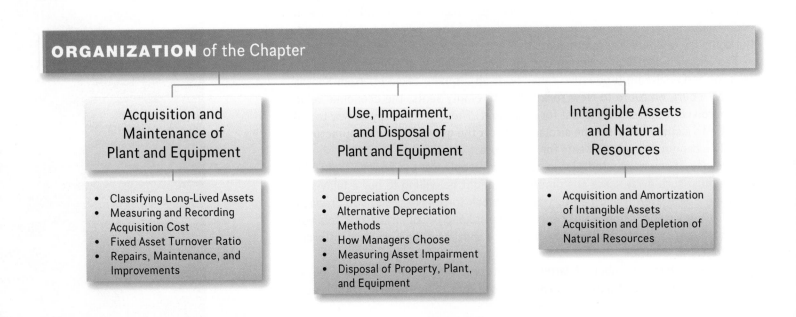

Acquisition and Maintenance of Plant and Equipment	Use, Impairment, and Disposal of Plant and Equipment	Intangible Assets and Natural Resources
• Classifying Long-Lived Assets • Measuring and Recording Acquisition Cost • Fixed Asset Turnover Ratio • Repairs, Maintenance, and Improvements	• Depreciation Concepts • Alternative Depreciation Methods • How Managers Choose • Measuring Asset Impairment • Disposal of Property, Plant, and Equipment	• Acquisition and Amortization of Intangible Assets • Acquisition and Depletion of Natural Resources

ACQUISITION AND MAINTENANCE OF PLANT AND EQUIPMENT

Exhibit 8.1 shows the asset section of the balance sheet from Southwest's annual report for the fiscal year ended December 31, 2011. Over 67 percent of Southwest's total assets are flight and ground equipment. Southwest also reports other assets with probable long-term benefits. Let's begin by classifying these assets.

Classifying Long-Lived Assets

The resources that determine a company's productive capacity are often called long-lived assets. These assets, which are listed as noncurrent assets on the balance sheet, may be either tangible or intangible and have the following characteristics:

1. Tangible assets have physical substance; that is, they can be touched. The three kinds of long-lived tangible assets are:

   a. **Land** used in operations. As is the case with Southwest, land often is not shown as a separate item on the balance sheet.

   b. **Buildings, fixtures, and equipment** used in operations. For Southwest, this category includes aircraft, ground equipment to service the aircraft, and office space. (*Note:* Land, buildings, fixtures, and equipment are also called **property, plant, and equipment** or **fixed assets.**)

   c. **Natural resources** used in operations. Southwest does not report any natural resources on its balance sheet. However, companies in other industries report natural resources such as timber tracts and silver mines.

2. Intangible assets are long-lived assets without physical substance that confer specific rights on their owner. Examples are patents, copyrights, franchises, licenses, and trademarks. Southwest reports $970 million of goodwill on its balance sheet.

Measuring and Recording Acquisition Cost

Under the cost principle, all reasonable and necessary expenditures made in acquiring and preparing an asset for use (or sale, as in the case of inventory) **should be recorded as the cost of the asset.** We say that the expenditures are **capitalized** when they are recorded as part of the cost of an asset instead of as expenses in the current period. Any sales taxes, legal

LONG-LIVED ASSETS are tangible and intangible resources owned by a business and used in its operations over several years.

TANGIBLE ASSETS have physical substance.

INTANGIBLE ASSETS have special rights but not physical substance.

Plant and Equipment as a Percent of Total Assets for Selected Focus Companies

National Beverage   30.3%

Chipotle Mexican Grill   55.8%

Harley-Davidson   8.4%

SOUTHWEST AIRLINES CO. Consolidated Balance Sheets (partial) December 31, 2011 and 2010		
Assets (*dollars in millions*)	**2011**	**2010**
Current assets: (*summarized*)	$ 4,345	$ 4,279
Property and equipment, at cost:		
Flight equipment	15,542	13,991
Ground property and equipment	2,423	2,122
Deposits on flight equipment purchase contracts	456	230
	18,421	16,343
Less allowance for depreciation and amortization	6,294	5,765
Total property and equipment	12,127	10,578
Goodwill	970	—
Other assets	626	606
Total assets	$18,068	$15,463

EXHIBIT 8.1

Southwest Airlines's Asset Section of the Balance Sheet

SOUTHWEST.COM

REAL WORLD EXCERPT
Annual Report

fees, transportation costs, and installation costs are then added to the purchase price of the asset. However, special discounts are subtracted and any interest charges associated with the purchase are expensed as incurred.

KEY RATIO ANALYSIS	Fixed Asset Turnover

Selected Focus Companies' Fixed Asset Turnover Ratios for 2011

Chipotle Mexican Grill   3.18

Deckers   19.96

Apple   17.26

❓ ANALYTICAL QUESTION

How effectively is management utilizing fixed assets to generate revenues?

% RATIO AND COMPARISONS

$$\text{Fixed Asset Turnover} = \frac{\text{Net Sales (or Operating Revenues)}}{\text{Average Net Fixed Assets*}}$$

The 2011 ratio for Southwest is (dollars in millions):

$$\text{Operating Revenues } \$15,658 \div [(\$10,578 + \$12,127) \div 2] = 1.38 \text{ times}$$

COMPARISONS OVER TIME			COMPARISONS WITH COMPETITORS	
Southwest Airlines			Delta	United Continental Holdings
2009	2010	2011	2011	2011
0.96	1.14	1.38	1.73	2.96

💡 INTERPRETATIONS

In General   The fixed asset turnover ratio measures the sales dollars generated by each dollar of fixed assets used. A high rate normally suggests effective management. An increasing rate over time signals more efficient fixed asset use. Creditors and security analysts use this ratio to assess a company's effectiveness in generating sales from its fixed assets.

Focus Company Analysis   Southwest's fixed asset turnover ratio increased between 2009 and 2011. Although at first glance it appears that Southwest is less efficient than perennial money losers Delta and United Continental Holdings, this is not the case. Their higher fixed asset turnover is due to the greater age of their fleet (a higher percentage has been depreciated) and the fact that more planes are leased in such a way that they do not appear as fixed assets on the balance sheet.

A Few Cautions   A lower or declining fixed asset turnover rate may indicate that a company is expanding (by acquiring additional productive assets) in anticipation of higher future sales. An increasing ratio could also signal that a firm has cut back on capital expenditures due to a downturn in business. This is not the case at Southwest, which continues to expand its fleet. As a consequence, appropriate interpretation of the fixed asset turnover ratio requires an investigation of related activities.

---

*[Beginning + Ending Fixed Asset Balance (net of accumulated depreciation)] ÷ 2.

LEARNING OBJECTIVE 8-2

Apply the cost principle to measure the acquisition and maintenance of property, plant, and equipment.

In addition to purchasing buildings and equipment, a company may acquire undeveloped land, typically with the intent to build a new factory or office building. When a company purchases land, all of the incidental costs of the purchase, such as title fees, sales commissions, legal fees, title insurance, delinquent taxes, and surveying fees, should be included in its cost.

Sometimes a company purchases an old building or used machinery for the business operations. Renovation and repair costs incurred by the company prior to the asset's use should be included as a part of its cost. Also, when purchasing land, building, and equipment as a group (known as a basket purchase), the total cost is allocated to each asset in proportion to the asset's market value relative to the total market value of the assets as a whole.

For the sake of illustration, let's assume that Southwest purchased a new 737 aircraft from Boeing on January 1, 2014 (the beginning of Southwest's fiscal year), for a list price of $78 million. Let's also assume that Boeing offered Southwest a discount of $4 million for signing the purchase agreement. That means the price of the new plane to Southwest would actually be $74 million. In addition, Southwest paid $200,000 to have the plane delivered and $800,000 to prepare the new plane for use. The amount recorded for the purchase, called the **acquisition cost,** is the net cash amount paid for the asset or, when noncash assets are used as payment, the fair value of the asset given or asset received, whichever can be more clearly determined (called the **cash equivalent price**). Southwest would calculate the acquisition cost of the new aircraft as follows:

> The ACQUISITION COST is the net cash equivalent amount paid or to be paid for the asset.

Invoice price	$78,000,000
Less: Discount from Boeing	4,000,000
Net cash invoice price	74,000,000
Add: Transportation charges paid by Southwest	200,000
Preparation costs paid by Southwest	800,000
Cost of the aircraft (added to the asset account)	$75,000,000

For Cash

Assuming that Southwest paid cash for the aircraft and related transportation and preparation costs, the transaction is recorded as follows:

	Debit	Credit
Flight Equipment (+A)	75,000,000	
Cash (−A)		75,000,000

Assets	=	Liabilities	+	Stockholders' Equity
Flight Equipment +75,000,000				
Cash −75,000,000				

It might seem unusual for Southwest to pay cash to purchase new assets that cost $75 million, but this is often the case. When it acquires productive assets, a company may pay with cash that was generated from operations or cash recently borrowed. It also is possible for the seller to finance the purchase on credit.

For Debt

Now let's assume that Southwest signed a note payable for the new aircraft and paid cash for the transportation and preparation costs. In that case, Southwest would record the following journal entry:

	Debit	Credit
Flight Equipment (+A)	75,000,000	
Cash (−A)		1,000,000
Notes Payable (+L)		74,000,000

Assets	=	Liabilities	+	Stockholders' Equity
Flight Equipment +75,000,000		Notes Payable +74,000,000		
Cash −1,000,000				

Commercial airlines often utilize financing schemes that include leasing aircraft. Shorter-term leases, called **operating leases,** provide airlines with flexibility in managing fleet size and obsolescence, which can occur with changes in environmental and noise-level laws in various countries. Operating leases are not reported on the balance sheet as liabilities and the assets are not included in fixed assets. On the other hand, longer-term leases, called **financing leases** or **capital leases,** are in essence the acquisition of assets that are reported on the balance sheet along with the lease obligations, allowing for companies to take advantage of tax benefits. At December 31, 2011, Southwest Airlines disclosed the following regarding its leasing commitments:

SOUTHWEST.COM

REAL WORLD EXCERPT
2011 Annual Report

NOTES TO CONSOLIDATED FINANCIAL STATEMENTS

8. Leases

The majority of the Company's and AirTran's terminal operations space, as well as 192 aircraft, were under operating leases at December 31, 2011 . . . Future minimum lease payments under capital leases and noncancelable operating leases with initial or remaining terms in excess of one year at December 31, 2011, were:

(in millions)	Capital leases	Operating leases
2012	$ 6	$ 640
2013	6	717
2014	6	642
2015	6	579
2016	6	489
Thereafter	26	2,516
Total minimum lease payments	$56	$5,583

Additional discussion of leases is provided in Chapter 9.

For Equity (or Other Noncash Considerations)

Noncash consideration, such as the company's common stock or a right given by the company to the seller to purchase the company's goods or services at a special price, might also be part of the transaction. When noncash consideration is included in the purchase of an asset, the cash-equivalent cost (fair value of the asset given or received) is determined.

Assume that Southwest gave Boeing 1,000,000 shares of its $1.00 par value common stock with a market value of $50 per share and paid the balance in cash. The journal entry and transaction effects follow:

	Debit	Credit
Flight Equipment (+A)	75,000,000	
Common Stock (+SE)		1,000,000
Additional Paid-In Capital (+SE)		49,000,000
Cash (−A)		25,000,000

1,000,000 shares × $1 par
1,000,000 shares × $49 excess
($50 market value − $1 par)

Assets		=	Liabilities	+	Stockholders' Equity	
Flight Equipment	+75,000,000				Common Stock	+1,000,000
Cash	−25,000,000				Additional Paid-In Capital	+49,000,000

By Construction

In some cases, a company may construct an asset for its own use instead of buying it from a manufacturer. When a company does so, the cost of the asset includes all the necessary costs associated with construction, such as labor, materials, and in most situations, a portion of the interest incurred during the construction period, called **capitalized interest.** The amount of interest expense that is capitalized is recorded by debiting the asset and crediting cash when the interest is paid. The amount of interest to be capitalized is a complex computation discussed in detail in other accounting courses.

Capitalizing labor, materials, and a portion of interest expense has the effect of increasing assets, decreasing expenses, and increasing net income. Let's assume Southwest constructed a new hangar, paying $600,000 in labor costs and $1,300,000 in supplies and materials. Southwest also paid $100,000 in interest expense during the year related to the construction project:

	Debit	Credit
Building (+A)	2,000,000	
Cash (−A)		2,000,000

Assets		=	Liabilities	+	Stockholders' Equity
Building	+2,000,000				
Cash	−2,000,000				

> **Capitalized Expenditures:**
> Wages paid $ 600,000
> Supplies paid   1,300,000
> Interest paid   100,000

US Airways includes a note on capitalized interest in a recent annual report:

> ### NOTES TO CONSOLIDATED FINANCIAL STATEMENTS
>
> **1. Basis of Presentation and Summary of Significant Accounting Policies:**
>
> *(g) Property and Equipment*
>
> Property and equipment are recorded at cost. Interest expense related to the acquisition of certain property and equipment, including aircraft purchase deposits, is capitalized as an additional cost of the asset or as a leasehold improvement if the asset is leased. Interest capitalized for the years ended December 31, 2011, 2010, and 2009 was $8 million, $4 million, and $10 million, respectively.

REAL WORLD EXCERPT
US Airways Group
2011 Annual Report

CAPITALIZED INTEREST refers to interest expenditures included in the cost of a self-constructed asset.

PAUSE FOR **FEEDBACK**

We just learned how to measure the cost of operational assets acquired under various methods. In general, all necessary and reasonable costs to ready the asset for its intended use are part of the cost of the asset. Assets can be acquired with cash, with debt, and/or with the company's stock (at market value).

SELF-STUDY **QUIZ**

It's your turn to apply these concepts by answering the following questions. In a recent year, McDonald's Corporation purchased property, plant, and equipment priced at $2.7 billion. Assume that the company also paid $216 million for sales tax; $20 million for transportation costs; $12 million for installation and preparation of the property, plant, and equipment before use; and $1 million in maintenance contracts to cover repairs to the property, plant, and equipment during use.

McDonald's Corporation

(continued)

1. Compute the acquisition cost for the property, plant, and equipment. *2.948 b*
2. How did you account for the sales tax, transportation costs, and installation costs? Explain.
3. Under the following independent assumptions, indicate the effects of the acquisition on the accounting equation. Use + for increase and − for decrease and indicate the accounts and amounts:

	ASSETS	LIABILITIES	STOCKHOLDERS' EQUITY
a. Paid 30 percent in cash and the rest by signing a note payable.	*+ PPE − cash*	*+ notepay*	
b. Issued 10 million shares of common stock ($0.01 per share par value) at a market price of $100 per share and paid the balance in cash.	*+PPE − cash*		*+ com stock paid-cap*

After you have completed your answers, check them with the solutions at the bottom of the page.

Repairs, Maintenance, and Improvements

Most assets require substantial expenditures during their lives to maintain or enhance their productive capacity. These expenditures include cash outlays for ordinary repairs and maintenance, major repairs, replacements, and additions. Expenditures that are made after an asset has been acquired are classified as follows:

ORDINARY REPAIRS AND MAINTENANCE are expenditures that maintain the productive capacity of the asset during the current accounting period only and are recorded as expenses.

1. **Ordinary repairs and maintenance** are expenditures that maintain the productive capacity of the asset during the current accounting period only. These expenditures are recurring in nature, involve relatively small amounts at each occurrence, and do not directly increase the productive life, operating efficiency, or capacity of the asset. These cash outlays are recorded as **expenses** in the current period.

In the case of Southwest Airlines, examples of ordinary repairs would include changing the oil in the aircraft engines, replacing the lights in the control panels, and fixing torn fabric on passenger seats. Although the cost of individual ordinary repairs is relatively small, in the aggregate these expenditures can be substantial. In 2011, Southwest paid $955 million for aircraft maintenance and repairs. This amount was reported as an expense on its income statement. The following summary entry represents how these expenditures would have been recorded by Southwest:

Solutions to

SELF-STUDY QUIZ

1. **Property, Plant, and Equipment (PPE)**

Acquisition cost	$2,700,000,000
Sales tax	216,000,000
Transportation	20,000,000
Installation	12,000,000
Total	$2,948,000,000

Because the maintenance contracts are not necessary to ready the assets for use, they are not included in the acquisition cost.

2. Sales tax and transportation and installation costs are capitalized because they are reasonable and necessary for getting the asset ready for its intended use.

3.

Assets		Liabilities		Stockholders' Equity	
a. PPE	+2,948,000,000	Note Payable	+2,063,600,000		
Cash	−884,400,000				
b. PPE	+2,948,000,000			Common Stock	+100,000
Cash	−1,948,000,000			Additional Paid-In Capital	+999,900,000

(in millions)	Debit	Credit
Maintenance and Repairs Expense (+E, −SE)	955	
Cash (−A)		955

Assets	=	Liabilities	+	Stockholders' Equity	
Cash −955				Maintenance and repairs expense (+E)	−955

2. **Improvements** are expenditures that increase the productive life, operating efficiency, or capacity of the asset. These **capital expenditures** are added to the appropriate asset accounts (that is, they are capitalized). They occur infrequently, involve large amounts of money, and increase an asset's economic usefulness in the future through either increased efficiency or longer life. Examples include additions, major overhauls, complete reconditioning, and major replacements and improvements, such as the complete replacement of an engine on an aircraft.

Assume that Southwest spent $300 million in 2011 to modify the exterior of its aircraft to reduce fuel consumption, resulting in 9 percent greater fuel efficiency and lower operating costs. The summary entry below represents how these expenditures would have been recorded by Southwest:

IMPROVEMENTS increase the productive life, operating efficiency, or capacity of the asset and are recorded as increases in asset accounts, not as expenses.

(in millions)	Debit	Credit
Flight Equipment (+A)	300	
Cash (−A)		300

Assets	=	Liabilities	+	Stockholders' Equity
Flight equipment +300				
Cash −300				

In many cases, no clear line distinguishes improvements (assets) from ordinary repairs and maintenance (expenses). In these situations, managers must exercise professional judgment and make a subjective decision. Capitalizing expenses will increase assets and net income in the current year, lowering future years' income by the amount of the annual depreciation. On the other hand, for tax purposes, expensing the amount in the current period will lower taxes immediately. Because the decision to capitalize or expense is subjective, auditors review the items reported as capital and revenue expenditures closely.

To avoid spending too much time classifying additions and improvements (capital expenditures) and repair expenses (revenue expenditures), some companies develop simple policies to govern the accounting for these expenditures. For

example, one large computer company expenses all individual items that cost less than $1,000. Such policies are acceptable because immaterial (relatively small dollar) amounts will not affect users' decisions when analyzing financial statements.

FINANCIAL ANALYSIS		WorldCom: Hiding Billions in Expenses through Capitalization

When expenditures that should be recorded as current period expenses are improperly capitalized as part of the cost of an asset, the effects on the financial statements can be enormous. In one of the largest accounting frauds in history, WorldCom (now part of Verizon) inflated its income and cash flows from operations by billions of dollars in just such a scheme. This fraud turned WorldCom's actual losses into large profits.

Over five quarters in 2001 and 2002, the company initially announced that it had capitalized $3.8 billion that should have been recorded as operating expenses. By early 2004, auditors discovered $74.4 billion in necessary restatements (reductions to previously reported pretax income) for 2000 and 2001.

Accounting for expenses as capital expenditures increases current income because it spreads a single period's operating expenses over many future periods as depreciation expense. It increases cash flows from operations by moving cash outflows from the operating section to the investing section of the cash flow statement.

PAUSE FOR **FEEDBACK**

Practice these applications for operational assets as they are used over time: repairing or maintaining (expensed in current period) and adding to or improving (capitalized as part of the cost of the asset).

SELF-STUDY **QUIZ**

A building that originally cost $400,000 has been used over the past 10 years and needs continual maintenance and repairs. For each of the following expenditures, indicate whether it should be expensed in the current period or capitalized as part of **the cost of the asset.**

Expense or Capitalize?

1. Major replacement of electrical wiring throughout the building.   *Capitalize*
2. Repairs to the front door of the building.   *expense*
3. Annual cleaning of the filters on the building's air conditioning system.   *expense*
4. Significant repairs due to damage from an unusual and infrequent flood.   ~~*expense*~~ *capitalize*

After you have completed your answers, check them with the solutions at the bottom of the page.

LEARNING OBJECTIVE 8-3

Apply various cost allocation methods as assets are held and used over time.

USE, IMPAIRMENT, AND DISPOSAL OF PLANT AND EQUIPMENT

Depreciation Concepts

Except for land, which is considered to have an unlimited life, a long-lived asset with a limited useful life, such as an airplane, represents the prepaid cost of a bundle of future services or benefits. The **expense matching principle** requires that a portion of an asset's cost be allocated as an expense in the same period that revenues are generated by its use. Southwest Airlines

---

Solutions to
SELF-STUDY QUIZ

1. Capitalize   2. Expense   3. Expense   4. Capitalize

earns revenue when it provides air travel service and incurs an expense when using its aircraft to generate the revenue.

The term used to identify the matching of the cost of using buildings and equipment with the revenues they generate is **depreciation.** Thus, depreciation is **the process of allocating the cost of buildings and equipment over their productive lives using a systematic and rational method.**

DEPRECIATION is the process of allocating the cost of buildings and equipment over their productive lives using a systematic and rational method.

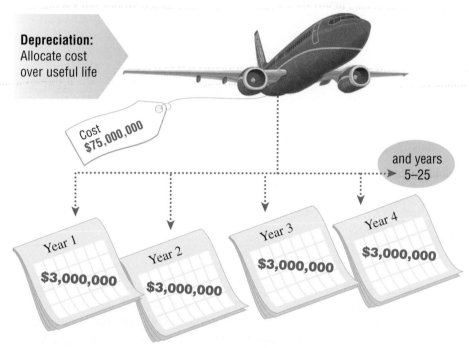

Using the asset→Depreciation Expense each year

Students often are confused by the concept of depreciation as accountants use it. In accounting, depreciation is a process of **cost allocation,** not a process of determining an asset's current market value or worth. When an asset is depreciated, the remaining balance sheet amount **probably does not represent its current market value.** On balance sheets subsequent to acquisition, the undepreciated cost is not measured on a market or fair value basis.

An adjusting journal entry is needed at the end of each period to reflect the use of buildings and equipment for the period:

	Debit	Credit
Depreciation Expense (+E, −SE)	x,xxx	
Accumulated Depreciation (+XA, −A)		x,xxx

Assets	=	Liabilities	+	Stockholders' Equity
Accumulated Depreciation (+XA) −x,xxx				Depreciation Expense (+E) −x,xxx

The amount of depreciation recorded during each period is reported on the income statement as **Depreciation Expense.** The amount of depreciation expense accumulated since the acquisition date is reported on the balance sheet as a contra-account, **Accumulated Depreciation,** and deducted from the related asset's cost. The net amount on the balance sheet is called **net book value** or **carrying value.** The **net book (or carrying) value** of a long-lived asset is its acquisition cost less the accumulated depreciation from the acquisition date to the balance sheet date.

NET BOOK (or CARRYING) VALUE is the acquisition cost of an asset less accumulated depreciation.

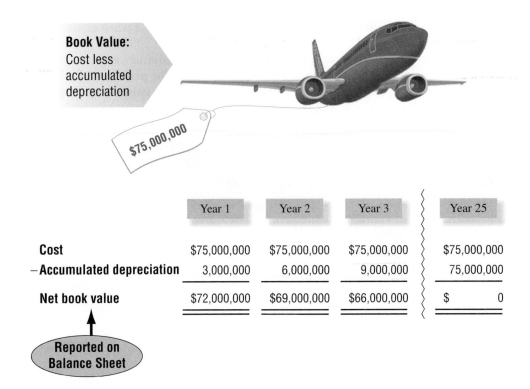

Book Value:
Cost less
accumulated
depreciation

$75,000,000

	Year 1	Year 2	Year 3	Year 25
Cost	$75,000,000	$75,000,000	$75,000,000	$75,000,000
−Accumulated depreciation	3,000,000	6,000,000	9,000,000	75,000,000
Net book value	$72,000,000	$69,000,000	$66,000,000	$ 0

Reported on Balance Sheet

From Exhibit 8.1 on page 383, we see that Southwest's acquisition cost for property and equipment is $18,421 million at the end of 2011. The accumulated depreciation and amortization on the property and equipment is $6,294 million. Thus, the book value is reported at $12,127 million. Southwest also reported depreciation and amortization expense of $715 million on its income statement for 2011.

FINANCIAL ANALYSIS	Book Value as an Approximation of Remaining Life

Book Value as a Percentage of Original Cost in 2011

Southwest   66%

United Continental   79%

JetBlue   83%

Some analysts compare the book value of assets to their original cost as an approximation of their remaining life. If the book value of an asset is 100 percent of its cost, it is a new asset; if the book value is 25 percent of its cost, the asset has about 25 percent of its estimated life remaining. In Southwest's case, the book value of its property and equipment is 66 percent of its original cost, compared to 79 percent for United Continental and 83 percent for JetBlue Airways.

This comparison suggests that Southwest's flight equipment is older than the equipment at JetBlue and United Continental. This comparison is only a rough approximation and is influenced by some of the accounting issues discussed in the next section.

To calculate depreciation expense, three amounts are required for each asset:

1. Acquisition cost.

2. Estimated useful life to the company.

3. Estimated residual (or salvage) value at the end of the asset's useful life to the company.

Notice that the asset's useful life and residual value are estimates. Therefore, **depreciation expense is an estimate.**

ESTIMATED USEFUL LIFE
is the expected service life of an asset to the present owner.

Estimated useful life represents management's estimate of the asset's useful **economic life** to the company rather than its total economic life to all potential users. The asset's expected physical life is often longer than the company intends to use the asset. Economic life may be expressed in terms of years or units of capacity, such as the number of hours a machine is expected to operate or the number of units it can produce. Southwest's aircraft fleet is expected to fly for more than 25 years, but Southwest wants to offer its customers a high level of service by replacing its older aircraft with modern equipment. For accounting purposes, Southwest uses a 23- to 30-year estimated useful life. The subsequent owner of the aircraft (likely a regional airline) would use an estimated useful life based on its own policies.

Differences in Estimated Lives within a Single Industry	FINANCIAL ANALYSIS

Notes to recent actual financial statements of various airline companies reveal the following estimates for the useful lives of flight equipment:

Company	Estimated Life (in years)
Southwest	23 to 30
United Continental	30
Singapore Airlines	15

The differences in the estimated lives may be attributed to a number of factors such as the type of aircraft used by each company, equipment replacement plans, operational differences, and the degree of management's conservatism. In addition, given the same type of aircraft, companies that plan to use the equipment over fewer years may estimate higher residual values than companies that plan to use the equipment longer. For example, Singapore Airlines uses a residual value of 10 percent over a relatively short useful life for its passenger aircraft, compared to 5 percent for Delta Air Lines over a 25-year useful life.

Differences in estimated lives and residual values of assets can have a significant impact on a comparison of the profitability of the competing companies. Analysts must be certain to identify the causes of differences in depreciable lives.

Residual (or salvage) value represents management's estimate of the amount the company expects to recover upon disposal of the asset at the end of its estimated useful life. The residual value may be the estimated value of the asset as salvage or scrap or its expected value if sold to another user. In the case of Southwest's aircraft, residual value may be the amount it expects to receive when it sells the asset to a small regional airline that operates older equipment. The notes to Southwest's financial statements indicate that the company estimates residual value to be between 0 and 15 percent of the cost of the asset, depending on the asset.

RESIDUAL (or SALVAGE) VALUE is the estimated amount to be recovered by the company at the end of the asset's estimated useful life.

Alternative Depreciation Methods

Because of significant differences among companies and the assets they own, accountants have not been able to agree on a single best method of depreciation. As a result, managers may choose from several acceptable depreciation methods that match depreciation expense with the revenues generated in a period. They may also choose different methods for specific assets or groups of assets. Once selected, the method should be applied consistently over time to enhance comparability of financial information. We will discuss the three most common depreciation methods:

1. Straight-line (the most common, used by more than 98 percent of companies surveyed for many or all of their assets).

2. Units-of-production.

3. Declining-balance.

To illustrate each method, let's assume that Southwest Airlines acquired a new service vehicle (ground equipment) on January 1, 2014. The relevant information is shown in Exhibit 8.2.

Percentage of 500 Companies Using Alternative Depreciation Methods*

Straight-line	98%
Units-of-production	3%
Declining-balance	2%
Others	6%

*Methods reported by companies sampled in *Accounting Trends & Techniques* (AICPA), 2012.

Data for Illustrating the
Computation of Depreciation
under Alternative Methods

SOUTHWEST AIRLINES
Acquisition of a New Service Vehicle

Cost, purchased on January 1, 2014	$62,500	
Estimated residual value	$ 2,500	
Estimated useful life		3 years **OR** 100,000 miles
Actual miles driven in:	Year 2014	30,000 miles
	Year 2015	50,000 miles
	Year 2016	20,000 miles

Straight-Line Method

The STRAIGHT-LINE DEPRECIATION method allocates the depreciable cost of an asset in equal periodic amounts over its useful life.

More companies, including Southwest, use **straight-line depreciation** in their financial statements than all other methods combined. Under the straight-line method, an equal portion of an asset's depreciable cost is allocated to each accounting period over its estimated useful life. Using the information in Exhibit 8.2, the formula to estimate annual depreciation expense follows:

Straight-Line Formula:

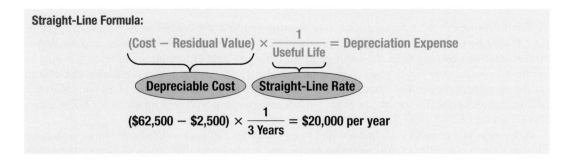

$$(\text{Cost} - \text{Residual Value}) \times \frac{1}{\text{Useful Life}} = \text{Depreciation Expense}$$

Depreciable Cost   Straight-Line Rate

$$(\$62,500 - \$2,500) \times \frac{1}{3 \text{ Years}} = \$20,000 \text{ per year}$$

In this formula, "Cost minus Residual Value" is the amount to be depreciated, also called the **depreciable cost.** The formula "1 ÷ Useful Life" is the **straight-line rate.** Using the data provided in Exhibit 8.2, the depreciation expense for Southwest's new truck would be $20,000 per year.

Companies often create a **depreciation schedule** that shows the computed amount of depreciation expense each year over the entire useful life of the machine. You can use computerized spreadsheet programs, such as Excel, to create the depreciation schedule. Using the data in Exhibit 8.2 and the straight-line method, Southwest's depreciation schedule follows:

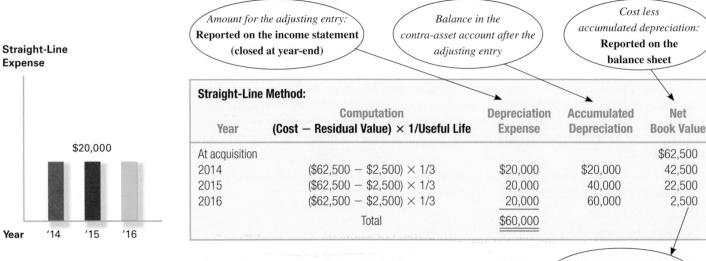

Straight-Line Expense

$20,000

Year   '14   '15   '16

Amount for the adjusting entry: **Reported on the income statement** *(closed at year-end)*

Balance in the contra-asset account after the adjusting entry

Cost less accumulated depreciation: **Reported on the balance sheet**

Straight-Line Method:

Year	Computation (Cost − Residual Value) × 1/Useful Life	Depreciation Expense	Accumulated Depreciation	Net Book Value
At acquisition				$62,500
2014	($62,500 − $2,500) × 1/3	$20,000	$20,000	42,500
2015	($62,500 − $2,500) × 1/3	20,000	40,000	22,500
2016	($62,500 − $2,500) × 1/3	20,000	60,000	2,500
	Total	$60,000		

Equal to estimated residual value at end of useful life

Notice that

- Depreciation expense is a constant amount each year.
- Accumulated depreciation increases by an equal amount each year.
- Net book value decreases by the same amount each year until it equals the estimated residual value.

This is the reason for the name **straight-line method.** Notice, too, that the adjusting entry can be prepared from this schedule, and the effect on the income statement and balance sheet are known. Southwest Airlines uses the straight-line method for all of its assets. The company reported depreciation expense in the amount of $715 million for 2011, equal to 5 percent of the airline's revenues for the year. Most companies in the airline industry use the straight-line method.

Units-of-Production Method

The **units-of-production depreciation** method relates depreciable cost to total estimated productive output. The formula to estimate annual depreciation expense under this method is as follows:

The UNITS-OF-PRODUCTION DEPRECIATION method allocates the depreciable cost of an asset over its useful life based on the relationship of its periodic output to its total estimated output.

Units-of-Production Formula:

$$\frac{(\text{Cost} - \text{Residual Value})}{\text{Estimated Total Production}} \times \frac{\text{Actual}}{\text{Production}} = \text{Depreciation Expense}$$

$$\frac{(\$62,500 - \$2,500)}{100,000 \text{ miles}} = \$0.60 \text{ per mile depreciation rate}$$

$$\$0.60 \text{ per mile} \times 30,000 \text{ actual miles in 2014} = \underline{\underline{\$18,000}} \text{ for 2014}$$

Dividing the depreciable cost by the estimated total production yields the **depreciation rate per unit of production,** which is then multiplied by the actual production for the period to determine depreciation expense. In our illustration, for every mile that the new vehicle is driven, Southwest would record depreciation expense of $0.60. Based on the information in Exhibit 8.2, the depreciation schedule for the truck under the units-of-production method would appear as follows:

Units-of-Production Expense

Units-of-Production Method:				
	Computation			
Year	**[(Cost − Residual Value)/Total Estimated Production] × Actual Production**	**Depreciation Expense**	**Accumulated Depreciation**	**Net Book Value**
At acquisition	RATE			$62,500
2014	$.60 per mile × 30,000 miles	$18,000	$18,000	44,500
2015	$.60 per mile × 50,000 miles	30,000	48,000	14,500
2016	$.60 per mile × 20,000 miles	12,000	60,000	2,500
	Total	$60,000		

Equal to estimated residual value at end of useful life

Notice that, from period to period, depreciation expense, accumulated depreciation, and book value vary directly with the units produced. In the units-of-production method, depreciation expense is a **variable expense** because it varies directly with production or use.

You might wonder what happens if the total estimated productive output differs from actual total output. Remember that the estimate is management's best guess of total output. If any difference occurs at the end of the asset's life, the final adjusting entry to depreciation expense should be for the amount needed to bring the asset's net book value equal to the asset's estimated residual value. For example, if, in 2016, Southwest's truck ran 25,000 actual miles, the same amount of depreciation expense, $12,000, would be recorded.

Although Southwest does not use the units-of-production method, the Exxon Mobil Corporation, a major energy company that explores, produces, transports, and sells crude oil and natural gas worldwide, does, as a note to the company's annual report explains.

ExxonMobil

REAL WORLD EXCERPT
2011 Annual Report

1. Summary of Accounting Policies

Property, Plant, and Equipment

Depreciation, depletion, and amortization, based on cost less estimated salvage value of the asset, are primarily determined under either the unit-of-production method or the straight-line method, which is based on estimated asset service life taking obsolescence into consideration . . . Unit-of-production rates are based on the amount of proved developed reserves of oil, gas, and other minerals that are estimated to be recoverable from existing facilities using current operating methods.

The units-of-production method is based on an estimate of an asset's total future productive capacity or output, which is difficult to determine. This is another example of the degree of subjectivity inherent in accounting.

Declining-Balance Method

If an asset is considered to be more efficient or productive when it is newer, managers might choose the **declining-balance depreciation** method to match a higher depreciation expense with higher revenues in the early years of an asset's life and a lower depreciation expense with lower revenues in the later years. We say, then, that this is an **accelerated depreciation** method. Although accelerated methods are seldom used for financial reporting purposes, the method that is used more frequently than others is the declining-balance method.

Declining-balance depreciation is based on applying a rate exceeding the straight-line rate to the asset's net book value over time. The rate is often double (two times) the straight-line rate and is termed the **double-declining-balance rate.** For example, if the straight-line rate is 10 percent ($1 \div 10$ years) for a 10-year estimated useful life, then the declining-balance rate is 20 percent ($2 \times$ the straight-line rate). Other typical acceleration rates are 1.5 times and 1.75 times. The double-declining-balance rate is adopted most frequently by companies employing an accelerated method, so we will use it in our illustration, with information from Exhibit 8.2.

The DECLINING-BALANCE DEPRECIATION method allocates the net book value (cost minus accumulated depreciation) of an asset over its useful life based on a multiple of the straight-line rate, thus assigning more depreciation to early years and less depreciation to later years of an asset's life.

Double-Declining-Balance Formula:

$$\text{(Cost} - \text{Accumulated Depreciation)} \times \frac{2}{\text{Useful Life}} = \text{Depreciation Expense}$$

Accumulated Depreciation increases over time

$$(\$62,500 - \$0 \text{ in 2014}) \times \frac{2}{3 \text{ years}} = \$41,667 \text{ in the first year}$$

There are two important differences between this method and the others described previously:

1. Notice that accumulated depreciation, not residual value, is included in the formula. Since accumulated depreciation increases each year, net book value (Cost minus Accumulated Depreciation) decreases. The double-declining rate is applied to a lower net book value each year, resulting in a decline in depreciation expense over time.

2. As with the other methods, the net book value should not be depreciated below the residual value:

- Occasionally, before the end of the estimated useful life, if the annual computation reduces net book value below residual value, only the amount of depreciation expense needed to make net book value equal to residual value is recorded, and no additional depreciation expense is computed in subsequent years.

- More likely, in the last year of the asset's estimated useful life, whatever amount is needed to bring net book value to residual value is recorded, regardless of the amount of the computation.

Computation of double-declining-balance depreciation expense is illustrated in the depreciation schedule:

Year	Computation [(Cost − Accumulated Depreciation) × 2/Useful Life]	Depreciation Expense	Accumulated Depreciation	Net Book Value
At acquisition				$62,500
2014	($62,500 − $0) × 2/3	$41,667	$41,667	20,833
2015	($62,500 − $41,667) × 2/3	13,889	55,556	6,944
2016	($62,500 − $55,556) × 2/3	4,629	60,185	2,315
		4,444	60,000	2,500
	Total	$60,000		

Computed amount is too large

Equal to estimated residual value at end of useful life

Double-Declining-Balance Expense

$41,667

$13,889

$4,444

Year   '14   '15   '16

The calculated depreciation expense for 2016 ($4,629) is not the same as the amount actually reported on the income statement ($4,444). An asset should never be depreciated below the point at which net book value equals its residual value. The asset owned by Southwest has an estimated residual value of $2,500. If depreciation expense were recorded in the amount of $4,629, the book value of the asset would be less than $2,500. The correct depreciation expense for year 2016 is therefore $4,444, the amount that will reduce the book value to exactly $2,500. To determine the amount to record in 2016, indicate the amount needed for net book value ($2,500), determine what the balance in accumulated depreciation should be to yield the $60,000 ($62,500 cost − $2,500 residual value), and compute the amount of depreciation expense necessary to increase the balance in accumulated depreciation to $60,000 ($60,000 balance needed in accumulated depreciation − $55,556 prior balance in accumulated depreciation).

Companies in industries that expect fairly rapid obsolescence of their equipment use the declining-balance method. Sony is one of the companies that uses this method, as a note to its annual report shows.

2. Summary of Significant Accounting Policies:

Property, Plant, Equipment and Depreciation

Property, plant and equipment are stated at cost. Depreciation of property, plant and equipment is computed on the declining-balance method for Sony Corporation and its Japanese subsidiaries, except for certain semiconductor manufacturing facilities and buildings whose depreciation is computed on the straight-line method over the estimated useful life of the assets. Depreciation of property, plant and equipment for foreign subsidiaries is also computed on the straight-line method. Useful lives for depreciation range from 2 to 50 years for buildings and from 1 to 17 years for machinery and equipment.

REAL WORLD EXCERPT

Sony Corporation

2011 Annual Report

As this note indicates, companies may use different depreciation methods for different classes of assets. Under the consistency principle, they are expected to apply the same methods to those assets over time.

In Summary

The three depreciation methods, computations, and the differences in depreciation expense over time for each method are summarized as follows:

Method	Computation	Depreciation Expense
Straight-line	(Cost − Residual Value) × 1/Useful Life	Equal amounts each year
Units-of-production	[(Cost − Residual Value)/Estimated Total Production] × Annual Production	Varying amounts based on production level
Double-declining-balance	(Cost − Accumulated Depreciation) × 2/Useful Life	Declining amounts over time

FINANCIAL ANALYSIS

Impact of Alternative Depreciation Methods

Summary Depreciation Expense

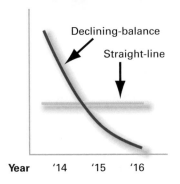

Year   '14   '15   '16

Assume that you are comparing two companies that are exactly the same, except that one uses accelerated depreciation and the other uses the straight-line method. Which company would you expect to report a higher net income? Actually, this question is a bit tricky. The answer is that you cannot say for certain which company's income would be higher.

The accelerated methods report higher depreciation and therefore lower net income during the early years of an asset's life. As the age of the asset increases, this effect reverses. Therefore, companies that use accelerated depreciation report lower depreciation expense and higher net income during the later years of an asset's life. The graph in the margin shows the pattern of depreciation over the life of an asset for the straight-line and declining-balance methods discussed in this chapter. When the curve for the accelerated method falls below the line for the straight-line method, the accelerated method produces a higher net income than the straight-line method. However, total depreciation expense by the end of the asset's life is the same for each method.

Users of financial statements must understand the impact of alternative depreciation methods used over time. **Differences in depreciation methods rather than real economic differences can cause significant variation in reported net incomes.**

PAUSE FOR **FEEDBACK**

The three cost allocation methods discussed in this section are:

- Straight-line (Cost − Residual Value) × 1/Useful Life
- Units-of-production [(Cost − Residual Value)/Estimated Total Production] × Annual Production
- Double-declining-balance (Cost − Accumulated Depreciation) × 2/Useful Life

Practice these methods using the following information.

SELF-STUDY **QUIZ**

Assume that Southwest has acquired new computer equipment at a cost of $240,000. The equipment has an estimated life of six years, an estimated operating life of 50,000 hours, and an estimated residual value of $30,000. Determine depreciation expense for the first full year under each of the following methods:

1. Straight-line method.
2. Units-of-production method (assume the equipment ran for 8,000 hours in the first year).
3. Double-declining-balance method.

After you have completed your answers, check them with the solutions at the bottom of the page.

GUIDED **HELP**

For additional step-by-step video instruction on using the three cost allocation methods discussed in this section, go to the URL or scan the QR code in the margin with your smartphone or iPad.

www.mhhe.com/libby8e

Increased Profitability Due to an Accounting Adjustment? Reading the Notes

Financial analysts are particularly interested in changes in accounting estimates because they can have a large impact on a company's before-tax operating income. In 2001, Singapore Airlines disclosed in its annual report that it had increased the estimated useful life of its aircraft from 10 to 15 years to reflect a change in its aircraft replacement policy. The change reduced depreciation expense for the year by $265 million and would reduce expenses by a similar amount each year over the remaining life of the aircraft. Analysts pay close attention to this number because it represents increased profitability due merely to an accounting adjustment.

SINGAPORE AIRLINES
A great way to fly

Component Allocation

INTERNATIONAL PERSPECTIVE

Under IFRS, the cost of an individual asset's components is allocated among each significant component and then depreciated separately over that component's useful life. For example, British Airways (now merged into International Airlines Group) separates the cost of an aircraft between its body and engines and interior cabin space. It then depreciates the body and engines over 18 to 25 years and the cabin interior over 5 years.

How Managers Choose

Financial Reporting

For financial reporting purposes, corporate managers must determine which depreciation method provides the best matching of revenues and expenses for any given asset. If the asset is expected to provide benefits evenly over time, then the straight-line method is preferred. Managers also find this method to be easy to use and to explain. If no other method is more systematic or rational, then the straight-line method is selected. Also, during the early years of an asset's life, the straight-line method reports higher income than the accelerated methods do. For these reasons, the straight-line method is, by far and away, the most common.

On the other hand, certain assets produce more revenue in their early lives because they are more efficient than in later years. In this case, managers select an accelerated method to allocate cost.

---

1. ($240,000 − $30,000) × 1/6 = $35,000
2. [($240,000 − $30,000) ÷ 50,000] × 8,000 = $33,600
3. ($240,000 − $0) × 2/6 = $80,000

Solutions to
SELF-STUDY QUIZ

Tax Reporting

Southwest Airlines, like most public companies, maintains two sets of accounting records. Both sets of records reflect the same transactions, but the transactions are accounted for using two different sets of measurement rules. One set is prepared under GAAP for reporting to stockholders. The other set is prepared to determine the company's tax obligation under the Internal Revenue Code. The reason that the two sets of rules are different is simple: The objectives of GAAP and the Internal Revenue Code differ.

Financial Reporting (GAAP)	Tax Reporting (IRC)
The objective of financial reporting is to provide economic information about a business that is useful in projecting future cash flows of the business. Financial reporting rules follow generally accepted accounting principles.	The objective of the Internal Revenue Code is to raise sufficient revenues to pay for the expenditures of the federal government. Many of the Code's provisions are designed to encourage certain behaviors that are thought to benefit society (e.g., contributions to charities are made tax deductible to encourage people to support worthy programs).

In some cases, differences between the Internal Revenue Code and GAAP leave the manager no choice but to maintain separate records. In other cases, the differences are the result of management choice. When given a choice among acceptable tax accounting methods, managers apply what is called the **least and the latest rule.** All taxpayers want to pay the lowest amount of tax that is legally permitted and at the latest possible date. If you had the choice of paying $100,000 to the federal government at the end of this year or at the end of next year, you would choose the end of next year. By doing so, you could invest the money for an extra year and earn a significant return on the investment.

A QUESTION OF ETHICS   **Two Sets of Books**

When they first learn that companies maintain two sets of books, some people question the ethics or legality of the practice. In reality, **it is both legal and ethical to maintain separate records for tax and financial reporting purposes. However, these records must reflect the same transactions.** Understating revenues or overstating expenses on a tax return can result in financial penalties and/or imprisonment. Accountants who aid tax evaders also can be fined or imprisoned and lose their professional licenses.

Similarly, by maintaining two sets of books, corporations can defer (delay) paying millions and sometimes billions of dollars in taxes. The following companies reported significant gross deferred tax obligations in 2011. Much of these deferrals were due to differences in asset cost allocation methods:

Company	Deferred Tax Liabilities	Percentage Due to Applying Different Cost Allocation Methods
Southwest Airlines	$3,621 million	98%
PepsiCo	7,816 million	32
Hertz	3,685 million	74
Marriott International	18 million	56

Most corporations use the IRS-approved Modified Accelerated Cost Recovery System (MACRS) to calculate depreciation expense for their tax returns. MACRS is similar to the declining-balance method and is applied over relatively short asset lives to yield high depreciation expense in the early years. The high depreciation expense reported under MACRS reduces a corporation's taxable income and therefore the amount it must pay in taxes. MACRS provides an incentive for corporations to invest in modern property, plant, and equipment in order to be competitive in world markets. However, **it is not acceptable for financial reporting purposes.**

Measuring Asset Impairment

As we discussed in Chapter 2, assets are defined as economic resources with probable future benefits acquired in an exchange transaction. On the date of the exchange, an asset is measured at historical cost. However, later in its useful life, when an asset is not expected to generate sufficient cash flows (probable future benefits) at least equal to its book value, we say the asset's book value is impaired. Corporations must review long-lived tangible and intangible assets for possible impairment. Two steps are necessary:

> **LEARNING OBJECTIVE 8-4**
> Explain the effect of asset impairment on the financial statements.

Step 1: Test for Impairment **Impairment** occurs when events or changed circumstances cause the estimated future cash flows (future benefits) of these assets to fall below their book value.

If net book value > Estimated future cash flows, then the asset is impaired.

Step 2: Computation of Impairment Loss For any asset considered to be impaired, companies recognize a loss for the difference between the asset's book value and its **fair value** (a market concept).

Impairment Loss = Net Book Value − Fair Value

That is, the asset is **written down** to fair value.

To illustrate measuring impairment losses, let's assume that Southwest did a review for asset impairment and identified an aircraft with the following information:

Step 1: Test	→ Net book value	$10,000,000 ←	
	→ Estimated future cash flows	8,000,000	Step 2: If impaired, loss
	Fair value	7,500,000 ←	

Step 1: Since the net book value of $10 million exceeds the estimated future cash flows of $8 million, then the asset is impaired because it is not expected to generate future benefits equal to its net book value. When impaired, proceed to Step 2.

Step 2: If impaired, the amount of the impairment loss is the difference between net book value and the asset's fair value. For Southwest, determining fair value includes using published sources and third-party bids to obtain the value of the asset. If the asset's fair value was $7,500,000, then the loss is calculated as $2,500,000 ($10,000,000 net book value less $7,500,000 fair value). The following journal entry would be recorded:

	Debit	Credit
Asset Impairment Loss (+Loss, −SE)	2,500,000	
Flight Equipment (−A)		2,500,000

Assets	=	Liabilities	+	Stockholders' Equity	
Flight Equipment −2,500,000				Asset Impairment Loss (+E) −2,500,000	

Although Southwest did not report asset impairment losses in its recent annual report, it did report in notes to the financial statements that it follows the practice of reviewing assets for impairment:

SOUTHWEST.COM

REAL WORLD EXCERPT
2011 Annual Report

> The Company evaluates its long-lived assets used in operations for impairment when events and circumstances indicate that the undiscounted cash flows to be generated by that asset are less than the carrying amounts of the asset and may not be recoverable. Factors that would indicate potential impairment include, but are not limited to, significant decreases in the market value of the long-lived asset(s), a significant change in the long-lived asset's physical condition, and operating or cash flow losses associated with the use of the long-lived asset. If an asset is deemed to be impaired, an impairment loss is recorded for the excess of the asset book value in relation to its estimated fair value.

Sears Holdings Corporation, which owns and operates approximately 4,000 Kmart and Sears stores in the United States and Canada, reported impairment losses on its fixed assets in its annual report for the fiscal year ended January 28, 2012:

Sears Holdings Corporation

REAL WORLD EXCERPT
2011 Annual Report

> ### NOTE 13—STORE CLOSING CHARGES, SEVERANCE COSTS AND IMPAIRMENTS
> *Long-Lived Assets*
>
> In accordance with accounting standards governing the impairment or disposal of long-lived assets, we performed an impairment test of certain of our long-lived assets (principally the value of buildings and other fixed assets associated with our stores) due to events and changes in circumstances during 2011 that indicated an impairment might have occurred. The impairment review was triggered by . . . a decline in operating performance at certain locations. As a result of this impairment testing, the Company recorded a $16 million impairment charge during 2011. This impairment charge was made up of a $10 million charge at Kmart and a $6 million charge at Sears Domestic.

The impairment loss in addition to a decline in revenues and an increase in expenses in fiscal year 2011 resulted in Sears Holdings Corporation reporting a net loss of over $3 billion, the first loss since Kmart and Sears merged in March 2005.

Disposal of Property, Plant, and Equipment

LEARNING OBJECTIVE 8-5

Analyze the disposal of property, plant, and equipment.

In some cases, a business may **voluntarily** decide not to hold a long-lived asset for its entire life. The company may drop a product from its line and no longer need the equipment that was used to produce it, or managers may want to replace a machine with a more efficient one. These disposals include sales, trade-ins, and retirements. When Southwest disposes of an old aircraft, the company may sell it to a cargo airline or regional airline. A business may also dispose of an asset **involuntarily,** as the result of a casualty such as a storm, fire, or accident.

Disposals of long-lived assets seldom occur on the last day of the accounting period. Therefore, depreciation must be recorded on the date of disposal for the amount of cost used since the last time depreciation was recorded. Therefore, the disposal of a depreciable asset usually requires two journal entries:

1. An adjusting entry to update the depreciation expense and accumulated depreciation accounts.

2. An entry to record the disposal. The cost of the asset **and** any accumulated depreciation at the date of disposal must be removed from the accounts. The difference between any resources received on disposal of an asset and its book value at the date of disposal is treated

as a gain or loss on the disposal of the asset. This gain (or loss) is reported on the income statement. It is not an operating revenue (or expense), however, because it arises from peripheral or incidental activities rather than from central operations. Gains and losses from disposals are usually shown as a separate item on the income statement.

Assume that at the end of year 17, Southwest sold an aircraft that was no longer needed because of the elimination of service to a small city. The aircraft was sold for $11 million cash. The original cost of the flight equipment of $30 million was depreciated using the straight-line method over 25 years with no residual value ($1.2 million depreciation expense per year). The last accounting for depreciation was at the end of year 16; thus, depreciation expense must be recorded for year 17. The computations are:

Cash received		$11,000,000
Original cost of flight equipment	$30,000,000	
Less: Accumulated depreciation ($1,200,000 × 17 years)	20,400,000	
Book value at date of sale		9,600,000
Gain on sale of flight equipment		$ 1,400,000

The entries and effects of the transaction on the date of the sale are as follows:

1. Update depreciation expense for year 17:

	Debit	Credit
Depreciation Expense (+E, −SE)	1,200,000	
Accumulated Depreciation (+XA, −A)		1,200,000

2. Record the sale:

	Debit	Credit
Cash (+A)	11,000,000	
Accumulated Depreciation (−XA, +A)	20,400,000	
Flight Equipment (−A)		30,000,000
Gain on Sale of Assets (+Gain, +SE)		1,400,000

Assets	=	Liabilities	+	Stockholders' Equity	
(1) Accumulated				Depreciation	
Depreciation (+XA) −1,200,000				Expense (+E)	−1,200,000
(2) Cash +11,000,000				Gain on Sale of Asset	+1,400,000
Flight Equipment −30,000,000					
Accumulated					
Depreciation (−XA) +20,400,000					

PAUSE FOR **FEEDBACK**

We learned that, when disposing of an operational asset, you must first record depreciation expense for usage of the asset since the last time it was recorded. Then eliminate the asset at cost and its related accumulated depreciation. The difference between the cash received, if any, and the net book value of the asset is either a gain or loss on disposal.

(*continued*)

SELF-STUDY QUIZ

Now let's assume the same facts as illustrated on the previous page except that the asset was sold for $2,000,000 cash. Prepare the two entries on the date of the sale:

1. Update depreciation expense for year 17:

	Debit	Credit

2. Record the sale:

	Debit	Credit

Assets	=	Liabilities	+	Stockholders' Equity

(1)

(2)

After you have completed your answers, check them with the solutions at the bottom of the page.

LEARNING OBJECTIVE 8-6

Apply measurement and reporting concepts for intangible assets and natural resources.

INTANGIBLE ASSETS AND NATURAL RESOURCES

Acquisition and Amortization of Intangible Assets

Intangible assets are increasingly important resources for organizations. An intangible asset, like any other asset, has value because of certain rights and privileges often conferred by law on its owner. Unlike tangible assets such as land and buildings, however, an intangible asset has no material or physical substance. Examples of intangible assets include patents, trademarks, and licenses. Most intangible assets usually are evidenced by a legal document. Accounting for intangible assets has become increasingly important due to the tremendous expansion in computer information systems and Web technologies and the frenzy in companies purchasing other

Solutions to
SELF-STUDY QUIZ

		Debit	Credit
(1)	Depreciation Expense (+E, −SE)	1,200,000	
	Accumulated Depreciation (+XA, −A).......................		1,200,000
(2)	Cash (+A)..	2,000,000	
	Accumulated Depreciation (−XA, +A).......................	20,400,000	
	Loss on Sale of Flight Equipment (+Loss, −SE)	7,600,000	
	Flight Equipment (−A)....................................		30,000,000

Assets		=	Liabilities	+	Stockholders' Equity	
(1) Accumulated Depreciation	−1,200,000				Depreciation Expense	−1,200,000
(2) Flight Equipment	−30,000,000				Loss on Sale of Asset	−7,600,000
Accumulated Depreciation	+20,400,000					
Cash	+2,000,000					

companies at high prices, with the expectation that these intangible resources will provide significant future benefits to the company.

Intangible assets are recorded **at historical cost only if they have been purchased.** If these assets are developed internally by the company, they are expensed when incurred. Upon acquisition of intangible assets, managers determine whether the separate intangibles have definite or indefinite lives:

- **Definite Life.** The cost of an intangible asset with a definite life is allocated on a **straight-line basis** each period over its useful life in a process called amortization that is similar to depreciation. Most companies do not estimate a residual value for their intangible assets. Amortization expense is included on the income statement each period and the intangible assets are reported at cost less accumulated amortization on the balance sheet.

> **AMORTIZATION** is the systematic and rational allocation of the acquisition cost of an intangible asset over its useful life.

Let's assume a company purchases a patent for $800,000 and intends to use it for 20 years. The adjusting entry to record $40,000 in patent amortization expense ($800,000 ÷ 20 years) is as follows:

	Debit	Credit
Patent Amortization Expense (+E, −SE)	40,000	
Patents (−A) (or Accumulated Amortization +XA, −A)[1]		40,000

Assets	=	Liabilities	+	Stockholders' Equity
Patents −40,000 (or Accumulated Amortization +XA)				Patent Amortization Expense (+E) −40,000

- **Indefinite Life.** Intangible assets with indefinite lives are **not amortized.** Instead, these assets must be reviewed at least annually for possible impairment of value by first using qualitative factors to determine whether it is more likely than not (that is, it is greater than a 50 percent likelihood) that the fair value of the indefinite-life intangible is less than its carrying amount. Qualitative factors can include, for example, negative effects due to increases in costs, decreases in cash flows beyond expectations, an economic downturn, or deterioration in the industry. If it is more likely, then the two-step process described on page 401 is followed to determine the amount of the impairment loss.

The AICPA's 2012 **Accounting Trends & Techniques** summarizes intangible assets most frequently disclosed by the 500 companies surveyed:

	Number of Companies	Percentage of 500
Goodwill recognized in a business combination	435	87%
Customer lists/relationships	320	64
Trademarks, brand names, copyrights	302	60
Technology	156	31
Patents, patent rights	134	27
Noncompete covenants	89	18
Contracts, agreements	81	16
Licenses, franchises, memberships	73	15
Other—described in the annual report	184	37

---

[1]Consistent with the procedure for recording depreciation, an accumulated amortization account may be used. In practice, however, most companies credit the asset account directly for periodic amortization. This procedure is also typically used for natural resources, which are discussed in the next section.

Goodwill

For accounting purposes, GOODWILL (COST IN EXCESS OF NET ASSETS ACQUIRED) is the excess of the purchase price of a business over the fair value of the business's assets and liabilities.

By far the most frequently reported intangible asset is goodwill (cost in excess of net assets acquired). The term **goodwill,** as used by most businesspeople, means the favorable reputation that a company has with its customers. Goodwill arises from factors such as customer confidence, reputation for good service or quality goods, location, outstanding management team, and financial standing. From its first day of operations, a successful business continually builds goodwill. In this context, the goodwill is said to be **internally generated** and is not reported as an asset (i.e., it was not purchased).

The only way to report goodwill as an asset is to purchase another business. Often the purchase price of the business exceeds the fair value of all of its net assets (assets minus liabilities). Why would a company pay more for a business as a whole than it would pay if it bought the assets individually? The answer is to obtain its goodwill. You could easily buy modern bottling equipment to produce and sell a new cola drink, but you would not make as much money as you would if you acquired the goodwill associated with Coke or Pepsi brand names.

For accounting purposes, goodwill is defined as the difference between the purchase price of a company as a whole and the fair value of its net assets. For example, in 2006, Cedar Fair, the Ohio-based owner and operator of numerous amusement and water parks and hotels throughout North America, bought five theme parks from Paramount Parks. The total purchase price that Cedar Fair agreed to pay ($1.2 billion) exceeded the fair value of Paramount's net assets ($890 million). As shown below, Cedar Fair paid this extra $310 million to acquire the goodwill associated with the theme parks' businesses.

Cedar Fair's Purchase of Paramount Parks	In Millions
Purchase price	**$1,200**
− Fair value of assets purchased and liabilities assumed:	
Current assets	70
Property and equipment	1,000
Intangible assets	80
Debt and other liabilities	(260)
Net assets, at fair value	**890**
Goodwill	**$ 310**

In many acquisitions, the amount recorded as Goodwill can be very large. For example, Cisco Systems, which designs, manufactures, and sells Internet-based networking and other products and services, has completed several acquisitions since 2009. Of the nearly $6.9 billion total cost of these acquisitions, $4.2 billion was recorded as Goodwill. That is nearly 25 percent of the $16,988 billion in Goodwill reported on Cisco's July 28, 2012, balance sheet and the second largest asset reported.

Goodwill is considered to have an indefinite life and must be tested for possible impairment as described on the previous page for indefinite-life intangibles. Cisco reported the following policy:

REAL WORLD EXCERPT

CISCO.
2012 Annual Report

2. Summary of Significant Accounting Policies

Goodwill and Purchased Intangible Assets

Goodwill is tested for impairment on an annual basis in the fourth fiscal quarter and, when specific circumstances dictate, between annual tests. When impaired, the carrying value of goodwill is written down to fair value.

Trademarks

A trademark is a special name, image, or slogan identified with a product or a company; it is protected by law. Trademarks are among the most valuable assets a company can own. For example, most of us cannot imagine the Walt Disney Company without Mickey Mouse. Similarly, you probably enjoy your favorite soft drink more because of the image that has been built up around its name than because of its taste. Many people can identify the shape of a corporate logo as quickly as they can recognize the shape of a stop sign. Although trademarks are valuable assets, they are rarely seen on balance sheets. The reason is simple; intangible assets are not recorded unless they are purchased. Companies often spend millions of dollars developing trademarks, but most of those expenditures are recorded as expenses rather than being capitalized as an intangible asset.

Copyrights

A copyright gives the owner the exclusive right to publish, use, and sell a literary, musical, or artistic piece for a period not exceeding 70 years after the author's death.[2] The book you are reading has a copyright to protect the publisher and authors. It is against the law, for example, for an instructor to copy several chapters from this book and hand them out in class. A copyright that is purchased is recorded at cost.

A **TRADEMARK** is an exclusive legal right to use a special name, image, or slogan.

A **COPYRIGHT** is the exclusive right to publish, use, and sell a literary, musical, or artistic work.

Technology

The number of companies reporting a technology intangible asset continues to rise. Computer software and Web development costs are becoming increasingly significant. In 2011, IBM Corporation reported $799 million in software on its balance sheet and disclosed the following in the notes to the financial statements:

TECHNOLOGY includes costs for computer software and Web development.

> **Note A: Significant Accounting Policies**
>
> *Software Costs*
>
> The company capitalizes certain costs that are incurred to purchase or to create and implement internal-use software programs, including software coding, installation, testing and certain data conversions. These capitalized costs are amortized on a straight-line basis over periods up to two years and are recorded in selling, general and administrative expense.

REAL WORLD EXCERPT
International Business Machines Corporation
2011 Annual Report

Patents

A patent is an exclusive right granted by the federal government for a period of 20 years, typically granted to a person who invents a new product or discovers a new process.[3] The patent enables the owner to use, manufacture, and sell both the subject of the patent and the patent itself. It prevents a competitor from simply copying a new invention or discovery until the inventor has had time to earn an economic return on the new product. Without the protection of a patent, inventors likely would be unwilling to search for new products.

A **PATENT** is granted by the federal government for an invention; it is an exclusive right given to the owner to use, manufacture, and sell the subject of the patent.

---

[2]In general, the limit is 70 years beyond the death of an author. For anonymous authors, the limit is 95 years from the first publication date. For more detail, go to lcweb.loc.gov/copyright.

[3]For more details, go to http://www.uspto.gov/web/offices/pac/doc/general/index.html#patent.

Patents are recorded at their purchase price or, if **developed internally,** at only their registration and legal costs because GAAP requires the immediate expensing of research and development costs.

Franchises

A FRANCHISE is a contractual right to sell certain products or services, use certain trademarks, or perform activities in a geographical region.

Franchises may be granted by the government or a business for a specified period and purpose. A city may grant one company a franchise to distribute gas to homes for heating purposes, or a company may sell franchises, such as the right to operate a KFC restaurant (owned by Yum! Brands). Franchise agreements are contracts that can have a variety of provisions. They usually require an investment by the franchisee; therefore, they should be accounted for as intangible assets. The life of the franchise agreement depends on the contract. It may be a single year or an indefinite period. For example, Papa John's International, a franchisor, has over 3,900 stores around the world, and about 84 percent are franchises. The franchise agreement covers a 10-year term that is renewable for another 10 years. In the United States, to obtain a new Papa John's franchise, a franchisee pays an initial franchise fee of $25,000 to Papa John's. This amount is then recorded by the franchisee as an intangible asset.

Licenses and Operating Rights

LICENSES AND OPERATING RIGHTS, obtained through agreements with governmental units or agencies, permit owners to use public property in performing their services.

Southwest Airlines's intangible assets are included on the balance sheet presented in Exhibit 8.1 as *other assets.* They primarily represent leasehold rights to airport-owned gates. Others include operating rights, which are authorized landing slots regulated by the government that are in limited supply at many airports. They are intangible assets that can be bought and sold by the airlines. Other types of licenses and operating rights that grant permission to companies include using airwaves for radio and television broadcasts and land for cable and telephone lines.

Research and Development Expense— Not an Intangible Asset under U.S. GAAP

If an intangible asset is developed internally, the cost of development normally is recorded as **research and development expense.** For example, Abbott Laboratories (a manufacturer of pharmaceutical and nutritional products) recently spent more than $4,129 million on research to discover new products. This amount was reported as an expense, not an asset, because research and development expenditures typically do not possess sufficient probability of resulting in measurable future cash flows. If Abbott Labs had spent an equivalent amount to purchase patents for new products from other drug companies, it would have recorded the expenditure as an asset.

INTERNATIONAL PERSPECTIVE

Differences in Accounting for Tangible and Intangible Assets

IFRS differs from GAAP somewhat in accounting for tangible and intangible assets. Two of the most significant differences are summarized below. IFRS allows companies the option of reporting these assets at fair value (e.g., appraisals), provided they use the fair value method consistently each year. The primary argument in favor of revaluation is that the historical cost of an asset purchased 15 to 20 years ago is not meaningful because of the impact of inflation. In contrast, GAAP requires tangible and intangible assets to be recorded at cost and not revalued for later increases in asset values. A primary argument against the revaluation is the lack of objectivity involved in estimating an asset's current cost.

IFRS also requires companies to capitalize the costs of developing intangible assets, such as prototypes for making new products or tools. GAAP, on the other hand, generally expenses such development costs because of the uncertainty of their value.

	GAAP	IFRS
Cost versus Fair Value	• Must record at **cost** • Adjust for depreciation/amortization and impairment • Do not record increases in value	• Choose between either **cost or fair value** • Adjust for depreciation/amortization and impairment • **If using fair value, record increases in value**
Research and Development	• **Expense all costs** of researching and developing intangible assets	• Expense research costs, but **capitalize measurable costs of developing intangible assets**

Until the United States adopts IFRS, you should carefully read the financial statement notes of any non–U.S. company you analyze. Euro Disney and LEGO reported in 2010 that they chose to use historical costs, but they could have chosen instead to use fair value.

Acquisition and Depletion of Natural Resources

You are probably most familiar with large companies that are involved in manufacturing (Ford, Black & Decker), distribution (Sears, Home Depot), or services (FedEx® Kinko's, Holiday Inn). A number of large companies, some of which are less well known, develop raw materials and products from **natural resources,** including mineral deposits such as gold or iron ore, oil wells, and timber tracts. These resources are often called **wasting assets** because they are depleted (i.e., physically used up). Companies that develop natural resources are critical to the economy because they produce essential items such as lumber for construction, fuel for heating and transportation, and food for consumption. Because of the significant effect they can have on the environment, these companies attract considerable public attention. Concerned citizens often read the financial statements of companies involved in the exploration for oil, coal, and various ores to determine the amount of money they spend to protect the environment.

> **NATURAL RESOURCES** are assets that occur in nature, such as mineral deposits, timber tracts, oil, and gas.

When natural resources are acquired or developed, they are recorded in conformity with the **cost principle.** As a natural resource is used up, its acquisition cost must be apportioned among the periods in which revenues are earned in conformity with the **expense matching principle.** The term **depletion** describes the process of allocating a natural resource's cost over the period of its exploitation.[4] The units-of-production method is often applied to compute depletion.

When a natural resource such as an oil well is depleted, the company obtains inventory (oil). Since depleting the natural resource is necessary to obtain the inventory, the depletion computed during a period is not expensed immediately, but is **capitalized** as part of the cost of the inventory. Only when the inventory is sold does the company record an expense (Cost of Goods Sold). Consider the following illustration:

> **DEPLETION** is the systematic and rational allocation of the cost of a natural resource over the period of its exploitation.

A timber tract costing $530,000 is depleted over its estimated cutting period based on a "cutting" rate of approximately 20 percent per year:

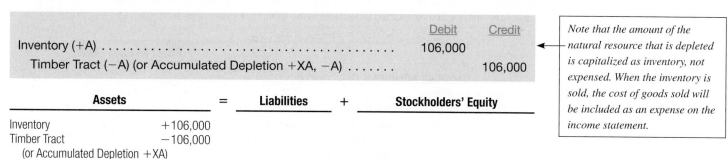

	Debit	Credit
Inventory (+A)	106,000	
Timber Tract (−A) (or Accumulated Depletion +XA, −A)		106,000

Assets		=	Liabilities	+	Stockholders' Equity
Inventory	+106,000				
Timber Tract	−106,000				
(or Accumulated Depletion +XA)					

> Note that the amount of the natural resource that is depleted is capitalized as inventory, not expensed. When the inventory is sold, the cost of goods sold will be included as an expense on the income statement.

---

[4]Consistent with the procedure for recording depreciation, an accumulated depletion account may be used. In practice, however, most companies credit the asset account directly for periodic depletion.

Following is an excerpt from the asset section of International Paper's 2011 balance sheet, along with the related footnote describing the accounting policies for the company's natural resource, forestland:

CONSOLIDATED BALANCE SHEET (DOLLARS IN MILLIONS)

	2011
Assets	
Cash	$3,994
. . .	
Forestlands	660

Notes to Consolidated Financial Statements:

Note 1. Summary of Business and Significant Accounting Policies

Forestlands

At December 31, 2011, International Paper and its subsidiaries owned or managed approximately 325,000 acres of forestlands in Brazil, and through licenses and forest management agreements, had harvesting rights on government-owned forestlands in Russia. Costs attributable to timber are charged against income as trees are cut. The rate charged is determined annually based on the relationship of incurred costs to estimated current merchantable volume.

FOCUS ON CASH FLOWS

 ## Productive Assets and Depreciation

LEARNING OBJECTIVE 8-7

Explain how the acquisition, use, and disposal of long-lived assets impact cash flows.

EFFECT ON STATEMENT OF CASH FLOWS

The indirect method for preparing the operating activities section of the statement of cash flows involves reconciling net income on the accrual basis (reported on the income statement) to cash flows from operations. This means that, among other adjustments, (1) revenues and expenses that do not involve cash and (2) gains and losses that relate to investing or financing activities (not operations) should be eliminated.

When depreciation is recorded, no cash payment is made (i.e., there is no credit to Cash). Since depreciation expense (a noncash expense) is subtracted in calculating net income on the income statement, it must be added back to net income to eliminate its effect. Likewise, since any gain (or loss) on the sale of long-lived assets (an investing activity) is added (or subtracted) to determine net income, it must be subtracted from (or added to) net income to eliminate its effect.

In General   The acquisition, sale, and depreciation of long-term assets are reflected on a company's cash flow statement as indicated in the following table:

	Effect on Cash Flows
Operating activities (indirect method)	
Net income	$xxx
Adjusted for: Depreciation and amortization expense	+
Gains on sale of long-lived assets	−
Losses on sale of long-lived assets	+
Losses due to asset impairment write-downs	+
Investing activities	
Purchase of long-lived assets	−
Sale of long-lived assets	+

Focus Company Analysis   The following is a condensed version of Southwest's statement of cash flows for 2011. Buying and selling long-lived assets are investing activities. In 2011, Southwest used $968 million in cash to purchase flight equipment and ground property and equipment. Southwest did not sell any flight or ground equipment during the year. Selling long-lived assets is not an operating activity. Therefore, any gains (losses) on sales of long-term assets that were included in net income must be deducted from (added to) net income in the operating activities section to eliminate the effect of the sale. Unless they are large, these gain and loss adjustments normally are not specifically highlighted on the statement of cash flows. Southwest did not list any gains or losses as adjustments in 2011.

In capital-intensive industries such as airlines, depreciation is a significant noncash expense. In Southwest's case, depreciation and amortization expense is usually the single largest adjustment to net income in determining cash flows from operations. For example, in 2011, the adjustment for depreciation and amortization expense was 52 percent of operating cash flows.

SOUTHWEST AIRLINES CO. **Consolidated Statement of Cash Flows (partial)** **For the Year Ended December 31, 2011** *(In millions)*	
	2011
Cash Flows from Operating Activities:	
Net income	$ 178
Adjustments to reconcile net income to cash provided by operating activities:	
Depreciation and amortization	715
Other (*summarized*)	492
Net cash provided by (used in) operating activities	1,385
Cash Flows from Investing Activities:	
Purchases of property and equipment, net	(968)
Other (*summarized*)	(83)
Net cash used in investing activities	(1,051)

A Misinterpretation

**FINANCIAL
ANALYSIS**

Some analysts misinterpret the meaning of a noncash expense, saying that "cash is provided by depreciation." Although depreciation is added in the operating section of the statement of cash flows, **depreciation is not a source of cash.** Cash from operations can be provided only by selling goods and services. A company with a large amount of depreciation expense does not generate more cash compared with a company that reports a small amount of depreciation expense, assuming that they are exactly the same in every other respect. While depreciation expense reduces the amount of reported net income for a company, it does not reduce the amount of cash generated by the company because it is a noncash expense. Remember that the effects of recording depreciation are a reduction in stockholders' equity and a reduction in fixed assets, not in cash. That is why, on the statement of cash flows, depreciation expense is added back to net income on an accrual basis to compute cash flows from operations (on a cash basis).

Although depreciation is a noncash expense, the **depreciation for tax purposes can affect a company's cash flows.** Depreciation is a deductible expense for income tax purposes. The higher the amount of depreciation recorded by a company for tax purposes, the lower the company's taxable income and the taxes it must pay. Because taxes must be paid in cash, a reduction in a company's results reduces the company's cash outflows (that is, lower net income leads to lower tax payments).

DEMONSTRATION   CASE A

(Resolve the requirements before proceeding to the suggested solution that follows.) Diversified Industries started as a residential construction company. In recent years, it has expanded into heavy construction, ready-mix concrete, construction supplies, and earth-moving services. The company completed the following transactions during 2013. Amounts have been simplified.

2013

Jan. 1   The management decided to buy a 10-year-old building for $175,000 and the land on which it was situated for $130,000. It paid $100,000 in cash and signed a mortgage note payable for the rest.

Jan. 12   Paid $38,000 in renovation costs on the building prior to use.

July 10   Paid $1,200 for ordinary repairs on the building.

Dec. 31   Year-end adjustments:

a. The building will be depreciated on a straight-line basis over an estimated useful life of 30 years. The estimated residual value is $33,000.

b. Diversified purchased another company several years ago at $100,000 over the fair value of the net assets acquired. The goodwill has an indefinite life.

c. At the beginning of the year, the company owned equipment with a cost of $650,000 and accumulated depreciation of $150,000. The equipment is being depreciated using the double-declining-balance method, with a useful life of 20 years and no residual value.

d. At year-end, the company tested its long-lived assets for possible impairment of their value. It identified a piece of old excavation equipment with a cost of $156,000 and remaining book value of $120,000. Due to its smaller size and lack of safety features, the old equipment has limited use. The future cash flows are expected to be $40,000 and the fair value is determined to be $35,000. Goodwill was found not to be impaired.

December 31, 2013, is the end of the annual accounting period.

Required:

1. Indicate the accounts affected and the amount and direction (+ for increase and − for decrease) of the effect of each of the preceding events (Jan. 1, Jan. 12, July 10, and adjustments a through d) on the financial statement categories at the end of the year. Use the following headings:

Date	Assets	=	Liabilities	+	Stockholders' Equity

2. Record the December 31 adjusting journal entries (a) and (c) only.

3. Show the December 31, 2013, balance sheet classification and amount reported for each of the following items:

   Fixed assets—land, building, and equipment

   Intangible asset—goodwill

4. Assuming that the company had sales of $1,000,000 for the year and a net book value of $500,000 for fixed assets at the beginning of the year, compute the fixed asset turnover ratio. Explain its meaning.

SUGGESTED SOLUTION

1. Effects of events (with computations):

Date	Assets		=	Liabilities		+	Stockholders' Equity	
Jan. 1	Cash Land Building	−100,000 +130,000 +175,000		Note Payable	+205,000			
Jan. 12 (1)	Cash Building	−38,000 +38,000						
July 10 (2)	Cash	−1,200					Repairs Expense	−1,200
Dec. 31 *a* (3)	Accumulated Depreciation (+XA)	−6,000					Depreciation Expense	−6,000
Dec. 31 *b* (4)	No entry							
Dec. 31 *c* (5)	Accumulated Depreciation (+XA)	−50,000					Depreciation Expense	−50,000
Dec. 31 *d* (6)	Equipment	−85,000					Loss Due to Asset Impairment	−85,000

(1) Capitalize the $38,000 expenditure because it is necessary to prepare the asset for use.

(2) This is an ordinary repair and should be expensed.

(3)

Cost of Building		Straight-Line Depreciation
Initial purchase price	$175,000	($213,000 cost − $33,000 residual value) ×
Repairs prior to use	38,000	1/30 years = **$6,000** annual depreciation
Acquisition cost	$213,000	

(4) Goodwill has an indefinite life and is therefore not amortized. We will test for impairment later.

(5) **Double-declining-balance depreciation**

($650,000 cost − $150,000 accumulated depreciation) × 2/20 years = **$50,000** depreciation for 2013.

(6) **Asset impairment**

Impairment Test: The book value of old equipment, $120,000, exceeds expected future cash flows, $40,000. The asset is impaired.

Impairment Loss	
Book value	$120,000
Less: Fair value	−35,000
Loss due to impairment	$ 85,000

2. Adjusting entries at December 31, 2013:

a.

Depreciation Expense (+E, −SE)	6,000	
Accumulated Depreciation (+XA, −A)		6,000

c.

Depreciation Expense (+E, −SE)	50,000	
Accumulated Depreciation (+XA, −A)		50,000

3. Partial balance sheet, December 31, 2013:

Assets		
Fixed assets		
Land		$130,000
Building	$213,000	
Less: Accumulated depreciation	6,000	207,000
Equipment	565,000	
Less: Accumulated depreciation	200,000	365,000
Total fixed assets		702,000
Intangible asset		
Goodwill		100,000

$650,000 − $85,000 ⟶ (Equipment)
$150,000 + $50,000 ⟶ (Less: Accumulated depreciation)

4. Fixed asset turnover ratio:

$$\frac{\text{Sales}}{(\text{Begining Net Fixed Asset Balance} + \text{Ending Net Fixed Asset Balance}) \div 2} = \frac{\$1,000,000}{(\$500,000 + 702,000) \div 2} = 1.66$$

This construction company is capital intensive. The fixed asset turnover ratio measures the company's efficiency at using its investment in property, plant, and equipment to generate sales.

DEMONSTRATION CASE B

In 2014, Diversified Industries, a residential construction company, acquired a gravel pit (designated Gravel Pit No. 1) to support its construction operations. The company completed the following transactions during 2014 related to the gravel pit. Amounts have been simplified and the company's fiscal year ends on December 31.

June 19	Bought Gravel Pit No.1 for $50,000 cash. It was estimated that 100,000 cubic yards of gravel could be removed.
Aug. 1	Paid $10,000 for costs of preparing the new gravel pit for exploitation.
Nov. 10	12,000 cubic yards of gravel were removed from Gravel Pit No. 1 to be used or sold in 2015.

Required:

Record the June 19, August 1, and November 10 transactions.

SUGGESTED SOLUTION

Date	Accounts	Debit	Credit
June 19	Gravel Pit No. 1 (+A)	50,000	
	Cash (−A)		50,000
Aug. 1	Gravel Pit No. 1 (+A)	10,000	
	Cash (−A)		10,000
Nov. 10*	Inventory − gravel (+A)	7,200	
	Gravel Pit No. 1 (−A)		7,200

*Cost of Gravel Pit

Initial purchase price	$50,000
Preparation costs	10,000
Total cost	$60,000

Units-of-Production Depletion

Depletion Rate: $60,000 cost ÷ 100,000 estimated production = $0.60 per unit

Depletion Expense: $0.60 per unit × 12,000 actual production = **$7,200**

Capitalize the depletion to gravel inventory.

Chapter Supplement

Changes in Depreciation Estimates

Depreciation is based on two estimates: useful life and residual value. These estimates are made at the time a depreciable asset is acquired. As experience with the asset accumulates, one or both of these initial estimates may need to be revised. In addition, any improvements that extend the asset's useful life may be added to the original acquisition cost at some time during the asset's use. When it is clear that either estimate should be revised to a material degree or that the asset's cost has changed, the undepreciated asset balance (less any residual value at that date) should be apportioned over the remaining estimated life from the current year into the future. This is called a prospective **change in estimate.**

To compute the new depreciation expense due to a change in estimate for any of the depreciation methods described here, substitute the net book value for the original acquisition cost, the new residual value for the original amount, and the estimated remaining life in place of the original estimated life. As an illustration, the formula using the straight-line method follows.

Original Straight-Line Formula Modified for a Change in Estimate:

$$(\text{Cost} - \text{Residual Value}) \times \frac{1}{\text{Useful Life}} = \text{Original Depreciation Expense}$$

$$(\text{Net Book Value} - \text{New Residual Value}) \times \frac{1}{\text{Remaining Life}} = \text{Revised Depreciation Expense}$$

Assume Southwest purchased an aircraft for $60,000,000 with an estimated useful life of 20 years and estimated residual value of $3,000,000. Shortly after the start of year 5, Southwest changed the initial

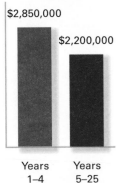

Straight-Line Depreciation Expense with a Change in Estimate

$2,850,000

$2,200,000

Years 1–4   Years 5–25

estimated life to 25 years and lowered the estimated residual value to $2,400,000. At the end of year 5, the computation of the new amount for depreciation expense is as follows:

Original depreciation expense

$$(\$60,000,000 - \$3,000,000) \times 1/20 = \$\ 2,850,000 \text{ per year}$$
$$\times\ 4\ \text{years}$$

Accumulated depreciation at the end of year 4: $11,400,000

Net book value at the end of year 4

Acquisition cost	$60,000,000
Less: Accumulated depreciation	11,400,000
Net book value	$48,600,000

Remaining Life

New estimated life	25 years
In the past	4 years
Remaining	21 years

Depreciation in years 5 through 25 based on changes in estimates

(Net Book Value − New Residual Value) × 1/Remaining Years = New Depreciation Expense

$$(\$48,600,000 - \$2,400,000) \times 1/21 \text{ years} = \$2,200,000 \text{ per year}$$

Companies may also change depreciation methods (for example, from declining balance to straight line). Such a change requires significantly more disclosure since it violates the consistency principle which requires that accounting information reported in the financial statements should be comparable across accounting periods. Under GAAP, changes in accounting estimates and depreciation methods should be made only when a new estimate or accounting method "better measures" the periodic income of the business.

PAUSE FOR **FEEDBACK**

When management changes an estimate used in a depreciation computation, the net book value at the time of the change minus any expected residual value is allocated over the remaining life of the asset.

SELF-STUDY **QUIZ**

Assume that Southwest Airlines owned a service truck that originally cost $100,000. When purchased at the beginning of 2009, the truck had an estimated useful life of 10 years with no residual value. At the beginning of 2014, after operating the truck for five years, Southwest determined that the remaining life was only two more years. Southwest uses the straight-line method.

1. What is the truck's net book value at the beginning of 2014?
2. Based on this change in estimate, what amount of depreciation should be recorded each year over the remaining life of the asset?

After you have completed your answers, check them with the solutions at the bottom of the page.

Solutions to SELF-STUDY QUIZ

1. (Cost $100,000 − Residual Value $0) × 1/10 = $10,000 Original Annual Depreciation
   $10,000 Annual Depreciation Expense × 5 years = $50,000 Accumulated Depreciation.
   Net Book Value After 5 Years = Cost $100,000 − Accumulated Depreciation $50,000 = $50,000.
2. (Net Book Value $50,000 − Residual Value $0) × 1/2 (remaining life) = $25,000 Depreciation Expense per Year.

8-1. Define, classify, and explain the nature of long-lived productive assets and interpret the fixed asset turnover ratio.   p. 383

 a. Productive assets are those that a business retains for long periods of time for use in the course of normal operations rather than for sale. They may be divided into tangible assets (land, buildings, equipment, natural resources) and intangible assets (including goodwill, patents, and franchises).

 b. The cost allocation method utilized affects the amount of net property, plant, and equipment that is used in the computation of the fixed asset turnover ratio. Accelerated methods reduce book value and increase the turnover ratio.

8-2. Apply the cost principle to measure the acquisition and maintenance of property, plant, and equipment.   p. 384

The acquisition cost of property, plant, and equipment is the cash-equivalent purchase price plus all reasonable and necessary expenditures made to acquire and prepare the asset for its intended use. These assets may be acquired using cash, debt, stock, or through self-construction. Expenditures made after the asset is in use are either additions and improvements or ordinary repairs (expenses):

 a. **Ordinary repairs and maintenance** provide benefits during the current accounting period only. Amounts are debited to appropriate current expense accounts when the expenses are incurred.

 b. **Improvements** provide benefits for one or more accounting periods beyond the current period. Amounts are debited to the appropriate asset accounts (they are capitalized) and depreciated, depleted, or amortized over their useful lives.

8-3. Apply various cost allocation methods as assets are held and used over time.   p. 390

Cost allocation methods: In conformity with the expense matching principle, cost less any estimated residual value is allocated to periodic expense over the periods benefited. Because of depreciation, the net book value of an asset declines over time and net income is reduced by the amount of the expense. Common depreciation methods include straight-line (a constant amount over time), units-of-production (a variable amount over time), and double-declining-balance (a decreasing amount over time).

 a. Depreciation—buildings and equipment.

 b. Amortization—intangibles.

 c. Depletion—natural resources.

8-4. Explain the effect of asset impairment on the financial statements. p. 401

When events or changes in circumstances reduce the estimated future cash flows of long-lived assets below their book value, the book values should be written down (by recording a loss) to the fair value of the assets.

8-5. Analyze the disposal of property, plant, and equipment.   p. 402

When assets are disposed of through sale or abandonment,

 a. Record additional depreciation since the last adjustment was made.

 b. Remove the cost of the old asset and its related accumulated depreciation, depletion, or amortization.

 c. Recognize the cash proceeds.

 d. Recognize any gain or loss when the asset's net book value is not equal to the cash received.

8-6. Apply measurement and reporting concepts for intangible assets and natural resources. p. 404

The cost principle should be applied in recording the acquisition of intangible assets and natural resources. Intangibles with definite useful lives are amortized using the straight-line method. Intangibles with indefinite useful lives, including goodwill, are not amortized, but are reviewed at least annually for impairment. Report intangibles at net book value on the balance sheet. Natural resources should be depleted (usually by the units-of-production method) usually with the amount of the depletion expense capitalized to an inventory account.

8-7. **Explain how the acquisition, use, and disposal of long-lived assets impact cash flows.   p. 410**

Depreciation expense is a noncash expense that has no effect on cash. It is added back to net income on the statement of cash flows to determine cash from operations. Acquiring and disposing of long-lived assets are investing activities.

In previous chapters, we discussed business and accounting issues related to the assets that a company holds. In Chapters 9, 10, and 11, we shift our focus to the other side of the balance sheet to see how managers finance business operations and the acquisition of productive assets. We discuss various types of liabilities in Chapters 9 and 10 and examine stockholders' equity in Chapter 11.

KEY **RATIO**

The **fixed asset turnover ratio** measures how efficiently a company utilizes its investment in property, plant, and equipment over time. Its ratio can then be compared to competitors' ratios. The fixed asset turnover ratio is computed as follows (p. 384):

$$\text{Fixed Asset Turnover} = \frac{\text{Net Sales (or Operating Revenues)}}{\text{Average Net Fixed Assets}}$$

FINDING **FINANCIAL INFORMATION**

Balance Sheet

Under Noncurrent Assets
Property, plant, and equipment (net of
     accumulated depreciation)
Natural resources (net of accumulated depletion)
Intangibles (net of accumulated amortization,
     if any)

Income Statement

Under Operating Expenses
Depreciation, depletion, and amortization
     expense **or** included in
Selling, general, and administrative expenses and
Cost of goods sold (with the amount for
     depreciation expense disclosed in a note)

Statement of Cash Flows

Under Operating Activities (indirect method)
Net income
+ Depreciation and amortization expense
− Gains on sales of assets
+ Losses on sales of assets

Under Investing Activities
+ Sales of assets for cash
− Purchases of assets for cash

Notes

Under Summary of Significant Accounting Policies
Description of management's choice for depreciation
     and amortization methods, including useful lives,
     and the amount of annual depreciation expense, if
     not listed on the income statement.

Under a Separate Footnote
If not specified on the balance sheet, a listing of the
     major classifications of long-lived assets at cost
     and the balance in accumulated depreciation,
     depletion, and amortization.

KEY **TERMS**

Acquisition Cost   p. 385
Amortization   p. 405
Capitalized Interest   p. 387
Copyright   p. 407

Declining-Balance Depreciation   p. 396
Depletion   p. 409
Depreciation   p. 391
Estimated Useful Life   p. 392

Franchise   p. 408
Goodwill (Cost in Excess of Net Assets
     Acquired)   p. 406
Improvements   p. 389

QUESTIONS

1. Define **long-lived assets.** Why are they considered to be a "bundle of future services"?
2. How is the fixed asset turnover ratio computed? Explain its meaning.
3. What are the classifications of long-lived assets? Explain each.
4. Under the cost principle, what amounts should be included in the acquisition cost of a long-lived asset?
5. Describe the relationship between the expense matching principle and accounting for long-lived assets.
6. Distinguish between ordinary repairs and improvements. How is each accounted for?
7. Distinguish among depreciation, depletion, and amortization.
8. In computing depreciation, three values must be known or estimated; identify and explain the nature of each.
9. The estimated useful life and residual value of a long-lived asset relate to the current owner or user rather than all potential users. Explain this statement.
10. What type of depreciation expense pattern is used under each of the following methods and when is its use appropriate?
    a. The straight-line method.
    b. The units-of-production method.
    c. The double-declining-balance method.
11. Over what period should an addition to an existing long-lived asset be depreciated? Explain.
12. What is **asset impairment**? How is it accounted for?
13. When equipment is sold for more than net book value, how is the transaction recorded? For less than net book value? What is **net book value**?
14. Define **intangible asset.** What period should be used to amortize an intangible asset with a definite life?
15. Define **goodwill.** When is it appropriate to record goodwill as an intangible asset?
16. Why is depreciation expense added to net income (indirect method) on the statement of cash flows?

MULTIPLE-CHOICE QUESTIONS

1. Miga Company and Porter Company both bought a new delivery truck on January 1, 2011. Both companies paid exactly the same cost, $30,000, for their respective vehicles. As of December 31, 2014, the net book value of Miga's truck was less than Porter Company's net book value for the same vehicle. Which of the following is an acceptable explanation for the difference in net book value?
   a. Miga Company estimated a lower residual value, but both estimated the same useful life and both elected straight-line depreciation.
   b. Both companies elected straight-line depreciation, but Miga Company used a longer estimated life.
   c. Because GAAP specifies rigid guidelines regarding the calculation of depreciation, this situation is not possible.
   d. Miga Company is using the straight-line method of depreciation, and Porter Company is using the double-declining-balance method of depreciation.
2. Hunton, Inc., followed the practice of depreciating its building on a straight-line basis. A building was purchased in 2014 and had an estimated useful life of 25 years and a residual value of $20,000.

The company's depreciation expense for 2014 was $15,000 on the building. What was the original cost of the building?

a. $395,000

b. $500,000

c. $520,000

d. Cannot be determined from the information given.

3. Maks, Inc., uses straight-line depreciation for all of its depreciable assets. Maks sold a used piece of machinery on December 31, 2015, that it purchased on January 1, 2014, for $10,000. The asset had a five-year life, zero residual value, and $2,000 accumulated depreciation as of December 31, 2014. If the sales price of the used machine was $7,500, the resulting gain or loss upon the sale was which of the following amounts?

a. Loss of $500   d. Gain of $1,500

b. Gain of $500   e. No gain or loss upon the sale.

c. Loss of $1,500

4. Under what method(s) of depreciation is an asset's **net book value** the depreciable base (the amount to be depreciated)?

a. Straight-line method   c. Units-of-production method

b. Declining-balance method   d. All of the above

5. What assets should be amortized using the straight-line method?

a. Intangible assets with definite lives   c. Natural resources

b. Intangible assets with indefinite lives   d. All of the above

6. A company wishes to report the highest earnings possible for financial reporting purposes. Therefore, when calculating depreciation,

a. It will follow the MACRS depreciation tables prescribed by the IRS.

b. It will select the shortest lives possible for its assets.

c. It will select the lowest residual values for its assets.

d. It will estimate higher residual values for its assets.

7. How many of the following statements regarding goodwill are true?

• Goodwill is not reported unless purchased in an exchange.

• Goodwill must be reviewed annually for possible impairment.

• Impairment of goodwill results in a decrease in net income.

a. Three   c. One

b. Two   d. None

8. Company X is going to retire equipment that is fully depreciated with no residual value. The equipment will simply be disposed of, not sold. Which of the following statements is *false*?

a. Total assets will not change as a result of this transaction.

b. Net income will not be impacted as a result of this transaction.

c. This transaction will not impact cash flow.

d. All of the above statements are true.

9. When recording depreciation, which of the following statements is *true*?

a. Total assets increase and stockholders' equity increases.

b. Total assets decrease and total liabilities increase.

c. Total assets decrease and stockholders' equity increases.

d. None of the above are true.

10. (Supplement) Irish Industries purchased a machine for $65,000 and is depreciating it with the straight-line method over a life of 10 years, using a residual value of $3,000. At the beginning of the sixth year, a major overhaul was made costing $5,000, and the total estimated useful life was extended to 13 years. Depreciation expense for year 6 is:

a. $1,885   d. $3,625

b. $2,000   e. $4,500

c. $3,250

For more practice with multiple-choice questions, go to the text website at **www.mhhe.com/libby8e.**

Classifying Long-Lived Assets and Related Cost Allocation Concepts

M8-1
LO8-1, 8-3, 8-6

For each of the following long-lived assets, indicate its nature and the related cost allocation concept. Use the following symbols:

Nature		Cost Allocation Concept	
L	Land	DR	Depreciation
B	Building	DP	Depletion
E	Equipment	A	Amortization
NR	Natural resource	NO	No cost allocation
I	Intangible	O	Other
O	Other		

Asset	Nature	Cost Allocation	Asset	Nature	Cost Allocation
(1) Tractors	_____	_____	(6) Operating license	_____	_____
(2) Land in use	_____	_____	(7) Production plant	_____	_____
(3) Timber tract	_____	_____	(8) Trademark	_____	_____
(4) Warehouse	_____	_____	(9) Silver mine	_____	_____
(5) New engine for old machine	_____	_____	(10) Land held for sale	_____	_____

Computing and Evaluating the Fixed Asset Turnover Ratio

M8-2
LO8-1

The following information was reported by Young's Air Cargo Service for 2011:

Net fixed assets (beginning of year)	$1,500,000
Net fixed assets (end of year)	2,300,000
Net sales for the year	3,600,000
Net income for the year	1,600,000

Compute the company's fixed asset turnover ratio for the year. What can you say about Young's ratio when compared to Southwest's 2011 ratio?

Identifying Capital Expenditures and Expenses

M8-3
LO8-2

For each of the following items, enter the correct letter to the left to show the type of expenditure. Use the following:

Type of Expenditure		Transactions
C	Capital expenditure	_____ (1) Purchased a patent, $4,300 cash.
E	Expense	_____ (2) Paid $10,000 for monthly salaries.
N	Neither	_____ (3) Paid cash dividends, $20,000.
		_____ (4) Purchased a machine, $7,000; gave a long-term note.
		_____ (5) Paid three-year insurance premium, $900.
		_____ (6) Paid for routine maintenance, $200, on credit.
		_____ (7) Paid $400 for ordinary repairs.
		_____ (8) Paid $6,000 for improvements that lengthened the asset's productive life.
		_____ (9) Paid $20,000 cash for addition to old building.

M8-4
LO8-3

Computing Book Value (Straight-Line Depreciation)

Calculate the book value of a three-year-old machine that has a cost of $31,000, an estimated residual value of $1,000, and an estimated useful life of five years. The company uses straight-line depreciation.

M8-5
LO8-3

Computing Book Value (Double-Declining-Balance Depreciation)

Calculate the book value of a three-year-old machine that has a cost of $55,000, an estimated residual value of $5,000, and an estimated useful life of five years. The company uses double-declining-balance depreciation. Round to the nearest dollar.

M8-6
LO8-3

Computing Book Value (Units-of-Production Depreciation)

Calculate the book value of a three-year-old machine that has a cost of $26,000, an estimated residual value of $1,000, and an estimated useful life of 50,000 machine hours. The company uses units-of-production depreciation and ran the machine 3,200 hours in year 1; 7,050 hours in year 2; and 7,500 hours in year 3.

M8-7
LO8-4

Identifying Asset Impairment

For each of the following scenarios, indicate whether an asset has been impaired (Y for yes and N for no) and, if so, the amount of loss that should be recorded.

	Book Value	Estimated Future Cash Flows	Fair Value	Is Asset Impaired?	Amount of Loss
a. Machine	$ 15,500	$ 10,000	$ 9,500		
b. Copyright	31,000	41,000	37,900		
c. Factory building	58,000	29,000	27,000		
d. Building	227,000	227,000	200,000		

M8-8
LO8-5

Recording the Disposal of a Long-Lived Asset (Straight-Line Depreciation)

As part of a major renovation at the beginning of the year, Bonham's Bakery sold shelving units (store fixtures) that were 10 years old for $1,800 cash. The original cost of the shelves was $6,500 and they had been depreciated on a straight-line basis over an estimated useful life of 12 years with an estimated residual value of $800. Record the sale of the shelving units.

M8-9
LO8-6

Computing Goodwill and Patents

Elizabeth Pie Company has been in business for 50 years and has developed a large group of loyal restaurant customers. Giant Bakery Inc. has made an offer to buy Elizabeth Pie Company for $5,000,000. The book value of Elizabeth Pie's recorded assets and liabilities on the date of the offer is $4,300,000 with a fair value of $4,500,000. Elizabeth Pie also (1) holds a patent for a pie crust fluting machine that the company invented (the patent with a fair value of $300,000 was never recorded by Elizabeth Pie because it was developed internally) and (2) estimates goodwill from loyal customers to be $310,000 (also never recorded by the company). Should Elizabeth Pie Company management accept Giant Bakery's offer of $5,000,000? If so, compute the amount of goodwill that Giant Bakery should record on the date of the purchase.

M8-10
LO8-7

Preparing the Statement of Cash Flows

Garrett Company had the following activities for the year ended December 31, 2015: Sold land that cost $20,000 for $20,000 cash; purchased $181,000 of equipment, paying $156,000 in cash and signing a note payable for the rest; and recorded $5,500 in depreciation expense for the year. Net income for the year was $18,000. Prepare the operating and investing sections of a statement of cash flows for the year based on the data provided.

Preparing a Classified Balance Sheet

The following is a list of account titles and amounts (dollars in millions) from a recent annual report of Hasbro, Inc., a leading manufacturer of games, toys, and interactive entertainment software for children and families:

E8-1
LO8-1

Hasbro, Inc.

Buildings and improvements	$202	Goodwill	$ 475
Prepaid expenses and other		Machinery and equipment	462
current assets	243	Accumulated depreciation	453
Allowance for doubtful accounts	24	Inventories	334
Other noncurrent assets	717	Other intangibles	1,089
Accumulated amortization		Land and improvements	7
(other intangibles)	622	Accounts receivable	1,059
Cash and cash equivalents	642		

Required:
Prepare the asset section of the balance sheet for Hasbro, Inc., classifying the assets into Current Assets, Property, Plant, and Equipment (net), and Other Assets.

Computing and Interpreting the Fixed Asset Turnover Ratio from a Financial Analyst's Perspective

The following data were included in a recent Apple Inc. annual report ($ in millions):

E8-2
LO8-1

Apple, Inc.

In millions	2008	2009	2010	2011
Net sales	$32,479	$36,537	$62,225	$108,249
Net property, plant, and equipment	2,455	2,954	4,768	7,777

Required:
1. Compute Apple's fixed asset turnover ratio for 2009, 2010, and 2011. Round your answers to two decimal points.
2. How might a financial analyst interpret the results?

Computing and Recording Cost and Depreciation of Assets (Straight-Line Depreciation)

Shahia Company bought a building for $82,000 cash and the land on which it was located for $107,000 cash. The company paid transfer costs of $9,000 ($3,000 for the building and $6,000 for the land). Renovation costs on the building were $21,000.

E8-3
LO8-2, 8-3

Required:
1. Give the journal entry to record the purchase of the property, including all expenditures. Assume that all transactions were for cash and that all purchases occurred at the start of the year.
2. Compute straight-line depreciation at the end of one year, assuming an estimated 10-year useful life and a $15,000 estimated residual value.
3. What would be the net book value of the property (land and building) at the end of year 2?

Determining Financial Statement Effects of an Asset Acquisition and Depreciation (Straight-Line Depreciation)

Ashkar Company ordered a machine on January 1, 2013, at an invoice price of $21,000. On the date of delivery, January 2, 2013, the company paid $6,000 on the machine, with the balance on credit at 10 percent interest due in six months. On January 3, 2013, it paid $1,000 for freight on the machine. On January 5, Ashkar paid installation costs relating to the machine amounting to $2,500. On July 1, 2013,

E8-4
LO8-2, 8-3

the company paid the balance due on the machine plus the interest. On December 31, 2013 (the end of the accounting period), Ashkar recorded depreciation on the machine using the straight-line method with an estimated useful life of 10 years and an estimated residual value of $4,000.

Required (round all amounts to the nearest dollar):

1. Indicate the effects (accounts, amounts, and + or −) of each transaction (on January 1, 2, 3, and 5 and July 1) on the accounting equation. Use the following schedule:

Date	Assets	=	Liabilities	+	Stockholders' Equity

2. Compute the acquisition cost of the machine.
3. Compute the depreciation expense to be reported for 2013.
4. What impact does the interest paid on the 10 percent note have on the cost of the machine? Under what circumstances can interest expense be included in acquisition cost?
5. What would be the net book value of the machine at the end of 2014?

E8-5
LO8-2, 8-3

Recording Depreciation and Repairs (Straight-Line Depreciation)

Hulme Company operates a small manufacturing facility as a supplement to its regular service activities. At the beginning of 2014, an asset account for the company showed the following balances:

Manufacturing equipment	$120,000
Accumulated depreciation through 2013	57,600

During 2014, the following expenditures were incurred for the equipment:

Routine maintenance and repairs on the equipment	$ 1,000
Major overhaul of the equipment that improved efficiency on January 2, 2014	13,000

The equipment is being depreciated on a straight-line basis over an estimated life of 15 years with a $12,000 estimated residual value. The annual accounting period ends on December 31.

Required:

1. Give the adjusting entry that was made at the end of **2013** for depreciation on the manufacturing equipment.
2. Starting at the beginning of **2014,** what is the remaining estimated life?
3. Give the journal entries to record the two expenditures during **2014.**

E8-6
LO8-2, 8-3

Determining Financial Statement Effects of Depreciation and Repairs (Straight-Line Depreciation)

Refer to the information in E8-5.

Required:
Indicate the effects (accounts, amounts, and + or −) of the following on the accounting equation.

Date	Assets	=	Liabilities	+	Stockholders' Equity

1. The adjustment for depreciation at the end of **2013.**
2. The two expenditures during **2014.**

E8-7
LO8-3

Computing Depreciation under Alternative Methods

Purity Ice Cream Company bought a new ice cream maker at the beginning of the year at a cost of $9,000. The estimated useful life was four years, and the residual value was $1,000. Assume that the estimated productive life of the machine was 16,000 hours. Actual annual usage was 5,500 hours in year 1; 3,800 hours in year 2; 3,200 hours in year 3; and 3,500 hours in year 4.

Required:

1. Complete a separate depreciation schedule for each of the alternative methods. Round your answers to the nearest dollar.
   a. Straight-line.
   b. Units-of-production (use four decimal places for the per unit output factor).
   c. Double-declining-balance.

Method: _____				
Year	Computation	Depreciation Expense	Accumulated Depreciation	Net Book Value
At acquisition				
1				
2				
etc.				

2. Assuming that the machine was used directly in the production of one of the products that the company manufactures and sells, what factors might management consider in selecting a preferable depreciation method in conformity with the expense matching principle?

Computing Depreciation under Alternative Methods

E8-8
LO8-3

Strong Metals Inc. purchased a new stamping machine at the beginning of the year at a cost of $950,000. The estimated residual value was $50,000. Assume that the estimated useful life was five years, and the estimated productive life of the machine was 300,000 units. Actual annual production was as follows:

Year	Units
1	70,000
2	67,000
3	50,000
4	73,000
5	40,000

Required:

1. Complete a separate depreciation schedule for each of the alternative methods. Round your answers to the nearest dollar.
   a. Straight-line.
   b. Units-of-production.
   c. Double-declining-balance.

Method: _____				
Year	Computation	Depreciation Expense	Accumulated Depreciation	Net Book Value
At acquisition				
1				
2				
etc.				

2. Assuming that the machine was used directly in the production of one of the products that the company manufactures and sells, what factors might management consider in selecting a preferable depreciation method in conformity with the expense matching principle?

E8-9
LO8-3

**General Motors
Corporation**

Explaining Depreciation Policy

The 2001 annual report for General Motors Corporation contained the following note:

Note 3. Significant Accounting Policies

Property, Net

Property, plant, and equipment, including internal use software, is recorded at cost. Major improvements that extend the useful life of property are capitalized. Expenditures for repairs and maintenance are charged to expense as incurred. At January 1, 2001, we adopted the straight-line method of depreciation for real estate, facilities, and equipment placed in service after that date. Assets placed in service before January 1, 2001, continue to be depreciated using accelerated methods. The accelerated methods accumulate depreciation of approximately two-thirds of the depreciable cost in the first half of the estimated useful lives of property groups as compared to the straight-line method, which allocates depreciable costs equally over the estimated useful lives of property groups.

Required:

Why do you think the company changed its depreciation method for real estate, facilities, and equipment placed in service after January 1, 2001, and subsequent years?

E8-10
LO8-3

FedEx

Interpreting Management's Choice of Different Depreciation Methods for Tax and Financial Reporting

A recent annual report for FedEx includes the following information:

For financial reporting purposes, we record depreciation and amortization of property and equipment on a straight-line basis over the asset's service life or related lease term if shorter. For income tax purposes, depreciation is computed using accelerated methods when applicable.

Required:

Explain why FedEx uses different methods of depreciation for financial reporting and tax purposes.

E8-11
LO8-3, 8-7

Computing Depreciation and Book Value for Two Years Using Alternative Depreciation Methods and Interpreting the Impact on Cash Flows

Schrade Company bought a machine for $96,000 cash. The estimated useful life was four years, and the estimated residual value was $6,000. Assume that the estimated useful life in productive units is 120,000. Units actually produced were 43,000 in year 1 and 45,000 in year 2.

Required:

1. Determine the appropriate amounts to complete the following schedule. Show computations, and round to the nearest dollar.

	Depreciation Expense for		Net Book Value at the End of	
Method of Depreciation	Year 1	Year 2	Year 1	Year 2
Straight-line				
Units-of-production				
Double-declining-balance				

2. Which method would result in the lowest EPS for year 1? For year 2?

3. Which method would result in the highest amount of cash outflows in year 1? Why?
4. Indicate the effects of (*a*) acquiring the machine and (*b*) recording annual depreciation on the operating and investing activities sections of the statement of cash flows (indirect method) for year 1 (assume the straight-line method).

Inferring Asset Impairment and Recording Disposal of an Asset

In a recent 10-K report, United Parcel Service states it "is the world's largest package delivery company, a leader in the U.S. less-than-truckload industry, and a global leader in supply chain management." The following note and data were reported:

E8-12
LO8-4, 8-5

United Parcel
Service Inc.

> **Note 1—Summary of Accounting Policies**
>
> *Impairment of Long-Lived Assets*
>
> . . . we review long-lived assets for impairment when circumstances indicate the carrying amount of an asset may not be recoverable based on the undiscounted future cash flows of the asset. . . .

	Dollars in Millions
Cost of property and equipment (beginning of year)	$33,611
Cost of property and equipment (end of year)	35,098
Capital expenditures during the year	2,636
Accumulated depreciation (beginning of year)	15,948
Accumulated depreciation (end of year)	16,833
Depreciation expense during the year	1,814
Cost of property and equipment sold during the year	1,040
Accumulated depreciation on property sold	929
Cash received on property sold	147

Required:
1. Reconstruct the journal entry for the disposal of property and equipment during the year.
2. Compute the amount of property and equipment that United Parcel wrote off as impaired during the year. (**Hint:** Set up T-accounts.)

Recording the Disposal of an Asset at Three Different Sale Prices

FedEx is the world's leading express-distribution company. In addition to the world's largest fleet of all-cargo aircraft, the company has more than 688 aircraft and 50,000 vehicles and trailers that pick up and deliver packages. Assume that FedEx sold a delivery truck that had been used in the business for three years. The records of the company reflected the following:

E8-13
LO8-5

FedEx

Delivery truck cost	$35,000
Accumulated depreciation	23,000

Required:
1. Give the journal entry for the disposal of the truck, assuming that the truck sold for
   a. $12,000 cash
   b. $12,400 cash
   c. $11,500 cash
2. Based on the three preceding situations, explain the effects of the disposal of an asset.

E8-14
LO8-5

Marriott
International, Inc.

Recording the Disposal of an Asset at Three Different Sale Prices

Marriott International is a worldwide operator and franchisor of hotels and related lodging facilities totaling over $1.1 billion in property and equipment. It also develops, operates, and markets time-share properties totaling nearly $2 billion. Assume that Marriott replaced furniture that had been used in the business for five years. The records of the company reflected the following regarding the sale of the existing furniture:

Furniture (cost)	$8,000,000
Accumulated depreciation	7,700,000

Required:
1. Give the journal entry for the disposal of the furniture, assuming that it was sold for
   a. $300,000 cash
   b. $900,000 cash
   c. $100,000 cash
2. Based on the three preceding situations, explain the effects of the disposal of an asset.

E8-15
LO8-3, 8-5

Inferring Asset Age and Recording Accidental Loss on a Long-Lived Asset (Straight-Line Depreciation)

On January 1, 2015, the records of Sitake Corporation showed the following regarding a truck:

Equipment (estimated residual value, $9,000)	$25,000
Accumulated depreciation (straight-line, three years)	6,000

On December 31, 2015, the delivery truck was a total loss as the result of an accident.

Required:
1. Based on the data given, compute the estimated useful life of the truck.
2. Give all journal entries with respect to the truck on December 31, 2015. Show computations.

E8-16
LO8-6

FREEPORT-McMoRan
COPPER & GOLD

Computing the Acquisition and Depletion of a Natural Resource

Freeport-McMoRan Copper & Gold Inc., headquartered in Phoenix, Arizona, is one of the world's largest copper, gold, and molybdenum mining and production companies, with its principal asset in natural resource reserves (approximately 119.7 billion pounds of copper, 33.9 million ounces of gold, 3.42 billion pounds of molybdenum, 330.3 million ounces of silver, and 0.86 billion pounds of cobalt, as of the end of 2011). Its annual revenues exceed $20.8 billion.

Assume that in February 2015, Freeport-McMoRan paid $800,000 for a mineral deposit in Indonesia. During March, it spent $70,000 in preparing the deposit for exploitation. It was estimated that 1,000,000 total cubic yards could be extracted economically. During 2015, 60,000 cubic yards were extracted. During January 2016, the company spent another $6,000 for additional developmental work that increased the estimated productive capacity of the mineral deposit.

Required:
1. Compute the acquisition cost of the deposit in 2015.
2. Compute depletion for 2015.
3. Compute the net book value of the deposit after payment of the January 2016 developmental costs.

E8-17
LO8-6

Computing and Reporting the Acquisition and Amortization of Three Different Intangible Assets

Trotman Company had three intangible assets at the end of 2013 (end of the accounting year):

a. Computer software and Web development technology purchased on January 1, 2012, for $70,000. The technology is expected to have a four-year useful life to the company.
b. A patent purchased from Ian Zimmer on January 1, 2013, for a cash cost of $6,000. Zimmer had registered the patent with the U.S. Patent Office five years ago.
c. An internally developed trademark registered with the federal government for $13,000 on November 1, 2013. Management decided the trademark has an indefinite life.

Required:
1. Compute the acquisition cost of each intangible asset.
2. Compute the amortization of each intangible at December 31, 2013. The company does not use contra-accounts.
3. Show how these assets and any related expenses should be reported on the balance sheet and income statement for 2013.

Computing and Reporting the Acquisition and Amortization of Three Different Intangible Assets

Springer Company had three intangible assets at the end of 2014 (end of the accounting year):

a. A copyright purchased on January 1, 2014, for a cash cost of $14,500. The copyright is expected to have a 10-year useful life to Springer.
b. Goodwill of $65,000 from the purchase of the Hartford Company on July 1, 2013.
c. A patent purchased on January 1, 2013, for $48,000. The inventor had registered the patent with the U.S. Patent Office on January 1, 2009.

Required:
1. Compute the acquisition cost of each intangible asset.
2. Compute the amortization of each intangible at December 31, 2014. The company does not use contra-accounts.
3. Show how these assets and any related expenses should be reported on the balance sheet and income statement for 2014. (Assume there has been no impairment of goodwill.)

E8-18
LO8-6

Recording Leasehold Improvements and Related Amortization

Starbucks Corporation is the leading roaster and retailer of specialty coffee, with over 17,000 company-operated and licensed stores worldwide. Assume that Starbucks planned to open a new store on Commonwealth Avenue near Boston University and obtained a 10-year lease starting January 1, 2015. The company had to renovate the facility by installing an elevator costing $325,000. Amounts spent to enhance leased property are capitalized as intangible assets called Leasehold Improvements. The elevator will be amortized over the useful life of the lease.

Required:
1. Give the journal entry to record the installation of the new elevator.
2. Give any adjusting entries required at the end of the annual accounting period on December 31, 2015, related to the new elevator. Show computations.

E8-19
LO8-6

Starbucks

Finding Financial Information as a Potential Investor

You are considering investing the cash gifts you received for graduation in various stocks. You have received several annual reports of major companies.

Required:
For each of the following, indicate where you would locate the information in an annual report. (**Hint:** The information may be in more than one location.)
1. Depreciation expense.
2. The detail on major classifications of long-lived assets.
3. Prior year's accumulated depreciation.
4. The accounting method(s) used for financial reporting purposes.
5. Net amount of property, plant, and equipment.
6. Whether the company had any capital expenditures for the year.
7. Policies on amortizing intangibles.
8. Any significant gains or losses on disposals of fixed assets.
9. The amount of assets written off as impaired during the year.

E8-20
LO8-1, 8-2, 8-3, 8-4, 8-5, 8-6, 8-7

(Supplement) Recording a Change in Estimate

Refer to E8-5.

Required:
Give the adjusting entry that should be made by Hulme Company at the end of 2014 for depreciation of the manufacturing equipment, assuming no change in the original estimated life or residual value. Show computations. Round answer to the nearest dollar.

E8-21
LO8-3

E8-22

LO8-2, 8-3

(Supplement) Recording and Explaining Depreciation, Improvements, and Changes in Estimated Useful Life and Residual Value (Straight-Line Depreciation)

At the end of the annual accounting period, December 31, 2014, O'Connor Company's records reflected the following for Machine A:

Cost when acquired	$30,000
Accumulated depreciation	10,200

During January 2015, the machine was renovated at a cost of $15,500. As a result, the estimated life increased from five years to eight years, and the residual value increased from $4,500 to $6,500. The company uses straight-line depreciation.

Required:
1. Give the journal entry to record the renovation.
2. How old was the machine at the end of 2014?
3. Give the adjusting entry at the end of 2015 to record straight-line depreciation for the year.
4. Explain the rationale for your entries in requirements 1 and 3.

E8-23

LO8-3, 8-7

(Supplement) Computing the Effect of a Change in Useful Life and Residual Value on Financial Statements and Cash Flows (Straight-Line Depreciation)

Burbank Company owns the building occupied by its administrative office. The office building was reflected in the accounts at the end of last year as follows:

Cost when acquired	$330,000
Accumulated depreciation (based on straight-line depreciation, an estimated life of 50 years, and a $30,000 residual value)	78,000

During January of this year, on the basis of a careful study, management decided that the total estimated useful life should be changed to 30 years (instead of 50) and the residual value reduced to $22,500 (from $30,000). The depreciation method will not change.

Required:
1. Compute the annual depreciation expense prior to the change in estimates.
2. Compute the annual depreciation expense after the change in estimates.
3. What will be the net effect of changing estimates on the balance sheet, net income, and cash flows for the year?

To practice with more exercises, go to the text website at **www.mhhe.com/libby8e.**

PROBLEMS

P8-1

LO8-1, 8-2

Explaining the Nature of a Long-Lived Asset and Determining and Recording the Financial Statement Effects of Its Purchase (AP8-1)

On January 2, 2015, Summers Company bought a machine for use in operations. The machine has an estimated useful life of eight years and an estimated residual value of $2,600. The company provided the following expenditures:

a. Invoice price of the machine, $85,000.
b. Freight paid by the vendor per sales agreement, $1,000.
c. Installation costs, $2,400 paid in cash.
d. Payment was made as follows:

On January 2:

• The installation costs were paid in cash.
• Summers Company common stock, par $1; 2,000 shares (market value, $3.50 per share).

- Note payable, $60,000; 11.5 percent due April 16, 2015 (principal plus interest).
- Balance of invoice price to be paid in cash. The invoice allows for a 3 percent discount for cash paid by January 12.

On January 15:

- Summers Company paid the balance due.

Required:
1. What are the classifications of long-lived assets? Explain their differences.
2. Record the purchase on January 2 and the subsequent payment on January 15. Show computations.
3. Indicate the accounts, amounts, and effects (+ for increase and − for decrease) of the purchase and subsequent cash payment on the accounting equation. Use the following structure:

Date	Assets	=	Liabilities	+	Stockholders' Equity

4. Explain the basis you used for any questionable items.

Analyzing the Effects of Repairs, an Addition, and Depreciation (AP8-2)

A recent annual report for FedEx included the following note:

P8-2
LO8-2, 8-3

FedEx

> **Property and Equipment**
>
> Expenditures for major additions, improvements, flight equipment modifications, and certain equipment overhaul costs are capitalized when such costs are determined to extend the useful life of the asset or are part of the cost of acquiring the asset. Maintenance and repairs are charged to expense as incurred . . .

Assume that FedEx made extensive repairs on an existing building and added a new wing. The building is a garage and repair facility for delivery trucks that serve the Denver area. The existing building originally cost $950,000, and by the end of 2013 (10 years), it was half depreciated on the basis of a 20-year estimated useful life and no residual value. Assume straight-line depreciation was used. During 2014, the following expenditures related to the building were made:

a. Ordinary repairs and maintenance expenditures for the year, $7,000 cash.
b. Extensive and major repairs to the roof of the building, $122,000 cash. These repairs were completed on December 31, 2014.
c. The new wing was completed on December 31, 2014, at a cash cost of $230,000.

Required:
1. Applying the policies of FedEx, complete the following, indicating the effects for the preceding expenditures. If there is no effect on an account, write NE on the line.

	Building	Accumulated Depreciation	Depreciation Expense	Repairs Expense	Cash
Balance January 1, 2014	$950,000	$475,000			
Depreciation for 2014		_____	_____		_____
Balance prior to expenditures	950,000	_____	_____		
Expenditure (*a*)	_____	_____	_____	_____	_____
Expenditure (*b*)	_____	_____	_____	_____	_____
Expenditure (*c*)	_____	_____	_____	_____	_____
Balance December 31, 2014	_____	_____	_____	_____	

2. What was the book value of the building on December 31, 2014?
3. Explain the effect of depreciation on cash flows.

P8-3
LO8-2, 8-3

www.mhhe.com/libby8e

Computing the Acquisition Cost and Recording Depreciation under Three Alternative Methods (AP8-3)

At the beginning of the year, Plummer's Sports Center bought three used fitness machines from Advantage, Inc. The machines immediately were overhauled, installed, and started operating. The machines were different; therefore, each had to be recorded separately in the accounts.

	Machine A	Machine B	Machine C
Amount paid for asset	$11,000	$30,000	$8,000
Installation costs	500	1,000	500
Renovation costs prior to use	2,500	1,000	1,500

By the end of the first year, each machine had been operating 4,800 hours.

Required:
1. Compute the cost of each machine.
2. Give the entry to record depreciation expense at the end of year 1, assuming the following:

Machine	ESTIMATES Life	ESTIMATES Residual Value	Depreciation Method
A	5 years	$1,000	Straight-line
B	60,000 hours	2,000	Units-of-production
C	4 years	1,500	Double-declining-balance

P8-4
LO8-1, 8-3

Best Buy

www.mhhe.com/libby8e

Inferring Depreciation Amounts and Determining the Effects of a Depreciation Error on Key Ratios (AP8-4)

Best Buy Co., Inc., headquartered in Richfield, Minnesota, is one of the leading consumer electronics retailers, operating more than 1,000 stores in the United States, Europe, Canada, China, and Mexico. The following was reported in a recent annual report:

CONSOLIDATED BALANCE SHEETS		
($ in millions)	February 26, 2011	February 27, 2010
ASSETS		
Property and Equipment		
Land and buildings	$ 766	$ 757
Leasehold improvements	2,318	2,154
Fixtures and equipment	4,701	4,447
Property under capital lease	120	95
	7,905	7,453
Less accumulated depreciation	4,082	3,383
Net property and equipment	3,823	4,070

Required:
1. Assuming that Best Buy did not sell any property, plant, and equipment in the current year, what was the amount of depreciation expense recorded during the current year?
2. Assume that Best Buy failed to record depreciation during the current year. Indicate the effect of the error (i.e., overstated or understated) on the following ratios:
   a. Earnings per share.
   b. Fixed asset turnover.
   c. Current ratio.
   d. Return on assets.

Evaluating the Effect of Alternative Depreciation Methods on Key Ratios from an Analyst's Perspective

P8-5
LO8-1, 8-3

www.mhhe.com/libby8e

You are a financial analyst for Ford Motor Company and have been asked to determine the impact of alternative depreciation methods. For your analysis, you have been asked to compare methods based on a machine that cost $106,000. The estimated useful life is 13 years, and the estimated residual value is $2,000. The machine has an estimated useful life in productive output of 200,000 units. Actual output was 20,000 in year 1 and 16,000 in year 2. (Round results to the nearest dollar.)

Required:

1. For years 1 and 2 only, prepare separate depreciation schedules assuming:
   a. Straight-line method.
   b. Units-of-production method.
   c. Double-declining-balance method.

Method: _____				
Year	Computation	Depreciation Expense	Accumulated Depreciation	Net Book Value
At acquisition				
1				
2				

2. Evaluate each method in terms of its effect on cash flow, fixed asset turnover, and EPS. Assuming that Ford Motor Company is most interested in reducing taxes and maintaining a high EPS for year 1, what would you recommend to management? Would your recommendation change for year 2? Why or why not?

Recording and Interpreting the Disposal of Three Long-Lived Assets (AP8-5)

P8-6
LO8-3, 8-5

www.mhhe.com/libby8e

During 2015, Merkley Company disposed of three different assets. On January 1, 2015, prior to their disposal, the accounts reflected the following:

Asset	Original Cost	Residual Value	Estimated Life	Accumulated Depreciation (straight line)
Machine A	$21,000	$3,000	8 years	$15,750 (7 years)
Machine B	50,000	4,000	10 years	36,800 (8 years)
Machine C	85,000	5,000	15 years	64,000 (12 years)

The machines were disposed of in the following ways:

a. Machine A: Sold on January 1, 2015, for $5,000 cash.
b. Machine B: Sold on December 31, 2015, for $10,500; received cash, $2,500, and a $8,000 interest-bearing (12 percent) note receivable due at the end of 12 months.
c. Machine C: On January 1, 2015, this machine suffered irreparable damage from an accident. On January 10, 2015, a salvage company removed the machine at no cost.

Required:

1. Give all journal entries related to the disposal of each machine in 2015.
2. Explain the accounting rationale for the way that you recorded each disposal.

P8-7

LO8-5, 8-7

Inferring Activities Affecting Fixed Assets from Notes to the Financial Statements and Analyzing the Impact of Depreciation on Cash Flows

Singapore Airlines reported the following information in the notes to a recent annual report (in Singapore dollars):

SINGAPORE AIRLINES

Notes to the Accounts

21. Property, Plant, and Equipment (in $ millions)
The Group

	Beginning of Year	Additions	Disposals/ Transfers	End of Year
Cost				
Aircraft	20,042.8	116.4	548.4	19,610.8
Other fixed assets (summarized)	4,566.8	1,118.0	1,069.9	4,614.9
	24,609.6	1,234.4	1,618.3	24,225.7

	Beginning of Year	Depreciation	Impairment Loss	Disposals/ Transfers	End of Year
Accumulated depreciation					
Aircraft	7,567.9	1,506.9	14.6	590.5	8,498.9
Other fixed assets (summarized)	1,977.8	164.8	1.1	294.5	1,849.2
	9,545.7	1,671.7	15.7	885.0	10,348.1

Singapore Airlines also reported the following cash flow details:

Cash Flow from Operating Activities (in $ millions)

	Current Year	Prior Year
Profit before taxation	1,419.0	285.5
Adjustments for		
Depreciation	1,671.7	1,713.8
Impairment loss	15.7	6.1
Surplus (gain) on disposal of fixed assets	(103.3)	(25.4)
Other adjustments (summarized)	282.1	(7.7)
Cash generated from operations	3,285.2	1,972.3

Required:

1. Reconstruct the information in Note 21 using T-accounts for Fixed Assets and Accumulated Depreciation:

Property, Plant, and Equipment		Accumulated Depreciation	
Beg. balance Acquisitions	Disposals/transfers	Disposal/transfers	Beg. balance Depreciation expense Impairment loss
End. balance			End. balance

2. Compute the amount of cash the company received for disposals and transfers for the current year. Show computations.

3. Compute the percentage of depreciation expense to cash flows from operations for the current year. What do you interpret from the result?

**Determining Financial Statement Effects of Activities Related to Various
Long-Lived Assets (AP8-6)**

During the 2013 annual accounting period, BSP Company completed the following transactions:

a. On January 1, 2013, purchased a patent for $28,000 cash (estimated useful life, seven years).

b. On January 1, 2013, purchased the assets (not detailed) of another business for $164,000 cash, including $10,000 for goodwill. The company assumed no liabilities. Goodwill has an indefinite life.

c. On December 31, 2013, constructed a storage shed on land leased from D. Heald. The cost was $15,600. The company uses straight-line depreciation. The lease will expire in three years. (Amounts spent to enhance leased property are capitalized as intangible assets called Leasehold Improvements.)

d. Total expenditures during 2013 for ordinary repairs and maintenance were $5,500.

e. On December 31, 2013, sold Machine A for $6,000 cash. Original cost on January 1, 2009, was $25,000; accumulated depreciation (straight line) to December 31, 2012, was $16,000 ($5,000 residual value and five-year useful life).

f. On December 31, 2013, paid $5,000 for a complete reconditioning of Machine B acquired on January 1, 2012. Original cost, $31,000; accumulated depreciation (straight line) to December 31, 2012, $1,600 ($7,000 residual value and 15-year useful life).

Required:

1. For each of these transactions, indicate the accounts, amounts, and effects (+ for increase and − for decrease) on the accounting equation. Use the following structure:

Date	Assets	=	Liabilities	+	Stockholders' Equity

2. For each of these assets, except the assets not detailed in (b), compute depreciation and amortization to be recorded at the end of the year on December 31, 2013.

**Computing Goodwill from the Purchase of a Business and Related Depreciation
and Amortization**

The notes to a recent annual report from Weebok Corporation included the following:

> **Business Acquisitions**
>
> During the current year, the Company acquired the assets of Sport Shoes, Inc. . . .

Assume that Weebok acquired Sport Shoes on January 5, 2013. Weebok acquired the name of the company and all of its assets for $750,000 cash. Weebok did not assume the liabilities. The transaction was closed on January 5, 2013, at which time the balance sheet of Sport Shoes reflected the following book values and an independent appraiser estimated the following market values for the assets:

Sport Shoes, Inc.		
January 5, 2010	Book Value	Market Value*
Accounts receivable (net)	$ 50,000	$ 50,000
Inventory	385,000	350,000
Fixed assets (net)	156,000	208,000
Other assets	4,000	10,000
Total assets	$595,000	
Liabilities	$ 75,000	*These values for the purchased assets were provided to Weebok by an independent appraiser.*
Stockholders' equity	520,000	
Total liabilities and stockholders' equity	$595,000	

Required:

1. Compute the amount of goodwill resulting from the purchase. (**Hint:** Assets are purchased at market value in conformity with the cost principle.)
2. Compute the adjustments that Weebok would make at the end of the annual accounting period, December 31, 2013, for the following:
   a. Depreciation of the fixed assets (straight line), assuming an estimated remaining useful life of 10 years and no residual value.
   b. Goodwill (an intangible asset with an indefinite life).

P8-10

LO8-3, 8-4, 8-6

Computing Amortization, Book Value, and Asset Impairment Related to Different Intangible Assets (AP8-7)

Starn Tool Company has five different intangible assets to be accounted for and reported on the financial statements. The management is concerned about the amortization of the cost of each of these intangibles. Facts about each intangible follow:

a. **Patent.** The company purchased a patent at a cash cost of $55,900 on January 1, 2014. The patent has an estimated useful life of 13 years.
b. **Copyright.** On January 1, 2014, the company purchased a copyright for $22,500 cash. It is estimated that the copyrighted item will have no value by the end of 10 years.
c. **Franchise.** The company obtained a franchise from McKenna Company to make and distribute a special item. It obtained the franchise on January 1, 2014, at a cash cost of $14,400 for a 10-year period.
d. **License.** On January 1, 2013, the company secured a license from the city to operate a special service for a period of five years. Total cash expended to obtain the license was $14,000.
e. **Goodwill.** The company started business in January 2011 by purchasing another business for a cash lump sum of $400,000. Included in the purchase price was "Goodwill, $40,000." Company executives stated that "the goodwill is an important long-lived asset to us." It has an indefinite life.

Required:

1. Compute the amount of amortization that should be recorded for each intangible asset at the end of the annual accounting period, December 31, 2014.
2. Give the book value of each intangible asset on December 31, 2015.
3. Assume that on January 2, 2016, the copyrighted item was impaired in its ability to continue to produce strong revenues. The other intangible assets were not affected. Starn estimated that the copyright would be able to produce future cash flows of $17,000. The fair value of the copyright was determined to be $16,000. Compute the amount, if any, of the impairment loss to be recorded.

P8-11

LO8-3

(Supplement) Analyzing and Recording Entries Related to a Change in Estimated Life and Residual Value

Rungano Corporation is a global publisher of magazines, books, and music and video collections and is a leading direct mail marketer. Many direct mail marketers use high-speed Didde press equipment to print their advertisements. These presses can cost more than $1 million. Assume that Rungano owns a Didde press acquired at an original cost of $400,000. It is being depreciated on a straight-line basis over a 20-year estimated useful life and has a $50,000 estimated residual value. At the end of 2013, the press had been depreciated for a full six years. In January 2014, a decision was made, on the basis of improved maintenance procedures, that a total estimated useful life of 25 years and a residual value of $73,000 would be more realistic. The accounting period ends December 31.

Required:

1. Compute (*a*) the amount of depreciation expense recorded in 2013 and (*b*) the book value of the printing press at the end of 2013.
2. Compute the amount of depreciation that should be recorded in 2014. Show computations (round amount to the nearest dollar).
3. Give the adjusting entry for depreciation at December 31, 2014.

Explaining the Nature of a Long-Lived Asset and Determining and Recording the Financial Statement Effects of Its Purchase (P8-1)

AP8-1

LO8-1, 8-2

On June 1, 2013, the Wallace Corp. bought a machine for use in operations. The machine has an estimated useful life of six years and an estimated residual value of $2,000. The company provided the following expenditures:

a. Invoice price of the machine, $60,000.
b. Freight paid by the vendor per sales agreement, $650.
c. Installation costs, $1,500.
d. Payment was made as follows:

On June 1:

- The installation costs were paid in cash.
- Wallace Corp. common stock, par $2; 2,000 shares (market value, $6 per share).
- Balance of the invoice price on a note payable, 12 percent due September 2, 2013 (principal plus interest).

On September 2:

- Wallace Corp. paid the balance and interest due on the note payable.

Required:
1. What are the classifications of long-lived assets? Explain their differences.
2. Record the purchase on June 1 and the subsequent payment on September 2. Show computations.
3. Indicate the accounts, amounts, and effects (+ for increase and − for decrease) of the purchase and subsequent cash payment on the accounting equation. Use the following structure:

Date	Assets	=	Liabilities	+	Stockholders' Equity

4. Explain the basis you used for any questionable items.

Analyzing the Effects of Repairs, an Addition, and Depreciation (P8-2)

AP8-2

LO8-2, 8-3

AMERCO

A recent annual report for AMERCO, the holding company for U-Haul International, Inc., included the following note:

Note 3: Accounting Policies

Property, Plant, and Equipment

Property, plant, and equipment are stated at cost. Interest expense incurred during the initial construction of buildings and rental equipment is considered part of cost. Depreciation is computed for financial reporting purposes using the straight-line or an accelerated method based on a declining balances formula over the following estimated useful lives: rental equipment 2–20 years and buildings and nonrental equipment 3–55 years. The Company follows the deferral method of accounting based in the AICPA's Airline Audit Guide for major overhauls in which engine overhauls are capitalized and amortized over five years and transmission overhauls are capitalized and amortized over three years. Routine maintenance costs are charged to operating expense as they are incurred.

AMERCO subsidiaries own property, plant, and equipment that are utilized in the manufacture, repair, and rental of U-Haul equipment and that provide offices for U-Haul. Assume that AMERCO made extensive repairs on an existing building and added a new wing. The building is a garage and repair facility for rental trucks that serve the Seattle area. The existing building originally cost $330,000, and by the end of 2014 (its fifth year), the building was one-quarter depreciated on the basis of a 20-year estimated useful life and no residual value. Assume straight-line depreciation. During 2015, the following expenditures related to the building were made:

a. Ordinary repairs and maintenance expenditures for the year, $6,000 cash.
b. Extensive and major repairs to the roof of the building, $17,000 cash. These repairs were completed on December 31, 2015.
c. The new wing was completed on December 31, 2015, at a cash cost of $70,000.

Required:
1. Applying the policies of AMERCO, complete the following, indicating the effects for the preceding expenditures. If there is no effect on an account, write NE on the line.

	Building	Accumulated Depreciation	Depreciation Expense	Repairs Expense	Cash
Balance January 1, 2015	$330,000	$82,500			
Depreciation for 2015					
Balance prior to expenditures	330,000				
Expenditure (*a*)					
Expenditure (*b*)					
Expenditure (*c*)					
Balance December 31, 2015					

2. What was the book value of the building on December 31, 2015?
3. Explain the effect of depreciation on cash flows.

AP8-3
LO8-2, 8-3

Computing the Acquisition Cost and Recording Depreciation under Three Alternative Methods (P8-3)

At the beginning of the year, Ramos Inc. bought three used machines from Santaro Corporation. The machines immediately were overhauled, installed, and started operating. The machines were different; therefore, each had to be recorded separately in the accounts.

	Machine A	Machine B	Machine C
Cost of the asset	$12,200	$32,500	$21,700
Installation costs	1,600	1,100	1,100
Renovation costs prior to use	600	1,400	1,600

By the end of the first year, each machine had been operating 7,000 hours.

Required:
1. Compute the cost of each machine.
2. Give the entry to record depreciation expense at the end of year 1, assuming the following:

Machine	ESTIMATES		Depreciation Method
	Life	Residual Value	
A	8 years	$1,000	Straight-line
B	33,000 hours	2,000	Units-of-production
C	5 years	1,400	Double-declining-balance

AP8-4
LO8-1, 8-3
The Gap, Inc.

Inferring Depreciation Amounts and Determining the Effects of a Depreciation Error on Key Ratios (P8-4)

The Gap, Inc., is a global specialty retailer of casual wear and personal products for women, men, children, and babies under the Gap, Banana Republic, Old Navy, Athleta, and Piperlime brands. As of

January 31, 2012, the Company operated 3,036 stores across the globe, as well as online. The following is a note from a recent annual report:

Note 1. Summary of Significant Accounting Policies:

Property and Equipment

Depreciation is computed using the straight-line method over the estimated useful lives of the related assets . . .

   The cost of assets sold or retired and the related accumulated depreciation are removed from the accounts with any resulting gain or loss included in operating expenses in the Consolidated Statements of Earnings. Maintenance and repairs are expensed as incurred.

   Interest related to assets under construction is capitalized during the construction period up to the amount of interest expense actually incurred.

Note 2. Additional Financial Statement Information

Property and Equipment

Property and equipment are stated at cost less accumulated depreciation and consist of the following:

($ in millions)	January 28, 2012	January 29, 2011
Leasehold improvements	$3,168	$3,066
Furniture and equipment	2,463	2,431
Land and buildings	1,096	1,093
Software	960	909
Construction-in-progress	96	74
Property and equipment, at cost	7,783	7,573
Less: Accumulated depreciation	(5,260)	(5,010)
Property and equipment, net of accumulated depreciation	$2,523	$2,563

Required:
1. Assuming that The Gap, Inc., did not have any asset impairment write-offs but did sell property, plant, and equipment in the most recent year with a cost of $501 million and an accumulated depreciation of $384 million, what was the amount of depreciation expense recorded in the current year?
2. Assume that The Gap, Inc., failed to record depreciation in the current year. Indicate the effect of the error (i.e., overstated or understated) on the following ratios:
   a. Earnings per share
   b. Fixed asset turnover
   c. Current ratio
   d. Return on assets

Recording and Interpreting the Disposal of Three Long-Lived Assets (P8-6)

AP8-5
LO8-3, 8-5

During 2014, Rank Company disposed of three different assets. On January 1, 2014, prior to their disposal, the accounts reflected the following:

Asset	Original Cost	Residual Value	Estimated Life	Accumulated Depreciation (straight line)
Machine A	$24,000	$2,000	5 years	$17,600 (4 years)
Machine B	16,500	5,000	20 years	4,025 (7 years)
Machine C	59,200	3,200	14 years	48,000 (12 years)

The machines were disposed of in the following ways:

a. Machine A: Sold on January 1, 2014, for $6,750 cash.
b. Machine B: Sold on December 31, 2014, for $8,000; received cash, $2,000, and a $6,000 interest-bearing (10 percent) note receivable due at the end of 12 months.
c. Machine C: On January 1, 2014, this machine suffered irreparable damage from an accident and was scrapped.

Required:

1. Give all journal entries related to the disposal of each machine.
2. Explain the accounting rationale for the way in which you recorded each disposal.

AP8-6

LO8-2, 8-3, 8-6

Determining Financial Statement Effects of Activities Related to Various Long-Lived Assets (P8-8)

During the 2015 annual accounting period, Nguyen Corporation completed the following transactions:

a. On January 1, 2015, purchased a license for $7,200 cash (estimated useful life, four years).
b. On January 1, 2015, repaved the parking lot of the building leased from H. Lane. The cost was $17,800; the estimated useful life was five years with no residual value. The lease will expire in 10 years. (Amounts spent to enhance leased property are capitalized as intangible assets called Leasehold Improvements.)
c. On July 1, 2015, purchased another business for $120,000 cash. The transaction included $115,000 for the assets and $24,000 for the liabilities assumed by Nguyen. The remainder was goodwill with an indefinite life.
d. On December 31, 2015, sold Machine A for $6,000 cash. Original cost, $21,500; accumulated depreciation (straight line) to December 31, 2014, $13,500 ($3,500 residual value and four-year life).
e. Total expenditures during 2015 for ordinary repairs and maintenance were $6,700.
f. On December 31, 2015, paid $8,000 for a complete reconditioning of Machine B acquired on January 1, 2012. Original cost, $18,000; accumulated depreciation (straight line) to December 31, 2014, $12,000 ($2,000 residual value and four-year life).

Required:

1. For each of these transactions, indicate the accounts, amounts, and effects (+ for increase and − for decrease) on the accounting equation. Use the following structure:

Date	Assets	=	Liabilities	+	Stockholders' Equity

2. For each of these assets, except the assets not detailed in (c), compute depreciation and amortization to be recorded at the end of the year on December 31, 2015.

AP8-7

LO8-3, 8-4, 8-6

Computing Amortization, Book Value, and Asset Impairment Related to Different Intangible Assets (P8-10)

Carey Corporation has five different intangible assets to be accounted for and reported on the financial statements. The management is concerned about the amortization of the cost of each of these intangibles. Facts about each intangible follow:

a. **Goodwill.** The company started business in January 2012 by purchasing another business for a cash lump sum of $650,000. Included in the purchase price was "Goodwill, $75,000." Company executives stated that "the goodwill is an important long-lived asset to us." It has an indefinite life.
b. **Patent.** The company purchased a patent at a cash cost of $18,600 on January 1, 2014. It is amortized over its expected useful life of 10 years.
c. **Copyright.** On January 1, 2014, the company purchased a copyright for $24,750 cash. It is estimated that the copyrighted item will have no value by the end of 30 years.
d. **Franchise.** The company obtained a franchise from Cirba Company to make and distribute a special item. It obtained the franchise on January 1, 2014, at a cash cost of $19,200 for a 12-year period.
e. **License.** On January 1, 2013, the company secured a license from the city to operate a special service for a period of seven years. Total cash expended to obtain the license was $21,700.

Required:

1. Compute the amount of amortization that should be recorded for each intangible asset at the end of the annual accounting period, December 31, 2014.
2. Give the book value of each intangible asset on January 1, 2017.

3. Assume that on January 2, 2017, the franchise was impaired in its ability to continue to produce strong revenues. The other intangible assets were not affected. Carey estimated that the franchise would be able to produce future cash flows of $13,500. The fair value of the franchise was determined to be $12,000. Compute the amount, if any, of the impairment loss to be recorded.

COMPREHENSIVE PROBLEM (CHAPTERS 6–8)

Complete the requirements for each of the following independent cases:

Case A. Dr Pepper Snapple Group, Inc., is a leading integrated brand owner, bottler, and distributor of nonalcoholic beverages in the United States, Canada, and Mexico. Key brands include Dr. Pepper, Snapple, 7-UP, Mott's juices, A&W root beer, Canada Dry ginger ale, Schweppes ginger ale, and Hawaiian Punch, among others.

COMP8-1

Dr Pepper Snapple Group, Inc.

The following represents selected data from recent financial statements of Dr Pepper Snapple Group (dollars in millions):

DR PEPPER SNAPPLE GROUP, INC.		
Consolidated Balance Sheets (partial)		
(in millions)	**December 31, 2011**	**December 31, 2010**
Assets		
Current assets:		
Cash and cash equivalents	$701	$315
Accounts receivable (net of allowances of $3 and $5, respectively)	585	536

Consolidated Statements of Income (partial)			
	For the Year Ended December 31		
(in millions)	**2011**	**2010**	**2009**
Net sales	$5,903	$5,636	$5,531
...			
Net income	$ 606	$ 528	$ 555

The company also reported bad debt expense of $4 million in 2011, $1 million in 2010, and $3 million in 2009.

1. Record the company's write-offs of uncollectible accounts for 2011.
2. Assuming all sales were on credit, what amount of cash did Dr Pepper Snapple Group collect from customers in 2011?
3. Compute the company's net profit margin for the three years presented. What does the trend suggest to you about Dr Pepper Snapple Group?

Case B. Samuda Enterprises uses the aging approach to estimate bad debt expense. At the end of 2014, Samuda reported a balance in accounts receivable of $620,000 and estimated that $12,400 of its accounts receivable would likely be uncollectible. The allowance for doubtful accounts has a $1,500 debit balance at year-end (that is, more was written off during the year than the balance in the account).

1. What amount of bad debt expense should be recorded for 2014?
2. What amount will be reported on the 2014 balance sheet for accounts receivable?

Case C. At the end of 2015, the unadjusted trial balance of Samuels, Inc., indicated $6,530,000 in Accounts Receivable, a credit balance of $9,200 in Allowance for Doubtful Accounts, and Sales Revenue (all on credit) of $155,380,000. Based on knowledge that the current economy is in distress, Samuels increased its bad debt rate estimate to 0.3 percent on credit sales.

1. What amount of bad debt expense should be recorded for 2015?
2. What amount will be reported on the 2015 balance sheet for accounts receivable?

Case D. Stewart Company reports the following inventory records for November 2014:

INVENTORY			
Date	Activity	# of Units	Cost/Unit
November 1	Beginning balance	100	$16
November 4	Purchase	300	19
November 7	Sale (@ $50 per unit)	200	
November 13	Purchase	500	21
November 22	Sale (@ $50 per unit)	500	

Selling, administrative, and depreciation expenses for the month were $16,000. Stewart's tax rate is 30 percent.

1. Calculate the cost of ending inventory and the cost of goods sold under each of the following methods:
   a. First-in, first-out.
   b. Last-in, first out.
   c. Weighted average (round unit cost to the nearest penny.)
2. Based on your answers in requirement (1)
   a. What is the gross profit percentage under the FIFO method?
   b. What is net income under the LIFO method?
   c. Which method would you recommend to Stewart for tax and financial reporting purposes? Explain your recommendation.
3. Stewart applied the lower of cost or market method to value its inventory for reporting purposes at the end of the month. Assuming Stewart used the FIFO method and that inventory had a market replacement value of $19.50 per unit, what would Stewart report on the balance sheet for inventory? Why?

Case E. Matson Company purchased the following on January 1, 2014:

- Office equipment at a cost of $60,000 with an estimated useful life to the company of three years and a residual value of $15,000. The company uses the double-declining-balance method of depreciation for the equipment.
- Factory equipment at an invoice price of $880,000 plus shipping costs of $20,000. The equipment has an estimated useful life of 100,000 hours and no residual value. The company uses the units-of-production method of depreciation for the equipment.
- A patent at a cost of $330,000 with an estimated useful life of 15 years. The company uses the straight-line method of amortization for intangible assets with no residual value.

1. Prepare a partial depreciation schedule for 2014, 2015, and 2016 for the following assets (round your answers to the nearest dollar):
   a. Office equipment.
   b. Factory equipment. The company used the equipment for 8,000 hours in 2014, 9,200 hours in 2015, and 8,900 hours in 2016.
2. On January 1, 2017, Matson altered its corporate strategy dramatically. The company sold the factory equipment for $700,000 in cash. Record the entry related to the sale of the factory equipment.
3. On January 1, 2017, when the company changed its corporate strategy, its patent had estimated future cash flows of $210,000 and a fair value of $190,000. What would the company report on the income statement (account and amount) regarding the patent on January 2, 2017? Explain your answer.

CASES **AND PROJECTS**

Annual Report Cases

Finding Financial Information

Refer to the financial statements of American Eagle Outfitters in Appendix B at the end of this book.

Required:

For each question, answer it and indicate where you located the information to answer the question. (**Hint:** Use the notes to the financial statements for some of these questions.)

1. How much did the company spend on property and equipment (capital expenditures) in fiscal 2011 (the year ended January 28, 2012)?
2. What is the typical estimated useful life of leasehold improvements for amortization purposes?
3. What was the original cost of fixtures and equipment held by the company at the end of the most recent reporting year?
4. What was the amount of depreciation and amortization reported as an expense for the current year? Compare this amount to the change in accumulated depreciation from fiscal year ended 2011 to fiscal year ended 2012. Why would these numbers be different?
5. What is the company's fixed asset turnover ratio for fiscal year ended 2012?

CP8-1
LO8-1, 8-2, 8-4, 8-6

AMERICAN EAGLE
OUTFITTERS, INC.

Finding Financial Information

Refer to the financial statements of Urban Outfitters given in Appendix C at the end of this book.

Required:

For each question, answer it and indicate where you located the information to answer the question. (**Hint:** Use the notes to the financial statements for many of these questions.)

1. What method of depreciation does the company use?
2. What is the amount of accumulated depreciation and amortization at the end of the most recent reporting year?
3. For depreciation purposes, what is the estimated useful life of furniture and fixtures?
4. What was the original cost of leasehold improvements owned by the company at the end of the most recent reporting year?
5. What amount of depreciation and amortization was reported as expense for the most recent reporting year?
6. What is the company's fixed asset turnover ratio for the most recent year? What does it suggest?

CP8-2
LO8-1, 8-2, 8-6

Comparing Companies within an Industry

Refer to the financial statements of American Eagle Outfitters (Appendix B) and Urban Outfitters (Appendix C) and the Industry Ratio Report (Appendix D) at the end of this book.

Required:

1. Compute the percentage of net fixed assets to total assets for both companies for the most recent year. Why do the companies differ?
2. Compute the percentage of gross fixed assets that has been depreciated for both companies for the most recent year. Why do you think the percentages differ?
3. Compute the fixed asset turnover ratio for the most recent year presented for both companies. Which company has higher asset efficiency? Why?
4. Compare the fixed asset turnover ratio for both companies to the industry average. Are these companies doing better or worse than the industry average in asset efficiency?

CP8-3
LO8-1, 8-3

AMERICAN EAGLE
OUTFITTERS, INC.

Financial Reporting and Analysis Cases

CP8-4
LO8-3

Sysco Corporation

Using Financial Reports: Analyzing the Age of Assets

In its recent annual report, Sysco Corporation noted it "is the largest North American distributor of food and related products primarily to the foodservice 'food-away-from-home' industry. We provide products and related services to approximately 400,000 customers, including restaurants, health-care, and educational facilities, lodging establishments, and other foodservice customers." A note to a recent annual report for Sysco contained the following information:

(in thousands)	Current Year
Land	$ 348,168
Buildings and improvements	3,227,340
Fleet and equipment	2,275,007
Computer hardware and software	897,712
	6,748,227
Less accumulated depreciation	3,235,838
	$3,512,389

Depreciation expense (in thousands of dollars) charged to operations was $374,000 in the current year. Depreciation generally is computed using the straight-line method for financial reporting purposes.

Required:
1. What is your best estimate of the average expected life for Sysco's depreciable assets?
2. What is your best estimate of the average age of Sysco's depreciable assets?

CP8-5
LO8-1, 8-6, 8-7

Using Financial Reports: Analyzing Fixed Asset Turnover Ratio and Cash Flows

Karl Company operates in both the beverage and entertainment industries. In June 2013, Karl purchased Good Time, Inc., which produces and distributes motion picture, television, and home video products and recorded music; publishes books; and operates theme parks and retail stores. The purchase resulted in $2.7 billion in goodwill. Since 2013, Karl has undertaken a number of business acquisitions and divestitures (sales of businesses) as the company expands into the entertainment industry. Selected data from a recent annual report are as follows (amounts are in U.S. dollars in millions):

Property, Plant, Equipment, and Intangibles From the Consolidated Balance Sheet	Current Year	Prior Year
Film costs, net of amortization	$1,272	$ 991
Artists' contracts, advances, and other entertainment assets	761	645
Property, plant, and equipment, net	2,733	2,559
Excess of cost over fair value of assets acquired	3,076	3,355
From the Consolidated Statement of Income		
Total revenues	$9,714	$10,644
From the Consolidated Statement of Cash Flows		
Income from continuing operations	$ 880	$ 445
Adjustments:		
Depreciation	289	265
Amortization	208	190
Other adjustments (summarized)	(1,618)	(256)
Net cash provided by continuing operations	(241)	644
From the Notes to the Financial Statements		
Accumulated depreciation on property, plant, and equipment	$1,178	$ 1,023

Required:

1. Compute the cost of the property, plant, and equipment at the end of the current year. Explain your answer.
2. What was the approximate age of the property, plant, and equipment at the end of the current year?
3. Compute the fixed asset turnover ratio for the current year. Explain your results.
4. What is "excess of cost over fair value of assets acquired"?
5. On the consolidated statement of cash flows, why are the depreciation and amortization amounts added to income from continuing operations?

Using Financial Reports: Inferring the Sale of Assets

A recent annual report for Eastman Kodak reported that the cost of property, plant, and equipment at the end of the current year was $5,485 million. At the end of the previous year, it had been $6,022 million. During the current year, the company bought $128 million worth of new equipment. The balance of accumulated depreciation at the end of the current year was $4,590 million; at the end of the previous year it was $4,985 million. Depreciation expense for the current year was $253 million. The company reported an $80 million gain on the disposition of property, plant, and equipment.

Required:

What amount of proceeds did Eastman Kodak receive when it sold property, plant, and equipment during the current year? (**Hint:** Set up T-accounts.)

CP8-6
LO8-1, 8-5, 8-7

Critical Thinking Cases

Making a Decision as a Financial Analyst: Interpreting the Impact of the Capitalization of Interest on an Accounting Ratio

Hess Corporation is a global energy company that explores, produces, refines, and markets crude oil and natural gas. The capitalization of interest associated with self-constructed assets was discussed in this chapter. A recent annual report for Hess Corporation disclosed the following information concerning capitalization of interest:

In Note 1:

> *Capitalized Interest:* Interest from external borrowings is capitalized on material projects using the weighted average cost of outstanding borrowings until the project is substantially complete and ready for its intended use, which for oil and gas assets is at first production from the field.

In Note 7:

> The Corporation capitalized interest of $13 million, $5 million, and $6 million in 2011, 2010, and 2009, respectively.

Required:

1. Explain why an analyst would calculate the interest coverage ratio.
2. Did Hess include the $13 million capitalized interest in the reported interest expense of $383 million? If not, should an analyst include it when calculating the interest coverage ratio? Explain.

CP8-7
LO8-2

Hess Corporation

Evaluating an Ethical Dilemma: A Real-Life Example

Assume you work as a staff member in a large accounting department for a multinational public company. Your job requires you to review documents relating to the company's equipment purchases. Upon verifying that purchases are properly approved, you prepare journal entries to record the equipment purchases in the accounting system. Typically, you handle equipment purchases costing $100,000 or less.

This morning, you were contacted by the executive assistant to the chief financial officer (CFO). She says that the CFO has asked to see you immediately in his office. Although your boss's boss has attended a few meetings where the CFO was present, you have never met the CFO during your three years with the company. Needless to say, you are anxious about the meeting.

CP8-8
LO8-1, 8-2

Upon entering the CFO's office, you are warmly greeted with a smile and friendly handshake. The CFO compliments you on the great work that you've been doing for the company. You soon feel a little more comfortable, particularly when the CFO mentions that he has a special project for you. He states that he and the CEO have negotiated significant new arrangements with the company's equipment suppliers, which require the company to make advance payments for equipment to be purchased in the future. The CFO says that, for various reasons that he didn't want to discuss, he will be processing the payments through the operating division of the company rather than the equipment accounting group. Given that the payments will be made through the operating division, they will initially be classified as operating expenses of the company. He indicates that clearly these advance payments for property and equipment should be recorded as assets, so he will be contacting you at the end of every quarter to make an adjusting journal entry to capitalize the amounts inappropriately classified as operating expenses. He advises you that a new account, called Prepaid Equipment, has been established for this purpose. He quickly wraps up the meeting by telling you that it is important that you not talk about the special project with anyone. You assume he doesn't want others to become jealous of your new important responsibility.

A few weeks later, at the end of the first quarter, you receive a voicemail from the CFO stating, "The adjustment that we discussed is $771,000,000 for this quarter." Before deleting the message, you replay it to make sure you heard it right. Your company generates over $8 billion in revenues and incurs $6 billion in operating expenses every quarter, but you've never made a journal entry for that much money. So, just to be sure there's not a mistake, you send an e-mail to the CFO confirming the amount. He phones you back immediately to abruptly inform you, "There's no mistake. That's the number." Feeling embarrassed that you may have annoyed the CFO, you quietly make the adjusting journal entry.

For each of the remaining three quarters in that year and for the first quarter in the following year, you continue to make these end-of-quarter adjustments. The "magic number," as the CFO liked to call it, was $560,000,000 for Q2, $742,745,000 for Q3, $941,000,000 for Q4, and $818,204,000 for Q1 of the following year. During this time, you've had several meetings and lunches with the CFO where he provides you the magic number, sometimes supported with nothing more than a Post-it note with the number written on it. He frequently compliments you on your good work and promises that you'll soon be in line for a big promotion.

Despite the CFO's compliments and promises, you are growing increasingly uncomfortable with the journal entries that you've been making. Typically, whenever an ordinary equipment purchase involves an advance payment, the purchase is completed a few weeks later. At that time, the amount of the advance is removed from an Equipment Deposit account and transferred to the appropriate equipment account. This hasn't been the case with the CFO's special project. Instead, the Prepaid Equipment account has continued to grow, now standing at over $3.8 billion. There's been no discussion about how or when this balance will be reduced, and no depreciation has been recorded for it.

Just as you begin to reflect on the effect the adjustments have had on your company's fixed assets, operating expenses, and operating income, you receive a call from the vice president for internal audit. She needs to talk with you this afternoon about "a peculiar trend in the company's fixed asset turnover ratio and some suspicious journal entries that you've been making."

Required:
1. Complete the following table to determine what the company's accounting records would have looked like had you not made the journal entries as part of the CFO's special project. Comment on how the decision to capitalize amounts, which were initially recorded as operating expenses, has affected the level of income from operations in each quarter.

(amounts in millions of U.S. dollars)	Q1 Year 1 (March 31)		Q2 Year 1 (June 30)		Q3 Year 1 (September 30)		Q4 Year 1 (December 31)		Q1 Year 2 (March 31)	
	With the Entries	Without the Entries	With the Entries	Without the Entries	With the Entries	Without the Entries	With the Entries	Without the Entries	With the Entries	Without the Entries
Property and equipment, net	$38,614	$	$35,982	$	$38,151	$	$38,809	$	$39,155	$
Sales revenues	8,825	8,825	8,910	8,910	8,966	8,966	8,478	8,478	8,120	8,120
Operating expenses	7,628		8,526		7,786		7,725		7,277	
Income from operations	1,197		384		1,180		753		843	

2. Using the publicly reported numbers (which include the special journal entries that you recorded), compute the fixed asset turnover ratio (rounded to two decimal places) for the periods ended Q2–Q4 of year 1 and Q1 of year 2. What does the trend in this ratio suggest to you? Is this consistent with the changes in operating income reported by the company?

3. Before your meeting with the vice president for internal audit, you think about the above computations and the variety of peculiar circumstances surrounding the "special project" for the CFO. What in particular might have raised your suspicion about the real nature of your work?

4. Your meeting with internal audit was short and unpleasant. The vice president indicated that she had discussed her findings with the CFO before meeting with you. The CFO claimed that he too had noticed the peculiar trend in the fixed asset turnover ratio, but that he hadn't had a chance to investigate it further. He urged internal audit to get to the bottom of things, suggesting that perhaps someone might be making unapproved journal entries. Internal audit had identified you as the source of the journal entries and had been unable to find any documents that approved or substantiated the entries. She ended the meeting by advising you to find a good lawyer. Given your current circumstances, describe how you would have acted earlier had you been able to foresee where it might lead you.

5. In the real case on which this one is based, the internal auditors agonized over the question of whether they had actually uncovered a fraud or whether they were jumping to the wrong conclusion. *The Wall Street Journal* mentioned this on October 30, 2002, by stating, "it was clear . . . that their findings would be devastating for the company. They worried about whether their revelations would result in layoffs. Plus, they feared that they would somehow end up being blamed for the mess." Beyond the personal consequences mentioned in this quote, describe other potential ways in which the findings of the internal auditors would likely be devastating for the publicly traded company and those associated with it.

Epilogue: This case is based on a fraud committed at WorldCom (now called Verizon). The case draws its numbers, the nature of the unsupported journal entries, and the CFO's role in carrying out the fraud from a report issued by WorldCom's bankruptcy examiner. Year 1 in this case was actually 2001 and year 2 was 2002. This case excludes other fraudulent activities that contributed to WorldCom's $11 billion fraud. The 63-year-old CEO was sentenced to 25 years in prison for planning and executing the biggest fraud in the history of American business. The CFO, who cooperated in the investigation of the CEO, was sentenced to five years in prison.

WorldCom

Evaluating the Impact of Capitalized Interest on Cash Flows and Fixed Asset Turnover from an Analyst's Perspective

CP8-9

LO8-1, 8-2, 8-7

Marriott International

You are a financial analyst charged with evaluating the asset efficiency of companies in the hotel industry. Recent financial statements for Marriott include the following note:

---

8. Property and Equipment

We record property and equipment at cost, including interest and real estate taxes incurred during development and construction. Interest capitalized as a cost of property and equipment totaled $12 million in 2011, $10 million in 2010, and $8 million in 2009. We capitalize the cost of improvements that extend the useful life of property and equipment when incurred.

Required:

1. Assume that Marriott followed this policy for a major construction project this year. How does Marriott's policy affect the following (use + for increase, − for decrease, and NE for no effect)?
   a. Cash flows.
   b. Fixed asset turnover ratio.

2. Normally, how would your answer to requirement (1*b*) affect your evaluation of Marriott's effectiveness in utilizing fixed assets?

3. If the fixed asset turnover ratio decreases due to interest capitalization, does this change indicate a real decrease in efficiency? Why or why not?

Financial Reporting and Analysis Team Project

CP8-10

LO8-1, 8-2, 8-3,
8-4, 8-6, 8-7

Team Project: Analysis of Long-Lived Assets

As a team, select an industry to analyze. *Yahoo!Finance* provides lists of industries at biz.yahoo.com/p/industries.html. Click on an industry for a list of companies in that industry. Alternatively, go to Google Finance at www.google.com/finance, search for a company you are interested in, and you will be presented with a list including that company and its competitors. Each team member should acquire the annual report or 10-K for one publicly traded company in the industry, with each member selecting a different company (the SEC EDGAR service at www.sec.gov or the company's investor relations website itself are good sources).

Required:

1. List the accounts and amounts of the company's long-lived assets (land, buildings, equipment, intangible assets, natural resources, and/or other) for the last three years.
   a. What is the percentage of each to total assets?
   b. What do the results of your analysis suggest about the strategy your company has followed with respect to investing in long-lived assets?
2. What cost allocation method(s) and estimates does the company use for each type of long-lived asset?
3. What percentage of the property, plant, and equipment has been used as of the end of the most recent year? (Accumulated Depreciation ÷ Cost)
4. What does the company disclose regarding asset impairment? What was its impairment loss, if any, in the most recent year?
5. Ratio analysis:
   a. What does the fixed asset turnover ratio measure in general?
   b. Compute the ratio for the last three years.
   c. What do your results suggest about the company?
   d. If available, find the industry ratio for the most recent year, compare it to your results, and discuss why you believe your company differs or is similar to the industry ratio.
6. What was the effect of depreciation expense on cash flows from operating activities? Compute the percentage of depreciation expense to cash flows from operating activities for each of the past three years.
7. From the statement of cash flows, what were capital expenditures over the last three years? Did the company sell any long-lived assets?

CONTINUING CASE

CC8-1

≋POOLCORP

Asset Acquisition, Depreciation, and Disposal

Pool Corporation, Inc., is the world's largest wholesale distributor of swimming pool supplies and equipment. Assume Pool Corporation purchased for cash new loading equipment for the warehouse on January 1, 2014, at an invoice price of $72,000. It also paid $2,000 for freight on the equipment, $1,300 to prepare the equipment for use in the warehouse, and $800 for insurance to cover the equipment during operation in 2014. The equipment was estimated to have a residual value of $3,300 and be used over three years or 24,000 hours.

Required:

1. Record the purchase of the equipment, freight, preparation costs, and insurance on January 1, 2014.
2. Create a depreciation schedule assuming Pool Corporation uses the straight-line method.
3. Create a depreciation schedule assuming Pool Corporation uses the double-declining-balance method. Round answers to the nearest dollar.
4. Create a depreciation schedule assuming Pool Corporation uses the units-of-production method, with actual production of 8,000 hours in 2014, 7,400 hours in 2015, and 8,600 hours in 2016.
5. On December 31, 2015, the equipment was sold for $22,500. Record the sale of the equipment assuming the company used the straight-line method.

Reporting and Interpreting Liabilities

Each week, Starbucks serves customers more than 50 million times. The company, founded in 1985, has more than 17,000 coffeehouses and does business in 55 international markets. The mission statement for the company is "to establish Starbucks as the premier purveyor of the finest coffees in the world." After a brief period of slower growth, store closures, and cost reductions, the company recently reported an 11% increase in sales and a 43% increase in stock price. This success is the result of increased emphasis on the company's core values.

To achieve its goals, Starbucks must focus on a number of activities. The annual report identifies several of them:

- Serve the finest cup of coffee in the world.
- Grow the company one customer at a time based on exceptional customer service.
- Make someone's day with a relaxing in-store experience including music, art, and high-speed wireless Internet access.

In addition to these operating activities, management must focus on a number of critical financing activities to ensure that the company remains profitable and is able to generate sufficient resources to maintain liquidity and eventually open new coffeehouses. The financing

Learning Objectives

After studying this chapter, you should be able to:

9-1 Define, measure, and report current liabilities. p. 453

9-2 Analyze the accounts payable turnover ratio. p. 454

9-3 Report notes payable and explain the time value of money. p. 458

9-4 Report contingent liabilities. p. 460

9-5 Explain the importance of working capital and its impact on cash flows. p. 462

9-6 Report long-term liabilities. p. 464

9-7 Compute present values. p. 466

9-8 Apply present value concepts to liabilities. p. 469

activities for Starbucks serve two important purposes. They generate funds to (1) finance the current operating activities of the business and (2) acquire long-term assets that will permit the company to grow in the future.

UNDERSTANDING THE BUSINESS

Businesses finance the acquisition of their assets from two external sources: funds supplied by creditors (debt) and funds provided by owners (equity). The mixture of debt and equity a business uses is called its *capital structure*. In addition to selecting a capital structure, management can select from a variety of sources from which to borrow money, as illustrated by the liability section of the balance sheet from Starbucks shown in Exhibit 9.1.

What factors do managers consider when they borrow money? Two key factors are risk and cost. From the firm's perspective, debt capital is more risky than equity because payments associated with debt are a company's legal obligation. If a company cannot meet a required debt payment (either principal or interest) because of a temporary cash shortage, creditors may force the company into bankruptcy and require the sale of assets to satisfy the debt. As with any business transaction, borrowers and lenders attempt to negotiate the most favorable terms possible. Managers devote considerable effort to analyzing alternative borrowing arrangements.

Companies that include debt in their capital structure must also make strategic decisions concerning the balance between short-term and long-term debt. To evaluate a company's capital structure, financial analysts calculate a

EXHIBIT 9.1

Starbucks Consolidated
Balance Sheets

STARBUCKS

REAL WORLD EXCERPT
Annual Report

STARBUCKS CORPORATION
Consolidated Balance Sheets
(in millions, except per share data)

	Oct. 2, 2011	Oct. 3, 2010
Liabilities		
Current liabilities:		
Accounts payable	$ 540.0	$ 282.6
Accrued compensation and related costs	364.4	400.0
Accrued occupancy costs	148.3	173.2
Accrued taxes	109.2	100.2
Insurance reserves	145.6	146.2
Other accrued liabilities	319.0	262.8
Deferred revenue	449.3	414.1
Total current liabilities	2,075.8	1,779.1
Long-term debt	549.5	549.4
Other long-term liabilities	347.8	375.1
Total liabilities	$2,973.1	$2,703.6

number of accounting ratios. In this chapter, we will discuss both short-term and long-term debt, as well as some important accounting ratios. We will also introduce present value concepts. In the next chapter, we discuss a special category of long-term debt, bonds payable.

ORGANIZATION of the Chapter

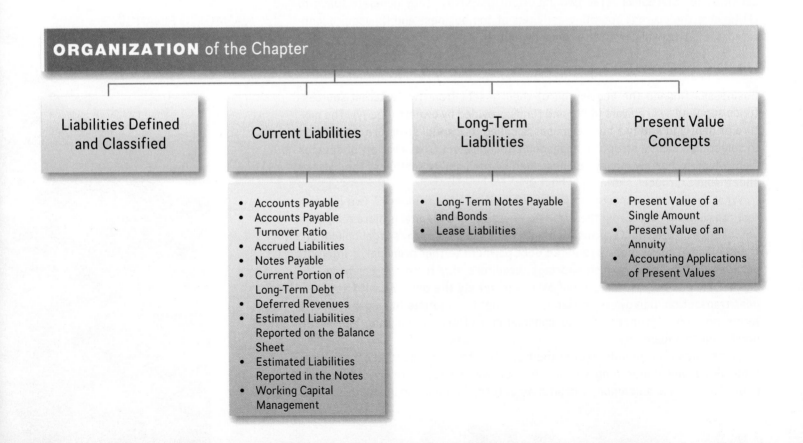

Liabilities Defined and Classified

Current Liabilities
- Accounts Payable
- Accounts Payable Turnover Ratio
- Accrued Liabilities
- Notes Payable
- Current Portion of Long-Term Debt
- Deferred Revenues
- Estimated Liabilities Reported on the Balance Sheet
- Estimated Liabilities Reported in the Notes
- Working Capital Management

Long-Term Liabilities
- Long-Term Notes Payable and Bonds
- Lease Liabilities

Present Value Concepts
- Present Value of a Single Amount
- Present Value of an Annuity
- Accounting Applications of Present Values

LIABILITIES DEFINED AND CLASSIFIED

Most people have a reasonable understanding of the definition of the word *liability*. Accountants formally define **liabilities** as probable debts or obligations of the entity that result from past transactions, which will be paid with assets or services. As Exhibit 9.1 shows, as of October 2, 2011, Starbucks had borrowed on a long-term basis $549.5 million. The company has a current obligation to pay cash to its creditors at some time in the future based on the borrowing agreements. Because of this obligation, Starbucks must record long-term debt.

When a liability is first recorded, it is measured in terms of its current cash equivalent, which is the cash amount a creditor would accept to settle the liability immediately. Although Starbucks borrowed $549.5 million, it will repay much more than that because the company must also pay interest on the debt. Interest that will be paid in the future is not included in the reported amount of the liability because it accrues and becomes a liability with the passage of time.

Like most businesses, Starbucks has several kinds of liabilities as well as a wide range of creditors. The list of liabilities on the balance sheet differs from one company to the next because different operating activities result in different types of liabilities. The liability section of the Starbucks report begins with the caption Current Liabilities. **Current liabilities** are defined as short-term obligations that will be paid within the current operating cycle of the business or within one year of the balance sheet date, whichever is longer. Because most companies have an operating cycle that is shorter than one year, current liabilities usually can be defined simply as liabilities that are due within one year. Noncurrent liabilities include all other liabilities.

Information about current liabilities is very important to managers and analysts because these obligations must be paid in the near future. Analysts say that a company has **liquidity** if it has the ability to meet its current obligations. A number of financial measures are useful in evaluating liquidity, including the current ratio (discussed in Chapter 2) and the dollar amount of working capital (defined as current assets minus current liabilities). Starbucks reported current assets of $3,794.9 (million), which results in working capital of $1,719.1 (million). Working capital is a margin of safety that ensures a company can meet its short-term obligations.

Working capital management involves a delicate balance. On one hand, working capital provides liquidity and a margin of safety. If sales activity slows, for example, working capital provides resources to maintain business operations during a period in which there are reduced cash inflows from customers. On the other hand, excess money tied up in a checking account or inventory is not productive because it does not generate profits. Companies have become very sophisticated in managing working capital to provide needed liquidity without tying up excessive amounts of money in nonproductive assets. One example is the just-in-time (JIT) inventory method, which uses statistical methods to maintain optimal levels of inventory based on forecasted needs.

LIABILITIES are probable debts or obligations that result from past transactions, which will be paid with assets or services.

CURRENT LIABILITIES are short-term obligations that will be paid within the current operating cycle or one year, whichever is longer.

LIQUIDITY is the ability to pay current obligations.

CURRENT LIABILITIES

Many current liabilities have a direct relationship to the operating activities of a business. In other words, specific operating activities are financed, in part, by a related current liability. Some examples from the Starbucks annual report (Exhibit 9.1) are:

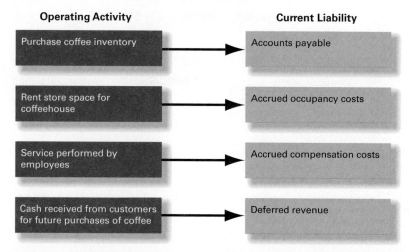

Operating Activity	Current Liability
Purchase coffee inventory	Accounts payable
Rent store space for coffeehouse	Accrued occupancy costs
Service performed by employees	Accrued compensation costs
Cash received from customers for future purchases of coffee	Deferred revenue

Early in this chapter, we mentioned that Starbucks is aggressively opening new stores each year. As a result, it must buy more inventory, rent more store space, and hire more employees. By understanding the relationship between operating activities and current liabilities, an analyst can easily explain changes in the various current liability accounts.

We will now discuss the current liability accounts that are found on most balance sheets.

Accounts Payable

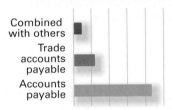

Accounts Payable Titles (sample of 600 companies)

Most companies do not produce all the goods and services that they use in their basic operating activities. Instead, they purchase some goods and services from other businesses. Typically, these transactions are made on credit with cash payments made after the goods and services have been provided. As a result, these transactions create accounts payable, also called **trade accounts payable.** *Accounting Trends & Techniques* (published by the AICPA) examined the reporting practices of 600 companies and found that most companies use the term **accounts payable.**[1]

For many companies, trade credit is a relatively inexpensive way to finance the purchase of inventory because interest does not normally accrue on accounts payable. As an incentive to encourage more sales, some vendors offer generous credit terms that may allow the buyer to resell merchandise and collect cash before payment must be made to the original vendor.

Some managers may be tempted to delay payment to suppliers as long as possible to conserve cash. This strategy normally is not advisable. Most successful companies develop positive working relationships with suppliers to ensure that they receive quality goods and services. A positive relationship can be destroyed by slow payment of debt. In addition, financial analysts become concerned if a business does not meet its obligations to trade creditors on a timely basis because such slowness often indicates that a company is experiencing financial difficulties. Both managers and analysts use the accounts payable turnover ratio to evaluate effectiveness in managing payables.

KEY RATIO ANALYSIS   **Accounts Payable Turnover**

LEARNING OBJECTIVE 9-2

Analyze the accounts payable turnover ratio.

? ANALYTICAL QUESTION

How efficient is management in meeting its obligations to suppliers?

% RATIO AND COMPARISONS

The accounts payable turnover ratio is computed as follows:

Accounts Payable Turnover = Cost of Goods Sold ÷ Average Accounts Payable

The 2011 accounts payable turnover ratio for Starbucks was:

$$\$4,949.3 \div \$411.3^* = 12.0$$

$$*(\$540.0 + \$282.6) \div 2 = \$411.3$$

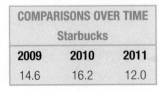

COMPARISONS OVER TIME			COMPARISONS WITH COMPETITORS	
Starbucks			Peet's Coffee	Caribou Coffee
2009	**2010**	**2011**	**2011**	**2011**
14.6	16.2	12.0	18.0	17.7

---

[1] Reprinted with permission from *Accounting Trends & Techniques.* Copyright © 2008 by the American Institute of Certified Public Accountants, Inc.

💡 INTERPRETATIONS

In General   The accounts payable turnover ratio measures how quickly management is paying trade accounts. A high accounts payable ratio normally suggests that a company is paying its suppliers in a timely manner. The ratio can be stated more intuitively by dividing it into the number of days in a year:

Average Age of Payables = 365 Days ÷ Turnover Ratio

The 2011 average age of payables for Starbucks was:

365 Days ÷ 12.0 = 30.4 Days

Focus Company Analysis   The accounts payable turnover for Starbucks is lower than both of its competitors and shows a fair amount of variation over time. Usually, a low ratio would raise questions concerning a company's liquidity. Starbucks, on average, pays its creditors within approximately 30 days, which represents normal credit terms. Analysts would consider this ratio to be strong.

A Few Cautions   The accounts payable turnover ratio is an average based on all accounts payable. The ratio might not reflect reality if a company pays some creditors on time but is late with others. The ratio is also subject to manipulation. Managers could be late in paying creditors during the entire year but catch up at year-end so that the ratio is at an acceptable level. As our focus company analysis indicates, a low turnover ratio can indicate either liquidity problems (i.e., the company is not able to generate sufficient cash to meet its obligations) or aggressive cash management (i.e., the company maintains only the minimum amount of cash necessary to support its operating activities). The first is a problem; the second is a strength. Analysts need to study other factors (such as the quick ratio and the amount of cash generated from operating activities) to determine which is the case.

Accrued Liabilities

In many situations, a business incurs an expense in one accounting period and makes the cash payment in another period. **Accrued liabilities** are expenses that have been incurred before the end of an accounting period but have not been paid. These expenses include items such as property taxes, electricity, and salaries. The balance sheet for Starbucks lists four of these items: accrued compensation and related costs, accrued occupancy costs (rent), accrued taxes, and other accrued expenses. Accrued liabilities are recorded as adjusting entries at year-end.

ACCRUED LIABILITIES are expenses that have been incurred but have not been paid at the end of the accounting period.

Accrued Taxes Payable

Like individuals, corporations must pay taxes on the income they earn. Corporate tax rates are graduated, with large corporations paying a top federal tax rate of 35 percent. Corporations may also pay state and local income taxes and, in some cases, foreign income taxes. The notes to the Starbucks annual report include the following information pertaining to taxes:

INCOME TAXES

Note 13:

Provision for income taxes (*in millions*):

Fiscal Year Ended	Oct. 2, 2011	Oct. 3, 2010	Sep. 27, 2009
Current taxes:			
Federal	$344.7	$457.5	$165.3
State	61.2	79.6	35.0
Foreign	37.3	38.3	26.3
Total deferred taxes	119.9	(86.7)	(58.2)
Total provision for income taxes	$563.1	$488.7	$168.4

STARBUCKS

REAL WORLD EXCERPT
Annual Report

The 2011 federal income tax for Starbucks ($344.7 million) was approximately 28 percent of its reported earnings. For most corporations, federal income taxes represent a major cost.

Accrued Compensation and Related Costs

At the end of each accounting period, employees usually have earned salaries that have not yet been paid. Unpaid salaries may be reported as part of accrued liabilities or as a separate item, as is the case with Starbucks (the amount shown on the balance sheet is $364.4 million). In addition to reporting salaries that have been earned but not paid, companies must report the cost of unpaid benefits, including retirement programs, vacation time, and health insurance.

Let's look at vacation time as an example. Typically, a business grants employees paid vacation time based on the number of months they have worked. Under the matching concept, the cost of vacation time must be recorded in the year employees perform a service rather than the year they actually take vacation. If Starbucks estimates the cost of accrued vacation time to be $125,000, accountants make the following adjusting entry at the end of the fiscal year:

Compensation expense (+E, −SE).	125,000	
Accrued vacation liability (+L).		125,000

Assets	=	Liabilities	+	Stockholders' Equity
		Accrued vacation liability +125,000		Compensation expense (+E) −125,000

When the vacations are taken (during the next summer), the accountants record the following:

Accrued vacation liability (−L).	125,000	
Cash (−A)		125,000

Assets		=	Liabilities	+	Stockholders' Equity
Cash	−125,000		Accrued vacation liability −125,000		

Starbucks does not separately disclose the amount of accrued vacation liability. Instead, the company reports this liability as part of accrued compensation. Apparently, the amount of accrued vacation liability is not material in management's opinion. Most analysts would probably agree.

Payroll Taxes

All payrolls are subject to a variety of taxes, including federal, state, and local income taxes, Social Security taxes, and federal and state unemployment taxes. Employees pay some of these taxes and employers pay others. While we will look at only the three largest deductions for most people, reporting is similar for each type of payroll tax.

Employee Income Taxes Employers are required to withhold income taxes for each employee. The amount of income tax withheld is recorded by the employer as a current liability between the date of the deduction and the date the amount is remitted to the government. Federal Income Tax Withheld is often referred to as **FITW.**

Employee and Employer FICA Taxes The Social Security taxes often are called **FICA taxes** because they are required by the Federal Insurance Contributions Act. These taxes are imposed in equal amounts on both the employee and the employer. Effective January 1, 2013, the Social Security tax rate was 6.2 percent on the first $113,700 paid to each employee during the year. In addition, a separate 1.45 percent

Medicare tax applies to all income. Therefore, the FICA tax rate is 7.65 percent on income up to $113,700 and 1.45 percent on all income above $113,700.

Employer Unemployment Taxes Employers are charged unemployment taxes through the Federal Unemployment Tax Act (FUTA) and State Unemployment Tax Acts (SUTA). These programs provide limited financial support to employees who lose their jobs through no fault of their own. Because the rate and specified amount of wages vary by state, we will focus on federal unemployment taxes. The FUTA specifies a federal tax rate of 6.2 percent on taxable wages up to the first $7,000 for each employee. Employers with a good payment history may receive a credit for taxes paid at the state level, up to 5.4 percent of taxable wages. For most large employers, the FUTA taxes are .8 percent of wages up to $7,000 for each employee.

Employee compensation expense includes all funds earned by employees as well as funds paid to others on behalf of employees. As a result, the cost of hiring employees is much more than the amount that those employees actually receive in cash.

To illustrate a payroll, let's assume that Starbucks accumulated the following information in its records for the first two weeks of June 2014:

Salaries and wages earned	$1,800,000
Income taxes withheld	275,000
FICA taxes (employees' share)	105,000
FUTA taxes	2,300

The entry to record the payroll is normally made with two entries. The first entry records amounts paid to employees or withheld from amounts they have earned:

Compensation expense (+E, −SE)...........................	1,800,000	
Liability for income taxes withheld (+L).....................		275,000
FICA payable (+L)..		105,000
Cash (−A)...		1,420,000

Assets	=	Liabilities	+	Stockholders' Equity
Cash −1,420,000		FICA payable +105,000		Compensation
		Liability for income		expense (+E) −1,800,000
		taxes withheld +275,000		

The second entry records the taxes that employers must pay from their own funds. These additional tax payments are required by federal and state law. The FICA tax amount is equal to the amount that is paid by employees:

Compensation expense (+E, −SE)...........................	107,300	
FICA payable (+L)..		105,000
FUTA payable (+L).......................................		2,300

Assets	=	Liabilities	+	Stockholders' Equity
		FICA payable +105,000		Compensation expense (+E) −107,300
		FUTA payable +2,300		

Accounting Trends & Techniques found that most companies in its sample of 600 companies report employee-related liabilities.[2]

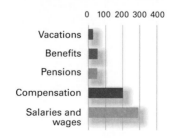

Types of Employee-Related Liabilities (sample of 600 companies)

0 100 200 300 400

Vacations
Benefits
Pensions
Compensation
Salaries and wages

---

[2]Reprinted with permission from *Accounting Trends & Techniques.* Copyright © 2008 by the American Institute of Certified Public Accountants, Inc.

Notes Payable

The TIME VALUE OF MONEY
is interest that is associated with
the use of money over time.

When a company borrows money, a formal written contract is usually prepared. Obligations supported by these contracts are called *notes payable.* A note payable specifies the amount borrowed, the date by which it must be repaid, and the interest rate associated with the borrowing.

Creditors are willing to lend cash because they will earn interest in return for giving up the use of their money for a period. This simple concept is called the **time value of money.** The longer borrowed money is held, the larger is the total dollar amount of interest expense. Interest at a given interest rate on a two-year loan is more than interest on a one-year loan. To the borrower, interest is an expense; to the creditor, it is revenue.

To calculate interest, three variables must be considered: (1) the principal (i.e., the cash that was borrowed), (2) the annual interest rate, and (3) the time period for the loan. The interest formula is:

$$\text{Interest} = \text{Principal} \times \text{Interest Rate} \times \text{Time}$$

To illustrate, assume that on November 1, 2014, Starbucks borrows $100,000 cash on a one-year, 12 percent note payable. The interest is payable on March 31, 2015, and October 31, 2015. The principal is payable at the maturity date, October 31, 2015. The note is recorded in the accounts as follows:

Cash (+A)	100,000	
Notes payable, short-term (+L).		100,000

Assets		=	Liabilities		+	Stockholders' Equity
Cash	+100,000		Notes payable	+100,000		

Interest is an expense of the period in which the money is used. Under the matching concept, interest expense is recorded when it is incurred rather than when the cash actually is paid. Because Starbucks uses the money for two months during 2014, it records interest expense in 2014 for two months, even though cash is not paid until March 31 of the following year.

The computation of interest expense for 2014 is as follows:

$$\text{Interest} = \text{Principal} \times \text{Interest Rate} \times \text{Time}$$
$$\$2,000 = \$100,000 \times \quad 12\% \quad \times \ 2/12$$

The entry to record interest expense on December 31, 2014, is:

Interest expense (+E, −SE)	2,000	
Interest payable (+L)		2,000

Assets	=	Liabilities		+	Stockholders' Equity	
		Interest payable	+2,000		Interest expense (+E)	−2,000

On March 31, 2015, Starbucks would pay $5,000 in interest, which includes the $2,000 accrued and reported in 2014 plus the $3,000 interest accrued in the first three months of 2015. The following journal entry would be made:

Interest expense (+E, −SE)	3,000	
Interest payable (−L).	2,000	
Cash (−A)		5,000

Assets		=	Liabilities		+	Stockholders' Equity	
Cash	−5,000		Interest payable	−2,000		Interest expense (+E)	−3,000

Current Portion of Long-Term Debt

The distinction between current and long-term debt is important for both managers and analysts. Because current debt must be paid within the next year, companies must have sufficient cash to repay it. To provide accurate information on its current liabilities, a company must reclassify its long-term debt as a current liability within a year of its maturity date. Assume that Starbucks signed a note payable of $5 million on January 1, 2014. Repayment is required on December 1, 2016. The December 31, 2014 and 2015, balance sheets would report the following:

December 31, 2014	
Long-term liabilities:	
Note payable	$5,000,000

December 31, 2015	
Current liabilities:	
Current portion of long-term note	$5,000,000

Note in Exhibit 9.1 that Starbucks did not report any current portion of long-term debt to be paid in full during the following accounting period. In some cases, companies will refinance debt when it comes due rather than pay out cash currently on hand.

Refinanced Debt: Current or Noncurrent?

FINANCIAL ANALYSIS

Instead of repaying a debt from current cash, a company may refinance it either by negotiating a new loan agreement with a new maturity date or by borrowing money from a new creditor and repaying the original creditor. If a company intends to refinance a currently maturing debt and has the ability to do so, should the debt be classified as a current or a long-term liability? Remember that analysts are interested in a company's current liabilities because those liabilities will generate cash outflows in the next accounting period. If a liability will not generate a cash outflow in the next accounting period, GAAP requires that it not be classified as current. This rule is illustrated by a note from the General Mills annual report.

> We have a revolving credit agreement that provides us with the ability to refinance short-term borrowing on a long-term basis. Therefore we have reclassified a portion of our notes payable to long-term debt.

GENERAL MILLS
Used with permission of General Mills Marketing Inc. (GMMI)

REAL WORLD EXCERPT
Annual Report

U.S. GAAP and IFRS differ with respect to the timing of the refinancing. In the case of IFRS, the actual refinancing must take place by the balance sheet date. Under GAAP, the ability to refinance must be in place before the financial statements are issued.

Deferred Revenues

In most business transactions, cash is paid after the product or service has been delivered. In some cases, cash is paid before delivery. You have probably paid for magazines that you will receive at some time in the future. The publisher collects money for your subscription in advance, before the magazine is published. When a company collects cash before the related revenue has been earned, the cash is called **deferred revenues.** The popular Starbucks card permits customers to pay in advance for their coffee. The advantage for the customer is convenience at the point of sale. The advantage for the company is that Starbucks is able to collect

DEFERRED REVENUES are revenues that have been collected but not earned; they are liabilities until the goods or services have been provided.

and use cash before customers actually buy the product. The Starbucks report shows that the company has collected $449.3 million from customers prior to providing them with coffee and explains the amount with the following note:

Revenues from the Company's stored value cards, such as the Starbucks Card, and gift certificates are recognized when tendered for payment, or upon redemption. Outstanding customer balances are included in "Deferred revenue" on the consolidated balance sheet.

Under the revenue principle, revenue cannot be recorded until it has been earned. Deferred revenues are reported as a liability because cash has been collected but the related revenue has not been earned by the end of the accounting period. The obligation to provide services or goods in the future still exists. These obligations are classified as current or long-term, depending on when they must be satisfied.

Estimated Liabilities Reported on the Balance Sheet

Some recorded liabilities are based on estimates because the exact amount will not be known until a future date. For example, an estimated liability is created when a company offers a warranty with the products it sells. The cost of providing future repair work must be estimated and recorded as a liability (and expense) in the period in which the product is sold.

Starbucks offers a warranty on coffee brewing and espresso equipment sold in its stores but does not record an estimated warranty liability at the time of sale. Rather than repairing brewing machines, the company gives the customer the right to return any defective product for a period of up to 24 months. The estimated amount of product that will be returned is reported as a reduction from sales revenue in the year the sales are recorded.

Estimated Liabilities Reported in the Notes

LEARNING OBJECTIVE 9-4
Report contingent liabilities.

A CONTINGENT LIABILITY
is a potential liability that has
arisen as the result of a past
event; it is not an effective
liability until some future event
occurs.

Each of the liabilities that we have discussed is reported on the balance sheet at a specific dollar amount because each involves the probable future sacrifice of economic benefits. Some transactions or events create only a reasonably possible (but not probable) future sacrifice of economic benefits. These situations create **contingent liabilities,** which are potential liabilities that are created as a result of a past event. A contingent liability may or may not become a recorded liability depending on future events. A situation that produces a contingent liability also causes a contingent loss.

Contingent Liability Examples

Lawsuits   Environmental   Product
                  problems   warranties

Whether a situation produces a recorded or a contingent liability depends on two factors: the probability of a future economic sacrifice and the ability of management to estimate the amount of the liability. The following table illustrates the possibilities:

	Probable	**Reasonably Possible**	**Remote**
Subject to estimate	Record as liability	Disclose in note	Disclosure not required
Not subject to estimate	Disclose in note	Disclose in note	Disclosure not required

The probabilities of occurrence are defined in the following manner:

1. Probable—The chance that the future event or events will occur is high.

2. Reasonably possible—The chance that the future event or events will occur is more than remote but less than likely.

3. Remote—The chance that the future event or events will occur is slight.

It's a Matter of Degree

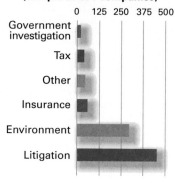

INTERNATIONAL PERSPECTIVE

The assessment of future probabilities is inherently subjective but both U.S. GAAP and IFRS provide some guidance. Under GAAP, "probable" has been defined as *likely,* which is interpreted as having a greater than 70 percent chance of occurring. In the case of IFRS, "probable" is defined as *more likely than not,* which would imply more than a 50 percent chance of occurring. This difference means that companies reporting under IFRS would record a liability when other companies reporting under GAAP would report the same event as a contingency.

In summary, (1) a liability that is both probable and capable of being reasonably estimated must be recorded and reported on the balance sheet, (2) a liability that is reasonably possible must be disclosed in a note in the financial statements whether it can be estimated or not, and (3) remote contingencies are not disclosed.

The notes to Starbucks's annual report include the following information about a loan guarantee:

STARBUCKS

REAL WORLD EXCERPT
Annual Report

> **Note 15: Commitments and Contingencies**
>
> We have unconditionally guaranteed the repayment of certain Japanese yen-denominated bank loans and related interest and fees of Starbucks Japan. The guarantees continue until the loans, including accrued interest and fees, have been paid in full. These guarantees expire in 2014. Our maximum exposure under this commitment as of October 2, 2011, was $1.0 million and is limited to the sum of unpaid principal and interest, as well as other related expenses. Since there has been no modification of these loan guarantees subsequent to the adoption of accounting requirements for guarantees, we have applied the disclosure provisions only and have not recorded the guarantees on our consolidated balance sheets.

Consistent with the chart shown earlier, Starbucks did not record a liability because the likelihood of a loss did not meet the threshold of "probable." Therefore, disclosure in a footnote was sufficient.

Accounting Trends & Techniques studied the financial statements of 600 companies and found that litigation was the most common type of contingent liability.[3]

Working Capital Management

Working capital is defined as the dollar difference between current assets and current liabilities. Working capital is important to both managers and financial analysts because it has a significant impact on the health and profitability of a company.

The working capital accounts are actively managed to achieve a balance between costs and benefits. If a business has too little working capital, it runs the risk of not being able to meet its obligations to creditors. On the other hand, too much working capital may tie up resources in unproductive assets and incur additional costs. Excess inventory, for example, ties up dollars that could be invested more profitably elsewhere in the business and incurs additional costs associated with storage and deterioration.

Changes in working capital accounts are also important to managers and analysts because they have a direct impact on the cash flows from operating activities reported on the statement of cash flows.

FOCUS ON CASH FLOWS	Working Capital and Cash Flows

Many working capital accounts have a direct relationship to income-producing activities. Accounts receivable, for example, are related to sales revenue: Accounts receivable increase when sales are made on credit. Cash is collected when the customer pays the bill. Similarly, accounts payable increase when an expense is incurred without a cash payment. A cash outflow occurs when the account is paid. Changes in working capital accounts that are related to income-producing activities must be considered when computing cash flows from operating activities.

EFFECT ON STATEMENT OF CASH FLOWS

In General   On the statement of cash flows, net income is adjusted (under the indirect method) to compute cash flows from operating activities. Changes in working capital accounts have the impact shown in the following table:

	Effect on Cash Flows
Operating activities (indirect method)	
Net income	$xxx
Adjusted for: Decreases in current assets*	
or increases in current liabilities	+
Adjusted for: Increases in current assets*	
or decreases in current liabilities	−

*Other than cash.

Focus Company Analysis   A segment of the Starbucks Consolidated Statements of Cash Flows, prepared using the indirect method, follows. Notice the significant amount of cash flows from operating activities from 2009 to 2011 (compared to the net earnings). These substantial cash flows are important for a company with the growth strategy that Starbucks is following.

---

[3]Reprinted with permission from *Accounting Trends & Techniques*. Copyright © 2008 by the American Institute of Certified Public Accountants, Inc.

STARBUCKS CORPORATION Consolidated Statements of Cash Flows (in millions)			
Fiscal Year Ended	**Oct. 2, 2011**	**Oct. 3, 2010**	**Sep. 27, 2009**
OPERATING ACTIVITIES:			
Net earnings including noncontrolling interests	$1,248.0	$ 948.3	$ 391.5
Adjustments to reconcile net earnings to net cash provided by operating activities:			
Depreciation and amortization	550.0	540.8	563.3
Gain on sale of properties	(30.2)	0.0	0.0
Provision for impairments and asset disposals	36.2	67.7	224.4
Deferred income taxes, net	106.2	(42.0)	(69.6)
Equity in income of investees	(118.5)	(108.6)	(78.4)
Distributions of income from equity investees	85.6	91.4	53.0
Gain resulting from acquisition of joint ventures	(55.2)	(23.1)	0.0
Stock-based compensation	145.2	113.6	83.2
Excess tax benefit from exercise of stock options	(103.9)	(36.9)	(15.9)
Other	(2.9)	7.8	5.4
Cash provided/(used) by changes in operating assets and liabilities:			
Accounts receivable	(88.7)	(33.4)	59.1
Inventories	(422.3)	123.2	28.5
Accounts payable	227.5	(3.6)	(53.0)
Accrued taxes	104.0	0.6	59.2
Deferred revenue	35.8	24.2	16.3
Other operating assets	(22.5)	17.3	61.4
Other operating liabilities	(81.9)	17.6	60.6
Net cash provided by operating activities	$1,612.4	$1,704.9	$1,389.0

PAUSE FOR **FEEDBACK**

Companies report two classifications of liabilities. We have discussed current liabilities and in the next section we will discuss long-term liabilities. Before you move on, complete the following questions to test your understanding of these concepts.

SELF-STUDY **QUIZ**

For each of the following events, state whether working capital will increase, decrease, or not change:

1. Starbucks incurs an account payable of $250,000 with no change in current assets.
2. The company borrows $1,000,000 in long-term debt.
3. The company pays taxes payable in the amount of $750,000.
4. The company finances a new building with long-term debt.

After you have completed your answers, check them with the solutions at the bottom of the page.

Working capital

1. Decrease   2. Increase   3. No change   4. No change

Solutions to
SELF-STUDY QUIZ

LONG-TERM LIABILITIES

LONG-TERM LIABILITIES
are all of the entity's obligations
not classified as current
liabilities.

Long-term liabilities include all obligations that are not classified as current liabilities, such as long-term notes payable and bonds payable. Typically, a long-term liability will require payment more than one year in the future. These obligations may be created by borrowing money, or they may result from other activities.

Most companies borrow money on a long-term basis in order to purchase operational assets. To reduce risk for creditors, some companies agree to use specific assets as security. If the liability is not satisfied, the creditor may take ownership of the asset. A liability supported by this type of agreement is called a **secured debt.** An unsecured debt is one for which the creditor relies primarily on the borrower's integrity and general earning power.

Long-Term Notes Payable and Bonds

Companies can raise long-term debt capital directly from a number of financial service organizations including banks, insurance companies, and pension plans. Raising debt from one of these organizations is known as **private placement.** This type of debt is often called a **note payable,** which is a written promise to pay a stated sum at one or more specified future dates called the **maturity date(s).**

In many cases, a company's need for debt capital exceeds the financial ability of any single creditor. In these situations, the company may issue publicly traded debt called **bonds.** The opportunity to sell a bond in established markets provides bondholders with an important benefit. They can sell their bonds to other investors prior to maturity if they have an immediate need for cash. Because bonds provide liquidity to investors, they are more likely to lend money to a company. Bonds will be discussed in detail in the next chapter.

Accounting for long-term debt is based on the same concepts used in accounting for short-term notes payable. A liability is recorded when the debt is incurred and interest expense is recorded with the passage of time.

Business operations are global in nature. Successful corporations market their products in many countries and locate manufacturing facilities around the world based on cost and productivity. The financing of corporations also has become international, even for companies that do not have international operations. Borrowing money in a foreign currency raises some interesting accounting and management issues.

INTERNATIONAL PERSPECTIVE	Borrowing in Foreign Currencies

Many corporations with foreign operations elect to finance those operations with foreign debt to lessen exchange rate risk. This type of risk exists because the relative value of each nation's currency varies on virtually a daily basis. As this book was being written, the British pound was worth approximately $1.50.

A U.S. corporation that conducts business operations in England might decide to borrow pounds to finance its operations there. The profits from the business, which will be in pounds, can be used to pay off the debt, which is in pounds. If this business earned profits in pounds but paid off debt in dollars, it would be exposed to exchange rate risk because the relative value of the dollar and the pound fluctuates.

Foreign corporations face this same problem. A note to a recent annual report from Toyota, a Japanese company that does significant business in the United States, stated:

Toyota

REAL WORLD EXCERPT

Annual Report

> Earnings declined in the current year ended, as the appreciation of the yen aggravated the adverse effects of sluggish demand. . . . The movement in exchange rates reduced operating income of the company. Losses on currency exchange thus offset most of the cost savings we achieved.

Toyota has borrowed a large amount of money in the United States to lessen the exchange rate risk it faces. The company also owns and operates many factories in the United States.

Even if a company does not have international operations, it may elect to borrow in foreign markets. Interest rates often are low in countries experiencing a recession. These situations give corporations the opportunity to borrow at a lower cost.

For reporting purposes, accountants must convert, or translate, foreign debt into U.S. dollars. Conversion rates for all major currencies are published in most newspapers. To illustrate foreign currency translation, assume that Starbucks borrowed 1 million pounds (£). For the Starbucks annual report, the accountant must use the conversion rate as of the balance sheet date, which we assume was £1.00 to $1.50. The dollar equivalent of the debt is $1,500,000 (£1,000,000 × 1.50). The dollar equivalent of foreign debt may change if the conversion rate changes even without any additional borrowings or repayments.

The notes to the balance sheet for Starbucks indicate that the company has borrowed money only in the United States. In contrast, many companies with international operations borrow in the local currency of the countries in which they operate. These companies often repay the foreign currency debt with earnings (in the same currency) from operations in the foreign country.

Lease Liabilities

Companies often lease assets rather than purchase them. For example, renting extra delivery trucks during a busy period is more economical than owning them if they are not needed during the rest of the year. When a company leases an asset on a short-term basis, the agreement is called an **operating lease.** No liability is recorded when an operating lease is created. Instead, a company records rent expense as it uses the asset. Assume that on December 15, 2014, Starbucks signed an operating lease contract to rent five large trucks during January 2015. No liability is recorded in 2014. Rent expense is recorded during January 2015 as the trucks are actually used.

For a number of reasons, a company may prefer to lease an asset on a long-term basis rather than purchase it. This type of lease is called a **capital lease.** In essence, a capital lease contract represents the purchase and financing of an asset even though it is legally a lease agreement. Unlike an operating lease, capital leases are accounted for as if an asset had been purchased by recording an asset and a liability. Because of the significant differences between operating and capital leases, GAAP specifies criteria to distinguish between them. If a lease meets any of the following four criteria, it is considered a capital lease:

An OPERATING LEASE does not meet any of the four criteria for a capital lease established by GAAP and does not cause the recording of an asset and liability.

A CAPITAL LEASE meets at least one of the four criteria established by GAAP and results in the recording of an asset and liability.

- The lease term is 75 percent or more of the asset's expected economic life.

- Ownership of the asset is transferred to the lessee at the end of the lease term.

- The lease contract permits the lessee to purchase the asset at a price that is lower than its fair market value.

- The present value of the lease payments is 90 percent or more of the fair market value of the asset when the lease is signed.

If managers have a choice of recording a lease as an operating or a capital lease, most would prefer to record it as an operating lease. By doing so, the company is able to report less debt on its balance sheet. In the notes to its financial statements, Starbucks reports capital lease obligations of $1.4 million, which are included on the balance sheet under the category "other long-term liabilities." Many financial analysts are concerned that companies can avoid reporting debt associated with capital leases by structuring the lease agreement in a manner that meets the requirements for recording it as an operating lease.

To record a capital lease, it is necessary to determine the current cash equivalent of the required lease payments. Assume that Starbucks signs a lease for new delivery trucks. The accountant has determined that the lease is a capital lease with a current cash equivalent of

$250,000. Once the lease is signed, the transaction would be recorded in a manner similar to the actual purchase of delivery trucks:

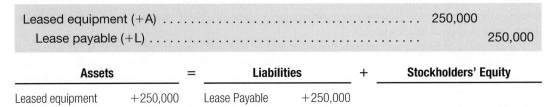

| Leased equipment (+A) | 250,000 | |
| Lease payable (+L) | | 250,000 |

Assets	=	Liabilities	+	Stockholders' Equity
Leased equipment +250,000		Lease Payable +250,000		

In this example, you were given the current cash equivalent of the lease. In the next section, on present value concepts, we will show you how this amount is computed.

PRESENT VALUE CONCEPTS

Our discussion of capital leases raises an interesting question about liabilities: Is the recorded amount of the liability the actual amount of cash that will be paid in the future? For example, if I agree to pay you $10,000 five years from now, should I report a liability of $10,000 on my personal balance sheet? To answer such questions, we will now introduce some relatively simple mathematics called **present value concepts.** These concepts will provide a foundation for our discussion of bond liabilities in the next chapter.

The concept of **present value** (PV) is based on the time value of money. Quite simply, money received today is worth more than money to be received one year from today (or at any other future date) because it can be used to earn interest. If you invest $1,000 today at 10 percent, you will have $1,100 in one year. In contrast, if you receive $1,000 one year from today, you will lose the opportunity to earn the $100 in interest revenue. The difference between the $1,000 and the $1,100 is the interest that can be earned during the year.

In one of your math classes, you have probably already solved some problems involving the time value of money. In the typical problem, you are told a certain dollar amount has been deposited in a savings account earning a specified rate of interest. You are asked to determine the dollar amount in the savings account after a certain number of years. In contrast, in this chapter we show you how to solve the opposite problem. In present value problems, you are told a dollar amount to be received in the future (such as the balance of a savings account after five years) and are asked to determine the present value of the amount (which is the amount that must be deposited in the savings account today).

The value of money changes over time because money can earn interest. In a present value problem, you know the dollar amount of a cash flow that will occur in the future and need to determine its value now. The opposite situation occurs when you know the dollar amount of a cash flow that occurs today and need to determine its value at some point in the future. These problems are called future value problems. Future value concepts are discussed in a supplement to this chapter.

Present Value of a Single Amount

The present value of a single amount is the worth to you today of receiving that amount some time in the future. For instance, you might be offered an opportunity to invest in a debt instrument that would pay you $10,000 in three years. Before you decided whether to invest, you would want to determine the present value of the instrument. Graphically, the present value of $1 due at the end of the third period with an interest rate of 10 percent can be represented as follows:

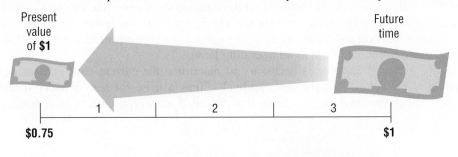

To compute the present value of an amount to be received in the future, we will subtract interest that is earned over time from the amount to be received in the future. For example, if you place $100 in a savings account that earns 5 percent, you will have $105 at the end of a year. In a present value problem, you will be told that you have $105 at the end of the year and must compute the amount to be deposited at the beginning of the year. To solve this type of problem, you must discount the amount to be received in the future at i interest rate for n periods. The formula to compute the present value of a single amount is

$$\text{Present value} = \frac{1}{(1 + i)^n} \times \text{Amount}$$

While the formula is not difficult to use, most analysts use present value tables, calculators, or Excel. We will illustrate how to use present value tables (an explanation of how to use Excel to compute present values is presented in a supplement to this chapter). Assume that today is January 1, 2014, and you have the opportunity to receive $1,000 cash on December 31, 2017. At an interest rate of 10 percent per year, how much is the $1,000 payment worth to you on January 1, 2014? You could discount the amount year by year[4] but it is easier to use Table A.1, Appendix A, Present Value of $1. For $i = 10\%$, $n = 3$, we find that the present value of $1 is 0.7513. The present value of $1,000 to be received at the end of three years can be computed as follows:

$$\$1,000 \times 0.7513 = \$751.30$$

> From Table A.1
> Interest rate = 10%,
> n = 3

Learning how to compute a present value amount is not difficult, but it is more important that you understand what it means. The $751.30 is the amount you would pay now to have the right to receive $1,000 at the end of three years, assuming an interest rate of 10 percent. Conceptually, you should be indifferent between having $751.30 today and receiving $1,000 in three years, because you can use financial institutions to convert dollars from the present value to the future value and vice versa. If you had $751.30 today but preferred $1,000 in three years, you could simply deposit the money in a savings account and it would grow to $1,000 in three years. Alternatively, if you had a contract that promised you $1,000 in three years, you could sell it to an investor for $751.30 in cash today because it would permit the investor to earn the difference in interest.

To compute the present value using Excel, enter:
= 1000/(1.10)^3

PAUSE FOR **FEEDBACK**

SELF-STUDY **QUIZ**

There are two types of payments when you compute present values. So far, we have discussed single payments. In the next section, we will discuss annuities. Before you move on, complete the following questions to test your understanding of these concepts.

1. If the interest rate in a present value problem increases from 8 percent to 10 percent, will the present value increase or decrease?
2. What is the present value of $10,000 to be received 10 years from now if the interest rate is 5 percent, compounded annually?

After you have completed your answers, check them with the solutions at the bottom of the next page.

---

[4]The detailed discounting is as follows:

Periods	Interest for the Year	Present Value*
1	$1,000 − ($1,000 × 1/1.10) = $90.91	$1,000 − $90.91 = $909.09
2	$909.09 − ($909.09 × 1/1.10) = $82.64	$909.09 − $82.64 = $826.45
3	$826.45 − ($826.45 × 1/1.10) = $75.15†	$826.45 − $75.15 = $751.30

*Verifiable in Table A.1.   † Adjusted for rounding.

Present Value of an Annuity

An ANNUITY is a series of periodic cash receipts or payments that are equal in amount each interest period.

Instead of a single payment, many business problems involve multiple cash payments over a number of periods. An **annuity** is a series of consecutive payments characterized by

1. An equal dollar amount each interest period.

2. Interest periods of equal length (year, half a year, quarter, or month).

3. An equal interest rate each interest period.

Examples of annuities include monthly payments on an automobile or home, yearly contributions to a savings account, and monthly pension benefits.

The present value of an annuity is the value now of a series of equal amounts to be received (or paid out) for some specified number of periods in the future. It is computed by discounting each of the equal periodic amounts. A good example of this type of problem is a retirement program that offers employees a monthly income after retirement. The present value of an annuity of $1 for three periods at 10 percent may be represented graphically as follows:

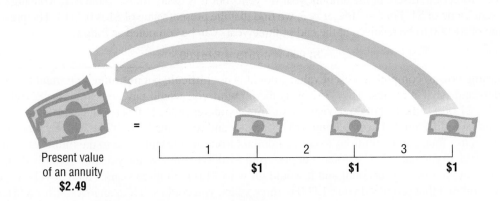

Present value
of an annuity
$2.49

Assume you are to receive $1,000 cash on each December 31, 2014, 2015, and 2016. How much would the sum of these three $1,000 future amounts be worth on January 1, 2014, assuming an interest rate of 10 percent per year? We could use Table A.1, Appendix A, to calculate the present value as follows:

Year	Amount		Factor from Table A.1, Appendix A, $i = 10\%$		Present Value
1	$1,000	×	0.9091 ($n = 1$)	=	$ 909.10
2	$1,000	×	0.8264 ($n = 2$)	=	826.40
3	$1,000	×	0.7513 ($n = 3$)	=	751.30
			Total present value	=	$2,486.80

We can compute the present value of this annuity more easily however, by using Table A.2, Appendix A, as follows:

From Table A.2, Interest rate = 10%, n = 3

$1,000 × 2.4869 = $2,487 (rounded)

To compute the present value using Excel, enter: $f_x = \text{PV}(0.10,3,-1000)$

Interest Rates and Interest Periods

The preceding illustrations assumed annual periods for compounding and discounting. Although interest rates are almost always quoted on an annual basis, most compounding

1. The present value will decrease.
2. $10,000 × 0.6139 = $6,139

periods encountered in business are less than one year. When interest periods are less than a year, the values of n and i must be restated to be consistent with the length of the interest period.

To illustrate, 12 percent interest compounded annually for five years requires the use of $n = 5$ and $i = 12\%$. If compounding is quarterly, however, the interest period is one quarter of a year (i.e., four periods per year), and the quarterly interest rate is one quarter of the annual rate (i.e., 3 percent per quarter). Therefore, 12 percent interest compounded quarterly for five years requires use of $n = 20$ and $i = 3\%$.

Truth in Advertising   A QUESTION OF ETHICS

Newspaper, magazine, and television advertisements are easy to misinterpret if the consumer does not understand present value concepts. For example, most car companies offer seasonal promotions with special financing incentives. A car dealer may advertise 4 percent interest on car loans when banks are charging 10 percent. Typically, the lower interest rate is not really an incentive because the dealer simply charges a higher price for cars the dealership finances. Borrowing from the bank and paying cash at the dealership may help the buyer to negotiate a lower price. Customers should use the present value concepts illustrated in this chapter to compare financing alternatives.

Another misleading advertisement, seen every January, promises magazine subscribers a chance to become an instant millionaire. The fine print discloses that the winner will receive $25,000 for 40 years, which amounts to $1,000,000 (40 × $25,000), but the present value of this annuity at 8 percent is only $298,000. While most winners are happy to get the money, they are not really millionaires.

Some consumer advocates argue that consumers should not have to study present value concepts to understand such advertisements. While some of these criticisms may be valid, the quality of information contained in advertisements that include interest rates has improved over time.

Accounting Applications of Present Values

Many business transactions require the use of future and present value concepts. So that you can enhance your understanding of these concepts, we provide three examples.

LEARNING OBJECTIVE 9-8
Apply present value concepts to liabilities.

Computing the Amount of a Liability with a Single Payment

On January 1, 2014, Starbucks bought some new delivery trucks. The company signed a note and agreed to pay $200,000 on December 31, 2015, an amount representing the cash equivalent price of the trucks plus interest for two years. The market interest rate for this note was 12 percent.

To record this transaction, the accountant must first compute the present value of a single amount paid in the future. In conformity with the cost principle, the cost of the trucks is their current cash equivalent price, which is the present value of the future payment. The problem can be shown graphically as follows:

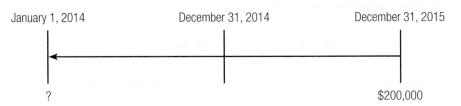

The present value of the $200,000 is computed as follows:

$$\$200,000 \times 0.7972 = \$159,440$$

From Table A.1,
Interest rate = 12%,
$n = 2$

Therefore, the journal entry is as follows:

To compute the present value using Excel, enter:
= 200000/(1.12)^2

| Delivery trucks (+A)... | 159,440 | |
| Note payable (+L)... | | 159,440 |

Assets	=	Liabilities	+	Stockholders' Equity
Delivery trucks	+159,440	Note payable	+159,440	

After the initial transaction is recorded, each year's interest expense is recorded in an adjusting entry as follows:

December 31, 2014	Interest expense (+E, −SE)	19,133*	
	Note payable (+L)		19,133
*$159,440 × 12% = $19,133			

Assets	=	Liabilities	+	Stockholders' Equity
		Note payable	+19,133	Interest expense (+E)	−19,133

December 31, 2015	Interest expense (+E, −SE)	21,429*	
	Note payable (+L)		21,429
*($159,440 + $19,133) × 12% = 21,429			

Assets	=	Liabilities	+	Stockholders' Equity
		Note payable	+21,429	Interest expense (+E)	−21,429

At the end of two years, the loan amount must be repaid. The amount owed is the balance of Note Payable, which is the same as the maturity amount on the due date. The journal entry to record full payment of the debt follows:

| Note payable (−L)... | 200,000 | |
| Cash (−A) .... | | 200,000 |

Assets	=	Liabilities	+	Stockholders' Equity
Cash	−200,000	Note payable	−200,000	

Computing the Amount of a Liability with an Annuity

On January 1, 2014, Starbucks bought new printing equipment. The company elected to finance the purchase with a note payable to be paid off in three years in annual installments of $163,686. Each installment includes principal plus interest on the unpaid balance at 11 percent per year. The annual installments are due on December 31, 2014, 2015, and 2016. This problem can be shown graphically as follows:

The amount of the note can be determined by computing the present value of each installment payment, $i = 11\%$ and $n = 3$. This is an annuity because payment is made in three equal installments. The amount of the note is computed as follows:

From Table A.2,
Interest rate = 11%,
n = 3

$$\$163,686 \times 2.4437 = \$400,000$$

The acquisition on January 1, 2014, is recorded as follows:

Printing equipment (+A)	400,000	
Note payable (+L)		400,000

To compute the present value using Excel, enter:
$f_x = \text{PV}(0.11, 3, -163,686)$

Assets		=	Liabilities		+	Stockholders' Equity
Printing equipment	+400,000		Note payable	+400,000		

Each year, the accountant must record the payments on this note as follows:

December 31, 2014			
	Note payable (−L).......................	119,686	
	Interest expense (+E, −SE)		
	($400,000 × 11%)....................	44,000	
	Cash (−A).........................		163,686

Assets		=	Liabilities		+	Stockholders' Equity	
Cash	−163,686		Note payable	−119,686		Interest expense (+E)	−44,000

December 31, 2015			
	Note payable (−L).......................	132,851	
	Interest expense (+E, −SE)		
	[($400,000 − 119,686) × 11%]..........	30,835	
	Cash (−A).........................		163,686

Assets		=	Liabilities		+	Stockholders' Equity	
Cash	−163,686		Note payable	−132,851		Interest expense (+E)	−30,835

December 31, 2016			
	Note payable (−L).......................	147,463	
	Interest expense (+E, −SE)	16,223*	
	Cash (−A).........................		163,686

*Interest: ($400,000 − $119,686 − $132,851) × 11% = $16,223 (rounded to accommodate rounding errors).

Assets		=	Liabilities		+	Stockholders' Equity	
Cash	−163,686		Note payable	−147,463		Interest expense (+E)	−16,223

Present Values Involving Both an Annuity and a Single Payment

In some business situations, a borrower may agree to make periodic payments (an annuity) in addition to a single payment at the end of the agreement. Assume Starbucks bought a new delivery truck and agreed to pay the truck dealership $1,000 per month for 20 months and an additional $40,000 at the end of 20 months. The dealership is charging 24 percent per year, or 2 percent per month.

In this type of problem, you can determine the present value of the total obligation by computing the present value of each part. In other words, you compute the present value of the annuity and the present value of the single payment, and add the two amounts together, as follows:

From Table A.2,
Interest rate = 2%,
n = 20

To compute the present value using Excel, enter:
$f_x = PV(0.02, 20, -1000)$

Step 1:   Compute the present value of the annuity by using Table A.2, Appendix A:

$$\$1,000 \times 16.3514 = \$16,351$$

Step 2:   Compute the present value of the single payment by using Table A.1, Appendix A:

$$\$40,000 \times 0.6730 = \$26,920$$

From Table A.1,
Interest rate = 2%,
n = 20

To compute the present value using Excel, enter:
$= 40,000/(1.02)^{20}$

Step 3:   Add the two amounts to determine the present value of the obligation:

$$
\begin{array}{r}
\$16,351 \\
+ \quad 26,920 \\
\hline
\$43,271
\end{array}
$$

The $43,271 is the present value of all the cash payments that Starbucks must make under this agreement. This amount would be recorded as a liability by Starbucks.

www.mhhe.com/libby8e

GUIDED **HELP**

For additional step-by-step video instruction, go to the URL or scan the QR code in the margin with your smartphone or Ipad.

Computing the Amount of a Lease Liability

On January 1, 2014, Starbucks signed a 20-year lease for coffee roasting equipment. The lease is based on an effective interest rate of 8 percent and requires annual payments of $10,000 on December 31 of each year. The term is 100 percent of the expected life of the equipment. As a result, this lease should be recorded as a capital lease. The amount of the liability is the present value of the lease payments, computed as follows:

$$\$10,000 \times 9.8181 = \$98,181$$

From Table A.2,
Interest rate = 8%,
n = 20

To compute the present value using Excel, enter:
$f_x = PV(0.08, 20, -10,000)$

The signing of the lease on January 1, 2014, is recorded as follows:

Roasting equipment (+A)	98,181	
Lease payable (+L)		98,181

Assets	=	Liabilities	+	Stockholders' Equity
Roasting equipment +98,181		Lease payable +98,181		

In the next chapter, we will use the present value techniques you have just learned to understand how to account for bonds.

DEMONSTRATION CASE

(Try to answer the questions before proceeding to the suggested solution that follows.) Muller Construction completed several transactions during the year. In each case, decide if a liability should be recorded and, if so, determine the amount. Assume the current date is December 31, 2014.

1. Employees earned salaries of $100,000 which have not been paid at year-end. The employer share of FICA is $7,000.

2. The company borrowed $100,000 on June 30th at 7 percent interest. No payments associated with this loan have been made.

3. A customer made a $75,000 down payment on a construction project. Work will begin next month.

4. The company lost a lawsuit for $250,000 but plans to appeal.

5. A new truck was leased for a period equal to 85 percent of the expected life of the truck.

6. On December 31, 2014, a bank lent money to Muller. The company agreed to repay the bank $100,000 on December 31, 2015. The bank charges 5 percent interest.

7. The company signed a loan agreement that requires it to pay $50,000 per year for 20 years. The interest rate is 8 percent.

SUGGESTED SOLUTION

1. A liability of $107,000 should be recorded.

2. The amount borrowed ($100,000) should be recorded as a liability on June 30th. In addition, interest accrued but not paid should be recorded as a liability at year-end. This amount is $100,000 × 7% × 6/12 = $3,500.

3. The customer deposit ($75,000) is a liability until work is performed and the related revenue earned.

4. Most likely, the $250,000 should be recorded as a liability, unless the grounds for appeal significantly reduce the probability that the $250,000 will eventually be paid.

5. Because the lease covers more than 75 percent of the estimated life of the truck, a liability should be recorded. The amount is the present value of the lease payments (which were not given in the problem).

6. A liability should be recorded for the present value of the obligation. The amount is determined by using the factor from Table A.1 for $n = 1$, $i = 5\%$: $100,000 × 0.9524 = $95,240.

7. A liability should be recorded for the present value of the obligation. The amount is determined by using the factor from Table A.2 for $n = 20$, $i = 8\%$: $50,000 × 9.8181 = $490,905.

Chapter Supplement A

Present Value Computations Using Excel

While the present value tables at the end of this book are useful for educational purposes, most present value problems in business are solved with calculators or Excel spreadsheets. Because of the widespread availability of Excel, we will show you how to solve present value problems using Excel. There are slightly different versions of Excel available, depending on the age of the computer.

Present Value of a Single Payment

The calculation of a present value amount is based on a fairly simple mathematical formula:

$$PV = Payment/(1 + i)^n$$

In this formula, *payment* is the cash payment made at some point in the future, i is the interest rate each period, and n is the number of periods in the problem. We could use this formula to solve all problems involving the present value of a single payment. It is, of course, easier to use a present value table (like the one at the end of this book) which is derived by solving the present value formula for various interest rates and numbers of periods. Unfortunately, a table that included all interest rates and numbers of periods actually encountered in business would be too large to work with. As a result, most accountants and analysts use Excel to compute a present value.

To compute the present value of a single payment in Excel, you enter the present value formula in a cell, using the format required by Excel. You should select a cell and enter the following formula:

$$= Payment/(1 + i)^{\wedge}n$$

To illustrate, if you wanted to solve for the present value of a $100,000 payment to be made in five years with an interest rate of 10 percent, you would enter the following in the function field:

$$= 100000/(1.10)^{\wedge}5$$

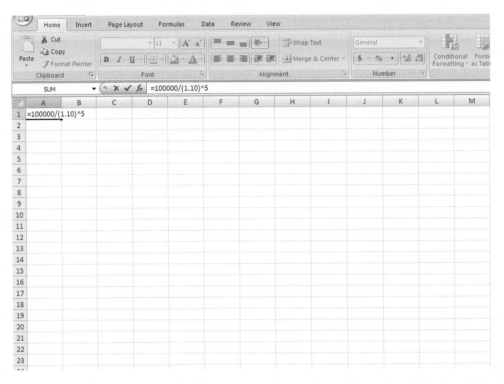

Based on this entry, Excel would compute a present value of $62,092.13. This answer is slightly different than the answer you would have if you used the present value tables at the end of the book. The tables in the book are rounded based on four digits. Excel does not round and, therefore, provides a more accurate computation.

Present Value of an Annuity

The formula for computing the present value of an annuity is a little more complicated than the present value of a single payment. As a result, Excel has been programmed to include the formula so that you do not have to enter it yourself.

To compute the present value of an annuity in Excel, select a cell and click on the insert function button (f_x). The following dropdown box will appear:

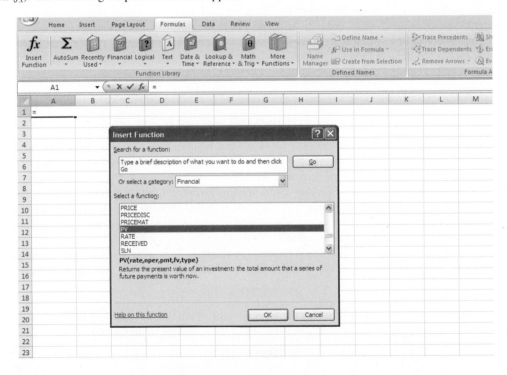

Under the "Select a Category" heading, you should pick "Financial." Next, under the "Select a Function" heading, scroll down and select "PV." Then, click on "OK" and a new dropdown box will appear:

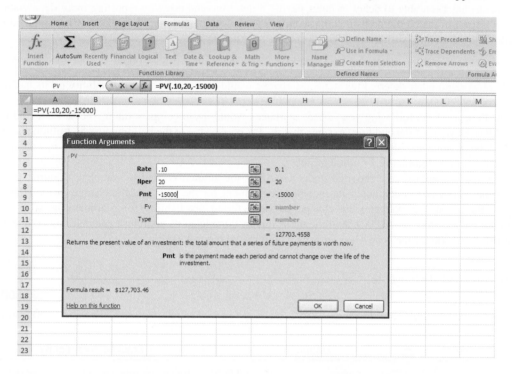

In this box, you should enter the interest rate, 10 percent in this example, under Rate. Notice that the rate must be entered as a decimal (i.e., 0.10) Enter the number of periods (20) under Nper. Excel has an unusual convention associated with the payment. It must be entered as a negative amount (−15000) under Pmt. Notice also that a comma should not be included in the amount you enter. When you click on OK, Excel will enter the present value in the cell you selected. In this example, the value determined by Excel is $127,703.46.

Chapter Supplement B

Deferred Taxes

Most companies report a large long-term liability called *deferred taxes.* The deferred tax liability for Starbucks is relatively small ($49.2 million) and is reported in the notes to its financial statements. Because separate rules govern the preparation of financial statements (GAAP) and tax returns (Internal Revenue Code), income tax expense and current taxes payable often differ in amount. To reflect this difference, companies establish a separate account called Deferred Taxes. In practice, deferred taxes can be either assets (such as taxes related to cash collected in advance from a customer, which is taxable before it is reported as a revenue on the income statement) or liabilities (such as taxes related to depreciation, which is reported on the tax return before it is reported on the income statement). Starbucks has deferred tax amounts reported as both assets and liabilities.

Deferred tax items exist because of timing differences in the reporting of revenues and expenses on the income statement and tax return. These **temporary differences** are caused by differences between GAAP, which governs financial statement preparation, and the Internal Revenue Code, which governs the preparation of tax returns.

Deferred tax amounts always reverse themselves. For example, at some point in the future the accelerated depreciation recorded on the tax return will be less than the straight-line depreciation reported on the income statement (recall from Chapter 8 that accelerated depreciation causes higher depreciation expense compared to straight line in the early years of an asset's life and lower depreciation in the later years). When a deferred tax liability reverses, the deferred tax amount is reduced, and the company pays more taxes to the IRS than the amount of income tax expense reported on the income statement.

Let's consider a simple example. Assume that in 2014, Starbucks owned a building that originally cost $10 million. The current book value (cost less accumulated depreciation) on the balance sheet is

DEFERRED TAX ITEMS exist because of timing differences caused by reporting revenues and expenses according to GAAP on a company's income statement and according to the Internal Revenue Code on the tax return.

TEMPORARY DIFFERENCES are timing differences that cause deferred income taxes and will reverse, or turn around, in the future.

$8.5 million. For tax purposes, the book value is $6.5 million. The $2 million difference is caused by using straight-line depreciation for financial reporting and accelerated depreciation for tax purposes. Starbucks has been able to delay or defer paying federal income taxes by reporting more depreciation on its tax return than it did on its income statement. The amount of deferred tax liability is computed by multiplying the timing difference by the corporate tax rate (34%):

$$\text{Deferred Tax Liability} = \$2 \text{ million} \times 34\% = \$680,000$$

If there were no other deferred tax items, Starbucks would report a deferred tax liability on its balance sheet of $680,000.

At the end of the following year, 2015, Starbucks would again compare the tax book value and the GAAP book value of the building. Assume that the tax book value of the building was $6 million and the GAAP book value was $8.2 million. The timing difference would be $2.2 million, resulting in a deferred tax liability of $748,000 ($2.2 million × 34%).

The income tax expense reported under GAAP is the amount needed to complete a journal entry once the company has computed its income tax payment for the year and the change in its deferred taxes. Based on our example, the change in the deferred tax liability for Starbucks in 2015 was $68,000 ($748,000 − $680,000). Assume the company completed its tax return and determined it owed the IRS $550,000 for the year. The company would record the following:

Income tax expense (+E, −SE).	618,000	
Deferred taxes (+L)		68,000
Income taxes payable (+L)		550,000

Assets	=	Liabilities		+	Stockholders' Equity	
		Deferred taxes	+68,000		Income tax expense (+E)	−618,000
		Income taxes payable	+550,000			

The computation of deferred taxes involves some complexities that are discussed in advanced accounting courses. At this point, you need to understand only that deferred tax assets and liabilities are caused by temporary differences between the income statement and tax return. Each temporary difference has an impact on the income statement in one accounting period and on the tax return in another.

Chapter Supplement C

Future Value Concepts

Future value problems are similar to present value problems in the sense that they are both based on the time value of money. As we saw earlier, a present value problem determines the current cash equivalent of an amount to be received in the future. In comparison, a **future value** is the sum to which an amount will increase as the result of compound interest. The following table illustrates the basic difference between present value and future value problems:

The FUTURE VALUE is the sum to which an amount will increase as the result of compound interest.

	Now	Future
Present value	?	$1,000
Future value	$1,000	?

Future Value of a Single Amount

In future value of a single amount problems, you are asked to calculate how much money you will have in the future as the result of investing a certain amount in the present. If you were to receive a gift of $10,000, for instance, you might decide to put it in a savings account and use the money as a down payment on a house after you graduate. The future value computation would tell you how much money would be available when you graduate.

To solve a future value problem, you need to know three items:

1. Amount to be invested.
2. Interest rate (*i*) the amount will earn.
3. Number of periods (*n*) in which the amount will earn interest.

Since the future value concept is based on compound interest, the amount of interest for each period is calculated by multiplying the principal plus any interest not paid out in prior periods. Graphically, the calculation of the future value of $1 for three periods and an interest rate of 10 percent may be represented as follows:

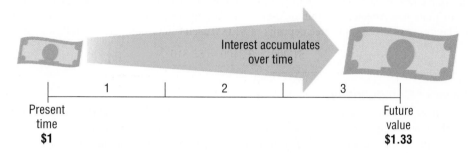

Assume that on January 1, 2014, you deposit $1,000 in a savings account at 10 percent annual interest, compounded annually. At the end of three years, the $1,000 will have increased to $1,331 as follows:

Year	Amount at Start of Year	+	Interest During the Year	=	Amount at End of Year
1	$1,000	+	$1,000 × 10% = $100	=	$1,100
2	1,100	+	1,100 × 10% = $110	=	1,210
3	1,210	+	1,210 × 10% = $121	=	1,331

We can avoid the detailed arithmetic by referring to Table A.3, Future Value of $1. For $i = 10\%, n = 3$, we find the value 1.331. We then compute the balance at the end of year 3 as follows:

$$\$1,000 \times 1.3310 = \$1,331$$

From Table A.3, Interest rate = 10%, n = 3

Note that the increase of $331 is due to the time value of money. It is interest revenue to the owner of the savings account and interest expense to the savings institution.

Future Value of an Annuity

If you are saving money for some purpose, such as to finance a new car or a trip to Europe, you might decide to deposit a fixed amount of money in a savings account each month. The future value of an annuity computation will tell you how much money will be in your savings account at some point in the future.

The future value of an annuity includes compound interest on each payment from the date of payment to the end of the term of the annuity. Each new payment accumulates less interest than prior payments, only because the number of periods remaining in which to accumulate interest decreases. The future value of an annuity of $1 for three periods at 10 percent may be represented graphically as:

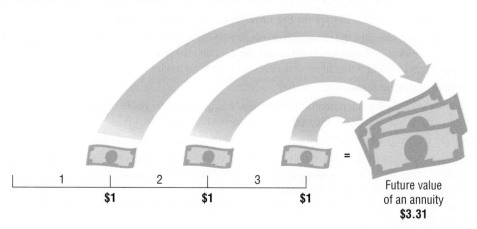

Assume that each year for three years, you deposit $1,000 cash in a savings account at 10 percent interest per year. You make the first $1,000 deposit on December 31, 2014, the second one on December 31, 2015, and the third and last one on December 31, 2016. The first $1,000 deposit earns compound interest for two years (for a total principal and interest of $1,210); the second deposit earns interest for one year (for a total principal and interest of $1,100). The third deposit earns no interest because it was made on the day that the balance is computed. Thus, the total amount in the savings account at the end of three years is $3,310 ($1,210 + $1,100 + $1,000).

To derive the future value of this annuity, we could compute the interest on each deposit. However, we can refer to Table A.4, Appendix A, Future Value of an Annuity of $1 for $i = 10\%$, $n = 3$ to find the value 3.3100. The future value of your three deposits of $1,000 each can be computed as follows:

$$\$1,000 \times 3.3100 = \$3,310$$

From Table A.4,
Interest rate = 10%,
n = 3

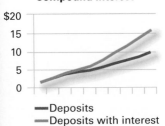

**Effects of
Compound Interest**

— Deposits
— Deposits with interest

The Power of Compounding

Compound interest is a remarkably powerful economic force. Indeed, the ability to earn interest on interest is the key to building economic wealth. If you save $1,000 per year for the first 10 years of your career, you will have more money when you retire than you would if you had saved $15,000 per year for the last 10 years of your career. This surprising outcome occurs because the money you save early in your career will earn more interest than the money you save at the end of your career. If you start saving money now, the majority of your wealth will not be the money you saved but the interest your money was able to earn.

The chart in the margin illustrates the power of compounding over a brief 10-year period. If you deposit $1 each year in an account earning 10 percent interest, at the end of just 10 years, only 64 percent of your balance will be made up of money you have saved; the rest will be interest you have earned. After 20 years, only 35 percent of your balance will be from saved money. The lesson associated with compound interest is clear: Even though saving money is difficult, you should start now.

CHAPTER TAKE-AWAYS

9-1. Define, measure, and report current liabilities.   p. 453

Strictly speaking, accountants define liabilities as probable future sacrifices of economic benefits that arise from past transactions. They are classified on the balance sheet as either current or long term. Current liabilities are short-term obligations that will be paid within the current operating cycle of the business or within one year of the balance sheet date, whichever is longer. Long-term liabilities are all obligations not classified as current.

9-2. Analyze the accounts payable turnover ratio.   p. 454

This ratio is computed by dividing cost of goods sold by average accounts payable. It shows how quickly management is paying its trade creditors and is considered to be a measure of liquidity.

9-3. Report notes payable and explain the time value of money.   p. 458

A note payable specifies the amount borrowed, when it must be repaid, and the interest rate associated with the debt. Accountants must report the debt and the interest as it accrues. The time value of money refers to the fact that interest accrues on borrowed money with the passage of time.

9-4. Report contingent liabilities.   p. 460

A contingent liability is a potential liability that has arisen as the result of a past event. Such liabilities are disclosed in a note if the obligation is reasonably possible.

9-5. Explain the importance of working capital and its impact on cash flows.   p. 462

Working capital is used to fund the operating activities of a business. Changes in working capital accounts affect the statement of cash flows. Cash flows from operating activities are increased by decreases in current assets (other than cash) or increases in current liabilities. Cash flows from operating activities are decreased by increases in current assets (other than cash) or decreases in current liabilities.

9-6. Report long-term liabilities.   p. 464

Usually, long-term liabilities will be paid in more than one year in the future. Accounting for long-term debt is based on the same concepts used in accounting for short-term debt.

9-7. Compute present values.   p. 466

The present value concept is based on the time value of money. Simply stated, a dollar to be received in the future is worth less than a dollar available today (present value). This concept can be applied either to a single payment or multiple payments called *annuities*. Either present value tables or Excel can be used to determine present values.

9-8. Apply present value concepts to liabilities.   p. 469

Accountants use present value concepts to determine the reported amounts of liabilities. A liability involves the payment of some amount at a future date. The reported liability is not the amount of the future payment. Instead, the liability is reported at the amount of the present value of the future payment.

In this chapter, we focused on current liabilities and introduced you to present value concepts. In the next chapter, we will use present value concepts to measure long-term liabilities. We will also discuss long-term liabilities in the context of the capital structure of the company.

KEY **RATIO**

Accounts payable turnover is a measure of how quickly a company pays its creditors. It is computed as follows (p. 454):

$$\text{Accounts Payable Turnover} = \frac{\text{Costs of Goods Sold}}{\text{Average Accounts Payable}}$$

FINDING **FINANCIAL INFORMATION**

Balance Sheet

Under Current Liabilities
Liabilities listed by account title, such as
  Accounts payable
  Accrued liabilities
  Notes payable
Current portion of long-term debt

Under Noncurrent Liabilities
Liabilities listed by account title, such as
  Long-term debt
  Deferred taxes
  Bonds

Statement of Cash Flows

Under Operating Activities (indirect method)
  Net income
  + Increases in most current liabilities
  − Decreases in most current liabilities

Under Financing Activities
  + Increases in long-term liabilities
  − Decreases in long-term liabilities

Income Statement

Liabilities are shown only on the balance sheet, never on the income statement. Transactions affecting liabilities often affect an income statement account. For example, accrued salary compensation affects an income statement account (compensation expense) and a balance sheet account (salaries payable).

Notes

Under Summary of Significant Accounting Policies
Description of pertinent information concerning accounting treatment of liabilities. Normally, there is minimal information.

Under a Separate Note
If not listed on the balance sheet, a listing of the major classifications of liabilities with information about maturities and interest rates. Information about contingent liabilities is reported in the notes.

KEY **TERMS**

QUESTIONS

1. Define *liability*. Differentiate between a current liability and a long-term liability.
2. How can external parties be informed about the liabilities of a business?
3. Liabilities are measured and reported at their current cash equivalent amount. Explain.
4. A *liability* is a known obligation of either a definite or an estimated amount. Explain.
5. Define *working capital*. How is it computed?
6. Define *accrued liability*. What type of entry usually reflects an accrued liability?
7. Define *deferred revenue*. Why is it a liability?
8. Define *note payable*. Differentiate between a secured and an unsecured note.
9. What is a contingent liability? How is a contingent liability reported?
10. Compute 2014 interest expense for the following note: face, $4,000; 12 percent interest; date of note, April 1, 2014.
11. Explain the concept of the time value of money.
12. Explain the basic difference between future value and present value.
13. If you hold a valid contract that will pay you $8,000 cash in 10 years and the going rate of interest is 10 percent, what is its present value? Show your computations.
14. What is an annuity?
15. Complete the following schedule:

	Table Values
Concept	$i = 5\%, n = 4; i = 10\%, n = 7; i = 14\%, n = 10$
PV of $1	
PV of annuity of $1	

16. You purchased an XIT auto for $18,000 by making a $3,000 cash payment and six semiannual installment payments for the balance at 12 percent interest. Determine the amount of each payment.

MULTIPLE-CHOICE **QUESTIONS**

1. What is the present value factor for an annuity of five periods and an interest rate of 10 percent?
   a. 1.6105
   b. 6.1051
   c. 3.7908
   d. 7.7217
2. The university spirit organization needs to buy a car to travel to football games. A dealership in Lockhart has agreed to the following terms: $4,000 down plus 20 monthly payments of $750. A dealership in Leander will agree to a $1,000 down payment plus 20 monthly payments of $850. The local bank is currently charging an annual interest rate of 12 percent for car loans. Which is the better deal, *and why*?

a. The Leander offer is better because the total payments of $18,000 are less than the total payments of $19,000 to be made to the Lockhart dealership.

b. The Lockhart offer is better because the cost in terms of present value is less than the present value cost of the Leander offer.

c. The Lockhart offer is better because the monthly payments are less.

d. The Leander offer is better because the cash down payment is less.

e. The Leander offer is better because the cost in terms of present value is less than the present value cost of the Lockhart offer.

3. Which of the following best describes *accrued liabilities*?

a. Long-term liabilities.

b. Current amounts owed to suppliers of inventory.

c. Current liabilities to be recognized as revenue in a future period.

d. Current amounts owed to various parties excluding suppliers of inventory.

4. Company X has borrowed $100,000 from the bank to be repaid over the next five years, with payments beginning next month. Which of the following best describes the presentation of this debt in the balance sheet as of today (the date of borrowing)?

a. $100,000 in the Long-Term Liability section.

b. $100,000 plus the interest to be paid over the five-year period in the Long-Term Liability section.

c. A portion of the $100,000 in the Current Liability section and the remainder of the principal in the Long-Term Liability section.

d. A portion of the $100,000 plus interest in the Current Liability section and the remainder of the principal plus interest in the Long-Term Liability section.

5. A company is facing a class-action lawsuit in the upcoming year. It is possible, but not probable, that the company will have to pay a settlement of approximately $2,000,000. How would this fact be reported in the financial statements to be issued at the end of the current month?

a. $2,000,000 in the Current Liability section.

b. $2,000,000 in the Long-Term Liability section.

c. In a descriptive narrative in the footnote section.

d. None because disclosure is not required.

6. Which of the following transactions would usually cause accounts payable turnover to increase?

a. Payment of cash to a supplier for merchandise previously purchased on credit.

b. Collection of cash from a customer.

c. Purchase of merchandise on credit.

d. None of the above.

7. How is working capital calculated?

a. Current assets multiplied by current liabilities.

b. Current assets plus current liabilities.

c. Current assets minus current liabilities.

d. Current assets divided by current liabilities.

8. The present value of an annuity of $10,000 per year for 10 years discounted at 8 percent is what amount?

a. $5,002   c. $53,349

b. $67,101   d. $80,000

9. Jacobs Company borrowed $100,000 at 8 percent interest for three months. How much interest does the company owe at the end of three months?

a. $8,000   c. $800

b. $2,000   d. $200

10. Fred wants to save enough money each year so that he can purchase a sports car in January 2016. Fred receives a large bonus from his employer every December 31. He anticipates that the car will cost $54,000 on January 1, 2016. Which of the following will Fred need to calculate how much he must save each December 31?

a. The anticipated interest rate and the present value of $1 table.

b. The anticipated interest rate and the future value of $1 table.

c. The anticipated interest rate and the present value table for annuities.

d. The anticipated interest rate and the future value table for annuities.

MINI-**EXERCISES**

M9-1
LO9-3

Computing Interest Expense

Kieso Company borrowed $600,000 on a 90-day note at 11 percent interest. The money was borrowed for 30 days in 2014 and 60 days in 2015; the note and interest were to be paid upon maturity in 2015. How much interest expense, if any, would be reported in 2014 and in 2015?

M9-2
LO9-3

Recording a Note Payable

Wygant Corporation borrowed $290,000 on October 1, 2014. The note carried a 10 percent interest rate with the principal and interest payable on May 1, 2015. Prepare the journal entry to record the note on October 1. Prepare the adjusting entry to record accrued interest on December 31.

M9-3
LO9-1, 9-2, 9-5

Finding Financial Information

For each of the following items, specify whether the information would be found in the balance sheet, the income statement, the statement of cash flows, the notes to the statements, or not at all.

1. The amount of working capital.
2. The total amount of current liabilities.
3. Information concerning company pension plans.
4. The accounts payable turnover ratio.
5. Information concerning the impact of changes in working capital on cash flows for the period.

M9-4
LO9-1

Computing Working Capital

The balance sheet for Stevenson Corporation reported the following: noncurrent assets, $240,000; total assets, $360,000; noncurrent liabilities, $176,000; total stockholders' equity, $94,000. Compute Stevenson's working capital.

M9-5
LO9-1

Analyzing the Impact of Transactions on Liquidity

Ospry, Inc., has working capital in the amount of $1,240,000. For each of the following transactions, determine whether working capital will increase, decrease, or remain the same.

a. Paid accounts payable in the amount of $50,000.
b. Recorded accrued salaries in the amount of $100,000.
c. Borrowed $250,000 from a local bank, to be repaid in 90 days.
d. Purchased $20,000 of new inventory on credit.

M9-6
LO9-4

Reporting Contingent Liabilities

Buzz Coffee Shops is famous for its large servings of hot coffee. After a famous case involving McDonald's, the lawyer for Buzz warned management (during 2014) that it could be sued if someone were to spill hot coffee and be burned: "With the temperature of your coffee, I can guarantee it's just a matter of time before you're sued for $1,000,000." Unfortunately, in 2015 the prediction came true when a customer filed suit. The case went to trial in 2016, and the jury awarded the customer $400,000 in damages, which the company immediately appealed. During 2017 the customer and the company settled their dispute for $150,000. What is the proper reporting of this liability each year?

M9-7
LO9-7

Computing the Present Value of a Single Payment

What is the present value of $500,000 to be paid in 10 years with an interest rate of 8 percent?

M9-8
LO9-7

Computing the Present Value of an Annuity

What is the present value of 10 equal payments of $15,000 with an interest rate of 10 percent?

M9-9
LO9-7

Computing the Present Value of a Complex Contract

As a result of a slowdown in operations, Global Stores is offering employees who have been terminated a severance package of $118,000 cash, another $129,000 to be paid in one year, and an annuity of $27,500 to be paid each year for six years beginning in one year. What is the present value of the package, assuming an interest rate of 5 percent?

Computing the Future Value of an Annuity (Supplement C)   **M9-10**

You plan to retire in 10 years. Would it be better for you to save $27,500 a year for the last five years before retirement or $16,250 for each of the 10 years? You are able to earn 9 percent interest on your investments.

Making a Complex Computation of a Future Value (Supplement C)   **M9-11**

You want a retirement fund of $125,000 when you retire in six years. You are able to earn 8 percent on your investments. How much should you deposit each year to build the retirement fund that you want?

 **EXERCISES**

Computing Working Capital; Explaining Working Capital   **E9-1**
LO9-1, 9-4, 9-5

Diane Corporation is preparing its 2015 balance sheet. The company records show the following selected amounts at the end of the accounting period, December 31, 2015:

Total assets	$530,000
Total noncurrent assets	362,000
Liabilities:	
Notes payable (8%, due in 5 years)	15,000
Accounts payable	56,000
Income taxes payable	14,000
Liability for withholding taxes	3,000
Rent revenue collected in advance	7,000
Bonds payable (due in 15 years)	90,000
Wages payable	7,000
Property taxes payable	3,000
Note payable (10%, due in 6 months)	12,000
Interest payable	400
Common stock	100,000

Required:
1. Compute working capital. Why is working capital important to management?
2. Would your computation be different if the company reported $250,000 worth of contingent liabilities in the notes to the statements? Explain.

Recording Payroll Costs   **E9-2**
LO9-1

Paul Company completed the salary and wage payroll for March 2014. The payroll provided the following details:

Salaries and wages earned	$200,000
Employee income taxes withheld	40,000
Insurance premiums withheld	1,000
FICA payroll taxes*	15,000

*$15,000 each for employer and employees.

Required:
1. Give the journal entry to record the payroll for March, including employee deductions.
2. Give the journal entry to record the employer's payroll taxes.
3. Give a combined journal entry to show the payment of amounts owed to governmental agencies.

E9-3

LO9-1

Computing Payroll Costs; Discussion of Labor Costs

Oaks Company has completed the payroll for January 2015, reflecting the following data:

Salaries and wages earned	$86,000
Employee income taxes withheld	10,000
FICA payroll taxes*	6,000

Assessed on both employer and employee (i.e., $6,000 each).

Required:

1. What amount of additional labor expense to the company was due to tax laws? What was the amount of the employees' take-home pay?
2. List the liabilities and their amounts reported on the company's January 31, 2015, balance sheet, assuming the employees have been paid.
3. Would employers react differently to a 10 percent increase in the employer's share of FICA than to a 10 percent increase in the basic level of salaries? Would financial analysts react differently?

E9-4

LO9-1, 9-3

Recording a Note Payable through Its Time to Maturity with Discussion of Management Strategy

Many businesses borrow money during periods of increased business activity to finance inventory and accounts receivable. Neiman Marcus is one of America's most prestigious retailers. Each Christmas season, Neiman Marcus builds up its inventory to meet the needs of Christmas shoppers. A large portion of these Christmas sales are on credit. As a result, Neiman Marcus often collects cash from the sales several months after Christmas. Assume that on November 1, 2014, Neiman Marcus borrowed $4.8 million cash from Texas Capital Bank for working capital purposes and signed an interest-bearing note due in six months. The interest rate was 8 percent per annum payable at maturity. The accounting period ends December 31.

Required:

1. Give the journal entry to record the note on November 1.
2. Give any adjusting entry required at the end of the annual accounting period.
3. Give the journal entry to record payment of the note and interest on the maturity date, April 30, 2015.
4. If Neiman Marcus needs extra cash during every Christmas season, should management borrow money on a long-term basis to avoid the necessity of negotiating a new short-term loan each year?

E9-5

LO9-1, 9-3

Determining Financial Statement Effects of Transactions Involving Notes Payable

Using the data from the previous exercise, complete the following requirements.

Required:

1. Determine the financial statement effects for each of the following: (*a*) issuance of the note on November 1, (*b*) the impact of the adjusting entry at the end of the accounting period, and (*c*) payment of the note and interest on April 30, 2015. Indicate the effects (e.g., cash + or −) using the schedule below.
2. If Neiman Marcus needs extra cash during every Christmas season, should management borrow money on a long-term basis to avoid the necessity of negotiating a new short-term loan each year?

Date	Assets	Liabilities	Stockholders' Equity

E9-6

LO9-1

Reporting Short-Term Borrowings

PepsiCo, Inc., manufactures a number of products that are part of our daily lives. Its businesses include Pepsi, Frito-Lay, Tropicana, Quaker, and Gatorade. The company's annual revenues exceed $22 billion. A recent PepsiCo annual report contained the following information:

> At the end of the current year, $3.6 billion of short-term borrowings were classified as long-term, reflecting PepsiCo's intent and ability to refinance these borrowings on a long-term basis, through either long-term debt issuances or rollover of existing short-term borrowings. The significant amount of short-term

borrowings classified as long-term, as compared to the end of the previous year when no such amounts were reclassified, primarily reflects the large commercial paper issuances in the current year but also resulted from a refined analysis of amounts expected to be refinanced beyond one year.

Required:
As an analyst, comment on the company's classification of short-term borrowings as long-term liabilities. What conditions should exist to permit a company to make this type of classification?

Using Working Capital

E9-7
LO9-1

Super Savers Department Store's balance sheet revealed the following information:

Current assets	$750,000
Noncurrent assets	450,000
Noncurrent liabilities	400,000
Stockholders' equity	380,000

Determine the amount of working capital reported in the balance sheet.

Determining the Impact of Transactions, Including Analysis of Cash Flows

E9-8
LO9-1, 9-3, 9-5

Vernon Company sells a wide range of goods through two retail stores operated in adjoining cities. Most purchases of goods for resale are on invoices. Occasionally, a short-term note payable is used to obtain cash for current use. The following transactions were selected from those occurring during 2015:

a. Purchased merchandise on credit, $18,000 on January 10, 2015; the company uses a periodic inventory system.
b. Borrowed $45,000 cash on March 1, 2015, from City Bank and gave an interest-bearing note payable: face amount, $45,000, due at the end of six months, with an annual interest rate of 10 percent payable at maturity.

Required:
1. Describe the impact of each transaction on the balance sheet equation. Indicate the effects (e.g., cash + or −), using the following schedule:

Date	Assets	Liabilities	Stockholders' Equity

2. What amount of cash is paid on the maturity date of the note?
3. Discuss the impact of each transaction on Vernon's cash flows.

Reporting a Liability

E9-9
LO9-6
McDonald's Corporation

McDonald's is one of the world's most popular fast-food restaurants, offering good food and convenient locations. Effective management of its properties is a key to its success. As the following note in its current annual report indicates, McDonald's both owns and leases property:

> The Company owns and leases real estate primarily in connection with its restaurant business. The Company identifies and develops sites that offer convenience to customers and long-term sales and profit potential to the Company. The Company generally owns the land and building or secures long-term leases for restaurant sites, which ensures long-term occupancy rights and helps control related costs.

Required:
Should McDonald's report lease obligations on its balance sheet? Explain. If the obligation should be reported as a liability, how should the amount be measured?

Evaluating Lease Alternatives

E9-10
LO9-6

As the new vice president for consumer products at Heffner Manufacturing, you are attending a meeting to discuss a serious problem associated with delivering merchandise to customers. Bob Smith, director of logistics, summarized the problem: "It's easy to understand, we just don't have enough delivery trucks given our recent growth." Barb Bader from the accounting department responded: "Maybe it's easy to understand but it's impossible to do anything. Because of Wall Street's concern about the amount of debt on our balance sheet, we're under a freeze and can't borrow money to acquire new assets. There's nothing we can do."

On the way back to your office after the meeting, your assistant offers a suggestion: "Why don't we just lease the trucks we need? That way we can get the assets we want without having to record a liability on the balance sheet."

How would you respond to this suggestion?

E9-11 Computing Deferred Income Tax (Supplement B)

The following information pertains to the Lewis Corporation.

	Year 2014	Year 2015
Income taxes payable	$250,000	$290,000
Increase in deferred tax liability	54,000	58,000

Required:
1. For each year, compute income tax expense (assume that no taxes have been paid).
2. Explain why tax expense is not simply the amount of cash paid during the year.

E9-12 Recording Deferred Income Tax (Supplement B)

The balance sheet for Nair Corporation provided the following summarized pretax data:

	Year 2014	Year 2015
Deferred tax liability	$355,000	$463,000

The income statement reported tax expense for 2015 in the amount of $580,000.

Required:
1. What was the amount of income taxes payable for 2015?
2. Why would management want to incur the cost of maintaining separate tax and financial accounting records?

E9-13 Reporting Deferred Income Taxes (Supplement B)

STARBUCKS

The annual report for Starbucks contains the following information (in millions):

Income Taxes

The provision for income taxes consisted of the following (in millions):

	2008	2007	2006
Current income taxes	$255.1	$423.2	$402.4
Deferred Taxes	(111.1)	(39.5)	(77.6)
Total	$144.0	$383.7	$324.8

Required:
1. Determine whether tax expense is higher or lower than taxes payable for each year.
2. Is the deferred tax liability reported on the 2008 balance sheet $111.1 million? Explain.

E9-14 Computing Four Present Value Problems

LO9-7

On January 1, 2014, Shannon Company completed the following transactions (assume a 10 percent annual interest rate):

a. Bought a delivery truck and agreed to pay $60,000 at the end of three years.
b. Rented an office building and was given the option of paying $10,000 at the end of each of the next three years or paying $28,000 immediately.
c. Established a savings account by depositing a single amount that will increase to $90,000 at the end of seven years.
d. Decided to deposit a single sum in the bank that will provide 10 equal annual year-end payments of $40,000 to a retired employee (payments starting December 31, 2014).

Required (show computations and round to the nearest dollar):
1. In (*a*), what is the cost of the truck that should be recorded at the time of purchase?
2. In (*b*), which option for the office building should the company select?
3. In (*c*), what single amount must be deposited in this account on January 1, 2014?
4. In (*d*), what single sum must be deposited in the bank on January 1, 2014?

Using Present Value Concepts for Decision Making

E9-15
LO9-7

You have just won the state lottery and have two choices for collecting your winnings. You can collect $100,000 today or receive $20,000 per year for the next seven years. A financial analyst has told you that you can earn 10 percent on your investments. Which alternative should you select?

Calculating a Retirement Fund

E9-16
LO9-7

You are a financial adviser working with a client who wants to retire in eight years. The client has a savings account with a local bank that pays 9 percent and she wants to deposit an amount that will provide her with $1,000,000 when she retires. Currently, she has $300,000 in the account. How much additional money should she deposit now to provide her with $1,000,000 when she retires?

Determining an Educational Fund

E9-17
LO9-7

Judge Drago has decided to set up an educational fund for his favorite granddaughter, Emma, who will start college in one year. The judge plans to deposit an amount in a savings account that pays 9 percent interest. He wants to deposit an amount that is sufficient to permit Emma to withdraw $20,000 starting in one year and continuing each year for a total of four years. How much should he deposit today to provide Emma with a fund to pay for her college tuition?

Computing a Present Value

E9-18
LO9-7

An investment will pay $20,000 at the end of the first year, $30,000 at the end of the second year, and $50,000 at the end of the third year. Determine the present value of this investment using a 10 percent interest rate.

Computing a Present Value

E9-19
LO9-7

An investment will pay $15,000 at the end of each year for eight years and a one-time payment of $150,000 at the end of the eighth year. Determine the present value of this investment using a 7 percent interest rate.

Determining Present Value Involving Annuity and a Single Payment

E9-20
LO9-7

The Jenkins Corporation has purchased an executive jet. The company has agreed to pay $200,000 per year for the next 10 years and an additional $1,000,000 at the end of the 10th year. The seller of the jet is charging 6 percent interest. Determine the liability that would be recorded by Jenkins.

Computing Present Value Involving Annuity and a Single Payment

E9-21
LO9-7

You have decided to buy a used car. The dealer has offered you two options:

a. Pay $500 per month for 20 months and an additional $10,000 at the end of 20 months. The dealer is charging 24 percent per annum.
b. When you buy the car, pay cash equal to the present value of the payments in option (a).

Determine how much cash the dealer would charge in option (b).

Computing Growth in a Savings Account: A Single Amount (Supplement C)

E9-22

On January 1, 2014, you deposited $6,000 in a savings account. The account will earn 10 percent annual compound interest, which will be added to the fund balance at the end of each year.

Required (round to the nearest dollar):
1. What will be the balance in the savings account at the end of 10 years?
2. What is the amount of interest earned during the 10 years?
3. How much interest revenue did the fund earn in 2014? 2015?

E9-23   **Computing Deposit Required and Accounting for a Single-Sum Savings Account (Supplement C)**

On January 1, 2014, Alan King decided to deposit $58,800 in a savings account that will provide funds four years later to send his son to college. The savings account will earn 8 percent, which will be added to the fund each year-end.

Required (show computations and round to the nearest dollar):
1. How much will be available in four years?
2. Give the journal entry that Alan should make on January 1, 2014.
3. What is the interest for the four years?
4. Give the journal entry that Alan should make on (*a*) December 31, 2014, and (*b*) December 31, 2015.

E9-24   **Recording Growth in a Savings Account with Equal Periodic Payments (Supplement C)**

On each December 31, you plan to deposit $2,000 in a savings account. The account will earn 9 percent annual interest, which will be added to the fund balance at year-end. The first deposit will be made December 31, 2014 (end of period).

Required (show computations and round to the nearest dollar):
1. Give the required journal entry on December 31, 2014.
2. What will be the balance in the savings account at the end of the 10th year (i.e., after 10 deposits)?
3. What is the interest earned on the 10 deposits?
4. How much interest revenue did the fund earn in 2015? 2016?
5. Give all required journal entries at the end of 2015 and 2016.

E9-25   **Computing Growth for a Savings Fund with Periodic Deposits (Supplement C)**

On January 1, 2014, you plan to take a trip around the world upon graduation four years from now. Your grandmother wants to deposit sufficient funds for this trip in a savings account for you. On the basis of a budget, you estimate that the trip currently would cost $15,000. To be generous, your grandmother decides to deposit $3,500 in the fund at the end of each of the next four years, starting on December 31, 2014. The savings account will earn 6 percent annual interest, which will be added to the savings account at each year-end.

Required (show computations and round to the nearest dollar):
1. How much money will you have for the trip at the end of year 4 (i.e., after four deposits)?
2. What is the interest for the four years?
3. How much interest revenue did the fund earn in 2014, 2015, 2016, and 2017?

For more practice with exercises, go to the text website at www.mhhe.com/libby8e.

PROBLEMS

P9-1
LO9-1

Recording and Reporting Current Liabilities

Vigeland Company completed the following transactions during 2014. The annual accounting period ends December 31, 2014.

Jan. 15	Purchased and paid for merchandise for resale at an invoice cost of $26,500; periodic inventory system.
Apr. 1	Borrowed $700,000 from Summit Bank for general use; executed a 10-month, 6 percent interest-bearing note payable.
June 14	Received a $15,000 customer deposit from Mark Muller for services to be performed in the future.
July 15	Performed $3,750 of the services paid for by Mr. Muller.
Dec. 12	Received electric bill for $27,860. The company will pay it in early January.
31	Determined wages of $15,000 earned but not yet paid on December 31 (disregard payroll taxes).

Required:
1. Prepare journal entries for each of these transactions.
2. Prepare all adjusting entries required on December 31, 2014.

Recording and Reporting Current Liabilities with Discussion of Cash Flow Effects

P9-2
LO9-1, 9-5

Rogers Company completed the following transactions during 2014. The annual accounting period ends December 31, 2014. (AP9-1)

Jan.	8	Purchased merchandise for resale on account at an invoice cost of $14,860; assume a periodic inventory system.
	17	Paid January 8 invoice.
Apr.	1	Borrowed $35,000 from National Bank for general use; executed a 12-month, 8 percent interest-bearing note payable.
June	3	Purchased merchandise for resale on account at an invoice cost of $17,420.
July	5	Paid June 3 invoice.
Aug.	1	Rented a small office in a building owned by the company and collected six months' rent in advance amounting to $6,000. (Record the collection in a way that will not require an adjusting entry at year-end.)
Dec.	20	Received a $100 deposit from a customer as a guarantee to return a large trailer "borrowed" for 30 days.
	31	Determined wages of $9,500 earned but not yet paid on December 31 (disregard payroll taxes).

Required:
1. Prepare journal entries for each of these transactions.
2. Prepare all adjusting entries required on December 31, 2014.
3. Show how all of the liabilities arising from these transactions are reported on the balance sheet at December 31, 2014.
4. For each transaction, state whether cash flow from operating activities is increased or decreased or whether there is no effect.

Determining Financial Effects of Transactions Affecting Current Liabilities with Discussion of Cash Flow Effects (AP9-2)

P9-3
LO9-1, 9-5

Using data from the previous problem, complete the following requirements.

Required:
1. For each transaction (including adjusting entries) listed in the previous problem, indicate the effects (e.g., cash + or −), using the following schedule:

Date	Assets	Liabilities	Stockholders' Equity

2. For each transaction, state whether cash flow from operating activities is increased, decreased, or remains the same.

Recording and Reporting Accrued Liabilities and Deferred Revenue with Discussion

P9-4
LO9-1

During 2015, Walnut Company completed the following two transactions. The annual accounting period ends December 31.

a. Paid and recorded wages of $130,000 during 2015; however, at the end of December 2015, three days' wages are unpaid and unrecorded because the weekly payroll will not be paid until January 6, 2016. Wages for the three days are $4,000.
b. Collected rent revenue on December 10, 2015, of $2,400 for office space that Walnut rented to another party. The rent collected was for 30 days from December 10, 2015, to January 10, 2016, and was credited in full to Rent Revenue.

Required:

1. Give (*a*) the adjusting entry required on December 31, 2015, and (*b*) the January 6, 2016, journal entry for payment of any unpaid wages from December 2015.
2. Give (*a*) the journal entry for the collection of rent on December 10, 2015, and (*b*) the adjusting entry on December 31, 2015.
3. Show how any liabilities related to these transactions should be reported on the company's balance sheet at December 31, 2015.
4. Explain why the accrual method of accounting provides more relevant information to financial analysts than the cash method.

P9-5
LO9-1

Determining Financial Statement Effects of Transactions Involving Accrued Liabilities and Deferred Revenue

Using the data from the previous exercise, complete the following requirements.

Required:

1. Determine the financial statement effects for each of the following: (*a*) the adjusting entry for accrued wages required on December 31, 2015, (*b*) the January 6, 2016, journal entry for payment of any unpaid wages from December 2015, (*c*) the journal entry for the collection of rent on December 10, 2015, and (*d*) the adjusting entry for rent on December 31, 2015. Indicate the effects (e.g., cash + or −) using the following schedule:

Date	Assets	Liabilities	Stockholders' Equity

2. Explain why the accrual method of accounting provides more relevant information to financial analysts than the cash method.

P9-6
LO9-1, 9-4
Dell

Determining Financial Statement Effects of Various Liabilities (AP9-3)

Dell Computers is a leader in the industry with over $56 billion in sales each year. A recent annual report for Dell contained the following note:

Warranty

We record warranty liabilities at the time of sale for the estimated costs that may be incurred under its limited warranty. Factors that affect our warranty liability include the number of installed units currently under warranty, historical and anticipated rates of warranty claims on those units, and cost per claim to satisfy our warranty obligation.

1. Assume that estimated warranty costs for 2014 were $500 million and that the warranty work was performed during 2015. Describe the financial statement effects for each year.

The Walt Disney Company

Walt Disney is a well-recognized brand in the entertainment industry with products ranging from broadcast media to parks and resorts. The following note is from a recent annual report:

Revenue Recognition

For non-expiring, multi-day tickets to our theme parks, we recognize revenue over a three-year period based on estimated usage patterns which are derived from historical usage patterns.

2. Assume that Disney collected $90 million in 2014 multi-day tickets that will be used in future years. For 2015, the company estimates that 60 percent of the tickets will be used. Describe the financial statement effects for each year.

BRUNSWICK

Brunswick Corporation is a multinational company that manufactures and sells marine and recreational products. A recent annual report for Brunswick contained the following information:

Litigation

A jury awarded $44.4 million in damages in a suit brought by Independent Boat Builders, Inc., a buying group of boat manufacturers and its 22 members. Under the antitrust laws, the damage award has been trebled, and the plaintiffs will be entitled to their attorney's fees and interest.

The Company has filed an appeal contending the verdict was erroneous as a matter of law, both as to liability and damages.

3. How should Brunswick account for this litigation?

Halliburton is a major corporation involved in the entire life cycle of oil and gas reserves, starting with exploration and development, moving through production, operations, maintenance, conversion, and refining to infrastructure and abandonment. A recent annual report for the company stated the following:

Halliburton

Environmental Expenditures

Our accrued liabilities from environmental matters were $50 million for the current year and $41 million for the previous year.

4. In your own words, explain Halliburton's accounting policy for environmental expenditures. What is the justification for this policy?

Making a Decision as Chief Financial Officer: Contingent Liabilities

P9-7
LO9-4

For each of the following situations, determine whether the company should (*a*) report a liability on the balance sheet, (*b*) disclose a contingent liability, or (*c*) not report the situation. Justify and explain your conclusions.

1. An automobile company introduces a new car. Past experience demonstrates that lawsuits will be filed as soon as the new model is involved in any accidents. The company can be certain that at least one jury will award damages to people injured in an accident.
2. A research scientist determines that the company's best-selling product may infringe on another company's patent. If the other company discovers the infringement and files suit, your company could lose millions.
3. As part of land development for a new housing project, your company has polluted a natural lake. Under state law, you must clean up the lake once you complete development. The development project will take five to eight years to complete. Current estimates indicate that it will cost $2 to $3 million to clean up the lake.
4. Your company has just been notified that it lost a product liability lawsuit for $1 million that it plans to appeal. Management is confident that the company will win on appeal, but the lawyers believe that it will lose.
5. A key customer is unhappy with the quality of a major construction project. The company believes that the customer is being unreasonable but, to maintain goodwill, has decided to do $250,000 in repairs next year.

Determining Cash Flow Effects (AP9-4)

P9-8
LO9-5

For each of the following transactions, determine whether cash flows from operating activities will increase, decrease, or remain the same:

a. Purchased merchandise on credit.
b. Paid an account payable in cash.
c. Accrued payroll for the month but did not pay it.
d. Borrowed money from the bank. The term of the note is 90 days.
e. Reclassified a long-term note as a current liability.
f. Paid accrued interest expense.
g. Disclosed a contingent liability based on a pending lawsuit.
h. Paid back the bank for money borrowed in (*d*). Ignore interest.
i. Collected cash from a customer for services that will be performed in the next accounting period (i.e., deferred revenues are recorded).

Analyzing the Reclassification of Debt (AP9-5)

P9-9
LO9-3

PepsiCo, Inc., is a $25 billion company in the beverage, snack food, and restaurant businesses. PepsiCo's annual report included the following note:

At year-end, $3.5 billion of short-term borrowings were reclassified as long-term, reflecting PepsiCo's intent and ability to refinance these borrowings on a long-term basis, through either long-term debt issuances or rollover of existing short-term borrowings.

As a result of this reclassification, PepsiCo's working capital position improved. Do you think the reclassification was appropriate? Why do you think management made the reclassification? As a financial analyst, would you use the working capital amount before the reclassification or after the reclassification to evaluate PepsiCo's liquidity?

P9-10

LO9-6

www.mhhe.com/libby8e

Recording and Reporting Deferred Income Tax: Depreciation (Supplement B)

Mansfield Corporation purchased a new warehouse at the beginning of 2014 for $1,000,000. The expected life of the asset is 20 years with no residual value. The company uses straight-line depreciation for financial reporting purposes and accelerated depreciation for tax purposes (assume 10 percent of original cost for this problem). The company's marginal federal income tax rate is 34 percent. The company determined its income tax obligation was as follows: 2014, $400,000; 2015, $625,000.

Required:
1. Compute the deferred income tax amount reported on the balance sheet for each year. Is the deferred income tax a liability or an asset? Explain.
2. Compute income tax expense for each year.

P9-11

LO9-7, 9-8

www.mhhe.com/libby8e

Computing Present Values (AP9-6)

On January 1, 2014, Boston Company completed the following transactions (use a 7 percent annual interest rate for all transactions):

a. Borrowed $115,000 for seven years. Will pay $6,000 interest at the end of each year and repay the $115,000 at the end of the 7th year.
b. Established a plant addition fund of $490,000 to be available at the end of year 8. A single sum that will grow to $490,000 will be deposited on January 1, 2014.
c. Agreed to pay a severance package to a discharged employee. The company will pay $75,000 at the end of the first year, $112,500 at the end of the second year, and $150,000 at the end of the third year.
d. Purchased a $170,000 machine on January 1, 2014, and paid cash, $34,000. A five-year note payable is signed for the balance. The note will be paid in five equal year-end payments starting on December 31, 2014.

Required (show computations and round to the nearest dollar):
1. In transaction (*a*), determine the present value of the debt.
2. In transaction (*b*), what single sum amount must the company deposit on January 1, 2014? What is the total amount of interest revenue that will be earned?
3. In transaction (*c*), determine the present value of this obligation.
4. In transaction (*d*), what is the amount of each of the equal annual payments that will be paid on the note? What is the total amount of interest expense that will be incurred?

P9-12

LO9-7

www.mhhe.com/libby8e

Comparing Options Using Present Value Concepts (AP9-7)

After hearing a knock at your front door, you are surprised to see the Prize Patrol from a large, well-known magazine subscription company. It has arrived with the good news that you are the big winner, having won $12.5 million. You discover that you have three options: (1) you can receive $1.25 million per year for the next 10 years, (2) you can have $10 million today, or (3) you can have $4 million today and receive $1 million for each of the next eight years. Your lawyer tells you that it is reasonable to expect to earn 10 percent on investments. Which option do you prefer? What factors influence your decision?

P9-13

www.mhhe.com/libby8e

Computing Future Values (Supplement C) (AP9-8)

On December 31, 2014, Mercury Company created a fund that will be used to pay the principal amount of a $120,000 debt due on December 31, 2017. The company will make four equal annual deposits on each December 31 in 2014, 2015, 2016, and 2017. The fund will earn 7 percent annual interest, which will be added to the balance at each year-end. The fund trustee will pay the loan principal (to the creditor) upon receipt of the last fund deposit. The company's accounting period ends December 31.

Required (show computations and round to the nearest dollar):
1. How much must be deposited each December 31?
2. What amount of interest will be earned?
3. How much interest revenue will the fund earn in 2014, 2015, 2016, and 2017?

Computing Future Values (Supplement C)   **P9-14**

On January 1, 2014, Spearfish Company completed the following transactions (use an 8 percent annual interest rate for all transactions):

a. Deposited $50,000 in a debt retirement fund. Interest will be computed at six-month intervals and added to the fund at those times (i.e., semiannual compounding). (*Hint:* Think carefully about *n* and *i.*)

b. Established a pension retirement fund to be available by the end of year 6 by making six annual deposits of $130,000 at year-end, starting on December 31, 2014.

c. Deposited $250,000 in a debt retirement fund. Interest will be computed annually and added to the fund at those times.

Required:

1. In transaction (*a*), what will be the balance in the fund at the end of year 3? What is the total amount of interest revenue that will be earned?

2. In transaction (*b*), what is the amount of the retirement fund at the end of year 6? What is the total amount of interest revenue that will be earned?

3. In transaction (*c*), what will be the balance in the fund at the end of year 6? What is the total amount of interest revenue that will be earned?

ALTERNATE **PROBLEMS**

Recording and Reporting Current Liabilities with Discussion of Cash Flow Effects (P9-2)   **AP9-1**
                                                                                              LO9-1, 9-5
Sturgis Company completed the following transactions during 2015. The annual accounting period ends December 31, 2015.

Jan.	15	Recorded tax expense for the year in the amount of $125,000. Current taxes payable were $93,000.
	31	Paid accrued interest expense in the amount of $52,000.
Apr.	30	Borrowed $550,000 from Commerce Bank; executed a 12-month, 12 percent interest-bearing note payable.
June	3	Purchased merchandise for resale at an invoice cost of $75,820, on account.
July	5	Paid June 3 invoice.
Aug.	31	Signed contract to provide security service to a small apartment complex and collected six months' fees in advance amounting to $12,000. (Record the collection in a way that will not require an adjusting entry at year-end.)
Dec.	31	Reclassified a long-term liability in the amount of $100,000 as a current liability.
	31	Determined salary and wages of $85,000 earned but not yet paid December 31 (disregard payroll taxes).

Required:

1. Prepare journal entries for each of these transactions.

2. Prepare all adjusting entries required on December 31, 2015.

3. Show how all of the liabilities arising from these transactions are reported on the balance sheet at December 31, 2015.

4. For each transaction, state whether cash flow from operating activities is increased or decreased or whether there is no effect.

Determining Financial Effects of Transactions Affecting Current Liabilities with Discussion   **AP9-2**
of Cash Flow Effects (P9-3)   LO9-1, 9-5

Using data from problem AP9-1, complete the following requirements.

Required:

1. For each transaction (including adjusting entries) listed in the previous problem, indicate the effects (e.g., cash + or −) using the following schedule:

Date	Assets	Liabilities	Stockholders' Equity

2. For each transaction, state whether cash flow from operating activities is increased or decreased or whether there is no effect.

AP9-3
LO9-1, 9-4

Determining Financial Statement Effects of Various Liabilities (P9-6)

Ford Motor Company is one of the world's largest companies with annual sales of cars and trucks in excess of $170 billion. A recent annual report for Ford contained the following note:

> **Warranties**
>
> Estimated warranty costs are accrued for at the time the vehicle is sold to a dealer. Estimates for warranty cost are made based primarily on historical warranty claim experience.

1. This year, Ford reported claims amounting to $4.0 billion and accrued expenses for warranties in the amount of $3.9 billion. Describe the financial statement effects for this year.

Bally

Bally Total Fitness Holding Corporation is the largest publicly traded commercial operator of fitness centers in North America in terms of members, revenues, and square footage of its facilities. The company operates 409 fitness centers primarily under the Bally Total Fitness name. The following note was contained in a recent annual report for Bally.

> **Revenue Recognition**
>
> As a general principle, revenue is recognized when the following criteria are met: (i) persuasive evidence of an arrangement exists, (ii) delivery has occurred and services have been rendered, (iii) the price to the buyer is fixed or determinable and, (iv) collectability is reasonably assured. Membership revenue is earned on a straight-line basis over the longer of the contractual term or the estimated membership term. The weighted average membership life is 39 months.

2. In your own words, explain how unearned revenue is reported in the balance sheet for Bally. Assume that the company collected $23 million in December 2014 for "New Year's Resolution" memberships starting January 1, 2015. What is the amount of unearned revenue that should be reported on the 2014 and 2015 balance sheets?

ExxonMobil

3. A recent annual report for ExxonMobil reported a significant decline in working capital. Based on this information, do you think that Exxon is experiencing financial difficulty? What other information would you want to consider in making this evaluation?

BRUNSWICK

Brunswick Corporation is a multinational company that manufactures and sells marine and recreational products. A recent annual report for Brunswick contained the following information:

> **Legal and Environmental**
>
> The company is involved in numerous environmental remediation and clean-up projects with an aggregate estimated exposure of approximately $21 million to $42 million. The Company accrues for environmental remediation-related activities for which commitments or clean-up plans have been developed and for which costs can be reasonably estimated.

4. In your own words, explain Brunswick's accounting policy for environmental expenditures. What is the justification for this policy?

AP9-4
LO9-5

Determining Cash Flow Effects (P9-8)

For each of the following transactions, determine whether cash flows from operating activities will increase, decrease, or remain the same:

a. Purchased merchandise for cash.
b. Paid salaries and wages for the last month of the previous accounting period.
c. Paid taxes to the federal government.
d. Borrowed money from the bank. The term of the note is two years.
e. Withheld FICA taxes from employees' paychecks and immediately paid to the government.
f. Recorded accrued interest expense.

g. Paid cash as the result of losing a lawsuit. A contingent liability associated with the liability had been recorded.

h. Paid salaries and wages for the current month in cash.

i. Performed services for a customer who had paid for them in the previous accounting period (i.e., deferred revenue is earned).

Analyzing the Reclassification of Debt (P9-9)

General Mills is a multibillion-dollar company that makes and sells products used in the kitchens of most American homes. The company's annual report included the following note:

> We have a revolving credit agreement expiring in two years that provides for a credit line (which permits us to borrow money when needed). This agreement provides us with the opportunity to refinance short-term borrowings on a long-term basis.

Should General Mills classify the short-term borrowings as current or noncurrent debt based on this ability to borrow money to refinance the debt if needed? If you were a member of the management team, explain what you would want to do and why? If you were a financial analyst, would your answer be different?

AP9-5
LO9-3

GENERAL MILLS

Computing Present Values (P9-11)

On January 1, 2014, Ellsworth Company completed the following transactions (use an 8 percent annual interest rate for all transactions):

a. Borrowed $2,000,000 to be repaid in five years. Agreed to pay $150,000 interest each year for the five years.

b. Established a plant addition fund of $1,000,000 to be available at the end of year 10. A single sum that will grow to $1,000,000 will be deposited on January 1, 2014.

c. Purchased a $750,000 machine on January 1, 2015, and paid cash, $400,000. A four-year note payable is signed for the balance. The note will be paid in four equal year-end payments starting on December 31, 2014.

Required (show computations and round to the nearest dollar):

1. In transaction (*a*), determine the present value of the obligation.
2. In transaction (*b*), what single amount must the company deposit on January 1, 2014? What is the total amount of interest revenue that will be earned?
3. In transaction (*c*), what is the amount of each of the equal annual payments that will be paid on the note? What is the total amount of interest expense that will be incurred?

AP9-6
LO9-7, 9-8

Comparing Options Using Present Value Concepts (P9-12)

After completing a long and successful career as senior vice president for a large bank, you are preparing for retirement. Visiting the human resources office, you find that you have several retirement options: (1) you can receive an immediate cash payment of $750,000, (2) you can receive $60,000 per year for life (you have a life expectancy of 20 years), or (3) you can receive $50,000 per year for 10 years and then $80,000 per year for life (this option is intended to give you some protection against inflation). You have determined that you can earn 6 percent on your investments. Which option do you prefer and why?

AP9-7
LO9-7

Computing Future Values (Supplement C) (P9-13)

On January 1, 2014, Austin Auto Company decided to accumulate a fund to build an addition to its plant. The company will deposit $320,000 in the fund at each year-end, starting on December 31, 2014. The fund will earn 9 percent interest, which will be added to the balance at each year-end. The accounting period ends December 31.

AP9-8

Required:

1. What will be the balance in the fund immediately after the December 31, 2016, deposit?
2. Complete the following fund accumulation schedule:

Date	Cash Payment	Interest Revenue	Fund Increase	Fund Balance
12/31/2014				
12/31/2015				
12/31/2016				
Total				

CASES **AND PROJECTS**

Annual Report Cases

CP9-1
LO9-1, 9-5, 9-6

AMERICAN EAGLE
OUTFITTERS, INC.

Finding Financial Information

Refer to the financial statements of American Eagle given in Appendix B at the end of this book.

Required:
1. What is the amount of accrued compensation and payroll taxes at the end of the most recent reporting year?
2. By what amount did accounts payable change over the most recent reporting year? How did this change in accounts payable affect cash flows from operating activities during the most recent reporting year?
3. What is the amount of long-term liabilities at the end of the most recent reporting year?

CP9-2
LO9-1, 9-5, 9-6

URBAN OUTFITTERS INC.

Finding Financial Information

Refer to the financial statements of Urban Outfitters given in Appendix C at the end of this book.

Required:
1. What is the amount of accrued compensation at the end of the most recent reporting year?
2. By what amount did accounts payable change over the most recent reporting year? How did this change in accounts payable affect cash flows from operating activities during the most recent reporting year?
3. What is the amount of long-term liabilities at the end of the most recent reporting year?

CP9-3
LO9-2

AMERICAN EAGLE
OUTFITTERS, INC.

URBAN OUTFITTERS INC.

Comparing Companies within an Industry

Refer to the financial statements of American Eagle (Appendix B) and Urban Outfitters (Appendix C) and the Industry Ratio Report (Appendix D) at the end of this book.

Required:
1. Compute the payable turnover ratio for each company for the most recent reporting year.
2. Compare the latest year payable turnover ratio for each company to the industry average from the Industry Ratio Report. Are these companies doing better or worse than the average company in their industry at paying trade creditors?

Financial Reporting and Analysis Case

CP9-4
LO9-7

Analyzing Hidden Interest in a Real Estate Deal: Present Value

Many advertisements contain offers that seem too good to be true. A few years ago, an actual newspaper ad offered "a $150,000 house with a zero interest rate mortgage" for sale. If the purchaser made monthly payments of $3,125 for four years ($150,000 ÷ 48 months), no interest would be charged. When the offer was made, mortgage interest rates were 12 percent. Present value for $n = 48$, and $i = 1\%$ is 37.9740.

Required:
1. Did the builder actually provide a mortgage at zero interest?
2. Estimate the true price of the home that was advertised. Assume that the monthly payment was based on an implicit interest rate of 12 percent.

Critical Thinking Case

CP9-5
LO9-7

Evaluating an Ethical Dilemma: Fair Advertising

The New York State Lottery Commission ran the following advertisement in a number of New York newspapers:

The Lotto jackpot for Wednesday, August 25, 2010, will be $3 million including interest earned over a 20-year payment period. Constant payments will be made each year.

Explain the meaning of this advertisement in your own words. Evaluate the "fairness" of this advertisement. Could anyone be misled? Do you agree that the lottery winner has won $3 million? If not, what amount is more accurate? State any assumptions you make.

Financial Reporting and Analysis Team Project

Team Project: Examining an Annual Report

As a team, select an industry to analyze. *Yahoo!Finance* provides lists of industries at <u>biz.yahoo.com/p/industries.html.</u> Click on an industry for a list of companies in that industry. Alternatively, go to Google Finance at <u>www.google.com/finance</u> and search for a company you are interested in. You will be presented with a list including that company and its competitors. Each team member should acquire the annual report or 10-K for one publicly traded company in the industry, with each member selecting a different company (the SEC EDGAR service at <u>www.sec.gov</u> or the company's investor relations website itself are good sources).

Required:
On an individual basis, each team member should write a short report answering the following questions about the selected company. Discuss any patterns across the companies that you as a team observe. Then, as a team, write a short report comparing and contrasting your companies.
1. List the accounts and amounts of the company's liabilities for the last three years.
    a. What is the percentage of each to the respective year's total liabilities?
    b. What do the results of your analysis suggest about the strategy your company has followed with respect to borrowed funds overall and over time?
    c. Does the company disclose any lease liabilities in the footnotes? If so, compute the percentage of lease commitments to total liabilities.
2. What, if any, contingent liabilities are reported by the company for the most recent year and what is your assessment of the risk of each after reading the footnote(s)?
3. Ratio Analysis:
    a. What does the accounts payable turnover ratio measure in general?
    b. Compute the ratio for the last three years.
    c. What do your results suggest about the company?
    d. If available, find the industry ratio for the most recent year, compare it to your results, and discuss why you believe your company differs from or is similar to the industry ratio.
4. What is the effect of the change in accounts payable on cash flows from operating activities for the most recent year (that is, did the change increase or decrease operating cash flows)? Explain your answer.

CP9-6
LO9-1, 9-2, 9-4, 9-5, 9-6

CONTINUING **CASE**

Recording and Reporting Liabilities

CC9-1

≋*POOLCORP*

Pool Corporation, Inc., is the world's largest wholesale distributor of swimming pool supplies and equipment. It is a publicly traded corporation that trades on the NASDAQ exchange under the symbol POOL. It sells these products to swimming pool repair and service businesses, swimming pool builders, and retail swimming pool stores. The majority of these customers are small, family-owned businesses. Pool Corporation completed the following transactions during 2014.The annual accounting period ends December 31, 2014.

Sept. 15 Purchased and paid for merchandise for resale at an invoice cost of $125,000; periodic inventory system.
Oct. 1 Borrowed $900,000 from Southwest Bank for general use; signed an 11-month, 5 percent interest-bearing note payable.
Oct. 5 Received a $40,000 customer deposit from Joe Lipscomb for services to be performed in the future.
Oct. 15 Performed $18,000 of the services paid for by Mr. Lipscomb.
Dec. 12 Received electric bill for $12,000. Pool will pay it in early January.
    31 Determined wages of $52,000 earned but not yet paid on December 31 (disregard payroll taxes).

Required:
1. Prepare journal entries for each of these transactions.
2. Prepare all adjusting entries required on December 31, 2014.

Reporting and Interpreting Bonds

In 1876, Alexander Graham Bell invented the telephone with the simple words "Watson, come here." Today's telecommunications industry carries a volume and variety of information that could not have been imagined by Mr. Bell. The AT&T network, for example, carries nearly 29 petabytes (equal to one quadrillion bytes) of data every day.

The technology and infrastructure necessary to support the telecommunications industry could not have been developed without billions of dollars of investment. One of the strengths of our economic system is the ability of corporations to raise large amounts of money from owners and creditors. In this chapter, we will discuss money raised from creditors by the issuance of bonds and in the next chapter, we will look at the issuance of stock to owners.

AT&T is a familiar name in the telecommunications industry. If you are one of the 103 million subscribers to its network, you may have already texted a message today using AT&T. The company is large by any measure. It offers network coverage in 225 countries, employs over 250,000 people, and reported over $125 billion in revenue last year. In order for AT&T to maintain its position as an industry leader, it must reinvest large amounts of money in its business. Last year alone, the company spent over $1 billion on research and development and $20 billion on capital improvements to its network.

Learning Objectives

After studying this chapter, you should be able to:

10-1   Describe the characteristics of bonds. p. 501

10-2   Report bonds payable and interest expense for bonds sold at par and analyze the times interest earned ratio. p. 505

10-3   Report bonds payable and interest expense for bonds sold at a discount. p. 508

10-4   Report bonds payable and interest expense for bonds sold at a premium. p. 513

10-5   Analyze the debt-to-equity ratio. p. 516

10-6   Report the early retirement of bonds. p. 517

10-7   Explain how financing activities are reported on the statement of cash flows. p. 518

Like most capital-intensive companies, AT&T has employed a mixture of debt and equity capital to fund its business. AT&T has disclosed detailed information concerning its long-term debt in the note shown in Exhibit 10.1. Much of the terminology in this note will be new to you. After studying this chapter, you will understand each of the terms used in the note.

UNDERSTANDING THE BUSINESS

Capital structure is the mixture of debt and equity a company uses to finance its operations. Almost all companies employ some debt in their capital structure. Indeed, large corporations need to borrow billions of dollars, which makes borrowing from individual creditors impractical. Instead, these corporations issue bonds to raise debt capital.

Bonds are securities that corporations and governmental units issue when they borrow large amounts of money. After bonds have been issued, they can be traded on established exchanges such as the New York Bond Exchange. The ability to sell a bond on the bond exchange is a significant advantage for creditors because it provides them with liquidity, or the ability to convert their investments into cash. If you lend money directly to a corporation for 20 years, you must wait that long before your cash investment is repaid. If you lend money by purchasing a bond, you can always sell it to another creditor if you need cash before it matures.

The liquidity of publicly traded bonds offers an important advantage to corporations. Because most creditors are reluctant to lend money for long periods

NOTE 8. DEBT

Long-term debt of AT&T and its subsidiaries, including interest rates and maturities, is summarized as follows at December 31 (in millions):

Notes and debentures			2011	2010
	Interest Rates	**Maturities**		
	0.35%–2.99%	2011–2016	**$ 5,500**	$ 2,250
	3.00%–4.99%	2011–2021	**8,659**	5,880
	5.00%–6.99%	2011–2095	**41,390**	43,506
	7.00%–9.10%	2011–2097	**8,471**	11,986
	Other		**3**	14
Fair value of interest rate swaps recorded in debt			**445**	435
			64,468	64,071
Unamortized premium, net of discount			**46**	185
Total notes and debentures			**64,514**	64,256
Capitalized teases			**239**	259
Total long-term debt, including current maturities			**64,753**	64,515
Current maturities of long-term debt			**(3,453)**	(5,544)
Total long-term debt			**$61,300**	$58,971

with no opportunity to receive cash prior to maturity, they demand a higher interest rate for long-term loans. By issuing more liquid debt, corporations can reduce the cost of long-term borrowing.

This chapter provides a basic understanding of the management, accounting, and financial issues associated with bonds. We begin with a description of bonds payable. Then we see how bond transactions are analyzed and recorded. The chapter closes with a discussion of the early retirement of debt.

ORGANIZATION of the Chapter

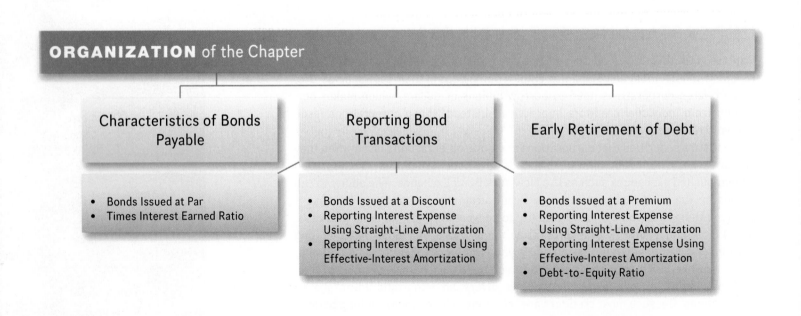

Characteristics of Bonds Payable
- Bonds Issued at Par
- Times Interest Earned Ratio

Reporting Bond Transactions
- Bonds Issued at a Discount
- Reporting Interest Expense Using Straight-Line Amortization
- Reporting Interest Expense Using Effective-Interest Amortization

Early Retirement of Debt
- Bonds Issued at a Premium
- Reporting Interest Expense Using Straight-Line Amortization
- Reporting Interest Expense Using Effective-Interest Amortization
- Debt-to-Equity Ratio

CHARACTERISTICS OF BONDS PAYABLE

Both stock and bonds are issued by corporations to raise money for long-term purposes. Several reasons why a corporation would want to issue bonds instead of stock are:

1. **Stockholders maintain control.** Bondholders do not vote or share in the company's earnings.

2. **Interest expense is tax-deductible.** The tax deductibility of interest expense reduces the net cost of borrowing. In contrast, dividends paid on stock are not tax deductible.

3. **The impact on earnings is positive.** Money can often be borrowed at a low interest rate and invested at a higher rate. Assume that Home Games, Inc., owns an electronic game rental store. The company has stockholders' equity of $100,000 invested in the store and earns net income of $20,000 per year. Management plans to open a new store that will also cost $100,000 and earn $20,000 per year. Should management issue new stock or borrow the money at an interest rate of 8 percent? The following analysis shows that the use of debt will increase the return to the owners:

LEARNING OBJECTIVE 10-1
Describe the characteristics of bonds.

	Option 1 Stock	Option 2 Debt
Income before interest and taxes	$ 40,000	$ 40,000
Interest (8% × $100,000)		8,000
Income before taxes	40,000	32,000
Income taxes (35%)	14,000	11,200
Net income	$ 26,000	$ 20,800
Stockholders' equity	$200,000	$100,000
Return on equity	13%	20.8%

Unfortunately, bonds carry higher risk than equity. The following are the major disadvantages associated with issuing bonds:

1. **Risk of bankruptcy.** Interest payments to bondholders are fixed charges that must be paid each period whether the corporation earns income or incurs a loss.

2. **Negative impact on cash flows.** Debt must be repaid at a specified time in the future. Management must be able to generate sufficient cash to repay the debt or have the ability to refinance it.

A bond usually requires the payment of interest over its life with repayment of principal on the maturity date. The **bond principal** is the amount (1) that is payable at the maturity date and (2) on which the periodic cash interest payments are computed. The principal is also called the **par value, face amount,** and maturity value. All bonds have a par value, which is the amount that will be paid when the bond matures. For most individual bonds, the par value is $1,000, but it can be any amount.

A bond always specifies a **stated rate** of interest and the timing of periodic cash interest payments, usually annually or semiannually. Each periodic interest payment is computed as principal times the stated interest rate. The selling price of a bond does not affect the periodic cash payment of interest. For example, a $1,000, 8 percent bond always pays cash interest of (1) $80 on an annual basis or (2) $40 on a semiannual basis.

Different types of bonds have different characteristics for good economic reasons. Individual creditors have different risk and return preferences. A retired person may be willing to receive a lower interest rate in return for greater security. This type of creditor might want a mortgage bond that pledges a specific asset as security in case the company cannot repay the bond. Another type of creditor might be willing to accept a low interest rate and an unsecured status in return for the opportunity to convert the bond into common stock at some point in the future. Companies try to design bond features that are attractive to different groups of creditors

The BOND PRINCIPAL is the amount (a) payable at the maturity of the bond and (b) on which the periodic cash interest payments are computed.

PAR VALUE is another name for bond principal, or the maturity amount of a bond.

FACE AMOUNT is another name for bond principal, or the maturity amount of the bond.

The STATED RATE is the rate of cash interest per period stated in the bond contract.

just as automobile manufacturers try to design cars that appeal to different groups of consumers. Some key types of bonds are shown in the illustration below.

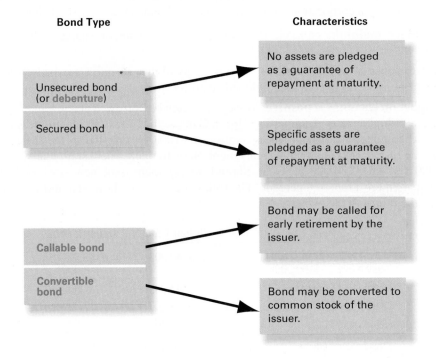

A DEBENTURE is an unsecured bond; no assets are specifically pledged to guarantee repayment.

A CALLABLE BOND may be called for early retirement at the option of the issuer.

A CONVERTIBLE BOND may be converted to other securities of the issuer (usually common stock).

An INDENTURE is a bond contract that specifies the legal provisions of a bond issue.

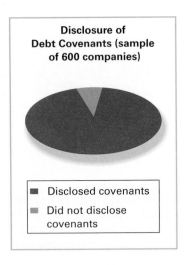

Disclosure of Debt Covenants (sample of 600 companies)

■ Disclosed covenants
■ Did not disclose covenants

When AT&T decides to issue new bonds, it prepares a bond **indenture** (bond contract) that specifies the legal provisions of the bonds. These provisions include the maturity date, the rate of interest to be paid, the date of each interest payment, and any conversion privileges. The indenture also contains covenants designed to protect the creditors. Typical indentures include limitations on new debt that the company might issue in the future, limitations on the payment of dividends, or requirements for minimums of certain accounting ratios, such as the current ratio. Because covenants may limit the company's future actions, management prefers those that are least restrictive. Creditors, however, prefer more restrictive covenants, which lessen the risk of the investment. As with any business transaction, the final result is achieved through negotiation.

Bond covenants are typically reported in the notes to the financial statements. *Accounting Trends & Techniques* (published by the AICPA) has reviewed the reporting practices of 600 companies.[1] The graph in the margin shows the percentage of companies that disclosed debt covenants. AT&T reported the following information about its debt covenants.

AT&T

REAL WORLD EXCERPT
Annual Report

Credit Agreement

The Agreement requires us to maintain a debt-to-EBITDA (earnings before interest, income taxes, depreciation and amortization) ratio of not more than 3-to-1, as of the last day of each fiscal quarter.

Defaults under the Agreement would permit the lenders to accelerate required repayment and would increase the interest by 2.00% per annum.

---

[1]Reprinted with permission from *Accounting Trends & Techniques.* Copyright © 2008 by the American Institute of Certified Public Accountants, Inc.

The bond issuer also prepares a prospectus, which is a legal document that is given to potential bond investors. The prospectus describes the company, the bonds, and how the proceeds of the bonds will be used. AT&T used the money it borrowed to increase working capital, make capital expenditures, and repurchase common stock.

When a bond is issued to an investor, the person receives a **bond certificate.** All bond certificates for a single bond issue are identical. The face of each certificate shows the same maturity date, interest rate, interest dates, and other provisions. An independent party, called the **trustee,** is usually appointed to represent the bondholders. A trustee's duties are to ascertain whether the issuing company has fulfilled all provisions of the bond indenture.

Because of the complexities associated with bonds, several agencies exist to evaluate the probability that a bond issuer will not be able to meet the requirements specified in the indenture. This risk is called *default risk.* Moody's and Standard & Poor's use letter ratings to specify the quality of a bond. Bonds with ratings above Baa/BBB are investment grade; bonds with ratings below that level are speculative and are often called *junk bonds.* Many banks, mutual funds, and trusts are permitted to invest only in investment-grade bonds. In addition to evaluating the risk of a specific bond, analysts also assess the overall risk of the issuer.

A BOND CERTIFICATE is the bond document that each bondholder receives.

A TRUSTEE is an independent party appointed to represent the bondholders.

Bond Information from the Business Press

Bond prices are reported each day in the business press based on transactions that have occurred on the bond exchange. The following is typical of the information you will find:

Bond	Yield	Volume	Close	Change
Safeway 6.0 13	6.8	58	97.2	−1/4
Sears 6.5 17	6.77	25	98.1	−3/8
AT&T 6.3 38	4.2	169	132.68	−1/4

This listing states that the AT&T bond has a coupon interest rate of 6.3 percent and will mature in the year 2038. The bond currently provides an effective interest yield of 4.2 percent and has a selling price of 132.68 percent of par, or $1,326.80. On this date, 169 bonds were sold, and the price fell 1/4 point from the closing price on the previous trading day (a point is 1 percent).

It is important to remember that these changes do not affect the company's financial statements. For financial reporting purposes, the company uses the interest rates that existed when the bonds were first sold to the public.

REPORTING BOND TRANSACTIONS

When AT&T issued its bonds, it specified two types of cash payment in the bond contract:

1. **Principal.** This amount is usually a single payment that is made when the bond matures. It is also called the **par value** or **face value.**

2. **Cash interest payments.** These payments, which represent an annuity, are computed by multiplying the principal amount times the interest rate stated in the bond contract. This interest is called the **contract, stated,** or **coupon rate** of interest. The bond contract specifies whether the interest payments are made quarterly, semiannually, or annually. When you are asked to work problems in which interest payments are made more frequently than once a year, you must adjust both the periodic interest rate and the number of periods. For example, a $1,000 (face value) bond with an annual interest rate of 6 percent and a life of 10 years would pay interest of $30 ($1,000 × 6% × 1/2) for 20 periods (every six months for 10 years, or 10 × 2).

The COUPON RATE is the stated rate of interest on bonds.

The issuing company does not determine the price at which the bonds sell. Instead, the market determines the price using the present value concepts introduced in the last chapter. To determine the present value of the bond, you compute the present value of the principal (a single payment) and the present value of the interest payments (an annuity) and add the two amounts.

Creditors demand a certain rate of interest to compensate them for the risks related to bonds, called the **market interest rate** (also known as the **yield** or **effective-interest rate**). Because the market rate is the interest rate on debt when it is incurred, it is the rate that should be used in computing the present value of a bond.

The present value of a bond may be the same as par, above par (**bond premium**), or below par (**bond discount**). If the stated and the market interest rates are the same, a bond sells at par; if the market rate is higher than the stated rate, a bond sells at a discount; and if the market rate is lower than the stated rate, the bond sells at a premium. This relationship can be shown graphically as follows:

The MARKET INTEREST RATE (or YIELD or EFFECTIVE-INTEREST RATE) is the current rate of interest on a debt when incurred.

BOND PREMIUM is the difference between the selling price and par when the bond is sold for more than par.

BOND DISCOUNT is the difference between the selling price and par when the bond is sold for less than par.

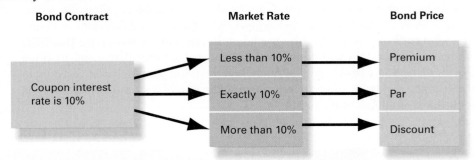

In commonsense terms, when a bond pays an interest rate that is less than the rate creditors demand, they will not buy it unless its price is reduced (i.e., a discount must be provided). When a bond pays more than creditors demand, they will be willing to pay a premium to buy it.

When a bond is issued at par, the issuer receives cash equal to its par value. When a bond is issued at a discount, the issuer receives less cash than the par value. When a bond is issued at a premium, the issuer receives more cash than the par value. Corporations and creditors do not care whether a bond is issued at par, at a discount, or at a premium because bonds are always priced to provide the market rate of interest. To illustrate, consider a corporation that issues three separate bonds on the same day. The bonds are the same except that one has a stated interest rate of 8 percent, another a rate of 10 percent, and a third a rate of 12 percent. If the market rate of interest were 10 percent, the first would be issued at a discount, the second at par, and the third at a premium. As a result, a creditor who bought any one of the bonds would earn the market interest rate of 10 percent.

During the life of the bond, its market price will change as market interest rates change. While this information is reported in the financial press, it does not affect the company's financial statements and the way its interest payments are accounted for from one period to the next.

In the next section of this chapter, we will see how to account for bonds issued at par, at a discount, and at a premium.

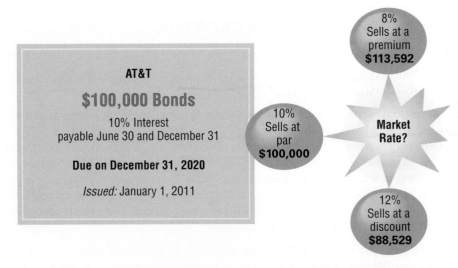

SELF-STUDY **QUIZ**

Your study of bonds will be easier if you understand the new terminology that has been introduced in this chapter. Let's review some of those terms. Define the following:

1. Market interest rate.
2. Coupon interest rate.
3. Synonyms for *coupon interest rate*.
4. Bond discount.
5. Bond premium.
6. Synonyms for *market interest rate*.

After you have completed your answers, check them with the solutions at the bottom of the page.

Bonds Issued at Par

Bonds sell at their par value when buyers are willing to invest in them at the interest rate stated in the bond contract. To illustrate, let's assume that on January 1, 2014, AT&T issued 10 percent bonds with a par value of $100,000 and received $100,000 in cash (which means that the bonds sold at par). The bonds were dated to start earning interest on January 1, 2014, and will pay interest each June 30 and December 31. The bonds mature in two years on December 31, 2015.

The amount of money a corporation receives when it sells bonds is the present value of the future cash flows associated with them. When AT&T issued its bonds, it agreed to make two types of payments in the future: a single payment of $100,000 when the bond matures in two years, and an annuity of $5,000 payable twice a year for two years. The bond payments can be shown graphically as follows:

> **LEARNING OBJECTIVE 10-2**
> Report bonds payable and interest expense for bonds sold at par and analyze the times interest earned ratio.

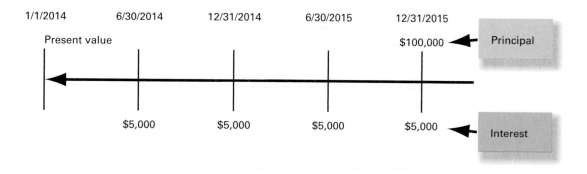

Solutions to
SELF-STUDY QUIZ

1. The market interest rate is the interest rate demanded by creditors. It is the rate used in the present value computations to discount future cash flows.
2. Coupon interest rate is the stated rate on the bonds.
3. Coupon interest rate is also called stated rate and contract rate.
4. A bond that sells for less than par is sold at a discount. This occurs when the coupon rate is lower than the market rate.
5. A bond that sells for more than par is sold at a premium. This occurs when the coupon rate is higher than the market rate.
6. Market interest rate is also called yield or effective-interest rate.

To compute the present value using Excel, enter:

$f_x = \text{PV}(0.05, 4, -5000, -100000)$

The present value of the bond payments can be computed with the tables contained in Appendix A using the factor for four periods and an interest rate of 5 percent per period:

	Present Value
a. Single payment: $100,000 × 0.8227	$ 82,270
b. Annuity: $5,000 × 3.5460	17,730
Issue (sale) price of bonds	$100,000

When the effective rate of interest equals the stated rate of interest, the present value of the future cash flows associated with a bond always equals the bond's par value amount. Remember a bond's selling price is determined by the present value of its future cash flows, not the par value. On the date of issue, bond liabilities are recorded at the present value of future cash flows on the date of issue, not the par value, as follows:

| Cash (+A) . . . . | 100,000 | |
| Bonds payable (+L) . . . . | | 100,000 |

Assets	=	Liabilities	+	Stockholders' Equity
Cash +100,000		Bonds payable +100,000		

Bonds may pay interest each month, each quarter, each half-year, or each year. In all cases, the present value of the bond is determined using the interest rate factor for the number of interest periods and the interest rate for each period.

PAUSE FOR **FEEDBACK**

SELF-STUDY **QUIZ**

Assume that AT&T issues $500,000 bonds that will mature in five years. The bonds pay interest at the end of each year at an annual rate of 8 percent. They are sold when the market rate is 8 percent. Compute the selling price of the bonds.

After you have completed your answer, check it with the solution at the bottom of the page.

Reporting Interest Expense on Bonds Issued at Par

Continuing with our example, the creditors who bought the AT&T bonds did so with the expectation that they would earn interest over the life of the bond. AT&T will pay interest at 10 percent per year on the par value of the bonds each June 30 and December 31 until the bond's maturity date. The amount of interest each period will be $5,000 (10% × $100,000 × 1/2). The entry to record each interest payment is as follows:

| Interest expense (+E, −SE) . . . . | 5,000 | |
| Cash (−A) . . . . | | 5,000 |

Assets	=	Liabilities	+	Stockholders' Equity
Cash −5,000				Interest expense (+E) −5,000

Solution to
SELF-STUDY QUIZ

1. $500,000 × 0.6806 = $340,300
($500,000 × 8%) × 3.9927 = 159,708
$500,000 (rounded)

Interest expense is reported on the income statement. Because interest is related to financing activities rather than operating activities, it is normally not included in operating expenses on the income statement. Instead, interest expense is reported as a deduction from "operating income." A portion of the income statement for AT&T shows how interest expense is usually reported.

AT&T INC. Consolidated Statements of Income (dollars in millions, except per share amounts)	2011	2010	2009
Other Income (Expense)			
Interest expense	(3,535)	(2,994)	(3,368)
Equity in net income of affiliates	784	762	734
Other income (expense) net	249	897	152
Total other income (expense)	(2,502)	(1,335)	(2,482)
Income from Continuing Operations Before			
Income Taxes	6,716	18,238	18,518
Income tax (benefit) expense	2,532	(1,162)	6,091
Income from Continuing Operations	4,184	19,400	12,427
Income from Discontinued Operations, net of tax	—	779	20
Net Income	4,184	20,179	12,447

AT&T

REAL WORLD EXCERPT
Annual Report

Bond interest payment dates rarely coincide with the last day of a company's fiscal year. Under the matching concept, interest expense that has been incurred but not paid must be accrued with an adjusting entry. If AT&T's fiscal year ended on May 31, the company would accrue interest for five months and record interest expense and interest payable.

Because interest payments are a legal obligation for the borrower, financial analysts want to be certain that a business is generating sufficient resources to meet its obligations. The times interest earned ratio is useful when making this assessment.

Times Interest Earned

KEY RATIO ANALYSIS

? ANALYTICAL QUESTION

Is the company generating sufficient resources from its profit-making activities to meet its current interest obligations?

% RATIO AND COMPARISONS

The times interest earned ratio is computed as follows:

$$\text{Times Interest Earned} = \frac{\text{Net Income} + \text{Interest Expense} + \text{Income Tax Expense}}{\text{Interest Expense}}$$

(continued)

The 2011 ratio for AT&T:

$$(\$3,944 + \$3,535 + \$2,532) \div \$3,535 = 2.8$$

COMPARISONS OVER TIME AT&T			COMPARISONS WITH COMPETITORS	
			Verizon	Sprint
2009	**2010**	**2011**	**2011**	**2011**
6.4	7.2	2.8	2.0	N/A

💡 INTERPRETATIONS

In General   A high times interest earned ratio is viewed more favorably than a low one. The ratio shows the amount of resources generated for each dollar of interest expense. A high ratio indicates an extra margin of protection in case profitability deteriorates. Analysts are particularly interested in a company's ability to meet its required interest payments because failure to do so could result in bankruptcy.

Focus Company Analysis   In 2011, profit-making activities for AT&T generated $2.80 for each dollar of interest, a reasonable safety margin. The ratio is significantly lower than previous years because AT&T's net income declined by approximately 80 percent during 2011. Nevertheless, AT&T is able to generate significant cash flows from its operating activities. Also, the ratio is in line with other companies in the industry. Required interest payments do not appear to be at risk. Notice that we are not able to compute a ratio for Sprint. The company reported a loss in 2011, which results in a meaningless ratio.

A Few Cautions   The times interest earned ratio is often misleading for new or rapidly growing companies, which tend to invest considerable resources to build their capacity for future operations. In such cases, the times interest earned ratio will reflect significant amounts of interest expense associated with the new capacity but not the income that will be earned with the new capacity. Analysts should consider the company's long-term strategy when using this ratio. Some analysts prefer to compare interest expense to the amount of cash a company can generate. Because creditors cannot be paid with "income" that is generated, they must be paid with cash.

Bonds Issued at a Discount

LEARNING OBJECTIVE 10-3
Report bonds payable and interest expense for bonds sold at a discount.

Bonds sell at a discount when the market rate of interest is higher than the stated interest rate on them. Let's assume that the market rate of interest was 12 percent when AT&T sold its bonds (which have a par value of $100,000). The bonds mature in two years and have a stated rate of 10 percent, payable twice a year on June 30 and December 31. Because the stated rate of interest was less than the market rate on the date of issue, the bonds sold at a discount.

To compute the cash issue price of the bonds, we can use the tables in Appendix A. As in the previous example, the number of periods is four and we use an interest rate of 6 percent per period, which is the market rate of interest. The cash issue price of the AT&T bonds is computed as follows:

To compute the present value using Excel, enter:
$f_x = \text{PV}(0.06, 4, -5000, -100000)$

	Present Value
a. Single payment: $100,000 × 0.7921	$79,210
b. Annuity: $5,000 × 3.4651	17,326
Issue (sale) price of bonds	$96,536*

The amount of the discount: $100,000 − $96,536 = $3,464.

The cash price of the bonds issued by AT&T is $96,536. Some people refer to this price as 96.5, which means that the bonds were sold at 96.5 percent of their par value ($96,536 ÷ $100,000).

When a bond is sold at a discount, the Bonds Payable account is credited for the par amount, and the discount is recorded as a debit to Discount on Bonds Payable. The issuance of the AT&T bonds at a discount is recorded as follows:

Cash (+A)	96,536	
Discount on bonds payable (+XL, −L)	3,464	
Bonds payable (+L)		100,000

Assets		=	Liabilities		+	Stockholders' Equity
Cash	+96,536		Bonds payable	+100,000		
			Discount on bonds	−3,464		

Note that the discount is recorded in a separate contra-liability account (Discount on Bonds Payable) as a debit. The balance sheet reports the bonds payable at their book value, which is their maturity amount less any unamortized discount. AT&T reports its discount as a net amount with its bond premium (explained in the next section). This approach is appropriate when the amount is small relative to other balance sheet amounts.

While AT&T received only $96,536 when it sold the bonds, it must repay $100,000 when the bonds mature. The extra cash that must be paid is an adjustment of interest expense to ensure that creditors earn the market rate of interest. To adjust interest expense, the borrower apportions or amortizes the bond discount to each interest period as an increase in interest expense. Therefore, the amortization of bond discount results in an increase in interest expense. Two amortization methods are often used by companies: (1) straight line and (2) effective interest. Many companies use straight-line amortization because it is easy to compute the required numbers. However, the effective-interest method is the method required by GAAP. You may wonder why companies are permitted to use a method that is not the one required by accounting rules. The answer is materiality. Companies are permitted to use the straight-line method because the results are normally not materially different from those computed using the effective-interest method. We will first discuss the straight-line method and then the effective-interest method.

Part A: Reporting Interest Expense on Bonds Issued at a Discount Using Straight-Line Amortization

To amortize the $3,464 bond discount over the life of AT&T bonds using **straight-line amortization,** we allocate an equal dollar amount to each interest period. AT&T bonds have four interest periods. The amortization of discount each period is: $3,464 ÷ 4 periods = $866. We add this amount to the cash payment of interest ($5,000) to compute interest expense for the period ($5,866). The interest payments on AT&T bonds each period are as follows:

STRAIGHT-LINE AMORTIZATION is a simplified method of amortizing a bond discount or premium that allocates an equal dollar amount to each interest period.

Interest expense (+E, −SE)	5,866	
Discount on bonds payable (−XL, +L)		866
Cash (−A)		5,000

Assets		=	Liabilities		+	Stockholders' Equity	
Cash	−5,000		Discount on bonds	+866		Interest expense (+E)	−5,866

Bonds payable are reported on the balance sheet at their book value. At the end of the first interest period (June 30, 2014), the book value of AT&T bonds is more than the original issue price. The book value increases to $97,402 ($96,536 + $866) because of the amortization of the discount. In each interest period, the book value of the bonds increases by $866 because the unamortized discount decreases by $866. At the maturity date of the bonds, the unamortized discount (i.e., the balance in the Discount on Bonds Payable account) is zero. At that time, the maturity amount of the bonds and the book value are the same (i.e., $100,000). This process can be seen in the following amortization schedule:

	AMORTIZATION SCHEDULE: BOND DISCOUNT (STRAIGHT-LINE)			
Date	(a) Interest to Be Paid (10% × $100,000 × 1/2)	(b) Interest Expense (a + c)	(c) Amortization ($3,464 ÷ 4 periods)	(d) Book Value Beginning Book Value + (c)
1/1/2014				$96,536
6/30/2014	$5,000	$5,866	$866	97,402
12/31/2014	5,000	5,866	866	98,268
6/30/2015	5,000	5,866	866	99,134
12/31/2015	5,000	5,866	866	100,000

PAUSE FOR **FEEDBACK**

SELF-STUDY **QUIZ**

Assume that AT&T issued $100,000 bonds that will mature in 10 years. The bonds pay interest at the end of each year at an annual rate of 5 percent. They were sold when the market rate was 6 percent at a price of $92,641. What amount of interest was paid at the end of the first year? What amount of interest expense would be reported at the end of the first year using straight-line amortization?

After you have completed your answers, check them with the solutions at the bottom of the page.

Part B: Reporting Interest Expense on Bonds Issued at a Discount Using Effective-Interest Amortization

EFFECTIVE–INTEREST AMORTIZATION is a method of amortizing a bond discount or premium on the basis of the effective-interest rate; it is the theoretically preferred method.

Under the **effective-interest amortization** method, interest expense for a bond is computed by multiplying the current unpaid balance times the market rate of interest that existed on the date the bonds were sold. The periodic amortization of a bond premium or discount is then calculated as the difference between interest expense and the amount of cash paid or accrued. This process can be summarized as follows:

Step 1: Compute interest expense

Unpaid Balance × Effective-Interest Rate × n/12

n = Number of Months in Each Interest Period

Step 2: Compute amortization amount

Interest Expense − Cash Interest

The first interest payment on AT&T bonds is made on June 30, 2014. Interest expense at the end of the first interest period (June 30, 2014) is calculated by multiplying the

1. $5,000 (5% × $100,000)
2. $5,736 [$5,000 + ($7,359 ÷ 10)]

unpaid balance of the debt by the market rate of interest ($96,536 × 12% × 1/2 = $5,792). The amount of cash paid is calculated by multiplying the principal by the stated rate of interest ($100,000 × 10% × 1/2 = $5,000). The difference between the interest expense and the cash paid (or accrued) is the amount of discount that has been amortized ($5,792 − $5,000 = $792).

Interest expense (+E, −SE)	5,792	
Discount on bonds payable (−XL, +L)		792
Cash (−A)		5,000

> *Effective-interest amortization causes these amounts to change each period.*

Assets	=	Liabilities	+	Stockholders' Equity	
Cash −5,000		Discount on bonds +792		Interest expense (+E) −5,792	

Each period, the amortization of the bond discount increases the bond's book value (or unpaid balance). The amortization of bond discount can be thought of as interest earned by the bondholders but not paid to them. During the first interest period, the bondholders earned interest of $5,792 but received only $5,000 in cash. The additional $792 was added to the book value of the bond and will be paid to bondholders when the bond matures.

Interest expense for the next interest period must reflect the change in the unpaid balance of bonds payable that occurred with amortization of the bond discount. The interest expense for the second half of 2014 is calculated by multiplying the unpaid balance ($96,536 + $792 = $97,328) on June 30, 2014, by the market rate of interest ($97,328 × 12% × 1/2 = $5,840). Thus amortization of the bond discount on December 31, 2014, is $840.

Interest expense (+E, −SE)	5,840	
Discount on bonds payable (−XL, +L)		840
Cash (−A)		5,000

Assets	=	Liabilities	+	Stockholders' Equity	
Cash −5,000		Discount on bonds +840		Interest expense (+E) −5,840	

Notice that interest expense for December 31, 2014, is more than interest expense for June 30, 2014. AT&T effectively borrowed more money during the second half of the year because of the unpaid interest. Because of the amortization of the bond discount, interest expense increases each year during the life of the bond. This process can be illustrated with the amortization schedule shown below:

	AMORTIZATION SCHEDULE: BOND DISCOUNT (EFFECTIVE-INTEREST)			
Date	(a) Interest to Be Paid (10% × $100,000 × 1/2)	(b) Interest Expense (12% × Beginning of Period Book Value × 1/2)	(c) Amortization (b) − (a)	(d) Book Value Beginning Book Value + (c)
1/1/2014				$ 96,536
6/30/2014	$5,000	$5,792	$792	97,328
12/31/2014	5,000	5,840	840	98,168
6/30/2015	5,000	5,890	890	99,058
12/31/2015	5,000	5,943	943	100,001*

This amount should be exactly $100,000. The $1 error is due to rounding.

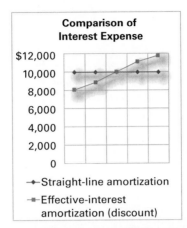

Comparison of Interest Expense

→ Straight-line amortization

→ Effective-interest amortization (discount)

Interest expense (column b) is computed by multiplying the market rate of interest by the book value of the bonds at the beginning of the period (column d). Amortization is computed by subtracting cash interest (column a) from interest expense (column b). The book value of the bonds (column d) is computed by adding amortization (column c) to the book value at the beginning of the period. In summary, under the effective-interest amortization method, interest expense changes each accounting period as the effective amount of the liability changes. Under the straight-line amortization method, interest expense remains constant over the life of the bond. The chart in the margin illustrates these differences.

PAUSE FOR **FEEDBACK**

SELF-STUDY **QUIZ**

Assume that AT&T issued $100,000 bonds that will mature in 10 years. The bonds pay interest at the end of each year at an annual rate of 5 percent. They were sold when the market rate was 6 percent at a price of $92,641. What amount of interest was paid at the end of the first year? What amount of interest expense would be reported at the end of the first year using effective-interest amortization?

After you have completed your answers, check them with the solutions at the bottom of the page.

| FINANCIAL ANALYSIS | Zero Coupon Bonds |

So far, we have discussed common bonds, which are issued by many corporations. For a number of reasons, corporations also may issue bonds with unusual features. The concepts you have learned will help you understand these bonds. For example, a corporation might issue a bond that does not pay periodic cash interest. These bonds are often called *zero coupon bonds*. Why would an investor buy a bond that did not pay interest? Our discussion of bond discounts has probably given you a good idea of the answer. The coupon interest rate on a bond can be virtually any amount and the price of the bond will be adjusted so that investors earn the market rate of interest. A bond with a zero coupon interest rate is simply a deeply discounted bond that will sell for substantially less than its maturity value.

Let's use the $100,000 AT&T bond to illustrate a zero coupon rate. Assume that the market rate is 10 percent and the bond pays no cash interest. The bond matures in five years. The selling price of the bond is the present value of the maturity amount because no other cash payments will be made over the life of the bond. We can compute the present value with the tables contained in Appendix A, using the factor for five periods and an interest rate of 10 percent:

To compute the present value using Excel, enter:
= 100000/(1.10)^5

	Present Value
Single payment: $100,000 × 0.6209	$62,090

Accounting for a zero coupon bond is no different from accounting for other bonds sold at a discount. However, the amount of the discount is much larger. For example, the

Solutions to
SELF-STUDY QUIZ

1. $5,000 (5% × $100,000)
2. $5,558 (6% × $92,641)

annual report for AT&T contained the following information concerning the company's zero coupon bonds:

AT&T INC. AND SUBSIDIARY DEBT DETAIL—MARCH 31, 2012
This chart shows the principal amount of AT&T Inc.'s and its subsidiaries' outstanding long-term debt issues as of the date above.

Entry (Original Issuer)	Amount Outstanding at Maturity	Coupon	Maturity Date	Total
BellSouth Telecommunications, Inc.	$ 115,968,616	6.300%	12/15/15	$ 115,968,616
Ameritech Capital Funding Corporation	$ 52,502,760	9.100%	6/1/16	$ 52,502,760
Various	$ 3,143,969	Various	Various	$ 3,143,969
BellSouth Corporation	$1,000,000,000	4.463%	4/26/21	$1,000,000,000
AT&T Inc.	$1,030,000,000	Zero	11/27/22	$ 616,127,631

While zero coupon bonds do not pay cash interest, they have been priced to provide the investor with a market rate of interest. Notice that the carrying value of the obligation ($616,127,631) is much lower than the maturity value ($1,000,000,000) because the payment has been discounted at the market rate of interest that existed on the issue date.

Bonds Issued at a Premium

Bonds sell at a premium when the market rate of interest is lower than their stated interest rate. Let's assume that the market rate of interest is 8 percent while the AT&T bonds pay cash interest of 10 percent. The bonds pay interest semiannually and mature in two years. They are issued on January 1, 2014.

The present value of AT&T 10 percent bonds can be computed from the tables contained in Appendix A using the factor for four periods and an interest rate of 4 percent per period:

LEARNING OBJECTIVE 10-4
Report bonds payable and interest expense for bonds sold at a premium.

To compute the present value using Excel, enter:
$f_x = PV(0.04, 4, -5000, -100000)$

	Present Value
a. Single payment: $100,000 × 0.8548	$ 85,480
b. Annuity: $5,000 × 3.6299	18,150
Issue (sale) price of bonds	$103,630*

The amount of the premium: $103,630 − $100,000 = $3,630.

When a bond is sold at a premium, the Bonds Payable account is credited for the par amount, and the premium is recorded as a credit to Premium on Bonds Payable. The January 1, 2014, issuance of AT&T bonds at a premium would be recorded as follows:

Cash (+A)	103,630	
Premium on bonds payable (+L)		3,630
Bonds payable (+L)		100,000

Assets		=	Liabilities		+	Stockholders' Equity
Cash	+103,630		Premium on bonds	+3,630		
			Bonds payable	+100,000		

The book value of the bond is the sum of the two accounts, Premium on Bonds Payable and Bonds Payable, or $103,630.

Part A: Reporting Interest Expense on Bonds Issued at a Premium Using Straight-Line Amortization

As with a discount, the recorded premium of $3,630 must be apportioned to each interest period. Using the straight-line method, the amortization of premium each annual interest period is $908 ($3,630 ÷ 4 periods). This amount is subtracted from the cash interest payment ($5,000) to calculate interest expense ($4,092). Thus, amortization of a bond premium decreases interest expense.

The payment of interest on the bonds is recorded as follows:

Interest expense (+E, −SE)	4,092	
Premium on bonds payable (−L).	908	
Cash (−A)		5,000

Assets		=	Liabilities		+	Stockholders' Equity	
Cash	−5,000		Premium on bonds	−908		Interest expense (+E)	−4,092

Notice that the $5,000 cash paid each period includes $4,092 interest expense and $908 premium amortization. Thus, the cash payment to investors includes the current interest they have earned plus a return of part of the premium they paid when they bought the bonds.

The book value of the bonds is the amount in the Bonds Payable account plus any unamortized premium. On June 30, 2014, the book value of the bonds is $102,722 ($100,000 + $3,630 − $908). A complete amortization schedule follows:

	AMORTIZATION SCHEDULE: BOND PREMIUM (STRAIGHT-LINE)			
Date	(a) Interest to Be Paid (10% × $100,000 × 1/2)	(b) Interest Expense (a − c)	(c) Amortization ($3,630 ÷ 4 periods)	(d) Book Value Beginning Book Value − (c)
1/1/2014				$103,630
6/30/2014	$5,000	$4,092	$908	102,722
12/31/2014	5,000	4,092	908	101,814
6/30/2015	5,000	4,092	908	100,906
12/31/2015	5,000	4,092	908	99,998*

This amount should be exactly $100,000. The $2 error is due to rounding.

At maturity, after the last interest payment, the bond premium is fully amortized and the maturity amount equals the book value of the bonds. When the bonds are paid off in full, the same entry will be made whether the bond was originally sold at par, at a discount, or at a premium. Exhibit 10.2 compares the effects of the amortization of a bond discount and a bond premium on a $1,000 bond.

PAUSE FOR FEEDBACK

SELF-STUDY QUIZ

Assume that AT&T issued $100,000 bonds that will mature in 10 years. The bonds pay interest at the end of each year at an annual rate of 9 percent. They were sold when the market rate was 8 percent at a price of $106,711. What amount of interest was paid at the end of the first year? What amount of interest expense would be reported at the end of the first year using straight-line amortization?

After you have completed your answers, check them with the solutions at the bottom of next page.

www.mhhe.com/libby8e

GUIDED **HELP**

For additional step-by-step video instruction, go to the URL or scan the QR code in the margin with your smartphone or Ipad.

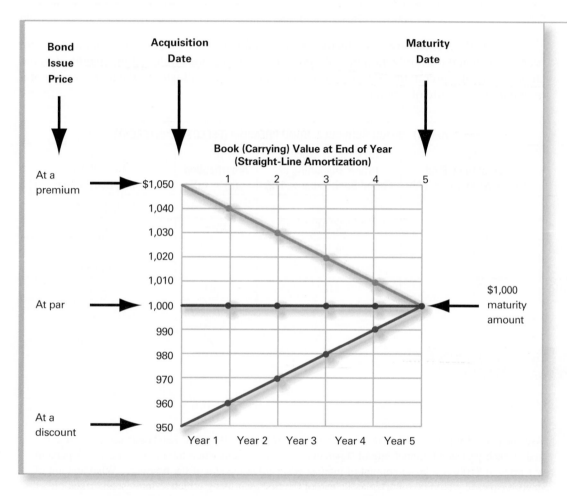

EXHIBIT 10.2

Amortization of Bond Discount and Premium Compared

Part B: Reporting Interest Expense on Bonds Issued at a Premium Using Effective-Interest Amortization

The effective-interest amortization method is basically the same for a discount or a premium. In either case, interest expense for a bond is computed by multiplying the current unpaid balance by the market rate of interest on the date the bonds were sold. The periodic amortization of a bond premium or discount is then calculated as the difference between interest expense and the amount of cash paid or accrued.

The first interest payment on AT&T bonds is made on June 30, 2014. The interest expense on that date is calculated by multiplying the unpaid balance of the debt by the market rate of interest ($103,630 × 8% × 1/2 = $4,145). The amount of cash paid is calculated by multiplying the principal by the stated rate of interest ($100,000 × 10% × 1/2 = $5,000). The difference between the interest expense and the cash paid (or accrued) is the amount of premium that has been amortized ($5,000 − $4,145 = $855).

---

1. $9,000 (9% × $100,000)
2. $8,329 [$9,000 − ($6,711 ÷ 10)]

Solutions to

SELF-STUDY QUIZ

Interest expense (+E, −SE)	4,145
Premium of bonds payable (−L)	855
Cash (−A)	5,000

Assets		=	Liabilities		+	Stockholders' Equity	
Cash	−5,000		Premium on bonds	−855		Interest expense (+E)	−4,145

The basic difference between effective-interest amortization of a bond discount and a bond premium is that the amortization of a discount increases the book value of the liability and the amortization of a premium reduces it. The following schedule illustrates the amortization of a premium over the life of a bond.

	AMORTIZATION SCHEDULE: BOND PREMIUM (EFFECTIVE-INTEREST)			
Date	(a) Interest to Be Paid (10% × $100,000 × 1/2)	(b) Interest Expense (8% × Beginning of Period Book Value × 1/2)	(c) Amortization (b) − (a)	(d) Book Value Beginning Book Value − (c)
1/1/2014				$103,630
6/30/2014	$5,000	$4,145	$855	102,775
12/31/2014	5,000	4,111	889	101,886
6/30/2015	5,000	4,075	925	100,961
12/31/2015	5,000	4,039*	961	100,000

*Rounded.

PAUSE FOR **FEEDBACK**

SELF-STUDY **QUIZ**

Assume that AT&T issued $100,000 bonds that will mature in 10 years. The bonds pay interest at the end of each year at an annual rate of 9 percent. They were sold when the market rate was 8 percent at a price of $106,711. What amount of interest was paid at the end of the first year? What amount of interest expense would be reported at the end of the first year using effective-interest amortization?

After you have completed your answers, check them with the solutions at the bottom of the page.

KEY RATIO ANALYSIS		Debt-to-Equity

LEARNING OBJECTIVE 10-5

Analyze the debt-to-equity ratio.

? **ANALYTICAL QUESTION**

What is the relationship between the amount of capital provided by owners and the amount provided by creditors?

% **RATIO AND COMPARISONS**

The debt-to-equity ratio is computed as follows:

Debt-to-Equity = Total Liabilities ÷ Stockholders' Equity

Solutions to
SELF-STUDY QUIZ

1. $9,000 (9% × $100,000)
2. $8,537 (8% × $106,711)

The 2011 ratio for AT&T is:

$$\$164,547 \div \$105,797 = 1.6$$

COMPARISONS OVER TIME AT&T			COMPARISONS WITH COMPETITORS	
2009	**2010**	**2011**	Verizon **2011**	Sprint **2011**
1.3	1.4	1.6	5.1	3.3

💡 INTERPRETATIONS

In General   A high ratio suggests that a company relies heavily on funds provided by creditors. Heavy reliance on creditors increases the risk that a company may not be able to meet its contractual financial obligations during a business downturn.

Focus Company Analysis   The debt-to-equity ratio for AT&T has increased slightly over the past few years. Most analysts would see this as an insignificant change, especially in light of the strength of the ratio compared to Sprint and Verizon.

A Few Cautions   The debt-to-equity ratio tells only part of the story with respect to the risks associated with debt. It does not help the analyst understand whether the company's operations can support its debt. Remember that debt carries an obligation to make cash payments for interest and principal. As a result, most analysts would evaluate the debt-to-equity ratio within the context of the amount of cash the company can generate from operating activities.

EARLY RETIREMENT OF DEBT

> **LEARNING OBJECTIVE 10-6**
> Report the early retirement of bonds.

Bonds are normally issued for long periods, such as 20 or 30 years. As mentioned earlier, bond-holders who need cash prior to the maturity date can simply sell the bonds to another investor. This transaction does not affect the books of the company that issued the bonds. In several situations, a corporation may decide to retire bonds before their maturity date. A bond with a call feature may be called in for early retirement at the issuer's option. Typically, the bond indenture includes a call premium for bonds retired before the maturity date, which often is stated as a percentage of par value.

Assume that several years ago, AT&T issued bonds in the amount of $1 million and that the bonds sold at par. If AT&T called the bonds in 2014 at 102 percent of par, the company's accountants would make the following journal entry:

Bonds payable (−L)	1,000,000	
Loss on bond call (+Loss, −SE)	20,000	
Cash (−A)		1,020,000

Assets		=	Liabilities		+	Stockholders' Equity	
Cash	−1,020,000		Bonds payable	−1,000,000		Loss	−20,000

The loss on the bond call is the amount over par that must be paid according to the bond indenture. This loss on the bond call would be reported on the income statement.

In some cases, a company may elect to retire debt early by purchasing it on the open market, just as an investor would. This approach is necessary when the bonds do not have a call feature. It might also be an attractive approach if the price of the bonds were to fall after the date of issue. What could cause the price of a bond to fall? The most common cause is a rise in interest rates. As you may have noticed during our discussion of present value concepts, bond prices move in the opposite direction of interest rates. If interest rates go up, bond prices fall, and vice versa. When interest rates have gone up, a company that wants to retire a bond before maturity may find buying the bond on the open market is less expensive than paying a call premium.

PAUSE FOR **FEEDBACK**

SELF-STUDY **QUIZ**

Which company has a higher level of risk: a company with a high debt-to-equity ratio and a high interest coverage ratio or a company with a low debt-to-equity ratio and a low interest coverage ratio?

After you have completed your answers, check it with the solution at the bottom of the page.

FOCUS ON CASH FLOWS

Bonds Payable

LEARNING OBJECTIVE 10-7

Explain how financing activities are reported on the statement of cash flows.

The issuance of a bond payable is reported as a cash inflow from financing activities on the statement of cash flows. The repayment of principal is reported as a cash outflow from financing activities. Many students are surprised to learn that the payment of interest is not reported in the Financing Activities section of the statement of cash flows. Interest expense is reported on the income statement and is related directly to the computation of net income. As a result, U.S. GAAP requires that interest payments be reported in the Cash Flows from Operating Activities section of the statement. Companies are also required to report the amount of cash paid for interest expense each accounting period. *Accounting Trends & Techniques* reports that companies disclose this information in a variety of locations.

EFFECT ON STATEMENT OF CASH FLOWS

In General As we saw in Chapter 9, transactions involving short-term creditors (e.g., accounts payable) affect working capital and are therefore reported in the Operating Activities section of the statement of cash flows. Cash received from long-term creditors is reported as an inflow from financing activities. Cash payments made to long-term creditors (with the exception of interest expense) are reported as outflows from financing activities. Examples are shown in the following table:

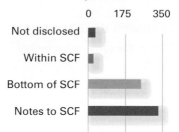

Disclosure of Cash Interest Payments (sample of 600 companies)

	0	175	350
Not disclosed			
Within SCF			
Bottom of SCF			
Notes to SCF			

Selected Company Comparisons: Cash Flows from Financing Activities (in millions)

General Mills	($102.3)
Outback	(54.7)
Home Depot	737.0

	Effect on Cash Flows
Financing activities	
Issuance of bonds	+
Debt retirement	−
Repayment of bond principal upon maturity	−

Focus Company Analysis A segment of AT&T's statement of cash flows follows. Several items pertain to issues discussed in this chapter. The remaining items will be discussed in other chapters. Notice that AT&T reports both payments on long-term debt and new borrowings. Although businesses normally borrow money to finance the acquisition of long-lived assets, they also borrow to rearrange their capital structure. In the case of AT&T, the company had outstanding debt with a high interest rate. The company was able to retire this debt by borrowing at a lower interest, saving the company a significant amount in annual interest cost.

Solution to SELF-STUDY QUIZ

A company can be forced into bankruptcy if it does not meet its interest obligations to creditors. Many successful companies borrow very large amounts of money without creating unreasonable risk because they generate sufficient funds from normal operations to meet their obligations. Even a small amount of debt can be a problem if a company does not generate funds to meet current interest obligations. Usually, the company with a high interest coverage ratio (even if it has a high debt-to-equity ratio) is viewed as being less risky than one with a low interest coverage ratio.

Analysts are particularly interested in the Financing Activities section of the statement of cash flows because it provides important insights about the future capital structure for a company. Rapidly growing companies typically report significant amounts of funds in this section of the statement.

AT&T INC. **Consolidated Statements of Cash Flows** **(dollars in millions)**			
	2011	**2010**	**2009**
Financing Activities			
Net change in short-term borrowings with original maturities			
of three months or less	$ **(1,625)**	$ 1,592	$ (3,910)
Issuance of long-term debt	**7,936**	2,235	8,161
Repayment of long-term debt	**(7,574)**	(9,294)	(8,652)
Issuance of treasury stock	**237**	50	28
Dividends paid	**(10,172)**	(9,916)	(9,670)
Other	**(452)**	(515)	(465)
Net Cash Used in Financing Activities	**$(11,650)**	$(15,848)	$(14,508)

DEMONSTRATION   CASE

(Try to answer the questions before proceeding to the suggested solution that follows.) To raise funds to build a new plant, Reed Company's management issued bonds. The bond indenture specified the following:

> Par value of the bonds: $100,000.
> Date of issue: January 1, 2014; due in 10 years.
> Interest rate: 12 percent per annum, payable semiannually on June 30 and December 31.

All the bonds were sold on January 1, 2014, at 106. The market rate of interest on the date of issue was 11 percent.

Required:

1. How much cash did Reed Company receive from the sale of the bonds payable? Show computations.

2. What was the amount of premium on the bonds payable?

3. Give the journal entry to record the sale and issuance of the bonds payable.

4. Give the journal entry for payment of interest and amortization of premium for the first interest payment.

SUGGESTED SOLUTION

1. Sale price of the bonds: $100,000 × 106% = $106,000.

2. Premium on the bonds payable: $106,000 − $100,000 = $6,000.

3. January 1, 2014 (issuance date):

Cash (+A)	106,000	
Premium on bonds payable (+L)		6,000
Bonds payable (+L)		100,000
To record sale of bonds payable at 106.		

4. Part A: straight-line amortization

June 30, 2014		
Interest expense (+E, −SE) ($6,000 − $300)	5,700	
Premium on bonds payable* (−L)	300	
Cash (−A) ($100,000 × 12% × 1/2)		6,000
To record payment of interest.		

*$6,000 ÷ 20 periods = $300

Part B: effective-interest amortization

June 30, 2014		
Interest expense* (+E, −SE)	5,830	
Premium on bonds payable (−L)	170	
Cash (−A) ($100,000 × 12% × 1/2)		6,000
To record payment of interest.		

*$106,000 × 11% × 1/2 = 5,830

Chapter Supplement A

Bond Calculations Using Excel

Instead of using the present value tables in Appendix A, most analysts and accountants use Excel to do the financial computations that are necessary when working with bonds. In Chapter 9, we showed you how to use Excel to compute the present value of both single payment and annuity problems. Because a bond involves both types of payments, you can use that process to compute the present value of each type of payment and add them together. Alternatively, you can use a single Excel process to compute the present value of a bond. We will illustrate the Excel process by using the bond example from this chapter. Assume that AT&T issued a $100,000 bond that matured in two years and paid $10,000 interest twice per year (4 payments of $5,000 each.) When the bond was issued, the market rate of interest was 12 percent. The present value of this bond can be computed as follows:

- **Determine the present value of a bond.** The present value of a bond can be computed using an Excel function (you don't have to enter the formula yourself). On the toolbar, click on the insert function button (f_x). A dropdown box called "insert function" will appear. You will be asked to "type a brief description of what you want to do and click 'go.'" You should enter "present value" and click the go button. A new screen will appear and you should highlight "PV," and click on the "ok" button. A new dropdown box will appear. Enter the amounts from the problem in this box: "Rate" is the market rate of interest per period. For this problem, enter 0.06. "Nper" is the number of periods. You should enter 4. "Pmt" is the cash interest payment per period, which is −5000 for this problem. "Fv" is the maturity value of the bond or −100000 in this case. Notice that when using Excel, amounts must be entered as negative numbers because they represent payments. Also, you should not enter a comma between the numbers. The final box is "type," which permits you to do problems involving payments at either the beginning or end of the period. Most problems involve payments at the end of the period, so you do not need to enter anything in this box because the default is for end-of-period problems. Once you have entered the required data, click on "ok" and Excel will compute this value as $96,534.89 and show it on your spreadsheet. Notice that this amount is slightly different from the amount computed using present value tables because the table numbers have been rounded. An Excel screen with the data entered follows:

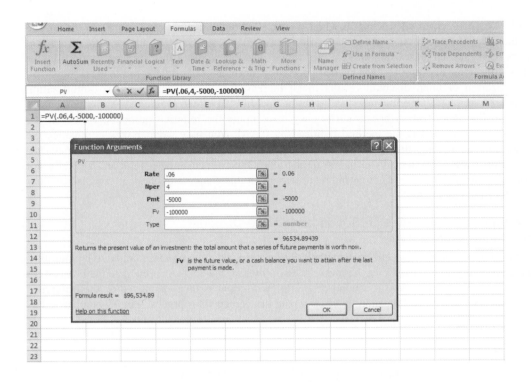

Chapter Supplement B

Bonds Issued at a Discount (Without Discount Account)

For financial reporting purposes, it is not necessary to use a discount or premium account when recording bonds sold at a discount or premium. This supplement is intended for use as an alternative to the discussion in the chapter, which shows the use of discount and premium accounts.

Bonds sell at a discount when the market rate of interest is higher than the stated interest rate on them. Let's assume that the market rate of interest was 12 percent when AT&T sold its bonds (which have a par value of $100,000). The bonds mature in two years and have a stated rate of 10 percent, payable twice a year on June 30 and December 31. Because the stated rate of interest was less than the market rate on the date of issue, the bonds sold at a discount.

To compute the cash issue price of the bonds, we can use the tables in Appendix A. As in the chapter example, the number of periods is four and we use an interest rate of 6 percent per period, which is the market rate of interest. The cash issue price of the AT&T bonds is computed as follows:

	Present Value
a. Single payment: $100,000 × 0.7921	$79,210
b. Annuity: $5,000 × 3.4651	17,326
Issue (sale) price of bonds	$96,536*

*The amount of the discount: $100,000 − $96,536 = $3,464.

To compute the present value using Excel, enter:
$f_x = \text{PV}(0.06, 4, -5000, -100000)$

The cash price of the bonds issued by AT&T is $96,536. Some people refer to this price as 96.5, which means that the bonds were sold at 96.5 percent of their par value ($96,536 ÷ $100,000).

The issuance of the AT&T bonds at a discount is recorded as follows:

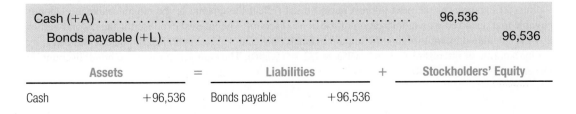

| Cash (+A) . . . . | 96,536 | |
| Bonds payable (+L). . . . . | | 96,536 |

Assets	=	Liabilities	+	Stockholders' Equity
Cash	+96,536	Bonds payable	+96,536	

While AT&T received only $96,536 when it sold the bonds, it must repay $100,000 when the bonds mature. The extra cash that must be paid is an adjustment of interest expense to ensure that creditors earn the market rate of interest. To adjust interest expense, the borrower apportions or amortizes the bond discount to each interest period as an increase in interest expense. Therefore, the amortization of bond discount results in an increase in interest expense. Two amortization methods are often used by companies: (1) straight line and (2) effective interest. Many companies use straight-line amortization because it is easy to compute the required numbers. However, the effective-interest method is the method required by GAAP. You may wonder why companies are permitted to use a method that is not the one required by accounting rules. The answer is materiality. Companies are permitted to use the straight-line method because the results are normally not materially different from the effective-interest method. In this chapter supplement, we discuss only the effective-interest method.

Reporting Interest Expense on Bonds Issued at a Discount Using Effective-Interest Amortization

Under the effective-interest amortization method, interest expense for a bond is computed by multiplying the current unpaid balance times the market rate of interest that existed on the date the bonds were sold. The periodic amortization of a bond premium or discount is then calculated as the difference between interest expense and the amount of cash paid or accrued. This process can be summarized as follows:

Step 1:   Compute interest expense

Unpaid Balance $\times$ Effective-Interest Rate $\times$ $n/12$

n = Number of Months in Each Interest Period

Step 2:   Compute amortization amount

Interest Expense $-$ Cash Interest

The first interest payment on AT&T bonds is made on June 30, 2014. Interest expense at the end of the first interest period (June 30, 2014) is calculated by multiplying the unpaid balance of the debt by the market rate of interest ($96,536 $\times$ 12% $\times$ 1/2 = $5,792). The amount of cash paid is calculated by multiplying the principal by the stated rate of interest ($100,000 $\times$ 10% $\times$ 1/2 = $5,000). The difference between the interest expense and the cash paid (or accrued) is the amount of discount that has been amortized ($5,792 $-$ $5,000 = $792).

Effective-interest amortization causes these amounts to change each period.

Interest expense (+E, −SE)	5,792	
Bonds payable (+L)...		792
Cash (−A)		5,000

Assets		=	Liabilities		+	Stockholders' Equity	
Cash	−5,000		Bonds payable	+792		Interest expense (+E)	−5,792

Each period, the amortization of the bond discount increases the bond's book value (or unpaid balance). The amortization of bond discount can be thought of as interest earned by the bondholders but not paid to them. During the first interest period, the bondholders earned interest of $5,792 but received only $5,000 in cash. The additional $792 was added to the principal of the bond and will be paid to bondholders when the bond matures.

Interest expense for the next interest period must reflect the change in the unpaid balance of bonds payable that occurred with amortization of the bond discount. The interest expense for the second half of 2014 is calculated by multiplying the unpaid balance ($96,536 + $792 = $97,328) on June 30, 2014, by the market rate of interest ($97,328 $\times$ 12% $\times$ 1/2 = $5,840). Thus amortization of the bond discount on December 31, 2014, is $840.

Interest expense (+E, −SE)	5,840	
Bonds payable (+L)..		840
Cash (−A)		5,000

Assets		=	Liabilities		+	Stockholders' Equity	
Cash	−5,000		Bonds payable	+840		Interest expense (+E)	−5,840

Notice that interest expense for December 31, 2014, is more than interest expense for June 30, 2014. AT&T effectively borrowed more money during the second half of the year because of the unpaid interest. Because of the amortization of the bond discount, interest expense increases each year during the life of the bond. This process can be illustrated with the amortization schedule shown below:

	AMORTIZATION SCHEDULE: BOND DISCOUNT (EFFECTIVE-INTEREST)			
Date	(a) Interest to Be Paid (10% × $100,000 × 1/2)	(b) Interest Expense (12% × Beginning of Period Book Value × 1/2)	(c) Amortization (b) − (a)	(d) Book Value Beginning Book Value + (c)
1/1/2014				$ 96,536
6/30/2014	$5,000	$5,792	$792	97,328
12/31/2014	5,000	5,840	840	98,168
6/31/2015	5,000	5,890	890	99,058
12/31/2015	5,000	5,943	943	100,001*

*This amount should be exactly $100,000. The $1 error is due to rounding.

Interest expense (column b) is computed by multiplying the market rate of interest by the book value of the bonds at the beginning of the period (column d). Amortization is computed by subtracting cash interest (column a) from interest expense (column b). The book value of the bonds (column d) is computed by adding amortization (column c) to the book value at the beginning of the period. In summary, under the effective-interest amortization method, interest expense changes each accounting period as the effective amount of the liability changes.

PAUSE FOR **FEEDBACK**

SELF-STUDY **QUIZ**

Assume that AT&T issued $100,000 bonds that will mature in 10 years. The bonds pay interest at the end of each year at an annual rate of 5 percent. They were sold when the market rate was 6 percent at a price of $92,641. What amount of interest was paid at the end of the first year? What amount of interest expense would be reported at the end of the first year using effective-interest amortization?

After you have completed your answers, check them with the solutions at the bottom of the page.

1. $5,000 (5% × $100,000)
2. $5,558 (6% × $92,641)

Solutions to
SELF-STUDY QUIZ

Zero Coupon Bonds

So far, we have discussed common bonds that are issued by many corporations. For a number of reasons, corporations may issue bonds with unusual features. The concepts you have learned will help you understand these bonds. For example, a corporation might issue a bond that does not pay periodic cash interest. These bonds are often called *zero coupon bonds*. Why would an investor buy a bond that did not pay interest? Our discussion of bond discounts has probably given you a good idea of the answer. The coupon interest rate on a bond can be virtually any amount and the price of the bond will be adjusted so that investors earn the market rate of interest. A bond with a zero coupon interest rate is simply a deeply discounted bond that will sell for substantially less than its maturity value.

Let's use the $100,000 AT&T bond to illustrate a zero coupon rate. Assume that market rate is 10 percent and the bond pays no cash interest. The bond matures in five years. The selling price of the bond is the present value of the maturity amount because no other cash payments will be made over the life of the bond. We can compute the present value with the tables contained in Appendix A, using the factor for five periods and an interest rate of 10 percent:

To compute the present value using Excel, enter:
= 100000/(1.10)^5

	Present Value
Single payment: $100,000 × 0.6209	$62,090

Accounting for a zero coupon bond is no different from accounting for other bonds sold at a discount. However, the amount of the discount is much larger. For example, the annual report for AT&T contained the following information concerning the company's zero coupon bonds:

AT&T

REAL WORLD EXCERPT
Annual Report

AT&T INC. AND SUBSIDIARY DEBT DETAIL—MARCH 31, 2012
This chart shows the principal amount of AT&T Inc.'s and its subsidiaries' outstanding long-term debt issues as of the date above.

Entry (Original Issuer)	Amount Outstanding at Maturity	Coupon	Maturity Date	Total
BellSouth Telecommunications, Inc.	$ 115,968,616	6.300%	12/15/15	$ 115,968,616
Ameritech Capital Funding Corporation	$ 52,502,760	9.100%	6/1/16	$ 52,502,760
Various	$ 3,143,969	Various	Various	$ 3,143,969
BellSouth Corporation	$1,000,000,000	4.463%	4/26/21	$1,000,000,000
AT&T Inc.	$1,030,000,000	Zero	11/27/22	$ 616,127,631

While zero coupon bonds do not pay cash interest, they have been priced to provide the investor with a market rate of interest. Notice that the carrying value of the obligation ($616,127,631) is much lower than the maturity value ($1,000,000,000) because the payment has been discounted at the market rate of interest that existed on the issue date.

Bonds Issued at a Premium (Without Premium Account)

Bonds sell at a premium when the market rate of interest is lower than their stated interest rate. Let's assume that the market rate of interest is 8 percent while the AT&T bonds pay cash interest of 10 percent. The bonds pay interest semiannually and mature in two years. They are issued on January 1, 2014.

The present value of AT&T 10 percent bonds can be computed from the tables contained in Appendix A using the factor for four periods and an interest rate of 4 percent per period:

	Present Value
a. Single payment: $100,000 × 0.8548	$ 85,480
b. Annuity: $5,000 × 3.6299	18,150
Issue (sale) price of bonds	$103,630*

The amount of the premium: $103,630 − $100,000 = $3,630.

To compute the present value using Excel, enter:

$f_x = PV(0.04, 4, -5000, -100000)$

When a bond is sold at a premium, the Bonds Payable account is credited for the present value of the bonds. The January 1, 2014, issuance of AT&T bonds at a premium would be recorded as follows:

Cash (+A)   103,630
   Bonds payable (+L).   103,630

Assets		=	Liabilities		+	Stockholders' Equity
Cash	+103,630		Bonds payable	+103,630		

Reporting Interest Expense on Bonds Issued at a Premium Using Effective-Interest Amortization

The effective-interest amortization method is basically the same for a discount or a premium. In either case, interest expense for a bond is computed by multiplying the current unpaid balance by the market rate of interest on the date the bonds were sold. The periodic amortization of a bond premium or discount is then calculated as the difference between interest expense and the amount of cash paid or accrued.

The first interest payment on AT&T bonds is made on June 30, 2014. The interest expense on that date is calculated by multiplying the unpaid balance of the debt by the market rate of interest ($103,630 × 8% × 1/2 = $4,145). The amount of cash paid is calculated by multiplying the principal by the stated rate of interest ($100,000 × 10% × 1/2 = $5,000). The difference between the interest expense and the cash paid (or accrued) is the amount of premium that has been amortized ($5,000 − $4,145 = $855).

Interest expense (+E, −SE)   4,145
Bonds payable (−L).   855
   Cash (−A)   5,000

Assets		=	Liabilities		+	Stockholders' Equity	
Cash	−5,000		Bonds payable	−855		Interest expense (+E)	−4,145

The basic difference between effective-interest amortization of a bond discount and a bond premium is that the amortization of a discount increases the book value of the liability and the amortization of a premium reduces it. The following schedule illustrates the amortization of a premium over the life of a bond.

	AMORTIZATION SCHEDULE: BOND PREMIUM (EFFECTIVE-INTEREST)			
Date	**(a) Interest to Be Paid (10% × $100,000 × 1/2)**	**(b) Interest Expense (8% × Beginning Book Value × 1/2)**	**(c) Amortization (b) − (a)**	**(d) Book Value Beginning Book Value − (c)**
1/1/2014				$103,630
6/30/2014	$5,000	$4,145	$855	102,775
12/31/2014	5,000	4,111	889	101,886
6/30/2015	5,000	4,075	925	100,961
12/31/2015	5,000	4,039*	961	100,000

*Rounded.

PAUSE FOR **FEEDBACK**

SELF-STUDY **QUIZ**

Assume that AT&T issued $100,000 bonds that will mature in 10 years. The bonds pay interest at the end of each year at an annual rate of 9 percent. They were sold when the market rate was 8 percent. The bonds were sold at a price of $106,711. What amount of interest was paid at the end of the first year? What amount of interest expense would be reported at the end of the first year using effective-interest amortization?

After you have completed your answers, check them with the solutions at the bottom of the page.

CHAPTER **TAKE-AWAYS**

10-1. Describe the characteristics of bonds.   p. 501

Bonds have a number of characteristics designed to meet the needs of both the issuing corporation and the creditor. A complete listing of bond characteristics is discussed in the chapter.

Corporations use bonds to raise long-term capital. Bonds offer a number of advantages compared to stock, including the ability to earn a higher return for stockholders, the tax deductibility of interest, and the fact that control of the company is not diluted. Bonds do carry additional risk, however, because interest and principal payments are not discretionary.

10-2. Report bonds payable and interest expense for bonds sold at par and analyze the times interest earned ratio.   p. 505

Three types of events must be recorded over the life of a typical bond: (1) the receipt of cash when the bond is first sold, (2) the periodic payment of cash interest, and (3) the repayment of principal at the maturity of the bond. Bonds are reported at the present value of the future cash flows specified in the bond contract. When the market interest rate and the coupon interest rate are the same, the bond will sell at par, which is the same as the maturity value of the bond.

The times interest earned ratio measures a company's ability to meet its interest obligations with resources from its profit-making activities. It is computed by comparing interest expense to earnings (including net income, interest expense, and income tax expense).

10-3. Report bonds payable and interest expense for bonds sold at a discount.   p. 508

Bonds are sold at a discount whenever the coupon interest rate is less than the market rate of interest. A discount is the dollar amount of the difference between the par value of the bond and its selling price. The discount is recorded as a contra-liability when the bond is sold and is amortized over the life of the bond as an adjustment to interest expense.

10-4. Report bonds payable and interest expense for bonds sold at a premium.   p. 513

Bonds are sold at a premium whenever the coupon interest rate is more than the market rate of interest. A premium is the dollar amount of the difference between the selling price of the bond and its par value. The premium is recorded as a liability when the bond is sold and is amortized over the life of the bond as an adjustment to interest expense.

10-5. Analyze the debt-to-equity ratio.   p. 516

The debt-to-equity ratio compares the amount of capital supplied by creditors to the amount supplied by owners. It is a measure of a company's debt capacity. It is an important ratio because of the high risk associated with debt capital that requires interest and principal payments.

10-6. Report the early retirement of bonds.   p. 517

A corporation may retire bonds before their maturity date. The difference between the book value and the amount paid to retire the bonds is reported as a gain or loss, depending on the circumstances.

Solutions to
SELF-STUDY QUIZ

1. $9,000 (9% × $100,000)
2. $8,537 (8% × $106,711)

10-7. Explain how financing activities are reported on the statement of cash flows. p. 518

Cash flows associated with transactions involving long-term creditors are reported in the Financing Activities section of the statement of cash flows. Interest expense is reported in the Operating Activities section.

KEY **RATIO**

Times interest earned ratio measures a company's ability to generate resources from current operations to meet its interest obligations. The ratio is computed as follows (p. 507):

$$\text{Times Interest Earned} = \frac{\text{Net Income} + \text{Interest Expense} + \text{Income Tax Expense}}{\text{Interest Expense}}$$

Debt-to-equity ratio measures the balance between debt and equity. Debt funds are viewed as being riskier than equity funds. The ratio is computed as follows (p. 516):

$$\text{Debt-to-Equity} = \frac{\text{Total Liabilities}}{\text{Stockholders' Equity}}$$

FINDING **FINANCIAL INFORMATION**

Balance Sheet

Under Current Liabilities
Bonds are normally listed as long-term liabilities. An exception occurs when the bonds are within one year of maturity. Such bonds are reported as current liabilities with the following title: Current Portion of Long-Term Debt

Under Noncurrent Liabilities
Bonds are listed under a variety of titles, depending on the characteristics of the bond. Titles include:
Bonds Payable
Debentures
Convertible Bonds

Income Statement

Bonds are shown only on the balance sheet, never on the income statement. Interest expense associated with bonds is reported on the income statement. Most companies report interest expense in a separate category on the income statement.

Statement of Cash Flows

Under Financing Activities
+ Cash inflows from long-term creditors
− Cash outflows to long-term creditors

Under Operating Activities
The cash outflow associated with interest expense is reported as an operating activity.

Notes

Under Summary of Significant Accounting Policies
Description of pertinent information concerning accounting treatment of liabilities. Normally, there is minimal information. Some companies report the method used to amortize bond discounts and premiums.

Under a Separate Note
Most companies include a separate note called "Long-Term Debt" that reports information about each major debt issue, including amount and interest rate. The note also provides detail concerning debt covenants.

KEY **TERMS**

Bond Certificate   p. 503
Bond Discount   p. 504
Bond Premium   p. 504
Bond Principal   p. 501
Callable Bonds   p. 502
Convertible Bonds   p. 502

Coupon Rate   p. 503
Debenture   p. 502
Effective-Interest Amortization   p. 510
Effective-Interest Rate   p. 504
Face Amount   p. 501
Indenture   p. 502

Market Interest Rate   p. 504
Par Value   p. 501
Stated Rate   p. 501
Straight-Line Amortization   p. 509
Trustee   p. 503
Yield   p. 504

QUESTIONS

1. What are the primary characteristics of a bond? For what purposes are bonds usually issued?
2. What is the difference between a bond indenture and a bond certificate?
3. Differentiate secured bonds from unsecured bonds.
4. Differentiate between callable and convertible bonds.
5. From the perspective of the issuer, what are some advantages of issuing bonds instead of capital stock?
6. As the tax rate increases, the net cost of borrowing money decreases. Explain.
7. At the date of issuance, bonds are recorded at their current cash equivalent amount. Explain.
8. Explain the nature of the discount and premium on bonds payable.
9. What is the difference between the stated interest rate and the effective-interest rate on a bond?
10. Differentiate among the stated and effective rates of interest on a bond (*a*) sold at par, (*b*) sold at a discount, and (*c*) sold at a premium.
11. What is the book value of a bond payable?
12. Explain the basic difference between the straight-line and the effective-interest methods of amortizing a bond discount or premium. Explain when each method should or may be used.

MULTIPLE-CHOICE **QUESTIONS**

1. Annual interest expense for a single bond issue continues to increase over the life of the bonds. Which of the following explains this?
   a. The market rate of interest has increased since the bonds were sold.
   b. The coupon rate of interest has increased since the bonds were sold.
   c. The bonds were sold at a discount.
   d. The bonds were sold at a premium.
2. Which of the following is **not** an advantage of issuing bonds when compared to issuing additional shares of stock in order to obtain additional capital?
   a. Stockholders maintain proportionate ownership percentages.
   b. Interest expense reduces taxable income.
   c. Timing flexibility associated with the payment of interest.
   d. All of the above are advantages associated with bonds.
3. A bond with a maturity value of $100,000 has a stated interest rate of 8 percent. The bond matures in 10 years. When the bond is issued, the market rate of interest is 10 percent. What amount should be reported when the bond is issued?
   a. $100,000   c. $49,157
   b. $87,707   d. $113,421
4. Which account would not be included in the debt-to-equity ratio calculation?
   a. Unearned Revenue.   c. Income Taxes Payable.
   b. Retained Earnings.   d. All of the above are included.

5. Which of the following is false when a bond is issued at a premium?
   a. The bond will issue for an amount above its par value.
   b. Bonds payable will be credited for the par value of the bond.
   c. Interest expense will exceed the cash interest payments.
   d. All of the above are false.
6. A bond with a face value of $100,000 was issued for $93,500 on January 1, 2014. The stated rate of interest was 8 percent and the market rate of interest was 10 percent when the bond was sold. Interest is paid annually. How much interest will be paid on December 31, 2014?
   a. $10,000   c. $7,480
   b. $8,000   d. $9,350
7. To determine whether a bond will be sold at a premium, discount, or at face value, one must know which of the following pairs of information?
   a. Par value and the coupon rate on the date the bond was issued.
   b. Par value and the market rate on the date the bond was issued.
   c. Coupon rate and the market rate on the date the bond was issued.
   d. Coupon rate and the stated rate on the date the bond was issued.
8. When using the effective-interest method of amortization, interest expense reported in the income statement is impacted by the
   a. Par value of the bonds.
   b. Coupon rate of interest stated in the bond certificate.
   c. Market rate of interest on the date the bonds were issued.
   d. Both (a) and (b).
9. A bond with a face value of $100,000 is sold on January 1. The bond has a stated interest rate of 10 percent and matures in 10 years. When the bond was issued the market rate of interest was 10 percent. On December 31, the market rate of interest increased to 11 percent. What amount should be reported on December 31 as the bond liability?
   a. $100,000   c. $94,460
   b. $94,112   d. $87,562
10. When using the effective-interest method of amortization, the book value of the bonds changes by what amount on each interest payment date?
    a. Interest expense   c. Amortization
    b. Cash interest payment   d. None of the above

For more practice with multiple-choice questions, go to the text website at **www.mhhe.com/libby8e.**

MINI-**EXERCISES**

Finding Financial Information

For each of the following items, specify whether the information would be found in the balance sheet, the income statement, the statement of cash flows, the notes to the statements, or not at all.
1. The amount of a bond liability.
2. Interest expense for the period.
3. Cash interest paid for the period.
4. Interest rates for specific bond issues.
5. The names of major holders of bonds.
6. The maturity date of specific bond issues.

M10-1
LO10-1, 10-2

Computing Bond Issuance Price

Willams Company plans to issue $600,000, 10-year bonds that pay 8 percent payable semiannually on June 30 and December 31. All of the bonds will be sold on January 1, 2014. Determine the issuance price of the bonds assuming a market yield of 8 percent.

M10-2
LO10-2

M10-3
LO10-3

Computing Bond Issuance Price

Trew Company plans to issue $900,000, 10-year, 6 percent bonds. Interest is payable semiannually on June 30 and December 31. All of the bonds will be sold on January 1, 2014. Determine the issuance price of the bonds assuming a market yield of 8.5 percent.

M10-4
LO10-3

Recording the Issuance of a New Bond and the Payment of Interest (Effective-Interest Amortization)

Coffman Company issued $1,000,000, 10-year, 10 percent bonds on January 1, 2014. The bonds sold for $940,000. Interest is payable semiannually each June 30 and December 31. Record the sale of the bonds on January 1, 2014, and the payment of interest on June 30, 2014, using effective-interest amortization. The yield on the bonds is 11 percent.

M10-5
LO10-3

Recording the Issuance of a New Bond and the Payment of Interest (Straight-Line Amortization)

Wefald Company issued $600,000, 10-year, 10 percent bonds on January 1, 2014. The bonds sold for $580,000. Interest is payable semiannually each June 30 and December 31. Record the sale of the bonds on January 1, 2014, and the payment of interest on June 30, 2014, using straight-line amortization.

M10-6
LO10-4

Computing Bond Issuance Price

Waterhouse Company plans to issue $500,000, 10-year, 10 percent bonds. Interest is paid semiannually on June 30 and December 31. All of the bonds will be sold on January 1, 2014. Determine the issuance price of the bonds, assuming a market yield of 8 percent.

M10-7
LO10-4

Recording the Issuance of a New Bond and the Payment of Interest (Straight-Line Amortization)

Ernst Company issued $600,000, 10-year, 9 percent bonds on January 1, 2014. The bonds sold for $620,000. Interest is payable annually each December 31. Record the sale of the bonds on January 1, 2014, and the payment of interest on December 31, 2014, using straight-line amortization.

M10-8
LO10-4

Recording the Issuance of a New Bond and the Payment of Interest (Effective-Interest Amortization)

RKO Company issued $850,000, 10-year, 8 percent bonds on January 1, 2014. The bonds sold for $910,000. Interest is payable annually each December 31. Record the sale of the bonds on January 1, 2014, and the payment of interest on December 31, 2014, using the effective-interest method of amortization. The yield on the bonds is 7 percent.

M10-9
LO10-2, 10-5

Understanding Financial Ratios

The debt-to-equity and times interest earned ratios were discussed in this chapter. Which is a better indicator of a company's ability to meet its required interest payment? Explain.

M10-10
LO10-6

Determining Financial Statement Effects of an Early Retirement of Debt

If interest rates fell after the issuance of a bond and the company decided to retire the debt, would you expect the company to report a gain or loss on debt retirement? Describe the financial statement effects of a debt retirement under these circumstances.

M10-11
LO10-7

Determining Cash Flow Effects

If a company issues a bond at a discount, will interest expense each period be more or less than the cash payment for interest? If another company issues a bond at a premium, will interest expense be more or less than the cash payment for interest? Is your answer to either question affected by the method used to amortize the discount or premium?

M10-12
LO10-7

Reporting Cash Flow Effects

In what section of the statement of cash flows would you find cash paid to retire bonds? In what section would you find cash paid for interest?

Bond Terminology: Fill in the Missing Blanks

1. The _____ is the amount (*a*) payable at the maturity of the bond and (*b*) on which the periodic cash interest payments are computed.
2. _____ is another name for bond principal, or the maturity amount of a bond.
3. _____ is another name for principal, or the principal amount of the bond.
4. The _____ is the rate of cash interest per period stated in the bond contract.
5. A _____ is an unsecured bond; no assets are specifically pledged to guarantee repayment.
6. _____ bonds may be called for early retirement at the option of the issuer.
7. _____ bonds may be converted to other securities of the issuer (usually common stock).

E10-1
LO10-1

Interpreting Information Reported in the Business Press

As this book was being written, the business press reported the following information concerning bonds issued by AT&T:

Bonds	Yield	Close
AT&T 6.5	7.3	89.5

Explain the meaning of the reported information. If you bought AT&T bonds with $10,000 face value, how much would you pay (based on the preceding information reported)? Assume that the bonds were originally sold at par. What impact would the decline in value have on the financial statements for AT&T?

E10-2
LO10-1

AT&T

Computing Issue Prices of Bonds for Three Cases

LaTanya Corporation is planning to issue $100,000, seven-year, 8 percent bonds. Interest is payable each December 31. All of the bonds will be sold on January 1, 2014.

Required:
Compute the issue (sale) price on January 1, 2014, for each of the following independent cases (show computations):

a. **Case A:** Market (yield) rate, 8 percent.
b. **Case B:** Market (yield) rate, 6 percent.
c. **Case C:** Market (yield) rate, 9 percent.

E10-3
LO10-2, 10-3, 10-4

Computing Issue Prices of Bonds for Three Cases

James Corporation is planning to issue $500,000 worth of bonds that mature in 10 years and pay 6 percent interest each June 30 and December 31. All of the bonds will be sold on January 1, 2014.

Required:
Compute the issue (sale) price on January 1, 2014, for each of the following independent cases (show computations):

a. **Case A:** Market (yield) rate, 4 percent.
b. **Case B:** Market (yield) rate, 6 percent.
c. **Case C:** Market (yield) rate, 8.5 percent.

E10-4
LO10-2, 10-3, 10-4

Analyzing Financial Ratios

You have just started your first job as a financial analyst for a large stock brokerage company. Your boss, a senior analyst, has finished a detailed report evaluating bonds issued by two different companies. She stopped by your desk and asked for help: "I have compared two ratios for the companies and found something interesting." She went on to explain that the debt-to-equity ratio for Applied Technologies, Inc., is much lower than the industry average and that the one for Innovative Solutions, Inc., is much higher. On the other hand, the times interest earned ratio for Applied Technologies is much higher than the industry average, and the ratio for Innovative Solutions is much lower. Your boss then asked you to think about

E10-5
LO10-2, 10-5

what the ratios indicate about the two companies so that she could include the explanation in her report. How would you respond to your boss?

E10-6

LO10-3

Computing the Issue Price of a Bond

GMAC Corporation issued a $250,000 bond that matures in five years. The bond has a stated interest rate of 6 percent. On January 1, 2014, when the bond was issued, the market rate was 8 percent. The bond pays interest twice per year, on June 30 and December 31. At what price was the bond issued?

E10-7

LO10-3

Recording Bond Issue and First Interest Payment with Discount (Straight-Line Amortization)

On January 1, 2014, Clearwater Corporation sold a $750,000, 8 percent bond issue (9 percent market rate). The bonds were dated January 1, 2014, pay interest each December 31, and mature in 10 years.

Required:
1. Give the journal entry to record the issuance of the bonds.
2. Give the journal entry to record the interest payment on December 31, 2014. Use straight-line amortization.
3. Show how the interest expense and the bonds payable should be reported on the December 31, 2014, annual financial statements.

E10-8

LO10-3

Recording Bond Issue and First Interest Payment with Discount (Effective-Interest Amortization)

On January 1, 2014, Park Corporation sold a $600,000, 7.5 percent bond issue (8.5 percent market rate). The bonds were dated January 1, 2014, pay interest each June 30 and December 31, and mature in four years.

Required:
1. Give the journal entry to record the issuance of the bonds.
2. Give the journal entry to record the interest payment on June 30, 2014. Use effective-interest amortization.
3. Show how the bond interest expense and the bonds payable should be reported on the June 30, 2014, income statement and balance sheet.

E10-9

(Supplement B) Recording Bond Issue and First Interest Payment with Discount (Effective-Interest Amortization with No Discount Account)

Using data from the previous exercise, complete each of the requirements in Exercise 10-8 without using a discount account.

E10-10

LO10-3

Recording Bond Issue: Entries for Issuance and Interest (Straight-Line Amortization)

Westover Corporation had $500,000, 10-year bonds outstanding on December 31, 2014 (end of the accounting period). Interest is payable each December 31. The bonds were issued on January 1, 2014. The company uses the straight-line method to amortize any premium or discount. The December 31, 2014, annual financial statements showed the following:

Income statement	
Bond interest expense	$ 23,100
Balance sheet	
Bonds payable (net liability)	481,100

Required (show computations):
1. What was the issue price of the bonds? Give the journal entry to record the issuance of the bonds.
2. Give the entry to record 2014 interest.

Analyzing a Bond Amortization Schedule: Reporting Bonds Payable

Santa Corporation sold a $1,000 bond on January 1, 2014. The bond specified an interest rate of 6 percent payable at the end of each year. The bond matures at the end of 2016. It was sold at a market rate of 8 percent per year. The following spreadsheet was completed:

	Cash Paid	Interest Expense	Amortization	Balance
January 1, 2014				$ 948
End of year 2014	$60	$76	$16	964
End of year 2015	60	77	17	981
End of year 2016	60	79	19	1,000

E10-11
LO10-3

Required:
1. What was the bond's issue price?
2. Did the bond sell at a discount or a premium? How much was the premium or discount?
3. What amount of cash was paid each year for bond interest?
4. What amount of interest expense should be shown each year on the income statement?
5. What amount(s) should be shown on the balance sheet for bonds payable at each year-end? (For year 2016, show the balance just before retirement of the bond.)
6. What method of amortization was used?
7. Show how the following amounts were computed for year 2015: (*a*) $60, (*b*) $77, (*c*) $17, and (*d*) $981.
8. Is the method of amortization that was used preferable? Explain.

Explaining Why Debt Is Sold at a Discount

The annual report of American Airlines contained the following note:

> The Company recorded the issuance of $775 million in bonds (net of $25 million discount) as long-term debt on the consolidated balance sheet. The bonds bear interest at fixed rates, with an average effective rate of 8.06 percent, and mature over various periods of time, with a final maturity in 2031.

After reading this note, an investor asked her financial advisor why the company didn't simply sell the notes for an effective yield of more than 8.06 percent and avoid having to account for a small discount over the next 20 years. Prepare a written response to this question.

E10-12
LO10-3

American Airlines

Evaluating Bond Features

You are a personal financial planner working with a married couple in their early 40s who have decided to invest $100,000 in corporate bonds. You have found two bonds that you think will interest your clients. One is a zero coupon bond issued by PepsiCo with an effective interest rate of 9 percent and a maturity date of 2020. It is callable at par. The other is a Walt Disney bond that matures in 2093. It has an effective interest rate of 9.5 percent and is callable at 105 percent of par. Which bond would you recommend and why? Would your answer be different if you expected interest rates to fall significantly over the next few years? Would you prefer a different bond if the couple were in their late 60s and retired?

E10-13
LO10-1, 10-3

Recording Bond Issue and First Interest Payment with Premium (Straight-Line Amortization)

On January 1, 2014, Victor Corporation sold a $1,400,000, 8 percent bond issue (6 percent market rate). The bonds were dated January 1, 2014, pay interest each June 30 and December 31, and mature in four years.

E10-14
LO10-4

Required:
1. Give the journal entry to record the issuance of the bonds.
2. Give the journal entry to record the interest payment on June 30, 2014. Use straight-line amortization.
3. Show how the bonds payable should be reported on the June 30, 2014, balance sheet and income statement.

E10-15
LO10-4

Recording Bond Issue and First Interest Payment with Premium (Effective-Interest Amortization)

On January 1, 2014, Frog Corporation sold a $2,000,000, 10 percent bond issue (8.5 percent market rate). The bonds were dated January 1, 2014, pay interest each June 30 and December 31, and mature in 10 years.

Required:
1. Give the journal entry to record the issuance of the bonds.
2. Give the journal entry to record the interest payment on June 30, 2014. Use effective-interest amortization.
3. Show how the bonds payable should be reported on the June 30, 2014, financial statements.

E10-16

(Supplement B) Recording Bond Issue and First Interest Payment with Premium (Effective-Interest Amortization with No Premium Account)

Using data from the previous exercise, complete each of the requirements in Exercise 10-15 without using a premium account.

E10-17
LO10-4

Preparing a Debt Payment Schedule with Effective-Interest Method of Amortization and Determining Reported Amounts

Houston Company issued a $10,000, three-year, 5 percent bond on January 1, 2014. The bond interest is paid each December 31. The bond was sold to yield 4 percent.

Required:
1. Complete a bond amortization schedule. Use the effective-interest method.
2. What amounts will be reported on the income statement and balance sheet at the end of 2014, 2015, and 2016?

E10-18
LO10-2, 10-4, 10-5, 10-7

Determining Financial Statement Effects for Bond Issue and First Interest Payment with Premium (Straight-Line Amortization)

Denver Corporation sold a $300,000, 6 percent bond issue on January 1, 2014, at a market rate of 3 percent. The bonds were dated January 1, 2014, with interest to be paid each December 31; they mature in 10 years. The company uses the straight-line method to amortize any discount or premium.

Required:
1. How are the financial statements affected by the issuance of the bonds? Describe the impact on the debt-to-equity and times interest earned ratios, if any.
2. How are the financial statements affected by the payment of interest on December 31? Describe the impact on the debt-to-equity and times interest earned ratios, if any.
3. Show how the bonds payable should be reported on the December 31, 2014, annual financial statements.

E10-19
LO10-4, 10-7

Computing the Issue Price of a Bond with Analysis of Income and Cash Flow Effects

Gateway Company issued a $1 million bond that matures in 10 years. The bond has a 9 percent stated rate of interest. When the bond was issued, the market rate was 8 percent. The bond pays interest each six months. Record the issuance of the bond on June 30. Notice that the company received more than $1 million when it issued the bond. How will this premium affect future income and future cash flows?

E10-20
LO10-6

Reporting the Early Retirement of a Bond

Several years ago, Walters Company issued a $1,000,000 bond at par value. As a result of declining interest rates, the company has decided to call the bond at a call premium of 5 percent. Record the retirement of the bonds.

Reporting the Early Retirement of a Bond with a Discount

The Mira Vista Company issued $1,200,000 in bonds at a discount five years ago. The current book value of the bonds is $1,125,000. The company now has excess cash on hand and plans to retire the bonds. The company must pay a 7 percent (of par) call premium to retire the bonds. Record the retirement of the bonds.

E10-21
LO10-6

Determining Effects on the Statement of Cash Flows

A number of events over the life of a bond have effects that are reported on the statement of cash flows. For each of the following events, determine whether the event affects the statement of cash flows. If so, describe the impact and specify where on the statement the effect is reported.

E10-22
LO10-7

Required:

1. A $1,000,000 bond is issued at a discount. The reported amount of the bond on the balance sheet is $960,000.
2. At year-end, $45,000 accrued interest payable is reported and $1,000 of the bond discount is amortized using the straight-line method.
3. Early in the second year, accrued interest is paid. At the same time, $12,000 interest that accrued in the second year is paid.
4. The company elects to retire the debt in the fifth year. At that time, the reported carrying value of the bonds is $935,000 and the company reports a $20,000 gain on the early retirement of debt.

For more practice with exercises, go to the text website at **www.mhhe.com/libby8e.**

  Mc Graw Hill **connect** |ACCOUNTING

PROBLEMS

Analyzing the Use of Debt

Arbor Corporation's financial statements for 2014 showed the following:

P10-1
LO10-1

Income Statement	
Revenues	$300,000
Expenses	(196,000)
Interest expense	(3,600)
Pretax income	100,400
Income tax (30%)	(30,120)
Net income	$ 70,280

Balance Sheet	
Assets	$360,000
Liabilities (average interest rate, 9%)	$ 40,000
Common stock, par $10	230,000
Retained earnings	90,000
	$360,000

Notice in these data that the company had a debt of only $40,000 compared with common stock outstanding of $230,000. A consultant recommended the following: debt, $90,000 (at 9 percent) and common stock outstanding of $180,000 (18,000 shares). That is, the company should finance the business with more debt and less owner contribution.

Required (round to nearest percent):

1. You have been asked to develop a comparison between (*a*) the actual results and (*b*) the results had the consultant's recommendation been followed. To do this, you develop the following schedule:

Item	Actual Results for 2014	Results with an Increase in Debt and Reduction in Equity
a. Total debt		
b. Total assets		
c. Total stockholders' equity		
d. Interest expense (total at 9 percent)		
e. Net income		
f. Return on total assets		
g. Earnings available to stockholders:		
(1) Amount		
(2) Per share		
(3) Return on stockholders' equity		

2. Based on the completed schedule in requirement (1), provide a comparative analysis and interpretation of the actual results and the consultant's recommendation.

P10-2
LO10-2

Reporting Bonds Issued at Par (AP10-1)

On January 1, 2014, Nowell Company issued $500,000 in bonds that mature in five years. The bonds have a stated interest rate of 8 percent and pay interest on June 30 and December 31 each year. When the bonds were sold, the market rate of interest was 8 percent.

Required:
1. What was the issue price on January 1, 2014?
2. What amount of interest expense should be recorded on (*a*) June 30, 2014? and (*b*) December 31, 2014?
3. What amount of cash interest should be paid on (*a*) June 30, 2014? and (*b*) December 31, 2014?
4. What is the book value of the bonds on (*a*) December 31, 2014? and (*b*) December 31, 2015?

P10-3
LO10-2, 10-3, 10-4

Completing Schedule Comparing Bonds Issued at Par, Discount, and Premium (Straight-Line Amortization) (AP10-2)

Barnett Corporation sold a $500,000, 7 percent bond issue on January 1, 2014. The bonds pay interest each June 30 and December 31 and mature 10 years from January 1, 2014. For comparative study and analysis, assume three separate cases. Use straight-line amortization and disregard income tax unless specifically required. Assume three independent selling scenarios:

Required:
Complete the following schedule as of December 31, 2014, to analyze the differences among the three cases.

	Case A (Par)	Case B (at 98)	Case C (at 103)
a. Cash received at issue			
b. Bond interest expense, pretax for 2014			
c. Bonds payable, 7 percent			
d. Unamortized discount			
e. Unamortized premium			
f. Net liability			
g. Stated interest rate			

P10-4
LO10-2, 10-3, 10-4

Comparing Bonds Issued at Par, Discount, and Premium (Straight-Line Amortization)

Akron Corporation, whose annual accounting period ends on December 31, issued the following bonds:

Date of bonds: January 1, 2014
Maturity amount and date: $100,000 due in 10 years
Interest: 10 percent per annum payable each June 30 and December 31
Date sold: January 1, 2014
Straight-line amortization is used.

Required:

1. Provide the following amounts to be reported on the December 31, 2014, financial statements:

	Issued at Par Case A	at 99 Case B	at 104 Case C
a. Interest expense	$	$	$
b. Bonds payable			
c. Unamortized premium or discount			
d. Net liability			
e. Stated rate of interest			
f. Cash interest paid			

2. Explain why items (*a*) and (*f*) in requirement (1) are different.

3. Assume that you are an investment adviser and a retired person has written to you asking, "Why should I buy a bond at a premium when I can find one at a discount? Isn't that stupid? It's like paying list price for a car instead of negotiating a discount." Write a brief letter in response to the question.

Determining Reported Amounts with Discussion of Management Strategy (Effective-Interest Amortization)

P10-5
LO10-2, 10-3, 10-5

On January 1, 2014, Cunningham Corporation issued $200,000 in bonds that mature in 10 years. The bonds have a stated interest rate of 6 percent and pay interest on December 31. When the bonds were sold, the market rate of interest was 8 percent. The company uses the effective-interest method. By December 31, 2014, the market rate of interest had increased to 10 percent.

Required:

1. What amount of bond liability is recorded on January 1, 2014?
2. What amount of interest expense is recorded on December 31, 2014?
3. As a manager of a company, would you prefer the straight-line or effective-interest method of amortization?
4. Determine the impact of these transactions at year-end on the debt-to-equity ratio and times interest earned ratio.

Reporting Bonds Issued at a Discount (Straight-Line Amortization) (AP10-3)

P10-6
LO10-3

On January 1, 2014, Antonio Company issued $700,000 in bonds that mature in 10 years. The bonds have a stated interest rate of 8 percent and pay interest on June 30 and December 31 each year. When the bonds were sold, the market rate of interest was 10 percent. The company uses the straight-line amortization method.

Required:

1. What was the issue price on January 1, 2014?
2. What amount of interest expense should be recorded on (*a*) June 30, 2014? and (*b*) December 31, 2014?
3. What amount of cash interest should be paid on (*a*) June 30, 2014? and (*b*) December 31, 2014?
4. What is the book value of the bonds on (*a*) June 30, 2014? and (*b*) December 31, 2014?

Reporting Bonds Issued at a Discount (Effective-Interest Amortization) (AP10-4)

P10-7
LO10-3

On January 1, 2014, TCU Utilities issued $1,000,000 in bonds that mature in 10 years. The bonds have a stated interest rate of 10 percent and pay interest on June 30 and December 31 each year. When the bonds were sold, the market rate of interest was 12 percent. The company uses the effective-interest amortization method.

Required:

1. What was the issue price on January 1, 2014?
2. What amount of interest expense should be recorded on (*a*) June 30, 2014? and (*b*) December 31, 2014?
3. What amount of cash interest should be paid on (*a*) June 30, 2014? and (*b*) December 31, 2014?
4. What is the book value of the bonds on (*a*) June 30, 2014? and (*b*) December 31, 2014?

P10-8

LO10-3, 10-5

www.mhhe.com/libby8e

Computing Amounts for Bond Issue and Comparing Amortization Methods

Electrolux Corporation manufactures electrical test equipment. The company's board of directors authorized a bond issue on January 1, 2014, with the following terms:

> Maturity (par) value: $800,000
> Interest: 8 percent per annum payable each December 31
> Maturity date: December 31, 2018
> Effective-interest rate when sold: 12 percent

Required:
1. Compute the bond issue price. Explain why both the stated and effective-interest rates are used in this computation.
2. Assume that the company used the straight-line method to amortize the discount on the bond issue. Compute the following amounts for each year (2014–2018):
   a. Cash payment for bond interest.
   b. Amortization of bond discount or premium.
   c. Bond interest expense.
3. Assume instead that the company used the effective-interest method to amortize the discount. Prepare an effective-interest bond amortization schedule similar to the one in the text. The effective-interest method provides a constant interest rate when interest expense is related to the net liability. Explain by referring to the bond amortization schedule.
4. Which method should the company use to amortize the bond discount? As a financial analyst, would you prefer one method over the other? If so, why?

P10-9

LO10-4

www.mhhe.com/libby8e

Reporting Bonds Issued at a Premium (Straight-Line Amortization) (AP10-5)

On January 1, 2014, Vigeland Corporation issued $2,000,000 in bonds that mature in 10 years. The bonds have a stated interest rate of 10 percent and pay interest on June 30 and December 31 each year. When the bonds were sold, the market rate of interest was 8 percent. The company uses the straight-line amortization method.

Required:
1. What was the issue price on January 1, 2014?
2. What amount of interest expense should be recorded on (*a*) June 30, 2014? and (*b*) December 31, 2014?
3. What amount of cash interest should be paid on (*a*) June 30, 2014? and (*b*) December 31, 2014?
4. What is the book value of the bonds on (*a*) June 30, 2014? and (*b*) December 31, 2014?

P10-10

LO10-4

Reporting Bonds Issued at a Premium (Effective-Interest Amortization) (AP10-6)

On January 1, 2014, Cron Corporation issued $700,000 in bonds that mature in five years. The bonds have a stated interest rate of 13 percent and pay interest on June 30 and December 31 each year. When the bonds were sold, the market rate of interest was 12 percent. The company uses the effective-interest amortization method.

Required:
1. What was the issue price on January 1, 2014?
2. What amount of interest expense should be recorded on (*a*) June 30, 2014? and (*b*) December 31, 2014?
3. What amount of cash interest should be paid on (*a*) June 30, 2014? and (*b*) December 31, 2014?
4. What is the book value of the bonds on (*a*) June 30, 2014? and (*b*) December 31, 2014?

P10-11

LO10-4

Recording Bond Issuance and Interest Payments (Straight-Line Amortization)

Commonwealth Company issued bonds with the following provisions:

> Maturity value: $300,000
> Interest: 11 percent per annum payable annually each December 31
> Terms: Bonds dated January 1, 2014, due five years from that date

The annual accounting period ends December 31. The bonds were sold on January 1, 2014, at a 10 percent market rate.

Required:

1. Compute the issue (sale) price of the bonds (show computations).
2. Give the journal entry to record the issuance of the bonds.
3. Give the journal entries at the following date (use straight-line amortization): December 31, 2014.
4. How much interest expense would be reported on the income statement for 2014? Show how the liability related to the bonds should be reported on the December 31, 2014, balance sheet.

Completing an Amortization Schedule (Effective-Interest Amortization)

P10-12
LO10-4

www.mhhe.com/libby8e

MBTA Corporation issued bonds and received cash in full for the issue price. The bonds were dated and issued on January 1, 2014. The stated interest rate was payable at the end of each year. The bonds mature at the end of four years. The following schedule has been completed (amounts in thousands):

Date	Cash	Interest	Amortization	Balance
January 1, 2014				$48,808
End of year 2014	$3,600	$3,417	$183	48,625
End of year 2015	3,600	?	?	48,429
End of year 2016	3,600	?	?	?
End of year 2017	3,600	?	?	48,000

Required:

1. Complete the amortization schedule.
2. What was the maturity amount of the bonds?
3. How much cash was received at the date of issuance (sale) of the bonds?
4. Was there a premium or a discount? If so, which and how much?
5. How much cash will be disbursed for interest each period and in total for the full life of the bond issue?
6. What method of amortization is being used? Explain.
7. What is the stated rate of interest?
8. What is the effective rate of interest?
9. What amount of interest expense should be reported on the income statement each year?
10. Show how the bonds should be reported on the balance sheet at the end of each year (show the last year immediately before retirement of the bonds).

Comparing Carrying Value and Market Value

P10-13
LO10-4

DIRECTV is the largest provider of direct-to-home digital television services and the second largest provider in the multichannel video programming distribution industry in the United States. It provides over 16 million subscribers with access to hundreds of channels of digital-quality video pictures and CD-quality audio programming that it transmits directly to subscribers' homes via high-powered geosynchronous satellites. The company's annual report contained the following note:

Long-Term Debt

The unamortized bond premium included in total debt for the current year was $2.8 million and $3.1 million for the prior year.

Required:

Explain why the unamortized premium is included in total debt and why the premium decreased in amount from one year to the next.

Reporting Bond Transactions on the Statement of Cash Flows

P10-14
LO10-7

Determine whether each of the following would be reported in the financing activities section of the statement of cash flows and, if so, specify whether it is a cash inflow or outflow.

1. Sale of bonds at a discount.
2. Payment of interest on a bond.
3. Early retirement of a bond with a 5 percent call premium.
4. Amortization of a bond discount.
5. Payment of bond principal upon maturity.
6. Sale of bond from one investor to another. Transaction was in cash.

ALTERNATE **PROBLEMS**

AP10-1
LO10-2

Reporting Bonds Issued at Par (P10-2)

On January 1, 2014, Trucks R Us Corporation issued $2,000,000 in bonds that mature in five years. The bonds have a stated interest rate of 10 percent and pay interest on June 30 and December 31 each year. When the bonds were sold, the market rate of interest was 10 percent.

Required:
1. What was the issue price on January 1, 2014?
2. What amount of interest expense should be recorded on (*a*) June 30, 2014? and (*b*) December 31, 2014?
3. What amount of cash interest should be paid on (*a*) June 30, 2014? and (*b*) December 31, 2014?
4. What is the book value of the bonds on (*a*) December 31, 2014? and (*b*) December 31, 2015?

AP10-2
LO10-2, 10-3, 10-4

Completing Schedule Comparing Bonds Issued at Par, Discount, and Premium (Straight-Line Amortization) (P10-3)

On January 1, 2014, Bidden Corporation sold and issued $100,000, five-year, 10 percent bonds. The bond interest is payable each June 30 and December 31. Assume three separate and independent selling scenarios: Case A, at par; Case B, at 95; and Case C, at 110.

Required:
Complete a schedule similar to the following for each separate case assuming straight-line amortization of discount and premium. Disregard income tax. Give all dollar amounts in thousands.

	At End of 2014	At End of 2015	At End of 2016	At End of 2017
Case A: Sold at par	$	$	$	$
Interest expense on income statement				
Net liability on balance sheet				
Case B: Sold at a discount				
Interest expense on income statement				
Net liability on balance sheet				
Case C: Sold at a premium				
Interest expense on income statement				
Net liability on balance sheet				

AP10-3
LO10-3

Reporting Bonds Issued at a Discount (Straight-Line Amortization) (P10-6)

On January 1, 2014, Kennedy Corporation issued $1,000,000 in bonds that mature in five years. The bonds have a stated interest rate of 7 percent and pay interest on December 31 each year. When the bonds were sold, the market rate of interest was 9 percent. The company uses the straight-line amortization method.

Required:
1. What was the issue price on January 1, 2014?
2. What amount of interest expense should be recorded on (*a*) December 31, 2014? and (*b*) December 31, 2015?
3. What amount of cash interest should be paid on (*a*) December 31, 2014? and (*b*) December 31, 2015?
4. What is the book value of the bonds on (*a*) December 31, 2014? and (*b*) December 31, 2015?

AP10-4
LO10-3

Reporting Bonds Issued at a Discount (Effective-Interest Amortization) (P10-7)

On January 1, 2014, Avaya Corporation issued $2,000,000 in bonds that mature in five years. The bonds have a stated interest rate of 6 percent and pay interest on December 31 each year. When the bonds were sold, the market rate of interest was 7 percent. The company uses the effective-interest amortization method.

Required:
1. What was the issue price on January 1, 2014?
2. What amount of interest expense should be recorded on (*a*) December 31, 2014? and (*b*) December 31, 2015?
3. What amount of cash interest should be paid on (*a*) December 31, 2014? and (*b*) December 31, 2015?
4. What is the book value of the bonds on (*a*) December 31, 2014? and (*b*) December 31, 2015?

Reporting Bonds Issued at a Premium (Straight-Line Amortization) (P10-9)

AP10-5
LO10-4

On January 1, 2014, Grand Isle Corporation issued $900,000 in bonds that mature in five years. The bonds have a stated interest rate of 10 percent and pay interest on December 31 each year. When the bonds were sold, the market rate of interest was 9 percent. The company uses the straight-line amortization method.

Required:
1. What was the issue price on January 1, 2014?
2. What amount of interest expense should be recorded on (*a*) December 31, 2014? and (*b*) December 31, 2015?
3. What amount of cash interest should be paid on (*a*) December 31, 2014? and (*b*) December 31, 2015?
4. What is the book value of the bonds on (*a*) December 31, 2014? and (*b*) December 31, 2015?

Reporting Bonds Issued at a Premium (Effective-Interest Amortization) (P10-10)

AP10-6
LO10-4

On January 1, 2014, Thomas Insurance Corporation issued $4,000,000 in bonds that mature in five years. The bonds have a stated interest rate of 9 percent and pay interest on December 31 each year. When the bonds were sold, the market rate of interest was 6 percent. The company uses the effective-interest amortization method.

Required:
1. What was the issue price on January 1, 2014?
2. What amount of interest expense should be recorded on (*a*) December 31, 2014? and (*b*) December 31, 2015?
3. What amount of cash interest should be paid on (*a*) December 31, 2014? and (*b*) December 31, 2015?
4. What is the book value of the bonds on (*a*) December 31, 2014? and (*b*) December 31, 2015?

CASES **AND PROJECTS**

Annual Report Cases

Finding Financial Information

CP10-1
LO10-1, 10-2

Refer to the financial statements of American Eagle Outfitters given in Appendix B at the end of this book.

AMERICAN EAGLE
OUTFITTERS, INC.

Required:
1. Did American Eagle repay a portion of its note payable during the year ended January 29, 2011? If so, what was the amount of the payment?
2. Explain why the company does not report bonds payable on its balance sheet.
3. Describe the company's established arrangements, if any, that permit it to borrow money if needed.

Finding Financial Information

CP10-2
LO10-1, 10-2

Refer to the financial statements of Urban Outfitters given in Appendix C at the end of this book.

URBAN OUTFITTERS INC.

Required:
1. Unlike most companies, Urban Outfitters does not report the amount of interest paid in cash during the most recent reporting year. Explain why you think the company has omitted this information.
2. Explain why the company does not report bonds payable on its balance sheet.
3. Describe the company's established arrangements, if any, that permit it to borrow money if needed.

CP10-3
LO10-2, 10-5, 10-7

AMERICAN EAGLE OUTFITTERS, INC.

URBN
URBAN OUTFITTERS INC.

www.mhhe.com/libby8e

CP10-4
LO10-3

JCPenney *Every Day Matters'*

CP10-5
LO10-1

CP10-6
LO10-1

CP10-7
LO10-1, 10-2, 10-3, 10-4, 10-5, 10-7

Comparing Companies within an Industry

Refer to the financial statements of American Eagle (Appendix B) and Urban Outfitters (Appendix C) and the Industry Ratio Report (Appendix D) at the end of this book. Most companies report some amounts of bonds payable on their balance sheets. It is somewhat surprising, therefore, that neither company reports any bond liabilities.

Required:
1. Examine the statements of cash flow for both companies. What is the primary source for cash flow for both companies?
2. Two financial ratios (the debt-to-equity ratio and the times interest earned ratio) are discussed in this chapter. Are they relevant for these companies? Explain.

Analyzing Zero Coupon Bonds from an Actual Company

JCPenney Company was one of the first companies to issue zero coupon bonds. It issued bonds with a face (maturity) value of $400 million due eight years after issuance. When the bonds were sold to the public, similar bonds paid 15 percent effective interest. An article in *Forbes* magazine discussed the JCPenney bonds and stated: "It's easy to see why corporations like to sell bonds that don't pay interest. But why would anybody want to buy that kind of paper [bond]?"

Required:
1. Explain why an investor would buy a JCPenney bond with a zero interest rate.
2. If investors could earn 15 percent on similar investments, how much did JCPenney receive when it issued the bonds with a face value of $400 million?

Critical Thinking Cases

Evaluating an Ethical Dilemma

You work for a small company that is considering investing in a new Internet business. Financial projections suggest that the company will be able to earn in excess of $40 million per year on an investment of $100 million. The company president suggests borrowing the money by issuing bonds that will carry a 7 percent interest rate. He says, "This is better than printing money! We won't have to invest a penny of our own money, and we get to keep $33 million per year after we pay interest to the bondholders." As you think about the proposed transaction, you feel a little uncomfortable about taking advantage of the creditors in this fashion. You feel that it must be wrong to earn such a high return by using money that belongs to other people. Is this an ethical business transaction?

Evaluating an Ethical Dilemma

Assume that you are a portfolio manager for a large insurance company. The majority of the money you manage is from retired school teachers who depend on the income you earn on their investments. You have invested a significant amount of money in the bonds of a large corporation and have just received a call from the company's president explaining that it is unable to meet its current interest obligations because of deteriorating business operations related to increased international competition. The president has a recovery plan that will take at least two years. During that time, the company will not be able to pay interest on the bonds and, she admits, if the plan does not work, bondholders will probably lose more than half of their money. As a creditor, you can force the company into immediate bankruptcy and probably get back at least 90 percent of the bondholders' money. You also know that your decision will cause at least 10,000 people to lose their jobs if the company ceases operations. Given only these two options, what should you do?

Financial Reporting and Analysis Team Project

Team Project: Examining an Annual Report

As a team, select an industry to analyze. *Yahoo!Finance* provides lists of industries at biz.yahoo.com/p/industries.html. Click on an industry for a list of companies in that industry. Alternatively, go to Google Finance at www.google.com/finance and search for a company you are interested in. You will be presented with a list including that company and its competitors. Each team member should acquire the annual report or 10-K for one publicly traded company in the industry, with each member selecting a different company (the SEC EDGAR service at www.sec.gov or the company's investor relations website itself are good sources).

Required:

On an individual basis, each team member should write a short report answering the following questions about the selected company. Discuss any patterns across the companies that you as a team observe. Then, as a team, write a short report comparing and contrasting your companies.

1. Has your company issued any long-term bonds or notes? If so, read the footnote and list any unusual features (e.g., callable, convertible, secured by specific collateral).
2. If your company issued any bonds, were they issued at either a premium or a discount? If so, does the company use the straight-line or effective-interest amortization method?
3. Ratio analysis:
   a. What does the debt-to-equity ratio measure in general?
   b. Compute the ratio for the last three years.
   c. What do your results suggest about the company?
   d. If available, find the industry ratio for the most recent year, compare it to your results, and discuss why you believe your company differs from or is similar to the industry ratio.
4. Ratio analysis:
   a. What does the times interest earned ratio measure in general?
   b. Compute the ratio for the last three years. If interest expense is not separately disclosed, you will not be able to compute the ratio. If so, state why you think it is not separately disclosed.
   c. What do your results suggest about the company?
   d. If available, find the industry ratio for the most recent year, compare it to your results, and discuss why you believe your company differs from or is similar to the industry ratio.
5. During the recent year, how much cash did the company receive on issuing debt? How much did it pay on debt principal? What does management suggest were the reasons for issuing and/or repaying debt during the year?

CONTINUING **CASE**

Recording and Reporting Liabilities

CC10-1

≋POOLCORP

Pool Corporation, Inc., is the world's largest wholesale distributor of swimming pool supplies and equipment. It is a publicly traded corporation that trades on the NASDAQ exchange under the symbol POOL. It sells these products to swimming pool repair and service businesses, swimming pool builders, and retail swimming pool stores. The majority of these customers are small, family-owned businesses. The current financial statements for Pool show that the company borrowed approximately $750,000,000 during 2011. For purposes of this case, assume that Pool borrowed the money on January 1, 2011, at an interest rate of 4 percent when the market rate was also 4 percent. The debt matures in 10 years. Pool pays interest on this debt on June 30th and December 31st each year.

Required:

1. What was the issue price on January 1, 2011?
2. What amount of interest should be recorded on June 30, 2011? How much on December 31, 2011?
3. What amount of cash interest should be paid on June 30, 2011? How much on December 31, 2011?
4. What is the book value of the bonds on December 31, 2011? What is the amount on December 31, 2012?

Reporting and Interpreting Owners' Equity

The Kroger Co. (Kroger) is a familiar name for U.S. consumers. The popular supermarket chain was founded in 1883 and now operates 2,435 supermarkets, 791 convenience stores, and 348 fine jewelry stores. The company is one of the largest retailers in the United States based on annual sales, ranking in the top 25 of the Fortune 100 list. The typical Kroger supermarket stocks approximately 14,000 individual items with 27 percent of its sales volume coming from private label merchandise, many of which are manufactured by Kroger. The Kroger Co.'s growth strategy is based on increasing sales by improving its existing store base through remodels. The company currently makes nearly $2 billion in capital expenditures each year. Through this strategy, management seeks to provide short-term results for shareholders while continuing to invest in the long-term growth of the company.

In this chapter, we study the role that stockholders' equity plays in building a successful business and strategies that managers use to maximize stockholders' wealth.

UNDERSTANDING THE BUSINESS

To some people, the words *corporation* and *business* are almost synonymous. You've probably heard friends refer to a career in business as "the corporate world." Equating business with

Learning Objectives

After studying this chapter, you should be able to:

11-1   Explain the role of stock in the capital structure of a corporation. p. 547

11-2   Analyze the earnings per share ratio. p. 549

11-3   Describe the characteristics of common stock and analyze transactions affecting common stock. p. 549

11-4   Discuss dividends and analyze transactions. p. 553

11-5   Analyze the dividend yield ratio. p. 553

11-6   Discuss the purpose of stock dividends and stock splits, and report transactions. p. 556

11-7   Describe the characteristics of preferred stock and analyze transactions affecting preferred stock. p. 560

11-8   Discuss the impact of capital stock transactions on cash flows. p. 562

FOCUS COMPANY:

The Kroger Co.

FINANCING CORPORATE
GROWTH WITH CAPITAL
SUPPLIED BY OWNERS

www.kroger.com

corporations is understandable because corporations are the dominant form of business organization in terms of volume of operations. If you were to write the names of 50 familiar businesses on a piece of paper, probably all of them would be corporations.

The popularity of the corporate form can be attributed to a critical advantage that corporations have over sole proprietorships and partnerships: They can raise large amounts of capital because both large and small investors can easily participate in their ownership. This ease of participation is related to several factors.

- Shares of stock can be purchased in small amounts. You could buy a single share of Kroger Co. stock for about $25 and become one of the owners of this successful company.
- Ownership interests can be easily transferred through the sale of shares on established markets such as the New York Stock Exchange.
- Stock ownership provides investors with limited liability. In the event of bankruptcy, creditors have claims against only the corporation's assets, not the assets of the individual owners.

Many Americans own stock either directly or indirectly through a mutual fund or pension program. Stock ownership offers them the opportunity to earn higher returns than they could on deposits to bank accounts or investments in corporate bonds. Unfortunately, stock ownership also involves higher risk. The proper balance between risk and the expected return on an investment depends on individual preferences.

EXHIBIT 11.1

Excerpt from Consolidated
Balance Sheets for
The Kroger Co.

REAL WORLD EXCERPT
Annual Report

THE KROGER CO.
Consolidated Balance Sheets
(on millions, except par values)

	January 28, 2012	January 29, 2011
Shareowners' Equity		
Preferred shares, $100 par per share, 5 shares authorized and unissued	—	—
Common shares, $1 par per share, 1,000 shares authorized; 959 shares issued in 2011 and 2010	959	959
Additional paid-in capital	3,427	3,394
Accumulated other comprehensive loss	(844)	(550)
Accumulated earnings	8,571	8,225
Common stock in treasury, at cost, 398 shares in 2011 and 339 shares in 2010	(8,132)	(6,732)
Total Shareowners' Equity—The Kroger Co.	$ 3,981	$ 5,296

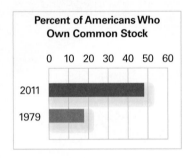

Percent of Americans Who Own Common Stock

	0 10 20 30 40 50 60
2011	
1979	

Exhibit 11.1 presents financial information from The Kroger Co.'s annual report. Notice that the stockholders' equity section of the balance sheet lists two primary sources of stockholders' equity:

1. Contributed capital from the sale of stock. This is the amount of money stockholders invested through the purchase of shares. For Kroger, contributed capital is the sum of common stock ($959 million) plus additional paid-in capital ($3,427 million).

2. Retained earnings (sometimes called accumulated earnings) generated by the company's profit-making activities. This is the cumulative amount of net income the corporation has earned since its organization less the cumulative amount of dividends paid since organization. While most companies call this amount retained earnings, Kroger uses the name accumulated earnings.

Most companies generate a significant portion of their stockholders' equity from retained earnings. In the case of The Kroger Co., retained earnings is actually more than the original capital invested by shareholders.

ORGANIZATION of the Chapter

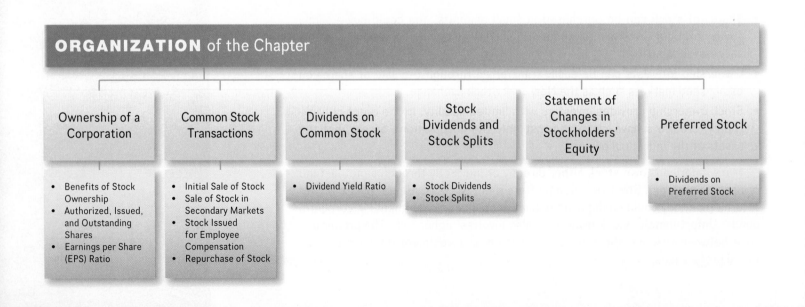

OWNERSHIP OF A CORPORATION

The corporation is the only business form the law recognizes as a separate entity. As a distinct entity, the corporation enjoys a continuous existence separate and apart from its owners. It may own assets, incur liabilities, expand and contract in size, sue others, be sued, and enter into contracts independently of its stockholder owners.

To protect everyone's rights, the creation and governance of corporations are tightly regulated by law. Corporations are created by application to a state government (not the federal government). On approval of the application, the state issues a charter, sometimes called the articles of incorporation. Corporations are governed by a board of directors elected by the stockholders.

Each state has different laws governing the organization of corporations created within its boundaries. The Kroger Co. has its headquarters in Ohio and it has elected to incorporate in the state of Ohio. You will find that an unusually large number of corporations are incorporated in Delaware even though their headquarters are located in a different state. Companies choose Delaware for incorporation because the state has some of the most favorable laws for establishing corporations.

Benefits of Stock Ownership

When you invest in a corporation, you are known as a stockholder or shareholder. As a stockholder, you receive shares of stock that you subsequently can sell on established stock exchanges. Owners of common stock receive a number of benefits:

> **LEARNING OBJECTIVE 11-1**
> Explain the role of stock in the capital structure of a corporation.

- **A voice in management.** You may vote in the stockholders' meeting on major issues concerning management of the corporation.
- **Dividends.** You receive a proportional share of the distribution of profits.
- **Residual claim.** You will receive a proportional share of the distribution of remaining assets upon the liquidation of the company.

Owners, unlike creditors, are able to vote at the annual stockholders' meeting with a number of votes equal to the number of shares owned. The following notice of the annual meeting of shareholders was recently sent to all owners of Kroger Co. stock:

NOTICE OF ANNUAL MEETING OF SHAREHOLDERS

Cincinnati, Ohio,
May 11, 2012

To All Shareholders of The Kroger Co.:

The annual meeting of shareholders of The Kroger Co. will be held at the MUSIC HALL BALLROOM, MUSIC HALL, 1241 Elm Street, Cincinnati, Ohio 45202, on June 21, 2012, at 11 a.m., eastern time, for the following purposes:

1. *To elect the directors for the ensuing year;*
2. *To consider and act upon an advisory vote to approve executive compensation;*
3. *To consider and act upon a proposal to ratify the selection of independent public accountants for the year 2012;*
4. *To act upon two shareholder proposals, if properly presented at the annual meeting; and*
5. *To transact such other business as may properly be brought before the meeting;*

all as set forth in the Proxy Statement accompanying this Notice. Holders of common shares of record at the close of business on April 23, 2012, will be entitled to vote at the meeting.

REAL WORLD EXCERPT
Notice of
Shareholders' Meeting

This notice also contained several pages of information concerning the people who were nominated to be members of the board of directors as well as a variety of financial information. Since most owners do not actually attend the annual meeting, the notice included a proxy card, which is similar to an absentee ballot. Owners may complete the proxy and mail it to the company, which includes it in the votes at the annual meeting.

Stockholders have ultimate authority in a corporation. The board of directors and, indirectly, all employees are accountable to the stockholders.

Authorized, Issued, and Outstanding Shares

The corporate charter specifies the maximum number of shares that can be sold to the public. The financial statements must report information concerning the number of shares that have been sold to date. Let's look at the share information reported by The Kroger Co. as of January 28, 2012, shown in Exhibit 11.1. For Kroger, the maximum number of common shares that can be sold, called the **authorized number of shares,** is 1,000,000,000. As of January 28, 2012, the company had sold 959,000,000 shares. Stock that has been sold to the public is called **issued shares.**

For a number of reasons, a company might want to buy back stock that already been sold to the public. Stock that has been bought back is called *treasury stock.* When a company buys back its stock, a difference is created between the number of issued shares and the number of **outstanding shares,** or shares currently held by individual stockholders. We can compute outstanding shares for The Kroger Co. using data from the January 28, 2012, balance sheet shown in Exhibit 11.1:

The **AUTHORIZED NUMBER OF SHARES** is the maximum number of shares of a corporation's capital stock that can be issued as specified in the charter.

ISSUED SHARES represent the total number of shares of stock that have been sold.

OUTSTANDING SHARES refer to the total number of shares of stock that are owned by stockholders on any particular date.

Issued shares	959,000,000
Less: Treasury stock	(398,000,000)
Outstanding shares	561,000,000

Notice that when treasury stock is held, the number of shares issued and the number of shares outstanding differ by the number of shares of treasury stock held (treasury stock is included in "issued" but not in "outstanding"). The number of shares outstanding is important to financial analysts who need to express certain dollar amounts on a per share basis. One example is the earnings per share ratio.

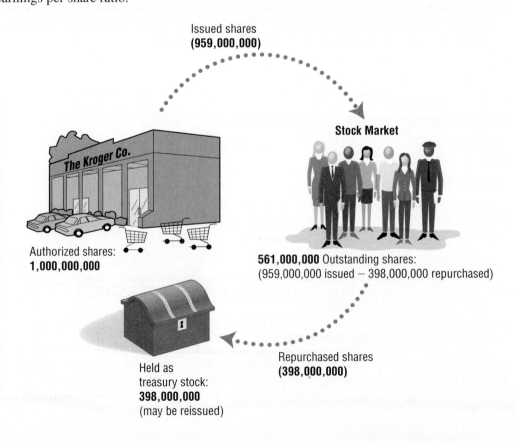

Issued shares
(959,000,000)

Stock Market

Authorized shares:
1,000,000,000

561,000,000 Outstanding shares:
(959,000,000 issued − 398,000,000 repurchased)

Held as
treasury stock:
398,000,000
(may be reissued)

Repurchased shares
(398,000,000)

Earnings Per Share (EPS)

? **ANALYTICAL QUESTION**

How well is a company performing?

% **RATIO AND COMPARISONS**

Earnings per share is computed as follows:

> **Earnings per Share = Net Income* ÷ Average Number of Common Shares Outstanding**
>
> *Preferred dividends, if any, should be subtracted from net income.

The 2012 ratio for The Kroger Co.:

$$\$602 \text{ million} \div 597 \text{ (million) shares*} = \$1.01$$

COMPARISONS OVER TIME			COMPARISONS WITH COMPETITORS	
Kroger			Whole Foods	Safeway
2010	2011	2012	2012	2012
$0.11	$1.75	$1.01	$1.96	$1.49

*As reported in the notes to the financial statements.

💡 **INTERPRETATIONS**

In General   All analysts and investors are interested in a company's earnings. You have probably seen newspaper headlines announcing a company's earnings. Notice that those news stories normally report earnings on an earnings per share (EPS) basis. EPS is a popular measure because income numbers are much easier to compare on a per share basis. For example, in 2012, The Kroger Co. earned income of $596 (million) compared to $1,249 (million) in the previous year, a very significant decrease. If we make that comparison on a per share basis, we see a similar decrease but a smaller percent. The EPS declined by a smaller percent because fewer shares were outstanding in 2012. EPS is also useful in comparing companies of different sizes. Whole Foods is a smaller company than Kroger, with income of $342.6 (million) in 2012. While net income for Whole Foods was less than 58 percent of the net income earned by The Kroger Co., EPS for Whole Foods was nearly twice the EPS for Kroger.

Focus Company Analysis   The Kroger Co. has a strategy of growth and reinvestment of earnings. Analysts are watching EPS to be sure the company will achieve its strategy. Kroger's EPS increased significantly between 2010 and 2012, indicating a strong level of growth considering the difficult economic environment during that period.

A Few Cautions   While EPS is an effective and widely used measure of profitability, it can be misleading if there are significant differences in the market values of the shares being compared. Two companies earning $1.50 per share might appear to be comparable, but if shares in one company cost $10 while shares of the other cost $175, they are not comparable. The stock price for Whole Foods is over $80 per share while the price for Kroger stock is $25. Obviously, investors expect a large EPS number for companies with higher stock prices.

COMMON STOCK TRANSACTIONS

Most corporations issue two types of stock, common stock and preferred stock. All corporations must issue common stock, but only some issue preferred stock. In this section, we discuss common stock and in a subsequent section, we discuss preferred stock.

Common stock is held by individuals who are often thought of as the "owners" of the corporation because they have the right to vote and share in the profitability of the business through dividends. Periodically, the board of directors declares dividends based on the company's profitability.

The fact that common stock dividends may increase with increases in the company's profitability helps to explain why investors can make money in the stock market. Basically, you

COMMON STOCK is the basic voting stock issued by a corporation.

can think of the price of a share of stock as the present value of all its future dividends. If a company's profitability improves so that it can pay higher dividends, the present value of its common stock will increase.

PAR VALUE is the nominal value per share of capital stock specified in the charter; serves as the basis for legal capital.

Common stock normally has a **par value,** a nominal value per share established in the corporate charter. Par value has no relationship to the market value of a stock. The annual report for The Kroger Co. states that the common stock has a par value of $1, while its market value is more than $20 per share.

Most states require stock to have a par value. The original purpose of this requirement was to protect creditors by specifying a permanent amount of capital that owners could not withdraw before a bankruptcy, which would leave creditors with an empty corporate shell. This permanent amount of capital is called **legal capital.** Today, this requirement has little importance because of other contractual protections for creditors.

LEGAL CAPITAL is the permanent amount of capital defined by state law that must remain invested in the business; serves as a cushion for creditors.

Some states require the issuance of **no-par value stock,** which does not have a specified amount per share. When a corporation issues no-par stock, legal capital is as defined by the state law.

NO-PAR VALUE STOCK is capital stock that has no par value specified in the corporate charter.

Initial Sale of Stock

Two names are applied to transactions involving the initial sale of a company's stock to the public. An **initial public offering,** or IPO, involves the very first sale of a company's stock to the public (i.e., when the company first "goes public"). You have probably heard stories of Internet stocks that have increased dramatically in value the day of the IPO. While investors sometimes earn significant returns on IPOs, they also take significant risks. Once a company's stock has been traded on established markets, additional sales of new stock to the public are called **seasoned new issues.**

Most sales of stock to the public are cash transactions. To illustrate the accounting for an initial sale of stock, assume that The Kroger Co. sold 100,000 shares of its $1 par value stock for $20 per share. The company would record the following journal entry:

Cash (+A) (100,000 × $20).............................	2,000,000	
Common stock (+SE) (100,000 × $1)..................		100,000
Capital in excess of par (+SE)		1,900,000

Assets		=	Liabilities	+	Stockholders' Equity	
Cash	+2,000,000				Common stock	+100,000
					Capital in excess of par	+1,900,000

Notice that the Common Stock account is credited for the number of shares sold times the par value per share, and the Capital in Excess of Par account is credited for the remainder. If the corporate charter does not specify a par value for the stock, the stated value is used in the same manner that par value is used. If there is no par or stated value, the entire proceeds from the sale will be entered in the common stock account.

Sale of Stock in Secondary Markets

When a company sells stock to the public, the transaction is between the issuing corporation and the buyer. Subsequent to the initial sale, investors can sell shares to other investors without directly affecting the corporation. For example, if investor Jon Drago sold 1,000 shares of The Kroger Co. stock to Jennifer Lea, The Kroger Co. would not record a journal entry on its books. Mr. Drago received cash for the shares he sold, and Ms. Lea received stock for the cash she paid. The Kroger Co. did not receive or pay anything.

Each business day, *The Wall Street Journal* reports the results of thousands of transactions between investors in secondary markets, such as the New York Stock Exchange (NYSE), the American Stock Exchange (AMEX), and the NASDAQ market. Managers of corporations closely follow the price movements of their company's stock. Stockholders expect to earn money on their investments through both dividends and increases in the stock price. In many instances, senior management has been replaced because of a stock's poor performance in the stock market. While managers watch the stock price on a daily basis, transactions between investors do not directly affect the company's financial statements.

Stock Issued for Employee Compensation

One of the advantages of the corporate form is the ability to separate the management of a business from its ownership. Separation can also be a disadvantage because some managers may not act in the owners' best interests. This problem can be overcome in a number of ways. Compensation packages can be developed to reward managers for meeting goals that are important to stockholders. Another strategy is to offer managers stock options, which permit them to buy stock at a fixed price.

The holder of a stock option has an interest in a company's performance just as an owner does. Stock option plans have become an increasingly common form of compensation over the past few years. Indeed, 98 percent of the companies surveyed by *Accounting Trends & Techniques*[1] now offer stock option plans to their employees.

The Kroger Co. offers employees stock options as part of their compensation. The options specify that shares may be bought at the then-current market price. Granting a stock option is a form of compensation, even if the grant price and the current stock price are the same. You can think of a stock option as a risk-free investment. If you hold a stock option and the stock price declines, you have lost nothing. If the stock price increases, you can exercise your option at the low grant price and sell the stock at the higher price for a profit.

Companies must estimate and report compensation expense associated with stock options. These procedures are discussed in more detail in intermediate accounting courses.

Repurchase of Stock

A corporation may want to repurchase its stock from existing stockholders for a number of reasons. One common reason is the existence of an employee bonus plan that provides workers with shares of the company's stock as part of their compensation. Because of Securities and Exchange Commission regulations concerning newly issued shares, most companies find it less costly to give employees repurchased shares than to issue new ones. Stock that has been reacquired and is held by the issuing corporation is called **treasury stock.** These shares have no voting, dividend, or other stockholder rights while they are held as treasury stock.

TREASURY STOCK is a corporation's own stock that has been issued but subsequently reacquired and is still being held by that corporation.

Most companies record the purchase of treasury stock based on the cost of the shares that were purchased. Assume that The Kroger Co. bought 100,000 shares of its stock in the open market when it was selling for $20 per share. Using the cost method, the company would record the following journal entry:

Treasury stock (+XSE, −SE) (100,000 × $20)	2,000,000	
Cash (−A)		2,000,000

Assets		=	Liabilities	+	Stockholders' Equity	
Cash	−2,000,000				Treasury stock	−2,000,000

Intuitively, many students expect the Treasury Stock account to be reported as an asset. Such is not the case because a company cannot create an asset by investing in itself. The Treasury

Ms. Lea   Stock   Mr. Drago

Cash

[1]Reprinted with permission from *Accounting Trends & Techniques.* Copyright © 2008 by the American Institute of Certified Public Accountants, Inc.

Treasury Stock

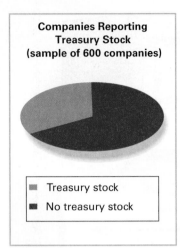

Companies Reporting Treasury Stock (sample of 600 companies)

■ Treasury stock
■ No treasury stock

Stock account is actually a contra-equity account, which means that it is subtracted from total stockholders' equity. This practice makes sense because treasury stock is stock that is no longer outstanding and therefore should not be included in stockholders' equity.

As the information in Exhibit 11.1 indicates, The Kroger Co. reported treasury stock in the amount of $8,132 (million) on its balance sheet as of January 28, 2012. The statement of stockholders' equity reports the same amount plus additional information.

When a company sells its treasury stock, it does not report an accounting profit or loss on the transaction, even if it sells the stock for more or less than it paid. GAAP does not permit a corporation to report income or losses from investments in its own stock because transactions with the owners are not considered normal profit-making activities. Based on the previous example, assume that The Kroger Co. re-sold 10,000 shares of treasury stock for $30 per share. Remember that the company had purchased the stock for $20 per share. Kroger would record the following journal entry:

Cash (+A) (10,000 × $30).	300,000	
Treasury stock (−XSE, +SE) (10,000 × $20)		200,000
Capital in excess of par (+SE)		100,000

Assets		=	Liabilities	+	Stockholders' Equity	
Cash	+300,000				Treasury stock	+200,000
					Capital in excess of par	+100,000

If treasury stock were sold at a price below its purchase price (i.e., at an economic loss), stockholders' equity would be reduced by the amount of the difference between the purchase price and the sale price. Assume that Kroger had sold the stock in the previous illustration for only $15 per share:

Cash (+A) (100,000 × $15).	150,000	
Capital in excess of par (−SE) (10,000 × $5).	50,000	
Treasury stock (−XSE, +SE) (10,000 × $20)		200,000

Assets		=	Liabilities	+	Stockholders' Equity	
Cash	+150,000				Treasury stock	+200,000
					Capital in excess of par	−50,000

PAUSE FOR FEEDBACK

We have looked at several transactions involving the sale and repurchase of common stock. In the next section, we will discuss dividends. Before you move on, complete the following questions to test your understanding of these concepts.

SELF-STUDY QUIZ

1. Assume that Applied Technology Corporation issued 10,000 shares of its common stock, par value $2, for $150,000 cash. Prepare the journal entry to record this transaction.
2. Assume that Applied Technology repurchased 5,000 shares of its stock in the open market when the stock was selling for $12 per share. Record this transaction.

After you have completed your answers, check them with the solutions at the bottom of the next page.

DIVIDENDS ON COMMON STOCK

LEARNING OBJECTIVE 11-4
Discuss dividends and analyze transactions.

Investors buy common stock because they expect a return on their investment. This return can come in two forms: stock price appreciation and dividends. Some investors prefer to buy stocks that pay little or no dividends because companies that reinvest the majority of their earnings tend to increase their future earnings potential, along with their stock price. Wealthy investors in high tax brackets prefer to receive their return in the form of higher stock prices because capital gains may be taxed at a lower rate than dividend income. Other investors, such as retired people who need a steady income, prefer to receive their return in the form of dividends. These people often seek stocks that will pay very high dividends, such as utility stocks. Because of the importance of dividends to many investors, analysts often compute the dividend yield ratio to evaluate a corporation's dividend policy.

Dividend Yield

KEY RATIO ANALYSIS

LEARNING OBJECTIVE 11-5
Analyze the dividend yield ratio.

❓ ANALYTICAL QUESTION

What is return on investment based on dividends?

% RATIO AND COMPARISONS

The dividend yield ratio is computed as follows:

Dividend Yield = Dividends per Share ÷ Market Price per Share

The 2012 ratio for The Kroger Co.:

$0.36 ÷ $22 = 1.6%

COMPARISONS OVER TIME			COMPARISONS WITH COMPETITORS	
Kroger			Whole Foods	Safeway
2010	2011	2012	2012	2012
1.0%	1.1%	1.6%	0.7%	4.6%

💡 INTERPRETATIONS

In General Investors in common stock earn a return from both dividends and capital appreciation (increases in the market price of the stock). Growth-oriented companies often rely mainly on increases in their market price to provide a return to investors. Others pay large dividends but have more stable market prices. Each type of stock appeals to different types of investors with different risk and return preferences.

Focus Company Analysis Like many companies, The Kroger Co. pays a modest dividend and reinvests the majority of its earnings in the company. The Kroger Co. also repurchases a significant amount of stock each year from current stockholders. Clearly, investors in The Kroger Co. hope to earn a significant return on the increased value of the company.

A Few Cautions Remember that the dividend yield ratio tells only part of the return on investment story. Often potential capital appreciation is a much more important consideration. The Kroger Co. is currently reinvesting a large portion of its earnings. Analysts should assess the future earnings potential of the company, not just its current dividend yield. Also, note that a high dividend yield may be the result of a large dividend or a low stock price. The yield for Safeway is much larger than the yield for its competitors, but it reflects a decline in the stock price from $35 four years ago to $15 today.

---

1. Cash (+A)...	150,000	
Common stock (+SE)...		20,000
Capital in excess of par (+SE)		130,000
2. Treasury stock (+XSE, −SE)..	60,000	
Cash (−A)...		60,000

Solutions to

SELF-STUDY QUIZ

The declaration and payment of a dividend involve several significant events. Let's review these events based on a dividend announcement reported by *Barron's*.

REAL WORLD EXCERPT
Dividend Announcement

The DECLARATION DATE is the date on which the board of directors officially approves a dividend.

The RECORD DATE is the date on which the corporation prepares the list of current stockholders as shown on its records; dividends can be paid only to the stockholders who own stock on that date.

The PAYMENT DATE is the date on which a cash dividend is paid to the stockholders of record.

> CINCINNATI, June 21, 2012/PRNewswire-FirstCall/—The Kroger Co. (NYSE: KR) announced today that its Board of Directors declared a quarterly dividend of $0.115 per share to be paid on September 1, 2012, to shareholders of record as of the close of business on August 15, 2012.

This announcement contains three important dates:

1. **Declaration date—June 21, 2012.** The declaration date is the date on which the board of directors officially approves the dividend. As soon as it makes the declaration, it creates a dividend liability.

2. **Date of record—August 15, 2012.** The record date follows the declaration; it is the date on which the corporation prepares the list of current stockholders based on its records. The dividend is payable only to those names listed on the record date. No journal entry is made on this date.

3. **Date of payment—September 1, 2012.** The payment date is the date on which the cash is disbursed to pay the dividend liability. It follows the date of record, as specified in the dividend announcement.

These three dates apply for all cash dividends and can be shown graphically as follows:

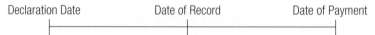

On the declaration date, a company records a liability related to the dividend. To illustrate, on June 21, The Kroger Co. records the following journal entry. Assuming 561 million shares are outstanding, the dividend amounts to $64,515,000 ($0.115 × 561,000,000):

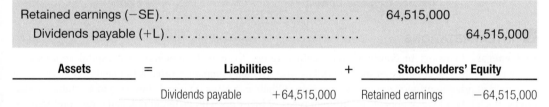

| Retained earnings (−SE).............................. | 64,515,000 | |
| Dividends payable (+L)............................. | | 64,515,000 |

Assets	=	Liabilities	+	Stockholders' Equity
		Dividends payable +64,515,000		Retained earnings −64,515,000

The payment of the liability on September 1 is recorded as follows:

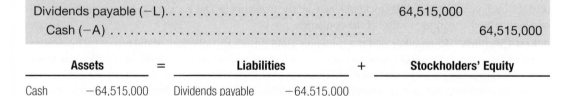

| Dividends payable (−L)............................. | 64,515,000 | |
| Cash (−A) .... | | 64,515,000 |

Assets	=	Liabilities	+	Stockholders' Equity
Cash −64,515,000		Dividends payable −64,515,000		

Notice that the declaration and payment of a cash dividend reduce assets (cash) and stockholders' equity (retained earnings) by the same amount. This observation explains the two fundamental requirements for payment of a cash dividend:

1. **Sufficient retained earnings.** The corporation must have accumulated a sufficient amount of retained earnings to cover the amount of the dividend. State incorporation laws often limit cash dividends to the balance in the Retained Earnings account.

2. **Sufficient cash.** The corporation must have sufficient cash to pay the dividend and meet the operating needs of the business. The mere fact that the Retained Earnings account

has a large credit balance does not mean that the board of directors can declare and pay a cash dividend. The cash generated in the past by earnings represented in the Retained Earnings account may have been expended to acquire inventory, buy operational assets, and pay liabilities. Consequently, no necessary relationship exists between the balance of retained earnings and the balance of cash on any particular date. Quite simply, retained earnings is not cash.

Investors should be careful to understand a company's dividend policy because in the United States, there is no legal obligation for companies to ever declare dividends. Many very successful companies have never paid dividends while others pay out a large percentage of their income each year. The dividend policy for a company is determined by the board of directors. In some other countries, dividend payments are not discretionary and are required by law. In Brazil, for example, companies are legally required to pay out at least 25 percent of their net income in dividends each year.

While companies are under no legal obligation to declare dividends, once the board of directors declares a dividend (i.e., creates a dividend payable) there is a legal obligation to pay that dividend. In the case of a corporate bankruptcy, dividends payable would be a legally enforceable claim against the company.

Impact of Dividends on Stock Price	**FINANCIAL ANALYSIS**

Another date that is important in understanding dividends has no accounting implications. The date two business days before the date of record is known as the *ex-dividend date.* This date is established by the stock exchanges to make certain that dividend checks are sent to the right people. If you buy stock before the ex-dividend date, you will receive the dividend. If you buy stock on the ex-dividend date or later, the previous owner will receive the dividend.

If you follow stock prices, you will notice that they often fall on the ex-dividend date. The stock is worth less on that date because it no longer includes the right to receive the next dividend.

PAUSE FOR FEEDBACK	

One of the reasons that investors buy common stock is to earn dividends. We have looked at dividends paid in cash. In the next section, we will look at dividends paid in stock. Before you move on, complete the following questions to test your understanding of these concepts.

(continued)

STOCK DIVIDENDS AND STOCK SPLITS

Stock Dividends

LEARNING OBJECTIVE 11-6

Discuss the purpose of stock dividends and stock splits, and report transactions.

A STOCK DIVIDEND is a distribution of additional shares of a corporation's own stock.

Without a qualifier, the term *dividend* means a cash dividend, but dividends can also be paid with additional shares of stock. A **stock dividend** is a distribution of additional shares of a corporation's own stock to its stockholders on a pro rata basis at no cost to the stockholder. The phrase *pro rata basis* means that each stockholder receives additional shares equal to the percentage of shares held. A stockholder with 10 percent of the outstanding shares would receive 10 percent of any additional shares issued as a stock dividend.

The term *stock dividend* is sometimes misused in annual reports and news articles. A recent *Wall Street Journal* headline announced that a particular company had just declared a "stock dividend." A close reading of the article revealed that the company had actually declared a cash dividend on the stock.

The value of a stock dividend is the subject of much debate. In reality, a stock dividend by itself has no economic value. All stockholders receive a pro rata distribution of shares, which means that each stockholder owns exactly the same portion of the company as before. The value of an investment is determined by the percentage of the company that is owned, not the number of shares held. If you get change for a dollar, you do not have more wealth because you hold four quarters instead of only one dollar. Similarly, if you own 10 percent of a company, you are not wealthier simply because the company declares a stock dividend and gives you (and all other stockholders) more shares of stock.

The stock market reacts immediately when a stock dividend is issued, and the stock price falls proportionally. Theoretically, if the stock price was $60 before a stock dividend and the number of shares is doubled, in the absence of events affecting the company, the price would fall to $30. Thus, an investor would own 100 shares worth $6,000 before the stock dividend (100 × $60) and 200 shares worth $6,000 after the stock dividend (200 × $30).

In reality, the fall in price is not exactly proportional to the number of new shares issued. In some cases, the stock dividend makes the stock more attractive to new investors. Many investors prefer to buy stock in round lots, which are multiples of 100 shares. An investor with $10,000 might not buy a stock selling for $150, for instance, because she cannot afford to buy 100 shares. She might buy the stock if the price were less than $100 as the result of a stock dividend. In other cases, stock dividends are associated with increases in cash dividends, which are attractive to some investors.

When a stock dividend occurs, the company must transfer an additional amount from the Retained Earnings account (or Capital in Excess of Par Value account, if there is not a sufficient balance in Retained Earnings) into the Common Stock account to reflect the additional shares issued. The amount transferred depends on whether the stock dividend is classified as

Size of Stock Dividends
(sample of 600 companies)

- Less than 50%
- 50%
- 100%
- More than 100%

large or small. Most stock dividends are classified as large. A large stock dividend involves the distribution of additional shares that amount to more than 20–25 percent of currently outstanding shares. A small stock dividend involves the distribution of shares that amount to less than 20–25 percent of the outstanding shares. If the stock dividend is classified as large, the amount transferred to the Common Stock account is based on the par value of the additional shares issued. If the stock dividend is small (i.e., less than 20–25 percent), the amount transferred should be the total market value of the shares issued, with the par value of the stock transferred to the Common Stock account and the excess transferred to the Capital in Excess of Par Value account. According to *Accounting Trends & Techniques,* most stock dividends are larger than 50 percent of the outstanding stock.[2]

Assume The Kroger Co. issued a large stock dividend. The company issued 400,000,000 shares and made the following journal entry:

Retained earnings (−SE) ($1 × 400,000,000).	400,000,000
Common stock (+SE)	400,000,000

Assets	=	Liabilities	+	Stockholders' Equity	
				Retained earnings	−400,000,000
				Common stock	+400,000,000

This journal entry moves an amount from Retained Earnings to the company's Common Stock account. Notice that the stock dividend did not change total stockholders' equity. It changed only the balances of some of the accounts that constitute stockholders' equity.

Stock Splits

Stock splits are not dividends. While they are similar to a stock dividend, they are quite different in terms of their impact on the stockholders' equity accounts. In a **stock split,** the total number of authorized shares is increased by a specified amount, such as 2-for-1. In this instance, each share held is called in and two new shares are issued in its place. Typically, a stock split is accomplished by reducing the par or stated value per share of all authorized shares, so that their total par value is unchanged. For instance, if The Kroger Co. executes a 2-for-1 stock split, it reduces the par value of its stock from $1 to $0.50 and doubles the number of shares outstanding. In contrast to a stock dividend, a stock split does not result in the transfer of a dollar amount to the Common Stock account. The reduction in the par value per share compensates for the increase in the number of shares, so that no transfer is needed.

In both a stock dividend and a stock split, the stockholder receives more shares of stock without having to invest additional resources to acquire the shares. A stock dividend requires a journal entry; a stock split does not but is disclosed in the notes to the financial statements. The comparative effects of a large stock dividend versus a stock split may be summarized as follows:

A STOCK SPLIT is an increase in the total number of authorized shares by a specified ratio; it does not decrease retained earnings.

STOCKHOLDERS' EQUITY

	Before	After a 100% Stock Dividend	After a 2-for-1 Stock Split
Number of shares outstanding	30,000	60,000	60,000
Par value per share	$ 10	$ 10	$ 5
Total par value outstanding	300,000	600,000	300,000
Retained earnings	650,000	350,000	650,000
Total stockholders' equity	950,000	950,000	950,000

---

[2]Reprinted with permission from *Accounting Trends & Techniques.* Copyright © 2008 by the American Institute of Certified Public Accountants, Inc.

PAUSE FOR FEEDBACK

We have concluded our discussion of common stock by looking at stock dividends and stock splits. In the next section, we will provide a brief introduction to the statement of changes in stockholders' equity and then proceed to examine preferred stock. Before you move on, complete the following questions to test your understanding of these concepts.

SELF-STUDY **QUIZ**

Barton Corporation issued 100,000 new shares of common stock (par value $10) in a stock dividend when the market value was $30 per share.

1. Record this transaction, assuming that it was a small stock dividend.
2. Record this transaction, assuming that it was a large stock dividend.
3. What journal entry would be required if the transaction were a stock split?

After you have completed your answers, check them with the solutions at the bottom of the page.

www.mhhe.com/libby8e

GUIDED **HELP**

For additional step-by-step video instruction, go to the URL or scan the QR code in the margin with your smartphone or iPad.

STATEMENT OF CHANGES IN STOCKHOLDERS' EQUITY

In the previous chapters, we have emphasized three financial statements: the income statement, the balance sheet, and the statement of cash flows. Under GAAP, these statements are required in addition to a fourth statement, the statement of changes in stockholders' equity. The purpose of this statement is to show changes in the key components of stockholders' equity, including common stock, paid-in capital, treasury stock, and retained earnings. The statement of changes in stockholders' equity for Kroger is shown in Exhibit 11.2. Under GAAP requirements, the statement must show three years of data but, for illustrative purposes, we show only the current year.

As you review Exhibit 11.2, you will observe many of the issues discussed in this chapter. Notice for example:

1. Treasury stock was purchased at a cost of $1,420 (million).

2. Cash dividends of $256 (million) were paid, which reduced retained earnings (in this statement, called *accumulated earnings*).

3. Net income (called *net earnings* in this statement) was reported in the amount of $602 million, which increased retained earnings.

The statement also contains a number of other changes that involve topics that will be covered in your next accounting course. Perhaps the most important one is accumulated other

1. Retained earnings..	3,000,000	
Common stock		1,000,000
Capital in excess of par..		2,000,000
2. Retained earnings..	1,000,000	
Common stock		1,000,000
3. No journal entry is required in the case of a stock split.		

EXHIBIT 11.2

Excerpt from Statement of
Changes in Stockholders'
Equity for The Kroger Co.

THE KROGER CO.
Consolidated Statement of Changes in Shareowners' Equity
(Years Ended January 28, 2012, January 29, 2011, and January 30, 2010)

(In millions, except per share amounts)	Common Stock Shares	Common Stock Amount	Additional Paid-In Capital	Treasury Stock Shares	Treasury Stock Amount	Accumulated Other Comprehensive Gain (Loss)	Accumulated Earnings	Noncontrolling Interest	Total
Balances at January 29, 2011	959	$959	$3,394	339	$(6,732)	$(550)	$8,225	$ 2	$ 5,298
Issuance of common stock:									
Stock options exercised	—	—	—	(5)	118	—	—	—	118
Restricted stock issued	—	—	(55)	(2)	34	—	—	—	(21)
Treasury stock activity:									
Treasury stock purchases, at cost	—	—	—	61	(1,420)	—	—	—	(1,420)
Stock options exchanged	—	—	—	5	(127)	—	—	—	(127)
Share-based employee compensation	—	—	81	—	—	—	—	—	81
Other comprehensive loss net of income tax of $(167)	—	—	—	—	—	(294)	—	—	(294)
Other	—	—	7	—	(5)	—	—	(11)	(9)
Cash dividends declared ($0.44 per common share)	—	—	—	—	—	—	(256)	—	(256)
Net earnings (loss) including noncontrolling interests	—	—	—	—	—	—	602	(6)	596
Balances at January 28, 2012	959	$959	$3,427	398	$(8,132)	$(844)	$8,571	$(15)	$ 3,966

comprehensive gain (loss), which is defined as net income plus certain items that bypass the income statement because they have not satisfied the revenue recognition criteria. Examples of items that bypass the income statement include:

1. *Unrealized hold gains or losses from available-for-sale securities.* These gains and losses occur when a company holds stock in another company and is prepared to sell them when cash is needed. Under GAAP, gains and losses are reported on the income statement only when the stock is sold. Unrealized gains and losses that occur before the stock is sold would be included in comprehensive income.

2. *Foreign currency translation gains and losses.* When a company invests in a foreign country, the investment is made in that country's currency. The exchange rate between the U.S. dollar and foreign currencies changes on a daily basis, resulting in foreign currency translation gains and losses. These gains and losses are not recorded on the income statement until the foreign currency is converted back into U.S. dollars, but the unrealized translation gains and losses are reported as a component of comprehensive income.

Comprehensive income will be discussed in greater detail in your next course. We have briefly introduced the topic at this point to give you a better understanding of the items included on the statement of changes in stockholders' equity.

PREFERRED STOCK

LEARNING OBJECTIVE 11-7
Describe the characteristics of preferred stock and analyze transactions affecting preferred stock.

PREFERRED STOCK is stock that has specified rights over common stock.

In addition to common stock, some corporations issue **preferred stock.** Notice in Exhibit 11.1 that The Kroger Co. is authorized to issue 5 (million) shares of preferred stock but has not done so. Kroger included this amount in its corporate charter so that it could raise additional funds, if needed, without having to amend its charter.

Preferred stock differs from common stock based on a number of rights granted to the stockholders. The most significant differences are:

- **Preferred stock does not grant voting rights.** As a result, preferred stock does not appeal to investors who want some control over the operations of a corporation. Indeed, this is one of the main reasons some corporations issue preferred stock to raise their equity capital: Preferred stock permits them to raise funds without diluting common stockholders' control. The chart in the margin shows the percentage of companies surveyed by *Accounting Trends & Techniques*[3] that include preferred stock in their capital structure.

- **Preferred stock is less risky.** Generally, preferred stock is less risky than common stock because holders receive priority payment of dividends and distribution of assets if the corporation goes out of business. Usually a specified amount per share must be paid to preferred stockholders upon dissolution, before any remaining assets can be distributed to the common stockholders.

- **Preferred stock typically has a fixed dividend rate.** For example, "6 percent preferred stock, par value $10 per share" pays an annual dividend of 6 percent of par, or $0.60 per share. If preferred stock had no par value, the preferred dividend would be specified as $0.60 per share. The fixed dividend is attractive to certain investors who want a stable income from their investments.

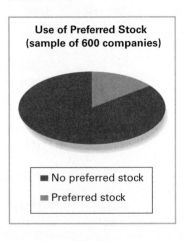

Use of Preferred Stock (sample of 600 companies)

- No preferred stock
- Preferred stock

INTERNATIONAL PERSPECTIVE

What's in a Name?

It is often confusing when different words are used to describe exactly the same thing. Such is the case with International Financial Accounting Standards (IFRS) and U.S. GAAP. The following table serves as a translation guide. Remember the actual elements are exactly the same. It is only their names that differ:

GAAP		IFRS
Capital stock	=	Issued capital or share capital
Paid-in capital	=	Share premium
Treasury stock	=	Treasury shares
Preferred stock	=	Preference shares

Dividends on Preferred Stock

Because investors who purchase preferred stock give up certain advantages that are available to investors in common stock, preferred stock offers a dividend preference. The two most common dividend preferences are current and cumulative.

---

[3]Reprinted with permission from *Accounting Trends & Techniques.* Copyright © 2008 by the American Institute of Certified Public Accountants, Inc.

Current Dividend Preference

The **current dividend preference** requires the current preferred dividend to be paid before any dividends are paid on the common stock. This preference is always a feature of preferred stock. After the current dividend preference has been met and if no other preference is operative, dividends can be paid to the common stockholders.

Declared dividends must be allocated between preferred stock and common stock. First, the preferred stock preference must be met; then the remainder of the total dividend can be allocated to the common stock. To illustrate, assume the Sophia Company has the following stock outstanding:

SOPHIA COMPANY
Preferred stock outstanding, 6%, par $20; 2,000 shares = $40,000 par
Common stock outstanding, par $10; 5,000 shares = $50,000 par

Assuming a current dividend preference only, dividends would be allocated as follows:

Example	Total Dividends	6% Preferred Stock*	Common Stock
No. 1	$ 3,000	$2,400	$ 600
No. 2	18,000	2,400	15,600

Preferred dividend preference, $40,000 × 6% = $2,400.

Cumulative Dividend Preference

The **cumulative dividend preference** states that if all or a part of the current dividend is not paid in full, the cumulative unpaid amount, known as **dividends in arrears**, must be paid before any common dividends can be paid. Of course, if the preferred stock is noncumulative, dividends can never be in arrears; any preferred dividends that are not declared are permanently lost. Because preferred stockholders are unwilling to accept this unfavorable feature, preferred stock is usually cumulative.

To illustrate the cumulative preference, assume that Sophia Company has the same amount of stock outstanding as in the last example. In this case, dividends have been in arrears for two years.

Example	Total Dividends	6% Preferred Stock*	Common Stock
No. 1	$ 8,000	$7,200	$ 800
No. 2	30,000	7,200	22,800

Current dividend preference, $40,000 × 6% = $2,400; dividends in arrears preference, $2,400 × 2 years = $4,800; current dividend preference plus dividends in arrears = $7,200.

CURRENT DIVIDEND PREFERENCE is the feature of preferred stock that grants priority on preferred dividends over common dividends.

CUMULATIVE DIVIDEND PREFERENCE is the preferred stock feature that requires specified current dividends not paid in full to accumulate for every year in which they are not paid. These cumulative preferred dividends must be paid before any common dividends can be paid.

DIVIDENDS IN ARREARS are dividends on cumulative preferred stock that have not been declared in prior years.

Restrictions on the Payment of Dividends

FINANCIAL ANALYSIS

Two common constraints on the ability of a corporation to pay dividends are the existence of loan covenants and preferred stock dividends in arrears. For additional security, some creditors include a loan covenant that limits the amount of dividends a corporation can pay. These debt covenants often also include a limit on borrowing and require a minimum balance of cash or working capital. If debt covenants are violated, the creditor can demand immediate repayment of the debt. The full-disclosure principle requires the disclosure of loan covenants, typically in a separate note to the financial statements.

The existence of dividends in arrears on preferred stock can also limit a company's ability to pay dividends to common stockholders and can affect a company's future cash flows. Because dividends are never an actual liability until the board of directors declares them, dividends in arrears are not reported

(continued)

on the balance sheet. Instead, they are disclosed in the notes to the statements. The following note from Lone Star Industries is typical:

Lone Star Industries

REAL WORLD EXCERPT

Annual Report

> The total of dividends in arrears on the $13.50 preferred stock at the end of the year was $11,670,000. The aggregate amount of such dividend must be paid before any dividends are paid on common stock.

Analysts are particularly interested in information concerning these restrictions because of the impact they have on the company's dividend policy and future cash flows.

FOCUS ON CASH FLOWS

Financing Activities

LEARNING OBJECTIVE 11-8

Discuss the impact of capital stock transactions on cash flows.

Transactions involving capital stock have a direct impact on the capital structure of a business. Because of the importance of these transactions, they are reported in the section of the statement of cash flows called Cash Flows from Financing Activities. Examples of cash flows associated with capital stock are included in the statement of cash flows for The Kroger Co. shown in Exhibit 11.3.

EFFECT ON STATEMENT OF CASH FLOWS

In General   Cash received from owners is reported as an inflow; cash payments made to owners are reported as outflows. See the following example:

Selected Focus Company Comparisons: Dividends Paid (in millions)

Lowe's $260

Starbucks $871

Home Depot $595

	Effect on Cash Flows
Financing activities	
Issuance of capital stock	+
Purchase of treasury stock	−
Sale of treasury stock	+
Payment of cash dividends	−

Focus Company Analysis   Notice that for each of the last three years, The Kroger Co. has paid out a significant amount of cash for purchases of treasury stock and has increased the cash paid out for dividends each year (see Exhibit 11.3).

EXHIBIT 11.3

Excerpt from Statement of Cash Flows for The Kroger Co.

REAL WORLD EXCERPT

Annual Report

THE KROGER CO.
Consolidated Statements of Cash Flows
Years Ended January 28, 2012, January 29, 2011, and January 30, 2010

(in millions)	2012 (52 weeks)	2011 (52 weeks)	2010 (52 weeks)
Cash Flows from Financing Activities:			
Proceeds from issuance of long-term debt	$ 453	$ 381	$ 511
Payments on long-term debt	(547)	(553)	(432)
Borrowings (payments) on credit facility	370	—	(129)
Proceeds from issuance of capital stock	118	29	51
Treasury stock purchases	(1,547)	(545)	(218)
Dividends paid	(257)	(250)	(238)
Investment in the remaining interest of a variable			
interest entity	—	(86)	—
Other	23	20	21
Net cash used by financing activities	$(1,387)	$(1,004)	$(434)

(Try to resolve the requirements before proceeding to the suggested solution that follows.)

This case focuses on the organization and operations for the first year of Owners' Club, Inc., which was organized by 10 local entrepreneurs on January 1, 2014, for the purpose of operating a business to operate a portfolio of exclusive vacation properties. The charter authorized the following capital stock:

Common stock, no-par value, 20,000 shares

Preferred stock, 5 percent, $100 par value, 5,000 shares

The laws of the state specify that the legal capital for no-par stock is the full sale amount.

The following summarized transactions, selected from 2014, were completed on the dates indicated:

a. Jan. Sold a total of 8,000 shares of common stock to the 10 entrepreneurs for cash at $50 per share. Credit the Common Stock account for the total issue amount.

b. Feb. Sold 2,000 shares of preferred stock at $102 per share; cash collected in full.

c. Mar. Declared cash dividend of $1 on common stock.

d. July Purchased 100 shares of preferred stock that had been sold and issued earlier. Owners' Club paid the stockholder $104 per share.

e. Aug. Sold 20 shares of the preferred treasury stock at $105 per share.

Required:

1. Give the appropriate journal entries with a brief explanation for each transaction.

2. Prepare the Stockholders' Equity section of the balance sheet for Owners' Club at December 31, 2014. Assume retained earnings is $23,000.

SUGGESTED SOLUTION

1. Journal entries:

a. Cash (+A)	400,000	
Common stock (+SE)		400,000
Sale of no-par common stock ($50 × 8,000 shares = $400,000).		
b. Cash (+A)	204,000	
Preferred stock (+SE)		200,000
Capital in excess of par, preferred stock (+SE).		4,000
Sale of preferred stock ($102 × 2,000 shares = $204,000).		
c. Retained earnings (−SE).	8,000	
Dividend payable (+L)		8,000
Declared cash dividend		
d. Treasury stock (+XSE, −SE).	10,400	
Cash (−A).		10,400
Purchased 100 shares of preferred stock ($104 × 100 shares = $10,400).		
e. Cash (+A)	2,100	
Treasury stock (−XSE, +SE)		2,080
Capital in excess of par, preferred stock (+SE).		20
Sold 20 shares of the preferred treasury stock at $105.		

2. Stockholders' equity section of the balance sheet:

OWNERS' CLUB, INC.
Partial Balance Sheet
At December 31, 2014

Stockholders' Equity

Contributed capital

Preferred stock, 5% (par value $100; authorized 5,000 shares,

    issued 2,000 shares of which 80 shares are held as treasury stock) $200,000

Capital in excess of par, preferred stock   4,020

Common stock (no-par value; authorized 20,000 shares,

    issued and outstanding 8,000 shares)   400,000

    Total contributed capital $604,020

Retained earnings   23,000

    Total contributed capital and retained earnings $627,020

Less cost of preferred treasury stock held (80 shares)   (8,320)

    Total stockholders' equity $618,700

Chapter Supplement

Accounting for Owners' Equity for Sole Proprietorships and Partnerships

Owners' Equity for a Sole Proprietorship

A *sole proprietorship* is an unincorporated business owned by one person. Only two owners' equity accounts are needed: (1) a capital account for the proprietor (J. Doe, Capital) and (2) a drawing (or withdrawal) account for the proprietor (J. Doe, Drawings).

The capital account of a sole proprietorship serves two purposes: to record investments by the owner and to accumulate periodic income or loss. The drawing account is used to record the owner's withdrawals of cash or other assets from the business. The drawing account is closed to the capital account at the end of each accounting period. Thus, the capital account reflects the cumulative total of all investments by the owner and all earnings of the entity less all withdrawals from the entity by the owner.

In most respects, the accounting for a sole proprietorship is the same as for a corporation. Exhibit 11.4 presents the recording of selected transactions of Doe Retail Store and the statement of owners' equity.

Because a sole proprietorship does not pay income taxes, its financial statements do not reflect income tax expense or income taxes payable. Instead, the net income of a sole proprietorship is taxed when it is included on the owner's personal income tax return. Likewise, the owner's salary is not recognized as an expense in a sole proprietorship because an employer/employee contractual relationship cannot exist with only one party involved. The owner's salary is therefore accounted for as a distribution of profits (i.e., a withdrawal).

Owners' Equity for a Partnership

The Uniform Partnership Act, which most states have adopted, defines a partnership as "an association of two or more persons to carry on as co-owners of a business for profit." Small businesses and professionals such as accountants, doctors, and lawyers often use the partnership form of business.

A partnership is formed by two or more persons reaching mutual agreement about the terms of the relationship. The law does not require an application for a charter as in the case of a corporation. Instead, the agreement between the partners constitutes a partnership contract. This agreement should specify matters such as division of periodic income, management responsibilities, transfer or sale of partnership interests,

EXHIBIT 11.4

Accounting for Owners' Equity for a Sole Proprietorship

Selected Entries during 2014
January 1, 2014
J. Doe started a retail store by investing $150,000 of personal savings. The journal entry follows:

Cash (+A)   150,000
   J. Doe, capital (+OE).   150,000

Assets		=	Liabilities	+	Owners' Equity	
Cash	+150,000				J. Doe, capital	+150,000

During 2014
Each month during the year, Doe withdrew $1,000 cash from the business for personal living costs. Accordingly, each month the following journal entry was made:

J. Doe, drawings (−OE)   1,000
   Cash (−A)   1,000

Assets		=	Liabilities	+	Owners' Equity	
Cash	−1,000				J. Doe, drawings	−1,000

Note: At December 31, 2014, after the last withdrawal, the drawings account reflected a debit balance of $12,000.

December 31, 2014
The usual journal entries for the year, including adjusting and closing entries for the revenue and expense accounts, resulted in an $18,000 net income, which was closed to the capital account as follows:

Individual revenue and expense accounts (−R&E).   18,000
   J. Doe, capital (+OE).   18,000

Assets		=	Liabilities	+	Owners' Equity	
					Revenues and expenses	−18,000
					J. Doe, capital	+18,000

December 31, 2014
The drawings account was closed as follows:

J. Doe, capital (−OE)   12,000
   J. Doe, drawings (+OE).   12,000

Assets		=	Liabilities	+	Owners' Equity	
					J. Doe, capital	−12,000
					J. Doe, drawings	+12,000

Balance Sheet December 31, 2014 (partial)	
Owners' equity	
J. Doe, capital, January 1, 2014	$150,000
Add: Net income for 2014	18,000
Total	168,000
Less: Withdrawals for 2014	(12,000)
J. Doe, capital, December 31, 2014	$156,000

disposition of assets upon liquidation, and procedures to be followed in case of the death of a partner. If the partnership agreement does not specify these matters, the laws of the resident state are binding.

The primary advantages of a partnership are (1) ease of formation, (2) complete control by the partners, and (3) lack of income taxes on the business itself. The primary disadvantage is the unlimited liability of each partner for the partnership's debts. If the partnership does not have sufficient assets to satisfy outstanding debt, creditors of the partnership can seize the partners' personal assets.

As with a sole proprietorship, accounting for a partnership follows the same underlying principles as any other form of business organization, except for those entries that directly affect owners' equity. Accounting for partners' equity follows the same pattern as for a sole proprietorship, except that separate capital and drawing accounts must be established for each partner. Investments by each partner are credited to that partner's capital account; withdrawals are debited to the respective partner's drawing account. The net income of a partnership is divided among the partners in accordance with the partnership agreement and credited to each account. The respective drawing accounts are closed to the partner capital accounts. After the closing process, each partner's capital account reflects the cumulative total of all of that partner's investments plus that partner's share of the partnership earnings less all that partner's withdrawals.

Exhibit 11.5 presents selected journal entries and partial financial statements for AB Partnership to illustrate the accounting for the distribution of income and partners' equity.

The financial statements of a partnership follow the same format as those for a corporation except that (1) the income statement includes an additional section entitled Distribution of Net Income, (2) the partners' equity section of the balance sheet is detailed for each partner, (3) the partnership has no income tax expense because partnerships do not pay income tax (partners must report their share of the partnership profits on their individual tax returns), and (4) salaries paid to the partners are not recorded as expenses but are treated as distributions of earnings.

EXHIBIT 11.5	**Selected Entries during 2014**
	January 1, 2014
Accounting for Partners' Equity	A. Able and B. Baker organized AB Partnership on this date. Able contributed $60,000 and Baker $40,000 cash to the partnership and agreed to divide net income (and net loss) 60 percent and 40 percent, respectively. The journal entry for the business to record the investment was as follows:

Cash (+A)	100,000	
A. Able, capital (+OE)		60,000
B. Baker, capital (+OE)		40,000

Assets		=	Liabilities	+	Owners' Equity	
Cash	+100,000				A. Able, capital	+60,000
					B. Baker, capital	+40,000

During 2014

The partners agreed that Able would withdraw $1,000 and Baker $650 per month in cash. Accordingly, each month the following journal entry was made:

A. Able, drawings (−OE)	1,000	
B. Baker, drawings (−OE)	650	
Cash (−A)		1,650

Assets		=	Liabilities	+	Owners' Equity	
Cash	−1,650				A. Able, drawings	−1,000
					B. Baker, drawings	−650

December 31, 2014

Assume that the normal closing entries for the revenue and expense accounts resulted in a net income of $30,000. The partnership agreement specified Able would receive 60 percent of earnings and Baker would receive 40 percent. The closing entry was as follows:

Individual revenue and expense accounts (−R&E).	30,000	
A. Able, capital (+OE)		18,000
B. Baker, capital (+OE)		12,000

Assets	=	Liabilities	+	Owners' Equity	
				Revenues and expenses	−30,000
				A. Able, capital	+18,000
				B. Baker, capital	+12,000

December 31, 2014

The journal entry required to close the drawing accounts follows:

A. Able, capital (−OE)	12,000	
B. Baker, capital (−OE)	7,800	
A. Able, drawings (+OE)		12,000
B. Baker, drawings (+OE)		7,800

Assets	=	Liabilities	+	Owners' Equity	
				A. Able, capital	−12,000
				B. Baker, capital	−7,800
				A. Able, drawings	+12,000
				B. Baker, drawings	+7,800

A separate statement of partners' capital, similar to the following, is customarily prepared to supplement the balance sheet:

AB PARTNERSHIP
Statement of Partners' Capital
For the Year Ended December 31, 2014

	A. Able	B. Baker	Total
Investment, January 1, 2014	$60,000	$40,000	$100,000
Add: Additional investments during the year	0	0	0
Net income for the year	18,000	12,000	30,000
Totals	78,000	52,000	130,000
Less: Drawings during the year	(12,000)	(7,800)	(19,800)
Partners' equity, December 31, 2014	$66,000	$44,200	$110,200

11-1.   Explain the role of stock in the capital structure of a corporation.   p. 547

The law recognizes corporations as separate legal entities. Owners invest in a corporation and receive capital stock that can be traded on established stock exchanges. Stock provides a number of rights, including the right to receive dividends.

11-2. Analyze the earnings per share ratio.   p. 549

The earnings per share ratio facilitates the comparison of a company's earnings over time or with other companies' earnings at a single point in time. By expressing earnings on a per share basis, differences in the size of companies become less important.

11-3. Describe the characteristics of common stock and analyze transactions affecting common stock.   p. 549

Common stock is the basic voting stock issued by a corporation. Usually it has a par value, but no-par stock also can be issued. Common stock offers some special rights that appeal to certain investors.

A number of key transactions involve capital stock: (1) initial sale of stock, (2) treasury stock transactions, (3) cash dividends, and (4) stock dividends and stock splits. Each is illustrated in this chapter.

11-4. Discuss dividends and analyze transactions.   p. 553

The return associated with an investment in capital stock comes from two sources: appreciation and dividends. Dividends are recorded as a liability when they are declared by the board of directors (i.e., on the date of declaration). The liability is satisfied when the dividends are paid (i.e., on the date of payment).

11-5. Analyze the dividend yield ratio.   p. 553

The dividend yield ratio measures the percentage of return on an investment from dividends. For most companies, the return associated with dividends is very small.

11-6. Discuss the purpose of stock dividends and stock splits, and report transactions.   p. 556

Stock dividends are pro rata distributions of a company's stock to existing owners. The transaction involves transferring an additional amount into the common stock account. A stock split also involves the distribution of additional shares to owners but no additional amount is transferred into the common stock account. Instead, the par value of the stock is reduced.

11-7. Describe the characteristics of preferred stock and analyze transactions affecting preferred stock.   p. 560

Preferred stock provides investors certain advantages, including dividend preferences and a preference on asset distributions in the event the corporation is liquidated.

11-8. Discuss the impact of capital stock transactions on cash flows.   p. 562

Both inflows (e.g., the issuance of capital stock) and outflows (e.g., the purchase of treasury stock) are reported in the Financing Activities section of the statement of cash flows. The payment of dividends is reported as an outflow in this section.

This chapter concludes a major section of the book. In the previous several chapters, we have discussed individual sections of the balance sheet. We will now shift our focus to a common business transaction that affects many accounts on each of the financial statements. For a number of strategic reasons, businesses often invest in other businesses. In the next chapter, you will see why companies invest in other companies and how those investments affect their financial statements.

KEY **RATIOS**

The **earnings per share ratio** states the net income of a corporation on a per share of common stock basis. The ratio is computed as follows (p. 549):

$$\text{Earnings per Share} = \frac{\text{Net Income}}{\text{Average Number of Shares of Common Stock Outstanding}}$$

The **dividend yield ratio** measures the dividend return on the current price of the stock. The ratio is computed as follows (p. 553):

$$\text{Dividend Yield} = \frac{\text{Dividends per Share}}{\text{Market Price per Share}}$$

FINDING **FINANCIAL INFORMATION**

Balance Sheet

Under Current Liabilities
Dividends, once declared by the board of directors, are reported as a liability (usually current).

Under Noncurrent Liabilities
Transactions involving capital stock do not generate noncurrent liabilities.

Under Stockholders' Equity
Typical accounts include
  Preferred stock
  Common stock
  Capital in excess of par
  Retained earnings
  Treasury stock

Statement of Changes in Stockholders' Equity

This statement reports detailed information concerning stockholders' equity, including
  (1) Amounts in each equity account,
  (2) Number of shares outstanding,
  (3) Impact of transactions such as earning income, payment of dividends, and purchase of treasury stock.
  (4) Information concerning comprehensive gain (loss).

Income Statement

Capital stock is never shown on the income statement. Dividends paid are not an expense. They are a distribution of income and are, therefore, not reported on the income statement.

Statement of Cash Flows

Under Financing Activities
+ Cash inflows from initial sale of stock
+ Cash inflows from sale of treasury stock
− Cash outflows for dividends
− Cash outflows for purchase of treasury stock

Notes

Under Summary of Significant Accounting Policies
Usually, very little information concerning capital stock is provided in this summary.

Under a Separate Note
Most companies report information about their stock option plans and information about major transactions such as stock dividends or significant treasury stock transactions. A historical summary of dividends paid per share is typically provided. Also, dividends in arrears on preferred stock, if any, would be reported as a note.

KEY **TERMS**

QUESTIONS

1. Define the term *corporation* and identify the primary advantages of this form of business organization.
2. What is the charter of a corporation?
3. Explain each of the following terms: (*a*) authorized capital stock, (*b*) issued capital stock, and (*c*) outstanding capital stock.

4. Differentiate between common stock and preferred stock.

5. Explain the distinction between par value and no-par value capital stock.

6. What are the usual characteristics of preferred stock?

7. What are the two basic sources of stockholders' equity? Explain each.

8. Owners' equity is accounted for by source. What does source mean?

9. Define treasury stock. Why do corporations acquire treasury stock?

10. How is treasury stock reported on the balance sheet? How is the "gain or loss" on treasury stock that has been sold reported on the financial statements?

11. What are the two basic requirements to support the declaration of a cash dividend? What are the effects of a cash dividend on assets and stockholders' equity?

12. Differentiate between cumulative and noncumulative preferred stock.

13. Define *stock dividend*. How does a stock dividend differ from a cash dividend?

14. What are the primary reasons for issuing a stock dividend?

15. Identify and explain the three important dates with respect to dividends.

16. Define *retained earnings*. What are the primary components of retained earnings at the end of each period?

MULTIPLE-CHOICE QUESTIONS

1. Katz Corporation has issued 400,000 shares of common stock and holds 20,000 shares in treasury. The charter authorized the issuance of 500,000 shares. The company has declared and paid a dividend of $1 per share. What is the total amount of the dividend?
   a. $400,000
   b. $20,000
   c. $380,000
   d. $500,000

2. Which statement regarding treasury stock is false?
   a. Treasury stock is considered to be issued but not outstanding.
   b. Treasury stock has no voting, dividend, or liquidation rights.
   c. Treasury stock reduces total equity on the balance sheet.
   d. None of the above are false.

3. Which of the following statements about stock dividends is true?
   a. Stock dividends are reported on the statement of cash flows.
   b. Stock dividends are reported on the statement of retained earnings.
   c. Stock dividends increase total equity.
   d. Stock dividends decrease total equity.

4. Which order best describes the largest number of shares to the smallest number of shares?
   a. Shares authorized, shares issued, shares outstanding.
   b. Shares issued, shares outstanding, shares authorized.
   c. Shares outstanding, shares issued, shares authorized.
   d. Shares in the treasury, shares outstanding, shares issued.

5. A company issued 100,000 shares of common stock with a par value of $1 per share. The stock sold for $20 per share. By what amount does stockholders' equity increase?
   a. $100,000
   b. $1,900,000
   c. $2,000,000
   d. No change in stockholders' equity

6. A journal entry is not recorded on what date?
   a. Date of declaration.
   b. Date of record.
   c. Date of payment.
   d. A journal entry is recorded on all of these dates.

7. A company has net income of $225,000 and declares and pays dividends in the amount of $75,000. What is the net impact on retained earnings?
   a. Increase of $225,000
   b. Decrease of $75,000
   c. Increase of $150,000
   d. Decrease of $150,000

8. Which statement regarding dividends is false?
   a. Dividends represent a sharing of corporate profits with owners.
   b. Both stock and cash dividends reduce retained earnings.
   c. Cash dividends paid to stockholders reduce net income.
   d. None of the above statements are false.
9. When treasury stock is purchased with cash, what is the impact on the balance sheet equation?
   a. No change: the reduction of the asset cash is offset with the addition of the asset treasury stock.
   b. Assets decrease and stockholders' equity increases.
   c. Assets increase and stockholders' equity decreases.
   d. Assets decrease and stockholders' equity decreases.
10. Does a stock dividend increase an investor's personal wealth immediately?
    a. No, because the stock price falls when a stock dividend is issued.
    b. Yes, because the investor has more shares.
    c. Yes, because the investor acquired additional shares without paying a brokerage fee.
    d. Yes, because the investor will receive more in cash dividends by owning more shares.

For more practice with multiple-choice questions, go to the text website at **www.mhhe.com/libby8e**.

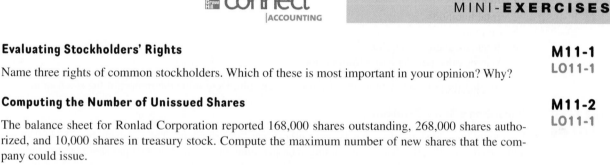

MINI-**EXERCISES**

Evaluating Stockholders' Rights

Name three rights of common stockholders. Which of these is most important in your opinion? Why?

M11-1
LO11-1

Computing the Number of Unissued Shares

The balance sheet for Ronlad Corporation reported 168,000 shares outstanding, 268,000 shares authorized, and 10,000 shares in treasury stock. Compute the maximum number of new shares that the company could issue.

M11-2
LO11-1

Recording the Sale of Common Stock

To expand operations, Aragon Consulting issued 170,000 shares of previously unissued stock with a par value of $1. The selling price for the stock was $21 per share. Record the sale of this stock. Would your answer be different if the par value was $2 per share? If so, record the sale of stock with a par value of $2.

M11-3
LO11-3

Comparing Common Stock and Preferred Stock

Your parents have just retired and have asked you for some financial advice. They have decided to invest $100,000 in a company very similar to Kroger. The company has issued both common and preferred stock. What factors would you consider in giving them advice? Which type of stock would you recommend?

M11-4
LO11-3, 11-7

Determining the Effects of Treasury Stock Transactions

Carbide Corporation purchased 20,000 shares of its own stock for $45 per share. The next year, the company sold 5,000 shares for $50 per share and the following year, it sold 10,000 shares for $37 per share. Determine the impact (increase, decrease, or no change) of each of these transactions on the following classifications:

1. Total assets
2. Total liabilities
3. Total stockholders' equity
4. Net income

M11-5
LO11-3

M11-6

LO11-4

Determining the Amount of a Dividend

Cole Company has 288,000 shares of common stock authorized, 260,000 shares issued, and 60,000 shares of treasury stock. The company's board of directors has declared a dividend of 65 cents per share. What is the total amount of the dividend that will be paid?

M11-7

LO11-4

Recording Dividends

On April 15, 2014, the board of directors for Auction.com declared a cash dividend of 65 cents per share payable to stockholders of record on May 20. The dividends will be paid on June 14. The company has 100,000 shares of stock outstanding. Prepare any necessary journal entries for each date.

M11-8

LO11-7

Determining the Amount of a Preferred Dividend

Lipscomb, Inc., has 200,000 shares of cumulative preferred stock outstanding. The preferred stock pays dividends in the amount of $2 per share but because of cash flow problems, the company did not pay any dividends last year. The board of directors plans to pay dividends in the amount of $1.4 million this year. What amount will go to the preferred stockholders?

M11-9

LO11-6

Determining the Impact of Stock Dividends and Stock Splits

Reliable Tools, Inc., announced a 100 percent stock dividend. Determine the impact (increase, decrease, no change) of this dividend on the following:

1. Total assets
2. Total liabilities
3. Common stock
4. Total stockholders' equity
5. Market value per share of common stock

Assume that the company announced a 2-for-1 stock split. Determine the impact of the stock split.

M11-10

LO11-6

Recording a Stock Dividend

University Food Systems, Inc., has issued a 40 percent stock dividend. The company has 752,000 shares authorized and 200,000 shares outstanding. The par value of the stock is $10 per share, and the market value is $130 per share. Record the payment of this stock dividend.

EXERCISES

E11-1

LO11-1

Philip Morris

Computing Shares Outstanding

The 2011 annual report for Philip Morris Companies, Inc., disclosed that 4 billion shares of common stock have been authorized. At the end of 2010, a total of 2,109,316,331 shares had been issued and the number of shares in treasury stock was 307,532,841. During the current year, no additional shares were issued, but additional shares were purchased for treasury stock and shares were sold from treasury stock. The net change was an increase of 75,874,824 shares of treasury stock. Determine the number of shares outstanding at the end of the current year.

E11-2

LO11-1, 11-3

Computing Number of Shares

The charter of Vista West Corporation specifies that it may issue 300,000 shares of common stock. Since the company was incorporated, it has sold a total of 160,000 shares to the public but bought back a total of 25,000. The par value of the stock is $3 and the stock was sold at an average price of $16. When the stock was bought back from the public, the market price was $40.

Required:
1. Determine the authorized shares.
2. Determine the issued shares.
3. Determine the outstanding shares.

Determining the Effects of the Issuance of Common and Preferred Stock

Tandy, Incorporated, was issued a charter on January 15, 2014, that authorized the following capital stock:

Common stock, no-par, 103,000 shares

Preferred stock, 9 percent, par value $8 per share, 4,000 shares

The board of directors established a stated value on the no-par common stock of $10 per share. During 2014, the following selected transactions were completed in the order given:

a. Sold and issued 20,000 shares of the no-par common stock at $16 cash per share.
b. Sold and issued 3,000 shares of preferred stock at $20 cash per share.
c. At the end of 2014, the accounts showed net income of $60,000.

Required:
1. Prepare the stockholders' equity section of the balance sheet at December 31, 2014.
2. Assume that you are a common stockholder. If Tandy needed additional capital, would you prefer to have it issue additional common stock or additional preferred stock? Explain.

E11-3
LO11-1, 11-3, 11-7

Reporting Stockholders' Equity

The financial statements for Highland Publications Corporation included the following selected information:

Common stock	$1,600,000
Retained earnings	$900,000
Net income	$1,000,000
Shares issued	90,000
Shares outstanding	80,000
Dividends declared and paid	$800,000

The common stock was sold at a price of $30 per share.

Required:
1. What is the amount of capital in excess of par?
2. What was the amount of retained earnings at the beginning of the year?
3. How many shares are in treasury stock?
4. Compute earnings per share.

E11-4
LO11-1, 11-2, 11-3

Reporting Stockholders' Equity and Determining Dividend Policy

Tarrant Corporation was organized in 2014 to operate a financial consulting business. The charter authorized the following capital stock: common stock, par value $10 per share, 11,500 shares. During the first year, the following selected transactions were completed:

a. Sold and issued 5,600 shares of common stock for cash at $20 per share.
b. Sold and issued 1,000 shares of common stock for cash at $25 per share.
c. At year-end, the accounts reflected income of $12,000.

Required:
1. Give the journal entry required for each of these transactions.
2. Prepare the stockholders' equity section as it should be reported on the year-end balance sheet.

E11-5
LO11-1, 11-3, 11-4

Finding Amounts Missing from the Stockholders' Equity Section

The stockholders' equity section on the balance sheet of Dillard's, a popular department store, is shown below. The company reported a net income of $463,909,000 and declared and paid dividends of $10,002,000 in 2012.

E11-6
LO11-1, 11-3

Dillard's

Stockholders' Equity (in thousands):	2012	2011
Common stock, Class A—118,529,925 and 117,706,523 shares issued; ? and ? shares outstanding	?	1,177
Common stock, Class B (convertible)—4,010,929 shares issued and outstanding	40	40
Additional paid-in capital	828,796	805,422
Retained earnings	3,107,344	?
Less treasury stock, at cost, Class A—73,099,319 and 61,740,439 shares	(1,846,312)	(1,355,526)

Required:

Complete the following statements and show your computations.

1. Common stock, class A at par value for 2012 was _____.
2. The number of shares of common stock outstanding was _____ in 2011 and _____ in 2012.
3. Retained earnings for 2011 was _____.
4. At the end of 2012, have the treasury stock transactions (*a*) increased corporate resources or (*b*) decreased resources? _____ By how much? _____.
5. During 2012, the treasury stock transactions increased (decreased) stockholders' equity by _____.
6. How much did the treasury stock cost per share? $_____.

E11-7
LO11-1, 11-3

Reporting Stockholders' Equity

Williamson Corporation was organized in 2014 to operate a tax preparation business. The charter authorized the following capital stock: common stock, par value $2 per share, 80,000 shares. During the first year, the following selected transactions were completed:

a. Sold and issued 50,000 shares of common stock for cash at $50 per share.
b. Bought 2,000 shares from a stockholder for cash at $52 per share.

Required:

1. Give the journal entry required for each of these transactions.
2. Prepare the stockholders' equity section as it should be reported on the year-end balance sheet.

E11-8
LO11-1, 11-3
Ruth's Chris Steakhouse

Reporting Stockholders' Equity

Ruth's Chris Steakhouse is the largest upscale steakhouse company in the United States, based on total company- and franchisee-owned restaurants. The company's menu features a broad selection of high-quality USDA prime grade steaks and other premium offerings. Currently, there are 100 Ruth's Chris restaurants, of which 50 are company-owned and 50 are franchisee-owned, including 10 international franchisee-owned restaurants in Mexico, Hong Kong, Taiwan, and Canada. Information from the company's annual report is shown below (dollar amounts in thousands, except share data):

a. Common stock, par value $0.01, 100,000,000 shares authorized, 33,981,509 issued and outstanding at December 31, 2010, 34,150,389 issued and outstanding at December 31, 2011.
b. Additional paid-in capital $198,304 in 2010 and $200,524 in 2011.
c. Accumulated deficit $118,282 in 2010.
d. Net income in 2011 was $19,549. No dividends were paid.

Required:

Prepare the stockholders' equity section of the balance sheet at December 31, 2011.

E11-9
LO11-1, 11-3, 11-7

Determining the Effects of Transactions on Stockholders' Equity

Quick Fix-it Corporation was organized in January 2014 to operate several car repair businesses in a large metropolitan area. The charter issued by the state authorized the following capital stock:

Common stock, $10 par value, 98,000 shares

Preferred stock, $50 par value, 8 percent, 59,000 shares

During January and February 2014, the following stock transactions were completed:

a. Sold 78,000 shares of common stock at $20 per share and collected cash.
b. Sold 20,000 shares of preferred stock at $80 per share; collected the cash and immediately issued the stock.
c. Bought 4,000 shares of common stock from a current stockholder for $20 per share.

Required:
Net income for 2014 was $210,000; cash dividends declared and paid at year-end were $50,000. Prepare the stockholders' equity section of the balance sheet at December 31, 2014.

Recording Stockholders' Equity Transactions

E11-10
LO11-3, 11-7

On-line Learning Corporation obtained a charter at the start of 2014 that authorized 52,000 shares of no-par common stock and 23,000 shares of preferred stock, par value $10. The corporation was organized by four individuals who purchased 20,000 shares of the common stock. The remaining shares were to be sold to other individuals at $37 per share on a cash basis. During 2014, the following selected transactions occurred:

a. Collected $20 per share cash from the four organizers and issued 5,000 shares of common stock to each of them.
b. Sold and issued 6,000 shares of common stock to an outsider at $40 cash per share.
c. Sold and issued 7,000 shares of preferred stock at $30 cash per share.

Required:
1. Give the journal entries indicated for each of these transactions.
2. Is it ethical to sell stock to outsiders at a higher price than the amount paid by the organizers?

Finding Amounts Missing from the Stockholders' Equity Section

E11-11
LO11-3, 11-7

The stockholders' equity section on the December 31, 2014, balance sheet of American Corporation follows:

Stockholders' Equity	
Contributed capital	
Preferred stock (par $10; authorized 10,000 shares, ? issued, of which 500 shares are held as treasury stock)	$100,000
Common stock (no-par; authorized 20,000 shares, issued and outstanding 8,000 shares)	600,000
Contributed capital (includes $1,500 from treasury stock transactions)	16,500
Retained earnings	34,000
Cost of treasury stock, preferred	(9,500)

Required:
Complete the following statements and show your computations.
1. The number of shares of preferred stock issued was _____.
2. The number of shares of preferred stock outstanding was _____.
3. The average sale price of the preferred stock when issued was $_____ per share.
4. Have the treasury stock transactions (a) increased corporate resources or (b) decreased resources? _____ By how much? _____.
5. The treasury stock transactions increased (decreased) stockholders' equity by _____.
6. How much did the treasury stock held cost per share? $_____.
7. Total stockholders' equity is $_____.
8. The average issue price of the common stock was $_____.

Finding Information Missing from an Annual Report

E11-12
LO11-1, 11-3, 11-4

P&G

Procter & Gamble is an $84 billion company that sells products that are part of most of our daily lives, including Mr. Clean, Cheer, Crest, Vicks, Scope, Pringles, Folgers, Vidal Sassoon, Zest, and Charmin. The annual report for P&G contained the following information:

a. Retained earnings at the end of 2011 totaled $70,682 million.
b. Net income for 2012 was $10,756 million.

c. Par value of the stock is $1 per share.

d. Cash dividends declared in 2012 were $1.45 per share.

e. The Common Stock, Par Value account totaled $4,008 million at the end of 2012 and $4,008 at the end of 2011.

Required (assume that no other information concerning stockholders' equity is relevant):

1. Estimate the number of shares outstanding at the end of 2012.

2. Estimate the amount of retained earnings at the end of 2012.

E11-13

LO11-3, 11-4

Analyzing the Repurchase of Stock

The business section of *The New York Times* recently contained the following article:

> Freeport-McMoRan Copper & Gold Inc., one of the world's largest copper producers, said yesterday that it would repurchase up to five million shares of its common stock in the open market and through private transactions. The company, based in Phoenix, said it recently completed a program announced last September to buy back 2.5 million shares. Freeport-McMoRan said the purchases were being made to enhance shareholders' value. The company has about 70.7 million shares outstanding. Shares of Freeport-McMoRan fell to $53.50 on the New York Stock Exchange yesterday.

Required:

1. Determine the impact of the stock repurchase on the financial statements.

2. Why do you think the board decided to repurchase the stock?

3. What impact will this purchase have on the company's future dividend obligations?

E11-14

LO11-1, 11-3, 11-4, 11-5

Preparing a Statement of Stockholders' Equity and Evaluating Dividend Policy

The following account balances were selected from the records of TEAC Corporation at December 31, 2014, after all adjusting entries were completed:

Common stock (par $20; authorized 100,000 shares, issued 34,000 shares, of which 2,000 shares are held as treasury stock)	$680,000
Capital in excess of par	163,000
Dividends declared and paid in 2014	16,000
Retained earnings, January 1, 2014	75,000
Treasury stock at cost (2,000 shares)	25,000

Net income for the year was $30,000. Restriction on retained earnings equal to the cost of treasury stock held is required by law in this state. The stock price is currently $22.29 per share.

Required:

1. Prepare the Stockholders' Equity section of the balance sheet at December 31, 2014.

2. Compute and evaluate the dividend yield ratio. Determine the number of shares of stock that received dividends.

E11-15

LO11-3

Recording Treasury Stock Transactions and Analyzing Their Impact

During 2014 the following selected transactions affecting stockholders' equity occurred for Orlando Corporation:

a. Apr. 1   Purchased in the market 200 shares of the company's own common stock at $20 per share.

b. Jun. 14   Sold 40 shares of treasury stock for $25 cash per share.

c. Sept. 1   Sold 30 shares of treasury stock for $15 cash per share.

Required:

1. Give journal entries for each of these transactions.

2. Describe the impact, if any, that these transactions have on the income statement.

Recording Treasury Stock Transactions and Analyzing Their Impact

During 2014 the following selected transactions affecting stockholders' equity occurred for TARP Corporation:

a.	Feb. 1	Purchased in the open market 160 shares of the company's own common stock at $20 cash per share.
b.	Jul. 15	Sold 80 of the shares purchased on February 1 for $21 cash per share.
c.	Sept. 1	Sold 50 more of the shares purchased on February 1 for $19 cash per share.

Required:
1. Give the indicated journal entries for each of the transactions.
2. What impact does the purchase of treasury stock have on dividends paid?
3. What impact does the sale of treasury stock for an amount higher than the purchase price have on net income and the statement of cash flows?

E11-16
LO11-3, 11-4, 11-8

Analyzing the Impact of Dividend Policy

Peters and Associates is a small manufacturer of electronic connections for local area networks. Consider three independent situations.

Case 1: Peters increases its cash dividends by 50 percent, but no other changes occur in the company's operations.

Case 2: The company's income and cash flows increase by 50 percent, but this does not change its dividends.

Case 3: Peters issues a 50 percent stock dividend, but no other changes occur.

Required:
1. How do you think each situation would affect the company's stock price?
2. If the company changed its accounting policies and reported higher net income, would the change have an impact on the stock price?

E11-17
LO11-4, 11-6

Computing Dividends on Preferred Stock and Analyzing Differences

The records of Hollywood Company reflected the following balances in the stockholders' equity accounts at December 31, 2013:

Common stock, par $12 per share, 50,000 shares outstanding

Preferred stock, 10 percent, par $10 per share, 5,000 shares outstanding

Retained earnings, $216,000

On September 1, 2014, the board of directors was considering the distribution of an $85,000 cash dividend. No dividends were paid during the previous two years. You have been asked to determine dividend amounts under two independent assumptions (show computations):

a. The preferred stock is noncumulative.
b. The preferred stock is cumulative.

Required:
1. Determine the total and per share amounts that would be paid to the common stockholders and to the preferred stockholders under the two independent assumptions.
2. Write a brief memo to explain why the dividends per share of common stock were less for the second assumption.
3. What factor would cause a more favorable per share result for the common stockholders?

E11-18
LO11-4, 11-7

Determining the Impact of Dividends

Service Corporation has the following capital stock outstanding at the end of 2014:

Preferred stock, 6 percent, par $15, outstanding shares, 8,000

Common stock, par $8, outstanding shares, 30,000

E11-19
LO11-4, 11-6, 11-7

On October 1, 2014, the board of directors declared dividends as follows:

> Preferred stock: Full cash preference amount, payable December 20, 2014
>
> Common stock: 50 percent common stock dividend issuable December 20, 2014

On December 20, 2014, the market prices were preferred stock, $40, and common stock, $32.

Required:

Explain the overall effect of each of the dividends on the assets, liabilities, and stockholders' equity of the company.

E11-20
LO11-4, 11-7

Sears Holdings Corporation

Recording the Payment of Dividends

A recent annual report for Sears Holdings Corporation disclosed that the company paid preferred dividends in the amount of $119.9 million. It declared and paid dividends on common stock in the amount of $2 per share. During the year, Sears had 1,000,000,000 shares of common authorized; 387,514,300 shares had been issued; 41,670,000 shares were in treasury stock. Assume that the transaction occurred on July 15.

Required:

Prepare a journal entry to record the declaration and payment of dividends.

E11-21
LO11-6

Analyzing Stock Dividends

At the beginning of the year, the stockholders' equity section of the balance sheet of Solutions Corporation reflected the following:

Common stock (par $12; authorized 65,000 shares,	
outstanding 30,000 shares)	$360,000
Capital in excess of par	120,000
Retained earnings	580,000

On February 1, 2014, the board of directors declared a 60 percent stock dividend to be issued April 30, 2014. The market value of the stock on February 1, 2014, was $15 per share.

Required:

1. For comparative purposes, prepare the Stockholders' Equity section of the balance sheet (*a*) immediately before the stock dividend and (*b*) immediately after the stock dividend. (*Hint:* Use two amount columns for this requirement.)
2. Explain the effects of this stock dividend on assets, liabilities, and stockholders' equity.

E11-22
LO11-3

P&G

Recording Dividends

Two billion times a day, Procter & Gamble (P&G) brands touch the lives of people around the world. The company has one of the largest and strongest portfolios of trusted, quality brands, including Pampers, Tide, Bounty, Pringles, Folgers, Charmin, Downy, Crest, and Clairol Nice 'n Easy. The P&G community consists of nearly 98,000 employees working in almost 80 countries worldwide. The company has 5,000 million shares of common stock authorized and 3,000 million shares issued and outstanding. Par value is $1 per share. In 2012, the company issued the following press release:

> CINCINNATI (Friday, April 13, 2012)—Today, the Procter & Gamble Company announced that its Board of Directors declared an increase in the quarterly dividend from $0.525 to $0.562 per share on its Common Stock payable on May 15, 2012, to Common Stock shareholders of record at the close of business on April 27, 2012. This represents a 7 percent increase compared to the prior quarterly dividend.

P&G has been paying a dividend for 122 consecutive years since its incorporation in 1890. This marks the 56th consecutive year that the Company has increased the dividend.

Required:

Prepare journal entries as appropriate for each date mentioned in the press release.

E11-23
LO11-6

Comparing Stock Dividends and Splits

On July 1, 2014, Davidson Corporation had the following capital structure:

Common stock (par $1)	$600,000
Capital in excess of par	900,000
Retained earnings	700,000
Treasury stock	–0–

Required:

Complete the following comparative tabulation based on two independent cases:

Case 1: The board of directors declared and issued a 50 percent stock dividend when the stock was selling at $12 per share.

Case 2: The board of directors voted a 6-to-5 stock split (i.e., a 20 percent increase in the number of shares). The market price prior to the split was $12 per share.

Items	Before Dividend and Split	After Stock Dividend	After Stock Split
Common stock account	$	$	$
Par per share	$1	$	$
Shares outstanding	#	#	#
Capital in excess of par	$900,000	$	$
Retained earnings	$700,000	$	$
Total stockholders' equity	$	$	$

Comparing Stock Dividends and Splits

E11-24
LO11-6

Weil Corporation has 80,000 shares of common stock (par value $8) outstanding.

Required:

Complete the following comparative tabulation based on two independent cases:

Case 1: The board of directors declared and issued a 40 percent stock dividend when the stock was selling at $25 per share. The dividend will be accounted for as a large stock dividend.

Case 2: The board of directors voted a 5-to-3 stock split (i.e., a 66.67 percent increase in the number of shares). The market price prior to the split was $25 per share.

Items	Before Dividend and Split	After Stock Dividend	After Stock Split
Common stock account	$	$	$
Par per share	$8	$	$
Shares outstanding	#	#	#
Capital in excess of par	$ 280,000	$	$
Retained earnings	$2,100,000	$	$
Total stockholders' equity	$	$	$

Evaluating Dividend Policy

E11-25
LO11-4

Ford Motor Company is an internationally known manufacturer of automobiles and trucks. The company recently lost over $12 billion in a single year of operations. Despite that staggering loss, the company issued the following press release:

> DEARBORN, Mich., July 13 /PRNewswire-FirstCall/—The Board of Directors of Ford Motor Company (NYSE: F) today declared a third quarter dividend of 5 cents per share on the company's common stock. The dividend, which is payable on Sept. 1 to shareholders of record on Aug. 2 is a reduction of 5 cents per share from the dividend paid in the second quarter.

Required:

1. Explain why Ford can pay dividends despite its loss.
2. What factors did the board of directors consider when it declared the dividends?

For more practice with exercises, go to the text website at **www.mhhe.com/libby8e**.

PROBLEMS

Finding Missing Amounts (AP11–1)

P11-1
LO11-2, 11-3, 11-4, 11-6

At December 31, 2014, the records of NCIS Corporation provided the following selected and incomplete data:

Common stock (par $10; no changes during the year).
Shares authorized, 200,000.

Shares issued, _____?_____ ; issue price $17 per share; cash collected in full, $2,125,000.
Shares held as treasury stock, 3,000 shares, cost $20 per share.
Net income, $240,340.
Dividends declared and paid, $123,220.
Retained earnings balance, January 1, 2014, $555,000.
The treasury stock was acquired after a stock split was issued.

Required:
1. Complete the following tabulation:
   Shares authorized _____.
   Shares issued _____.
   Shares outstanding _____.
2. The balance in the Capital in Excess of Par account appears to be $_____.
3. Earnings per share is $_____.
4. Dividend paid per share of common stock is $_____.
5. Treasury stock should be reported on the balance sheet under the major caption _____ in the amount of $_____.
6. Assume that the board of directors voted a 100 percent stock split (the number of shares will double). After the stock split, the par value per share will be $_____, and the number of outstanding shares will be _____.
7. Assuming the stock split mentioned above, give any journal entry that should be made. If none, explain why.
8. Disregard the stock split (assumed above). Assume instead that a 10 percent stock dividend was declared and issued when the market price of the common stock was $21. Give any journal entry that should be made.

P11-2

LO11-3, 11-7

www.mhhe.com/libby8e

Preparing the Stockholders' Equity Section of the Balance Sheet

Witt Corporation received its charter during January 2014. The charter authorized the following capital stock:

Preferred stock: 10 percent, par $10, authorized 21,000 shares

Common stock: par $8, authorized 50,000 shares

During 2014, the following transactions occurred in the order given:

a. Issued a total of 40,000 shares of the common stock to the four organizers at $12 per share.
b. Sold 5,500 shares of the preferred stock at $16 per share.
c. Sold 3,000 shares of the common stock at $15 per share and 1,000 shares of the preferred stock at $26.
d. Net income for the year was $96,000.

Required:
Prepare the Stockholders' Equity section of the balance sheet at December 31, 2014.

P11-3

LO11-3, 11-7

Recording Transactions Affecting Stockholders' Equity (AP11-2)

King Corporation began operations in January 2014. The charter authorized the following capital stock:

Preferred stock: 10 percent, $10 par, authorized 40,000 shares

Common stock: $5 par, authorized 85,000 shares

During 2014, the following transactions occurred in the order given:

a. Issued 22,000 shares of common stock to each of the three organizers and collected $9 cash per share from each of them.
b. Sold 9,000 shares of the preferred stock at $20 per share.
c. Sold 1,000 shares of the preferred stock at $20 and 2,500 shares of common stock at $10 per share.

Required:
Give the journal entries indicated for each of these transactions.

P11-4

LO11-1, 11-3

Recording Transactions and Comparing Par and No-Par Stock

The following press release was issued by Haynes International:

NEW YORK, March 19 (Reuters)—Haynes International Inc., a producer of high-performance nickel and cobalt-based alloys, on Monday raised $136.5 million with a U.S. initial public offering that was priced above the forecast range.

HAYNES
International

The 2.1-million-share offering was sold for $65 per share, compared with a $61 to $64 forecast range.

Required:
1. Record the issuance of stock, assuming the stock was no-par value common stock.
2. Record the issuance of stock, assuming the common stock had a par value of $2 per share.
3. Should a stockholder care whether a company issues par or no-par value stock? Explain.

Preparing the Stockholders' Equity Section after Selected Transactions (AP11-3)

P11-5
LO11-1, 11-3

United Resources Company obtained a charter from the state in January 2014, which authorized 200,000 shares of common stock, $1 par value. During the first year, the company earned $590,000 and the following selected transactions occurred in the order given:

a. Sold 100,000 shares of the common stock in an initial public offering at $12 per share.
b. Repurchased 20,000 shares of the previously issued shares at $15 cash per share for treasury stock.
c. Resold 5,000 of the shares of the treasury stock at $18 cash per share.

Required:
Prepare the stockholders' equity section of the balance sheet at December 31, 2014.

Analyzing Stockholders' Equity Transactions, Including Treasury Stock

P11-6
LO11-3, 11-4, 11-6

1. Compare a stock dividend with a cash dividend.
2. Compare a large stock dividend with a small stock dividend.
3. Describe the impact of the sale of treasury stock for more than cost on the income statement and the statement of cash flows.
4. Explain why a company might purchase treasury stock.

Analyzing Treasury Stock Transactions

P11-7
LO11-3, 11-8

RadioShack Corporation primarily engages in the retail sale of consumer electronics goods and services through 4,467 company-operated stores under the RadioShack brand, located throughout the United States, as well as in Puerto Rico and the U.S. Virgin Islands. These stores are located in major shopping malls and strip centers, as well as individual storefronts. The company's statement of cash flows contained the following information (in millions):

RadioShack Corporation

	2011	2010	2009
Cash flows from financing activities:			
Purchases of treasury stock	(113.3)	(398.8)	-0-

Required:
1. Record the purchase of treasury stock in 2011.
2. Record the sale of treasury stock in 2012. Assume the stock had been purchased at a cost of $9 million and the company sold the stock for $10 million.

Comparing Stock and Cash Dividends (AP11-4)

P11-8
LO11-4, 11-6, 11-7

Chicago Company had the following stock outstanding and retained earnings at December 31, 2014:

Common stock (par $8; outstanding, 35,000 shares)	$280,000
Preferred stock, 10% (par $15; outstanding, 8,000 shares)	120,000
Retained earnings	281,000

The board of directors is considering the distribution of a cash dividend to the two groups of stockholders. No dividends were declared during the previous two years. Three independent cases are assumed:

Case A: The preferred stock is noncumulative; the total amount of dividends is $31,000.

Case B: The preferred stock is cumulative; the total amount of dividends is $35,000.

Case C: Same as Case B, except the amount is $90,000.

Required:

1. Compute the amount of dividends, in total and per share, that would be payable to each class of stockholders for each case. Show computations.
2. Assume the company issued a 30 percent common stock dividend on the outstanding shares when the market value per share was $24. Complete the following comparative schedule including explanation of the comparative differences.

	AMOUNT OF DOLLAR INCREASE (DECREASE)	
Item	Cash Dividend—Case C	Stock Dividend
Assets	$	$
Liabilities	$	$
Stockholders' equity	$	$

P11-9

LO11-4, 11-8

Dell

Analyzing Dividend Policy

Heather and Scott, two young financial analysts, were reviewing financial statements for Dell, one of the world's largest manufacturers of personal computers. Scott noted that the company did not report any dividends in the Financing Activity section of the statement of cash flows and said, "I have heard that Dell is one of the best performing companies. If it's so good, I wonder why it isn't paying any dividends." Heather wasn't convinced that Scott was looking in the right place for dividends but didn't say anything.

Scott continued the discussion by noting, "Sales for Dell are up nearly 35 percent over the previous two years. While net income is up over $500 million compared to last year, cash flow from operating activities declined by nearly $500 million compared to the previous year."

At that point, Heather noted that the statement of cash flows reported that Dell had repurchased nearly $3 billion in common stock. She also was surprised to see that inventory and accounts receivable had decreased by nearly $2 billion in the previous year. "No wonder it can't pay dividends. With cash flows declining by $500 million, the Board is probably reluctant to obligate itself to dividends."

Required:

1. Correct any misstatements that either Heather or Scott made. Explain.
2. Which of the factors presented in the case help you understand Dell's dividend policy?

P11-10

LO11-4, 11-6, 11-7

Determining the Financial Statement Effects of Dividends

Uno Company has outstanding 52,000 shares of $10 par value common stock and 25,000 shares of $20 par value preferred stock (8 percent). On December 1, 2014, the board of directors voted an 8 percent cash dividend on the preferred stock and a 30 percent stock dividend on the common stock. At the date of declaration, the common stock was selling at $35 and the preferred at $20 per share. The dividends are to be paid, or issued, on February 15, 2015. The annual accounting period ends December 31.

Required:

Explain the comparative effects of the two dividends on the assets, liabilities, and stockholders' equity (*a*) through December 31, 2014, (*b*) on February 15, 2015, and (*c*) overall, from December 1, 2014, through February 15, 2015. A schedule similar to the following might be helpful:

	COMPARATIVE EFFECTS EXPLAINED	
Item	Cash Dividend on Preferred	Stock Dividend on Common
1. Through December 31, 2014: Assets, etc.		

P11-11

LO11-4, 11-6

P&G

Recording Dividends

Procter & Gamble is a well-known consumer products company that owns a variety of popular brands. A recent news article contained the following information:

CINCINNATI, March 9 /PRNewswire-FirstCall/—The Procter & Gamble Company (NYSE: PG) today said that earnings per share for the January through March quarter as well as the fiscal year is expected to exceed current consensus estimates by $0.01 to $0.02. The increased earnings are being driven by continued strong organic volume growth.

Stock Dividend

The company also announced today that its board of directors approved a 10% stock dividend to shareholders of record on May 21. This move does not change the proportionate interest a shareholder maintains in the company. The additional shares will be distributed on June 18. In a separate action, the board declared an increase in the annual rate of its common stock dividend from $1.82 to $2.00 per share.

Required:

1. Prepare any journal entries that P&G should make as the result of information in the preceding report. Assume that the company has 2,500 million shares outstanding, the par value is $1.00 per share, and the market value is $50 per share.
2. What do you think happened to the company's stock price after the announcement?
3. What factors did the board of directors consider in making this decision?

(Chapter Supplement) Comparing Stockholders' Equity Sections for Alternative Forms of Organization

P11-12

Assume for each of the following independent cases that the annual accounting period ends on December 31, 2014, and that the revenue and expense accounts at that date reflect a loss of $20,000.

Case A: Assume that the company is a *sole proprietorship* owned by Proprietor A. Prior to the closing entries, the capital account reflects a credit balance of $52,000 and the drawing account shows a balance of $9,000.

Case B: Assume that the company is a *partnership* owned by Partner A and Partner B. Prior to the closing entries, the owners' equity accounts reflect the following balances: A, Capital, $43,000; B, Capital, $43,000; A, Drawings, $5,000; and B, Drawings, $7,000. Profits and losses are divided equally.

Case C: Assume that the company is a *corporation*. Prior to the closing entries, the stockholders' equity accounts show the following: Common Stock, par $10, authorized 30,000 shares, outstanding 14,000 shares; Capital in Excess of Par, $9,000; Retained Earnings, $62,000.

Required:

1. Give all the closing entries indicated at December 31, 2014, for each of the separate cases.
2. Show how the owners' equity section of the balance sheet would appear at December 31, 2014, for each case.

ALTERNATE **PROBLEMS**

Finding Missing Amounts (P11-1)

At December 31, 2014, the records of Duo Corporation provided the following selected and incomplete data:

AP11-1
LO11-2, 11-3, 11-4, 11-6

Common stock (par $1; no changes during the year).
Shares authorized, 5,000,000.
Shares issued, _____?_____ ; issue price $80 per share.
Shares held as treasury stock, 100,000 shares, cost $60 per share.
Net income, $4,800,000.
Common stock account, $1,500,000.
Dividends declared and paid, $2 per share.
Retained earnings balance, January 1, 2014, $82,900,000.

Required:

1. Complete the following tabulation:
   Shares issued _____.
   Shares outstanding _____.
2. The balance in the Capital in Excess of Par account appears to be $_____.
3. EPS on net income is $_____.
4. Total dividends paid on common stock during 2014 is $_____.
5. Treasury stock should be reported on the balance sheet under the major caption _____ in the amount of $_____.

Recording Transactions Affecting Stockholders' Equity (P11-3)

Granderson Company was granted a charter that authorized the following capital stock:

AP11-2
LO11-3, 11-7

Common stock: 100,000 shares, par value per share is $40

Preferred stock: 8 percent; par $5; 20,000 shares

During the first year, 2014, the following selected transactions occurred in the order given:

a. Sold 30,000 shares of the common stock at $40 cash per share and 5,000 shares of the preferred stock at $26 cash per share.

b. Issued 2,000 shares of preferred stock when the stock was selling at $32.

c. Repurchased 3,000 shares of the common stock sold earlier; paid cash, $38 per share.

Required:
Give journal entries for each of these transactions.

AP11-3

LO11-1, 11-3

Preparing the Stockholders' Equity Section After Selected Transactions (P11-5)

Luther Company obtained a charter from the state in January 2014 which authorized 1,000,000 shares of common stock, $5 par value. During the first year, the company earned $429,000, and the following selected transactions occurred in the order given:

a. Sold 700,000 shares of the common stock at $54 per share. Collected the cash and issued the stock.

b. Purchased 25,000 shares at $50 cash per share to use as stock incentives for senior management.

Required:
Prepare the Stockholders' Equity section of the balance sheet at December 31, 2014.

AP11-4

LO11-4, 11-6, 11-7

Comparing Stock and Cash Dividends (P11-8)

Carlton Company had the following stock outstanding and retained earnings at December 31, 2014:

Common stock (par $1; outstanding, 500,000 shares)	$500,000
Preferred stock, 8% (par $10; outstanding, 21,000 shares)	210,000
Retained earnings	900,000

The board of directors is considering the distribution of a cash dividend to the two groups of stockholders. No dividends were declared during the previous two years. Three independent cases are assumed:

Case A: The preferred stock is noncumulative; the total amount of dividends is $25,000.

Case B: The preferred stock is cumulative; the total amount of dividends is $25,000.

Case C: Same as Case B, except the amount is $75,000.

Required:

1. Compute the amount of dividends, in total and per share, payable to each class of stockholders for each case. Show computations.

2. Assume that the company issued a 40 percent common stock dividend on the outstanding shares when the market value per share was $50. Complete the following comparative schedule, including an explanation of the comparative differences.

	AMOUNT OF DOLLAR INCREASE (DECREASE)	
Item	Cash Dividend—Case C	Stock Dividend
Assets	$	$
Liabilities	$	$
Stockholders' equity	$	$

COMPREHENSIVE **PROBLEM (CHAPTERS 9–11)**

Complete the following requirements for each independent case.

Case A: The charter for Rogers, Incorporated, authorized the following capital stock:

Common stock, par $10, 103,000 shares

Preferred stock, 9 percent, par value $8 per share, 4,000 shares

The company sold 40,000 shares of common stock and 3,000 shares of preferred stock. During 2014, the following selected transactions were completed in the order given:

1. Rogers declared and paid dividends in the amount of $10,000. How much was paid to the holders of preferred stock? How much was paid to the common stockholders?

2. Rogers purchased 5,000 shares for treasury stock. After this transaction, how many shares of common stock were outstanding?

3. Describe the financial statement effects if Rogers sold 1,000 shares of treasury stock for $5 more than it paid.
4. Describe the financial statement effects if Rogers declared and issued a 2-for-1 stock split.

Case B: Ospry, Inc., has working capital in the amount of $960,000. For each of the following transactions, determine whether working capital will increase, decrease, or remain the same.

1. Paid accounts payable in the amount of $10,000.
2. Recorded rent payable in the amount of $22,000.
3. Collected $5,000 in accounts receivable.
4. Purchased $20,000 of new inventory for cash.

Case C: James Corporation is planning to issue $1,000,000 worth of bonds that mature in 10 years and pay 5 percent interest each December 31. All of the bonds will be sold on January 1, 2014.

Required:
Compute the issue (sale) price on January 1, 2014, for each of the following independent cases (show computations):
1. Market (yield) rate, 5 percent.
2. Market (yield) rate, 4 percent.
3. Market (yield) rate, 6 percent.

Case D: Miller Enterprises is a national chain of upscale bicycle shops. The company has followed a successful strategy of locating near major universities. Miller has the opportunity to expand into several new markets but must raise additional capital. The company has engaged in the following transactions:

- Issued 45,000 additional shares of common stock. The stock has a par value of $1 and sells in the market for $25 per share.
- Issued bonds. These bonds have a face value of $1,000,000 and mature in 10 years. The bonds pay 10 percent interest, semiannually. The current market rate of interest is 8 percent.

Required:
1. Record the sale of the bonds.
2. Record the issuance of the stock.

CASES **AND PROJECTS**

Annual Report Cases

Finding Financial Information

Refer to the financial statements of American Eagle Outfitters given in Appendix B at the end of this book.

Required:
1. Does the company have any treasury stock? If so, how much?
2. Does the company pay dividends? If so, how much per share?
3. Did the company buy treasury stock from the public during the current year?
4. What is the par value of the common stock?

CP11-1
LO11-1, 11-3, 11-4

AMERICAN EAGLE
OUTFITTERS, INC.

Finding Financial Information

Refer to the financial statements of Urban Outfitters given in Appendix C at the end of this book.

Required:
1. How many shares of common stock are authorized at the end of the current year? How many shares are issued and outstanding at the end of the current year?
2. Did the company pay dividends during the most recent reporting year? If so, what was the total amount of dividends paid and how much were they per share?
3. Does the company have any treasury stock? If so, how much?
4. Has the company issued a stock dividend or a stock split over the past three reporting years? If so, describe.
5. Does the company's common stock have a par value? If it does, what is the par value?

CP11-2
LO11-1, 11-3, 11-4, 11-6

URBAN OUTFITTERS INC.

CP11-3

LO11-4, 11-5, 11-6

AMERICAN EAGLE
OUTFITTERS, INC.

URBAN OUTFITTERS INC.

www.mhhe.com/libby8e

Comparing Companies within an Industry

Refer to the financial statements of American Eagle (Appendix B) and Urban Outfitters (Appendix C).

Required:
1. A few years ago, American Eagle Outfitters split its stock. Describe the impact that the split would have on the market value of the stock compared to a company that did not split its stock. Why do some companies elect to split their stock?
2. Calculate the dividend yield ratios for Urban Outfitters (assume the market price of the stock is $37) and American Eagle (assume the market price of the stock is $21) for the most recent reporting year.
3. Why would an investor choose to invest in a stock that does not pay dividends?
4. Using the information from the following table, compare the dividend-related industry average ratios for the retail apparel industry to the pharmaceutical industry and the telecommunications industry. What type of investor would be interested in buying stock in a utility instead of a retail store? Why?

DIVIDEND RATIOS FOR VARIOUS INDUSTRIES			
	Retail	Pharmaceuticals	Telecommunications
Dividend yield	2.3%	3.8%	4.8%
Example company	Walmart	Pfizer	AT&T

Financial Reporting and Analysis Case

CP11-4

LO11-4

Halliburton

Computing Dividends for an Actual Company

A recent annual report for Halliburton Company contained the following information (in millions of dollars):

Stockholders' Equity	Current Year	Previous Year
Common stock, par value $2.50, authorized 2,000 shares	$ 298.3	$ 298.4
Paid-in capital in excess of par	130.5	129.9
Retained earnings	2,080.8	2,052.3
Less 12.8 and 13.0 treasury stock, at cost	382.2	384.7

In the current year, Halliburton declared and paid cash dividends of $1 per share. What would be the total amount of dividends declared and paid if they had been based on the amount of stock outstanding at the end of the year?

Critical Thinking Cases

CP11-5

LO11-4, 11-6

Evaluating an Ethical Dilemma

You are a member of the board of directors of a large company that has been in business for more than 100 years. The company is proud of the fact that it has paid dividends every year it has been in business. Because of this stability, many retired people have invested large portions of their savings in your common stock. Unfortunately, the company has struggled for the past few years as it tries to introduce new products and is considering not paying a dividend this year. The president wants to skip the dividend in order to have more cash to invest in product development: "If we don't invest this money now, we won't get these products to market in time to save the company. I don't want to risk thousands of jobs." One of the most senior board members speaks next: "If we don't pay the dividend, thousands of retirees will be thrown into financial distress. Even if you don't care about them, you have to recognize our stock price will crash when they all sell." The company treasurer proposes an alternative: "Let's skip the cash dividend and pay a stock dividend. We can still say we've had a dividend every year." The entire board now turns to you for your opinion. What should the company do?

CP11-6

LO11-4

Evaluating an Ethical Dilemma

You are the president of a very successful Internet company that has had a remarkably profitable year. You have determined that the company has more than $10 million in cash generated by operating activities not needed in the business. You are thinking about paying it out to stockholders as a special dividend. You discuss the idea with your vice president, who reacts angrily to your suggestion:

"Our stock price has gone up by 200 percent in the last year alone. What more do we have to do for the owners? The people who really earned that money are the employees who have been working 12 hours a day, six or seven days a week, to make the company successful. Most of them didn't even take vacations last year. I say we have to pay out bonuses and nothing extra for the stockholders."

As president, you know that you are hired by the board of directors, which is elected by the stockholders. What is your responsibility to both groups? To which group would you give the $10 million?

Financial Reporting and Analysis Team Project

Team Project: Examining an Annual Report

As a team, select an industry to analyze. *Yahoo!Finance* provides lists of industries at <u>biz.yahoo.com/p/industries.html</u>. Click on an industry for a list of companies in that industry. Alternatively, go to Google Finance at <u>www.google.com/finance</u> and search for a company you are interested in. You will be presented with a list including that company and its competitors. Each team member should acquire the annual report or 10-K for one publicly traded company in the industry, with each member selecting a different company (the SEC EDGAR service at <u>www.sec.gov</u> or the company's investor relations website itself are good sources).

CP11-7
LO11-1, 11-3, 11-4, 11-6, 11-7

Required:
On an individual basis, each team member should write a short report answering the following questions about the selected company. Discuss any patterns across the companies that you as a team observe. Then, as a team, write a short report comparing and contrasting your companies.
  1. *a.* List the accounts and amounts of the company's stockholders' equity.
     b. From the footnotes, identify any unusual features in its contributed capital accounts (e.g., convertible preferred, nonvoting common, no par value), if any.
  2. What amount of stock was issued in the most recent year? (You will need to refer to the statement of cash flows for the cash proceeds and the statement of stockholders' equity for the amounts in the capital accounts.)
     a. What was the average market value per share of the issuance?
     b. Recreate the journal entry for the issuance.
  3. What amount of treasury stock, if any, did the company purchase during the year?
  4. What types of dividends, if any, did the company declare during the year? How much was paid in cash?

CONTINUING **CASE**

Recording and Reporting Stockholders' Equity Transactions

Pool Corporation, Inc., is the world's largest wholesale distributor of swimming pool supplies and equipment. It is a publicly traded corporation that trades on the NASDAQ exchange under the symbol POOL. It sells these products to swimming pool repair and service businesses, swimming pool builders, and retail swimming pool stores. The majority of these customers are small, family-owned businesses. The company issued the following press release:

CC11-1

≋POOLCORP

> *COVINGTON, La., Aug. 2, 2012 (GLOBE NEWSWIRE)—Pool Corporation (Nasdaq: POOL) announced today that its Board of Directors has authorized a new $100.0 million share repurchase program for the purchase of the Company's common stock in the open market at prevailing market prices.*
> *The Company also announced that the Board has declared a quarterly cash dividend of $0.16 per share. The dividend will be payable on August 29, 2012, to holders of record on August 13, 2012.*

Required:
  1. Record the repurchase of shares by Pool.
  2. Prepare all necessary entries associated with the dividend. Pool has 100 million shares authorized with 49.4 million issued and 49.2 million outstanding. Assume that the dividend was paid before the repurchase of shares took place.

Statement of Cash Flows

In the highly competitive beverage market dominated by giants Coca-Cola and PepsiCo, National Beverage aims at value-conscious consumers seeking flavor variety. With over 50 different flavors available in its well-known Shasta and Faygo carbonated soft drinks, combined with Everfresh juices, LaCroix waters, and Rip It energy products, National Beverage can meet all of the beverage needs of a wide variety of consumers and retailers. For its value strategy to earn profits for shareholders, National Beverage must also be a cost-effective producer. It maintains product quality and cost discipline through centralized purchasing and by owning and operating all of its production and bottling facilities. Its 12 plants, strategically located near customer distribution centers in different markets, reduce distribution costs and allow National Beverage to tailor its products and media promotions to regional tastes. Through difficult economic times, sales and profits at National Beverage continue to grow. As Nick Caporella, chairman and CEO of the company since its founding, said in a recent annual report, the keys to the company's strong performance are:

- Brands that sparkle in tough times
- Fortress balance sheet
- Investor focus that yields appreciation
- Investor cash—returned appropriately

Although it may seem puzzling, growing profitable operations do not always ensure positive cash flow. As we have seen in earlier chapters, this occurs because the timing of revenues and expenses does not always match cash inflows and outflows. As a consequence, National Beverage

Learning Objectives

After studying this chapter, you should be able to:

12-1 Classify cash flow statement items as part of net cash flows from operating, investing, and financing activities. p. 590

12-2 Report and interpret cash flows from operating activities using the indirect method. p. 597

12-3 Analyze and interpret the quality of income ratio. p. 603

12-4 Report and interpret cash flows from investing activities. p. 604

12-5 Analyze and interpret the capital acquisitions ratio. p. 606

12-6 Report and interpret cash flows from financing activities. p. 607

12-7 Understand the format of the cash flow statement and additional cash flow disclosures. p. 609

chapter 12

FOCUS COMPANY:

National Beverage Corp.

PRODUCING VALUE FOR CUSTOMERS AND CASH FLOWS FOR SHAREHOLDERS IN TOUGH TIMES

www.nationalbeverage.com

must carefully manage cash flows as well as profits. For the same reasons, financial analysts must consider the information provided in National Beverage's cash flow statement in addition to its income statement and balance sheet.

UNDERSTANDING THE BUSINESS

Clearly, net income is important, but cash flow is also critical to a company's success. Cash flow permits a company to expand operations, replace worn assets, take advantage of new investment opportunities, and pay dividends to its owners. Some Wall Street analysts go so far as to say "Cash flow is king." Both managers and analysts need to understand the various sources and uses of cash that are associated with business activity.

The cash flow statement focuses attention on a firm's ability to generate cash internally, its management of operating assets and liabilities, and the details of its investments and its external financing. It is designed to help both managers and analysts answer important cash-related questions such as these:

- Will the company have enough cash to pay its short-term debts to suppliers and other creditors without additional borrowing?
- Is the company adequately managing its accounts receivable and inventory?
- Has the company made necessary investments in new productive capacity?
- Did the company generate enough cash flow internally to finance necessary investments, or did it rely on external financing?
- Is the company changing the makeup of its external financing?

We begin our discussion with an overview of the statement of cash flows. Then we examine the information reported in each section of the statement in depth. The chapter ends with a discussion of additional cash flow disclosures.

ORGANIZATION of the Chapter

Classifications of the Statement of Cash Flows	Reporting and Interpreting Cash Flows from Operating Activities	Reporting and Interpreting Cash Flows from Investing Activities	Reporting and Interpreting Cash Flows from Financing Activities	Completing the Statement and Additional Disclosures
• Cash Flows from Operating Activities • Cash Flows from Investing Activities • Cash Flows from Financing Activities • Net Increase (Decrease) in Cash • Relationships to the Balance Sheet and Income Statement • Preliminary Steps in Preparing the Cash Flow Statement	• Reporting Cash Flows from Operating Activities— Indirect Method • Interpreting Cash Flows from Operating Activities • Quality of Income Ratio	• Reporting Cash Flows from Investing Activities • Interpreting Cash Flows from Investing Activities • Capital Acquisitions Ratio	• Reporting Cash Flows from Financing Activities • Interpreting Cash Flows from Financing Activities	• Statement Structure • Noncash Investing and Financing Activities • Supplemental Cash Flow Information

LEARNING OBJECTIVE 12-1

Classify cash flow statement items as part of net cash flows from operating, investing, and financing activities.

A CASH EQUIVALENT is a short-term, highly liquid investment with an original maturity of less than three months.

CLASSIFICATIONS OF THE STATEMENT OF CASH FLOWS

Basically, the statement of cash flows explains how the amount of cash on the balance sheet at the beginning of the period has become the amount of cash reported at the end of the period. For purposes of this statement, the definition of cash includes cash and cash equivalents. **Cash equivalents** are short-term, highly liquid investments that are both

1. Readily convertible to known amounts of cash, and

2. So near to maturity there is little risk that their value will change if interest rates change.

Generally, only investments with original maturities of three months or less qualify as a cash equivalent under this definition.[1] Examples of cash equivalents are Treasury bills (a form of short-term U.S. government debt), money market funds, and commercial paper (short-term notes payable issued by large corporations).

As you can see in Exhibit 12.1, the statement of cash flows reports cash inflows and outflows in three broad categories: (1) operating activities, (2) investing activities, and (3) financing

---

[1]**Original maturity** means original maturity to the entity holding the investment. For example, both a three-month Treasury bill and a three-year Treasury note purchased three months from maturity qualify as cash equivalents. A Treasury note purchased three years ago, however, does not become a cash equivalent when its remaining maturity is three months.

EXHIBIT 12.1

Consolidated Statement
of Cash Flows

REAL WORLD EXCERPT
Annual Report

NATIONAL BEVERAGE CORP.
Consolidated Statement of Cash Flows
Year Ended April 30, 2011
(amounts in thousands)

Cash flows from operating activities:	
Net income	$ 40,754
Adjustments to reconcile net income to cash flow from operating activities:	
Depreciation and amortization	10,771
Changes in assets and liabilities:	
Accounts receivable	(2,078)
Inventory	1,319
Prepaid expenses	(4,219)
Accounts payable	829
Accrued expenses	3,049
Net cash provided by operating activities	50,425
Cash flows from investing activities:	
Purchases of property, plant, and equipment	(11,389)
Proceeds from disposal of property, plant, and equipment	77
Purchase of short-term investments	(6,532)
Proceeds from sale of short-term investments	8,406
Net cash used in investing activities	(9,438)
Cash flows from financing activities:	
Repayment of principal on long-term debt	(191)
Proceeds from issuance of long-term debt	—
Purchase of treasury stock	—
Proceeds from issuance of stock	4,324
Payment of cash dividends	(106,314)
Net cash used in financing activities	(102,181)
Net decrease in cash and cash equivalents:	(61,194)
Cash and cash equivalents at beginning of period	68,566
Cash and cash equivalents at end of period	$ 7,372

Certain amounts have been adjusted for pedagogical purposes.

activities. Together, these three cash flow categories explain the change in cash from the beginning balance to the ending balance on the balance sheet.

Cash Flows from Operating Activities

Cash flows from operating activities (cash flows from operations) are the cash inflows and outflows that relate directly to revenues and expenses reported on the income statement. There are two alternative approaches for presenting the operating activities section of the statement:

1. The **direct method** reports the components of cash flows from operating activities as gross receipts and gross payments.

Inflows	Outflows
Cash received from	**Cash paid for**
Customers	Purchase of services (electricity, etc.)
Dividends and interest on investments	and goods for resale
	Salaries and wages
	Income taxes
	Interest on liabilities

CASH FLOWS FROM OPERATING ACTIVITIES (cash flows from operations) are cash inflows and outflows directly related to earnings from normal operations.

The **DIRECT METHOD** of presenting the operating activities section of the cash flow statement reports components of cash flows from operating activities as gross receipts and gross payments.

The difference between the inflows and outflows is called **net cash inflow (outflow) from operating activities.** National Beverage experienced a net cash inflow of $50,425 (all amounts in thousands) from its operations for the fiscal year ended April 30, 2011 (hereafter 2011). Though the FASB recommends the direct method, it is rarely used in the United States. Many financial executives have reported that they do not use it because it is more expensive to implement than the indirect method. Both the FASB and the IASB are considering a proposal to require this method, but intense opposition from the preparer community continues.

2. The **indirect method** starts with net income from the income statement and then eliminates noncash items to arrive at net cash inflow (outflow) from operating activities.

Net income
+/− Adjustments for noncash items
Net cash inflow (outflow) from operating activities

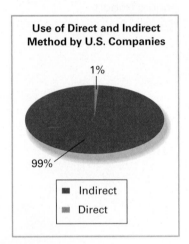

Use of Direct and Indirect Method by U.S. Companies

1%

99%

■ Indirect
■ Direct

Ninety-nine percent of large U.S. companies, including National Beverage, use the indirect method.[2] Notice in Exhibit 12.1 that in the year 2011, National Beverage reported positive net income of $40,754 but generated positive cash flows from operating activities of $50,425. Why should income and cash flows from operating activities differ? Remember that on the income statement, revenues are recorded when they are earned, without regard to when the related cash inflows occur. Similarly, expenses are matched with revenues and recorded without regard to when the related cash outflows occur.

For now, the most important thing to remember about the two methods is that they are simply alternative ways to arrive at the same number. The total amount of **cash flows from operating activities is always the same** (an inflow of $50,425 in National Beverage's case), **regardless of whether it is computed using the direct or indirect method,** as illustrated below.

Direct		Indirect	
Cash collected from customers	$ 598,115	Net income	$40,754
Cash payments for interest	1,119	Depreciation	10,771
Cash payments to suppliers	(379,391)	Changes in operating assets and liabilities	(1,100)
Cash payments for other expenses	(145,234)		
Cash payments for income taxes	(21,896)		
Net cash provided by operating activities	$ 50,425	Net cash provided by operating activities	$50,425

Cash Flows from Investing Activities

Cash flows from investing activities are cash inflows and outflows related to the purchase and disposal of long-lived productive assets and investments in the securities of other companies. Typical cash flows from investing activities include:

Inflows	Outflows
Cash received from	**Cash paid for**
Sale or disposal of property, plant, and equipment	Purchase of property, plant, and equipment
Sale or maturity of investments in securities	Purchase of investments in securities

The difference between these cash inflows and outflows is called **net cash inflow (outflow) from investing activities.**

[2]*Accounting Trends & Techniques* (New York: American Institute of CPAs, 2012).

For National Beverage, this amount was an outflow of $9,438 for the year 2011. Most of the activity was related to purchases and sales of short-term investments and the purchase and sale of property, plant, and equipment. Since total purchases exceeded cash collected from sales, there was a net cash outflow.

Cash Flows from Financing Activities

Cash flows from financing activities include exchanges of cash with creditors (debtholders) and owners (stockholders). Usual cash flows from financing activities include the following:

Inflows	Outflows
Cash received from	**Cash paid for**
Borrowing on notes, mortgages, bonds, etc., from creditors	Repayment of principal to creditors (excluding interest, which is an operating activity)
Issuing stock to owners	Repurchasing stock from owners
	Dividends to owners

CASH FLOWS FROM FINANCING ACTIVITIES are cash inflows and outflows related to external sources of financing (owners and creditors) for the enterprise.

The difference between these cash inflows and outflows is called **net cash inflow (outflow) from financing activities.**

National Beverage experienced a net cash outflow from financing activities of $102,181 for the year 2011. The Financing Activities section of its statement shows that National Beverage paid $191 in principal on long-term debt and $106,314 in dividends, and it received $4,324 for new stock issuances.[3]

Net Increase (Decrease) in Cash

The combination of **the net cash flows from operating activities, investing activities, and financing activities must equal the net increase (decrease) in cash** for the reporting period. For the year 2011, National Beverage reported a net decrease in cash of $61,194, which explains the change in cash on the balance sheet from the beginning balance of $68,566 to the ending balance of $7,372.

Net cash provided by operating activities	$ 50,425
Net cash used in investing activities	(9,438)
Net cash used in financing activities	(102,181)
Net decrease in cash and cash equivalents	(61,194)
Cash and cash equivalents at beginning of period	68,566
Cash and cash equivalents at end of period	$ 7,372

} *Beginning and ending balances from the balance sheet*

PAUSE FOR FEEDBACK

We just discussed the three main sections of the cash flow statement: Cash Flows from Operating Activities, which are related to earning income from normal operations; Cash Flows from Investing Activities, which are related to the acquisition and sale of productive assets; and Cash Flows from Financing Activities, which are related to external financing of the enterprise. The net cash inflow or outflow for the year is the same amount as the increase or decrease in cash and cash equivalents for the year on the balance sheet. To make sure you understand the appropriate classifications of the different cash flows, answer the following questions before you move on.

(continued)

[3]This description was simplified to eliminate discussion of stock options and cash flow hedges.

SELF-STUDY **QUIZ**

Dr Pepper Snapple Group

Dr Pepper Snapple Group is the third largest nonalcoholic beverage company in the world. A listing of some of its cash flows follows. Indicate whether each item is disclosed in the Operating Activities (O), Investing Activities (I), or Financing Activities (F) section of the statement of cash flows.

_____ 1. Proceeds from issuance of long-term debt.

_____ 2. Collections from customers.

_____ 3. Payment of interest on debt.

_____ 4. Purchase of property, plant, and equipment.

_____ 5. Proceeds from disposal of investment securities.

After you have completed your answers, check them with the solutions at the bottom of the page.

To give you a better understanding of the statement of cash flows, we now discuss National Beverage's statement in more detail, including the way in which it relates to the balance sheet and income statement. Then we examine how each section of the statement describes a set of important decisions made by National Beverage's management. Last, we examine how financial analysts use each section to evaluate the company's performance.

Relationships to the Balance Sheet and Income Statement

Preparing and interpreting the cash flow statement requires an analysis of the balance sheet and income statement accounts that relate to the three sections of the cash flow statement. In previous chapters, we emphasized that companies record transactions as journal entries that are posted to T-accounts, which are used to prepare the income statement and the balance sheet. But companies cannot prepare the statement of cash flows using the amounts recorded in the T-accounts because those amounts are based on accrual accounting. Instead, they must analyze the numbers recorded under the accrual method and adjust them to a cash basis. To prepare the statement of cash flows, they need the following data:

1. **Comparative balance sheets** used in calculating the cash flows from all activities (operating, investing, and financing).
2. A **complete income statement** used primarily in calculating cash flows from operating activities.
3. **Additional details** concerning selected accounts where the total change amount in an account balance during the year does not reveal the underlying nature of the cash flows.

Our approach to preparing and understanding the cash flow statement focuses on the changes in the balance sheet accounts. It relies on a simple manipulation of the balance sheet equation:

$$\text{Assets} = \text{Liabilities} + \text{Stockholders' Equity}$$

First, assets can be split into cash and noncash assets:

$$\text{Cash} + \text{Noncash Assets} = \text{Liabilities} + \text{Stockholders' Equity}$$

If we move the noncash assets to the right side of the equation, then:

$$\text{Cash} = \text{Liabilities} + \text{Stockholders' Equity} - \text{Noncash Assets}$$

Solutions to
SELF-STUDY QUIZ

1. F, 2. O, 3. O, 4. I, 5. I

Category	Transaction	Cash Effect	Other Account Affected
Operating	Collect accounts receivable	+Cash	−Accounts Receivable (A)
	Pay accounts payable	−Cash	−Accounts Payable (L)
	Prepay rent	−Cash	+Prepaid Rent (A)
	Pay interest	−Cash	−Retained Earnings (SE)
	Sale for cash	+Cash	+Retained Earnings (SE)
Investing	Purchase equipment for cash	−Cash	+Equipment (A)
	Sell investment securities for cash	+Cash	−Investments (A)
Financing	Pay back debt to bank	−Cash	−Notes Payable—Bank (L)
	Issue stock for cash	+Cash	+Common Stock and Additional Paid-in-Capital (SE)

EXHIBIT 12.2

Selected Cash Transactions and Their Effects on Other Balance Sheet Accounts

Given this relationship, the changes (Δ) in cash between the beginning and the end of the period must equal the changes (Δ) in the amounts on the right side of the equation between the beginning and the end of the period:

$$\Delta\ Cash = \Delta\ Liabilities + \Delta\ Stockholders'\ Equity - \Delta\ Noncash\ Assets$$

Thus, **any transaction that changes cash must be accompanied by a change in liabilities, stockholders' equity, or noncash assets.** Exhibit 12.2 illustrates this concept for selected cash transactions.

Preliminary Steps in Preparing the Cash Flow Statement

Based on this logic, we use the following preliminary steps to prepare the cash flow statement:

1. Determine the change in each balance sheet account. From this year's ending balance, subtract this year's beginning balance (i.e., last year's ending balance).

2. Classify each change as relating to operating (O), investing (I), or financing (F) activities by marking them with the corresponding letter. Use Exhibit 12.3 as a guide.

The balance sheet accounts related to earning income (operating items) should be marked with an O. These accounts are often called **operating assets and liabilities.** The accounts that should be marked with an O include the following:

- Most current assets (other than short-term investments, which relate to investing activities, and cash).[4]

- Most current liabilities (other than amounts owed to investors and financial institutions,[5] all of which relate to financing activities).

- Retained Earnings because it increases by the amount of net income, which is the starting point for the operating section. (Retained Earnings also decreases by dividends declared and paid, which is a financing outflow noted by an F.)

In Exhibit 12.3, all of the relevant current assets and liabilities have been marked with an O. These items include:

- Accounts Receivable

- Inventories

---

[4]Certain noncurrent assets such as long-term receivables from customers and noncurrent liabilities such as postretirement obligations to employees are considered to be operating items. These items are covered in more advanced accounting classes.

[5]Examples of the accounts excluded are Dividends Payable, Short-Term Debt to Financial Institutions, and Current Maturities of Long-Term Debt. Current maturities of long-term debt are amounts of debt with an original term of more than one year that are due within one year of the statement date. Certain noncurrent liabilities involving payables to suppliers, employees, or for taxes are also considered to be operating liabilities. These items are covered in more advanced accounting classes.

EXHIBIT 12.3

Comparative Balance Sheet
and Current Income
Statement

REAL WORLD EXCERPT
Annual Report

NATIONAL BEVERAGE CORP.
Consolidated Balance Sheet
(dollars in thousands)

	Related Cash Flow Section		April 30, 2011	April 30, 2010	*Change*
	Change in Cash	**Assets**			
		Current assets:			
	I	Cash and cash equivalents	$ 7,372	$ 68,566	−61,194
	O	Short-term investments	1,493	3,367	−1,874
	O	Accounts receivable	55,912	53,834	+2,078
	O	Inventories	33,353	34,672	−1,319
		Prepaid expenses	8,403	4,184	+4,219
		Total current assets	106,533	164,623	
	I†	Property, plant, and equipment, net	76,277	75,736	+541
		Total assets	$182,810	$240,359	
		Liabilities and Stockholders' Equity			
		Current liabilities:			
	O	Accounts payable	$ 49,257	$ 48,428	+829
	O	Accrued expenses	26,346	23,297	+3,049
		Total current liabilities	75,603	71,725	
	F	Long-term debt	26,871	27,062	−191
		Stockholders' equity:			
	F	Contributed capital	15,129	10,805	+4,324
	O and F	Retained earnings	65,207	130,767	−65,560
		Total stockholders' equity	80,336	141,572	
		Total liabilities and stockholders' equity	$182,810	$240,359	

NATIONAL BEVERAGE CORP.
Consolidated Statement of Income
For the Fiscal Year Ended April 30, 2011
(dollars in thousands)

Net sales	$600,193
Cost of sales	381,539
Gross profit	218,654
Operating expenses:	
Selling, general, and administrative expense	144,114
Depreciation and amortization expense	10,771
Total operating expenses	154,885
Operating income	63,769
Interest expense	(1,119)
Income before provision for income taxes	62,650
Provision for income taxes	21,896
Net income	$ 40,754

Certain balances have been adjusted to simplify the presentation.
†The Accumulated Depreciation account is also related to operations because it relates to depreciation.

- Prepaid Expenses
- Accounts Payable
- Accrued Expenses

As we have noted, retained earnings is also relevant to operations.

The balance sheet accounts related to investing activities should be marked with an I. These include all of the remaining assets on the balance sheet. In Exhibit 12.3 these items include:

- Short-term Investments
- Property, Plant, and Equipment, net

The balance sheet accounts related to financing activities should be marked with an F. These include all of the remaining liability and stockholders' equity accounts on the balance sheet. In Exhibit 12.3 these items include:

- Long-term Debt
- Contributed Capital (which includes common stock and additional paid-in capital)
- Retained Earnings (for decreases resulting from dividends declared and paid)

Next, we use this information to prepare each section of the statement of cash flows.

REPORTING AND INTERPRETING CASH FLOWS FROM OPERATING ACTIVITIES

As noted above, the operating section can be prepared in two formats, and virtually all U.S. companies choose the indirect method. As a result, we discuss the indirect method here and the direct method in Supplement A at the end of the chapter.
Recall that:

1. Cash flow from operating activities is always the **same** regardless of whether it is computed using the direct or indirect method.

2. The investing and financing sections are always presented in the **same** manner regardless of the format of the operating section.

Reporting Cash Flows from Operating Activities—Indirect Method

Exhibit 12.3 shows National Beverage's comparative balance sheet and income statement. Remember that the indirect method starts with net income and converts it to cash flows from operating activities. This involves adjusting net income for the differences in the timing of accrual basis net income and cash flows. The general structure of the operating activities section is:

> **Operating Activities**
> Net income
>   Adjustments to reconcile net income to cash
>   flow from operating activities:
>   +Depreciation and amortization expense
>   −Gain on sale of investing asset
>   +Loss on sale of investing asset
>   +Decreases in operating assets
>   +Increases in operating liabilities
>   −Increases in operating assets
>   −Decreases in operating liabilities
> **Net Cash Flow from Operating Activities**

LEARNING OBJECTIVE 12-2
Report and interpret cash flows from operating activities using the indirect method.

To keep track of all the additions and subtractions made to convert net income to cash flows from operating activities, it is helpful to set up a schedule to record the computations. We will construct a schedule for National Beverage in Exhibit 12.4.

EXHIBIT 12.4		

National Beverage Corp.:
Schedule for Net Cash Flow
from Operating Activities,
Indirect Method (dollars in
thousands)

CONVERSION OF NET INCOME TO NET CASH FLOW FROM OPERATING ACTIVITIES

Items	Amount	Explanation
Net income, accrual basis	$40,754	From income statement.
Add (subtract) to convert to cash basis:		
Depreciation and amortization	+10,771	Add back because depreciation and amortization expense does not affect cash.
Accounts receivable increase	−2,078	Subtract because cash collected from customers is less than accrual basis revenues.
Inventory decrease	+1,319	Add because purchases are less than cost of goods sold expense.
Prepaid expense increase	−4,219	Subtract because cash prepayments for expenses are more than accrual basis expenses.
Accounts payable increase	+829	Add because cash payments to suppliers are less than amounts purchased on account (borrowed from suppliers).
Accrued expenses increase	+3,049	Add because cash payments for expenses are less than accrual basis expenses.
Net cash provided by operating activities	$50,425	Reported on the statement of cash flows.

We begin our schedule presented in Exhibit 12.4 with net income of $40,754 taken from National Beverage's income statement (Exhibit 12.3). Completing the operating section using the indirect method involves two steps:

Step 1: **Adjust net income for depreciation and amortization expense and gains and losses on sale of investing assets such as property, plant, and equipment and investments.** Recording depreciation and amortization expense does not affect the cash account (or any other operating asset or liability). It affects a noncurrent investing asset (Property, plant, and equipment, net). **Since depreciation and amortization expense are subtracted in computing net income but do not affect cash, we always add each back** to convert net income to cash flow from operating activities. In the case of National Beverage, we need to remove the effect of depreciation and amortization expense by adding back $10,771 to net income (see Exhibit 12.4).

If National Beverage had sold property, plant, and equipment at a gain or loss, the amount of cash received would be classified as an investing cash inflow. Since all of the cash received is an investing cash flow, an adjustment must also be made in the operating activities section to avoid double counting the gain or loss. **Gains on sales of property, plant, and equipment are subtracted and losses on such sales are added** to convert net income to cash flow from operating activities. We illustrate the relevant computations and adjustments for gains and losses on the sale of long-term assets in Supplement B at the end of the chapter.[6]

Step 2: **Adjust net income for changes in assets and liabilities marked as operating (O).** Each **change** in operating assets (other than cash and short-term investments) and liabilities (other than amounts owed to owners and financial institutions) causes a difference between net income and cash flow from operating activities.[7] When converting net income to cash flow from operating activities, apply the following general rules:

---

[6]Other similar additions and subtractions are discussed in more advanced accounting courses.

[7]As noted earlier, certain noncurrent assets, such as long-term receivables from customers, and noncurrent liabilities, such as postretirement obligations to employees, are considered to be operating items. These items are covered in more advanced accounting classes.

- Add the change when an operating asset decreases or an operating liability increases.
- Subtract the change when an operating asset increases or an operating liability decreases.

Understanding what makes these assets and liabilities increase and decrease is the key to understanding the logic of these additions and subtractions.

Change in Accounts Receivable

We illustrate this logic with the first operating item (O) listed on National Beverage's balance sheet (Exhibit 12.3), accounts receivable. Remember that the income statement reflects sales revenue, but the cash flow statement must reflect cash collections from customers. As the following accounts receivable T-account illustrates, when sales revenues are recorded, accounts receivable increases, and when cash is collected from customers, accounts receivable decreases.

Accounts Receivable (A)			
Beginning balance	53,834		
Sales revenue (on account)	600,193	Collections from customers	598,115
Ending balance	55,912		

Change $2,078 (bracket for Beginning balance, Sales revenue, Ending balance)

In the National Beverage example, sales revenue reported on the income statement is greater than cash collections from customers by $600,193 − $598,115 = $2,078. Since less money was collected from customers, this amount must be subtracted from net income to convert to cash flows from operating activities. Note that this amount is also the same as the **change** in the accounts receivable account:

Ending balance	$55,912
− Beginning balance	53,834
Change	$ 2,078

This same underlying logic is used to determine adjustments for the other operating assets and liabilities.

To summarize, the income statement reflects revenues of the period, but cash flow from operating activities must reflect cash collections from customers. Sales on account increase the balance in accounts receivable, and collections from customers decrease the balance.

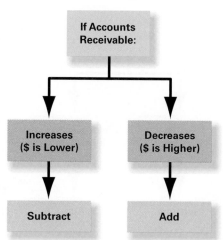

Accounts Receivable (A)		
Beg.	53,834	
Increase	2,078	
End.	55,912	

The balance sheet for National Beverage Corp. (Exhibit 12.3) indicates an **increase** in accounts receivable of $2,078 for the period, which means that cash collected from customers is lower than revenue. To convert to cash flows from operating activities, the amount of the increase (the reduced collections) must be **subtracted** in Exhibit 12.4. (A decrease is added.)

Change in Inventory

The income statement reflects merchandise sold for the period, whereas cash flow from operating activities must reflect cash purchases. As shown in the Inventories T-account, purchases of goods increase the balance in inventory, and recording merchandise sold decreases the balance in inventory.

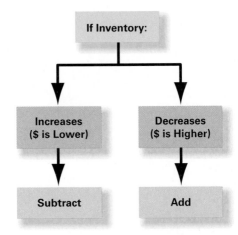

Inventories (A)	
Beg. bal.	Cost of goods sold
Purchases	
End. bal.	

Inventories (A)			
Beg.	34,672		
		Decrease	1,319
End.	33,353		

National Beverage's balance sheet (Exhibit 12.3) indicates that inventory **decreased** by $1,319, which means that the amount of purchases is less than the amount of merchandise sold. The decrease (the extra goods sold) must be added to net income to convert to cash flow from operating activities in Exhibit 12.4. (An increase is subtracted.)

Change in Prepaid Expenses

The income statement reflects expenses of the period, but cash flow from operating activities must reflect the cash payments. Cash prepayments increase the balance in prepaid expenses, and recording of expenses decreases the balance in prepaid expenses.

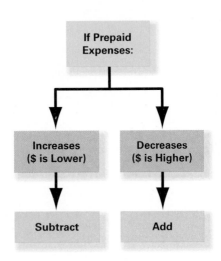

Prepaid Expenses (A)	
Beg. bal.	Services used (expense)
Cash prepayments	
End. bal.	

Prepaid Expenses (A)		
Beg.	4,184	
Increase	4,219	
End.	8,403	

The National Beverage balance sheet (Exhibit 12.3) indicates a $4,219 **increase** in prepaid expenses, which means that new cash prepayments are more than the amount of expenses. The increase (the extra prepayments) must be subtracted from net income in Exhibit 12.4.

Change in Accounts Payable

Cash flow from operations must reflect cash purchases, but not all purchases are for cash. Purchases on account increase accounts payable and cash paid to suppliers decreases accounts payable.

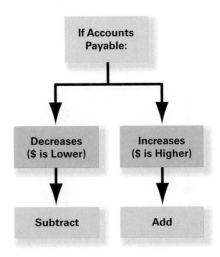

Accounts Payable (L)	
Cash payments	Beg. bal.
	Purchases on account
	End. bal.

Accounts Payable (L)		
Beg.	48,428	
Increase	829	
End.	49,257	

National Beverage's accounts payable **increased** by $829, which means that cash payments were less than purchases on account. This increase (the extra purchases on account) must be **added** in Exhibit 12.4. (A decrease is subtracted.)

Change in Accrued Expenses

The income statement reflects all accrued expenses, but the cash flow statement must reflect actual payments for those expenses. Recording accrued expenses increases the balance in the liability accrued expenses and cash payments for the expenses decrease accrued expenses.

Accrued Expenses (L)	
Pay off accruals	Beg. bal.
	Accrued expenses
	End. bal.

Accrued Expenses (L)		
Beg.	23,297	
Increase	3,049	
End.	26,346	

National Beverage's accrued expenses (Exhibit 12.3) **increased** by $3,049, which indicates that cash paid for the expenses is less than accrual basis expenses. The increase (the lower cash paid) must be **added** in Exhibit 12.4. (A decrease is subtracted.)

Summary

We can summarize the typical additions and subtractions that are required to reconcile net income with cash flow from operating activities as follows:

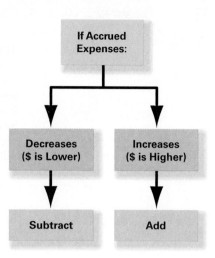

	ADDITIONS AND SUBTRACTIONS TO RECONCILE NET INCOME TO CASH FLOW FROM OPERATING ACTIVITIES	
Item	**When Item Increases**	**When Item Decreases**
Depreciation and amortization	+	NA
Gain on sale of long-term asset	−	NA
Loss on sale of long-term asset	+	NA
Accounts receivable	−	+
Inventory	−	+
Prepaid expenses	−	+
Accounts payable	+	−
Accrued expense liabilities	+	−

Notice again in this table that to reconcile net income to cash flows from operating activities, you must:

- **Add the change when an operating asset decreases or operating liability increases.**

- **Subtract the change when an operating asset increases or operating liability decreases.**

The cash flow statement for National Beverage (Exhibit 12.1) shows the same additions and subtractions to reconcile net income to cash flows from operating activities described in Exhibit 12.4.

Classification of Interest on the Cash Flow Statement

INTERNATIONAL PERSPECTIVE

U.S. GAAP and IFRS differ in the cash flow statement treatment of interest received and interest paid as follows:

	Interest Received	**Interest Paid**
U.S. GAAP	Operating	Operating
IFRS	Operating or Investing	Operating or Financing

Under U.S. GAAP, interest paid and received are both classified as operating cash flows, because the related revenue and expense enter into the computation of net income. This makes it easier to compare net income to cash flow from operations. It also benefits the financial statement user by ensuring comparability across companies. IFRS, on the other hand, allows interest received to be classified as either operating or investing and interest paid to be classified as either operating or financing. This recognizes that interest received results from investing activities and interest paid, like dividends paid, are payments to providers of financing. However, the alternative classifications may be confusing to financial statement readers. These differences are currently on the agenda of the joint FASB/IASB financial statement presentation project.

PAUSE FOR **FEEDBACK**

The indirect method for reporting cash flows from operating activities reports a conversion of net income to net cash flow from operating activities. The conversion involves additions and subtractions for (1) expenses (such as depreciation expense) and revenues that do not affect current assets or current liabilities and (2) changes in each of the individual current assets (other than cash and short-term investments) and current liabilities (other than short-term debt to financial institutions and current maturities of long-term debt, which relate to financing), which reflect differences in the timing of accrual basis net income and cash flows. To test whether you understand these concepts, answer the following questions before you move on.

SELF-STUDY **QUIZ**

Dr Pepper Snapple Group

Indicate which of the following items taken from Dr Pepper Snapple Group's cash flow statement would be added (+), subtracted (−), or not included (NA) in the reconciliation of net income to cash flow from operations.

_____ 1. Increase in inventories.   _____ 4. Decrease in accounts receivable.

_____ 2. Proceeds from issuance of notes payable.   _____ 5. Increase in accounts payable.

_____ 3. Amortization expense.   _____ 6. Increase in prepaid expenses.

After you have completed your answers, check them with the solutions at the bottom of the page.

www.mhhe.com/libby8e

GUIDED **HELP**

For additional step-by-step video instruction on preparing the operating section of the statement of cash flows using the indirect method, go to the URL or scan the QR code in the margin with your smartphone or iPad.

Interpreting Cash Flows from Operating Activities

The operating activities section of the cash flow statement focuses attention on the firm's ability to generate cash internally through operations and its management of current assets and current liabilities (also called **working capital**). Most analysts believe that this is the most important section of the statement because, in the long run, operations are the only source of cash. That is, investors will not invest in a company if they do not believe that cash generated from operations will be available to pay them dividends or expand the company. Similarly, creditors will not lend money if they do not believe that cash generated from operations will be available to pay back the loan. For example, many dot-com companies crashed when investors lost faith in their ability to turn business ideas into cash flows from operations.

A common rule of thumb followed by financial and credit analysts is to avoid firms with rising net income but falling cash flow from operations. Rapidly rising inventories or receivables often predict a slump in profits and the need for external financing. A true understanding of the meaning of the difference requires a detailed understanding of its causes.

In the year 2011, National Beverage reported that cash flow from operations was higher than net income. What caused this relationship? To answer these questions, we must carefully analyze how National Beverage's operating activities are reported in its cash flow statement. To properly interpret this information, we also must learn more about the beverage industry. National Beverage normally reports higher cash flow from operations than net income because of the effect of depreciation and amortization, which reduces income but is not a cash outflow. At the same time, it carefully manages the assets and liabilities that enter into the operating cash flow calculation, keeping those total changes to a minimum. Many analysts compute the quality of income ratio as a general sign of the ability to generate cash through operations.

Solutions to
SELF-STUDY QUIZ

1. −,   2. NA,   3. +,   4. +,   5. +,   6. −.

Quality of Income Ratio	KEY RATIO ANALYSIS

? **ANALYTICAL QUESTION**

How much cash does each dollar of net income generate?

% **RATIO AND COMPARISONS**

$$\text{Quality of Income Ratio} = \frac{\text{Cash Flow from Operating Activities}}{\text{Net Income}}$$

National Beverage Corp.'s ratio for the year 2011 was:

$$\frac{\$50,425}{\$40,754} = 1.24\ (124\%)$$

COMPARISONS OVER TIME			COMPARISONS WITH COMPETITORS	
National Beverage			Coca-Cola	PepsiCo
2009	2010	2011	2011	2011
1.43	1.66	1.24	1.10	1.38

LEARNING OBJECTIVE 12-3
Analyze and interpret the quality of income ratio.

Selected Focus Company Comparisons

Home Depot	1.71
Starbucks	1.29
Apple	1.71

💡 **INTERPRETATIONS**

In General   The quality of income ratio measures the portion of income that was generated in cash. All other things equal, a higher quality of income ratio indicates greater ability to finance operating and other cash needs from operating cash inflows. A higher ratio also indicates that it is less likely that the company is using aggressive revenue recognition policies to increase net income, and therefore is less likely to experience a decline in earnings in the future. When this ratio does not equal 1.0, analysts must establish the sources of the difference to determine the significance of the findings. There are four potential causes of any difference:

1. **The corporate lifecycle (growth or decline in sales).** When sales are increasing, receivables and inventory normally increase faster than accounts payable. This often reduces operating cash flows below income, which, in turn, reduces the ratio. When sales are declining, the opposite occurs, and the ratio increases.

2. **Seasonality.** Seasonal (from quarter to quarter) variations in sales and purchases of inventory can cause the ratio to deviate from 1.0 during particular quarters.

3. **Changes in revenue and expense recognition.** Aggressive revenue recognition or failure to accrue appropriate expenses will inflate net income and reduce the ratio.

4. **Changes in management of operating assets and liabilities.** Inefficient management will increase operating assets and decrease liabilities, reducing operating cash flows and the quality of income ratio. More efficient management, such as shortening of payment terms, will have the opposite effect.

Focus Company Analysis   During the past three years, National Beverage's quality of income ratio has ranged from 1.24 to 1.66. Its ratio is above that of Coca-Cola but below that of PepsiCo. National Beverage's high ratio would generally be viewed positively by analysts and would prompt them to read the management's discussion and analysis section of the annual report to determine its causes.

A Few Cautions   The quality of income ratio can be interpreted based only on an understanding of the company's business operations and strategy. For example, a low ratio for a quarter can be due simply to normal seasonal changes. However, it also can indicate obsolete inventory, slowing sales, or failed expansion plans. To test for these possibilities, analysts often analyze this ratio in tandem with the accounts receivable turnover and inventory turnover ratios.

Fraud and Cash Flows from Operations

The cash flow statement often gives outsiders the first hint that financial statements may contain errors and irregularities. The importance of this indicator as a predictor is receiving more attention in the United States and internationally. *Investors Chronicle* recently reported on an accounting fraud at a commercial credit company, suggesting that

REAL WORLD EXCERPT

Investors Chronicle

> . . . a look at Versailles's cash flow statement—an invaluable tool in spotting creative accounting—should have triggered misgivings. In the company's last filed accounts . . . Versailles reported operating profits of . . . $25 million but a cash outflow from operating activities of $24 million . . . such figures should . . . have served as a warning. After all, what use is a company to anyone if it reports only accounting profits which are never translated into cash?

As noted in earlier chapters, unethical managers sometimes attempt to reach earnings targets by manipulating accruals and deferrals of revenues and expenses to inflate income. Since these adjusting entries do not affect the cash account, they have no effect on the cash flow statement. A growing difference between net income and cash flow from operations can be a sign of such manipulations. This early warning sign has signaled some famous bankruptcies, such as that of W. T. Grant in 1975. The company had inflated income by failing to make adequate accruals of expenses for uncollectible accounts receivable and obsolete inventory. The more astute analysts noted the growing difference between net income and cash flow from operations and recommended selling the stock long before the bankruptcy.

Source: James Chapman, "Creative Accounting: Exposed!" *Investors Chronicle.*

LEARNING OBJECTIVE 12-4

Report and interpret cash flows from investing activities.

REPORTING AND INTERPRETING CASH FLOWS FROM INVESTING ACTIVITIES

Reporting Cash Flows from Investing Activities

Preparing this section of the cash flow statement requires an analysis of the accounts related to property, plant, and equipment; intangible assets; and investments in the securities of other companies. Normally, the relevant balance sheet accounts include Short-Term Investments and long-term asset accounts such as Long-Term Investments and Property, Plant, and Equipment. The following relationships are the ones that you will encounter most frequently:

Related Balance Sheet Account(s)	Investing Activity	Cash Flow Effect
Property, plant, and equipment and intangible assets (patents, etc.)	Purchase of property, plant, and equipment or intangible assets for cash	Outflow
	Sale of property, plant, and equipment or intangible assets for cash	Inflow
Short- or long-term investments (stocks and bonds of other companies)	Purchase of investment securities for cash	Outflow
	Sale (maturity) of investment securities for cash	Inflow

Remember this:

- **Only purchases paid for with cash or cash equivalents are included.**
- **The amount of cash that is received from the sale of assets is included, regardless of whether the assets are sold at a gain or loss.**

Items	Cash Inflows (Outflows)	Explanation
Purchase of property, plant, and equipment	$(11,389)	Payment in cash for equipment
Proceeds from disposal of property, plant, and equipment	77	Receipt of cash from sale of equipment
Purchase of short-term investments	(6,532)	Payment in cash for new investments
Proceeds from sale of short-term investments	8,406	Receipt of cash from sale of investments
Net cash inflow (outflow) from investing activities	$ (9,438)	Reported on the statement of cash flows

EXHIBIT 12.5

National Beverage Corp.:
Schedule for Net Cash Flow
from Investing Activities
(dollars in thousands)

In National Beverage's case, the balance sheet (Exhibit 12.3) shows two investing assets (noted with an I) that have changed during the period: Property, Plant, and Equipment, Net, and Short-Term Investments. To determine the causes of these changes, accountants need to search the related company records.

Property, Plant, and Equipment, Net

Analysis of National Beverage Corp.'s records reveals that the company purchased new property, plant, and equipment for $11,389 in cash, which is a cash outflow. The company also sold old equipment for $77 in cash, an amount equal to its net book value. This is a cash inflow. These investing items are listed in the schedule of investing activities in Exhibit 12.5. These items, less the amount of depreciation expense added back in the Operations section ($10,771), explain the increase in property, plant, and equipment, net, of $541.

Property, Plant, and Equipment, Net (A)			
Beg.	75,736	Sold	77
Purchased	11,389	Depreciation	10,771
End.	76,277		

Investments

National Beverage's records indicate that it purchased $6,532 in short-term investments during the year for cash, which is an investing cash outflow. The company also sold short-term investments for $8,406, an amount equal to their net book value. These investing items are listed in the schedule of investing activities in Exhibit 12.5. They explain the $1,874 decrease in short-term investments reported on the balance sheet. Changes in long-term investments would be treated in the same fashion.

Short-Term Investments (A)			
Beg.	3,367		
Purchased	6,532	Sold	8,406
End.	1,493		

The net cash flow from investing activities resulting from these four items is a $9,438 outflow (see Exhibit 12.5).

Interpreting Cash Flows from Investing Activities

Two common ways to assess a company's ability to internally finance its expansion needs are the capital acquisitions ratio and free cash flow.

KEY RATIO ANALYSIS	Capital Acquisitions Ratio

ANALYTICAL QUESTION

To what degree was the company able to finance purchases of property, plant, and equipment with cash provided by operating activities?

% RATIO AND COMPARISONS

$$\text{Capital Acquisitions Ratio} = \frac{\text{Cash Flow from Operating Activities}}{\text{Cash Paid for Property, Plant, and Equipment}}$$

National Beverage's ratio for 2011 was

$$\frac{\$50{,}425}{\$11{,}389} = 4.43$$

Examine the ratio using two techniques:

COMPARISONS OVER TIME			COMPARISONS WITH COMPETITORS	
National Beverage			Coca-Cola	PepsiCo
2009	2010	2011	2011	2011
5.33	6.51	4.43	3.24	2.68

INTERPRETATIONS

In General The capital acquisitions ratio reflects the portion of purchases of property, plant, and equipment financed from operating activities (without the need for outside debt or equity financing or the sale of other investments or fixed assets). A high ratio indicates less need for outside financing for current and future expansion. It benefits the company because it provides the company opportunities for strategic acquisitions, avoids the cost of additional debt, and reduces the risk of bankruptcy that comes with additional leverage (see Chapter 10).

Focus Company Analysis National Beverage's capital acquisitions ratio has ranged from 4.43 to 6.51 in recent years. It generates more than sufficient cash to meet its investing needs. This is all part of the company's strategy discussed at the beginning of the chapter: To maintain a "fortress balance sheet." As a consequence, when credit markets tightened during the recent financial meltdown, National Beverage's investment plans were unaffected. National Beverage has even maintained a ratio that is higher than its larger competitors, Coca-Cola and PepsiCo.

A Few Cautions Since the needs for investment in plant and equipment differ dramatically across industries (for example, airlines versus pizza delivery restaurants), a particular firm's ratio should be compared only with its prior years' figures or with other firms in the same industry. Also, a high ratio may indicate a failure to update plant and equipment, which can limit a company's ability to compete in the future.

LEARNING OBJECTIVE 12-5
Analyze and interpret the capital acquisitions ratio.

Selected Focus Company Comparisons

Deckers	0.54
Washington Post	1.82
Apple	8.81

FINANCIAL ANALYSIS	Free Cash Flow

Managers and analysts often calculate **free cash flow**[8] as a measure of a firm's ability to pursue long-term investment opportunities. Free cash flow is normally calculated as follows:

$$\text{Free Cash Flow} = \text{Cash Flow from Operating Activities} \\ - \text{Dividends} - \text{Capital Expenditures}$$

FREE CASH FLOW equals Cash Flows from Operating Activities − Dividends − Capital Expenditures.

---

[8]An alternative definition that does not subtract dividends and interest is often called the **total cash flow of the firm** in finance.

Any positive free cash flow is available for additional capital expenditures, investments in other companies, and mergers and acquisitions without the need for external financing or reductions in dividends to shareholders. While free cash flow is considered a positive sign of financial flexibility, it also can represent a hidden cost to shareholders. Sometimes managers use free cash flow to pursue unprofitable investments just for the sake of growth or to obtain perquisites (such as fancy offices and corporate jets) that do not benefit the shareholders. In these cases, the shareholders would be better off if free cash flow were paid as additional dividends or used to repurchase the company's stock on the open market.

REPORTING AND INTERPRETING CASH FLOWS FROM FINANCING ACTIVITIES

Reporting Cash Flows from Financing Activities

Financing activities are associated with generating capital from creditors and owners. This section of the cash flow statement reflects changes in two current liabilities, Notes Payable to Financial Institutions (often called short-term debt) and Current Maturities of Long-Term Debt, as well as changes in long-term liabilities and stockholders' equity accounts. These balance sheet accounts relate to the issuance and retirement of debt and stock and the payment of dividends. The following relationships are the ones that you will encounter most frequently:

> **LEARNING OBJECTIVE 12-6**
> Report and interpret cash flows from financing activities.

Related Balance Sheet Account(s)	Financing Activity	Cash Flow Effect
Short-term debt (notes payable)	Borrowing cash from banks or other financial institutions	Inflow
	Repayment of loan principal	Outflow
Long-term debt	Issuance of bonds for cash	Inflow
	Repayment of bond principal	Outflow
Common stock and additional paid-in capital	Issuance of stock for cash	Inflow
	Repurchase (retirement) of stock with cash	Outflow
Retained earnings	Payment of cash dividends	Outflow

Remember this:

- **Cash repayments of principal are cash flows from financing activities.**
- **Interest payments are cash flows from operating activities.** Since interest expense is reported on the income statement, the related cash flow is shown in the operating section.
- **Dividend payments are cash flows from financing activities.** Dividend payments are not reported on the income statement because they represent a distribution of income to owners. Therefore, they are shown in the financing section.
- **If debt or stock is issued for other than cash, it is not included in this section.**

To compute cash flows from financing activities, you should review changes in debt and stockholders' equity accounts. In the case of National Beverage Corp., the analysis of changes in the balance sheet (Exhibit 12.3) finds that only long-term debt and contributed capital changed during the period (noted with an F).

Short- and Long-Term Debt

When there is additional borrowing or principal repayments on long-term debt owed to financial institutions and investors, those amounts are financing cash flows. The appropriate amounts are determined by analyzing the long-term debt account. For 2011, the company repaid $191

EXHIBIT 12.6

National Beverage Corp.:
Schedule for Net Cash Flow
from Financing Activities
(dollars in thousands)

Items	Cash Inflows (Outflows)	Explanation
Cash flows from financing activities:		
Repayment of principal on long-term debt	(191)	Cash payments of principal on long-term debt
Proceeds from issuance of long-term debt	—	Cash proceeds from issuing long-term debt
Purchase of treasury stock	—	Cash payments to repurchase common stock
Proceeds from issuance of stock	4,324	Cash proceeds from issuing common stock
Payment of cash dividends	(106,314)	Cash payments of dividends to shareholders
Net cash used in financing activities	(102,181)	Reported on the statement of cash flows

in principal on long-term debt. This amount is listed in the schedule of financing activities in Exhibit 12.6. There were no additional borrowings on long-term debt.

Long-Term Debt (L)			
		Beginning	27,062
Retire (repay)	191	Issue (borrow)	0
		Ending	26,871

If the company had borrowed or repaid short-term debt to financial institutions, it would be treated in the same fashion.

Contributed Capital

National Beverage's change in contributed capital resulted from two decisions. National Beverage did not repurchase any outstanding stock during the year. But the company did issue common stock to employees and others for $4,324 in cash, which is a financing cash inflow.[9] This accounts for the $4,324 increase in contributed capital (the sum of common stock and additional paid-in capital). The amount is listed as an inflow in the schedule of financing activities in Exhibit 12.6.

Contributed Capital (SE)			
		Beg.	10,805
Repurchase	0	Issue	4,324
		End.	15,129

Retained Earnings

Finally, retained earnings should be analyzed. Retained earnings rise when income is earned and fall when dividends are declared and paid. National Beverage earned $40,754 in income and paid $106,314 in dividends during 2011. National Beverage's dividend payment is listed on the schedule of financing activities in Exhibit 12.6.

Retained Earnings (SE)			
		Beg.	130,767
Dividends	106,314	Net Income	40,754
		End.	65,207

---

[9]This description was simplified to eliminate discussion of stock options and cash flow hedges.

Interpreting Cash Flows from Financing Activities

The long-term growth of a company is normally financed from three sources: internally generated funds (cash from operating activities), the issuance of stock, and money borrowed on a long-term basis. As we discussed in Chapter 10, companies can adopt a number of different capital structures (the balance of debt and equity). The financing sources that management uses to fund growth will have an important impact on the firm's risk and return characteristics. The statement of cash flows shows how management has elected to fund its growth. This information is used by analysts who wish to evaluate the capital structure and growth potential of a business.

PAUSE FOR FEEDBACK

As we just discussed, the investing section of the statement of cash flows includes cash payments to acquire fixed assets and short- and long-term investments and cash proceeds from the sale of fixed assets and short- and long-term investments. Cash inflows from financing activities include cash proceeds from the issuance of short- and long-term debt and common stock. Cash outflows include cash principal payments on short- and long-term debt, cash paid for the repurchase of the company's stock, and cash dividend payments. Check your understanding of these concepts by answering the following questions before you move on.

SELF-STUDY **QUIZ**

Dr Pepper Snapple Group

Indicate which of the following items taken from the cash flow statement of Dr Pepper Snapple Group would be reported in the Investing section (I) or the Financing section (F) and whether the amount would be an inflow (+) or an outflow (−).

_____ 1. Purchases of short-term investments.

_____ 2. Proceeds from issuance of note payable (to bank).

_____ 3. Cash dividends paid.

_____ 4. Proceeds from issuance of common stock.

_____ 5. Proceeds from sale of property, plant, and equipment.

After you have completed your answers, check them with the solutions at the bottom of the page.

COMPLETING THE STATEMENT AND ADDITIONAL DISCLOSURES

Statement Structure

Refer to the formal statement of cash flows for National Beverage Corp. shown in Exhibit 12.1. As you can see, it is a simple matter to construct the statement after the detailed analysis of the accounts and transactions has been completed (shown in Exhibits 12.4, 12.5, and 12.6). Exhibit 12.7 summarizes the general structure of the statement for companies that use the indirect method. As you can see, when the **net increase or decrease in cash and cash equivalents** is added to the cash and cash equivalents taken from the beginning of the period balance sheet, it equals the cash and cash equivalents amount reported on the end of the period balance sheet. Companies also must provide two other disclosures related to the cash flow statement.

> **LEARNING OBJECTIVE 12-7**
> Understand the format of the cash flow statement and additional cash flow disclosures.

1. I−,   2. F +,   3. F−,   4. F +,   5. I +.

EXHIBIT 12.7

Structure of the Statement of Cash Flows (Indirect Method)

Statement of Cash Flows (Indirect Method)

Operating Activities:
Net Income
+Depreciation and amortization expense
−Gain on sale of long-term asset
+Loss on sale of long-term asset
+Decreases in operating assets
+Increases in operating liabilities
−Increases in operating assets
−Decreases in operating liabilities
Net Cash Flow from Operating Activities

Investing Activities:
−Purchase of property, plant, and equipment or intangible assets
+Sale of property, plant, and equipment or intangible assets
−Purchase of investment securities
+Sale (maturity) of investment securities
Net Cash Flow from Investing Activities

Financing Activities:
+Borrowing from bank or other financial institution
−Repayment of loan principal
+Issuance of bonds for cash
−Repayment of bond principal
+Issuance of stock
−Repurchase (retirement) of stock
−Payment of (cash) dividends
Net Cash Flow from Financing Activities

Net increase or decrease in cash and cash equivalents
Cash and cash equivalents at beginning of period
Cash and cash equivalents at end of period

Noncash Investing and Financing Activities

NONCASH INVESTING AND FINANCING ACTIVITIES are transactions that do not have direct cash flow effects; they are reported as a supplement to the statement of cash flows in narrative or schedule form.

Certain transactions are important investing and financing activities but have no cash flow effects. These are called **noncash investing and financing activities.** For example, the purchase of a $100,000 building with a $100,000 mortgage given by the former owner does not cause either an inflow or an outflow of cash. As a result, these noncash activities are not listed in the three main sections of the cash flow statement. However, supplemental disclosure of these transactions is required, in either narrative or schedule form. National Beverage's statement of cash flows does not list any noncash investing and financing activities. However, when US Airways purchases airplanes, the manufacturer provides some of the financing for those purchases. These amounts are disclosed as follows at the bottom of its cash flow statement:

REAL WORLD EXCERPT

US AIRWAYS

Annual Report

11. Supplemental Cash Flow Information

Supplemental disclosure of cash flow information and non-cash investing and financing activities are as follows (in millions):

	YEAR ENDED DECEMBER 31,		
	2011	2010	2009
Non-cash transactions:			
Note payables issued for aircraft purchases	—	$118	$333

Supplemental Cash Flow Information

Companies that use the indirect method of presenting cash flows from operations also must provide two other figures: **cash paid for interest** and **cash paid for income taxes.** These are normally listed at the bottom of the statement or in the notes.

Epilogue

Our more detailed analysis of National Beverage's cash flow indicates the causes of the difference between net income and cash flows from operations. In fact, it was a normal consequence of depreciation and amortization as well as careful management of operating assets and liabilities. Our further analysis of National Beverage's investing and financing activities indicates that the cash needs to maintain its investment strategy should continue to be more than met by operations. The ongoing success of its product value and strong balance sheet strategy is evident in its continued success in the first quarter of fiscal 2012. Check the company's latest quarterly reports to update this information.

DEMONSTRATION   CASE

During an earlier year (ended April 30), National Beverage Corp. reported net income of $24,742 (all numbers in thousands of dollars). The company also reported the following activities:

a. Purchased equipment for $6,658 in cash.

b. Disposed of equipment for $167 in cash, its net book value on the date of sale.

c. Purchased short-term investments for $109,450.

d. Sold short-term investments for $112,450, their net book value on the date of sale.

e. Issued stock for $950 in cash.

f. Repurchased treasury stock for $305 in cash.

g. Depreciation of equipment was $8,891 for the year.

Its comparative balance sheet is presented below.

BALANCE SHEET Year ended April 30		
(dollars in thousands)	Current Year	Prior Year
Assets		
Current assets:		
Cash and cash equivalents	$ 84,140	$ 51,497
Short-term investments	—	3,000
Accounts receivable	53,735	49,186
Inventories	39,612	38,754
Prepaid expenses	5,552	12,009
Total current assets	183,039	154,446
Equipment, net	79,381	81,781
Total assets	$262,420	$236,227
Liabilities and Stockholders' Equity		
Current liabilities:		
Accounts payable	$ 48,005	$ 49,803
Accrued expenses	44,403	41,799
Total current liabilities	92,408	91,602
Stockholders' equity:		
Contributed capital	9,803	9,158
Retained earnings	160,209	135,467
Total stockholders' equity	170,012	144,625
Total liabilities and stockholders' equity	$262,420	$236,227

Required:

Based on this information, prepare the cash flow statement using the indirect method. Evaluate cash flows reported in the statement.

SUGGESTED SOLUTION

NATIONAL BEVERAGE CORP.
Statement of Cash Flows
Year ended April 30
(dollars in thousands)

Cash flows from operating activities:	
Net income	$ 24,742
Adjustments to reconcile net income to cash flow from operating activities:	
Depreciation and amortization	8,891
Changes in assets and liabilities:	
Accounts receivable	(4,549)
Inventory	(858)
Prepaid expenses	6,457
Accounts payable	(1,798)
Accrued expenses	2,604
Net cash provided by operating activities	35,489
Cash flows from investing activities:	
Purchases of property, plant, and equipment	(6,658)
Proceeds from disposal of property, plant, and equipment	167
Purchase of short-term investments	(109,450)
Proceeds from sale of short-term investments	112,450
Net cash used in investing activities	(3,491)
Cash flows from financing activities:	
Purchase of treasury stock	(305)
Proceeds from issuance of stock	950
Net cash provided by financing activities	645
Net increase in cash and cash equivalents	32,643
Cash and cash equivalents at beginning of period	51,497
Cash and cash equivalents at end of period	$ 84,140

National Beverage reported positive profits and even higher cash flows from operations for the year. This difference between the two is caused primarily by decreases in prepaid expenses and depreciation. This also suggests that National Beverage is carefully managing its current assets and current liabilities so that it has more than sufficient cash on hand to cover the costs of purchases of additional equipment without the need to borrow additional funds. This cash can be used for future expansion or to pay future dividends to stockholders.

Chapter Supplement A

Reporting Cash Flows from Operating Activities—Direct Method

The **direct method** presents a summary of all operating transactions that result in either a debit or a credit to cash. It is prepared by adjusting each item on the income statement from an accrual basis to a cash basis. We will complete this process for all of the revenues and expenses reported in National Beverage's income statement in Exhibit 12.3 and accumulate them in a new schedule in Exhibit 12.8.

Converting Revenues to Cash Inflows

When sales are recorded, accounts receivable increases, and when cash is collected, accounts receivable decreases. Thus, the following formula will convert sales revenue amounts from the accrual basis to the cash basis:

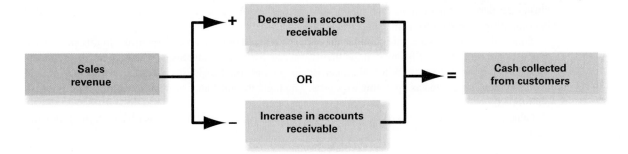

Using information from National Beverage's income statement and balance sheet presented in Exhibit 12.3, we can compute cash collected from customers as follows:

		Accounts Receivable (A)	
Net sales	$600,193	Beg.	53,834
− Increase in accounts receivable	(2,078)	Increase	2,078
Cash collected from customers	$598,115	End.	55,912

Converting Cost of Goods Sold to Cash Paid to Suppliers

Cost of goods sold represents the cost of merchandise sold during the accounting period. It may be more or less than the amount of cash paid to suppliers during the period. In National Beverage's case, inventory decreased during the year because the company bought less merchandise from suppliers than it sold to customers. If the company paid cash to suppliers of inventory, it must have paid less cash to suppliers than the amount of cost of goods sold, so the decrease in inventory must be subtracted to compute cash paid to suppliers.

Typically, companies owe their suppliers money (an accounts payable balance will appear on the balance sheet). To convert cost of goods sold to cash paid to suppliers, the borrowing and repayments represented by the accounts payable must also be considered. Borrowing increases cash and accounts payable and repayment decreases cash and accounts payable, so National Beverage's increase in accounts payable must also be subtracted in the computation. Cost of goods sold can therefore be converted to a cash basis in the following manner:

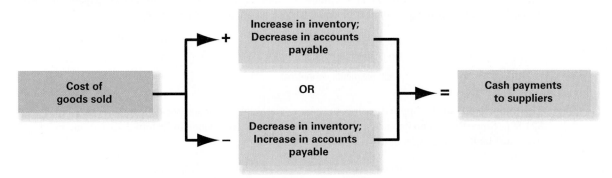

Using information from Exhibit 12.3, we can compute cash paid to suppliers as follows:

Inventories (A)				Cost of goods sold	$381,539	Accounts Payable (L)		
Beg.	39,672			− Decrease in inventory	(1,319)		Beg.	48,428
		Decrease	1,319	− Increase in accounts payable	(829)		Increase	829
End.	33,353			Cash payments to suppliers	$379,391		End.	49,257

Converting Operating Expenses to a Cash Outflow

The total amount of an expense on the income statement may differ from the cash outflow associated with that activity. Some expenses are paid before they are recognized as expenses (e.g., prepaid rent). When prepayments are made, the balance in the asset prepaid expenses increases; when expenses are recorded, prepaid expenses decreases. When National Beverage's prepaid expenses increased by $4,219 during the period, it paid more cash than it recorded as operating expenses. The increase must be added in computing cash paid for expenses.

Some other expenses are paid for after they are recognized (e.g., accrued expenses). In this case, when expenses are recorded, the balance in the liability accrued expenses increases; when payments are made, accrued expenses decreases. When National Beverage's accrued expenses increased by $3,049, it paid less cash than it recorded as operating expenses. The increase must also be subtracted in computing cash paid for expenses.

Generally, other expenses can be converted from the accrual basis to the cash basis in the following manner:

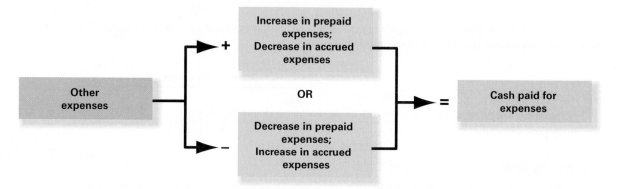

Using information from Exhibit 12.3, we can compute cash paid for expenses for National Beverage as follows:

Prepaid Expenses (A)			Selling, general, and administrative expense	$144,114		Accrued Expenses (L)		
Beg.	4,184		+ Increase in prepaid expenses	4,219		Beg.	23,297
Increase	4,219		− Increase in accrued expenses	(3,049)		Increase	3,049
End.	8,403		Cash payments for other expenses	$145,284		End.	26,346

National Beverage also reports $1,119 of interest expense.[10] Since there is no interest payable balance, we can see that interest expense must be equal to cash payments for interest expense.

Interest expense	$1,119
No changes in interest payable	0
Cash payments for interest	$1,119

The same logic can be applied to income taxes. National Beverage presents income tax expense of $21,896. Since there is no balance in Income Taxes Payable (or change in Deferred Taxes), income taxes paid must be the same as income tax expense.

Income tax expense	$21,896
No change in taxes payable	0
Cash payments for income taxes	$21,896

These amounts of the operating cash inflows and outflows are accumulated in Exhibit 12.8.

---

[10]Certain amounts have been adjusted to simplify the presentation.

Cash flows from operating activities	
Cash collected from customers	$ 598,115
Cash payments to suppliers	(379,391)
Cash payments for other expenses	(145,284)
Cash payments for interest	(1,119)
Cash payments for income taxes	(21,896)
Net cash provided by operating activities	$ 50,425

EXHIBIT 12.8

National Beverage Corp.:
Schedule for Net Cash Flow
from Operating Activities,
Direct Method (dollars in
thousands)

To summarize, the following adjustments must commonly be made to convert income statement items to the related operating cash flow amounts:

Income Statement Account	+/− Change in Balance Sheet Account(s)	= Operating Cash Flow
Sales revenue	+Decrease in Accounts Receivable (A) −Increase in Accounts Receivable (A)	= Collections from customers
Interest/Dividend revenue	+Decrease in Interest/Dividends Receivable (A) −Increase in Interest/Dividends Receivable (A)	= Collections of interest/dividends on investments
Cost of goods sold	+Increase in Inventory (A) −Decrease in Inventory (A) −Increase in Accounts Payable (L) +Decrease in Accounts Payable (L)	= Payments to suppliers of inventory
Other expenses	+Increase in Prepaid Expenses (A) −Decrease in Prepaid Expenses (A) −Increase in Accrued Expenses (L) +Decrease in Accrued Expenses (L)	= Payments to suppliers of services (e.g., rent, utilities, wages, interest)
Income tax expense	+Increase in Prepaid Income Taxes (Deferred Taxes) (A) −Decrease in Prepaid Income Taxes (Deferred Taxes) (A) −Increase in Income Taxes Payable (Deferred Taxes) (L) +Decrease in Income Taxes Payable (Deferred Taxes) (L)	= Payments of income taxes

It is important to note again that the net cash inflow or outflow is the same regardless of whether the direct or indirect method of presentation is used (in National Beverage's case, an inflow of $50,425). The two methods differ only in terms of the details reported on the statement.

PAUSE FOR **FEEDBACK**

SELF-STUDY **QUIZ**

Indicate which of the following line items taken from the cash flow statement would be added (+), subtracted (−), or not included (NA) in the cash flow from operations section when the **direct method** is used.

_____ 1. Increase in inventories.
_____ 2. Payment of dividends to stockholders.
_____ 3. Cash collections from customers.
_____ 4. Purchase of plant and equipment for cash.
_____ 5. Payments of interest to debtholders.
_____ 6. Payment of taxes to the government.

After you have completed your answers, check them with the solutions at the bottom of the page.

1. NA,   2. NA,   3. +,   4. NA,   5. −,   6. −.

Solutions to
SELF-STUDY QUIZ

Chapter Supplement B

Adjustment for Gains and Losses on Sale of Long-Term Assets—Indirect Method

As noted earlier, the Operating Activities section of the cash flow statement prepared using the indirect method may include an adjustment for gains and losses on the sale of long-term assets reported on the income statement. As discussed in Chapter 8, when property, plant, and equipment with an original cost of $10,000 and accumulated depreciation of $4,000 is sold for $8,000 cash, the following entry is made.

$8,000 Investing cash inflow

$2,000 subtraction in the Operating section

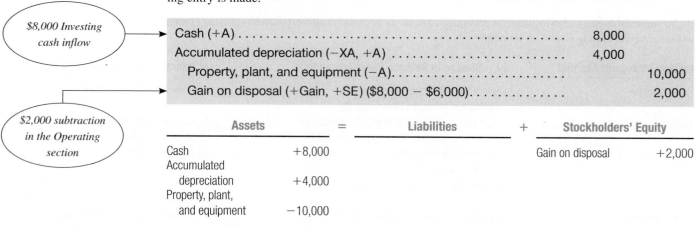

Cash (+A)	8,000	
Accumulated depreciation (−XA, +A)	4,000	
Property, plant, and equipment (−A).		10,000
Gain on disposal (+Gain, +SE) ($8,000 − $6,000).		2,000

Assets		=	Liabilities	+	Stockholders' Equity	
Cash	+8,000				Gain on disposal	+2,000
Accumulated depreciation	+4,000					
Property, plant, and equipment	−10,000					

The $8,000 inflow of cash is an investing cash inflow, but the reported gain of $2,000 is also shown on the income statement. Because the gain is included in the computation of income, it is necessary to remove (subtract) the $2,000 gain from the Operating Activities section of the statement to avoid double counting.

Cash flows from operating activities
Net income	40,754
Adjustments to reconcile net income to cash flow from operating activities:	
. . .	. . .
Gain on disposal of property, plant, and equipment	(2,000)
. . .	. . .
Net cash flow provided by operating activities	. . .

Cash flows from investing activities
Purchases of property, plant, and equipment	. . .
Proceeds from disposal of property, plant, and equipment	8,000
. . .	. . .
Net cash used in investing activities	. . .

If the company had sold the same asset for $5,000 cash, the following entry would be made:

$5,000 Investing cash inflow

$1,000 addition in the Operating section

Cash (+A)	5,000	
Accumulated depreciation (−XA, +A)	4,000	
Loss on disposal (−Loss, −SE) ($5,000 − $6,000)	1,000	
Property, plant, and equipment (−A).		10,000

Assets		=	Liabilities	+	Stockholders' Equity	
Cash	+5,000				Loss on disposal	−1,000
Accumulated depreciation	+4,000					
Property, plant, and equipment	−10,000					

On the cash flow statement, the loss of $1,000 must be removed (added back) in the computation of cash from operating activities, and the total cash collected of $5,000 must be shown in the investing activities section of the statement.

Cash flows from operating activities	
Net income	$40,754
Adjustments to reconcile net income to cash flow from operating activities:	
. . .	. . .
Loss on disposal of property, plant, and equipment	1,000
. . .	. . .
Net cash flow provided by operating activities	. . .
Cash flows from investing activities	
Purchases of property, plant, and equipment	. . .
Proceeds from disposal of property, plant, and equipment	5,000
. . .	. . .
Net cash used in investing activities	. . .

Chapter Supplement C

T-Account Approach (Indirect Method)

When we began our discussion of preparing the statement of cash flows, we noted that changes in cash must equal the sum of the changes in all other balance sheet accounts. Based on this idea, we used the following three steps to prepare the statement of cash flows:

1. Determine the change in each balance sheet account. From this year's ending balance, subtract this year's beginning balance (i.e., last year's ending balance).
2. Identify the cash flow category or categories to which each account relates.
3. Create schedules that summarize operating, investing, and financing cash flows.

Instead of creating separate schedules for each section of the statement, many accountants prefer to prepare a single large T-account to represent the changes that have taken place in cash subdivided into the three sections of the cash flow statement. Such an account is presented in Panel A of Exhibit 12.9. The cash account in Panel A shows increases in cash as debits and decreases in cash as credits. Note how each section matches the three schedules that we prepared for National Beverage's cash flows presented in Exhibits 12.4, 12.5, and 12.6. Panel B includes the same T-accounts for the noncash balance sheet accounts we used in our discussion of each cash flow statement section in the body of the chapter. Note how each change in the noncash balance sheet accounts has a number referencing the change in the cash account that it accompanies. The statement of cash flows presented in Exhibit 12.1 can be prepared in proper format based on the information in the cash flow T-account.

CHAPTER **TAKE-AWAYS**

12-1. **Classify cash flow statement items as part of net cash flows from operating, investing, and financing activities.   p. 590**

The statement has three main sections: Cash Flows from Operating Activities, which are related to earning income from normal operations; Cash Flows from Investing Activities, which are related to the acquisition and sale of productive assets; and Cash Flows from Financing Activities, which are related to external financing of the enterprise. The net cash inflow or outflow for the year is the same amount as the increase or decrease in cash and cash equivalents for the year on the balance sheet. Cash equivalents are highly liquid investments with original maturities of three months or less.

12-2. **Report and interpret cash flows from operating activities using the indirect method.   p. 597**

The indirect method for reporting cash flows from operating activities reports a conversion of net income to net cash flow from operating activities. The conversion involves additions and subtractions for (1) noncurrent accruals including expenses (such as depreciation expense) and revenues that do not affect current assets or current liabilities and (2) changes in each of the

EXHIBIT 12.9	T-Account Approach to Preparing the Statement of Cash Flows (Indirect Method)

Panel A: Changes in Cash Account

Cash (A)			
Operating			
(1) Net Income	40,754	2,078	(3) Accounts Receivable
(2) Depreciation and Amortization	10,771	4,219	(5) Prepaid Expense
(4) Inventory	1,319		
(6) Accounts Payable	829		
(7) Accrued Expenses	3,049		
Net cash flow provided by operating activities	50,425		
Investing			
(9) Disposals of Property, Plant & Equipment	77	11,389	(8) Purchased Property, Plant & Equipment
(11) Sales of Short-term Investments	8,406	6,532	(10) Purchased Short-term Investments
		9,438	**Net cash used in investing activities**
Financing			
(13) Proceeds from Stock Issuance	4,324	191	(12) Payment of Long-term Debt
		106,314	(14) Payment of Dividends
		102,181	**Net cash used by financing activities**
		61,194	**Net decrease in cash and cash equivalents**

Panel B: Changes in Noncash Accounts

Accounts Receivable (A)		
Beg. bal.	53,834	
(3) Increase	2,078	
End. bal.	55,912	

Inventories (A)		
Beg. bal.	34,672	
		(4) Decrease 1,319
End. bal.	33,353	

Prepaid Expenses (A)		
End. bal.	4,184	
(5) Increase	4,219	
End. bal.	8,403	

Accounts Payable (L)		
	Beg. bal.	48,428
	(6) Increase	829
	End. bal.	49,257

Accrued Expenses (L)		
	Beg. bal.	23,297
	(7) Increase	3,049
	End. bal.	26,346

Property, Plant & Equipment, Net (A)			
End. bal.	75,736	(2) Depreciation	10,771
(8) Purchases	11,389	(9) Disposals	77
End. bal.	76,277		

Short-term Investments		
Beg. bal.	3,367	
(10) Purchases 6,532	(11) Disposals 8,406
End. bal.	1,493	

Long-term Debt (L)		
(12) Payments 191	Beg. bal.	27,062
	Borrowings	0
	End. bal.	26,871

Contributed Capital (SE)		
	Beg. bal.	10,805
Stock repurchased 0	(13) Stock issued 4,324
	End. bal.	15,129

Retained Earnings (SE)		
	Beg. bal.	130,767
(14) Dividends 106,314	(1) Net income	40,754
	End. bal.	65,207

individual current assets (other than cash and short-term investments) and current liabilities (other than short-term debt to financial institutions and current maturities of long-term debt, which relate to financing), which reflect differences in the timing of accrual basis net income and cash flows.

12-3.   Analyze and interpret the quality of income ratio.   p. 603

The quality of income ratio (Cash Flow from Operating Activities ÷ Net Income) measures the portion of income that was generated in cash. A higher quality of income ratio indicates greater ability to finance operating and other cash needs from operating cash inflows. A higher ratio also indicates that it is less likely that the company is using aggressive revenue recognition policies to increase net income.

12-4.   Report and interpret cash flows from investing activities.   p. 604

Investing activities reported on the cash flow statement include cash payments to acquire fixed assets, intangibles, and short- and long-term investments and cash proceeds from the sale of fixed assets, intangibles, and short- and long-term investments.

12-5.   Analyze and interpret the capital acquisitions ratio.   p. 606

The capital acquisitions ratio (Cash Flow from Operating Activities ÷ Cash Paid for Property, Plant, and Equipment) reflects the portion of purchases of property, plant, and equipment financed from operating activities without the need for outside debt or equity financing or the sale of other investments or fixed assets. A high ratio benefits the company because it provides the company with opportunities for strategic acquisitions.

12-6.   Report and interpret cash flows from financing activities.   p. 607

Cash inflows from financing activities include cash proceeds from the issuance of short- and long-term debt and common stock. Cash outflows include cash principal payments on short- and long-term debt, cash paid for the repurchase of the company's stock, and cash dividend payments. Cash payments associated with interest are a cash flow from operating activities.

12-7.   Understand the format of the cash flow statement and additional cash flow disclosures.   p. 609

The statement of cash flows splits transactions that affect cash into three categories: Operating, Investing, and Financing Activities. The operating section is most often prepared using the indirect method that begins with Net Income and adjusts the amount to eliminate noncash transactions. Noncash investing and financing activities are investing and financing activities that do not involve cash. They include, for example, purchases of fixed assets with long-term debt or stock, exchanges of fixed assets, and exchanges of debt for stock. These transactions are disclosed only as supplemental disclosures to the cash flow statement along with cash paid for taxes and interest under the indirect method.

Throughout the preceding chapters, we emphasized the conceptual basis of accounting. An understanding of the rationale underlying accounting is important for both preparers and users of financial statements. In Chapter 13, we bring together our discussion of the major users of financial statements and how they analyze and use them. We discuss and illustrate many widely used analytical techniques discussed in earlier chapters, as well as additional techniques. As you study Chapter 13, you will see that an understanding of accounting rules and concepts is essential for effective analysis of financial statements.

KEY **RATIOS**

The **quality of income ratio** indicates what portion of income was generated in cash. It is computed as follows (p. 603):

$$\text{Quality of Income Ratio} = \frac{\text{Cash Flow from Operating Activities}}{\text{Net Income}}$$

The **capital acquisitions ratio** measures the ability to finance purchases of plant and equipment from operations. It is computed as follows (p. 606):

$$\text{Capital Acquisitions Ratio} = \frac{\text{Cash Flow from Operating Activities}}{\text{Cash Paid for Property, Plant, and Equipment}}$$

FINDING **FINANCIAL INFORMATION**

Balance Sheet
Changes in Assets, Liabilities, and Stockholders' Equity

Income Statement
Net Income and Noncurrent Accruals

Statement of Cash Flows
Cash Flows from Operating Activities

Cash Flows from Investing Activities

Cash Flows from Financing Activities

Separate Schedule (or note):
Noncash investing and financing activities
Interest and taxes paid

Notes
Under Summary of Significant
Accounting Policies:
Definition of cash equivalents

Under Separate Note
if not listed on cash flow statement:
Noncash investing and financing activities
Interest and taxes paid

KEY **TERMS**

Cash Equivalent   p. 590
Cash Flows from Financing
Activities   p. 593
Cash Flows from Investing
Activities   p. 592

Cash Flows from Operating
Activities (Cash Flows from
Operations)   p. 591
Direct Method   p. 591
Free Cash Flow   p. 606

Indirect Method   p. 592
Noncash Investing and Financing
Activities   p. 610

QUESTIONS

1. Compare the purposes of the income statement, the balance sheet, and the statement of cash flows.
2. What information does the statement of cash flows report that is not reported on the other required financial statements?
3. What are cash equivalents? How are purchases and sales of cash equivalents reported on the statement of cash flows?
4. What are the major categories of business activities reported on the statement of cash flows? Define each of these activities.
5. What are the typical cash inflows from operating activities? What are the typical cash outflows from operating activities?
6. Under the indirect method, depreciation expense is added to net income to report cash flows from operating activities. Does depreciation cause an inflow of cash?
7. Explain why cash paid during the period for purchases and for salaries is not specifically reported on the statement of cash flows, indirect method, as cash outflows.
8. Explain why a $50,000 increase in inventory during the year must be included in developing cash flows from operating activities under both the direct and indirect methods.
9. Compare the two methods of reporting cash flows from operating activities in the statement of cash flows.
10. What are the typical cash inflows from investing activities? What are the typical cash outflows from investing activities?
11. What are the typical cash inflows from financing activities? What are the typical cash outflows from financing activities?
12. What are noncash investing and financing activities? Give two examples. How are they reported on the statement of cash flows?
13. How is the sale of equipment reported on the statement of cash flows using the indirect method?

1. In what order do the three sections of the statement of cash flows usually appear when reading from top to bottom?
   a. Financing, Investing, Operating
   b. Investing, Operating, Financing
   c. Operating, Financing, Investing
   d. Operating, Investing, Financing

2. Total cash inflow in the operating section of the statement of cash flows should include which of the following?
   a. Cash received from customers at the point of sale.
   b. Cash collections from customer accounts receivable.
   c. Cash received in advance of revenue recognition (unearned revenue).
   d. All of the above.

3. If the balance in prepaid expenses has increased during the year, what action should be taken on the statement of cash flows when following the indirect method, and why?
   a. The change in the account balance should be subtracted from net income because the net increase in prepaid expenses did not impact net income but did reduce the cash balance.
   b. The change in the account balance should be added to net income because the net increase in prepaid expenses did not impact net income but did increase the cash balance.
   c. The net change in prepaid expenses should be subtracted from net income to reverse the income statement effect that had no impact on cash.
   d. The net change in prepaid expenses should be added to net income to reverse the income statement effect that had no impact on cash.

4. Consider the following: Net income = $10,000, depreciation expense = $2,000, accounts receivable increased by $800, inventory decreased by $100, and accounts payable increased by $500. Based on this information alone, what is cash flow from operating activities?
   a. $12,000
   b. $11,600
   c. $11,800
   d. $13,400

5. Which of the following would **not** appear in the investing section of the statement of cash flows?
   a. Purchase of inventory.
   b. Sale of obsolete equipment used in the factory.
   c. Purchase of land for a new office building.
   d. All of the above would appear.

6. Which of the following items would **not** appear in the financing section of the statement of cash flows?
   a. The repurchase of the company's own stock.
   b. The receipt of dividends.
   c. The repayment of debt.
   d. The payment of dividends.

7. Which of the following is **not** added to net income when computing cash flows from operations under the indirect method?
   a. The net increase in accounts payable.
   b. The net decrease in accounts receivable.
   c. Depreciation expense reported on the income statement.
   d. All of the above are added to net income.

8. Consider the following: Issued common stock for $18,000, sold office equipment for $1,200, paid cash dividends $4,000, purchased investments for $2,000, paid accounts payable of $4,000. What was the net cash inflow (outflow) from financing activities?
   a. $20,000
   b. $14,000
   c. ($20,000)
   d. ($14,000)

9. Consider the following: Issued common stock for $18,000, sold office equipment for $1,200, paid cash dividends $4,000, purchased investments for $2,000, purchased new equipment for $4,000. What was the net cash inflow (outflow) from investing activities?
   a. $20,200
   b. ($2,800)
   c. ($10,800)
   d. ($4,800)

10. The **total** change in cash as shown near the bottom of the statement of cash flows for the year should agree with which of the following?
    a. The difference in retained earnings when reviewing the comparative balance sheet.
    b. Net income or net loss as found on the income statement.
    c. The difference in cash when reviewing the comparative balance sheet.
    d. None of the above.

MINI-**EXERCISES**

M12-1
LO12-1

Matching Items Reported to Cash Flow Statement Categories (Indirect Method)

MillerCoors Brewing Company is the world's fifth largest brewer. In the United States, its tie to the magical appeal of the Rocky Mountains is one of its most powerful trademarks. Some of the items included in its recent annual consolidated statement of cash flows presented using the **indirect method** are listed here. Indicate whether each item is disclosed in the Operating Activities (O), Investing Activities (I), or Financing Activities (F) section of the statement or use (NA) if the item does not appear on the statement. (**Note:** This is the exact wording used on the actual statement.)

_____ 1. Purchase of stock. [This involves repurchase of the company's own stock.]
_____ 2. Principal payment on long-term debt.
_____ 3. Proceeds from sale of properties.
_____ 4. Inventories (decrease).
_____ 5. Accounts payable (decrease).
_____ 6. Depreciation, depletion, and amortization.

M12-2
LO12-2

Determining the Effects of Account Changes on Cash Flow from Operating Activities (Indirect Method)

Indicate whether each item would be added ($+$) or subtracted ($-$) in the computation of cash flow from operating activities using the indirect method.

_____ 1. Accrued expenses (increase).
_____ 2. Inventories (increase).
_____ 3. Accounts receivable (decrease).
_____ 4. Accounts payable (decrease).
_____ 5. Depreciation, depletion, and amortization.

M12-3
LO12-1

Lion

Matching Items Reported to Cash Flow Statement Categories (Direct Method)

Lion Nathan, brewer of XXXX, Toohey's, and other well-known Australian brands, has net revenue of more than $2 billion (Australian). Some of the items included in its recent annual consolidated statement of cash flows presented using the **direct method** are listed here. Indicate whether each item is disclosed in the Operating Activities (O), Investing Activities (I), or Financing Activities (F) section of the statement or use (NA) if the item does not appear on the statement. (**Note:** This is the exact wording used on the actual statement.)

_____ 1. Receipts from customers.
_____ 2. Dividends paid.
_____ 3. Payment for share buy-back.
_____ 4. Proceeds from sale of property, plant, and equipment.
_____ 5. Repayments of borrowings (bank debt).
_____ 6. Net interest paid.

M12-4
LO12-3

Analyzing the Quality of Income Ratio

Casey Corporation reported net income of $102,000, depreciation expense of $2,000, and cash flow from operations of $86,500. Compute the quality of income ratio. What does the ratio tell you about the company's ability to finance operating and other cash needs from operating cash inflows?

M12-5
LO12-4

Computing Cash Flows from Investing Activities

Based on the following information, compute cash flows from investing activities.

Cash collections from customers	$550
Sale of used equipment	400
Depreciation expense	200
Purchase of short-term investments	635

Computing Cash Flows from Financing Activities

Based on the following information, compute cash flows from financing activities.

Purchase of short-term investments	$ 500
Dividends paid	700
Interest paid	300
Additional short-term borrowing from bank	1,200

M12-6
LO12-6

Reporting Noncash Investing and Financing Activities

Which of the following transactions qualify as noncash investing and financing activities?

_____ Purchase of building with mortgage payable.
_____ Additional short-term borrowing from bank.
_____ Dividends paid in cash.
_____ Purchase of equipment with short-term investments.

M12-7
LO12-7

EXERCISES

Matching Items Reported to Cash Flow Statement Categories (Indirect Method)

Reebok International Ltd. is a global company that designs and markets sports and fitness products, including footwear, apparel, and accessories. Some of the items included in its recent annual consolidated statement of cash flows presented using the **indirect method** are listed here.

Indicate whether each item is disclosed in the Operating Activities (O), Investing Activities (I), or Financing Activities (F) section of the statement or (NA) if the item does not appear on the statement. (**Note:** This is the exact wording used on the actual statement.)

_____ 1. Dividends paid.
_____ 2. Repayments of long-term debt.
_____ 3. Depreciation and amortization.
_____ 4. Proceeds from issuance of common stock to employees.
_____ 5. [Change in] Accounts payable and accrued expenses.
_____ 6. Cash collections from customers.
_____ 7. Net repayments of notes payable to banks.
_____ 8. Net income.
_____ 9. Payments to acquire property and equipment.
_____ 10. [Change in] Inventory.

E12-1
LO12-1
Reebok

Matching Items Reported to Cash Flow Statement Categories (Direct Method)

EMC Corporation helps store, manage, protect, analyze, and secure information for companies that use Cloud Computing. Some of the items included in its recent annual consolidated statement of cash flows presented using the **direct method** are listed here.

Indicate whether each item is disclosed in the Operating Activities (O), Investing Activities (I), or Financing Activities (F) section of the statement or (NA) if the item does not appear on the statement. (**Note:** This is the exact wording used on the actual statement.)

_____ 1. Sales of short- and long-term available-for-sale securities (investments).
_____ 2. Interest paid.
_____ 3. Additions to property, plant, and equipment.
_____ 4. Income taxes paid.
_____ 5. Issuance of EMC's common stock.
_____ 6. Payment of long-term and short-term obligations.
_____ 7. Dividends and interest received.
_____ 8. Cash received from customers.
_____ 9. Purchases of short- and long-term available-for-sale securities.
_____ 10. Net income.

E12-2
LO12-1
EMC

E12-3
LO12-1

Determining Cash Flow Statement Effects of Transactions

Stanley Furniture Company is a Virginia-based furniture manufacturer. For each of the following first-year transactions, indicate whether **net cash inflows (outflows)** from operating activities (NCFO), investing activities (NCFI), or financing activities (NCFF) are affected and whether the effect is an inflow (+) or outflow (−), or (NE) if the transaction has no effect on cash. (**Hint:** Determine the journal entry recorded for the transaction. The transaction affects net cash flows *if and only if* the account Cash is affected.)

_____ 1. Recorded an adjusting entry to record accrued salaries expense.
_____ 2. Paid cash to purchase new equipment.
_____ 3. Collected payments on account from customers.
_____ 4. Recorded and paid interest on debt to creditors.
_____ 5. Declared and paid cash dividends to shareholders.
_____ 6. Sold used equipment for cash at book value.
_____ 7. Prepaid rent for the following period.
_____ 8. Repaid principal on revolving credit loan from bank.
_____ 9. Purchased raw materials inventory on account.
_____ 10. Made payment to suppliers on account.

E12-4
LO12-1

Hewlett-Packard

Determining Cash Flow Statement Effects of Transactions

Hewlett-Packard is a leading manufacturer of computer equipment for the business and home markets. For each of the following recent transactions, indicate whether **net cash inflows (outflows)** from operating activities (NCFO), investing activities (NCFI), or financing activities (NCFF) are affected and whether the effect is an inflow (+) or outflow (−), or (NE) if the transaction has no effect on cash. (**Hint:** Determine the journal entry recorded for the transaction. The transaction affects net cash flows *if and only if* the account Cash is affected.)

_____ 1. Purchased raw materials inventory on account.
_____ 2. Prepaid rent for the following period.
_____ 3. Purchased new equipment by signing a three-year note.
_____ 4. Recorded an adjusting entry for expiration of a prepaid expense.
_____ 5. Recorded and paid income taxes to the federal government.
_____ 6. Purchased investment securities for cash.
_____ 7. Issued common stock for cash.
_____ 8. Collected payments on account from customers.
_____ 9. Sold equipment for cash equal to its net book value.
_____ 10. Issued long-term debt for cash.

E12-5
LO12-1

Comparing the Direct and Indirect Methods

To compare statement of cash flows reporting under the direct and indirect methods, enter check marks to indicate which items are used with each method.

Cash Flows (and Related Changes)	STATEMENT OF CASH FLOWS METHOD	
	Direct	Indirect
1. Accounts payable increase or decrease		
2. Payments to employees		
3. Cash collections from customers		
4. Accounts receivable increase or decrease		
5. Payments to suppliers		
6. Inventory increase or decrease		
7. Wages payable, increase or decrease		
8. Depreciation expense		
9. Net income		
10. Cash flows from operating activities		
11. Cash flows from investing activities		
12. Cash flows from financing activities		
13. Net increase or decrease in cash during the period		

Reporting Cash Flows from Operating Activities (Indirect Method)

The following information pertains to Peak Heights Company:

Income Statement for 2015		
Sales		$93,000
Expenses		
Cost of goods sold	$51,875	
Depreciation expense	6,000	
Salaries expense	12,000	69,875
Net income		$23,125
Partial Balance Sheet	**2015**	**2014**
Accounts receivable	$10,500	$11,000
Inventory	13,000	8,000
Salaries payable	2,250	800

Required:
Present the operating activities section of the statement of cash flows for Peak Heights Company using the indirect method.

Reporting and Interpreting Cash Flows from Operating Activities from an Analyst's Perspective (Indirect Method)

Rodriguez Company completed its income statement and balance sheet for 2015 and provided the following information:

Income Statement for 2015		
Service revenue		$54,000
Expenses		
Salaries	$46,000	
Depreciation	4,500	
Amortization of copyrights	200	
Other expenses	9,700	60,400
Net loss		$ (6,400)
Partial Balance Sheet	**2015**	**2014**
Accounts receivable	$ 8,000	$13,000
Salaries payable	12,000	1,000
Other accrued liabilities	1,000	2,800

In addition, Rodriguez bought a small service machine for $5,000.

Required:
1. Present the operating activities section of the statement of cash flows for Rodriguez Company using the indirect method.
2. What were the major reasons that Rodriguez was able to report a net loss but positive cash flow from operations? Why are the reasons for the difference between cash flow from operations and net income important to financial analysts?

E12-8

LO12-2

Reporting and Interpreting Cash Flows from Operating Activities with Loss on Sale of Equipment (Indirect Method)

Parra Company completed its income statement and balance sheet for 2014 and provided the following information:

Service revenue		$125,000
Expenses:		
Salaries	$92,000	
Depreciation	8,500	
Utilities	8,000	
Loss on sale of equipment	2,500	111,000
Net income		$ 14,000

Partial Balance Sheet	2014	2013
Accounts receivable	$14,000	$ 24,000
Salaries payable	19,000	8,000
Other accrued liabilities	7,000	9,000
Land	52,000	57,000

Required:

Present the operating activities section of the statement of cash flows for Parra Company using the indirect method.

E12-9

LO12-2

Time Warner Inc.

Reporting and Interpreting Cash Flows from Operating Activities from an Analyst's Perspective (Indirect Method)

Time Warner Inc. is a leading media and entertainment company with businesses in television networks, filmed entertainment, and publishing. The company's 2011 annual report contained the following information (dollars in millions):

Net loss	$(13,402)
Depreciation, amortization, and impairments	34,790
Decrease in receivables	1,245
Increase in inventories	5,766
Decrease in accounts payable	445
Additions to equipment	4,377

Required:

1. Based on this information, compute cash flow from operating activities using the indirect method.
2. What were the major reasons that Time Warner was able to report a net loss but positive cash flow from operations? Why are the reasons for the difference between cash flow from operations and net income important to financial analysts?

E12-10

LO12-2

The Colgate-Palmolive Company

Inferring Balance Sheet Changes from the Cash Flow Statement (Indirect Method)

A recent statement of cash flows for Colgate-Palmolive reported the following information (dollars in millions):

Operating Activities	
Net income	$2,554
Depreciation	421
Cash effect of changes in	
Receivables	(130)
Inventories	(130)
Other current assets	54
Payables	199
Other	(72)
Net cash provided by operations	$2,896

Required:

Based on the information reported on the statement of cash flows for Colgate-Palmolive, determine whether the following accounts increased or decreased during the period: Receivables, Inventories, Other Current Assets, and Payables.

Inferring Balance Sheet Changes from the Cash Flow Statement (Indirect Method)

E12-11
LO12-2

A recent statement of cash flows for Apple contained the following information (dollars in millions):

Apple, Inc.

Operations	
Net income	$25,922
Depreciation	1,814
Changes in assets and liabilities	
Accounts receivable	143
Inventories	275
Other current assets	(1,391)
Accounts payable	2,515
Deferred revenue	1,654
Other current liabilities	4,495
Other adjustments	2,102
Cash generated by operations	$37,529

Required:

For each of the asset and liability accounts listed on the statement of cash flows, determine whether the account balances increased or decreased during the period.

(Supplement B) Computing and Reporting Cash Flow Effects of Sale of Plant and Equipment

E12-12

During two recent years Perez Construction, Inc., disposed of the following plant and equipment:

	Year 1	Year 2
Plant and equipment (at cost)	$ 75,000	$13,500
Accumulated depreciation on equipment disposed of	40,385	3,773
Cash received	17,864	12,163
Gain (loss) on sale	(16,751)	2,436

Required:

1. Determine the cash flow from the sale of property for each year that would be reported in the investing activities section of the cash flow statement.
2. Perez uses the indirect method for the operating activities section of the cash flow statement. What amounts related to the sales would be added or subtracted in the computation of Net Cash Flows from Operating Activities for each year?

(Supplement B) Computing and Reporting Cash Flow Effects of the Sale of Equipment

E12-13

During the period, Sanchez Company sold some excess equipment at a loss. The following information was collected from the company's accounting records:

From the Income Statement	
Depreciation expense	$ 1,500
Loss on sale of equipment	2,300
From the Balance Sheet	
Beginning equipment	82,500
Ending equipment	72,000
Beginning accumulated depreciation	43,000
Ending accumulated depreciation	41,000

No new equipment was bought during the period.

Required:

1. For the equipment that was sold, determine its original cost, its accumulated depreciation, and the cash received from the sale. (Use the equipment and accumulated depreciation T-accounts to infer the book value of the equipment sold.)
2. Sanchez Company uses the indirect method for the Operating Activities section of the cash flow statement. What amount related to the sale would be added or subtracted in the computation of Net Cash Flows from Operating Activities?
3. What amount related to the sale would be added or subtracted in the computation of Net Cash Flows from Investing Activities?

E12-14

LO12-2, 12-3

Analyzing Cash Flows from Operating Activities; Interpreting the Quality of Income Ratio

A recent annual report for PepsiCo contained the following information for the period (dollars in millions):

Net income	$6,462
Depreciation and amortization	2,737
Increase in accounts receivable	666
Increase in inventory	331
Increase in prepaid expense	27
Increase in accounts payable	520
Decrease in taxes payable	340
Increase in other current liabilities	589
Cash dividends paid	3,157
Treasury stock purchased	2,489

Required:

1. Compute cash flows from operating activities for PepsiCo using the indirect method.
2. Compute the quality of income ratio.
3. What were the major reasons that PepsiCo's quality of income ratio did not equal 1.0?

E12-15

LO12-4, 12-6

Reporting Cash Flows from Investing and Financing Activities

Oering's Furniture Corporation is a Virginia-based manufacturer of furniture. In a recent year, it reported the following activities:

Net income	$ 5,135
Purchase of property, plant, and equipment	1,071
Borrowings under line of credit (bank)	1,117
Proceeds from issuance of stock	11
Cash received from customers	37,164
Payments to reduce long-term debt	46
Sale of marketable securities	219
Proceeds from sale of property and equipment	6,894
Dividends paid	277
Interest paid	90
Purchase of treasury stock (stock repurchase)	2,583

Required:

Based on this information, present the cash flows from investing and financing activities sections of the cash flow statement.

E12-16

LO12-2, 12-4, 12-6

Preparing a Statement of Cash Flows (Indirect Method)

Shallow Waters Company was started several years ago by two diving instructors. The company's comparative balance sheets and income statement are presented below, along with additional information.

	2015	2014
Balance Sheet at December 31		
Cash	$ 3,900	$4,500
Accounts receivable	1,300	800
Prepaid expenses	100	250
Equipment	700	0
	$ 6,000	$5,550
Wages payable	$ 650	$1,100
Contributed capital	1,600	1,400
Retained earnings	3,750	3,050
	$ 6,000	$5,550
Income Statement for 2015		
Lessons revenue	$34,550	
Wages expense	30,200	
Other expenses	3,650	
Net income	$ 700	

Additional Data:
a. Prepaid expenses relate to rent paid in advance.
b. Other expenses were paid in cash.
c. Purchased equipment for $700 cash at the end of 2015 to be used starting in 2016.
d. An owner contributed capital by paying $200 cash in exchange for the company's stock.

Required:
Prepare the statement of cash flows for the year ended December 31, 2015, using the indirect method.

Reporting and Interpreting Cash Flows from Investing and Financing Activities with Discussion of Management Strategy

E12-17
LO12-4, 12-5, 12-6

Gibraltar Industries is a Buffalo, New York–based manufacturer of high-value-added steel products. In a recent year, it reported the following activities:

Gibraltar Industries

Acquisitions (investments in other companies)	$(109,248)
Increase in inventories	(10,101)
Depreciation and amortization	26,181
Long-term debt reduction	(76,658)
Net cash provided by operating activities	46,695
Net income	16,523
Net proceeds from issuance of common stock	34
Net proceeds from sale of property and equipment	1,226
Proceeds from long-term debt	73,849
Proceeds from sale of other equity investments	69,368
Purchases of property, plant, and equipment	(11,552)

Required:
1. Based on this information, present the cash flows from investing and financing activities sections of the cash flow statement.
2. Compute the capital acquisitions ratio. What does the ratio tell you about Gibraltar's ability to finance purchases of property, plant, and equipment with cash provided by operating activities?
3. What do you think was Gibraltar management's plan for the use of the cash generated by selling other equity investments?

E12-18

LO12-5, 12-7

Reporting Noncash Transactions on the Statement of Cash Flows; Interpreting the Effect on the Capital Acquisitions Ratio

An analysis of Courtney Corporation's operational asset accounts provided the following information:

a. Acquired a large machine that cost $36,000, paying for it by giving a $15,000, 12 percent interest-bearing note due at the end of two years and 500 shares of its common stock, with a par value of $10 per share and a market value of $42 per share.

b. Acquired a small machine that cost $12,700. Full payment was made by transferring a tract of land that had a book value of $12,700.

Required:
1. Show how this information should be reported on the statement of cash flows.
2. What would be the effect of these transactions on the capital acquisitions ratio? How might these transactions distort one's interpretation of the ratio?

E12-19

(Supplement A) Reporting Cash Flows from Operating Activities from an Analyst's Perspective (Direct Method)

Refer to the information for Peak Heights Company in Exercise 12-6.

Required:
Present the operating activities section of the statement of cash flows for Peak Heights Company using the direct method.

E12-20

(Supplement A) Reporting and Interpreting Cash Flows from Operating Activities from an Analyst's Perspective (Direct Method)

Refer to the information for Rodriguez Company in Exercise 12-7.

Required:
1. Present the operating activities section of the statement of cash flows for Rodriguez Company using the direct method. Assume that other accrued liabilities relate to other expenses on the income statement.
2. What were the major reasons that Rodriguez was able to report a net loss but positive cash flow from operations? Why are the reasons for the difference between cash flow from operations and net income important to financial analysts?

E12-21

(Supplement A) Reporting and Interpreting Cash Flows from Operating Activities from an Analyst's Perspective (Direct Method)

Refer to the following summarized income statement and additional selected information for Trumansburg, Inc.:

Income Statement	
Revenues	$150,800
Cost of sales	55,500
Gross margin	95,300
Salary expense	55,400
Depreciation and amortization	33,305
Other expense	9,600
Net loss before tax	(3,005)
Income tax expense	1,500
Net loss	$ (4,505)

Other information:	
Decrease in receivables	$ 800
Decrease in inventories	230
Increase in prepaid expenses	1,500
Increase in accounts payable	1,750
Decrease in accrued liabilities	602
Increase in income taxes payable	1,280

Required:
1. Based on this information, compute cash flow from operating activities using the direct method. Assume that prepaid expenses and accrued liabilities relate to other expense.

2. What were the major reasons that Trumansburg was able to report a net loss but positive cash flow from operations? Why are the reasons for the difference between cash flows from operations and net income important to financial analysts?

(Supplement C) Preparing a Statement of Cash Flows, Indirect Method: T-Account Method   **E12-22**

Golf Universe is a regional and online golf equipment retailer. The company reported the following for the current year:

Purchased a long-term investment for cash, $15,000.

Paid cash dividend, $12,000.

Sold equipment for $6,000 cash (cost, $21,000, accumulated depreciation, $15,000).

Issued shares of no-par stock, 500 shares at $12 per share cash.

Net income was $20,200.

Depreciation expense was $3,000.

Its comparative balance sheet is presented below.

	Balances 12/31/2013	Balances 12/31/2012
Cash	$ 19,200	$ 20,500
Accounts receivable	22,000	22,000
Merchandise inventory	75,000	68,000
Investments	15,000	0
Equipment	93,500	114,500
Accumulated depreciation	(20,000)	(32,000)
Total	$204,700	$193,000
Accounts payable	$ 14,000	$ 17,000
Wages payable	1,500	2,500
Income taxes payable	4,500	3,000
Notes payable	54,000	54,000
Contributed capital	106,000	100,000
Retained earnings	24,700	16,500
Total	$204,700	$193,000

Required:

1. Following Supplement C, complete a T-account worksheet to be used to prepare the statement of cash flows for the current year.

2. Based on the T-account worksheet, prepare the statement of cash flows for the current year in proper format.

For more practice with exercises, go to the text website at **www.mhhe.com/libby8e**.

PROBLEMS

Preparing a Statement of Cash Flows (Indirect Method) (AP12-1)

Sharp Screen Films, Inc., is developing its annual financial statements at December 31, 2015. The statements are complete except for the statement of cash flows. The completed comparative balance sheets and income statement are summarized as follows:

P12-1
LO12-1, 12-2, 12-4, 12-6

www.mhhe.com/libby8e

	2015	2014
Balance sheet at December 31		
Cash	$ 73,250	$ 63,500
Accounts receivable	15,250	21,350
Merchandise inventory	23,450	18,000
Property and equipment	209,250	160,350
Less: Accumulated depreciation	(57,450)	(45,750)
	$263,750	$217,450

Accounts payable	$ 16,500	$ 19,000
Wages payable	2,000	2,700
Note payable, long-term	56,300	71,000
Contributed capital	103,950	65,900
Retained earnings	85,000	58,850
	$263,750	$217,450
Income statement for 2015		
Sales	$205,000	
Cost of goods sold	123,500	
Depreciation expense	11,700	
Other expenses	43,000	
Net income	$ 26,800	

Additional Data:

a. Bought equipment for cash, $48,900.
b. Paid $14,700 on the long-term note payable.
c. Issued new shares of stock for $38,050 cash.
d. Dividends of $650 were declared and paid.
e. Other expenses all relate to wages.
f. Accounts payable includes only inventory purchases made on credit.

Required:

1. Prepare the statement of cash flows using the indirect method for the year ended December 31, 2015.
2. Based on the cash flow statement, write a short paragraph explaining the major sources and uses of cash by Sharp Screen Films during 2015.

P12-2

LO12-1, 12-2, 12-4, 12-6

Preparing a Statement of Cash Flows (Indirect Method) (AP12-2)

BG Wholesalers is developing its annual financial statements at December 31, 2016. The statements are complete except for the statement of cash flows. The completed comparative balance sheets and income statement are summarized:

	2016	2015
Balance sheet at December 31		
Cash	$ 37,000	$ 29,000
Accounts receivable	32,000	28,000
Merchandise inventory	41,000	38,000
Property and equipment	132,000	111,000
Less: Accumulated depreciation	(41,000)	(36,000)
	$201,000	$170,000
Accounts payable	$ 36,000	$ 27,000
Accrued wage expense	1,200	1,400
Note payable, long-term	38,000	44,000
Contributed capital	88,600	72,600
Retained earnings	37,200	25,000
	$201,000	$170,000
Income statement for 2016		
Sales	$120,000	
Cost of goods sold	70,000	
Other expenses	37,800	
Net income	$ 12,200	

Additional Data:

a. Bought equipment for cash, $21,000.

b. Paid $6,000 on the long-term note payable.

c. Issued new shares of stock for $16,000 cash.

d. No dividends were declared or paid.

e. Other expenses included depreciation, $5,000; wages, $20,000; taxes, $6,000; other, $6,800.

f. Accounts payable includes only inventory purchases made on credit. Because there are no liability accounts relating to taxes or other expenses, assume that these expenses were fully paid in cash.

Required:

1. Prepare the statement of cash flows for the year ended December 31, 2016, using the indirect method.

2. Based on the cash flow statement, write a short paragraph explaining the major sources and uses of cash during 2016.

(Supplement A) Preparing a Statement of Cash Flows (Direct Method) (AP12-3)

P12-3

Use the information concerning Sharp Screen Films, Inc., provided in Problem 12-1 to fulfill the following requirements.

Required:

1. Prepare the statement of cash flows using the direct method for the year ended December 31, 2015.

2. Based on the cash flow statement, write a short paragraph explaining the major sources and uses of cash by Sharp Screen Films during 2015.

(Supplement A) Comparing Cash Flows from Operating Activities (Direct and Indirect Methods)

P12-4

Omega Company's accountants have just completed the income statement and balance sheet for the year and have provided the following information (dollars in thousands):

INCOME STATEMENT		
Sales revenue		$22,600
Expenses		
Cost of goods sold	$10,500	
Depreciation expense	2,000	
Salaries expense	4,070	
Rent expense	3,200	
Insurance expense	1,100	
Utilities expense	850	
Interest expense on bonds	450	
Loss on sale of investments	650	22,820
Net loss		$ (220)

SELECTED BALANCE SHEET ACCOUNTS		
	2015	2016
Merchandise inventory	$ 65	$150
Accounts receivable	620	440
Accounts payable	212	285
Salaries payable	23	38
Rent payable	10	4
Prepaid rent	7	6
Prepaid insurance	4	17

Other Data:

The company issued $30,000, 8 percent bonds payable at par during the year.

Required:

1. Prepare the cash flows from operating activities section of the statement of cash flows using the direct method.
2. Prepare the cash flows from operating activities section of the statement of cash flows using the indirect method.

P12-5
LO12-2, 12-4, 12-6

(Supplement B) Preparing a Statement of Cash Flows with Gain on Sale of Equipment (Indirect Method)

XS Supply Company is developing its annual financial statements at December 31, 2014. The statements are complete except for the statement of cash flows. The completed comparative balance sheets and income statement are summarized:

	2014	2013
Balance sheet at December 31		
Cash	$ 34,000	$ 29,000
Accounts receivable	35,000	28,000
Merchandise inventory	41,000	38,000
Property and equipment	121,000	100,000
Less: Accumulated depreciation	(30,000)	(25,000)
	$201,000	$170,000
Accounts payable	$ 36,000	$ 27,000
Wages payable	1,200	1,400
Note payable, long-term	38,000	44,000
Contributed capital	88,600	72,600
Retained earnings	37,200	25,000
	$201,000	$170,000
Income statement for 2014		
Sales	$120,000	
Gain on sale of equipment	1,000	
Cost of goods sold	70,000	
Other expenses	38,800	
Net income	$ 12,200	

Additional Data:

a. Bought equipment for cash, $31,000.
   Sold equipment with original cost of $10,000, accumulated depreciation of $7,000, for $4,000 cash.
b. Paid $6,000 on the long-term note payable.
c. Issued new shares of stock for $16,000 cash.
d. No dividends were declared or paid.
e. Other expenses included depreciation, $12,000; wages, $13,000; taxes, $6,000; and other, $7,800.
f. Accounts payable includes only inventory purchases made on credit. Because there are no liability accounts relating to taxes or other expenses, assume that these expenses were fully paid in cash.

Required:

1. Prepare the statement of cash flows for the year ended December 31, 2014, using the indirect method.
2. Evaluate the statement of cash flows.

(Supplement C) Preparing a Statement of Cash Flows, Indirect Method, Using the T-Account Approach

P12-6

www.mhhe.com/libby8e

Hanks Company is developing its annual financial statements at December 31, 2016. The statements are complete except for the statement of cash flows. The completed comparative balance sheets and income statement are summarized as follows:

	2016	2015
Balance sheet at December 31		
Cash	$ 33,000	$ 18,000
Accounts receivable	26,000	28,000
Merchandise inventory	39,000	36,000
Fixed assets (net)	80,000	72,000
	$178,000	$154,000
Accounts payable	$ 27,000	$ 21,000
Wages payable	1,500	1,000
Note payable, long-term	42,000	48,000
Common stock, no par	78,500	60,000
Retained earnings	$29,000	24,000
	$178,000	$154,000
Income statement for 2016		
Sales	$ 80,000	
Cost of goods sold	(43,000)	
Expenses	(30,000)	
Net income	$ 7,000	

Additional Data:
a. Bought fixed assets for cash, $12,000.
b. Paid $6,000 on the long-term note payable.
c. Sold unissued common stock for $18,500 cash.
d. Declared and paid a $2,000 cash dividend.
e. Incurred the following expenses: depreciation, $4,000; wages, $12,000; taxes, $2,000; and other, $12,000.

Required:
1. Prepare statement of cash flows T-accounts using the indirect method to report cash flows from operating activities.
2. Prepare the statement of cash flows.
3. Prepare a schedule of noncash investing and financing activities if necessary.

ALTERNATE **PROBLEMS**

Preparing a Statement of Cash Flows (Indirect Method) (P12-1)

AP12-1
LO12-1, 12-2, 12-4, 12-6

Ingersol Construction Supply Company is developing its annual financial statements at December 31, 2015. The statements are complete except for the statement of cash flows. The completed comparative balance sheets and income statement are summarized as follows:

	2015	2014
Balance sheet at December 31		
Cash	$ 34,000	$ 29,000
Accounts receivable	45,000	28,000
Merchandise inventory	32,000	38,000
Property and equipment	121,000	100,000
Less: Accumulated depreciation	(30,000)	(25,000)
	$202,000	$170,000

Accounts payable	$ 36,000	$ 27,000
Wages payable	2,200	1,400
Note payable, long-term	40,000	46,000
Contributed capital	86,600	70,600
Retained earnings	37,200	25,000
	$202,000	$170,000
Income statement for 2015		
Sales	$135,000	
Cost of goods sold	70,000	
Other expenses	37,800	
Net income	$ 27,200	

Additional Data:

a. Bought equipment for cash, $21,000.

b. Paid $6,000 on the long-term note payable.

c. Issued new shares of stock for $16,000 cash.

d. Dividends of $15,000 were declared and paid in cash.

e. Other expenses included depreciation, $5,000; wages, $20,000; taxes, $6,000; and other, $6,800.

f. Accounts payable includes only inventory purchases made on credit. Because there are no liability accounts relating to taxes or other expenses, assume that these expenses were fully paid in cash.

Required:

1. Prepare the statement of cash flows using the indirect method for the year ended December 31, 2015.

2. Evaluate the statement of cash flows.

AP12-2
LO12-1, 12-2, 12-4, 12-6

Preparing a Statement of Cash Flows (Indirect Method) (P12-2)

Audio House, Inc., is developing its annual financial statements at December 31, 2016. The statements are complete except for the statement of cash flows. The completed comparative balance sheets and income statement are summarized as follows:

	2016	2015
Balance sheet at December 31		
Cash	$ 64,000	$ 65,000
Accounts receivable	15,000	20,000
Inventory	22,000	20,000
Property and equipment	210,000	150,000
Less: Accumulated depreciation	(60,000)	(45,000)
	$251,000	$210,000
Accounts payable	$ 8,000	$ 19,000
Taxes payable	2,000	1,000
Note payable, long-term	86,000	75,000
Contributed capital	75,000	70,000
Retained earnings	80,000	45,000
	$251,000	$210,000
Income statement for 2016		
Sales	$190,000	
Cost of goods sold	90,000	
Other expenses	60,000	
Net income	$ 40,000	

Additional Data:

a. Bought equipment for cash, $60,000.

b. Borrowed an additional $11,000 and signed an additional long-term note payable.

c. Issued new shares of stock for $5,000 cash.

d. Dividends of $5,000 were declared and paid in cash.

e. Other expenses included depreciation, $15,000; wages, $20,000; and taxes, $25,000.

f. Accounts payable includes only inventory purchases made on credit.

Required:

1. Prepare the statement of cash flows for the year ended December 31, 2016, using the indirect method.
2. Based on the cash flow statement, write a short paragraph explaining the major sources and uses of cash during 2016.

(Supplement A) Preparing a Statement of Cash Flows (Direct Method) (P12-3)

AP12-3

Use the information concerning Ingersol Construction Supply Company provided in Alternate Problem 12-1 to fulfill the following requirements.

Required:

1. Prepare the statement of cash flows using the direct method for the year ended December 31, 2015.
2. Evaluate the statement of cash flows.

CASES **AND** PROJECTS

Annual Report Cases

Finding Financial Information

Refer to the financial statements of American Eagle Outfitters given in Appendix B at the end of this book.

CP12-1
LO12-2, 12-4, 12-6

AMERICAN EAGLE
OUTFITTERS, INC.

Required:

1. On the statement of cash flows, what was the largest item (in absolute value) listed under "Adjustments to reconcile net income to net cash provided by operating activities"? What was the largest "Changes in assets and liabilities" in the operating section of the cash flow statement? Explain the direction of the effect of each in the reconciliation.
2. Examine American Eagle Outfitters's investing and financing activities. List the company's three largest uses of cash over the past three years. List two major sources of cash for these activities.
3. What was free cash flow for the year ended January 28, 2012? What does this imply about the company's financial flexibility?

Finding Financial Information

Refer to the financial statements of Urban Outfitters given in Appendix C at the end of this book.

CP12-2
LO12-2, 12-4, 12-6

URBAN OUTFITTERS INC.

Required:

1. Does Urban Outfitters use the direct or indirect method to report cash flows from operating activities?
2. What amount of tax payments did the company make during the most recent reporting year? (**Hint:** The statement of cash flows may be helpful to answer this question.)
3. Explain why the "share-based compensation" and "depreciation and amortization" items were added in the reconciliation of net income to net cash provided by operating activities.
4. Has the company paid cash dividends during the last three years? How do you know?
5. What was free cash flow for the year ended January 31, 2012?

Comparing Companies within an Industry

Refer to the financial statements of American Eagle Outfitters (Appendix B) and Urban Outfitters (Appendix C) and the Industry Ratio Report (Appendix D) at the end of this book.

CP12-3
LO 12-3, 12-5

AMERICAN EAGLE
OUTFITTERS, INC.

URBAN OUTFITTERS INC.

Required:

1. Compute the quality of income ratio for both companies for the most recent reporting year. Which company has a better quality of income ratio?
2. Compare the quality of income ratio for both companies to the industry average. Are these companies producing more or less cash from operating activities relative to net income than the average company in the industry?
3. Compute the capital acquisitions ratio for both companies for the most recent reporting year. Compare their abilities to finance purchases of property, plant, and equipment with cash provided by operating activities.
4. Compare the capital acquisitions ratio for both companies to the industry average. How does each company's ability to finance the purchase of property, plant, and equipment with cash provided by operating activities compare with that of other companies in the industry?

Financial Reporting and Analysis Cases

CP12-4

LO12-1, 12-2, 12-4, 12-6

Rocky Mountain
Chocolate Factory

Preparing a Complex Statement of Cash Flows (Indirect Method)

Rocky Mountain Chocolate Factory manufactures an extensive line of premium chocolate candies for sale at its franchised and company-owned stores in malls throughout the United States. Its balance sheet for the first quarter of a recent year is presented along with an analysis of selected accounts and transactions:

ROCKY MOUNTAIN CHOCOLATE FACTORY, INC.
Balance Sheets

Assets	May 31 (Unaudited)	February 29
Current assets		
Cash and cash equivalents	$ 921,505	$ 528,787
Accounts and notes receivable—trade, less allowance for doubtful accounts of $43,196 at May 31 and $28,196 at February 29	1,602,582	1,463,901
Inventories	2,748,788	2,504,908
Deferred tax asset	59,219	59,219
Other	581,508	224,001
Total current assets	5,913,602	4,780,816
Property and equipment—at cost	14,010,796	12,929,675
Less accumulated depreciation and amortization	(2,744,388)	(2,468,084)
	11,266,408	10,461,591
Other assets		
Notes and accounts receivable due after one year	100,206	111,588
Goodwill and other intangibles, net of accumulated amortization of $259,641 at May 31 and $253,740 at Feb. 29	330,359	336,260
Other	574,130	624,185
	1,004,695	1,072,033
	$18,184,705	$16,314,440
Liabilities and Equity		
Current liabilities		
Short-term debt	$ 0	$ 1,000,000
Current maturities of long-term debt	429,562	134,538
Accounts payable—trade	1,279,455	998,520
Accrued liabilities	714,473	550,386
Income taxes payable	11,198	54,229
Total current liabilities	2,434,688	2,737,673
Long-term debt, less current maturities	4,193,290	2,183,877
Deferred income taxes	275,508	275,508
Stockholders' Equity		
Common stock—authorized 7,250,000 shares, $.03 par value; issued 3,034,302 shares at May 31 and at Feb. 29	91,029	91,029
Additional paid-in capital	9,703,985	9,703,985
Retained earnings	2,502,104	2,338,267
	12,297,118	12,133,281
Less common stock held in treasury, at cost—129,153 shares at May 31 and at February 29	1,015,899	1,015,899
	11,281,219	11,117,382
	$18,184,705	$16,314,440

The accompanying notes are an integral part of these statements.

Analysis of Selected Accounts and Transactions:

a. Net income was $163,837. Notes and accounts receivable due after one year relate to operations.

b. Depreciation and amortization totaled $282,205.

c. No "other" noncurrent assets (which relate to investing activities) were purchased this period.

d. No property, plant, and equipment were sold during the period. No goodwill was acquired or sold.

e. Proceeds from issuance of long-term debt were $4,659,466, and principal payments were $2,355,029. (Combine the current maturities with the long-term debt in your analysis.)

f. No dividends were declared or paid.

g. Ignore the "deferred tax asset" and "deferred income taxes" accounts.

Required:
Prepare a statement of cash flows using the indirect method for the year.

Making a Decision as a Financial Analyst: Analyzing Cash Flow for a New Company

Carlyle Golf, Inc., was formed in September of last year. The company designs, contracts for the manufacture of, and markets a line of men's golf apparel. A portion of the statement of cash flows for Carlyle follows:

CP12-5
LO12-2

Carlyle Golf, Inc.

CURRENT YEAR	
Cash flows from operating activities	
Net income	$(460,089)
Depreciation	3,554
Noncash compensation (stock)	254,464
Deposits with suppliers	(404,934)
Increase in prepaid assets	(42,260)
Increase in accounts payable	81,765
Increase in accrued liabilities	24,495
Net cash flows	$(543,005)

Management expects a solid increase in sales in the near future. To support the increase in sales, it plans to add $2.2 million to inventory. The company did not disclose a sales forecast. At the end of the current year, Carlyle had less than $1,000 in cash. It is not unusual for a new company to experience a loss and negative cash flows during its start-up phase.

Required:
As a financial analyst recently hired by a major investment bank, you have been asked to write a short memo to your supervisor evaluating the problems facing Carlyle. Emphasize typical sources of financing that may or may not be available to support the expansion.

Critical Thinking Case

Ethical Decision Making: A Real-Life Example

In a February 19, 2004, press release, the Securities and Exchange Commission described a number of fraudulent transactions that Enron executives concocted in an effort to meet the company's financial targets. One particularly well-known scheme is called the "Nigerian barge" transaction, which took place in the fourth quarter of 1999. According to court documents, Enron arranged to sell three electricity-generating power barges moored off the coast of Nigeria. The "buyer" was the investment banking firm of Merrill Lynch. Although Enron reported this transaction as a sale in its income statement, it turns out this was no ordinary sale. Merrill Lynch didn't really want the barges and had only agreed to buy them because Enron guaranteed, in a secret side deal, that it would arrange for the barges to be bought back from Merrill Lynch within six months of the initial transaction. In addition, Enron promised to pay Merrill Lynch a hefty fee for doing the deal. In an interview on National Public Radio on August 17, 2002, Michigan Senator Carl Levin declared, "(T)he case of the Nigerian barge transaction was, by any definition, a loan."

CP12-6
LO12-1, 12-2, 12-6

Enron

Required:
1. Discuss whether the Nigerian barge transaction should have been considered a loan rather than a sale. As part of your discussion, consider the following questions. Doesn't the Merrill Lynch payment to Enron at the time of the initial transaction automatically make it a sale, not a loan? What aspects of the transaction are similar to a loan? Which aspects suggest that the four criteria for revenue recognition (summarized near the end of Chapter 3) were not fulfilled?
2. The income statement effect of recording the transaction as a sale rather than a loan is fairly clear: Enron was able to boost its revenues and net income. What is somewhat less obvious, but nearly as important, are the effects on the statement of cash flows. Describe how recording the transaction as a sale rather than as a loan would change the statement of cash flows.
3. How would the two different statements of cash flows (described in your response to requirement 2) affect financial statement users?

Financial Reporting and Analysis Team Project

CP12-7

LO12-1, 12-2, 12-3, 12-4, 12-5, 12-6

Team Project: Analyzing Cash Flows

As a team, select an industry to analyze. *Yahoo!Finance* provides lists of industries at biz.yahoo.com/p/industries.html. Click on an industry for a list of companies in that industry. Alternatively, go to Google Finance at www.google.com/finance and search for a company you are interested in. You will be presented with a list including that company and its competitors. Each team member should acquire the annual report or 10-K for one publicly traded company in the industry, with each member selecting a different company (the SEC EDGAR service at www.sec.gov or the company's investor relations website itself are good sources).

Required:
On an individual basis, each team member should write a short report answering the following questions about the selected company. Discuss any patterns across the companies that you as a team observe. Then, as a team, write a short report comparing and contrasting your companies.
1. Which of the two basic reporting approaches for cash flows from operating activities did the company adopt?
2. What is the quality of income ratio for the most current year? What were the major causes of differences between net income and cash flow from operations?
3. What is the capital acquisitions ratio for the three-year period presented in total? How is the company financing its capital acquisitions?
4. What portion of the cash from operations in the current year is being paid to stockholders in the form of dividends?

CONTINUING **CASE**

CC12-1

≈POOLCORP

Preparing the Statement of Cash Flows (Indirect Method)

Presented in alphabetical order below are the line items including the subtotals and totals from Pool Corporation's recent statement of cash flows prepared using the indirect method. Using these line items, prepare Pool Corporation's statement of cash flows in good form for the year ended December 31 following the format presented in Exhibit 12.1.

Accounts payable	$	6,402
Accrued expenses and other current liabilities		20,682
Acquisition of businesses		(5,934)
Amortization		1,559
Cash and cash equivalents at beginning of year		9,721
Cash and cash equivalents at end of year		17,487
Change in cash and cash equivalents		7,766
Depreciation		9,746
Loss on sale of property and equipment		263
Net cash provided by operating activities		75,103
Net cash used in financing activities		(41,759)
Net cash used in investing activities		(25,578)
Net income		71,993
Other financing activities		944
Other operating assets		8,635
Payments of cash dividends		(26,470)
Payments on long-term debt and other long-term liabilities		(149)
Payments on revolving line of bank credit		(700,749)
Prepaid expenses		(2,951)
Proceeds from revolving line of bank credit		749,349
Proceeds from stock issued under share-based compensation plans		13,085
Product inventories		(35,339)
Purchases of property and equipment		(19,844)
Purchases of treasury stock		(77,769)
Receivables		(5,887)
Sale of property and equipment		200

Analyzing Financial Statements

The history of The Home Depot is an unusual success story. Founded in 1978 in Atlanta, The Home Depot has grown to be America's largest home improvement retailer, with over 2,200 stores in the United States, Canada, China, and Mexico. According to *Fortune* magazine, The Home Depot is one of the nation's 30 largest retailers. Financial statements for The Home Depot are presented in Exhibit 13.1. As you can see, The Home Depot's rapid growth has resumed after a few years of slower growth due primarily to a difficult economic environment. Sales revenue for the year ended January 29, 2012, was 3.5 percent more than the previous year and income increased 16 percent.

With the recent improvement in the company's financial results, would you want to invest in The Home Depot? A number of professional analysts think you should, including those who work for Edward Jones, a large brokerage firm. In a report in which they recommended holding stock in The Home Depot, they wrote: "We expect market share growth, continued cost management and share repurchases to drive opportunities for earnings per share growth. We find Home Depot's market dominance, earnings growth outlook, and attractive dividend yield reasons to hold the shares."

Learning Objectives

After studying this chapter, you should be able to:

13-1 Explain how a company's business strategy affects financial analysis. p. 649

13-2 Discuss how analysts use financial statements. p. 650

13-3 Compute and interpret component percentages. p. 652

13-4 Compute and interpret profitability ratios. p. 653

13-5 Compute and interpret liquidity ratios. p. 659

13-6 Compute and interpret solvency ratios. p. 663

13-7 Compute and interpret market test ratios. p. 665

chapter 13

The Home Depot

FINANCIAL ANALYSIS:
BRINGING IT ALL TOGETHER

www.homedepot.com

Professional analysts consider a large number of factors in developing the type of recommendation contained in the Edward Jones report, including information reported in a company's financial statements. In this chapter, we use accounting information and a variety of analytical tools to study The Home Depot and its major competitor, Lowe's.

UNDERSTANDING THE BUSINESS

Companies spend billions of dollars each year preparing, auditing, and publishing their financial statements. These statements are then mailed to current and prospective investors. Most companies also make financial information available to investors on the Internet. The Home Depot has a particularly interesting home page (http://www.homedepot.com) that contains current financial statements, recent news articles about the company, and a variety of relevant information.

The reason that The Home Depot and other companies spend so much money to provide information to investors is simple: Financial statements help people make better economic decisions. In fact, published financial statements are designed primarily to meet the needs of external decision makers, including present and potential owners, investment analysts, and creditors.

EXHIBIT 13.1

The Home Depot Financial Statements

THE HOME DEPOT, INC., AND SUBSIDIARIES
Consolidated Statements of Earnings
(amounts in millions, except per share data)

	Fiscal Year Ended		
	January 29, 2012	January 30, 2011	January 31, 2010
NET SALES	$70,395	$67,997	$66,176
Cost of Sales	46,133	44,693	43,764
Gross Profit	24,262	23,304	22,412
Operating Expenses:			
Selling, General and Administrative	16,028	15,849	15,902
Depreciation and Amortization	1,573	1,616	1,707
Total Operating Expenses	17,601	17,465	17,609
Operating Income	6,661	5,839	4,803
Interest and Other (Income) Expense:			
Interest and Investment Income	(13)	(15)	(18)
Interest Expense	606	530	676
Other	—	51	163
Interest and Other, net	593	566	821
Earnings from Continuing Operations before			
Provision for Income Taxes	6,068	5,273	3,982
Provision for Income Taxes	2,185	1,935	1,362
Earnings from Continuing Operations	3,883	3,338	2,620
Earnings from Discontinued Operations, Net of Tax	—	—	41
Net Earnings	$ 3,883	$ 3,338	$ 2,661
Weighted Average Common Shares	1,562	1,648	1,683
Basic Earnings per Share from Continuing			
Operations	$ 2.49	$ 2.03	$ 1.56
Basic Earnings per Share from Discontinued			
Operations	$ —	$ —	$ 0.02
Basic Earnings per Share	$ 2.49	$ 2.03	$ 1.58
Diluted Weighted Average Common Shares	1,570	1,658	1,692
Diluted Earnings per Share from Continuing			
Operations	$ 2.47	$ 2.01	$ 1.55
Diluted Earnings per Share from Discontinued			
Operations	$ —	$ —	$ 0.02
Diluted Earnings per Share	$ 2.47	$ 2.01	$ 1.57

EXHIBIT 13.1

continued

THE HOME DEPOT, INC., AND SUBSIDIARIES
Consolidated Balance Sheets
(amounts in millions, except share and per share data)

	January 29, 2012	January 30, 2011
ASSETS		
Current Assets:		
Cash and Cash Equivalents	$ 1,987	$ 545
Receivables, net	1,245	1,085
Merchandise Inventories	10,325	10,625
Other Current Assets	963	1,224
Total Current Assets	14,520	13,479
Property and Equipment, at cost:		
Land	8,480	8,497
Buildings	17,737	17,606
Furniture, Fixtures, and Equipment	10,040	9,687
Leasehold Improvements	1,372	1,373
Construction in Progress	758	654
Capital Leases	588	568
	38,975	38,385
Less Accumulated Depreciation and Amortization	14,527	13,325
Net Property and Equipment	24,448	25,060
Notes Receivable	135	139
Goodwill	1,120	1,187
Other Assets	295	260
Total Assets	$40,518	$40,125
LIABILITIES AND STOCKHOLDERS' EQUITY		
Current Liabilities:		
Accounts Payable	$ 4,856	$ 4,717
Accrued Salaries and Related Expenses	1,372	1,290
Sales Taxes Payable	391	368
Deferred Revenue	1,147	1,177
Income Taxes Payable	23	13
Current Installments of Long-Term Debt	30	1,042
Other Accrued Expenses	1,557	1,515
Total Current Liabilities	9,376	10,122
Long-Term Debt, excluding current installments	10,758	8,707
Other Long-Term Liabilities	2,146	2,135
Deferred Income Taxes	340	272
Total Liabilities	22,620	21,236

continued

EXHIBIT 13.1

continued

STOCKHOLDERS' EQUITY

Common Stock, par value $0.05; authorized: 10 billion shares; issued: 1.733 billion shares at January 29, 2012, and 1.722 billion shares at January 30, 2011; outstanding: 1.537 billion shares at January 29, 2012, and 1.623 billion shares at January 30, 2011

January 30, 2011	87	86
Paid-In Capital	6,966	6,556
Retained Earnings	17,246	14,995
Accumulated Other Comprehensive Income	293	445
Treasury Stock, at cost, 196 million shares at January 29, 2012, and 99 million shares at January 30, 2011	(6,694)	(3,193)
Total Stockholders' Equity	17,898	18,889
Total Liabilities and Stockholders' Equity	**$40,518**	**$40,125**

THE HOME DEPOT, INC., AND SUBSIDIARIES
Consolidated Statements of Cash Flows
(amounts in millions)

	Fiscal Year Ended		
	January 29, 2012	January 30, 2011	January 31, 2010
CASH FLOWS FROM OPERATING ACTIVITIES:			
Net Earnings	$ 3,883	$ 3,338	$2,661
Reconciliation of Net Earnings to Net Cash Provided by Operating Activities:			
Depreciation and Amortization	1,682	1,718	1,806
Impairment of Investment	—	—	163
Stock-Based Compensation Expense	215	214	201
Changes in Assets and Liabilities, net of the effects of acquisition and disposition:			
Receivables, net	(170)	(102)	(23)
Merchandise Inventories	256	(355)	625
Other Current Assets	159	12	4
Accounts Payable and Accrued Expenses	422	(133)	59
Deferred Revenue	(29)	10	(21)
Income Taxes Payable	14	(85)	(174)
Deferred Income Taxes	170	104	(227)
Other Long-Term Liabilities	(2)	(61)	(19)
Other	51	(75)	70
Net Cash Provided by Operating Activities	6,651	4,585	5,125
CASH FLOWS FROM INVESTING ACTIVITIES:			
Capital Expenditures, net of $25, $62, and $10 of non-cash capital expenditures in fiscal 2011, 2010, and 2009, respectively	(1,221)	(1,096)	(966)
Proceeds from Sale of Business, net	101	—	—
Payments for Business Acquired, net	(65)	—	—
Proceeds from Sales of Property and Equipment	56	84	178
Proceeds from Sales and Maturities of Investments	—	—	33
Net Cash Used in Investing Activities	(1,129)	(1,012)	(755)

continued

CASH FLOWS FROM FINANCING ACTIVITIES:			
Proceeds from Long-Term Borrowings, net of discount	**1,994**	998	—
Repayments of Long-Term Debt	**(1,028)**	(1,029)	(1,774)
Repurchases of Common Stock	**(3,470)**	(2,608)	(213)
Proceeds from Sales of Common Stock	**306**	104	73
Cash Dividends Paid to Stockholders	**(1,632)**	(1,569)	(1,525)
Other Financing Activities	**(218)**	(347)	(64)
Net Cash Used in Financing Activities	**(4,048)**	(4,451)	(3,503)
Change in Cash and Cash Equivalents	**1,474**	(878)	867
Effect of Exchange Rate Changes on Cash and Cash Equivalents	**(32)**	2	35
Cash and Cash Equivalents at Beginning of Year	**545**	1,421	519
Cash and Cash Equivalents at End of Year	**$ 1,987**	$ 545	$ 1,421
SUPPLEMENTAL DISCLOSURE OF CASH PAYMENTS MADE FOR:			
Interest, net of interest capitalized	**$ 580**	$ 579	$ 664
Income Taxes	**$ 1,865**	$ 2,067	$ 2,082

EXHIBIT 13.1

concluded

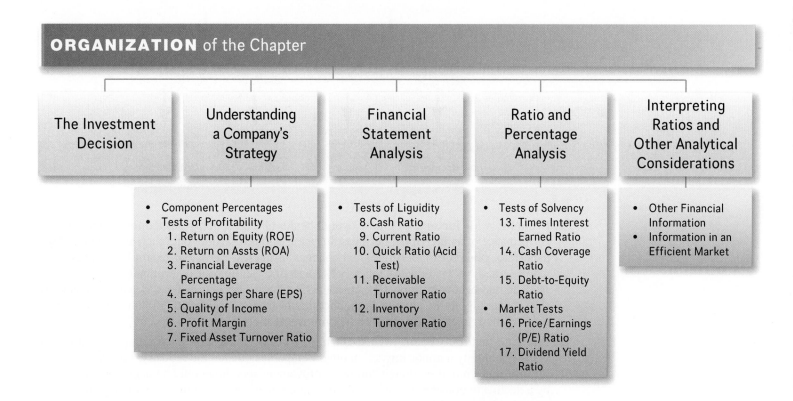

ORGANIZATION of the Chapter

The Investment Decision

Understanding a Company's Strategy
- Component Percentages
- Tests of Profitability
  1. Return on Equity (ROE)
  2. Return on Assts (ROA)
  3. Financial Leverage Percentage
  4. Earnings per Share (EPS)
  5. Quality of Income
  6. Profit Margin
  7. Fixed Asset Turnover Ratio

Financial Statement Analysis
- Tests of Liquidity
  8. Cash Ratio
  9. Current Ratio
  10. Quick Ratio (Acid Test)
  11. Receivable Turnover Ratio
  12. Inventory Turnover Ratio

Ratio and Percentage Analysis
- Tests of Solvency
  13. Times Interest Earned Ratio
  14. Cash Coverage Ratio
  15. Debt-to-Equity Ratio
- Market Tests
  16. Price/Earnings (P/E) Ratio
  17. Dividend Yield Ratio

Interpreting Ratios and Other Analytical Considerations
- Other Financial Information
- Information in an Efficient Market

THE INVESTMENT DECISION

Of the people who use financial statements, investors are perhaps the single largest group. They often rely on the advice of professional analysts, who develop recommendations on widely held stocks such as The Home Depot. Most individual investors use analysts' reports and track their recommendations. As this book was being written, professional analysts issued the following investment recommendations for The Home Depot:

ANALYST OPINIONS

Rating	Number of Analysts
Buy	13
Outperform	1
Hold	9
Underperform	0
Sell	0

Source: Quicken.com/investments/.

Perhaps the most important thing to notice about this summary of investment recommendations is the degree of disagreement. Currently, 13 analysts recommend buying more Home Depot stock, while 9 others recommend holding Home Depot stock only if one already owns it. This level of disagreement shows that financial analysis is part art and part science.

In considering an investment in stock, investors should evaluate the company's future income and growth potential on the basis of three factors:

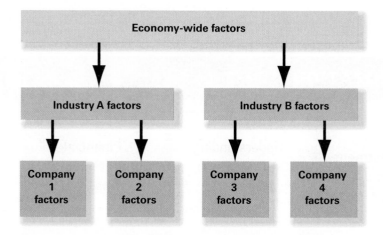

1. **Economy-wide factors.** Often the overall health of the economy has a direct impact on the performance of an individual business. Investors should consider data such as the unemployment rate, general inflation rate, and changes in interest rates. For example, in a research report issued by the Edward Jones brokerage firm, an analyst determined "rising interest rates could negatively impact Home Depot's sales." The reason for a negative impact on sales, according to the analyst, is the fact that nearly one-third of the dollars saved on refinancing mortgages are spent on home improvement projects.

2. **Industry factors.** Certain events can have a major impact on each company within an industry but only a minor impact on other companies outside the industry. For example, the Edward Jones report predicted "home-improvement spending could be negatively impacted by a decline in housing turnover and difficult comparisons from the recent period of unsustainable high growth."

3. **Individual company factors.** To properly analyze a company, good analysts do not rely only on the information contained in the financial statements. They visit the company, buy its products, and read about it in the business press. If you evaluate McDonald's, it is equally important to assess the quality of its balance sheet and the quality of its Big Mac. An example of company-specific information is contained in the Edward Jones report: New managers have been hired because the management skills "that grew Home Depot to 1,000 stores [were] probably different from the skill set needed as the company grows beyond 2,000 stores."

Besides considering these factors, investors should understand a company's business strategy when evaluating its financial statements. Before discussing analytical techniques, we will show how business strategy affects financial statement analysis.

UNDERSTANDING A COMPANY'S STRATEGY

Financial statement analysis involves more than just "crunching numbers." Before you start looking at numbers, you should know what you are looking for. While financial statements report on transactions, each of those transactions is the result of a company's operating decisions as it implements its business strategy.

LEARNING OBJECTIVE 13-1
Explain how a company's business strategy affects financial analysis.

The **DuPont model** helps us analyze the profitability of a business and demonstrates that a variety of strategies can result in high levels of profitability. The model follows:

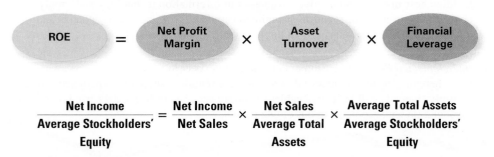

$$\frac{\text{Net Income}}{\text{Average Stockholders' Equity}} = \frac{\text{Net Income}}{\text{Net Sales}} \times \frac{\text{Net Sales}}{\text{Average Total Assets}} \times \frac{\text{Average Total Assets}}{\text{Average Stockholders' Equity}}$$

A key insight provided by the DuPont model is that companies can be profitable by achieving high profit margins or a rapid turnover of assets (or a combination of both). Businesses can earn a high rate of return by following different strategies. These are two fundamental strategies:

1. **Product differentiation.** Under this strategy, companies offer products with unique benefits, such as high quality or unusual style or features. These unique benefits allow a company to charge higher prices. In general, higher prices yield higher profit margins, which lead to higher returns on equity (as shown in the DuPont model).

2. **Cost differentiation.** Under this strategy, companies attempt to operate more efficiently than their competitors, which permits them to offer lower prices to attract customers. The efficient use of resources is captured in the asset turnover ratio, and as the DuPont model illustrates, a higher asset turnover ratio leads to higher return on investment.

You can probably think of a number of companies that have followed one of these two basic strategies. Here are some examples:

Differentiation on Quality	Differentiation on Cost
Cars:	**Cars:**
Lexus	Ford Focus
Mercedes	Chevrolet Aveo
BMW	Kia Rio
Retail Stores:	**Retail Stores:**
Nordstrom	Kmart
Tiffany	Walmart
Saks	Dollar General

The best place to start financial analysis is with a solid understanding of a company's business strategy. To evaluate how well a company is doing, you must know what managers are trying to do. You can learn a great deal about a company's business strategy by reading its annual report, especially the letter from the president. It also is useful to read articles about the company in the business press.

The Home Depot's business strategy is described in its 10-K report as follows:

REAL WORLD EXCERPT
10-K Report

Operating Strategy

In fiscal 2011, we continued to execute on our strategy focused on the following key initiatives:

- *Customer Service.* To enhance customer service, we introduced new information technology and optimized certain elements of our supply chain to eliminate tasks and give associates more time with customers. We also sought to maintain competitive wages and incentive opportunities to attract, retain and motivate our associates.
- *Productivity and Efficiency.* Our productivity and efficiency initiative is advanced through building best-in-class competitive advantages in information technology and supply chain. We continued our focus on disciplined capital allocation, expense control and increasing shareholder returns, both through share repurchases and increased dividend payments.
- *Interconnected Retail.* As customers increasingly expect to be able to buy how, when and where they want, we believe that providing a seamless shopping experience across multiple channels will be a key enabler for future success. In fiscal 2011, we focused in particular on enhancements to our online presence.

This description of The Home Depot's strategy serves as a guide for our financial analysis. By understanding what management is trying to accomplish, we are better able to evaluate its progress in meeting its goals.

With these implications in mind, we can attach more meaning to the information contained in The Home Depot's financial statements.

FINANCIAL STATEMENT ANALYSIS

LEARNING OBJECTIVE 13-2
Discuss how analysts use financial statements.

Analyzing financial data without a basis for comparison is impossible. For example, would you be impressed with a company that earned $1 million last year? You are probably thinking, "It depends." A $1 million profit might be very good for a company that lost money the year before but not good for a company that made $500 million the preceding year. It might be good for a small company but not for a very large company. And it might be considered good if all the other companies in the industry lost money the same year but not good if they all earned much larger profits.

As you can see from this simple example, financial results cannot be evaluated in isolation. To properly analyze the information reported in financial statements, you must develop appropriate comparisons. The task of finding appropriate benchmarks requires judgment and is not always easy. Financial analysis is a sophisticated skill, not a mechanical process.

There are two methods for making financial comparisons, times series analysis and comparisons with similar companies.

1. **Time series analysis.** In this type of analysis, information on a single company is compared over time. For example, a key measure of performance for most companies is the change in sales volume each year. The time series chart on the next page shows that The Home Depot's sales have been volatile over the past few years. Analysts would want to

examine this trend. The notes to the financial statements help us understand the improvement in sales in the current year:

The positive comparable store sales for the fiscal year reflect a number of factors including the execution of our key initiatives, economic growth and favorable weather conditions. We experienced positive comparable store sales in 12 of our 14 departments. The increase in comparable store sales also reflects a 2.6% increase in our comparable store average ticket and an 0.8% increase in our comparable store customer transactions.

In the current environment, The Home Depot is experiencing more customers in its stores and those customers are spending more money on their average purchase. Notice that our understanding of the reported numbers is directly tied to understanding The Home Depot's business strategy.

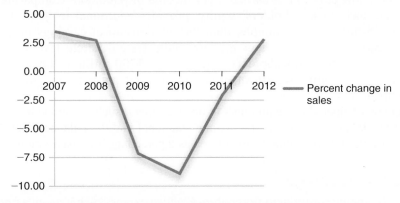

2. **Comparison with similar companies.** We have seen that financial results are often affected by industry and economy-wide factors. By comparing a company with another one in the same line of business, an analyst can gain better insight into its performance. The comparison of various measures for The Home Depot and Lowe's (in the following graph) shows similar results, suggesting that both companies are being affected by industry factors. The gross profit percentage is essentially the same for both companies but income as a percentage of sales is significantly higher for The Home Depot, indicating more efficient business operations. Also growth in sales is stronger for The Home Depot. This comparison suggests that The Home Depot has been successful in implementing its business strategy.

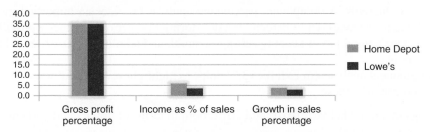

Finding comparable companies is often very difficult. Fortune Brands, for example, is a well-known company that each year sells more than $9 billion worth of distilled spirits, home improvement products, office products, and golf equipment. No other company sells exactly that group of products. Care must be exercised in selecting comparable companies from the same basic industry. Days Inn, La Quinta, Hilton, Four Seasons, Marriott, and Mirage Resorts are all well-known companies in the hotel industry, but not all could be considered comparable companies for purposes of financial analysis. These hotels offer different levels of quality and appeal to different types of customers.

The federal government has developed the North American Industry Classification System (NAICS) for use in reporting economic data. The system assigns a specific industry code to each corporation based on its business operations. Analysts often use these six-digit codes to identify companies that have similar business operations. In addition, financial information services such as Robert Morris Associates provide averages for many common accounting ratios for various industries defined by the industrial classification codes. Because of the diversity of companies included in each industry classification, however, these data should be used with great care. For this reason, some analysts prefer to compare two companies that are very similar instead of using industry-wide comparisons.

RATIO AND PERCENTAGE ANALYSIS

RATIO (PERCENTAGE) ANALYSIS is an analytical tool that measures the proportional relationship between two financial statement amounts.

All financial analysts use **ratio analysis** or **percentage analysis** when they review companies. A ratio or percentage expresses the proportionate relationship between two different amounts, allowing for easy comparisons. Assessing a company's profitability is difficult if you know only that it earned a net income of $500,000. Comparing income to other numbers, such as stockholders' equity, provides additional insights. If stockholders' equity is $5 million, for example, then the relationship of earnings to investment is $500,000 ÷ $5,000,000 = 10%. This measure indicates a different level of performance than would be the case if stockholders' equity were $250 million. Ratio analysis helps decision makers to identify significant relationships and make meaningful comparisons between companies.

LEARNING OBJECTIVE 13-3
Compute and interpret component percentages.

Ratios may be computed using amounts in one statement, such as the income statement, or in two different statements, such as the income statement and the balance sheet. In addition, amounts on a single statement may be expressed as a percentage of a base amount.

COMPONENT PERCENTAGES express each item on a particular financial statement as a percentage of a single base amount.

Component Percentages

Analysts often compute **component percentages,** which express each item on a financial statement as a percentage of a single base amount (the ratio's denominator). To compute component percentages for the income statement, the base amount is net sales revenue. Each expense is expressed as a percentage of net sales revenue. On the balance sheet, the base amount is total assets; each balance sheet account is divided by total assets.

Exhibit 13.2 shows a component percentage analysis for The Home Depot's income statement (see the consolidated statements of earnings in Exhibit 13.1). If you simply reviewed the dollar amounts on the income statement, you might miss important insights. For example, selling, general, and administrative expense increased by $179 million between 2011 and 2012. This increase might seem to reflect a decline in operating efficiency until it is compared with sales productivity. A component percentage analysis provides an important insight: This expense category decreased as a percent of sales during that period. In other words, The Home Depot has done a good job of keeping selling, general, and administrative expense in line with its sales activity.

The component analysis (in Exhibit 13.2) helps to highlight several additional issues for The Home Depot, such as these:

1. Earnings increased between 2010 and 2012, both in terms of dollars and percent of sales.

2. Some of the percentage changes may seem small, but they each show improved efficiency, a key part of The Home Depot strategy.

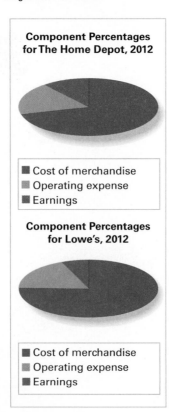

Component Percentages for The Home Depot, 2012

- Cost of merchandise
- Operating expense
- Earnings

Component Percentages for Lowe's, 2012

- Cost of merchandise
- Operating expense
- Earnings

Many analysts use graphics software in their study of financial results. Graphic representation is especially useful when communicating findings during meetings or in printed form. The charts in the margin summarize key 2012 data from Exhibit 13.2, along with comparable data from Lowe's, a key competitor.

In addition to component percentages, analysts use ratios to compare related items from the financial statements. Of the many ratios that can be computed from a single set of

Income Statement	COMPONENT PERCENTAGES*		
	2012	2011	2010
Net sales	100.0%	100.0%	100.0%
Cost of sales	65.5	65.7	66.1
Gross profit	34.5	34.3	33.9
Operating expenses			
Selling, general, and administrative	22.8	23.3	24.0
Depreciation and amortization	2.2	2.4	2.6
Total operating expenses	25.0	25.7	26.6
Operating income	9.5	8.6	7.3
Interest and investment income	0.0	0.0	0.0
Interest expense and other	0.9	0.8	1.3
Interest, net	0.9	0.8	1.3
Earnings, before taxes	8.6	7.8	6.0
Income taxes	3.1	2.8	2.0
Earnings from discontinued operations	0.0	0.0	0.0
Net earnings	5.5	4.9	4.0

*Numbers are rounded.

EXHIBIT 13.2

Component Percentages for
The Home Depot

financial statements, analysts use only those that can be helpful in a given situation. Comparing cost of goods sold to property, plant, and equipment is never useful because these items have no natural relationship. Instead, an analyst will often compute certain widely used ratios and then decide which additional ratios could be relevant to a particular decision. Research and development costs as a percentage of sales is not a commonly used ratio, for example, but it is useful when analyzing companies that depend on new products, such as drug or computer firms.

When you compute ratios, remember a basic fact about financial statements: Balance sheet amounts relate to a moment in time while income statement amounts relate to an entire period. In comparing an income statement amount to a balance sheet amount, you should express the balance sheet as an average of the beginning and ending balances. In practice, many analysts simply use the ending balance sheet amount, an approach that is appropriate only if no significant changes have occurred in the balance sheet amounts. For consistency, we always use average amounts.

Financial statement analysis is a judgmental process; not all ratios are helpful in a given situation. We will discuss several ratios that are appropriate to most situations. They can be grouped into the categories shown in Exhibit 13.3.

Tests of Profitability

Profitability is a primary measure of the overall success of a company. Indeed, it is necessary for a company's survival. Several **tests of profitability** focus on measuring the adequacy of income by comparing it to other items reported on the financial statements. Return on equity is a widely used measure of profitability.

1. Return on Equity (ROE)

Return on equity relates income earned to the investment made by the owners. This ratio reflects the simple fact that investors expect to earn more money if they invest more money. Two investments that offer a return of $10,000 are not comparable if one requires a $100,000

LEARNING OBJECTIVE 13-4
Compute and interpret
profitability ratios.

TESTS OF PROFITABILITY
are ratios that compare income
with one or more primary
activities.

	Ratio	Basic Computation

EXHIBIT 13.3

Widely Used Accounting Ratios

Tests of Profitability

1. Return on equity (ROE)

$$\frac{\text{Net Income}}{\text{Average Stockholders' Equity}}$$

2. Return on assets (ROA)

$$\frac{\text{Net Income} + \text{Interest Expense (net of tax)}}{\text{Average Total Assets}}$$

3. Financial leverage percentage

Return on Equity − Return on Assets

4. Earnings per share (EPS)

$$\frac{\text{Net Income}}{\text{Average Number of Shares of Common Stock Outstanding}}$$

5. Quality of income

$$\frac{\text{Cash Flows from Operating Activities}}{\text{Net Income}}$$

6. Profit margin

$$\frac{\text{Net Income}}{\text{Net Sales Revenue}}$$

7. Fixed asset turnover ratio

$$\frac{\text{Net Sales Revenue}}{\text{Average Net Fixed Assets}}$$

Tests of Liquidity

8. Cash ratio

$$\frac{\text{Cash} + \text{Cash Equivalents}}{\text{Current Liabilities}}$$

9. Current ratio

$$\frac{\text{Current Assets}}{\text{Current Liabilities}}$$

10. Quick ratio

$$\frac{\text{Quick Assets}}{\text{Current Liabilities}}$$

11. Receivable turnover ratio

$$\frac{\text{Net Credit Sales}}{\text{Average Net Receivables}}$$

12. Inventory turnover ratio

$$\frac{\text{Cost of Goods Sold}}{\text{Average Inventory}}$$

Tests of Solvency

13. Times interest earned ratio

$$\frac{\text{Net Income} + \text{Interest Expense} + \text{Income Tax Expense}}{\text{Interest Expense}}$$

14. Cash coverage ratio

$$\frac{\text{Cash Flows from Operating Activities (before interest and taxes paid)}}{\text{Interest Paid}}$$

15. Debt-to-equity ratio

$$\frac{\text{Total Liabilities}}{\text{Stockholders' Equity}}$$

Market Tests

16. Price/earnings (P/E) ratio

$$\frac{\text{Market Price per Share}}{\text{Earnings per Share}}$$

17. Dividend yield ratio

$$\frac{\text{Dividends per Share}}{\text{Market Price per Share}}$$

investment and the other requires a $250,000 investment. The return on equity ratio is computed as follows:[1]

$$\text{Return on Equity} = \frac{\text{Net Income}}{\text{Average Stockholders' Equity}}$$

$$\text{Home Depot 2012} = \frac{\$3,883}{\$18,394^{*}} = 21.1\%$$

*($17,898 + $18,889) ÷ 2 = $18,394

The Home Depot earned 21.1 percent on the owners' investment. Was that return good or bad? We can answer this question by comparing The Home Depot's return on equity with the ratio for a similar company. Return on equity for Lowe's was 11.1 percent in 2012. Clearly, The Home Depot produced a much better return than its strongest competitor.

We can gain additional insight by examining The Home Depot's ROE over time:

	2012	2011	2010
ROE	21.1%	18.0%	14.2%

This comparison indicates consistent improvement in The Home Depot's performance as measured by its ROE. As mentioned earlier, The Home Depot's performance was affected by stronger customer demand and effective implementation of an improved business strategy.

2. Return on Assets (ROA)

Another test of profitability compares income to the total assets (i.e., total investment) used to earn the income. Many analysts consider the return on assets ratio to be a better measure (compared to ROE) of management's ability to utilize assets effectively because it is not affected by the way in which the assets have been financed. For example, the return on equity could be very high for a company that has borrowed a large amount of debt compared to a company that has earned the same return on the same amount of assets but borrowed less money. Return on assets is computed as follows:

$$\text{Return on Assets} = \frac{\text{Net Income} + \text{Interest Expense (net of tax)}^{\dagger}}{\text{Average Total Assets}}$$

$$\text{Home Depot 2012} = \frac{\$3,883 + (\$606 \times 66\%)}{\$40,322^{\ddagger}} = 10.6\%$$

†This illustration assumes a corporate tax rate of 34 percent.
‡($40,518 + $40,125) ÷ 2 = $40,322.

Note that interest expense has been added to net income in the numerator of the ratio. Because the denominator of the ratio includes resources provided by both owners and creditors, the numerator must include the return that was available to each group. Interest expense is added back because it was previously deducted in the computation of net income. Note, too, that interest expense is measured net of income tax. This amount is used because it represents the net cost to the corporation for the funds provided by creditors.

---

[1]The figures for The Home Depot used throughout the following examples are taken from the financial statements in Exhibit 13.1.

The return on assets for Lowe's was 6.1 percent, lower than the ROA for The Home Depot. This comparison is another indication that The Home Depot is utilizing its assets more effectively than Lowe's.

3. Financial Leverage Percentage

Financial leverage percentage measures the advantage or disadvantage that occurs when a company's return on equity differs from its return on assets (i.e., ROE − ROA). In the DuPont model discussed earlier in this chapter, **financial leverage** was defined as the proportion of assets acquired with funds supplied by owners. The ratio **financial leverage percentage** measures a related but different concept. This ratio describes the relationship between the return on equity and the return on assets. Leverage is positive when the rate of return on a company's assets exceeds the average after-tax interest rate on its borrowed funds. Basically, the company borrows at one rate and invests at a higher rate of return. Most companies have positive leverage.

Financial leverage percentage can be measured by comparing the two return ratios as follows:

$$\text{Financial Leverage Percentage} = \text{Return on Equity} - \text{Return on Assets}$$

$$\text{Home Depot 2012} = 21.1\% - 10.6\% = 10.5\% \text{ (positive leverage)}$$

When a company borrows funds at an after-tax interest rate and invests those funds to earn a higher after-tax rate of return, the difference accrues to the benefit of the owners. The notes to The Home Depot's annual report indicate that the company borrowed money at rates ranging from 3.75 percent to 5.875 percent and invested it in assets earning 10.6 percent. The difference between the income earned on the money it has borrowed and the interest it has paid to creditors is available for the owners of The Home Depot. This benefit of financial leverage is the primary reason most companies obtain a significant amount of their resources from creditors rather than from the sale of capital stock. Note that financial leverage can be enhanced either by investing effectively (i.e., earning a high return on investment) or by borrowing effectively (i.e., paying a low rate of interest).

Lowe's financial leverage ratio (5.0 percent) is lower than The Home Depot's. Lowe's ratio is lower because it utilizes comparatively less debt in its capital structure and it is not earning as high a return on its assets, compared to The Home Depot.

4. Earnings per Share (EPS)

The earnings per share ratio is a measure of return on investment that is based on the number of shares outstanding instead of the dollar amounts reported on the balance sheet. In simple situations,[2] EPS is computed as follows:

$$\text{Earnings per Share} = \frac{\text{Net Income}}{\text{Average Number of Shares of Common Stock Outstanding}}$$

$$\text{Home Depot 2012} = \frac{\$3,883}{1,562} = \$2.49 \text{ per share}$$

Earnings per share is probably the single most widely watched ratio. Analysts develop their own estimates of EPS and the stock price of a company may change significantly if the actual EPS differs from the estimate.

---

[2]The EPS number we calculate in this section is the same as the one reported by The Home Depot on its income statement shown in Exhibit 13.1. Normally, that will not be the case due to additional complexities discussed in intermediate accounting courses.

5. Quality of Income

Most financial analysts are concerned about the quality of a company's earnings because some accounting procedures can be used to report higher income. For example, a company that uses LIFO and short estimated lives for depreciable assets will report lower earnings than a similar company that uses FIFO and longer estimated lives. One method of evaluating the quality of a company's earnings is to compare its reported earnings to its cash flows from operating activities, as follows:

$$\text{Quality of Income} = \frac{\text{Cash Flows from Operating Activities}}{\text{Net Income}}$$

$$\text{Home Depot 2012} = \frac{\$6,651}{\$3,883} = 1.71$$

A quality of income ratio that is higher than 1 is considered to indicate high-quality earnings, because each dollar of income is supported by one dollar or more of cash flow. A ratio that is below 1 represents lower-quality earnings.

A research report from Edward Jones discusses the issue of quality of earnings for The Home Depot:

Net income historically grew in line with cash flows from operating activities. But over the past three years, Home Depot has become much more efficient with its working capital, driving down net income as a percentage of cash flows from operating activities. Also, the company is using more conservative accounting methodology.

REAL WORLD EXCERPT
Edward Jones

6. Profit Margin

The profit margin measures the percentage of each sales dollar, on average, that represents profit. It is computed as follows:

$$\text{Profit Margin} = \frac{\text{Net Income}}{\text{Net Sales Revenue}}$$

$$\text{Home Depot 2012} = \frac{\$3,883}{\$70,395} = 5.5\%$$

For 2012, each dollar of The Home Depot's sales generated 5.5 cents of profit. In comparison, Lowe's earned 3.7 cents for each dollar of sales. This is a fairly significant difference for two companies in the same industry. It represents a significant advantage for The Home Depot.

While profit margin is a good measure of operating efficiency, care must be used in analyzing it because it does not consider the resources (i.e., total investment) needed to earn income. It is very difficult to compare profit margins for companies in different industries. For example, profit margins are low in the food industry while profit margins in the jewelry business are high. Both types of business can be quite profitable, however, because a high sales volume can compensate for a low profit margin. Grocery stores have low profit margins, but they generate a high sales volume from their relatively inexpensive stores and inventory. Although jewelry stores earn comparatively more profit from each sales dollar, they require a large investment in luxury stores and very expensive inventory.

The trade-off between profit margin and sales volume can be stated in simple terms: Would you prefer to have 5 percent of $1,000,000 or 10 percent of $100,000? As you can see, a larger profit margin is not always better.

7. Fixed Asset Turnover Ratio

Another measure of operating efficiency is the fixed asset turnover ratio, which compares sales volume with a company's investment in fixed assets. The term *fixed assets* is synonymous with property, plant, and equipment. The ratio is computed as follows:

$$\text{Fixed Asset Turnover Ratio} = \frac{\text{Net Sales Revenue}}{\text{Average Net Fixed Assets}}$$

$$\text{Home Depot 2012} = \frac{\$70,395}{\$24,754^*} = 2.84$$

*($24,448 + $25,060) ÷ 2 = $24,754.

In 2012, The Home Depot's fixed asset turnover ratio was better than Lowe's (2.28). In simple terms, this means that The Home Depot had a competitive advantage over Lowe's in terms of its ability to effectively utilize its fixed assets to generate revenue. For each dollar The Home Depot invested in property, plant, and equipment, the company was able to earn $2.84 in sales revenue, while Lowe's could earn only $2.28. This comparison is extremely important because it indicates that the management of The Home Depot was able to operate more efficiently than its main competitor.

The fixed asset turnover ratio is widely used to analyze capital-intensive companies such as airlines and electric utilities. For companies that hold large amounts of inventory and accounts receivable, analysts often prefer to use the *asset turnover ratio,* which is based on total assets rather than fixed assets:

$$\text{Asset Turnover Ratio} = \frac{\text{Net Sales Revenue}}{\text{Average Total Assets}}$$

$$\text{Home Depot 2012} = \frac{\$70,395}{\$40,322^*} = 1.75$$

*($40,518 + $40,125) ÷ 2 = $40,322.

In 2012, The Home Depot was able to generate $1.75 in revenue for each dollar invested in assets. In comparison, Lowe's asset turnover ratio was 1.49. Both turnover ratios show that The Home Depot was able to operate more efficiently than Lowe's. This comparison is important because operating efficiency has a significant impact on profitability, as shown by the DuPont model (presented earlier in this chapter).

PAUSE FOR **FEEDBACK**

SELF-STUDY **QUIZ**

We have discussed several measures of profitability. Next we will discuss tests of liquidity. Before you move on, complete the following questions to test your understanding of these concepts.

Show how to compute the following ratios:

1. Return on equity =
2. Return on assets =
3. Profit margin =

After you have completed your answers, check them with the solutions at the bottom of the next page.

Tests of Liquidity

Liquidity refers to a company's ability to meet its currently maturing debts. **Tests of liquidity** focus on the relationship between current assets and current liabilities. The ability to pay current liabilities is an important factor in evaluating a company's short-term financial strength. A company that does not have cash available to pay for purchases on a timely basis will lose its cash discounts and run the risk of having its credit discontinued by vendors. In this section, we discuss five ratios that are used to measure liquidity: the cash ratio, the current ratio, the quick ratio, the receivable turnover ratio, and the inventory turnover ratio.

LEARNING OBJECTIVE 13-5
Compute and interpret liquidity ratios.

TESTS OF LIQUIDITY are ratios that measure a company's ability to meet its currently maturing obligations.

8. Cash Ratio

Cash is the lifeblood of a business. Without cash, a company cannot pay its employees or meet its obligations to creditors. Even a profitable business will fail without sufficient cash. One measure of the adequacy of available cash, called the *cash ratio,* is computed as follows:

$$\text{Cash Ratio} = \frac{\text{Cash} + \text{Cash Equivalents}}{\text{Current Liabilities}}$$

$$\text{Home Depot 2012} = \frac{\$1,987}{\$9,376} = 0.21 \text{ to } 1$$

In 2012, Lowe's cash ratio was 0.13, indicating that its cash reserve was somewhat less than that indicated by the cash ratio for The Home Depot. The Home Depot ratio of 0.21 means that the company has on hand 21 cents of cash for each $1 of current liabilities. Would analysts be concerned about this fairly low margin of safety? In this case, the answer is no because there are other factors to consider. For example, The Home Depot's statement of cash flows shows that the company generated a large amount of cash from its operating activities. As a result, it did not need to keep a large amount of cash on hand to meet unexpected needs. Indeed, most analysts believe the cash ratio should not be too high because holding excess cash is usually uneconomical. It is far better to invest the cash in productive assets or reduce debt.

Some analysts do not use the cash ratio because they see it as too stringent a test of liquidity and it is very sensitive to small events. The collection of a large account receivable, for example, could have a significant impact on a company's cash ratio. The current ratio and the quick ratio are much less sensitive to the timing of such transactions.

9. Current Ratio

The current ratio measures the relationship between total current assets and total current liabilities on a specific date. It is computed as follows:

$$\text{Current Ratio} = \frac{\text{Current Assets}}{\text{Current Liabilities}}$$

$$\text{Home Depot 2012} = \frac{\$14,520}{\$9,376} = 1.55$$

The current ratio measures the cushion of working capital that companies maintain to allow for the inevitable unevenness in the flow of funds through the working capital accounts. At the end of

Solutions to
SELF-STUDY QUIZ

1. $\dfrac{\text{Net Income}}{\text{Average Stockholders' Equity}}$

2. $\dfrac{\text{Net Income} + \text{Interest Expense (net of tax)}}{\text{Average Total Assets}}$

3. $\dfrac{\text{Net Income}}{\text{Net Sales Revenue}}$

2012, The Home Depot had $1.55 in current assets for each $1 in current liabilities. Most analysts would judge that ratio to be very strong, given The Home Depot's ability to generate cash.

To properly use the current ratio, analysts must understand the nature of a company's business. Many manufacturing companies have developed sophisticated systems to minimize the amount of inventory they must hold. These systems, called *just-in-time inventory,* are designed to have an inventory item arrive just when it is needed. While these systems work well in manufacturing processes, they do not work as well in retailing. Customers expect to find merchandise in the store when they want it, and it has proven difficult to precisely forecast consumer behavior. As a result, most retailers have comparatively high current ratios because they must carry large inventories. The Home Depot, for example, maintains an inventory of 50,000 different products in each store.

Analysts consider a current ratio of 2 to be financially conservative. Indeed, most companies have current ratios that are below 2. The optimal level of the current ratio depends on the business environment in which a company operates. If cash flows are predictable and stable (as they are for a utility company), the current ratio can be low, even less than 1. For example, Procter & Gamble, a strong and fiscally conservative company, has a current ratio of 0.88. When cash flows are highly variable, a higher current ratio is desirable.

Analysts become concerned if a company's current ratio is high compared to that of other companies in its industry. A firm is operating inefficiently when it ties up too much money in inventory or accounts receivable. There is no reason, for instance, for a Home Depot store to hold 1,000 hammers in stock if it sells only 100 hammers a month.

10. Quick Ratio (Acid Test)

The quick ratio is a more stringent test of short-term liquidity than is the current ratio. The quick ratio compares quick assets, defined as *cash and near-cash assets,* to current liabilities. Quick assets include cash, short-term investments, and accounts receivable (net of the allowance for doubtful accounts). Inventory is omitted from quick assets because of the uncertainty of the timing of cash flows from its sale. Prepaid expenses are also excluded from quick assets. The quick ratio is computed as follows:

$$\text{Quick Ratio} = \frac{\text{Quick Assets}}{\text{Current Liabilities}}$$

$$\text{Home Depot 2012} = \frac{\$3,232^*}{\$9,376} = 0.35 \text{ to } 1$$

*($1,987 + $1,245) = $3,232.

The quick ratio is a measure of the safety margin that is available to meet a company's current liabilities. The Home Depot has 35 cents in cash and near-cash assets for every $1 in current liabilities. This margin of safety is typical of the retail industry and would be considered a good margin in light of the large amount of cash The Home Depot generates from its operating activities. In comparison, the quick ratio for Lowe's is less than Home Depot (0.17 to 1).

11. Receivable Turnover Ratio

Accounts receivable are closely related to both short-term liquidity and operating efficiency. A company that can quickly collect cash from its customers has good liquidity and does not needlessly tie up funds in unproductive assets. The receivable turnover ratio is computed as follows:

$$\text{Receivable Turnover Ratio} = \frac{\text{Net Credit Sales}^*}{\text{Average Net Receivables}}$$

$$\text{Home Depot 2012} = \frac{\$70,395}{\$1,165^\dagger} = 60.4 \text{ Times}$$

*When the amount of credit sales is not known, total sales may be used as a rough approximation.
†($1,245 + $1,085) ÷ 2 = $1,165.

A high receivable turnover ratio suggests that a company is effective in its credit-granting and collection activities. Granting credit to poor credit risks and ineffective collection efforts will produce a low receivable turnover ratio. While a very low ratio is obviously a problem, a very high ratio also can be troublesome because it suggests an overly stringent credit policy that could cause lost sales and profits.

The receivable turnover ratio is often converted to a time basis known as the *average age of receivables*. The computation is as follows:

$$\text{Average Age of Receivables} = \frac{\text{Days in a Year}}{\text{Receivable Turnover Ratio}}$$

$$\text{Home Depot 2012} = \frac{365}{60.4} = 6.0 \text{ Average Days to Collect}$$

The effectiveness of credit and collection activities is sometimes judged by the rule of thumb that the average days to collect should not exceed 1.5 times the credit terms. For example, if the credit terms require payment in 30 days, the average days to collect should not exceed 45 days (i.e., not more than 15 days past due). Like all rules of thumb, this one has many exceptions.

Although the receivable turnover ratio normally provides useful insights, the one for The Home Depot is not meaningful. It is highly unlikely that The Home Depot collects cash from its credit customers in just 6 days, on average. Because we did not know the amount of The Home Depot's credit sales, we used total sales as an approximation. In this case, the approximation is not reasonable. Think about the last time you watched a customer buying merchandise on credit in a retail store. Most customers use a bank credit card such as MasterCard or Visa. From the seller's perspective, a sales transaction involving a bank credit card is recorded in virtually the same manner as a cash sale. In other words, the money a customer owes on a credit card sale is owed to the credit card company, not the seller (in this case, The Home Depot). In practice, the majority of The Home Depot's credit sales involve bank credit cards. As a result, The Home Depot's receivable turnover ratio is not meaningful. This situation illustrates that ratio analysis involves more than the mere computation of numbers. Analysts must evaluate the results based on their understanding of the business.

12. Inventory Turnover Ratio

Like the receivable turnover ratio, the inventory turnover ratio is a measure of both liquidity and operating efficiency. This ratio reflects the relationship of inventory to the volume of goods sold during the period. It is computed as follows:

$$\text{Inventory Turnover Ratio} = \frac{\text{Cost of Goods Sold}}{\text{Average Inventory}}$$

$$\text{Home Depot 2012} = \frac{\$46,133}{\$10,475^*} = 4.4 \text{ Times}$$

*($10,325 + $10,625) ÷ 2 = $10,475.

Because a company normally realizes profit each time inventory is sold, an increase in this ratio is usually favorable. If the ratio is too high, however, it may be an indication that sales were lost because desired items were not in stock. The cost of a lost sale is often much higher than the lost profit. When a business is out of stock on an item desired by a customer, the individual will often go to a competitor to find it. That visit may help the competitor establish a business relationship with the customer. Thus, the cost of being out of stock may be all future profits on sales to a lost customer.

On average, The Home Depot's inventory was acquired and sold to customers 4.4 times during the year. The inventory turnover ratio is critical for The Home Depot because of its business strategy. It wants to be able to offer customers the right product when they need it at a price that beats the competition. If The Home Depot does not effectively manage its inventory levels, it will incur extra costs that must be passed on to the customer.

Inventory turnover for Lowe's was 3.9. Historically, The Home Depot has enjoyed a significant advantage over Lowe's in terms of inventory management. The Home Depot's effectiveness in inventory management means that the company is able to tie up less money in carrying inventory compared to Lowe's.

Turnover ratios vary significantly from one industry to the next. Companies in the food industry (grocery stores and restaurants) have high inventory turnover ratios because their inventory is subject to rapid deterioration in quality. Companies that sell expensive merchandise (automobiles and high-fashion clothes) have much lower ratios because although sales of those items are infrequent, customers want to have a selection to choose from when they do buy.

The inventory turnover ratio is often converted to a time basis called the *average days' supply in inventory*. The computation is:

$$\text{Average Days' Supply in Inventory} = \frac{\text{Days in Year}}{\text{Inventory Turnover Ratio}}$$

$$\text{Home Depot 2012} = \frac{365}{4.4} = 83 \text{ Average Days' Supply in Inventory}$$

Using Ratios to Analyze the Operating Cycle In Chapter 3, we introduced the concept of the operating cycle, which is the time it takes for a company to pay cash to its suppliers, sell goods to its customers, and collect cash from its customers. Analysts are interested in the operating cycle because it helps them evaluate a company's cash needs and is a good indicator of management efficiency.

The operating cycle for most companies involves three distinct phases: the acquisition of inventory, the sale of the inventory, and the collection of cash from the customer. We have discussed several ratios that are helpful when evaluating a company's operating cycle:

Ratio	Operating Activity
Accounts payable turnover ratio*	Purchase of inventory
Inventory turnover ratio	Sale of inventory
Receivable turnover ratio	Collection of cash from customers

*Discussed in Chapter 9.

Each of the ratios measures the number of days it takes, on average, to complete an operating activity. We have already computed two of the needed ratios for The Home Depot, so if we compute the accounts payable turnover ratio, we can analyze the operating cycle:

$$\text{Accounts Payable Turnover Ratio} = \frac{\text{Cost of Goods Sold}}{\text{Average Accounts Payable}}$$

$$\text{Home Depot 2012} = \frac{\$46,133}{\$4,786^*} = 9.6 \text{ Times}$$

*($4,856 + $4,717) ÷ 2 = $4,786.

$$\text{Average Age of Payables} = \frac{\text{Days in Year}}{\text{Payable Turnover Ratio}}$$

$$\text{Home Depot 2012} = \frac{365}{9.6} = 38 \text{ Average Days to Pay Suppliers}$$

The length of the component parts for The Home Depot's operating cycle are:

Ratio	Time
Average age of payables	38.0 days
Average days' supply of inventory	83.0 days
Average age of receivables	6.0 days

The component parts of the operating cycle help us understand the cash needs of the company. The Home Depot, on average, pays for its inventory 38 days after it receives it. It takes, on average, 89 days (83 + 6.0) for it to sell and for the company to collect cash from the customer. Therefore, The Home Depot must invest cash in its operating activities for just over 51 days between the time it pays its vendors and the time it collects from its customers. Companies prefer to minimize the time between paying vendors and collecting cash from customers because it frees up cash for other productive purposes. The Home Depot could reduce this time by slowing payments to creditors or by increasing the inventory turnover.

PAUSE FOR **FEEDBACK**

SELF-STUDY **QUIZ**

We have discussed several measures of liquidity. Next we will discuss tests of solvency. Before you move on, complete the following questions to test your understanding of these concepts.
Show how to compute the following ratios:

1. Current ratio =
2. Quick ratio =
3. Cash ratio =

After you have completed your answers, check them with the solutions at the bottom of the page.

Tests of Solvency

Solvency refers to a company's ability to meet its long-term obligations. **Tests of solvency,** which are measures of a company's ability to meet these obligations, include the times interest earned, cash coverage, and debt-to-equity ratios.

> **LEARNING OBJECTIVE 13-6**
> Compute and interpret solvency ratios.

13. Times Interest Earned Ratio

Interest payments are a fixed obligation. If a company fails to make required interest payments, creditors may force it into bankruptcy. Because of the importance of meeting interest payments, analysts often compute a ratio called *times interest earned:*

> TESTS OF SOLVENCY are ratios that measure a company's ability to meet its long-term obligations.

$$\text{Times Interest Earned} = \frac{\text{Net Income} + \text{Interest Expense} + \text{Income Tax Expense}}{\text{Interest Expense}}$$

$$\text{Home Depot 2012} = \frac{\$3{,}883 + \$606 + \$2{,}185}{\$606} = 11.0 \text{ Times}$$

The times interest earned ratio compares the income a company generated in a period to its interest obligation for the same period. It represents a margin of protection for creditors.

Solutions to
SELF-STUDY QUIZ

1. $\dfrac{\text{Current Assets}}{\text{Current Liabilities}}$

2. $\dfrac{\text{Quick Assets}}{\text{Current Liabilities}}$

3. $\dfrac{\text{Cash + Cash Equivalents}}{\text{Current Liabilities}}$

In 2012, The Home Depot generated $11.00 in income for each $1 of interest expense, a high ratio that indicates a secure position for creditors.

Some analysts prefer to calculate the times interest earned ratio based on all contractually required payments, including principal and rent payments. Others believe that the ratio is flawed because interest expense and other obligations are paid in cash, not with net income. These analysts prefer to use the cash coverage ratio.

14. Cash Coverage Ratio

Given the importance of cash flows and required interest payments, it is easy to understand why many analysts use the cash coverage ratio. It is computed as follows:

$$\text{Cash Coverage Ratio} = \frac{\text{Cash Flows from Operating Activities before Interest and Taxes Paid}}{\text{Interest Paid (from statement of cash flows)}}$$

$$\text{Home Depot 2012} = \frac{\$6,651 + \$580 + \$1,865}{\$580} = 15.7$$

The cash coverage ratio compares the cash generated by a company to its cash obligations for the period. Remember that analysts are concerned about a company's ability to make required interest payments. The Home Depot's cash coverage ratio shows that the company generated $15.70 in cash for every $1 of interest paid, which is strong coverage. Note that the cash coverage ratio uses **interest paid** and **income taxes paid** from the statement of cash flows instead of **interest expense** and **income tax expense** from the income statement. Accrued interest and interest payments, as well as income tax expense and income tax payments, are normally similar in amount but are not always the same.

15. Debt-to-Equity Ratio

The debt-to-equity ratio expresses a company's debt as a proportion of its stockholders' equity. It is computed as follows:

$$\text{Debt-to-Equity Ratio} = \frac{\text{Total Liabilities}}{\text{Stockholders' Equity}}$$

$$\text{Home Depot 2012} = \frac{\$22,620}{\$17,898} = 1.26$$

In 2012, for each $1 of stockholders' equity, The Home Depot had $1.26 worth of liabilities. By comparison, Lowe's debt-to-equity ratio was 1.03.

Debt is risky for a company because specific interest payments must be made even if the company has not earned sufficient income to pay them. In contrast, dividends are always at the company's discretion and are not legally enforceable until they are declared by the board of directors. Thus, equity capital is usually considered much less risky than debt.

Despite the risk associated with debt, however, most companies obtain significant amounts of resources from creditors because of the advantages of financial leverage discussed earlier. In addition, interest expense is a deductible expense on the corporate income tax return. In selecting a capital structure, a company must balance the higher returns available through leverage against the higher risk associated with debt. Because of the importance of the risk-return relationship, most analysts consider the debt-to-equity ratio a key part of any company evaluation.

Market Tests

Several ratios, often called **market tests,** relate the current price per share of stock to the return that accrues to investors. Many analysts prefer these ratios because they are based on the current value of an owner's investment in a company.

16. Price/Earnings (P/E) Ratio

The price/earnings (P/E) ratio measures the relationship between the current market price of a stock and its earnings per share. Recently, when the price of The Home Depot stock was $60 per share, EPS for The Home Depot was $2.49. The P/E ratio for The Home Depot is computed as follows:

$$\text{Price/Earnings Ratio} = \frac{\text{Market Price per Share}}{\text{Earnings per Share}}$$

$$\text{Home Depot 2012} = \frac{\$60}{\$2.49} = 24.1$$

This P/E ratio indicates that The Home Depot's stock was selling at a price that was 24.1 times its earnings per share. The P/E ratio reflects the stock market's assessment of a company's future performance. A high ratio indicates that earnings are expected to grow rapidly. The Home Depot's P/E ratio is higher compared to previous years and is higher than Lowe's, which reported a P/E ratio of 21. The P/E ratio for The Home Depot suggests that the market believes that The Home Depot has good potential to increase its income from current levels. This projected increase in income will most likely come from the company's strategy of improving operating efficiencies.

In economic terms, the value of a stock is related to the present value of the company's future earnings. Thus, a company that expects to increase its earnings in the future is worth more than one that cannot grow its earnings (assuming other factors are the same). However, while a high P/E ratio and good growth prospects are considered favorable, there are risks. When a company with a high P/E ratio does not meet the level of earnings expected by the market, the negative impact on its stock can be dramatic.

17. Dividend Yield Ratio

When investors buy stock, they expect two kinds of return: dividend income and price appreciation. The dividend yield ratio measures the relationship between the dividends per share paid to stockholders and the current market price of the stock. The Home Depot paid dividends of $1.16 per share when the market price of its stock was $60 per share. Its dividend yield ratio is computed as follows:

$$\text{Dividend Yield Ratio} = \frac{\text{Dividends per Share}}{\text{Market Price per Share}}$$

$$\text{Home Depot 2012} = \frac{\$1.16}{\$60} = 1.9\%$$

In recent years, the dividend yield for The Home Depot has been less than 2 percent. The ratio increased to 3.5% in 2009 because of a lower stock price. The dividend yield for most stocks is not high compared to alternative investments. Investors are willing to accept low dividend yields if they expect that the price of a stock will increase while they own it. Clearly, investors who bought The Home Depot stock did so with the expectation that its price would increase. In contrast, stocks with low growth potential tend to offer much higher dividend yields than do stocks with high growth potential. These stocks often appeal to retired investors who need current income rather than future growth potential.

The dividend yield for Lowe's is similar to that for The Home Depot, 2.1 percent in 2012. The chart in the margin shows dividend yields for some companies in other industries.

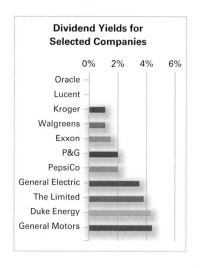

Dividend Yields for Selected Companies

SELF-STUDY **QUIZ**

We have discussed several measures of solvency and two market tests. Next we will discuss important analytical considerations. Before you move on, complete the following questions to test your understanding of these concepts.

Show how to compute the following ratios:

1. Current ratio =
2. Inventory turnover ratio =
3. Price/earnings ratio =

After you have completed your answers, check them with the solutions at the bottom of the page.

GUIDED **HELP**

For additional step-by-step video instruction, go to the URL or scan the QR code in the margin with your smartphone or iPad.

Define the following:

1. Time series analysis
2. Component percentages
3. Liquidity
4. Solvency
5. Return on equity
6. Debt-to-equity ratio

www.mhhe.com/libby8e

INTERPRETING RATIOS AND OTHER ANALYTICAL CONSIDERATIONS

Except for earnings per share, the computation of financial ratios has not been standardized by either the accounting profession or security analysts. Thus, users of financial statements should compute the various ratios in accordance with their decision objectives. Before using ratios computed by others, they should determine the computational approach that was used.

As we have seen, ratios can be interpreted only by comparing them to other ratios or to some optimal value. Some ratios, by their very nature, are unfavorable at either very high or very low values. For example, a very low current ratio may indicate an inability to meet maturing debts, while a very high current ratio may indicate an unprofitable use of funds. Furthermore, an optimal ratio for one company may not be optimal for another. Comparisons among the ratios for different companies are appropriate only if the companies are comparable in terms of their industry, operations, size, and accounting policies.

Because ratios are based on the aggregation of information, they may obscure underlying factors that are of interest to the analyst. For example, a current ratio that is considered optimal can obscure a short-term liquidity problem in a company with a large amount of inventory but a minimal amount of cash with which to pay debts as they mature. Careful analysis can uncover this type of problem.

Solutions to
SELF-STUDY QUIZ

1. $\dfrac{\text{Current Assets}}{\text{Current Liabilities}}$

2. $\dfrac{\text{Cost of Goods Sold}}{\text{Average Inventory}}$

3. $\dfrac{\text{Market Price per Share}}{\text{Earnings per Share}}$

YEARS BEFORE BANKRUPTCY				
5	**4**	**3**	**2**	**1**
Current ratio 1.8	1.7	1.7	1.2	1.2
Debt-to-equity ratio 1.6	1.8	2.0	5.0	5.6

EXHIBIT 13.4

Selected Financial Ratios
for Hechinger

In other cases, analysis cannot uncover obscured problems. For example, consolidated statements include financial information about a parent company and its subsidiaries. The parent company could have a high current ratio and the subsidiary a low one, but when their statements are consolidated, their current ratios are in effect averaged and can fall within an acceptable range. The fact that the subsidiary could have a serious liquidity problem is obscured.

Despite limitations, ratio analysis is a useful analytical tool. For instance, financial ratios are effective for predicting bankruptcy. Exhibit 13.4 presents the current and debt-to-equity ratios for Hechinger, a former competitor of The Home Depot, for the five years before its recent bankruptcy. Notice the progressive deterioration of these ratios. Analysts who studied these ratios probably were not surprised when Hechinger filed for bankruptcy.

Financial statements provide information to all investors, both sophisticated and unsophisticated. However, users who understand basic accounting principles and terminology are able to more effectively analyze the information contained in financial statements. For example, some unsophisticated users who do not understand the cost principle believe that assets are reported on the balance sheet at their fair market value. Interpreting accounting numbers correctly without an understanding of the concepts that were used to develop them is impossible.

In analyzing different companies, you will find that they rarely use exactly the same accounting policies. Comparisons among companies are appropriate only if the analyst who is making them understands the impact of different accounting alternatives. For example, one company may use conservative accounting alternatives such as accelerated depreciation and LIFO while another may use income-maximizing alternatives such as straight-line depreciation and FIFO. Analysts who do not understand the different effects of these accounting methods could misinterpret financial results. Perhaps the most important first step in analyzing financial statements is a review of the company's accounting policies, which are disclosed in a note to the statements.

Other Financial Information

The ratios we have discussed are useful for most analytical purposes. Because each company is different, however, you must exercise professional judgment when you conduct a financial analysis. To illustrate, let's look at some special factors that could affect our analysis of The Home Depot.

1. **Rapid growth.** Growth in total sales volume does not always indicate that a company is successful. Sales volume from new stores may obscure the fact that existing stores are not meeting customer needs and are experiencing declines in sales. The family pizza chain Chuck-E-Cheese appeared to be a success when it reported rapid growth in total sales revenue by opening new restaurants. Unfortunately, the novelty of the new Chuck-E-Cheese restaurants proved to be short-lived, and their sales volume fell quickly. Because its older restaurants were unprofitable, Chuck-E-Cheese was forced to reorganize. In contrast, The Home Depot's annual report shows that the company's stores posted sales increases ranging from 3 percent to 15 percent in each of the previous 10 years. Clearly, The Home Depot can generate sales increases from both new and existing stores.

2. **Uneconomical expansion.** Some growth-oriented companies will open stores in less desirable locations if good locations cannot be found. These poor locations can cause a company's average productivity to decline. One measure of productivity in the retail industry is

sales volume per square foot of selling space. For The Home Depot, productivity results are improving after several years of significant declines:

Year	Sales per Square Foot
2012	$299
2011	289
2010	279
2009	298
2008	332
2007	357
2006	375

Sales per square foot reached a peak of over $400 in the 1990s. Management explains the slowdown in growth is a direct result of its strategy:

REAL WORLD EXCERPT
Annual Report

> We strategically open stores near market areas served by existing stores ("cannibalize") to gain incremental sales and increase market penetration. New stores cannibalized approximately 5% of our existing stores and reduced sales volume by approximately 1%.

As the note indicates, The Home Depot is willing to accept lower productivity at certain existing stores in order to achieve high sales levels in a region. Despite the explanation, the rapid decline in sales per square foot represents a significant operating challenge for The Home Depot.

3. Subjective factors. Remember that vital information about a company is not contained in the annual report. The best way to evaluate The Home Depot's strategy of being a price leader, for instance, is to visit its stores and those of competitors. An analyst who studied The Home Depot for Smith Barney did exactly that:

REAL WORLD EXCERPT
Smith Barney
Research Report

> On July 15, we surveyed the Boca Raton, Florida, market. The Home Depot store is about two years old and was particularly impressive with respect to its in-stock position, customer service, and total store presentation. We were able to compare Home Depot's pricing on 20 sample items. Our price analysis revealed that Home Depot is the price leader in the market by an average of 11 percent below the average total price of our 20-item market basket. Given The Home Depot's low cost structure, we believe that it will remain the price leader in this important market.

As these examples illustrate, no single approach can be used to analyze all companies. Furthermore, an effective analyst will look beyond the information contained in an annual report.

A QUESTION OF ETHICS Insider Information

Financial statements are an important source of information for investors. The announcement of unexpected information can cause a substantial movement in the price of a company's stock.

A company's accountants often are aware of important financial information before it is made available to the public. This is called *insider information*. Some people might be tempted to buy or sell stock based on insider information, but to do so is a serious criminal offense. The Securities and Exchange Commission has brought a number of cases against individuals who traded on insider information. Their convictions resulted in large fines and time served in jail.

In some cases, determining whether something is insider information is difficult. For example, an individual could overhear a comment made in the company elevator by two executives. A well-respected Wall Street investment banker offers good advice on dealing with such situations: "If you are not sure if something is right or wrong, apply the newspaper headline test. Ask yourself how you would feel to have your family and friends read about what you had done in the newspaper." Interestingly, many people who have spent time in jail and lost small fortunes in fines because of insider trading say that the most difficult part of the process was telling their families.

To uphold the highest ethical standard, many public accounting firms have adopted rules that prevent their staff from investing in companies that the firms audit. Such rules are designed to ensure that a company's auditors will not be tempted to engage in insider trading.

Information in an Efficient Market

Considerable research has been performed on the way in which stock markets react to new information. Much of this evidence supports the view that the markets react very quickly to new information in an unbiased manner (that is, the market does not systematically overreact or underreact to new information). A market that reacts to information in this manner is called an **efficient market.** In an efficient market, the price of a security fully reflects all available information.

EFFICIENT MARKETS are securities markets in which prices fully reflect available information.

It is not surprising that the stock markets react quickly to new information. Many professional investors manage stock portfolios valued in the hundreds of millions of dollars. These investors have a financial incentive to discover new information about a company and to trade quickly based on that information.

The research on efficient markets has important implications for financial analysts. It probably is not beneficial to study old information (say an annual report that was released six months earlier) in an effort to identify an undervalued stock. In an efficient market, the price of a stock reflects all information contained in the annual report shortly after its release. In an efficient market, moreover, a company cannot manipulate the price of its stock by manipulating its accounting policy. The market should be able to differentiate between a company whose earnings are increasing due to improved productivity and one whose earnings have increased simply because of changes in accounting policies.

CHAPTER **TAKE-AWAYS**

13-1. Explain how a company's business strategy affects financial analysis.   p. 649

In simple terms, a business strategy establishes the objectives a business is trying to achieve. Performance is best evaluated by comparing the financial results to the objectives that the business was working to achieve. In other words, an understanding of a company's strategy provides the context for conducting financial statement analysis.

13-2. Discuss how analysts use financial statements.   p. 650

Analysts use financial statements to understand present conditions and past performance as well as to predict future performance. Financial statements provide important information to help users understand and evaluate corporate strategy. The data reported on statements can be used for either time series analysis (evaluating a single company over time) or in comparison with similar companies at a single point in time. Most analysts compute component percentages and ratios when using statements.

13-3. Compute and interpret component percentages.   p. 652

To compute component percentages for the income statement, the base amount used is net sales revenue. Each expense is expressed as a percentage of net sales revenue. On the balance sheet, the base amount is total assets; each balance sheet account is divided by total assets. Component percentages are evaluated by comparing them over time for a single company or by comparing them with percentages for similar companies.

13-4. Compute and interpret profitability ratios.   p. 653

Several tests of profitability focus on measuring the adequacy of income by comparing it to other items reported on the financial statements. Exhibit 13.3 lists these ratios and shows how to compute them. Profitability ratios are evaluated by comparing them over time for a single company or by comparing them with ratios for similar companies.

13-5. Compute and interpret liquidity ratios.   p. 659

Tests of liquidity measure a company's ability to meet its currently maturing debt. Exhibit 13.3 lists these ratios and shows how to compute them. Liquidity ratios are evaluated by comparing them over time for a single company or by comparing them with ratios for similar companies.

13-6. Compute and interpret solvency ratios.   p. 663

Solvency ratios measure a company's ability to meet its long-term obligations. Exhibit 13.3 lists these ratios and shows how to compute them. Solvency ratios are evaluated by comparing them over time for a single company or by comparing them with ratios for similar companies.

13-7. Compute and interpret market test ratios.   p. 665

Market test ratios relate the current price of a stock to the return that accrues to investors. Exhibit 13.3 lists these ratios and shows how to compute them. Market test ratios are evaluated by comparing them over time for a single company or by comparing them with ratios for similar companies.

FINDING **FINANCIAL INFORMATION**

Balance Sheet

Ratios are not reported on the balance sheet, but analysts use balance sheet information to compute many ratios. Most analysts use an average of the beginning and ending amounts for balance sheet accounts when comparing the account to an income statement account.

Income Statement

Earnings per share is the only ratio that is required to be reported on the financial statements. It is usually reported at the bottom of the income statement.

Statement of Cash Flows

Ratios are not reported on this statement, but some analysts use amounts from this statement to compute some ratios.

Statement of Stockholders' Equity

Ratios are not reported on this statement, but analysts use amounts from this statement to compute some ratios.

Notes

Under Summary of Significant Accounting Policies
This note has no information pertaining directly to ratios, but it is important to understand accounting differences if you are comparing two companies.

Under a Separate Note
Most companies include a 10-year financial summary as a separate note. These summaries include data for significant accounts, some accounting ratios, and nonaccounting information.

KEY **TERMS**

Component Percentage   p. 652
Efficient Markets   p. 669
Market Tests   p. 665

Ratio (Percentage)
  Analysis   p. 652
Tests of Liquidity   p. 659

Tests of Profitability   p. 653
Tests of Solvency   p. 663

QUESTIONS

1. What are some of the primary items on financial statements about which creditors usually are concerned?
2. Why are the notes to the financial statements important to decision makers?
3. What is the primary purpose of comparative financial statements?
4. Why are statement users interested in financial summaries covering several years? What is the primary limitation of long-term summaries?
5. What is ratio analysis? Why is it useful?
6. What are component percentages? Why are they useful?
7. Explain the two concepts of return on investment.
8. What is financial leverage? How is it measured as a percentage?
9. Is profit margin a useful measure of profitability? Explain.
10. Compare and contrast the current ratio and the quick ratio.
11. What does the debt-to-equity ratio reflect?
12. What are market tests?
13. Identify two factors that limit the effectiveness of ratio analysis.

MULTIPLE-CHOICE QUESTIONS

1. A company has total assets of $500,000 and noncurrent assets of $400,000. Current liabilities are $40,000. What is the current ratio?
   a. 12.5
   b. 10.0
   c. 2.5
   d. Cannot be determined without additional information.
2. Which of the following would **not** change the receivables turnover ratio for a retail company?
   a. Increases in the retail prices of inventory.
   b. A change in credit policy.
   c. Increases in the cost incurred to purchase inventory.
   d. None of the above.
3. Which of the following ratios is used to analyze liquidity?
   a. Earnings per share.   c. Current ratio.
   b. Debt-to-equity ratio.   d. Both (a) and (c).
4. Positive financial leverage indicates
   a. Positive cash flow from financing activities.
   b. A debt-to-equity ratio higher than 1.
   c. A rate of return on assets exceeding the interest rate on debt.
   d. A profit margin in one year exceeding the previous year's profit margin.
5. If a potential investor is analyzing three companies in the same industry and wishes to invest in only one, which ratio is least likely to affect the investor's decision?
   a. Quick ratio.   c. Price to earnings ratio.
   b. Earnings per share.   d. Dividend yield ratio.
6. A company has quick assets of $300,000 and current liabilities of $150,000. The company purchased $50,000 in inventory on credit. After the purchase, the quick ratio would be
   a. 2.0   c. 1.5
   b. 2.3   d. 1.75
7. The average days' supply in inventory for Natural Foods Stores is 14.6 days. The company reported cost of goods sold in the amount of $1,500,000 and total sales of $2,500,000. What is the average amount of inventory for Natural Foods?
   a. $102,740   c. $100,000
   b. $171,233   d. $60,000

8. Given the following ratios for four companies, which company is least likely to experience problems paying its current liabilities promptly?

	Quick Ratio	Receivable Turnover Ratio
a.	1.2	58
b.	1.2	45
c.	1.0	55
d.	.5	60

9. A decrease in selling and administrative expenses would impact what ratio?
   a. Fixed asset turnover ratio.   c. Debt-to-equity ratio.
   b. Times interest earned ratio.   d. Current ratio.

10. A creditor is least likely to use what ratio when analyzing a company that has borrowed funds on a long-term basis?
   a. Cash coverage ratio.   c. Times interest earned ratio.
   b. Debt-to-equity ratio.   d. Profit margin.

For more practice with multiple-choice questions, go to the text website at **www.mhhe.com/libby8e.**

MINI-**EXERCISES**

M13-1
LO13-3

Inferring Financial Information Using Component Percentages

A large retailer reported revenue of $1,665,000. The company's gross profit percentage was 44 percent. What amount of cost of goods sold did the company report?

M13-2
LO13-3

Inferring Financial Information Using Component Percentages

A consumer products company reported a 5.4 percent increase in sales from 2014 to 2015. Sales in 2014 were $29,600. In 2015, the company reported cost of goods sold in the amount of $9,107. What was the gross profit percentage in 2015?

M13-3
LO13-4

Computing the Return on Owners' Equity Ratio

Compute the return on equity ratio for 2015 given the following data:

	2015	2014
Net income	$ 183,000	$ 159,000
Stockholders' equity	1,100,000	1,250,000
Total assets	2,460,000	2,630,000
Interest expense	42,000	32,000

M13-4
LO13-4

Inferring Financial Information

Compute the financial leverage percentage for 2015 given the following data:

	2015	2014
Return on equity	21%	26%
Return on assets	6	8
Profit margin	12	12

M13-5
LO13-5

Analyzing the Inventory Turnover Ratio

A manufacturer reported an inventory turnover ratio of 8.6 during 2014. During 2015, management introduced a new inventory control system that was expected to reduce average inventory levels by 25 percent without affecting sales volume. Given these circumstances, would you expect the inventory turnover ratio to increase or decrease during 2015? Explain.

M13-6
LO13-5

Inferring Financial Information Using a Ratio

Stacy Company reported total assets of $1,400,000 and noncurrent assets of $480,000. The company also reported a current ratio of 3.5. What amount of current liabilities did the company report?

Analyzing Financial Relationships

Ramesh Company has prepared draft financial results now being reviewed by the accountants. You notice that the financial leverage percentage is negative. You also note that the current ratio is 2.4 and the quick ratio is 3.7. You recognize that these financial relationships are unusual. Does either imply that a mistake has been made? Explain.

M13-7
LO13-4, 13-5

Inferring Financial Information Using a Ratio

In 2014, Pringle Company reported earnings per share of $9.50 when its stock was selling for $228. In 2015, its earnings increased by 13 percent. If all other relationships remain constant, what is the price of the stock?

M13-8
LO13-7

Inferring Financial Information Using a Ratio

An Internet company earned $6.50 per share and paid dividends of $3.50 per share. The company reported a dividend yield of 5 percent. What was the price of the stock?

M13-9
LO13-7

Analyzing the Impact of Accounting Alternatives

Youngstown Corporation is considering changing its inventory method from FIFO to LIFO and wants to determine the impact on selected accounting ratios. In general, what impact would you expect on the following ratios: profit margin, fixed asset turnover ratio, current ratio, and quick ratio?

M13-10
LO13-7

EXERCISES

Using Financial Information to Identify Mystery Companies

The following selected financial data pertain to four unidentified companies:

E13-1
LO13-1, 13-2, 13-3,
13-5, 13-6

	COMPANIES			
	1	2	3	4
Balance Sheet Data				
(component percentage)				
Cash	3.5	4.7	8.2	11.7
Accounts receivable	16.9	28.9	16.8	51.9
Inventory	46.8	35.6	57.3	4.8
Property and equipment	18.3	21.7	7.6	18.7
Income Statement Data				
(component percentage)				
Gross profit	22.0	22.5	44.8	N/A*
Profit before taxes	2.1	0.7	1.2	3.2
Selected Ratios				
Current ratio	1.3	1.5	1.6	1.2
Inventory turnover ratio	3.6	9.8	1.5	N/A*
Debt-to-equity ratio	2.6	2.6	3.2	3.2

*N/A = Not applicable.

This financial information pertains to the following companies:

a. Retail fur store
b. Advertising agency
c. Wholesale candy company
d. Car manufacturer

Required:
Match each company with its financial information.

E13-2

LO13-1, 13-2, 13-3, 13-5, 13-6

Using Financial Information to Identify Mystery Companies

The following selected financial data pertain to four unidentified companies:

	COMPANIES			
	1	2	3	4
Balance Sheet Data				
(component percentage)				
Cash	7.3	21.6	6.1	11.3
Accounts receivable	28.2	39.7	3.2	22.9
Inventory	21.6	0.6	1.8	27.5
Property and equipment	32.1	18.0	74.6	25.1
Income Statement Data				
(component percentage)				
Gross profit	15.3	N/A*	N/A*	43.4
Profit before taxes	1.7	3.2	2.4	6.9
Selected Ratios				
Current ratio	1.5	1.2	0.6	1.9
Inventory turnover ratio	27.4	N/A*	N/A*	3.3
Debt-to-equity ratio	1.7	2.2	5.7	1.3

N/A = Not applicable.

This financial information pertains to the following companies:

a. Travel agency
b. Hotel
c. Meat packer
d. Drug company

Required:
Match each company with its financial information.

E13-3

LO13-1, 13-2, 13-3, 13-5, 13-6

Using Financial Information to Identify Mystery Companies

The following selected financial data pertain to four unidentified companies:

	COMPANIES			
	1	2	3	4
Balance Sheet Data				
(component percentage)				
Cash	5.1	8.8	6.3	10.4
Accounts receivable	13.1	41.5	13.8	4.9
Inventory	4.6	3.6	65.1	35.8
Property and equipment	53.1	23.0	8.8	35.7
Income Statement Data				
(component percentage)				
Gross profit	N/A*	N/A*	45.2	22.5
Profit before taxes	0.3	16.0	3.9	1.5
Selected Ratios				
Current ratio	0.7	2.2	1.9	1.4
Inventory turnover ratio	N/A*	N/A*	1.4	15.5
Debt-to-equity ratio	2.5	0.9	1.7	2.3

N/A = Not applicable.

This financial information pertains to the following companies:

a. Cable TV company
b. Grocery store
c. Accounting firm
d. Retail jewelry store

Required:
Match each company with its financial information.

Using Financial Information to Identify Mystery Companies

E13-4
LO13-1, 13-2, 13-3, 13-5, 13-6

The following selected financial data pertain to four unidentified companies:

| | COMPANIES | | | |
	1	2	3	4
Balance Sheet Data				
(component percentage)				
Cash	11.6	6.6	5.4	7.1
Accounts receivable	4.6	18.9	8.8	35.6
Inventory	7.0	45.8	65.7	26.0
Property and equipment	56.0	20.3	10.1	21.9
Income Statement Data				
(component percentage)				
Gross profit	56.7	36.4	14.1	15.8
Profit before taxes	2.7	1.4	1.1	0.9
Selected Ratios				
Current ratio	0.7	2.1	1.2	1.3
Inventory turnover ratio	30.0	3.5	5.6	16.7
Debt-to-equity ratio	3.3	1.8	3.8	3.1

This financial information pertains to the following companies:

a. Full-line department store
b. Wholesale fish company
c. Automobile dealer (both new and used cars)
d. Restaurant

Required:
Match each company with its financial information.

Matching Each Ratio with Its Computational Formula

E13-5
LO13-4, 13-5, 13-6, 13-7

Match each ratio or percentage with its computation.

Ratios or Percentages	Definitions
1. Profit margin	A. Net Income (before extraordinary items) ÷ Net Sales
2. Inventory turnover ratio	B. Days in Year ÷ Receivable Turnover Ratio
3. Average collection period	C. Net Income ÷ Average Stockholders' Equity
4. Dividend yield ratio	D. Net Income ÷ Average Number of Shares of Common Stock Outstanding
5. Return on equity	
6. Current ratio	E. Return on Equity − Return on Assets
7. Debt-to-equity ratio	F. Quick Assets ÷ Current Liabilities
8. Price/earnings ratio	G. Current Assets ÷ Current Liabilities
9. Financial leverage percentage	H. Cost of Goods Sold ÷ Average Inventory
10. Receivable turnover ratio	I. Net Credit Sales ÷ Average Net Receivables
11. Average days' supply of inventory	J. Days in Year ÷ Inventory Turnover Ratio
12. Earnings per share	K. Total Liabilities ÷ Stockholders' Equity
13. Return on assets	L. Dividends per Share ÷ Market Price per Share
14. Quick ratio	M. Market Price per Share ÷ Earnings per Share
15. Times interest earned	N. [Net Income + Interest Expense (net of tax)] ÷ Average Total Assets
16. Cash coverage ratio	
17. Fixed asset turnover ratio	O. Cash from Operating Activities (before interest and taxes) ÷ Interest Paid
	P. Net Sales Revenue ÷ Net Fixed Assets
	Q. (Net Income + Interest Expense + Income Tax Expense) ÷ Interest Expense

E13-6

LO13-3

Lowe's

Preparing a Schedule Using Component Percentages

Lowe's is a leading retailer in the home improvement field. Complete the component percentage analysis on the company's income statement that follows. Discuss any insights provided by this analysis.

LOWE'S COMPANIES, INC.
Consolidated Statements of Earnings
(in millions, except per share and percentage data)

	Fiscal Years Ended on					
	February 3, 2012	% Sales	January 28, 2011	% Sales	January 29, 2010	% Sales
Net sales	$50,208	100.00%	$48,815	100.00%	$47,220	100.00%
Cost of sales	32,858		31,663		30,757	
Gross margin	**17,350**		**17,152**		**16,463**	
Expenses:						
Selling, general, and administrative	12,593		12,006		11,737	
Depreciation	1,480		1,586		1,614	
Interest—net	371		332		287	
Total expenses	**14,444**		**13,924**		**13,638**	
Pre-tax earnings	2,906		3,228		2,825	
Income tax provision	1,067		1,218		1,042	
Net earnings	**$ 1,839**		**$ 2,010**		**$ 1,783**	

E13-7

LO13-5

Analyzing the Impact of Selected Transactions on the Current Ratio

Current assets totaled $120,000 and the current ratio was 1.5. Assume that the following transactions were completed: (1) purchased merchandise for $40,000 on short-term credit and (2) purchased a delivery truck for $25,000, paid $3,000 cash, and signed a two-year interest-bearing note for the balance.

Required:
Compute the cumulative current ratio after each transaction.

E13-8

LO13-5

The Bombay Company

Analyzing the Impact of Selected Transactions on the Current Ratio

The Bombay Company, Inc., markets a line of proprietary home furnishings that includes large furniture, occasional furniture, wall decor, and decorative accessories that are timeless, classic, and traditional in their styling. Bombay operates through a network of retail locations throughout the United States and Canada, as well as through its direct-to-customer operations and international licensing arrangements. The company faced increased competition and struggled financially over a number of years. It was forced to file for bankruptcy and was liquidated. In its last financial statement prior to bankruptcy, Bombay reported current assets of $161,604,000 and current liabilities of $113,909,000.

Required:
Determine the impact of the following transactions on the current ratio for Bombay:
1. Sold long-term assets that represented excess capacity.
2. Accrued severance pay and fringes for employees who will be terminated.
3. Wrote down the carrying value of certain inventory items that were deemed to be obsolete.
4. Acquired new inventory; supplier was not willing to provide normal credit terms, so an 18-month interest-bearing note was signed.

Analyzing the Impact of Selected Transactions on Receivable and Inventory Turnover

Procter & Gamble is a multinational corporation that manufactures and markets many products that are probably in your home. Last year, sales for the company were $83,680 (all amounts in millions). The annual report did not disclose the amount of credit sales, so we will assume that 90 percent of sales were on credit. The average gross profit rate was 52 percent on sales. Account balances follow:

	Beginning	Ending
Accounts receivable (net)	$6,275	$6,068
Inventory	7,379	6,721

E13-9
LO13-5

P&G

Required:
Compute the turnover for the accounts receivable and inventory, the average age of receivables, and the average days' supply of inventory.

Inferring Financial Information

Dollar General Corporation operates general merchandise stores that feature quality merchandise at low prices to meet the needs of middle-, low-, and fixed-income families. All stores are located in the United States, predominantly in small towns in 24 midwestern and southeastern states. In a recent year, the company reported average inventories of $1,456,414,000 and an inventory turnover ratio of 5.0. Average total fixed assets were $1,218,874,000, and the fixed asset turnover ratio was 7.5. Determine the gross profit for Dollar General.

E13-10
LO13-3, 13,4, 13,5

Dollar General Corporation

Computing Selected Ratios

Sales for the year for Victor Company were $1,000,000, 70 percent of which were on credit. The average gross profit rate was 40 percent on sales. Account balances follow:

	Beginning	Ending
Accounts receivable (net)	$45,000	$60,000
Inventory	70,000	25,000

E13-11
LO13-5

Required:
Compute the turnover for the accounts receivable and inventory, the average age of receivables, and the average days' supply of inventory.

Analyzing the Impact of Selected Transactions on the Current Ratio

Current assets for Mayfair Corporation totaled $410,000 and the current ratio was 2.0. Assume that the following transactions were completed: (1) sold $11,000 in merchandise on short-term credit, (2) declared but did not pay dividends of $50,000, (3) paid prepaid rent in the amount of $12,000, (4) paid previously declared dividends in the amount of $50,000, (5) collected an account receivable in the amount of $11,000, and (6) reclassified $45,000 of long-term debt as a short-term liability.

E13-12
LO13-5

Required:
Compute the cumulative current ratio after each transaction.

Computing Liquidity Ratios

Cintas designs, manufactures, and implements corporate identity uniform programs that it rents or sells to customers throughout the United States and Canada. The company's stock is traded on the NASDAQ and has provided investors with significant returns over the past few years. Selected information from the company's balance sheet follows. For 2012, the company reported sales revenue of $4,102,000 and cost of goods sold of $1,648,551.

E13-13
LO13-5

CINTAS		
Balance Sheet		
(in thousands)		
	2012	**2011**
Cash	$339,825	$438,106
Marketable securities	—	87,220
Accounts receivable	450,861	429,131
Inventories	251,205	249,658
Prepaid expense and other	24,704	23,481
Accounts payable	94,840	110,279
Accrued compensation and related liabilities	91,214	79,834
Accrued liabilities	256,642	242,691
Accrued tax liability	2,559	—
Long-term debt due within one year	225,636	1,335

Required:

Compute the current ratio, inventory turnover ratio, and accounts receivable turnover ratio (assuming that 60 percent of sales were on credit).

For more practice with exercises, go to the text website at **www.mhhe.com/libby8e.**

PROBLEMS

P13-1

LO13-5, 13-6, 13-7

Analyzing an Investment by Comparing Selected Ratios (AP13-1)

You have the opportunity to invest $10,000 in one of two companies from a single industry. The only information you have follows. The word *high* refers to the top third of the industry; *average* is the middle third; *low* is the bottom third. Which company would you select? Write a brief paper justifying your recommendation.

Ratio	Company A	Company B
Current	High	Average
Quick	Low	Average
Debt-to-equity	High	Average
Inventory turnover	Low	Average
Price/earnings	Low	Average
Dividend yield	High	Average

P13-2

LO13-5, 13-6, 13-7

Analyzing an Investment by Comparing Selected Ratios (AP13-2)

You have the opportunity to invest $10,000 in one of two companies from a single industry. The only information you have is shown here. The word *high* refers to the top third of the industry; *average* is the middle third; *low* is the bottom third. Which company would you select? Write a brief paper justifying your recommendation.

Ratio	Company A	Company B
Current	Low	Average
Quick	Average	Average
Debt-to-equity	Low	Average
Inventory turnover	High	Average
Price/earnings	High	Average
Dividend yield	Low	Average

Identifying Companies Based on the Price/Earnings Ratio

P13-3
LO13-7

The price/earnings ratio provides important information concerning the stock market's assessment of the growth potential of a business. The following are price/earnings ratios for selected companies as of the date this book was written. Match the company with its ratio and explain how you made your selections. If you are not familiar with a company, you should visit its website.

Company	Price/Earnings Ratio
1. Commerce Bank	A. 33
2. Duke Energy	B. 12
3. Ford	C. 15
4. The Home Depot	D. Not applicable (no earnings)
5. Motorola	E. 20
6. Starbucks	F. 13
7. PepsiCo	G. 99
8. Continental Airlines	H. 8

Analyzing Ratios (AP13-3)

P13-4
LO13-1, 13-2, 13-3,
13-4, 13-5, 13-6, 13-7

Sears Holdings
Corporation

Sears Holdings Corporation and JCPenney are two giants of the retail industry. Both offer full lines of moderately priced merchandise. Annual sales for Sears total $53 billion. JCPenney is smaller, with $20 billion in revenues. Compare the two companies as a potential investment based on the following ratios:

Ratio	Sears	JCPenney
P/E	15.0	10.9
Gross profit margin	28.6	39.3
Profit margin	2.8	5.7
Current ratio	1.5	1.9
Debt-to-equity	1.4	2.0
Return on equity	12.0	27.8
Return on assets	5.2	9.3
Dividend yield	0.0	1.4
Earnings per share	$9.17	$5.20

Comparing Alternative Investment Opportunities (AP13-4)

P13-5
LO13-3, 13-4,
13-5, 13-6, 13-7

www.mhhe.com/libby8e

The 2015 financial statements for the Ernst and Young companies are summarized here:

	Ernst Company	Young Company
Balance Sheet		
Cash	$ 41,000	$ 21,000
Accounts receivable (net)	38,000	31,000
Inventory	99,000	40,000
Operational assets (net)	140,000	401,000
Other assets	84,000	305,000
Total assets	$402,000	$798,000
Current liabilities	$99,000	$49,000
Long-term debt (10%)	65,000	60,000
Capital stock (par $10)	148,000	512,000
Contributed capital in excess of par	29,000	106,000
Retained earnings	61,000	71,000
Total liabilities and stockholders' equity	$402,000	$798,000

continued

	Ernst Company	Young Company
Income Statement		
Sales revenue (1/3 on credit)	$447,000	$802,000
Cost of goods sold	(241,000)	(400,000)
Expenses (including interest and income tax)	(161,000)	(311,000)
Net income	$ 45,000	$ 91,000
Selected data from the 2014 statements		
Accounts receivable (net)	$ 18,000	$ 38,000
Inventory	94,000	44,000
Long-term debt	60,000	48,000
Other data		
Per share price at end of 2015 (offering price)	$ 22	$ 15
Average income tax rate	30%	30%
Dividends declared and paid in 2015	$ 33,000	$148,000

The companies are in the same line of business and are direct competitors in a large metropolitan area. Both have been in business approximately 10 years, and each has had steady growth. The management of each has a different viewpoint in many respects. Young is more conservative, and as its president has said, "We avoid what we consider to be undue risk." Neither company is publicly held. Ernst Company has an annual audit by a CPA but Young Company does not.

Required:
1. Complete a schedule that reflects a ratio analysis of each company. Compute the ratios discussed in the chapter.
2. A client of yours has the opportunity to buy 10 percent of the shares in one or the other company at the per share prices given and has decided to invest in one of the companies. Based on the data given, prepare a comparative written evaluation of the ratio analyses (and any other available information) and give your recommended choice with the supporting explanation.

P13-6
LO13-3

Analyzing Comparative Financial Statements Using Percentages (AP13-5)

The comparative financial statements prepared at December 31, 2015, for Prince Company showed the following summarized data:

	2015	2014
Income Statement		
Sales revenue	$190,000*	$167,000
Cost of goods sold	112,000	100,000
Gross profit	78,000	67,000
Operating expenses and interest expense	56,000	53,000
Pretax income	22,000	14,000
Income tax	8,000	4,000
Net income	$ 14,000	$ 10,000
Balance Sheet		
Cash	$ 4,000	$ 7,000
Accounts receivable (net)	14,000	18,000
Inventory	40,000	34,000
Operational assets (net)	45,000	38,000
	$103,000	$ 97,000
Current liabilities (no interest)	$ 16,000	$ 17,000
Long-term liabilities (10% interest)	45,000	45,000
Common stock (par $5)	30,000	30,000
Retained earnings	12,000	5,000
	$103,000	$ 97,000

One-third was credit sales.

Required:
1. Complete the following columns for each item in the preceding comparative financial statements:

INCREASE (DECREASE) 2015 OVER 2014	
Amount	Percent

2. By what amount did working capital change?

Analyzing Comparative Financial Statements Using Percentages and Selected Ratios (AP13-6)

P13-7
LO13-3, 13-4, 13-6

Use the data given in P13-6 for Prince Company.

Required:
1. Present component percentages for 2015 only.
2. Respond to the following for 2015:
   a. What was the average gross profit?
   b. What was the average income tax rate?
   c. Compute the profit margin. Was it a good or poor indicator of performance? Explain.
   d. What percentage of total resources was invested in operational assets?
   e. Compute the debt-to-equity ratio. Does it look good or bad? Explain.
   f. What was the return on equity?
   g. What was the return on assets?
   h. Compute the financial leverage percentage. Was it positive or negative? Explain.

Analyzing Financial Statements Using Ratios

P13-8
LO13-3, 13-4, 13-5, 13-6, 13-7

Use the 2015 data in P13-6 for Prince Company. Assume a stock price of $28 per share. Compute the appropriate ratios.

Analyzing the Impact of Alternative Inventory Methods on Selected Ratios

P13-9
LO13-4, 13-5, 13-6

Company A uses the FIFO method to cost inventory, and Company B uses the LIFO method. The two companies are exactly alike except for the difference in inventory costing methods. Costs of inventory items for both companies have been rising steadily in recent years, and each company has increased its inventory each year. Each company has paid its tax liability in full for the current year (and all previous years), and each company uses the same accounting methods for both financial reporting and income tax reporting.

Required:
Identify which company will report the higher amount for each of the following ratios. If it is not possible to determine, explain why.
1. Current ratio.
2. Quick ratio.
3. Debt-to-equity ratio.
4. Return on equity.
5. Earnings per share.

Analyzing Financial Statements Using Appropriate Ratios

P13-10
LO13-3, 13-4, 13-5, 13-6, 13-7

California Pizza Kitchen

California Pizza Kitchen opened its first restaurant in Beverly Hills in 1985. Almost immediately after the first location opened, it expanded from California to more than 250 locations in more than 30 states and 11 countries. California Pizza Kitchen completed an initial public offering in August 2000 and traded on the NASDAQ National Market under the ticker symbol CPKI. On July 7, 2011, Golden Gate Capital completed the acquisition of California Pizza Kitchen and, as a result of the acquisition, the company's common stock is no longer publicly traded.

Compute the following ratios using information from the company annual report that was issued before California Pizza Kitchen was acquired.

a. Current ratio
b. Quick ratio

c. Profit margin
d. Return on equity
e. Inventory turnover
f. Debt-to-equity ratio
g. Earnings per share

CALIFORNIA PIZZA KITCHEN, INC., AND SUBSIDIARIES			
Consolidated Statements of Operations			
Years ended January 2, 2011, January 3, 2010, and December 28, 2008			
(amounts in thousands, except for per share data)			
	2010	2009	2008
Revenues:			
Restaurant sales	$630,606	$652,185	$665,616
Royalties from licensing agreement	6,122	7,739	6,580
Domestic franchise revenues	3,100	2,684	2,757
International franchise revenues	2,403	2,078	2,121
Total revenues	642,231	664,686	677,074
Costs and expenses:			
Food, beverage, and paper supplies	148,732	154,181	165,526
Labor	237,133	247,350	247,276
Direct operating and occupancy	142,420	141,973	140,367
Cost of sales	528,285	543,504	553,169
General and administrative	50,731	50,791	51,642
Depreciation and amortization	37,006	40,181	40,299
Pre-opening costs	3,269	1,843	4,478
Loss on impairment of property and equipment	18,702	22,941	13,336
Store closure costs	1,708	539	1,033
Litigation, settlement, and other costs	8,759	1,609	736
Total costs and expenses	648,460	661,408	664,693
Operating (loss)/income	(6,229)	3,278	12,381
Interest expense, net	(16)	(788)	(1,324)
(Loss)/income before income tax (benefit)/provision	(6,245)	2,490	11,057
Income tax (benefit)/provision	(5,839)	(2,091)	2,395
Net (loss)/income	$ (406)	$ 4,581	$ 8,662
Net (loss)/income per common share:			
Basic	$ (0.02)	$ 0.19	$ 0.34
Diluted	$ (0.02)	$ 0.19	$ 0.34
Weighted average shares used in calculating net (loss)/income per common snare:			
Basic	24.488	24,064	25,193
Diluted	24.488	24,143	25,211

CALIFORNIA PIZZA KITCHEN, INC., AND SUBSIDIARIES
Consolidated Balance Sheets
January 2, 2011, and January 3 2010
(in thousands, except for share data)

	2010	2009
Assets		
Current assets:		
Cash and cash equivalents	$ 21,230	$ 21,424
Other receivables	11,594	12,541
Inventories	5,827	5,557
Current deferred tax asset, net	8,225	7,076
Prepaid rent	231	4,957
Other prepaid expenses	2,518	2,031
Total current assets	49,625	53,586
Property and equipment, net	241,446	255,416
Noncurrent deferred tax asset, net	22,101	25,011
Goodwill	4,622	4,622
Other intangibles, net	4,837	4,714
Other assets	8,313	6.909
Total assets	$330,944	$350,258
Liabilities and Stockholders' Equity		
Current liabilities:		
Accounts payable	$ 17,075	$ 11,263
Accrued compensation and benefits	23,273	23,201
Accrued rent	20,424	19,287
Deferred rent credits	4,058	3,745
Other accrued liabilities	13,690	10,915
Gift card liability	14,577	20,640
Store closure reserve	54	326
Total current liabilities	93,151	89,377
Long-term debt	—	22,300
Other liabilities	9,886	7,728
Deferred rent credits, net of current portion	33,177	32,478
Income taxes payable, net of current portion	319	9,125
Commitments and contingencies		
Stockholders' equity:		
Common stock—$0.01 par value, 80,000,000 shares authorized, 24,579,797 and 24,195,800 shares issued and outstanding at January 2, 2011, and January 3, 2010, respectively	246	242
Additional paid-in capital	179,563	174,000
Retained earnings	14,602	15,008
Total stockholders' equity	194,411	189,250
Total liabilities and stockholders' equity	$330,944	$350,258

ALTERNATE **PROBLEMS**

AP13-1

LO13-4, 13-5, 13-6, 13-7

Analyzing an Investment by Comparing Selected Ratios (P13-1)

You have the opportunity to invest $10,000 in one of two companies from a single industry. The only information you have is shown here. The word *high* refers to the top third of the industry; *average* is the middle third; *low* is the bottom third. Which company would you select? Write a brief paper justifying your recommendation.

Ratio	Company A	Company B
EPS	High	Low
ROA	Low	High
Debt-to-equity	High	Average
Current	Low	Average
Price/earnings	Low	High
Dividend yield	High	Average

AP13-2

LO13-4, 13-5, 13-6, 13-7

Analyzing an Investment by Comparing Selected Ratios (P13-2)

You have the opportunity to invest $10,000 in one of two companies from a single industry. The only information you have is shown here. The word *high* refers to the top third of the industry; *average* is the middle third; *low* is the bottom third. Which company would you select? Write a brief paper justifying your recommendation.

Ratio	Company A	Company B
ROA	High	Average
Profit margin	High	Low
Financial leverage	High	Low
Current	Low	High
Price/earnings	High	Average
Debt-to-equity	High	Low

AP13-3

LO13-1, 13-2, 13-3, 13-4, 13-5, 13-6, 13-7

Coca-Cola

Analyzing Ratios (P13-4)

Coke and Pepsi are well-known international brands. Coca-Cola sells more than $13 billion worth of beverages each year while annual sales of PepsiCo products exceed $22 billion. Compare the two companies as a potential investment based on the following ratios:

Ratio	Coca-Cola	PepsiCo
P/E	65.0	26.5
Gross profit margin	69.3	58.4
Profit margin	12.2	8.8
Quick	0.4	0.7
Current	0.6	1.1
Debt-to-equity	0.7	0.4
Return on equity	27.4	29.1
Return on assets	28.0	16.6
Dividend yield	1.0	1.6
Dividend payout	65.0	41.0

AP13-4

LO13-3, 13-4, 13-5, 13-6, 13-7

Analyzing Financial Statements Using Ratios (P13-5)

Summer Corporation has just completed its comparative statements for the year ended December 31, 2015. At this point, certain analytical and interpretive procedures are to be undertaken. The completed statements (summarized) are as follows:

	2015	2014
Income Statement		
Sales revenue	$453,000*	$447,000*
Cost of goods sold	250,000	241,000
Gross profit	203,000	206,000
Operating expenses (including interest on bonds)	167,000	168,000
Pretax income	36,000	38,000
Income tax	10,800	11,400
Net income	$ 25,200	$ 26,600
Balance Sheet		
Cash	$ 6,800	$ 3,900
Accounts receivable (net)	42,000	29,000
Merchandise inventory	25,000	18,000
Prepaid expenses	200	100
Operational assets (net)	130,000	120,000
	$204,000	$171,000
Accounts payable	$ 17,000	$ 18,000
Income taxes payable	1,000	1,000
Bonds payable (10% interest rate)	70,000**	50,000
Common stock (par $10)	100,000†	100,000
Retained earnings	16,000‡	2,000
	$204,000	$171,000

Credit sales totaled 40 percent.
***$20,000 of bonds were issued on 1/2/2015. Assume the tax rate is 30%.*
†The market price of the stock at the end of 2015 was $18 per share.
‡During 2015, the company declared and paid a cash dividend of $9,000.

Required:
1. Compute appropriate ratios for 2015 and explain the meaning of each.
2. Respond to the following for 2015:
   a. Evaluate the financial leverage. Explain its meaning using the computed amount(s).
   b. Evaluate the profit margin amount and explain how a stockholder might use it.
   c. Explain to a stockholder why the current ratio and the quick ratio are different. Do you observe any liquidity problems? Explain.
   d. Assuming that credit terms are 1/10, n/30, do you perceive an unfavorable situation for the company related to credit sales? Explain.

Analyzing Financial Statements Using Ratios and Percentage Changes (P13-6)

AP13-5
LO13-3, 13-4, 13-5, 13-6, 13-7

Tabor Company has just prepared the following comparative annual financial statements for 2015:

TABOR COMPANY
Comparative Income Statement
For the Years Ended December 31, 2015, and 2014

	2015	2014
Sales revenue (one-half on credit)	$110,000	$99,000
Cost of goods sold	52,000	48,000
Gross profit	$ 58,000	$51,000
Expenses (including $4,000 interest expense each year)	40,000	37,000
Pretax income	$ 18,000	$14,000
Income tax on operations (30%)	5,400	4,200
Net income	$ 12,600	$ 9,800

	2015	2014
TABOR COMPANY		
Comparative Balance Sheet		
At December 31, 2015, and 2014		
Assets		
Cash	$ 49,500	$ 18,000
Accounts receivable (net; terms 1/10, n/30)	37,000	32,000
Inventory	25,000	38,000
Operational assets (net)	95,000	105,000
Total assets	$206,500	$193,000
Liabilities		
Accounts payable	$ 42,000	$ 35,000
Income taxes payable	1,000	500
Note payable, long-term	40,000	40,000
Stockholders' equity		
Capital stock (par $5)	90,000	90,000
Retained earnings	33,500	27,500
Total liabilities and stockholders' equity	$206,500	$193,000

Required (round percentages and ratios to one decimal place):

1. For 2015, compute the tests of (*a*) profitability, (*b*) liquidity, (*c*) solvency, and (*d*) market. Assume that the quoted price of the stock was $23 for 2015. Dividends declared and paid during 2015 were $6,750.
2. Respond to the following for 2015:
   a. Compute the percentage changes in sales, net income, cash, inventory, and debt.
   b. What appears to be the pretax interest rate on the note payable?
3. Identify at least two problems facing the company that are suggested by your responses to requirements (1) and (2).

AP13-6

LO13-3, 13-4, 13-5

Using Ratios to Analyze Several Years of Financial Data (P13-7)

The following information was contained in the annual financial statements of Cone Company, which started business January 1, 2014 (assume account balances only in Cash and Capital Stock on this date; all amounts are in thousands of dollars).

	2014	2015	2016	2017
Accounts receivable (net; terms n/30)	$11	$12	$18	$ 24
Merchandise inventory	12	14	20	30
Net sales (3/4 on credit)	44	66	80	100
Cost of goods sold	28	40	55	62
Net income (loss)	(8)	5	12	11

Required (show computations):

1. Complete the following tabulation

Items	2014	2015	2016	2017
a. Profit margin percentage				
b. Gross profit ratio				
c. Expenses as percentage of sales, excluding cost of goods sold				
d. Inventory turnover ratio				
e. Days' supply in inventory				
f. Receivable turnover ratio				
g. Average days to collect				

2. Evaluate the results of the related ratios *a, b,* and *c* to identify the favorable or unfavorable factors. Give your recommendations to improve the company's operations.
3. Evaluate the results of the last four ratios (*d, e, f,* and *g*) and identify any favorable or unfavorable factors. Give your recommendations to improve the company's operations.

CASES **AND PROJECTS**

Annual Report Cases

Analyzing Financial Statements

Refer to the financial statements of American Eagle Outfitters given in Appendix B at the end of this book. Compute the following ratios for the most recent reporting year for which you have available information: return on equity, earnings per share, profit margin, current ratio, inventory turnover, debt/equity ratio, price/earnings ratio, and dividend yield. Assume the stock price is $20.

CP13-1
LO13-4, 13-5, 13-6, 13-7

AMERICAN EAGLE
OUTFITTERS, INC.

Analyzing Financial Statements

Refer to the financial statements of Urban Outfitters given in Appendix C at the end of this book. Compute the following ratios for the most recent reporting year for which you have available information: return on equity, earnings per share, profit margin, current ratio, inventory turnover, debt/equity ratio, price/earnings ratio, and dividend yield. Assume the stock price is $35.

CP13-2
LO13-4, 13-5, 13-6, 13-7

URBAN OUTFITTERS INC.

Comparing Companies within an Industry

Refer to the financial statements of American Eagle (Appendix B) and Urban Outfitters (Appendix C) and the Industry Ratio Report (Appendix D) at the end of this book. Compute the following ratios for the most recent reporting year for which you have available information: return on equity, earnings per share, profit margin, current ratio, inventory turnover, debt/equity ratio, price/earnings ratio, and dividend yield. Assume the stock price is $35 for Urban Outfitters and $20 for American Eagle. Compare the ratios for each company to the industry average ratios.

CP13-3
LO13-4, 13-5, 13-6, 13-7
AMERICAN EAGLE
OUTFITTERS, INC.

URBAN OUTFITTERS INC.

www.mhhe.com/libby8e

Financial Reporting and Analysis Cases

Inferring Information from the ROE Model

CP13-4
LO13-1

In this chapter, we discussed the ROE profit driver (or DuPont model). Using that framework, find the missing amount in each case that follows:

Case 1: ROE is 10 percent; net income is $200,000; asset turnover ratio is 5; and net sales are $1,000,000. What is the amount of average stockholders' equity?
Case 2: Net income is $1,500,000; net sales are $8,000,000; average stockholders' equity is $12,000,000; ROE is 22 percent; and asset turnover ratio is 8. What is the amount of average total assets?
Case 3: ROE is 15 percent; net profit margin is 10 percent; asset turnover ratio is 5; and average total assets are $1,000,000. What is the amount of average stockholders' equity?
Case 4: Net income is $500,000; ROE is 15 percent; asset turnover ratio is 5; net sales are $1,000,000; and financial leverage is 2. What is the amount of average total assets?

Interpreting Financial Results Based on Corporate Strategy

CP13-5
LO13-1

In this chapter, we discussed the importance of analyzing financial results based on an understanding of the company's business strategy. Using the ROE model, we illustrated how different strategies could earn high returns for investors. Assume that two companies in the same industry adopt fundamentally different strategies. One manufactures high-quality consumer electronics. Its products employ state-of-the-art technology, and the company offers a high level of customer service both before and after the sale. The other company emphasizes low cost with good performance. Its products utilize well-established technology but are never innovative. Customers buy these products at large, self-service warehouses and are expected to install the products using information contained in printed brochures. Which of the ratios discussed in this chapter would you expect to differ for these companies as a result of their different business strategies?

Critical Thinking Case

CP13-6
LO13-5

Evaluating an Ethical Dilemma

Barton Company requested a sizable loan from First Federal Bank to acquire a large tract of land for future expansion. Barton reported current assets of $1,900,000 ($430,000 in cash) and current liabilities of $1,075,000. First Federal denied the loan request for a number of reasons, including the fact that the current ratio was below 2:1. When Barton was informed of the loan denial, the comptroller of the company immediately paid $420,000 that was owed to several trade creditors. The comptroller then asked First Federal to reconsider the loan application. Based on these abbreviated facts, would you recommend that First Federal approve the loan request? Why? Are the comptroller's actions ethical?

Financial Reporting and Analysis Team Project

CP13-7
LO13-3, 13-4, 13-5,
13-6, 13-7

Team Project: Examining an Annual Report

As a team, select an industry to analyze. *Yahoo!Finance* provides lists of industries at <u>biz.yahoo.com/p/industries.html.</u> Click on an industry for a list of companies in that industry. Alternatively, go to Google Finance at <u>www.google.com/finance</u> and search for a company you are interested in. You will be presented with a list including that company and its competitors. Each team member should acquire the annual report or 10-K for one publicly traded company in the industry, with each member selecting a different company. (the SEC EDGAR service at <u>www.sec.gov</u> or the company's investor relations website itself are good sources).

Required:
On an individual basis, each team member should write a short report providing the following information about the selected company. Discuss any patterns across the companies that you as a team observe. Then, as a team, write a short report comparing and contrasting your companies.

Compute and interpret each of the ratios discussed in this chapter. The most frequently used sections will be the financial statements. Also, you may want to review the footnotes, the summary of financial information (usually for the past five years or longer), and management's discussion and analysis.

CONTINUING **CASE**

CC13-1

≋POOLCORP

Recording and Reporting Stockholders' Equity Transactions

Pool Corporation, Inc., is the world's largest wholesale distributor of swimming pool supplies and equipment. It is a publicly traded corporation which trades on the NASDAQ exchange under the symbol POOL. It sells these products to swimming pool repair and service businesses, swimming pool builders, and retail swimming pool stores. The majority of these customers are small, family-owned businesses.

Required:
1. Using the SEC EDGAR service at <u>www.sec.gov,</u> download the current annual report for pool.
2. Compute the following ratios:
    a. Return on assets
    b. Profit margin
    c. Current ratio
    d. Inventory ratio
    e. Cash coverage ratio
    f. Debt-to-equity ratio
    g. Price/earnings ratio (*Hint:* You will need to go to another source to get the current market price per share)

TABLE A.1

Present Value of $1

Periods	2%	3%	3.75%	4%	4.25%	5%	6%	7%	8%
1	0.9804	0.9709	0.9639	0.9615	0.9592	0.9524	0.9434	0.9346	0.9259
2	0.9612	0.9426	0.9290	0.9246	0.9201	0.9070	0.8900	0.8734	0.8573
3	0.9423	0.9151	0.8954	0.8890	0.8826	0.8638	0.8396	0.8163	0.7938
4	0.9238	0.8885	0.8631	0.8548	0.8466	0.8227	0.7921	0.7629	0.7350
5	0.9057	0.8626	0.8319	0.8219	0.8121	0.7835	0.7473	0.7130	0.6806
6	0.8880	0.8375	0.8018	0.7903	0.7790	0.7462	0.7050	0.6663	0.6302
7	0.8706	0.8131	0.7728	0.7599	0.7473	0.7107	0.6651	0.6227	0.5835
8	0.8535	0.7894	0.7449	0.7307	0.7168	0.6768	0.6274	0.5820	0.5403
9	0.8368	0.7664	0.7180	0.7026	0.6876	0.6446	0.5919	0.5439	0.5002
10	0.8203	0.7441	0.6920	0.6756	0.6595	0.6139	0.5584	0.5083	0.4632
20	0.6730	0.5537	0.4789	0.4564	0.4350	0.3769	0.3118	0.2584	0.2145

Periods	9%	10%	11%	12%	13%	14%	15%	20%	25%
1	0.9174	0.9091	0.9009	0.8929	0.8850	0.8772	0.8696	0.8333	0.8000
2	0.8417	0.8264	0.8116	0.7972	0.7831	0.7695	0.7561	0.6944	0.6400
3	0.7722	0.7513	0.7312	0.7118	0.6931	0.6750	0.6575	0.5787	0.5120
4	0.7084	0.6830	0.6587	0.6355	0.6133	0.5921	0.5718	0.4823	0.4096
5	0.6499	0.6209	0.5935	0.5674	0.5428	0.5194	0.4972	0.4019	0.3277
6	0.5963	0.5645	0.5346	0.5066	0.4803	0.4556	0.4323	0.3349	0.2621
7	0.5470	0.5132	0.4817	0.4523	0.4251	0.3996	0.3759	0.2791	0.2097
8	0.5019	0.4665	0.4339	0.4039	0.3762	0.3506	0.3269	0.2326	0.1678
9	0.4604	0.4241	0.3909	0.3606	0.3329	0.3075	0.2843	0.1938	0.1342
10	0.4224	0.3855	0.3522	0.3220	0.2946	0.2697	0.2472	0.1615	0.1074
20	0.1784	0.1486	0.1240	0.1037	0.0868	0.0728	0.0611	0.0261	0.0115

TABLE A.2

Present Value of Annuity of $1

Periods*	2%	3%	3.75%	4%	4.25%	5%	6%	7%	8%
1	0.9804	0.9709	0.9639	0.9615	0.9592	0.9524	0.9434	0.9346	0.9259
2	1.9416	1.9135	1.8929	1.8861	1.8794	1.8594	1.8334	1.8080	1.7833
3	2.8839	2.8286	2.7883	2.7751	2.7620	2.7232	2.6730	2.6243	2.5771
4	3.8077	3.7171	3.6514	3.6299	3.6086	3.5460	3.4651	3.3872	3.3121
5	4.7135	4.5797	4.4833	4.4518	4.4207	4.3295	4.2124	4.1002	3.9927
6	5.6014	5.4172	5.2851	5.2421	5.1997	5.0757	4.9173	4.7665	4.6229
7	6.4720	6.2303	6.0579	6.0021	5.9470	5.7864	5.5824	5.3893	5.2064
8	7.3255	7.0197	6.8028	6.7327	6.6638	6.4632	6.2098	5.9713	5.7466
9	8.1622	7.7861	7.5208	7.4353	7.3513	7.1078	6.8017	6.5152	6.2469
10	8.9826	8.5302	8.2128	8.1109	8.0109	7.7217	7.3601	7.0236	6.7101
20	16.3514	14.8775	13.8962	13.5903	13.2944	12.4622	11.4699	10.5940	9.8181

*There is one payment each period.

TABLE A.2   *(continued)*

Present Value of Annuity of $1

Periods*	9%	10%	11%	12%	13%	14%	15%	20%	25%
1	0.9174	0.9091	0.9009	0.8929	0.8550	0.8772	0.8696	0.8333	0.8000
2	1.7591	1.7355	1.7125	1.6901	1.6681	1.6467	1.6257	1.5278	1.4400
3	2.5313	2.4869	2.4437	2.4018	2.3612	2.3216	2.2832	2.1065	1.9520
4	3.2397	3.1699	3.1024	3.0373	2.9745	2.9137	2.8550	2.5887	2.3616
5	3.8897	3.7908	3.6959	3.6048	3.5172	3.4331	3.3522	2.9906	2.6893
6	4.4859	4.3553	4.2305	4.1114	3.9975	3.8887	3.7845	3.3255	2.9514
7	5.0330	4.8684	4.7122	4.5638	4.4226	4.2883	4.1604	3.6046	3.1611
8	5.5348	5.3349	5.1461	4.9676	4.7988	4.6389	4.4873	3.8372	3.3289
9	5.9952	5.7590	5.5370	5.3282	5.1317	4.9464	4.7716	4.0310	3.4631
10	6.4177	6.1446	5.8892	5.6502	5.4262	5.2161	5.0188	4.1925	3.5705
20	9.1285	8.5136	7.9633	7.4694	7.0248	6.6231	6.2593	4.8696	3.9539

*There is one payment each period.

TABLE A.3

Future Value of $1

Periods	2%	3%	3.75%	4%	4.25%	5%	6%	7%	8%
0	1.	1.	1.	1.	1.	1.	1.	1.	1.
1	1.02	1.03	1.0375	1.04	1.0425	1.05	1.06	1.07	1.08
2	1.0404	1.0609	1.0764	1.0816	1.0868	1.1025	1.1236	1.1449	1.1664
3	1.0612	1.0927	1.1168	1.1249	1.1330	1.1576	1.1910	1.2250	1.2597
4	1.0824	1.1255	1.1587	1.1699	1.1811	1.2155	1.2625	1.3108	1.3605
5	1.1041	1.1593	1.2021	1.2167	1.2313	1.2763	1.3382	1.4026	1.4693
6	1.1262	1.1941	1.2472	1.2653	1.2837	1.3401	1.4185	1.5007	1.5869
7	1.1487	1.2299	1.2939	1.3159	1.3382	1.4071	1.5036	1.6058	1.7138
8	1.1717	1.2668	1.3425	1.3686	1.3951	1.4775	1.5938	1.7182	1.8509
9	1.1951	1.3048	1.3928	1.4233	1.4544	1.5513	1.6895	1.8385	1.9990
10	1.2190	1.3439	1.4450	1.4802	1.5162	1.6289	1.7908	1.9672	2.1589
20	1.4859	1.8061	2.0882	2.1911	2.2989	2.6533	3.2071	3.8697	4.6610

Periods	9%	10%	11%	12%	13%	14%	15%	20%	25%
0	1.	1.	1.	1.	1.	1.	1.	1.	1.
1	1.09	1.10	1.11	1.12	1.13	1.14	1.15	1.20	1.25
2	1.1881	1.2100	1.2321	1.2544	1.2769	1.2996	1.3225	1.4400	1.5625
3	1.2950	1.3310	1.3676	1.4049	1.4429	1.4815	1.5209	1.7280	1.9531
4	1.4116	1.4641	1.5181	1.5735	1.6305	1.6890	1.7490	2.0736	2.4414
5	1.5386	1.6105	1.6851	1.7623	1.8424	1.9254	2.0114	2.4883	3.0518
6	1.6771	1.7716	1.8704	1.9738	2.0820	2.1950	2.3131	2.9860	3.8147
7	1.8280	1.9487	2.0762	2.2107	2.3526	2.5023	2.6600	3.5832	4.7684
8	1.9926	2.1436	2.3045	2.4760	2.6584	2.8526	3.0590	4.2998	5.9605
9	2.1719	2.3579	2.5580	2.7731	3.0040	3.2519	3.5179	5.1598	7.4506
10	2.3674	2.5937	2.8394	3.1058	3.3946	3.7072	4.0456	6.1917	9.3132
20	5.6044	6.7275	8.0623	9.6463	11.5231	13.7435	16.3665	38.3376	86.7362

TABLE A.4

Future Value of Annuity of $1

Periods*	2%	3%	3.75%	4%	4.25%	5%	6%	7%	8%
1	1.	1.	1.	1.	1.	1.	1.	1.	1.
2	2.02	2.03	2.0375	2.04	2.0425	2.05	2.06	2.07	2.08
3	3.0604	3.0909	3.1139	3.1216	3.1293	3.1525	3.1836	3.2149	3.2464
4	4.1216	4.1836	4.2307	4.2465	4.2623	4.3101	4.3746	4.4399	4.5061
5	5.2040	5.3091	5.3893	5.4163	5.4434	5.5256	5.6371	5.7507	5.8666
6	6.3081	6.4684	6.5914	6.6330	6.6748	6.8019	6.9753	7.1533	7.3359
7	7.4343	7.6625	7.8386	7.8983	7.9585	8.1420	8.3938	8.6540	8.9228
8	8.5830	8.8923	9.1326	9.2142	9.2967	9.5491	9.8975	10.2598	10.6366
9	9.7546	10.1591	10.4750	10.5828	10.6918	11.0266	11.4913	11.9780	12.4876
10	10.9497	11.4639	11.8678	12.0061	12.1462	12.5779	13.1808	13.8164	14.4866
20	24.2974	26.8704	29.0174	29.7781	30.5625	33.0660	36.7856	40.9955	45.7620

Periods*	9%	10%	11%	12%	13%	14%	15%	20%	25%
1	1.	1.	1.	1.	1.	1.	1.	1.	1.
2	2.09	2.10	2.11	2.12	2.13	2.14	2.15	2.20	2.25
3	3.2781	3.3100	3.3421	3.3744	3.4069	3.4396	3.4725	3.6400	3.8125
4	4.5731	4.6410	4.7097	4.7793	4.8498	4.9211	4.9934	5.3680	5.7656
5	5.9847	6.1051	6.2278	6.3528	6.4803	6.6101	6.7424	7.4416	8.2070
6	7.5233	7.7156	7.9129	8.1152	8.3227	8.5355	8.7537	9.9299	11.2588
7	9.2004	9.4872	9.7833	10.0890	10.4047	10.7305	11.0668	12.9159	15.0735
8	11.0285	11.4359	11.8594	12.2997	12.7573	13.2328	13.7268	16.4991	19.8419
9	13.0210	13.5975	14.1640	14.7757	15.4157	16.0853	16.7858	20.7989	25.8023
10	15.1929	15.9374	16.7220	17.5487	18.4197	19.3373	20.3037	25.9587	33.2529
20	51.1601	57.2750	64.2028	72.0524	80.9468	91.0249	102.4436	186.6880	342.9447

*There is one payment each period.

UNITED STATES SECURITIES AND EXCHANGE COMMISSION
Washington, D.C. 20549

Form 10-K

☑ **ANNUAL REPORT PURSUANT TO SECTION 13 OR 15(d)
OF THE SECURITIES EXCHANGE ACT OF 1934**

For the Fiscal Year Ended January 28, 2012

OR

☐ **TRANSITION REPORT PURSUANT TO SECTION 13 OR 15(d)
OF THE SECURITIES EXCHANGE ACT OF 1934**

Commission File Number: 1-33338

American Eagle Outfitters, Inc.

(Exact name of registrant as specified in its charter)

Delaware	**No. 13-2721761**
(State or other jurisdiction of incorporation or organization)	*(I.R.S. Employer Identification No.)*
77 Hot Metal Street, Pittsburgh, PA	**15203-2329**
(Address of principal executive offices)	*(Zip Code)*

Registrant's telephone number, including area code:
(412) 432-3300

Securities registered pursuant to Section 12(b) of the Act:

Common Shares, $0.01 par value	New York Stock Exchange
(Title of class)	*(Name of each exchange on which registered)*

Securities registered pursuant to Section 12(g) of the Act:
None

Indicate by check mark if the registrant is a well-known seasoned issuer, as defined in Rule 405 of the Securities Act. YES ☑ NO ☐

Indicate by check mark if the registrant is not required to file reports pursuant to Section 13 or Sections 15(d) of the Act. YES ☐ NO ☑

Indicate by check mark whether the registrant (1) has filed all reports required to be filed by Section 13 or 15(d) of the Securities Exchange Act of 1934 during the preceding 12 months (or for such shorter period that the registrant was required to file such reports), and (2) has been subject to the filing requirements for at the past 90 days. YES ☑ NO ☐

Indicate by check mark whether the registrant has submitted electronically and posted on its corporate Web site, if any, every Interactive Data File required to be submitted and posted pursuant to Rule 405 of Regulation S-T (§232.405 of this chapter) during the preceding 12 months (or for such shorter period that the registrant was required to submit and post such files). YES ☑ NO ☐

Indicate by check mark if disclosure of delinquent filers pursuant to Item 405 of Regulation S-K (§229.405 of this chapter) is not contained herein, and will not be contained, to the best of registrant's knowledge, in definitive proxy or information statements incorporated by reference in Part III of this Form 10-K or any amendment to this Form 10-K. ☐

Indicate by check mark whether the registrant is a large accelerated filer, an accelerated filer, a non-accelerated filer, or a smaller reporting company. See the definitions of "large accelerated filer," "accelerated filer" and "smaller reporting company" in Rule 12b-2 of the Exchange Act. (Check one):

Large accelerated filer ☑ Accelerated filer ☐ Non-accelerated filer ☐ Smaller reporting company ☐
(Do not check if a smaller reporting company)

Indicate by check mark whether the registrant is a shell company (as defined in Rule 12b-2 of the Act). YES ☐ NO ☑

The aggregate market value of voting and non-voting common equity held by non-affiliates of the registrant as of July 30, 2011 was $2,334,798,008.

Indicate the number of shares outstanding of each of the registrant's classes of common stock, as of the latest practicable date: 194,539,858 Common Shares were outstanding at March 12, 2012.

DOCUMENTS INCORPORATED BY REFERENCE

Part III — Proxy Statement for 2012 Annual Meeting of Stockholders, in part, as indicated.

ITEM 1. *BUSINESS.*

General

American Eagle Outfitters, Inc., a Delaware corporation (the "Company"), operates under the American Eagle®, aerie® by American Eagle®, and 77kids by american eagle® brands. The Company operated the MARTIN+OSA® brand ("M+O") until its closure during Fiscal 2010.

Founded in 1977, American Eagle Outfitters® is a leading specialty retailer that operates more than 1,000 retail stores in the U.S. and Canada, and online at ae.com®. Through our family of brands, American Eagle Outfitters, Inc., offers high quality, on-trend clothing, accessories and personal care products at affordable prices. Our online business, AEO Direct, ships to 77 countries worldwide.

As used in this report, all references to "we," "our" and the "Company" refer to American Eagle Outfitters, Inc. ("AEO, Inc.") and its wholly-owned subsidiaries. "American Eagle Outfitters," "American Eagle," "AE" and the "AE Brand" refer to our U.S. and Canadian American Eagle Outfitters® stores. "AEO Direct" refers to our e-commerce operations, ae.com®, aerie.com and 77kids.com. "MARTIN+OSA" or "M+O" refers to the MARTIN+OSA stores and e-commerce operation which we operated until its closure during Fiscal 2010.

Our financial year is a 52/53 week year that ends on the Saturday nearest to January 31. As used herein, "Fiscal 2012" refers to the 53 week period ending February 2, 2013. "Fiscal 2011," "Fiscal 2010," "Fiscal 2009," "Fiscal 2008," and "Fiscal 2007" refer to the 52 week periods ended January 28, 2012, January 29, 2011, January 30, 2010, January 31, 2009, and February 2, 2008, respectively. "Fiscal 2006" refers to the 53 week period ended February 3, 2007.

On March 5, 2010, our Board of Directors (the "Board") approved management's recommendation to proceed with the closure of the M+O brand. We completed the closure of M+O stores and its e-commerce operation during the second quarter of Fiscal 2010. The Consolidated Financial Statements reflect the presentation of M+O as a discontinued operation. Refer to Note 15 to the Consolidated Financial Statements for additional information regarding the discontinued operations of M+O.

As of January 28, 2012, we operated 911 American Eagle Outfitters stores, 158 aerie stand-alone stores and 21 77kids stores. We also had 21 franchised stores operated by our franchise partners in 10 countries.

Information concerning our segments and certain geographic information is contained in Note 2 of the Consolidated Financial Statements included in this Form 10-K and is incorporated herein by reference. Additionally, a five-year summary of certain financial and operating information can be found in Part II, Item 6, Selected Consolidated Financial Data, of this Form 10-K. See also Part II, Item 8, Financial Statements and Supplementary Data.

Growth Strategy

Our primary growth strategies are focused on the following key areas of opportunity:

AE Brand

The American Eagle Outfitters® brand targets 15- to 25-year-old men and women. Denim is the cornerstone of the American Eagle® product assortment, which is complemented by other key categories including sweaters, graphic t-shirts, fleece, outerwear and accessories. American Eagle® is honest, real, individual and fun. American Eagle® is priced to be worn by everyone, everyday, delivering value through quality and style.

Gaining market share in key categories, such as knit tops and fleece, is a primary focus within the AE Brand. In addition, we will build upon our leading position in denim. Delivering value, variety and versatility to our customers remains a top priority. We will offer value at all levels of the assortment, punctuated with promotions. We are reducing production lead-times, which enables us to react more quickly to emerging trends. Finally, we continue to innovate our store experience to be more impactful from front to back.

aerie by American Eagle

In the fall of 2006, the Company launched aerie® by American Eagle® ("aerie"), a collection of Dormwear®, intimates and personal care products for the AE® girl. The collection is available in 158 stand-alone aerie stores throughout the United States and Canada, online at aerie.com and at select American Eagle® stores. aerie, with intimates at the core, is beautiful, feminine, soft, sensuous, yet comfortable.

77kids by american eagle

Introduced in October of 2008 as an online-only brand, 77kids by american eagle® ("77kids") offers on-trend, high-quality clothing and accessories for kids ages two to 14 and babies under the brand name little77 ™. 77kids is available in 21 stores throughout the United States. The brand draws from the strong heritage of American Eagle Outfitters®, with a point-of-view that is thoughtful, playful and real. Like American Eagle® clothing, 77kids focuses on great fit, value and style. All 77kids® clothing is backed by the brand's 77wash™ and 77soft™ guarantees to maintain size, shape and quality and to be extremely soft and comfortable through dozens of washes.

AEO Direct

We sell merchandise via our e-commerce operations, ae.com®, aerie.com and 77kids.com, which are extensions of the lifestyle that we convey in our stores. We currently ship to 77 countries. In addition to purchasing items online, customers can experience AEO Direct in-store through Store-to-Door. Store-to-Door enables store associates to sell any item available online to an in-store customer in a single transaction. Customers are taking advantage of Store-to-Door by purchasing extended sizes that are not available in-store, as well as finding a certain size or color that happens to be out-of-stock at the time of their visit. The ordered items are shipped to the customer's home free of charge. We accept PayPal® and Bill Me Later® as a means of payment from our ae.com®, aerie.com and 77kids.com customers. We are continuing to focus on the growth of AEO Direct through various initiatives, including improved site efficiency and faster check-out, expansion of sizes and styles, on-line specialty shops and targeted marketing strategies.

Real Estate

We continue to remain focused on the real-estate strategies that we have in place to grow our business and strengthen our financial performance utilizing our most productive formats.

We continue the expansion of our brands throughout the United States. At the end of Fiscal 2011, we operated in all 50 states, Puerto Rico and Canada. During Fiscal 2011, we opened 33 new stores, consisting of 11 AE stores, 10 aerie stores and 12 77kids stores. These store openings, partially offset by 29 store closings, increased our total store base to 1,090 stores.

Our stores average approximately 5,870 gross square feet and approximately 4,690 on a selling square foot basis. Our gross square footage increased by approximately 1% during Fiscal 2011, with approximately 54% attributable to the incremental square footage from store remodels and the remaining 46% attributable to new store openings.

During Fiscal 2011, we remodeled and refurbished a total of 106 AE stores. Five stores were remodeled with an expansion to their existing locations, 10 stores were relocated to a larger space within the mall, two stores were remodeled within their existing locations and 89 stores were refurbished as discussed below.

Remodeling of our AE stores into our current store format is important to enhance our customer's shopping experience. In order to maintain a balanced presentation and to accommodate additional product categories, we selectively enlarge our stores during the remodeling process to an average of 6,400 gross square feet, either within their existing location or by upgrading the store location within the mall. We believe the larger format can better accommodate our expansion of merchandise categories. We select stores for expansion or relocation based on market demographics and store volume forecasts.

We maintain a cost effective store refurbishment program targeted towards our lower volume stores, typically located in smaller markets. Stores selected as part of this program maintain their current location and size but are updated to include certain aspects of our current store format, including paint and new fixtures.

In Fiscal 2012, we plan to open approximately 14 AE and one 77kids store. We also plan to remodel and refurbish approximately 100 existing AE stores and close approximately 20 to 30 stores. Our square footage growth is expected to decrease slightly in Fiscal 2012. We believe that there are attractive retail locations where we can continue to open American Eagle stores and our other brands in enclosed regional malls, urban areas and lifestyle centers.

The table below shows certain information relating to our historical store growth from continuing operations.

	Fiscal 2011	Fiscal 2010	Fiscal 2009	Fiscal 2008	Fiscal 2007
Consolidated stores at beginning of period	1,086	1,075	1,070	968	906
Consolidated stores opened during the period	33	34	29	112	66
Consolidated stores closed during the period	(29)	(23)	(24)	(10)	(4)
Total consolidated stores at end of period	**1,090**	**1,086**	**1,075**	**1,070**	**968**

	Fiscal 2011	Fiscal 2010	Fiscal 2009	Fiscal 2008	Fiscal 2007
AE Brand stores at beginning of period	929	938	954	929	903
AE Brand stores opened during the period	11	14	8	35	30
AE Brand stores closed during the period	(29)	(23)	(24)	(10)	(4)
Total AE Brand stores at end of period	**911**	**929**	**938**	**954**	**929**

	Fiscal 2011	Fiscal 2010	Fiscal 2009	Fiscal 2008	Fiscal 2007
aerie stores at beginning of period	148	137	116	39	3
aerie stores opened during the period	10	11	21	77	36
aerie stores closed during the period	—	—	—	—	—
Total aerie stores at end of period	**158**	**148**	**137**	**116**	**39**

	Fiscal 2011	Fiscal 2010	Fiscal 2009	Fiscal 2008	Fiscal 2007
77kids stores at beginning of period	9	—	—	—	—
77kids stores opened during the period	12	9	—	—	—
77kids stores closed during the period	—	—	—	—	—
Total 77kids stores at end of period	**21**	**9**	**—**	**—**	**—**

Consolidated Store Locations

As of January 28, 2012, we operated 1,090 stores in the United States and Canada under the American Eagle Outfitters, aerie and 77kids brands as shown below:

United States, including the Commonwealth of Puerto Rico — 994 stores

Alabama	17	Indiana	22	Nebraska	7	Rhode Island	4
Alaska	5	Iowa	12	Nevada	4	South Carolina	17
Arizona	16	Kansas	9	New Hampshire	9	South Dakota	3
Arkansas	8	Kentucky	14	New Jersey	28	Tennessee	25
California	71	Louisiana	14	New Mexico	3	Texas	73
Colorado	11	Maine	5	New York	70	Utah	11
Connecticut	20	Maryland	19	North Carolina	31	Vermont	3
Delaware	5	Massachusetts	35	North Dakota	4	Virginia	28
Florida	52	Michigan	34	Ohio	37	Washington	19
Georgia	32	Minnesota	22	Oklahoma	12	West Virginia	9
Hawaii	4	Mississippi	8	Oregon	12	Wisconsin	19
Idaho	4	Missouri	19	Pennsylvania	65	Wyoming	2
Illinois	34	Montana	2	Puerto Rico	5		

Canada — 96 stores

Alberta	13	New Brunswick	4	Ontario	49
British Columbia	13	Newfoundland	1	Quebec	9
Manitoba	2	Nova Scotia	3	Saskatchewan	2

International Expansion

We have entered into franchise agreements with multiple partners to expand our brands internationally. Through these franchise agreements, we plan to open and operate a series of American Eagle stores in the Middle East, Northern Africa, Eastern Europe, Hong Kong, China, Israel and Japan. As of January 28, 2012, we had 21 franchised stores operated by our franchise partners in 10 countries. These franchise agreements do not involve a capital investment from AEO and require minimal operational involvement. We continue to evaluate additional opportunities to expand internationally. International franchise stores are not included in the consolidated store data or the total gross square feet calculation.

Purchasing

We purchase merchandise from suppliers who either manufacture their own merchandise, supply merchandise manufactured by others or both. During Fiscal 2011, we purchased a majority of our merchandise from non-North American suppliers.

All of our merchandise suppliers receive a vendor compliance manual that describes our quality standards and shipping instructions. We maintain a quality control department at our distribution centers to inspect incoming merchandise shipments for uniformity of sizes and colors and for overall quality of manufacturing. Periodic inspections are also made by our employees and agents at manufacturing facilities to identify quality problems prior to shipment of merchandise.

Corporate Responsibility

The Company is firmly committed to the principle that the people who make our clothes should be treated with dignity and respect. We seek to work with apparel suppliers throughout the world who share our commitment to providing safe and healthy workplaces. At a minimum, we require our suppliers to maintain a workplace environment that complies with local legal requirements and meets universally-accepted human rights standards.

Our Vendor Code of Conduct (the "Code"), which is based on universally-accepted human rights principles, sets forth our expectations for suppliers. The Code must be posted in every factory that manufactures our clothes in the local language of the workers. All suppliers must agree to abide by the terms of our Code before we will place production with them.

We maintain an extensive factory inspection program, through our Hong Kong compliance office, to monitor compliance with our Code. The Hong Kong team validates the inspection reporting of our third-party vendor compliance auditors and works with new and existing factories on remediation of issues. New garment factories must pass an initial inspection in order to do business with us. Once new factories are approved, we then strive to re-inspect them at least once a year. We review the outcome of these inspections with factory management with the goal of helping them to continuously improve their performance. Although our primary goal is to remediate issues and build long term relationships with our vendors, in cases where a factory is unable or unwilling to meet our standards, we will take steps up to and including the severance of our business relationship.

In September 2011, we published our first publicly available Corporate Responsibility Report, AE Better World, on our website at www.ae.com. This Report focuses on four key areas of our company: Supply Chain, Environment, Associates and Communities. Where possible, the report references relevant indicators from the Global Reporting Initiative ("GRI") G3 Guidelines and GRI Apparel & Footwear Sector Supplement.

Security Compliance

During recent years, there has been an increasing focus within the international trade community on concerns related to global terrorist activity. Various security issues and other terrorist threats have brought increased demands from the Bureau of Customs and Border Protection ("CBP") and other agencies within the Department of Homeland Security that importers take responsible action to secure their supply chains. In response, we became a certified member of the Customs - Trade Partnership Against Terrorism program ("C-TPAT") during 2004. C-TPAT is a voluntary program offered by CBP in which an importer agrees to work with CBP to strengthen overall supply chain security. Our internal security procedures were reviewed by CBP during February 2005 and a validation of processes with respect to our external partners was completed in June 2005 and then re-evaluated in June 2008. We received formal written validations of our security procedures from CBP during Fiscal 2006 and Fiscal 2008, each indicating the highest level of benefits afforded to C-TPAT members.

Historically, we took significant steps to expand the scope of our security procedures, including, but not limited to: a significant increase in the number of factory audits performed; a revision of the factory audit format to include a review of all critical security issues as defined by CBP; and a requirement that all of our international logistics partners, including forwarders, consolidators, shippers and brokers be certified members of C-TPAT. In Fiscal 2007, we further increased the scope of our inspection program to strive to include pre-inspections of all potential production facilities. In Fiscal 2009, we again expanded the program to require all suppliers that have passed pre-inspections and reached a satisfactory level of security compliance through annual factory re-audits to provide us with security self-assessments on at least an annual basis. Additionally, in Fiscal 2009, we began evaluating additional oversight options for high-risk security countries and among other things, implemented full third-party audits on an annual basis.

Trade Compliance

We act as the importer of record for substantially all of the merchandise we purchase overseas from foreign suppliers. Accordingly, we have an affirmative obligation to comply with the rules and regulations established for importers by the CBP regarding issues such as merchandise classification, valuation and country of origin. We have developed and implemented a comprehensive series of trade compliance procedures to assure that we adhere to all CBP requirements. In its most recent review and audit of our import operations and procedures, CBP found no material, unacceptable risks of non-compliance.

Product Safety

We are strongly committed to the safety and well-being of our customers. We require our products to meet U.S. state and federal and Canadian national laws and regulations. In certain cases, we also voluntarily adopt industry standards and best practices that may be higher than legally required or where no clear laws exist.

To ensure compliance with our product safety standards, we maintain an extensive set of testing protocols for each category of products. All of the products we sell are tested by an independent testing laboratory in accordance with applicable regulatory requirements. In rare cases where a safety issue has been discovered in a product that has reached our store shelves, we respond with a comprehensive recall process for all of our brands. In accordance with Consumer Product Safety Commission requirements, we publicly maintain a list of product recalls conducted on our e-commerce website.

Merchandise Inventory, Replenishment and Distribution

Merchandise is generally shipped directly from our vendors and routed through third-party transloaders at key ports of entry to our three U.S. distribution centers, one in Warrendale, Pennsylvania, and the other two in Ottawa, Kansas, or to our Canadian distribution center in Mississauga, Ontario. Additionally, certain product is eligible to be shipped directly to stores, by-passing our distribution centers.

Upon receipt at one of our distribution centers, merchandise is processed and prepared for shipment to the stores or forwarded to a warehouse holding area to be used as store replenishment goods. The allocation of merchandise among stores varies based upon a number of factors, including geographic location, customer demographics and store size. Merchandise is shipped to our stores two to five times per week depending upon the season and store requirements.

The expansion of our Kansas distribution center in Fiscal 2007 enabled us to bring fulfillment services for AEO Direct in-house. The second phase of this expansion was completed in Fiscal 2008 to enhance operating efficiency and support our future growth.

Customer Credit and Returns

We offer a co-branded credit card (the "AEO Visa Card") and a private label credit card (the "AEO Credit Card") under the AE, aerie and 77kids brands. These credit cards are issued by a third-party bank (the "Bank"), and we have no liability to the Bank for bad debt expense, provided that purchases are made in accordance with the Bank's procedures. Once a customer is approved to receive the AEO Visa Card or the AEO Credit Card and the card is activated, the customer is eligible to participate in our credit card rewards program. Customers who make purchases at AE, aerie and 77kids earn discounts in the form of savings certificates when certain purchase levels are reached. Also, AEO Visa Card customers who make purchases at other retailers where the card is accepted earn additional discounts. Savings certificates are valid for 90 days from issuance. AEO Credit Card holders will also receive special promotional offers and advance notice of all American Eagle in-store sales events. The AEO Credit Card is accepted at all of our U.S. stores and at ae.com, aerie.com and 77kids.com. The AEO Visa Card is accepted in all of our stores and AEO Direct sites as well as merchants worldwide that accept Visa®.

Customers in our U.S. and Canada stores may also pay for their purchases with American Express®, Discover®, MasterCard®, Visa®, bank debit cards, cash or check. Our AEO Direct customers may pay for their purchases using American Express®, Discover®, MasterCard® and Visa®. They may also pay for their purchases using PayPal® and Bill Me Later®.

Customers may also use gift cards to pay for their purchases. AE, aerie and 77kids gift cards can be purchased in our American Eagle, aerie and 77kids stores, respectively, and can be used both in-store and online. In addition, AE, aerie and 77kids gift cards are available for purchase through ae.com, aerie.com or 77kids.com. When the recipient uses the gift card, the value of the purchase is electronically deducted from the card and any remaining value can be used for future purchases. Our gift cards do not expire and we do not charge a service fee on inactive gift cards.

We offer our retail customers a hassle-free return policy. We believe that our competitors offer similar credit card and customer service policies.

Competition

The retail apparel industry, including retail stores and e-commerce, is highly competitive. We compete with various individual and chain specialty stores, as well as the casual apparel and footwear departments of department stores and discount retailers, primarily on the basis of quality, fashion, service, selection and price.

Trademarks and Service Marks

We have registered AMERICAN EAGLE OUTFITTERS®, AMERICAN EAGLE®, AE® and AEO® with the United States Patent and Trademark Office. We have also registered or have applied to register these trademarks with the registries of the foreign countries in which our stores and/or manufacturers are located and/or where our product is shipped.

We have registered AMERICAN EAGLE OUTFITTERS® and AMERICAN EAGLE® with the Canadian Intellectual Property Office. In addition, we are exclusively licensed in Canada to use AE™ and AEO® in connection with the sale of a wide range of clothing products.

In the United States and around the world, we have also registered, or have applied to register, a number of other marks used in our business, including aerie®, 77kids by american eagle® and little77 by american eagle®.

These trademarks are renewable indefinitely and their registrations are properly maintained in accordance with the laws of the country in which they are registered. We believe that the recognition associated with these trademarks makes them extremely valuable and, therefore, we intend to use and renew our trademarks in accordance with our business plans.

Employees

As of January 28, 2012, we had approximately 39,600 employees in the United States and Canada, of whom approximately 33,100 were part-time and seasonal hourly employees. We consider our relationship with our employees to be good.

Seasonality

Historically, our operations have been seasonal, with a large portion of net sales and operating income occurring in the third and fourth fiscal quarters, reflecting increased demand during the back-to-school and year-end holiday selling seasons, respectively. As a result of this seasonality, any factors negatively affecting us during the third and fourth fiscal quarters of any year, including adverse weather or unfavorable economic conditions, could have a material adverse effect on our financial condition and results of operations for the entire year. Our quarterly results of operations also may fluctuate based upon such factors as the timing of certain holiday seasons, the number and timing of new store openings, the acceptability of seasonal merchandise offerings, the timing and level of markdowns, store closings and remodels, competitive factors, weather and general economic conditions.

Available Information

Our Annual Reports on Form 10-K, Quarterly Reports on Form 10-Q, Current Reports on Form 8-K and amendments to those reports are available, free of charge, under the "About AEO, Inc." section of our website at www.ae.com. These reports are available as soon as reasonably practicable after such material is electronically filed with the Securities and Exchange Commission (the "SEC").

Our corporate governance materials, including our corporate governance guidelines, the charters of our audit, compensation, and nominating and corporate governance committees, and our code of ethics may also be found under the "About AEO, Inc." section of our website at www.ae.com. Any amendments or waivers to our code of ethics will also be available on our website. A copy of the corporate governance materials is also available upon written request.

Additionally, our investor presentations are available under the "About AEO, Inc." section of our website at www.ae.com. These presentations are available as soon as reasonably practicable after they are presented at investor conferences.

Certifications

As required by the New York Stock Exchange ("NYSE") Corporate Governance Standards Section 303A.12(a), on July 5, 2011, our Chief Executive Officer submitted to the NYSE a certification that he was not aware of any violation by the Company of NYSE corporate governance listing standards. Additionally, we filed with this Form 10-K, the Principal Executive Officer and Principal Financial Officer certifications required under Sections 302 and 906 of the Sarbanes-Oxley Act of 2002.

ITEM 1A.   *RISK FACTORS*

Our ability to anticipate and respond to changing consumer preferences, fashion trends and a competitive environment in a timely manner

Our future success depends, in part, upon our ability to identify and respond to fashion trends in a timely manner. The specialty retail apparel business fluctuates according to changes in the economy and customer preferences, dictated by fashion and season. These fluctuations especially affect the inventory owned by apparel retailers because merchandise typically must be ordered well in advance of the selling season. While we endeavor to test many merchandise items before ordering large quantities, we are still susceptible to changing fashion trends and fluctuations in customer demands.

In addition, the cyclical nature of the retail business requires that we carry a significant amount of inventory, especially during our peak selling seasons. We enter into agreements for the manufacture and purchase of our private label apparel well in advance of the applicable selling season. As a result, we are vulnerable to changes in consumer demand, pricing shifts and the timing and selection of merchandise purchases. The failure to enter into agreements for the manufacture and purchase of merchandise in a timely manner could, among other things, lead to a shortage of inventory and lower sales. Changes in fashion trends, if unsuccessfully identified, forecasted or responded to by us, could, among other things, lead to lower sales, excess inventories and higher markdowns, which in turn could have a material adverse effect on our results of operations and financial condition.

The effect of economic pressures and other business factors

The success of our operations depends to a significant extent upon a number of factors relating to discretionary consumer spending, including economic conditions affecting disposable consumer income such as employment, consumer debt, interest rates, increases in energy costs and consumer confidence. There can be no assurance that consumer spending will not be further negatively affected by general or local economic conditions, thereby adversely impacting our continued growth and results of operations.

Our ability to react to raw material, labor and energy cost increases

Increases in our costs, such as raw materials, labor and energy, may reduce our overall profitability. Specifically, fluctuations in the price of cotton that is used in the manufacture of merchandise we purchase from our suppliers has negatively impacted our cost of sales. We have strategies in place to help mitigate the rising cost of raw materials and our overall profitability depends on the success of those strategies. Additionally, increases in other costs, including labor and energy, could further reduce our profitability if not mitigated.

Our ability to grow through new store openings and existing store remodels and expansions

Our continued growth and success will depend in part on our ability to open and operate new stores and expand and remodel existing stores on a timely and profitable basis. During Fiscal 2012, we plan to open approximately 14 new American Eagle stores in the U.S. and Canada and one 77kids store. Additionally, we plan to remodel and refurbish approximately 100 existing American Eagle stores during Fiscal 2012. Accomplishing our new and existing store expansion goals will depend upon a number of factors, including the ability to obtain suitable sites for new and expanded stores at acceptable costs, the hiring and training of qualified personnel, particularly at the store management level, the integration of new stores into existing operations and the expansion of our buying and inventory capabilities. There can be no assurance that we will be able to achieve our store expansion goals, manage our growth effectively, successfully integrate the planned new stores into our operations or operate our new and remodeled stores profitably.

Our ability to achieve planned store financial performance

The results achieved by our stores may not be indicative of long-term performance or the potential performance of stores in other locations. The failure of stores to achieve acceptable results could result in additional store asset impairment charges, which could adversely affect our continued growth and results of operations.

Our ability to grow through the internal development of new brands

We launched our new brand concepts, aerie and 77kids, during Fiscal 2006 and Fiscal 2008, respectively. Our ability to succeed in these new brands requires significant expenditures and management attention. Additionally, any new brand is subject to certain risks including customer acceptance, competition, product differentiation, the ability to attract and retain qualified personnel, including management and designers, and the ability to obtain suitable sites for new stores at acceptable costs. There can be no assurance that these new brands will grow or become profitable. If we are unable to succeed in developing profitable new brands, this could adversely impact our continued growth and results of operations.

Our international merchandise sourcing strategy

Substantially all of our merchandise is purchased from foreign suppliers. Although we purchase a significant portion of our merchandise through a single foreign buying agent, we do not maintain any exclusive commitments to purchase from any vendor. Since we rely on a small number of foreign sources for a significant portion of our purchases, any event causing the disruption of imports, including the insolvency of a significant supplier or a significant labor dispute, could have an adverse effect on our operations. Other events that could also cause a disruption of imports include the imposition of additional trade law provisions or import restrictions, such as increased duties, tariffs, anti-dumping provisions, increased CBP enforcement actions, or political or economic disruptions.

We have a Vendor Code of Conduct (the "Code") that provides guidelines for all of our vendors regarding working conditions, employment practices and compliance with local laws. A copy of the Code is posted on our website, www.ae.com, and is also included in our vendor manual in English and multiple other languages. We have a factory compliance program to audit for compliance with the Code. However, there can be no assurance that our factory compliance program will be fully effective in discovering all violations. Publicity regarding violation of our Code or other social responsibility standards by any of our vendor factories could adversely affect our sales and financial performance.

We believe that there is a risk of terrorist activity on a global basis, and such activity might take the form of a physical act that impedes the flow of imported goods or the insertion of a harmful or injurious agent to an imported shipment. We have instituted policies and procedures designed to reduce the chance or impact of such actions including, but not limited to, factory audits and self-assessments, including audit protocols on all critical security issues; the review of security procedures of our other international trading partners, including forwarders, consolidators, shippers and brokers; and the cancellation of agreements with entities who fail to meet our security requirements. In addition, the United States CBP has recognized us as a validated, tier three member of the Customs - Trade Partnership Against Terrorism program, a voluntary program in which an importer agrees to work with customs to strengthen overall supply chain security. However, there can be no assurance that terrorist activity can be prevented entirely and we cannot predict the likelihood of any such activities or the extent of their adverse impact on our operations.

Our reliance on external vendors

Given the volatility and risk in the current markets, our reliance on external vendors leaves us subject to certain risks should one or more of these external vendors become insolvent. Although we monitor the financial stability of our key vendors and plan for contingencies, the financial failure of a key vendor could disrupt our operations and have an adverse effect on our cash flows, results of operations and financial condition.

Seasonality

Historically, our operations have been seasonal, with a large portion of net sales and operating income occurring in the third and fourth fiscal quarters, reflecting increased demand during the back-to-school and year-end holiday selling seasons, respectively. As a result of this seasonality, any factors negatively affecting us during the third and fourth fiscal quarters of any year, including adverse weather or unfavorable economic conditions, could have a material adverse effect on our financial condition and results of operations for the entire year. Our quarterly results of operations also may fluctuate based upon such factors as the timing of certain holiday seasons, the number and timing of new store openings, the acceptability of seasonal merchandise offerings, the timing and level of markdowns, store closings and remodels, competitive factors, weather and general economic conditions.

Our reliance on our ability to implement and sustain information technology systems

We regularly evaluate our information technology systems and are currently implementing modifications and/or upgrades to the information technology systems that support our business. Modifications include replacing legacy systems with successor systems, making changes to legacy systems or acquiring new systems with new functionality. We are aware of inherent risks associated with replacing and modifying these systems, including inaccurate system information and system disruptions. We believe we are taking appropriate action to mitigate the risks through testing, training, staging implementation and in-sourcing certain processes, as well as securing appropriate commercial contracts with third-party vendors supplying such replacement and redundancy technologies. Information technology system disruptions and inaccurate system information, if not anticipated and appropriately mitigated, could have a material adverse effect on our results of operations.

Our ability to safeguard against any security breach with respect to our information technology systems

During the course of business, we regularly obtain and transmit confidential customer information through our information technology systems. If our information technology systems are breached, an unauthorized third party may obtain access to confidential customer information. Any compromise or breach of our systems that results in unauthorized access to confidential customer information could cause us to incur significant legal and financial liabilities, damage to our reputation and a loss of customer confidence. These impacts could have a material adverse effect on our business and results of operations.

Our reliance on key personnel

Our success depends to a significant extent upon the continued services of our key personnel, including senior management, as well as our ability to attract and retain qualified key personnel and skilled employees in the future. Our operations could be adversely affected if, for any reason, one or more key executive officers ceased to be active in our management.

Failure to comply with regulatory requirements

As a public company, we are subject to numerous regulatory requirements. Our policies, procedures and internal controls are designed to comply with all applicable laws and regulations, including those imposed by the Sarbanes-Oxley Act of 2002, the SEC and the NYSE. Failure to comply with such laws and regulations could have a material adverse effect on our reputation, financial condition and on the market price of our common stock.

Our ability to obtain and/or maintain our credit facilities

We believe that we have sufficient cash flows from operating activities to meet our operating requirements. In addition, the banks participating in our various credit facilities are currently rated as investment grade, and all of the amounts under the credit facilities are currently available to us at the discretion of the respective financial institutions. We draw on our credit facilities to increase our cash position to add financial flexibility. Although we expect to continue to generate positive cash flow despite the current economy, there can be no assurance that we will be able to successfully generate positive cash flow in the future. Continued negative trends in the credit markets and/or continued financial institution failures could lead to lowered credit availability as well as difficulty in obtaining financing. In the event of limitations on our access to credit facilities, our liquidity, continued growth and results of operations could be adversely affected.

Our efforts to expand internationally

We have entered into franchise agreements with multiple franchisees to open and operate stores throughout the Middle East, Northern Africa, Eastern Europe, Hong Kong, China, Israel and Japan over the next several years. While the franchise arrangements do not involve a capital investment from us and require minimal operational involvement, the effect of these arrangements on our business and results of operations is uncertain and will depend upon various factors, including the demand for our products in new markets internationally. Furthermore, although we provide store operation training, literature and support, to the extent that the franchisee does not operate its stores in a manner consistent with our requirements regarding our brand and customer experience standards, the value of our brand could be negatively impacted. A failure to protect the value of our brand or any other adverse actions by a franchisee could have an adverse effect on our results of operations and our reputation.

Other risk factors

Additionally, other factors could adversely affect our financial performance, including factors such as: our ability to successfully acquire and integrate other businesses; any interruption of our key infrastructure systems; any disaster or casualty resulting in the interruption of service from our distribution centers or in a large number of our stores; any interruption of our business related to an outbreak of a pandemic disease in a country where we source or market our merchandise; changes in weather patterns; the effects of changes in current exchange rates and interest rates; and international and domestic acts of terror.

The impact of any of the previously discussed factors, some of which are beyond our control, may cause our actual results to differ materially from expected results in these statements and other forward-looking statements we may make from time-to-time.

ITEM 6.   *SELECTED CONSOLIDATED FINANCIAL DATA.*

The following Selected Consolidated Financial Data should be read in conjunction with "Management's Discussion and Analysis of Financial Condition and Results of Operations" included under Item 7 below and the Consolidated Financial Statements and Notes thereto, included in Item 8 below. Most of the selected data presented below is derived from our Consolidated Financial Statements, if applicable, which are filed in response to Item 8 below. The selected Consolidated Statement of Operations data for the years ended January 31, 2009, and February 2, 2008, and the selected Consolidated Balance Sheet data as of January 30, 2010, January 31, 2009, and February 2, 2008, are derived from audited Consolidated Financial Statements not included herein.

	For the Years Ended(1)				
	January 28, 2012	January 29, 2011	January 30, 2010	January 31, 2009	February 2, 2008
	(In thousands, except per share amounts, ratios and other financial information)				
Summary of Operations(2)					
Net sales	$3,159,818	$2,967,559	$2,940,269	$2,948,679	$3,041,158
Comparable store sales increase (decrease)(3)	3%	(1)%	(4)%	(10)%	1%
Gross profit	$1,128,341	$1,170,959	$1,173,430	$1,197,186	$1,438,236
Gross profit as a percentage of net sales	35.7%	39.5%	39.9%	40.6%	47.3%
Operating income	$ 231,136	$ 317,261	$ 310,392	$ 382,797	$ 652,201
Operating income as a percentage of net sales	7.3%	10.7%	10.6%	13.0%	21.4%
Income from continuing operations	$ 151,705	$ 181,934	$ 213,398	$ 229,984	$ 433,507
Income from continuing operations as a percentage of net sales	4.8%	6.1%	7.3%	7.8%	14.3%
Per Share Results					
Income from continuing operations per common share — basic	$ 0.78	$ 0.91	$ 1.04	$ 1.12	$ 2.01
Income from continuing operations per common share — diluted	$ 0.77	$ 0.90	$ 1.02	$ 1.11	$ 1.97
Weighted average common shares outstanding — basic	194,445	199,979	206,171	205,169	216,119
Weighted average common shares outstanding — diluted	196,314	201,818	209,512	207,582	220,280
Cash dividends per common share	$ 0.44	$ 0.93	$ 0.40	$ 0.40	$ 0.38
Balance Sheet Information					
Total cash and short-term investments	$ 745,044	$ 734,695	$ 698,635	$ 483,853	$ 619,939
Long-term investments	$ 847	$ 5,915	$ 197,773	$ 251,007	$ 165,810
Total assets	$1,950,802	$1,879,998	$2,138,148	$1,963,676	$1,867,680
Short-term debt	$ —	$ —	$ 30,000	$ 75,000	$ —
Long-term debt	$ —	$ —	$ —	$ —	$ —
Stockholders' equity	$1,416,851	$1,351,071	$1,578,517	$1,409,031	$1,340,464
Working capital	$ 882,087	$ 786,573	$ 758,075	$ 523,596	$ 644,656
Current ratio	3.18	3.03	2.85	2.30	2.71
Average return on stockholders' equity	11.0%	9.6%	11.3%	13.0%	29.0%

| | For the Years Ended(1) | | | | |
	January 28, 2012	January 29, 2011	January 30, 2010	January 31, 2009	February 2, 2008
	(In thousands, except per share amounts, ratios and other financial information)				
Other Financial Information(2)					
Total stores at year-end	1,090	1,086	1,075	1,070	968
Capital expenditures	$ 100,135	$ 84,259	$ 127,080	$ 243,564	$ 249,640
Net sales per average selling square foot(4)	$ 545	$ 524	$ 526	$ 563	$ 644
Total selling square feet at end of period	5,115,770	5,067,489	4,981,595	4,920,285	4,492,198
Net sales per average gross square foot(4)	$ 436	$ 420	$ 422	$ 452	$ 522
Total gross square feet at end of period	6,398,034	6,339,469	6,215,355	6,139,663	5,581,769
Number of employees at end of period	39,600	39,900	38,800	36,900	38,400

(1)   All fiscal years presented include 52 weeks.

(2)   All amounts presented are from continuing operations and exclude MARTIN+OSA's results of operations for all periods. Refer to Note 15 to the accompanying Consolidated Financial Statements for additional information regarding the discontinued operations of MARTIN+OSA.

(3)   The comparable store sales increase for the period ended February 2, 2008, is compared to the corresponding 52 week period in Fiscal 2006.

(4)   Net sales per average square foot is calculated using retail store sales for the year divided by the straight average of the beginning and ending square footage for the year.

ITEM 8. *FINANCIAL STATEMENTS AND SUPPLEMENTARY DATA.*

Report of Independent Registered Public Accounting Firm

The Board of Directors and Stockholders of
American Eagle Outfitters, Inc.

We have audited the accompanying consolidated balance sheets of American Eagle Outfitters, Inc. (the Company) as of January 28, 2012, and January 29, 2011, and the related consolidated statements of operations, comprehensive income, stockholders' equity, and cash flows for each of the three years in the period ended January 28, 2012. These financial statements are the responsibility of the Company's management. Our responsibility is to express an opinion on these financial statements based on our audits.

We conducted our audits in accordance with the standards of the Public Company Accounting Oversight Board (United States). Those standards require that we plan and perform the audit to obtain reasonable assurance about whether the financial statements are free of material misstatement. An audit includes examining, on a test basis, evidence supporting the amounts and disclosures in the financial statements. An audit also includes assessing the accounting principles used and significant estimates made by management, as well as evaluating the overall financial statement presentation. We believe that our audits provide a reasonable basis for our opinion.

In our opinion, the financial statements referred to above present fairly, in all material respects, the consolidated financial position of American Eagle Outfitters, Inc. at January 28, 2012, and January 29, 2011, and the consolidated results of its operations and its cash flows for each of the three years in the period ended January 28, 2012, in conformity with U.S. generally accepted accounting principles.

We also have audited, in accordance with the standards of the Public Company Accounting Oversight Board (United States), American Eagle Outfitters, Inc.'s internal control over financial reporting as of January 28, 2012, based on criteria established in Internal Control — Integrated Framework issued by the Committee of Sponsoring Organizations of the Treadway Commission and our report dated March 15, 2012, expressed an unqualified opinion thereon.

/s/   Ernst & Young LLP

Pittsburgh, Pennsylvania
March 15, 2012

AMERICAN EAGLE OUTFITTERS, INC.

CONSOLIDATED BALANCE SHEETS

	January 28, 2012	January 29, 2011
	(In thousands, except per share amounts)	
Assets		
Current assets:		
Cash and cash equivalents	$ 719,545	$ 667,593
Short-term investments	25,499	67,102
Merchandise inventory	378,426	301,208
Accounts receivable	40,310	36,721
Prepaid expenses and other	74,947	53,727
Deferred income taxes	48,761	48,059
Total current assets	1,287,488	1,174,410
Property and equipment, at cost, net of accumulated depreciation	582,162	643,120
Intangible assets, at cost, net of accumulated amortization	39,832	7,485
Goodwill	11,469	11,472
Non-current deferred income taxes	13,467	19,616
Other assets	16,384	23,895
Total assets	$1,950,802	$1,879,998
Liabilities and Stockholders' Equity		
Current liabilities:		
Accounts payable	$ 183,783	$ 167,723
Accrued compensation and payroll taxes	42,625	34,954
Accrued rent	76,921	70,390
Accrued income and other taxes	20,135	32,468
Unredeemed gift cards and gift certificates	44,970	41,001
Current portion of deferred lease credits	15,066	16,203
Other liabilities and accrued expenses	21,901	25,098
Total current liabilities	405,401	387,837
Non-current liabilities:		
Deferred lease credits	71,880	78,606
Non-current accrued income taxes	35,471	38,671
Other non-current liabilities	21,199	23,813
Total non-current liabilities	128,550	141,090
Commitments and contingencies	—	—
Stockholders' equity:		
Preferred stock, $0.01 par value; 5,000 shares authorized; none issued and outstanding	—	—
Common stock, $0.01 par value; 600,000 shares authorized; 249,566 and 249,566 shares issued; 193,848 and 194,366 shares outstanding, respectively	2,496	2,496
Contributed capital	552,797	546,597
Accumulated other comprehensive income	28,659	28,072
Retained earnings	1,771,464	1,711,929
Treasury stock, 55,718 and 55,200 shares, respectively, at cost	(938,565)	(938,023)
Total stockholders' equity	1,416,851	1,351,071
Total liabilities and stockholders' equity	$1,950,802	$1,879,998

Refer to Notes to Consolidated Financial Statements

AMERICAN EAGLE OUTFITTERS, INC.

CONSOLIDATED STATEMENTS OF OPERATIONS

	For the Years Ended		
	January 28, 2012	January 29, 2011	January 30, 2010
	(In thousands, except per share amounts)		
Net sales	$3,159,818	$2,967,559	$2,940,269
Cost of sales, including certain buying, occupancy and warehousing expenses	2,031,477	1,796,600	1,766,839
Gross profit	1,128,341	1,170,959	1,173,430
Selling, general and administrative expenses	735,828	713,197	725,278
Loss on impairment of assets	20,730	—	—
Depreciation and amortization expense	140,647	140,501	137,760
Operating income	231,136	317,261	310,392
Realized loss on sale of investment securities	—	(24,426)	(2,749)
Other income (expense), net	5,874	2,249	(3,268)
Income before income taxes	237,010	295,084	304,375
Provision for income taxes	85,305	113,150	90,977
Income from continuing operations	151,705	181,934	213,398
Loss from discontinued operations, net of tax	—	(41,287)	(44,376)
Net income	$ 151,705	$ 140,647	$ 169,022
Basic income per common share:			
Income from continuing operations	$ 0.78	$ 0.91	$ 1.04
Loss from discontinued operations	—	$ (0.21)	$ (0.22)
Basic net income per common share	$ 0.78	$ 0.70	$ 0.82
Diluted income per common share:			
Income from continuing operations	$ 0.77	$ 0.90	$ 1.02
Loss from discontinued operations	—	(0.20)	(0.21)
Diluted net income per common share	$ 0.77	$ 0.70	$ 0.81
Weighted average common shares outstanding — basic	194,445	199,979	206,171
Weighted average common shares outstanding — diluted	196,314	201,818	209,512

Refer to Notes to Consolidated Financial Statements

AMERICAN EAGLE OUTFITTERS, INC.

CONSOLIDATED STATEMENTS OF COMPREHENSIVE INCOME

	For the Years Ended		
	January 28, 2012	January 29, 2011	January 30, 2010
		(In thousands)	
Net income	$ 151,705	$ 140,647	$ 169,022
Other comprehensive income:			
Temporary (impairment) recovery related to investment securities, net of tax	—	(1,140)	14,506
Reclassification adjustment for realized losses in net income related to investment securities, net of tax	—	7,541	940
Foreign currency translation gain	587	4,833	15,781
Other comprehensive income	587	11,234	31,227
Comprehensive income	$ 152,292	$ 151,881	$ 200,249

Refer to Notes to Consolidated Financial Statements

AMERICAN EAGLE OUTFITTERS, INC.
CONSOLIDATED STATEMENTS OF STOCKHOLDERS' EQUITY

	Shares Outstanding (1)	Common Stock	Contributed Capital	Retained Earnings	Treasury Stock(2)	Accumulated Other Comprehensive Income (Loss)	Stockholders' Equity
			(In thousands, except per share amounts)				
Balance at January 31, 2009	**205,281**	**$ 2,485**	**$513,574**	**$1,694,161**	**$ (786,800)**	**$ (14,389)**	**$ 1,409,031**
Stock awards	41	1	39,903	—	—	—	39,904
Repurchase of common stock from employees	(18)	—	—	—	(247)	—	(247)
Reissuance of treasury stock	1,528	—	—	(15,228)	27,792	—	12,564
Net income	—	—	—	169,022	—	—	169,022
Other comprehensive income, net of tax	—	—	—	—	—	31,227	31,227
Cash dividends and dividend equivalents ($0.40 per share)	—	—	922	(83,906)	—	—	(82,984)
Balance at January 30, 2010	**206,832**	**$ 2,486**	**$ 554,399**	**$1,764,049**	**$ (759,255)**	**$ 16,838**	**$1,578,517**
Stock awards	997	10	36,229	—	—	—	36,239
Repurchase of common stock as part of publicly announced programs	(15,500)	—	—	—	(216,070)	—	(216,070)
Repurchase of common stock from employees	(1,035)	—	—	—	(18,041)	—	(18,041)
Reissuance of treasury stock	3,072	—	(45,841)	(7,791)	55,343	—	1,711
Net income	—	—	—	140,647	—	—	140,647
Other comprehensive income, net of tax	—	—	—	—	—	11,234	11,234
Cash dividends and dividend equivalents ($0.93 per share)	—	—	1,810	(184,976)	—	—	(183,166)
Balance at January 29, 2011	**194,366**	**$ 2,496**	**$ 546,597**	**$1,711,929**	**$ (938,023)**	**$ 2 8,072**	**$1,351,071**
Stock awards	—	—	10,532	—	—	—	10,532
Repurchase of common stock as part of publicly announced programs	(1,365)	—	—	—	(15,160)	—	(15,160)
Repurchase of common stock from employees	(145)	—	—	—	(2,189)	—	(2,189)
Reissuance of treasury stock	992	—	(5,997)	(4,261)	16,807	—	6,549
Net income	—	—	—	151,705	—	—	151,705
Other comprehensive income, net of tax	—	—	—	—	—	587	587
Cash dividends and dividend equivalents ($0.44 per share)	—	—	1,665	(87,909)	—	—	(86,244)
Balance at January 28, 2012	**193,848**	**$ 2,496**	**$552,797**	**$1,771,464**	**$ (938,565)**	**$ 28,659**	**$ 1,416,851**

(1)   600,000 authorized, 249,566 issued and 193,848 outstanding, $0.01 par value common stock at January 28, 2012; 600,000 authorized, 249,566 issued and 194,366 outstanding, $0.01 par value common stock at January 29, 2011; 600,000 authorized, 249,561 issued and 206,832 outstanding (excluding 992 shares of non-vested restricted stock), $0.01 par value common stock at January 30, 2010; The Company has 5,000 authorized, with none issued or outstanding, $0.01 par value preferred stock at January 28, 2012, January 29, 2011, and January 30, 2010.

(2)   55,718 shares, 55,200 shares, and 41,737 shares at January 28, 2012, January 29, 2011, and January 30, 2010, respectively. During Fiscal 2011, Fiscal 2010 and Fiscal 2009, 992 shares, 3,072 shares and 1,528 shares, respectively, were reissued from treasury stock for the issuance of share-based payments.

Refer to Notes to Consolidated Financial Statements

AMERICAN EAGLE OUTFITTERS, INC.
CONSOLIDATED STATEMENTS OF CASH FLOWS

| | For the Years Ended | | |
	January 28, 2012	January 29, 2011	January 30, 2010
	(In thousands)		
Operating activities:			
Net income	$ 151,705	$ 140,647	$ 169,022
Loss from discontinued operations, net of tax	—	41,287	44,376
Income from continuing operations	$ 151,705	$ 181,934	$ 213,398
Adjustments to reconcile net income to net cash provided by operating activities			
Depreciation and amortization	143,156	145,548	139,832
Share-based compensation	12,341	25,457	34,615
Provision for deferred income taxes	4,207	11,885	(36,027)
Tax benefit from share-based payments	356	15,648	7,995
Excess tax benefit from share-based payments	(373)	(12,499)	(2,812)
Foreign currency transaction (gain) loss	(325)	117	6,477
Loss on impairment of assets	20,730	—	—
Realized investment losses	—	25,674	3,689
Changes in assets and liabilities:			
Merchandise inventory	(77,311)	18,713	(33,699)
Accounts receivable	(3,589)	(3,790)	6,656
Prepaid expenses and other	(21,261)	(9,045)	12,916
Other assets	2,444	(1,380)	1,146
Accounts payable	17,934	5,232	8,358
Unredeemed gift cards and gift certificates	3,979	1,713	(3,591)
Deferred lease credits	(7,837)	(7,451)	4,667
Accrued compensation and payroll taxes	7,677	(19,618)	25,841
Accrued income and other taxes	(15,515)	11,999	12,858
Accrued liabilities	938	12,457	(1,993)
Total adjustments	87,551	220,660	186,928
Net cash provided by operating activities from continuing operations	**239,256**	**402,594**	**400,326**
Investing activities:			
Capital expenditures for property and equipment	(100,135)	(84,259)	(127,080)
Acquisition of intangible assets	(34,187)	(2,801)	(2,003)
Purchase of available-for-sale securities	(193,851)	(62,797)	—
Sale of available-for-sale securities	240,797	177,472	80,353
Net cash (used for) provided by investing activities from continuing operations	**(87,376)**	**27,615**	**(48,730)**
Financing activities:			
Payments on capital leases	(3,256)	(2,590)	(2,015)
Repayment of note payable	—	(30,000)	(45,000)
Repurchase of common stock as part of publicly announced programs	(15,160)	(216,070)	—
Repurchase of common stock from employees	(2,189)	(18,041)	(247)
Net proceeds from stock options exercised	5,098	7,272	9,044
Excess tax benefit from share-based payments	373	12,499	2,812
Cash used to net settle equity awards	—	(6,434)	(1,414)
Cash dividends paid	(85,592)	(183,166)	(82,985)
Net cash used for financing activities from continuing operations	**(100,726)**	**(436,530)**	**(119,805)**
Effect of exchange rates on cash	798	1,394	3,030
Cash flows of discontinued operations			
Net cash used for operating activities	—	(21,434)	(13,864)
Net cash used for investing activities	—	(6)	(339)
Net cash used for financing activities	—	—	—
Effect of exchange rates on cash	—	—	—
Net cash used for discontinued operations	**—**	**(21,440)**	**(14,203)**
Net increase (decrease) in cash and cash equivalents	**51,952**	**(26,367)**	**220,618**
Cash and cash equivalents — beginning of period	667,593	693,960	473,342
Cash and cash equivalents — end of period	$ 719,545	$ 667,593	$ 693,960

Refer to Notes to Consolidated Financial Statements

AMERICAN EAGLE OUTFITTERS, INC.
NOTES TO CONSOLIDATED FINANCIAL STATEMENTS
FOR THE YEAR ENDED JANUARY 28, 2012

1.   Business Operations

American Eagle Outfitters, Inc. (the "Company"), a Delaware corporation, operates under the American Eagle® ("AE"), aerie® by American Eagle® ("aerie"), and 77kids by american eagle® ("77kids") brands. The Company operated the MARTIN+OSA® brand ("M+O") until its closure during Fiscal 2010.

Founded in 1977, American Eagle Outfitters is a leading apparel and accessories retailer that operates more than 1,000 retail stores in the U.S. and Canada, and online at ae.com. Through its family of brands, the Company offers high quality, on-trend clothing, accessories and personal care products at affordable prices. The Company's online business, AEO Direct, ships to 77 countries worldwide.

Merchandise Mix

The following table sets forth the approximate consolidated percentage of net sales attributable to each merchandise group for each of the periods indicated:

	For the Years Ended		
	January 28, 2012	January 29, 2011	January 30, 2010
Men's apparel and accessories	40%	40%	40%
Women's apparel and accessories (excluding aerie)	51%	51%	51%
aerie	8%	9%	9%
Kid's apparel and accessories	1%	—%	—%
Total	100%	100%	100%

2.   Summary of Significant Accounting Policies

Principles of Consolidation

The Consolidated Financial Statements include the accounts of the Company and its wholly-owned subsidiaries. All intercompany transactions and balances have been eliminated in consolidation. At January 28, 2012, the Company operated in one reportable segment.

On March 5, 2010, the Company's Board of Directors (the "Board") approved management's recommendation to proceed with the closure of the M+O brand. The Company completed the closure of the M+O stores and e-commerce operation during Fiscal 2010. These Consolidated Financial Statements reflect the results of M+O as a discontinued operation for all periods presented.

Fiscal Year

The Company's financial year is a 52/53 week year that ends on the Saturday nearest to January 31. As used herein, "Fiscal 2012" refers to the 53 week period ending February 2, 2013. "Fiscal 2011," "Fiscal 2010," "Fiscal 2009," "Fiscal 2008" and "Fiscal 2007" refer to the 52 week periods ended January 28, 2012, January 29, 2011, January 30, 2010, January 31, 2009, and February 2, 2008, respectively.

Estimates

The preparation of financial statements in conformity with accounting principles generally accepted in the United States of America ("GAAP") requires the Company's management to make estimates and assumptions that affect the reported amounts of assets and liabilities and disclosure of contingent assets and liabilities at the date of the financial statements and the reported amounts of revenues and expenses during the reporting period. Actual results could differ from those estimates. On an ongoing basis, our management reviews its estimates based on currently available information. Changes in facts and circumstances may result in revised estimates.

Recent Accounting Pronouncements

In June 2011, the Financial Accounting Standards Board ("FASB") issued Accounting Standards Update ("ASU") 2011-05, *Presentation of Comprehensive Income* ("ASU 2011-05"). ASU 2011-05 requires that all non-owner changes in stockholders' equity be presented either in a single continuous statement of comprehensive income or in two separate but consecutive statements. In the two-statement approach, the first statement should present total net income and its components followed consecutively by a second statement that should present total other comprehensive income, the components of other comprehensive income and the total of comprehensive income. In December 2011, the FASB issued ASU 2011-12, *Deferral of the Effective Date for Amendments to the Presentation of Reclassifications of Items Out of Accumulated Other Comprehensive Income* ("ASU 2011-12"). ASU 2011-12 defers the requirement to present reclassifications out of accumulated other comprehensive income as required by ASU 2011-05. For public entities, the amendments in ASU 2011-05 and ASU 2011-12 are effective for fiscal years, and interim periods within those years, beginning after December 15, 2011, and are to be applied retrospectively, with early adoption permitted. The Company is currently evaluating the impact of ASU 2011-05 and ASU 2011-12 on its financial statement presentation of comprehensive income and will adopt in Fiscal 2012.

AMERICAN EAGLE OUTFITTERS, INC.

NOTES TO CONSOLIDATED FINANCIAL STATEMENTS — (Continued)

In September 2011, the FASB issued ASU 2011-08, *Testing Goodwill for Impairment* ("ASU 2011-08"). ASU 2011-08 permits an entity to first assess qualitative factors to determine whether it is more likely than not that the fair value of a reporting unit is less than its carrying amount as a basis for determining whether it is necessary to perform the two-step goodwill impairment test. ASU 2011-08 applies to all companies that have goodwill reported in their financial statements. The provisions of ASU 2011-08 are effective for annual and interim goodwill impairment tests performed for fiscal years beginning after December 15, 2011. The Company will adopt ASU 2011-08 in Fiscal 2012. As a result of the adoption, the Company does not expect an impact to its Consolidated Financial Statements.

Foreign Currency Translation

The Canadian dollar is the functional currency for the Canadian business. In accordance with Accounting Standards Codification ("ASC") 830, *Foreign Currency Matters*, assets and liabilities denominated in foreign currencies were translated into U.S. dollars (the reporting currency) at the exchange rate prevailing at the balance sheet date. Revenues and expenses denominated in foreign currencies were translated into U.S. dollars at the monthly average exchange rate for the period. Gains or losses resulting from foreign currency transactions are included in the results of operations, whereas, related translation adjustments are reported as an element of other comprehensive income in accordance with ASC 220, *Comprehensive Income* (refer to Note 11 to the Consolidated Financial Statements).

Cash and Cash Equivalents, Short-term Investments and Long-term Investments

Cash includes cash equivalents. The Company considers all highly liquid investments purchased with a remaining maturity of three months or less to be cash equivalents.

As of January 28, 2012, short-term investments include treasury bills purchased with a maturity of greater than three months, but less than one year. It also includes auction rate securities ("ARS") classified as available for sale that the Company expects to be redeemed at par within 12 months.

As of January 28, 2012, long-term investments include the Company's ARS Call Option related to investment sales during Fiscal 2010. Long-term investments are included within other assets on the Company's Consolidated Balance Sheets. The ARS Call Option expires on October 29, 2013.

Unrealized gains and losses on the Company's available-for-sale securities are excluded from earnings and are reported as a separate component of stockholders' equity, within accumulated other comprehensive income, until realized. The components of other-than-temporary impairment ("OTTI") losses related to credit losses are considered by the Company to be realized and are recorded in earnings. When available-for-sale securities are sold, the cost of the securities is specifically identified and is used to determine any realized gain or loss.

Refer to Note 3 to the Consolidated Financial Statements for information regarding cash and cash equivalents, short-term investments and long-term investments.

Other-than-Temporary Impairment

The Company evaluates its investments for impairment in accordance with ASC 320, *Investments — Debt and Equity Securities* ("ASC 320"). ASC 320 provides guidance for determining when an investment is considered impaired, whether impairment is other-than-temporary, and measurement of an impairment loss. An investment is considered impaired if the fair value of the investment is less than its cost. If, after consideration of all available evidence to evaluate the realizable value of its investment, impairment is determined to be other-than-temporary, then an impairment loss is recognized in the Consolidated Statement of Operations equal to the difference between the investment's cost and its fair value. Additionally, ASC 320 requires additional disclosures relating to debt and equity securities both in the interim and annual periods as well as requires the Company to present total OTTI with an offsetting reduction for any non-credit loss impairment amount recognized in other comprehensive income ("OCI").

There was no net impairment loss recognized in earnings during Fiscal 2011. During Fiscal 2010, there was $1.2 million of net impairment loss recognized in earnings which consisted of gross other-than-temporary losses of $5.0 million, partially offset by $3.8 million of OTTI losses recognized in other comprehensive income. During Fiscal 2009, there was $0.9 million of net impairment loss recognized in earnings which consisted of gross other-than-temporary losses of $4.4 million, partially offset by $3.5 million of OTTI losses recognized in other comprehensive income.

Refer to Note 4 to the Consolidated Financial Statements for additional information regarding net impairment losses recognized in earnings.

Merchandise Inventory

Merchandise inventory is valued at the lower of average cost or market, utilizing the retail method. Average cost includes merchandise design and sourcing costs and related expenses. The Company records merchandise receipts at the time merchandise is delivered to the foreign shipping port by the manufacturer (FOB port). This is the point at which title and risk of loss transfer to the Company.

The Company reviews its inventory levels to identify slow-moving merchandise and generally uses markdowns to clear merchandise. Additionally, the Company estimates a markdown reserve for future planned permanent markdowns related to current inventory. Markdowns may occur when inventory exceeds customer demand for reasons of style, seasonal adaptation, changes in customer preference, lack of consumer acceptance of fashion items, competition, or if it is determined that the inventory in stock will not sell at its currently ticketed price. Such markdowns may have a material adverse impact on earnings, depending on the extent and amount of inventory affected. The Company also estimates a shrinkage reserve for the period between the last physical count and the balance sheet date. The estimate for the shrinkage reserve, based on historical results, can be affected by changes in merchandise mix and changes in actual shrinkage trends.

AMERICAN EAGLE OUTFITTERS, INC.

NOTES TO CONSOLIDATED FINANCIAL STATEMENTS — (Continued)

Property and Equipment

Property and equipment is recorded on the basis of cost with depreciation computed utilizing the straight-line method over the assets' estimated useful lives. The useful lives of our major classes of assets are as follows:

Buildings	25 years
Leasehold improvements	Lesser of 10 years or the term of the lease
Fixtures and equipment	5 years

In accordance with ASC 360, *Property, Plant, and Equipment*, the Company's management evaluates the value of leasehold improvements and store fixtures associated with retail stores, which have been open for a period of time sufficient to reach maturity. The Company evaluates long-lived assets for impairment at the individual store level, which is the lowest level at which individual cash flows can be identified. Impairment losses are recorded on long-lived assets used in operations when events and circumstances indicate that the assets might be impaired and the undiscounted cash flows estimated to be generated by those assets are less than the carrying amounts of the assets. When events such as these occur, the impaired assets are adjusted to their estimated fair value and an impairment loss is recorded separately as a component of operating income under loss on impairment of assets.

During Fiscal 2011, the Company recorded asset impairment charges of $20.7 million consisting of 59 retail stores, largely related to the aerie brand, which is recorded as a loss on impairment of assets in the Consolidated Statements of Operations. Based on the Company's review of the operating performance and projections of future performance of these stores, the Company determined that they would not be able to generate sufficient cash flow over the life of the related leases to recover the Company's initial investment in them.

During Fiscal 2010, the Company recorded asset impairment charges of $18.0 million related to the impairment of 18 M+O stores. Additionally, during Fiscal 2009, the Company recorded asset impairment charges of $18.0 million related primarily to the impairment of 10 M+O stores. The asset impairment charges in Fiscal 2010 and Fiscal 2009 related to the 28 M+O stores are recorded within loss from discontinued operations, net of tax in the Consolidated Statements of Operations.

Refer to Note 15 to the Consolidated Financial Statements for additional information regarding the discontinued operations for M+O.

When the Company closes, remodels or relocates a store prior to the end of its lease term, the remaining net book value of the assets related to the store is recorded as a write-off of assets within depreciation and amortization expense.

Refer to Note 7 to the Consolidated Financial Statements for additional information regarding property and equipment.

Goodwill

The Company's goodwill is primarily related to the acquisition of its importing operations and Canadian business. In accordance with ASC 350, *Intangibles- Goodwill and Other* ("ASC 350"), the Company evaluates goodwill for possible impairment on at least an annual basis and last performed an annual impairment test as of January 28, 2012. As a result of the Company's annual goodwill impairment test, the Company concluded that its goodwill was not impaired.

Intangible Assets

Intangible assets are recorded on the basis of cost with amortization computed utilizing the straight-line method over the assets' estimated useful lives. The Company's intangible assets, which primarily include trademark assets, are amortized over 15 to 25 years.

The Company evaluates intangible assets for impairment in accordance with ASC 350 when events or circumstances indicate that the carrying value of the asset may not be recoverable. Such an evaluation includes the estimation of undiscounted future cash flows to be generated by those assets. If the sum of the estimated future undiscounted cash flows are less than the carrying amounts of the assets, then the assets are impaired and are adjusted to their estimated fair value. No intangible asset impairment charges were recorded during Fiscal 2011, Fiscal 2010 or Fiscal 2009.

Refer to Note 8 to the Consolidated Financial Statements for additional information regarding intangible assets.

Deferred Lease Credits

Deferred lease credits represent the unamortized portion of construction allowances received from landlords related to the Company's retail stores. Construction allowances are generally comprised of cash amounts received by the Company from its landlords as part of the negotiated lease terms. The Company records a receivable and a deferred lease credit liability at the lease commencement date (date of initial possession of the store). The deferred lease credit is amortized on a straight-line basis as a reduction of rent expense over the term of the original lease (including the pre-opening build-out period) and any subsequent renewal terms. The receivable is reduced as amounts are received from the landlord.

Self-Insurance Liability

The Company is self-insured for certain losses related to employee medical benefits and worker's compensation. Costs for self-insurance claims filed and claims incurred but not reported are accrued based on known claims and historical experience. Management believes that it has adequately reserved for its self-insurance liability, which is capped through the use of stop loss contracts with insurance companies. However, any significant variation of future claims from historical trends could cause actual results to differ from the accrued liability.

AMERICAN EAGLE OUTFITTERS, INC.

NOTES TO CONSOLIDATED FINANCIAL STATEMENTS — (Continued)

Co-branded Credit Card and Customer Loyalty Program

The Company offers a co-branded credit card (the "AEO Visa Card") and a private label credit card (the "AEO Credit Card") under the AE, aerie and 77kids brands. These credit cards are issued by a third-party bank (the "Bank"), and the Company has no liability to the Bank for bad debt expense, provided that purchases are made in accordance with the Bank's procedures. Once a customer is approved to receive the AEO Visa Card or the AEO Credit Card and the card is activated, the customer is eligible to participate in the credit card rewards program. Customers who make purchases at AE, aerie and 77kids earn discounts in the form of savings certificates when certain purchase levels are reached. Also, AEO Visa Card customers who make purchases at other retailers where the card is accepted earn additional discounts. Savings certificates are valid for 90 days from issuance.

Points earned under the credit card rewards program on purchases at AE, aerie and 77kids are accounted for by analogy to ASC 605-25, Revenue Recognition, *Multiple Element Arrangements* ("ASC 605-25"). The Company believes that points earned under its point and loyalty programs represent deliverables in a multiple element arrangement rather than a rebate or refund of cash. Accordingly, the portion of the sales revenue attributed to the award points is deferred and recognized when the award is redeemed or when the points expire. Additionally, credit card reward points earned on non-AE, aerie or 77kids purchases are accounted for in accordance with ASC 605-25. As the points are earned, a current liability is recorded for the estimated cost of the award, and the impact of adjustments is recorded in cost of sales.

The Company offers its customers the AEREWARD$℠ loyalty program (the "Program"). Under the Program, customers accumulate points based on purchase activity and earn rewards by reaching certain point thresholds during three-month earning periods. Rewards earned during these periods are valid through the stated expiration date, which is approximately one month from the mailing date of the reward. These rewards can be redeemed for a discount on a purchase of merchandise. Rewards not redeemed during the one-month redemption period are forfeited. The Company determined that rewards earned using the Program should be accounted for in accordance with ASC 605-25. Accordingly, the portion of the sales revenue attributed to the award credits is deferred and recognized when the awards are redeemed or expire.

Income Taxes

The Company calculates income taxes in accordance with ASC 740, *Income Taxes* ("ASC 740"), which requires the use of the asset and liability method. Under this method, deferred tax assets and liabilities are recognized based on the difference between the Consolidated Financial Statement carrying amounts of existing assets and liabilities and their respective tax bases as computed pursuant to ASC 740. Deferred tax assets and liabilities are measured using the tax rates, based on certain judgments regarding enacted tax laws and published guidance, in effect in the years when those temporary differences are expected to reverse. A valuation allowance is established against the deferred tax assets when it is more likely than not that some portion or all of the deferred taxes may not be realized. Changes in the Company's level and composition of earnings, tax laws or the deferred tax valuation allowance, as well as the results of tax audits, may materially impact the Company's effective income tax rate.

The Company evaluates its income tax positions in accordance with ASC 740, which prescribes a comprehensive model for recognizing, measuring, presenting and disclosing in the financial statements tax positions taken or expected to be taken on a tax return, including a decision whether to file or not to file in a particular jurisdiction. Under ASC 740, a tax benefit from an uncertain position may be recognized only if it is "more likely than not" that the position is sustainable based on its technical merits.

The calculation of the deferred tax assets and liabilities, as well as the decision to recognize a tax benefit from an uncertain position and to establish a valuation allowance require management to make estimates and assumptions. The Company believes that its assumptions and estimates are reasonable, although actual results may have a positive or negative material impact on the balances of deferred tax assets and liabilities, valuation allowances or net income.

Revenue Recognition

Revenue is recorded for store sales upon the purchase of merchandise by customers. The Company's e-commerce operation records revenue upon the estimated customer receipt date of the merchandise. Shipping and handling revenues are included in net sales. Sales tax collected from customers is excluded from revenue and is included as part of accrued income and other taxes on the Company's Consolidated Balance Sheets.

Revenue is recorded net of estimated and actual sales returns and deductions for coupon redemptions and other promotions. The Company records the impact of adjustments to its sales return reserve quarterly within net sales and cost of sales. The sales return reserve reflects an estimate of sales returns based on projected merchandise returns determined through the use of historical average return percentages.

	For the Years Ended		
	January 28, 2012	January 29, 2011	January 30, 2010
	(In thousands)		
Beginning balance	$ 3,691	$ 4,690	$ 3,981
Returns	(77,656)	(70,789)	(71,705)
Provisions	76,896	69,790	72,414
Ending balance	$ 2,931	$ 3,691	$ 4,690

AMERICAN EAGLE OUTFITTERS, INC.

NOTES TO CONSOLIDATED FINANCIAL STATEMENTS — (Continued)

Revenue is not recorded on the purchase of gift cards. A current liability is recorded upon purchase, and revenue is recognized when the gift card is redeemed for merchandise. Additionally, the Company recognizes revenue on unredeemed gift cards based on an estimate of the amounts that will not be redeemed ("gift card breakage"), determined through historical redemption trends. Gift card breakage revenue is recognized in proportion to actual gift card redemptions as a component of net sales. For further information on the Company's gift card program, refer to the Gift Cards caption below.

The Company recognizes royalty revenue generated from its franchise agreements based upon a percentage of merchandise sales by the franchisee. This revenue is recorded as a component of net sales when earned.

The Company sells off end-of-season, overstock, and irregular merchandise to a third-party. The proceeds from these sales are presented on a gross basis, with proceeds and cost of sell-offs recorded in net sales and cost of sales, respectively.

	For the Years Ended		
	January 28, 2012	January 29, 2011	January 30, 2010
	(In thousands)		
Proceeds from sell-offs	$17,556	$25,593	$29,347
Marked-down cost of merchandise disposed of via sell-offs	$ 17,441	$ 24,728	$ 29,023

Cost of Sales, Including Certain Buying, Occupancy and Warehousing Expenses

Cost of sales consists of merchandise costs, including design, sourcing, importing and inbound freight costs, as well as markdowns, shrinkage and certain promotional costs (collectively "merchandise costs") and buying, occupancy and warehousing costs. Buying, occupancy and warehousing costs consist of compensation, employee benefit expenses and travel for our buyers and certain senior merchandising executives; rent and utilities related to our stores, corporate headquarters, distribution centers and other office space; freight from our distribution centers to the stores; compensation and supplies for our distribution centers, including purchasing, receiving and inspection costs; and shipping and handling costs related to our e-commerce operation. Merchandise profit is the difference between net sales and merchandise costs. Gross profit is the difference between net sales and cost of sales.

Selling, General and Administrative Expenses

Selling, general and administrative expenses consist of compensation and employee benefit expenses, including salaries, incentives and related benefits associated with our stores and corporate headquarters. Selling, general and administrative expenses also include advertising costs, supplies for our stores and home office, communication costs, travel and entertainment, leasing costs and services purchased. Selling, general and administrative expenses do not include compensation, employee benefit expenses and travel for our design, sourcing and importing teams, our buyers and our distribution centers as these amounts are recorded in cost of sales.

Advertising Costs

Certain advertising costs, including direct mail, in-store photographs and other promotional costs are expensed when the marketing campaign commences. As of January 28, 2012, and January 29, 2011, the Company had prepaid advertising expense of $7.7 million and $5.4 million, respectively. All other advertising costs are expensed as incurred. The Company recognized $73.1 million, $64.9 million and $60.9 million in advertising expense during Fiscal 2011, Fiscal 2010 and Fiscal 2009, respectively.

Design Costs

The Company has certain design costs, including compensation, rent, depreciation, travel, supplies and samples, which are included in cost of sales as the respective inventory is sold.

Store Pre-Opening Costs

Store pre-opening costs consist primarily of rent, advertising, supplies and payroll expenses. These costs are expensed as incurred.

Other Income (Expense), Net

Other income (expense), net consists primarily of interest income/expense, foreign currency transaction gain/loss and realized investment gains/losses other than those realized upon the sale of investment securities, which are recorded separately on the Consolidated Statements of Operations.

Gift Cards

The value of a gift card is recorded as a current liability upon purchase and revenue is recognized when the gift card is redeemed for merchandise. The Company estimates gift card breakage and recognizes revenue in proportion to actual gift card redemptions as a component of net sales. The Company determines an estimated gift card breakage rate by continuously evaluating historical redemption data and the time when there is a remote likelihood that a gift card will be redeemed. The company recorded gift card breakage of $6.5 million, $5.5 million and $6.8 million during Fiscal 2011, Fiscal 2010 and Fiscal 2009, respectively.

AMERICAN EAGLE OUTFITTERS, INC.

NOTES TO CONSOLIDATED FINANCIAL STATEMENTS — (Continued)

Legal Proceedings and Claims

The Company is subject to certain legal proceedings and claims arising out of the conduct of its business. In accordance with ASC 450, *Contingencies* ("ASC 450"), the Company records a reserve for estimated losses when the loss is probable and the amount can be reasonably estimated. If a range of possible loss exists and no anticipated loss within the range is more likely than any other anticipated loss, the Company records the accrual at the low end of the range, in accordance with ASC 450. As the Company believes that it has provided adequate reserves, it anticipates that the ultimate outcome of any matter currently pending against the Company will not materially affect the consolidated financial position, results of operations or consolidated cash flows of the Company.

Supplemental Disclosures of Cash Flow Information

The table below shows supplemental cash flow information for cash amounts paid during the respective periods:

| | For the Years Ended | | |
	January 28, 2012	January 29, 2011	January 30, 2010
	(In thousands)		
Cash paid during the periods for:			
Income taxes	$99,756	$45,737	$61,869
Interest	$ —	$ 191	$ 1,879

Segment Information

In accordance with ASC 280, *Segment Reporting* ("ASC 280"), the Company has identified four operating segments (American Eagle® Brand US and Canadian stores, aerie® by American Eagle® retail stores, 77kids by american eagle® retail stores and AEO Direct) that reflect the basis used internally to review performance and allocate resources. All of the operating segments have been aggregated and are presented as one reportable segment, as permitted by ASC 280.

The following tables present summarized geographical information:

| | For the Years Ended | | |
	January 28, 2012	January 29, 2011	January 30, 2010
	(In thousands)		
Net sales:			
United States	$ 2,849,248	$ 2,675,992	$ 2,665,655
Foreign(1)	310,570	291,567	274,614
Total net sales	$3,159,818	$2,967,559	$2,940,269

(1) Amounts represent sales from American Eagle and aerie Canadian retail stores, AEO Direct sales that are billed to and/or shipped to foreign countries and international franchise revenue.

	January 28, 2012	January 29, 2011
	(In thousands)	
Long-lived assets, net:		
United States	$580,161	$615,049
Foreign	53,302	47,028
Total long-lived assets, net	$633,463	$662,077

Reclassifications

Certain reclassifications have been made to the Consolidated Financial Statements for prior periods in order to conform to the current period presentation.

AMERICAN EAGLE OUTFITTERS, INC.

NOTES TO CONSOLIDATED FINANCIAL STATEMENTS — (Continued)

3.   Cash and Cash Equivalents, Short-term Investments and Long-term Investments

The following table summarizes the fair market value of our cash and marketable securities, which are recorded on the Consolidated Balance Sheets:

	January 28, 2012	January 29, 2011
	(In thousands)	
Cash and cash equivalents:		
Cash	$548,728	$122,578
Money-market	131,785	397,440
Commercial Paper	29,998	40,884
Treasury bills	9,034	102,996
Corporate bonds	—	3,695
Total cash and cash equivalents	$719,545	$667,593
Short-term investments:		
Treasury bills	$ 19,999	$ —
State and local government ARS	5,500	3,700
Term-deposits	—	63,402
Total short-term investments	$ 25,499	$ 67,102
Long-term investments:		
ARS Call Option	$ 847	$ 415
State and local government ARS	—	5,500
Total long-term investments	$ 847	$ 5,915
Total	$745,891	$740,610

Proceeds from the sale of available-for-sale securities were $240.8 million, $177.5 million and $80.4 million for Fiscal 2011, Fiscal 2010 and Fiscal 2009, respectively. The purchases of available-for-sale securities for Fiscal 2011 and Fiscal 2010 were $193.9 million and $62.8 million, respectively. There were no purchases of available-for-sale securities during Fiscal 2009. At January 28, 2012, and January 29, 2011, the fair value of all available-for-sale securities approximated par, with no gross unrealized holding gains or losses.

During Fiscal 2010, the Company liquidated ARS investments with $191.4 million of carrying value for proceeds of $177.5 million and a realized loss of $24.4 million (of which $10.9 million had previously been included in OCI on the Company's Consolidated Balance Sheets). The ARS securities sold during Fiscal 2010 included $119.7 million of par value ARS securities whereby the Company entered into a settlement agreement under which a financial institution (the "purchaser") purchased the ARS at a discount to par, plus accrued interest. Additionally, under this agreement, the Company retained a right (the "ARS Call Option"), for a period ending October 29, 2013, to: (a) repurchase any or all of the ARS securities sold at the agreed upon purchase prices received from the purchaser plus accrued interest; and/or (b) receive additional proceeds from the purchaser upon certain redemptions of the ARS securities sold. The ARS Call Option is cancelable by the purchaser for additional cash consideration.

The Company is required to assess the value of the ARS Call Option at the end of each reporting period, with any changes in fair value recorded within the Consolidated Statement of Operations. Upon origination, the Company determined that the fair value was $0.4 million. The fair value of the ARS Call Option was included as an offsetting amount within the net loss on liquidation of $24.4 million referenced above. As of January 28, 2012, the Company determined that the fair value of the ARS Call Option, which is classified as a long-term investment, was $0.8 million.

4.   Fair Value Measurements

ASC 820, *Fair Value Measurement Disclosures* ("ASC 820"), defines fair value, establishes a framework for measuring fair value in accordance with GAAP, and expands disclosures about fair value measurements. Fair value is defined under ASC 820 as the exit price associated with the sale of an asset or transfer of a liability in an orderly transaction between market participants at the measurement date.

Financial Instruments

Valuation techniques used to measure fair value under ASC 820 must maximize the use of observable inputs and minimize the use of unobservable inputs. In addition, ASC 820 establishes this three-tier fair value hierarchy, which prioritizes the inputs used in measuring fair value. These tiers include:

- *Level 1* — Quoted prices in active markets for identical assets or liabilities.

- *Level 2* — Inputs other than Level 1 that are observable, either directly or indirectly, such as quoted prices for similar assets or liabilities; quoted prices in markets that are not active; or other inputs that are observable or can be corroborated by observable market data for substantially the full term of the assets or liabilities.

- *Level 3* — Unobservable inputs (i.e., projections, estimates, interpretations, etc.) that are supported by little or no market activity and that are significant to the fair value of the assets or liabilities.

As of January 28, 2012, and January 29, 2011, the Company held certain assets that are required to be measured at fair value on a recurring basis. These include cash equivalents and short and long-term investments, including ARS.

AMERICAN EAGLE OUTFITTERS, INC.

NOTES TO CONSOLIDATED FINANCIAL STATEMENTS — (Continued)

In accordance with ASC 820, the following tables represent the fair value hierarchy for the Company's financial assets (cash equivalents and investments) measured at fair value on a recurring basis as of January 28, 2012, and January 29, 2011:

| | Carrying Amount | Fair Value Measurements at January 28, 2012 | | |
		Quoted Market Prices in Active Markets for Identical Assets (Level 1)	Significant Other Observable Inputs (Level 2)	Significant Unobservable Inputs (Level 3)
		(In thousands)		
Cash and cash equivalents				
Cash	$548,728	$548,728	$ —	$ —
Money-market	131,785	131,785	—	—
Commercial paper	29,998	29,998	—	—
Treasury bills	9,034	9,034	—	—
Total cash and cash equivalents	$719,545	$719,545	$ —	$ —
Short-term investments				
Treasury bills	$ 19,999	$ 19,999	$ —	$ —
State and local government ARS	5,500	—	—	5,500
Total short-term investments	$ 25,499	$ 19,999	$ —	$ 5,500
Long-term investments				
ARS Call Option	$ 847	$ —	$ —	$ 847
Total long-term investments	$ 847	$ —	$ —	$ 847
Total	$745,891	$739,544	$ —	$ 6,347

| | Carrying Amount | Fair Value Measurements at January 29, 2011 | | |
		Quoted Market Prices in Active Markets for Identical Assets (Level 1)	Significant Other Observable Inputs (Level 2)	Significant Unobservable Inputs (Level 3)
		(In thousands)		
Cash and cash equivalents				
Cash	$122,578	$122,578	$ —	$ —
Money-market	397,440	397,440	—	—
Treasury bills	102,996	102,996	—	—
Commercial paper	40,884	40,884	—	—
Corporate bonds	3,695	3,695	—	—
Total cash and cash equivalents	$667,593	$667,593	$ —	$ —
Short-term investments				
Term deposits	$ 63,402	$ 63,402	$ —	$ —
State and local government ARS	3,700	—	—	3,700
Total short-term investments	$ 67,102	$ 63,402	$ —	$ 3,700
Long-term investments				
State and local government ARS	$ 5,500	$ —	$ —	$ 5,500
ARS Call Option	415	—	—	415
Total long-term investments	$ 5,915	$ —	$ —	$ 5,915
Total	$740,610	$730,995	$ —	$ 9,615

The Company uses a discounted cash flow ("DCF") model to value its Level 3 investments. For Fiscal 2011, the assumptions in the Company's model for Level 3 investments, excluding the ARS Call Option, included a recovery period of five months, a discount factor for yield of 0.1% and illiquidity of 0.5%. For Fiscal 2010, the assumptions in the Company's model included different recovery periods, ranging from five to 17 months depending on the type of security, and discount factors for yield of 0.2% and illiquidity of 0.5%. These assumptions are subjective and are based on the Company's current judgment and view of current market conditions. The use of different assumptions would not result in a material change to the valuation.

As a result of the discounted cash flow analysis, no impairment loss on investment securities was recorded for Fiscal 2011. For Fiscal 2010, the Company recognized net impairment loss of $0.6 million ($0.4 million, net of tax), which increased the total cumulative impairment recognized in OCI from $10.3 million ($6.4 million, net of tax) at the end of Fiscal 2009 to $10.9 million ($6.8 million, net of tax) prior to the Company's liquidation of auction rate securities during the third quarter of Fiscal 2010. Additionally, during Fiscal 2010, as a result of a credit rating downgrade on student-load backed ARS, the Company recorded a net impairment loss in earnings of $1.2 million, which is recorded within Other Expense on the Consolidated Statements of Operations.

The fair value of the ARS Call Option described in Note 3 to the Consolidated Financial Statements was also estimated using a discounted cash flow model. The model considered potential changes in yields for securities with similar characteristics to the underlying ARS and evaluated possible future

AMERICAN EAGLE OUTFITTERS, INC.

NOTES TO CONSOLIDATED FINANCIAL STATEMENTS — (Continued)

refinancing opportunities for the issuers of the ARS. The analysis then assessed the likelihood that the options would be exercisable as a result of the underlying ARS being redeemed or traded in a secondary market at an amount greater than the exercise price prior to the end of the option term. Future changes in the fair values of the ARS Call Option will be recorded within the Consolidated Statements of Operations.

The reconciliation of our assets measured at fair value on a recurring basis using unobservable inputs (Level 3) is as follows:

| | | Level 3 (Unobservable inputs) | | | |
	Total	Auction-Rate Municipal Securities	Student Loan-Backed Auction-Rate Securities	Auction-Rate Preferred Securities	ARS Call Option
			(In thousands)		
Balance at January 30, 2010	$ 202,448	$ 40,244	$ 149,431	$ 12,773	$ —
Settlements	(177,472)	(29,101)	(141,246)	(7,125)	—
Gains and (losses):					
Reported in earnings	(25,674)	(2,399)	(16,755)	(6,935)	415
Reported in OCI	10,313	456	8,570	1,287	—
Balance at January 29, 2011	$ 9,615	$ 9,200	$ —	$ —	$ 415
Settlements	(3,700)	(3,700)	—	—	—
Gains and (losses):					
Reported in earnings	432	—			432
Balance at January 28, 2012	$ 6,347	$ 5,500	$ —	$ —	$ 847

Non-Financial Assets

The Company's non-financial assets, which include goodwill, intangible assets and property and equipment, are not required to be measured at fair value on a recurring basis. However, if certain triggering events occur, or if an annual impairment test is required and the Company is required to evaluate the non-financial instrument for impairment, a resulting asset impairment would require that the non-financial asset be recorded at the estimated fair value. As a result of the Company's annual goodwill impairment test performed as of January 28, 2012, the Company concluded that its goodwill was not impaired.

Certain long-lived assets were measured at fair value on a nonrecurring basis using Level 3 inputs as defined in ASC 820. During Fiscal 2011, certain long-lived assets related to the Company's retail stores were determined to be unable to recover their respective carrying values and were written down to their fair value, resulting in a loss of $20.7 million, which is recorded as a loss on impairment of assets within the Consolidated Statements of Operations.

Additionally, based on the Company's decision to close all M+O stores in Fiscal 2010, the Company determined that the M+O stores not previously impaired would not be able to generate sufficient cash flow over the life of the related leases to recover the Company's initial investment in them. Therefore, during Fiscal 2010, the M+O stores not previously impaired were written down to their fair value, resulting in a loss on impairment of assets of $18.0 million. During Fiscal 2009, certain long-lived assets primarily related to M+O stores were determined to be unable to recover their respective carrying values and were written down to their fair value, resulting in a loss on impairment of assets of $18.0 million. The loss on impairment of M+O assets for all periods presented is included within Loss from Discontinued Operations.

The fair value of the Company's stores were determined by estimating the amount and timing of net future cash flows and discounting them using a risk-adjusted rate of interest. The Company estimates future cash flows based on its experience and knowledge of the market in which the store is located.

Refer to Note 15 to the Consolidated Financial Statements for additional information regarding the discontinued operations for M+O.

5.   Earnings per Share

The following is a reconciliation between basic and diluted weighted average shares outstanding:

| | For the Years Ended | | |
	January 28, 2012	January 29, 2011	January 30, 2010
	(In thousands, except per share amounts)		
Weighted average common shares outstanding:			
Basic number of common shares outstanding	194,445	199,979	206,171
Dilutive effect of stock options and non-vested restricted stock	1,869	1,839	3,341
Dilutive number of common shares outstanding	196,314	201,818	209,512

Equity awards to purchase approximately 7.2 million, 7.9 million and 6.6 million shares of common stock during the Fiscal 2011, Fiscal 2010 and Fiscal 2009, respectively, were outstanding, but were not included in the computation of weighted average diluted common share amounts as the effect of doing so would have been anti-dilutive.

AMERICAN EAGLE OUTFITTERS, INC.

NOTES TO CONSOLIDATED FINANCIAL STATEMENTS — (Continued)

Additionally, for Fiscal 2011, Fiscal 2010 and Fiscal 2009, approximately 1.9 million, 0.7 million and 0.4 million shares, respectively, of performance-based restricted stock awards were not included in the computation of weighted average diluted common share amounts because the number of shares ultimately issued is contingent on the Company's performance compared to pre-established performance goals.

ASC 260-10-45, *Participating Securities and the Two-Class Method* ("ASC 260-10-45"), addresses whether awards granted in unvested share-based payment transactions that contain non-forfeitable rights to dividends or dividend equivalents (whether paid or unpaid) are participating securities and therefore are included in computing earnings per share under the two-class method, as described in ASC 260, *Earnings Per Share*. Participating securities are securities that may participate in dividends with common stock and the two-class method is an earnings allocation formula that treats a participating security as having rights to earnings that would otherwise have been available to common shareholders. Under the two-class method, earnings for the period are allocated between common shareholders and other shareholders, based on their respective rights to receive dividends. Restricted stock awards granted to certain employees under the Company's 2005 Plan are considered participating securities as these employees receive non-forfeitable dividends at the same rate as common stock. There were no participating securities outstanding during Fiscal 2011. During Fiscal 2010 and Fiscal 2009, the allocation of earnings to participating securities was not significant. For Fiscal 2011, Fiscal 2010 and Fiscal 2009, the application of ASC 260-10-45 resulted in no material change to basic or diluted income from continuing operations per common share.

Refer to Note 12 to the Consolidated Financial Statements for additional information regarding share-based compensation.

6.   Accounts Receivable

Accounts receivable are comprised of the following:

	January 28, 2012	January 29, 2011
	(In thousands)	
Franchise receivable	$ 20,108	$ 5,183
Marketing cost reimbursements	4,182	3,553
Gift card receivable	4,113	3,567
Landlord construction allowances	3,672	11,739
Insurance claims receivable	2,071	4,374
Merchandise sell-offs	1,955	4,539
Taxes	1,076	1,239
Other	3,133	2,527
Total	$ 40,310	$36,721

7.   Property and Equipment

Property and equipment consists of the following:

	January 28, 2012	January 29, 2011
	(In thousands)	
Land	$ 6,364	$ 6,364
Buildings	153,538	152,984
Leasehold improvements	638,496	624,479
Fixtures and equipment	656,337	647,346
Construction in progress	3,787	1,629
Property and equipment, at cost	$1,458,522	$1,432,802
Less: Accumulated depreciation	(876,360)	(789,682)
Property and equipment, net	$ 582,162	$ 643,120

Depreciation expense is summarized as follows:

	For the Years Ended		
	January 28, 2012	January 29, 2011	January 30, 2010
	(In thousands)		
Depreciation expense	$137,934	$139,169	$137,045

Additionally, during Fiscal 2011, Fiscal 2010 and Fiscal 2009, the Company recorded $3.4 million, $2.7 million and $2.3 million, respectively, related to asset write-offs within depreciation and amortization expense.

AMERICAN EAGLE OUTFITTERS, INC.

NOTES TO CONSOLIDATED FINANCIAL STATEMENTS — (Continued)

8.   Intangible Assets

Intangible assets include costs to acquire and register the Company's trademark assets. During the Fiscal 2011, the Company purchased $34.2 million of trademark assets primarily to support its international expansion strategy. The following table represents intangible assets as of January 28, 2012, and January 29, 2011:

	January 28, 2012	January 29, 2011
	(In thousands)	
Trademarks, at cost	$ 44,142	$ 9,967
Less: Accumulated amortization	(4,310)	(2,482)
Intangible assets, net	$ 39,832	$ 7,485

Amortization expense is summarized as follows:

	For the Years Ended		
	January 28, 2012	January 29, 2011	January 30, 2010
	(In thousands)		
Amortization expense	$ 1,828	$ 625	$ 509

The table below summarizes the estimated future amortization expense for intangible assets existing as of January 28, 2012, for the next five Fiscal Years:

	Future Amortization
	(In thousands)
2012	$ 1,961
2013	1,956
2014	1,956
2015	1,956
2016	1,911

9.   Other Credit Arrangements

The Company has borrowing agreements with four separate financial institutions under which it may borrow an aggregate of $245.0 million United States dollars ("USD") and $25.0 million Canadian dollars ("CAD"). Of this amount, $135.0 million USD can be used for letter of credit issuances, $50.0 million USD and $25.0 million CAD can be used for demand line borrowings and the remaining $60.0 million USD can be used for either letters of credit or demand line borrowings at the Company's discretion. These lines are provided at the discretion of the respective financial institutions and are subject to their periodic review.

As of January 28, 2012, the Company had outstanding letters of credit of $25.2 million USD and no demand line borrowings.

The availability of any future borrowings is subject to acceptance by the respective financial institutions.

Refer to Note 17 to the Consolidated Financial Statements for a subsequent event footnote related to the Company's credit facilities.

AMERICAN EAGLE OUTFITTERS, INC.

NOTES TO CONSOLIDATED FINANCIAL STATEMENTS — (Continued)

10. Leases

The Company leases all store premises, some of its office space and certain information technology and office equipment. The store leases generally have initial terms of 10 years and are classified as operating leases. Most of these store leases provide for base rentals and the payment of a percentage of sales as additional contingent rent when sales exceed specified levels. Additionally, most leases contain construction allowances and/or rent holidays. In recognizing landlord incentives and minimum rent expense, the Company amortizes the items on a straight-line basis over the lease term (including the pre-opening build-out period).

A summary of fixed minimum and contingent rent expense for all operating leases follows:

	For the Years Ended		
	January 28, 2012	January 29, 2011	January 30, 2010
	(In thousands)		
Store rent:			
Fixed minimum	$251,504	$230,277	$218,785
Contingent	7,618	8,182	7,873
Total store rent, excluding common area maintenance charges, real estate taxes and certain other expenses	$259,122	$238,459	$226,658
Offices, distribution facilities, equipment and other	17,405	16,722	17,391
Total rent expense	$276,527	$255,181	$244,049

In addition, the Company is typically responsible under its store, office and distribution center leases for tenant occupancy costs, including maintenance costs, common area charges, real estate taxes and certain other expenses.

The table below summarizes future minimum lease obligations, consisting of fixed minimum rent, under operating leases in effect at January 28, 2012:

Fiscal years:	Future Minimum Lease Obligations
	(In thousands)
2012	$ 255,576
2013	241,878
2014	222,931
2015	207,248
2016	183,881
Thereafter	612,557
Total	$1,724,071

AMERICAN EAGLE OUTFITTERS, INC.

NOTES TO CONSOLIDATED FINANCIAL STATEMENTS — (Continued)

11.   Other Comprehensive Income (Loss)

The accumulated balances of other comprehensive (loss) income included as part of the Consolidated Statements of Stockholders' Equity follow:

	Before Tax Amount	Tax Benefit (Expense)	Accumulated Other Comprehensive (Loss) Income
		(In thousands)	
Balance at January 31, 2009	**$(27,835)**	**$ 13,446**	**$(14,389)**
Temporary reversal of impairment related to ARS	24,041	(9,535)	14,506
Reclassification adjustment for realized losses in net income related to investment securities	940	—	940
Foreign currency translation gain	15,781	—	15,781
Balance at January 30, 2010	**$ 12,927**	**$ 3,911**	**$ 16,838**
Temporary impairment related to ARS	(1,830)	690	(1,140)
Reclassification adjustment for realized losses in net income related to investment securities	12,142	(4,601)	7,541
Foreign currency translation gain	4,833	—	4,833
Balance at January 29, 2011	**$ 28,072**	**$ —**	**$ 28,072**
Foreign currency translation gain	587	—	587
Balance at January 28, 2012	**$ 28,659**	**$ —**	**$ 28,659**

Accumulated other comprehensive income consists only of foreign currency translation adjustment as of January 28, 2012, and January 29, 2011.

12.   Share-Based Payments

The Company accounts for share-based compensation under the provisions of ASC 718, *Compensation — Stock Compensation* ("ASC 718"), which requires the Company to measure and recognize compensation expense for all share-based payments at fair value. Total share-based compensation expense included in the Consolidated Statements of Operations for Fiscal 2011, Fiscal 2010 and Fiscal 2009 was $12.3 million ($7.6 million, net of tax), $25.5 million ($15.7 million, net of tax) and $34.6 million ($21.4 million, net of tax), respectively.

ASC 718 requires recognition of compensation cost under a non-substantive vesting period approach for awards containing provisions that accelerate or continue vesting upon retirement. Accordingly, for awards with such provisions, the Company recognizes compensation expense over the period from the grant date to the date retirement eligibility is achieved, if that is expected to occur during the nominal vesting period. Additionally, for awards granted to retirement eligible employees, the full compensation cost of an award must be recognized immediately upon grant.

At January 28, 2012, the Company had awards outstanding under three share-based compensation plans, which are described below.

Share-based compensation plans

1994 Stock Option Plan

On February 10, 1994, the Company's Board adopted the American Eagle Outfitters, Inc., 1994 Stock Option Plan (the "1994 Plan"). The 1994 Plan provided for the grant of 12.2 million incentive or non-qualified options to purchase common stock. The 1994 Plan was subsequently amended to increase the shares available for grant to 24.3 million shares. Additionally, the amendment provided that the maximum number of options that may be granted to any individual may not exceed 8.1 million shares. The options granted under the 1994 Plan were approved by the Compensation Committee of the Board, primarily vest over five years, and expire 10 years from the date of grant. The 1994 Plan terminated on January 2, 2004, with all rights of the optionees and all unexpired options continuing in force and operation after the termination.

1999 Stock Incentive Plan

The 1999 Stock Option Plan (the "1999 Plan") was approved by the stockholders on June 8, 1999. The 1999 Plan authorized 18.0 million shares for issuance in the form of stock options, stock appreciation rights ("SAR"), restricted stock awards, performance units or performance shares. The 1999 Plan was subsequently amended to increase the shares available for grant to 33.0 million. Additionally, the 1999 Plan provided that the maximum number of shares awarded to any individual may not exceed 9.0 million shares. The 1999 Plan allowed the Compensation Committee to determine which employees and consultants received awards and the terms and conditions of these awards. The 1999 Plan provided for a grant of 1,875 stock options quarterly (not to be adjusted for stock splits) to each director who is not an officer or employee of the Company starting in August 2003. The Company ceased making these quarterly stock option grants in June 2005. Under this plan, 33.2 million non-qualified stock options and 6.7 million shares of restricted stock were granted to employees and certain non-employees (without considering cancellations to date of awards for 9.7 million shares). Approximately 33% of the options granted were to vest over eight years after the date of grant but were accelerated as the Company met annual performance goals. Approximately 34% of the options granted under the 1999 Plan vest over three years, 23% vest over five years and the remaining grants vest over one year. All options expire after 10 years. Performance-based restricted stock was earned if the Company met established performance goals. The 1999 Plan terminated on June 15, 2005, with all rights of the awardees and all unexpired awards continuing in force and operation after the termination.

AMERICAN EAGLE OUTFITTERS, INC.

NOTES TO CONSOLIDATED FINANCIAL STATEMENTS — (Continued)

2005 Stock Award and Incentive Plan

The 2005 Plan was approved by the stockholders on June 15, 2005. The 2005 Plan authorized 18.4 million shares for issuance, of which 6.4 million shares are available for full value awards in the form of restricted stock awards, restricted stock units or other full value stock awards and 12.0 million shares are available for stock options, SAR, dividend equivalents, performance awards or other non-full value stock awards. The 2005 Plan was subsequently amended in Fiscal 2009 to increase the shares available for grant to 31.9 million without taking into consideration 9.1 million non-qualified stock options, 2.9 million shares of restricted stock and 0.2 million shares of common stock that had been previously granted under the 2005 plan to employees and directors (without considering cancellations as of January 31, 2009, of awards for 2.9 million shares). The 2005 Plan provides that the maximum number of shares awarded to any individual may not exceed 6.0 million shares per year for options and SAR and no more than 4.0 million shares may be granted with respect to each of restricted shares of stock and restricted stock units plus any unused carryover limit from the previous year. The 2005 Plan allows the Compensation Committee of the Board to determine which employees receive awards and the terms and conditions of the awards that are mandatory under the 2005 Plan. The 2005 Plan provides for grants to directors who are not officers or employees of the Company, which are not to exceed 20,000 shares per year (not to be adjusted for stock splits). Through January 28, 2012, 14.4 million non-qualified stock options, 8.0 million shares of restricted stock and 0.5 million shares of common stock had been granted under the 2005 Plan to employees and directors (without considering cancellations to date of awards for 7.5 million shares). Approximately 99% of the options granted under the 2005 Plan vest over three years and 1% vest over five years. Options were granted for ten and seven year terms. Approximately 62% of the restricted stock awards are performance-based and are earned if the Company meets established performance goals. The remaining 38% of the restricted stock awards are time-based and vest over three years.

Stock Option Grants

The Company grants both time-based and performance-based stock options under the 2005 Plan. Time-based stock option awards vest over the requisite service period of the award or to an employee's eligible retirement date, if earlier. Performance-based stock option awards vest over three years and are earned if the Company meets pre-established performance goals during each year.

A summary of the Company's stock option activity under all plans for Fiscal 2011 follows:

	For the Year Ended January 28, 2012			
	Options	Weighted-Average Exercise Price	Weighted-Average Remaining Contractual Term	Aggregate Intrinsic Value
	(In thousands)		(In years)	(In thousands)
Outstanding — January 29, 2011	12,124	$15.25		
Granted	47	$15.02		
Exercised(1)	(544)	$9.38		
Cancelled	(430)	$21.18		
Outstanding — January 28, 2012	11,197	$15.31	2.2	$29,567
Vested and expected to vest — January 28, 2012	11,077	$15.33	2.2	$29,303
Exercisable — January 28, 2012(2)	3,691	$6.87	1.5	$26,264

(1) Options exercised during Fiscal 2011 ranged in price from $4.54 to $12.30.

(2) Options exercisable represent "in-the-money" vested options based upon the weighted average exercise price of vested options compared to the Company's stock price at January 28, 2012.

The weighted-average grant date fair value of stock options granted during Fiscal 2011, Fiscal 2010 and Fiscal 2009 was $4.73, $5.19 and $3.86, respectively. The aggregate intrinsic value of options exercised during Fiscal 2011, Fiscal 2010 and Fiscal 2009 was $2.8 million, $11.7 million and $11.7 million, respectively. Cash received from the exercise of stock options and the actual tax benefit realized from share-based payments was $5.1 million and $0.4 million, respectively, for Fiscal 2011. Cash received from the exercise of stock options and the actual tax benefit realized from share-based payments was $7.3 million and $15.6 million, respectively, for Fiscal 2010. Cash received from the exercise of stock options and the actual tax benefit realized from share-based payments was $9.0 million and $8.0 million, respectively, for Fiscal 2009.

The fair value of stock options was estimated at the date of grant using a Black-Scholes option pricing model with the following weighted-average assumptions:

	For the Years Ended		
Black-Scholes Option Valuation Assumptions	January 28, 2012	January 29, 2011	January 30, 2010
Risk-free interest rates(1)	2.1%	2.3%	1.7%
Dividend yield	2.6%	2.1%	3.4%
Volatility factors of the expected market price of the Company's common stock(2)	42.7%	40.2%	56.9%
Weighted-average expected term(3)	5.0 years	4.5 years	4.1 years
Expected forfeiture rate(4)	8.0%	8.0%	8.0%

AMERICAN EAGLE OUTFITTERS, INC.

NOTES TO CONSOLIDATED FINANCIAL STATEMENTS — (Continued)

(1)   Based on the U.S. Treasury yield curve in effect at the time of grant with a term consistent with the expected life of our stock options.

(2)   Based on a combination of historical volatility of the Company's common stock and implied volatility.

(3)   Represents the period of time options are expected to be outstanding. The weighted average expected option term for the years ended January 28, 2012, January 29, 2011, and January 30, 2010, were determined based on historical experience.

(4)   Based on historical experience.

As of January 28, 2012, there was $1.3 million of unrecognized compensation expense related to nonvested stock option awards that is expected to be recognized over a weighted average period of 11 months.

Restricted Stock Grants

Time-based restricted stock awards are comprised of time-based restricted stock units. These awards vest over three years; however, they may be accelerated to vest over one year if the Company meets pre-established performance goals in the year of grant. Time-based restricted stock units receive dividend equivalents in the form of additional time-based restricted stock units, which are subject to the same restrictions and forfeiture provisions as the original award.

Performance-based restricted stock awards include performance-based restricted stock units. These awards cliff vest at the end of a three year period based upon the Company's achievement of pre-established goals throughout the term of the award. Performance-based restricted stock units receive dividend equivalents in the form of additional performance-based restricted stock units, which are subject to the same restrictions and forfeiture provisions as the original award.

The grant date fair value of all restricted stock awards is based on the closing market price of the Company's common stock on the date of grant.

A summary of the activity of the Company's restricted stock is presented in the following tables:

	Time-Based Restricted Stock Units For the year ended January 28, 2012		Performance-Based Restricted Stock Units For the year ended January 28, 2012	
	Shares	Weighted-Average Grant Date Fair Value	Shares	Weighted-Average Grant Date Fair Value
	(Shares in thousands)			
Nonvested — January 29, 2011	877	$17.45	630	$12.59
Granted	1,406	15.03	1,240	15.03
Vested	(372)	17.45	—	—
Cancelled/Forfeited	(127)	16.04	(108)	12.64
Nonvested — January 28, 2012	1,784	$15.73	1,762	$ 14.23

As of January 28, 2012, there was $17.3 million of unrecognized compensation expense related to nonvested time-based restricted stock unit awards that is expected to be recognized over a weighted average period of 1.8 years. The total fair value of restricted stock awards vested during Fiscal 2011, Fiscal 2010 and Fiscal 2009 was $5.6 million, $46.2 million and $0.6 million, respectively.

As of January 28, 2012, the Company had 25.3 million shares available for all equity grants.

13. Retirement Plan and Employee Stock Purchase Plan

The Company maintains a profit sharing and 401(k) plan (the "Retirement Plan"). Under the provisions of the Retirement Plan, full-time employees and part-time employees are automatically enrolled to contribute 3% of their salary if they have attained 20 1/2 years of age. In addition, full-time employees need to have completed 60 days of service and part-time employees must complete 1,000 hours worked to be eligible. Individuals can decline enrollment or can contribute up to 50% of their salary to the 401(k) plan on a pretax basis, subject to IRS limitations. After one year of service, the Company will match 100% of the first 3% of pay plus an additional 50% of the next 3% of pay that is contributed to the plan. Contributions to the profit sharing plan, as determined by the Board, are discretionary. The Company recognized $9.1 million, $11.7 million and $5.9 million in expense during Fiscal 2011, Fiscal 2010 and Fiscal 2009, respectively, in connection with the Retirement Plan.

The Employee Stock Purchase Plan is a non-qualified plan that covers all full-time employees and part-time employees who are at least 18 years old and have completed 60 days of service. Contributions are determined by the employee, with the Company matching 15% of the investment up to a maximum investment of $100 per pay period. These contributions are used to purchase shares of Company stock in the open market.

AMERICAN EAGLE OUTFITTERS, INC.

NOTES TO CONSOLIDATED FINANCIAL STATEMENTS — (Continued)

14. Income Taxes

The components of income before income taxes from continuing operations were:

	For the Years Ended		
	January 28, 2012	January 29, 2011	January 30, 2010
	(In thousands)		
U.S.	$218,153	$258,408	$269,932
Foreign	18,857	36,676	34,443
Total	$237,010	$295,084	$304,375

The significant components of the Company's deferred tax assets and liabilities were as follows:

	January 28, 2012	January 29, 2011
	(In thousands)	
Deferred tax assets:		
Deferred compensation	$ 31,379	$ 30,801
Rent	27,642	25,145
Foreign tax credits	22,302	25,498
Capital loss carryforward	18,440	20,381
Inventories	11,734	10,432
Foreign and state income taxes	6,723	7,575
Employee compensation and benefits	6,345	4,942
State tax credits	6,105	5,866
Other	9,650	8,547
Gross deferred tax assets	140,320	139,187
Valuation allowance	(18,440)	(20,381)
Total deferred tax assets	$ 121,880	$118,806
Deferred tax liabilities:		
Property and equipment	$ (55,503)	$ (47,852)
Prepaid expenses	(4,149)	(3,279)
Total deferred tax liabilities	$(59,652)	$ (51,131)
Total deferred tax assets, net	$ 62,228	$ 67,675
Classification in the Consolidated Balance Sheet:		
Current deferred tax assets	$ 48,761	$ 48,059
Noncurrent deferred tax assets	13,467	19,616
Total deferred tax assets	$ 62,228	$ 67,675

The net decrease in deferred tax assets and liabilities was primarily due to an increase in the deferred tax liability for property and equipment basis differences.

Significant components of the provision for income taxes from continuing operations were as follows:

	For the Years Ended		
	January 28, 2012	January 29, 2011	January 30, 2010
	(In thousands)		
Current:			
Federal	$63,631	$ 89,110	$ 92,074
Foreign taxes	6,621	13,429	14,526
State	10,841	9,610	13,575
Total current	81,093	112,149	120,175
Deferred:			
Federal	$ 7,158	$ (310)	$ (32,361)
Foreign taxes	(1,120)	(991)	6,513
State	(1,826)	2,302	(3,350)
Total deferred	4,212	1,001	(29,198)
Provision for income taxes	$85,305	$113,150	$ 90,977

AMERICAN EAGLE OUTFITTERS, INC.

NOTES TO CONSOLIDATED FINANCIAL STATEMENTS — (Continued)

As a result of additional tax deductions related to share-based payments, tax benefits have been recognized as contributed capital for Fiscal 2011, Fiscal 2010 and Fiscal 2009 in the amounts of $0.4 million, $15.6 million and $8.0 million, respectively.

During Fiscal 2009, the Company approved and repatriated $91.7 million from its Canadian subsidiaries. The proceeds from the repatriation were used for general corporate purposes. The Company plans to indefinitely reinvest accumulated earnings of our Canadian subsidiaries outside of the United States to the extent not repatriated in Fiscal 2009. Accordingly, no provision for U.S. income taxes has been provided thereon. Upon distribution of those earnings in the form of dividends or otherwise, the Company would be subject to income and withholding taxes offset by foreign tax credits. As of January 28, 2012, and January 29, 2011, the unremitted earnings of our Canadian subsidiaries were $72.0 million (USD) and $57.1 million (USD), respectively.

As of January 28, 2012, the gross amount of unrecognized tax benfits was $31.6 million, of which $22.8 million would affect the effective income tax rate if recognized. The gross amount of unrecognized tax benefits as of January 29, 2011, was $31.1 million, of which $22.7 million would affect the effective income tax rate if recognized.

The following table summarizes the activity related to our unrecognized tax benefits:

	For the Years Ended		
	January 28, 2012	January 29, 2011	January 30, 2010
	(In thousands)		
Unrecognized tax benefits, beginning of the year balance	$ 31,108	$31,649	$ 41,080
Increases in tax positions of prior periods	932	1,069	1,679
Decreases in tax positions of prior periods	(2,106)	(3,801)	(13,457)
Increases in current period tax positions	2,782	2,707	14,842
Settlements	(1,073)	(6)	(6,204)
Lapse of statute of limitations	(65)	(510)	(6,291)
Unrecognized tax benefits, end of the year balance	$31,578	$ 31,108	$31,649

Unrecognized tax benefits increased by $0.5 million during Fiscal 2011 and decreased by $0.5 million during Fiscal 2010. Over the next twelve months the Company believes that it is reasonably possible that unrecognized tax benefits may decrease by approximately $2.9 million due to settlements, expiration of statute of limitations or other changes in unrecognized tax benefits.

The Company records accrued interest and penalties related to unrecognized tax benefits in income tax expense. Accrued interest and penalties related to unrecognized tax benefits included in the Consolidated Balance Sheet were $7.9 million and $7.6 million as of January 28, 2012, and January 29, 2011, respectively. During Fiscal 2009, the Company recognized a net benefit of $3.3 million in the provision for income taxes related to the reversal of accrued interest and penalties primarily due to federal and state income tax settlements. An immaterial amount of interest and penalties were recognized in the provision for income taxes during Fiscal 2011 and Fiscal 2010.

The Company and its subsidiaries file income tax returns in the U.S. federal jurisdiction and various state and foreign jurisdictions. The Internal Revenue Service ("IRS") examination of the Company's U.S. federal income tax returns for the tax years ended July 2008 and January 2009 was completed in April of 2011. Accordingly, all years prior to January 2010 are no longer subject to U.S. federal income tax examinations by tax authorities. An IRS examination of the January 2010 federal income tax return is scheduled to be completed in Fiscal 2012. The Company does not anticipate that any adjustments will result in a material change to its financial position, results of operations or cash flow. With respect to state and local jurisdictions and countries outside of the United States, with limited exceptions, generally, the Company and its subsidiaries are no longer subject to income tax audits for tax years before 2005. Although the outcome of tax audits is always uncertain, the Company believes that adequate amounts of tax, interest and penalties have been provided for any adjustments that are expected to result from these years.

The Company has foreign tax credit carryovers in the amount of $22.3 million and $25.5 million as of January 28, 2012, and January 29, 2011 respectively. The foreign tax credit carryovers expire in Fiscal 2019 to the extent not utilized. No valuation allowance has been recorded on the foreign tax credit carryovers as the Company believes it is more likely than not the foreign tax credits will be utilized prior to expiration.

The Company has been certified to qualify for nonrefundable incentive tax credits in Kansas for additional expenditures related to the Ottawa, Kansas, distribution center. As a result, the Company has a deferred tax asset related to Kansas tax credit carryforwards of $6.1 million (net of federal income taxes) as of January 28, 2012. These tax credits can be utilized to offset future Kansas income taxes and have a carryforward period of 10-16 years. They will begin to expire in Fiscal 2018. Due to a favorable incentive agreement with the Kansas Department of Commerce in Fiscal 2010, the Company released a $5.0 million valuation allowance that had been previously recorded related to the Company's Kansas tax credit carryforward.

During Fiscal 2010 and 2009, the Company recorded a valuation allowance against deferred tax assets arising from the disposition or other than temporary impairment of certain investment securities. The disposition of the investment securities results in a capital loss that can only be utilized to the extent of capital gains. These capital losses are subject to a three year carryback period and a five year carryforward period for tax purposes. The capital losses generally will expire in Fiscal 2014 through Fiscal 2015. Due to the contingencies related to the future use of these capital losses, we believe it is more likely than not that the full benefit of this asset will not be realized within the carryforward period. Thus, the Company has recorded a valuation allowance against the deferred tax assets arising from the other than temporary impairment or disposition of these investment securities. The valuation allowance related to these investment securities was $18.4 million and $20.4 million as of January 28, 2012, and January 29, 2011, respectively.

AMERICAN EAGLE OUTFITTERS, INC.

NOTES TO CONSOLIDATED FINANCIAL STATEMENTS — (Continued)

A reconciliation between the statutory federal income tax rate and the effective income tax rate from continuing operations follows:

	For the Years Ended		
	January 28, 2012	January 29, 2011	January 30, 2010
Federal income tax rate	35%	35%	35%
State income taxes, net of federal income tax effect	3	3	3
Valuation allowance changes, net	(1)	1	1
Tax settlements	(1)	(1)	(4)
Canadian earnings repatriation	—	—	(5)
	36%	38%	30%

15. Discontinued Operations

On March 5, 2010, the Company's Board approved management's recommendation to proceed with the closure of the M+O brand. The Company completed the closure of the M+O stores and e-commerce operation during the second quarter of Fiscal 2010. These Consolidated Financial Statements reflect the results of M+O as discontinued operations for all periods presented.

Costs associated with exit or disposal activities are recorded when incurred. A summary of the exit and disposal costs recognized within Loss from Discontinued Operations on the Consolidated Income Statement for Fiscal 2010 are included in the table as follows. There were no exit or disposal costs recognized in Fiscal 2011 or Fiscal 2009. The Loss from Discontinued Operations for Fiscal 2010 and Fiscal 2009 includes pre-tax asset impairment charges of $18.0 million in both years.

	For the Year Ended January 29, 2011
	(In thousands)
Non-cash charges	
Asset impairments	$17,980
Cash charges	
Lease-related charges(1)	15,377
Inventory charges	2,422
Severence charges	7,660
Total charges	$43,439

(1)   Presented net of the reversal of non-cash lease credits.

The table below presents the significant components of M+O's results included in Loss from Discontinued Operations on the Consolidated Statements of Operations for the years ended January 29, 2011, and January 30, 2010, respectively. There was no loss from discontinued operations for the year ended January 28, 2012.

	For the Years Ended	
	January 29, 2011	January 30, 2010
	(In thousands)	
Net sales	$ 21,881	$ 50,251
Loss from discontinued operations, before income taxes	$(66,959)	$(71,984)
Income tax benefit	25,672	27,608
Loss from discontinued operations, net of tax	$ (41,287)	$ (44,376)
Loss per common share from discontinued operations:		
Basic	$ (0.21)	$ (0.22)
Diluted	$ (0.20)	$ (0.21)

There were no assets or liabilities included in the Consolidated Balance Sheets for M+O as of January 28, 2012, or January 29, 2011.

AMERICAN EAGLE OUTFITTERS, INC.

NOTES TO CONSOLIDATED FINANCIAL STATEMENTS — (Continued)

16.   Quarterly Financial Information — Unaudited

The sum of the quarterly EPS amounts may not equal the full year amount as the computations of the weighted average shares outstanding for each quarter and the full year are calculated independently.

	Fiscal 2011 Quarters Ended			
	April 30, 2011	July 30, 2011	October 29, 2011	January 28, 2012
	(In thousands, except per share amounts)			
Net sales	$609,562	$675,703	$831,826	$1,042,727
Gross profit	$231,761	$232,061	$308,967	$355,552
Income from continuing operations	28,325	19,669	52,427	51,284
Loss from discontinued operations	—	—	—	—
Net income	$ 28,325	$ 19,669	$ 52,427	$ 51,284
Basic per common share amounts:				
Income from continuing operations	$ 0.15	$ 0.10	$ 0.27	$ 0.26
Loss from discontinued operations	—	—	—	—
Basic net income per common share	$ 0.15	$ 0.10	$ 0.27	$ 0.26
Diluted per common share amounts:				
Income from continuing operations	$ 0.14	$ 0.10	$ 0.27	$ 0.26
Loss from discontinued operations	—	—	—	—
Diluted net income per common share	$ 0.14	$ 0.10	$ 0.27	$ 0.26

	Fiscal 2010 Quarters Ended			
	May 1, 2010	July 31, 2010	October 30, 2010	January 29, 2011
	(In thousands, except per share amounts)			
Net sales	$648,462	$651,502	$751,507	$916,088
Gross profit	$257,696	$239,708	$312,309	$361,246
Income from continuing operations	35,862	25,843	33,191	87,038
Loss from discontinued operations	(24,940)	(16,180)	(167)	—
Net income	$ 10,922	$ 9,663	$ 33,024	$ 87,038
Basic per common share amounts:				
Income from continuing operations	$ 0.17	$ 0.13	$ 0.17	$ 0.45
Loss from discontinued operations	(0.12)	(0.08)	—	—
Basic net income per common share	$ 0.05	$ 0.05	$ 0.17	$ 0.45
Diluted per common share amounts:				
Income from continuing operations	$ 0.17	$ 0.13	$ 0.17	$ 0.44
Loss from discontinued operations	(0.12)	(0.08)	—	—
Diluted net income per common share	$ 0.05	$ 0.05	$ 0.17	$ 0.44

17.   Subsequent Events

On March 2, 2012, the Company entered into a five-year, $150.0 million syndicated, unsecured, revolving credit agreement (the "Credit Agreement"). The primary purpose of the Credit Agreement is to provide additional access to capital for general corporate purposes and the issuance of letters of credit. The Credit Agreement replaced the uncommitted demand lines in the aggregate amount of $110.0 million USD and $25.0 million CAD.

The Credit Agreement will mature on March 2, 2017. Stand-by letters of credit totaling approximately $8.5 million were outstanding under the Credit Agreement on March 15, 2012. No borrowings were outstanding under the Credit Agreement on March 15, 2012.

Refer to Note 9 to the Consolidated Financial Statements for additional information regarding other credit arrangements.

UNITED STATES
SECURITIES AND EXCHANGE COMMISSION
Washington, DC 20549

FORM 10-K

☒ **ANNUAL REPORT PURSUANT TO SECTION 13 OR 15(d) OF THE SECURITIES EXCHANGE ACT OF 1934**

For the fiscal year ended January 31, 2012

☐ **TRANSITION REPORT PURSUANT TO SECTION 13 OR 15(d) OF THE SECURITIES EXCHANGE ACT OF 1934**

For the transition period from   to

Commission File No. 000-22754

URBAN OUTFITTERS, INC.
(Exact Name of Registrant as Specified in Its Charter)

Pennsylvania	**23-2003332**
(State or Other Jurisdiction of Incorporation or Organization)	(I.R.S. Employer Identification No.)
5000 South Broad Street, Philadelphia, PA	**19112-1495**
(Address of Principal Executive Offices)	(Zip Code)

Registrant's telephone number, including area code: (215) 454-5500
Securities registered pursuant to Section 12(b) of the Act:

Title of Each Class	Name of Exchange on Which Registered
Common Shares, $.0001 par value	**The NASDAQ Global Select Market LLC**

Securities registered pursuant to Section 12(g) of the Act: None

Indicate by checkmark if the registrant is a well-known seasoned issuer, as defined in Rule 405 of the Securities Act.   Yes ☒   No ☐

Indicate by checkmark if the registrant is not required to file reports pursuant to Section 13 or Section 15(d) of the Act.   Yes ☐   No ☒

Indicate by checkmark whether the registrant (1) has filed all reports required to be filed by Section 13 or 15(d) of the Securities Exchange Act of 1934 during the preceding 12 months (or for such shorter period that the registrant was required to file such reports), and (2) has been subject to such filing requirements for the past 90 days.   Yes ☒   No ☐

Indicate by check mark whether the registrant has submitted electronically and posted on its corporate website, if any, every Interactive Data File required to be submitted and posted pursuant to Rule 405 of Regulation S-T during the preceding 12 months (or for such shorter period that the registrant was required to submit and post such files).   Yes ☒   No ☐

Indicate by checkmark if disclosure of delinquent filers pursuant to Item 405 of Regulation S-K is not contained herein, and will not be contained, to the best of Registrant's knowledge, in definitive proxy or information statements incorporated by reference in Part III of this Form 10-K or any amendment to this Form 10-K. ☒

Indicate by checkmark whether the registrant is a large accelerated filer, an accelerated filer, a non-accelerated filer, or a smaller reporting company. See the definitions of "large accelerated filer," "accelerated filer" and "smaller reporting company" in Rule 12b-2 of the Exchange Act.

Large accelerated filer ☒   Accelerated filer ☐
Non-accelerated filer ☐ (Do not check if a smaller reporting company   Smaller reporting company ☐

Indicate by a checkmark whether the registrant is a shell company (as defined in Rule 12b-2 of the Act).   Yes ☐   No ☒

The aggregate market value of the voting and non-voting common equity held by non-affiliates computed by reference to the price at which the common equity was last sold, or the average bid and asked price of such common equity, as of the last business day of the registrant's most recently completed second fiscal quarter, was $3,956,641,654.

The number of shares outstanding of the registrant's common stock on March 27, 2012, was 144,706,907.

DOCUMENTS INCORPORATED BY REFERENCE

Certain information required by Items 10, 11, 12, 13 and 14 is incorporated by reference into Part III hereof from portions of the Proxy Statement for the registrant's 2012 Annual Meeting of Shareholders.

REPORT OF INDEPENDENT REGISTERED PUBLIC ACCOUNTING FIRM

To the Board of Directors and Shareholders of
Urban Outfitters, Inc.
Philadelphia, Pennsylvania

We have audited the accompanying consolidated balance sheets of Urban Outfitters, Inc., and subsidiaries (the "Company") as of January 31, 2012, and 2011, and the related consolidated statements of income, shareholders' equity, and cash flows for each of the three years in the period ended January 31, 2012. These financial statements are the responsibility of the Company's management. Our responsibility is to express an opinion on these financial statements based on our audits.

We conducted our audits in accordance with the standards of the Public Company Accounting Oversight Board (United States). Those standards require that we plan and perform the audit to obtain reasonable assurance about whether the financial statements are free of material misstatement. An audit includes examining, on a test basis, evidence supporting the amounts and disclosures in the financial statements. An audit also includes assessing the accounting principles used and significant estimates made by management, as well as evaluating the overall financial statement presentation. We believe that our audits provide a reasonable basis for our opinion.

In our opinion, such consolidated financial statements present fairly, in all material respects, the financial position of Urban Outfitters, Inc., and subsidiaries as of January 31, 2012, and 2011, and the results of their operations and their cash flows for each of the three years in the period ended January 31, 2012, in conformity with accounting principles generally accepted in the United States of America.

We have also audited, in accordance with the standards of the Public Company Accounting Oversight Board (United States), the Company's internal control over financial reporting as of January 31, 2012, based on the criteria established in *Internal Control—Integrated Framework* issued by the Committee of Sponsoring Organizations of the Treadway Commission and our report dated April 2, 2012, expressed an unqualified opinion on the Company's internal control over financial reporting.

/s/ DELOITTE & TOUCHE LLP

Philadelphia, Pennsylvania
April 2, 2012

URBAN OUTFITTERS, INC.

Consolidated Balance Sheets
(in thousands, except share and per share data)

	January 31,	
	2012	2011
ASSETS		
Current assets:		
Cash and cash equivalents	$ 145,273	$ 340,257
Marketable securities	89,854	116,420
Accounts receivable, net of allowance for doubtful accounts of $1,614 and $1,015, respectively	36,673	36,502
Inventories	250,073	229,561
Prepaid expenses and other current assets	69,876	66,886
Deferred taxes	5,243	14,351
Total current assets	596,992	803,977
Property and equipment, net	684,979	586,346
Marketable securities	126,913	351,988
Deferred income taxes and other assets	74,824	52,010
Total Assets	$1,483,708	$1,794,321
LIABILITIES AND SHAREHOLDERS' EQUITY		
Current liabilities:		
Accounts payable	$ 95,754	$ 82,904
Accrued compensation	15,630	20,212
Accrued expenses and other current liabilities	122,082	107,908
Total current liabilities	233,466	211,024
Deferred rent and other liabilities	183,974	171,749
Total Liabilities	417,440	382,773
Commitments and contingencies (see Note 12)		
Shareholders' equity:		
Preferred shares; $.0001 par value, 10,000,000 shares authorized, none issued	—	—
Common shares; $.0001 par value, 200,000,000 shares authorized, 144,633,007 and 164,413,427 issued and outstanding, respectively	15	17
Additional paid-in capital	—	27,603
Retained earnings	1,077,765	1,394,190
Accumulated other comprehensive loss	(11,512)	(10,262)
Total Shareholders' Equity	1,066,268	1,411,548
Total Liabilities and Shareholders' Equity	$1,483,708	$1,794,321

The accompanying notes are an integral part of these consolidated financial statements.

URBAN OUTFITTERS, INC.

Consolidated Statements of Income
(in thousands, except share and per share data)

	Fiscal Year Ended January 31,		
	2012	2011	2010
Net sales	$ 2,473,801	$ 2,274,102	$ 1,937,815
Cost of sales, including certain buying, distribution and occupancy costs	1,613,265	1,337,482	1,151,670
Gross profit	860,536	936,620	786,145
Selling, general and administrative expenses	575,811	522,417	447,161
Income from operations	284,725	414,203	338,984
Interest income	5,120	4,669	6,290
Other income	553	486	463
Other expenses	(1,567)	(2,150)	(1,331)
Income before income taxes	288,831	417,208	344,406
Income tax expense	103,580	144,250	124,513
Net income	$ 185,251	$ 272,958	$ 219,893
Net income per common share:			
Basic	$ 1.20	$ 1.64	$ 1.31
Diluted	$ 1.19	$ 1.60	$ 1.28
Weighted average common shares outstanding:			
Basic	154,025,589	166,896,322	168,053,502
Diluted	156,191,289	170,333,550	171,230,245

The accompanying notes are an integral part of these consolidated financial statements.

URBAN OUTFITTERS, INC.

Consolidated Statements of Shareholders' Equity
(in thousands, except share data)

	Compre-hensive Income	Common Shares		Additional Paid-in Capital	Retained Earnings	Accumulated Other Compre-hensive Loss	Total
		Number of Shares	Par Value				
Balances as of January 31, 2009		167,712,088	$ 17	$ 170,166	$ 901,339	$ (17,747)	$1,053,775
Net income	$219,893	—	—	—	219,893	—	219,893
Foreign currency translation	7,173	—	—	—	—	7,173	7,173
Unrealized gains on marketable securities, net of tax	1,480	—	—	—	—	1,480	1,480
Comprehensive income	$228,546						
Share-based compensation		—	—	4,766	—	—	4,766
Stock options and awards		846,283	—	3,250	—	—	3,250
Tax effect of share exercises		—	—	6,438	—	—	6,438
Balances as of January 31, 2010		168,558,371	$ 17	$ 184,620	$1,121,232	$ (9,094)	$1,296,775
Net income	$272,958	—	—	—	272,958	—	272,958
Foreign currency translation	(429)	—	—	—	—	(429)	(429)
Unrealized losses on marketable securities, net of tax	(739)	—	—	—	—	(739)	(739)
Comprehensive income	$271,790						
Share-based compensation		—	—	10,725	—	—	10,725
Stock options and awards		2,256,273	—	24,129	—	—	24,129
Tax effect of share exercises		—	—	12,847	—	—	12,847
Share repurchases		(6,401,217)	—	(204,718)	—	—	(204,718)
Balances as of January 31, 2011		164,413,427	$ 17	$ 27,603	$1,394,190	$ (10,262)	$1,411,548
Net income	$185,251	—	—	—	185,251	—	185,251
Foreign currency translation	(2,285)	—	—	—	—	(2,285)	(2,285)
Unrealized gains on marketable securities, net of tax	1,035	—	—	—	—	1,035	1,035
Comprehensive income	$184,001						
Share-based compensation		—	—	3,068	—	—	3,068
Stock options and awards		993,923	—	4,134	—	—	4,134
Tax effect of share exercises		—	—	8,995	—	—	8,995
Share repurchases		(20,774,343)	(2)	(43,800)	(501,676)	—	(545,478)
Balances as of January 31, 2012		144,633,007	$ 15	$ —	$1,077,765	$ (11,512)	$1,066,268

The accompanying notes are an integral part of these consolidated financial statements.

URBAN OUTFITTERS, INC.

Consolidated Statements of Cash Flows
(in thousands)

	Fiscal Year Ended January 31,		
	2012	2011	2010
Cash flows from operating activities:			
Net income	$ 185,251	$ 272,958	$ 219,893
Adjustments to reconcile net income to net cash provided by operating activities:			
Depreciation and amortization	108,112	101,105	92,350
Provision for deferred income taxes	(12,150)	(8,727)	2,161
Excess tax benefit on share-based compensation	(8,995)	(12,847)	(6,438)
Share-based compensation expense	3,068	10,725	4,766
Loss on disposition of property and equipment, net	857	119	339
Changes in assets and liabilities:			
Receivables	(251)	1,835	(1,825)
Inventories	(20,817)	(43,372)	(15,544)
Prepaid expenses and other assets	6,317	14,825	(25,619)
Accounts payable, accrued expenses and other liabilities	21,310	48,492	55,311
Net cash provided by operating activities	282,702	385,113	325,394
Cash flows from investing activities:			
Cash paid for property and equipment	(190,010)	(143,642)	(109,260)
Cash paid for marketable securities	(169,467)	(463,129)	(806,546)
Sales and maturities of marketable securities	414,769	571,236	421,040
Net cash provided by (used in) investing activities	55,292	(35,535)	(494,766)
Cash flows from financing activities:			
Exercise of stock options	4,136	24,129	3,250
Excess tax benefit from stock option exercises	8,995	12,847	6,438
Share repurchases	(545,478)	(204,718)	—
Net cash (used in) provided by financing activities	(532,347)	(167,742)	9,688
Effect of exchange rate changes on cash and cash equivalents	(631)	(603)	2,673
(Decrease) increase in cash and cash equivalents	(194,984)	181,233	(157,011)
Cash and cash equivalents at beginning of period	340,257	159,024	316,035
Cash and cash equivalents at end of period	$ 145,273	$ 340,257	$ 159,024
Supplemental cash flow information:			
Cash paid during the year for:			
Income taxes	$ 120,847	$ 121,341	$ 137,490
Non-cash investing activities—Accrued capital expenditures	$ 21,955	$ 8,077	$ 12,960

The accompanying notes are an integral part of these consolidated financial statements.

URBAN OUTFITTERS, INC.

NOTES TO CONSOLIDATED FINANCIAL STATEMENTS
(in thousands, except share and per share data)

1. Nature of Business

Urban Outfitters, Inc. (the "Company" or "Urban Outfitters"), which was founded in 1970 and originally operated by a predecessor partnership, was incorporated in the Commonwealth of Pennsylvania in 1976. The principal business activity of the Company is the operation of a general consumer product retail and wholesale business selling to customers through various channels including retail stores, nine websites and five catalogs. As of January 31, 2012, and 2011, the Company operated 429 and 372 stores, respectively. Stores located in the United States totaled 381 as of January 31, 2012, and 334 as of January 31, 2011. Operations in Europe and Canada included 33 stores and 15 stores as of January 31, 2012, respectively and 24 stores and 14 stores as of January 31, 2011, respectively. In addition, the Company's wholesale segment sold and distributed apparel to approximately 1,400 better department and specialty retailers worldwide.

2. Summary of Significant Accounting Policies

Fiscal Year-End

The Company operates on a fiscal year ending January 31 of each year. All references to fiscal years of the Company refer to the fiscal years ended on January 31 in those years. For example, the Company's fiscal 2012 ended on January 31, 2012.

Principles of Consolidation

The Consolidated Financial Statements include the accounts of Urban Outfitters, Inc., and all of its subsidiaries. All inter-company transactions and accounts have been eliminated in consolidation.

Use of Estimates

The preparation of financial statements, in conformity with accounting principles generally accepted in the United States, requires management to make estimates and assumptions that affect the reported amounts of assets and liabilities and disclosure of contingent assets and liabilities at the date of the financial statements and the reported amounts of net sales and expenses during the reporting period. Actual results could differ from those estimates.

Cash and Cash Equivalents

Cash and cash equivalents are defined as cash and short-term highly liquid investments with maturities of less than three months at the time of purchase. These short-term highly liquid investments are both readily convertible to known amounts of cash and so near their maturity that they present insignificant risk of changes in value because of changes in interest rates. As of January 31, 2012, and 2011, cash and cash equivalents included cash on hand, cash in banks and money market accounts.

Marketable Securities

All of the Company's marketable securities as of January 31, 2012, and 2011, are classified as available-for-sale and are carried at fair value, which approximates amortized cost. Interest on these securities, as well as the amortization of discounts and premiums, is included in interest income in the Consolidated Statements of Income. Unrealized gains and losses on these securities are considered temporary and therefore are excluded from earnings and are reported in accumulated other comprehensive loss in shareholders' equity until realized. Other than temporary impairment losses related to credit losses are considered to be realized losses. When available-for-sale securities are sold, the cost of the securities is specifically identified and is used to determine the realized gain or loss. Securities classified as current have maturity dates of less than one year from the balance sheet date. Securities classified as non-current have maturity dates greater than one year from the balance sheet date. Available-for-sale securities, such as Auction Rate Securities ("ARS") that fail at auction and do not liquidate in the normal course, are classified as non-current assets.

The Company's ARS represent interests in municipal and student loan related collateralized debt obligations, all of which are rated "A" or better and are guaranteed by either government agencies and/or insured by private insurance agencies up to 97% or greater of par value. The Company's ARS had a fair value of $20.2 million as of January 31, 2012, and $29.5 million as of January 31, 2011. As of and subsequent to the end of the current fiscal year, all of the ARS held by the Company failed to liquidate at auction due to a lack of market demand. Liquidity for these ARS was historically provided by an auction process that resets the applicable interest rate at pre-determined intervals, usually 7, 28, 35 or 90 days. The principal associated with these failed auctions will not be available until a successful auction occurs, the bond is called by the issuer, a buyer is

URBAN OUTFITTERS, INC.

NOTES TO CONSOLIDATED FINANCIAL STATEMENTS—(Continued)
(in thousands, except share and per share data)

found from outside the auction process, or the debt obligation reaches its maturity. Based on review of credit quality, collateralization, final stated maturity, estimates of the probability of being called or becoming illiquid prior to final maturity, redemptions of similar ARS, previous market activity for same investment security, impact due to extended periods of maximum auction rates and valuation models, the Company has recorded $2.8 million and $3.8 million of temporary impairment on its ARS as of January 31, 2012, and January 31, 2011, respectively. To date the Company has collected all interest receivable on outstanding ARS when due and has not been informed by the issuers that accrued interest payments are currently at risk. The Company does not have the intent to sell the underlying securities prior to their recovery and the Company believes it is not likely that it will be required to sell the underlying securities prior to their anticipated recovery of full amortized cost. As a result of the current illiquidity, the Company has classified all ARS as non-current assets under marketable securities. The Company continues to monitor the market for ARS and consider the impact, if any, on the fair value of its investments.

Accounts Receivable

Accounts receivable primarily consists of amounts due from our wholesale customers as well as credit card receivables outstanding with third-party credit card vendors. The activity of the allowance for doubtful accounts for the years ended January 31, 2012, 2011, and 2010 was as follows:

	Balance at beginning of year	Additions	Deductions	Balance at end of year
Year ended January 31, 2012	$1,015	3,920	(3,321)	$1,614
Year ended January 31, 2011	$1,284	2,397	(2,666)	$1,015
Year ended January 31, 2010	$1,229	1,791	(1,736)	$1,284

Inventories

Inventories, which consist primarily of general consumer merchandise held for sale, are valued at the lower of cost or market. Cost is determined on the first-in, first-out method and includes the cost of merchandise and import related costs, including freight, import taxes and agent commissions. A periodic review of inventory is performed in order to determine if inventory is properly stated at the lower of cost or market. Factors related to current inventories such as future expected consumer demand and fashion trends, current aging, current and anticipated retail markdowns or wholesale discounts, and class or type of inventory are analyzed to determine estimated net realizable value. Criteria utilized by the Company to quantify aging trends include factors such as average selling cycle and seasonality of merchandise, the historical rate at which merchandise has sold below cost during the average selling cycle, and the value and nature of merchandise currently priced below original cost. A provision is recorded to reduce the cost of inventories to the estimated net realizable values, if appropriate. The majority of inventory at January 31, 2012, and 2011 consisted of finished goods. Unfinished goods and work-in-process were not material to the overall net inventory value.

Adjustments to reserves related to the net realizable value of inventories are primarily based on the market value of the Company's physical inventories, cycle counts and recent historical trends. The Company's physical inventories for fiscal 2012 were performed as of June 2011 and January 2012. The Company's estimates generally have been accurate and its reserve methods have been applied on a consistent basis. The Company expects the amount of its reserves and related inventories to increase over time as it expands its store base and increases direct-to-consumer sales.

Property and Equipment

Property and equipment are stated at cost and primarily consist of store-related leasehold improvements, buildings and furniture and fixtures. Depreciation is typically computed using the straight-line method over five years for furniture and fixtures, the lesser of the lease term or useful life for leasehold improvements, three to ten years for other operating equipment and 39 years for buildings. Major renovations or improvements that extend the service lives of our assets are capitalized over the extension period or life of the improvement, whichever is less.

URBAN OUTFITTERS, INC.

NOTES TO CONSOLIDATED FINANCIAL STATEMENTS—(Continued)
(in thousands, except share and per share data)

The Company reviews long-lived assets for possible impairment whenever events or changes in circumstances indicate the carrying amount may not be recoverable. This determination includes evaluation of factors such as future asset utilization and future net undiscounted cash flows expected to result from the use of the assets. Management believes there has been no material impairment of the Company's long-lived assets as of January 31, 2012.

Deferred Rent

Rent expense from leases is recorded on a straight-line basis over the lease period. The net excess of rent expense over the actual cash paid is recorded as deferred rent. In addition, certain store leases provide for contingent rentals when sales exceed specified break-point levels that are weighted based upon historical cyclicality. For leases where achievement of these levels is considered probable based on cumulative lease year revenue versus the established breakpoint at any given point in time, the Company accrues a contingent rent liability and a corresponding rent expense.

Operating Leases

The Company leases its retail stores under operating leases. Many of the lease agreements contain rent holidays, rent escalation clauses and contingent rent provisions or some combination of these items.

The Company recognizes rent expense on a straight-line basis over the lease period commencing on the date that the premise is available from the landlord. The lease period includes the construction period required to make the leased space suitable for operating during which time the Company is not permitted to occupy the space. For purposes of calculating straight-line rent expense, the commencement date of the lease term reflects the date the Company takes possession of the building for initial construction and setup.

The Company classifies tenant improvement allowances in its consolidated financial statements under deferred rent and amortizes them on a straight-line basis over the related lease period. Tenant improvement allowance activity is presented as part of cash flows from operating activities in the accompanying Consolidated Statements of Cash Flows.

Revenue Recognition

Revenue is recognized at the point-of-sale for retail store sales or when merchandise is shipped to customers for wholesale and direct-to-consumer sales, net of estimated customer returns. Revenue is recognized at the completion of a job or service for landscape sales. Revenue is presented on a net basis and does not include any tax assessed by a governmental or municipal authority. Payment for merchandise at stores and through the Company's direct-to-consumer channel is tendered by cash, check, credit card, debit card or gift card. Therefore, the Company's need to collect outstanding accounts receivable for its retail and direct-to-consumer channel is negligible and mainly results from returned checks or unauthorized credit card transactions. The Company maintains an allowance for doubtful accounts for its wholesale and landscape service accounts receivable, which management reviews on a regular basis and believes is sufficient to cover potential credit losses and billing adjustments. Deposits for custom orders are recorded as a liability and recognized as a sale upon delivery of the merchandise to the customer. These custom orders, typically for upholstered furniture, are not material. Deposits for landscape services are recorded as a liability and recognized as a sale upon completion of service. Landscape services and related deposits are not material.

The Company accounts for a gift card transaction by recording a liability at the time the gift card is issued to the customer in exchange for consideration from the customer. A liability is established and remains on the Company's books until the card is redeemed by the customer, at which time the Company records the redemption of the card for merchandise as a sale or when it is determined the likelihood of redemption is remote, based on historical redemption patterns. Revenues attributable to gift card liabilities relieved after the likelihood of redemption becomes remote are included in sales and are not material. The Company's gift cards do not expire.

URBAN OUTFITTERS, INC.

NOTES TO CONSOLIDATED FINANCIAL STATEMENTS—(Continued)
(in thousands, except share and per share data)

Sales Return Reserve

The Company records a reserve for estimated product returns where the sale has occurred during the period reported, but the return is likely to occur subsequent to the period reported and may otherwise be considered in-transit. The reserve for estimated in-transit product returns is based on the Company's most recent historical return trends. If the actual return rate or experience is materially higher than the Company's estimate, additional sales returns would be recorded in the future. The activity of the sales returns reserve for the years ended January 31, 2012, 2011, and 2010 was as follows:

	Balance at beginning of year	Additions	Deductions	Balance at end of year
Year ended January 31, 2012	$11,367	41,034	(41,434)	$10,967
Year ended January 31, 2011	$ 9,912	41,692	(40,237)	$11,367
Year ended January 31, 2010	$ 7,547	33,889	(31,524)	$ 9,912

Cost of Sales, Including Certain Buying, Distribution and Occupancy Costs

Cost of sales, including certain buying, distribution and occupancy costs includes the following: the cost of merchandise; merchandise markdowns; obsolescence and shrink provisions; store occupancy costs including rent and depreciation; customer shipping costs for direct-to-consumer orders; in-bound and outbound freight; U.S. Customs related taxes and duties; inventory acquisition and purchasing costs; warehousing and handling costs and other inventory acquisition related costs.

Selling, General and Administrative Expenses

Selling, general and administrative expenses includes expenses such as: direct selling and selling supervisory expenses; marketing expenses; various corporate expenses such as information systems, finance, loss prevention, talent acquisition, and executive management expenses; and other associated general expenses.

Shipping and Handling Fees and Costs

The Company includes shipping and handling revenues in net sales and shipping and handling costs in cost of sales. The Company's shipping and handling revenues consist of amounts billed to customers for shipping and handling merchandise. Shipping and handling costs include shipping supplies, related labor costs and third-party shipping costs.

Advertising

The Company expenses the costs of advertising when the advertising occurs, except for direct-to-consumer advertising, which is capitalized and amortized over its expected period of future benefit. Advertising costs primarily relate to our direct-to-consumer marketing expenses which are comprised of web marketing, catalog printing, paper, postage and other costs related to production of photographic images used in our catalogs and on our websites. The catalog printing, paper, postage and other costs are amortized over the period in which the customer responds to the marketing material determined based on historical customer response trends to a similar season's advertisement. Amortization rates are reviewed on a regular basis during the fiscal year and may be adjusted if the predicted customer response appears materially different than the historical response rate. The Company has the ability to measure the response rate to direct marketing early in the course of the advertisement based on its customers' reference to a specific catalog or by product placed and sold. The average amortization period for a catalog and related items are typically three months. If there is no expected future benefit, the cost of advertising is expensed when incurred. Advertising costs reported as prepaid expenses were $3,586 and $3,323 as of January 31, 2012, and 2011, respectively. Advertising expenses were $71,684, $58,336 and $46,827 for fiscal 2012, 2011 and 2010, respectively.

Start-up Costs

The Company expenses all start-up and organization costs as incurred, including travel, training, recruiting, salaries and other operating costs.

URBAN OUTFITTERS, INC.

NOTES TO CONSOLIDATED FINANCIAL STATEMENTS—(Continued)
(in thousands, except share and per share data)

Website Development Costs

The Company capitalizes applicable costs incurred during the application and infrastructure development stage and expenses costs incurred during the planning and operating stage. During fiscal 2012, 2011 and 2010, the Company did not capitalize any internal-use software development costs because substantially all costs were incurred during the planning and operating stages, and costs incurred during the application and infrastructure development stage were not material.

Income Taxes

The Company utilizes a balance sheet approach to provide for income taxes. Under this method, deferred tax assets and liabilities are recognized for the expected future tax consequences of net operating loss carryforwards and temporary differences between the carrying amounts and the tax bases of assets and liabilities. The Company files a consolidated United States federal income tax return (see Note 8 for a further discussion of income taxes).

Net Income Per Common Share

Basic net income per common share is computed by dividing net income by the weighted average number of common shares outstanding. Diluted net income per common share is computed by dividing net income by the weighted average number of common shares and common share equivalents outstanding. Common share equivalents include the effect of stock options, stock appreciation rights ("SARs"), restricted stock units ("RSUs") and performance share units ("PSUs").

Accumulated Other Comprehensive Loss

Comprehensive income is comprised of two subsets—net income and accumulated other comprehensive loss. Amounts included in accumulated other comprehensive loss relate to foreign currency translation adjustments and unrealized gains or losses on marketable securities. The foreign currency translation adjustments are not adjusted for income taxes because these adjustments relate to non–U.S. subsidiaries for which foreign earnings have been designated as permanently reinvested. Accumulated other comprehensive loss consisted of foreign currency translation losses of $10,037 and $7,752 as of January 31, 2012, and January 31, 2011, respectively, and unrealized losses, net of tax, on marketable securities of $1,475 and $2,510 as of January 31, 2012, and January 31, 2011, respectively. Gross realized gains and losses are included in other income in the Consolidated Statements of Income and were not material to the Company's Consolidated Financial Statements for all three years presented.

Foreign Currency Translation

The financial statements of the Company's foreign operations are translated into U.S. dollars. Assets and liabilities are translated at current exchange rates as of the balance sheet date, equity accounts at historical exchange rates, while revenue and expense accounts are translated at the average rates in effect during the year. Translation adjustments are not included in determining net income, but are included in accumulated other comprehensive loss within shareholders' equity. As of January 31, 2012, 2011 and 2010, foreign currency translation adjustments resulted in accumulated losses of $10,037 and $7,752, respectively.

Concentration of Credit Risk

Financial instruments that potentially subject the Company to concentrations of credit risk consist principally of cash, cash equivalents, marketable securities and accounts receivable. The Company manages the credit risk associated with cash, cash equivalents and marketable securities by investing in high-quality securities held with reputable trustees and, by policy, limiting the amount of credit exposure to any one issuer or issue, as well as providing limitations on investment maturities. The Company's investment policy requires that the majority of its cash, cash equivalents and marketable securities are invested in corporate and municipal bonds rated "A" or better and federally insured or guaranteed investment vehicles such as federal government agencies, irrevocable pre-refunded municipal bonds and United States treasury bills. Receivables from third-party credit cards are processed by financial institutions, which are monitored for financial stability. The Company periodically evaluates the financial condition of its wholesale segment customers. The Company's allowance for doubtful accounts reflects current market conditions and management's assessment regarding the collectability of its accounts receivable. The Company maintains cash accounts that, at times, may exceed federally insured limits. The Company has not experienced any losses from maintaining cash accounts in excess of such limits. Management believes that it is not exposed to any significant risks related to its cash accounts.

URBAN OUTFITTERS, INC.

NOTES TO CONSOLIDATED FINANCIAL STATEMENTS—(Continued)
(in thousands, except share and per share data)

Recently Issued Accounting Pronouncements

In January 2010, the Financial Accounting Standards Board ("FASB") issued an accounting standards update that amended fair value measurements and disclosures and aimed to improve the transparency of financial reporting of assets and liabilities measured at fair value. The update required new disclosures for transfers in and out of Level 1 and Level 2 and the basis for such transfers. Also required are disclosures for activity in Level 3, including purchase, sale, issuance and settlement information. Lastly, it clarified guidance regarding disaggregation and disclosure of information about valuation techniques and inputs used to measure fair value for both recurring and non-recurring fair value measurements in Level 2 and Level 3 categories. The Company adopted the provisions of this accounting standards update effective February 1, 2010, except for the requirement to disclose purchases, sales, issuances, and settlements related to Level 3 measurements, which we adopted February 1, 2011. This adoption had no impact on the Company's financial condition, results of operations or cash flows.

In May 2011, the FASB issued an additional update that amended fair value measurements and disclosures. This amendment provides that the inputs and measures used to value assets that fall within Level 3 of the valuation hierarchy be quantitatively presented. Application is required prospectively for interim and annual periods beginning after December 15, 2011. The Company is required to adopt the provisions of this update in the first quarter of fiscal 2013. Other than the change in presentation, this accounting standards update will not have an impact on the Company's financial position and results of operations.

In June 2011, the FASB issued an accounting standards update that requires an increase in the prominence of other comprehensive income and its components within the financial statements. The update provides entities the option to present the components of net income and other comprehensive income in either one or two consecutive financial statements. It also eliminates the option to present other comprehensive income in the statements of shareholders' equity. Application is to be applied retrospectively and is effective for interim and annual periods beginning after December 15, 2011. The Company is required to adopt the provisions of this update in the first quarter of fiscal 2013. Other than the change in presentation, this accounting standards update will not have an impact on the Company's financial position and results of operations.

URBAN OUTFITTERS, INC.

NOTES TO CONSOLIDATED FINANCIAL STATEMENTS—(Continued)
(in thousands, except share and per share data)

3. Marketable Securities

During all periods shown, marketable securities are classified as available-for-sale. The amortized cost, gross unrealized gains (losses) and fair values of available-for-sale securities by major security type and class of security as of January 31, 2012, and 2011 are as follows:

	Amortized Cost	Unrealized Gains	Unrealized (Losses)	Fair Value
As of January 31, 2012				
Short-term Investments:				
Corporate bonds	$ 34,899	$ 7	$ (28)	$ 34,878
Municipal and pre-refunded municipal bonds	41,519	135	(10)	41,644
Certificate of deposit	5,225	—	—	5,225
Federal government agencies	4,513	2	—	4,515
Commercial paper	3,580	12	—	3,592
	89,736	156	(38)	89,854
Long-term Investments:				
Corporate bonds	60,852	277	(72)	61,057
Municipal and pre-refunded municipal bonds	18,410	186	(6)	18,590
Auction rate securities	22,975	—	(2,778)	20,197
Treasury bills	14,982	6	—	14,988
Certificate of deposit	6,970	—	(1)	6,969
Federal government agencies	5,111	2	(1)	5,112
	129,300	471	(2,858)	126,913
	$219,036	$ 627	$ (2,896)	$216,767
As of January 31, 2011				
Short-term Investments:				
Municipal and pre-refunded municipal bonds	$ 42,996	$ 48	$ (9)	$ 43,035
Treasury bills	7,004	4	—	7,008
Federal government agencies	40,842	80	—	40,922
FDIC insured corporate bonds	23,489	66	—	23,555
Variable rate demand notes	1,900	—	—	1,900
	116,231	198	(9)	116,420
Long-term Investments:				
Corporate bonds	137,540	173	(154)	137,559
Municipal and pre-refunded municipal bonds	143,711	216	(558)	143,369
Auction rate securities	33,250	—	(3,788)	29,462
Treasury bills	23,311	34	—	23,345
Federal government agencies	18,225	30	(2)	18,253
	356,037	453	(4,502)	351,988
	$472,268	$ 651	$ (4,511)	$468,408

Proceeds from the sale and maturities of available-for-sale securities were $414,769, $571,236 and $421,040 in fiscal 2012, 2011 and 2010, respectively. The Company included in interest income, in the Consolidated Statements of Income, a net realized gain of $1,171 during fiscal 2012, a net realized loss of $30 during fiscal 2011 and a net realized gain of $1,075 during fiscal 2010. Amortization of discounts and premiums, net, resulted in a reduction to interest income of $7,373, $8,702 and $6,204 for fiscal years 2012, 2011, and 2010, respectively.

URBAN OUTFITTERS, INC.

NOTES TO CONSOLIDATED FINANCIAL STATEMENTS—(Continued)
(in thousands, except share and per share data)

The following tables show the gross unrealized losses and fair value of the Company's marketable securities with unrealized losses that are not deemed to be other-than-temporarily impaired aggregated by the length of time that individual securities have been in a continuous unrealized loss position, at January 31, 2012, and January 31, 2011, respectively.

| | January 31, 2012 | | | | | |
| | Less Than 12 Months | | 12 Months or Greater | | Total | |
Description of Securities	Fair Value	Unrealized Losses	Fair Value	Unrealized Losses	Fair Value	Unrealized Losses
Corporate bonds	45,089	(100)	—	—	45,089	(100)
Municipal and pre-refunded municipal bonds	9,985	(9)	2,954	(7)	12,939	(16)
Auction rate securities	—	—	20,197	(2,778)	20,197	(2,778)
Treasury bills	1,039	—	—	—	1,039	—
Certificates of deposit	1,489	(1)	—	—	1,489	(1)
Federal government agencies	1,099	(1)	—	—	1,099	(1)
Total	58,701	(111)	23,151	(2,785)	81,852	(2,896)

| | January 31, 2011 | | | | | |
| | Less Than 12 Months | | 12 Months or Greater | | Total | |
Description of Securities	Fair Value	Unrealized Losses	Fair Value	Unrealized Losses	Fair Value	Unrealized Losses
FDIC-insured corporate bonds	67,359	(154)	—	—	67,359	(154)
Municipal and pre-refunded municipal bonds	103,090	(567)	—	—	103,090	(567)
Auction rate securities	—	—	29,462	(3,788)	29,462	(3,788)
Federal government agencies	1,397	(2)	—	—	1,397	(2)
Total	171,846	(723)	29,462	(3,788)	201,308	(4,511)

As of January 31, 2012, and 2011, there were a total of 76 and 128 issued securities with unrealized loss positions within the Company's portfolio, respectively. The total unrealized loss position due to the impairment of ARS held by the Company that have experienced auction failures as of January 31, 2012, and 2011 was $2,778 and $3,788, respectively. The Company deemed all of these securities as temporarily impaired. The unrealized loss positions were primarily due to auction failures of the ARS held and fluctuations in the market interest rates for remaining securities. The Company believes it has the ability to realize the full value of all of these investments upon maturity or redemption.

As of January 31, 2012, the par value of our ARS was $22,975 and the estimated fair value was $20,197. Our ARS portfolio consists of "A" or better rated ARS that represent interests in municipal and student loan related collateralized debt obligations, all of which are guaranteed by either government agencies and/or insured by private insurance agencies at 97% or greater of par value. To date, we have collected all interest payable on outstanding ARS when due and have not been informed by the issuers that accrued interest payments are currently at risk. The Company does not have the intent to sell the underlying securities prior to their recovery and the Company believes it is not likely that it will be required to sell the underlying securities prior to their anticipated recovery of full amortized cost.

4. Fair Value

The Company utilizes a hierarchy that prioritizes fair value measurements based on the types of inputs used for the various valuation techniques (market approach, income approach and cost approach that relate to its financial assets and financial liabilities). The levels of the hierarchy are described as follows:

- Level 1: Observable inputs such as quoted prices in active markets for identical assets or liabilities.

- Level 2: Inputs other than quoted prices that are observable for the asset or liability, either directly or indirectly; these include quoted prices for similar assets or liabilities in active markets and quoted prices for identical or similar assets or liabilities in markets that are not active.

- Level 3: Unobservable inputs that reflect the Company's own assumptions.

URBAN OUTFITTERS, INC.

NOTES TO CONSOLIDATED FINANCIAL STATEMENTS—(Continued)
(in thousands, except share and per share data)

Management's assessment of the significance of a particular input to the fair value measurement requires judgment and may affect the valuation of financial assets and liabilities and their placement within the fair value hierarchy. The Company's financial assets that are accounted for at fair value on a recurring basis are presented in the table below:

| | Marketable Securities Fair Value as of January 31, 2012 | | | |
	Level 1	Level 2	Level 3	Total
Assets:				
Corporate bonds	$ 95,935	$ —	$ —	$ 95,935
Municipal and pre-refunded municipal bonds	—	60,234	—	60,234
Auction rate securities	—	—	20,197	20,197
Treasury bills	14,988	—	—	14,988
Certificates of deposit	—	12,194	—	12,194
Federal government agencies	9,627	—	—	9,627
Commercial paper	—	3,592	—	3,592
	$120,550	$76,020	$20,197	$216,767

| | Marketable Securities Fair Value as of January 31, 2011 | | | |
	Level 1	Level 2	Level 3	Total
Assets:				
Corporate bonds	$137,559	$ —	$ —	$137,559
Municipal and pre-refunded municipal bonds	—	186,404	—	186,404
Auction rate securities	—	—	29,462	29,462
Treasury bills	30,353	—	—	30,353
Federal government agencies	59,175	—	—	59,175
FDIC insured corporate bonds	23,555	—	—	23,555
Variable rate demand notes	—	1,900	—	1,900
	$250,642	$188,304	$29,462	$468,408

Level 2 assets consist of financial instruments whose value has been based on quoted prices for similar assets and liabilities in active markets as well as quoted prices for identical or similar assets or liabilities in markets that are not active.

Level 3 consists of financial instruments where there was no active market as of January 31, 2012, and 2011. As of January 31, 2012, and 2011 all of the Company's level 3 financial instruments consisted of failed ARS of which there was insufficient observable market information to determine fair value. The Company estimated the fair values for these securities by incorporating assumptions that market participants would use in their estimates of fair value. Some of these assumptions included credit quality, collateralization, final stated maturity, estimates of the probability of being called or becoming liquid prior to final maturity, redemptions of similar ARS, previous market activity for the same investment security, impact due to extended periods of maximum auction rates and valuation models. As a result of this review, the Company determined its ARS to have a temporary impairment of $2,778 and $3,788 as of January 31, 2012, and January 31, 2011, respectively. The estimated fair values could change significantly based on future market conditions. The Company will continue to assess the fair value of its ARS for substantive changes in relevant market conditions, changes in its financial condition or other changes that may alter its estimates described above.

URBAN OUTFITTERS, INC.

NOTES TO CONSOLIDATED FINANCIAL STATEMENTS—(Continued)
(in thousands, except share and per share data)

Below is a reconciliation of the beginning and ending ARS securities balances that the Company valued using a Level 3 valuation for the fiscal years ended January 31, 2012, and 2011.

	Fiscal Year Ended January 31, 2012	Fiscal Year Ended January 31, 2011
Balance at beginning of period	$ 29,462	$ 33,505
Total gains (losses) realized/unrealized:		
Included in earnings	—	—
Included in comprehensive income	1,010	332
Settlements	(10,275)	(4,375)
Transfers in and/or out of Level 3	—	—
Balance at end of period	$ 20,197	$ 29,462
Unrealized losses included in accumulated other comprehensive loss related to assets still held at reporting date	$ (2,778)	$ (3,788)
Total gains for the period included in earnings attributable to the change in unrealized gains or losses related to assets still held at reporting date	$ —	$ —

5. Property and Equipment

Property and equipment is summarized as follows:

	January 31,	
	2012	2011
Land	$ 5,801	$ 2,387
Buildings	118,050	117,982
Furniture and fixtures	306,020	273,621
Leasehold improvements	676,644	606,020
Other operating equipment	103,818	81,856
Construction-in-progress	91,433	29,295
	1,301,766	1,111,161
Accumulated depreciation	(616,787)	(524,815)
Total	$ 684,979	$ 586,346

Depreciation expense for property and equipment for fiscal years ended 2012, 2011 and 2010 was $100,739, $92,403 and $86,146, respectively.

6. Accrued Expenses and Other Current Liabilities

Accrued expenses and other current liabilities consist of the following:

	January 31,	
	2012	2011
Gift certificates and merchandise credits	$ 34,331	$ 30,866
Accrued construction	21,866	8,103
Accrued income taxes	14,462	22,466
Sales return reserve	10,967	11,367
Accrued rents and estimated property taxes	9,118	9,329
Accrued sales taxes	9,089	7,780
Other current liabilities	22,249	17,997
Total	$122,082	$107,908

URBAN OUTFITTERS, INC.

NOTES TO CONSOLIDATED FINANCIAL STATEMENTS—(Continued)
(in thousands, except share and per share data)

7. Line of Credit Facility

On April 25, 2011, the Company amended its line of credit facility (the "Line") with Wells Fargo Bank, National Association. This amendment extended the term of the Line for three years, increased the accordion feature from $100 million to $175 million, reduced the interest rate margin for certain cash advances and modified certain financial covenants and terms. The Line contains a sub-limit for borrowings by the Company's European subsidiaries that are guaranteed by the Company. Cash advances bear interest at LIBOR plus 0.50% to 1.50% based on the Company's achievement of prescribed adjusted debt ratios. The Line subjects the Company to various restrictive covenants, including maintenance of certain financial ratios such as adjusted debt. The covenants also include limitations on the Company's capital expenditures, ability to repurchase shares and the payment of cash dividends. On October 31, 2011, the Company further amended the Line to revise certain financial covenants which included removing the limitation on share repurchases, as well as to join certain subsidiaries of the Company as additional borrowers and guarantors and release certain others. As of and for the year ended January 31, 2012, there were no borrowings under the Line. Outstanding letters of credit and stand-by letters of credit under the Line totaled approximately $59,685 as of January 31, 2012. The available credit, including the accordion feature, under the Line was $115,315 as of January 31, 2012.

8. Income Taxes

The components of income before income taxes are as follows:

	Fiscal Year Ended January 31,		
	2012	2011	2010
Domestic	$261,214	$374,777	$333,824
Foreign	27,617	42,431	10,582
	$288,831	$417,208	$344,406

The components of the provision for income tax expense are as follows:

	Fiscal Year Ended January 31,		
	2012	2011	2010
Current:			
Federal	$ 93,244	$127,390	$107,350
State	14,199	19,492	13,216
Foreign	8,287	6,095	1,786
	115,730	152,977	122,352
Deferred:			
Federal	(11,292)	(6,698)	2,960
State	124	(1,906)	(365)
Foreign	(982)	(123)	(434)
	(12,150)	(8,727)	2,161
	$103,580	$144,250	$124,513

The Company's effective tax rate was different than the statutory U.S. federal income tax rate for the following reasons:

	Fiscal Year Ended January 31,		
	2012	2011	2010
Expected provision at statutory U.S. federal tax rate	35.0%	35.0%	35.0%
State and local income taxes, net of federal tax benefit	3.2	3.2	2.3
Foreign taxes	(2.1)	(2.1)	(0.6)
Federal rehabilitation tax credits	—	(0.8)	—
Other	(0.2)	(0.7)	(0.5)
Effective tax rate	35.9%	34.6%	36.2%

URBAN OUTFITTERS, INC.

NOTES TO CONSOLIDATED FINANCIAL STATEMENTS—(Continued)
(in thousands, except share and per share data)

The significant components of deferred tax assets and liabilities as of January 31, 2012, and 2011 are as follows:

	January 31,	
	2012	2011
Deferred tax liabilities:		
Prepaid expenses	$ (1,402)	$ (1,551)
Depreciation	(4,761)	(15,922)
Gross deferred tax liabilities	(6,163)	(17,473)
Deferred tax assets:		
Deferred rent	37,024	43,005
Inventories	3,093	5,434
Accounts receivable	1,166	747
Net operating loss carryforwards	5,684	5,123
Tax uncertainties	7,651	4,433
Accrued salaries and benefits	13,786	13,496
Other temporary differences	4,437	—
Gross deferred tax assets, before valuation allowances	72,841	72,238
Valuation allowances	(2,754)	(2,622)
Net deferred tax assets	$63,924	$ 52,143

Net deferred tax assets are attributed to the jurisdictions in which the Company operates. As of January 31, 2012, and 2011, respectively, $48,762 and $37,170 were attributable to U.S. federal, $12,374 and $13,546 were attributed to state jurisdictions and $2,788 and $1,427 were attributed to foreign jurisdictions.

As of January 31, 2012, certain non–U.S. subsidiaries of the Company had net operating loss carryforwards for tax purposes of approximately $10,503 that do not expire and certain U.S. subsidiaries of the Company had state net operating loss carryforwards for tax purposes of approximately $9,114 that expire from 2016 through 2032. As of January 31, 2011, the Company had a full valuation allowance for certain foreign and state net operating loss carryforwards where it was uncertain the carryforwards would be utilized. The Company had no valuation allowance for certain other foreign and state net operating loss carryforwards where management believes it is more likely than not the tax benefit of these carryforwards will be realized. As of January 31, 2012, and 2011, the non-current portion of net deferred tax assets aggregated $58,681 and $37,789, respectively.

The cumulative amount of the Company's share of undistributed earnings of non–U.S. subsidiaries for which no deferred taxes have been provided was $130,219 as of January 31, 2012. These earnings are deemed to be permanently re-invested to finance growth programs.

A reconciliation of the beginning and ending balances of the total amounts of gross unrecognized tax benefits is as follows:

	January 31,		
	2012	2011	2010
Balance at the beginning of the period	$ 7,758	$7,532	$ 7,509
Increases in tax positions for prior years	3,466	43	948
Decreases in tax positions for prior years	(310)	(592)	(116)
Increases in tax positions for current year	360	1,000	1,894
Settlements	(2,259)	(40)	(924)
Lapse in statute of limitations	(351)	(185)	(1,779)
Balance at the end of the period	$ 8,664	$7,758	$ 7,532

URBAN OUTFITTERS, INC.

NOTES TO CONSOLIDATED FINANCIAL STATEMENTS—(Continued)
(in thousands, except share and per share data)

The total amount of net unrecognized tax benefits that, if recognized, would impact the Company's effective tax rate were $3,874 and $6,677 at January 31, 2012, and 2011, respectively. The Company accrues interest and penalties related to unrecognized tax benefits in income tax expense in the Consolidated Statements of Income, which is consistent with the recognition of these items in prior reporting periods. During the years ended January 31, 2012, 2011 and 2010, the Company recognized a benefit of $1,334, $437 and $427 in interest and penalties. The Company accrued $2,529 and $3,620 for the payment of interest and penalties as of January 31, 2012, and 2011, respectively.

The Company files income tax returns in the U.S. federal jurisdiction and various state and foreign jurisdictions. During the year ended January 31, 2012, the Company settled its Internal Revenue Service examination for the periods ended January 31, 2005, through 2008. The Company has recognized the tax effect of this settlement for previous and future periods in the end of year balances. The Company also began a new Internal Revenue audit for periods ended January 31, 2009, and 2010. State and foreign jurisdictions that remain subject to examination range from fiscal 2002 to 2011 with few exceptions. It is possible that the Federal or any state examination may be resolved within twelve months. Due to the potential for resolution of Federal audit and state examinations, and the expiration of various statutes of limitation, it is possible that the Company's gross unrecognized tax benefits balance may change within the next twelve months by a range of zero to $3,340.

9. Share-Based Compensation

The Company's 2008 and 2004 Stock Incentive Plans each authorize up to 10,000,000 common shares, which can be granted as RSUs, unrestricted shares, incentive stock options, nonqualified stock options, PSUs or as SARs. Awards under these plans generally expire seven or ten years from the date of grant, thirty days after termination of employment or six months after the date of death or termination due to disability of the grantee. As of January 31, 2012, there were 6,951,650 and 902,516 common shares available to grant under the 2008 and 2004 Stock Incentive Plans, respectively.

A Lattice Binomial pricing model ("Model") was used to estimate the fair value of stock options and SARs. The Model allows for assumptions such as the risk-free rate of interest, volatility and exercise rate to vary over time reflecting a more realistic pattern of economic and behavioral occurrences. The Company uses historical data on exercise timing to determine the expected life assumption. The risk-free rate of interest for periods within the contractual life of the award is based on U.S. Government Securities Treasury Constant Maturities over the expected term of the equity instrument. The expected volatility is based on a weighted average of the implied volatility and the Company's most recent historical volatility.

Based on the Company's historical experience, it has assumed an annualized forfeiture rate of 5% for its non-vested share based awards granted during the fiscal years ended January 31, 2012, and 2011. For share based awards granted in previous years that remain non-vested, an annualized forfeiture rate of 2% has been assumed. The Company will record additional expense if the actual forfeiture rate is lower than it estimated, and will record a recovery of prior expense if the actual forfeiture is higher than estimated.

Share based compensation expense, included in the Consolidated Statements of Income, for the fiscal years ended January 31, 2012, 2011 and 2010 was as follows:

	Fiscal Year Ended January 31,		
	2012	2011	2010
Stock Options	$2,886	$ 4,331	$2,975
Stock Appreciation Rights	1,111	463	—
Performance Share Units (1)	(959)	5,929	1,349
Restricted Shares	30	2	442
Total	$3,068	$10,725	$4,766

(1) Includes the reversal of $8,800 of previously recognized compensation expense in fiscal 2012, related to 1,054,466 PSUs, granted to a former executive officer of the Company, that will not vest due to the service requirement not being met.

URBAN OUTFITTERS, INC.

NOTES TO CONSOLIDATED FINANCIAL STATEMENTS—(Continued)
(in thousands, except share and per share data)

Stock Options

The Company grants stock options which generally vest over a period of three to five years. Stock options become exercisable over the vesting period in installments determined by the administrator, which can vary depending upon each individual grant. Stock options granted to non-employee directors generally vest over a period of one year. The following weighted average assumptions were used in the Model to estimate the fair value of stock options at the date of grant:

	Fiscal 2012	Fiscal 2011	Fiscal 2010
Expected life, in years	3.5	4.3	4.2
Risk-free interest rate	0.9%	1.8%	2.0%
Volatility	50.0%	49.9%	51.4%
Dividend rate	—	—	—

The following table summarizes the Company's stock option activity:

	Fiscal Year Ended January 31, 2012			
	Shares	Weighted Average Exercise Price	Weighted Average Remaining Contractual Term (years)	Aggregate Intrinsic Value
Awards outstanding at beginning of year	8,330,683	$ 24.31		
Granted	100,000	36.07		
Exercised	(1,912,967)	14.17		
Forfeited or Expired	(487,066)	35.01		
Awards outstanding at end of year	6,030,650	26.86	3.5	$23,918
Awards outstanding expected to vest	5,980,827	26.86	3.5	$23,344
Awards exercisable at end of year	5,140,725	$ 25.63	3.3	$23,377

The following table summarizes other information related to stock options during the years ended January 31, 2012, 2011 and 2010:

	Fiscal Year Ended January 31,		
	2012	2011	2010
Weighted-average grant date fair value—per share	$ 10.36	$ 12.07	$ 8.35
Intrinsic value of awards exercised	$22,615	$55,100	$16,613
Net cash proceeds from the exercise of stock options	$ 4,136	$24,129	$ 3,250
Actual income tax benefit realized from stock option exercises	$ 8,995	$12,847	$ 6,390

The Company recognized tax benefits, related to stock options of $953, $1,336 and $1,034, in the accompanying Consolidated Statements of Income for the fiscal years ended January 31, 2012, 2011 and 2010, respectively. Total unrecognized compensation cost of stock options granted but not yet vested, as of January 31, 2012, was $6,044, which is expected to be recognized over the weighted average period of 2.09 years.

URBAN OUTFITTERS, INC.

NOTES TO CONSOLIDATED FINANCIAL STATEMENTS—(Continued)
(in thousands, except share and per share data)

The following table summarizes information concerning outstanding and exercisable stock options as of January 31, 2012:

Range of Exercise Prices	Awards Outstanding			Awards Exercisable	
	Amount Outstanding	Wtd. Avg. Remaining Contractual Life	Wtd. Avg. Exercise Price	Amount Exercisable	Wtd. Avg. Exercise Price
$ 0.00–$ 3.96	41,900	0.2	$ 2.86	41,900	$ 2.86
$ 3.97–$ 7.92	630,500	1.4	4.72	630,500	4.72
$11.87–$15.83	579,000	2.4	14.38	579,000	14.38
$15.84–$19.79	138,750	4.2	19.12	80,000	19.77
$19.80–$23.75	119,000	4.0	22.06	115,000	22.07
$23.76–$27.71	497,000	3.6	25.62	472,000	25.65
$27.72–$31.66	2,512,500	3.7	31.06	2,505,375	31.06
$31.67–$35.62	494,600	4.5	32.98	161,960	32.62
$35.63–$39.58	1,017,400	4.0	37.60	554,990	37.78
	6,030,650	3.5	$26.86	5,140,725	$25.63

Stock Appreciation Rights

The Company granted SARs during fiscal 2012 and 2011. There were no SARs issued or outstanding during fiscal 2010. These SARs generally vest over a five year period. Each vested SAR entitles the holder the right to the differential between the value of the Company's common share price at the date of exercise and the value of the Company's common share price at the date of grant. As of January 31, 2012, none of these SARs had vested. The following weighted average assumptions were used in the Model to estimate the fair value of SARs at the date of grant:

	Fiscal Year Ended January 31,	
	2012	2011
Expected life, in years	4.8	5.3
Risk-free interest rate	0.8%	1.6%
Volatility	48.8%	47.9%
Dividend rate	—	—

The following table summarizes the Company's SAR activity:

	Fiscal Year Ended January 31, 2012			
	Awards	Weighted Average Exercise Price	Weighted Average Remaining Contractual Term (years)	Aggregate Intrinsic Value
Awards outstanding at beginning of year	488,800	$ 32.84		
Granted	208,500	26.89		
Exercised	—	—		
Forfeited or Expired	(46,500)	32.80		
Awards outstanding at end of year	650,800	30.91	7.0	$ —
Awards outstanding expected to vest	618,260	$ 30.91	7.0	$ —
Awards exercisable at end of year	—	—	—	$ —
Weighted average grant date fair value—per share	$ 9.50			

Total unrecognized compensation cost of SARs granted, but not yet vested as of January 31, 2012, was $5,589, which is expected to be recognized over the weighted average period of 3.7 years.

URBAN OUTFITTERS, INC.

NOTES TO CONSOLIDATED FINANCIAL STATEMENTS—(Continued)
(in thousands, except share and per share data)

Performance Share Units

The Company grants PSUs which vest based on the achievement of various company performance targets and external market conditions. The fair value of the PSUs are determined using a Monte Carlo simulation. Once the Company determines that it is probable that the performance targets will be met, compensation expense is recorded for these awards. If any of these performance targets are not met, the awards are forfeited. Each PSU is equal to one common share with varying maximum award value limitations. PSUs typically vest over a five year period.

The following table summarizes the Company's PSU activity for the fiscal year ended January 31, 2012:

	Shares	Weighted Average Fair Value
Non-vested awards outstanding at beginning of year	1,441,366	$ 24.57
Granted	2,198,450	16.21
Vested	—	—
Forfeited	(1,115,866)	24.76
Non-vested awards outstanding at end of year	2,523,950	17.23

The aggregate grant date fair value of PSUs awarded during fiscal 2012, 2011 and 2010 was $35,629, $9,621 and $26,932, respectively. No PSUs vested during fiscal year 2012. The aggregate grant date fair value of PSUs vested during fiscal year 2011 was $1,060. No PSUs vested during fiscal year 2010. Unrecognized compensation cost related to non-vested PSUs as of January 31, 2012, was $35,978, which is expected to be recognized over a weighted average period of 4.3 years.

Restricted Stock Units

The Company grants RSUs which vest based on the achievement of specified service and external market conditions. RSUs typically vest over a three to five year period.

The following table summarizes the Company's RSUs activity for the fiscal year ended January 31, 2012:

	Shares	Weighted Average Fair Value
Non-vested awards outstanding at beginning of year	1,000	$36.64
Granted	10,000	20.08
Vested	(334)	36.64
Exercised	—	—
Forfeited / Cancelled	—	—
Non-vested awards outstanding at end of year	10,666	21.11

The aggregate grant date fair value of RSUs awarded during fiscal 2012 and 2011 was $201 and $37, respectively. There were no RSUs awarded in fiscal 2010. The aggregate grant date fair value of RSUs vested during fiscal year 2012 was $12. No RSUs vested during fiscal years 2011 and 2010. Total unrecognized compensation cost for non-vested RSUs granted as of January 31, 2012, was $195, which is expected to be recognized over the weighted average period of 4.2 years.

10. Shareholders' Equity

On February 28, 2006, the Company's Board of Directors approved a stock repurchase program which authorized the Company to repurchase up to 8,000,000 common shares. On November 16, 2010, and August 25, 2011, the Company's Board of Directors approved two separate stock repurchase authorizations of 10,000,000 additional common shares. These additional authorizations supplemented the Company's 2006 stock repurchase program.

URBAN OUTFITTERS, INC.

NOTES TO CONSOLIDATED FINANCIAL STATEMENTS—(Continued)
(in thousands, except share and per share data)

During the fiscal years ended January 31, 2012, and 2011 the Company repurchased and subsequently retired 20,491,530 and 6,288,447 common shares at a total cost of $538,311 and $200,732, respectively. There were no share repurchases during the fiscal year ended January 31, 2010. The average cost per share of the repurchases for the fiscal years ended January 31, 2012, and 2011 was $26.27 and $31.92, respectively, including commissions. As of January 31, 2012, there were no common shares available for repurchase under the program.

In addition to shares repurchased under the stock repurchase program, during the fiscal years ended January 31, 2012, and 2011, the Company settled and subsequently retired 282,813 and 112,770 common shares at a total cost of $7,167 and $3,986, respectively, from employees to meet minimum statutory tax withholding requirements.

As a result of the share repurchase activity noted above, the Company reduced the balance of additional paid-in-capital to zero. Subsequent share repurchase activity was recorded as a reduction of retained earnings. During the fiscal year ended January 31, 2012, the Company reduced retained earnings by $501,676 related to these share repurchases.

11. Net Income per Common Share

The following is a reconciliation of the weighted average common shares outstanding used for the computation of basic and diluted net income per common share:

	Fiscal Year Ended January 31,		
	2012	2011	2010
Basic weighted average shares outstanding	154,025,589	166,896,322	168,053,502
Effect of dilutive options, non-vested shares and stock appreciation rights	2,165,700	3,437,228	3,176,743
Diluted weighted average common shares outstanding	156,191,289	170,333,550	171,230,245

For the fiscal years ended January 31, 2012, 2011 and 2010, awards to purchase 3,836,838 common shares ranging in price from $26.85 to $39.58, 1,324,238 awards to purchase common shares ranging in price from $32.89 to $39.58 and 4,331,650 awards to purchase common shares ranging in price from $16.58 to $37.51, were excluded from the calculation of diluted net income per common share because the impact would be anti-dilutive.

As of January 31, 2012, 2,533,950 contingently issuable awards were excluded from the calculation of diluted net income per common share as they did not meet certain performance criteria.

12. Commitments and Contingencies

Leases

The Company leases its stores under non-cancelable operating leases. The following is a schedule by year of the future minimum lease payments for operating leases with original terms in excess of one year:

Fiscal Year	
2013	$ 185,047
2014	183,374
2015	175,947
2016	160,574
2017	139,948
Thereafter	544,113
Total minimum lease payments	$1,389,003

URBAN OUTFITTERS, INC.

NOTES TO CONSOLIDATED FINANCIAL STATEMENTS—(Continued)
(in thousands, except share and per share data)

Amounts noted above include commitments for 36 executed leases for stores not opened as of January 31, 2012. The majority of our leases allow for renewal options between five and ten years upon expiration of the initial lease term. The store leases generally provide for payment of direct operating costs including real estate taxes. Certain store leases provide for contingent rentals when sales exceed specified levels. Additionally, the Company has entered into store leases that require a percentage of total sales to be paid to landlords in lieu of minimum rent.

Rent expense consisted of the following:

	Fiscal Year Ended January 31,		
	2012	2011	2010
Minimum and percentage rentals	$165,901	$143,919	$125,651
Contingent rentals	5,403	5,836	3,327
Total	$171,304	$149,755	$128,978

The Company also has commitments for unfulfilled purchase orders for merchandise ordered from our vendors in the normal course of business, which are liquidated within 12 months, of $315,890. The majority of the Company's merchandise commitments are cancellable with no or limited recourse available to the vendor until merchandise shipping date. The Company also has commitments related to contracts with construction contractors, fully liquidated upon the completion of construction, which is typically within 12 months, of $16,292.

Benefit Plan

Full and part-time U.S.–based employees who are at least 18 years of age are eligible after three months of employment to participate in the Urban Outfitters 401(k) Savings Plan (the "Plan"). Under the Plan, employees can defer 1% to 25% of compensation as defined. The Company makes matching contributions in cash of $0.25 per employee contribution dollar on the first 6% of the employee contribution. The employees' contribution is 100% vested while the Company's matching contribution vests at 20% per year of employee service. The Company's contributions were $1,365, $1,308 and $1,171 for fiscal years 2012, 2011 and 2010, respectively.

Contingencies

The Company is party to various legal proceedings arising from normal business activities. Management believes that the ultimate resolution of these matters will not have a material adverse effect on the Company's financial position, results of operations or cash flows.

13. Related Party Transactions

Drinker Biddle & Reath LLP ("DBR"), a law firm, provided general legal services to the Company. Fees paid to DBR during fiscal 2012, 2011 and 2010 were $2,509, $2,707 and $1,732, respectively. Harry S. Cherken, Jr., a director of the Company, is a partner at DBR. Fees due to DBR for the fiscal years ended January 31, 2012, 2011 and 2010 were approximately $273, $251 and $251, respectively.

The McDevitt Company, a real estate company, acted as a broker in substantially all of the Company's new real estate transactions during fiscal 2012, 2011 and 2010. The Company has not paid any compensation to The McDevitt Company for such services, but the Company has been advised that The McDevitt Company has received commissions from other parties to such transactions. Wade L. McDevitt is the president and the sole shareholder of The McDevitt Company and brother-in-law of Scott A. Belair, one of the Company's directors. There were no amounts due to The McDevitt Company as of January 31, 2012, and January 31, 2011. Mr. McDevitt's wife, Wendy B. McDevitt, is an executive officer of the Company, serving as President of the Terrain Brand.

The Addis Group ("Addis"), an insurance brokerage and risk management consulting company, acted as the Company's commercial insurance broker and risk management consultant for the years ended January 31, 2012, 2011 and 2010. The Company has not paid any compensation to Addis for such services, but has been advised that Addis has received commissions from other parties to such transactions. Scott Addis, the brother-in-law of Richard A. Hayne, Chief Executive Officer, President and Chairman of the Board of the Company, is the President of The Addis Group. There were no amounts due to or from Addis as of January 31, 2012, and January 31, 2011.

URBAN OUTFITTERS, INC.

NOTES TO CONSOLIDATED FINANCIAL STATEMENTS—(Continued)
(in thousands, except share and per share data)

14. Segment Reporting

The Company is a global retailer of lifestyle-oriented general merchandise with two reporting segments—"Retail" and "Wholesale." The Company's Retail segment consists of the aggregation of its five brands operating through 429 stores under the retail names "Urban Outfitters," "Anthropologie," "Free People," "Terrain" and "BHLDN" and includes their direct marketing campaigns which consist of five catalogs and nine websites as of January 31, 2012. Our Retail stores and their direct marketing campaigns are considered an operating segment. Net sales from the Retail segment accounted for more than 94% of total consolidated net sales for the years ended January 31, 2012, 2011 and 2010. The remainder is derived from the Company's Wholesale segment that distributes apparel to its retail segment and to approximately 1,400 better department and specialty retailers worldwide.

The Company has aggregated its retail stores and associated direct marketing campaigns into a Retail segment based upon their shared management, customer base and economic characteristics. Reporting in this format provides management with the financial information necessary to evaluate the success of the segments and the overall business. The Company evaluates the performance of the segments based on the net sales and pre-tax income from operations (excluding inter-company charges) of the segment. Corporate expenses include expenses incurred and directed by the corporate office that are not allocated to segments. The principal identifiable assets for each operating segment are inventories and property and equipment. Other assets are comprised primarily of general corporate assets, which principally consist of cash and cash equivalents, marketable securities, and other assets, and which are typically not allocated to the Company's segments. The Company accounts for inter-segment sales and transfers as if the sales and transfers were made to third parties making similar volume purchases.

URBAN OUTFITTERS, INC.

NOTES TO CONSOLIDATED FINANCIAL STATEMENTS—(Continued)
(in thousands, except share and per share data)

The accounting policies of the operating segments are the same as the policies described in Note 2, "Summary of Significant Accounting Policies." Both the retail and wholesale segments are highly diversified. No customer comprises more than 10% of sales. A summary of the information about the Company's operations by segment is as follows:

	Fiscal Year		
	2012	2011	2010
Net sales			
Retail operations	$2,340,794	$2,153,792	$1,833,733
Wholesale operations	140,657	124,768	109,269
Intersegment elimination	(7,650)	(4,458)	(5,187)
Total net sales	$2,473,801	$2,274,102	$1,937,815
Income from operations			
Retail operations	$ 276,581	$ 418,403	$ 338,114
Wholesale operations	26,919	23,372	22,164
Intersegment elimination	(709)	(389)	(202)
Total segment operating income	302,791	441,386	360,076
General corporate expenses	(18,066)	(27,183)	(21,092)
Total income from operations	$ 284,725	$ 414,203	$ 338,984
Depreciation expense for property and equipment			
Retail operations	$ 99,645	$ 91,267	$ 85,077
Wholesale operations	1,094	1,136	1,069
Total depreciation expense for property and equipment	$ 100,739	$ 92,403	$ 86,146
Inventories			
Retail operations	$ 237,825	$ 213,420	
Wholesale operations	12,248	16,141	
Total inventories	$ 250,073	$ 229,561	
Property and equipment, net			
Retail operations	$ 681,501	$ 582,241	
Wholesale operations	3,478	4,105	
Total property and equipment, net	$ 684,979	$ 586,346	
Cash paid for property and equipment			
Retail operations	$ 189,311	$ 142,791	$ 107,941
Wholesale operations	699	851	1,319
Total cash paid for property and equipment	$ 190,010	$ 143,642	$ 109,260

The Company has foreign operations in Europe and Canada. Revenues and long-lived assets, based upon the Company's domestic and foreign operations, are as follows:

	Fiscal Year		
	2012	2011	2010
Net sales			
Domestic operations	$2,169,976	$2,027,074	$1,752,787
Foreign operations	303,825	247,028	185,028
Total net sales	$2,473,801	$2,274,102	$1,937,815
Property and equipment, net			
Domestic operations	$ 557,512	$ 497,521	
Foreign operations	127,467	88,825	
Total property and equipment, net	$ 684,979	$ 586,346	

INDUSTRY RATIO REPORT
Retail Family Clothing Stores

Liquidity

Current Ratio	2.67
Quick Ratio	1.48

Activity

Inventory Turnover	4.92
Days to Sell Inventory	100.82 days
Receivables Turnover	97.49
Average Collection Period	12.63 days
Fixed Asset Turnover	7.43
Total Asset Turnover	1.75
Accounts Payable Turnover	11.55

Profitability

Gross Profit Margin	42.47%
Operating Profit Margin	12.37%
Net Profit Margin	5.40%
Return on Equity	13.61%
Return on Assets	9.09%
Quality of Income	1.81

Leverage

Times Interest Earned	92.35
Total Debt/Total Equity	0.70
Total Assets/Total Equity	1.70

Dividends

Dividend Payout	15.24%
Dividend Yield	1.49%

Other

Advertising-to-Sales	5.55%
Sales Growth	8.87%
Capital Acquisitions Ratio	2.62
Price/Earnings	16.10

COMPANIES USED IN INDUSTRY ANALYSIS

Company Name	Ticker Symbol
Abercrombie & Fitch	ANF
Aeropostale Inc.	ARO
American Eagle Outfitters	AEO
Ascena Retail Group Inc.	ASNA
Brown Shoe Company	BWS
Chico's FAS Inc.	CHS
Collective Brands Inc.	PSS
Dillard's Inc.	DDS
DSW Inc.	DSW
Foot Locker Inc.	FL
Genesco Inc.	GCO
Guess? Inc.	GES
Jos. A. Bank Clothiers Inc.	JOSB
Saks Inc.	SKS
Signet Jewelers Ltd.	SIG
Stage Stores Inc.	SSI
The Buckle Inc.	BKE
The Children's Place	PLCE
The Finish Line Inc.	FINL
The Men's Wearhouse Inc.	MW
Urban Outfitters	URBN

Reporting and Interpreting Investments in Other Corporations

The Washington Post Company is best known for publishing the most important newspaper in our nation's capital. However, the company does much more. It owns television stations, *Newsweek* magazine, Cable One (a TV cable company), and a variety of community newspapers. Many users of this text have already been Post Company customers without knowing it. The company also owns Kaplan, Inc., the king of admissions test preparation services that will help you prepare for the SAT, GMAT, Certified Public Accountant, or Chartered Financial Analyst exams. The Post Company also recognizes that new technologies bring increased efficiency to its operations while expanding business opportunities. For example, it publishes electronic versions of *The Washington Post* and *Newsweek,* and it shares news resources with NBC News and MSNBC.

The company has achieved its diversity in part by investing in the stock of other companies. For example, it spent over $1.1 billion over the last decade to purchase other companies, including the online magazine *Slate* and a variety of private education companies around the world. It jointly owns one of the major providers of the paper *The Washington Post* is printed on. In addition, the company's investment portfolio consists of almost $350 million worth of stock of other companies.

UNDERSTANDING THE BUSINESS

Many strategic factors motivate managers to invest in securities. A company that has extra cash and simply wants to earn a return on the idle funds can invest those funds in the stocks and bonds of other companies, either long or short term. We say these investments are

Learning Objectives

After studying this material, you should be able to:

E-1 Analyze and report investments in debt securities held to maturity. p. E-4

E-2 Analyze and report passive investments in securities using the fair value method. p. E-5

E-3 Analyze and report investments involving significant influence using the equity method. p. E-13

E-4 Analyze and report investments in controlling interests. p. E-18

FOCUS COMPANY:

The Washington
Post Company

INVESTMENT STRATEGIES IN
THE MEDIA INDUSTRY

www.washpostco.com

passive because the managers are not interested in influencing or controlling the other companies. Washington Post's 2010 and 2011 comparative balance sheet, shown in Exhibit E.1, includes the short-term account, "Investments in Available-for-Sale Securities."

Sometimes a company decides to invest in another company with the purpose of influencing that company's policies and activities. Washington Post's balance sheet reports these types of investments as "Investments in Affiliates." Finally, managers may determine that controlling another company, either by purchasing it directly or becoming the majority shareholder, is desirable. If the acquired company goes out of existence, its assets and liabilities are added at fair value to the assets and liabilities of the buyer. If the acquired company continues as a separate legal entity, the two companies' financial reports are combined into consolidated financial statements, as Washington Post has done (see the title to its **consolidated** balance sheet).

In this appendix, we discuss the accounting for four types of investments. First, we discuss using the amortized cost method to account for passive investments in bonds. Second, we examine the fair value method of accounting for passive investments. Third, we present the equity method used to account for stock investments involving significant influence. The appendix closes with a discussion of accounting for mergers and consolidated statements.

EXHIBIT E.1

The Washington Post
Company Consolidated
Balance Sheet (Condensed)

THE WASHINGTON POST COMPANY
Consolidated Balance Sheets

	As of	
(in millions)	**December 31 2011**	**January 2 2011**
Assets		
Current assets		
Cash and cash equivalents	$ 381	$ 438
Investments in available-for-sale securities	339	374
Other current assets	526	550
Total current assets	1,246	1,362
Property, plant, and equipment, net	1,152	1,201
Investments in affiliates	17	32
Goodwill and other intangible assets, net	2,000	1,968
Other noncurrent assets	602	595
Total assets	$5,017	$5,158
Liabilities and Equity		
Current liabilities	$ 996	$1,008
Long-term debt	452	397
Other noncurrent liabilities	949	921
Total liabilities	2,397	2,326
Redeemable preferred stock and noncontrolling interest		
Common Stockholders' Equity:	18	17
Common stock	20	20
Capital in excess of par value	253	250
Retained earnings	4,562	4,520
Accumulated other comprehensive income, net of taxes:		
Cumulative foreign currency translation adjustment	21	38
Unrealized gain on available-for-sale securities	80	71
Unrealized gain (loss) on pensions	64	74
Treasury stock	(2,398)	(2,158)
Total equity	2,602	2,815
Total liabilities and equity	$5,017	$5,158

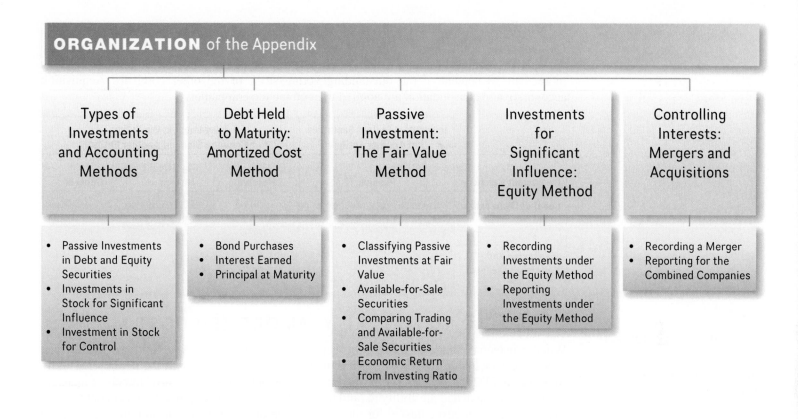

TYPES OF INVESTMENTS AND ACCOUNTING METHODS

The accounting methods used to record investments are directly related to how much is owned and how long management intends to hold the investments. The investment categories and the appropriate measuring and reporting methods are summarized as follows.

Passive Investments in Debt and Equity Securities

Passive investments are made to earn a return on funds that may be needed for future short-term or long-term purposes. This category includes both investments in debt (bonds and notes) and equity securities (stock). Debt securities are always considered passive investments. If the company intends to hold the securities until they reach maturity, the investments are measured and reported at amortized cost. If they are to be sold before maturity, they are reported using the fair value method.

For investments in equity securities, the investment is presumed passive if the investing company owns less than 20 percent of the outstanding voting shares of the other company. The fair value method is used to measure and report the investments.

Investments in Stock for Significant Influence

Significant influence is the ability to have an important impact on the operating, investing, and financing policies of another company. Significant influence is presumed if the investing company owns from 20 to 50 percent of the outstanding voting shares of the other company. However, other factors may also indicate that significant influence exists, such as membership on the board of directors of the other company, participation in the policy-making processes, evidence of material transactions between the two companies, an interchange of management personnel, or technological dependency. The equity method is used to measure and report this category of investments.

Investments in Stock for Control

Control is the ability to determine the operating and financing policies of another company through ownership of voting stock. Control is presumed when the investing company owns more than 50 percent of the outstanding voting stock of the other company. Acquisition accounting and consolidation are applied to combine the companies.

	Investment in Debt Securities of Another Entity		Investment in the Voting Common Stock of Another Entity		
Investment Category	**Passive**		**Passive**	**Significant Influence**	**Control**
Level of Ownership	Held to maturity	Not held to maturity	< 20% of outstanding shares	20–50% of outstanding shares	> 50% of outstanding shares
Measuring and Reporting Method	Amortized cost method	Fair value method		Equity method	Acquisition accounting and consolidation

DEBT HELD TO MATURITY: AMORTIZED COST METHOD

LEARNING OBJECTIVE E-1

Analyze and report investments in debt securities held to maturity.

HELD-TO-MATURITY INVESTMENTS are investments in debt securities that management has the intent and ability to hold until maturity.

The **AMORTIZED COST METHOD** reports investments in debt securities held to maturity at cost minus any premium or plus any discount.

When management plans to hold a debt security (such as a bond or note) until its maturity date (when the principal is due), it is reported in an account appropriately called **held-to-maturity investments.** Debt securities should be classified as held-to-maturity investments if management has the intent and the ability to hold them until maturity. These investments in debt instruments are listed at cost adjusted for the amortization of any discount or premium (**amortized cost method**), not at their fair value. We now illustrate accounting for investments in bonds issued by another company.

Bond Purchases

On the date of purchase, a bond may be acquired at the maturity amount (at **par**), for less than the maturity amount (at a **discount**), or for more than the maturity amount (at a **premium**).[1] The total cost of the bond, including all incidental acquisition costs such as transfer fees and broker commissions, is debited to the Held-to-Maturity Investments account.

To illustrate accounting for bond investments, assume that on July 1, 2013, Washington Post paid the par value of $100,000 for 8 percent bonds that mature on June 30, 2018.[2] Interest at 8 percent is paid each June 30 and December 31. Management plans to hold the bonds for five years, until maturity.

The journal entry to record the purchase of the bonds follows:

	Debit	Credit
Held-to-Maturity Investments (+A)	100,000	
Cash (−A)		100,000

Assets	=	Liabilities	+	Stockholders' Equity
Held-to-Maturity				
Investments +100,000				
Cash −100,000				

---

[1]The determination of the price of the bond is based on the present value techniques discussed in Chapter 9. Many analysts refer to a bond price as a **percentage of par.** For example, *The Wall Street Journal* might report that an ExxonMobil bond with a par value of $1,000 is selling at 82.97. This means it would cost $829.70 (82.97 percent of $1,000) to buy the bond.

[2]When bond investors accept a rate of interest on a bond investment that is the same as the stated rate of interest on the bonds, the bonds will sell at par (i.e., at 100 or 100% of face value). For illustration of the journal entries of a bond purchased at other than par value, see Supplement A at the end of this appendix.

Interest Earned

The bonds in this illustration were purchased at par or face value. Since no premium or discount needs to be amortized, the book value remains constant over the life of the investment. In this situation, revenue earned from the investment each period is measured as the amount of interest collected in cash or accrued at year-end. The following journal entry records the receipt of interest on December 31:

	Debit	Credit
Cash (+A) [$100,000 × .08 × 6/12]	4,000	
Interest Revenue (+R, +SE)		4,000

Assets		=	Liabilities	+	Stockholders' Equity	
Cash	+4,000				Interest Revenue (+R)	+4,000

The same entry is made on succeeding interest payment dates.

Principal at Maturity

When the bonds mature on June 30, 2018, the journal entry to record receipt of the principal payment would be:

	Debit	Credit
Cash (+A)	100,000	
Held-to-Maturity Investments (−A)		100,000

Assets		=	Liabilities	+	Stockholders' Equity
Cash	+100,000				
Held-to-Maturity					
Investments	−100,000				

If the bond investment must be sold before maturity, any difference between market value (the proceeds from the sale) and net book value would be reported as a gain or loss on sale. If management **intends** to sell the bonds before the maturity date, they are treated in the same manner as investments in stock classified as available-for-sale securities, which we discuss in the next section.

PASSIVE INVESTMENTS: THE FAIR VALUE METHOD

When the investing company owns debt securities or less than 20 percent of the outstanding voting stock of another company, the investment is considered passive. Among the assets and liabilities on the balance sheet, only passive investments in marketable securities (other than debt held to maturity) are **required** to be reported using the **fair value method** on the date of the balance sheet. Fair value is a security's current market value (the amount that would be received in an orderly sale). Before we discuss the specific accounting for these investments, we should consider the implications of using fair value:

1. **Why are passive investments reported at fair value on the balance sheet?** Two primary factors determine the answer to this question:
   - **Relevance.** Analysts who study financial statements often attempt to forecast a company's future cash flows. They want to know how a company can generate cash for purposes such as expansion of the business, payment of dividends, or survival during a prolonged economic downturn. One source of cash is the sale of securities from its passive investments portfolio. The best estimate of the cash that could be generated by the sale of these securities is their current fair value.

> **LEARNING OBJECTIVE E-2**
> Analyze and report passive investments in securities using the fair value method.

> The FAIR VALUE METHOD is used to report securities at their current market value (the amount that would be received in an orderly sale).

UNREALIZED HOLDING GAINS OR LOSSES are amounts associated with price changes of securities that are currently held.

- **Measurability.** Accountants record only items that can be measured in dollar terms with a high degree of reliability (an unbiased and verifiable measurement). Determining the fair value of most assets is very difficult because they are not actively traded. For example, Washington Post's balance sheet reports its headquarters building in terms of its original cost less accumulated depreciation in part because of the difficulty in determining an objective fair value for it. Contrast the difficulty of determining the value of a building with the ease of determining the value of Berkshire Hathaway stock owned by Washington Post. A quick look at *The Wall Street Journal* or an Internet financial service is all that is necessary to determine the current price because these securities are traded each day on established stock exchanges.

2. **When the investment account is adjusted to reflect changes in fair value, what other account is affected when the asset account is increased or decreased?** Under the double-entry method of accounting, every journal entry affects at least two accounts. One account is the investment account. The other account affected is for unrealized holding gains or losses that are recorded whenever the fair value of investments changes. These are unrealized because no actual sale has taken place; simply by holding the security, the value has changed. If the value of the investments increases by $100,000 during the year, an adjusting journal entry records the increase in the investment account and an unrealized holding gain for $100,000. If the value of the investments decreases by $75,000 during the year, an adjusting journal entry records the decrease in the investment account and an unrealized holding loss of $75,000. The financial statement treatment of the unrealized holding gains or losses depends on the classification of the passive investments.

Classifying Passive Investments at Fair Value

Depending on management's intent, passive investments at fair value may be classified as trading securities or available-for-sale securities.

Trading Securities

TRADING SECURITIES are all investments in stocks or bonds held primarily for the purpose of active trading (buying and selling) in the near future (classified as short term).

Trading securities are actively traded with the objective of generating profits on short-term changes in the price of the securities. This approach is similar to the one taken by many mutual funds. The portfolio manager actively seeks opportunities to buy and sell securities. Trading securities are classified as **current assets** on the balance sheet.

Available-for-Sale Securities

AVAILABLE-FOR-SALE SECURITIES are all passive investments other than trading securities and debt held to maturity (classified as short or long term).

Most companies do not actively trade the securities of other companies. Instead, they invest to earn a return on funds they may need for future operating purposes. Other than debt securities to be held to maturity, these debt and equity investments are called available-for-sale securities. They are classified as current or noncurrent assets on the balance sheet depending on whether management intends to sell the securities during the next year.

Trading securities (TS for short) are most commonly reported by financial institutions that actively buy and sell short-term investments to maximize returns. Most corporations, however, invest in short- and long-term available-for-sale securities (AFS, for short). We will focus on this category in the next section by analyzing Washington Post's investing activities.

Available-for-Sale Securities

As shown in Exhibit E.1, Washington Post's Investments in Available-for-Sale Securities accounts are reported for the year 2010 at $374 million for current assets. In 2011, the account shows a balance of $339 million for current assets. The notes to Washington Post's annual report contain the following information concerning this investment portfolio:

B. Summary of Significant Accounting Policies

Investments in Available-for-Sale Securities. The Company's investments in marketable equity securities are classified as available-for-sale and, therefore, are recorded at fair value in the Consolidated Financial Statements, with the change in fair value during the period excluded from earnings and recorded net of income taxes as a separate component of other comprehensive income. If the fair value of a marketable equity security declines below its cost basis and the decline is considered other than temporary, the Company will record a write-down, which is included in earnings.

THE WASHINGTON POST COMPANY

REAL WORLD EXCERPT
Annual Report

For simplification, let's assume that Washington Post had no passive investments at the end of 2011. In the following illustration, we will apply the accounting policy used by Washington Post for 2012, 2013, and 2014.

Purchase of Securities

At the beginning of 2012, Washington Post purchases for cash 15,000 shares of Internet News[3] (INews for short) common stock for $10 per share (a total of $150,000). There were 100,000 outstanding shares, so Washington Post owns 15 percent of INews (15,000 shares ÷ 100,000 shares), which is treated as a passive investment. Such investments are recorded initially at cost:

	Debit	Credit
Investments in AFS Securities (+A).	150,000	
Cash (−A)		150,000

Assets	=	Liabilities	+	Stockholders' Equity
Investments in AFS				
Securities +150,000				
Cash −150,000				

Dividends Earned

Investments in equity securities earn a return from two sources: (1) dividend income and (2) price increases. Dividends earned are reported as investment income on the income statement and are included in the computation of net income for the period. Washington Post received a $1 per share cash dividend from INews totaling $15,000 ($1 ×15,000 shares).

	Debit	Credit
Cash (+A)	15,000	
Dividend Revenue (+R, +SE)		15,000

Assets	=	Liabilities	+	Stockholders' Equity
Cash +15,000				Dividend Revenue (+R) +15,000

This entry is the same for both the trading securities and available-for-sale securities. Price increases (or decreases) are analyzed both at year-end and when a security is sold.

---

[3]Internet News is a fictitious company.

Year-End Valuation

At the end of the accounting period, these passive investments are reported on the balance sheet at fair value, the amount that would be received in an orderly sale.

For 2012   Assume that INews had an $8 per share fair value at the end of the year. That is, the investment had lost value ($10 − $8 = $2 per share) for the year. However, since the investment has not been sold, the loss is an unrealized loss, not a realized loss.

Reporting the AFS investment at fair value requires adjusting the asset Investments in AFS Securities **up or down** to fair value at the end of each period.[4] The gain is credited or the loss is debited to the Net Unrealized Gains (Losses) account to complete the entry. For available-for-sale securities, the Net Unrealized Gains (Losses) account is reported in the stockholders' equity section of the balance sheet under **Other Comprehensive Income** (denoted as **OCI**). Thus, the balance sheet remains in balance. Only when the security is sold are any realized gains or losses included in net income.

The following chart is used to compute any unrealized gain or loss in the AFS portfolio:

Net Unrealized Gains (Losses) (SE)	
1/1/12 0	
AJE 30,000	
12/31/12 30,000	

Year	Fair Value	−	Book Value before Adjustment	=	Amount for Adjusting Entry
2012	$120,000	−	$150,000	=	($30,000)
	($8 × 15,000)		($10 × 15,000)		An **unrealized loss** for the period

The adjusting entry (AJE) at the end of 2012 is recorded as follows:

Investments in AFS Securities (A)	
1/1/12 150,000	
	30,000 AJE
12/31/12 120,000	

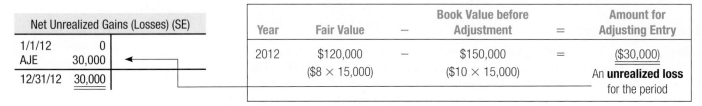

	Debit	Credit
Net Unrealized Gains (Losses) (−OCI, −SE)	30,000	
Investments in AFS Securities (−A)		30,000

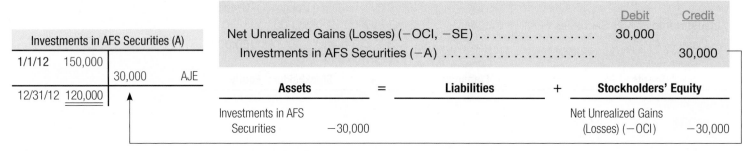

Assets	=	Liabilities	+	Stockholders' Equity
Investments in AFS Securities −30,000				Net Unrealized Gains (Losses) (−OCI) −30,000

On the 2012 Balance Sheet:	
Assets	
Investments in AFS Securities	$120,000
Stockholders' Equity	
Other Comprehensive Income:	
Net unrealized gains (losses)	(30,000)

On the 2012 balance sheet under Other Investments, Washington Post would report an investment in available-for-sale securities of $120,000. It would also report under Other Comprehensive Income its net unrealized loss on available-for-sale securities of $30,000. The only item reported on the income statement for 2012 would be investment income of $15,000 from the dividends earned, classified under Other Items.

For 2013   Now let's assume that the INews securities were held through the next year, 2013. At the end of 2013, the stock had an $11 per share fair value. The adjustment for 2013 would be computed as follows:

Net Unrealized Gains (Losses) (SE)	
1/1/12 0	
AJE 30,000	
12/31/12 30,000	
45,000 AJE	
15,000 12/31/13	

Year	Fair Value	−	Book Value before Adjustment	=	Amount for Adjusting Entry
2013	$165,000	−	$120,000	=	$45,000
	($11 × 15,000)		($8 × 15,000)		An **unrealized gain** for the period

---

[4]Companies often keep the asset value at cost and record the change in fair value in a related valuation allowance which is added or subtracted from the asset. This does not change the financial statement presentation.

The adjusting entry at the end of 2013 would be:

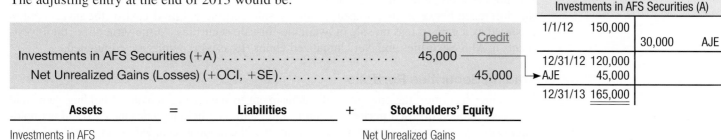

	Debit	Credit
Investments in AFS Securities (+A)	45,000	
Net Unrealized Gains (Losses) (+OCI, +SE).		45,000

Assets	=	Liabilities	+	Stockholders' Equity
Investments in AFS				Net Unrealized Gains
Securities +45,000				(Losses) (+OCI) +45,000

On the 2013 balance sheet, Washington Post would report under Assets an investment in available-for-sale securities of $165,000 and under Other Comprehensive Income its net unrealized gain on available-for-sale securities of $15,000 (fair value − cost).

On the 2013 Balance Sheet:
Assets
Investments in AFS
Securities $165,000
Stockholders' Equity
Other Comprehensive
Income:
Net unrealized gains
(losses)   15,000

Sale of Securities

When available-for-sale securities are sold, Cash is increased and **two** accounts on the balance sheet are eliminated:

- Investments in AFS Securities (A)
- Net Unrealized Gains (Losses) (OCI, SE)

Let's assume that at the end of 2014 Washington Post sold all of its AFS securities investment in INews for $13 per share. The company would receive $195,000 in cash ($13 × 15,000 shares) for stock it paid $150,000 for in 2012 ($10 × 15,000 shares). The gain or loss on sale is computed as follows:

Proceeds from sale − Investment cost = Gain if positive (Loss if negative)

In our example, a gain on sale of $45,000 (proceeds of $195,000 − cost of $150,000) would be recorded and reported on the income statement. The Investment in AFS securities of $165,000 and the credit balance of $15,000 in Net Unrealized Gains (Losses) would be eliminated.

	Debit	Credit
Cash (+A)	195,000	
Net Unrealized Gains (Losses) (−OCI, −SE)	15,000	
Investment in AFS Securities (−A)		165,000
Gain on Sale of Investments (+Gain, +SE)		45,000

Assets	=	Liabilities	+	Stockholders' Equity
Investments in AFS				Net Unrealized Gains
Securities −165,000				(Losses) (−OCI) −15,000
				Gain on Sales of
Cash +195,000				Investment (+Gain) +45,000

Comparing Trading and Available-for-Sale Securities

The reporting impact of unrealized holding gains or losses depends on whether the investment is classified as an available-for-sale security or a trading security.

Available-for-Sale Portfolio

As we learned in the previous section, for available-for-sale securities, the balance in net unrealized holding gains and losses is reported as a separate **component of stockholders' equity** (under Other Comprehensive Income, as illustrated in Exhibit E.1 for Washington Post).

It is not reported on the income statement and does not affect net income. At the time of sale, the difference between the proceeds from the sale and the **original cost** of the investment is recorded as a gain or loss on sale of available-for-sale securities. At the same time, the Investments in AFS Securities and Net Unrealized Gains (Losses) accounts are eliminated.

Trading Securities Portfolio

For trading securities, the amount of the adjustment to record net unrealized holding gains and losses is **included on each period's income statement.** Net holding gains increase and net holding losses decrease net income. This also means that the amount recorded as net unrealized gains and losses on trading securities is closed to Retained Earnings at the end of the period. Thus, when selling a trading security, Cash and only *one* other balance sheet account are affected: Investments

---

EXHIBIT E.2	Comparison of Accounting for Trading Securities and Available-for-Sale Portfolios

PART A: ENTRIES

	TRADING SECURITIES			AVAILABLE-FOR-SALE SECURITIES		
2012:						
• Purchase (for $150,000 cash)	Investments in TS (+A) .... Cash (−A)	150,000	150,000	Investments in AFS Securities (+A) .... Cash (−A)	150,000	150,000
• Receipt of dividends ($15,000 cash)	Cash (+A) .... Dividend Revenue (+R, +SE)	15,000	15,000	Cash (+A) .... Dividend Revenue (+R, +SE)	15,000	15,000

• Year-end adjustment to fair value (= $120,000)	Net unrealized loss
	     (+Loss, −SE) ....
	         Investments in TS (−A) ....
		30,000	30,000	Net unrealized gains (losses)
				     (−OCI, −SE) ....
				         Investments in AFS
				             Securities (−A) ....
					30,000	30,000

2013:						

• Year-end adjustment to fair value (= $165,000)	Investments in TS (+A) ....
	     Net unrealized gain
	         (+Gain, +SE) ....
		45,000	45,000	Investments in AFS Securities (+A) ....
				     Net unrealized gains (losses)
				         (+OCI, +SE) ....
					45,000	45,000

2014:						

• Sale (for $195,000)	*One balance sheet account is eliminated:*
	 Cash (+A) ....
	     Investments in TS (−A) ....
	     Gain on sale of investments
	         (+Gain, +SE) ....
		195,000	165,000
			
			 30,000
				Two balance sheet accounts are eliminated:
				 Cash (+A) ....
				 Net unrealized gains (losses)
				     (−OCI, −SE) ....
				         Investments in AFS
				             Securities (−A) ....
				     Gain on sale of investments
				         (+Gain, +SE) ....
					195,000
					
					 15,000
						
						 165,000
						
						 45,000

PART B: FINANCIAL REPORTING

	TRADING SECURITIES				AVAILABLE-FOR-SALE SECURITIES			
• **Balance Sheet:**	**Assets**	**2014**	**2013**	**2012**	**Assets**	**2014**	**2013**	**2012**
	Investments in TS	0	165,000	120,000	Investments in AFS Securities	0	165,000	120,000

					Stockholders' Equity
					 Other comprehensive income:
					     Net unrealized
					         gains (losses)
						
						 0
							
							 15,000
								
								 (30,000)

• **Income Statement:**		**2014**	**2013**	**2012**		**2014**	**2013**	**2012**
	Dividend revenue	0	0	15,000	Dividend revenue	0	0	15,000
	Gain on sale	30,000	—	—	Gain on sale	45,000	—	—
	Net unrealized gains (losses)		45,000	(30,000)				

in TS. Also, only the difference between the cash proceeds from the sale and the **book value** (not cost) of the Investments in TS is recorded as a gain or loss on sale of trading securities. In the illustration above, assuming the investment was in trading securities, the realized gain from the sale of the investments in 2013 would be $30,000 ($195,000 proceeds − $165,000 book value). **Note that total income reported for the three years is the same $60,000 for both trading securities and available-for-sale securities. Only the allocation across the three periods differs.**

Income in	Trading Securities	Available-for-Sale Securities
2012	$15,000 dividend revenue	$15,000 dividend revenue
	(30,000) unrealized loss	—
2013	45,000 unrealized gain	—
2014	30,000 realized gain	45,000 realized gain
Total	$60,000	$60,000

Exhibit E.2 provides comparative journal entries and financial statement balances for the transactions illustrated for Washington Post from 2012 to 2014.

Reporting the Fair Value of Investments

FINANCIAL ANALYSIS

Accounting standards require that companies disclose the measurements used to determine the fair values of assets on the balance sheet. The fair value of an asset is the amount that would be received in an orderly sale. The standard recognizes three approaches in order of decreasing reliability:

Fair Value

- Level 1: Quoted prices in active markets for identical assets.
- Level 2: Estimates based on other observable inputs (e.g., prices for similar assets).
- Level 3: Estimates based on unobservable estimates (the company's own estimates of factors that market participants would consider).

Fair value should be determined using the **most** reliable method available (Level 1 if possible). The reporting company must then disclose the amounts determined under each approach in a note to the financial statements. The following is the note provided in the most recent annual report of The Buckle.

The Company's financial assets measured at fair value on a recurring basis subject to the disclosure requirements of SFAS 157 as of January 28, 2012, were as follows:

	Fair Value Measurements at Reporting Date Using			
	Quoted Prices in Active Markets for Identical Assets (Level 1)	Significant Observable Inputs (Level 2)	Significant Unobservable Inputs (Level 3)	Total
Assets:				
Available-for-sale securities	$ 26	$2,920	$11,220	$14,166
Trading securities	8,581	—	—	8,581
Totals	$8,607	$2,920	$11,220	$22,747

REAL WORLD EXCERPT
The Buckle
Annual Report

Companies also have the option of accounting for other financial assets (such as notes receivable) and financial liabilities (such as bonds payable) at fair value. Thus far, application of this **fair value option** has been limited mostly to banks and other financial institutions.

PAUSE FOR **FEEDBACK**

Passive investments other than debt held to maturity are recorded at cost and adjusted to **fair value** at year-end. The resulting unrealized gain or loss is recorded.

- For trading securities, the net unrealized gains and losses are reported in net income.
- For available-for-sale securities, the net unrealized gains and losses are reported as a component of stockholders' equity in other comprehensive income.

Any dividends earned are reported as revenue, and any gains or losses on sales of passive investments are reported on the income statement. To see if you understand passive investments accounting and reporting, answer the following questions.

SELF-STUDY **QUIZ**

In 2013, Rosa Food Corporation acquired 5,000 shares (10%) of the outstanding voting equity shares of another company for $100,000 to be held as long-term available-for-sale securities. At the end of 2013, the fair value of the stock was $22 per share. At the end of 2014, the fair value of the stock was $17 per share. On January 2, 2015, Rosa Food sold the entire investment for $120,000 cash.

1. Record the purchase.	
2. Record the adjusting entry at the end of 2013.	
a. What would be reported on the balance sheet for the investment? b. What would be reported on the income statement for the investment?	
3. Record the adjusting entry at the end of 2014.	
4. Record the sale in 2015.	

5. If the investment was held as trading securities,
   a. What would be reported on the balance sheet for the investment at the end of 2013?
   b. What would be reported on the 2013 income statement for the investment?	

After you have completed your answers, check them with the solutions at the bottom of the page.

GUIDED **HELP**

www.mhhe.com/libby8e

For additional step-by-step video instruction on accounting for and reporting available-for-sale securities as investments at fair value, go to the URL or scan the QR code in the margin with your smartphone or iPad.

Solutions to
SELF-STUDY QUIZ

1. Investments in AFS securities (+A)............... 100,000
   Cash (−A) 100,000
2. Investments in AFS securities (+A) 10,000
   Net unreal. gains (losses) (+OCI, +SE).......... 10,000   [$110,000 fair value − $100,000 cost = +$10,000]

   a. Under noncurrent assets: Investments in AFS securities $110,000
      Under stockholders' equity
      (other comprehensive income):   Net unrealized gain $ 10,000
   b. No dividend revenue or realized gains and losses from sales of investments would be reported on the income statement.
3. Net unrealized gains (losses) (−OCI, −SE) 25,000   [($17 × 5,000 shares) − $110,000
   Investments in AFS securities (−A) 25,000   book value = −$25,000]
4. Cash (+A) 120,000
   Investments in AFS securities (−A) 85,000
   Net unrealized gains (losses) (+OCI, +SE) 15,000
   Gain on sale of investments (+Gain, +SE)........ 20,000
5. *a.* Under current assets: Investments in AFS securities $110,000
   b. Under other items: Net unrealized gain $ 10,000
      There were no dividends reported.

Economic Return from Investing

Both corporate and individual investors need to monitor the performance of their securities portfolios. Normally, this is done using the economic return from investing ratio, which provides a percentage of what was earned plus any realized and/or unrealized gains or losses on the portfolio.

? ANALYTICAL QUESTION

During the period, how much was earned per dollar invested in securities?

% RATIO AND COMPARISONS

$$\text{Economic Return from Investing} = \frac{\text{Dividends and Interest Received} + \text{Change in Fair Value*}}{\text{Fair Value of Investments (beginning of period)}}$$

*Ending balance of Investments − Beginning balance of Investments

The 2012 ratio for our hypothetical investment:

$$\frac{\$15{,}000 \text{ Dividends} - \$30{,}000 \text{ Unrealized Loss}}{\$150{,}000} = -0.10 \ (-10.0\%)$$

The 2013 ratio for our hypothetical investment:

$$\frac{\$0 \text{ Dividends} + \$45{,}000 \text{ Unrealized Gain}}{\$120{,}000} = +0.375 \ (+37.5\%)$$

The 2014 ratio for our hypothetical investment:

$$\frac{\$0 \text{ Dividends} - \$15{,}000 \text{ Unrealized Loss} + \$45{,}000 \text{ Realized Gain}}{\$165{,}000} = +0.182 \ (18.2\%)$$

💡 INTERPRETATIONS

In General   Economic investment returns contain two parts: the effect of dividends received, called the *dividend yield,* and the effect of the change in fair value, called the *capital gain* or *loss.* Note that from an economic standpoint, you have earned the capital gain or loss whether you have sold the securities or not since you had the opportunity to convert the gain or loss into cash by selling. If you look at the numerator of the ratio each year, you will see that it matches the amount of income reported each year under trading securities in Exhibit E.2, Part B. This is why many analysts believe that the accounting for trading securities better reflects the economics of investing.

A Few Cautions   Computations for realistic portfolios are more complex if securities are bought and sold throughout the year. This affects the computation of the denominator of the ratio.

INVESTMENTS FOR SIGNIFICANT INFLUENCE: EQUITY METHOD

LEARNING OBJECTIVE E-3
Analyze and report investments involving significant influence using the equity method.

When Washington Post invests cash in securities that are reported on its balance sheet as Investments in Available-for-Sale Securities, it is a passive investor. However, when the company reports Investments in Affiliates on its balance sheet, it is taking a more active role as an investor. For a variety of reasons, an investor may want to exert influence (presumed by owning 20 to 50 percent of the outstanding voting stock) without becoming the controlling shareholder (presumed when owning more than 50 percent of the voting stock). Examples follow:

- A retailer may want to influence a manufacturer to be sure that it can obtain certain products designed to its specifications.

- A manufacturer may want to influence a computer consulting firm to ensure that it can incorporate the consulting firm's cutting-edge technology in its manufacturing processes.

- A manufacturer may recognize that a parts supplier lacks experienced management and could prosper with additional managerial support.

THE WASHINGTON POST COMPANY

REAL WORLD EXCERPT

Annual Report

The **equity method** must be used when an investor can exert significant influence over an affiliate. On the balance sheet these long-term investments are classified as **investments in affiliates** (or **associated companies**). Washington Post reported investments in affiliates in its 2011 annual report.

Notes to Financial Statements

B. Summary of Significant Accounting Policies

Investments in Affiliates. The Company uses the equity method of accounting for its investments in and earnings or losses of affiliates that it does not control, but over which it does exert significant influence . . .

D. Investments

Investments in Affiliates. At the end of 2011, the Company's investments in affiliates include a 49% interest in the common stock of Bowater Mersey Paper Company Limited, which owns and operates a newsprint mill in Nova Scotia. The Company also holds a 16.5% interest in Classified Ventures, LLC, which owns and operates several leading businesses in the online classified advertising space, and several other investments.

Recording Investments under the Equity Method

Under the equity method, the investor's 20 to 50 percent ownership of a company presumes significant influence over the affiliate's process of earning income. As a consequence, the investor reports its portion of the affiliate's net income as its income and increases the investment account by the same amount. Similarly, the receipt of dividends by the investor is treated as a reduction of the investment account, not revenue. A summary follows:

- *Net income of affiliates:* If affiliates report positive results of operations for the year, the investor then records investment income equal to its percentage share of the affiliates' net income and increases its asset account Investments in Affiliates (or Associated Companies). If the affiliates report net losses, the investor records the opposite effect.

- *Dividends paid by affiliates:* If affiliates declare and pay dividends during the year (a financing decision), the investor reduces its investment account and increases cash when it receives its share of the dividends.

Investments in Affiliates (A)	
Beginning balance Purchases	Sales
Company's % share of affiliates' net income (credit Equity in Affiliate Earnings [↑ income])	Company's % share of affiliates' net losses (debit Equity in Affiliate Losses [↓ income]
	Company's % share of affiliates' dividends declared for the period (debit Cash)
Ending balance	

Purchase of Stock

For simplification, let's assume that, at the beginning of 2013, Washington Post had no long-term investments in companies over which it exerted significant influence. In 2013, Washington Post purchased 40,000 shares of the outstanding voting common stock of Internet News (INews) for $400,000 in cash. Since INews had 100,000 shares of common stock outstanding, Washington Post acquired 40 percent and was presumed to have significant influence over the affiliate. Therefore, Washington Post must use the equity method to account for this investment. The purchase of the asset would be recorded at cost.

	Debit	Credit
Investments in Affiliates (+A)	400,000	
Cash (−A)		400,000

Assets	=	Liabilities	+	Stockholders' Equity
Investments in Affiliates +400,000				
Cash −400,000				

Earnings of Affiliates

Because the investor can influence the process of earning income for the affiliates, the investor company bases its investment income on the affiliates' earnings rather than the dividends affiliates pay. During 2013, INews reported a net income of $500,000 for the year. Washington Post's percentage share of INews's income was $200,000 (40% × $500,000) and is recorded as follows:

	Debit	Credit
Investments in Affiliates (+A)	200,000	
Equity in Affiliate Earnings (+R, +SE)......................		200,000

Assets	=	Liabilities	+	Stockholders' Equity
Investments in Affiliates +200,000				Equity in Affiliate Earnings (+R) +200,000

If the affiliates report a net loss for the period, the investor records its percentage share of the loss by decreasing the investment account and recording Equity in Affiliate Loss. The Equity in Affiliate Earnings (or Loss) is reported in the Other Items section of the income statement, with interest revenue, interest expense, and gains and losses on sales of assets.

Dividends Received

Because Washington Post can influence the dividend policies of its equity-method investments, any dividends it receives should **not** be recorded as investment income. Instead, dividends received reduce its investment account. During 2013, INews declared and paid a cash dividend of $1 per share to stockholders. Washington Post received $40,000 in cash ($1 × 40,000 shares) from INews.

	Debit	Credit
Cash (+A)	40,000	
Investments in Affiliates (−A).............................		40,000

Assets	=	Liabilities	+	Stockholders' Equity
Investments in Affiliates −40,000				
Cash +40,000				

In summary, the effects for 2013 are reflected in the following T-accounts:

Investments in Affiliates (A)				Equity in Affiliate Earnings (R)		
1/1/13	0				0	1/1/13
Purchase	400,000					
Share of affiliate's net earnings	200,000	40,000	Share of affiliate's dividends		200,000	Share of affiliate's net earnings
12/31/13	560,000				200,000	12/31/13

Reporting Investments under the Equity Method

The Investments in Affiliates account is reported on the balance sheet as a long-term asset. However, as these last two entries show, the investment account does not reflect either cost or fair value. Instead, the following occurs:

- The investment account is increased by the cost of shares that were purchased and the proportional share of the affiliates' net income.

- The account is reduced by the amount of dividends received from the affiliate companies and the proportional share of any affiliates' net losses.

At the end of the accounting period, accountants **do not adjust the investment account to reflect changes in the fair value** of the securities that are held.[5] When the securities are sold, the difference between the cash received and the book value of the investment is recorded as a gain or loss on the sale of the investment and is reported on the income statement in the Other Items section.

PAUSE FOR **FEEDBACK**

If between 20 and 50 percent of the outstanding voting shares are owned, significant influence over the affiliate firm's operating and financing policies is presumed, and the equity method is applied. Under the **equity method,** the investor records the investment at cost on the acquisition date. Each period thereafter, the investment amount is increased (or decreased) by the proportionate interest in the income (or loss) reported by the affiliate corporation and decreased by the proportionate share of the dividends declared by the affiliate corporation.

SELF-STUDY **QUIZ**

To test your understanding of these concepts, answer the following questions.

At the beginning of 2014, Weld Company purchased 30 percent (20,000 shares) of the outstanding voting stock of another company for $600,000 cash. During 2014, the affiliate declared and paid $50,000 in dividends. For 2014, the affiliate reported net income of $150,000. The stock had a fair value of $34 per share on December 31, 2014. Answer the following questions.

1. Record the purchase.	
2. Record the receipt of dividends in 2014.	
3. Record Weld's equity in the affiliate's earnings for 2014.	
4. Record any year-end adjustment to the investments account.	
5. What would be reported on the balance sheet for the investment in the affiliate at the end of 2014? (*Hint:* Construct a T-account.)	
6. What would be reported on the 2014 income statement for the investment in the affiliate?	

After you have completed your answers, check them with the solutions at the bottom of the next page.

---

[5]FAS 159 (ASC 825-10) does allow companies to elect fair value treatment for equity method investments, but few companies are expected to take the election.

Transaction Structuring: Selecting Accounting Methods for Minority Investments

Managers can choose freely between LIFO and FIFO or accelerated depreciation and straight-line depreciation. In the case of minority (≤ 50% owned) investments, investments of less than 20 percent of a company's outstanding stock are usually accounted for under the fair value method and investments of 20 to 50 percent are accounted for under the equity method.

However, managers may be able to structure the acquisition of stock in a manner that permits them to use the accounting method that they prefer. For example, a company that wants to use the fair value method could purchase only 19.9 percent of the outstanding stock of another company and achieve the same investment goals as it would with a 20 percent investment. Why might managers want to avoid using the equity method? Most managers prefer to minimize variations in reported earnings. If a company were planning to buy stock in a firm that reported large earnings in some years and large losses in others, it might want to use the fair value method to avoid reporting its share of the affiliate's earnings and losses.

Analysts who compare several companies must understand management's reporting choices and the way in which differences between the fair value and equity methods can affect earnings.

INVESTMENTS

Many of the effects of applying the fair value method to passive investments and the equity method to investments held for significant influence affect net income but not cash flow. These items require adjustments under the indirect method when converting net income to cash flows from operating activities.

In General   Investments have a number of effects on the statement of cash flows:

1. The cash resulting from the sale or purchase is reflected in the Investing Activities section.

2. In the Operating Activities section, there are a number of adjustments to net income:

   a. Any gain (loss) on the sale is subtracted from (added to) net income.

   b. Any unrealized holding gain (loss) on trading securities is subtracted from (added to) net income.

   c. Equity in affiliate earnings (losses) is subtracted from (added to) net income because no cash was involved in the recording of the revenue under the equity method.

   d. Any dividends received from an affiliate are added to net income because, when cash was received, no revenue was recorded under the equity method.

(continued)

---

1. Investments in Affiliates (+A)   600,000
      Cash (−A)   600,000

2. Cash (+A)   15,000   [$50,000 total
      Investments in Affiliates (−A)   15,000   dividends × 30%]

3. Investments in Affiliates (+A)   45,000
      Equity in Affiliate Earnings (+R, +SE)   45,000   [$150,000 net
          income × 30%]

4. There is no other year-end adjustment related to the stock's fair value under the equity method.

5. Under Long-Term Assets: Investments in Affiliates $630,000

6. Under Other Items on Weld's
        income statement: Equity in Affiliate Earnings $45,000

Investments in Affiliates (A)			
1/1/14	0		
Purchase	600,000		
Share of affiliate's net earnings	45,000	15,000	Share of affiliate's dividends
12/31/14	630,000		

EFFECT ON THE STATEMENT OF CASH FLOWS	
	Effect on Cash Flows
Operating activities	
Net income	$xxx
Adjusted for	
Gains/losses on sale of investments	−/+
Net unrealized holding gains/losses on trading securities	−/+
Equity in net earnings/losses of affiliated companies	−/+
Dividends received from affiliated companies	+
Investing Activities	
Purchase of investments	−
Sale of investments	+

LEARNING OBJECTIVE E-4
Analyze and report investments in controlling interests.

CONTROLLING INTERESTS: MERGERS AND ACQUISITIONS

Before we discuss financial reporting issues for situations in which a company owns more than 50 percent of the outstanding common stock of another corporation, we should consider management's reasons for acquiring this level of ownership. The following are some of the reasons for acquiring control of another corporation:

1. **Vertical integration.** In this type of acquisition, a company acquires another at a different level in the channels of distribution. For example, Washington Post owns a newsprint company that provides raw materials.

2. **Horizontal growth.** These acquisitions involve companies at the same level in the channels of distribution. For example, Washington Post has expanded internationally by creating or acquiring companies in major international markets.

3. **Synergy.** The operations of two companies together may be more profitable than the combined profitability of the companies as separate entities. Washington Post has created or purchased a number of broadcast and Internet services. Merging these companies and sharing news content may create more profits than operating separate entities could.

Understanding why one company has acquired control over other companies is a key factor in understanding the company's overall business strategy.

Recording a Merger

A MERGER occurs when one company purchases all of the assets and liabilities of another and the acquired company goes out of existence.

The simplest way to understand the statements that result from the purchase of another company is to consider the case of a simple merger where one company purchases all of the assets and liabilities of another and the acquired company goes out of existence as a separate corporation. We will consider the case where Washington Post acquires all of the assets and liabilities of INews for $1,000,000 cash.

The ACQUISITION METHOD records assets and liabilities acquired in a merger or acquisition at their fair value on the transaction date.

The acquisition method is the only method allowed by U.S. GAAP and IFRS for recording a merger or acquisition. It requires that the assets and liabilities of INews be recorded by Washington Post on its books at their **fair value** on the date of the merger. So the acquiring company, in this case Washington Post, must go through a two-step process, often called the **purchase price allocation,** to determine how to record the acquisition:

GOODWILL (COST IN EXCESS OF NET ASSETS ACQUIRED) is the excess of the purchase price of a business over the fair value of the acquired company's assets and liabilities.

Step 1: **Estimate the fair value of the acquired company's tangible assets, identifiable intangible assets, and liabilities.** This includes all assets and liabilities, regardless of whether and at what amount they were recorded on the books of the acquired company.

Step 2: **Compute goodwill, the excess of the total purchase price over the fair value of the assets minus the liabilities listed in Step 1.**

For our example, assume that INews owned two assets (equipment and a patent) and had one liability (a note payable). Washington Post followed the two steps and produced the following:

Step 1:   Estimate the fair value of the acquired company's tangible assets, identifiable intangible assets, and liabilities.

Fair value of INews's—	Equipment	$350,000	}	$950,000 total assets
	Patents	600,000		
	Note Payable	100,000		

Step 2:   Compute goodwill as follows:

Purchase price for INews	$1,000,000
Less: Fair value of assets ($950,000) minus liabilities ($100,000)	−850,000
Goodwill purchased	$ 150,000

Washington Post would then account for the merger by recording the assets and liabilities listed above and reducing cash for the amount paid as follows:

	Debit	Credit
Equipment (+A)	350,000	
Patents (+A)	600,000	
Goodwill (+A)	150,000	
Note Payable (+L)		100,000
Cash (−A)		1,000,000

Assets		=	Liabilities		+	Stockholders' Equity
Equipment	+350,000		Note Payable	+100,000		
Patents	+600,000					
Goodwill	+150,000					
Cash	−1,000,000					

In summary, when performing a purchase price allocation, it is important to remember two points:

- The book values on the acquired company's balance sheet are irrelevant unless they represent fair value.
- Goodwill is reported only if it is acquired in a merger or acquisition transaction.

In a recent annual report, Washington Post describes GAAP for recording mergers and acquisitions in the following note:

B. Summary of Significant Accounting Policies

Business Combinations—The purchase price of an acquisition is allocated to the assets acquired, including intangible assets, and liabilities assumed, based on their respective fair values at the acquisition date. The excess of the cost of an acquired entity over the net of the amounts assigned to the assets acquired and liabilities assumed is recognized as goodwill. The net assets and results of operations of an acquired entity are included in the Company's consolidated financial statements from the acquisition date.

THE WASHINGTON
POST COMPANY

REAL WORLD EXCERPT
Annual Report

Reporting for the Combined Companies

After the merger, Washington Post will treat the acquired assets and liabilities in the same manner as if they were acquired individually. For example, the company will depreciate the $350,000 added to equipment over its remaining useful life and amortize the $600,000 for patents over their remaining useful life. As we noted in Chapter 8, goodwill is considered to have an indefinite life. As a consequence, it is not amortized, but, like all long-lived assets, goodwill is reviewed for possible impairment of value. Recording an impairment loss would increase expenses for the period and reduce the amount of goodwill on the balance sheet.

When a company acquires another, and both companies continue their separate legal existence, **consolidated financial statements** must be presented. The parent company is the company that gains control over the other company. The subsidiary company is the company that the parent acquires. When the parent buys 100 percent of the subsidiary, the resulting consolidated financial statements look the same as they would if the companies were combined into one in a simple merger as discussed above. The procedures involved in preparation of consolidated statements are discussed in advanced accounting courses.

 PAUSE FOR **FEEDBACK**

Mergers and ownership of a controlling interest in another corporation (more than 50 percent of the outstanding voting shares) must be accounted for using the acquisition method. The acquired company's assets and liabilities are measured at their fair values. Any amount paid above the fair value of the net assets is reported as goodwill by the buyer. To make sure you understand how to apply these concepts, answer the following questions.

SELF-STUDY **QUIZ**

Lexis Corporation purchased 100 percent of Nexis Company for $10 and merged Nexis into Lexis. On the date of the merger, the fair value of Nexis's other assets was $11 and the fair value of Nexis's liabilities was $4. What amounts would be added to Lexis's balance sheet as a result of the merger for:

1. Goodwill?
2. Other Assets (excluding Goodwill)?

After you have completed your answers, check them with the solutions at the bottom of the page.

DEMONSTRATION   **CASE A**

PASSIVE INVESTMENTS USING FAIR VALUE METHOD

(Try to resolve the requirements before proceeding to the suggested solution that follows.) Howell Equipment Corporation sells and services a major line of farm equipment. Both sales and service operations have been profitable. The following transactions affected the company during 2013:

a. Jan.   1   Purchased 2,000 shares of common stock of Dear Company at $40 per share to be held as available-for-sale securities. This purchase represented 1 percent of the shares outstanding.

b. Dec. 28   Received $4,000 cash dividend on the Dear Company stock.

c. Dec. 31   Determined that the current market price of the Dear stock was $39.

Solutions to
SELF-STUDY QUIZ

1. Purchase Price ($10) − Fair Value of Net Assets ($11 − $4) = Goodwill $3.
2. Nexis's other assets (at fair value) = $11.

Required:

1. Prepare the journal entry for each of these transactions.

2. What accounts and amounts will be reported on the balance sheet at the end of 2013? On the income statement for 2013?

3. Assuming management intends to trade these shares actively instead of holding them as available-for-sale securities, what accounts and amounts will be reported on the balance sheet at the end of 2013? On the income statement for 2013?

SUGGESTED SOLUTION FOR CASE A

1.

a. Jan. 1 Investments in AFS securities (+A).	80,000	
Cash (−A) [2,000 shares × $40 per share]		80,000
b. Dec. 28 Cash (+A)	4,000	
Dividend revenue (+R, +SE).		4,000
c. Dec. 31 Net unrealized gains (losses) (−OCI, −SE).	2,000	
Investments in AFS securities (−A).		2,000

Year	Fair Value	−	Book Value before Adjustment	=	Amount for Adjusting Entry
2013	$78,000 ($39 × 2,000 shares)	−	$80,000	=	($2,000) An unrealized loss for the period

2. On the Balance Sheet:

Current or Noncurrent Assets
Investments in AFS securities
($80,000 cost − $2,000 adjustment) $78,000

Stockholders' Equity
Other comprehensive income:
Net unrealized gain (loss)   (2,000)

On the Income Statement:

Other Items
Dividend revenue $4,000

3. Assuming trading securities—
On the Balance Sheet:

Current Assets
Investments in TS
($80,000 cost − $2,000 adjustment) $78,000

On the Income Statement:

Other Items
Dividend revenue $4,000
Net unrealized gain (loss)   (2,000)

DEMONSTRATION   CASE B

INVESTMENTS WITH SIGNIFICANT INFLUENCE USING EQUITY METHOD

On January 1, 2013, Connaught Company purchased 40 percent of the outstanding voting shares of London Company on the open market for $85,000 cash. London declared and paid $10,000 in cash dividends on December 1 and reported net income of $60,000 for the year.

Required:

1. Prepare the journal entries for 2013.

2. What accounts and amounts were reported on Connaught's balance sheet at the end of 2013? On Connaught's income statement for 2013?

SUGGESTED SOLUTION FOR CASE B

1.

Jan. 1	Investments in affiliates (+A)	85,000	
	Cash (−A)		85,000
Dec. 1	Cash (+A) (40% × $10,000)	4,000	
	Investments in affiliates (−A)		4,000
Dec. 31	Investments in affiliates (+A) (40% × $60,000) . .	24,000	
	Equity in affiliate earnings (+R, +SE)		24,000

2. On the Balance Sheet:

Noncurrent Assets
Investments in affiliates
($85,000 − $4,000 + $24,000) $105,000

On the Income Statement:

Other Items
Equity in affiliate earnings $24,000

DEMONSTRATION CASE C

MERGER USING ACQUISITION METHOD

On January 1, 2013, Ohio Company purchased 100 percent of the outstanding voting shares of Allegheny Company in the open market for $85,000 cash and Allegheny was merged into Ohio Company. On the date of acquisition, the fair value of Allegheny Company's plant and equipment was $89,000 and the fair value of a note payable was $10,000. Allegheny had no other assets or liabilities.

Required:

1. Analyze the merger to determine the amount of goodwill purchased.

2. Give the journal entry that Ohio Company should make on the date of the acquisition. If none is required, explain why.

3. Should Allegheny Company's assets be included on Ohio's balance sheet at book value or fair value? Explain.

SUGGESTED SOLUTION FOR CASE C

1.

Purchase price for Allegheny Company	$85,000	
Less: Fair value of net assets purchased	79,000	($89,000 − $10,000)
Goodwill	$ 6,000	

2.

Jan. 1, 2013 Plant and Equipment (+A)	89,000	
Goodwill (+A)	6,000	
Notes Payable (+L)		10,000
Cash (−A)		85,000

3. Allegheny Company's assets should be included on the postmerger balance sheet at their fair values as of the date of acquisition. The cost principle applies as it does with all asset acquisitions.

CHAPTER **TAKE-AWAYS**

E-1. Analyze and report investments in debt securities held to maturity.   p. E-4

When management intends to hold an investment in a debt security (such as a bond or note) until it matures, the held-to-maturity security is recorded at cost when acquired and reported at amortized cost on the balance sheet. Any interest earned during the period is reported on the income statement.

E-2. Analyze and report passive investments in securities using the fair value method.   p. E-5

Acquiring debt securities not held to maturity or less than 20 percent of the outstanding voting shares of another company's common stock is presumed to be a passive investment. Passive investments may be classified as:

- Trading securities (which are actively traded to maximize return) **or**
- Available-for-sale securities (which earn a return but are not as actively traded), depending on management's intent.

The investments are recorded at cost and adjusted to **fair value** at year-end. The resulting unrealized gain or loss is recorded as follows:

- For trading securities, the net unrealized gains and losses are reported in net income.
- For available-for-sale securities, the net unrealized gains and losses are reported as a component of stockholders' equity in other comprehensive income.

Any dividends earned are reported as revenue, and any gains or losses on sales of passive investments are reported on the income statement.

E-3. Analyze and report investments involving significant influence using the equity method.   p. E-13

If between 20 and 50 percent of the outstanding voting shares are owned, significant influence over the affiliate firm's operating and financing policies is presumed, and the equity method is applied. Under the **equity method,** the investor records the investment at cost on the acquisition date. Each period thereafter, the investment amount is increased (or decreased) by the proportionate interest in the income (or loss) reported by the affiliate corporation and decreased by the proportionate share of the dividends declared by the affiliate corporation.

E-4. Analyze and report investments in controlling interests.   p. E-18

Mergers occur when one company purchases all of the net assets of another and the target company ceases to exist as a separate legal entity. Mergers and ownership of a controlling interest of another corporation (more than 50 percent of the outstanding voting shares) must be accounted for using the acquisition method. The acquired company's assets and liabilities are measured at their fair values on the date of the transaction. Any amount paid above the fair value of the assets less liabilities is reported as goodwill by the buyer.

Each year, many companies report healthy profits but file for bankruptcy. Some investors consider this situation to be a paradox, but sophisticated analysts understand how this situation can occur. These analysts recognize that the income statement is prepared under the accrual concept (revenue is reported when earned and the related expense is matched with the revenue). The income statement does not report cash collections and cash payments. Troubled companies usually file for bankruptcy because they cannot meet their cash obligations (for example, they cannot pay their suppliers or meet their required interest payments). The income statement does not help analysts assess the cash flows of a company. The statement of cash flows, discussed in Chapter 12, is designed to help statement users evaluate a company's cash inflows and outflows.

Chapter Supplement A

Held-to-Maturity Bonds Purchased at Other than Par Value: Amortized Cost Method

Bond Purchases

On the date of purchase, a bond may be acquired at the maturity amount (at par), for less than the maturity amount (at a discount), or for more than the maturity amount (at a premium). The total cost of the bond, including all incidental acquisition costs such as transfer fees and broker commissions, is debited to the Held-to-Maturity Investments account.

To illustrate accounting for bond investments acquired **at other than par,** assume that on July 1, 2013, Washington Post paid $92,277 cash for an 8 percent, 5-year $100,000 bond that paid interest semi-annually (on June 30 and December 31). The bond's yield was 10 percent. The $92,277 represents the present value of the bond on the purchase date, computed as follows:

Present value of the bond investment = Present value of the face + Present value of the interest annuity

$92,277 = ($100,000 × .6139) + ($4,000 × 7.7217)

[*n* = 10 periods; interest rate = 5%]

Management intends to hold the bonds until maturity. The journal entry to record the purchase of the bonds follows:

	Debit	Credit
Held-to-Maturity Investments (+A)...........................	92,277	
Cash (−A)		92,277

Assets	=	Liabilities	+	Stockholders' Equity
Held-to-Maturity Investments +92,277				
Cash −92,277				

Interest Earned

The bonds in this illustration were purchased at a discount that will need to be amortized over the life of the investment. Using the effective interest amortization method (discussed in Chapter 10), the cash received is based on the face amount of the bond ($100,000) multiplied by the stated rate of interest for half of a year (4 percent). Revenue earned is computed by multiplying the present value of the bond times the market rate for half of a year (5 percent). The following journal entry records the receipt of interest on December 31, 2013:

	Debit	Credit
Cash (+A)	4,000	
Held-to-Maturity Investments (+A)...........................	614	
Interest Revenue (+R, +SE)		4,614

Assets	=	Liabilities	+	Stockholders' Equity
Held-to-Maturity Investments +614				Interest Revenue (+R) +4,614
Cash +4,000				

The amount reported on the balance sheet at December 31, 2013, is $92,891 ($92,277 + $614), which will be the present value of the bond used in determining interest revenue on the next payment date of June 30, 2014. If the bond investment must be sold before maturity, any difference between market value on the date of sale and net book value would be reported as a gain or loss on sale.

KEY **RATIO**

Economic return from investing measures the performance of a company's securities portfolios. Investment returns include both dividends received and any change in the fair value. A high or rising ratio suggests that a firm's securities portfolio is improving. It is computed as follows (p. E-13):

$$\text{Economic Return from Investing} = \frac{\text{Dividends and Interest Received + Change in Fair Value*}}{\text{Fair Value of Investments (beginning of period)}}$$

*Ending Balance of Investments − Beginning Balance of Investments

FINDING **FINANCIAL INFORMATION**

Balance Sheet

Current Assets:
Investment in trading securities
Investment in available-for-sale securities

Noncurrent Assets:
Investment in available-for-sale securities
Investment in affiliates (or associated companies)
Investments held to maturity

Stockholders' Equity
Other comprehensive income:
   Net unrealized gains (losses) (on
      available-for-sale securities)

Statement of Cash Flows

Operating Activities:
Net income adjusted for:
   Gains/losses on sale of investments
   Equity in earnings/losses of affiliates
   Dividends received from affiliates
   Net unrealized gains (losses) on trading securities

Investing Activities:
Purchase/sale of investments

Income Statement

Under "Other Items":
Dividend (and interest) revenue
Loss or gain on sale of investments
Net unrealized gains (losses) (on
   trading securities)
Equity in affiliate earnings/losses

Notes

In Various Notes:
Accounting policies for investments
Details on securities held as trading and
   available-for-sale securities and
   investments in affiliates

KEY **TERMS**

Acquistion Method   p. E-18
Amortized Cost Method   p. E-4
Available-for-Sale Securities   p. E-16
Equity Method   p. E-14
Fair Value Method   p. E-5

Goodwill (Cost in Excess of Net
   Assets Acquired)   p. E-18
Held-to-Maturity Investments   p. E-4
Investments in Affiliates (or Associated
   Companies)   p. E-14

Merger   p. E-18
Trading Securities   p. E-6
Unrealized Holding Gains or Losses
   p. E-6

QUESTIONS

1. Explain the difference between a short-term investment and a long-term investment.
2. Explain the difference in accounting methods used for passive investments, investments in which the investor can exert significant influence, and investments in which the investor has control over another entity.
3. Explain how bonds held to maturity are reported on the balance sheet.
4. Explain the application of the cost principle to the purchase of capital stock in another company.
5. Under the fair value method, when and how does the investor company measure revenue?
6. Under the equity method, why does the investor company measure revenue on a proportionate basis when income is reported by the affiliate company rather than when dividends are declared?
7. Under the equity method, dividends received from the affiliate company are not recorded as revenue. To record dividends as revenue involves double counting. Explain.
8. When one company acquires control of another, how are the acquired company's assets and liabilities recorded?
9. What is goodwill?

MULTIPLE-CHOICE **QUESTIONS**

1. Company X owns 40 percent of Company Y and exercises significant influence over the management of Company Y. Therefore, Company X uses what method of accounting for reporting its ownership of stock in Company Y?
   a. The amortized cost method.
   b. The equity method.
   c. The fair value method.
   d. Consolidation of the financial statements of companies X and Y.

2. Company W purchases 10 percent of Company Z and Company W intends to hold the stock for at least five years. At the end of the current year, how would Company W's investment in Company Z be reported on Company W's December 31 (year-end) balance sheet?
   a. At the December 31 fair value in the long-term assets section.
   b. At original cost in the current assets section.
   c. At the December 31 fair value in the current assets section.
   d. At original cost in the long-term assets section.

3. Dividends received from stock that is reported as an available-for-sale security in the long-term assets section of the balance sheet are reported as which of the following?
   a. An increase to cash and a decrease to the investment in stock account.
   b. An increase to cash and an increase to revenue.
   c. An increase to cash and an unrealized gain on the income statement.
   d. An increase to cash and an unrealized gain on the balance sheet.

4. Realized gains and losses are recorded on the income statement for which of the following transactions in trading securities and available-for-sale securities?
   a. When adjusting a trading security to its fair value.
   b. Only when recording the sale of a trading security.
   c. When adjusting an available-for-sale security to its fair value.
   d. When recording the sale of either a trading security or an available-for-sale security.

5. When recording dividends received from a stock investment accounted for using the equity method, which of the following statements is true?
   a. Total assets are increased and net income is increased.
   b. Total assets are increased and total stockholders' equity is increased.
   c. Total assets and total stockholders' equity do not change.
   d. Total assets are decreased and total stockholders' equity is decreased.

6. When using the equity method of accounting, when is revenue recorded on the books of the investor company?
   a. When a dividend is received from the affiliate.
   b. When the fair value of the affiliate stock increases.
   c. When the affiliate company reports net income.
   d. Both (a) and (c).

7. Bott Company acquired 500 shares of stock of Barus Company at $53 per share as a long-term investment. This represents 10 percent of the outstanding voting shares of Barus. During the year, Barus paid stockholders $3 per share in dividends. At year-end, Barus reported net income of $60,000. Barus's stock price at the end of the year was $55 per share. For Bott Company, the amount of investments reported on the balance sheet at year-end and the amount reported on the income statement for the year are:

	Balance Sheet	Income Statement
a.	$26,500	$1,500
b.	$27,500	$1,500
c.	$27,500	$6,000
d.	$26,500	$6,000

8. Bott Company acquired 500 shares of stock of Barus Company at $53 per share as a long-term investment. This represents 40 percent of the outstanding voting shares of Barus. During the year, Barus paid stockholders $3 per share in dividends. At year-end, Barus reported net income of $60,000. Barus's stock price at the end of the year was $55 per share. For Bott Company, the amount

of investments reported on the balance sheet at year-end and the amount reported on the income statement for the year are:

	Balance Sheet	Income Statement
a.	$27,500	$ 0
b.	$27,500	$ 0
c.	$27,500	$24,000
d.	$49,000	$24,000

9. Which of the following is true regarding the economic return from investing ratio?
   a. This ratio is used to evaluate how efficiently a company manages its total assets.
   b. This ratio is used to evaluate the efficiency of a company given the capital contributed by owners.
   c. This ratio is used to evaluate the financing strategy of a company.
   d. This ratio is used to evaluate the performance of a company's investment portfolio.

10. Lamichael Company purchased 100 percent of the outstanding voting shares of Darrell Corporation in the open market for $230,000 cash and Darrell was merged into Lamichael Company. On the date of acquisition, the fair value of Darrell Corporation's property and equipment was $300,000 and the fair value of its long-term debt was $130,000. Darrell has no other assets or liabilities. What amount of goodwill would Lamichael record related to the purchase of Darrell Corporation?
    a. No goodwill should be recorded by Lamichael.
    b. $170,000
    c. $60,000
    d. $40,000

For more practice with multiple-choice questions, go to the text website at **www.mhhe.com/libby8e.**

MINI-EXERCISES

Matching Measurement and Reporting Methods

ME-1
LO E-1, E-2, E-3, E-4

Match the following. Answers may be used more than once:

Measurement Method	
A. Amortized cost	____ 1. Less than 20 percent ownership.
B. Equity method	____ 2. Current fair value.
C. Acquisition method and consolidation	____ 3. More than 50 percent ownership.
D. Fair value method	____ 4. At least 20 percent but not more than 50 percent ownership.
	____ 5. Bonds held to maturity.
	____ 6. Original cost less any amortization of premium or discount with the purchase.
	____ 7. Original cost plus proportionate part of the income of the affiliate less proportionate part of the dividends declared by the affiliate.

Recording a Bond Investment

ME-2
LO E-1

James Company purchased $800,000, 8 percent bonds issued by Heidi Company on January 1, 2014. The purchase price of the bonds was $900,000. Interest is payable semiannually each June 30 and December 31. Record the purchase of the bonds on January 1, 2014.

Recording Available-for-Sale Securities Transactions

ME-3
LO E-2

During 2014, James Company acquired some of the 50,000 outstanding shares of the common stock, par $12, of Andrew Corporation as available-for-sale investments. The accounting period for both companies ends December 31. Give the journal entries for each of the following transactions that occurred during 2014:

Dec. 2	Purchased 6,250 shares of Andrew common stock at $15 per share.
Dec. 15	Andrew Corporation declared and paid a cash dividend of $2 per share.
Dec. 31	Determined the current market price of Andrew stock to be $12 per share.

ME–4

LO E-2

Recording Trading Securities Transactions

Using the data in ME-3, assume that James Company purchased the voting stock of Andrew Corporation for the trading securities portfolio instead of the available-for-sale securities portfolio. Give the journal entries for each of the transactions listed.

ME–5

LO E-2

Determining Financial Statement Effects of Available-for-Sale Securities Transactions

Using the following categories, indicate the effects of the transactions listed in ME-3 assuming the securities are available for sale. Use + for increase and − for decrease and indicate the amounts.

	Balance Sheet			Income Statement		
Transaction	Assets	Liabilities	Stockholders' Equity	Revenues/ Gains	Expenses/ Losses	Net Income

ME–6

LO E-2

Determining Financial Statement Effects of Trading Securities Transactions

Using the following categories, indicate the effects of the transactions listed in ME-3 assuming the securities are trading securities. Use + for increase and − for decrease and indicate the amounts.

	Balance Sheet			Income Statement		
Transaction	Assets	Liabilities	Stockholders' Equity	Revenues/ Gains	Expenses/ Losses	Net Income

ME–7

LO E-3

Recording Equity Method Securities Transactions

On January 1, 2014, PurchaseAgent.com acquired 35 percent (800,000 shares) of the common stock of E-Transaction Corporation. The accounting period for both companies ends December 31. Give the journal entries for each of the following transactions that occurred during 2014 for PurchaseAgent.com:

July	2	E-Transaction declared and paid a cash dividend of $5 per share.
Dec. 31		E-Transaction reported net income of $400,000.

ME–8

LO E-3

Determining Financial Statement Effects of Equity Method Securities

Using the following categories, indicate the effects of the transactions listed in ME-7. Use + for increase and − for decrease and indicate the amounts.

	Balance Sheet			Income Statement		
Transaction	Assets	Liabilities	Stockholders' Equity	Revenues/ Gains	Expenses/ Losses	Net Income

ME–9

LO E-4

Recording a Merger

England Textile Company acquired Belgium Fabric Company for $660,000 cash when Belgium's only assets, property and equipment, had a book value of $660,000 and a fair value of $750,000. England also assumed Belgium's bonds payable of $175,000. After the merger, Belgium would cease to exist as a separate legal entity. Record the acquisition.

ME–10

LO E-2

Computing and Interpreting Economic Return from Investing Ratio

N.M.S. Company held available-for-sale securities and reported the following information at the end of each year:

Year	Dividend Revenue	Ending Fair Value of Investments
2014	$1,500	$64,000
2015	3,000	70,000
2016	4,200	82,000
2017	3,500	80,000

Compute the economic return from investing ratio for 2015, 2016, and 2017. What do the results suggest about N.M.S. Company?

Interpreting Goodwill Disclosures

The Walt Disney Company owns theme parks, movie studios, television and radio stations, newspapers, and television networks, including ABC and ESPN. Its balance sheet recently reported goodwill in the amount of $24 billion, which is almost 35 percent of the company's total assets. This percentage is very large compared to that of most companies. Explain why you think Disney has such a large amount of goodwill reported on its balance sheet.

ME-11
LO E-4

The Walt Disney Company

EXERCISES

Recording Bonds Held to Maturity

Macy's, Inc., operates nearly 850 Macy's and Bloomingdale's department stores nationwide. The company does more than $24 billion in sales each year.

Assume that as part of its cash management strategy, Macy's purchased $12 million in bonds at par for cash on July 1, 2015. The bonds pay 8 percent interest annually with payments June 30 and December 31 and mature in 10 years. Macy's plans to hold the bonds until maturity.

Required:
1. Record the purchase of the bonds on July 1, 2015.
2. Record the receipt of interest on December 31, 2015.

EE-1
LO E-1

Macy's, Inc.

Comparing Fair Value and Equity Methods

Company A purchased a certain number of Company B's outstanding voting shares at $20 per share as a long-term investment. Company B had outstanding 20,000 shares of $10 par value stock. Complete the following table relating to the measurement and reporting by Company A after acquisition of the shares of Company B stock.

EE-2
LO E-2, E-3

Questions	Fair Value Method	Equity Method
a. What level of ownership by Company A of Company B is required to apply the method?	_____%	_____%

For *b, e, f,* and *g,* assume the following:		
Number of shares acquired of Company B stock	2,500	7,000
Net income reported by Company B in first year	$59,000	$59,000
Dividends declared by Company B in first year	$12,000	$12,000
Market price at end of first year, Company B stock	$ 17	$ 17

	Fair Value Method	Equity Method
b. At acquisition, the investment account on the books of Company A should be debited at what amount?	$_____	$_____
c. When should Company A recognize revenue earned on the stock of Company B? Explanation required.	_____	_____
d. After the acquisition date, how should Company A change the balance of the investment account with respect to the stock owned in Company B (other than for disposal of the investment)? Explanation required.	_____	_____
e. What is the balance in the investment account on the balance sheet of Company A at the end of the first year?	$_____	$_____
f. What amount of revenue from the investment in Company B should Company A report at the end of the first year?	$_____	$_____
g. What amount of unrealized loss should Company A report at the end of the first year?	$_____	$_____

EE-3
LO E-2

Recording Transactions in the Available-for-Sale Securities Portfolio

On June 30, 2014, Slick Rocks, Inc., purchased 7,000 shares of Sandstone stock for $15 per share. Management recorded the stock in the available-for-sale securities portfolio. The following information pertains to the price per share of Sandstone stock:

	Price
12/31/2014	$17
12/31/2015	14
12/31/2016	18

Slick Rocks sold all of the Sandstone stock on February 14, 2017, at a price of $20 per share. Prepare any journal entries that are required by the facts presented in this case.

EE-4
LO E-2

Recording Transactions in the Trading Securities Portfolio

Using the data in EE-3, assume that Slick Rocks management purchased the Sandstone stock for the trading securities portfolio instead of the available-for-sale securities portfolio. Prepare any journal entries that are required by the facts presented in the case.

EE-5
LO E-2

Reporting Gains and Losses in the Available-for-Sale Securities Portfolio

On March 10, 2014, Dearden, Inc., purchased 15,000 shares of Jaffa stock for $35 per share. Management recorded it in the available-for-sale securities portfolio. The following information pertains to the price per share of Jaffa stock:

	Price
12/31/2014	$33
12/31/2015	36
12/31/2016	32

Dearden sold all of the Jaffa stock on September 12, 2017, at a price of $30 per share. Prepare any journal entries that are required by the facts presented in this case.

EE-6
LO E-2

Reporting Gains and Losses in the Trading Securities Portfolio

Using the data in EE-5, assume that Dearden management purchased the Jaffa stock for the trading securities portfolio instead of the available-for-sale securities portfolio. Prepare any journal entries that are required by the facts presented in the case.

EE-7
LO E-3

Recording and Reporting an Equity Method Investment

Gioia Company acquired some of the 65,000 shares of outstanding common stock (no par) of Tristezza Corporation during 2014 as a long-term investment. The annual accounting period for both companies ends December 31. The following transactions occurred during 2014:

> Jan. 10   Purchased 17,875 shares of Tristezza common stock at $11 per share.
> Dec. 31   *a.* Received the 2011 financial statements of Tristezza Corporation that reported net income of $80,000.
> *b.* Tristezza Corporation declared and paid a cash dividend of $0.60 per share.
> *c.* Determined the market price of Tristezza stock to be $10 per share.

Required:
1. What accounting method should the company use? Why?
2. Give the journal entries for each of these transactions. If no entry is required, explain why.
3. Show how the long-term investment and the related revenue should be reported on the 2014 financial statements (balance sheet and income statement) of the Gioia Company.

Interpreting the Effects of Equity Method Investments on Cash Flow from Operations

Using the data in EE-7, answer the following questions.

Required:
1. On the current year cash flow statement, how would the investing section of the statement be affected by the preceding transactions?
2. On the current year cash flow statement (indirect method), how would the equity in the earnings of the affiliated company and the dividends from the affiliated company affect the operating section? Explain the reasons for the effects.

EE-8
LO E-3

Determining the Appropriate Accounting Treatment for an Acquisition

The notes to recent financial statements of Colgate-Palmolive contained the following information (dollar amounts in millions):

EE-9
LO E-4

The Colgate-Palmolive Company

> **3. Acquisitions and Divestitures**
>
> On June 20, 2011, the Company . . . finalized the Company's acquisition from Unilever of the Sanex personal care business . . . for an aggregate purchase price of $966 . . . This strategic acquisition is expected to strengthen Colgate's personal care business in Europe, primarily in the liquid body cleansing and deodorants business. Total purchase price consideration of $966 has been allocated to the net assets acquired based on their respective fair values at June 20, 2011 . . .

Assume that Colgate-Palmolive acquired 100 percent of the fair value of the net assets of Sanex in a recent year for $1,377 million in cash. Sanex's assets at the time of the acquisition had a book value of $625 million and a fair value of $1,036 million. Colgate-Palmolive also assumed Sanex's liabilities of $70 million (books value and fair value of the liabilities are the same). Prepare the entry on the date of acquisition as a merger.

Analyzing and Interpreting the Economic Return from Investing Ratio

Kukenberger, Inc., reported the following in its portfolio of available-for-sale securities:

EE-10
LO E-2

Year	Dividends Received	Ending Fair Value of Investment Portfolio
2013	$24,550	$836,451
2014	23,906	759,999
2015	24,399	806,345
2016	25,538	845,160

Required:
1. Determine the economic return from investing ratio for the years 2014, 2015, and 2016.
2. What do your results suggest about Kukenberger's investment portfolio?

(Supplement) Recording Bonds Held to Maturity (Purchased at a Premium)

Macy's, Inc., operates nearly 850 Macy's and Bloomingdale's department stores nationwide. The company does more than $24 billion in sales each year.

Assume that, as part of its cash management strategy, Macy's purchased as a long-term investment $12 million in 10-year bonds for $13,785,600 cash on July 1, 2014. The bonds pay 8 percent interest semiannually on June 30 and December 31. The market rate on the bonds on the date of purchase was 6 percent.

EE-11
LO E-1

Required:
1. Record the purchase of the bonds on July 1, 2014.
2. Record the receipt of interest on December 31, 2014 (including applying the effective interest amortization method).

PROBLEMS

PE-1
LO E-1

Starbucks

Determining Financial Statement Effects for Bonds Held to Maturity (APE-1)

Starbucks is a global company that provides high-quality coffee products. Assume that as part of its expansion strategy, Starbucks plans to open numerous new stores in Mexico in three years. The company has $7 million to support the expansion and has decided to invest the funds in corporate bonds until the money is needed. Assume that Starbucks purchased bonds with $7 million face value at par for cash on July 1, 2015. The bonds pay 7 percent interest each June 30 and December 31 and mature in three years. Starbucks plans to hold the bonds until maturity.

Required:
1. What accounts are affected when the bonds are purchased on July 1, 2015?
2. What accounts are affected when interest is received on December 31, 2015?
3. Should Starbucks prepare a journal entry if the fair value of the bonds decreased to $6,000,000 on December 31, 2015? Explain.

PE-2
LO E-2

www.mhhe.com/libby8e

Recording Passive Investments (APE-2)

On March 1, 2014, Rain Technology purchased 20,000 shares of Lightyear Services Company for $10 per share. The following information applies to the stock price of Lightyear Services:

	Price
12/31/2014	$ 8
12/31/2015	14
12/31/2016	17

Required:
1. Prepare journal entries to record the facts in the case, assuming that Rain purchased the shares for the trading securities portfolio.
2. Prepare journal entries to record the facts in the case, assuming that Rain purchased the shares for the available-for-sale securities portfolio.

PE-3
LO E-2

Recording Passive Investments

Below are selected T-accounts for the RunnerTech Company.

Balance Sheet Accounts

(In Other Investments) Investments in AFS Securities			
1/1	5,587		
Purchase	19,000		
AJE	?	15,239	Sale
12/31	14,558		

(In Other Comprehensive Income) Net Unrealized Gains (Losses)—AFS			
		1,565	1/1
Sale	?	?	AJE
		5,683	12/31

Income Statement Accounts

Dividend Revenue		
	?	Earned
	7,771	12/31

Gain on Sale of Investments		
	2,384	Sale
	2,384	12/31

Required:
Complete the following journal entries and answer the following questions:
a. Purchased available-for-sale securities for cash. Prepare the journal entry.
b. Received cash dividends on the investments. Prepare the journal entry.
c. Sold AFS investments at a gain. Prepare the journal entry.
d. At year-end, the AFS portfolio had a fair value of $14,558. Prepare the adjusting entry.

e. What would be reported on the balance sheet related to the AFS investments on December 31?

f. What would be reported on the income statement for the year?

g. How would year-end reporting change if the investments were categorized as trading securities instead of available-for-sale securities?

Reporting Passive Investments (APE-3)

PE-4
LO E-2

During January 2014, Optimum Glass Company purchased the following securities as its long-term available-for-sale securities investment portfolio:

D Corporation Common Stock: 14,000 shares (95,000 outstanding) at $11 per share

F Corporation Bonds: $400,000 (20-year, 7 percent) purchased at par (not to be held to maturity)

Subsequent to acquisition, the following data were available:

	2014	2015
Net income reported at December 31:		
D Corporation	$ 31,000	$ 41,000
F Corporation	$360,000	$550,000
Dividends and interest paid during the year:		
D Corporation common stock cash dividends (per share)	$ 0.50	$ 0.70
F Corporation bonds interest	$ 28,000	$ 28,000
Fair value at December 31:		
D Corporation common stock (per share)	$ 10.00	$ 11.50
F Corporation bonds	$375,000	$385,000

Required:

1. What accounting method should be used for the investment in D common stock? F bonds? Why?
2. Give the journal entries for the company for each year in parallel columns (if none, explain why) for each of the following:
   a. Purchase of the investments.
   b. Income reported by D and F Corporations.
   c. Dividends and interest received from D and F Corporations.
   d. Fair value effects at year-end.
3. For each year, show how the following amounts should be reported on the financial statements:
   a. Long-term investments.
   b. Stockholders' equity—net unrealized losses/gains.
   c. Revenues.

Recording Passive Investments and Investments for Significant Influence

PE-5
LO E-2, E-3

On August 4, 2015, Jeffrey Corporation purchased 2,000 shares of Kevin Company for $180,000. The following information applies to the stock price of Kevin Company:

	Price
12/31/2015	$85
12/31/2016	91
12/31/2017	94

www.mhhe.com/libby8e

Kevin Company declares and pays cash dividends of $3.50 per share on June 1 of each year.

Required:

1. Prepare journal entries to record the facts in the case, assuming that Jeffrey purchased the shares for the trading securities portfolio.
2. Prepare journal entries to record the facts in the case, assuming that Jeffrey purchased the shares for the available-for-sale securities portfolio.
3. Prepare journal entries to record the facts in the case, assuming that Jeffrey used the equity method to account for the investment. Jeffrey owns 30 percent of Kevin and Kevin reported $30,000 in income each year.

PE-6

LO E-2, E-3

www.mhhe.com/libby8e

Comparing Methods to Account for Various Levels of Ownership of Voting Stock

Company T had outstanding 25,000 shares of common stock, par value $10 per share. On January 1, 2014, Company P purchased some of these shares as a long-term investment at $25 per share. At the end of 2014, Company T reported the following: income, $45,000, and cash dividends declared and paid during the year, $16,500. The fair value of Company T stock at the end of 2014 was $22 per share.

Required:
1. For each of the following cases (in the tabulation), identify the method of accounting that Company P should use. Explain why.
2. Give the journal entries for Company P at the dates indicated for each of the two independent cases, assuming that the investments will be held long term. If no entry is required, explain why. Use the following format:

Tabulation of Items	Case A: 3,000 Shares Purchased	Case B: 8,750 Shares Purchased
1. Accounting method?		
2. Journal entries:		
a. To record the acquisition at January 1, 2014.		
b. To recognize the income reported by Company T for 2014.		
c. To recognize the dividends declared and paid by Company T.		
d. To recognize fair value effect at end of 2014.		

3. Complete the following schedule to show the separate amounts that should be reported on the 2014 financial statements of Company P:

	DOLLAR AMOUNTS	
	Case A	Case B
Balance sheet		
Investments		
Stockholders' equity		
Income statement		
Dividend revenue		
Equity in earnings of affiliate		

4. Explain why assets, stockholders' equity, and revenues for the two cases are different.

PE-7

LO E-2, E-3

www.mhhe.com/libby8e

Comparing the Fair Value and Equity Methods (APE-4)

Surge Corporation had outstanding 120,000 shares of no-par common stock. On January 10, 2014, Crash Company purchased a block of these shares in the open market at $25 per share for long-term investment purposes. At the end of 2014, Surge reported net income of $175,000 and cash dividends of $1.00 per share. At December 31, 2014, Surge stock was selling at $23 per share. This problem involves two separate cases:

Case A: Purchase of 15,000 shares of Surge common stock.

Case B: Purchase of 48,000 shares of Surge common stock.

Required:
1. For each case, identify the accounting method that the company should use. Explain why.
2. For each case, in parallel columns, give the journal entries for each of the following (if no entry is required, explain why):
    a. Acquisition.
    b. Revenue recognition.
    c. Dividends received.
    d. Fair value effects.
3. For each case, show how the following should be reported on the 2014 financial statements:
    a. Long-term investments.
    b. Stockholders' equity.
    c. Revenues.
4. Explain why the amounts reported in requirement (3) are different for the two cases.

Recording Investments for Significant Influence

PE-8
LO E-3

Below are selected T-accounts for William Company.

Investments in Affiliates			
1/1	56,432		
Purchase	15,685		
Share of			Share of
affiliate net			affiliate
income	?	8,564	dividends
12/31	67,450		

Equity in Affiliate Earnings	
	0	1/1
	Share of
	affiliate net
?	income
3,897	12/31

Required:

Complete the following journal entries and answer the following questions:

a. Purchased additional investments in affiliated companies for cash. Prepare the journal entry.

b. Received cash dividends on the investments. Prepare the journal entry.

c. At year-end, the investments in affiliates account had a fair value of $62,000; the affiliate also reported $8,120 in net income for the year. Prepare the adjusting entry.

d. What would be reported on the balance sheet related to the investments in affiliates on December 31?

e. What would be reported on the income statement for the year?

Determining Cash Flow Statement Effects of Investments for Significant Influence (APE-5)

PE-9
LO E-3

During 2014, Bradford Company purchased some of the 90,000 shares of common stock, par $6, of Hall, Inc., as a long-term investment. The annual accounting period for each company ends December 31. The following transactions occurred during 2014:

Jan. 7	Purchased 40,500 shares of Hall stock at $30 per share.
Dec. 31	a. Received the 2014 financial statements of Hall, which reported net income of $215,000.
	b. Hall declared and paid a cash dividend of $1.50 per share.
	c. Determined that the current market price of Hall stock was $41 per share.

Required:

Indicate how the Operating Activities and Investing Activities sections of the cash flow statement (indirect method) will be affected by each transaction.

Analyzing Goodwill and Reporting a Merger (APE-6)

PE-10
LO E-4

On January 4, 2014, David Company acquired all of the net assets (assets and liabilities) of William Company for $145,000 cash. The two companies merged, with David Company surviving. On the date of acquisition, William's balance sheet included the following.

Balance Sheet at January 4, 2014	William Company
Cash	$23,000
Property and equipment (net)	70,000
Total assets	$93,000
Liabilities	$16,000
Common stock (par $5)	41,000
Retained earnings	36,000
Total liabilities and stockholders' equity	$93,000

The property and equipment had a fair value of $85,000. William also owned an internally developed patent with a fair value of $3,000. The book values of the cash and liabilities were equal to their fair values.

Required:

1. How much goodwill was involved in this merger? Show computations.

2. Give the journal entry that David would make to record the merger on January 4, 2014.

PE-11

LO E-2

Apple, Inc.

Interpreting the Economic Return from Investing Ratio

Apple, Inc., designs and markets innovative hardware, software, peripherals, and services, including the iPhone,® iPad,® Mac,® iPod,® and Apple TV.® The following information was reported in the company's 2012 annual report for available-for-sale securities:

	(DOLLARS IN MILLIONS)	
	2012	2011
AFS investment portfolio	$121,251*	$81,570
Investment income	522	415

*The increase in the portfolio was due to $1,031 fair value change and $38,650 in additional purchases of AFS securities acquired on the last day of the year.

Required:
1. Compute the economic return from investing ratio for 2012.
2. What do the results in requirement (1) suggest about Apple, Inc.?

ALTERNATE PROBLEMS

APE-1

LO E-1

Determining Financial Statement Effects for Bonds Held to Maturity (PE-1)

Sonic Corp. operates and franchises a chain of quick-service drive-in restaurants in most of the United States. Customers order at a drive thru, dine on the patio, or drive up to a canopied parking space. A carhop then delivers the food to the customer. Assume that Sonic has $15 million in cash to support future expansion and has decided to invest the funds in corporate bonds until the money is needed. Sonic purchases bonds with $15 million face value for $15.7 million cash on January 1, 2014. The bonds pay 9 percent interest annually with payments each June 30 and December 31 and mature in four years. Sonic plans to hold the bonds until maturity.

Required:
1. What accounts were affected when the bonds were purchased on January 1, 2014?
2. What accounts were affected when interest was received on June 30, 2014?
3. Should Sonic prepare a journal entry if the fair value of the bonds increased to $16,300,000 on December 31, 2014? Explain.

APE-2

LO E-2

Recording Passive Investments (PE-2)

On September 15, 2014, Hill-Nielson Corporation purchased 7,000 shares of Community Communications Company for $32 per share. The following information applies to the stock price of Community Communications:

	Price
12/31/2014	$34
12/31/2015	25
12/31/2016	21

Required:
1. Prepare journal entries to record the facts in the case, assuming that Hill-Nielson purchased the shares for the trading securities portfolio.
2. Prepare journal entries to record the facts in the case, assuming that Hill-Nielson purchased the shares for the available-for-sale securities portfolio.

APE-3

LO E-2

Reporting Passive Investments (PE-4)

During January 2014, Pentagon Company purchased 12,000 shares of the 200,000 outstanding common shares (no-par value) of Square Corporation at $25 per share. This block of stock was purchased as a long-term investment. Assume that the accounting period for each company ends December 31. Subsequent to acquisition, the following data were available:

	2014	2015
Income reported by Square Corporation at December 31	$40,000	$60,000
Cash dividends declared and paid by Square Corporation during the year	$60,000	$80,000
Market price per share of Square common stock on December 31	$ 28	$ 27

Required:
1. What accounting method should Pentagon Company use? Why?
2. Give the journal entries for the company for each year (use parallel columns) for the following (if none, explain why):
   a. Acquisition of Square Corporation stock.
   b. Net income reported by Square Corporation.
   c. Dividends received from Square Corporation.
   d. Fair value effects at year-end.
3. For each year, show how the following amounts should be reported on the financial statements:
   a. Long-term investments.
   b. Stockholders' equity—net unrealized loss/gain.
   c. Revenues.

Comparing the Fair Value and Equity Methods (PE-7)

APE-4
LO E-2, E-3

Cardinal Company purchased, as a long-term investment, some of the 200,000 shares of the outstanding common stock of Arbor Corporation. The annual accounting period for each company ends December 31. The following transactions occurred during 2015:

Jan. 10   Purchased shares of common stock of Arbor at $12 per share as follows:
   Case A—30,000 shares
   Case B—80,000 shares
Dec. 31   *a.* Received the 2015 financial statements of Arbor Corporation; the reported net income was $90,000.
   b. Received a cash dividend of $0.60 per share from Arbor Corporation.
   c. Determined that the current market price of Arbor stock was $9 per share.

Required:
1. For each case, identify the accounting method that the company should use. Explain why.
2. Give the journal entries for each case for these transactions. If no entry is required, explain why. (**Hint:** Use parallel columns for Case A and Case B.)
3. Give the amounts for each case that should be reported on the 2015 financial statements. Use the following format:

	Case A	Case B
Balance sheet (partial)		
Investments		
Investments in common stock, Arbor Corporation		
Stockholders' equity		
Net unrealized gain or loss		
Income statement (partial)		
Dividend revenue		
Equity in earnings of affiliate		

Determining Cash Flow Statement Effects of Passive Investments and Investments for Significant Influence (PE-9)

APE-5
LO E-2, E-3

For each of the transactions in APE-4, indicate how the operating activities and investing activities sections of the cash flow statement (indirect method) will be affected.

APE-6

LO E-4

Analyzing Goodwill and Reporting a Merger (PE-10)

On June 1, 2014, Gamma Company acquired all of the net assets of Pi Company for $140,000 cash. The two companies merged, with Gamma Company surviving. On the date of acquisition, Pi Company's balance sheet included the following:

Balance Sheet at June 1, 2014	Pi Company
Inventory	$ 13,000
Property and equipment (net)	165,000
Total assets	$178,000
Liabilities	$ 82,000
Common stock (par $1)	65,000
Retained earnings	31,000
Total liabilities and stockholders' equity	$178,000

On the date of acquisition, the inventory had a fair value of $12,000 and the property and equipment had a fair value of $180,000. The fair value of the liabilities equaled their book value.

Required:
1. How much goodwill was involved in this merger? Show computations.
2. Give the journal entry that Gamma Company would make to record the merger on June 1, 2014.

CASES AND PROJECTS

Annual Report Cases

CPE-1

LO E-1, E-2, E-4

AMERICAN EAGLE OUTFITTERS, INC.

Finding Financial Information

Refer to the financial statements of American Eagle Outfitters in Appendix B at the end of this book.

Required:
1. What types of securities are included in the short-term investments and the long-term investments reported on the company's balance sheet as of the end of fiscal 2011 (statement dated January 28, 2012)? (**Hint:** The notes to the financial statements may be helpful for this question.)
2. What is the balance of goodwill reported by the company at January 28, 2012? What does the change in goodwill from January 29, 2011, imply about corporate acquisition activities in the 2011 fiscal year? Do the notes to the financial statements indicate any acquisition or disposition activity in either fiscal 2010 or 2011? If so, what were the activities?

CPE-2

LO E-1, E-2

URBAN OUTFITTERS INC.

Finding Financial Information

Refer to the financial statements of Urban Outfitters in Appendix C at the end of this book.

Required:
1. What is the balance in short-term and long-term marketable securities reported by the company on January 31, 2012? What types of securities are included in these accounts? (**Hint:** The notes to the financial statements may be helpful for this question.)
2. How much cash did the company use to purchase marketable securities during the year ended January 31, 2012?

Financial Reporting and Analysis Cases

Using Financial Reports: Analyzing the Financial Effects of the Fair Value and Equity Methods

CPE-3
LO E-2, E-3

On January 1, 2015, Sheena Company purchased 30 percent of the outstanding common stock of Maryn Corporation at a total cost of $485,000. Management intends to hold the stock for the long term. On the December 31, 2015, balance sheet, the investment in Maryn Corporation was $556,000, but no additional Maryn stock was purchased. The company received $90,000 in cash dividends from Maryn. The dividends were declared and paid during 2015. The company used the equity method to account for its investment in Maryn. The market price of Sheena Company's share of Maryn stock increased during 2015 to a total value of $550,000.

Required:
1. Explain why the investment account balance increased from $485,000 to $556,000 during 2015.
2. What amount of revenue from the investment was reported during 2015?
3. If Sheena did not have significant influence over Maryn and used the fair value method, what amount of revenue from the investment should have been reported in 2015?
4. If Sheena did not have significant influence over Maryn and used the fair value method, what amount should be reported as the investment in Maryn Corporation on the December 31, 2015, balance sheet?

Using Financial Reports: Interpreting International Goodwill Disclosures

CPE-4
LO E-4

Diageo

Diageo is a major international company located in London, best known for its Smirnoff, Johnnie Walker, and Guinness brands of spirits. Its financial statements are accounted for under IFRS. A recent annual report contained the following information concerning its accounting policies.

> Acquired brands and other intangible assets are recognised when they are controlled through contractual or other legal rights, or are separable from the rest of the business, and the fair value can be reliably measured.
> Intangible assets that are regarded as having limited useful economic lives are amortised on a straight-line basis over those lives and reviewed for impairment whenever events or circumstances indicate that the carrying amount may not be recoverable. Goodwill and intangible assets that are regarded as having indefinite useful economic lives are not amortised. These assets are reviewed for impairment at least annually or when there is an indication that the assets may be impaired. To ensure that assets are not carried at above their recoverable amounts . . . Amortisation and any impairment writedowns are charged to other operating expenses in the income statement.

Required:
Discuss how this accounting treatment compares with procedures used in this country.

Critical Thinking Cases

Evaluating an Ethical Dilemma: Using Inside Information

CPE-5
LO E-4

Assume that you are on the board of directors of a company that has decided to buy 80 percent of the outstanding stock of another company within the next three or four months. The discussions have convinced you that this company is an excellent investment opportunity, so you decide to buy $10,000 worth of the company's stock for your personal portfolio. Is there an ethical problem with your decision? Would your answer be different if you planned to invest $500,000? Are there different ethical considerations if you don't buy the stock but recommend that your brother do so?

CPE-6
LO E-4

Evaluating an Acquisition from the Standpoint of a Financial Analyst

Assume that you are a financial analyst for a large investment banking firm. You are responsible for analyzing companies in the retail sales industry. You have just learned that a large West Coast retailer has acquired a large East Coast retail chain for a price more than the net book value of the acquired company. You have reviewed the separate financial statements for the two companies before the announcement of the acquisition. You have been asked to write a brief report explaining what will happen when the financial results of the companies are consolidated under the acquisition method.

Financial Reporting and Analysis Team Project

CPE-7
LO E-2, E-3, E-4

Team Project: Examining an Annual Report

As a team, select an industry to analyze. *Yahoo! Finance* provides lists of industries at biz.yahoo.com/p/industries.html. Click on an industry for a list of companies in that industry. Alternatively, go to Google Finance at www.google.com/finance and search for a company you are interested in. You will be presented with a list including that company and its competitors. Each team member should acquire the annual report or 10-K for one publicly traded company in the industry, with each member selecting a different company (the SEC EDGAR service at www.sec.gov or the company's investor relations website itself are good sources).

Required:
On an individual basis, each team member should write a short report answering the following questions about the selected company. Discuss any patterns across the companies that you as a team observe. Then, as a team, write a short report comparing and contrasting your companies.

On an individual basis, each team member should write a short report that answers the following questions:
1. Determine whether the company prepared consolidated financial statements. If so, did it use the acquisition method? How do you know?
2. Does the company use the equity method for any of its investments?
3. Does the company hold any investments in securities? If so, what is their fair value? Does the company have any unrealized gains or losses?
4. Identify the company's lines of business. Why does management want to engage in these business activities?

CONTINUING **CASE**

CCE-1

≋POOLCORP

Accounting for Passive Investments

Pool Corporation, Inc., is the world's largest wholesale distributor of swimming pool supplies and equipment. Assume Pool Corporation purchased for cash 400,000 shares of The Walt Disney Company on November 21, 2012, at $48 per share as an investment. The following information applies to the stock price of Disney:

	Price per Share
12/31/2012	$45
12/31/2013	41
12/31/2014	49

On September 15, 2015, Pool Corporation sold all of the Disney securities at $50 per share.

Required:
1. Prepare journal entries to record the facts in the case, assuming that Pool Corporation purchased the shares for the trading securities portfolio.
2. Prepare journal entries to record the facts in the case, assuming that Pool Corporation purchased the shares for the available-for-sale securities portfolio.

A

Account A standardized format that organizations use to accumulate the dollar effect of transactions on each financial statement item. (48)

Accounting A system that collects and processes (analyzes, measures, and records) financial information about an organization and reports that information to decision makers. (4)

Accounting Cycle The process used by entities to analyze and record transactions, adjust the records at the end of the period, prepare financial statements, and prepare the records for the next cycle. (54)

Accounting Entity The organization for which financial data are to be collected. (6)

Accounting Period The time period covered by the financial statements. (9)

Accounts Receivable (Trade Receivables, Receivables) Open accounts owed to the business by trade customers. (283)

Accrual Basis Accounting Records revenues when earned and expenses when incurred, regardless of the timing of cash receipts or payments. (105)

Accrued Expenses Previously unrecorded expenses that need to be adjusted at the end of the accounting period to reflect the amount incurred and its related payable account. (167)

Accrued Liabilities Expenses that have been incurred but have not been paid at the end of the accounting period. (455)

Accrued Revenues Previously unrecorded revenues that need to be adjusted at the end of the accounting period to reflect the amount earned and its related receivable account. (170)

Acquisition Cost The net cash equivalent amount paid or to be paid for an asset. (385)

Acquisition Method Records assets and liabilities acquired in a merger or acquisition at their fair value on the transaction date. (E-18)

Additional Paid-In Capital (Paid-In Capital, Contributed Capital in Excess of Par) The amount of contributed capital less the par value of the stock. (51)

Adjusting Entries Entries necessary at the end of the accounting period to measure all revenues and expenses of that period. (163)

Aging of Accounts Receivable Method Estimates uncollectible accounts based on the age of each account receivable. (288)

Allowance for Doubtful Accounts (Allowance for Bad Debts, Allowance for Uncollectible Accounts) Contra-asset account containing the estimated uncollectible accounts receivable. (284)

Allowance Method Bases bad debt expense on an estimate of uncollectible accounts. (284)

Amortization Systematic and rational allocation of the acquisition cost of an intangible asset over its useful life. (405)

Amortized Cost Method Reports investments in debt securities held to maturity at cost minus any premium or plus any discount. (E-4)

Annuity A series of periodic cash receipts or payments that are equal in amount each interest period. (468)

Assets Probable future economic benefits owned by the entity as a result of past transactions. (45)

Audit An examination of the financial reports to ensure that they represent what they claim and conform with generally accepted accounting principles. (20)

Authorized Number of Shares The maximum number of shares of a corporation's capital stock that can be issued as specified in the charter. (548)

Available-for-Sale Securities All passive investments other than trading securities and debt held to maturity (classified as either short term or long term). (E-6)

Average Cost Method Uses the weighted average unit cost of the goods available for sale for both cost of goods sold and ending inventory. (337)

B

Bad Debt Expense (Doubtful Accounts Expense, Uncollectible Accounts Expense, Provision for Uncollectible Accounts) Expense associated with estimated uncollectible accounts receivable. (284)

Balance Sheet (Statement of Financial Position) Reports the amount of assets, liabilities, and stockholders' equity of an accounting entity at a point in time. (6)

Bank Reconciliation Process of verifying the accuracy of both the bank statement and the cash accounts of a business. (295)

Bank Statement A monthly report from a bank that shows deposits recorded, checks cleared, other debits and credits, and a running bank balance. (294)

Basic Accounting Equation (Balance Sheet Equation) Assets = Liabilities + Stockholders' Equity. (6)

Board of Directors Elected by the shareholders to represent their interests; its audit committee is responsible for maintaining the integrity of the company's financial reports. (228)

Bond Certificate The bond document that each bondholder receives. (503)

Bond Discount The difference between the selling price and par when a bond is sold for less than par. (504)

Bond Premium The difference between the selling price and par when a bond is sold for more than par. (504)

Bond Principal The amount (a) payable at the maturity of the bond and (b) on which the periodic cash interest payments are computed. (501)

C

Callable Bonds Bonds that may be called for early retirement at the option of the issuer. (502)

Capital Lease Meets at least one of the four criteria established by GAAP and results in the recording of an asset and liability. (465)

Capitalized Interest Interest expenditures included in the cost of a self-constructed asset. (387)

Cash Money or any instrument that banks will accept for deposit and immediate credit to a company's account, such as a check, money order, or bank draft. (293)

Cash Basis Accounting Records revenues when cash is received and expenses when cash is paid. (105)

Cash Equivalents Short-term investments with original maturities of three months or less that are readily convertible to cash and whose value is unlikely to change. (293, 590)

Cash Flows from Financing Activities Cash inflows and outflows related to external sources of financing (owners and creditors) for the enterprise. (593)

Cash Flows from Investing Activities Cash inflows and outflows related to the acquisition or sale of productive facilities and investments in the securities of other companies. (592)

Cash Flows from Operating Activities (Cash Flows from Operations) Cash inflows and outflows directly related to earnings from normal operations. (591)

Closing Entries Made at the end of the accounting period to transfer balances in temporary accounts to Retained Earnings and to establish a zero balance in each of the temporary accounts. (181)

Common Stock The basic voting stock issued by a corporation. (51, 549)

Component Percentage Expresses each item on a particular financial statement as a percentage of a single base amount. (652)

Contingent Liability A potential liability that has arisen as the result of a past event; it is not an effective liability until some future event occurs. (460)

Continuity (Going-Concern) Assumption States that businesses are assumed to continue to operate into the foreseeable future. (44)

Contra-Account An account that is an offset to, or reduction of, the primary account. (169)

Contributed Capital Cash (and sometimes other assets) provided from the owners to the business. (45)

Convertible Bonds Bonds that may be converted to other securities of the issuer (usually common stock). (502)

Copyright Exclusive right to publish, use, and sell a literary, musical, or artistic work. (407)

Corporate Governance The procedures designed to ensure that the company is managed in the interests of the shareholders. (225)

Cost Effectiveness Requires that the benefits of accounting for and reporting information should outweigh the costs. (231)

Cost of Goods Sold Equation BI + P − EI = CGS. (332)

Coupon Rate The stated rate of interest on bonds. (503)

Credit The right side of an account. (55)

Credit Card Discount Fee charged by the credit card company for its services. (279)

Cumulative Dividend Preference The preferred stock feature that requires specified current dividends not paid in full to accumulate for every year in which they are not paid. These cumulative preferred dividends must be paid before any common dividends can be paid. (561)

Current Assets Assets that will be used or turned into cash within one year. Inventory is always considered a current asset regardless of the time needed to produce and sell it. (45)

Current Dividend Preference The feature of preferred stock that grants priority on preferred dividends over common dividends. (561)

Current Liabilities Short-term obligations that will be paid in cash (or other current assets) within the current operating cycle or one year, whichever is longer. (45, 453)

D

Debenture An unsecured bond; no assets are specifically pledged to guarantee repayment. (502)

Debit The left side of an account. (55)

Declaration Date The date on which the board of directors officially approves a dividend. (554)

Declining-Balance Depreciation Method that allocates the net book value (cost minus accumulated depreciation) of an asset over its useful life based on a multiple of the straight-line rate, thus assigning more depreciation to early years and less depreciation to later years of an asset's life. (396)

Deferred Expenses Previously acquired assets that need to be adjusted at the end of the accounting period to reflect the amount of expense incurred in using the asset to generate revenue. (167)

Deferred (Unearned) Revenues Previously recorded liabilities that need to be adjusted at the end of the accounting period to reflect the amount of revenue earned; on the balance sheet, revenues that have been collected but not earned; liabilities until the goods or services have been provided. (166, 459)

Deferred Tax Items Timing differences caused by reporting revenues and expenses according to GAAP on a company's income statement and according to the Internal Revenue Code on the tax return. (475)

Depletion Systematic and rational allocation of the cost of a natural resource over the period of its exploitation. (409)

Depreciation The process of allocating the cost of buildings and equipment over their productive lives using a systematic and rational allocation of the cost of property, plant, and equipment (but not land) over their useful lives. (391)

Direct Labor The earnings of employees who work directly on the products being manufactured. (331)

Direct Method A method of presenting the operating activities section of the statement of cash flows that reports components of cash flows from operating activities as gross receipts and gross payments. (591)

Dividends in Arrears Dividends on cumulative preferred stock that have not been paid in prior years. (561)

E

Earnings Forecasts Predictions of earnings for future accounting periods, prepared by financial analysts. (229)

Effective-Interest Amortization Amortizes a bond discount or premium on the basis of the effective-interest rate; it is the theoretically preferred method. (510)

Effective-Interest Rate (Yield) The current rate of interest on a debt when incurred; also called the market interest rate. (504)

Efficient Markets Securities markets in which prices fully reflect available information. (669)

Equity Method Used when an investor can exert significant influence over an affiliate; the method permits recording the investor's share of the affiliate's income. (E-14)

Estimated Useful Life The expected service life of an asset to the present owner. (392)

Expense Matching Principle Requires that expenses be recorded when incurred in earning revenue. (109)

Expenses Decreases in assets or increases in liabilities from ongoing operations incurred to generate revenues during the period. (103)

F

Face Amount Another name for bond principal or the maturity amount of a bond. (501)

Factory Overhead Manufacturing costs that are not raw material or direct labor costs. (331)

Fair Value Method Reports securities at their current market value (the amount that would be received in an orderly sale). (E-5)

Faithful Representation Requires that the information be complete, neutral, and free from error. (44)

Financial Accounting Standards Board (FASB) The private sector body given the primary responsibility to work out the detailed rules that become generally accepted accounting principles. (227)

Finished Goods Inventory Manufactured goods that are complete and ready for sale. (329)

First-In, First-Out (FIFO) Method An inventory costing method that assumes that the first goods purchased (the first in) are the first goods sold. (335)

Form 8-K The report used by publicly traded companies to disclose any material event not previously reported that is important to investors. (234)

Form 10-K The annual report that publicly traded companies must file with the SEC. (233)

Form 10-Q The quarterly report that publicly traded companies must file with the SEC. (234)

Franchise A contractual right to sell certain products or services, use certain trademarks, or perform activities in a geographical region. (408)

Free Cash Flow Cash Flows from Operating Activities less Dividends less Capital Expenditures. (606)

Future Value The sum to which an amount will increase as the result of compound interest. (476)

G

Gains Increases in assets or decreases in liabilities from peripheral transactions. (104)

Generally Accepted Accounting Principles (GAAP) The measurement and disclosure rules used to develop the information in financial statements. (16)

Goods Available for Sale The sum of beginning inventory and purchases (or transfers to finished goods) for the period. (332)

Goodwill (Cost in Excess of Net Assets Acquired) For accounting purposes, the excess of the purchase price of a business over the fair value of the acquired business's assets and liabilities. (406, E-18)

Gross Profit (Gross Margin) Net sales less cost of goods sold. (236)

H

Held-to-Maturity Investments Investments in debt securities that management has the ability and intent to hold until maturity. (E-4)

I

Improvements Expenditures that increase the productive life, operating efficiency, or capacity of an asset and are recorded as increases in asset accounts, not as expenses. (389)

Income before Income Taxes (Pretax Earnings) Revenues minus all expenses except income tax expense. (236)

Income Statement (Statement of Income, Statement of Earnings, Statement of Operations, Statement of Comprehensive Income) Reports the revenues less the expenses of the accounting period. (9)

Indenture A bond contract that specifies the legal provisions of a bond issue. (502)

Indirect Method A method of presenting the operating activities section of the statement of cash flows that adjusts net income to compute cash flows from operating activities. (592)

Institutional Investors Managers of pension, mutual, endowment, and other funds that invest on the behalf of others. (231)

Intangible Assets Assets that have special rights but not physical substance. (383)

Internal Controls Processes by which a company provides reasonable assurance regarding the reliability of the company's financial reporting, the effectiveness and efficiency of its operations, and its compliance with applicable laws and regulations. (293)

Inventory Tangible property held for sale in the normal course of business or used in producing goods or services for sale. (329)

Investments in Affiliates (or Associated Companies) Investments in stock held for the purpose of influencing the operating and financing strategies of the entity for the long term. (E-14)

Issued Shares The total number of shares of stock that have been sold; shares outstanding plus treasury shares held. (548)

J

Journal Entry An accounting method for expressing the effects of a transaction on accounts in a debits-equal-credits format. (57)

L

Last-In, First-Out (LIFO) Method An inventory costing method that assumes that the most recently purchased units (the last in) are sold first. (336)

Legal Capital The permanent amount of capital defined by state law that must remain invested in the business; serves as a cushion for creditors. (550)

Lenders (Creditors) Suppliers and financial institutions that lend money to companies. (231)

Liabilities Probable debts or obligations of the entity that result from past transactions, which will be paid with assets or services. (45, 453)

Licenses and Operating Rights Obtained through agreements with governmental units or agencies; permit owners to use public property in performing their services. (408)

LIFO Liquidation A sale of a lower-cost inventory item from beginning LIFO inventory. (352)

LIFO Reserve A contra-asset for the excess of FIFO over LIFO inventory. (345)

Liquidity The ability to pay current obligations. (453)

Long-Lived Assets Tangible and intangible resources owned by a business and used in its operations over several years. (383)

Long-Term Liabilities All of the entity's obligations that are not classified as current liabilities. (464)

Losses Decreases in assets or increases in liabilities from peripheral transactions. (104)

Lower of Cost or Market (LCM) Valuation method departing from the cost principle; it serves to recognize a loss when replacement cost or net realizable value drops below cost. (342)

M

Market Interest Rate The current rate of interest on a debt when incurred; also called *yield* or *effective-interest rate*. (504)

Market Tests Ratios that tend to measure the market worth of a share of stock. (665)

Material Amounts Amounts that are large enough to influence a user's decision. (231)

Merchandise Inventory Goods held for resale in the ordinary course of business. (329)

Merger Occurs when one company purchases all of the net assets of another and the acquired company goes out of existence. (E-18)

Mixed-Attribute Measurement Model Applied to measuring different assets and liabilities of the balance sheet. (44)

N

Natural Resources Assets occurring in nature, such as mineral deposits, timber tracts, oil, and gas. (409)

Net Book Value (Book Value, Carrying Value) The acquisition cost of an asset less accumulated depreciation, depletion, or amortization. (169, 391)

Net Realizable Value The expected sales price less selling costs (e.g., repair and disposal costs). (342)

Net Sales The top line reported on the income statement. Net Sales = Sales Revenue − (Credit card discounts + Sales discounts + Sales returns and allowances). (281)

Noncash Investing and Financing Activities Transactions that do not have direct cash flow effects; reported as a supplement to the statement of cash flows in narrative or schedule form. (610)

No-Par Value Stock Capital stock that has no par value specified in the corporate charter. (550)

Notes (Footnotes) Provide supplemental information about the financial condition of a company, without which the financial statements cannot be fully understood. (16)

Notes Receivable Written promises that require another party to pay the business under specified conditions (amount, time, interest). (283)

O

Operating (Cash-to-Cash) Cycle The time it takes for a company to pay cash to suppliers, sell goods and services to customers, and collect cash from customers. (101)

Operating Income (Income from Operations) Net sales less cost of goods sold and other operating expenses. (236)

Operating Lease Does not meet any of the four criteria for a capital lease established by GAAP and does not cause the recording of an asset and liability. (465)

Ordinary Repairs and Maintenance Expenditures that maintain the productive capacity of an asset during the current accounting period only and are recorded as expenses. (388)

Outstanding Shares The total number of shares of stock that are owned by stockholders on any particular date. (548)

P

Paid-In Capital (Additional Paid-in Capital, Contributed Capital in Excess of Par) The amount of contributed capital less the par value of the stock. (51)

Par Value (1) The nominal value per share of capital stock established by the board of directors; serves as the basis for legal capital; it establishes the minimum amount a stockholder must contribute and has no relationship to the market price of the stock. (2) Also, another name for bond principal, or the maturity amount of a bond. (51, 501, 550)

Patent Granted by the federal government for an invention; gives the owner the exclusive right to use, manufacture, and sell the subject of the patent. (407)

Payment Date The date on which a cash dividend is paid to the stockholders of record. (554)

Percentage of Credit Sales Method Bases bad debt expense on the historical percentage of credit sales that result in bad debts. (287)

Periodic Inventory System An inventory system in which ending inventory and cost of goods sold are determined at the end of the accounting period based on a physical inventory count. (334)

Permanent (Real) Accounts The balance sheet accounts that carry their ending balances into the next accounting period. (181)

Perpetual Inventory System An inventory system in which a detailed inventory record is maintained, recording each purchase and sale during the accounting period. (334)

Post-Closing Trial Balance Prepared as an additional step in the accounting cycle to check that debits equal credits and all temporary accounts have been closed. (184)

Preferred Stock Stock that has specified rights over common stock. (560)

Present Value The current value of an amount to be received in the future; a future amount discounted for compound interest. (466)

Press Release A written public news announcement normally distributed to major news services. (232)

Primary Objective of Financial Reporting to External Users To provide useful economic information about a business to help external parties make sound financial decisions. (43)

Private Investors Individuals who purchase shares in companies. (231)

Public Company Accounting Oversight Board (PCAOB) The private sector body given the primary responsibility to work out detailed auditing standards. (227)

Purchase Discount Cash discount received for prompt payment of an account. (355)

Purchase Returns and Allowances A reduction in the cost of purchases associated with unsatisfactory goods. (354)

R

Ratio (Percentage) Analysis An analytical tool that measures the proportional relationship between two financial statement amounts. (652)

Raw Materials Inventory Items acquired for the purpose of processing into finished goods. (329)

Record Date The date on which the corporation prepares the list of current stockholders as shown on its records; dividends can be paid only to the stockholders who own stock on that date. (554)

Relevant Information Information that can influence a decision; it is timely and has predictive and/or feedback value. (44)

Replacement Cost The current purchase price for identical goods. (342)

Residual (or Salvage) Value The estimated amount to be recovered by the company, less disposal costs, at the end of an asset's estimated useful life. (393)

Retained Earnings Cumulative earnings of a company that are not distributed to the owners and are reinvested in the business. (46)

Revenue Realization Principle Revenues are recognized when (1) goods or services are delivered, (2) there is evidence of an arrangement for customer payment, (3) the price is fixed or determinable, and (4) collection is reasonably assured. (106)

Revenues Increases in assets or settlements of liabilities from ongoing operations. (102)

S

Sales (or Cash) Discount Cash discount offered to encourage prompt payment of an account receivable. (280)

Sales Returns and Allowances A reduction of sales revenues for return of or allowances for unsatisfactory goods. (280)

Sarbanes-Oxley Act A law that strengthens U.S. financial reporting and corporate governance regulations. (226)

Securities and Exchange Commission (SEC) The U.S. government agency that determines the financial statements that public companies must provide to stockholders and the measurement rules that they must use in producing those statements. (227)

Separate-Entity Assumption States that business transactions are separate from the transactions of the owners. (44)

Specific Identification Method An inventory costing method that identifies the cost of the specific item that was sold. (335)

Stable Monetary Unit Assumption States that accounting information should be measured and reported in the national monetary unit without any adjustment for changes in purchasing power. (44)

Stated Rate The rate of cash interest per period specified in the bond contract. (501)

Statement of Cash Flows (Cash Flow Statement) Reports inflows and outflows of cash during the accounting period in the categories of operating, investing, and financing. (13)

Statement of Stockholders' Equity Reports the way that net income and the distribution of dividends affected the financial position of the company during the accounting period. (11)

Stock Dividend A distribution of additional shares of a corporation's own stock. (556)

Stock Split An increase in the total number of authorized shares by a specified ratio; it does not decrease retained earnings. (557)

Stockholders' Equity (Shareholders' or Owners' Equity) The financing provided by the owners and the operations of the business. (45)

Straight-Line Amortization A simplified method of amortizing a bond discount or premium that allocates an equal dollar amount to each interest period. (509)

Straight-Line Depreciation Method that allocates the depreciable cost of an asset in equal periodic amounts over its useful life. (394)

T

T-account A tool for summarizing transaction effects for each account, determining balances, and drawing inferences about a company's activities. (58)

Tangible Assets Assets that have physical substance. (383)

Technology Includes costs for computer software and Web development. (407)

Temporary (Nominal) Accounts Income statement (and sometimes dividends declared) accounts that are closed to Retained Earnings at the end of the accounting period. (181)

Temporary Differences Timing differences that cause deferred income taxes and will reverse, or turn around, in the future. (475)

Tests of Liquidity Ratios that measure a company's ability to meet its currently maturing obligations. (659)

Tests of Profitability Ratios that compare income with one or more primary activities. (653)

Tests of Solvency Ratios that measure a company's ability to meet its long-term obligations. (663)

Time Period Assumption The long life of a company can be reported in shorter time periods. (101)

Time Value of Money Interest that is associated with the use of money over time. (458)

Trademark An exclusive legal right to use a special name, image, or slogan. (407)

Trading Securities All investments in stocks or bonds that are held primarily for the purpose of active trading (buying and selling) in the near future (classified as short term). (E-6)

Transaction (1) An exchange between a business and one or more external parties to a business or (2) a measurable internal event such as the use of assets in operations. (47)

Transaction Analysis The process of studying a transaction to determine its economic effect on the business in terms of the accounting equation. (49)

Treasury Stock A corporation's own stock that has been issued but subsequently reacquired and is still being held by that corporation. (551)

Trial Balance A list of all accounts with their balances to provide a check on the equality of the debits and credits. (64)

Trustee An independent party appointed to represent the bondholders. (503)

U

Units-of-Production Depreciation Method that allocates the depreciable cost of an asset over its useful life based on the relationship of its periodic output to its total estimated output. (395)

Unqualified (Clean) Audit Opinion Auditor's statement that the financial statements are fair presentations in all material respects in conformity with GAAP. (228)

Unrealized Holding Gains or Losses Amounts associated with price changes of securities that are currently held. (E-6)

W

Work in Process Inventory Goods in the process of being manufactured. (329)

Working Capital The dollar difference between total current assets and total current liabilities. (462)

Y

Yield (Effective-Interest Rate) The current rate of interest on a debt when incurred; also called the *market interest rate*. (504)

American Eagle Outfitters logo courtesy of American Eagle Outfitters, Inc.
Urban Outfitters logo courtesy of Urban Outfitters, Inc.
POOLCORP logo used courtesy of Pool Corporation.

Chapter 8

Opener: © Le Desk/Alamy.
Page 389: © AP Photo/Ted S. Warren.
Page 403: © Juan Silva/Iconica/Getty Images.
Page 407: © D. Hurst/Alamy.
Southwest logo is a trademark of Southwest Airlines Co. and is used with permission.
Exxon logo is a registered trademark of ExxonMobil Corporation and is used with permission.
Singapore Airlines logo is a trademark of Singapore Airlines Limited and is used with permission.
Cisco Systems logo courtesy of Cisco Systems, Inc. Used with permission.
International Paper logo courtesy of International Paper Company. All rights reserved.
Kodak is a trademark of Eastman Kodak Company. Used with permission.
Ford logo is a trademark of Ford Motor Company and is used with permission.
Freeport-McMoRan logo is a trademark of Freeport-McMoRan Copper & Gold Inc. and is used with permission.
American Eagle Outfitters logo courtesy of American Eagle Outfitters, Inc.
Urban Outfitters logo courtesy of Urban Outfitters, Inc.
POOLCORP logo used courtesy of Pool Corporation.

Chapter 9

Opener: © The McGraw-Hill Companies, Inc./Jill Braaten, photographer.
Page 456: AP Photos/Kevin P. Casey.
Page 460: © Mark Richards/Photo Edit.
General Mills logo is a registered trademark of General Mills, Inc. and is used with permission of General Mills Marketing Inc. (GMMI).
Pepsi logo—this material contains valuable trademarks owned and used by PepsiCo, Inc. and its subsidiaries and affiliates to distinguish products and services of outstanding quality. Used with permission.
Ford logo is a trademark of Ford Motor Company and is used with permission.
Exxon logo is a registered trademark of ExxonMobil Corporation and is used with permission.
Brunswick logo used courtesy of Brunswick Corporation.

American Eagle Outfitters logo courtesy of American Eagle Outfitters, Inc.
Urban Outfitters logo courtesy of Urban Outfitters, Inc.
POOLCORP logo used courtesy of Pool Corporation.

Chapter 10

Opener: © Andrew Harrer/Bloomberg via Getty Images.
Page 503: © Artville/Getty.
Pepsi logo—this material contains valuable trademarks owned and used by PepsiCo, Inc. and its subsidiaries and affiliates to distinguish products and services of outstanding quality. Used with permission.
DIRECTV logo used courtesy of DIRECTV, LLC.
General Mills logo is a registered trademark of General Mills, Inc. and is used with permission of General Mills Marketing Inc. (GMMI).
JCPenney logo is a trademark of JCPenney Company Inc. and is used with permission.
American Eagle Outfitters logo courtesy of American Eagle Outfitters, Inc.
Urban Outfitters logo courtesy of Urban Outfitters, Inc.
POOLCORP logo used courtesy of Pool Corporation.

Chapter 11

Opener: © Daniel Acker/Bloomberg via Getty Images.
Page 555: © epa european pressphoto agency b.v./Alamy.
Page 556: © Joel Gordon.
Kroger logo is a registered trademark of The Kroger Co. of Michigan and is used with permission.
Dillard's logo courtesy of Dillard's.
P&G logo courtesy of Procter & Gamble Corporation.
Freeport-McMoRan logo is a trademark of Freeport-McMoRan Copper & Gold Inc. and is used with permission.
Ford logo is a trademark of Ford Motor Company and is used with permission.
Haynes International is a trademark of Haynes International Corp. and is used with permission.
American Eagle Outfitters logo courtesy of American Eagle Outfitters, Inc.
Urban Outfitters logo courtesy of Urban Outfitters, Inc.
POOLCORP logo used courtesy of Pool Corporation.

Chapter 12

Opener: Courtesy of National Beverage Corp.
Page 602: © mauritius images GmbH/Alamy.

National Beverage logo is a registered trademark of National Beverage Corporation and is used with permission.
Stanley Furniture logo courtesy of Stanley Furniture Company.
MillerCoors logo is a registered trademark of MillerCoors Properties and is used with permission of MillerCoors LLC.
Pepsi logo—this material contains valuable trademarks owned and used by PepsiCo, Inc. and its subsidiaries and affiliates to distinguish products and services of outstanding quality. Used with permission.
American Eagle Outfitters logo courtesy of American Eagle Outfitters, Inc.
Urban Outfitters logo courtesy of Urban Outfitters, Inc.
POOLCORP logo used courtesy of Pool Corporation.

Chapter 13

Opener: © EPA/Joshua Gates Weisberg/Corbis.
Page 655: © Jim McIsaac/Getty Images.
Page 660: © Erik S. Lesser/Bloomberg via Getty Images.
Home Depot THE HOME DEPOT and the Home Depot logo are trademarks of Licensor TLC, Inc., used under license.
P&G logo courtesy of Procter & Gamble Corporation.
Cintas logo is a registered trademark of Cintas Corporation and is used with permission.
JCPenney logo is a trademark of JCPenney Company Inc. and is used with permission.
Pepsi logo – this material contains valuable trademarks owned and used by PepsiCo, Inc. and its subsidiaries and affiliates to distinguish products and services of outstanding quality. Used with permission.
American Eagle Outfitters logo courtesy of American Eagle Outfitters, Inc.
Urban Outfitters logo courtesy of Urban Outfitters, Inc.
POOLCORP logo used courtesy of Pool Corporation.

Appendix E

Page E-1: © Alliance Images/Alamy.
Page E-6: © Studio 101/Alamy.
Sonic, America's Drive-In logo is a trademark of Sonic Corporation and is used with permission.
American Eagle Outfitters logo courtesy of American Eagle Outfitters, Inc.
Urban Outfitters logo courtesy of Urban Outfitters, Inc.
POOLCORP logo used courtesy of Pool Corporation.

COMPANY INDEX

Ratios Used for Financial Analyses

Ratio		Basic Computation	Chapter
Current Ratio	=	$\dfrac{\text{Current Assets}}{\text{Current Liabilities}}$	2
Net Profit Margin	=	$\dfrac{\text{Net Income}}{\text{Net Sales}}$	3
Total Asset Turnover	=	$\dfrac{\text{Sales (or Operating) Revenues}}{\text{Average Total Assets}}$	4
Return on Assets (ROA)*	=	$\dfrac{\text{Net Income}}{\text{Average Total Assets}}$	5
Gross Profit Percentage	=	$\dfrac{\text{Gross Profit}}{\text{Net Sales}}$	5
Receivables Turnover	=	$\dfrac{\text{Net Sales}}{\text{Average Net Trade Accounts Receivable}}$	6
Inventory Turnover	=	$\dfrac{\text{Cost of Goods Sold}}{\text{Average Inventory}}$	7
Fixed Asset Turnover	=	$\dfrac{\text{Net Sales}}{\text{Average Net Fixed Assets}}$	8
Accounts Payable Turnover	=	$\dfrac{\text{Cost of Goods Sold}}{\text{Average Accounts Payable}}$	9
Debt-to-Equity	=	$\dfrac{\text{Total Liabilities}}{\text{Stockholders' Equity}}$	10
Times Interest Earned	=	$\dfrac{\text{Net Income + Interest Expense + Income Tax Expense}}{\text{Interest Expense}}$	10
Earnings per Share	=	$\dfrac{\text{Net Income**}}{\text{Average Number of Shares of Common Stock Outstanding During the Period}}$	11
Dividend Yield	=	$\dfrac{\text{Dividend per Share}}{\text{Market Price per Share}}$	11
Quality of Income	=	$\dfrac{\text{Cash Flow from Operating Activities}}{\text{Net Income}}$	12
Capital Acquisitions	=	$\dfrac{\text{Cash Flow from Operating Activities}}{\text{Cash Paid for Property, Plant, and Equipment}}$	12
Economic Return from Investing	=	$\dfrac{\text{Dividends and Interest Received + Change in Fair Value***}}{\text{Fair Value of Investments (beginning of period)}}$	E

*As shown in Chapter 13, in most complex analytical situations, interest expense net of tax is added back to net income in the numerator of the ratio.

**If there are preferred dividends, the amount is subtracted from the Net Income in the numerator.

***Beginning Balance of Investments—Ending Balance of Investments

	Chapter Title	Focus Company	Managerial Focus	Contrast Companies	Key Ratios
1	Financial Statements and Business Decisions	**LE-NATURE'S** Beverage company	Valuing an acquisition	Pier 1 Imports	
2	Investing and Financing Decisions and the Accounting System	CHIPOTLE Restaurant chain (food service)	Investing and financing decisions	Panera Bread Yum! Brands Fiesta Restaurant Group The Wendy's Company	**Current Ratio**
3	Operating Decisions and the Accounting System	CHIPOTLE Restaurant chain	Operating decisions	GlaxoSmithKline Unilever Parmalat BMW Group Papa John's Pizza Mattel Panera Bread Fiesta Restaurant Group	**Net Profit Margin**
4	Adjustments, Financial Statements, and the Quality of Earnings	CHIPOTLE Restaurant chain	Year-end accounting activities	Panera Bread Fiesta Restaurant Group Toys R Us	**Total Asset Turnover**
5	Communicating and Interpreting Accounting Information	**APPLE** Computer manufacturer	Corporate communication	Dell Lenovo Microsoft Corporation Hewlett-Packard	**Return on Assets Gross Profit Percentage**
6	Reporting and Interpreting Sales Revenue, Receivables, and Cash	**DECKERS** outdoor corporation Shoe manufacturer and clothing merchandiser	Marketing strategy	Skechers U.S.A. Crocs, Inc.	**Receivables Turnover**
7	Reporting and Interpreting Cost of Goods Sold and Inventory	**HARLEY-DAVIDSON, INC.** Motorcycle manufacturer and clothing merchandiser	Inventory management	Dell Deere & Company Caterpillar Polaris Honda Motor	**Inventory Turnover**
8	Reporting and Interpreting Property, Plant, and Equipment; Intangibles; and Natural Resources	**SOUTHWEST.COM** Major air carrier	Planning productive capacity	Delta Air Lines United Continental Holdings Singapore Airlines International Paper ExxonMobil Corporation IBM Corporation Cisco Systems Cedar Fair Sears Holdings Corporation	**Fixed Asset Turnover**